Marriages
and
Families

Changes, Choices, and Constraints

FIFTH EDITION

Nijole V. Benokraitis
University of Baltimore

PEARSON

Prentice
Hall

Upper Saddle River, New Jersey 07458

Library of Congress Cataloging-in-Publication Data

Benokraitis, Nijole V. (Nijole Vaicaitis)
    Marriages and families: changes, choices, and constraints /
Nijole V. Benokraitis.— 5th ed. p. cm.
    Includes bibliographical references and index.
    ISBN 0-13-130516-6
    1. Family—United States.   2. Marriage—United States.   I. Title.
HQ536.45 2003
306.8'0973—dc22   2003053678

AVP, Publisher: Nancy Roberts
Executive Editor: Christopher DeJohn
VP, Director of Production and Manufacturing:
    Barbara Kittle
Prepress and Manufacturing Manager: Nick Sklitsis
Prepress and Manufacturing Buyer: Mary Ann Gloriande
Production Editor: Cheryl Keenan
Copyeditor: Carol Peschke
Supplements Editor: Erin Katchmar
Proofreader: Susan Plog
Editorial Assistant: Veronica D'Amico
Director of Marketing: Beth Mejia
Senior Marketing Manager: Marissa Feliberty
Marketing Assistant: Adam Laitman

Creative Design Director: Leslie Osher
Senior Art Director: Anne Bonanno Nieglos
Interior and Cover Design: Susan Walrath
Production/Art Manger: Guy Ruggiero
Illustrator (Interior): Mirella Signoretto
Director Image Resource Center:: Melinda Reo
Manager, Rights and Permissions: Zina Arabia
Interior Image Specialist: Beth Brenzel
Image Permission Coordinator: Carolyn Gauntt
Photo Researcher: Beaura K. Ringrose
Cover Image Specialist: Karen Sanatar
Cover Art: Mike Quon/Stock Illustration Source, Inc.
Media Editor: Kate Ramunda
Media Production Manager: Lynn Pearlman

This book was set in 10/11.5 Sabon by Lithokraft, and was printed and bound by RR Donnelley and Sons Company. The cover was printed by The Lehigh Press, Inc.

For permission to use copyrighted material, grateful acknowledgment is made to the copyright holders listed on page 589, which is considered an extension of this copyright page.

Pearson Education LTD.
Pearson Education Singapore, Pte. Ltd
Pearson Education, Canada, Ltd
Pearson Education–Japan
Pearson Education Australia PTY, Limited

Pearson Education North Asia Ltd
Pearson Educación de Mexico, S.A. de C.V
Pearson Education Malaysia, Pte. Ltd
Pearson Education, Upper Saddle River, New Jersey

10 9 8 7 6 5 4 3

ISBN 0-13-130516-6

To Andrius and Gema

BRIEF CONTENTS

CONTENTS

CHAPTER 7
Sexuality and Sexual Expression throughout Life   *166*

PART THREE:
Individual and Marital Commitments

CHAPTER 8
Choosing Others: Dating and Mate Selection   *202*

BOXED FEATURES

CROSS**CULTURAL AND** MULTI**CULTURAL**

ASK**YOURSELF**

A FEW WORDS TO STUDENTS

In the last few years, I've started asking my students how many read the Preface, in this textbook or others. About one out of fifty raises her or his hand.

You're welcome to read the Preface, of course, because I write it with the student in mind. If you're like many of my students and will skip the Preface, however, I wanted to say a few things to all of you before you plunge into the assigned readings.

You're going to enjoy your marriage and family course. Because the family is something *all* of us have in common, it's always one of the liveliest courses I teach. In fact, you'll probably remember this course as one of the most important and interesting that you've taken in college.

I hope that this textbook will be one of the reasons that your marriage and family course will be informative and memorable. Here are a few comments I've received from my own students and others outside our university:

"You not only present the material in a clear way but also do it humorously."

"I especially appreciate your in-depth coverage of ethnic issues and the tremendous diversity of family styles and patterns in America, past and present."

"I looked forward to reading the chapters each week. I enjoyed reading the book and have recommended it to many of my friends—to help give them a dose of reality and the facts concerning the stages of dating, mating, marriage, separation, divorce, remarriage and aging."

"I found the online tests very helpful. It was a good way to review the material in each chapter. Professor (X) used similar essay questions for exams, so I was really ready!"

"I liked the Web links a lot. I used some of them for research projects in other classes."

"I know more about families and culture and how to deal better with relationships. Your book gave me a positive outlook on family life."

"I have a better knowledge of my family. I now understand why we have some of the problems we do."

"When we were driving to Florida during Spring break, I brought this book along to study for an exam. I read some of the passages to my husband to keep him awake because it was a 12-hour drive. We started discussing some issues about our marriage for the first time. It was great!"

"I talked about some of the stuff in the textbook with my teenage son when I was studying. We had some interesting conversations. Believe it or not, he read several of the chapters, and on his own!"

"This is the most interesting book I've had in college. It's not as good as a mystery novel :-), but I never dozed off in the middle of a chapter."

"I'm not afraid of figures and tables any more."

Even if you shudder every time you see figures and tables, you'll enjoy this textbook. You may not agree with everything (and neither do I as I summarize the most recent research), but the material will help you think about your own family or marriage, reflect on ways to improve your current relationships, get out of bad relationships, make better decisions in the future, and understand the diversity of families in the United States and other countries.

I hope all of you enjoy your course and this textbook. The "About the Author" page provides my e-mail address if you'd like to contact me. I'm *always* happy to hear from students.

Have a good semester. And for those of you who are graduating this year, congratulations!

Dr. B (as my students call me)

PREFACE

Welcome to the fifth edition of *Marriages and Families: Changes, Choices, and Constraints*. Having recently crossed into the new millennium, we're experiencing more unprecedented changes than ever before that affect marriages and families. The shift in the racial and ethnic composition of the U.S. population continues to transform families. As the number and variety of immigrants increase, the way we relate to each other becomes both more interesting and more complex.

Medical technology is also altering lifespans. As this book goes to press, for example, medical researchers are experimenting with new ways to help infertile couples and performing innovative surgery on infants still in a mother's womb. At the other end of the life course, the number of people age 85 and over is surging, and promising new drugs are helping people who suffer from Alzheimer's disease. Living longer means that many of us will enjoy multigenerational families but will also have numerous elderly relatives who will need care.

Other recent changes have also affected families. A booming economy in the late 1990s plummeted in the early 2000s: Many dot-coms crashed, retirement portfolios dwindled, and an unprecedented number of people were laid off. Families in the high socioeconomic brackets still flourished, but many other families became poorer than ever.

Some important gay rights issues also made the headlines during the early 2000s. In 2003, for example, a U.S. Supreme Court decision struck down state sodomy laws (*Lawrence vs. Texas*). Despite the recent election of an openly gay Anglican bishop in the United States, the ruling will probably call into question a host of other laws, including same-sex marriage, that most gay rights advocates endorse but gay rights opponents resist. Thus, the debates continue.

Scholarly Work, Comprehensiveness, and Readability

This revision has almost 1400 new references. Most come from scholarly research that has been published since 2001. And, whenever possible, I provide Web links, rather than hard copy citations, for faculty and students who want to access the material quickly and avoid traveling to a library.

Marriages and Families offers students a comprehensive introduction to many issues facing families in the twenty-first century. Although written from a sociological perspective, the book incorporates material from other disciplines: history, economics, social work, psychology, law, biology, medicine, and anthropology. The material also encompasses family studies, women's studies, and gay and lesbian studies, as well as both quantitative and qualitative studies. Nationally representative and longitudinal data are supplemented with insights from clinical, case, and observational studies.

Readability continues to be one of this textbook's most attractive features. A major reason why this textbook has been successful is that it discusses theories and recent studies that students find very interesting. As one of my students once said, "This is the first textbook I've had where I don't count how many more pages I have to read while I'm still on the first page."

In addition, reviewers have consistently described the writing as "very clear" and "excellent." According to one reviewer, for example, "The interesting anecdotes and quotes help to maintain the student's interest while also providing examples of the subject under discussion."

Continuity of Major Themes on the Contemporary Family

Marriages and Families continues to be distinguished from other textbooks in several important ways. It offers comprehensive coverage of the field, allowing instructors to select chapters that best suit their needs. It balances theoretical and empirical discussions with practical examples and applications.

It highlights important contemporary *changes* in society and the family. It explores the *choices* that are available to family members and the *constraints* that often limit our choices. It examines the diversity of U.S. families, using *cross-cultural and multicultural* material to encourage students to think about the many critical issues that confront the family of the twenty-first century.

More Changes

Changes that affect the structure and functioning of today's family inform the pages of every chapter of this book. In addition, several chapters focus on some major transformations in American society. Chapter 4, for example, examines the growing cultural diversity of the United States, focusing on African American, American Indian, Latino, Asian American, Middle Eastern, and interracial marriages and families.

Chapter 17 discusses the ways in which the rapid "graying of America" has affected adult children, grandchildren, and even great-grandchildren, family members' roles as caregivers, and family relations in general. And Chapter 18 analyzes some of the social policy changes that affect the family.

More Choices

On the individual level, family members have many more choices today than ever before. People feel freer to postpone marriage, to cohabit, or to raise children as single parents. As a result, household forms vary greatly, ranging from commuter marriages to those in which several generations live together under the same roof.

As reproductive technology becomes increasingly sophisticated, many infertile couples can now have children. Some states offer "covenant marriages" and mediation to stem the high divorce rates. And as the U.S. population continues to age, many elderly family members are participating in innovative housing arrangements (such as senior communes), and they are demanding legislation that allows them to die with dignity. Although some of these issues are very controversial, they increase the options that family members have now and will enjoy in the future.

More Constraints

Although family members' choices are more varied today, we also face greater macro-level constraints. Our options are increasingly limited, for example, by government policies that ignore the need for national health insurance coverage for families and child care resources for middle-class and lower-class households.

Family life is often shaped by economic changes and not vice versa. Political and legal institutions also have a major impact on most families in terms of tax laws, welfare reform, and even in defining what a family is. Because laws, public policies, and religious groups affect our everyday lives, I have framed many discussions of individual choices within the larger picture of the institutional constraints that limit our choices.

Cross-Cultural and Multicultural Diversity in the United States

Because contemporary American marriages and families vary greatly in terms of structure, dynamics, and cultural heritage, discussions of gender roles, class, race, ethnicity, age, and sexual orientation are integrated throughout this book. To further strengthen students' understanding of the growing diversity among today's families, I have also included a series of boxes that focus on families from many cultures. Both text and boxed materials should encourage students to think about the many forms families may take and the different ways in which family members interact.

Encouraging Students to Think More Critically

All editions of this textbook have prodded students to think about themselves and their families in the "Ask Yourself" boxes. In this edition, I'm prodding even more than before **by adding two new features:**

- **Making Connections:** At several points in each chapter, these questions ask students to connect the material to their own lives by relating it to a personal experience, by integrating it with scholarly studies discussed in the chapter, or by "connecting" with classmates who might be sitting next to them in a class.

- **Stop and Think:** These critical thinking questions follow important issues in boxes throughout the textbook. These items encourage reflective thought about current topics, both personally and across other cultures.

New and Expanded Topics

- **Chapter 4 on Racial and Ethnic families:** This groundbreaking chapter has been moved from later in the textbook to earlier, reflecting the growing impact of this topic on all of the facets of relationships and families.

- **New U.S. Census Bureau data:** Pulling from recent releases from the U.S. Census Bureau, *Marriages and Families* has unparalleled currency. Numerous statistics from 2002 and 2003 offer a current picture of families in America not found in other books.

- **New coverage of Middle Eastern American families:** Unlike other textbooks, Chapter 4 covers Middle Eastern families, their increased numbers, their prominence, and the benefits and the problems they face in today's U.S. diverse society.

- **A new "Investigate with Research Navigator™" feature ends each chapter:** Providing students with key search terms that can be used to search the three databases of Prentice Hall's Research Navigator™. Please see the writeup on Resarch Navigator™ in the supplements listed later in the preface for more details.

  In most chapters, "a global view" adds new material to the *Data Digest* or text. In addition, many chapters include more examples from the popular culture (television, videos, movies) to which students relate. Specifically, new, updated, and expanded coverage includes the following:

- Updated material on economic security, marriage movements, children's time with parents, recent changes in the nuclear family, social class and racial and ethnic variations in using technological innovations, and a map on U.S. diversity. I've also provided new "Ask Yourself" boxes on how much students know about contemporary marriage and family life and whether Uncle Sam should be a matchmaker for low-income women (**Chapter 1**).

- Revised section of ecological theory, family life course development theory, and a new discussion of experimental research designs. In addition, a new "Ask Yourself" box queries students about how much they know about accessing medical sites. I've also rewritten the "Politics of Sex Research" box to include the most recent research and have updated the discussion of research and ethical issues (**Chapter 2**).

- New material on misconceptions about slavery and on the "modern family" (**Chapter 3**).

- New concepts that include assimilation and racial socialization. This chapter includes a heavily revised section on immigrant families, interracial and interethnic marriages, and multicultural children. Middle Eastern families are a new topic in this chapter, and I've updated all the tables, figures, and other material on racial and ethnic minority families. There's also a new box on the increasing number of Mexican day laborers in the United States (**Chapter 4**).

- New content on feminist theories in explaining gender roles, revised material on parents and socialization, and a rewritten section on the global variations in gender roles cross-culturally. Also, a new "Ask Yourself" box challenges students to find out how much they know about gender differences (**Chapter 5**).

- New sections on friendship and love, narcissism and love, and the relationship between love and physical health. I've also revised and updated the material on jealousy, the evolutionary perspectives on love, cyberstalking, and the global view of love (**Chapter 6**).

- Recent research on homosexuality in non-Western countries, sexual scripts in terms of gender and race, and a revised discussion of what adolescents and young adults don't know about sex. There's a revised discussion on sex education and abstinence. New topics include "outercourse," cybersex, online infidelity, unmarried sexual infidelity, and preventing sexually transmitted diseases (**Chapter 7**).

- New material on hooking up, dating in later life, and speed dating. Updated material on the functions of dating, equity theory, global mate selection, and breaking up (**Chapter 8**).

- Rewritten text on individual reasons for postponing marriage, sex ratios, the global view on cohabitation, and older singles who "age in place." New discussions include being home alone, the impact of cohabitation on children, social class and cohabitation, and a new "Ask Yourself" box on singles (**Chapter 9**).

- New data on prenuptial agreements, marital success and happiness, and marriage and health. Also included is a new section on why people marry, "wifework," and a box for students to consider whether they're ready to tie the knot (**Chapter 10**).

- New research on fertility patterns worldwide, unmarried older mothers, relative income and fertility, and new reproductive technologies (such as preimplantation genetic diagnosis). I've also revised this material in terms of racial and ethnic variations in fertility, the types of and reasons for adoption, same-sex adoptions, and postponing parenthood (**Chapter 11**).

- New content on the contradictions of gender roles and parenting, bed sharing between children and parents, role overload, socioeconomic status and parenting, raising biracial children, how much time parents spend with children, and parenting adolescents (**Chapter 12**).

- New material on the recent increase of stay-at-home moms. There are also revised and updated sections on pregnancy discrimination, the increasing gender wage gap, social class and family inequality, and recent data on stay-at-home dads (**Chapter 13**).

- New section on infant homicide, and updates on elder abuse, adolescent abuse, and preventing family violence (**Chapter 14**).

- New sections on being separated but not divorced, family abductions, and updated material on custody battles and child-support payments (**Chapter 15**).

- More inclusive definition of stepfamily, an updated discussion of the myths about remarriage, and recent theoretical explanations of the effects of stepfamilies on children (**Chapter 16**).

- New content on centenarians, dementia, Social Security benefits by sex and race, and divorcing grandparents. A new box examines how Mexican American families deal with death. I have also revised and updated the information on Alzheimer's disease and grandparenting styles (**Chapter 17**).

- Updated sections on national health insurance, the Canadian health-care system, the 1996 welfare reforms, some results of Oregon's assisted suicide legislation, and new data on the aging world (**Chapter 18**).

Features in the Fifth Edition

Much of *Marriages and Families* has been revised to incorporate new research (both in print and on the Internet), recent surveys, the U.S. Census, and current examples and illustrations from the media. I have maintained several popular features such as the *Data Digest* and the author's files quotations. In response to student and reviewer comments, I have revised some figures and the end-of-chapter materials, including the *Taking It Further* sections.

Data Digest

I introduced the *Data Digest* in the second edition because "all those numbers" from the Census Bureau, empirical studies, and demographic trends often overwhelmed students (both mine and others'). Because this has been a popular feature, I've updated the U.S. statistics and have included information from other countries. The *Data Digest* that introduces each chapter not only provides students with a thought-provoking overview of current statistics and trends but makes all those numbers more interesting and digestible.

The first question from my students is usually "Will this material be on the exam?" Not in my classes. I see the *Data Digest* as piquing student curiosity about the chapter rather than providing a lot of numbers for them to memorize. Some faculty tell me that their students have used the *Data Digest* to develop class presentations or course papers.

Material from the Author's Files

Many faculty who reviewed previous editions of *Marriages and Families,* and many students as well, liked the anecdotes and personal experiences with which I illustrate sometimes "dry" theories and abstract concepts. In this new edition I weave more of this material into the text. Thus, many examples discussions in my own classes are included (cited as "author's files") to enliven theoretical perspectives and abstract concepts.

Figures

Many students tend to skip over figures and tables because they're afraid of numbers, they don't trust statistics (see Chapter 2), or the material seems boring or complicated. Regardless of what textbooks I use and in *all* the courses I teach, I routinely go over a number of figures in class. As I tell my students, a good figure or table may be more important (or at least more memorable) than the author's explanation. To encourage students to look at data, I have streamlined many figures and often provide brief summaries to accompany the figures.

Taking It Further

A common question from my own students has been, "Can't we do something about [issue X]?" And sometimes students have asked me for practical information: "How can I find a good child care center?" or "Can anyone help my sister get out of an abusive marriage?" The *Taking It Further* section addresses such questions and concerns.

It tells students how to get information on particular topics, how to get personal assistance such as counseling or therapy for themselves or others, how to contact organizations that deal with specific problems and provides URLs for a wealth of Internet sites that delve deeper into topics discussed in each chapter. Some of the Web sites are fun (such as those on love and dating), some provide up-to-date information (especially many of the U.S. Census Bureau and Centers for Disease Control sites), and others offer practical advice and community resources on the workplace, family research, aging, sex and sexually transmitted diseases, gender, sexual orientation, and many other family-related topics.

What is on the Internet today may be gone tomorrow. Therefore, I have tried to include only the Web sites that have been around for a while and will not vanish overnight.

Pedagogical Features

The pedagogical features in *Marriages and Families* have been designed specifically to capture students' attention and to help them understand and recall the material. Some of these features are familiar from the earlier editions, but some are new. Each has been carefully crafted to ensure that it ties in clearly to the text material, enhancing its meaning and applicability.

Informative and Engaging Illustration Program

Many chapters contain figures that, in bold and original artistic designs, demonstrate such concepts as the exchange theory of dating, romantic versus lasting love, and theories of mating, as well as presenting simple statistics in innovative and visually appealing ways. Many of the photographs are new. We have taken great care to select substantive photographs (rather than what I call "pretty postcards") that illustrate the text.

Thought-Provoking Box Series

Reflecting and reinforcing the book's primary themes, three categories of boxes focus on the changes, choices, and constraints that confront today's families. A fourth category discusses cultural differences, and a fifth, self-assessment quizzes, helps students evaluate their own knowledge and acquire insights about family life.

- **Changes boxes**—some historical, some anecdotal, and some empirically based—show how marriages and families have been changing or are expected to change in the future. For example, a box in Chapter 13 describes how the role of the working mother has evolved over the years.

- **Choices boxes** illustrate the kinds of decisions families can make to improve their well-being, often highlighting options that family members may be unaware of. In Chapter 11, for instance, a box shows what mothers and fathers can do to increase the likelihood of having healthy babies.

- **Constraints boxes** illustrate some of the obstacles that limit our options. They highlight the fact that although most of us are raised to believe that we can do whatever we want, we are often constrained by macro-level socioeconomic, demographic, and cultural factors. For example, a box on the ten biggest myths about the African American family reveals some of the stereotypes that black families confront on a daily basis.

- **Cross-Cultural and Multicultural boxes** illustrate the richness of varying family structures and dynamics, both in the United States and in other countries. For example, one box contrasts the American style of dating with arranged courtship and marriage in Muslim societies.

- **Ask Yourself** self-assessment quiz boxes not only encourage students to think about and to evaluate their knowledge about marriage and the family but also help them to develop guidelines for action, both on their own and others' behalf. For example, "If This Is Love, Why Do I Feel So Bad?" helps the reader evaluate and make the decision to leave an abusive relationship.

Outlines

Each chapter contains an opening outline. The outlines help students organize their learning by focusing on the main topics of each chapter.

Key Terms and Glossary

Important terms and concepts are boldfaced and defined in the text and listed at the end of each chapter. All key terms and their definitions are repeated in the Glossary at the end of the book.

Supplements

The supplement package for this textbook is of exceptional quality. Each component has been meticulously crafted to amplify and illuminate materials in the text.

Study Guide

This helpful guide offers students the opportunity to review material presented in the text. Each chapter consists of chapter summaries, definitions of key terms, critical thinking exercises geared to the questions in the text, and a self-test question page referenced to the text.

Family Notes

This innovative guide with perforated pages allows students to bring together the best of the textbook with the best of your lecture. Combining PowerPoint presentations with lines for note taking on the same printed page, FamilyNotes allows students to organize their study time with one easy resource.

Instructor's Resource Manual with Tests

This essential instructor's tool includes detailed chapter outlines, teaching objectives, discussion questions, classroom activities, *Study Tips,* and almost 1900 multiple-choice, true-or-false, fill-in, and essay questions that are page referenced to the text.

Test-Gen-EQ

This software allows instructors to create their own personalized exams, to edit the existing test questions, and to add new questions. Other special features of this program include random generation of an item set, creation of alternative versions of the same test, scrambling question sequence, and test preview before printing.

ABCNEWS ABC News and Prentice Hall Video Library for Marriage and the Family

Video is the most dynamic supplement you can use to enhance a class, but the quality of the video material and how well it relates to your course still make all the difference. Prentice Hall and ABC News are now working together to bring you the best and most comprehensive video ancillaries available in the college market.

Through its wide variety of award-winning programs—*Nightline, Business World, 20/20,* and *World News Tonight*—ABC News offers a resource for feature and documentary-style videos related to the chapters in *Marriages and Families.* The programs have extremely high production quality, present substantial content, and are hosted by well-versed, well-known anchors.

Prentice Hall and its authors and editors have selected videos and topics that will work well with this course and text and have include notes on how to use them in the classroom.

Transparency Acetates for Marriages and Families, Series IV

Taken from graphs, diagrams, and tables in this text and other sources, more than 50 full-color transparencies offer an effective way to illustrate lecture topics.

Prentice Hall Marriages and Families PowerPoint Slides

This PowerPoint slide set combines graphics and text in a colorful format to help you convey principles in a new and exciting way. Created in PowerPoint, an easy-to-use and widely available software program, this set contains more than 200 content slides keyed to each chapter.

Companion Website™: www.prenhall.com/benokraitis

More than an online study guide, the Prentice Hall *Companion Website™* for *Marriages and Families* is a truly integrated, text-specific resource. The site offers

- **Self-grading quizzes** where students can test their knowledge of key concepts and obtain instant feedback

- **Web destinations** with chapter-by-chapter links that will help launch your students' exploration on the Web.

- **Key word searches** that are easy to use with built-in search engines

- **And a whole lot more**

Research Navigator™

The goal of Research Navigator™ is to help students understand the steps in the research process so they can more confidently and efficiently complete research assignments. In addition, Research Navigator™ offers students three exclusive databases of scholarly and reliable source content to help them focus their research efforts and get the research process started.

Students and faculty can access Research Navigator™ through an access code found in the front of *The Prentice Hall Guide to Evaluating Online Resources.* This guide can be wrapped with *Marriages and Families, 5th Edition,* at no additional cost.

Research Navigator™ includes three databases of scholarly and reliable source material:

EBSCO's ContentSelect Academic Journal Database

EBSCO's ContentSelect™ Academic Journal Database, organized by subject, contains more than 100 of the leading academic journals grouped by discipline. Instructors and students can search the online journals by key word, topic, or multiple topics. Articles include abstract and citation information and can be cut, pasted, e-mailed, or saved for later use.

 The New York Times Search-by-Subject Archive, specific to sociology, is searchable by key word or multiple key words. Instructors and students can view full-text articles from the world's leading journalists from *The New York Times.*

 Link Library offers editorially selected "**Best of the Web**" sites for each discipline. Link Libraries are continually scanned and kept up to date, providing the most relevant and accurate links for research assignments.

Acknowledgments

A number of people have contributed to this edition of *Marriages and Families: Changes, Choices, and Constraints*. First, I would like to thank my students. Their lively and passionate exchanges during class and in online discussions always help me refocus some of my research and writing.

Linda Fair, our division's administrative guru, is always good-natured and responsive in solving everyday office-related glitches, expediting correspondence, and making sure that our computer equipment is serviced quickly. Our graduate research assistants, Sheriea Waters and Flo Combs, helped track down some of the research.

Many thanks to the reference and circulation staff at the University of Baltimore's Langsdale Library for their continuous support. Brian Chetelet, James Foster, Carole Mason, Lyle Nash, Delores Redman, and Tammy Taylor kept track of hundreds of books checked out from a dozen Maryland system libraries. They facilitated my research and resolved all problems patiently and graciously. "I can't" isn't part of their vocabulary.

Carol Vaeth is extraordinary in accessing materials from a variety of academic and public libraries. Carol's amazing interlibrary skills have provided me with many of the articles and books I've needed to research and revise this edition of *Marriages and Families*.

Other reference librarians—Lucy Holman, Jack Lattimore, Jeanne Lauber, Susan Wheeler, and Joan Wolk—have always been quick to respond. They have trained my students on the Internet and article databases, have spent hours helping me track down elusive information, and have *always* willingly provided instruction when I ran into Internet or online problems. Their average turn-around time in helping me locate materials online is about 10 minutes. I've worked at a dozen academic libraries and consider our reference librarians among the most helpful I've ever met.

Colleagues play a critical role in revisions. For this edition, I received valuable input from

Sandra L. Caron, University of Maine
Katherine Clifton, Edison Community College
Lovberta A. Cross, Southwest Tennessee Community College
Maureen Semans Davey, University of Georgia
Keith F. Durkin, Ohio Northern University
Wanda Kaluza, Camden County College
Cynthia K. S. Reed, Tarrant County College
Barbara Seater, Raritan Valley Community College
Glenn M. Van Metre, Wichita State University
Xiaohe Xu, Mississippi State University

At Prentice Hall, I am grateful to Chris DeJohn, executive editor for sociology, who guided the book's development enthusiastically and creatively, resolving a variety of snags quickly and astutely. Veronica D'Amico, Chris's superb editorial assistant, handled many tasks efficiently and amiably. Susan Moss, development editor, provided numerous insightful suggestions during the book's revisions. Cheryl Keenan, an excellent production editor, kept track of myriad details and deadlines and played a major role in making sure that the figures and text were clear. Carol Anne Peschke, copyeditor, made the book even more engaging and reader-friendly.

I also want to thank others at Prentice Hall for their high-quality contributions to this edition of *Marriages and Families:* Marissa Feliberty, marketing manager; Beth Mejia, director of marketing; Kathleen Karcher, permissions; Susan Walrath, designer; and Beaura K. Ringrose, photo researcher.

I thank my family for their unfaltering patience and sense of humor throughout life's little stresses, especially my research and writing. Throughout our 37 years of marriage, Vitalius, my husband, has always been my greatest supporter, a sympathetic sounding board, and an incredibly patient high-tech consultant.

Andrius, our son, helps me maintain my sanity by keeping my computer humming, regardless of where he is during business trips. He cheers me up in the middle of the night with humorous Instant Messenger quips and conversations. Gema, our daughter, manages to drag me away from the monitor and into the sunshine despite my "But I have so much to do!" protests. Her healthful meals and sense of humor replenish both body and soul. I also want to thank my brother, Casimir Vaicaitis, for his numerous computer-related gifts that facilitate my research and writing.

Last, but not least, I have benefited greatly from the suggestions of faculty and students who have contacted me during the last few years. I have incorporated many of their reactions in the fifth edition and look forward to future comments.

Thank you, one and all.

ABOUT THE AUTHOR

Nijole V. Benokraitis, professor of sociology at the University of Baltimore, has taught the marriage and family course for more than 20 years and says it's her favorite class, although her courses in racial and ethnic relations and gender roles run a close second. Professor Benokraitis received a B.A. in sociology and English from Emmanuel College, an M.A. in sociology from the University of Illinois at Urbana, and a doctorate in sociology from the University of Texas at Austin.

She is a strong proponent of applied sociology and requires her students to enhance their study through interviews, direct observation, and other hands-on learning methods. She also enlists her students in community service activities such as tutoring and mentoring inner-city high school students, writing to government officials and other decision makers about specific social problems, and volunteering research services to nonprofit organizations.

Professor Benokraitis, who immigrated to the United States from Lithuania with her family when she was 6 years old, is bilingual and bicultural. She has authored, co-authored, edited, or coedited *Contemporary Ethnic Families in the United States: Characteristics, Variations, and Dynamics* (Prentice Hall, 2001); *Feuds about Families: Conservative, Centrist, Liberal, and Feminist Perspectives* (Prentice Hall, 2000); *Subtle Sexism: Current Practices and Prospects for Change* (1997); *Marriages and Families: Changes, Choices, and Constraints* (Prentice Hall, 2002, 4/e); *Modern Sexism: Blatant, Subtle, and Covert Discrimination* (Prentice Hall, 1995, 2/e); *Seeing Ourselves: Classic, Contemporary, and Cross-Cultural Readings in Sociology* (Prentice Hall, 2004, 6/e); and *Affirmative Action and Equal Opportunity: Action, Inaction, and Reaction* (1978).

Professor Benokraitis has published numerous articles and book chapters on such topics as institutional racism, discrimination against women in government and higher education, fathers in two-earner families, displaced homemakers, and family policy. She has served as both chair and graduate program director of the University of Baltimore's Department of Sociology and has chaired numerous university committees.

She has received grants and fellowships from many institutions, including the National Institute of Mental Health, the Ford Foundation, the American Educational Research Association, the Administration on Aging, and the National Endowment for the Humanities. She has for some time served as a consultant in the areas of sex and race discrimination to women's commissions, business groups, colleges and universities, and federal government programs. She has also made several appearances on radio and television on gender communication differences and single-sex educational institutions. She currently serves on the editorial board of *Women & Criminal Justice*.

Professor Benokraitis lives in Maryland with her husband, Dr. Vitalius Benokraitis, director of Graduate Studies in Computer Science and Software Engineering, Loyola College in Maryland. They have two children, Gema and Andrius.

The author looks forward (and always responds) to comments on the 5th Edition of *Marriages and Families: Changes, Choices and Constraints*. She can be contacted at

University of Baltimore
Division of Criminology,
    Criminal Justice
    and Social Policy
1420 North Charles Street
Baltimore, MD 21201
Voice mail: 410-837-5294
Fax: 410-837-5061

E-mail: nbenokraitis@ubalt.edu

The Changing Family

DATADIGEST

- The **"traditional" family** (where the husband is the breadwinner and the wife is a full-time mother) declined from 60 percent in 1972 to 30 percent in 2001.

- Almost 19 million people aged 25 to 34 years have **never been married**, representing 41 percent of all people in that age group.

- Today the **median age at first marriage** is higher than at any time in the twentieth century: 26.8 years for men, 25.1 years for women.

- On average, **first marriages that end in divorce** last 7 to 8 years.

- The percentage of children under age 18 **living with one parent** rose from 11 percent in 1970 to 27 percent in 2000.

SOURCES: Fields, 2001; Fields and Casper, 2001; Smith, 2001; Kreider and Fields, 2002; U.S. Census Bureau, 2002.

Two generations ago, the typical American family consisted of a father, a mother, and three or four children. In a recent survey on what constitutes a family, in contrast, a woman in her 60s wrote the following:

My boyfriend and I have lived together with my youngest son for several years. However, our family (with whom we spend holidays and special events) also includes my ex-husband and his wife and child; my boyfriend's ex-mother-in-law and her sister; his ex-wife and her boyfriend; my oldest son who lives on his own; my mom and stepfather; and my stepbrother and his wife, their biological child, adopted child, and "Big Sister" child. Needless to say, introductions to outsiders are confusing (Cole, 1996: 12, 14).

Clearly, contemporary family arrangements are more fluid than in the past. Does this shift reflect changes in individual preferences, as people often assume? Or are other forces at work? As this chapter shows, although individual choices have altered some family structures, many of these changes reflect adaptations to larger societal transformations.

You will also see that, despite both historical and recent evidence to the contrary, we continue to cling to a number of myths about the family. Before we examine these and other issues, we need to define what we mean by *marriage* and *family*. First, test your knowledge about current U.S. family trends by taking the quiz on p. 4.

What Is Marriage?

Defined broadly, **marriage** is a socially approved mating relationship that is expected to be stable and enduring. Marriage forms vary across many different groups because the members of a society construct its **norms,** or culturally defined rules for behavior. Norms

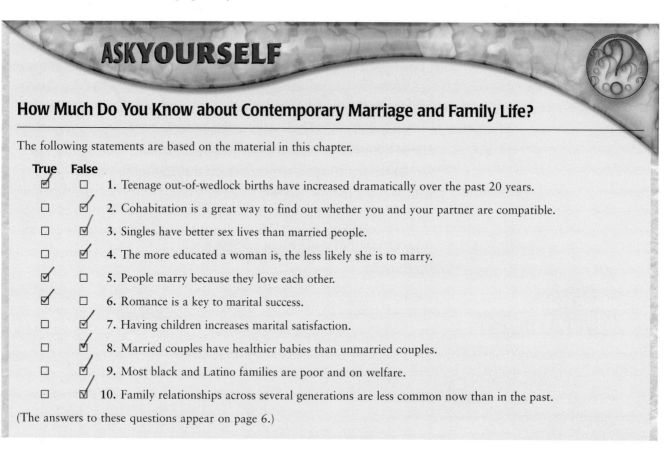

How Much Do You Know about Contemporary Marriage and Family Life?

The following statements are based on the material in this chapter.

True	False	
☑	☐	**1.** Teenage out-of-wedlock births have increased dramatically over the past 20 years.
☐	☑	**2.** Cohabitation is a great way to find out whether you and your partner are compatible.
☐	☑	**3.** Singles have better sex lives than married people.
☐	☑	**4.** The more educated a woman is, the less likely she is to marry.
☑	☐	**5.** People marry because they love each other.
☑	☐	**6.** Romance is a key to marital success.
☐	☑	**7.** Having children increases marital satisfaction.
☐	☑	**8.** Married couples have healthier babies than unmarried couples.
☐	☑	**9.** Most black and Latino families are poor and on welfare.
☐	☑	**10.** Family relationships across several generations are less common now than in the past.

(The answers to these questions appear on page 6.)

that define marriage include formal laws and religious doctrines. To be legally married, for example, we must meet specified requirements in every state, such as a minimal age. Although the laws are rarely enforced, 31 states prohibit marriage between first cousins. And because the Catholic Church forbids the dissolution of what it considers the holy sacrament of marriage, devout Catholics may seek annulments but not divorces.

Despite numerous societal and cultural variations, marriages in most Western industrialized countries have some common characteristics. In general, married couples are expected to share economic responsibilities, to engage in sexual activity only with their spouses, and to bear and raise children.

In the United States, laws governing marriage have changed more rapidly than social customs or regional practices. In 1967, for example, the U.S. Supreme Court declared miscegenation laws, which prohibit interracial marriages, unconstitutional. However, local customs and attitudes among many groups still discourage interracial marriages (see Chapter 4). And as recent violent outbursts in white neighborhoods in Massachusetts, New York, and New Jersey have

shown, intolerance of interracial dating is not limited to the South or to rural areas (see Chapter 8).

Marriages in the United States are legally defined as either ceremonial or nonceremonial. A *ceremonial* marriage is one in which the couple must follow procedures specified by the state or other jurisdiction, such as buying a license, getting blood tests, and being married by an authorized official. Some states also recognize **common-law marriage**, a *nonceremonial* form of marriage that people establish by cohabitation (living together) or evidence of *consummation* (sexual intercourse). Common-law marriages are recognized as legal in 14 states and the District of Columbia. In both kinds of marriage, the parties must meet minimal age requirements, and they cannot engage in **bigamy**, that is, marrying a second person while a first marriage is still legal.

When common-law relationships break up, the legal problems can be complex, including the child's inheritance rights and the father's responsibility to pay child support. Even when common-law marriage is considered legal, ceremonial marriage provides more advantages (such as health benefits and social approval).

What Is a Family?

Although it may seem unnecessary to define familiar terms such as *family*, meanings vary between groups of people and change over time. The definitions also have important consequences for policy decisions, often determining family members' rights and obligations by legal and other social institutions. Under Social Security laws, for example, only a worker's spouse, dependent parents, and children can claim benefits based on the worker's record. And in most adoptions, a child is not legally a member of an adopting family until social service agencies and the courts have approved the adoption. Thus, definitions of family affect people's lives by limiting their options.

Traditionally, *family* has been defined as a unit made up of two or more people who are related by blood, marriage, or adoption and who live together, form an economic unit, and bear and raise children. The U.S. Census Bureau defines the family simply as two or more people living together who are related by birth, marriage, or adoption.

Many social scientists have challenged such traditional definitions because they exclude a number of diverse groups who also consider themselves families. Social scientists have asked, Are childless couples families? What about cohabiting couples? Foster parents and their charges? Elderly sisters living together? Gay and lesbian couples, with or without children? Grandparents raising grandchildren?

There is no universal definition of the family because contemporary household arrangements are very complex. For our purposes, a **family** is as an intimate environment in which two or more people: (1) live together in a committed relationship, (2) see their identity as importantly attached to the group, and (3) share close emotional ties and functions. However, not all social scientists will agree with this definition because it does not explicitly include legalized marriage, procreation, or child rearing.

Definitions may become even more complicated—and more controversial—in the future. As reproductive technology advances, a baby might have several "parents": an egg donor, a sperm donor, a woman who carries the baby during a pregnancy, and the couple who intends to raise the child. If that's not confusing enough, the biological father may be dead for years by the time the child is actually conceived because his sperm can be frozen and stored (see Chapter 11).

Some believe that definitions of the family should emphasize affection and mutual cooperation among people who are living together. Particularly in African American and Latino communities, ties with **fictive kin,** or nonrelatives who are accepted as part of the family, may be stronger and more lasting than the ties

Gilmore Girls, a popular show, portrays the Gilmores as a non-traditional family.

established by blood or marriage (Dilworth-Anderson et al., 1993). James, one of my black students now in his forties, still fondly recalls Mike, a fictive kin, who was a boarder in their home:

> *Mike was an older gentleman who lived with us from my childhood to my teenage years. We considered him part of the family. He was like a grandfather to me. He taught me how to ride a bike, took me fishing, and always told me stories. He was very close to me and my family until he died. When the family gets together, we still talk about old Mike because he was just like family and we still miss him dearly (Author's files).*

A recent variation of fictive kin among Unitarian congregations is "intentional families," made up primarily of white, professional people. They are separated by distance or estrangement from their own relatives but yearn for familial closeness. Intentional families live apart but meet regularly for meals, holidays, and milestones. They also plan outings together, help each other during crises, and sometimes find stand-in grandparents (E. Graham, 1996).

MAKING CONNECTIONS

■ Ask three of your friends to define *family*. Are their definitions the same as yours? Or different?

■ According to one of my students, "I never view my biological family as 'my family' because my parents were abusive and didn't love me." Do you agree that people should be able to choose whomever they want to be their family?

Answers to How Much Do You Know about Contemporary Marriage and Family Life?

All of the answers are **false**:

1. Teenage out-of-wedlock births have decreased over the past 20 years, especially in the early 2000s (see Chapters 10 and 11).

2. Couples who are living together and plan to marry each other *shortly* have a good chance of staying together after a marriage. In most cases, however, "shacking up" decreases the likelihood of marriage (see Chapter 9).

3. Compared with singles, married people have more and better sex and enjoy it more, both physically and emotionally (see Chapter 7).

4. College-educated women postpone marriage but are more likely to marry, over a lifetime, than their non–college-educated peers (see Chapters 9 and 10).

5. Love is not the major or even only reason for getting married. Other reasons include societal expectations, economic insecurity, or a fear of loneliness (see Chapters 6, 10, 16, and 17).

6. The best indicators of long-term marital success include hard work, sharing compatible values and interests, and resolving conflicts in a "civilized" manner (see Chapters 10, 14, and 15).

7. The arrival of a first baby typically pushes mothers and fathers apart. Generally, child rearing lowers marital satisfaction for both partners (see Chapters 11, 12, and 16).

8. Social class is a more important factor than marital status in a baby's health. Low-income mothers are less likely to have healthy babies than high-income mothers, whether they are married or not (see Chapters 11–14).

9. Although many black and Latino families live below the poverty level, in 2001 almost 28 percent of African American families and 31 percent of Latino families had annual incomes of $50,000 or more (see Chapters 4, 12, and 13).

10. Family relationships across several generations are more common and more important now than in the past. People live longer and get to know their kin, aging parents and grandparents often provide financial and child care support, and many relatives maintain their ties after a divorce or remarriage (see Chapters 3, 4, 12, 16, and 17).

Family Structure and Social Change

For nearly a century, the nation's family structure remained remarkably stable. Between 1880 and 1970, about 85 percent of all children lived in two-parent households. Then, in the next two decades, the number of divorces and single-parent families skyrocketed. By 1996, almost one in four children was living in mother-only homes (see *Figure 1.1*). Some people have been concerned that the **nuclear family**—made up of a husband, a wife, and their biological or adopted children—has dwindled. Some groups were very optimistic when the nuclear family "rebounded" from 51 percent in 1991 to 56 percent in 1996 (Fields, 2001).

Despite the recent increase in the number of nuclear families, many social scientists contend that using the nuclear family as the only "normal" or "natural" type of family ignores many other prevalent household forms. One researcher, for example, has identified 23 types of family structures, and some include only friends or group-home members (Wu, 1996). Various family structures exist not only across cultures and eras but also within any particular culture or historical period (see Chapter 3).

As reflected in many television shows, diverse family households are more acceptable today than ever before (see *Table 1.1* on page 8). At the same time, the lineup of shows is rarely representative of "real" families. For example, at least 11 shows have focused on single-father households, but only 4 have portrayed single-mother households. In real life, only 3 percent of all children live in father-only families (see *Figure 1.1*). The star of the only show that featured an unwed mother—*Murphy Brown*—was white, upper middle class, and a successful professional. In real life, most unwed mothers are poor and have little education (Fields and Casper, 2001; see also Chapter 9). And although the number of traditional families has decreased since the 1970s (see "Data Digest"), such programs increased during prime time in the early 2000s (for example, *The Hughleys, 7th Heaven, Everybody Loves Raymond, American Dreams,* and *Yes, Dear*).

MAKING CONNECTIONS

You may not even remember some of the television shows that came and went in the 1990s. Some, such as *Married . . . with Children, Mad about You, Home Improvement,* and *The Bill Cosby Show,* are now syndicated. Television shows have portrayed a wide variety of family structures.

■ How many of these programs are *really* representative of most U.S. families today? Or of your own family?

■ How do these shows shape our ideas about how families should relate to one another?

Functions of the Family

Although family structures differ, most contemporary families fulfill five important functions. They legitimize sexual activity, bear and raise children, provide economic security, offer emotional support, and establish family members' places in society. As you read this section, think about your own family. How does its structure—whether nuclear, divorced, stepfamily, or another form—fulfill these functions?

Regulation of Sexual Activity

Every society has norms regarding who may engage in sexual relations, with whom, and under what circumstances. One of the oldest rules is the **incest taboo,** cultural norms and laws that forbid sexual intercourse between close blood relatives, such as brother and sister, father and daughter, uncle and niece, or grandparent and grandchild.

Incest Taboos Sexual relations between close relatives can increase the incidence of inherited genetic diseases and abnormalities by about 3 percent (Bennett et al., 2002). Incest taboos have primarily social bases, however, and probably arose to maintain the family for several reasons:

■ Incest taboos minimize jealousies and destructive sexual competition that might interfere with the functioning of the family circle.

■ Incest taboos ensure a group's survival. If family members who are sexual partners lose interest in each other, for example, they may avoid mating.

■ Because incest taboos ensure that mating will take place outside the family, a wider circle of people can band together in cooperative efforts (such as hunting), in the face of danger, or in war (Ellis, 1963).

■ By controlling the mother's sexuality, incest taboos prevent doubt about the legitimacy of her offspring and their property rights, titles, or inheritance.

Most social scientists believe that incest taboos are universal. There have been exceptions, however. The rulers of the Incan empire, the native Hawaiian royalty,

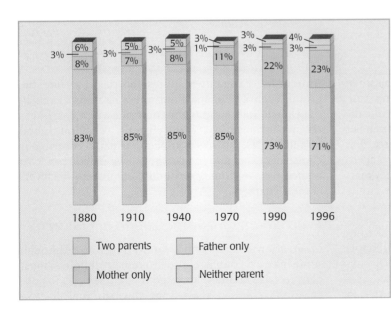

FIGURE 1.1 **Where Children Live: Selected Years, 1880–1996**

SOURCE: Fields, 2001, Figure 7.

TABLE 1.1

Family Structure According to 1990s and Early 2000s Television

Family Structure	Television Show
Married couple with children; father as breadwinner	*Married . . . with Children, The Simpsons, Dave's World, Everybody Loves Raymond, 7th Heaven, The Hughleys, The PJs, Family Guy, That '70s Show, American Dreams, Yes, Dear*
Married couple with children; two earners	*The Cosby Show, Roseanne, Home Improvement, Mad about You, Malcolm in the Middle, My Wife and Kids, George Lopez, Still Standing, Life with Bonnie*
Married couple with no children	*Dharma and Greg, My Big Fat Greek Life*
Married couple with children and related adults	*Under One Roof, All-American Girl, Family Matters*
Male householder with children	*Soul Man, Smart Guy, Blossom, One on One*
Male householder with children and unrelated adults	*Full House, The Nanny*
Male householder with children and related adults	*Me and the Boys, The Gregory Hines Show*
Male householder with children and grandchildren	*Thunder Alley*
Male householder with unmarried adult children	*Empty Nest, Providence*
Female householder with children	*Grace under Fire, Cybill, Gilmore Girls, The Parkers*
Married couple with stepchildren	*True Colors, Major Dad*
Married couple with biological or nonbiological children	*Fresh Prince of Bel Air, Step by Step, The Bernie Mac Show, One World, Moesha*
Children, no adults present	*On Our Own, Party of Five*
Unmarried mother	*Murphy Brown*
Related adults	*Head over Heels, Between Brothers, Charmed*
Related and unrelated adults	*Frasier*
Unrelated adults	*Living Single, Friends, 3rd Rock from the Sun, George and Leo, Men Behaving Badly, Girlfriends, Sex and the City, Will and Grace, Real World*
Single-person households	*Seinfeld, Ellen, Ally McBeal*
Retired couple or roommates	*Cosby, The Golden Girls*

the ancient Persian rulers, and the Ptolemaic dynasty in Egypt practiced incest while it was forbidden to commoners. Cleopatra, for example, was purportedly the issue of at least 11 generations of incest and married her younger brother. Some anthropologists speculate that wealthy Egyptian families practiced sibling marriage to prevent losing or fragmenting their land. If a sister married a brother, the property would remain in the family in cases of divorce or death (Parker, 1996).

Endogamy and Exogamy   Two other cultural rules define the "right" marriage partner. The principle of **endogamy** requires that people marry or have sexual relations within a certain group, such as Jews marrying Jews or African Americans marrying African

Americans. **Exogamy** requires marriage outside the group, such as not marrying one's relatives. Even in the United States and other countries where marriages are not arranged, societal, religious, subcultural, and familial rules, however implicit, usually govern our choice of sexual and life partners. (We will discuss two related terms—*homogamy* and *heterogamy*—in several later chapters.)

Procreation and Socialization of Children

Procreation is an essential family function. Although some married couples choose to remain childless, most plan to raise families. Some go to great lengths to conceive the children they want through reproductive technologies (see Chapter 11). Once a couple becomes parents, the family embarks on socialization, another critical function.

Through **socialization,** children acquire language, absorb the accumulated knowledge, attitudes, beliefs, and values of their culture, and learn the social and interpersonal skills needed to function effectively in society. Some of our socialization is unconscious and may be unintentional, such as teaching culturally accepted stereotypical gender traits (see Chapter 5). Much of the socialization is both conscious and deliberate, however, such as carefully selecting preschoolers' playmates or raising children in a specific religion.

We are socialized through **roles,** the obligations and expectations attached to a particular situation or position. Families are important role-teaching agents because they delineate relationships between mothers and fathers, siblings, parents and children, and other relatives and non-family members.

Some of the rights and responsibilities associated with our roles are not always clear because family structures shift and change. For example, if you or your parents have experienced divorce or remarriage, have some of the new role expectations been fuzzy or even contradictory? Children often are torn between their allegiance to a biological parent and that to a stepparent because stepparent–stepchild roles are often ambiguous (see Chapter 16).

Some claim that the family is less powerful today in socializing its young than it was in the past. With more mothers of young children in the work force, for example, child-care centers and preschool programs are playing an increasingly important role in socialization. Especially on such politically charged issues as sex education, some parents feel that schools have become too intrusive in socializing their children and have undermined parental authority (see Chapter 7).

Economic Security

The family is an important economic unit that provides financial security and stability. Families supply food, shelter, clothing, and other material resources for their members. If such economic cooperation did not exist, a family's survival would be jeopardized. There is a large number of homeless families (see Chapter 13). They often wind up on the streets or in shelters not because the parents are mentally ill or drug users but simply because they can't produce the income to purchase some of life's basic necessities such as housing and food.

In traditional families, the male is the breadwinner and the female does the housework and cares for the children. Increasingly, however, many mothers are entering the labor force. Among married couples with

The family provides love, comfort, and emotional support that children need to develop into happy, healthy, and secure adults.

children under 18, the proportion of traditional homes has declined significantly (see "Data Digest"). The traditional family, where Mom stays home to raise the kids, is a luxury that most families today can't afford. Because of high unemployment rates, depressed wages and salaries, and a lack of job security, many mothers must work outside the home whether they want to or not (see Chapter 13).

Emotional Support

American sociologist Charles Horton Cooley (1864–1929) explored the concept of **primary groups,** those characterized by close, long-lasting, intimate, and face-to-face interaction. Later writers introduced the notion of **secondary groups,** those characterized by impersonal and short-term relationships where people work together on common tasks or activities. The family is a critical primary group because it provides the nurturance, love, and emotional sustenance that people need to be happy, healthy, and secure.

In contrast, secondary groups have few emotional ties, and its members typically leave the group after attaining a specific goal. While you're taking this course, for example, you, most of your classmates (except for a few close friends, perhaps), and your instructor make up a secondary group. You've all come together for a quarter or a semester to study marriage and the family. Once the course is over, most of you may never see each other again.

You might discuss your course with other secondary groups, such as co-workers. They might listen politely, especially if you're the boss, but they probably won't care how you feel about a class. Such primary groups as your family and close friends, in contrast, usually will listen sympathetically, drive you to class or your job when your car breaks down, offer to do your laundry during exams, and console you if you don't get that much-deserved "A" in a course or a promotion at work.

A simple test distinguishes my primary and secondary groups. I don't hesitate to call the former at 3:00 A.M. to pick me up at the airport, for example, because I know they'll be happy (or at least willing) to do so.

Social Class Placement

A **social class** is a category of people who have a similar standing or rank based on wealth, education, power, prestige, and other valued resources. People in the same social class tend to have similar attitudes, values, and leisure interests.

Social class affects many aspects of family life. There are class variations in terms of when we marry, how many children we have, how parents socialize their children, and even how partners and spouses relate to each other. Middle-class couples are more likely than their working-class counterparts to share more equally in housework and child rearing, for example (see Chapters 10, 12, and 13). And as you will see in later chapters, families on the lower rungs of the socioeconomic ladder face a greater risk than their middle-class counterparts of adolescent nonmarital childbearing, dropping out of high school, committing street crimes, neglecting their children, and domestic violence.

Diversity in Marriages, Families, and Kinship Systems

Although the basic family functions you have just read about are common to most cultures, each society has its own norms that specify acceptable marriage and family forms. Thus, there is much diversity among families both across and within cultures.

Most people are born into a biological family, or *family of origin.* If the person is raised in this family or is adopted, it is her or his **family of orientation.** By leaving this family to marry or cohabit, the individual becomes part of the **family of procreation,** the family a person forms by marrying and having or adopting children. This term is somewhat dated, however, because in several types of households—such as childless or gay and lesbian families—procreation may not be part of the relationship.

Each type of family is part of a larger **kinship system,** or network of people who are related by blood, marriage, or adoption. In much of the preindustrial

world, which contains most of the world's population, the most common family form is the **extended family,** in which two or more generations (such as the family of orientation and the family of procreation) live together or in adjacent dwellings.

Some researchers predict that in industrialized societies where the numbers of single-parent families are increasing, extended families living together or nearby may become more common. Such families can make it much easier for a single parent to work outside the home, raise children, and perform household tasks. Because remarriage rates are high, however, it remains to be seen whether extended families will become widespread.

A variety of formal laws and informal norms regulate inheritance rights, define the pool of eligible marital partners, and determine whether children will take the surname of the father, the mother, or both. There are also worldwide variations in the types of marriages and residential patterns that characterize families and kinship systems.

Types of Marriage

Several types of marriage—including monogamy, polygamy, or a combination—are common in most societies. One anthropologist concluded that only about 20 percent of societies are strictly monogamous. Others permit either polygamy or combinations of polygamy and monogamy (Murdock, 1967).

Monogamy In **monogamy,** one person is married exclusively to another person. Because divorce and remarriage rates are high in the United States and in many European countries, residents of these countries practice **serial monogamy.** That is, they marry several people, but one at a time—they marry, divorce, remarry, redivorce, and so on.

Polygamy Polygamy, in which a man or woman has two or more spouses, is subdivided into *polygyny* (one man married to two or more women) and *polyandry* (one woman with two or more husbands). In group marriage, two or more men and two or more women live together and have sexual relations with each other. Polygyny is common in many societies, especially in Africa, South America, and the Mideast. In Saudi Arabia, for example, some wealthy men have as many as 11 wives and 54 children (Dickey and McGinn, 2001). No one knows the actual figures of polygamy worldwide, however, because "accurate censuses of polygyny are generally unavailable" (Hern, 1992: 504).

Although industrial societies forbid polygamy, there are small pockets of polygynous groups. The

Tom Green from Snake Valley, Utah, is shown here with his 5 wives and some of their 29 children. Green was found guilty in 2002 of polygamy, having sex with one of his wives when she was just 13 years old, and welfare fraud.

Mormon Church banned polygamy in the late 1800s. Still, an estimated 300,000 families are headed by fundamentalist men in the Rocky Mountain states and Canada. The men maintain that they practice polygamy according to nineteenth-century Mormon religious beliefs. Marriages often are performed in secret ceremonies, and some girls as young as 11 are married off at the first sign of menstruation (Divoky, 2002; Madigan, 2003).

Wives who have recently escaped from plural families have raised allegations of forced marriage, sexual abuse, pedophilia, and incest (Cart, 2002). Why don't these girls refuse to marry or try to escape? They can't. Among other things, they're typically isolated from outsiders: They live in remote rural areas, and their education is cut off when they're about 10 years old. Their parents support the marriages because elderly men, the patriarchs, have brainwashed them to believe that "This is what the heavenly father wants." In addition, the girls can't run away because there is no place to go and because Utah law enforcement agencies rarely prosecute polygamists (Janofsky, 2003).

Polygynous marriages can be either formal or informal. In a study of marriage forms in Nigeria, Karanja (1987) differentiates between an inside wife and an outside wife. An "inside wife," who marries in a church or civil ceremony, typically subscribes to the Christian ideal of monogamy in marriage. Under native law and custom, however, her husband may also "marry" (no official ceremony is performed) an "outside wife."

As the box "The Outside Wife" on page 12 shows, the outside wife has regular sexual relations with her "husband," establishes an autonomous residence that the husband pays for, and has children that the man acknowledges as his. Outside wives, however, have limited social recognition and status and much less political and legal recognition. When a well-known Nigerian businessman and politician died at age 60 a few years ago, he had four official wives (because "under Muslim law, a man may have four wives") and more than 40 unofficial wives (Vick, 1998:A9). Some African families that immigrate to Europe continue to live in polygymous families (Randle, 1998).

Some of my students, especially women, become angry when they read about polygynous marriages. They contend that polygyny benefits men at the expense of women because a man has many wives who care for him and his children from birth to death. This may be true, but polygyny is widespread for other reasons. In a study of South Africa, for example, Anderson (2002) concluded that there is often a shortage of men (often because of war), that poor women prefer to marry a rich polygamist than a poor monogamist, that the wives often pool income and cooperative child care, and that the rural wives often contact urban wives when they're looking for jobs. Thus, polygyny is functional because it meets many women's needs.

The very rare practice of polyandry is illustrated by the Todas, a small pastoral tribe that flourished in south India until the late nineteenth century. The Toda woman who married one man became the wife of his brothers—including brothers born after the marriage—and all lived in the same household. When one of the brothers was with the wife, "he placed his cloak and staff outside the hut as a warning to the rest not to disturb him" (Queen et al., 1985: 19). Marital privileges rotated among the brothers, there was no evidence of sexual jealousy, and one of the brothers, usually the oldest, was the legal father of the first two or three children. Another brother could become the legal father of children born later.

According to some anthropologists, polyandry exists in societies where property is difficult to amass. Because there is a limited amount of available land, the kinship group is more likely to survive in harsh

CROSSCULTURAL

The Outside Wife

Temi, 38 years old, is a British-trained doctor in private practice in Lagos, Nigeria. Her father (now retired) was a university professor, and her mother was a high school teacher. Temi's first church marriage, in which she had two children, ended in divorce. She is now an outside wife of an eminent business-man, with whom she has a child. She lives in a flat rented by her husband on Victoria Island, said to be where the who's-who of Nigeria live.

Temi sees no contradiction in her way of life:

Look, I lived in England for years and I know there you are expected to be monogamously married. Well, I am not in England now, am I? (She laughs.) My first husband was a fine gentleman, but, let's face it, he had no money. Most of our spare time was spent bickering over who was going to pay the bills. It was intolerable. In the end I decided to quit.

Financial straits for me are history. My children are in school abroad. My hus-band recently bought me a Mercedes Benz, and I am building a house here in Lagos with his help. We also plan to buy a home in the U.S.

Temi's "husband" has two other wives. The church wife, or inside wife, is also a doctor; the other outside wife is an attorney who practices and lives in Lagos (Karanja, 1987: 255–56).

---

environments if more than one husband contributes to food production (Cassidy and Lee, 1989).

Residential Patterns

Families also vary in terms of where they live. In the *patrilocal* residential pattern, newly married couples live with the husband's family. In a *matrilocal* pattern, newly married couples live with the wife's family. A *neolocal* residence is one in which the newly mar-ried couple sets up its own residence. Around the world families tend to be extended rather than nuclear, and the most common pattern is residence with the husband's family.

In modern industrial societies, married couples typically establish their own residences. Since the early 1990s, however, the tendency for young married adults to live with the parents of either the wife or husband— or sometimes with the grandparents of one of the part-ners—has increased. At least half of all families starting out cannot afford a medium-priced house because they don't have the cash for a downpayment and the clos-ing costs (Conley, 1999). Divorced mothers and their children often live with parents or grandparents for economic reasons (see Chapters 12 and 15).

Clearly, there is much diversity in family arrange-ments both in the United States and around the world. As families change, however, we sometimes get bogged down with idealized images of what a "good" family looks like. Our unrealistic expectations can result in dissatisfaction and anger. Instead of enjoying our

families as they are, we might waste a lot of time and energy searching for family relationships that exist only in fairy tales and TV sitcoms.

Myths about Marriage and the Family

Ask yourself the following questions:

- Were families happier in the past than now?
- Is marrying and having children the "natural" thing to do?
- Are "good" families self-sufficient, whereas "bad" families depend on welfare?
- Is the family a bastion of love and support?
- Should all of us strive to be as perfect as possible in our families?

If you answered "yes" to any of these questions, you—like most people in the United States—believe in several myths about marriage and the family. Although most myths are dysfunctional, some can be functional.

Myths Can Be Dysfunctional

Myths can be *dysfunctional* when they result in nega-tive (although often unintended) consequences that disrupt a family. The myth of the perfect family can make us miserable. We may feel there is something wrong with *us* if we do not live up to some ideal scenario. Instead of accepting our current families, we might pressure our children to become what we want them to be or spend a lifetime waiting for our parents or in-laws to accept us. We may become very critical of family members or withdraw emotionally because they don't fit into a mythical mold.

Myths can also divert our attention from widespread social problems that generate family crises. If people blame themselves for the gap they perceive between image and reality, they may not recognize the external forces, such as social policies, that create difficulties on the individual level. For example, if we believe that only bad, sick, or maladjusted people beat their children, we will search for solutions at the individual level, such as counseling, support groups, and therapy. As we will see in later chapters, however, many family crises result from large-scale problems such as racism, poverty, and unemployment.

Myths Can Be Functional

Not all myths are harmful. Some are *functional* because they bring people together and promote social solidarity (Guest, 1988). If myths give us hope that we can have a good marriage and family life, for example, we won't give up at the first sign of problems. In this sense, myths can help us maintain our emotional balance during crises. Myths can also free us from guilt or shame. For instance, "We fell out of love" is a more face-saving explanation for getting a divorce than "I made a stupid mistake" or "I married an alcoholic."

The same myth may be both functional and dysfunctional. A belief in the decline of the family has been functional in generating social policies (such as child-support legislation) that try to keep children of divorced families from sinking into poverty, for example. But this same myth is also dysfunctional if people become unrealistically preoccupied with finding self-fulfillment and happiness.

Myths about the Past

We often hear that in the "good old days" there were fewer problems, people were happier, and families were stronger. Because of the widespread influence of movies and television, many of us cherish romantic notions of the frontier days. These highly unrealistic images of the family have been portrayed in John Wayne films, the antebellum South of *Gone with the Wind*, and the strong, poor, but loving rural family presented in such television shows as *The Waltons* and *Little House on the Prairie* in the 1970s, *Dr. Quinn, Medicine Woman* in the late 1990s, and *7th Heaven* most recently.

Many historians maintain that such golden ages never existed. We glorify them only because we know so little about the past (Coontz, 1992). Even in the 1800s, many families experienced desertion by a parent or out-of-wedlock births (Demos, 1986). Family life in the "good old days" was filled with deprivation, loneliness, and dangers, as the "Diary of a Pioneer Daughter" box on page 14 illustrates. Families worked very hard and often were decimated by accidents, illness, and disease. Until the mid-1940s, a much shorter life expectancy meant that parental death often led

Like these Nebraska homesteaders, many families in the so-called "good old days" lived in dugouts like this one, made from sod cut from the prairies.

CHANGES

Diary of a Pioneer Daughter

Many scholars point out that life on the old frontier was anything but romantic. Malaria and cholera were widespread. Because of their darkness, humidity, and warmth, as well as their gaping windows and doors, pioneer cabins were ideal environments for mosquitoes. Women and children have been described as doing household tasks with "their hands and arms flailing the air" against hordes of attacking mosquitoes (Faragher, 1986: 90).

Historian Joanna Stratton examined the letters, diaries, and other documents of pioneer women living on the Kansas prairie between 1854 and 1890. The following selection is from a diary of a 15-year-old girl:

A man by the name of Johnson had filed on a claim just west of us and had built a sod house. He and his wife lived there 2 years, when he went to Salina to secure work. He was gone 2 or 3 months and wrote home once or twice, but his wife grew very homesick for her folks in the east and would come over to our house to visit mother.

Mother tried to cheer her up, but she continued to worry until she got bedfast with the fever. At night she was frightened because the wolves would scratch on the door, on the sod, and on the windows, so my mother and I started to sit up nights with her. I would bring my revolver and ammunition and ax and some good-sized clubs.

The odor from the sick woman seemed to attract the wolves, and they grew bolder and bolder. I would step out, fire off the revolver, and they would settle back for a while when they would start a new attack.

Finally the woman died and mother laid her out. Father took some wide boards that we had in our loft and made a coffin for her. Mother made a pillow and trimmed it with black cloth, and we also painted the coffin black.

After that the wolves were more determined than ever to get in. One got his head in between the door casing, and as he was trying to wriggle through, mother struck him in the head with an ax and killed him. I shot one coming through the window. After that they

quieted down for about half an hour, when they came back again. Their howling was awful. We fought these wolves five nights in succession . . . .

When Mr. Johnson arrived home and found his wife dead and his house badly torn down by wolves he fainted away. After the funeral he sold out and moved away (Stratton, 1981: 81).

Rebecca Bryan Boone, wife of the legendary pioneer Daniel Boone, endured months and sometimes even years of solitude when Boone hunted in the woods or went on trading trips.

Besides household chores, she chopped wood, cultivated the fields, harvested the crops, and hunted for small game in the woods near her cabin. Although Rebecca was a strong and resourceful woman, she told a traveling preacher that she felt "frequent distress and fear in her heart" (Peavy and Smith, 1994: xi).

---

to child placements in extended families, foster care, or orphanages. Thus, the chances of not growing up in an intact family were actually greater in the past than they are now (Walsh, 1993).

People who have the "nostalgia bug" aren't aware of several facts. For example, teenage pregnancy rates were higher in the 1950s than they are today, even though a higher proportion of teen mothers were married (many because of "shotgun marriages"). Until the 1970s, few people ever talked or wrote about child abuse, incest, domestic violence, marital unhappiness, sexual harassment, or gay bashing. Many families lived in silent misery and quiet desperation because these issues, were largely invisible. In addition, parents spend more time with their children today than in "the good old days" (see Chapter 12).

Myths about What Is Natural

Many people have strong opinions about what is "natural" or "unnatural" in marriages and families. Although remaining single is more acceptable today than in the past, there is still a lingering suspicion that something is wrong with a person who doesn't marry (see Chapter 9).

We sometimes have misgivings about childless marriages or about other committed relationships. We often hear, for instance, that "It's only natural to want to get married and have children" or that "Gays are violating human nature." Other beliefs, also surviving from so-called simpler times, claim that family life is "natural" and that women are "natural" mothers (see Chapter 5).

The problem with such thinking is that if motherhood is natural, why do many women choose not to have children? If homosexuality is unnatural, how do we explain its existence since time immemorial? If getting married and creating a family are natural, why do millions of men refuse to marry their pregnant partners or abandon their children?

Myths about the Self-sufficient Family

Some of our most cherished values in the United States idealize individual achievement, self-reliance, and self-sufficiency. The numerous best-selling self-help books on such topics as parenting, combining work and marriage, and having "good sex" also reflect our belief that we should improve ourselves, that we can pull ourselves up by our bootstraps.

Although we have many choices in our personal lives, few families—past or present—have been entirely self-sufficient. Most of us need some kind of help at one time or another. Because of unemployment, underemployment, and recessions, the poverty rate has increased by 40 percent since 1970, and many of the working poor are two-parent families (see Chapter 13). From time to time, these families need assistance to survive.

The United States has a higher infant mortality rate than many other countries. Among industrialized countries, the United States ranks only twenty-ninth in terms of child well-being, slipping from its twentieth rank in 1995. The plight of black children is even worse. Nationally, black infant mortality rates are more than twice those of whites, largely because of poverty (Kent and Mather, 2002). In our nation's capital, black infant mortality is higher than that in 56 nations, including low-income countries such as Bahamas, Barbados, Dominican Republic, and Oman ("It's Time for New Voices . . .," 2002). Thus, millions of American families are far from self-sufficient in maintaining their children's well-being.

The middle class isn't self-sufficient, either. In the 1950s and 1960s, for example, many middle-class families were able to prosper not because of family savings or individual enterprise but as a result of federal housing loans, education payments, and publicly financed roads that provided suburbanites with inexpensive travel to their jobs in the city (Coontz, 1992).

Currently, poor and rich alike receive Medicare, and the government provides numerous tax cuts for middle-income and affluent families (see Chapters 13 and 18). Even if you're middle class, you or other family members have probably collected unemployment payments after being laid off from a job. In addition, state-based merit scholarships are more likely to subsidize the college costs of rich rather than poor and minority families. Georgia, for example, spends only $5 million per year on merit scholarships for needy students, compared with $40 million for middle- and upper-income families (Heller and Marin, 2002).

The Myth of the Family as a Loving Refuge

The family has been described as a "haven in a heartless world" (Lasch, 1977: 8). One of the major functions of the family is to provide love, nurturance, and emotional support. The home can also be one of the most physically and psychologically brutal settings in society. An alarming number of children suffer from physical and sexual abuse from family members, and there is a high rate of violence between married and cohabiting partners (see Chapter 14).

Many parents experience stress while balancing the demands of work and family responsibilities. Furthermore, concern about crime, drugs, and unemployment has made many parents pessimistic about their children's future. In one national poll—and at the height of an unprecedented economic boom in the late 1990s—33 percent of those surveyed said they expect their children to have a lower quality of life and to be worse off financially than they, the parents, are (Ladd, 1999). The worry that underlies such responses is bound to affect family dynamics.

Sometimes family members are unrealistic about the daily strains that they encounter. For example, if people expect family interactions to always be cheery and pleasant, the level of tension may surge even when routine problems arise. And especially for families with health or economic problems, the home may be loving, but it's hardly a "haven in a heartless world."

Myths about the Perfect Marriage, the Perfect Family

Here's how one woman described the clash between marital expectations and reality:

> *Marriage is not what I had assumed it would be. One premarital assumption after another has crashed down on my head. . . . Marriage is like taking an airplane to Florida for a relaxing vacation in January, and when you get off the plane you find you're in the Swiss Alps. There is cold and snow instead of swimming and sunshine. Well, after you buy winter clothes and learn how to ski and learn how to talk a new foreign language, I guess you can have just as good a vacation in the Swiss Alps as you can in Florida. But I can tell you, doctor, it's one hell of a surprise when you get off that marital airplane and find that everything is far different from what one had assumed (Lederer and Jackson, 1968: 39).*

Even if partners live together and feel they know each other, many couples may find themselves in the Swiss Alps instead of Florida after tying the knot. Numerous marriages dissolve because we cling to myths about conjugal life. After the perfect wedding, the perfect couple must be everything to one another: good providers, fantastic sexual partners, best friends, sympathetic confidantes, stimulating companions, and spiritual soulmates (Rubin, 1985). Are such expectations realistic?

Fables about the perfect family are just as pervasive as those about the perfect marriage. According to historian John Gillis (1996), we all have two families: one that we live *with* (the way families really are) and another that we live *by* (the way we would like families to be). Gillis maintains that people have been imagining and reimagining family since at least the late Middle Ages because the families we are born and marry into have been too fragile to satisfy most people's need for a sense of continuity, belonging, unity, and rootedness.

Making Connections

■ How do media images of family affect our own perceptions? When you watch some TV shows, for example, do you feel disappointed in your own family?

■ Do you believe any (or all) of the myths about marriage and the family that you just read about? If so, are these beliefs functional or dysfunctional in your life?

Family Values: Three Perspectives on the Changing Family

I introduced this chapter with several definitions of the family. Then we examined the functions of the family, the ways families vary, and some myths about family life. Now we are ready to look at the major theme of this chapter: how the family is changing.

Numerous surveys show that we place a high value on marriage and family. In a recent poll, for example, Americans ranked their family as the most important aspect of life, above health, work, money, and even religion (see *Figure 1.2*). One national survey found that "almost 8 out of 10 married Americans said they would give their marriage an A grade, with the bulk of the rest saying they would give their marriage a B" (Newport, 1996: 18). There were few Cs, Ds, or Fs. In a recent poll, only 3 percent of the respondents felt that morality and family values were problematic (Walczak et al., 2000). In another study, people cited traffic, urban sprawl, and crime as the biggest problems in their lives. Only 6 percent felt that child and teen issues were a major concern (Knickerbocker, 2000).

Despite these upbeat views, a number of writers worry that the family is falling apart. Quite commonly, journalists and scholars refer to the "vanishing" family, "troubled" marriages, and "appalling" divorce statistics as sure signs that the family is disintegrating. Some claim that our most urgent social problem is the disappearance of many fathers because of divorce or unmarried relationships that break up (Blankenhorn,

FIGURE 1.2 **How Important Is Family Life?**

Note: Results of Gallup Poll conducted December 5–8, 2002.

SOURCE: David W. Moore, 2003, Gallup Poll Analysis.

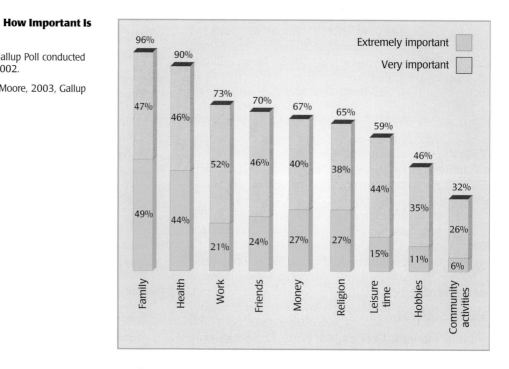

1995). Others contend that we have a "marriage problem" because marriage is now a convenient promise that is easily made and just as easily broken (Wilson, 2002).

Who's right? The status of the family continues to spark debate between three schools of thought. One group contends that the family is deteriorating, a second argues that the family is changing but not deteriorating, and a third, smaller group maintains that the family is stronger than ever.

The Family Is Deteriorating

More than 100 years ago, the *Boston Quarterly Review* issued a dire warning: "The family, in its old sense, is disappearing from our land, and not only are our institutions threatened, but the very existence of our society is endangered" (cited in Rosen, 1982: 299). In the late 1920s, E. R. Groves (1928), a well-known social scientist, warned that marriages were in "extreme collapse." Some of his explanations for what he called the "marriage crisis" and high divorce rates have a surprisingly modern ring: self-indulgence, too much luxury, extreme independence, financial strain, and incompatible personalities.

Even those who were optimistic a decade ago have become more pessimistic because of recent data on family "decay." Some of these data include high rates of divorce and children born out of wedlock, millions of "latchkey children," an increase in the number of people deciding not to get married, unprecedented numbers of single-parent families, and a decline of parental authority in the home.

Why have these changes occurred? Those who feel the family is in trouble echo Groves, citing such reasons as a lack of individual responsibility, a lack of commitment to the family, and just plain selfishness. Many conservative politicians and influential academics argue that the family is deteriorating because most people put their own needs over family duties (see Benokraitis, 2000, for a discussion of these perspectives). This school of thought claims that many men and women are unwilling to invest their psychological and financial resources in their children or that they give up on marriages too quickly when there are problems (Gallagher, 1996; Popenoe, 1996 Wilson, 2002).

Many of those who believe that the family is deteriorating are headed by *communitarians*, people who are politically more moderate than conservatives on some family issues. For example, they accept the idea that many mothers have to work outside the home for economic reasons. Communitarians claim, however, that because many adults focus almost exclusively on their personal gratification, such traditional family functions as the early care and socialization of children have become a low priority (Glenn, 1996). They contend that there has been a general increase in a sense of entitlement (what people believe they should receive from others) and a decline in a sense of duty (what people believe they should give to others).

The family-decline adherents point out that marriage exists for the sake of the children and not just adults. Simply telling children we love them is not enough. Instead of wasting our money on divorce, the argument goes, we should be investing in children by maintaining a stable marriage:

> A large divorce industry made up of lawyers, investigative accountants; real estate appraisers and salespeople; pension specialists; therapists and psychologists; expert witnesses; and private collectors of child support has sprung up to harvest the fruits of family discord. However necessary their services, these professionals are the recipients of family income that might, in happier circumstances . . . [be] invested in children (Whitehead, 1996: 11).

Many who endorse the "family is deteriorating" perspective blame most of the family's problems on mothers who work outside the home. If mothers stayed at home and took care of their children, these writers maintain, we would have less delinquency, fewer high school dropouts, and more children who are disciplined. Gallagher (1996: 184) argues for example, that if women spent more time finding good provider husbands, they could "devote their talents and education and energy to the rearing of their children, the nurturing of family relationships, and the building of community and neighborhood." The implication is that the deteriorating family could be shored up if fathers were breadwinners and mothers were homemakers.

The Family Is Changing, Not Deteriorating

In contrast, other scholars argue that the family has not deteriorated as much as we think. Instead, they say, the changes we are experiencing are extensions of long-standing family patterns.

Although more women have entered the labor force since 1970, the mother who works outside the home is not a new phenomenon. Mothers sold dairy products and woven goods during colonial times, took in boarders around the turn of the twentieth century, and held industrial jobs during World War II (see Chapter 3). The number of married women in the labor force doubled between 1930 and 1980 but *quadrupled* between 1900 and 1904 (Stannard, 1979).

Many family scholars contend that family problems such as desertion, out-of-wedlock birth, and child abuse have *always* existed. Family literature published in the 1930s, for example, included studies that dealt with such issues as divorce, desertion, and family crises due to discord, delinquency, and depression (Broderick, 1988).

Similarly, there have always been single-parent families. The percentage of single-person households has doubled in the last three decades, but this number *tripled* between 1900 and 1950 (Stannard, 1979). Divorce began to be more common in the eighteenth century, parents had less control over their adult married children because there was little land or other property to inherit, and the importance of romantic love increased (Cott, 1976).

There is no question, however, that a greater proportion of people divorce today than in the past and that more early marriages are ending in divorce (see Chapter 15). As a result, the decision of many singles to postpone marriage until they are older, more mature and have stable careers may often be a sound one (see Chapter 9).

Families are changing but are also remarkably resilient, despite numerous adversities. They cope with everyday stresses and protect their most vulnerable members: the young, old, ill, or disabled (Patterson, 2002). They overcome financial hardships. They handle everyday conflict and tension as children make a bumpy transition to adolescence and then to early adulthood (Conger and Conger, 2002).

Most poor families have stable and loving relationships despite constant worries and harsh economic environments (Seccombe, 2002). And many gay and lesbian families, despite their rejection by much of "mainstream" society, are also resilient and resourceful in developing successful family relationships (Oswald, 2002). Thus, according to many researchers, there is little empirical evidence that family change is synonymous with family decline.

The Family Is Stronger than Ever

Do our nostalgic myths about the past misinterpret the contemporary family as weak and on the decline? Some writers think so, asserting that modern family life is much more loving than in the past. Consider the treatment of women and children in colonial days: If they disobeyed strict male authority, they were often severely punished. And, in contrast to some of our sentimental notions, only a small number of white, middle-class families enjoyed a life that was both gentle and genteel:

> For *every nineteenth-century middle-class family that protected its wife and child within the family circle . . . there was an Irish or a German girl scrubbing floors in that middle-class home, a Welsh boy mining coal to keep the home-baked*

goodies warm, a black girl doing the family laundry, a black mother and child picking cotton to be made into clothes for the family, and a Jewish or an Italian daughter in a sweatshop making "ladies" dresses or artificial flowers for the family to purchase (Coontz, 1992: 11–12).

Some social scientists argue that despite myriad problems, families are happier today than in the past because of the increase in multigenerational relationships. Many people have living grandparents, feel closer to them, and often receive both emotional and economic support from these family members. The recent growth of the older segment of the population has produced four-generation families. On the one hand, more adults in their 60s may be stressed out because they are caring for 80- to 100-year-old parents. On the other hand, more children and grandchildren grow up knowing and enjoying their older relatives (see Chapter 17).

Families are stronger now than in the past, some claim, because they have more equitable roles at home and are more tolerant of diverse family forms (such as single-parent homes, unmarried couple homes, and families with adopted children). And most Americans believe that marriage is a lifetime commitment that should end only under extreme circumstances, such as domestic violence (Thornton and Young-DeMarco, 2001).

Despite a sharp increase in the number of two-income families, in 1997 children between the ages of 3 and 12 spent, on average, about 3 to 5 more hours a week with their parents than they did in 1981. The time spent together included activities such as reading, playing, conversing, and being in the same room while a parent did household tasks. Thus, contrary to popular belief, children spend more time with parents today than several decades ago, and despite women's greater participation in the labor force (Sandberg and Hofferth, 2001).

Parents often feel guilty about not spending enough time with their children. In reality, what has changed is not the amount of family time, but the pace of family life when both parents work. Parents have to squeeze in household chores between jobs and attending their children's activities, and children often have highly scheduled lives because of numerous school and extracurricular activities (Daly, 2001).

Each of the three schools of thought provides evidence for its position. How, then, can we decide which perspective to believe? Is the family weak, or is it strong? The answer depends largely on how we define, measure, and interpret family "weakness" and family "strength," issues we address in Chapter 2. For better or worse, the family has never been static and continues to change.

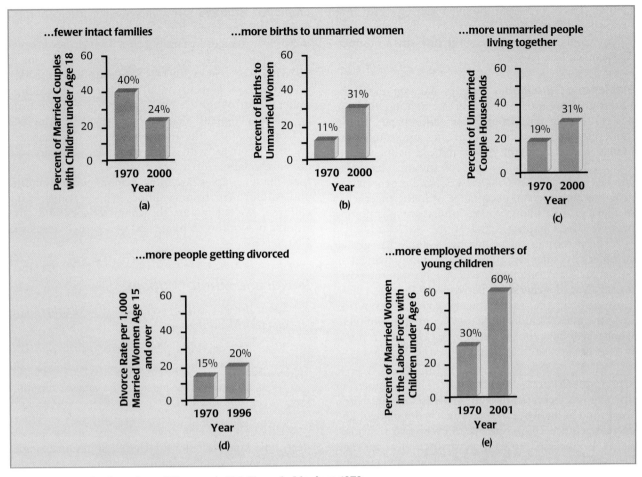

FIGURE 1.3 **An Overview of Changes in U.S. Households since 1970**

SOURCES: Bachu and O'Connell, 2001; Fields and Casper, 2001; Labor Force Statistics, stats.bls.gov/news.release/famee.t04.htm (accessed March 1, 2003).

Trends in Changing Families

The family is clearly changing. But how? And why? Demographic transitions, shifts in the racial and ethnic composition of families, and economic transformations have all played a role in these changes.

Demographic Changes

Two demographic changes have had especially far-reaching consequences for family life. First, fertility rates have declined (see Chapter 11). Since the end of the eighteenth century, most American women have been bearing fewer children, having them closer together, and finishing child rearing at an earlier age. Second, the average age of the population has risen from 17 in the mid-1800s to nearly 36 in 2001 (Kinsella and Velkoff, 2001). Both these shifts mean that a larger proportion of the U.S. population now experiences the "empty-nest syndrome"—the departure of grown children from the home—at an earlier age, as well as earlier grandparenthood and prolonged widowhood (see Chapters 17 and 18).

We see other changes in the composition of households as well: a large number of singles and cohabitants, higher rates of marriage and divorce, more one-parent families and working mothers, and a rapid increase in the number of stepfamilies (see *Figure 1.3*). We'll look at these changes briefly now and examine them more closely in later chapters.

Changes in Family and Nonfamily Households The Census Bureau divides households into two categories: family and nonfamily. A *family household* consists of the two or more people living together who are related through marriage, birth, or adoption. *Nonfamily households* include people who live alone or with non-relatives (roommates, boarders, or cohabitants). In 2000, 31 percent of all households were nonfamily households, a substantial increase from 19 percent in 1970 (Fields and Casper, 2001).

As *Figure 1.3a* shows, the percentage of married-couple households with children under age 18 declined from 40 percent in 1970 to 24 percent in 2000. The percentage of children under age 18 living in one-parent families has more than doubled during this same period (see "Data Digest"). Part of the increase in one-parent families is due to the surge of births to unmarried women (see *Figure 1.3b*).

Singles and Cohabitants Singles make up one of the fastest-growing groups. The decrease in household size has resulted in part from fewer children per family, more one-parent families, and greater age segregation, that is, the tendency of young and old people to live separately. The number of cohabitants has also climbed since 1970 (see *Figure 1.3c*) and is expected to grow because societal acceptance of living together is increasing, and many young adults are postponing marriage (see Chapters 8 and 9).

The percentage of people living alone has grown considerably since 1970. For baby-boom women in particular (**baby boomers** are people born in the post–World War II generation between 1946 and 1964), more divorces, increased longevity, and shaky retirement incomes could mean that fewer midlife and older women will have the option of living alone even if this is their preference (see Chapters 17 and 18).

Marriage–Divorce–Remarriage The number of divorces has increased over the years (see *Figure 1.3d*). Even though divorce rates have reached a plateau and decreased since 2000, one out of every two first marriages is expected to end in divorce (Kreider and Fields, 2002; see also Chapter 15). Teen marriages and marriages entered into because the woman became pregnant are especially likely to unravel.

Stepfamilies are becoming much more common. About 17 percent of all children live in a stepfamily (Fields, 2001). Whether or not a couple has children seems to have little effect on divorce or remarriage. Women with lower educational levels are more likely to divorce and to remarry than are those with college degrees. This suggests that age and maturation are important factors in lasting marriages. We'll examine marriage, divorce, and remarriage more extensively in Chapters 10, 15, and 16.

One-Parent Families As more adults remain single into their 30s and as divorce rates increase, the number of children living with one parent also increases. The number of one-parent families has almost tripled, from 9 percent in 1960 to nearly 32 percent in 2000 (Fields and Casper, 2001).

The proportion of children living with a never-married parent has also increased, from 4 percent in 1960 to 42 percent in 2000. Of all one-parent families, 83 percent are mother–child families (Fields and Casper, 2001; Hobbs and Stoops, 2002). We'll look at one-parent households in several later chapters.

Employed Mothers The increased participation of mothers in the labor force has been one of the most important changes in family roles. Two-earner couples with children under age 18 rose from 31 percent in 1976 to 70 percent in 2001 (U.S. Census Bureau, 2002).

About 55 percent of all mothers with children under 1 year of age are in the labor force, down from an all-time high of 59 percent in 1998 (Bachu and O'Connell, 2001). In addition, six out of every ten married women with children under 6 years old are in the labor force (see *Figure 1.3e*). This means that many couples are now coping with domestic and employment responsibilities while raising young children. We'll examine the characteristics and constraints of working mothers and two-earner couples in Chapter 13.

Racial and Ethnic Changes

What do you call a person who speaks three languages? Multilingual.

What do you call a person who speaks two languages? Bilingual.

What do you call a person who speaks one language? American.

Although, as this joke suggests, many people stereotype (and ridicule) the United States as a single-language and a single-culture society, it's the most multicultural country in the world. Diversity is booming, ethnic groups speak many languages, and foreign-born families live in all states.

Ethnic Families Are Booming In 2002, almost 12 percent of the U.S. population was foreign-born, up from 8 percent in 1990. Only one-sixth—about 5 million—are from Europe and Canada. The other 24 million come from South America, Latin America, Central America (including Mexico), Asia, and the Caribbean (Schmidley, 2003). Because of huge immigration waves and high birth rates, 1 in 5 people are either foreign-born or first-generation U.S. residents (Bernstein, 2002). Our multicultural rainbow includes about 150 distinct ethnic or racial groups among the almost 285 million people living in the United States today.

By 2025 only 62 percent of the U.S. population will be white, down from 86 percent in 1950 (see *Figure 1.4*). For the first time, in 2003 Latinos edged past African Americans as the nation's largest minority. The Latino population is now 37 million, whereas blacks number 36.2 million (Bernstein, 2003). Chinese, Filipinos, and Japanese still rank as the largest Asian American groups. Since 1990, however, Southeast Asians, Indians, Koreans, Pakistanis, and Bangladeshis have registered

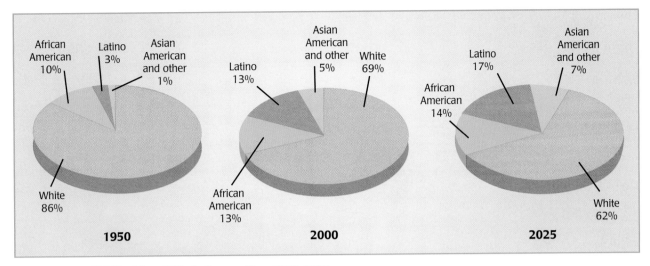

FIGURE 1.4 **U.S. Racial and Ethnic Composition, 1950–2025**

SOURCES: U.S. Census Bureau, www.census.gov/population/www.pop-profile/nat-proj.html
(accessed October 24, 1997); U.S. Census Bureau, www.census.gov/population/cen2000/phc-t08/phc-t-08.pdf
(accessed March 4, 2003).

much faster growth. Mexicans, Puerto Ricans, and Cubans are the largest groups among Latinos, but people from Central and South American countries—such as El Salvador, Guatemala, Colombia, and Honduras—have been immigrating in very high numbers.

Ethnic Families Speak Many Languages Despite the earlier joke about Americans speaking only one language, 18 percent—almost 47 million people—speak a language other than English at home. The largest group, 11 percent, is Latinos. Then the number drops to Chinese (0.8 percent); French (0.6 percent); Portuguese, German, and Tagalog (0.5 percent each); Italian and Vietnamese (0.4 percent each); and myriad other languages such as Greek, Hebrew, Arabic, Russian, Navajo, Korean, Japanese, and Hindi (*Language Spoken at Home*, 2000).

In some states—especially California, New York, New Jersey, Texas, and Florida—the percentages of people who *don't* speak English are higher than those who *do* speak English. At the county level, for instance, a large proportion of residents speak Spanish rather than English: Hidalgo County, Texas (84 percent); Miami–Dade County, Florida (68 percent); Hudson County, New Jersey (54 percent); Los Angeles County, California; and Bronx County, New York (54 percent each) (*Speaking a Language Other Than English*, 2001).

Nationwide, the Asian-language market includes more than 300 newspapers (92 dailies), 50 radio programs, 75 television shows, and miscellaneous products such as phone directories. By the mid-1990s one Orange County, California, station was broadcasting in Vietnamese 18 hours a day, and another southern California station was entirely Korean-language (Trumbull, 1995). One company publishes a Chinese-language Yellow Pages for New York City (Dortch, 1997).

Where Ethnic Families Live By 2000, foreign-born groups surpassed the national average of 10 percent in nine states: California (26 percent), New York (20 percent), Florida (18 percent), Hawaii (16 percent), Nevada and New Jersey (15 percent each), Arizona (13 percent), and Massachusetts and Texas (12 percent each) (Schmidley, 2001).

Except for some parts of the Midwest, ethnic families live in all parts of the country but tend to cluster in certain regions (see *Figure 1.5* on page 22). Such clustering reflects job opportunities and established immigrant communities that can help newcomers find housing and jobs. In other cases, past federal government policies have encouraged some communities to accept refugees from Southeast Asia, forced many American Indians to live on reservations, and implemented a variety of exclusionary immigration laws that concentrated some Asian groups to specific geographic areas. Overall,

■ Approximately 53 percent of blacks live in the South, about 10 percent are in the West, and the remaining 37 percent are split evenly between the Midwest and Northeast.

■ More than half of Latinos, many of whom are from Mexico, reside in California and Texas. Nearly 60 percent of recent Latino immigrants in Washington, D.C., identify themselves as Central Americans, and about 31 describe themselves as Salvadorans.

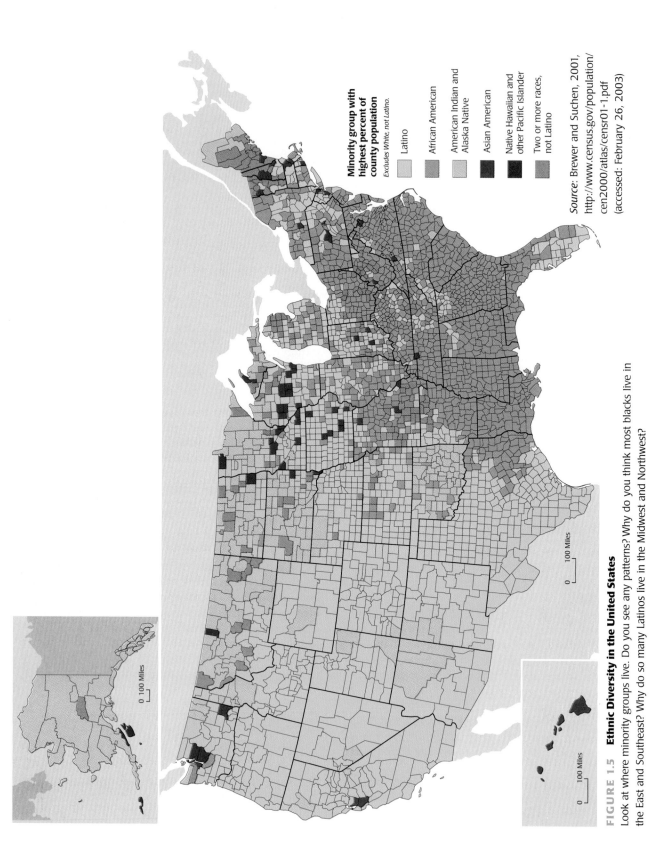

Minority group with highest percent of county population

Excludes White, not Latino.

- Latino
- African American
- American Indian and Alaska Native
- Asian American
- Native Hawaiian and other Pacific Islander
- Two or more races, not Latino

Source: Brewer and Suchen, 2001, http://www.census.gov/population/cen2000/atlas/censr01-1.pdf (accessed: February 26, 2003)

0   100 Miles

0   100 Miles

0   100 Miles

FIGURE 1.5   Ethnic Diversity in the United States

Look at where minority groups live. Do you see any patterns? Why do you think most blacks live in the East and Southeast? Why do so many Latinos live in the Midwest and Northwest?

- A majority of Asians and Pacific Islanders (57 percent) live in just three states: California, New York, and Hawaii.

- More than 60 percent of Chinese Americans live in California or New York. About two-thirds of Filipinos and Japanese live in California or Hawaii. Asian Indian and Korean families are somewhat less concentrated geographically, although large numbers live in a handful of states that include Illinois, New Jersey, Texas, California, and New York.

- About 48 percent of American Indians, Eskimos, and Aleuts are concentrated in the West. Many (13 percent) live in Oklahoma. The next most likely states of residence include Arizona, California, New Mexico, and Alaska (Benokraitis, 2002).

This brief overview shows that ethnic families are numerous and increasing, speak many languages (though primarily Spanish), and live in practically every state. We'll examine ethnic families in every chapter, especially Chapter 4.

Why Are Families Changing?

Clearly, we are seeing changes in the family. These changes reflect both the choices people make (such as choosing to marry later or to divorce) and the constraints that limit those choices (such as economic problems or caring for elderly parents).

To study people's choices, social scientists often take a **micro-level perspective**, focusing on individuals' social interaction in specific settings. To understand the constraints that limit people's options, social scientists use a **macro-level perspective**, focusing on large-scale patterns that characterize society as a whole. Both perspectives and how they interact are crucial in understanding the family.

Micro-level Influences on the Family

Consider the following scenario: Two students meet in college, fall in love, marry after graduation, find well-paying jobs, and live the good life, feasting on brie and lobster, driving a Corvette, and the like. Then they have an unplanned child. The wife quits her job to take care of the baby, the husband loses his job, and the wife goes to work part time. She has difficulty balancing her multiple roles of mother, wife, and employee. The stress and arguments between the partners increase, and the marriage ends.

When I ask my students what went wrong, most of them take a micro viewpoint and criticize the individuals: "They should have saved some money," "They didn't need a Corvette," "Haven't they heard about contraceptives?" and so on. Almost all my students blame the divorce on the two people involved because they were unrealistic or immature or made "lousy" decisions.

On the one hand, there's much to be said for micro-level perspectives. As you will see throughout this book, some of the biggest societal changes that have had a major impact on families began with the efforts of one person who took a stand on an issue. For example, Mary Beth Whitehead refused to give up her right to see the baby she bore as a surrogate mother. The ensuing court battles created national debates about the ethics of the new reproductive technologies. As a result, many states have instituted surrogacy legislation (see Chapter 11).

On the other hand, micro explanations should be kept in perspective. Many marriage and family textbooks and pop psychology books stress the importance of individual choices but ignore macro-level variables. Micro analyses are limited. They cannot explain some of the things over which families have very little control. For these broader analyses, we must turn to macro explanations.

Macro-level Influences on the Family

Constraints such as economic forces, technological innovations, popular culture, social movements, and family policies limit our choices. These are broad social issues that require macro-level explanations.

Economic Forces   The Industrial Revolution and urbanization sparked widespread changes that affected the family (see Chapter 3). By the late eighteenth century, factories replaced the local industries that had employed large numbers of women and children. As families became less self-sufficient and family members worked outside the home, parents' control over their children diminished.

In the latter half of the twentieth century, many corporations moved their companies to developing countries to increase their profits. Such moves resulted in relocations and unemployment for many U.S. workers. These changes created job dissatisfaction, unemployment, and financial distress that disrupted many marital relationships and families.

Many African Americans have been concerned that immigration, another external factor, is diminishing their job opportunities. As you've just read, Latinos and Asians constitute the fastest-growing groups in the United States. A large proportion of African Americans are employed in skilled and semiskilled blue-collar jobs. The influx of new immigrants, who are also competing for such jobs, constitutes a serious economic threat to many working-class blacks and, consequently, to their families (see Chapters 4 and 13).

As the U.S. economy has shifted, millions of low-paying service jobs have replaced higher-paying manufacturing jobs. This has wrought havoc with many families' finances, contributing to the rise in the number of employed mothers. At the other end of the continuum, the high-tech sector requires people to spend more time learning new skills. Learning new skills often means postponing marriage and having children (see Chapters 9 and 11).

Technological Innovations Advances in medical and other health-related technologies have led to a decline in birth rates and to a longer life. On the one hand, the invention and availability of the birth-control pill in the early 1960s meant that women could prevent unwanted pregnancies, pursue a higher education, and seek long-term jobs. Improved prenatal and postnatal care has also released women from the need to bear six or seven children so that one or two will survive.

On the other hand, because the average man or woman can now expect to live into his or her 80s and beyond, poverty after retirement is more likely. Medical services can eat up savings, and the middle-aged—sometimes called the "sandwich generation"—cope with both raising their own children and helping their aged parents (see Chapters 12, 17, and 18).

Televisions, videocassette recorders (VCRs), digital video discs (DVDs), microwave ovens, and personal computers (PCs) have also affected families positively and negatively. On the negative side, for example, multiple television sets in a home often dilute parental control and supervision of programs that young children watch.

On the positive side, television can enhance children's intellectual development. For example, children aged 2 to 7 who spend a few hours a week watching educational programs such as *Sesame Street, Mister Rogers' Neighborhood, Reading Rainbow, Captain Kangaroo, Mr. Wizard's World,* and *3-2-1 Contact* have higher academic test scores three years later than those who didn't watch such educational programs. Children who watch many hours of entertainment programs and cartoons have lower test scores than those who rarely watch such programs.

The positive effects of educational programming are strongest for children aged 2 and 3. TV may have a greater impact on young children because they are less likely than older children to have formal preschool instruction (Wright et al., 2001). During adolescence, television provides a common source of interest that peers discuss and can share with their parents. Television

also provides useful information about other cultures and a variety of work roles.

Some people feel that electronic mail (e-mail) and discussion lists are intrusive because enthusiasts replace close offline relationships with superficial but time-consuming online relationships. College students who spend four to seven hours a day online for nonacademic reasons may earn low grades and experience the risk of dismissal, poorer health because of sleep loss, and greater social isolation. Among other problems, frequent Internet usage decreases participation in extracurricular activities and opportunities to meet new people (Reisberg, 2000). In the general population, people who spend more than ten hours a week on the Internet report a decrease in social activities and less time talking on the phone to friends and family (Nie and Erbring, 2000).

On the other hand, e-mail has encouraged long-distance conversations between parents, children, and relatives that might otherwise not occur because of busy schedules or high telephone costs. Family members who are scattered coast to coast can become more connected by exchanging photos on their own Web pages (including background music and voice commentary), organizing family reunions, tracking down distant relatives, or tracing their ancestral roots (Kanaley, 2000).

Popular Culture Popular culture—which includes television, pop music, magazines, radio, advertising, sports, hobbies, fads, fashions, and movies—is one of our major sources of information *and* misinformation about our values, roles, and family life. Television is especially influential in transmitting both facts and fictions. According to TV-Free America, a national nonprofit organization, in a 65-year lifetime the average American spends 9 years in front of a TV set (www.tvturnoff.org).

Compared with even five years ago, today there are many programs on black families (see *Table 1.1*). Even though Asian and Latino families are huge consumers of prime-time television, they're almost invisible, except for an occasional show such as *George Lopez*. In the music industry, some Latino singers such as Ricky Martin, Marc Anthony, Jennifer Lopez, and Shakira are "hot." Nonetheless, they have nothing to do with family shows. And, to my knowledge, there isn't a single family program that features Asian or Middle Eastern families. We'll examine the effect of popular culture on families in Chapter 5.

Social Movements Over the years, a number of social movements have changed family life. These macro-level movements include the civil rights movement, the women's movement, gay rights movement, and, most recently, a marriage movement.

The *civil rights movement* of the 1960s had a great impact on most U.S. families, black and white. Because of affirmative action legislation, many African Americans and Latinos were able to take advantage of educational and economic opportunities that improved their families' socioeconomic status (see Chapter 4). As a result, many black and Latino students got into privileged colleges and universities, families received money for small businesses, and a number of bright employees were promoted (see Chapter 13).

The *women's movements*—in the late 1800s and especially in the 1970s—transformed many women's roles and, consequently, family life. As women gained more rights in law, education, and employment, many became less financially dependent on men and started questioning traditional assumptions about gender roles.

The upside of this is that women—particularly white, middle-class women—enjoyed more personal and professional options and provided their children with less stereotypical female role models. The downside, according to many scholars, is that when women became sexually "liberated," they entered willingly into nonmarital sexual relationships (see Chapter 7). The result was more out-of-wedlock children who were not supported by their biological fathers.

The *gay rights movement* that began in the 1970s challenged discriminatory laws in such areas as housing, adoption, and employment. Many lesbian women and gay men (as well as sympathetic heterosexuals) feel that the challenges have resulted in very modest changes so far. There has been progress, however. Children with gay or lesbian parents, for example, are less likely to be as stigmatized as they were a decade ago. Many companies now provide benefits to the gay or lesbian partners of employees, a number of adoption agencies assist lesbians and gays who want to become parents, and numerous municipalities or states now recognize civil unions (see Chapters 8–12).

People who are alarmed by marital dissolution and the increase in cohabitation rates are joining a burgeoning *marriage movement*. Among other things, the marriage movement seeks to repeal no-fault divorce laws, to reduce the rates and state benefits for out-of-wedlock children, to promote abstinence among young people, to increase funding on marriage-supportive research, and to embrace women's homemaker roles.

In addition, the marriage movement encourages proponents to lobby lawmakers to pass state "covenant marriage" laws requiring couples to take mandatory premarital counseling classes and "marital skills" programs (see Chapter 9). As the box titled "Should Uncle Sam Be a Matchmaker?" on page 26 shows, however, many people feel that the government should stay out of people's private lives.

Communitarians, a group that you met earlier in this chapter, support the marriage movement and similar organizations. They believe that most current social problems (such as juvenile delinquency, high divorce rates, and high out-of-wedlock birth rates) could be solved by promoting "traditional" family values. These values include enhancing marital stability, reinforcing parental responsibility, reining in children's premature sexualization, and curbing the excessive societywide individualism that endangers many children's well-being (see Elshtain et al., 1993). In contrast, many liberals believe that numerous family problems are due to macro-level forces, such as government policies that subsidize middle-class families but penalize poor and working-class families.

Family Policies Government policy affects practically every aspect of family life. Thousands of rules and regulations, both civil and criminal—at the local, state, and federal levels—govern domestic matters: laws about when and whom we can marry, how to dissolve a marriage, how children will fare after a divorce, how we treat one another in the home, and even how we dispose of our dead.

Families do not just passively accept policy changes, however. Parents have played critical roles in such major social policy changes as the education of disabled children and joint custody of children after divorce. Chapter 18 and sections of several other chapters examine the effects of government policy on families in greater detail.

A Cross-Cultural and Global Perspective

Why does this textbook include material on U.S. subcultures (American Indians, African Americans, Asian Americans, Middle Eastern Americans, and Latinos) and on cultures in other countries? First, unless you are a full-blooded American Indian, your kin were slaves or immigrants to this country. They contributed their cultural beliefs, and their practices shaped current family institutions. Modern U.S. families are a mosaic of many cultural, religious, ethnic, racial, and socioeconomic groups. A traditional white, middle-class model is not adequate for understanding our marriages and families.

A second reason for this multicultural and cross-cultural approach is that the world is shrinking. Compared with even ten years ago, more people are traveling outside the United States, more students

Should Uncle Sam Be a Matchmaker?

In 1996, President Clinton signed new welfare legislation, the Personal Responsibility and Work Opportunity Reconciliation Act (see Chapter 18). One of the goals of the act was to "encourage the formation and maintenance of two-parent families."

In 2003, Congress passed a bill that allotted $1.5 billion over five years to promote marriage as part of welfare reform. The money would be used for a variety of promarriage initiatives, including the following:

• Encouraging caseworkers to counsel pregnant women to marry the fathers
• Judging a state's success based on reductions in out-of-wedlock births
• Teaching about the value of marriage in high schools
• Providing divorce counseling for the poor
• Sponsoring experiments to see what programs might produce more marriages

Conservatives initiated these and similar proposals. They believe that the "breakdown of the family"—remaining single, having children outside of marriage, and divorce—is a major "cause" of poverty (see "The Family Is Deteriorating" section earlier in this chapter).

A very vocal marriage movement enthusiastically endorses such laws. According to many of its members, government programs should encourage cohabiting parents to marry and discourage married parents from divorce (Lichter and Crowley, 2002).

Some of the proponents justify marriage initiatives by pointing to the economic costs—from welfare to child support enforcement—that states incur because of high divorce and out-of-wedlock birth rates. Others, such as conservative religious groups (many of which belong to marriage movements), also support promarriage legislation. They maintain that the government should pass policies to support and strengthen marriage because "marriage and family are institutions ordained by God" (Wilcox, 2002).

Promoting matrimony is not a novel idea. A number of states have been using federal welfare money for several years to foster wedlock. West Virginia, for example, gives couples on public assistance an additional $100 a month if they marry or stay married. Some states provide premarital classes. And Oklahoma paid $250,000 to "a couple of gurus to hold 'relationship rallies' on campuses around the state" (Goodman, 2003).

There is a growing consensus among social scientists that two-parent homes are best for children. Compared with children raised in two-parent homes, children raised in single-parent homes are at greater risk of poverty, school dropouts, delinquency, teen pregnancy, and adult joblessness (see Chapters 11–13). Researchers don't know, however, how many people are poor because they are unmarried and how many are unmarried because they are poor.

Many poor couples want to marry. Often, though, single mothers are reluctant to tie the knot if their partners cannot or do not work or if the man seems disinterested in or abusive with the mother's or couple's children (Ooms, 2002).

Feminists point out that matrimony doesn't guarantee economic benefits such as a steady income from a male breadwinner. A husband's income is often too low to lift a family out of poverty (see Chapter 13). In addition, critics charge, promoting marriage for low-income women stigmatizes them (but not high-income unmarried mothers) and compels them to stay in abusive or unhappy relationships.

Some directors of fatherhood programs are also opposed to promarriage legislation. They believe that marriage is not a "quick fix" because many poor men have a lot of problems. As Robert Brady of the Young Fathers Program in Denver observed, "I wonder if these conservatives would be so dedicated to marriage promotion if it was their daughters they were trying to marry these guys off to" (Starr, 2001: 68). In addition, critics of the promarriage initiatives feel that the government should stay out of people's private matters.

STOP AND THINK . . .

• Should the government pressure low-income mothers to marry? Do you think that such strategies will work in reducing poverty?

• Are there other ways to decrease the economic stresses that plague poor households and poor children?

from abroad attend North American colleges and universities, and more exchange programs for students and scholars are offered at all educational levels. In the late twentieth century, the Internet changed our communication processes significantly, shrinking our modern world. As members of the global community, we should be aware of family practices and customs in other cultures.

On Mother's Day in May, 2000, hundreds of thousands of women across the United States and all walks of life, converged on Washington, D.C. for the Million Mom March. The purpose of the march was to protest lenient gun-control laws that result in the deaths of children and teenagers through suicide, accidents, and homicides in urban neighborhoods and shooting sprees in suburban schools.

A third reason for this text's perspective is that U.S. businesses are continuing to recognize the importance of understanding cross-cultural differences. Since the late 1980s, more companies have been requiring their employees to take crash courses about other cultures before they are sent abroad. For example, one of my students who won a job with a Fortune 500 company felt she had gained an edge over some very tough competition because of her knowledge of Portuguese and of Brazil's cultural institutions.

The business sector is not the only one that has learned to appreciate diversity. Many educators believe that multicultural competence is essential to the professional preparation of researchers, faculty, counselors, and therapists who will study and interact with people from many different socioeconomic and national backgrounds in the twenty-first century.

Finally, understanding the customs of other countries challenges our notion that U.S. marriage forms are "natural" or inevitable. According to Hutter (1998: 12), "Americans have been notorious for their lack of understanding and ignorance of other cultures. This is compounded by their gullible ethnocentric belief in the superiority of all things American and not only has made them unaware of how others live and think but also has given them a distorted picture of their own life." Hutter's perspective—and that of this book—is that understanding other people helps us understand ourselves.

Conclusion

Families are transforming rather than destroying themselves. Although there have been *changes* in family structures, families of all kinds want caring, supportive, comforting, and enduring relationships. There is nothing inherently better about one type of family form over another. Family structures don't appear by themselves. People create families that meet their needs for love and security.

These greatly expanded *choices* in family structure and function mean that the definition of family no longer reflects the interests of any one social class, gender, or ethnic group. This fluidity generates new questions. Who, for example, will ensure that our children will grow up to be healthy and responsible adults if both parents must work outside the home? Is it possible to pursue personal happiness without sacrificing our obligations to other family members?

Our choices often are limited by *constraints*, especially at the macro level, because of economic and political policies. To deal with changes, choices, and constraints, we need as much information as possible about the family. In the next chapter we will see how scientists conduct research on families, gathering data that make it possible for us to track the trends described in this and other chapters and to make informed decisions about our choices.

SUMMARY

1. Although the nuclear family—composed of husband, wife, and children—is still predominant in U.S. society, the definition of *family* has been challenged to include such less traditional arrangements as single parents, childless couples, foster parents, and siblings sharing a home. Advances in reproductive technology have opened up the possibility of still more varied redefinitions of the family.

2. The family continues to fulfill basic functions such as producing and socializing children, providing family members with emotional support, legitimizing and regulating sexual activity, and placing family members in society.

3. Marriages, families, and kinship systems vary in terms of whether marriages are monogamous or polygamous, whether familial authority is vested in the man or in the woman or both share power, and whether a new family resides with the family of the man or of the woman or creates its own home.

4. The many deep-rooted myths about the family include erroneous beliefs about how the family was in "the good old days," the "naturalness" of marriage and family as human interpersonal and social arrangements, the self-sufficiency of the family, the family as a refuge from outside pressures, and the "perfect family."

5. Social scientists generally agree that the family is changing. They disagree, however, as to whether it is changing in drastic and essentially unhealthy ways, whether it is simply continuing to adapt and adjust to changing circumstances, or whether it is changing in ways that will ultimately make the family stronger.

6. Many changes are occurring in U.S. families: There is more racial and ethnic diversity, membership is more varied than the traditional nuclear family, and there are more single-parent families, stepfamilies, and families in which the mother works outside the home.

7. The reasons for changes in the family can be analyzed on two levels. Micro-level explanations emphasize individual behavior: the choices that people make and the personal and interpersonal factors that influence these choices. Macro-level explanations focus on large-scale patterns that characterize society as a whole and often constrain individual options. Some constraints arise from economic factors, technological advances, the popular culture, social movements, and government policies that affect families.

8. Understanding the family requires an appreciation of racial, gender, ethnic, religious, and cultural diversity, both at home and around the world.

KEY TERMS

marriage 3
norm 3
common-law marriage 4
bigamy 4
family 5
fictive kin 5
nuclear family 6
incest taboo 7
endogamy 8
exogamy 8
socialization 9

roles 9
primary groups 9
secondary groups 9
social class 10
family of orientation 10
family of procreation 10
kinship system 10
extended family 10
monogamy 10

serial monogamy 10
polygamy 10
baby boomers 20
micro-level
    perspective 23
macro-level
    perspective 23

TAKING IT FURTHER

Examine U.S. and Global Family Trends

Does your instructor want you to compare family trends and patterns in the United States and worldwide? Here are a few sites to get you started:

The **United Nations Statistics Division** maintains a list of statistical bureaus of nations to help you find family and household information for other countries.

unstats.un.org/unsd/methods/inter-natlinks/sd_natstat.htm

International Data Base at the U.S. Census Bureau offers a variety of country-level data, including marital status, family planning, ethnicity, religion, labor force, and employment.

www.census.gov/ftp/pub/ipc/www/idbnew.html

Statistical Abstract of the United States, also from the U.S. Census Bureau, provides a wealth of information about marriage, remarriage, family characteristics, living arrangements, divorce, and hundreds of other variables.

www.census.gov/statab/www

The Population Reference Bureau maintains four sites that may be valuable in your research.

www.prb.org, the main Website, offers excerpts or full text of many of the Population Reference Bureau's publications on U.S. and international issues.

www.popnet.org allows the visitor to view a clickable world map and provides a comprehensive directory of population-related Websites.

www.ameristat.org gives summaries, in graphics and text, of 14 demographic characteristics of the U.S. population, including marriage and family, income and poverty, fertility, and race and ethnicity.

www.measurecommunication.org is devoted to disseminating information and data on population, health, and nutrition in developing countries.

The Internet Scout Project, an invaluable research resource, offers weekly summaries of recent sites on many family-related issues.

www.scout.cs.wisc.edu

And more: If your instructor assigns a "do-whatever-interests-you" project, look at www.prenhall.com/benokraitis for Websites that include a variety of ethnic families, black communities, social movements, global statistics, liberal and conservative think tanks about the family, the social and economic implications of information technologies, groups that endorse and denounce polygamy, and an online comic strip of a middle-class Latino family.

INVESTIGATE WITH RESEARCH NAVIGATOR

Welcome to the Research Navigator™ feature that will end each chapter of this textbook. To access the Research Navigator™ Website, please find the access code on the inside front cover of your *Evaluating Online Resources Guide.* (If your textbook was not packaged with an *Evaluating Online Resources Guide,* you can purchase an access code at the Research Navigator™ site.) Visit the Research Navigator™ site at http://www.researchnavigator.com and click on REGISTER under the New Users tab. Enter your access code and relevant information to create your own LOGIN NAME and PASSWORD. After registering, you can return to this site and fill in the LOGIN NAME and PASSWORD on the initial page.

On the opening page, you have three relevant search engines to begin your research. They include:

1) **ContentSelect**™—a collection of peer-reviewed academic journals organized by discipline; 2) *New York Times* Search-by-Subject archive that includes an 18-month database of articles from the New York Times; and 3) *Best of the Web* Link Library—a wealth of links divided by topic. At the end of each chapter you will find key words as a starting point for your research. Enter these words into the various search fields while selecting the appropriate databases.

Please search the Research Navigator™ site using the following key search terms:

monogamy
kinship
patriarchy

Studying Marriage and the Family

DATADIGEST

- **A typical interview can cost about $75 an hour,** including training, pretesting, transportation, wages, and follow-up interviews.

- The **return of census questionnaires** has decreased over the years: 78 percent in 1970, 75 percent in 1980, and 65 percent in 1990 and 2000.

- During the 2000 census, the **cost per individual mailing was $2, compared with $36** every time a census worker visited a nonrespondent's home as part of a follow-up when the form wasn't filled out.

- **People are less trusting of some types of surveys** than of others. In a recent study, 81 percent of respondents were willing to rely on scientific studies that describe the causes of disease, 63 percent believed consumer survey reports of how many people like a particular product, but only 54 percent said they trusted the results of general public opinion polls.

- From 2000 to 2001, businesses increased their spending on **online survey research** by 53 percent, to $400 million.

Sources: Crossen, 1994; Edmonston, 1999; Libbon, 2000; Wellner, 2003.

When my mother died recently, the funeral director called *twice* to confirm the information before submitting it to Maryland's Division of Vital Statistics. Even though I provided the same, and accurate, information both times, the death certificate had three errors. First, my mother died at age 87, not 88. Second, she had completed ten years of education, not eight. Third, because my mother never smoked, tobacco did *not* contribute to the cause of her death.

When I saw the mistakes, I winced. Here's a good example, I thought, of why many people—including my students—often distrust statistics. "Statistics mean never having to say you're certain," some quip. Others firmly believe the well-known quote, "There are three kinds of lies: lies, damned lies, and statistics."

Data collection isn't perfect. Nonetheless, it's a far better source of information on families and other topics than personal opinions, experiential anecdotes, or other nonscientific ways of understanding our world.

This chapter will help you evaluate the enormous amount of information we encounter on a daily basis. It will also help you to understand how the researchers cited in this text collected their data. Let's begin with a discussion of why a basic understanding of family theory and research is important.

Why Are Theories and Research Important in Our Everyday Lives?

The very words *theory* and *research* often intimidate people. Many of us may distrust statistics because they often challenge generally accepted beliefs. Most of my students, for example, believe that cohabitation decreases the chance of divorce. They are surprised when the studies that show this is not the case (see Chapter 9).

Should I Consult Dr. Web?

A team of 34 physician-reviewers evaluated almost 20,000 printed pages in English-language sites and more than 2000 pages from Spanish-language sites on four medical conditions on the Web. All of the reviewers were board-certified in family medicine, pediatrics, internal medicine, and other specializations. What did they find?

The researchers concluded that

- Many sites contain contradictory information. In the case of depression, for example, some sites recommend St. John's wort, whereas others state that St. John's wort is ineffective. In fact, St. John's wort, if consumed with other medications such as Prozac, can sometimes be fatal.
- Some sites recommend investigating a breast lump only if it doesn't change over time. Others urge consumers to

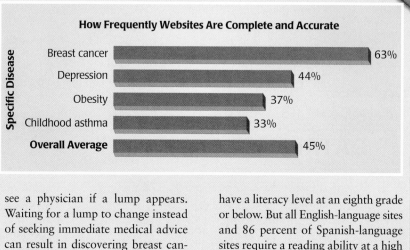

see a physician if a lump appears. Waiting for a lump to change instead of seeking immediate medical advice can result in discovering breast cancer that might be inoperable.

- Many online users may not be able to read the information they find. Nearly half of adults in the United States have a literacy level at an eighth grade or below. But all English-language sites and 86 percent of Spanish-language sites require a reading ability at a high school level or higher.

Source: Adapted from Berland et al., 2001a, 2001b.

There are three very practical reasons why theory and research are important to us: 1) what we don't know can hurt us, 2) theories and research help us understand ourselves and our families, and 3) they improve our ability to think more critically and make informed decisions in our own marriages and families.

What We Don't Know Can Hurt Us

Millions of people use the Internet to buy products, do research for their jobs, and get information on family issues. When people are perplexed by problems involving divorce and stepfamilies, for example, they often seek help online and offline.

There are numerous reputable online sources of information (see the "Taking It Further" section at the end of this chapter). Many Web sites, however, are maintained by people who know next to nothing about family issues but are looking to make a profit. Some of these sites charge consumers up to $5000 each to become "certified stepfamily counselors" even though there is no such certification process in the United States. Other sites charge people $500 for eight hours of audiotapes on running marriage workshops (Siwolop, 2002).

Needless to say, no one can become knowledgeable about leading such workshops after listening to only a few hours of audiotapes.

An estimated 100 million Americans go online to search for health information. About 75 percent say that what they find influences their decisions about treatment (Rainie and Packel, 2001; Baker et al., 2003). How accurate is the health information on the Web? As the box "Should I Consult Dr. Web?" shows, less than half of the sites offer both complete and accurate information on problems such as depression and childhood obesity, especially on the Spanish-language sites. As a result, the misinformation we get from the Internet can shorten our lives.

Theories and Research Help Us Understand Our Family Life

Theoretical perspectives and research can illuminate many aspects of our everyday family lives. For example, does spanking correct misbehavior? Suppose a 2-year-old throws a temper tantrum at a family barbecue. One adult comments, "What that kid needs is a good smack on the behind." Another person immediately disagrees: "All kids go through this stage. Just ignore it."

CHOICES

Popular Magazines and Self-Help Books: Let the Reader Beware

Authors of self-help books are extremely well-adjusted, free of phobias and anxieties, and bursting with self-esteem. Right? Wrong. A best-selling book on phobias, for example, lacks the author's photo because he has a phobia about having his picture taken (Quick, 1992). Husband and wife co-authors of a two-volume textbook on divorce have been involved in "'the divorce from Hell'—a very public, bitter blizzard of litigation that has spawned nearly 400 legal filings," including arguments about ownership of a low-number auto tag (Ringle, 1999: C1).

Some of the most ardent marriage movement (see Chapter 1) leaders have been divorced at least once. And Dr. Benjamin Spock, a best-selling baby book author and family expert for at least 50 years, agreed with his estranged sons, just before he died at age 94, that he had been too career-driven to spend much time with his family (Maier, 1998).

Many self-help books and articles in popular magazines are bogus because they are based on personal opinion and experience rather than on scholarly research.

Perhaps the single best thing about some magazine articles is that they encourage people to try to change their lives. But they also "violate commonly accepted standards of scholarship" (Rosenblatt and Phillips, 1975). As a result, self-help books and articles can create three serious problems:

1. **They can threaten relationships.** Many articles encourage the reader to make new demands on a spouse or children. Such one-sided changes can increase conflict that the family may not be able to handle.
2. **They can make partners feel inadequate.** Many popular writers tie a person's feelings of adequacy to family relationships. This ignores the satisfaction and self-confidence that people can get from work, friendships, participation in organizations, and solitary pursuits.
3. **They may oversimplify complex problems.** Many popular writers gloss over complicated factors in family relationships. Reduced frequency of sexual intercourse can lead

to depression, some "experts" claim. In fact, many factors may trigger depression, and sex isn't at the top of the list (see Chapters 7 and 10).

STOP AND THINK . . .

As you read articles and books about the family, ask yourself the following questions:

- *Does the writer cite research or clinical experience or only anecdotal material as sources? If the writer cites himself or herself, are the references scholarly or only personal stories? According to one scholar, "If modern science has learned anything in the past century, it is to distrust anecdotal evidence" (Park, 2003: B20).*
- *Does the author describe only a few families with problems but generalize the "findings" to all families?*
- *Does the writer make it sound as though life is exceedingly simple and easy to understand, such as following ten steps for marital happiness? Family interaction and behavior are much more complex than throwing a few ingredients into the pot and stirring.*

Who's right? In fact, empirical studies show that neither ignoring a problem nor inflicting physical punishment stops bad behavior (see Chapter 12).

Theory and research are also important to family practitioners. If counselors, clinicians, and other professionals rely exclusively on anecdotal and personal experiences, their effectiveness will be limited. Instead, successful intervention requires understanding cultural and socioeconomic variations and having a firm grasp of research results that show what works in helping children and families (McGoldrick and Giordano, 1996; Hanson, 1998).

Theories and Research Help Us Think Critically and Make Informed Decisions

Our world is becoming more quantitative. We rarely pick up a magazine or newspaper without coming across

numbers that affect some aspect of our lives. We listen numbly to the probabilities of dying earlier than expected because of our genetic inheritance, lifestyle, or environment. We are inundated with information on the importance of exercising, lowering cholesterol levels, and not smoking.

One of the largest growth industries is parenting materials. Amazon.com lists almost 11,000 titles under the category "Parenting and Families" (Gardner, 2002). If you key in "parenting magazines" using www.google.com, you'll get several million hits.

Some of the information is sound, but much is biased, inaccurate, or generated by unlicensed, self-proclaimed "experts." They whip up anxieties and then sell solutions that include their own books and "consulting" services. As the box "Popular Magazines and Self-Help Books: Let the Reader Beware" shows, one of the best ways to protect yourself against quacks and con artists is to be informed.

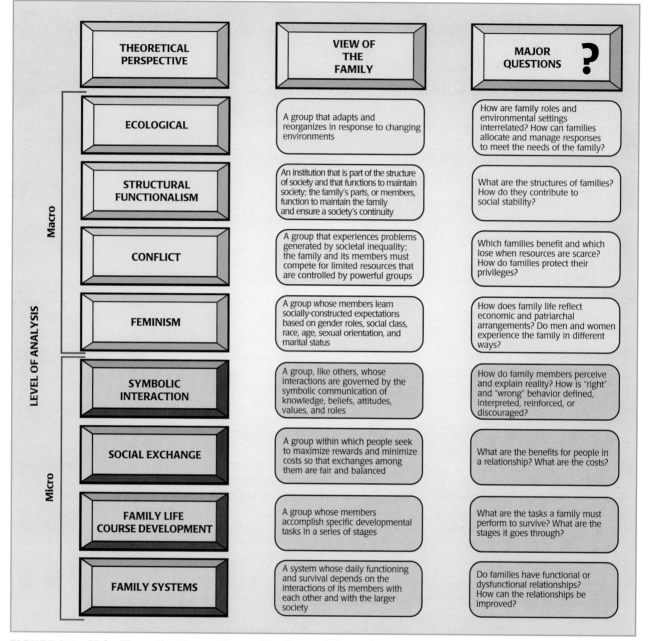

FIGURE 2.1 **Major Theoretical Perspectives on Marriage and the Family**

Students in family courses in which faculty incorporate scientific studies often feel that they and their instructors are on different planets. At the beginning of a semester, for example, I've heard my students grumble, "I took this course to find out how to avoid a divorce after I get married. Who cares about divorce studies!" In fact, by learning something about scientific evidence, you will be able to make more informed decisions about finding a suitable mate and, quite possibly, protect yourself against a divorce. In addition, knowing something about *how* social scientists study families will enhance your ability to think more critically and to vote intelligently on family policy issues (see Chapter 18).

In scholarly journals, peers review research before it is published. In contrast, the mass media are largely immune to criticism, even when their reports are biased, simplistic, or wrong (Gans, 1979). As a result, many people who rely exclusively on the media for information often get a very skewed picture of marriages, families, and other aspects of life.

This chapter will not transform you into a researcher, but it will help you ask some of the right questions when you are deluged with popular nonsense. Let's begin with the most influential theories of marriage and the family that guide social science investigation.

Theoretical Frameworks for Understanding Families

Someone once observed, "I used to have six theories about parenting and no children. Now I have six children and no theories." This quip suggests that there is no relationship between theory and practice. As you saw in Chapter 1, however, theories about families are often translated into policies and laws that affect all of us.

Ideas have consequences. People who theorize that the family is disintegrating might propose such micro-level solutions as cutting off welfare benefits for unmarried mothers. In contrast, those who theorize that the family is changing might propose such macro-level remedies as providing girls and young women with good schooling and jobs that discourage early sexual involvement and pregnancy (see Chapter 11).

As people struggle to understand family-related processes, they develop theories. A **theory** is a set of statements that explains why a phenomenon occurs. Theories drive research, help us to analyze our findings, and, ideally, offer solutions for family problems.

One family sociologist compares theories to the fable of the six blind men who felt different parts of an elephant and arrived at different explanations of what elephants were like. The man who felt the side of the elephant compared it to a massive and immovable wall. The man who felt the trunk thought the elephant was like a rope that could move large objects. Similarly, different theories explain different aspects of the elephant (Burr, 1995).

There are eight influential marriage and the family theories: four macro-level theories (ecological, structural-functional, conflict, and feminist perspectives) and four micro-level theories (symbolic interaction, social exchange, family life course development, and family systems perspectives) (see *Figure 2.1*). Researchers typically use more than one theory in examining any marriage and family topic, and the theories overlap. For greater clarity, let's look at each perspective separately.

The Ecological Perspective

Ecological theory stresses the importance of understanding the relationships between individuals and the social environments that shape human development.

Urie Bronfenbrenner (1979, 1986), a major advocate of ecological theory, proposed four interlocking systems that mold our developmental growth.

As *Figure 2.2* on page 36 illustrates, these systems range from the most "immediate" settings, such as the family and peer group, to more "remote" contexts in which the child is not involved directly, such as technological changes and ideological beliefs:

- The *microsystem* is made up of the interconnected behaviors, roles, and relationships that influence a child's daily life (such as parents' teaching a child toilet training).

- The *mesosystem* comprises the relationships between settings (the home, a day-care center, and schools). Parents interact with teachers and religious groups, children interact with peers, and health-care providers interact with both children and parents.

- The *exosystem* consists of settings or events that a child does not experience directly but that can affect her or his development (such as parents' employment).

- The *macrosystem* reflects complex ideological systems (such as beliefs and values) within a culture or subculture that also affect the child. For example, children who live in an inner-city ghetto often grow up with a different set of values and beliefs than children in an affluent suburb.

All four of these embedded systems, or environments, can help or hinder a child's development and a family's functioning. Successful drug-prevention programs, for example, should be multifaceted: They must understand the teenager's specific family dynamics, address the unique needs of a particular neighborhood, and involve all the citizens (such as local churches, businesses, and colleges) to offer alternatives to high-risk behavior. Such alternatives include not selling alcohol to adolescents, providing parent education and family support, and involving youth in meaningful community projects (Bogenschneider, 1996).

Critique Although many family scientists endorse ecological perspectives, others note several weaknesses. Ecological theories try to explain how growth comes about because of changes in the environment, but explanations of decay or disintegration (such as aging) are "notably absent." In addition, it is not always apparent exactly how and when environments produce changes in individuals and families (White and Klein, 2002). Finally, it is unclear how the interactions between microsystems, mesosystems, exosystems, and macrosystems affect such nontraditional families as stepfamilies, gay and lesbian households, and intergenerational families living under one roof (Ganong et al., 1995).

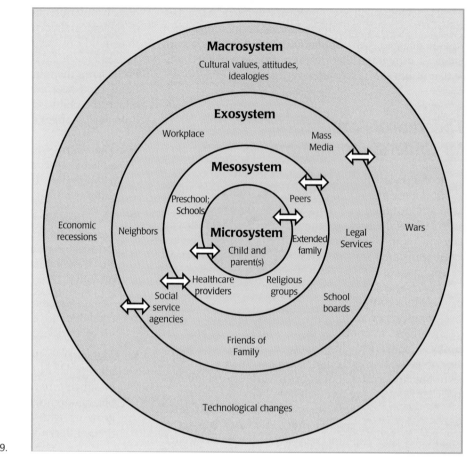

FIGURE 2.2 An Ecological Model of Development

SOURCE: Based on Bronfenbrenner, 1979.

The Structural-Functional Perspective

Structural-functional theory examines the relationship between the family and the larger society. When social scientists study family structure, they examine how the parts work together to fulfill the functions or tasks necessary for the family's survival. Adult family tasks are best accomplished when spouses carry out distinct and specialized roles, one called *instrumental*, the other *expressive* (Parsons and Bales, 1955).

The husband or father, the "breadwinner," plays the instrumental role. Playing the **instrumental role** means providing food and shelter for the family and, at least theoretically, being hardworking, tough, and competitive. Assuming the expressive role, the wife or mother is the homemaker. Playing the **expressive role** means providing the emotional support and nurturing qualities that sustain the family unit and support the husband or father. These family roles characterize what social scientists call the *traditional family*, a family form that many conservative groups would like to resurrect (see Chapter 1).

These and other roles that family members play are *functional*. That is, they preserve order, stability, and

equilibrium. They also provide the physical shelter and emotional support that ensure a family's health and survival. Anything that interferes with these tasks is seen as *dysfunctional* because it jeopardizes the family's smooth functioning. For example, the abuse of one member by another is dysfunctional because the negative physical and emotional consequences threaten the family's continuity.

There are two kinds of functions. **Manifest functions** are intended and recognized; they are present and clearly evident. **Latent functions** are unintended and unrecognized; they are present but not immediately obvious. Consider the wedding. The primary manifest function of the marriage ceremony is to publicize the formation of a new family unit and to legitimize sexual intercourse (see Chapter 1). Its latent functions communicate a "hands-off" message to past or prospective sweethearts, outfit the new couple with household goods and products, and redefine family boundaries to include in-laws or stepfamily members.

Finally, structural functionalists note that the family affects and is affected by such other interrelated institutions as law, politics, and the economy. For example, politicians (many of whom are lawyers and businessmen) play a major role in setting policies that determine, among other things, whether a marriage is legal, who can and cannot adopt a child, and which family members can claim Social Security payments (see Chapter 1).

Critique Structural functionalism, a dominant perspective in the 1950s and 1960s, later came under attack for being so conservative in its emphasis on order and stability that it ignored social change. For example, this perspective typically sees divorce as dysfunctional and as signaling the disintegration of the family rather than indicating positive change (such as individuals leaving an unhappy relationship). Nor does this perspective show how families interact on a daily basis, "up close and personal." Structural functionalism has also been criticized for seeing the family narrowly, through white, male, middle-class lenses (Andersen, 2000).

The Conflict Perspective

A third macro theory, the conflict perspective, has a long history. It became popular in the late 1960s, when African Americans and feminists started to challenge structural functionalism as the dominant explanation of marriage and the family.

Conflict theory examines the ways in which groups disagree, struggle over power, and compete for scarce resources (such as wealth and prestige). In contrast to structural functionalists, conflict theorists see conflict and the resulting changes in traditional roles as natural, inevitable, and often desirable.

According to conflict theory, many family difficulties result from widespread societal problems. For example, shifts in the U.S. economy have led to a decline in manufacturing and the loss of many well-paying blue-collar jobs. This has had a profound influence on many families, sending some into a spiral of downward mobility. Racial discrimination also has a negative impact on many families, diminishing access to health services, education, and employment (see Chapters 4, 13, and 18).

Conflict theorists see society not as cooperative and stable but as a system of widespread inequality. There is continuous tension between the "haves" and the "have-nots." The latter are mainly children, women, minorities, and the poor. Much research based on conflict theory focuses on how those in power—typically white, middle-aged, wealthy, Protestant, Anglo-Saxon males—dominate political and economic decision making in American society.

Critique Some social scientists criticize conflict theory for overemphasizing clashes and coercion at the expense of order and stability. They believe that conflict theory presents a negative view of human nature while neglecting the importance of love and self-sacrifice, which are essential to family relationships. Some critics also feel that the conflict perspective is less useful than other approaches because it emphasizes institutional processes rather than personal choices and constraints in everyday family life.

Feminist Perspectives

Conflict theories provided a springboard for feminist theories, the fourth macro approach. **Feminist theories** include a wide range of perspectives and research procedures. The theories examine, for example, how gender roles (expectations about how men and women should behave) shape relations between women and men in such institutions as politics, the economy, religion, education, and the family.

Despite some widespread misconceptions, feminists are not always women or lesbians. Any person—male or female, straight or gay—who believes that *both* sexes should have equal political, educational, economic, and other rights is a feminist, even if he or she refuses to self-identify with this "label." According to Rebecca West, an English journalist and novelist who died in 1983, "I myself have never been able to find out precisely what feminism is; I only know that people call me a feminist whenever I express sentiments that differentiate me from a doormat."

A second misconception is that feminists hate men. What *is* true is that many feminists are angry about the injustices perpetrated against women in the workplace and the family and have proposed such "radical" changes as equal pay for equal work and men's greater participation in raising children.

There are many types of feminisms (see, for example, Elliot and Mandell, 1995; Kemp and Squires, 1997; Lindsey, 1997). *Liberal feminism* emphasizes social and legal reform to create equal opportunities for women. *Radical feminism* considers male domination a major cause of women's inequality. *Global feminism* focuses on how the intersection of gender with race, social class, and colonization has exploited women in the developing world.

Feminist theory has had a significant impact on our understanding of family life. Since the early 1980s, feminist scholars (women and men) have contributed to family theory and social change in several ways:

- They have pointed out that family life is diverse and should include families from many cultures and ethnic groups as well as those with single parents, lesbian and gay families, stepfamilies, and grandparent–grandchild households.

According to the symbolic interaction perspective, we interact verbally and through gestures. Besides using facial expressions, signing is a "visual language" that helps people who can't hear to communicate.

■ They have initiated legislation on family violence. Feminists have also supported stiffer penalties for men who assault children and women.

■ They have endorsed greater equality between husbands and wives. Feminists have also worked for legislation that provides employed women and men with parental leave rights (see Chapters 5 and 13).

■ They have refocused much of the research to include fathers as involved, responsible, and nurturant family members who have a profound effect on children and the family (see Chapters 4 and 12).

Critique Feminists have challenged discriminatory peer review processes that have routinely excluded women from the "old boy network" (Wenneras and Wold, 1997). However, many feminists are part of an "old girl network." This network has not always welcomed conflicting points of view from African American, Latina, Asian American, American Indian, Muslim, lesbian, working-class, and disabled women in both research and therapeutic settings (Almeida, 1994; Lynn and Todoroff, 1995; S.A. Jackson, 1998).

Another criticism is that much feminist research uses qualitative methods to the exclusion of quantitative methods. In **quantitative research,** researchers assign numbers to qualitative (i.e., nonnumeric) observations by counting and measuring attitudes or behavior. In Chapter 1, for example, all of the figures are based on quantitative research. In **qualitative research,** in contrast, researchers rely on observation and interviews and report their data from the respondents' point of view.

Many feminists maintain that quantitative methods, which emphasize detachment and "objectivity," fail to convey the respondents' experiences on such topics as everyday communication and gender power differences (see Adams and Sydie, 2002, for an analysis of some of this literature). Some critics argue, however, that findings based on quantitative methods have important political implications (Maynard, 1994). For example, policy makers are more likely to take feminist research seriously if the studies show the widespread prevalence—rather than just the subjects' personal feelings—of such problems as wife abuse, children's poverty, and gender discrimination in the workplace.

The Symbolic Interaction Perspective

In contrast to the macro-level structural-functionalist, ecological, conflict, and feminist theories, **symbolic interaction theory** is a micro-level theory that looks at the everyday behavior of individuals. Symbolic interactionists examine how our ideas, beliefs, and attitudes shape our daily lives. To the symbolic interactionist, a father's batting practice with his daughter is not simply batting practice. It is an interaction that conveys such messages as "I enjoy spending time with you" or "Girls can be good baseball players."

The symbolic interaction perspective looks at subjective, interpersonal meanings and how we communicate using *symbols*: words, gestures, or pictures that stand for something. If we are to interact effectively, our symbols must have *shared meanings,* or agreed-upon definitions.

One of the most important of these shared meanings is the *definition of the situation,* that is, the way we perceive reality and react to it. Relationships often break up, for example, because partners have different definitions of the meaning of dating, love, communication, and sex (see Chapters 6–9). As one of my students observed, "We broke up because Dave wanted sex. I wanted intimacy and conversation." We typically learn our definitions of the situation through interaction with **significant others**—people in our primary groups, such as parents, friends, relatives, and teachers—who play an important role in our socialization (see Chapters 1 and 5).

According to symbolic interaction theory, each family member plays more than one role. A man, for example, may be a husband, father, grandfather, brother, son, uncle, and so on. Roles are also *reciprocal*. Even before a baby is born, the prospective parents begin to take on parenting roles (see Chapters 11 and 12).

Roles require different behaviors both within and outside the family, and people modify and adjust their roles as they interact with other role players. For example, you probably interact differently with Mom, Grandma, and Uncle Ned than with your brothers and sisters. And you probably interact still differently when you're talking to a classmate, a professor, or an employer.

Critique One of the most common criticisms of symbolic interaction theory is that it ignores macro-level factors that affect family relationships. As conflict theorists point out, much of our individual behavior and decision making is limited by macro-level or demographic factors such as ethnicity, social class, gender, age, and a variety of laws (see Chapters 1, 4, 5, 13, and 17).

Some believe that symbolic interaction theory overlooks the irrational and unconscious aspects of human behavior (LaRossa and Reitzes, 1993). That is, people don't always behave as reflectively as symbolic interactionists assume. We often act impulsively or make hurtful comments, for instance, without weighing the consequences of our actions or words.

And because symbolic interactionists often study only white, middle-class families—those most likely to cooperate in research—the findings are rarely representative of a wide range of racial, ethnic, and lower socioeconomic groups (Winton, 1995). As a result, according to some critics, symbolic interactionists often have an unrealistic view of everyday life.

The Social Exchange Perspective

The fundamental premise of **social exchange theory**, another micro theory, is that any social interaction between two or more people is based on the efforts of each person to maximize rewards and minimize costs. As a result, most people will continue in a relationship only as long as it is more rewarding than costly to do so.

We bring a variety of resources to a relationship—some tangible, some intangible—such as energy, money, material goods, status, intelligence, good looks, youth, power, talent, fame, or affection. People "trade" these resources for more, better, or different assets that another person possesses. And as long as costs are equal to or lower than benefits, the exchanges will seem fair or balanced (see Chapters 8, 10, and 14).

From a social exchange perspective, when the costs of a marriage outweigh the rewards, the spouses may separate or divorce because one or both partners feel that they're not getting anything out of the relationship. On the other hand, many people stay in unhappy marriages

The Beatles' Paul McCartney is 26 years older than his second wife, Heather. Such marriages usually reflect an exchange of the man's money and fame for the woman's youth, physical attractiveness, and ability to bear children.

because the rewards seem equal to the costs: "It's better than being alone," "I don't want to hurt the kids," or "It could be worse."

Although some of our cost–reward decisions are conscious, others are not. Much of the research on wife abuse, for example, shows that women stay in abusive relationships because their self-esteem has eroded after years of criticism, put-downs, and ridicule by their parents, spouses, or partners ("You'll be lucky if anyone marries you," "You're dumb," "You're ugly," and so on). As a result, abused girls and women rarely recognize that they have the right to expect a rewarding relationship.

Critique Some critics have accused exchange theorists of putting too much weight on rational behavior. People don't always calculate the potential cost and reward of every decision. For example, Linda, one of my students, spent every Saturday (the only day she wasn't working or in class), driving from Baltimore to Philadelphia to visit a grandmother who was showing early symptoms of Alzheimer's disease (see Chapter 17). Linda's mother and several nurses' aides were giving the grandmother, who often didn't recognize Linda, good care. Nonetheless, Linda gave up her "dating evening" because "I just want to make sure Grandma is OK." In this and other cases, genuine love and concern for others can override "sensible" cost–benefit decisions.

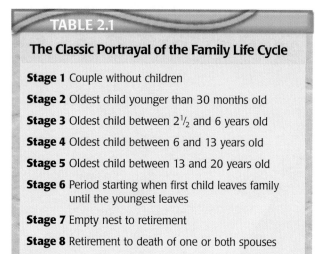

TABLE 2.1

The Classic Portrayal of the Family Life Cycle

Stage 1 Couple without children

Stage 2 Oldest child younger than 30 months old

Stage 3 Oldest child between 2½ and 6 years old

Stage 4 Oldest child between 6 and 13 years old

Stage 5 Oldest child between 13 and 20 years old

Stage 6 Period starting when first child leaves family until the youngest leaves

Stage 7 Empty nest to retirement

Stage 8 Retirement to death of one or both spouses

Exchange theory is also limited to explaining behavior that is motivated by immediate costs or rewards. In many ethnic groups, family responsibilities take precedence over individual rights. Traditional Asian cultures stress filial piety, which obligates children, especially sons, to make sacrifices for the well-being of their parents and siblings (Hurh, 1998; Do, 1999). Many Middle Eastern families, similarly, teach children to value family harmony rather than "me first" benefits (see Chapters 4, 5, and 12).

The Family Life Course Development Perspective

A third micro-level perspective, **family life course development theory,** examines the changes that families experience over the lifespan. This is the only theoretical perspective that emerged out of a specific interest in families. Other theories, such as exchange theory and conflict theory, can be applied to a variety of groups, such as labor–management relations and those between husbands and wives. The family life course development framework, in contrast, focuses exclusively on the family (White and Klein, 2002).

As family members progress through various stages and events over the life course, they accomplish **developmental tasks.** That is, they learn to fulfill role expectations and responsibilities such as showing affection and support for family members and socializing with people outside the family.

Many family development tasks are important in keeping the group going. According to our development stage, we learn to interact and handle different "hassles" as we grow older. For example, young children must deal with teasing, children aged 6 to 10 must cope with getting bad grades, older children face pressure to

use drugs, and 16- to 22-year olds report that the biggest hassles are trouble at work and school. For adults, the greatest source of stress is fighting between family members. For the elderly, the biggest problems include paying for prescriptions and other living expenses (Ellis et al., 2001; see also Chapters 17 and 18).

We also learn many developmental tasks in response to a community's pressures for conformity. For example, teachers expect even very young children to accomplish such developmental tasks as paying attention and obeying the teacher. As a child gets older, a failure to comply with school standards, such as skipping classes or being disruptive, can give parents a bad reputation and lead to intervention by public authorities such as the police (Aldous, 1996).

Family life course development theory evolved over many decades (see White and Klein, 2002, for a description of this evolution). One of the earliest variations, which is still popular, is Duvall's (1957) model of the life cycle. The **family life cycle** consists of the transitions that a family makes as it moves through a series of stages and events from the early days of marriage to the death of one or both partners. According to this classic model and others like it, the family life cycle begins with marriage and continues through child rearing, seeing the children leave home, retirement, and the death of one or both spouses (see *Table 2.1*).

Over time, developmental theories became more sophisticated. They now propose, for example, that developmental stages and tasks vary in different kinds of families, such as single-parent families, childless couples, stepfamilies, and grandparent–grandchild families.

Also, the complex situations and problems that confront families in an aging society are multigenerational (Jerrome, 1994). If a couple divorces, for instance, the ex-spouses aren't the only ones who must learn new developmental tasks in relating to their children and each other. Grandparents and even great-grandparents may also have to forge different ties with their grandchildren, an ex-son-in-law or ex-daughter-in-law, and grand-stepchildren if either of the divorced partners remarries.

Finally, the nature of the family life course may differ greatly between poor, minority families and white, middle-class families. As the box "Kinscripts: Ensuring Family Survival in Tough Situations" on page 42 shows, to keep their members together throughout the life cycle, poor families must be more creative and resilient than others.

Critique Family life course development theories have generated a great deal of research, especially on the internal dynamics of marital and family interaction. Although almost all of the studies are micro-level, a few scholars have used the developmental approach to examine patterns of family change cross-culturally and historically (see Thornton, 2001). The family life course development perspective is especially useful for therapists and practitioners who counsel families on problem solving.

Critics point out several limitations. First, some believe that the stages are artificial because "the processes of life are not always so neatly and cleanly segmented" (Winton, 1995: 39). Second, despite the recent work on kinscripts and extended families, developmental theories generally are limited to examining nuclear, heterosexual, and stable families. Gay and lesbian households generally are excluded from family life cycle stages (Laird, 1993). Third, some question why developmental theories ignore sibling relationships, which are among the most important emotional resources we have throughout life and especially after the last parent dies (McGoldrick et al., 1993). Thus, according to Burr (1995: 81), family life course development theory still "deals with a fairly small part of the elephant."

The Family Systems Perspective

Family systems theory, the final micro perspective we consider, views the family as a functioning unit that solves problems, makes decisions, and achieves collective goals (Day, 1995). The emphasis is not on individual family members but on how the members interact within the family system. Many of the research and therapeutic models emphasize how family members communicate, how family patterns evolve, and how individual personalities affect family members (Rosenblatt, 1994).

Family systems analysts are interested in the implicit or explicit rules that hold families together. For example, how do family members influence each other during stressful times such as illness, unemployment, and the death of a loved one? As the boundaries of the family change—through birth, divorce, or remarriage, for example—the focus of the analysis may shift from family members to the relationship between family members and outside groups (Broderick, 1993).

Family theorists sometimes combine systems theory with the family life course development perspective. In her systemic family development model, for example, Tracey Laszloffy (2002) uses a cake metaphor to illustrate the complexity and the interactional and intergenerational richness of most families. Once the cake ingredients (for example, butter, milk, flour, eggs) are mixed and baked, what emerges is a unique product. The same is true of families. If we stir together all the ingredients (the individuals), we get a unique entity.

And if we slice a piece of the cake, which is similar to freezing a family's moment in the life cycle, we see the various multigenerational layers made of individuals. The individuals within each generation are experiencing different developmental tasks (such as leaving home for college) and coping with different stressors and crises (such as divorce or retirement).

Critique Some critics maintain that family systems theory has generated a lot of terminology but little insight into how the family functions (Holman and Burr, 1980; Nye and Berardo 1981). Because the perspective originated in the study of dysfunctional families in clinical settings, some question whether the theory can be applied to healthy families. Finally, because some of the findings on boundaries and interaction patterns come from case studies, the results are limited because they can't be generalized to larger groups (Day, 1995).

Conclusion

Although I've discussed the eight major theories of marriage and the family separately, researchers and clinicians often combine several of these perspectives to interpret data or choose intervention strategies. For example, a counselor who is helping a couple with marital problems might draw on social exchange, symbolic interaction, life course developmental, and systems theories to shed light on the couple's situation.

Counselors who work with children with attention deficit hyperactivity disorders (ADHD) typically combine ecological and family systems perspectives in assessments and intervention (Bernier and Siegel, 1994). Instead of simply focusing on the child or the family, clinicians usually observe the child in his or her natural environment, involve the child's teacher, and educate grandparents about ADHD. Thus, both researchers and practitioners often rely on several theories to explain or respond to family-related issues.

We've examined some of the most influential theoretical perspectives that guide researchers and practitioners in their work. We turn next to the ways in which researchers, guided by these theoretical perspectives, design studies and collect information about marriages and families.

MAKING CONNECTIONS

■ Return to **Table 2.1** for a moment. Does this model illustrate your family of orientation? What about your family of procreation? If not, how have the stages been different?

■ Consider the cake metaphor that describes family life course development. Does your family resemble a piece of cake? Has it shed old layers or added new ones recently?

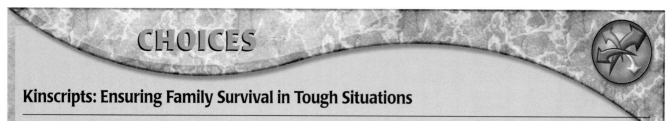

CHOICES

Kinscripts: Ensuring Family Survival in Tough Situations

Family life cycle patterns differ markedly in terms of needs, resources, gender roles, migration patterns, education, and attitudes toward family and aging (McGoldrick et al., 1993). Studying low-income African American families, Burton and Stack (1993) proposed the concept of the *kinscript* to explain the life courses of many multigenerational families. The kinscript arises in response to both extreme economic need and intense commitment by family members to the survival of future generations, and it requires family interaction in three domains: kin-work, kin-time, and kin-scription.

Kin-work is the collective labor that families share to endure over time. It includes family help during childbirth, intergenerational care for children or dependents, and support for other relatives. For example, a 76-year old widower parented three preschool children after their mother started "running the streets":

There ain't no other way. I have to raise these babies, else the service people will take 'em away. This is my family. Family has to take care of family else we won't

be no more (Burton and Stack, 1993: 105).

Kin-time is the shared understanding among family members of when and in what sequence kin-work should be performed. Kin-time provides for learning developmental tasks during such transitions as marriage, childbearing, and grandparenthood and includes temporal guides for assuming family leadership roles and caregiving responsibilities. A woman receiving assistance from her mother and other female kin describes the complex but cooperative pattern that characterizes the care of her child:

Well, on the days Damen has school, my mother picks him up at night and keeps him at her home. And then when she goes to work in the morning, she takes him to my grandmother's house. And when my little sister gets out of school, she picks him up and takes him back to my mother's house. And then I go and pick him up (Jarrett, 1994: 41–42).

Kin-scription is the process by which kin-work is assigned to specific family

members, most often women and children. Women often find it difficult to refuse kin demands. One woman, who had lost her first love 14 years earlier at the age of 21, provides an example of the interplay of family power, kin-scription, and the role of women:

When Charlie died, it seemed like everyone said, since she's not getting married, we have to keep her busy. Before I knew it, I was raising kids, giving home to long-lost kin, and even helping the friends of my mother. Between doing all of this, I didn't have time to find another man (Burton and Stack, 1993: 107).

Many people believe that poor families or those on welfare are doomed to pass dependency down from generation to generation (Hill et al., 1993). As the kinscript framework suggests, however, many low-income, multigenerational families have well-defined family scripts that enable family members to survive by depending on kin rather than on public assistance.

Rebecca Anderson, 54-years-old and battling lupus, became a mother again when she took in five nieces and nephews, whose three sets of parents could not care for them. Anderson's husband, Alton, who does not live with Rebecca, helps with the children occasionally, but provides no financial support.

Methods in Family Research

Why are we attracted to some people and not others? Why are young people postponing marriage? Why have divorce rates recently declined? Social scientists use six major research methods to answer these and other questions about the family: surveys, clinical research, field research, secondary analysis, experiments, and evaluation research.

Surveys

Researchers use **surveys** to systematically collect data from respondents by a mailed questionnaire or an interview. In social science research, a *population* is any well-defined group of people about whom we want to know something specific (say, all adolescents who practice sexual abstinence).

For various reasons, obtaining information from populations is problematic. The population may be so large that it would be too expensive and time-consuming to conduct the research. In other cases—such as obtaining the membership lists of religious groups or social clubs—it may be impossible even to identify the population we would like to study. Researchers, therefore, typically draw a *sample*, a group of people (or things) that are representative of the population they want to study.

Television news, newsmagazines, and entertainment shows often provide a toll-free number or an Internet site and encourage viewers to "vote" on an issue. How representative are these voters of the general population? And how many enthusiasts "stuff the ballot box" by voting more than once? According to one observer, most Internet polls are "good for a few laughs" but are little more than "the latest in a long series of junk masquerading as indicators of public opinion because the participants aren't representative of everyone's opinion" (Witt, 1998: 23).

But what if 100,000 people cast their vote on an issue? Don't such large numbers reflect how most people think? No. Because the respondents are self-selected, the pollster simply has "junk" from a very large number of people.

Since the mid-1990s, the amount of social science research, including polls, has boomed. Are the studies legitimate? The box "The Prospects and Pitfalls of Internet Surveys" on page 44 examines some of the benefits and costs of online research that relies on surveys to collect data.

Questionnaires and Interviews Researchers collect survey data using questionnaires, face-to-face or telephone interviews, or a combination of these techniques. Questionnaires can be mailed, used during an interview, or self-administered to large groups of respondents. Student course evaluations are good examples of self-administered questionnaires.

www.benitaepstein.com

© Benita Epstein 1996

"I already wrote the paper. That's why it's so hard to get the right data."

In interviews, the researcher and the respondent interact directly, either face to face or by telephone. The latter approach is very popular because it is an inexpensive way to collect data.

Researchers obtain representative samples through *random-digit dialing*, which involves selecting area codes and exchanges followed by four random digits. In the procedure called *computer-assisted telephone interviewing (CATI)*, the interviewer uses a computer to select random telephone numbers and then keys the replies into the computer.

Focus Groups Marketing companies have traditionally used *focus groups* to get people's reactions to a new or a "new and improved" product. Family researchers also use focus groups to explore issues before launching a large survey project (Morgan, 1993; Krueger, 1994). Usually 6 to 12 members of a focus group participate in a guided discussion of a particular topic.

Although a focus group can become an unstructured bull session, it often provides important information. In a study using 11 focus groups across the country, for example, Stone and Waszak (1992) found that teenage participants, aged 13 to 19, had strong opinions about the topic of abortion but said that their parents or teachers had never discussed the students' attitudes about abortion. Regardless of how one feels about abortion personally, such focus groups are invaluable in exploring controversial issues that have been largely untapped by previous studies.

Strengths Surveys are usually inexpensive, simple to administer, and have a fast turnaround rate. With assurance that their answers will remain anonymous, respondents are generally willing to answer questions on such sensitive topics as income, sexual behavior, and drug use.

Face-to-face interviews have high response rates (up to 99 percent) compared with other data-collection techniques. Interviewers can also record the respondent's body language, facial expressions, and intonations, which can sometimes be as useful as the verbal response.

If a respondent does not understand a question or is reluctant to answer, the interviewer can clarify, probe, or keep the respondent from digressing. An astute interviewer can also gather information on such variables as social class by observing the respondent's home and neighborhood.

Like questionnaires, telephone surveys are relatively inexpensive and a quick means of gathering information. Telephone interviews provide a nearly unlimited pool of respondents because more than 98 percent of all homes have at least one telephone. These interviews often elicit more honest responses on controversial issues than face-to-face interviews. In addition, researchers have more control over interviewer procedures (such as probing a respondent's vague answers).

Weaknesses One of the major limitations of surveys that use mailed questionnaires is a low response rate, often well under 50 percent. If the questions are unclear, complicated, or offensive, a respondent may simply throw the questionnaire away. A number of studies have found that anywhere from a third to half of survey respondents offer opinions on subjects they know nothing about, such as fictitious legislation or nonexistent political figures (see Bishop et al., 1980).

Moreover, those who respond to questionnaires may be very different from those who do not. Some of the least representative surveys tap self-selected respondents such as readers of particular magazines. How many times have *you* taken the time to complete and return such questionnaires? Norman Bradburn of the National Opinion Research Center calls these surveys SLOPS, for "Self-Selected Opinion Polls" (cited in Tanur, 1994).

Another problem is that people may skip or lie about questions that they feel are "too nosy." In the 2000 census, for example, a third of the people who received the 53-question long form felt that none of the questions was too personal. However, 53 percent viewed

The Prospects and Pitfalls of Internet Surveys

One of the greatest benefits of the Internet is the ability to reach large numbers of people at a very low cost. Hundreds of Websites invite visitors to participate in a variety of studies that resemble scientific research, including personality tests and opinion surveys. How scientific are the studies? And should you or your family members—especially children under age 18—participate?

A nationally representative study of 1305 parents and their children (aged 10 to 17) found that almost two out of three children are willing to divulge private information to online marketers in exchange for a free gift (such as a sweepstakes prize). Some of this information includes the names of parents' favorite stores, parents' weekend activities, the number of parent absences from work, and whether or not the family drinks beer or wine with dinner (Turow and Nir, 2000).

The Children's Online Privacy Protection Act now bars sites from collecting information from users under age 13 without their parents' consent. Enforcement is practically nonexistent, however. In addition, many preteens can figure out ways to get around such precautions or even forge their parents' permission electronically.

What about legitimate academic Internet surveys: Should you or your family members participate? Empirical studies conducted on the Internet, though scientific, reflect a variety of problems.

In face-to-face or telephone interviews, researchers can see or sense whether participants have a negative reaction to an item. The researcher can stop the interview or answer a respondent's questions. Internet surveys can't provide such safeguards, even if there are "warnings" that some of the questions may be sensitive or intrusive.

Institutional review boards try to ensure that paper-and-pencil studies comply with legal and ethical standards (a topic we address later in this chapter). So far, however, there are no established guidelines for online research. Therefore, Internet users should investigate a site before participating even in scientific studies.

STOP AND THINK . . .

- *Have you ever participated in an online survey? Why or why not?*
- *Should parents block teenagers' access to some Internet sites? Or should teenagers be trusted to make their own decisions?*

CHOICES

Can I Trust This Survey?

Surveys are often used in public opinion polls and are reported on television and in newspapers. Asking a few basic questions about the survey will help you evaluate its credibility:

- *Who sponsored the survey?* A government agency, a nonprofit partisan organization, a business, or a group that's lobbying for change?

- *What is the purpose of the survey?* To provide objective information, to promote an idea or a political candidate, or to get attention through sensationalism?

- *How was the sample drawn?* Randomly? Or was it a SLOP (see text)?

- *How were the questions worded?* Were they clear, objective, loaded, or

biased? If the survey questions are not provided, why not?

- *How did the researchers report their findings?* Were they objective, or did they make value judgments?

---

questions about income as intrusive, and 32 percent felt the same way about questions on physical or mental disabilities (Cohn, 2000). If respondents lie or omit questionnaire items about their income or other family characteristics, the data will be invalid, or the researcher may have to scrap a key variable (such as income).

Unlike questionnaires and telephone surveys, face-to-face interviews can be very expensive (see "Data Digest"). And because people have become oversaturated with marketing research, many use caller I.D. or answering machines to avoid telephone surveys.

Because the survey is the research approach you will encounter most often, it is important to be an informed consumer. As the box "Can I Trust This Survey?" shows, you can't simply assume that the survey is accurate or representative of a larger population.

Clinical Research

Unlike survey research, which explores large-scale social processes and changes, **clinical research** studies individuals or small groups of people who seek help from mental health professionals and other scientists (Miller and Crabtree, 1994). Many clinical researchers focus on conflict in family relationships and intervene in traumatic situations such as marital rape and incest. They try to change dysfunctional interactions such as hostile communication patterns between spouses or those in the family environment that might create eating disorders.

Clinical research often relies on the *case study method*, a traditional approach used by social workers, psychologists, clinical sociologists, and marriage counselors. A case study provides in-depth information and detailed and vivid descriptions of family life (see LaRossa, 1984, for good examples of case studies across

the life course). Clinical practitioners work with families or individuals on a one-to-one basis, but they often use several techniques, including interviews, record analysis, and direct observation.

Strengths Case studies are typically linked with long-term counseling, which is beneficial for many individuals and families. Useful intervention strategies can be disseminated fairly quickly to thousands of other practitioners. Clinicians may also offer insights about family dynamics that can enrich theories such as symbolic interaction or general systems perspectives. Researchers can then incorporate these insights into larger or more representative studies that use surveys or other data-collection methods.

Weaknesses Clinical research and case studies are usually time-consuming and expensive. Clinicians typically see only those with severe problems or people who are willing and financially able to seek help. Therefore, the results are not representative of the average family or even of other troubled families.

Another problem is that clinical studies are subjective and rarely ask "Where's the evidence?" If a client complains that he has a terrible mother, for example, clinicians try to make the patient feel better instead of meeting the mother. As a result, some critics contend, clinical "opinions" are widespread despite empirical evidence to the contrary. It is *not* true, for instance, that low self-esteem causes aggression, drug use, and low achievement. How parents treat a child in the first years of life does *not* determine a child's later intellectual and emotional success (see Chapter 12). Nor do abused children inevitably become abusive parents, causing a "cycle of abuse" (Tavris, 2003).

Researchers often study development by observing children in natural settings.

Field Research

In **field research,** researchers collect data by systematically observing people in their natural surroundings. Field research usually is highly structured. It typically involves carefully designed projects in which the data are recorded and then converted to quantitative summaries. The studies examine complex communication patterns, measure the frequency of acts (such as the number of nods or domineering statements), and note the duration of a particular behavior (such as the length of eye contact) (Stillars, 1991). Thus, field research is much more elaborate and sophisticated than it appears to be to the general public or to an inexperienced researcher.

Field research includes several types of observation. In *participant observation,* researchers interact naturally with the people they are studying but do not reveal their identities as researchers. For example, if you quietly note interaction patterns between the "stars" and the "black sheep" during a Thanksgiving dinner, you are engaging in participant observation.

In *nonparticipant observation,* researchers study phenomena without being part of the situation. For example, child psychologists, clinicians, and sociologists often study young children in classrooms or playgrounds. (For a discussion of other variations in observation research, see Adler and Adler, 1994.)

In many studies, researchers combine both participant and nonparticipant observation. For example, sociologist Elijah Anderson has devoted much of his research to examining households in West Philadelphia, an inner-city black community with high crime rates. Although Anderson teaches at the University of Pennsylvania, he "hangs out" in West Philadelphia to learn why some poor residents take extraordinary measures to conform to mainstream values (such as maintaining a strong family life) whereas others engage in crime and violence (Anderson, 1999).

Strengths Field research provides an in-depth understanding of behavior that other approaches often lack. In her study of families in Saudi Arabia, for example, Soraya Altorki (1988) established rapport with the women in the community. They invited her to their homes, where Altorki could observe everyday interaction, behavior, and activities.

Field research is more flexible than some other methods. For instance, the researcher can decide to interview (rather than just observe) key people after beginning the data collection.

Most important, field research does not disrupt a "natural" setting. Therefore, the subjects aren't influenced by the researcher's presence. For example, Phillip Davis (1996) and some of his graduate research assistants have observed adults' verbal aggression and corporal punishment of children in public settings such as indoor shopping malls, zoos, amusement parks, flea markets, city streets, rapid transit stations, bus depots, and toy stores.

Weaknesses If a researcher needs elaborate recording equipment, must travel far or often, or lives in a different society or community for a long time, field research can be very expensive. Researchers who study other cultures often spend several years learning a new language or adjusting to different cultural norms. A researcher doing fieldwork in a country experiencing civil wars may be abducted or even killed (Garland, 1999).

It may also be very difficult to balance the role of participant and observer. In Anderson's studies in West Philadelphia cited earlier, he became personally involved with some of his research subjects. Instead of being a detached observer, Anderson hired an ex-drug dealer as a part-time research assistant, found community members lawyers or jobs, encouraged his respondents to stay out of crime, and even lent them money (Cose, 1999). Thus, the researcher may bias the research by succumbing to the impulse to fix a problem and to protect subjects from harm (Fine, 1993).

A final problem with field research is the observer's ability to recognize and address her or his biased point of view. Because observation is very personal and subjective, it is often difficult to maintain one's objectivity while collecting and interpreting the data.

Secondary Analysis Besides using surveys, clinical studies, and field research, family researchers rely heavily on secondary analysis. In **secondary analysis,** researchers use data that were collected by someone else. Such data may be historical materials (such as court proceedings), personal documents (such as letters and diaries), public records (such as federal information on immigration or state or county archives on births, marriages, and deaths), and official statistics (such as Census Bureau publications).

Many of the statistics in this textbook come from secondary analysis. The information includes the U.S. Census Bureau and other government agencies, reputable nonprofit organizations, and university research centers (see Greenstein, 2001, for a good summary of the major sources of secondary analysis in family research).

Strengths In most cases, secondary analysis is accessible, convenient, and inexpensive. Census Bureau information on topics such as household income, the number of children in single-parent families, and immigration is readily available at college and university libraries and, most recently, on the Internet (see the "Taking It Further" section in Chapter 1).

Because secondary data often are *longitudinal* (information collected at two or more points in time) rather than *cross-sectional* (information collected at one point in time), there is the added advantage of examining trends (such as age at first marriage) over time. And increasingly, both longitudinal and cross-sectional publications provide the reader with colorful pie charts and other figures that are easy to read, understand, and incorporate into slide presentations.

Another advantage of secondary analysis is the high quality of the data. Nationally known survey organizations have huge budgets, well-trained staff, and experts who can quickly handle any data-collection problems. Because the samples are representative of larger populations, you can be more confident about the study's generalizability to larger groups.

Weaknesses Secondary analysis has several drawbacks. First, secondary data may not provide all of the information needed. For example, some of the statistics on remarriages and redivorces have been collected only since the early 1990s. Therefore, it is impossible for a researcher to make comparisons over time.

Second, secondary analysis may be difficult because the documents may be fragile, housed in only a few libraries in the country, or part of private collections.

In some isolated locations, census takers must often travel to places that are inaccessible by road or without conventional postal addresses. In the 2000 census, for example, Harold Johnson transported Census Director Kenneth Prewitt into town by dog sled. Unalakdeet, a village of about 800, is on the Bering Sea 400 miles northwest of Anchorage.

Determining the accuracy and authenticity of historical materials also may be difficult.

A third limitation of secondary analysis is that the data may not include information the researcher is looking for. If you wanted to examine some of the characteristics of couples who are separated but not divorced, for example, you'd find no national data. Consequently, you'd have to rely on studies with small and nonrepresentative samples or collect such information yourself.

Experiments

Unlike surveys, clinical research, field research, and secondary analysis, an **experiment** investigates cause-and-effect relationships under strictly controlled conditions. A researcher tests a prediction, or *hypothesis*, that one variable "causes" another. According to many of my students, for example, heavy course assignments "cause" cheating because students don't have enough time to prepare for exams, work part-time (or full time), and have other interests. To test this hypothesis, a researcher would compare the cheating results of students who have both heavy and light course loads and compare other factors such as employment, class attendance, and amount of time devoted to studying.

Experimental designs are rare in family research but are considered a powerful research tool in psychological and medical research. Using specially designed laboratories, psychologists investigate such family-related issues as infants' attention spans, children's problem-solving techniques, and adults' interaction with each other. In medicine, researchers routinely try to establish cause–effect relationships between many variables, such as diet and blood pressure or stress and physical illness (see Chapter 6).

In the social sciences, psychologist John Gottman has used the experimental method to study marital discord and conflict (see Chapters 10 and 15). And, in a recent study, psychologists Rachel Ebling and Robert Levenson (2003) investigated whether people with professional training or personal marital experience could predict marital satisfaction and marital stability in others. The researchers recruited 177 participants who viewed short videotapes of the marital interaction of ten couples. The participants then rated the couples on their marital satisfaction and the likelihood of divorce. (The researchers found that people who were happily married or recently divorced were more accurate in their ratings than those with professional training, such as marital therapists and marital researchers, in judging marital satisfaction. This suggests that the "experts" aren't as savvy about interpersonal relationships as they or we expect.)

Strengths The major advantage of the controlled (laboratory) experiment lies in its isolation of the "causal" variable. For example, if students who get information in sex education classes show attitudinal changes toward casual sex, a school might decide to provide such information for all of its students.

Another strength of experimental designs is their low expense. In general, there's no need to purchase special equipment, and participants expect little or no compensation. Also, experiments usually are less time-consuming than data-collection techniques such as surveys and field research.

A third advantage of experiments is that they can be replicated over many years and with different subjects. Such replication strengthens the researchers' confidence in the *validity*, or accuracy, and *reliability*, or consistency, of the research findings.

Weaknesses One major disadvantage of experimental designs is their reliance on student volunteers or paid subjects. Students often feel obligated to participate as part of a grade, or they may fear antagonizing an instructor who's conducting a study. Students might give "acceptable" answers that they think the instructor expects. In the case of paid subjects, often only those with serious financial problems will participate in experiments.

A second and related disadvantage is that experimental study results can't be generalized to a larger population because they come from small or self-selected samples. For example, college students who participate in experiments aren't necessarily representative of other college students, much less people who aren't in college.

A third limitation is that experiments, especially those in laboratories, are very artificial. People *know* that they're being observed and may behave very differently than they would in a natural setting.

Finally, many experiments gauge attitudes rather than behavior. Like surveys, some experiments tell researchers only what the subjects *say* they'll do rather than how they *really* behave. Medical experiments probably are more accurate because they measure physiological variables (weight, blood pressure, medications). Even here, however, subjects can lie about their medical history or lifestyles. In addition, there are many variables that medical researchers can't take into account. That's one of the reasons why consumers often get mixed advice (for example, drinking tea is healthy versus drinking tea has little effect on one's health).

Evaluation Research

In **evaluation research,** which relies on all of the standard methodological techniques described in this section, researchers assess the efficiency and the effectiveness of social programs in both the public and private sectors. Many government and nonprofit agencies provide services that affect the family both directly and indirectly. Programs to prevent or deal with teenage pregnancy, work-training programs, and drug rehabilitation programs are examples.

Because local, state, and national governments have cut social service budgets since the early 1980s, service delivery groups have become increasingly concerned about doing more with less. As you saw in the "Should Uncle Sam be a Matchmaker?" box in Chapter 1, caseworkers are now required to provide counseling for which they have no training. Nonetheless, there is an increasing emphasis on evaluations to advise agencies how to achieve the best results at the lowest possible costs (Kettner et al., 1999).

Like clinical research, evaluation research is *applied*. It assesses a specific social program for a specific agency or organization, evaluating that program's achievements in terms of its original goals (Weiss, 1998). Administrators often use the final reports to improve a program or to initiate a new service such as an after-school program.

Strengths and Weaknesses Evaluation research is one of the most valuable research approaches because it examines actual efforts to deal with problems that confront many families. And if researchers use secondary analysis rather than collecting new data, the expenses can be modest.

TABLE 2.2

Six Common Data Collection Methods in Family Research

Method	Strengths	Weaknesses
Surveys	Fairly inexpensive and simple to administer; interviews have high response rates; findings often are generalizable.	Mailed questionnaires may have low response rates; respondents may be self-selected; interviews usually are expensive.
Clinical research	Helps subjects with family problems; offers insights for theory development.	Usually time-consuming and expensive; findings are not generalizable.
Field research	Flexible; offers deeper understanding of family behavior; usually inexpensive.	Difficult to quantify and to maintain observer–subject boundaries; the observer may be biased or judgmental; findings are not generalizable.
Secondary analysis	Usually accessible, convenient, and inexpensive; often longitudinal and historical.	Information may be incomplete; some documents may be inaccessible; some data cannot be collected over time.
Experiment	Attempts to demonstrate cause and effect; usually inexpensive; plentiful availability of subjects; can be replicated.	Volunteers and paid subjects aren't representative of larger populations; artificial laboratory setting; measures attitudes rather than behavior.
Evaluation research	Usually inexpensive; valuable in real-life applications.	Often political; may entail training many staff members.

In addition, the research findings can be very valuable to program directors or agency heads. Managers are able to keep a program on course because the findings highlight discrepancies between the original objectives and the way the program is actually working (Peterson et al., 1994).

Evaluation research can also be frustrating. Politics often play an important role in what is evaluated and for whom the research is done. Even though supervisors typically solicit the research, they may ignore the results if the study shows that the program isn't tapping the neediest groups, that the administrators are wasting money, or that caseworkers are making serious mistakes.

Finally, some evaluations are inadequate because they rely on small and unrepresentative samples. So-called marriage preparation programs have mushroomed since the early 1990s. However, we know little about their effectiveness because the evaluations have been limited to "young, well-adjusted, middle-class volunteers," most of whom are white (Silliman and Schumm, 2000: 138). Therefore, no one really knows whether marriage preparation programs are useful or just a waste of money.

Conclusion

Researchers have to weigh the benefits and limitations of each research approach in designing their studies (see

Table 2.2). Often, they use a combination of strategies to achieve their research objectives. Despite the researcher's commitment to objectivity, ethical debates and politically charged disagreements can influence much family research.

MAKING CONNECTIONS

■ If you get information off the Internet, how do you judge whether the material is accurate?

■ When you get questionnaires in the mail, do you answer them? If you respond, do you ignore some questions? If so, which ones? ◯◯

The Ethics and Politics of Family Research

Researchers don't work in a vacuum. Many people have very strong opinions about family issues (see Chapter 1). There is also pressure in universities, for example, to supplement shrinking budgets with outside funding sources. It is not surprising, then, that researchers may encounter ethical and political dilemmas.

Ethical Issues

In a recent experiment, researchers found that an AIDS vaccine worked especially well for African Americans who volunteered to participate. Researchers are having problems recruiting black volunteers for further studies. Why?

In the Tuskegee Syphilis Study, conducted by the federal government between 1932 and 1972, researchers withheld medical treatment from poor black men in Macon County, Alabama. The men were not told they had syphilis and were not treated, even after penicillin became available, because the researchers wanted to study the progression of the disease. By the time the study was exposed in the early 1990s, 128 men had died of syphilis or related complications.

Decades after the Tuskegee Study, and even though blacks represent about half of new HIV cases (see Chapter 7), many are suspicious of scientists and researchers: "Even though people may or may not know the specifics of the Tuskegee trials, they know that there are health disparities and that blacks often get inferior treatment based on race" ("Black volunteers . . .," 2003: 5A).

Because so much research relies on human subjects, the federal government and many professional organizations have devised ethics codes to protect research participants.

Researchers are responsible for the ethical behavior of everyone involved in their own research. Among other professional organizations, the National Council on Family Relations and the American Sociological Association publish a detailed set of Ethical Code guidelines for researchers. The key elements of these codes, regardless of the discipline or type of research used, appear in *Table 2.3*.

Ethical violations affect all families. For example, a researcher at the University of Illinois at Chicago admitted that she had fabricated research data and submitted the false information to the director of a study on prenatal care (P. W. Campbell, 1999). In other cases, businesses pressure scientists to withhold negative findings. Recently, for instance, in the *Journal of the American Medical Association*, one of the world's most highly respected medical journals, University of California researchers reported that in clinical trials, an anti-HIV drug, Remune, was no more effective than a placebo (sugar pill). The pharmaceutical company sued the university, demanding that it pay $7–10 million in damages, but later dropped the suit (Van Der Werf, 2001).

Ethically, it is important for researchers to state whether something works. However, businesses that pay for research would rather not reveal findings that can cut into their profits or decrease the value of their stock. As a result, ethical guidelines may sometimes buckle under the weight of academic pressure to avoid discussing topics that challenge the status quo, to bring in as many grants as possible, or to please corporations that sponsor the research.

To please corporations, some researchers violate conflict-of-interest policies. A few years ago, for example, the prestigious *New England Journal of Medicine* admitted that, between 1997 and 1999, its editors published 18 articles of which the researchers also served as consultants to or received "major research support" from pharmaceutical companies (Angell et al., 2000).

As these examples illustrate, some researchers engage in unethical behavior. For the most part, however, research errors are unintentional. They result from ignorance of statistical procedures, simple arithmetic mistakes, or inadequate supervision. These kinds of honest errors often are caught by referees who review academic articles and books before publication or by scholars who evaluate funding requests.

Some data-collection methods are more susceptible to ethical violations than others. Surveys are less vulnerable than observation, for example, because researchers do not interact directly with subjects, interpret their behavior, or become personally involved with the respondents.

TABLE 2.3

Some Basic Principles of Ethical Family Research

- Obtain all subjects' consent to participate and their permission to quote from their responses, particularly if the research concerns sensitive issues or if subjects' comments will be quoted extensively.

- Do not exploit subjects or research assistants involved in the research for personal gain.

- Never harm, humiliate, abuse, or coerce participants, either physically or psychologically. This includes the withholding of medications or other services or programs that might benefit subjects.

- Honor all guarantees to participants of privacy, anonymity, and confidentiality.

- Use the highest methodological standards and be as accurate as possible.

- Describe the limitations and shortcomings of the research in published reports.

CONSTRAINTS

The Politics of Sex Research

In 2002, the Bush administration quietly removed scientific material from several federal Websites that conflicted with the administration's political position on sexual behavior. As this book goes to press, the sites haven't been restored.

Abortion and Breast Cancer

In one case, the NIH removed the National Cancer Institute's reports of findings that abortion does not increase a woman's risk of developing breast cancer. Originally, the National Cancer Institute's document said, "The current body of scientific evidence suggests that women who have had either induced or spontaneous abortion have the same risk as other women for developing breast cancer." The Website now says that the evidence for the relationship between abortions and breast cancer is "inconclusive."

The major reason for this change is that conservative administrations frown on abortion. However, liberals worry that instead of getting a legal abortion, many women (including unmarried teens) may bear unwanted children because they'll fear that abortion "causes" breast cancer ("National Cancer Institute . . .," 2003).

Sex Education and Sexual Activity

In another case, the NIH and CDC removed information about the effectiveness of condoms and a sex education curriculum titled "Programs That Work." Originally, both sites promoted condom usage to decrease unwanted pregnancies. Because the Bush administration sees abstinence as the only "acceptable" sex education program, it expunged material on how using condoms protects against HIV and other sexually transmitted diseases (STDs).

The Bush administration also deleted CDC materials showing that education about condom use does not lead to earlier or increased sexual activity, especially among teens. The new CDC version, in boldface, now advocates abstinence instead of condom use:

The surest way to avoid transmission of sexually transmitted diseases is to abstain from sexual intercourse, or to be in a long-term mutually monogamous relationship with a partner who has been tested and you know is uninfected. . . . Correct and consistent use of the male latex condom can reduce the risk of S.T.D. transmission. However, no protective method is 100 percent effective, and condom use cannot guarantee absolute protection against any S.T.D.

SOURCES: Clymer, 2002; "Daily Reproductive Health Report," 2002; "Male latex condoms . . .," 2002.

STOP AND THINK . . .

- *Should the government endorse sexual abstinence—especially for teens—to prevent out-of-wedlock pregnancies, HIV, and other STDs?*

- *Or should the government provide the results of scientific studies and let people decide how to behave sexually, whether they act responsibly or not?*

Political Pressures

Former Senator William Proxmire became famous (or infamous, some feel) for his "Golden Fleece" awards to social research projects that he ridiculed as wasting taxpayer money. Some of the most recent examples include studies on stress and why people fall in love. The legitimacy of social science research becomes especially suspect to political and religious groups when the studies focus on sensitive social, moral, and political issues.

One of the most controversial research topics is human sexuality. Alfred Kinsey and his colleagues carried out the first widely publicized research on sexuality in the late 1940s and early 1950s. Although there were methodological limitations (see Chapter 7), many social scientists consider Kinsey's research to be the major springboard that launched scientific investigations of human sexuality in subsequent decades.

Many people are still suspicious of research on sex, however. In 1992, for example, Congress withdrew the funding for two projects on adolescent and adult sexual behavior that had already been peer-reviewed, approved, and funded by the National Institutes of Health (NIH) and the Centers for Disease Control and Prevention (CDC). Congress dumped the projects because a number of conservative Christian groups complained that the research would "liberalize" opinions and laws regarding homosexuality, pedophilia, anal and oral sex, sex education, and teenage pregnancy and undermine "traditional family values" (Fiester, 1993; Udry, 1993).

More recently, the Bush administration has purged material from federal Internet sites that violate the administration's ideological stance on sexual abstinence. As "The Politics of Sex Research" box shows, politicians have the power to revise or delete information about sexual behavior on Websites, regardless of what scientific studies show (see also Chapter 7).

Politicians tinker with other data—not just sexuality—that might decrease their popularity or chances of being re-elected. During the 2002 recession, for example, President Bush's Council of Economic Advisers yanked off its Website a study that predicted mediocre job growth after Bush's proposed $674-billion economic stimulus plan. In addition, the Bureau of Labor Statistics quietly announced that it would no longer publish the mass-layoff statistics it had been putting out since 1994 (Coy and Cohn, 2003). Without such information, states find it much harder to plan for job-training and other programs.

In its most extreme form, doing research on topics that politicians don't like may jeopardize a scholar's current or future employment. Even a tenured professor at a large research university can come close to being fired by a Republican governor who disapproves of the research on abstinence education, for example (Bailey et al., 2002).

MAKING CONNECTIONS

■ Some researchers violate ethical guidelines to bring in more money for their institutions. Is this acceptable, especially if the grants can reduce class sizes, provide much-needed computer labs, and increase library staff and student services?

■ On a number of sites (such as www.pickaprof.com and www.ratemyprofessors.com), students can say anything they want about faculty. Should students identify themselves instead of submitting the "evaluations" anonymously? Are the comments representative of all students in a course? Should faculty set up similar public sites and evaluate students by name?

Conclusion

As this chapter shows, understanding marriage and the family is *not* an armchair activity dominated by ivory-tower philosophers. Quite to the contrary, and like the family itself, the study of the family reflects *changes* in the evolution of theories and *constraints* due to the limitations of research designs. There has been much progress in family research, and researchers have more *choices* in methodology. At the same time, "there is plenty of reason for marriage and family scholars to be modest about what they know and humble about what they do not" (Miller, 1986: 110).

Research explanations sometimes are inadequate because social scientists ignore the historical context that has shaped the contemporary family. We look at some of these historical processes in the next chapter.

SUMMARY

1. Although many people are suspicious of statistics, data of all kinds are becoming increasingly important in our daily lives. Information derived from social science research affects much of our everyday behavior, shapes family policy, and provides explanations for social change.

2. Both theory and research are critical in our understanding marriages and families.

3. The most influential theories of marriage and the family include four macro-level perspectives (ecological, structural-functional, conflict, and feminist theories) and four micro-level theories (symbolic interaction, social exchange, family life course and development, and family systems). Researchers and clinicians often use several theoretical perspectives in interpreting data or choosing intervention strategies.

4. The survey is one of the most common data-collection methods in family research. Surveys rely on questionnaires, interviews, or a combination. Both questionnaires and interviews have advantages and limitations that researchers consider in designing their studies.

5. Clinical research and case studies provide a deeper understanding of behavior because attitudes and behavior can be studied intensively and over time. Such research, however, is also time-consuming and limited to small groups of people.

6. Field research offers a deeper understanding of behavior and is usually inexpensive. The results of this type of research are difficult to quantify, however, and the researcher may experience difficulty in maintaining a balance between observation and participation.

7. Experiments try to establish cause-effect explanations. It is impossible to "prove" such associations, however, because experiments are usually conducted in artificial settings that don't represent people's behavior in natural environments.

8. Secondary analysis uses data collected by other researchers (such as historical documents and official government statistics). It is usually an accessible, convenient,

and inexpensive source of data but may not provide information on the variables that a researcher wants to examine.

9.   Evaluation research, an applied research technique, often assesses the effectiveness and efficiency of social programs that offer services to families and other groups. If the results are unflattering, however, politicians and administrators may ignore the findings and never publish the reports.

10.   Social scientists must adhere to professional ethical standards, both in conducting research and in reporting the results. Because political issues often affect research, however, collecting data is not as simple as it seems.

KEY TERMS

theory *35*
ecological theory *35*
structural-functional theory *36*
instrumental role *36*
expressive role *36*
manifest functions *36*
latent functions *36*
conflict theory *37*
feminist theories *37*

quantitative research *38*
qualitative research *38*
symbolic interaction theory *38*
significant others *38*
social exchange theory *39*
family life course development
    theory *40*
developmental tasks *40*
family life cycle *40*

family systems theory *41*
surveys *43*
clinical research *45*
field research *46*
secondary analysis *47*
experiments *47*
evaluation research *48*

TAKING IT FURTHER

Do Your Research Online

Here are some Internet sites that are especially germane to this chapter:

WWW Virtual Library: Sociology is a comprehensive site that offers a good overview of many sociology resources, including chat rooms that discuss family issues.
www.mcmaster.ca/socscidocs/w3virtsoclib/resource.htm

Social Science Information Gateway contains an excellent Internet catalog that includes thousands of online resources, browsable or searchable by subject topics such as *family*, *theory*, and *research methods*. Its Social Science Search Engine (sosig.ac.uk/harvester.html) indexes a database of more than 50,000 social science Web pages.
sosig.ac.uk

Academic Survey Research Centers provide links to and information about survey research centers in the United States and other countries, some include family studies.
www.princeton.edu/~abelson/xsrcs.html

Bill Trochim's Center for Social Research Methods "is for people involved in applied social research and evaluation." This site offers an online statistical adviser and links to Internet data and research methods sites.
trochim.human.cornell.edu/index.html

The **Inter-University Consortium for Political and Social Research (ICPSR)** is the largest data warehouse in the world that holds secondary data on social issues.
http://www.icpsr.umich.edu

Human Development & Family Life Education Resource Center offers research and practical information for professionals, educational resources, reviews of information technology developments that affect family life education, and online bulletins on evaluating family life Websites.
www.hec.ohio-state.edu/famlife

And more: www.prenhall.com/benokraitis provides URLs for theory sites, practical tips for evaluating a variety of online resources, sites of major research institutions, audio clips of Studs Terkel's interviews, studies of human development across the lifespan, the rejuvenated Golden Fleece award sites, online journals on qualitative research, cybersociology, "mundane" behavior, and more.

INVESTIGATE WITH RESEARCH NAVIGATOR

Please go to www.researchnavigator.com and enter your LOGIN NAME and PASSWORD. For instructions on registering for the first time, please view the detailed instructions at the end of the Chapter 1. Please search the Research Navigator™ site using the following key search terms:

feminism or feminist theory
social exchange theory
family systems theory

The Family in Historical Perspective

DATADIGEST

- During the **Great Depression,** the Southern Pacific Railroad threw more than half a million transients—200,000 of whom were adolescent males—off its boxcars in a single year.

- The fathers of **nearly 183,000 children were killed during World War II.**

- Of the almost 7 million women who **worked outside their homes** during World War II, 75 percent were married.

- African American women made some of the greatest **employment gains** during World War II.

Those working as servants fell from 72 to 48 percent, and the proportion employed in factories grew from 7 percent to almost 20 percent.

- **Divorce rates surged** from 321,000 in 1942 to 610,000 in 1946, after the end of the war. By 1950, a million veterans had been divorced.

- Overall, 62 percent of Americans **attend a family reunion** every year.

Sources: Chafe, 1972; Tuttle, 1993; Mergenbagen, 1996; Fetto, 2001.

In 1890, Joel Coleman, a recent Jewish immigrant to New York City, wrote home:

Dear Father, I can tell You very little about my great achievements. I am not yet a wealthy man, but for sure not a beggar either. . . . Right now, during the winter, work is very slow. It happens every winter; therefore, we see to it that we have put something aside for those winter months. On the whole my life here is not bad and I cannot complain about America, except for one thing—my health was better at home, in Poland, where the air was better. Here I often get sick, but I prefer not to write about it (Wtulich, 1986:218).

Immigrants' letters often spoke of loneliness, low wages, hard and unsteady work, language barriers, poverty, and numerous hardships. Life was difficult and unpredictable in the "land of plenty."

When social scientists examine the past, they find that "the good old days" never existed for most people. Historians, especially, have raised some interesting questions: Were the colonists as virtuous as we were taught in grade school? Did people really pull together to help each other during the Depression? Were the 1950s as fabulous as many people insist?

The Colonial Family

Although colonial families differed from modern ones in terms of social class, religious practices, and geographic dispersion, such factors as family roles and family structure were very similar. The diversity that characterizes modern families also existed in colonial times.

Family Structure

The nuclear family was the most prevalent family form both in England and in the first settlements in the

United States. An elderly grandparent or an apprentice sometimes lived with or near the family, but few households were made up of extended families for long periods of time (Goode, 1963; Laslett, 1971). Although families typically started out with six or seven children, high infant mortality rates left household sizes small, with large age differences between children.

The Puritans—Protestant colonists who adhered to strict moral and religious values—believed that the community had a right to intervene in families that did not perform their duties properly. In the 1670s, for example, the Massachusetts General Court directed towns to appoint "tithingmen" to ensure that marital relations were harmonious and that parents disciplined unruly children (Mintz and Kellogg, 1988).

Unlike in later times, few people survived outside the family during the colonial period. Most of the settlements were small (fewer than 100 families), and each family was considered a "little commonwealth" that performed a variety of functions. The family was

- a self-sufficient *business* that produced and exchanged goods, in which all family members worked together

- a *school* that taught children to read

- a *vocational institute* that instructed children and prepared them for jobs through apprenticeships

- a miniature *church* that guided its members in daily prayers, personal meditation, and formal worship in the community

- a *house of correction* where the courts sentenced idle or criminal people to be servants in reputable families

- a *welfare institution* where families gave their members medical and other care and provided a home for other relatives who were orphaned, aging, sick, or homeless (Demos, 1970).

As you'll see later in this chapter, all of these functions changed considerably with the onset of industrialization.

Sexual Relations

The Puritans tried to prevent premarital intercourse in several ways. One was **bundling,** a New England custom in which a fully dressed young man and woman spent the night in a bed together, separated by a wooden board.

The custom was adopted because it was difficult for the young suitor, who had traveled many miles, to return home the same night, especially during harsh winters. Because the rest of the family shared the room, it was considered quite proper for the bundled young man

and woman to continue their conversations after the fire was out (McPharlin, 1946).

Despite such safeguards as bundling, premarital and extramarital sex were common. According to some historians, between 20 and 33 percent of colonial women were pregnant at the time of marriage (Hawke, 1988; Demos, 1970). Keep in mind, however, that sexual activity was generally confined to engaged couples. The idea of a casual meeting that included sexual intercourse would have been utterly foreign to the Puritans.

Out-of-wedlock births were fairly common among young women who immigrated to the southern colonies as indentured (contracted) servants. They typically came to the United States alone because they were from poor families that could not afford to migrate together. Because these very young (under age 15) women were alone and vastly outnumbered by men in the colonies, they were vulnerable to sexual attacks by their employers and other men (Harari and Vinovskis, 1993).

The Puritan community condemned adultery and illegitimacy because they threatened the family structure. Sometimes local newspapers denounced a straying spouse publicly:

> *Catherine Treen, the wife of the subscriber, behaved in the most disgraceful manner, by leaving her own place of abode, and living in a criminal state with a certain William Collins, a plaisterer, under whose bed she was last night, discovered, endeavoring to conceal herself. Her much injured husband thinks it absolutely necessary to forewarn all persons from trusting after such flagrant proof of her prostitution, to pay no debts of her contracting (cited in Lantz, 1976: 14).*

Few records, however, documented men's extramarital affairs. Although frowned upon, a husband's infidelity was considered "normal." And because the courts did not enforce a father's economic obligation to a child born out of wedlock, it was women who paid the costs of bearing and raising illegitimate children (Ryan, 1983). As you can see, the double standard (which we discuss later) is not a modern invention.

Husbands and Wives

Husbands and wives worked together to make sure that the family survived. Like modern society, colonial America expected spouses to have strong personal economic relationships. Inequalities, however, were very much a part of early American family life.

In Personal Relationships In general, women were subordinate to men; the wife's chief duty was obedience to her husband. New England clergymen often referred to male authority as a "government" that women must accept as "law." In the southern colonies, husbands often denounced assertive wives as "impertinent" (Ryan, 1983). A woman's social status and her power and prestige in the community came from the patriarchal head of the household: her husband or her father.

At the same time, the "well-ordered" family was based on a number of mutual spousal responsibilities. Husbands and wives were expected to love each other and to show "a very great affection." They should be chaste and faithful to each other, and they were instructed to be patient and to help each other: "If the one is sick, pained, troubled, distressed, the other should manifest care, tenderness, pity, compassion, and afford all possible relief and succour" (Scott and Wishy, 1982: 86).

In Plymouth, women had the right to transfer land. In 1646, for example, when one man wanted to sell his family's land, the court called in his wife to make sure that she approved. The courts also granted liquor and other business licenses to women (Demos, 1970). And they sometimes offered a woman protection from a violent husband. The Plymouth court ordered a whipping for a man who kicked his wife off a stool and into a blazing fireplace (Mintz and Kellogg, 1988). Such protections were not typical in the colonies outside Plymouth, however.

In a few cases, the local courts permitted divorce. The acceptable grounds were limited to desertion, adultery, bigamy, and impotence. Incompatibility was recognized as a problem but not as serious enough to warrant divorce. It was not until about 1765, when romantic love emerged as a basis for marriage, that "loss of affection" was mentioned as a reason for divorce (Cott and Pleck, 1979).

At Work and in the Economy

Men were expected to be industrious, hardworking, ambitious, and responsible for the family's economic survival. Husbands and wives often worked side by side. Men, women, and children all produced, cultivated, and processed goods for the family's consumption. When necessary, men cared for and disciplined the children while women worked in the fields.

Much of women's work was directed toward meeting the needs of others. In his 1793 *Female Guide*, a New Hampshire pastor defined a woman's role as "piety to God—reverence to parents—love and obedience to their husbands—tenderness and watchfulness over their children—justice and humanity to their dependents" (quoted in Cott, 1977: 22–23).

Although both sexes were praised for being wealthy and industrious, men were expected to initiate economic activity, and women were expected to support men and to be frugal. In 1692, Cotton Mather, an

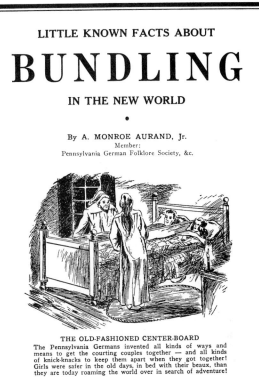

Illustrated Edition **25c**

LITTLE KNOWN FACTS ABOUT

BUNDLING

IN THE NEW WORLD

•

By A. MONROE AURAND, Jr.
Member:
Pennsylvania German Folklore Society, &c.

THE OLD-FASHIONED CENTER-BOARD
The Pennsylvania Germans invented all kinds of ways and means to get the courting couples together — and all kinds of knick-knacks to keep them apart when they got together! Girls were safer in the old days, in bed with their beaux, than they are today roaming the world over in search of adventure!

The Pennsylvania Germans invented various ways of keeping courting couples apart when they were together. What do you suppose might have happened to the "centerboard" shown in this sketch after the young woman's parents went to bed? The couple could hope that the family members—who typically slept in the same room—were sound sleepers.

influential minister and author, described women's economic role as being only "to spend (or save) what others get" (Cott, 1977).

In some cases, unmarried women, especially widows and those who had been deserted by their husbands, turned their homemaking activities into self-supporting businesses. Some used their homes as inns, restaurants, or schools and sold homemade foods. Others made a living by washing, mending, nursing, midwifery, or producing cure-all and beauty potions.

Some widows continued their husbands' businesses in such "masculine" areas as chocolate and mustard production, soap making, cutlery, coach making, rope making, publishing, printing, horseshoeing, net making, whaling, and running grocery stores, bookstores, drugstores, and hardware stores. And some of these businesswomen placed ads, on a regular basis, in the local newspapers (Matthaei, 1982).

In general, however, the economic roles of women, especially wives, were severely limited. Women had little access to credit, could not sue to collect debts, were not allowed to own property, and were rarely chosen as executors of wills, especially if their husbands had complicated estates (Ryan, 1983).

Children's Lives

Poor sanitation, crude housing, limited hygiene, and dangerous physical environments characterized colonial America. Infant and child mortality rates were high. Between 10 and 30 percent of all children died before their first birthday, and fewer than two out of three children lived to see their tenth birthday. Cotton Mather fathered 14 children, but only 1 outlived his father: 7 died shortly after birth, 1 died at age 2, and 5 died in their early 20s (Stannard, 1979).

Children in colonial times were dominated by the concepts of repression, religion, and respect (Adams, 1980). The Puritans believed that children were born with original sin and were inherently stubborn, willful, selfish, and corrupt. The entire community—parents, school, church, and neighbors—worked together to keep children "in their place."

Compared with contemporary children, colonial children were expected to be extraordinarily well behaved, obedient, and docile (*Figure 3.1*). Within 40 years of their arrival in Plymouth, however, many colonists worried that their families were disintegrating, that parents were becoming less responsible, and that children were losing respect for authority. Ministers repeatedly warned parents that their children were frequenting taverns, keeping "vicious company," and "tending to dissoluteness (unrestrained and immoral behavior)" (Mintz and Kellogg, 1988: 17). These concerns sound pretty modern, don't they?

Wealthy southern families were more indulgent with their children than were well-to-do families in the northern colonies, but child labor was nearly universal throughout the colonies in less affluent families. Even very young children worked hard in their own homes, as indentured servants, or as slaves. For example, several shiploads of "friendless boys and girls," kidnapped in England, were sent to the Virginia colony to provide cheap and submissive labor for the American planters (Queen et al., 1985).

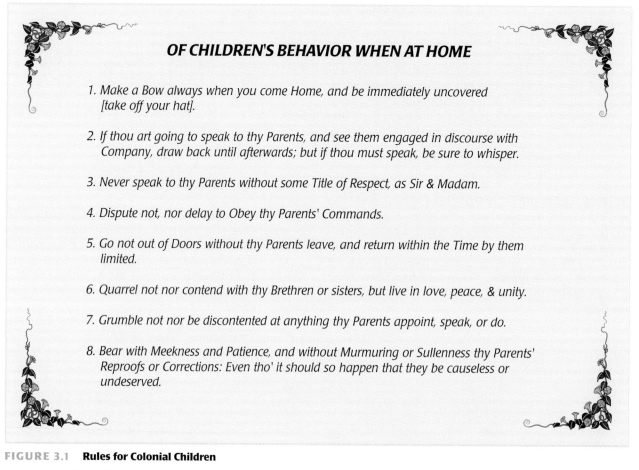

OF CHILDREN'S BEHAVIOR WHEN AT HOME

1. Make a Bow always when you come Home, and be immediately uncovered [take off your hat].

2. If thou art going to speak to thy Parents, and see them engaged in discourse with Company, draw back until afterwards; but if thou must speak, be sure to whisper.

3. Never speak to thy Parents without some Title of Respect, as Sir & Madam.

4. Dispute not, nor delay to Obey thy Parents' Commands.

5. Go not out of Doors without thy Parents leave, and return within the Time by them limited.

6. Quarrel not nor contend with thy Brethren or sisters, but live in love, peace, & unity.

7. Grumble not nor be discontented at anything thy Parents appoint, speak, or do.

8. Bear with Meekness and Patience, and without Murmuring or Sullenness thy Parents' Reproofs or Corrections: Even tho' it should so happen that they be causeless or undeserved.

FIGURE 3.1 **Rules for Colonial Children**

SOURCE: Adapted from Wadsworth, 1712, in Scott and Wishy, 1982.

Because girls were expected to be homemakers, their formal education was meager. The New England colonies educated boys, but girls were generally banned from education. They were commonly admitted to the public schoolhouse only during the hours and seasons when boys were occupied with other affairs or were needed in the fields. As one farmer stated, "In winter it's too far for girls to walk; in summer they ought to stay at home to help in the kitchen" (quoted in Earle, 1899: 96). Women who succeeded in getting an education were often ridiculed:

> John Winthrop—the first governor of the Massachusetts Bay Colony—maintained that such intellectual exertion [as education and writing books] could rot the female mind. He attributed the madness of Ann Hopkins, wife of the Connecticut governor, to her intellectual curiosity: "If she had attended her household affairs and such things as belong to women and not gone out of her way to meddle in the affairs of men whose minds are stronger, she'd have kept her wits and might have improved them usefully" (Ryan, 1983: 57).

Social Class and Regional Differences

The colonial family's experiences were not the same across all groups; there were a number of regional and social class variations. In a study of Salem families between 1790 and 1810, Farber (1972) found three social classes with very different socialization patterns that supported the economic structure.

In the *merchant class*, or the upper class, the patriarchs typically were shipping and commercial entrepreneurs. The oldest son continued the commercial enterprises and invested the family's profits in other high-paying ventures. Family businesses were inherited, and partnerships were expanded through first-cousin marriages.

Highly skilled occupations, apprenticeship systems, and cooperation among relatives characterized the *artisan class*, or the middle class. Children were encouraged to be upwardly mobile and to find secure jobs.

The *laboring class*, or the working class, was made up mainly of migrants in the community. These people, who had no voting privileges and little education, provided much of the necessary unskilled labor for the merchant class.

Colonial families also differed across regions. In the northern colonies people settled in villages; in the southern colonies people settled on isolated plantations and farms. There was an especially rigid stratification system among wealthy families, poor whites, indentured servants, and black slaves in the southern colonies.

Early American Families from Non-European Cultures

European explorers and settlers who invaded the North American continent in the sixteenth and seventeenth centuries pushed the original inhabitants—American Indians and Mexicans—out of their territories. Except for people who arrived in the colonies as servants—and in general they *chose* to indenture themselves—African Americans are the only people who did not come to America voluntarily. The experiences of these three peoples were quite different. Some families and tribes fared better than others, and there was considerable diversity within each group.

American Indians

Many anthropologists believe that American Indians migrated to North America from northeastern Asia over a period of 30,000 years (Greenberg and Ruhlen, 1992). By the time European settlers arrived, there were almost 18 million Indians living in North America, speaking approximately 300 languages. About 175 distinct languages are still spoken in the United States (Trimble and Medicine, 1993; Pierre, 2003). American Indians were enormously diverse racially, culturally, and linguistically. This variation was reflected in kinship and family systems, as well as in interpersonal relations.

Kinship and Family Systems Family structures and customs varied across Indian societies. For example, polygyny was common in more than 20 percent of marriages among Indians of the Great Plains and the northwest coast. In contrast, monogamy was the norm among such agricultural groups as the Hopi, Iroquois, and Huron. Among the agricultural tribes in eastern and southwestern America, where women played a major role in food production, inheritance through the mother's side was common, and young couples often lived with the woman's family.

In many American Indian groups, the most important stages of the life cycle were birth, puberty, marriage, and death. Again, however, there were many variations, some formal and some more casual, that governed marriage, relations with in-laws, and religious rituals (Price, 1981).

Approximately 25 percent of North American Indian tribes were **matrilineal,** which meant that children traced their family descent through the mother's line rather than that of the father (**patrilineal**). The women owned all the houses, the household furnishings, the fields and gardens, the work tools, and the livestock, and all of this property was passed on to their female heirs (Mathes, 1981). Some groups, such as the Creek society, allowed polygyny. Few men took more than one wife, however,

MULTICULTURAL

American Indian Women: Chiefs, Physicians, Politicians, and Warriors

Many American Indian women and men had egalitarian relationships. Besides being wives and mothers, many Indian women were also chiefs, physicians, politicians, and warriors.

Chiefs: In some cases, women became chiefs because of their achievements on the battlefield. In other cases, they replaced husbands who died. Like men, female chiefs could declare war, resolve disputes in the community, and punish offenders.

Physicians: Women could be medicine women, or shamans, the Indian equivalent of doctors. In many Indian cultures, women played crucial spiritual leadership roles.

Politicians: Because many tribes were matrilineal and matrilocal, many women were powerful politically.

Among the Lakota, for example, a man owned only his clothing, a horse for hunting, weapons, and spiritual items. Homes, furnishings, and other property belonged to women. In many tribes, women were influential decision makers in the community.

Warriors: Among the Apache, some women warriors were as courageous as the men, and Cheyenne women distinguished themselves in war. Lakota women maintained warrior societies, and among the Cherokee, one of the fiercest warriors was a woman who also headed a women's military society. Women could stop war parties by refusing to supply the necessary food for the journey. An Iroquois woman could initiate a war party by demanding that a captive replace any murdered member of her

Delaware nation council chief and educator Linda Poolaw was asked to choose works for an exhibition for the Smithsonian's National Muesuem of the American Indian. Poolaw's ancestors once lived on Manhattan Island in New York.

clan. Creek women often were responsible for raising "war fervor" against enemies (Mathes, 1981; Braund, 1990; Stockel, 1991; Jaimes and Halsey, 1992).

---

because only the best hunters could support more than one wife and one set of children (Braund, 1990).

Historians say that Indian women were often better off than their white counterparts. In contrast to film-makers' stereotypes of the passive Indian woman and docile "squaw," Indian women actually wielded considerable power and commanded respect in many bands and tribes. The box "American Indian Women: Chiefs, Physicians, Politicians, and Warriors" describes some of the societal roles that Indian women of colonial times played.

Marriage and Divorce   Most American Indian women typically married between ages 12 and 15, after reaching puberty. Men married at slightly older ages, between 15 and 20, usually after they had shown an ability to hunt and to provide for a family. Some families arranged their children's marriages; others allowed young men and women to choose their own spouses.

Family structures and customs also varied. Among the Shoshone there were no formal marriage ceremonies; the families simply exchanged gifts. Also, there were

no formal rules of residence. The newly married couple could live with the family of either the groom or the bride or establish its own independent unit.

Mohave marriages were also casual: There was no dowry, gift exchange, or wedding ceremony. To prevent incest, a man could not marry a woman who was a direct blood relative from his mother's or father's side or who was a member of his own clan. Divorce was simple—either partner could initiate the separation—and fairly common among young adults, who remarried easily.

Among the Zuñi of the Southwest, marriages were arranged casually, and the groom moved into the bride's household. Divorce was easy in the Zuñi and other groups. If a wife was fed up with a demanding husband, she would simply put his belongings outside their home, and they were no longer married. The man accepted the dismissal and returned to his mother's household. If a husband sought a divorce, he would tell his wife he was going hunting and then never return (Stockel, 1991).

In the Great Plains, most Teton parents arranged marriages, but some were based on romantic love. Marriages were often lifetime associations, but divorce was easy and fairly common. A man could divorce a wife for adultery, laziness, or even excessive nagging. Both parties usually agreed to divorce, but a man could humiliate a wife by casting her off publicly at a dance or other ceremony. Instead of literally cutting off his unfaithful wife's nose and demanding a payment from her lover, a truly generous husband would force the couple to leave the band and even provide them with a horse and other property to show his magnanimous nature.

Children   Most Indian families were small because of high infant and child death rates. In addition, mothers nursed their children for several years, often abstaining from sexual relations until the child was weaned. Throughout most American Indian groups, childhood was considered to be a happy time, and parents were generally kind and loving. Mohave parents, for example, were indulgent; children were carefree, and disciplinary methods were rare and mild. Similarly, the Zuñi treated children with kindness and little physical discipline. Children were taught to be polite and gentle. Unruly children were frightened into conformity by stories of religious bogeymen rather than by physical punishment. The grandparents on both sides of the family played an active role in educating children and telling stories that inculcated the tribe's values.

Puberty   In most Indian societies, puberty rites were more elaborate for girls than for boys. Among the Alaskan Nabesna, for example, the menstruating girl was secluded, observed strict food taboos, was forbidden to touch her own body with her hands (lest sores break out), and was forbidden to travel with the tribe. Among the Navajo, girls underwent elaborate rites with an all-night "sing" on the fourth ceremonial night. In contrast, among the Mohave, the observance of a girl's puberty was a private family matter that did not include any community rituals.

Among the Teton, a boy's puberty was marked by a series of events, such as his first successful bison hunt, his first war party, his first capture of enemy horses, and other deeds, all of which his father commemorated with feasts and gifts to others. Some tribes also emphasized the *vision quest*, a supernatural experience in which a "familiar spirit" suggested the course the boy's adult life would take. The young boy fasted for four days before leaving the tribe's camp and took ritual purifying sweat baths in a small, dome-shaped sweat lodge. On leaving the camp, the boy found an isolated place, often a butte top or other elevated spot, where he waited for four days and nights or until he experienced a vision in which a supernatural being instructed him on his future responsibilities (Spencer and Jennings, 1977).

The Impact of European Cultures   The French, Spanish, Portuguese, and British played a major role in destroying much American Indian culture. Europeans exploited the abundant North American resources of gold, land, and fur. Missionaries, determined to convert the "savages" to Christianity, were responsible for some of the cultural destruction. Disregarding important cultural values and beliefs, missionaries tried to eliminate religious ceremonies and such practices as polygyny and matrilineal inheritance (Price, 1981).

Indian tribes coped with military slaughter, enslavement, forced labor, land confiscation, coerced mass migration, and involuntary religious conversions (Collier, 1947). By the end of the seventeenth century, staggering numbers of American Indians in the East had died from such new diseases as influenza, measles, smallpox, and typhus. The Plymouth colony was located in a deserted Indian village whose inhabitants had been devastated by epidemics brought by Europeans.

By the 1670s, only 10 percent of the original American Indian population of New England survived. At least 50 tribes became extinct as a result of disease and massacre. In the eighteenth and nineteenth centuries, the diversity of American Indian family practices was reduced even further through ongoing missionary activities, intrusive federal land policies, and marriage with outside groups (John, 1988).

African Americans

One colonist wrote in his journal that on August 20, 1619, at the Jamestown settlement in Virginia, "there came . . . a Dutch man-of-warre that sold us 20 negars." These first African Americans were brought over as indentured servants. After their terms of service, they were free to buy land, marry, and hire their own labor.

These rights were short-lived. By the mid-1660s, the southern colonies had passed laws prohibiting blacks from testifying in court, owning property, making contracts, traveling without permission, congregating in public places, and marrying. The slave trade grew in both the northern and the southern colonies over several decades.

Some early statesmen, such as Thomas Jefferson, publicly denounced slavery but supported it privately. In 1809, for example, Jefferson maintained that "the Negro slave in America must be removed beyond the reach of mixture" for the preservation of the "dignity" and "beauty" of the white race (Bergman, 1969). At the same time, Jefferson had a slave mistress, Sally Hemmings, and fathered children with her. Inconsistent to the end, he freed five of his slaves in his will but left the rest to his heirs.

Marriage   Throughout the colonies, it was difficult for a slave to find a spouse. In northern cities, most slaves

CONSTRAINTS

A Slave Auction

In the mid-1970s, Alex Haley, a journalist who had taught himself to read and write during a 20-year career in the U.S. Coast Guard, was catapulted to fame when his book *Roots: The Saga of an American Family* (1976) became a best-seller and was made into one of the first miniseries on television. In the book, Haley traced the six generations of his ancestors, the first of whom was abducted at age 16 from Gambia, West Africa, in 1767. The following excerpt is an equally powerful description of how African families were destroyed by slavery:

During the day a number of sales were made. David and Caroline were purchased together by a Natchez planter. They left us, grinning broadly, and in a most happy state of mind, caused by the fact of their not being separated. Sethe was sold to a planter of Baton Rouge, her eyes flashing with anger as she was led away.

The same man also purchased Randall. The little fellow was made to jump, and run across the floor, and perform many other feats, exhibiting his activity and condition. All the time the trade was

going on, Eliza was crying aloud and wringing her hands. She besought the man not to buy him, unless he also bought herself and Emily. She promised, in that case, to be the most faithful slave that ever lived.

The man answered that he could not afford it, and then Eliza burst into a paroxysm of grief, weeping plaintively. Freeman turned round to her, savagely, with his whip in his uplifted hand, ordering her to stop her noise, or he would flog her. Unless she ceased that minute, he would take her to the yard and give her a hundred lashes. . . . Eliza shrunk before him and tried to wipe away her tears, but it was all in vain. She wanted to be with her children, she said, the little time she had to live.

All the frowns and threats of Freeman could not wholly silence the afflicted mother. She kept on begging and beseeching them, most piteously, not to separate the three. Over and over again she told them how she loved her boy. A great many times she repeated her former promises—how very faithful and obedient she would be, how hard she would

labor day and night, to the last moment of her life, if he would only buy them all together.

But it was of no avail; the man could not afford it. The bargain was agreed upon, and Randall must go alone. Then Eliza ran to him, embraced him passionately, kissed him again and again, told him to remember her—all the while her tears falling in the boy's face like rain.

Freeman damned her, calling her a blubbering, bawling wench, and ordered her to go to her place, and behave herself, and be somebody. . . . He would soon give her something to cry about, if she was not mighty careful, and that she might depend on.

The planter from Baton Rouge, with his new purchase, was ready to depart. "Don't cry, mama. I will be a good boy. Don't cry," said Randall, looking back, as they passed out of the door.

What has become of the lad, God knows. It was a mournful scene indeed. I would have cried myself if I had dared.

SOURCE: Adapted from Solomon Northrup, cited in Meltzer (1964: 87–89).

---

lived with their masters and were not allowed to associate with other slaves. In the southern colonies, most slaves lived on plantations that had fewer than ten slaves. Because the plantations were far apart, it was difficult for slave men and women to find a spouse of roughly the same age. In addition, overwork and high death rates due to widespread disease meant that marriages did not last very long (Mintz and Kellogg, 1988).

To ensure that slaves would remain on the plantations, many owners recognized familial relationships among slaves, encouraged them to have large families, and provided living quarters. Yet slave marriages were fragile. As the box "A Slave Auction" shows, owners often separated slave families. Studies of slave families in Mississippi, Tennessee, and Louisiana show that such auctions ended 35 to 40 percent of marriages (Gutman, 1976; Matthaei, 1982).

Family Structure   Until the 1970s, sociologists and historians maintained that slavery had emasculated black fathers, forced black mothers to be family matriarchs, and destroyed the African American family. Historian Herbert Gutman (1983) dispelled many of these beliefs with his study of 21 urban and rural communities in the South between 1855 and 1880. Gutman found that 70 to 90 percent of African American households were made up of a husband and wife or a single parent.

Most women were heads of households because their husbands had died, not because they had never married. They usually had only one or two children. Thus, according to Gutman, in the nineteenth century black families were stable, intact, and resilient.

Husbands and Fathers   Several black scholars have also noted that white, male, middle-class historians and sociologists have misrepresented the slave family structure (McAdoo, 1986; Staples, 1988). One example is the portrayal of slave husbands and fathers. In contrast to popular conceptions of the African American male as powerless, adult male slaves provided important role models for boys:

> *Trapping wild turkeys required considerable skill; not everyone could construct a "rabbit gum" equal to the guile of the rabbits; and running down the quick, battling raccoon took pluck. For a boy growing up, the moment when his father thought him ready to join in the hunting and to learn to trap was a much-sought recognition of his own manhood (Genovese, 1981: 239–40).*

These activities increased families' nutritional intake and supplemented monotonous and inadequate diets.

African male slaves often served as surrogate fathers to many children, blood relatives and others. Black preachers, whose eloquence and morality commanded the respect of the entire community, were also influential role models. Men made shoes, wove baskets, constructed furniture, and cultivated the tiny household garden plots allotted to families by the master (Jones, 1985).

Some male slaves were also apprenticed in skilled jobs, promoted to better jobs, and granted cash bonuses for loyal service (Ryan, 1983). They were excluded, however, from political, economic, and educational institutions.

Wives and Mothers   Many historians describe African American women as survivors who resisted the slave system. For example, one proud daughter recalls, "My mother was the smartest black woman in Edes. . . . She would do anything. She made as good a field hand as she did a cook. She was a demon, loud and boisterous, high-spirited and independent. I tell you she was a captain" (quoted in Ryan, 1983: 162–63).

Mothers raised the children, cooked, made clothes for their families, maintained the slave cabin, and toiled in the fields. Because the African American woman was often both a "mammy" to the plantation owner's children and a mother to her own, she experienced the exhausting *double day*—a full day of domestic chores plus a full day of work outside the home—at least a century before middle-class white women coined the term.

Black women got little recognition for such grueling schedules and were often subjected to physical punishment. Pregnant slaves were sometimes forced to lie facedown in a specially dug depression in the ground, which protected the fetus while the mother was beaten, and some nursing mothers were whipped until "blood and milk flew mingled from their breasts" (Jones, 1985: 20).

In the South, children as young as 2 or 3 were put to work. They fetched things or carried the train of a mistress's dress. Masters often "gave" slave children as gifts to their own offspring (Schwartz, 2000). Only a few female slaves worked in the master's house, known as "the big house." Most females over 10 years of age worked in the field, sunup to sundown, six days a week, and mothers struggled to maintain a semblance of family life:

> *Occasionally, women were permitted to leave the fields early on Saturday to perform some chores around the slave quarters. Their homes were small cabins of one or two rooms, which they usually shared with their mate and their children, and perhaps another family secluded behind a crude partition (Ryan, 1983: 159).*

Popular films such as *Gone with the Wind* often portray house slaves as doing little more than adjusting Miss Scarlett's petticoats and announcing male suitors. In reality, domestic work was as hard as fieldwork. Fetching wood and water, preparing three meals a day over a smoky fireplace, and pressing clothes for an entire family was backbreaking labor. Female servants sometimes had to sleep on the floor at the foot of the mistress's bed. They were often forced into sexual relations with the master. Injuries were common, minor infractions met with swift and severe punishment, and servants suffered abuse ranging from jabs with pins to beatings that left them disfigured for life (Jones, 1985).

Economic Survival   *Ethnic Notions*, a memorable documentary, shows that many Hollywood movies, books, and newspapers have portrayed slaves as helpless, passive, and dependent people who couldn't care for themselves. Recent evidence is shattering such stereotypes. An archaeological team excavating Virginia plantations, for example, has found that some enslaved Africans were "entrepreneurs": They traded fish and game for children's toys, dishes, and other household items.

Also, many slaves hid important personal possessions and items stolen from plantation owners in underground storage areas (Wheeler, 1998). Many slaves were hardly meek or submissive. Instead, slaves used such effective tactics as breaking tools to slow their pace of work and negotiating with masters over assigned tasks (Berlin, 1998; Morgan, 1998).

After Emancipation   After slavery was abolished in 1863, many mothers set out to find children from whom they had been separated many years earlier (King, 1996). Numerous slaves formalized their marriages, even though the one-dollar fee for the marriage license cost about two weeks' pay for most. A legal marriage was an important status symbol, and a wedding was a festive event (Degler, 1981; Staples, 1988).

By permission of John L. Hart FLP, and Creators Syndicate, Inc.

Some writers have claimed that the African American family, already disrupted by slavery, was further weakened by urban migration to the North in the late 1800s (Frazier, 1939; Moynihan, 1970). However, many black migrants tried to maintain contact with their kin and families in the South. When black men migrated alone, "a constant flow of letters containing cash and advice between North and South facilitated the gradual migration of whole clans and even villages" (Jones, 1985: 159). Others returned home frequently to join in community celebrations or to help with planting and harvesting on the family farm. Thus, many African American families remained resilient despite difficult conditions.

Mexican Americans

After 30 years of war and conflict, in 1848 the United States annexed territory that was originally Mexican. Despite the provisions of the Treaty of Guadalupe Hidalgo, which guaranteed security of their property, the federal government confiscated the land of most Mexican families. Land speculators defrauded countless other landowners. Most of the Mexicans and their descendants became laborers. The loss of land, an important economic base, has had long-term negative effects on Mexican American families (see Chapter 4).

Work and Gender Whether they lived and grew up in the United States or migrated from Mexico, Mexican laborers were essential to the prosperity of southwestern businesses. Even though many had done skilled work in Mexico, employers purposely refrained from hiring Mexicans for skilled jobs because "they are available in such [great] numbers and . . . they [would] do the most disagreeable work at the lowest wages" (Feldman, 1931: 115).

During the 1800s, most women and children worked as almond pickers and shellers. Men typically worked on the railroads, mining, agriculture, ranching, or low-level urban occupations (such as dishwasher). Women worked as domestics, cooks, live-in house servants, and laundresses, as well as in canning and packing houses, and in agriculture (Camarillo, 1979).

By the 1930s, Mexican women made up a major portion of the labor pool of the garment manufacturing sweatshops in the Southwest. Even though American labor codes stipulated a pay rate of $15 a week, Mexican women were paid less than $5, and some earned as little as 50 cents a week. If the women protested, they lost their jobs. Illegal migrants were especially vulnerable because they were intimidated by threats of deportation (Acuna, 1988). Despite the economic exploitation, many Mexican families preserved traditional family structure, child rearing, and family roles.

Family Structure Mexican society was characterized by **familism**; that is, family relationships took precedence over individual well-being. (You will see in Chapter 4 that familism still characterizes much of contemporary Latino culture, including Mexican Americans.) The nuclear family often embraced an extended family of several generations, including cousins, where the relationships were both emotionally and financially supportive.

A key factor in conserving Mexican culture was the concept and practice of **compadrazgo,** in which parents, children, and the children's godparents established and maintained close relationships. The *compadres,* or co-parents, were godparents who enlarged family ties, similar to the fictive kin described in Chapter 1. Godparents were close family friends who had strong ties with their godchildren throughout life and participated in such rites of passage as baptism, confirmation, first communion, and marriage.

The godparents in the *compadrazgo* network provided both discipline and support. They expected obedience, respect, and love from their godchildren. They were also warm and affectionate and helped the children financially whenever possible. For girls, who led cloistered and protected lives, visiting godparents' families was a major form of recreation (Williams, 1990).

Children The handful of available diaries, letters, and other writings suggests that, at least in middle- and upper-class families, children were socialized according to gender. Although boys did some of the same domestic chores as their sisters, they had much more freedom than girls. Young girls were severely restricted in their social relationships outside the home. A girl was expected to learn how to be a good mother and wife—a refuge for the husband, a virtuous example for her children, and the "soul of society" (del Castillo, 1984: 81).

According to the diary of a teenage girl who lived on the outskirts of San Antonio from 1889 to 1892, her brother was responsible for helping with such family tasks as laundry and chopping wood. He was allowed to go into town on errands and to travel around the countryside on his horse. In contrast, she was not allowed to go into town with her father and brother or to attend chaperoned dances in the town. She could not visit neighbors, and she attended only one social event in a six-month period when her family traveled into town to visit her aunt during Christmas (del Castillo, 1984).

Many middle-class Mexican American children who were born in the United States had a prolonged adolescence, living with their parents until young adulthood. This was because, in general, Mexican American families believed in protecting children as long as possible. The practice was more common among affluent families, where children stayed at home to learn to take care of any inherited land and wealth. In contrast, working-class children left home earlier to seek wage-paying jobs.

Family Roles Women were the cultural guardians of family traditions, even though many mothers worked outside the home because of economic necessity. Despite the disruptions caused by migratory work, women nurtured Mexican culture through folklore, songs, baptisms, weddings, and celebrations of birthdays and saints' days (Garcia, 1980). In the traditional family, women defined their roles primarily as homemakers and mothers.

In the Mexican American family, the male head of the family had all the authority. Masculinity was expressed in the concept of **machismo,** which stresses such male attributes as dominance, assertiveness, pride, and sexual prowess. (Chapter 4 discusses some of the controversy surrounding the interpretation of *machismo*.)

This notion of male preeminence carried with it the clear implication of a double standard. Men could engage in premarital and extramarital sex, for example, but women were expected to remain virgins, to be faithful to their husbands, and to limit their social relationships, even after marriage, to family and female friends (Mirande, 1985; Moore and Pachon, 1985).

The European Influence Although they suffered less physical and cultural destruction than American Indians, Mexican Americans endured a great deal at the

hands of European frontiersmen, land speculators, and politicians. By the mid-1800s, when most Mexican Americans were beginning to experience widespread exploitation, new waves of European immigrant families were also harnessed under the yoke of industrialization.

Industrialization, Urbanization, and European Immigration: 1820 to 1930

The lives of many U.S. families changed dramatically from about 1820 to 1930 because of two massive waves of immigration from Europe. More than 10 million immigrants—mostly English, Irish, Scandinavian, and German—arrived during the first wave, from 1830 to 1882. During the second wave, 1882 to 1930, immigrants were predominantly Russian, Greek, Polish, Italian, Austrian, Hungarian, and Slavic.

The Industrial Revolution brought about extensive mechanization, which shifted home manufacturing to large-scale factory production. As the economic structure changed, a small group of white, Anglo-Saxon, Protestant (often referred to as WASP), upper-class families prospered from the backbreaking labor of Mexicans, Asians, European immigrants, and many American-born whites. European immigrants endured some of the most severe pressures on family life.

Family Life

As farming became large scale and commercial and as factories developed, families lost many of their production functions. Most family members had to work outside the home to purchase goods and services. Although it is not clear exactly how it happened, family life changed.

In the middle classes, husbands and wives developed separate spheres of activity. The husband went out to work (the "breadwinner"), and the wife stayed home to care for the children (the "housewife") (see Chapters 2 and 5). Couples had more freedom in choosing partners in terms of compatibility and personal attraction because romantic love became the basis for marriage.

As households became more private, ties with the larger community became more tenuous, and spouses turned to each other for affection and happiness much more than in the past (Skolnick, 1991). New attitudes about the "true woman" became paramount in redefining the role of the wife as nurturer and caregiver rather than workmate. In the lower socioeconomic classes, many mothers worked outside the home in low-paying jobs. Children often dropped out of school to work and to help support their families. Most spouses had little time to show love and affection to children or to each other.

CHANGES

Characteristics of "True Womanhood"

One author describes nineteenth-century working-class women as "without corsets, matrons with their breasts unrestrained, their armpits damp with sweat, with their hair all over the place, blouses dirty or torn, and stained skirts" (Barret-Ducrocq, 1991: 11). Expectations for upper-class women (whom middle-class women tried to emulate) were quite different.

For "true women," the loss of purity was worse than death. In *The Young Lady's Friend* (1837), Eliza Farrar gave practical advice about staying out of trouble: "Sit not with another in a place that is too narrow; read not out of the same book; let not your eagerness to see anything induce you to place your head close to another person's."

"True women" were expected to be gentle, passive, submissive, childlike, weak, dependent, and protected. Unlike men, they should work silently, unseen, and only for affection, not for money or ambition. Women should marry, but not for money. They should choose "only the high road of true love and not truckle to the values of a materialistic society." A woman should stifle her own talents and devote herself "to sustain her husband's genius and aid him in his arduous career."

Domesticity was a woman's most prized virtue. One of the most important functions of a woman as comforter was her role as nurse. The sickroom needed her "higher qualities" of patience, mercy, gentleness, and housewifely arts.

Home was supposed to be a cheerful place, so that brothers, husbands, and sons would not go elsewhere for a good time. Women were the "highest adornment of civilization" and should keep busy at "morally uplifting tasks." Housework was seen as uplifting. For example, making beds was good exercise, the repetitiveness of routine tasks inculcated patience and perseverance, and proper management of the home was a surprisingly complex art: "There is more to be learned about pouring out tea and coffee than most young ladies are willing to believe."

The true woman was expected to love flowers, to write letters ("an activity particularly feminine since it had to do with the outpourings of the heart"), and to practice singing and playing an instrument. If a woman had to read, she should choose spiritually uplifting books from a list of "morally acceptable authors," preferably religious biographies.

Source: Welter, 1966: 151–74.

The Debut of "True Womanhood" By the late eighteenth century, a small group of northern merchants had monopolized the import business, and wealthy southern planters had greatly expanded their landholdings and crop production. The wives and daughters of these elite business leaders devoted much of their energy to "a conspicuous display of personal adornment and social graces" (Ryan, 1983: 85).

The women spent much of their time socializing, throwing lavish parties, and adorning their homes and themselves. "The upkeep of her appearance might involve preparation of the cosmetic base, aqua vitae, a potion requiring 30 ingredients, 2 months' cultivation, and an impossible final step: 'shake the bottle incessantly for 10 to 12 hours'" (quoted in Ryan, 1983: 85–86).

By the early 1800s, most men's work was totally separated from the household, and family life became oriented around the man's struggle to make a living. The "good" wife made the home a comfortable retreat from the pressures that the man faced in the workplace.

Between 1820 and 1860, women's magazines and religious literature defined and applauded the attributes of "true womanhood." Women were judged as "good" if they displayed four cardinal virtues: piety, purity, submissiveness, and domesticity (Welter, 1966). As the box "Characteristics of 'True Womanhood'" demonstrates, working-class women were not "true women" because, like men, most worked outside the home.

Children and Adolescents Fathers' control over children began to erode even before the onset of the Industrial Revolution. By the end of the seventeenth century, fathers had less land to divide among sons. This meant that fathers had less authority over their children's (especially sons') sexual behavior and choice of a marriage partner. The percentage of women who were pregnant at the time of marriage shot up to more than 40 percent by the mid-eighteenth century, suggesting that parents had become less effective in preventing premarital intercourse (Mintz and Kellogg, 1988).

Because a marriage became less likely to involve agreements about the distribution of family land and property, children were less dependent on their fathers for economic support. Moreover, new opportunities for nonagricultural work and labor shortages in cities prompted many children to leave home and to escape strict fathers.

Perhaps the biggest change was that, largely in the middle class, children began to be perceived and treated not just as small adults but as individuals in a particular stage of life. Around 1800, the concept of original sin—which decrees that children are inherently bad—gave way to the notion that children were innocent creatures with the capacity for either good or bad.

Children began to spend more time playing than working, and adolescence gained recognition as another stage of life that had no adult responsibilities. People published more books for and about children. Adults began to recognize children's individuality by giving them names that were different from their father's or mother's. In the nineteenth century, people began for the first time to celebrate birthdays, especially those of children. There was also a decline in physical punishment, and physicians and others now recognized the early onset of sexual feelings in children (Aries, 1962; Degler, 1981; Demos, 1986).

Among the working classes and the poor in the nineteenth century, however, child labor was widespread, and children made a critical contribution to their families' survival. In a Massachusetts survey of working-class families in 1875, for example, children under age 15 contributed nearly 20 percent of their families' income (Mintz and Kellogg, 1988).

The Impact of Immigration and Urbanization

Immigration played a key role in the Industrial Revolution in the United States. Immigrants provided a large pool of unskilled and semi-skilled labor that fueled emerging industries and gave investors huge profits.

In the first large waves of immigration in the late 1800s, paid middlemen arranged for the shipment of immigrants to waiting industries. For example, Asians were channeled into the western railroads, Italians were funneled into public works projects and used as strikebreakers, and Hungarians were directed toward the Pennsylvania mines. Later immigrants followed these established paths into industrial America (Bodnar, 1985).

Work Very few immigrant families escaped dire poverty. Because men's wages were low, most married women were also in the labor force. Some worked at home making artificial flowers, threading wires through tags, or crocheting over curtain rings. Some were cleaning women or seamstresses, did laundry, or sold cakes. Others took in boarders and lodgers, especially after their children had left home (Hareven, 1984; Weatherford, 1986).

These Pennsylvania miners and "breaker boys"—youngsters who sorted the mined coal into traded categories—worked as many as fourteen hours a day for very low pay. Like most miners of this period, they were immigrants who provided backbreaking labor during the U.S. Industrial Revolution.

Like the men, women of different ethnic groups tended to move into specific jobs. For example, Italian women were more likely than Polish or Greek women to reject domestic labor, which would take them out of the Italian community and into other people's homes. Consequently, they were more likely to work as seasonal laborers for fruit and vegetable processing companies (Squier and Quadagno, 1988). By the turn of the nineteenth century, as *Figure* 3.2 on page 68 shows, a woman's occupation was usually associated with her race and ethnicity.

Women and Work in Nineteenth-Century America

By 1890, all but 9 of the 369 industries listed by the U.S. Census Bureau employed women. Many of these industries were especially eager to hire "greenhorns" and women "just off the boat" who would work for low wages. Greenhorns were often underpaid or not paid at all. In some cases, employers delayed wage payments for several months and then closed up the shops, disappearing overnight (Manning, 1970).

By the late 1800s, Irish girls as young as 11 were leaving home to work as servants; 75 percent of all Irish teenage girls were domestic servants. Even though they were hired only for housekeeping, many had to care for

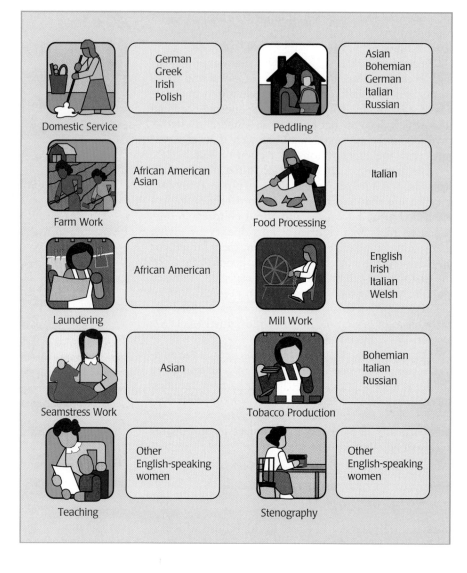

FIGURE 3.2 Women and Work in Nineteenth-Century America
As you can see, women who worked outside the home in the 1800s tended to cluster in certain low-paying jobs. Only those who spoke English well were hired as office workers or teachers.

children, were sexually assaulted by their male employers, and were not paid their full wages (Ryan, 1983).

Most manufacturing jobs were segregated by sex. In the tobacco industry, for example, even though cigar rolling traditionally had been a woman's task in Slavic countries, men filled this well-paying job. Immigrant women were relegated to damp and smelly basements, where they stripped the tobacco that was then rolled by men who worked "upstairs" under better conditions. In the metal trades, men worked with lighter and more intricate sand cores (devices used in molding steel) and had high-paying jobs. In contrast, immigrant women hauled heavy sand cores through dusty shops to fuming ovens (Ryan, 1983).

Housing One of the biggest problems for immigrant families was the lack of decent housing in densely populated cities. One Philadelphia tenement house, for example, housed 30 families in 34 rooms. A Lithuanian couple and their five children lived in a tiny closet of a home that contained only slightly more air space than the law required for one adult. The buildings were jammed together so that the immigrant population of one block in New York City was equal to that of an entire town. Women increased their kitchen wall space by reaching out the window and hanging utensils on the outside of the house next door (Weatherford, 1986).

Health Epidemics and disease were rampant among immigrant families. A cholera epidemic that barely touched the rest of New York City killed nearly 20 percent of the residents of a crowded immigrant neighborhood. Because a third of tenement rooms had no windows or ventilation, many immigrants contracted tuberculosis. In Lawrence, Massachusetts, where the population was 90 percent immigrant, a third of the

CROSSCULTURAL

Stereotypes about European Immigrants

On October 28, 1886, President Grover Cleveland dedicated the Statue of Liberty in New York Harbor on whose pedestal are inscribed Emma Lazarus's famous welcoming words: "Give me your tired, your poor, your huddled masses yearning to breathe free." As the following examples show, however, Lazarus's poem did not reflect the reality:

1886: The U.S. consul in Budapest advised that Hungarian immigrants were not "a desirable acquisition" because, he claimed, they lacked ambition and they would work as cheaply as the Chinese, which would interfere "with a civilized laborer's earning a 'white' laborer's wages."

1891: Congressman Henry Cabot Lodge called for a restriction of immigration because (referring especially to Jewish and Polish immigrants) the immigrants represented the "lowest and most illiterate classes," which were "alien to the body of the American people."

1910: Members of the eugenics movement promoted "improving" the human species by controlling hereditary factors in mating. They contended that through intermarriage, immigration would contaminate the "old stock" with feeblemindedness, criminality, and pauperism. Many eugenicists, such as Robert DeCouncey Ward from Harvard, were faculty in privileged eastern universities.

1914: Edward A. Ross, a prominent sociologist at the University of Wisconsin and a self-proclaimed immigration watchdog wrote, "that the Mediterranean people are morally below the races of northern Europe is as certain as any social fact."

1922: Kenneth L. Roberts, a Cornell graduate, served as a correspondent for the *Saturday Evening Post* on immigration questions. He warned that "if a few more million members of the Alpine, Mediterranean, and Semitic races are poured among us, the result must inevitably be a hybrid race of people as worthless and futile as the good-for-nothing mongrels of Central America and Southeastern Europe."

1946: After World War II, the immigration of displaced persons revived old fears. Such influential senators as Pat McCurran and James Eastland argued that political immigrants should not be permitted to enter the United States because of their "alien philosophies" and "biological incompatibility with Americans' parent stocks."

SOURCE: Carlson and Colburn, 1972: 311–50.

STOP AND THINK . . .

- *Look at* Figure 3.1 *again. Some of my students feel that such rules for colonial children were ridiculous. Others think that we should resurrect some of these practices because many parents are too permissive. What do you think?*

- *Did your ancestors experience prejudice and discrimination? Did their past shape how you and your parents were raised? If you're a recent immigrant, what kinds of prejudice and discrimination have you and your family encountered?*

spinners in the textile mills died of respiratory diseases, such as pneumonia and tuberculosis, before they had worked ten years. These diseases were triggered by the lint, dust, and machine fumes of the unventilated mills. Furthermore, the excruciating noise of the mills often resulted in deafness, and many workers were injured by faulty machines (Weatherford, 1986).

Family Conflict   Dilapidated urban housing and epidemics were not the only problems that immigrant families faced. Most immigrants suffered many of the ills that come with poverty and isolation in a strange and often hostile new environment: a breakdown of marital and family relations, crime, delinquency among their children, and general demoralization. Living quarters

shared with relatives put additional pressures on already strained marital ties (Thomas and Znaniecki, 1927).

Prejudice and Discrimination   Like the American Indians, Mexicans, and blacks before them, most European immigrants met with enormous prejudice, discrimination, and economic exploitation. Much of the inequality was created and reinforced by high-ranking, highly respected, and influential people who had been educated in the most prestigious colleges and universities in the United States (see the box "Stereotypes about European Immigrants").

Despite the stereotypes and discrimination, most immigrant families overcame enormous obstacles.

Rarely complaining, they worked at low-status jobs with low-paying wages and encouraged their children to achieve and move up.

The "Modern" Family Emerges

The economic depression of the 1930s, World War II in the 1940s, the baby boom of the 1950s, and the increasing economic and political unrest of the years since the 1960s have all influenced the American family—sometimes for better, sometimes for worse.

Some social scientists maintain that the "modern" family emerged around 1830. At this time, courtship was more open, marriages were often based on affection rather than financial considerations, and parents centered more of their attention on children (Degler, 1983). Others believe that the modern family emerged at the beginning of the twentieth century, especially with the rise of the "companionate family" (Burgess et al., 1963).

Rise of the Companionate Family (1900–1930)

At the turn of the twentieth century, married couples increasingly stressed the importance of sexual attraction and compatibility in their relationships. Particularly in the middle classes, the notion of companionship, or the *companionate family,* also included a couple's children. Affection between parents and children was more intimate and more open, and adolescents enjoyed greater freedom from parental supervision.

This new independence generated criticism, however. Many of the popular magazines, such as *The Atlantic Monthly, The Ladies' Home Journal,* and the *New Republic,* worried about "young people's rejection of genteel manners, their defiant clothing and hairstyles, their slang-filled language, and their 'lewd' pastimes . . . (such as smoking, attending petting parties, and going out on school nights). Public condemnation and moral outrage were widespread" (Mintz and Kellogg, 1988: 119). Do any of these complaints about young people sound familiar?

The Great Depression (1929–1939)

There was nothing great about the Great Depression. Still, families had a vast variety of experiences, influenced largely by factors such as residence, social class, gender, race, and ethnicity.

Urban and Rural Residence Among tenant farmers, many people who farmed the land owned by others could not pay the rent either in cash or in a share of the crops. Husbands sometimes left their families to search for jobs. Some women who could not cope with such

desertion took drastic steps to end their misery. In 1938, for example, a Nebraska farm mother of 13 children committed suicide by walking into the side of a train because "she had had enough" (Fink, 1992: 172).

Even when husbands remained at home, some families lost their land and personal possessions. Parents made enormous sacrifices to feed their children. As one jobless Oregon father stated, "We do not dare to use even a little soap when it will pay for an extra egg or a few more carrots for our children" (McElvaine, 1993: 172).

To help support their families, many young men and women raised on farms moved to cities to find work. Young women were more likely to find jobs because there was a demand for low-paying domestic help. What they sent home from their $10 or so weekly wages helped their families buy clothes and other necessities.

Social Class The most devastating impact of the Great Depression fell on working-class and poor families. More than half of all married women—especially those in the poorest southern states such as South Carolina, Mississippi, Louisiana, Georgia, and Alabama—were employed in low-paying jobs, such as domestic and personal service and apparel and canning factories (Cavan and Ranck, 1938; Chafe, 1972).

In contrast to middle-class children, children from working classes did not have carefree teenage years in the 1930s. Boys, especially, were expected to work after school or to leave school entirely to supplement their family's meager income. When mothers found jobs, older children, especially girls, looked after their younger brothers and sisters and often had to drop out of school to do so (McElvaine, 1993).

Some working-class children became part of the "transient army" that drifted from town to town looking for work. Most slept in lice-ridden and rat-infested housing when they could afford to pay the 10 or 15 cents for a urine-stained mattress on the floor. Others slept on park benches, under park shrubbery and bridges, in doorways, in packing crates, or in abandoned automobiles (Watkins, 1993).

As blue-collar employment in the male-dominated industrial sectors decreased, white-collar clerical and government jobs expanded. Women took many of these jobs. The wages of white, middle-class women enabled their families, even during the Depression, to maintain the standard of living and consumer habits that they enjoyed during the affluent 1920s (Ryan, 1983).

Upper-middle-class families fared even better. Fairly affluent families made only minor sacrifices. Some families cut down on entertainment, did not renew country club memberships, and decreased such outside family services as domestic help. Few reported problems in food budgets, however, and many of these families continued to take summer vacations. In fact, the number of families that owned radios, musical instruments, and new cars increased (Morgan, 1939).

Race Although the Depression was an economic disaster for many people, African Americans suffered even more. Unemployment was much higher among blacks than whites. As layoffs began in late 1929 and accelerated in the following years, blacks were often the first to be fired. By 1932, black unemployment had reached approximately 50 percent nationwide. As the economic situation deteriorated, many whites demanded that white workers replace blacks in such occupations as garbage collector, elevator operator, waiter, bellhop, and street cleaner.

In some government jobs, employers set an unofficial quota of 10 percent black, on the theory that this represented, roughly, the percentage of African Americans in the general population. In fact, though, the government employed only about 6 percent. Even those who were able to keep their jobs faced great hardship. A 1935 study in Harlem, for instance, found that from the onset of the Depression, the wages of skilled black workers dropped nearly 50 percent (McElvaine, 1993; Watkins, 1993).

Gender Roles In many families, unemployment wreaked havoc on gender roles. The position of the husband and father was based on his occupation and his role as provider. If he lost his job, he often suffered a decline in status within the family. Understandably, men were despondent: "Sometimes the father did not go to bed but moved from chair to chair all night long" (Cavan and Ranck, cited in Griswold, 1993: 148).

Men who could not provide for their families became depressed, preoccupied, abusive, drank more, or spent much of their time searching for jobs. As fathers became physically and emotionally distant, their authority in the family and their children's respect often decreased. Adolescents became more independent and more rebellious (Griswold, 1993).

In 1932, a federal executive order decreed that only one spouse could work for the federal government. The widespread unemployment of men therefore put pressure on women, especially married women, to resign from some occupations. In addition, school boards fired married female teachers, and some companies dismissed married women. More than 77 percent of the school districts in the United States would not hire married women, and 50 percent had a policy of firing women who got married (Milkman, 1976; McElvaine, 1993).

When women did work, the federal government endorsed lower pay rates for women than men and promoted sex discrimination. For example, men on Works

Many women worked in American factories, steel mills, and shipyards during WW II. Although many women found it hard to give up their new-found jobs and financial independence, most were replaced by men who returned from the war in 1945.

Progress Administration (WPA) projects were paid $5 per day; women received only $3.

World War II (1939–1945)

World War II triggered even greater changes in work roles and family life. These changes began to be felt in 1941, after the United States entered the war.

Work Roles Workers were scarce when the United States entered World War II, especially in the defense and manufacturing industries, because many able-bodied men had been drafted.

Initially, employers were unwilling to recruit women for traditionally male jobs. And many women, especially white middle-class women, were reluctant to violate traditional gender roles.

In 1942, however, prompted by both the Women's Bureau of the U.S. Department of Labor and organized women's groups, employers began attempting to fill many jobs, especially those in nontraditional positions, with women. The government, supported by the mass media, was enormously successful in convincing both men and women that a "woman's place is in the workplace" and not the home:

In all the media, women at work were pictured and praised, and the woman who did not at least . . . work as a volunteer for the Red Cross was made to feel guilty. . . . Even the movies joined in. The wife or sweetheart who stayed behind and went to work . . . became as familiar a figure as the valiant soldier-lover for whom she waited (Banner, 1984: 219).

Millions of women, including middle-aged mothers and even grandmothers, worked in shipyards, steel mills, and ammunition factories (see "Data Digest"). They welded, dug ditches, and operated forklifts. For the first time, black women were recruited into high-paying jobs, making some of the greatest economic gains.

Hundreds of thousands of domestic servants and farm workers left their jobs for much better paying positions in the defense and other industries. In the superb documentary film *The Life and Times of Rosie the Riveter*, black women describe the pride and exhilaration they felt in having well-paying jobs that they genuinely enjoyed.

Because of the labor shortages, this was the only time when even working-class women were praised for working outside the home. Two of the best-selling magazines during that time, the *Saturday Evening Post* and *True Story*, supported the government's propaganda efforts during World War II by casting working-class women in very positive roles:

Stories and advertisements glorified factory work as psychologically rewarding, as emotionally exciting, and as leading to success in love. Both magazines combated class prejudice against factory work by portraying working-class men and women as diligent, patriotic, wholesome people. . . . Working-class women were resourceful, respectable, warmhearted, and resilient (Honey, 1984: 186–87).

Family Life   Although divorce rates had been increasing slowly since the turn of the century, they reached a new high in 1946, a year after the end of World War II. The war had a direct, negative effect on many families. Some wives and mothers who had worked during the war enjoyed their newfound economic independence and decided to end unhappy marriages.

In other cases, families disintegrated because of the strains of living with a man who returned partially or completely incapacitated. Alcoholism, which was rampant among veterans, was believed to be the major cause of the upward spiral of postwar divorces (Tuttle, 1993).

For some people, the war deferred rather than caused divorce. Some couples, caught up in war hysteria, courted briefly and married impulsively (Mowrer,

1972). In many cases, both the bride and the young soldier matured during the husband's prolonged absence and had little in common when they were reunited.

Perhaps one of the greatest difficulties that many families faced was the children's reaction to fathers they barely knew or had never even seen. As the box "Daddy's Coming Home!" shows, despite widespread rejoicing over the end of the war, a father's return was unsettling for many children.

The "Golden" Fifties

After World War II, when women were no longer needed in the workplace because returning veterans needed jobs, the propaganda about family roles changed almost overnight. Ads now depicted happy housewives totally engrossed in using vacuum cleaners and the latest consumer products. Heroines in short stories and women's magazines were no longer the nurses dying at the front but mothers who devoted themselves exclusively to cooking, caring for their children, and pleasing their husbands. In the 1950s, many people moved to the suburbs, and middle-class people, especially, became absorbed with their families.

Gender Roles   Movies and television shows celebrated two stereotypical portrayals of women: sweet, innocent virgins, such as Doris Day and Debbie Reynolds, or sexy bombshells such as Marilyn Monroe and Jayne Mansfield. Television applauded domesticity on such popular shows as *I Love Lucy, Ozzie and Harriet, Leave It to Beaver,* and *Father Knows Best.* Marriage manuals and child-care experts, such as Dr. Benjamin Spock, told women to please their husbands and to be full-time homemakers. By the mid-1950s, 60 percent of female undergraduates were dropping out of college to marry (Banner, 1984).

As you saw in Chapter 1, the post–World War II generation experienced a baby boom. Family plans that had been disrupted by the war were renewed. Although women continued to enter the job market, many middle-class families, spurred by the mass media, sought a traditional family life in which the husband worked and the wife played the domestic role.

The editor of *Mademoiselle* echoed a widespread belief that women in their teens and twenties should avoid careers and instead raise as many children as the "good Lord gave them." Many magazines and newspaper articles encouraged families to participate in "creative" activities such as outdoor barbecues and cross-country camping trips (Chafe, 1972).

Moving to the Suburbs   Suburbs mushroomed, accounting for nearly two-thirds of the population increase in the fifties. The interest in moving to the suburbs reflected structural and attitudinal changes.

CHANGES

Daddy's Coming Home!

Soldiers returning from World War II encountered numerous problems, including unemployment and high divorce rates (Mowrer, 1972). Historian William M. Tuttle, Jr. (1993) solicited 2500 letters from men and women, then in their 50s and 60s, who were children during World War II. What most of these people had in common were the difficulties they and their families experienced in adjusting to the return of their fathers from military service.

Some children feared that their fathers would not stay and therefore avoided becoming too attached. Some were bitter that their fathers had left in the first place. Others, especially those who were preschoolers at the time, were frightened of the strange men who suddenly moved into their homes. One woman remembered watching "the stranger with the big white teeth" come toward her. As he did, the 4-year-old ran upstairs in terror and hid under a bed.

Some recalled anger because their fathers' return disrupted their lives. Grandparents had often pampered children they helped to raise. In contrast, the returning father, fresh from military experience, was often a strict disciplinarian and saw the child as "a brat." If the children had been very close to their mothers, they became resentful of fathers for displacing them. Others were disappointed when the idealized images they had constructed of "Daddy" did not match reality or when fathers who had been described as kind, sensitive, and gentle returned troubled or violent.

Readjustment was difficult for both children and fathers. Although some households adjusted to the changes, in

The "G.I. Bill" enabled many WW II veterans to go to school and improve their job opportunities. But for many vets with families, like William Oskay, Jr., and his wife and daughter, daily life required many sacrifices and hardships.

many families the returning fathers and their children never developed a close relationship.

The federal government, fearful of a return to economic depression, underwrote the construction of homes in the suburbs (Rothman, 1978). The general public got low-interest mortgages, and veterans were offered the added incentive of purchasing a home with a $1 downpayment.

Massive highway construction programs enabled people to commute from the city to the suburbs. Families wanted more room, seclusion, and an escape from city noise, crime, dirt, and crowding. The larger space offered more privacy for both children and parents: "The spacious master bedroom, generally set apart from the rooms of the children, was well-suited to a highly sexual relationship. And wives anticipated spending many evenings alone with their husbands, not with family or friends" (Rothman, 1978: 225–26).

The suburban way of life added a new dimension to the traditional role of women:

The duties of child-rearing underwent expansion. Suburban mothers volunteered for library work in the school, took part in PTA activities, and chauffeured their children from music lessons to scout *meetings. Perhaps most important, the suburban wife was expected to make the home an oasis of comfort and serenity for her harried husband (Chafe, 1972: 217–18).*

The Blissful 1950s?   Were such changes desirable? And did they really take place in most families? Some writers have argued that many of these presumed shifts in people's beliefs and behavior are actually myths, not reality. "Contrary to popular opinion," notes historian Stephanie Coontz (1992: 29) "*Leave It to Beaver* was not a documentary." In fact, the "golden fifties" were riddled with many family problems, and people had fewer choices than they do today. Here are some examples:

- *Consumerism* was limited primarily to middle- and upper-class families. In 1950, a supermarket stocked an average of 3750 items; in the 1990s, most markets carried more than 17,000 items. Until the 1990s, *many prepared foods were loaded with lard, salt, sugar, and harmful preservatives.*

Suburbs boomed during the 1950s. Levittown, on Long Island, New York, represented the ideal image of middle-class life. These small, detached, single-family houses all looked the same but offered affordable housing to returning GIs and their young families.

- Black and other ethnic families faced *severe discrimination* in employment, education, housing, and access to recreational activities.

- *Domestic violence and child abuse,* though widespread, were invisible (see Chapter 14).

- Many young people were forced into *"shotgun" marriages* because of premarital conception; young women were pressured to give up their babies for adoption.

- About 20 percent of mothers had *paying jobs.* Although child-care services are still inadequate today, they were practically nonexistent in the 1950s.

- Many people, including housewives, tried to escape from their unhappy lives through *alcohol or drugs.* The consumption of tranquilizers, largely unheard of in 1955, soared to almost 1.2 million pounds in 1959 (Coontz, 1992; Crispell, 1992; Reid, 1993).

The Family since the 1960s

In the 1970s, families had lower birth rates and higher divorce rates, and larger numbers of women entered colleges and graduate programs. In the 1980s, more people over age 25 postponed marriage. Many who were already married delayed having children.

Out-of-wedlock births, especially among teenage girls, declined in the late 1990s, but the number of one-parent households increased precipitously (see Chapters 7 and 9). Two-income families burgeoned, along with adult children who continued to live at home with their parents because of financial difficulties (see Chapter 12).

The twenty-first century began with numerous problems that affected families. The stock market plunged. Many older people had to go back to work because their retirement portfolios shrank by at least 50 percent (see Chapters 17 and 18). Many young adults were laid off from promising high-tech jobs and scurried to find *any* employment above a minimum wage (see Chapter 13).

Health-care costs skyrocketed. And, because of terrorist attacks on September 11, 2001, federal and state governments funneled billions of dollars into "homeland security" and the war in Iraq. As a result, agencies gutted many family programs and services, especially for poor and working-class families.

MAKING CONNECTIONS

- Many of your grandparents or parents probably lived through the Great Depression and World War II. How did they survive these turbulent periods? If your kin were poor, how did these eras shape their attitudes and values about jobs, money, food, and other issues?

- Many people are nostalgic about the "golden fifties." Were these years really "golden" for you, your parents, or your grandparents? Or did your family experience hardships because of racial, ethnic, social class, gender, and sexual orientation prejudice and discrimination?

- If you grew up in the suburbs, how have they changed over the years? If you grew up in the city, has the ethnic composition changed? What are the advantages and disadvantages of living in either area?

Conclusion

If we examine the family in a historical context, we see that *change,* rather than stability, has been the norm. Furthermore, families differed by region and social class even during colonial times.

We also see that the experiences and *choices* open to American Indians, African Americans, Mexican Americans, and many European immigrants were very different from those of "middle America," experiences that were romanticized by many television programs in the 1950s.

Such macro-level constraints as wars and shifting demographic characteristics have also influenced families.

Many families survived despite enormous hardships, disruptions, and dislocations.

They are still coping with such macro-level constraints as an unpredictable economy and such micro-level variables as greater *choices* in family roles. The next chapter, on racial and ethnic families, examines some of the ongoing changes, choices, and constraints.

SUMMARY

1. Historical factors have played an important role in shaping the contemporary family. The early exploitation of American Indian, African American, and Mexican families has had long-term economic effects on these groups in U.S. society.

2. The colonial family was a self-sufficient unit that performed a wide variety of functions. Children were part of the family work force and were expected to be docile and well behaved. Premarital sex was fairly common, wives' work was subordinate to that of husbands, and family practices varied across social classes and geographic regions.

3. American Indian families were extremely diverse in function, structure, sexual relations, puberty rites, and child-rearing patterns. European armies, adventurers, and missionaries played major roles in destroying many tribes and much of American Indian culture.

4. Contrary to popular belief, many slave households had two parents, men played important roles as fathers or surrogate fathers, and most women worked as hard in the fields as the men. Instead of succumbing to subordination, many slaves were resourceful and resilient in maintaining their families.

5. Most Mexican American families lost their lands to European American settlers. Despite severe economic exploitation, many families survived through cohesive family networks and strong family bonds.

6. By the nineteenth century, industrialization had changed some aspects of the family. Marriages were

based more on love and choice rather than on economic considerations, and parental roles in the family became more sex segregated. In the upper and middle classes the "true woman," who devoted most of her time to looking beautiful and pleasing her husband, emerged.

7. Millions of European immigrants who worked in labor-intensive jobs at very low wages fueled the rapid advance of industrialization. Many immigrants, including women and children, endured severe social and economic discrimination, dilapidated housing conditions, and chronic health problems.

8. Working-class families felt the most devastating effects of the Great Depression. Whereas middle-class families cut back on some luxuries, working-class men experienced widespread unemployment, and their wives worked in the most menial and low-paying jobs.

9. World War II had a mixed effect on families. For the first time, many women, especially black mothers, found jobs that paid a decent salary. However, death and divorce disrupted many families.

10. After the war, suburbs boomed and birth rates surged. The family roles of white middle-class women expanded to include full-time nurturance of children and husbands. Husbands' roles were largely limited to work. The "golden fifties" reflects a mythical portrayal of the family in that decade.

KEY TERMS

bundling 56
matrilineal 59

patrilineal 59
familism 64

compadrazgo 64
machismo 65

TAKING IT FURTHER

Research Your Family Tree and Other Families

I've listed several dozen genealogy sites in www. prenhall.com/benokraitis. One of the most interesting and unusual is **Find a Grave**. Visitors can search almost 4 million burial records, free of charge, and sometimes even find photographs of dead relatives.

www.findagrave.com

The **Gilder Lehrman Institute of American History** offers excellent information about families from colonial periods to the present day. Some of the most delightful links include love letters by young couples and the fathers' attempts to dampen their daughters' romances.

www.gliah.uh.edu/index.cfm

The **Pilgrims in American Culture: Thanksgiving** site will help dispel many of our current myths about this holiday. If you want to duplicate the "first" Thanksgiving, you'll enjoy the recipes for roast fowl (not turkey), seethed cod, and hominy pudding.

www.plimoth.org/Library/Thanksgiving/thanksgi.htm

Documenting the American South: North American Slave Narratives, Beginnings to 1920, provided by the University of North Carolina at Chapel Hill, offers a collection of eighteenth-, nineteenth-, and early-twentieth-century slave narratives and an extensive bibliography.

docsouth.unc.edu/neh/neh.html

Westward by Sea: A Maritime Perspective on American Expansion, 1820–1890 is a site that presents pictorial and textual material about the California Gold Rush, the roles of women, the immigrant experience, whaling life, and native populations. It includes materials about California, Texas, Hawaii, and the Pacific Northwest.

memory.loc.gov:8081/ammem/award99/mymhihtml/
mymhihome.html

Levittown: Documents of an Ideal American Suburb provides a social, cultural, and visual history of the epitome of suburban living after World War II and the town's evolution over the past 50 years.

tigger.uic.edu/%7Epbhales/Levittown.html

And more: www.prenhall.com/benokraitis provides sites on topics that include a bibliography on North American Indians, interviews with former slaves, a Women of the West Museum, documentary materials from the original Plymouth Colony, photographs and oral histories on American Indian traders in the Southwest, key events in the history of slavery, World War II posters featuring women, a documentary of Levittown (the "ideal American suburb"), World War II's "victory gardens," an immigrant tenement museum in New York City, and much more.

INVESTIGATE WITH RESEARCH NAVIGATOR

Please go to www.researchnavigator.com and enter your LOGIN NAME and PASSWORD. For instructions on registering for the first time, please view the detailed instructions at the end of the Chapter 1. Please search the Research Navigator™ site using the following key search terms:

family structure
matrilineal
machismo

Racial and Ethnic Families:
Strengths and Stresses

DATADIGEST

- Most of the world's immigrants live in Europe (56 million), Asia (50 million), and the United States and Canada (41 million). Almost **one person in every ten living in affluent nations is an immigrant**.

- In 2001, 34 percent of whites, 26 percent of Asian Americans, 15 percent of Latinos, and only 9 percent of blacks thought that **we have overcome the major problems facing racial minorities in the country**.

- In 2000, **married-couple households across racial and ethnic groups** were as follows: 81 percent for whites, 80 percent for Asian and Pacific Islanders, 65 percent each for Latinos and American Indians, and 47 percent for African Americans.

- In 2000, the largest number of **people with Middle Eastern roots who immigrated to the United States** came from Pakistan (14,500), Iran (8500), Egypt (4500), and Jordan (3900).

- Of the 281.4 million people counted in the 2000 census, about 6.8 million (2.4 percent) **identified with two or more races**.

SOURCES: United Nations, 2002; *Race and Ethnicity . . .*, 2001; U.S. Census Bureau, 2002; Jones and Smith, 2001.

Yolanda Zambrano married her Colombian sweetheart, already living in the United States, in 1990. After she arrived in Worcester, Massachusetts, Yolanda volunteered in the community, including a travel agency, to learn English and as much as possible about her new country. The owner of the travel agency, tired of the business, suggested that Yolanda might like to buy it.

Although she had only $2000 in savings at the time, Yolanda maxed out her credit cards and secured a small loan plus the $20,000 needed for her license. She hired and trained a bilingual staff and focused on providing top-quality, personalized service for people traveling to Latin America for business or recreation. By 2001, her company had grown to $7 million in annual sales, and she won an award from the Small Business Administration as the Minority Small Business Person of the Year for New England (Lampman, 2001: 15).

Yolanda's story is typical of many immigrants who arrive on American soil and work hard to turn opportunities into successes. Not all immigrants have been as successful, of course, but millions of non-European immigrants have made significant contributions to U.S. society.

Chapter 3 discussed some of the history of white immigrants and several minority families. In this chapter we focus on contemporary African American, American Indian, Latino, Asian American, and Middle Eastern families. We'll also examine marriage and other relationships across racial and ethnic lines. Let's begin with an overview of the growing diversity of American families.

The Increasing Diversity of U.S. Families

As you saw in Chapter 1, U.S. households are becoming more diverse in terms of racial and ethnic composition. As the number and variety of immigrants increase, the ways we relate to each other become more complex.

To understand some of this complexity, think of a continuum. At one end of the continuum is **assimilation**, or the conformity of ethnic group members to the culture of the dominant group, including intermarriage. At the other end of the continuum is **cultural pluralism**, or maintaining many aspects of one's original culture—including language and marrying within one's own ethnic group—while living peacefully with the host culture.

Still others—those in the middle of the continuum—blend into U.S. society through acculturation. **Acculturation** is the process of adopting the language, values, beliefs, roles, and other characteristics of a host culture (such as attaining high educational levels and securing good jobs). Like cultural pluralism, acculturation does not include intermarriage, but the newcomers merge into the host culture in most other ways.

Changes in the Immigration Mosaic

The United States is largely a country of immigrants. One in five Americans either was born abroad or born of parents who were born abroad (Bernstein, 2002). The current proportion of foreign-born U.S. residents is small by historical standards, however.

In 1900, about 15 percent of the total U.S. population was foreign-born, compared with 11 percent in 2000. Since the turn of the twentieth century, there has been a significant shift in many immigrants' country of origin. In 1900, almost 85 percent of immigrants came from Europe. In 2002, in contrast, Europeans made up only 14 percent of all new immigrants. Today, immigrants come primarily from Asia (mainly China and the Philippines) and Latin America (mainly Mexico) (see *Figure 4.1*).

In the last decade, the largest foreign-born population growth occurred in the South and Southwest (Fix and Capps, 2002). Immigration increased in these regions because of the development of high-tech companies that relied on highly skilled and highly educated "outsiders" or because the newcomers were willing to work for low wages in semi-skilled and unskilled jobs (Foust et al., 2002).

Attitudes about Immigration How do Americans feel about immigration? Most are uneasy. According to a recent poll, for example, 55 percent favor reducing immigration (up from 41 percent in 2001), 27 percent want to keep it at the same level, and only 15 percent favor increasing current immigration rates (Dillin, 2001; Chicago Council on Foreign Relations, 2002).

Compared with most other countries, the United States welcomes immigrants. Japan, for instance, historically has had very low immigration rates simply because it doesn't want to become "an immigrant country." In 2001, 44 percent of high-income countries and 39 percent of middle-income countries initiated policies to lower immigration levels (*International Migration Report*, 2002).

Since 2001, almost every nation in Europe, from the Scandinavian countries to Spain, has implemented laws

FIGURE 4.1 **Origins of U.S. Immigrants: 1900 and 2002**

SOURCE: Based on data in U.S. Department of Commerce, 1993, and Schmidley, 2003.

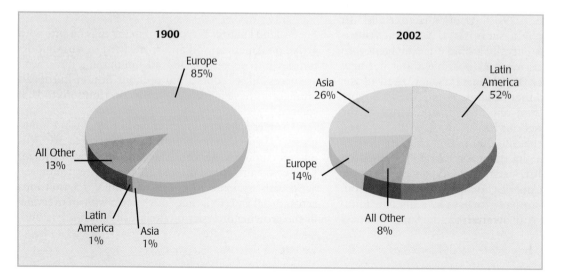

Every year, millions of immigrants become U.S. citizens. Here, a Vietnamese man and some of his family members participate in a naturalization ceremony.

to decrease the number of immigrants. Some countries have become aggressive about expelling illegal immigrants. Mexico deported 160,000 undocumented migrants from Guatemala, and arrests climbed 25 percent higher in 2001. India has cracked down on illegal Bangladeshis along its borders (Dillin, 2001; MacKenzie, 2002; Francis, 2003; Sharma, 2003).

The Costs and Benefits of Immigration   Many countries are curtailing immigration for a number of reasons: fears about security, concerns about diluting national identity, and worries about displacing U.S.-born employees. Some American immigration critics point out that low-skilled workers depress wages, reduce the standard of living, and overload schools and welfare systems. Others note that because immigrants are younger, poorer, and less well-educated than the native population, they use more government services and pay less in taxes. By some estimates, hospitals spend $2 billion a year to treat illegal immigrants who are ineligible for Medicaid (Canedy, 2002; Martin and Midgley, 2003).

In some cases, U.S. multinational corporations use an obscure visa called the L-1 to transfer high-tech employees within companies "to dump high-paid Americans in favor of cheaper workers from abroad." Such practices displace high-tech American employees who are paid three times as much as their replacements (Grow and Kripalani, 2003).

Immigrants themselves, both legal and illegal, also endure costs. At the low end of the pay scale, recruiters promise people good jobs and training. Instead, the immigrants often find themselves living in abject poverty. The federal government has prosecuted Tyson Foods, the nation's largest meat producer and processor, for helping illegal immigrants from Mexico and Central America to obtain false documents such as Social Security cards, for cheating workers out of wages, and for violating child labor laws that have resulted in serious injuries and deaths of children under 16 (Reardon-Anderson et al., 2002; Roche and Mariano, 2002; Day, 2003; "Tyson Foods . . .," 2003).

On the other hand, immigrants provide many benefits for their host countries. Immigrants clean homes and business offices, toil as nannies and busboys, serve as nurses' aides, and pick fruit, all at low wages and in jobs that most American-born workers don't want to do. Recent immigrants have also rejuvenated many other employment sectors, working in professional, administrative, sales, and blue-collar occupations (Sum et al., 2002).

Without immigrants, many rural towns would shrivel or experience a severe shortage of young workers. For example, Mason City, Iowa, has imported workers who are taxpaying members of the community at both ends of the employment spectrum:

> *Mercy Medical has brought in a pediatrician from the Philippines to complement a staff that also includes doctors from India, South Africa, and Latin America. A local cement factory has brought in engineers from Argentina and elsewhere. A local meat-processing facility employs a number of Bosnians who have moved to Mason City (Belsie, 2001: 4).*

Many demographers predict that countries with low immigration rates will experience severe problems in the future. As populations in industrialized countries age and birth rates plunge, there will be fewer workers to keep economies from shrinking (see Chapter 18). Even maintaining current inflows, the United States is likely to face labor shortages by 2010. To avoid people working well into their 70s, Germany would have to boost immigration twentyfold and Japan fiftyfold (Baker, 2002).

Race and Ethnicity Still Matter

Social scientists routinely describe Latino, African American, Asian American, Middle Eastern, and American Indian families as minority groups. A **minority group** is a group of people who may be treated differently or unequally because of their physical or cultural characteristics, such as gender, sexual orientation, religion, or skin color. Even though minority groups may outnumber a dominant group, they have less power, privilege, and social status in a society.

What kinds of physical and cultural characteristics differentiate minority groups from a dominant group? Two of the most important are race and ethnicity.

Race   A **racial group** is a category of people who share physical characteristics, such as skin color, that members of a society consider socially important. Both sociologists and anthropologists see race as a social label rather than a biological trait. Many biologists, similarly, view race as a social rather than a biological or scientific concept because possibly only 6 of the body's estimated 35,000 genes determine the color of a person's skin (Graves, 2001).

If it's a meaningless concept, why are we so obsessed with race? There are two main reasons. First, biologists note that some diseases are more prevalent in some populations, such as Tay–Sachs disease among Ashkenazi Jews, cystic fibrosis among people of northern European descent, and cardiovascular disease among blacks. Do some of the health disparities result from a common ancestral tree? Unhealthy lifestyles? Living in toxic environments where disease-causing traits are transmitted from generation to generation? No one knows. According to some scientists, discarding race as a category could result in not developing medical treatments, even when the causes are social (Duster, 2001; Cooper et al., 2003).

The second reason why the concept of race is important is that physical characteristics, such as skin color and eye shape, are easily observed and mark groups for unequal treatment. As you'll see in this and other chapters, as long as we sort ourselves into racial categories and act on the basis of these characteristics, our life experiences will differ in terms of access to jobs and other resources and how people treat us.

Ethnicity   An **ethnic group** (from the Greek word *ethnos*, meaning "nation") is a set of people who identify with a common national origin or cultural heritage. The cultural heritage includes language, geographic roots, customs, traditions, and religion. Ethnic groups in the United States include Puerto Ricans, Chinese, Serbs, blacks, and a variety of white ethnic groups such as Italians, Swedes, Hungarians, Jews, and many others.

Even though the U.S. government acknowledges that race is a social, not biological concept, it considers race and ethnicity to be separate in people's self-identification. The Census 2000 question on race included 15 separate response categories, three areas where respondents could write in a more specific race group, and a question on "ancestry or ethnic origin." Someone who's Latino, for example, could answer questions on both ethnicity and race.

Like race, ethnicity—an individual's or group's cultural or national identity—can be a basis for unequal treatment. As you saw in Chapter 3, many white European immigrants experienced discrimination because of their ethnic roots when they came to the United States.

Racial-Ethnic Group   Sociologists often refer to a set of people who have distinctive physical and cultural characteristics as a **racial-ethnic** group. All of the families we examine in this chapter are examples of racial-ethnic groups because both physical and cultural attributes are central features of their heritage.

Although some people use the terms interchangeably, remember that *race* is a social concept that refers to physical characteristics, whereas *ethnicity* describes cultural characteristics. The term *racial-ethnic* incorporates both physical and cultural traits (Murry et al., 2001b). Making these distinctions becomes complicated because people prefer some "labels" to others, and these labels change over time.

The Labeling Issue   Although *Hispanic* and *Latino* are often used interchangeably, the labels reflect regional usage and cultural background. *Hispanic* is preferred in New York and Florida, whereas *Latino* is most popular in California and Texas. The label *Chicano* (*Chicana* for women) arose in the 1970s and is still used to refer to those of Mexican origin born in the United States. *Hispano* is favored to emphasize unity with Spain rather than Mexico. And a small group in southern California prefers *Mexica* to stress indigenous Indian roots in Mexico.

Labels for blacks have also changed over time, from hurtful racial epithets to *colored*, *Negro*, and *Afro-American* (Kennedy, 2002). Currently, most people, including African American scholars, use *black* and *African American* interchangeably. I find the same results when I poll my black students informally. Some are vehement about using *African American* to emphasize their African ancestry; others prefer *black* (with or without the capitalization) because "black is beautiful."

We see similar variations in the usage of *Native Americans* and *American Indians*. Although these groups prefer their tribal identities (such as Cherokee, Apache, and Lumbi), people often dispute whether an American Indian is full-blooded or mixed blood, belongs to a tribe or not, or is simply a "wannabe" after several centuries of intermarriage rather than being a "real" Indian (Snipp, 2002).

Prejudice and Discrimination

Race and ethnicity affect whether we and our family members will experience prejudice and discrimination. Generally, prejudice is less harmful than discrimination because it's in our heads rather than our actions.

Prejudice Prejudice is an *attitude* that prejudges people, usually in a negative way, who are different from us in terms of race, ethnicity, or religion. If an employer assumes, for example, that white workers will be more productive than their black or Latino counterparts, she or he is prejudiced.

Sometimes my students, especially minorities, argue that prejudice is one-sided: They maintain that it is directed against racial and ethnic groups by those in power, the dominant group. In fact, prejudice is typically two-sided. Antiwhite sentiment has decreased in black communities since 1992. Still, almost one-third of the black respondents in a recent survey said that "almost all" or "many" blacks dislike whites (Saad, 2002). The point is that *all* of us can be prejudiced. However, minorities, rather than whites, are typically targets of discrimination.

Discrimination Discrimination is behavior that treats people unequally or unfairly. Discrimination encompasses all sorts of actions, ranging from social slights (such as inviting only white kids in a child's class to a birthday party) to rejection of job applications and hate crimes.

In a recent survey, researchers asked people whether they had encountered any discrimination in the previous 30 days. Among African Americans, 42 percent said they were discriminated against once (and 12 percent said it happened two or more times). Asian Americans ranked second (31 percent) and then Latinos (16 percent). Only 13 percent of whites said they experienced discrimination because of race. The minority respondents complained of being followed around suspiciously or not being able to get the attention of salesclerks. Asian Americans said they experienced the most unfair treatment at restaurants (Smith, 2000).

Discrimination also occurs *within* racial-ethnic groups. In a recent national poll, for example, 83 percent

of Latinos said that they had experienced discrimination from other Latinos. The most recent immigrants, especially Colombians and Dominicans, said that they had encountered unequal treatment in employment and income from U.S.-born Latinos (Brodie et al., 2002).

Thousands of books and scholarly articles document widespread discriminatory practices, all of which hurt racial-ethnic families. Discrimination in mortgage loans is one example. About 72 percent of whites own homes, compared with 53 percent of Asian Americans and 46 percent of African Americans and Latinos (Mather, 2002). Although the discrimination against blacks and Latinos seeking to buy a home has declined more than 25 percent since 1989, inequality persists. Both groups, for example, are more likely than whites to encounter mortgage lending discrimination and "racial steering" (where real estate agents show units only in minority neighborhoods) and are not encouraged to make an offer for a house or to meet with a real estate agent (Turner et al., 2002).

Yet homeownership is important. Besides being an American dream come true, children who live in homes that their parents own rather than rent experience safer and healthier environments: better lighting, play areas, stability (because parents are less likely to move), and neighborhood activities (such as Halloween parties) in which both parents and children participate (Haurin et al., 2002).

Heath care provides another example of widespread discriminatory practices. For example,

- Minorities are less likely than whites to receive appropriate heart medicine or undergo bypass surgery, kidney dialysis or transplants, cancer treatment, or the newest treatments for AIDS.

- Minorities, even those with private health insurance, receive lower-quality care than whites. This inferior treatment contributes to higher death rates and shorter lifespans.

- Black children under age 18 suffer more disabilities—such as asthma, diabetes, mental retardation, and learning difficulties—than their white counterparts because black children are more likely to grow up in poverty (Swift, 2002; Newacheck et al., 2003).

Although education and employment opportunities have improved since the mid-1960s, racial-ethnic families have to deal, often on a daily basis, with prejudice and discrimination. However, African American, American Indian, Latino, Asian American, and Middle Eastern families also have strengths despite ongoing inequality. We now turn to a closer examination of each of these five groups.

CONSTRAINTS

The Ten Biggest Myths about the African American Family

There are many misconceptions about the African American family, most of which can be reduced to the following ten myths (see also Chapter 3):

Myth 1. Black family bonds were destroyed during slavery. Historical studies show that most slaves lived in families headed by a father and a mother. Many slave couples lived in long marriages, some for 30 years or more (Bennett, 1989).

Myth 2. The black family collapsed after emancipation. In 1865, the roads of the South were clogged with black men and women searching for long-lost family. Most freed slaves, some of them elderly, remained with their mates. Few renounced their slave vows or sought new partners.

Myth 3. The black family has always been a matriarchy characterized by domineering women and weak or absent men. Black America has produced a long line of extraordinary fathers and many mothers and fathers working, loving, and living together (Billingsley, 1992).

Myth 4. Most black families are poor and on welfare. Although 23 percent of African Americans live below the poverty level, in 2001 almost 28 percent of black families had annual incomes of $50,000 or more (DeNavas-Walt and Cleveland, 2002).

Myth 5. The major problem of black families is loose morals. In reality, black America has always condemned unrestrained sexual expression and has insisted on stable mating patterns. Children are valued, whether born in or out of wedlock (Hill et al., 1993).

Myth 6. Most black single-parent families are dysfunctional. Given the obstacles they face, many single-parent

families are remarkably resilient. They are raising highly motivated children who graduate from college and who become quite successful (Toliver, 1998).

Although such films as *Boyz'n the Hood* offer a realistic portrayal of some working-class black neighborhoods, these negative images should not be generalized to all black communities (Gaiter, 1994).

Myth 7. Black parents avoid work, fail to motivate their children, and teach them to rely on handouts. For most of the twentieth century, blacks were more likely to work than whites. Until the mid-1990s, for instance, proportionally more black mothers than white mothers were in the labor force. At many Fortune 1000 companies, blacks make up 2 to 26 percent of managers and board members (Hickman, 2002).

Myth 8. Black men can't sustain stable relationships. Many unmarried African American fathers maintain ties with their children and the mothers of their children (see Chapter 12). Middle-class black fathers are often more family-oriented than middle-class white fathers (Taylor, 2000).

Myth 9. Black families no longer face widespread job and housing discrimination. In a recent poll, 34 percent of white respondents, compared with only 6 percent of black respondents, said that "blacks have achieved racial equality" (Bobo et al., 2001).

In fact, blacks report everyday discrimination in a variety of settings, from dealings with the police to local shop owners (Barnes, 2000; "The color line—still," 2001).

Almost 75 percent of white respondents said that "blacks have as

good a chance as white people in my community to get any kind of job for which they are qualified" (Wheeler, 1993). In fact, qualified blacks are still less likely to be hired than their white counterparts (Thornton et al., 1992).

And although high-interest mortgage loans are illegal, they are five times more likely in black neighborhoods than in white neighborhoods (Hoerlyck, 2003).

Myth 10. The African American family owes its survival to white generosity and government welfare. Most blacks survived because of the support of the extended family, house rent parties, church suppers, and black schools and churches, not handouts or welfare. In fact, African Americans have made enormous contributions in education, music, business, and other areas (Kunjufu, 1987; McWhorter, 2001).

STOP AND THINK...

- *In Chapter 1, you recall, we considered how myths are functional and dysfunctional. How are myths about African American families functional? How are they dysfunctional?*

- *What other myths might you add to the ones in this box?*

MAKING CONNECTIONS

■ Do you think the United States should change its immigration levels? What do you think would be the costs and benefits of increasing or decreasing current immigration rates?

■ Have you, your family members, or friends ever experienced racial-ethnic discrimination? Also, list examples of situations in which a person who is prejudiced might not discriminate and in which a person who discriminates may not necessarily be prejudiced. ◎

African American Families

Contrary to what many people seem to think, there is no such thing as "the" African American family. Such families, like other American families, vary in terms of kinship structure, values, lifestyles, and social class (Allen and James, 1998). Yet profound stereotypes still exist (see the box on "The Ten Biggest Myths about the African American Family").

Family Structure

E. Franklin Frazier (1937) was one of the first sociologists to point out that there are several types of black family structures: families with matriarchal patterns, traditional families similar to those of middle-class whites, and families, usually of mixed racial origins, that have been relatively isolated from the main currents of African American life. Over time, black family structures have changed, adapting to the pressures of society as a whole (Billingsley, 1992). When men become jobless, for example, some nuclear families expand to include extended families. Others welcome nonrelatives, such as fictive kin, as members of the household (see Chapter 1).

Until 1980, married-couple families were the norm. Since then, black children have been more likely to grow up with only one parent, usually a mother, than children in other racial-ethnic groups (see *Figure 4.2*). This shift reflects a number of social and economic developments: postponement of marriage, high divorce and separation rates, low remarriage rates, male unemployment, and out-of-wedlock births (see Chapters 9–13, 15, and 16). Although almost 68 percent of all black children under age 18 live in two-parent homes, "the formation of African-American households often originates not in marriage but in the birth of a child" (Barbarin and McCandies, 2003: 52).

Husbands and Wives

In the late 1980s, many black men criticized the movie *The Color Purple*, based on Alice Walker's novel, for depicting them as sadistic, exploitive, and brutal. In contrast, many black women felt the film realistically portrayed black women as supporting one another and their families.

Although African American families are often stereotyped as matriarchal, the egalitarian family pattern, where both men and women share equal authority, is a more common arrangement. Black husbands are more likely than their white counterparts to share in the household chores (John and Shelton, 1997; Xu et al., 1997). The more equal sharing of housework and child care probably reflects black husbands' willingness to "pitch in" because many of their wives are employed. Also, many grew up in families in which mothers worked outside the home and many black men were "active participants" in domestic labor (Penha-Lopes, 1995).

The division of domestic work is not equal, however. Black married women are still more likely than men to do most of the traditional chores, such as cooking, cleaning, and laundry, and to be overworked. Some of the instability in black marriages, as in white marriages, has been a result of conflict when wives demand that men do more of the "traditionally female" domestic tasks (Hatchett, 1991; Hatchett et al., 1995).

FIGURE 4.2 Where Children Live

SOURCE: Based on Fields, 2001, Figure 1.

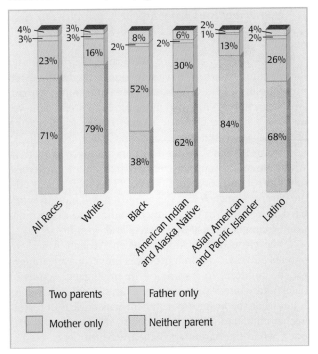

Overall, black couples report lower marital happiness and satisfaction than white couples (Glenn and White, 2003). It's not clear why this is the case. Some researchers speculate that greater economic stress among African American couples increases marital conflict and discontent, especially when parents must also deal with relationships with rebellious adolescent children (Gutman and Eccles, 1999; McLoyd et al., 2001).

Others feel that racial discrimination decreases the quality of marital relationships. As psychological stressors pile up at work, for example, black parents may become more anxious, depressed, and angry. As a result, spouses might argue more and be less nurturing with their children (Murry et al., 2001a).

Parents and Children

Most African American parents play important roles in their children's development. Married middle-class black parents, especially, are very similar to their counterparts in other groups. If anything, they are more flexible in family roles. Many black fathers make a conscious effort to be involved with their children because their own fathers were aloof. Others emulate fathers who participated actively in father–child activities. Still others are simply devoted to their kids:

> [My older son and I] do everything together. I learned to roller-skate so that I could teach him and then go skating together. I'm the one who picks him up from school. I'm one of his Sunday school teachers, so he spends Sundays with me at church while my wife stays at home with our two-month-old son (Penha-Lopes, 1995: 187–88).

Black parents are more likely than their white and Latino counterparts to have someone in the family teach preschoolers letters, words, numbers, and songs. African American parents are also more likely to stress achievement in school to children about to enter kindergarten (Toth and Xu, 1999; Wagemaar and Coates, 1999). Black, Latino, and Asian American parents are more likely than white parents to emphasize that their children exercise self-control and succeed in school. This may reflect ethnic parents' concern that their children will have to work harder in school to overcome prejudice and discrimination (Julian et al., 1994; Thomas and Speight, 1999).

The close relationship between African American parents and their children produces numerous advantages for the children. In a study of the intelligence scores of black and white 5-year-olds, for example, the researchers found that the home environment was critical in fostering a child's development. Even if the family was poor, when the parents provided warmth (as caressing, kissing, or cuddling the child) and stimulated the child's learning (as reading to the child at least three times a week), there were no differences between white and black children in intelligence scores (Brooks-Gunn et al., 1996).

Despite many African American children's positive outcomes, parents must deal with a variety of obstacles. Three of the most important include racism, neighborhood violence, and absent fathers.

Racism Most black children first learn to cope with **racism**, a belief that people of one race are superior or inferior to others, in the family. Daniel and Daniel (1999) compare teaching children about racism to exclaiming "No!" when toddlers inch toward a hot stove.

Race awareness occurs at about 2 to 3 years of age. Some African American parents talk about race with their children, but others feel that such discussions will make the child feel inferior (McAdoo, 2002). Because blacks, more than any other group, experience racism on an everyday basis, many parents engage in **racial socialization**, a process where parents teach their children to negotiate race-related barriers and experiences in a racially stratified society and to take pride in their ancestry (Hughes and Johnson, 2001).

Is racial socialization effective? The data are inconclusive. Some researchers argue that a child's self-esteem and educational achievement depend heavily on a strong sense of her or his racial or ethnic identity (Oyserman et al., 1995; Phinney, 1996). Others have concluded that there is no overall relationship between racial socialization and children's identity, school achievement, or dealing with racial and ethnic stereotyping and discrimination (McLoyd et al., 2001). Teaching children self-esteem is important, but this cuts across all racial-ethnic groups and social classes (see Chapter 12).

Neighborhood Violence African American families—especially those in inner cities—are more likely than those of other racial-ethnic groups to face violence or the threat of violence on an almost daily basis. According to a recent study of fourth- and fifth-grade children living in inner cities, 89 percent reported that they regularly heard the sound of gunfire, and more than 25 percent said that they had seen someone stabbed or shot. Many of the mothers weren't aware of their children's being victimized (beaten up, punched, or chased by gangs) or witnessing violence. The researchers found that exposure to such violence was associated with the children's psychological distress: stomachaches or headaches, bad dreams, troubled sleep, difficulty paying attention in school, and feeling "jumpy" (Ceballo et al., 2001).

Absent Fathers According to one black journalist, "America makes shirking daddy duty easy" (Dawsey, 1996: 112). Some black men simply dump girlfriends

Family reunions, like this birthday celebration for John Garrett (seated wearing white cap) of New Jersey not only bring extended families together but also remind family members of closeness and shared family history.

who become pregnant. The men don't want a relationship or a long-term commitment or don't have the money to support a child. Others may die young, are in jail, or are involved in crime and drugs. Some out-of-wedlock fathers visit their children, play with them, and care for young children while the mothers are working. Although the numbers of such fathers are increasing, they're still low (see Chapters 9 and 12).

Intergenerational Families

About one of five black children under 15 years old lives in an extended family. This rate is lower than in Latino families but higher than in American Indian and Asian American families (see Chapter 12). Both black and white unwed mothers have a higher probability of living in an extended household than do their married counterparts. In some African American households, and especially during emergencies, three generations often depend on one another for support (see Chapter 1).

Mothers of black teenage parents are especially important in helping adolescent mothers achieve educational and economic goals (Hogan et al., 1990; Dickerson, 1995). In low-income families, many grandmothers provide child-care assistance to teenage mothers age 16 and younger. Tension may arise, however, if a grandmother agrees to provide support such as free room and board only under specific conditions, such as the mother's promising not to see the baby's father or agreeing to work to help support the child (Cramer and McDonald, 1996; East and Felice, 1996).

Caregivers in intergenerational families meet the needs of family members across the lifespan in three ways. First, they help socialize and parent the children

of adolescent mothers. Second, they provide extensive instrumental aid (such as baby-sitting, financial assistance, and housing), and emotional support to all family members. Finally, they meet the daily needs, such as bathing and feeding, of family members who cannot care for themselves—especially frail elderly parents, disabled children and older adults, or drug-addicted young adults.

What may appear to be a broken African American home to outsiders may be a strong extended family network of fathers and mothers, grandfathers and grandmothers, brothers and sisters, uncles and aunts, and cousins. Black family members visit and contact one another frequently and emphasize special family occasions and rituals. Such supportive family networks are common in close-knit families at both low and high socioeconomic levels (Hatchett and Jackson, 1993; Kim and McKenry, 1998).

Economic Well-being

The median family income of African Americans is the lowest of all racial-ethnic groups (see *Figure 4.3* on page 88). Those with little education who are lucky enough to find work are disproportionately employed in low-wage jobs. Typically, they work in industries such as manufacturing and construction that are sensitive to recessions. Because of uneven job histories, black employees may not be covered by benefit programs and seniority. The high levels of poverty and unemployment have led many African American men, especially high school dropouts, to pursue illegal ways of making money (Holzer, 2001).

The percentage of black families with annual incomes of $50,000 or more has increased. Still, more

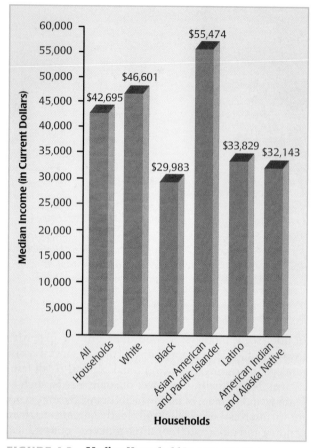

than two-thirds of African Americans (compared with less than one-third of whites) have no financial assets such as stocks and bonds. Black families inherit less wealth. This means that parents often cannot afford to give young adults money for college, large cash gifts for weddings, and downpayments for their first homes (Oliver and Shapiro, 2001).

Despite these and other economic problems, many African Americans are optimistic about the future. For example more than 61 percent of blacks (compared with 46 percent of whites) feel that their children will enjoy a higher standard of living (*Race and Ethnicity . . .*, 2001).

Strengths of the African American Family

Black families have numerous strengths: strong kinship bonds, an ability to adapt family roles to outside pressures, a strong work ethic despite recessions and unemployment, a determination to succeed in education, and an unwavering spirituality that helps people cope with adversity (Taylor, 2000; McAdoo, 2002). Single-parent

families headed by mothers, especially, show enormous fortitude and coping skills (Edin and Lein, 1997).

Numerous self-help institutions (churches, voluntary associations, neighborhood groups, and extended family networks) enhance the resilience of black families even in the poorest communities (Hill, 1998). In the last decade, for example, many black men across the country have organized mentoring and self-help groups for adolescents and young fathers.

Despite much economic adversity, many African Americans see their families as cohesive, love their children, provide a strong religious foundation, and teach their children to be proud of their cultural heritage and to contribute to their community. Other strengths include imbuing children with self-respect, teaching them how to be happy, and stressing cooperation in the family (Brissett-Chapman and Issacs-Shockley, 1997; St. Jean and Feagin, 1998).

American Indian Families

American Indians used to be called the "vanishing Americans." Since the 1980s, however, this population has "staged a surprising comeback" because of higher birth rates, a longer life expectancy, and better health services (Snipp, 1996). There are 4.1 million American Indians and Alaska Natives in the United States. They make up 1.5 percent of the total population. Of this group, 0.6 percent report being multiracial (Ogunwole, 2002).

American Indian families are very heterogeneous. A Comanche–Kiowa educator cautions that "lumping all Indians together is a mistake. Tribes . . . are sovereign nations and are as different from another tribe as Italians are from Swedes" (Pewewardy, 1998: 71).

Of about 175 native American Indian languages still spoken in the United States, only about 20 are being passed on to the next generation. Some linguists are working with tribes to preserve their languages because some of the last speakers, now elderly, are dying off (Pierre, 2003).

Family Structure

About 94 percent of the nation's American Indian and Alaska Native children live with at least one parent. Of all families, 62 percent are maintained by married couples, 30 percent by women with no husband present, and 2 percent by men with no wife present. Almost 24 percent of all children—as in black, Asian American, and Pacific Islander households—live in extended families (Fields, 2001).

Extended families are typical among American Indians, especially those living on reservations. Their frequent contact with family members provides a buffer

Gaming profits from the Mystic Lake Casino owned and operated by the Shakopee Mdewakanton Sioux Indians in Minnesota have enabled them to endow a program in Native American Studies at Augsburg College and to support Indian arts and the American Indian Dance Theatre. The casino also provides jobs for non-Indians who make up more than half of its employees.

under stressful emotional and economic circumstances. Supportive family networks are especially important if families are isolated geographically because they migrate to urban areas to find jobs (MacPhee et al., 1996).

In many American Indian languages, there is no distinction between blood and married relatives. Among some groups, aunts and uncles are considered intimate family members. Sometimes the father's brothers are called "father," uncles and aunts refer to nieces and nephews as "son" or "daughter," and a great-uncle may be referred to as "grandfather" (Sutton and Broken Nose, 1996).

Husbands and Wives

Studies of contemporary American Indian families, husbands and wives, and gender roles are virtually nonexistent (Kawamoto, 2001). One exception is a study of 28 off-reservation Navajo families. Here, Hossain (2001) found that mothers spent significantly more time than did fathers in cleaning, food-related work, and child-care responsibilities.

Compared to fathers in other cultural groups, the Navajo fathers' involvement in household labor and child-related tasks was high—between 2 to 3 hours per day. The wives reported higher levels of commitment (always pitching in), cohesion (making sacrifices for others), and communication (expressing concerns and feelings). Both husbands and wives, however, felt equally competent in solving family problems and coping with everyday issues.

Parents and Children

Children are important family members. Parents spend considerable time and effort in making items for children to play with or to use in popular activities and ceremonies (such as costumes for special dances, looms for weaving, and tools for gardening, hunting, and fishing). Many tribes teach spiritual values and emphasize special rituals and ceremonies (Yellowbird and Snipp, 1994).

Most adults teach children to show respect for authority figures by listening and not interrupting. As one tribal leader reportedly noted, "You have two ears and one mouth for a reason" (Gose, 1994). Mothers, especially—both urban and those living on reservations—strive to transmit their cultural heritage to their children. They emphasize the importance of listening to and observing adults to learn about their identity (Dalla and Gamble, 1997; Cheshire, 2001).

American Indian families emphasize such values as cooperation, sharing, personal integrity, generosity, harmony with nature, and spirituality—values quite different from the individual achievement, competitiveness, and drive toward accumulation emphasized by many in the white community. Families teach children that men and women may have different roles but that both should be respected for their contributions to the family (Stauss, 1995; MacPhee et al., 1996; Kawamoto and Cheshire, 1997).

Sometimes American Indian parents feel they are losing control over their children's behavior, especially hanging around with friends and drinking. Researchers suggest that there is a relationship between American Indian adolescents' risk-taking behavior (such as using drugs and dropping out of school) and fragile family connections. That is, migration off reservations has weakened the extended family, a principal mechanism for transmitting values and teaching accountability (Machamer and Gruber, 1998).

Elders and Grandparents

American Indian children are taught to respect their elders. Old age is a "badge of honor"—a sign that one has done the right things and has pleased the creator.

Elders have traditionally occupied a central role in a family's decision making. Because of the Indian emphasis on family unity and cooperation, family members and tribal officials often offer elders assistance without having to ask for it (Kawamoto and Cheshire, 1997). According to the Navajo, for example, the life cycle consists of three stages: "being cared for," "preparing to care for," and "assuming care of" (Bahr and Bahr, 1995). Thus, caring for each other and elderly family members is a cultural value passed on to children.

In their research on Navajo and Apache reservations, Bahr and Bahr (1995: 248) found that many grandmothers and grandchildren rely on each other:

> *Grandchildren may help their grandmothers gather cattails to harvest yellow pollen, "pick" worms to sell to fishermen, catch fish to help supplement the family diet, or make tortillas. The grandmothers encourage the children in their schoolwork, and many of the grandchildren help with household chores, chopping wood, sweeping floors and washing dishes.*

CONSTRAINTS

American Indians and Alcohol Use: Facts and Fictions

American Indians have forbidden the sale of alcohol on two-thirds of all reservations, but alcohol consumption remains a serious problem. The rate of alcohol-related deaths is six times higher among American Indians than among whites (Kington and Nickens, 2001). American Indians under age 35 are about ten times more likely than other U.S. residents to die from alcohol-related problems (such as liver disease). They are also about three times more likely to commit suicide because of alcohol use (Brenneman et al., 2000; Wissow, 2000). In addition, more than half of violent crimes among American Indians involve drinking by both the victim and the offender (Greenfeld and Smith, 1999).

Although alcohol abuse is a problem in any community, May (1999) notes that there are many stereotypes and myths about "the drunken Indian." In reality,

- There is wide variation in the prevalence of drinking from one tribal group to another.

- About 75 percent of alcohol-related deaths are due to sporadic binge drinking rather than chronic alcoholism.
- Serious injuries (such as car accidents) due to alcohol often result in death because many Indians live in rural, remote environments where medical care is far away or unavailable.
- Although the media have publicized that "one in three" Indian babies are born with fetal alcohol syndrome (FAS), the rates range from a high of 190 per 1000 children to a low of 1.3 per 1000 children, depending on the community's socioeconomic characteristics and drinking patterns.

According to many tribal leaders, several major beer companies have specifically targeted American Indians with their marketing strategies. The poorest reservations often accept sponsorship from major brewing companies for annual tribal fairs and rodeos.

Some American Indian tribes, including the Cherokee Nation, have stopped accepting brewery money for cultural events. Tribal communities that try to prohibit alcohol sales run into obstacles, however. When the governing body of the Yakama Nation in Washington State passed a resolution to ban the sale and possession of alcohol on the reservation, they were met with protest. The owners of 48 businesses that sell alcohol—most of them non–American Indians who own land within tribal boundaries—argued that they'd lose their businesses and that many American Indians would lose their jobs (Greene, 2000).

STOP AND THINK . . .

- *Should businesses that sell alcohol be banned in American Indian communities that don't want them? Or do such restrictions jeopardize "free enterprise"?*
- *Alcohol commercials dominate most television sports programs. Should they also be banned?*

As families move off reservations in search of decent housing and better employment and educational opportunities, some grandparents play the role of "cultural conservators" (Weibel-Orlando, 1990). Conservator grandparents try to have their grandchildren live with them whenever possible. By taking their grandchildren to church meetings, tribal hearings, dances in full regalia at powwows, and other reservation activities, the grandparents hope to familiarize their grandchildren with native history and wisdom.

As more women work outside the home, they are especially likely to turn their children over to the grandmother for care (Schweitzer, 1999). Today many American Indian college students return to work or teach on reservations or in other American Indian communities because "they long for mothers, fathers, sisters, brothers, and perhaps most of all, their grandparents" (Garrod and Larimore, 1997: xi).

Health and Economic Well-being

Two significant issues that tribal leaders have begun to address are mental health problems (especially depression) and the physical and sexual abuse of children. Suicide rates are high among American Indians, especially among teenagers and men under age 40. Alcohol-related violence is another problem and is related to depression, high suicide rates, and crime (see the box "American Indians and Alcohol Use: Facts and Fictions").

Many American Indians believe that one of the reasons for the high alcoholism rate, especially among youth, has been the gradual erosion of American Indian culture. Urban American Indian children have a particularly hard time maintaining their cultural identity and often feel like outsiders in both the American Indian and white cultures. In response, hundreds of programs nationwide are fighting addiction by reinforcing American Indian cultural practices and values (Sanchez-Way and Johnson, 2000; Sagiri, 2001).

American Indians have consistently been one of the poorest groups in American society. One out of four lives below the poverty level. American Indians have higher joblessness rates than do other racial-ethnic groups. On many reservations, unemployment rates run about 50 percent and sometimes up to 90 percent (Vanderpool, 2002).

Substandard housing is common, especially on reservations. Many homes are overcrowded and lack kitchen facilities (including stoves and refrigerators) and indoor plumbing (Bonnette, 1995a, 1995b).

Many people believed that the ritzy gambling casinos springing up on American Indian reservations across the nation would lift poor American Indians out of poverty. They were wrong. Only half of the 561 federally

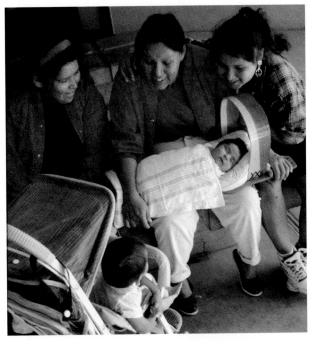

Among many American Indian tribes some people preserve traditional ways while others adopt the practices and products of the majority culture. These differences can be seen even within extended families.

recognized tribes operate the nearly 300 casinos that generate $13 billion a year in revenue. A few tribes near big cities have hit the jackpot. Some members haul in as much $900,000 annually and still get up to $20,000 of federal aid per person. But 80 percent of American Indians haven't received a penny (Bartlett and Steele, 2002a, 2002b).

Why not? Some large tribes such as the Navajo oppose gambling for religious reasons. In other cases, the council of tribal leaders that controls official membership sometimes refuses to recognize tribal members to increase their own profits. Non–American Indian investors have become billionaires by underwriting the initial costs of buying land and starting up the casinos and are pocketing 40 percent of the profits (Barlett and Steele, 2002a, 2002b).

Some argue that despite the greed and corruption, casinos have created jobs, economic stability, and political power. Among other benefits, gambling profits have enabled tribes to fund needed health clinics, new schools, sanitation systems, services for the elderly and youth, and similar programs. In addition, some tribes have used gambling revenues to build or run enterprises such as malls, concert halls, vacation resorts, community colleges, apparel companies, timber operations, and power plants and to provide housing for low-income families (Gerdes et al., 1998; Fixico, 2001).

Strengths of the American Indian Family

American Indian family strengths include "relational bonding," a core behavior that is built on widely shared values such as respect, generosity, and sharing across the tribe, band, clan, and kin group. Harmony and balance include putting community and family needs above individual achievements. Another strength is a spirituality that sustains the family's identity and place in the world (Stauss, 1995; Cross, 1998).

In some cases, tribal members have worked patiently over several generations to develop self-sufficient industries. In the remote village of Mekoryuk, Alaska, for example, Inuit women collaborated with an anthropologist at the University of Alaska–Fairbanks to begin a knitting cooperative that transforms the downy wool of musk oxen into warm and lightweight clothes.

The knitting began in 1968. Since then, member-knitters, ranging in age from 9 to 90, work from home in several villages and sell the products through mail order. The women don't get rich, but the knitting keeps them out of poverty and passes traditional skills on to younger generations, as the women incorporate ancient patterns from traditional and Inuit culture into the knitting (Watkins, 2002).

MAKING CONNECTIONS

▨ Many American Indian languages are becoming extinct. Is this a normal part of a group's acculturation with a host society that should be accepted? Or should the languages be preserved?

▨ American Indians run tax-free gambling enterprises. Should African Americans have the same opportunities, especially because they lost their inheritances when they were shipped from Africa? ◎

Latino Families

Latino families are diverse. Some trace their roots to the Spanish and Mexican settlers who established homes and founded cities in the Southwest before the arrival of the Pilgrims. Others are immigrants or children of immigrants who arrived in large numbers by the turn of the twentieth century (see Chapter 3).

Spanish-speaking people from Mexico, Ecuador, the Dominican Republic, and Spain differ in their customs and experiences in U.S. society. We focus here primarily on characteristics that Latino families share, noting intergroup variations where possible.

Family Structure

About 68 percent of Latino children live in two-parent families, down from 78 percent in 1970 (Lugaila, 1998; Fields, 2001). About 26 percent of Latino children live in mother-only families, compared with 16 percent in white families and 52 percent in black families (see *Figure 4.2*).

Shifting social norms, economic changes, and immigration patterns have altered the structure of many Latino families. Couples are more likely to divorce, and there are more out-of-wedlock births (del Pinal and Singer, 1997; see also Chapters 11 and 15). In addition, some young Latino children may be more likely to live with relatives than parents because new immigrants depend on family sponsors until they can become self-sufficient (Garcia, 2002).

Gender Roles and Parenting

Among Latino families, gender and parenting roles vary in terms of such factors as how long a family has lived in the United States, whether the wife or mother works outside the home, and the degree of acculturation. Many Latino families, especially new immigrants, must grapple with new gender and parenting roles that are very different from those in their homeland.

Gender Roles   Latino men often bear the stereotype of *machismo*, a concept of masculinity that emphasizes characteristics such as dominance, aggression, and womanizing (see Chapter 3). The mainstream press often ignores such positive elements of *machismo* as courage, honor, *respeto* (a respect for authority, tradition, and family), *dignidad* (avoiding a loss of dignity in front of others), and close ties with the extended family. The female counterpart of *machismo* is *marianismo*. *Marianismo*, associated with the Virgin Mary in Catholicism, expects women to remain virgins until marriage and to be self-sacrificing and unassuming (De La Cancela, 1994; Mayo, 1997; see also Chapters 5 and 7).

Some scholars contend that *machismo* is a ludicrous stereotype about Latino men and their domestic roles. There are many good role models among U.S. Latino men who participate in domestic work and child rearing, but they are often overlooked in favor of the macho tough guy or the domineering husband and father (Gonzalez, 1996). Among recent Dominican immigrants, for example, many husbands share some housework and discuss how to spend their money (Pessar, 1995).

On the other hand, some researchers report that even wives who work outside the home are often subordinate to men and are expected to follow traditional family roles. In a study of Puerto Rican families, for example, Toro-Morn (1998) found that working mothers were primarily

Migrant families at the lower socioeconomic level like this family in Texas frequently rely on their children to help in the often-backbreaking labor they perform on America's farmlands.

responsible for the care of the home and the children. And in a study of Central American workers, Repak (1995) found that men in working-class households balked at sharing household responsibilities and child care even when women worked full time outside the home.

If a woman holds a professional or middle-class job, her husband is less likely to exhibit *machismo*. Two-earner, middle-class, Mexican American married couples, for example, are likely to share some of the housework if the wife earns as much as or more than her husband (Coltrane, 1996).

Parenting The available literature shows that most Latino parents, like other parents, are caring and affectionate and expect their children to be successful. Most Latino parents teach their children to be obedient, honest, and respectful, both at home and outside the home. There are socioeconomic differences, however. Middle-class Latinos who have acculturated, for instance, tend to be more permissive—like their white counterparts—in raising their children (Harwood et al., 2002).

Even when they're in the labor force, Latinas devote much of their lives to bearing and rearing children. As one Latina said, "To be valued [in our community] we have to be wives and mothers first" (Segura, 1994). Parenting and marital conflicts might erupt, however, because Latina mothers are often overloaded in caring for families and working outside the home (DeBiaggi, 2002).

Latino fathers don't do nearly as much parenting as mothers (see Chapter 12). Nonetheless, they're warm and loving with children. And compared with white fathers, Latino fathers are more likely to supervise and restrict their children's TV viewing, regulate the types of programs they watch, and require them to finish their homework before going outside to play (Toth and Xu, 2002).

Familism and Extended Families

For many Latino households, familism and the strength of the extended family have traditionally provided emotional and economic support. In a national poll, for example, 82 percent of Latinos, compared with 67 percent of the general U.S. population, said that relatives are more important than friends ("The ties that bind," 2000).

Familism Familism refers to family relationships that take precedence over individual well-being. The family serves as a critical support system for emotional and economic help. Sharing and cooperation are key values. Familism is often a response to historical conditions of economic deprivation. Many Mexican American families, for example, survive only because they have the support of earlier immigrants (Baca Zinn and Wells, 2000).

Many researchers who have relied on small samples or anecdotal information maintain that Latino families are more familistic than white families. They also claim that social support increases with each generation living in the United States (see Hurtado, 1995, and Vega, 1995, for a summary of some of this literature).

Others suggest that familism may be decreasing because of high separation and divorce rates, a decrease in married-couple families, and a lack of economic resources that erode support networks (Taylor, 2002).

Extended Families Many Latino families include aunts and uncles, grandparents, cousins, in-laws, godparents, and even close friends. The extended family exchanges a wide range of goods and services, including child care, temporary housing, personal advice, nursing, and emotional support (DeBord and de Atiles, 1999; López, 1999). Some Mexicans have practiced a kind of "chain migration," in which those already in the United States find employment and housing for other kin who are leaving Mexico (Ramirez and Arce, 1981; Sarmiento, 2002).

Typically, Latino grandparents are welcome to live with the family. In many Mexican American families, the elderly often have *plactitas*, or "talks," with their children or grandchildren and pass on religious beliefs to the younger members of their families. Grandmothers, especially, serve as role models and often take care of the children while the parents are working (Carrasquillo, 1991; Paz, 1993).

Again, there may be variations by residence and social class. In a study of Mexican families in Texas, Williams (1990: 137) concluded that "among economically advantaged Mexican Americans in urban centers, the extended family is not central to the routines of everyday life." In very poor communities where the family has been decimated by unemployment, drugs, or AIDS, social agencies and community-based organizations sometimes become the new extended family, taking the place of grandparents and other family members (Abalos, 1993).

Among many recent immigrant families, young children often have more responsibilities than U.S.-born children. Because children learn English faster than their parents, they often assume adult roles. According to one researcher,

> I see a lot of situations where [Salvadoran and Guatemalan] parents will take a young child to get their gas installed, to ask why their services were shut off, to pay the bill. . . . In that sense the children play a different role from other children because they are secretaries or assistants to their parents in order for the family to function (Dorrington, 1995: 121).

Acculturation can be a source of tension between parents and children and can erode traditionally strong intergenerational ties. Even when they speak Spanish, for example, Mexican American grandchildren who are more acculturated than their grandparents report less frequent interaction and a decline of affection over time. Grandchildren whose cultural values resemble those of their grandparents (such as celebrating Mexican holidays and marrying Mexican Americans) retain strong emotional ties and contact (Silverstein and Chen, 1999).

FIGURE 4.4 **Families with Annual Incomes of $50,000 or More, 2001**

SOURCE: Based on DeNavas-Walt and Cleveland, 2002, Table A-1.

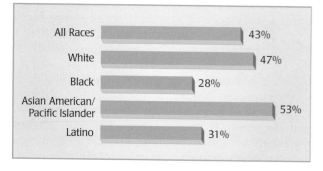

Economic Well-being and Poverty

Many Latinos are successful. Minorities own more than 3 million, or 15 percent, of all U.S. businesses. Of these, Latinos own 40 percent (*Summary*, 2001). According to historian Kevin Starr, "The economy of the Sun Belt and California would collapse without Hispanics. They are doing the work of the entire culture," from harvesting the nation's food supply to manning hotels, restaurants, and construction sites (cited in Chaddock, 2003: 1, 3).

Economic Success Like that of black families, the number of middle-class Latino families has increased. Almost one in three earns $50,000 a year or more (see *Figure 4.4*), up considerably from 7 percent in 1972. Keep in mind that there is a great deal of variation among Latino families. Almost 40 percent of Cuban families earn this much, compared with only 28 percent of Mexican American families and 26 percent of Puerto Rican families (U.S. Census Bureau, 2002).

Economic success depends on a number of interrelated factors, including U.S. immigration policies and political relations with the country of origin, timing of migration, the skills that immigrants bring with them, and the deterioration of major metropolitan areas that are open to development.

In the case of Cuban immigrants, all of these variables were just right in the late 1950s. The U.S. government, hoping to weaken Fidel Castro's power, extended Cuban exiles a "generous welcome." Unlike *any* other group of immigrants in history, Cuban refugees received government subsidies, magnanimous refugee programs, college scholarships, and other resources (Suro, 1998).

Many of the Cubans came from a middle- or upper-middle-class background. They had human capital (such as high educational levels and entrepreneurial skills), worked hard to develop rundown and abandoned Miami neighborhoods, and became politically active (Pérez, 1992). In contrast, none of the other Latino immigrants have received such assistance, regardless of their human capital resources.

This doesn't mean that all Cuban Americans are wealthy and all other Latinos are poor. There is wide variation across Latino subgroups. About 20 percent of all Latino families live below the poverty line. Of these, 67 percent are Mexicans, 12 percent are Puerto Ricans, 12 percent are Central and South Americans, and only 4 percent are Cubans (U.S. Census Bureau, 2002).

Poverty In many cases, according to one Latino researcher, "The family that is doing the right thing is still falling behind. We have people working, people married and yet we see poverty increasing" (Fletcher, 1997).

Why do many Latino families have high poverty rates? Many recent immigrants who were professionals in their native land find only low-paying jobs (delivering

MULTICULTURAL

Mexican Day Laborers in America

Angelo earned $100 for 16 hours of work at a Los Angeles construction site. Antonio stacked boxes at a Chicago warehouse for 10 hours and wasn't paid at all. Both Angelo and Antonio are *los jornaleros*, Mexican slang for "day laborers." Day laborers are people who get paid for work on a daily or short-term basis. Day laborers often congregate on street corners and wait for employers to drive by and offer them work. The term also includes those who are employed by temporary staffing agencies that assign work on a daily basis.

Day laborers are a common sight in California and the Southwest. A study of day laborers in southern California estimated their numbers to be as high as 20,000 in one metropolitan area. Increasingly, they are also working in Chicago and other cities and suburbs in the Midwest. Day labor offers no health benefits, no job security, no overtime, and payment in cash. The employers get cheap labor, tax-free. And the workers get work.

Day laborers are overwhelmingly Mexican men who speak little English and have no more than a sixth-grade education. The 80 percent who are illegal immigrants are especially vulnerable to unscrupulous smugglers, employers, home owners, and contractors. Most are underpaid, are paid less than they were promised, or don't get paid at all. Day laborers can earn as much as $1069 in a good month and as little as $341 in a typical bad month. Many send a large portion of the earnings home; others use the money to smuggle relatives across the U.S. border.

Day laborers handle toxic materials without proper safety equipment, perform dangerous work, and suffer injuries on the job. They possess the very traits that we celebrate—self-reliance, hard work, and raising income for their families—yet they are "widely used, abused, and despised" (Valenzuela, 2000; Schlosser, 2002: 72; Rectanus and Gomez, 2002).

STOP AND THINK . . .

- *The police know that most day laborers are illegal immigrants. Why aren't they arrested?*

- *Because they work hard and in jobs that most Americans don't want, why do you think that day laborers are "widely used, abused, and despised"?*

food for restaurants, cleaning buildings, or working as cashiers in retail stores). They don't have time both to work and to learn the language that would help them gain the accreditation they need to practice as doctors, lawyers, and accountants ("Living humbled . . .," 1996).

Other recent entrants and U.S.-born Latinos have low educational levels. Almost one-third don't have a high school degree (U.S. Census Bureau, 2002). Some drop out of high school because they're failing; some work to support their families. Others say they drop out because public schools marginalize them, disrespect their culture, and make them feel "like a dumb Mexican" (Headden, 1997).

A number of Latinos have few skills and work experience that employers want. Therefore, they are likely to earn entry-level salaries in lower-skilled jobs. During recessions, including that of the early twenty-first century, even second-generation young Latinos suffered unemployment rates as high as 10 percent (Lowell, 2002). Darker-skinned Latinos, especially, face discrimination in the labor market (Espino and Franz, 2002). Day laborers are among the most abused workers in America (see the box "Mexican Day Laborers in America").

Strengths of the Latino Family

Despite their economic vulnerability, many Latino families have been resilient and adaptive. Family networks protect their members' health and emotional well-being. Many immigrants demonstrate incredible internal resources in coping with economic hardship, learning a new language, and shaping their own solutions in adjusting to a new environment.

The ability of Latino families to transmit traditional values about familism has often offset the negative impact of prejudice and discrimination, drug use, and other risky behavior among many adolescents (Rodriguez and Kosloski, 1998; Strait, 1999; Quintana and Vera, 1999). As in black families, parental socialization of ethnic pride and identity protects many Latino children from anger, depression, and, in some cases, violence (Oyserman et al., 1995; Phinney et al., 1997, 2001a).

Asian American Families

Asian Americans encompass a broad swath of cultures and traditions. They come from at least 26 countries of East and Southeast Asia (including China, Taiwan,

Korea, Japan, Vietnam, Laos, Cambodia, and the Philippines) and South Asia (including India, Pakistan, and Sri Lanka). They follow different religions, speak different languages, and use different alphabets. Asian Americans also include Native Hawaiians and other Pacific Islanders from Guam and Samoa.

Chinese are the largest Asian American group (2.3 million), followed by Filipinos (1.9 million) and Asian Indians (1.7 million). Combined, these three groups account for 58 percent of all Asian Americans (Barnes and Bennett, 2002).

Regardless of the country of origin, Asian American families feel pressure to adapt to U.S. culture. Some of the changes they experience are in family structure, gender roles, parent–child relationships, and intergenerational interaction.

Family Structure

Asian American family structures vary widely depending on their original roots, their time of arrival, past and current immigration policies, whether the families are immigrants or refugees, and the parents' original socioeconomic status. The average family size for Asian Americans and Pacific Islanders is larger (3.96 people) than for Latinos (3.81), American Indians (3.50), blacks (3.34), and whites (3.01). Almost 11 percent have six or more household members, compared with 5 percent of families nationally. Household size varies across groups: 5.1 for Cambodians, Hmong, and Laotians, for example, but only 2.5 for Japanese families (McLoyd et al., 2001).

Asian American households are likely to be extended rather than nuclear families. They might include parents, children, unmarried siblings, and grandparents. Most children grow up in two-parent homes (see *Figure 4.2*). Female-headed homes, whether because of divorce or out-of-wedlock birth, are much less common than in other groups.

Husbands and Wives

Many Asian Americans follow Confucianism, which endorses a patriarchal structure. This structure instructs women to obey fathers, husbands, and the oldest son. The woman thus derives her status through her role as a wife, mother, or daughter-in-law. The man, in contrast, is the head of household, principal provider, decision maker, and disciplinarian (Segal, 1991; Yu, 1995; Chan, 1997).

Women are more likely to be equal partners in some groups than others. Filipino culture historically has had a less patriarchal gender role structure: Husbands and wives share financial and domestic decision making. Generally, Filipino husbands and wives tend to have egalitarian relationships (Espiritu, 1995).

In contrast, Korean, Asian Indian, Hmong, and Vietnamese families, among others, follow traditional gender roles, even if the wife is in the labor force. Large numbers of Asian American mothers are employed because a double income is necessary for economic survival. In some cases, a woman may work outside the home to support the family while the man pursues an education or job training (Kibria, 2002b; Min, 2002; Purkayastha, 2002).

In many cases, working outside the home has not decreased the wife's homemaker role. The wife is still expected to cook, clean the house, and take care of the children. She bears these double roles regardless of length of residence in the United States (Hurh, 1998; Kim and Kim, 1998; Chen, 1999; Kim, 1999).

Tensions often arise as the husband's traditional role of breadwinner shifts. Especially in working-class families, two-paycheck couples may be working more than one job or irregular hours. There is little time for each other, their children, or household tasks, and stress builds (Fong, 2002).

Parents and Children

In many Asian American families, the strongest family ties are between parent and child rather than between spouses. Parents sacrifice personal needs in the interests of their children. In return, they expect *filial piety:* respect and obedience toward one's parents (Chan, 1997).

Family Values   As with the Latino emphasis on familism, to Asian Americans the family is more important than the individual. Among Indian Asian families, traditional Hindu values regard kinship ties as more important than individual interests (Chekki, 1996).

In a similar vein, the Vietnamese saying *mot giot mau dao hon ao nuoc la* ("one drop of blood is much more precious than a pond full of water") reflects the belief that family solidarity is more important than outside relationships. Even when extended kin don't live together, they may cooperate in running a common family business, pool income, and share certain domestic functions, such as meal preparation (Glenn and Yap, 1994).

Filipino ideology teaches that revealing a family problem to an "outsider"—whether a friend, teacher, or counselor—creates gossip and brings shame (*hiya*) and embarrassment to the family. Such "confessions" imply that parents are doing a bad job of raising their children. On the other hand, bottling up problems may lead to loneliness, depression, and suicidal thoughts (Wolf, 1997).

Discipline   Asian American parents exercise more control over their children's lives than non–Asian American parents. They use guilt and shame rather

MULTICULTURAL

How to Be a Perfect Taiwanese Kid

Many immigrant parents—Latino, Middle Eastern, and African—emphasize education as the route to upward mobility and success. The value of education is embodied in the Chinese proverb, "If you are planning for a year, sow rice; if you are planning for a decade, plant trees; if you are planning for a lifetime, educate people." For many Asian American parents, securing a good education for their children is a top priority (Zhou and Bankston, 1998; Hurh, 1998; Pollard and O'Hare, 1999).

By excelling in school, the child brings honor to the family. Educational and occupational successes further enhance the family's social status and ensure its economic well-being as well as that of the next generation (Chan, 1999). The following tongue-in-cheek observations about how to be the perfect Taiwanese kid (Ng, 1998: 42) from the parents' perspective would apply to many other Asian American families as well:

1. Score 1600 on the SAT [Scholastic Aptitude Test].
2. Play the violin or piano at the level of a concert performer.
3. Apply to and be accepted by 27 colleges.
4. Have three hobbies: studying, studying, and studying.
5. Go to a prestigious Ivy League university and win a scholarship to pay for it.
6. Love classical music and detest talking on the phone.
7. Become a Westinghouse, Presidential, and eventually a Rhodes Scholar.
8. Aspire to be a brain surgeon.
9. Marry a Taiwanese American doctor and have perfect, successful children (grandkids for *ahma* and *ahba*).
10. Love to hear stories about your parents' childhood, especially the one about walking 7 miles to school without shoes.

than physical abuse to keep their children in line and to reinforce the children's strong obligations to the family (Fong, 2002). In Chinese American families, for example, *guan* ("to govern") has a positive connotation. *Guan* also means "to care for" or "to love." Therefore, "parental care, concern, and involvement are synonymous with a firm control and governance of the child" (Chao and Tseng, 2002: 75).

Many Asian American parents are indulgent, tolerant, and permissive with infants and toddlers. As the child approaches school age, however, parents expect greater discipline and responsibility for grooming, dressing, and completing chores (Chan, 1997). Most parents don't tolerate aggressive behavior and sibling rivalry and expect older children to serve as role models for their younger siblings. Parents also teach their children to conform to societal expectations because they are concerned about what other people think, both within and outside the Asian American community.

Many parents not only pressure their children to excel in school but also may endure extreme hardships—even selling their house—to ensure the best college opportunities for their children (Fong, 2002). The box "How to Be a Perfect Taiwanese Kid" describes the emphasis on academic achievement.

Gender Roles Gender-role socialization is still very traditional in many Asian American families. In Chinese American families, for example, many parents rely more heavily on girls than boys to perform domestic chores (Fuligni et al., 1999). Vietnamese parents expect obedience from both sons and daughters. Parents enforce discipline more strongly among girls than among boys, however, even in the use of corporal punishment. The Vietnamese ideal of "the virtuous woman" expects girls, but not boys, to live up to higher behavioral standards (Zhou and Bankston, 1998; Saito, 2002).

Intergenerational Relationships

What often keeps many new immigrant families together is tradition, religion, and cultural bonds brought with them from their homeland. As children become more assimilated, their attitudes about marriage and family life differ from those of their parents. This creates the potential for greater generational and cultural conflicts.

Intergenerational conflicts vary across groups in terms of length of residence, degree of acculturation, and self-identity (being "Chinese" versus "Chinese American," for instance). In a study of Japanese Americans and Asian Indians in California, for example, both Asian Indian parents and their second-generation children said that the single greatest source of conflict was dating and marriage partners. Compared with Japanese American respondents who have been in the United States for many generations, Asian Indian parents were more concerned that their children might marry people from different religious and ethnic backgrounds (Kar et al., 1998).

Because of the traditional value of filial responsibility, it has long been assumed that Asian American adults feel more obligated to their parents, provide them with more financial aid, and interact more frequently with their parents than do other racial-ethnic groups. In reality, filial obligations vary widely across Chinese, Japanese, and Korean families because of a number of structural and economic factors. Korean American adults, for example, are more likely to provide emotional and financial support to their parents—compared to their Chinese and Japanese counterparts—only when the elderly parents are recent immigrants. In addition, only adult children who have stable financial resources assist their elderly parents (Ishii-Kuntz, 1997). And although many Asian American grandparents transmit cultural values to their grandchildren, they can also create conflict by "meddling" or criticizing adult children and grandchildren who have become Americanized (Pettys and Balgopal, 1998; Kibria, 2002a).

As a group, Asian American families have maintained much of their cultural identity and have remained cohesive despite assimilation and intergenerational differences. Ironically, their ability to succeed despite historical discrimination and exclusion has created other problems. Their reputation for being a "model minority," for example, has both helped and hindered their progress.

The Model Minority: Fictions and Facts

Recently, a *Washington Post* article heralded the opening of a Korean-owned Super H Mart, which was "Northern Virginia's newest supermarket extraordinaire." Among other things, it would compete with the big chain grocers, expand Korean-owned stores outside mom-and-pop inner-city ethnic enclaves, and prove that hardworking immigrants can be successful in U.S. society (Cho, 2003). Do you think such stories encourage its readers to stereotype *all* Asian American families as the "model minority"?

Fictions about the Model Minority Asian American families have the highest median income in the country (see *Figure 4.3*). Such figures are misleading, however. Many Asian American households are larger than average, as you saw earlier, and include more workers. In addition, more than 60 percent of all Asian Americans live in three states that have both high incomes and high costs of living: California, Hawaii, and New York (Barnes and Bennett, 2002).

Many Asian Americans arrive in the United States with few skills and low educational levels. Lumping all

Asian Americans together as a "model minority" ignores many subgroups that are not doing well because of low educational levels and language barriers.

The most successful Asian Americans are those who speak English relatively well *and* have high educational levels. As in the case of Latinos, many recent Asian American immigrants who have top-notch credentials from their homeland often experience underemployment in the United States. For example, some Korean doctors work as hospital orderlies and nurses' assistants because they can't support a family at the same time as they prepare for the English-language test and the medical exam in their field of specialization (Jo, 1999).

Even when Asian Americans are employed in professional jobs—as architects, engineers, computer system analysts, teachers, and pharmacists—they are not in the upper management levels (Hope and Jacobson, 1995). The box "Dangers of the Model Minority Myth" describes some negative effects of the "model minority" image on Asian Americans and on American society at large.

Facts about the Model Minority Why have many Asian American families become successful? Let's take a look at two major factors.

First, the U.S. Immigration and Naturalization Service screens immigrants, allowing entry primarily to those who are the "cream of the crop." For example, nearly 66 percent of Filipino immigrants are professionals, usually nurses and other medical personnel, and nearly two-thirds of all Asian American Indian professionals in the United States have advanced degrees. Foreign-born professionals are willing to work the long hours demanded by public hospitals and to work for lower salaries (Suro, 1998; Adler, 2003).

Second, the mixture of Buddhist and Confucian values and traditions resembles traditional middle-class prerequisites for success in America. All three ideologies emphasize hard work, education, achievement, self-reliance, sacrifice, steadfast purpose, and long-term goals.

Asian American and American traditions differ in at least one important way, however. Whereas American values stress individualism, competition, and independence, Buddhist and Confucian traditions emphasize interdependence, harmony, cooperation, and pooling of resources (Chan, 1997). Thus, for example, many Korean immigrants have been able to secure capital to start a small business through *kae* (or *kye*), a credit rotation system in which about a dozen families donate $1000 or more to help a shopkeeper set up a new business (Yoon, 1997).

The rotating savings and credit organization is common to many ethnic groups: Ethiopians call it *ekub*, Bolivians call it *pasanaqu* (to "pass from hand to hand"), and Cambodians call it *tong-tine*. All operate on the same

MULTICULTURAL

Dangers of the Model Minority Myth

In recent years, many Asian American and other scholars have debunked the stereotypical notion of Asian Americans as a "model minority." Petersen (1966: 21) first used the phrase "model minority" when he described Japanese Americans as an unparalleled success story:

By any criterion that we choose, the Japanese Americans are better than any other group in our society, including U.S.-born whites. They have established this remarkable record, moreover, by their own almost totally unaided effort. Every attempt to hamper this progress resulted only in enhancing their determination to succeed.

Do (1999: 118–22) presents six dangers closely associated with the model minority image. Although Do is referring to Vietnamese Americans, the negative effects of the model minority myth apply to other Asian Americans as well:

Danger #1: The model minority image distorts and ignores the differences within Asian American communities. Although Vietnamese Americans, for example, share many cultural characteristics and customs, they are a diverse group in terms of their time of arrival, educational levels, English proficiency, and support after landing on U.S. shores.

Danger #2: The model minority stereotype creates tension and antagonism within and across Asian American subgroups. If recently arrived immigrants aren't as successful as their predecessors, there must be something wrong with them. Other immigrants have done very well, after all.

Danger #3: Model minority images can lead to verbal and physical assaults. White supremacist groups, who resent many Asian Americans' educational and occupational accomplishments, often target Asian Americans in hate crimes that include homicide.

Danger #4: The model minority myth camouflages ongoing racial discrimination in U.S. society by blaming the victim. If some groups—such as blacks, Latinos, and American Indians—don't succeed, it must be their own fault rather than U.S. policies or racism.

Danger #5: As with any stereotype, the model minority image denies its members their individuality. Although many Asian American students are interested in teaching, social work, dance, and theater, they are often pressured to pursue careers in law, medicine, engineering, dentistry, computer science, or the biological sciences.

Danger #6: The model minority myth deprives individuals of necessary social services and monetary support. Asian Americans typically are excluded from corrective civil rights policies, such as affirmative action programs, because they are labeled as "achievers" (Ancheta, 1998).

STOP AND THINK . . .

- *Why do you think that these myths about Asian Americans as a model minority are so widespread?*

- *How do such myths and stereotypes affect our interpersonal relationships with many Asian Americans in classes, at work, and in Asian American–owned businesses?*

basic principles: Organize a group of close friends, agree on how much and how often to pay into the kitty, and determine how the money will be apportioned, whether by lottery or need. The winner can use the funds to start a business, pay for a wedding, put down a deposit for a home, or pay for college tuition (Suro, 1998).

Many Asian American students work harder and longer than their non–Asian American counterparts. They are active in many extracurricular activities—such as school clubs, athletics, and community service—but typically spend twice as much time on homework and less time watching television, socializing with friends, and working after school (Saito, 2002).

Strengths of the Asian American Family

As in the case of Latino families, researchers continuously emphasize that Asian American families vary significantly in terms of country of origin, timing of immigration, ability to speak English, and other factors. Generally, however, the strengths of Asian American families include stable households where parents encourage children to remain in school and offer personal support that reduces stress against discrimination and leads to better emotional health (Barringer et al., 1993; Leonard, 1997). Although many traditional families are changing, many young adults want to maintain the close-knit

Most Middle Eastern families, including the Muslim women shown here, demonstrated solidarity with other Americans after the September 11, 2001 terrorist attacks on the United States.

character of their family life that emphasizes cooperation, caring, and self-sacrifice (Kibria, 1994; Zhou and Bankston, 1998).

Middle Eastern Families

What do the following well-known people have in common: consumer advocate Ralph Nader, singer Paula Abdul, deejay Casey Kasem, heart surgeon Michael De Bakey, Heisman Trophy winner Doug Flutie, former Secretary of Health Donna Shalala, and senators George Mitchell and John Sununu? All are Middle Eastern Americans of Arab origin.

The term *Middle East* refers to "one of the most diverse and complex combinations of geographic, historical, religious, linguistic, and even racial places on Earth" (Sharifzadeh, 1997: 442). The Middle East encompasses about 30 countries. They include Turkey, Israel, Iran, Afghanistan, Pakistan, and a number of Arab nations (such as Algeria, Egypt, Iraq, Jordan, Kuwait, Lebanon, Palestine, Saudi Arabia, Syria, and the United Arab Emirates).

Of the almost 19 million people in the United States who speak a language other than English or Spanish at home, almost 11 percent speak such Middle Eastern languages as Armenian, Arabic, Hebrew, Persian, or Urdu (U.S. Census Bureau, 2003). As in the case of Asian American families, Middle Eastern families make up a heterogeneous population that is a "multicultural, multiracial, and multiethnic mosaic" (Abudabbeh, 1996: 333).

Despite the growing numbers of Middle Eastern families in the United States, we know little about them. A study of the four most prominent family science journals over a 14-year period found that only 16 percent of the almost 2800 articles focused on ethnic groups (Bean et al., 2002). Middle Eastern families weren't even mentioned. There are some books and chapters in books on Middle Eastern families. Most, however, and as you'll see in this section, were published in the 1990s or earlier.

Family Structure

As in other ethnic groups, family structures vary. However, there are some common attitudes toward having children and the role of kin.

Family Size "Wealth and children are the ornaments of this life," says the Qur'an, the sacred book of Muslims. In traditional Middle Eastern societies, not having children is a reason for great unhappiness. In a study of a working-class Arab American community in Dearborn, Michigan, Aswad (1994) found that 38 percent had five or more children.

The number declines, however, among people who are U.S. born and in higher socioeconomic classes. U.S.-born Arab American women have low fertility rates: just under two children per lifetime (which is lower than the average among U.S. women). Many postpone childbearing and have fewer children because they pursue college and professional degrees and have high employment rates (Kulczycki and Lobo, 2001).

Nuclear and Extended Families Most Middle Eastern children (84 percent) live with both parents, compared with 71 percent of all American children. Middle Eastern families frown on divorce. Iranians, for example, view divorce as a calamity (*bala*) and equate it with an "unfortunate fate" that should be avoided at all costs. Although divorce rates among U.S.-born Middle Eastern families are increasing, the percentages are much lower than the national average (almost half of all marriages). Unless a parent is a widow or a widower, single parenthood is seen as abnormal (Aswad, 1997; Hojat et al., 2000; Kulczycki and Lobo, 2001).

Nuclear families are the norm, but extended family ties are important. "The typical Lebanese," for example, "views family as an extension of him or herself" (Richardson-Bouie, 2003: 528). Households composed of parents and children maintain close contact with their relatives. These relationships include financial, social, and emotional support.

Whenever possible, Middle Eastern families try to bring relatives from their homelands to stay with them over long periods of time to attend U.S. colleges and universities, to work, or just to visit. According to a young Algerian woman, her 26-year-old female cousin lived with their family for six years while attending school. Both women had strict curfews (Shakir, 1997). One of my Turkish students told his classmates that his American-born parents "kicked me down to the basement" because a visiting uncle was to use his bedroom for the next year or so. The students were appalled. He simply shrugged: "Relatives are important in Turkish families."

Husbands and Wives

Many Middle Eastern families value close and reciprocal ties between husbands and wives. Marriage is often a "family affair," and gender role expectations are clearly delineated.

Marriage Marriage is endogamous (see Chapter 1), favoring marriage between cousins in some groups and between people from the same national group. Marriage is a sacred ceremony and is regarded as central to the family unit.

Marriage is usually a contract between two families and is rarely based on the Western concept of romantic love. Marriages are often arranged or semi-arranged in the sense that children can turn down parents' choices of a suitable mate. Some of these practices are changing and vary across groups. Among Iranians, Lebanese, and Palestinians, for example, and especially those from upper and middle-class families, young adults tend to choose their own marital partners but usually seek parental approval (Jalali, 1996). Others visit their homelands to meet prospective partners that their kin (especially mothers and aunts) have singled out for marriage.

Gender Roles Cultural attitudes mandate distinct gender role expectations. Men have been socialized to be the family providers and to protect their wives, children, and female kin. A "good" husband, then, supports his family and makes decisions that promote the family's well-being. In most cases, the husband is the highest authority in the family and has the final decision on any family issues (Aswad, 1999; Joseph, 1999).

Women anchor a family's identity. A "good" wife takes care of the home and children, obeys her husband, and gets along with in-laws. She doesn't challenge her husband, especially in public, and doesn't work outside

the home, especially when the children are young. Although men have many privileges, women have considerable influence and status in the domestic area (Simon, 1996).

A wife should always act honorably and do nothing that humiliates her husband and kin. Premarital sex and extramarital affairs are out of the question because they bring shame to the family and the extended kin. According to some young women, such gender role expectations are comforting rather than restrictive because they protect women from assaults and competition for dates (Shakir, 1997).

Gender roles are changing, however. Many Middle Eastern women must work out of economic necessity while raising children. As a result, they have more power in financial decisions. Divorce rates are low but increasing. And as families become more Americanized, there are more conflicts between parents and children.

Parents and Children

According to an Arabic saying, "To satisfy God is to satisfy parents." Satisfying parents means following the family's customs and traditions, respecting one's cultural identity, and living up to gender role expectations.

Ethnic Identity Parents and children usually have strong bonds. In a study of Arab Canadian teenagers, for example, nine out of ten respondents said that they talk to their parents, usually the mother, about their personal lives and problems (Abu-Laban and Abu-Laban, 1999). This trust and confidence reflects Middle Eastern values that parents are a resource. Parents also teach their children to feel a lifelong responsibility to their siblings and parents and to respect their aunts, uncles, cousins, and grandparents (Ajrouch, 1999; Joseph, 1999).

Parents also reinforce ethnic identity by encouraging their children to associate with peers from their own culture. Armenian children, for example, attend language schools on weekends. Here adolescents not only learn their language but also associate with Armenian peers who have similar cultural values (Phinney et al., 2001b).

Because many Middle East parents see education as a ladder for success, they expect their children to do well. Parents encourage their children to spend time on homework instead of watching television and hanging out with schoolmates (Abu-Laban and Abu-Laban, 1999).

Gender Role Expectations Many Middle Eastern parents have a double standard for girls' and boys' behavior in terms of dating and curfews. Girls have many more restrictions in both areas. Girls are guarded because husbands want a virgin bride and not "damaged goods" (see Chapter 1). Brothers have every right to scold or threaten their sisters if they "misbehave" or act in any way that could tarnish the family name (Ajrouch, 1999).

Although boys are expected to marry within their ethnic group, they have much more freedom to date, both inside and outside their group. According to a Lebanese mother, "We just feel the boy can take care of himself. If a boy goes out with a girl, nobody's going to point a finger at him." In contrast, a girl who dates or who dresses "the wrong way" will ruin her reputation and dishonor the family's name (Simon, 1996; Ajrouch, 1999).

Girls are expected to perform traditional domestic chores and serve men. Some girls accept these roles, but others complain. According to a young Lebanese woman,

> *So many times I would be asked to fix my brother's bed. I was told, "He is a boy." And I would say, "He has arms and legs." Or sometimes he would be sitting, and he would say, "Go get me a glass of water." I would say, "Never! Get your own." My family would say to me, "Your head is so strong, it cannot be broken with a hammer" (Shakir, 1997: 166).*

The double standards create conflict between daughters and their parents. Middle Eastern teenage girls who spend much time with their American friends, especially, balk at the restrictions on dating. These and other disagreements can strain intergenerational relationships.

Intergenerational Relationships

The relationships across generations are usually strong. As with Mexican American families, many Middle Eastern families practice chain migration: A son immigrates to the United States, establishes himself, and then brings other members of the family until many relatives have settled together (Aswad, 1997).

Families respect elderly relatives. According to an Iranian saying, "Children are like canes in the hands of old parents" (Sharifzadeh, 1997: 454). If Middle Eastern families have the resources, they visit their elderly parents, aunts, and uncles overseas regularly. Even in the case of intermarriages, affluent Turkish fathers visit their kin annually or send their children to Turkey during the summer to visit their grandparents and other relatives (Bilgé, 1996). Thus, older generations reinforce many cultural attitudes and behaviors.

Prejudice and Discrimination

All ethnic families have experienced prejudice and discrimination (see Chapter 3). Middle Eastern families, however, have suffered a large share of verbal and physical assaults because of the U.S. government's combative relations with the Middle East, the September 11, 2001, terrorist attacks, and, most recently, the war against Iraq.

Finding acceptance is difficult. When Alia first came to the United States, her new classmates teased her about being Palestinian: "What do you have in your bag, a bomb?" (Shakir, 1997: 144). The number of workplace discrimination complaints to the Equal Employment Opportunity Commission more than quadrupled three months after the September 11 terrorist attacks. The complainants, many of whom were Arab Americans, said that they had been fired without any notice or explanation (Breslau, 2001; Conlin, 2001; Grimsley, 2001).

Still others experienced harassment, hate crimes, and even death:

- An Arab American citizen, father of eight children, was shot to death at a convenience store where he worked in Fresno, California. This was one of five murders that the Arab-American Anti-Discrimination Committee attributed to the September 11 attacks.

- Muslim American and Arab American women—many recognizable by their distinctive head scarves, or *hijabs*—became targets of violence even though they were middle-class professionals. For example, a young cashier at a Staples store in Westbury, New York, threw a credit card back at an Arab American woman.

- Some teachers implied that all Muslims are terrorists. Some classmates harassed U.S.-born Middle Eastern children with comments such as "Go back where you belong." As a result, many children were afraid to identify their Middle Eastern heritage (Shakir, 1997; Benet, 2001; Breslau, 2001).

All of these and other prejudices and discrimination have a negative impact on parents and their children. Nonetheless, Middle Eastern families—like African Americans, American Indians, Latinos, and Asian Americans—show an enormous resilience in overcoming obstacles.

Strengths of the Middle Eastern Family

In many ways, Middle Eastern children have the best of two worlds. Because they're bicultural (and many are bilingual), they understand their own and American culture. When ethnic identity, strong family ties, and religion secure children to their communities, they can cope with prejudice and discrimination. Most importantly, perhaps, many Middle East families have extended kin networks and relatives on whom they can count during hard times (Shakir, 1997; Ajrouch, 1999; Hayani, 1999).

MAKING CONNECTIONS

■ How do the media reinforce the image of the model minority?

■ How do children's and adult movies (like *Aladdin* and *The Mummy*) portray Middle Eastern people, especially Arabs?

Interracial and Interethnic Relationships and Marriages

In 1997, professional golfer Tiger Woods said he was "Cablinasian," a word he'd made up as a boy, because he was one-eighth Caucasian, one-fourth black, one-eighth American Indian, one-fourth Thai, and one-fourth Chinese. Many blacks were upset that Woods seemed to downplay his African American roots, but Woods maintained that he was embracing all parts of his multicultural heritage. Even former President Bill Clinton announced that he, too, was a multiracial American because some of his ancestors were American Indians.

Interracial and Interethnic Relationships

One of the big news stories from the 2000 Census was that California is now a "minority majority" state, meaning that whites make up less than one-half the state population (Kent et al., 2001). Not all people identify themselves with only one race, however.

Growing Multiracial Diversity As you saw earlier in this chapter, the 2000 Census allowed people to mark more than one race for the first time. The federal government added this option because of increasing rates of interracial marriage and the growing population that identifies with more than one race, especially among children. Checking more than one race offered 126 categories and combinations.

Almost 98 percent reported only one race. But one in 40 Americans calls herself or himself the product of two or more racial groups. About 4 percent of children under age 18 were identified as multiracial, compared with 2 percent of adults. Almost a third of those reporting two or more races were Latinos (Jones and Smith, 2001). The next highest percentages included combinations of whites and other racial-ethnic identities (see *Figure 4.5*).

According to an Italian and Irish man and his black wife who live in Hawaii and have a biracial daughter, "You ask a Hawaiian what race they are and you'd get

20 different races" (Fears, 2001: A8). That's an exaggeration, but Hawaii has the largest proportion of people—21 percent—who identify themselves as two or more races, followed by Alaska and California (5 percent each), Puerto Rico (4 percent), and Arizona and Washington (almost 4 percent each). In terms of numbers, about 40 percent of the people who identify themselves as two or more races live in just three states: California (1.6 million), New York (590,000), and Texas (515,000) (Jones and Smith, 2001).

Reactions to Interracial Relationships Of all the people who reported being more than one race, 42 percent were children under age 18 (Jones and Smith, 2001). These "mixies," as they sometimes call themselves, experience emotions ranging from self-confidence to self-hatred (see Chapter 12).

Interracial dating is fairly common (see Chapter 8). Nonetheless, interracial couples encounter everything from discrimination to acceptance. In a recent survey, whites were more likely than other groups to feel that people should marry only within their own race. There were striking differences by age, however. Only 17 percent of people between ages 18 to 29, compared to 68 percent of those ages 65 and over, felt that it's better to marry someone of your own race (*Race and Ethnicity. . .*, 2001).

There are several reasons for the greater acceptance of biracial marriages by younger people. Some are the offspring of biracial casual sex, dating, cohabitation, or marriage. Also many young people are more accepting of interracial relationships than their parents. In fact, 82 percent of high school students said they would date people of other races (Dutton, 2001).

FIGURE 4.5 **Percentage of Americans Who Identify with More Than One Race, 2000**

Note: Of the 281.4 million population in 2000, 2.4 percent identified themselves with two or more races. Only 0.1 percent said they were three or more races.

SOURCE: Based on Jones and Smith, 2001, Tables 4 and 5.

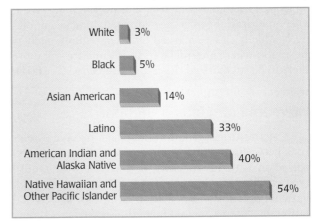

TABLE 4.1

Racial-Ethnic Intermarriages by Race and Sex: 2000

Racial Group	Men	Women
White		
Number	43.8 million	43.6 million
Percentage married out	3.4	2.9
Black		
Number	4.1 million	3.9 million
Percentage married out	8.4	3.3
Latino		
Number	5.2 million	5.3 million
Percentage married out	15.0	17.2
Asian American		
Number	1.9 million	2.2 million
Percentage married out	9.9	21.3
American Indian		
Number	351,000	371,000
Percentage married out	52.3	53.9
Total		
Number	55,352,000	55,352,000
Percentage married out	5.4	5.4

Note: These data tabulate the race of spouses for persons married and living with a spouse. For example, 43.8 million white men and 43.6 million white women were married and living with a spouse in 2000.

SOURCE: Adapted from Farley, 2002, Table 1.1.

These are attitudes. What about behavior: How do people react to dating or marring across racial and ethnic lines? When a national survey asked couples how often they encountered discriminatory behavior such as stares or pointing, 25 percent of black–white couples said "never," compared with 9 percent of Latino–white couples and 5 percent of Asian–white couples. Such behavior varies greatly by region, however. In the West, where multiracial percentages are high, biracial couples are less likely to be "marked" than in regions, such as the South, where interracial relationships are still more likely to be stigmatized (*Race and Ethnicity . . .*, 2001).

Interracial and Interethnic Marriages

Laws against miscegenation (marriage or sexual relations between a man and a woman of different races) existed in America as early as 1661. It wasn't until 1967, in the U.S. Supreme Court's *Loving v. Virginia* decision, that antimiscegenation laws were overturned nationally. Interracial and interethnic marriages reflect

exogamy: marrying outside of one's particular group (see Chapters 1 and 8).

Prevalence of Racial-Ethnic Intermarriages The rates of racial-ethnic intermarriages have increased slowly, from 0.7 percent in 1970 to 5.4 percent of all married couples in 2000 (Fields and Casper, 2001). Thus, about 95 percent of all couples still marry someone of the same race or ethnicity.

When people think about racial intermarriage, they generally assume that it's between blacks and whites. This is a misconception. Of the 3 million racial-ethnic intermarriages, the outmarriage rates are lower for whites and blacks than for Latinos, Asian American and Pacific Islanders, and American Indians (see *Table 4.1*). Whereas black men are more likely to marry white women than women in other racial-ethnic groups, white men are more likely to marry Latino, Asian American, and American Indian women (and in that order) than African American women (Fields and Casper, 2001).

There are large variations by sex both across and within racial-ethnic groups. The outmarriage rates are lower for black and white women than for Latino, Asian American, and American Indian women. Across groups, more than half of American Indian men and women marry out, compared with much lower proportions of other groups (see *Table 4.1*).

In terms of within-group variations, some Asian Americans are more likely to intermarry than others. Japanese Americans, especially men, are much more likely to marry out than are Chinese or Asian American Indians (Hwang et al., 1997; Foreman and Nance, 1999).

Why have racial-ethnic intermarriages increased? And why do the rates vary across and within racial-ethnic boundaries? There are a number of reasons.

Proximity We tend to date and marry people whom we see on a regular basis (see Chapter 8). Greater opportunity for interracial contact through housing, schools, work, and leisure activities may result in more racial-ethnic intermarriages (Kalmijn, 1998).

For example, the military, one of the most integrated of U.S. institutions, seems to set the stage for dating and interracial marriage. White men who have served in the military are three times more likely to marry black women than white men who have never served. White women who have served are seven times more likely to marry outside their racial group than those who have never served ("Interracial marriages . . .," 1997).

Availability of Potential Spouses We sometimes marry outside of our racial-ethnic groups because of a shortage of potential spouses. Because the population is so small, for example, an overwhelming 80 percent of U.S.-born Arabs have non-Arab spouses (Kulczycki and Lobo, 2002). In contrast, intermarriage rates among Latinos and Asian Americans have decreased since 1990—for both women and men—because the influx of new immigrants has provided a larger pool of eligible mates (Farley, 2002).

Some demographers predict, however, that by 2100 more than half of all Asian Americans, Pacific Islanders, and Latinos will have intermarried (Edmonston et al., 2002). Because many people are multiracial, the racial divides that exist now will presumably be much less important in the future.

Acculturation   Racial-ethnic groups that are the most acculturated are also the most likely to intermarry. Asian Americans who are less likely to out-marry are those who live in ethnic enclaves, do not speak fluent English, and have lived in the United States a short time (Shinagawa and Pang, 1996).

Among Japanese Americans, in contrast, intermarriage rates are high because many families have been in the country for four or five generations, have acculturated, and are generally more accepting of intermarriage. In addition, the number of Japanese Americans is small compared with those of other Asian American groups. This decreases their chances of finding a desirable mate within their own group (Hwang et al., 1994; Rosenfeld, 2002).

Upward Mobility   Many of my black female students often complain that successful black men are marrying white women. This reduces the marriage market, they maintain, even for well-educated, attractive, and successful African American women.

This perspective is only partly correct. Interracial marriage is certainly a source of upward mobility for many women. A study of marriages between black men and white women in 33 states found, for example, that in most of these unions the men were of higher status than the women (Kalmijn, 1993).

Interracial marriage can also provide upward mobility for men. Successful black men have a large pool of eligible partners, including black women. In a racially stratified society, however, skin color is a "resource" that increases or decreases one's status. High-status black men can compensate for their lower racial status by marrying lower-status white women, who have a higher racial status (Fu, 2001).

Asian American men and women with high socioeconomic status are more likely to marry other Asian Americans because they can compete successfully for the available marital partners. In contrast, those at lower socioeconomic levels "may be forced to settle for a less desirable choice outside of the group," including groups that they see as having a lower racial status (Hwang et al., 1997: 770).

Changing Attitudes   An increase in interracial marriages also reflects changing attitudes. American approval of interracial marriage rose from 4 percent in 1958 to 65 percent in 2002 (*Marriage between Blacks and Whites*, 2002).

Whites are less accepting of all racial-ethnic intermarriages than other groups, however. According to a recent survey, 46 percent of white respondents said that people should "marry someone of their own race," compared to 21 percent of African Americans, 29 percent of Latinos, and 30 percent of Asian Americans (*Race and Ethnicity*, 2001). An Ohio pastor refused to allow a wedding in his church when he learned that the white bride's groom was black ("Interracial wedding . . .," 2000). And, according to one recent white bride, her parents accepted her Puerto Rican husband because they thought he was Italian (Fears and Deane, 2001).

Even though, as a group, African Americans are more accepting than whites of interracial marriages (including those between whites and blacks), many disapprove. With a significant shortage of marriageable African American men, many black women feel betrayed or deserted when a black man marries a white woman. Some black leaders also feel that mixed marriages weaken black solidarity (see Chapter 8).

Asian American parents also have mixed feelings about outmarriages. They often encourage their children to marry within their own group to preserve "lineage purity" and to avoid a clash of values (about child rearing, hard work, and respect for elders, for example) that intermarriage with "mainstream America" often brings.

Asian American parents who object to their children's marrying outside of their specific ethnic group are more accepting of those within Asian American groups. According to a Chinese American writer and artist, for example, his mother's initial dismay that he was dating a non-Chinese woman evaporated when the mother learned that her son was seeing a Korean American woman. The mother saw Koreans as physically similar to the Chinese and felt that many of the values would be similar (Kibria, 1997).

MAKING CONNECTIONS

■ One of every five babies born in Sacramento, California, is multiracial. Could we conclude, then, that Sacramento is one of America's most integrated cities? Or not?

■ Do racial-ethnic intermarriages decrease our race consciousness? Or dilute cultural heritages?

Conclusion

The racial and ethnic composition of American families is *changing*. There has been an influx of immigrants from many non-European countries. The growth of African American, American Indian, Asian American, Latino, and Middle Eastern families is expected to continue in the future.

As you've seen in this chapter, there are many variations both between and within racial-ethnic groups in terms of family structure, extended kinship networks, and parenting styles. This means that families have more *choices* outside the traditional, white, middle-class family model.

These choices often are steeped in *constraints*, however. Even middle-class racial-ethnic minorities confront stereotypes and discrimination on a daily basis. Because many children are multiracial, they must live in at least two worlds. These worlds become even more complicated, as you'll see in the next chapter, because gender roles also play an important role in every family's daily life.

SUMMARY

1. U.S. households are becoming more diverse in terms of racial and ethnic composition. Demographers project that if current immigration and birth rate trends continue, by 2050 only half of the U.S. population will be white.

2. Many Americans are ambivalent about the high immigration rates. Some are grateful that immigrants provide important work at low-wage and professional levels. Others worry about national security and "diluting our national identity."

3. Latino, African American, Asian American, Middle Eastern, and American Indian families are considered minority groups. One of the most important characteristics of a minority group is its lack of economic and political power.

4. Black families are very heterogeneous in terms of lifestyle. They also vary in kinship structure, values, and social class. Despite such variations, African American families are the subject of many myths.

5. American Indian families are complex and diverse. They speak many languages, practice different religions and customs, and maintain a variety of economic and political styles. Because of assimilation, a number of tribes are losing their language and customs.

6. Latino families vary in a number of respects, including when they settled in the United States, where they came from, and how they adapted to economic and political situations. In addition, family structure and dynamics vary greatly by social class and degree of assimilation.

7. Asian American families are even more diverse than American Indian and Latino families. Asian American family structures vary depending on the family's origin, when the immigrants arrived, whether their homeland was ravaged by war, and the socioeconomic status of the parents.

8. Middle Eastern families come from about 30 countries. Although they speak many languages and practice different religions, most place a high value on nuclear and extended families, teach traditional gender roles, and reinforce their children's ethnic identity.

9. The number of multiracial Americans is increasing. Much of this population is children under age 18.

10. The rates of interracial and interethnic marriage have been increasing slowly since 1967. Some of the reasons for the growing number of these marriages include proximity in school and workplaces, a greater public acceptance of racial-ethnic intermarriages, acculturation, and a shrinking pool of eligible marriage partners among some groups.

KEY TERMS

assimilation   *80*
cultural pluralism   *80*
acculturation   *80*
minority group   *82*

racial group   *82*
ethnic group   *82*
racial-ethnic group   *82*
prejudice   *83*

discrimination   *83*
racism   *86*
racial socialization   *86*

TAKING IT FURTHER

Race and Ethnicity Resources on the Internet

The first site, **American Studies Web,** is very comprehensive, containing national and international materials on groups such as African Americans, Asian Americans, American Indians, and Latinos. The other URLs provide links to specific racial-ethnic groups.

American Studies Web

www.georgetown.edu/crossroads/asw/index.html

WWW Virtual Library: American Indians

www.hanksville.org/NAresources

Asian American Studies WWW Virtual Library

coombs.anu.edu.au/WWWVL-Asian Americanstudies.html

Black/African Related Resources

www.sas.upenn.edu/African_Studies/Home_Page/mcgee.html

Arab-American Affairs Homepage

www.arab-american-affairs.net

Hispanic Resources on the Web

www.hartfordpl.lib.ct.us/hispanic.htm

Interracial Voice

www.webcom.com/~intvoice

And more: www.prenhall.com/benokraitis provides sites on teaching tolerance, international migration, minority health, civil rights legislation, hate sites, and numerous URLs on ethnic minority groups in the United States.

INVESTIGATE WITH RESEARCH NAVIGATOR

Please go to www.researchnavigator.com and enter your LOGIN NAME and PASSWORD. For instructions on registering for the first time, please view the detailed instructions at the end of the Chapter 1. Please search the Research Navigator™ site using the following key search terms:

acculturation
prejudice
discrimination

Gender Roles and Socialization

Norman Rockwell, *The Shiner*. Printed by permission of the Norman Rockwell Family Agency. Copyright © 1953 The Norman Rockwell Family Entities.

DATADIGEST

- Nearly a billion people in the world are illiterate; **two-thirds are women**.

- In only 22 countries do women represent 25 percent or more of elected legislators, and this number has decreased since the early 1990s. In 2003, the **United States figures (14 percent) were lower** than those of many other countries: Sweden, 45 percent; Denmark, 38 percent; Finland, 37 percent; Norway, 36 percent; Costa Rica, 35 percent; Cuba, 28 percent; Austria and Vietnam, 27 percent each; and Mexico, 16 percent. Two countries—Kuwait and the United Arab Emirates, had no women in their legislative bodies.

- White men make up only **33 percent of the U.S. population.** Yet they make up 97 percent of school superintendents, 93 percent of the U.S. Congress, 90 percent of daily newspaper editors, 88 percent of college presidents, 87 percent of Fortune 500 chief executive officers, 86 percent of the U.S. House of Representatives, 86 percent of the Fortune 1000 board seats, 85 percent of partners in law firms, 85 percent of tenured professors, and 80 percent of state governors.

SOURCES: Schemo, 2002; Strupp, 2002; Strauss, 2002; Walsh, 2002; Caiazza, 2002–03; Jones, 2003; Seager, 2003; Tanner, 2003; *State of the World's Mothers*, 2003.

D o you know what would have happened if there had been Three Wise Women instead of Three Wise Men? They would have asked for directions, arrived on time, helped deliver baby Jesus, cleaned the stable, made a casserole, brought practical gifts, and there would be peace on Earth. Does this anecdote stereotype women and men? Or do you think that it has a kernel of truth?

In this chapter we examine gender roles: how we learn them and how they affect our everyday marriage and family relations. We begin with a look at gender myths and some of the nature–nurture debates that often fuel such myths. First, however, take the gender quiz in the "Ask Yourself" box on page 110 to see how much you already know about women and men.

Gender Myths and Biological Puzzles

Many Americans think that men and women are very different. Both sexes often describe men as aggressive, courageous, and ambitious. In contrast, they see women as emotional, talkative, patient, and affectionate (*Table 5.1* on page 111). Do these traits characterize your family members and friends? Probably not. Your mom may be aggressive and ambitious and your dad emotional and talkative. Or both may be aggressive, emotional, or talkative, depending on the situation. And either or both parents may change over the years.

We tend to associate stereotypically female characteristics with weakness and stereotypically male characteristics with strength. We may criticize women for being "emotional," for example, but praise men for

109

ASKYOURSELF

A Gender Quiz: Are Women and Men Different?

	True	False
1. Women are the weaker sex.	☐	☑
2. Boys are more group-centered, active, and aggressive than girls.	☑	☐
3. Women are more emotional than men.	☐	☑
4. Women talk more than men.	☑✗	☑
5. Women suffer more from depression.	☑	☑
6. Women are more likely than men to divulge personal information.	☐	☑
7. Men smile more often than women.	☐	☑
8. Women and men don't care whether a baby is a boy or a girl ("Just as long as it's healthy").	☑	☐
9. Smoking is more harmful to men than to women.	☐	☑
10. A heart attack is more likely to be fatal for a man than for a woman.	☑	☐

(The answers to this quiz are on p. 113.)

being "aggressive." Consider, also, how often we describe the same behavior differently for women and men: He's firm, but she's stubborn; he's careful about details, but she's picky; he's honest, but she's opinionated; he's raising good points, but she's bitching; and he's a man of the world, but she's "been around."

Why do these stereotypes persist? Because we don't differentiate between sex and gender, we often ignore the importance of the social context that produces and maintains these stereotypes. All of these misconceptions promote and sustain cultural myths that are harmful to both men and women.

The Difference between Sex and Gender

Although many people use the terms *sex* and *gender* interchangeably, the terms have distinct meanings. Sex and gender are highly related, but sex is a biological designation, whereas gender is a social creation that teaches us to be masculine or feminine in playing our roles.

Sex Sex refers to the biological characteristics with which we are born: our chromosomal, anatomical, hormonal, and other physical and physiological attributes. Such biological characteristics determine whether you have male or female genitalia, whether you will menstruate, how much bodily hair you will have and

where it will grow, whether you're able to bear children, and so on.

Although sex *influences* our behavior (such as shaving beards and buying bras), it does not *determine* how we think, feel, and act. We learn to be feminine or masculine through gender, a much more complex concept than sex.

Gender Gender consists of learned attitudes and behaviors that characterize people of one sex or the other. Gender is based on social and cultural expectations rather than on physical traits. Thus, whereas we are *born* either male or female, we *learn* to be either women or men because we associate conventional patterns of behavior with each sex.

If you've shopped for baby cards, you might have noticed that most of the cards for girls are pink, whereas those for boys are blue. The cards usually portray the baby girls as playing with their toes, in a bubble bath, or gazing at a mobile above their cribs. The cards for boys usually include sports such as baseballs, toys such as train sets, and even laptops. You also might have noticed how many baby cards describe female infants as "dear," "sweet," "cute," or "cuddly," whereas male infants are described as "a special joy," "a pride," and "a precious gift." What's the message in these cards? Female infants are passive and ornamental; male infants are active and more valued.

Gender Roles One of the functions of the family is to teach its members appropriate social roles (see Chapter 1). Among the most important are **gender roles**: the characteristics, attitudes, feelings, and behaviors that society expects of females and males. We learn to become male or female through interaction with family members and the larger society. In most societies, for example, men are expected to provide shelter, food, and clothing for their families; women are expected to nurture their children and to tend to the family's everyday needs (see Chapters 12 and 13).

Social scientists often describe our roles as gendered. *Gendered* refers to the process of treating and evaluating males and females differently because of their sex:

> *To the extent that women and men dress, talk, or act differently because of societal expectations, their behavior is gendered. To the extent that an organization assigns some jobs to women and others to men on the basis of their assumed abilities, that organization is gendered. And to the extent that professors treat a student differently because that student is a man or a woman, their interaction is gendered (Howard and Hollander, 1997: 11).*

The fact that we learn gender roles doesn't mean that we can't change them. As you'll see in this and later chapters, women and men have challenged and changed many conventional rules about our "proper" behavior. Many women now pursue college degrees and contribute to the family's finances; men participate more in raising children and doing housework.

Gender Identity Early in life, children develop a **gender identity**, or a perception of themselves as either masculine or feminine. Most cultures teach gender identity early. Indian and Mexican baby girls have pierced ears, for example, and toddler hairstyles and clothing differ by sex. Gender identity, which typically corresponds to a person's biological sex, is learned in early childhood and usually remains fixed throughout life.

The Nature–Nurture Debate: Is Anatomy Destiny?

Most social scientists differentiate between sex, gender, and gender roles. If gender roles are learned, these scientists argue, they can also be unlearned. However, other social scientists and biologists believe that the differences in the ways women and men behave reflect their innate, biological characteristics, not social and cultural expectations. This difference of opinion is often called the nature–nurture debate (*Table 5.2* on page 112).

How Important Is Nature?

Those who argue that nature shapes behavior point to four kinds of relevant evidence: developmental and health differences between men and women, research on the effects of sex hormones, sex differences in some parts of the human brain, and unsuccessful attempts at sex reassignment. Let's look at each of these briefly.

TABLE 5.1

The Top Ten Personality Traits Ascribed to Men and Women

Trait	More True of Men	More True of Women
1. Aggressive	68%	20%
2. Courageous	50	27
3. Ambitious	44	33
4. Easygoing	55	48
5. Intelligent	21	36
6. Creative	15	65
7. Patient	19	72
8. Talkative	10	78
9. Affectionate	5	86
10. Emotional	3	90

SOURCE: Newport, 2001: 34.

TABLE 5.2	
The Nature–Nurture Debate	
Nature	**Nurture**
Differences in male and female beliefs, attitudes, and behavior are	**Differences in male and female beliefs, attitudes, and behavior are**
Innate	Learned
Biological, physiological	Psychological, social, cultural
Due largely to heredity	Due largely to environment
Fairly fixed	Very changeable

Developmental and Health Differences There are some documented biological differences between men and women. Here are a few examples:

- Boys have more genetic disorders, such as night blindness, myopia (nearsightedness), hemophilia, and glaucoma.

- Senses of smell and taste are more acute in women than in men, and hearing is better and lasts longer in women than in men.

- Although women are better than men at warding off viral and bacterial infections, they are much more susceptible to autoimmune diseases such as lupus.

- Women have a higher risk than men of developing diabetes (a major contributor to endometrial cancer, adult blindness, and cardiovascular disease).

- Some conditions such as migraine headaches predominate in women, whereas others, including some kinds of skin cancer, are more common in men (McDonald, 1999; Sugg, 2000; Kreeger, 2002a, 2002b).

Effects of Sex Hormones Scientists don't know why women and men differ but believe that hormones provide part of the explanation. All males and females share three sex **hormones:** chemical substances secreted into the bloodstream by glands of the endocrine system. They are *estrogen* (dominant in females and produced by the ovaries), *progesterone* (present in high levels during pregnancy and also secreted by the ovaries), and *testosterone* (dominant in males, where it is produced by the testes). All of these hormones are produced in minute quantities in both sexes before puberty.

After puberty, varying levels of these hormones in males and females produce different physiological changes. For example, testosterone, the dominant male sex hormone, strengthens muscles but threatens the heart. It triggers production of low-density lipoprotein, which clogs blood vessels. Therefore, men are at twice the risk of coronary heart disease as are (premenopausal) women. The dominant female sex hormones, especially estrogen, make blood vessels more elastic and strengthen the immune system, making females more infection resistant (Wizeman and Pardue, 2001).

Sex Differences in the Brain In some cases, gender identity may be inconsistent with a person's biological sex. *Transsexuals* are people who feel that their gender identity is out of sync with their anatomical sex. Transsexuals often describe themselves as feeling "trapped in the wrong body" (Devor, 1997).

About one person in 350,000 believes she or he was born the wrong sex (Gorman, 1995). Some undergo surgery (which costs about $60,000), but others opt for only hormonal treatments. In one of the earliest and most publicized cases in the 1970s, Richard Raskind, a married man with two children who was a highly ranked tennis player and a respected ophthalmologist, underwent surgery and became Renee Richards.

No one knows the reasons for transsexualism. Autopsies of six male-to-female transsexuals found that a tiny brain structure that controls sexual function was more like that of a woman than that of a man. Some researchers suggest that structures in the brain, or nature, may account for transsexualism (Zhou et al., 1995). Others argue that transsexuals are usually gay men who are so feminine that they want to become women. According to this perspective, sex differences in the brain have nothing to do with transsexualism (Bailey, 2003).

Unsuccessful Sex Reassignment Some scientists point to unsuccessful attempts at sex reassignment as another example favoring the nature-over-nurture argument. Since the 1960s, John Money, a highly respected psychologist, has published numerous articles and books that maintain that gender identity is not firm at birth but is determined as much by culture and nurture as it is by hormones (see, for example, Money and Ehrhardt, 1972).

Several scientists have challenged such conclusions, however. As the box "The Case of John/Joan" on page 114 shows, Money's most famous sex reassignment experiment does not support his contention that infants born as biological males can be raised successfully as females.

How Important Is Nurture?

Most social scientists maintain that culture, or nurture, shapes human behavior. They often point to three data sources: cross-cultural variations in gender roles, international differences in male violence rates, and successful sex assignment cases.

Cross-cultural Variations in Gender Roles

In a classic study, anthropologist Margaret Mead (1935) studied three tribes that lived within short distances of each other in New Guinea and found three combinations of gender roles. Among the Arapesh, both men and women were nurturant with their children. The men were cooperative and sensitive, and they rarely engaged in warfare.

The Mundugumors were just the opposite. Both men and women were competitive and aggressive. Neither parent showed much tenderness, and both often used physical punishment to discipline the children.

The Tchumbuli demonstrated the reverse of Western gender roles. The women were the economic providers, whereas the men took care of children, sat around gossiping, and spent a lot of time decorating themselves for tribal festivities. Mead concluded that attributes long considered either masculine or feminine (such as nurturance) were culturally—rather than biologically—determined.

Contemporary cultures and subcultures also vary widely in gender roles. As you saw in Chapter 4, for example, black couples are more egalitarian than white couples or recent immigrants from Asia or the Middle East.

Cross-cultural Variations in Male Violence

If men were biologically aggressive, their violent acts, such as homicide, would be similar across societies. This is not the case. Male homicide rates vary widely across countries (*Figure 5.1* on page 115). In addition, the rates of deadly assault can change over time because they reflect factors such as attitudes about crime, law enforcement policies, and, especially, the degree of a country's poverty. Most violence-related deaths occur in low-income countries (Krug et al., 2002).

This does not mean that all men are aggressive and all women are nonviolent. For example, archaeologists have excavated burial mounds of fifth-century B.C. nomads in Russia and found that 14 percent of the graves were those of women buried with daggers, arrowheads, swords, and other artifacts. Both the artifacts and bent arrowheads in some of the women's body cavities suggest that the women were warriors and that some had been killed in battle (Davis-Kimball, 1997).

Answers to "A Gender Quiz: Are Women and Men Different?"

1. **False.** Although infant mortality rates vary by race and ethnicity, the death rate for male infants is 22 percent higher than for female infants. And, on average, women live about five years longer than men do.

2. **True.** Boys' play is typically hierarchical, group-centered, competitive, physical, and aggressive. Girls engage in more reciprocal, verbal, and cooperative kinds of play.

3. **False.** Both sexes are equally emotional but express their feelings differently. Men may "churn" more internally whereas women "externalize" their emotions through facial and verbal expressions.

4. **False.** In most situations, men tend to talk more and at greater length than women.

5. **True.** Women are two to three times more likely than men to suffer from depression. Women's societal roles affect their happiness, and, in turn, unhappiness can affect brain functions. In addition, women's brains produce less of the feel-good chemical serotonin.

6. **False.** Both sexes self-disclose by divulging personal information but are more comfortable in doing so with women than with men.

7. **False.** Women smile significantly more than men. It is a woman's task to do "emotion work." Smiling is one way to restore harmony and reduce tension.

8. **False.** According to a recent Gallup poll, 55 percent of men but only 32 percent of women said that, if they could have only one child, they would prefer a boy.

9. **False.** Women smokers are 20 to 70 percent more likely than men to develop lung cancer and heart disease. Smoking is also deadlier for women because it increases the chances of infertility, pregnancy complications, low-weight babies, problems with menstrual function, and cervical cancer.

10. **False.** A heart attack is more likely to be fatal for a woman than for a man. Women with heart disease are less likely than men to be diagnosed correctly or treated promptly and are less likely to be sent for cardiac rehabilitation.

SOURCES: Tannen, 1994; McDonald, 1999; Sugg, 2000; Martel, 2001; Misra, 2001; *Women and Smoking . . .*, 2001; Lippa, 2002; Mathews et al., 2002; Vaccarino et al., 2002; Vakili et al., 2002; Wood, 2002; Gupta, 2003; LaFrance et al., 2003.

CHOICES

The Case of John/Joan

In 1963, twin boys were being circumcised. The penis of one of the infants was accidentally burned off. Encouraged by John Money, a medical psychologist at Johns Hopkins Hospital, the parents agreed to reassign and raise "John" as "Joan." Joan's testicles were removed a year later to facilitate feminization, and further surgery would construct a full vagina when Joan was older.

For many years, medical texts and social science writings reported that masculine and feminine behavior could be altered despite a person's genes at conception and anatomy. Money had reported that the twins were growing into happy, well-adjusted children of the opposite sex. The case set a precedent for sex reassignment as the standard treatment for 15,000 newborns with similarly injured genitals (Colapinto, 1997).

In the mid-1990s, however, Milton Diamond, a biologist at the University of Hawaii, and Keith Sigmundson, a psychiatrist with the Canadian Ministry of Health, conducted a follow-up of Joan's progress and showed that the sex reassignment had *not* been successful. Almost from the beginning, Joan refused to be treated like a girl. When Joan's mother dressed her in frilly clothes as a toddler, Joan tried to rip them off. She preferred to play with boys and stereotypical boys' toys such as machine guns. People in the community said that she "looks like a boy, talks like a boy" (Colapinto, 1997: 70). Joan had no friends, and no one would play with her. "Every day I was picked on, every day I was teased, every day I was threatened" (Diamond and Sigmundson, 1997: 300).

When she was 14, Joan rebelled and stopped living as a girl: "She refused to wear dresses and now favored a tattered jean jacket, ragged cords and work boots. Her hair was unwashed, uncombed and matted" (Colapinto, 1997: 73). She urinated standing up, refused vaginal surgery, and decided she would either commit suicide or live as a male.

When her father finally told her the true story of her birth and sex change, John recalls that "all of a sudden everything clicked. For the first time things made sense and I understood who and what I was" (Diamond and Sigmundson, 1997: 300). Joan had a mastectomy at the age of 14 and underwent several operations to reconstruct a penis. He is able to ejaculate but experiences little "erotic sensitivity." At age 25 he married a woman several years older than he and adopted her three children.

In contrast to Money's theories, then, Diamond and Sigmundson maintain that John's case is evidence that gender identity and sexual orientation are largely inborn. Nature, they argue, is stronger than nurture in shaping a person's sexual identity.

STOP AND THINK . . .

- *Do parents and physicians have a right to "reassign" a baby's sex?*
- *What would you do if you had to make a decision about a child's sex reassignment?*

Several campuses have suspended *sorority* (not just fraternity) chapters because hazing incidents included beating and physically injuring pledges (Geraghty, 1997). Many people were shocked by a recent hazing incident in which high school girls in "picture-perfect" suburban Northbrook, Illinois, were shown "kicking, punching, and dousing each other with all manner of foul substances, from fish guts to feces" (Paulson, 2003: 4).

Some women abuse children and engage in domestic violence (see Chapter 14). For example, wives or girlfriends killed 4 percent of male victims in 2001 (Rennison, 2003). Although women's violence rates are much lower than men's, such data show that women are not innately nurturant.

Male violence and aggression are most likely in patriarchal societies. In a **matriarchy**, women control cultural, political, and economic resources and, consequently, have power over men. In a **patriarchy**, in contrast, men hold the positions of power and authority—political, economic, legal, religious, educational, military, and domestic.

Scholars doubt that truly matriarchal societies—where women have power over men—have ever existed. Some cultures, however, exercise much more control than others over women's behavior. In some Middle Eastern countries, for example, women (but not men) are killed if they dishonor the family by engaging in premarital or extramarital sex (see Chapter 7). As the box "The Worldwide War against Women" on page 116 shows, patriarchal societies practice discrimination and violence against women because cultural and religious values, customs, and laws promote women's second-class citizenship.

Successful Sex Assignment As you saw earlier, some scientists cite the John/Joan case as evidence of the biological imprint on gender roles and identity. Others maintain that the successful sex assignments of hermaphrodites demonstrate the powerful effects of culture.

Hermaphrodites—also known as intersexuals—are people born with both male and female sex organs (internal and/or external). The incidence of ambiguous genitalia—where the sex of the newborn is not immediately apparent—is about 1 in every 8000 to 10,000 births (O'Mara, 1997).

Typically, parents choose a sex for the child and pursue surgical and hormonal treatment to change the ambiguous genital organs. The parents raise the child in the selected gender role: The name is male or female, the clothes are masculine or feminine, and the child is taught to behave in gender-appropriate ways. Such sex assignments suggest that socialization is more important than biology in determining a child's gender identity.

What Can We Conclude about the Nature–Nurture Debate?

What does all this information tell us, ultimately, about the nature–nurture debate? Several things. First, women and men do exhibit some sex-related genetic differences. Boys, for example, are more likely to have genetic defects, physical disabilities, mental retardation, reading disabilities, and school and emotional problems. There is no evidence, however, that boys' (or girls') hormones *cause* physical or behavioral maladies.

Second, cross-cultural research shows much variation in sex differences, such as aggression, that are typically ascribed to men (see *Figure 5.1*). Gender roles may be the result of a cascade of biological, genetic, family, and peer influences that vary widely across cultures and subcultures within a society (Lippa, 2002).

Finally, nature and nurture interact to explain our behavior. Parenting, for example, has a strong effect on children's behavior despite genetic makeup. A child with a difficult temperament—irritability, hostility, or aggressiveness—can become more sociable and learn self-control if parents are continuously patient, affectionate, and loving (see Chapter 12). In effect, many researchers contend, genes are turned on or off by socialization: "A particular gene can have a different effect, depending on the environment" (Sapolsky, 2000: 68). In this sense, our minds and bodies are connected.

Living Gendered Lives

There are more similarities than differences between the sexes. Males and females have similar cognitive skills,

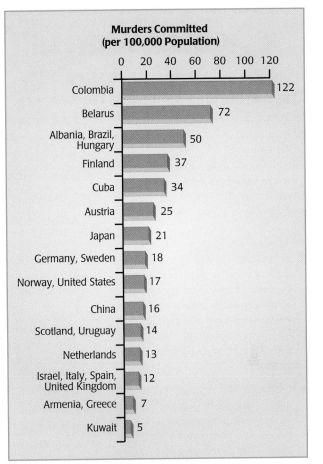

FIGURE 5.1   Deadly Assaults by Males in Selected Countries

Note: These figures reflect the most recent year available between 1995 and 2000.

Source: Based on Krug et al., 2002, Table A-7.

similar memory abilities, and similar abstract problem-solving aptitudes, and parents express affection and love to their children in very similar ways (Day, 2002). Despite these similarities and regardless of our personal preferences or abilities, most of us accommodate our behavior to gender-role expectations, in a process that West and Zimmerman (1987) called "doing gender."

We "do gender," sometimes consciously and sometimes unconsciously, by adjusting our behavior and our perceptions depending on the gender and age of the person with whom we are working or talking. By adulthood, there are vast society-wide inequalities such as unequal incomes, unequal responsibilities in child care, and significant differences in political power. There are more similarities than differences between men and women, so why is this the case? Gender socialization theories provide some of the answers.

CONSTRAINTS

The Worldwide War against Women

Women make up half the world's population, do two-thirds of the world's work, earn one-tenth of the world's income, and own one-hundredth of the world's property. Women are widely mistreated in many countries around the world:

- *Afghanistan:* In the countryside, tribal leaders deploy religious police to enforce stringent controls on women's behavior. Many girls cannot attend school, and laws dictate that families murder their own women if they have been "dishonored" by rape during a war. One in seven mothers dies in childbirth.

- *China:* A culture that values boys more than girls, China has used advances in sonogram technology to help prospective parents identify—and abort—female fetuses. Despite official government condemnation of the practice, the gap between the number of male and female births is widening (see Chapters 7 and 8).

- *Nigeria:* The penal code allows a man to "correct" his wife as long as the "correction" does not leave a scar or necessitate a stay of 21 days or more in the hospital.

- *India and Pakistan:* If a groom and his family decide a bride's dowry is too small, she may be persecuted or burned to death. Aborting female fetuses is still widespread in India.

- *Kuwait:* Although Kuwaiti women are now allowed to drive and no longer have rigid dress codes, they still cannot vote. Household maids, many from the Philippines, are often victims of abuse and murder.

- *Latin America:* A macho culture pervades most countries in Latin America, unofficially condoning wife abuse, rape, and other forms of violence against women.

- *Morocco:* If a woman commits adultery, the law permits the husband to maim or kill her as punishment. Adulterous husbands are not punished.

- *Norway:* Even though women dominate the political scene, they are still hired last, fired first, paid less than men, and held back from the top jobs.

- *Pakistan:* In some regions, tribal council elders order (and sometimes participate in) gang-rapes of girls to avenge a brother's (real or imagined) crime. Domestic violence, acid throwing, burning, "honor" killings, and sex trafficking of young girls are common.

- *Russia:* Wife-beating is not against the law; husbands kill approximately 15,000 wives each year.

- *Saudi Arabia:* A divorced woman may keep her children until they are 7 years old. Although she may visit them, the father's relatives then raise the children.

- *South Africa:* A woman is raped every 83 seconds. Domestic work is the primary occupation for black women, and the average salary is about $80 a month.

- *Thailand:* Young rural women are kidnapped or bought from their parents for prostitution. An estimated 1 million women work in Thai brothels.

- *Turkey:* In some regions, young girls are killed by their fathers or brothers because they shame the family by going out with boys or marrying someone from a different sect.

- *United States:* On average, women earn 75 percent of what men earn in the same jobs, and a woman with a college degree earns about the same as a man who has completed one year of high school. Among single mothers, about 60 percent live in or near poverty (see Chapter 13).

- In war-torn countries around the world, hundreds of thousands of women and children have been victims of mass rape, torture, and genital mutilation (for example, in *Bangladesh, Burundi, Cambodia, Liberia, Peru, Rwanda, Somalia,* and *Uganda*). In some cases, a woman was raped more than a hundred times. Reports of large-scale organized rape have come from the countries that made up the former *Yugoslavia,* where at least 20,000 women and girls were raped during the first few months of the war that followed the country's dissolution in 1992.

SOURCES: Berry, 1997; Neft and Levine, 1997; Goodsmith, 2000; Moore, 2001; Dauer, 2002; Itano, 2002b; "Pakistani girl describes . . .," 2002; Gall, 2003; *State of the World's Mothers,* 2003.

STOP AND THINK . . .

- *Why do women in many countries, including the United States, tolerate violence and inequality?*

- *Why do soldiers rape women and girls, for example, instead of torturing and killing boys and elderly men?*

How We Learn Gender Roles

A common misconception is that our gender roles are carved in stone by about age 4. In fact, gender roles change throughout the life course. Before we can understand how such change occurs, we need to examine, briefly, three of the major perspectives on gender-role learning: social learning theory, cognitive development theory, and feminist approaches.

Social Learning Theory

In contrast to biological theories, social learning theorists see behavior not as fixed at an early age but as changing throughout the life course. The central notion in **social learning theory** is that people learn attitudes, beliefs, and behaviors through social interaction. The learning occurs through reinforcement or imitation and modeling (Bandura and Walters, 1963; Lynn, 1969).

In terms of reinforcement, we learn some gender-role behaviors by direct or indirect rewards or punishments. A little girl who puts on her mother's makeup may be told she is cute, but her brother who does the same will be scolded ("boys don't wear makeup"). Children also learn gender roles through indirect reinforcement. For example, if a little boy's male friends are punished for crying, he will learn that "boys don't cry."

Children also learn to behave as boys or girls by observing and imitating the behavior of others. Although children may not be directly rewarded or punished for "behaving like boys" or "behaving like girls," they learn about gender by watching who does what in families. A father who is rarely at home because he's always working sends the message that men are supposed to earn money. A mother who is always complaining about being too fat sends the message that women are supposed to be thin.

Because parents are very visible and emotionally important to children, they are typically the most powerful role models. Other role models include caregivers, friends, and celebrities. According to a multiethnic study of Los Angeles adolescents, for example, teenagers who said that their role model was someone they knew (a parent, relative, friend, or doctor outside the family) had higher self-esteem, higher grades, and lower substance use than their peers whose role models were sports figures, singers, or other media characters. The researchers concluded that role model selection can have a positive or negative outcome on a teenager's psychosocial development (Yancey et al., 2002).

An absence of role models also affects learning gender roles. Although women earn almost 60 percent of all bachelor's degrees, they account for only 27 percent of those degrees in computer and information sciences, down from a peak of 37 percent in 1985 (U.S. Census

Cooking with his dad teaches a young boy that domestic work is an acceptable activity for men. Such activities also increase interaction and closer relationships between fathers and their children.

Bureau, 2002). Some feel that this decrease results largely from a lack of role models, especially in prestigious corporations. Even during the boom years of the high-tech industry in the late 1990s, for instance, most women were office workers rather than managers or engineers (Guido, 2003).

Cognitive Development Theory

In contrast to social learning theories, **cognitive development theory** argues that children acquire female or male values on their own by thinking, reasoning, and interpreting information in their environment. According to this perspective, children pass through developmental stages in learning gender-appropriate attitudes and behavior. By the age of 3 or 4, the girl knows she is a girl and prefers "girl things" to "boy things" simply because she likes what is familiar or similar to herself. By age 5, most children anticipate disapproval from their peers for playing with opposite-sex toys and don't do so.

© Judy Horacek from *Life on the Edge* (Spinifex Press, Melbourne, 1992).

After acquiring masculine or feminine values, the child tends to identify with same-sex people. A child's movement through the developmental stages depends on the child's age as well as cognitive, intellectual, and maturity level (Kohlberg, 1969; Maccoby, 1990; Bussey and Bandura, 1992).

Gender schema theory extended cognitive development theory by focusing on how children actively construct for themselves what it means to be female or male. A *schema* is a cognitive (or mental) information-processing category that organizes and guides a person's perceptions of a vast array of cultural stimuli (Bem, 1983).

By observing the distinctions between the sexes, girls and boys learn the specific content of femininity and masculinity. For example, when a girl realizes that cultural expectations of femininity include being affectionate, understanding, and emotional, she incorporates these perceptions into her emerging gender schema and adjusts her behavior accordingly. Similarly, a boy incorporates such masculine gender schema as being brave, forceful, and tough.

Children use gender schemas to evaluate the behavior of others as either gender appropriate ("good") or gender inappropriate ("bad"). Eventually, children become sex-typed because they accept cultural definitions of gender appropriateness and reject behavior that does not match their sex (Bem, 1993).

Gender schemas may become more rigid during adolescence. At that time, young people often feel compelled to conform to peers' **gender-role stereotypes**—the belief and expectation that both women and men display definite traditional gender-role characteristics. Gender-role stereotypes may become more flexible again during adulthood. Generally, however, people who have internalized sex-typed standards tend to expect stereotypical behavior from others (Hudak, 1993; Renn and Calvert, 1993).

Feminist Approaches

Feminist perspectives analyze socially constructed expectations, including gender roles (see Chapter 2). Feminist theories are similar to social learning theories and cognitive development theories because all of these approaches focus on how we learn gender roles.

Feminist theories differ from other perspectives in several important ways, however. First, many academic feminists view gender as a social role that is taught carefully and repeatedly. Consequently, one's gender role script becomes "so natural as to be seen as an integral part of oneself" (Fox and Murry, 2001: 382). In a study of preschoolers, Martin (1998) concluded that educational institutions gender children's behavior. Even though boys' play often was much noisier than girls', for example, the teachers told girls three times more often than boys to be quiet or use a "nicer" voice.

Second, feminists argue that gender scripts result, over time, in macro-level power differences and inequality in the home and elsewhere. Because many parents follow traditional gender scripts, they interact differently with sons and daughters. In a study of middle-class parents and their sixth- and eighth-grade sons and daughters, for example, the parents—especially fathers—used less scientific language with their daughters than their sons. Even though the girls and boys said they were equally interested in science, were confident about their abilities, and earned the same grades in the subjects, the parents assumed that the sons were more interested in science (Tenenbaum and Leaper, 2003). Thus, boys are more privileged because they have more access to resources, including parents' supportive expectations.

Finally, feminists maintain that if people change women's and men's traditional roles, behavior will also change. If, for example, boys are taught to cook and clean, they are more likely to do so in adulthood. If girls are taught to be independent, they are more likely to fend for themselves instead of relying on a man for economic support.

MAKING CONNECTIONS

■ Drawing on your experiences and your knowledge of both sexes, do you think that women and men are similar? Or different?

■ Think about how you were raised. Who played a major role in teaching you what it means to be "masculine" or "feminine"? What happened, if anything, when you broke "the rules"?

Who Teaches Gender Roles?

We learn gender roles from a variety of sources. The most important are parents (and other adult caregivers), peers, teachers, books, and the popular culture.

Parents are important socialization agents. This three-year-old may be inspired to follow in his father's occupational footsteps.

Parents

Parents usually are the first and most influential socialization agents. Many parents begin to treat infants differently from birth. They hold girls more gently and cuddle them more. Fathers, especially, are more likely to jostle and play in a more rough-and-tumble way with boys (Parke, 1996). Parents influence their children's gender development through differential treatment in several important ways: talking, setting expectations, and providing opportunities for various activities.

Talking Parents often communicate differently with boys and girls, starting at a very early age. Both mothers and fathers use more words about feelings and emotions with female than male toddlers. Parents also encourage daughters to be emotionally expressive. It isn't clear, however, whether this is because of gender typing or because many girls begin to talk earlier than boys and thereby evoke more "emotion talk" from their parents (Flannagan and Perese, 1998; Brody, 2000; Fivush and Buckner, 2000).

Fathers tend to use more directives ("Bring that over here") and more threatening language ("If you do that again, you'll be sorry") with their sons than with their daughters. Mothers tend to ask for compliance rather than demand it ("Could you bring that to me, please?"). By the time they start school, many boys use threatening, commanding, and dominating language ("If you do that one more time, I'll sock you"). In contrast, many girls emphasize agreement and cooperation ("Can I play, too?") (Shapiro, 1990).

Setting Expectations When parents *expect* their daughters to be better in English and their sons to excel in math and sports, parents provide the support and advice to enable children to do so. This sex-stereotypical encouragement builds up the children's confidence in their abilities and helps them master the various skills (Eccles et al., 2000).

The ways that parents divide up household tasks also influence gender typing. Even when mothers work outside the home and parents try to be egalitarian, household chores are gendered—between parents themselves and between children. Parents typically assign child care and cleaning to daughters and maintenance work to sons. Girls also get these duties much earlier in childhood and adolescence than boys (Leaper, 2002). These gender-stereotyped responsibilities provide training for later role differences in adulthood (as you'll see shortly).

Mothers start criticizing their children's—especially daughters'—weight and physical appearance in elementary school. And throughout adolescence, fathers make more appearance-related comments to daughters than to sons (Schwartz et al., 1999; Smolak et al., 1999). Such gender-typed expectations may result in girls' having negative body images and eating disorders (see Chapter 14).

Providing Opportunities During childhood and adolescence, parents provide children with activities and opportunities that our culture defines as gender appropriate. Boys often get toys that demand more space (such as trains and car sets), whereas girls receive dolls or dollhouses, which take up less space. Also, boys' toys (such as footballs and basketballs) encourage leaving the home; girls' toys (such as play vacuum cleaners, play ovens) are designed to be used in the home (Knapp and Hall, 1992).

Many parents systematically restrict opportunities for fun and learning when they pressure children to choose "girls' stuff" or "boys' stuff." Because, in general, "boys' stuff" is more interesting than "girls' stuff," parental pressure for girls to play with sex-stereotypical toys diminishes their cognitive skills and dampens their interest in "active" toys and activities.

Fathers, especially, are still more likely to stress the importance of a career or occupational success for sons than for daughters. As a result, parents are more likely to provide opportunities for sons than daughters to attend computer summer camps, to explain science exhibits to sons than to daughters, and to pressure boys to attend college (Crowley et al., 2001; Kladko, 2002).

Toys, Sports, and Peers

Toys, sports, and peer groups are also important socialization sources. Few encourage gender-neutral attitudes and behavior.

Toys From an early age, play is generally sex-typed. Girls' sections of catalogs and toy stores are swamped with cosmetics, dolls and accessories, arts and crafts kits, and housekeeping and cooking wares. In contrast, boys' sections feature sports equipment, building toys, workbenches, construction equipment, and toy guns. Although 67 percent of parents in one large study said it was "never OK" for a parent to let a child play with toy guns, those who allowed their children to do so were typically white fathers with male children (Cheng et al., 2003).

War, violence, aggression, and sexism have been the hallmarks of many computer games geared to young boys. Some of the most popular video software aimed at young men in their late teens emphasizes "a nasty streak of violence" that includes blood, gore, and "mature sexual themes." (Blasko, 2002c) In the phenomenally popular *Theft Auto III*, for example, "You get to shoot whomever you want, including cops. You get to beat women to death with baseball bats. You get to have sex with prostitutes and then kill them" (Herbert, 2002: 35A).

There is no evidence that viewing violence in video games *causes* aggressive behavior. Researchers are finding, however, that such material desensitizes children to violence and makes it seem "normal." Violent video games are especially harmful—compared with television and movies—because they are interactive and engrossing and require the player to identify with the aggressor. Violent

video games also encourage male-to-female violence because most of the assaults are directed at women (Dietz, 1998; Anderson and Dill, 2000; "Key facts: TV violence," 2003).

Barbie was the top-selling toy in the twentieth century (Austin, 1999). An estimated 99 percent of all U.S. girls between the ages of 3 and 10 own at least one Barbie doll, and the average girl owns a total of eight (Greenwald, 1996). According to many critics, the problem with Barbie dolls is that they idealize unrealistic body images (such as enormous breasts, a tiny waist, and extremely long legs) that many girls and women try to achieve through diets and cosmetic surgery (Lord, 1994; Tosa, 1998; M. F. Rogers, 1999).

The only acceptable dolls for boys are action figures such as GI Joe and "The Punisher." GI Joes are rugged, macho fighting men that come with a wardrobe of Army fatigues and such accessories as M–1 rifles. The creator of GI Joe has described it as "a doll that's okay for boys to play with" because "even dads don't mind" (Oldenburg, 1996). Several boys on the toys.com site enthusiastically described The Punisher as an "outstanding" action figure because it comes with "a load of weapons" that have "superb detail" and a bulletproof vest.

Male action figures have grown increasingly muscular over the years. GI Joes, for example, have biceps that are twice as large as those of a typical man and larger than those of any known bodybuilder (Pope et al., 1999). These action figures (and comic strip heroes) put boys at risk of developing the "Barbie syndrome"—unrealistic expectations for their bodies. As a result, some researchers maintain, increasing numbers of men may become obsessively preoccupied with working out and taking dangerous drugs, such as anabolic steroids (see Chapter 14).

Sports Many parents encourage sports for both daughters and sons because athletic activities are healthy, give children a chance to develop self-confidence and team skills, and may provide a chance at college athletic scholarships. A survey of girls aged 9 to 13 found that 77 percent play sports or sports video games, 80 percent watch sports on TV, and 79 percent talk about or play sports with friends (compared with 89 percent, 93 percent, and 86 percent for their male counterparts, respectively) (Gardyn, 2001). Thus, millions of young girls are sports enthusiasts.

There are certainly more women's teams in middle schools and high schools today than in the past. Almost 3 million high school girls are active in sports today, compared with only 300,000 in 1971 but this rate is still lower than the 4 million boys who participate in sports. (Richey, 1997; "Participation sets record . . .," 2002).

The share of women among all intercollegiate athletes increased from 28 percent in 1982 to almost 42 percent in 2001 (Clayton, 2002). Some people complain that men's teams are being wiped out to provide more athletics for women under Title IX (the landmark 1972 federal law that mandated gender equality in education, including sports). According to a General Accounting Office report, however, the number of men's teams increased slightly between 1981 and 1999 (Bellis and Pfeiffer, 2001). Women's gymnastics lost 83 teams, for example, whereas 36 additional men's teams were formed in sports like basketball and football (Bradley-Doppes, 2002; Flores, 2002).

Despite considerable progress, female athletes still face numerous institutional barriers in college athletics. They play in inferior facilities, stay in lower-caliber hotels on the road, eat in cheaper restaurants, get smaller promotional budgets, and have fewer assistant coaches (Zimbalist, 2000).

The visibility of such tennis superstars as Serena and Venus Williams gives the impression that minority girls and women have unprecedented opportunities in sports. This is not the case. Often, black women don't play sports at all and have access primarily to basketball and track because they don't grow up in suburban neighborhoods or schools that offer lacrosse, soccer, rowing, swimming, or a variety of other sports. Even then, less than 3 percent of minority female athletes receive scholarships to play sports in the top schools and divisions (Suggs, 2001).

Asian American, American Indian, and Latina athletes are even less likely to participate in college sports. Many Latinas grow up in communities where girls and women are expected to avoid unfeminine endeavors like competitive sports. Some exceptions—athletes such as softball players Kristy Aguirre, Felicia Delgado, Laura Rodriguez, and Shannon Soles—credit their athletic success to their parents, especially their fathers, who enrolled them in church sports programs as preschoolers and encouraged their athletic development (Williams, 2002).

Only a handful of women and minority men own professional leagues or serve as athletic directors or coaches. A recent study gave colleges an "F" for not hiring female and minority athletic directors. Women now coach only 45 percent of women's teams, down from 99 percent in the 1970s. In the Division I colleges (those with the highest sports sponsorship, sports attendance records, and financial aid awards), only 5 percent of the athletic directors were members of minority groups, and only 7 percent were women (Lapchick, 2003). Thus, female and minority male athletes have few role models.

Peers By as early as age 2, most toddlers are learning to interact with peers—pulling or being pulled in a wagon, exchanging toys (or refusing to do so and not "playing nice"), and learning new skills by imitating children their own age.

Few things are more important to children than acceptance by their peers. Peers play an important role in helping a child develop self-esteem. During childhood and adolescence, peers often offer support, a sense of belonging, and a chance to develop interpersonal skills. On the negative side, peers can also involve children, especially adolescents, in risk-taking behavior such as sexual intercourse and drug use (see Chapter 12).

One of the most widely recognized social characteristics of childhood is young children's preference for same-sex play partners. The more time boys spend with other boys, the greater the likelihood that they learn to be rougher, more aggressive, more competitive, and more active. The more time that girls spend with other girls, the more likely they are to be cooperative rather than aggressive, to play quiet games, and to be less physical in their play. Thus, the more both girls and boys play with same-sex partners, the more likely they are to participate in gender-typed play (Martin and Fabes, 2001).

By adolescence, and especially when hormones kick in, adolescents develop a strong interest in members of the opposite sex. In our society, being "popular" is critical. Being disliked by one's peers may lead to strong feelings of social isolation, loneliness, and alienation (Cassidy and Asher, 1992). Trying to be popular can also have negative effects. Boys and girls who hang out with peers who bully, for example, tend to do more bullying themselves. If girls want to join the "inner circle" of the "queen bees," they may bully even their closest friends by tormenting them with gossip and sarcastic comments (Wiseman, 2002; Espelage et al., 2003).

Parents also affect children's peer relationships. Until about age 15, for instance, mothers often influence their daughters' peer relationships by chauffeuring, and fathers may be involved with their sons and their sons' peers (Updegraff et al., 2001). After children begin driving and have more independence, however, parental supervision, monitoring, and influence decrease considerably (see Chapters 7 and 12).

Teachers and Schools

Teachers and schools send a number of gender-related messages to children. These messages follow boys and girls from preschool, especially from elementary school, to college.

Elementary and Middle Schools In elementary and middle schools, boys usually get more time to talk in class, are called on more often, and receive more positive feedback. Teachers are more likely to give answers to girls or to do the problems for them but to expect boys to find the answers themselves (Sadker and Sadker, 1994). Expecting more from boys increases their problem-solving abilities, decision-making skills, and self-confidence in finding answers on their own.

TATJANA CAN'T WAIT TO TEST THE CORSA'S ALL ROUND SAFETY CAGE.

Much of the advertising in the United States and other Western countries uses sexy images of women to sell everything from cars to toothpaste. As the graffiti on this London poster illustrates, many people are offended by sterotypical advertising that demeans women.

Despite our current era of "grrl power" and breaking gender stereotypes, girls still write stories about romance whereas boys write about action and adventure. In a study of eighth-grade students, for example, Peterson (2002) found that both sexes expected girls to write about "mushy stuff" and the boys to write about sports and violence. Although the study was conducted at a school that encouraged egalitarian gender roles, the teachers didn't admonish the boys for demeaning the girls' romance writing or ridiculing a male student's story about a gay relationship.

Teachers often treat boys and girls differently in the classroom. Even when their behavior is disruptive, "problem girls" often receive less attention than do either boys or "problem boys." Moreover, teachers tend to emphasize "motherwork" skills for girls, such as nurturance and emotional support. Although both girls and boys are evaluated on academic criteria, such as work habits and knowledge, teachers are more likely to also evaluate girls on such nonacademic criteria as grooming, personal qualities such as politeness, and appearance (Martin, 1998).

High School In high school, guidance counselors, who play an important role in helping students make career choices, are particularly guilty of sex stereotyping. Even well-intentioned counselors often steer girls into vocational training, such as secretarial work or data processing, rather than college preparatory programs. In some Michigan high schools, girls aren't allowed to operate equipment in vocational education classes without a male student supervising. And during summer vacations, the teachers and counselors often help the boys, but not the girls, find jobs (Gerber, 2002).

Counselors and teachers often encourage girls who are in college preparatory programs to take courses in the social sciences and humanities rather than mathematics or the sciences (Renzetti and Curran, 1995). Talented young women may be squeezed out of the "science achievement pipeline" because they are less likely than their male counterparts to have fathers who keep track of their progress in school and parents who attend PTA meetings and parent–teacher conferences (Hanson, 1996).

According to Dr. Suzanne Franks, the founding director of the Women in Engineering and Science Program at Kansas State University, some middle schools and high schools simply dismiss nontraditional opportunities for girls as inappropriate:

> We contacted a school in Western Kansas to notify them of an opportunity to send some of their middle school girls on an industry tour we were sponsoring, where the girls could meet women engineers and scientists and see what they did for a living. We were flatly turned down, with the explanation being "I can assure you that none of our girls would be interested in such a thing" (Personal correspondence, October 9, 2002).

College Women make up 56 percent of all higher education students (Knapp et al., 2002). Despite the higher enrollments, most women still focus on traditional female-dominated disciplines such as social work, teaching, and nursing. Some people argue that women pursue these low-paying areas because they want to do so. Others maintain that women don't get the necessary science and math courses that might pique their interest in male-dominated fields like engineering and computer science (Margolis and Fisher, 2002).

Books and Textbooks

In children's books, female characters are still overwhelmingly portrayed as using household objects (cooking utensils, brooms, sewing needles), whereas male characters are expected to master outside-the-home tools (shovels, plows, construction equipment) (Crabb and Bielawski, 1994). Although many of these books were published from the 1950s to the 1990s, they are still popular with young readers and reinforce sex-stereotypical images of women and men.

Nonstereotypical books are more readily available than ever before, especially for preschoolers. Very young children are generally open to stories that describe nontraditional male roles, such as boys playing with dolls (Etaugh and Liss, 1992). If parents or teachers tend to stereotype gender roles, however, children will not be exposed to these resources.

Early exposure to gender-neutral information is critical in removing gender blinders because many educational materials still depict men's and women's roles very narrowly. As the box "Do Books and Textbooks Stereotype Women and Men?" shows, for example, high school and college textbooks are still gendered in their portrayal of the sexes.

Popular Culture and the Media

Media myths and unrealistic images assault our gender identity on a daily basis. The research in this area has boomed in the last decade and is too extensive to discuss fully here. A few examples from advertising, newspapers and magazines, television, and music videos will illustrate how the media reinforce sex stereotyping from childhood to adulthood.

Advertising Much of the advertising aimed at children creates and strengthens stereotypes. Ethnic children are often a face in a crowd, or they promote

CONSTRAINTS

Do Books and Textbooks Stereotype Women and Men?

A few years ago, a teacher in an affluent and progressive suburban high school invited me to discuss gender issues with an advanced class of juniors. I examined their history textbook to see what issues had received the least coverage. To my surprise, the textbook offered only two paragraphs on women: One discussed the women's rights movement in the 1960s; the other described the Equal Rights Amendment.

Many textbooks in colleges and professional schools also ignore women or present them in stereotypical ways. Mendelsohn and her associates (1994) analyzed more than 4000 illustrations in 12 anatomy and physical diagnosis textbooks used in medical schools.

The anatomy textbooks used illustrations of male bodies more than twice as often as female bodies. In the texts on physical diagnosis, the illustrations of women were largely confined to chapters on reproduction, falsely implying that female and male physiology differs only in respect to their reproductive organs.

The researchers concluded that "women are dramatically underrepresented in illustrations of normal, nonreproductive anatomy" and that "males continue to be depicted as the norm or the standard. As a result, students may develop an incomplete knowledge of normal female anatomy" (p. 1269).

A self-proclaimed "teacher and therapist" maintains that nature intends girls primarily for having and nurturing children. By 10-years-old, he claims, a girl's brain is concerned about being pretty and popular, and she has a "natural" drive to "connect" with others.

The author declares unequivocally that the structure of most girls' brains makes it too hard for them to grasp subjects such as calculus and physics and that women lack natural technical ability. He argues that if they put too much emphasis on achievement and careers, girls will suffer lifelong misery (Gurian, 2002). Teachers have been "lining up" to buy his books (Rivers, 2002).

In a study of the ten best-selling self-help books, the researchers found that half of the books promoted stereotypical behavior. The books proclaim that female independence and assertiveness could jeopardize their relationships with men. The books also describe men as being inherently success or achievement oriented and rarely advise men to improve their relationships (Zimmerman et al., 2001).

STOP AND THINK . . .

- *Think about your high school and college history textbooks. How many discussed gender issues? How many described men's lives beyond wars, politics, and inventions?*

- *If teachers believe that girls' brains are hardwired for relationships and men's for success, how do such beliefs shape girls' and boys' behavior?*

According to some researchers (see text), some of the Walt Disney G-rated films, such as Aladdin, portray high levels of violence.

products as "cool" or trendy. Black children routinely appear in commercials that plug sports and music, reinforcing the stereotype that African Americans are "natural" in sports and music—and, by default, "not natural" in educational and other pursuits (Bang and Reece, 2003).

To decrease advertisers' influence on children under age 12, many European countries now ban ads before, during, and after children's television programs. Greek TV forbids toy ads altogether (Ford, 1999).

Many media critics maintain that magazine ads are more sexist than ever, especially during televised sporting events. In beer commercials, for example, half of the camera shots focus on women's breasts, buttocks, and crotches—instead of their entire bodies (Hall and Crum, 1994). The ability to alter photographs with computers—to elongate bodies or put one woman's head with another woman's body—makes the "perfect woman" even less attainable (Kilbourne, 1999).

One result of such ads is that women are unhappy with their bodies. Almost 250,000 American women underwent costly breast augmentation (about $6000 on average) in 2002. More than 5000 were 18 or younger. Not only are women choosing implants, but they are choosing ever-larger models. Between 1985 and 2000, the Food and Drug Administration (FDA) received almost 130,000 adverse reports on breast implants that sometimes resulted in deaths due to blood loss and other surgery problems ("Breast implants," 2002; Kaufman, 2002).

Newspapers and Magazines Newspapers routinely ignore women. A survey of the front-page stories of 104 national and local newspapers found that of the 3500 front-page stories, male sources outnumbered female sources almost three to one. Men were more likely to be quoted in stories about politics, business, parenting, religion, and science. Women were more likely to be quoted

in stories about health, home, food, fashion, travel, and ordinary people ("Newspaper content . . .," 2001). Thus, even though women have the greatest responsibility for child rearing, men are quoted as the parenting "experts."

Most magazines also reinforce gender stereotypes. Magazines aimed at adolescent boys for example, emphasize success in sports and improving their mechanical and computer skills. Magazines for adolescent girls are full of articles and ads on being more popular, thin, and beautiful. Almost 61 percent of all teen girls (and 76 percent of Latina teens) read such beauty magazines as *Seventeen* on a regular basis (Weissman, 1999a).

Magazines that emphasize women's appearance (such as *Cosmopolitan, Glamour,* and *Vogue*) hold the largest share of the magazine market. About 60 percent or women read such "women's magazines" during the year, compared with just 7 percent who read business or financial magazines. Although ad pages and ad dollars for all magazines have declined, they have increased for the top women's magazines (Wellner, 2002). In effect, then, women are exposed to more beauty ads and traditional images of femininity than ever before.

Television and Other Screen Media Children spend much more time in front of the television set and other screen media (video games, videotapes, DVDs, computers, and movies) than they do interacting with parents, family members, teachers, or friends. According to two national studies, the typical American child spends almost seven hours *a day* watching television. Twenty-eight percent of preschool children aged 2 to 5 and 60 percent of adolescents have television sets in their bedrooms (Roberts et al., 1999; Woodard and Gridina, 2000).

What do children see about gender roles when they watch movies and videotapes? In a study of 74 animated movies rated G (for general audiences) released between

1937 and 1999 and available on videocassette, the researchers found that the amount and duration of violence had increased, especially in the films released in the 1990s. The total duration of violent acts ranged from 6 seconds (*My Neighbor Totoro*, 1993) to 24 minutes (*Quest for Camelot*, 1998) (Yokota and Thompson, 2000). Although the researchers didn't specify assailants and victims by sex, most of the films cast male characters as the aggressors.

Some media critics have praised the Disney Corporation for finally producing, in 2001, the first African-American hero in the animated feature film *Atlantis: The Lost Empire*. Others have applauded Disney for depicting girls in *Lilo & Stitch* more realistically than the hourglass, Barbie-like figures and highly sensual features of female characters in *The Little Mermaid* and *Pocahontas* (Elder, 2002). *Lilo & Stitch* and *Atlantis* are exceptions, however.

How do children react to gender and ethnic images in the media? In a national study of 1200 children and nine focus groups, the children felt that whites overwhelmingly appear in positive roles compared with other groups. As *Figure 5.2* shows, the children believed that Latinos, especially, are portrayed in negative ways.

Across all races, the children felt that white characters on television were presented as having wealth, education, leadership qualities, academic success, and intelligence. In contrast, ethnic characters—especially blacks and Latinos—were typically portrayed as lawbreakers, poor, lazy, and "goofy." One teenage Asian girl complained that when Asians do appear, they are shown as "kind of book smart . . . wearing thick glasses and taking notes . . . or they're like the Kung Fu Master." American Indian children felt that media stereotypes about American Indians were widespread. They saw themselves characterized as "poor," "drunk and beating up on each other," "living on reservations," "selling fireworks," and "fighting over land" (Children Now, 1998).

The National Organization for Women (NOW) sees few reasons to celebrate most of television's prime-time portrayals of women, minorities, and other "outsiders." After examining all of the prime-time programs on ABC, CBS, FOX, NBC, UPN, and WB, the NOW study concluded, among other things, that

- **White men rule television.** As in real life, in television men are the heads of government (*24*, *Spin City*, *The West Wing*), the military (*JAG*), investigative agencies (*The Agency*, *Alias*, *The X-Files*), police departments (*The District*, *Law & Order: Criminal Intent*, *Law & Order: Special Victims Unit*, *NYPD Blue*), crime labs (*Crossing Jordan*, *CSI*), law officers (*Girlfriends*, *The Guardian*, *The Practice*), hospitals (*ER*, *Scrubs*), radio stations (*Frasier*, *Once & Again*), magazines (*Just Shoot Me*), schools (*Boston Public*, *The Simpsons*), factories (*George Lopez*), department

stores (*The Drew Carey Show*), and space exploration (*Enterprise*).

- **Studios follow the "Jennifer Aniston Rule."** At least 140 women on TV are white, young, model-thin, and conventionally beautiful, compared with just 31 women who appear to wear a size 10 or larger.

- **Blacks, whites, and others are segregated.** Aside from the handful of shows centered on black families, racial and ethnic diversity in prime time is minimal. Only *George Lopez* includes Latinos, and four Asian American actresses play supporting roles in other shows. There are no regular characters portrayed by American Indian or Middle Eastern actors.

- **U.S. women are very similar.** If you are a middle-aged woman, a lesbian, a Latina, a woman with a disability, a fat woman, or a low-income mom struggling to get by, "good luck finding programming that even pretends to reflect your life" (Bennett, 2002).

The gender role and minority depictions in movies are more mixed. In 2002, black actors Halle Berry and

FIGURE 5.2 How Children View Racial-Ethnic Groups on TV Percentage of children aged 10–17 who responded to the question "Are TV characters shown in a mostly positive way, a mostly negative way, or both?"

SOURCE: Based on Children Now, *A Different World: Children's Perceptions of Race and Class in the Media, 1998*, www.childrennow.org/redesigns/media/mc98/MC98page6.html (accessed August 24, 2000).

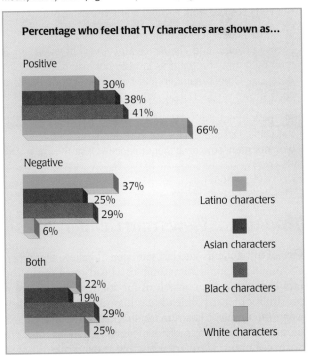

Percentage who feel that TV characters are shown as...

Positive
- 30%
- 38%
- 41%
- 66%

Negative
- 37%
- 25%
- 29%
- 6%

Both
- 22%
- 19%
- 29%
- 25%

Latino characters
Asian characters
Black characters
White characters

Denzel Washington won Oscars for best actress and actor, and Hollywood honored Sidney Poitier for his lifetime acting achievement. It was a historical evening in recognizing black talent. On the other hand, some writers point out that black actors—including Berry and Washington—are rarely portrayed in romances and science fiction movies, fantasy films, and musicals (Farley, 2002).

Music Videos Another dominant source of much sex-stereotypical programming is music videos. From the advent of Music Television (MTV), a number of researchers have found that music videos are rife with sex, sexism, drugs, and violence (Strasburger and Wilson, 2002). For example, a study of the 20 most popular music videos on MTV found that more than 25 percent of the videos emphasized female breasts, legs, or torsos. Almost two-thirds of the videos featured women as props, like background dancers. Whereas half of the female props were seminude or dressed in revealing clothes, 75 percent of the male props were fully dressed ("Boys to Men . . .," 1999). Moreover, violent music lyrics don't cause but increase aggressive thoughts and feelings, especially among males (Anderson et al., 2003).

MAKING CONNECTIONS

▓ Has equality in sports gone too far? For example, should well-established men's teams in wrestling and track and field—even though they produce little revenue—be supported instead of adding women's teams in sports such as golf, rowing, and gymnastics?

▓ Some people feel that sitcoms (such as *Everybody Loves Raymond* and *The Bernie Mac Show*) degrade men by portraying them as lovable but insensitive doofuses. Others maintain that most viewers don't take such shows very seriously. What's your position?

▓ Think about the MTV videos you've watched over the years. Did they influence your thoughts about women, men, sex, drugs, or violence? Or not? ◎

Traditional Views and Gender Roles

One of my students said last semester, "I believe that when a woman attempts to assume the head position in the family without the consent of the man, there is a good possibility that it will lead to a loss of order and stability in the family." His remark sparked some lively class discussion, but such traditional views of gender roles are fairly common. Here are a few more examples:

▓ The Southern Baptist Convention doctrine opposes female pastors and says wives should submit to their husbands. An official recently sent 25 missionaries a deadline to sign this document or face dismissal.

▓ In a national study, 50 percent of recent Latino immigrants and 23 percent of the "highly assimilated" felt that "the husband should have the final say in family matters."

▓ Kansas state senator Kay O'Conner, an elected official, stirred up a controversy when she said that there was no reason to celebrate passage of the Nineteenth Amendment, which allowed women to vote. She believes that mothers should stay home to rear their children and that "the man should be the head of the family."

▓ Several best-selling pop psychologists maintain that women have a "primal need" to be mothers and to be supported by men and that wives should "surrender themselves" to their husbands because a man should be the boss of the family (Deane et al., 2000; Doyle, 2001; Pierre, 2001; Gurian, 2002; "Baptist missionaries . . .," 2003).

Instrumental and Expressive Roles

Social scientists often describe traditional gender roles as instrumental or expressive (see Chapter 2). Although there is a great deal of variation in everyday life, the characteristics of instrumental and expressive role players are useful in understanding some of the differences between traditional and nontraditional gender roles.

Instrumental Roles Conceptually, *instrumental role players* (husbands and fathers) must be "real men." A "real man" is a procreator, a protector, and a provider. He must produce children because this will prove his virility, and having boys is especially important to carry on his family name. The procreator must also be a protector. He must be strong and powerful in ensuring his family's physical safety. The provider keeps working hard even if he is overwhelmed by multiple roles, such as "the responsible breadwinner," "the devoted husband," and "the dutiful son" (Gaylin, 1992; Betcher and Pollack, 1993).

If the traditional man is a "superman," the traditional woman is an only slightly more modern version of the "true woman" you met in Chapter 3. Many women have internalized gender expectations and try to live up to them. In a study of two middle schools, for example, Orenstein (1994) found that intelligent female students—regardless of social class and across all racial groups—lived up to the traditional definition of girls: pretty and polite but not too aggressive, not too outspoken, and not too smart. Young women often "dumb down" to be popular with male and female peers and with some teachers.

Expressive Roles *Expressive role players* (wives and mothers) provide the emotional support and nurturing qualities that sustain the family unit and support the husband/father. They should be warm, sensitive, and sympathetic. For example, the expressive role player consoles a teenage daughter when she breaks up with her boyfriend, encourages her son to try out for the Little League baseball team, and is always ready to comfort a husband who has had a bad day at work.

A good example of women's expressive roles is that of kinkeeper. The role is often passed down from mother to daughter. Kinkeepers are important communication links between family members. They spend a lot of time maintaining contact with family members, visiting friends and families, and organizing or holding gatherings during the holidays or for special events like birthdays and anniversaries. They also often act as the family helper, problem solver, or mediator (Rosenthal, 1985).

The Benefits and Costs of Traditional Gender Roles

Traditional gender roles have both benefits and costs. These roles may be chosen consciously, or they may be a product of habit, custom, or socialization. Remember, too, that traditional relationships vary. In some, partners feel loving and committed; in others, people feel as though they are trapped or sleepwalking.

Benefits Traditional gender roles promote stability, continuity, and predictability. Because each person knows what is expected of him or her, rights and responsibilities are clear. Men and women do not have to argue over who does what: If the house is clean, she is a "good wife"; if the bills are paid, he is a "good husband."

Using the exchange model (see Chapter 2), if the costs and benefits of the relationship are fairly balanced and each partner is relatively happy, traditional gender roles can work well. As long as both partners live up to their role expectations, they are safe in assuming that they will take care of each other financially, emotionally, and sexually.

Some women stay in traditional relationships because they don't have to make decisions or assume responsibility when things go wrong. An accommodating wife can enjoy both power and prestige through her husband's accomplishments. A good mother not only controls and dominates her children but can also be proud of guiding and enriching their lives (Harris, 1994).

When a traditional husband complained about his traditional wife's spending too much money, the wife composed and gave her husband the following "help wanted" ad:

I need someone full time who is willing to be on call 24 hours a day, seven days a week. Sick leave only

when hospitalization is required. Must be able to cook, clean house, do laundry, care for children, feed and clean up after dog, do yard work, mow lawn, shovel snow, do shopping, do menu planning, take out trash, pay bills, answer phone and run errands. Must be able to pinch pennies. Also must be a friend and companion. Must be patient and cannot complain. If you are interested, please leave a message. I will contact you when I feel like talking. Speak only when you have something to say that might interest me. Otherwise, shut up and get to work.—C. L. in Utah ("Want ad proves . . .," 1997).

This "ad" provides a good example of how men benefit from traditional marriages. That is, traditional wives protect their husbands from the pressure of doing domestic work while meeting job-related responsibilities. In addition, the wives themselves don't have the tension of being pulled in many directions such as juggling jobs and housework. Such clearly designated duties can decrease both partners' stress.

But traditional roles are changing. Only 18 percent of women describe themselves as full-time "homemakers" ("Americans' Lifestyles," 2002). The percentage of women who would prefer to stay home and take care of a house and family decreased from 60 percent in 1974 to 44 percent in 1999 ("*Choices,*" 2000). Many women don't have the option of being a traditional wife and mother, however. Most women work outside the home because millions of men have lost their jobs to downsizing, automation, and global job restructuring (see Chapter 13).

Costs Traditional gender roles have their drawbacks. Although many traditional families try to scale down their standard of living, a sole breadwinner is under a lot of economic pressure: "When mothers quit work to care for babies, fathers must shoulder unbearable stress to provide for more dependents" (Alton, 2001: 20). Because many men's definitions of themselves are based on the breadwinner role, losing a job can send some men into severe depression, frustrated rages that end in violence, and even suicide (Liu, 2002).

In terms of costs, a traditional wife can expect little relief from never-ending tasks that may be exhausting, monotonous, and boring. She may also be taken for granted by her husband and children. And what are her options if she's miserable? If she's been out of the work force for a number of years, she might be worse off after a divorce (see Chapter 15). Or a woman who has left all the money matters to her husband may find, after his death, that he did little estate planning and that their finances are in disarray.

Another cost of traditional gender roles is loneliness. A strong but unemotional man may be hard to live with if he does not communicate. Sometimes the seemingly

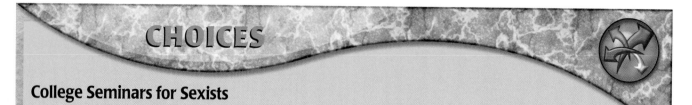

CHOICES

College Seminars for Sexists

In the last few years, a number of messages have appeared over the Internet either challenging or reinforcing gender-role stereotypes. Some Net lists have suggested that colleges establish a graduation requirement of specific and parallel seminars for men and women. Here are some of the suggested courses:

Seminars for Men

1. You, Too, Can Do Housework
2. Easy Laundry Techniques
3. Get a Life—Learn to Cook
4. Spelling—Even You Can Get It Right
5. How to Stay Awake after Sex
6. Garbage—Getting It to the Curb
7. How to Put the Toilet Seat Down
8. Combating Stupidity

Seminars for Women

1. You, Too, Can Change the Oil
2. Elementary Map Reading
3. Get a Life—Learn to Kill Spiders
4. Checkbook Balancing—Even You Can Get It Right
5. How to Stay Awake after Sex
6. Shopping in Less Than 16 Hours
7. How to Close the Garage Door
8. Combating the Impulse to Nag

distant man is quiet because he is continuously worried about the family's economic well-being (Kaufman, 1993). The dutiful worker, husband, and father may feel overwhelmed by his responsibilities and may be unhappy with his life. A traditional man may believe that he never quite lives up to the standard of manhood. Although he has not failed completely, he may feel that he has not succeeded, either (Gaylin, 1992). On the female side, such traditional values as being nurturant, dependent, and submissive can discourage some women from leaving abusive relationships (see Chapter 14).

Gender-role stereotypes reflect another cost of traditional roles. The box "College Seminars for Sexists" offers a tongue-in-cheek look at such stereotypes. Traditional roles have been idealized for so long that many of us think they are normal.

Why do traditional gender roles persist? First, they are profitable for business. The unpaid work that women do at home (such as housework, child rearing, and emotional support) means that companies don't have to pay for child-care services or counseling for stressed-out male employees. And if there is only one breadwinner, many men may work extra hours without additional pay to keep their jobs. Thus, companies increase their profits. If women feel that their place is in the home, they will take part-time jobs that have no benefits, will work for less pay, and will not complain. This increases the corporate world's pool of exploitable and expendable low-paid workers (Kendall, 1999).

Second, traditional roles maintain male privilege and power. If women are seen as not having leadership qualities (see *Table 5.1*), men can dominate political and legal institutions. They can shape laws and policies to maintain their vested interests without being challenged by women who are unhappy with the status quo.

Finally, traditional roles save taxpayers money. After decades of demands by the National Housewives' Federation, Italy started a state-aided pension plan for housewives and househusbands at age 57 who have made social security contributions for five years ("Italy promises . . .," 1996). The United States isn't even discussing such progressive legislation.

A Bubbling Contradiction about Traditional Gender Roles?

In a national survey, many people wanted to return to the romanticized "good old days": 42 percent of the women and 35 percent of the men felt that it would be "better for the country if men and women went back to the traditional roles they had in the 1950s." About two-thirds of both women and men embraced the idea that although mothers often *have* to work for economic reasons, it would be better if they stayed at home and took care of the house and kids (Hugick, 1999:10).

In contrast, a survey of adolescents aged 13 to 17 found that many teenage girls "envision a family-work model that stands tradition on its head." On the one hand, twice as many girls as boys saw themselves staying home to raise their children (52 percent of girls compared with 25 percent of boys). Thus, about half of adolescent girls still see raising children as "women's work." On the other hand, although half of the teenage boys expected their wife to stay home with the kids, 38 percent of the girls believed *it would be their husband* who stays home with the children while the girls work outside the home (Roper Youth Report, 1999).

These findings suggest an interesting dilemma. Whereas parents (and grandparents) might encourage their offspring to reclaim traditional gender roles, nearly two in five teen girls expect their future spouses to be stay-at-home dads. Thus, in the future there may be a significant gap between the roles that women and men expect their partners to play in the home.

Contemporary Gender Roles in Adulthood

In 1993, the Ms. Foundation for Women launched "Take Our Daughters to Work Day" to encourage girls to expand their career aspirations. In 2003, the foundation decided to include boys and implemented "Take Our Daughters and Sons to Work Day." Why the change? To urge both sexes—as well as employers—to think about ways to balance work and family life. According to the president of the Ms. Foundation, "Women are not going to get equality in public life until men can participate equally in private life" (Tergesen, 2003: 105).

Many women's private and public roles have changed dramatically in the last two decades. Nearly three out of four married mothers are in the labor force, compared with two out of four in 1970. Women now earn 46 percent of law degrees, 43 percent of medical degrees, and 44 percent of all doctorates (U.S. Census Bureau, 2002). They own half of all businesses in the United States that generate $2.3 trillion a year in revenue (Center for Women's Business Research, 2003).

Despite such changes, or because of them, men—especially working-class and middle-class white men—feel that they are being attacked from all sides. Such complaints are not supported by the data. White males make up just 33 percent of the population, but they

hold most of the power (see "Data Digest"). In fact, 39 percent of women and 33 percent of men say that there are more advantages to being a man, citing such reasons as better-paying jobs, more opportunities and choices in jobs, and quick promotions. In contrast, only 7 percent of women and 10 percent of men feel that there are more advantages in being a woman (Roper Starch Worldwide, 1996).

Gender Roles at Home: Who Does the Work?

Because many mothers work outside the home, there is more pressure on fathers to share in child rearing and housework. Some fathers report that it took them some time to be more "tuned in" to their children. Others have become more understanding of the drudgery involved in housework and are more willing to buy expensive appliances (such as dishwashers) to make housework easier (Coltrane, 1998). Such purchases, however, don't always lighten women's domestic work.

The "Second Shift"   In most cases, one of the major sources of tension is that many fathers do not participate in the "second shift"—the household work and child care many mothers face after coming home from work. Increasingly, more couples say that they share tasks, especially cooking and grocery shopping, about equally. In terms of shopping for groceries and children's clothing, for example, men were the principal purchasers in 21 percent of all households in 2002, up from 13 percent in 1985 (Fetto, 2002).

In these and other areas, however, there's still quite a difference between women and men. According to the

Increasing numbers of women are attending college part time while working and raising their children. Others are pursuing college degrees in their later years.

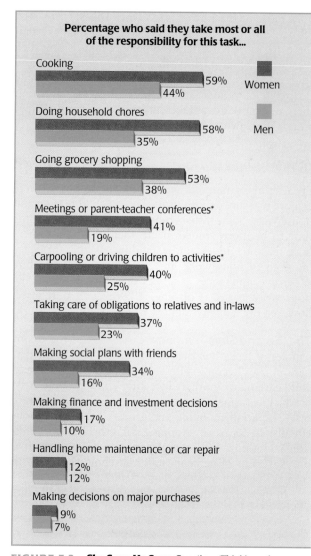

Percentage who said they take most or all of the responsibility for this task...

■ Women
■ Men

Cooking
Women 59%
Men 44%

Doing household chores
Women 58%
Men 35%

Going grocery shopping
Women 53%
Men 38%

Meetings or parent-teacher conferences*
Women 41%
Men 19%

Carpooling or driving children to activities*
Women 40%
Men 25%

Taking care of obligations to relatives and in-laws
Women 37%
Men 23%

Making social plans with friends
Women 34%
Men 16%

Making finance and investment decisions
Women 17%
Men 10%

Handling home maintenance or car repair
Women 12%
Men 12%

Making decisions on major purchases
Women 9%
Men 7%

FIGURE 5.3   She Says, He Says Question: "Thinking of your relationship with your spouse or partner, I'd like to ask you about your roles with respect to a number of responsibilities in your relationship. For each item I read, please tell me whether you take all the responsibility for that item, you take most but not all the responsibility, or your spouse or partner takes all the responsibility . . ."

Note: All questions were asked of respondents who are part of a couple in a household.

*Asked of respondents who are part of a couple in a household and they have children.

Source: Survey by Peter D. Hart Research Associates for Shell Oil, January 7–13, 2000. Adapted from table in *Public Perspective,* July/August 2000, p. 27.

feminine tasks, whereas men do household labor on a more sporadic basis (Bianchi et al., 2000). For the most part, however, neither employed women nor full-time housewives are doing as much housework (Robinson and Godbey, 1999). Instead, most of us have adapted to messier and dustier homes.

It's surprising that men do any housework at all because women's magazines continue to promote domestic work as if it were a gender-specific task. *Martha Stewart Living*—a magazine targeted at women—has published special editions devoted entirely to tips on laundering, ironing, and properly storing clothes. And the lead cover story of a recent issue of *Real Simple* magazine devoted space to instructing women (not men) on how to get a more sparkling sink (McGrath, 2003).

In terms of child care, women's hours decreased from 6 to 5 hours a week between 1965 and 1995, mainly because employed mothers use child care services. Men's child care hours are much the same—about 2 hours a week. As you'll see in Chapter 12, many men still believe that child care is "women's work."

There is also a discrepancy in women's and men's perceptions of their domestic contributions. As *Figure 5.3* shows, many men don't feel that women have as much responsibility for household tasks as women say they do. Conflict over who does how much may lead to communication problems or, ultimately, to separation and divorce (see Chapters 10 and 15).

Even when men share some of the work, women feel more responsible for caring for the home and children:

> *More women than men kept track of doctor's appointments and arranged for kids' playmates to come over. More mothers than fathers worried about a child's Halloween costume or a birthday present for a school friend. They were more likely to think about their children while at work and to check in by phone with the babysitter (Hochschild and Machung, 1989: 24).*

In addition, women sometimes complain that men's participation is peripheral and superficial:

> *I'm always amused when my husband says that he'll "help" me make our bed. I guess he "helps" because he feels making the bed is my responsibility, not his, even though we both sleep in it. When I mow the lawn, it's no big deal. But when he occasionally helps make the bed or does the dishes, he expects a litany of thank-you's and hugs (Author's files).*

Housework combined with full employment means that women often experience greater stress than men. Because they have either more responsibility or a greater share of the domestic work, women often multitask, such as writing checks while returning phone calls. In

best and most recent estimates, women spend almost twice as much time in family care as men. Women's weekly housework declined from 27 hours in 1965 to less than 16 hours in 1995, whereas men's increased from 5 to 10 hours. Wives still perform the core of traditionally

As more women enlist in the military forces, gender roles are changing. In Parris Island, South Carolina, for example, women recruits in the U.S. Marine Corps trudge through mud and rain, carry 50 pounds of gear, and respond to "barking drill instructors" during daily training maneuvers.

"household" matters. And women often feel that they have to postpone or forgo having children to pursue a career.

We'll examine family and work roles at some length in Chapter 13. Here we'll briefly consider sex discrimination and sexual harassment—two work-related gender inequities that affect women, men, their partners, and families.

Sex Discrimination   Often, even women in managerial or professional jobs are denied the opportunities and benefits offered to men in comparable jobs. One example of the glass ceiling is a highly publicized case at the Massachusetts Institute of Technology's School of Science. A female professor of molecular biology spent several years collecting information on the unequal resources provided to male and to female scientists—including salaries, research funds, and laboratory space. The university admitted that the discrimination existed but that it had not been "conscious or deliberate" and implemented some remedies such as salary increases, more desirable teaching assignments, and greater support for research (Wilson, 1999).

In 2001, the Colorado Supreme Court ruled that the University of Northern Colorado had committed sex discrimination when it fired a female parking service director, a highly paid woman, to protect the jobs of two men (Mulhauser, 2001). In another case, a federal jury in Minneapolis awarded a former home health care executive $1 million in lost wages and punitive damages. The jury agreed that the company, Mallinckrodt Inc., paid the woman less than her male counterparts but gave her heavier workloads (Cruz, 2003).

Female physicians are more likely than their male counterparts to teach in medical schools but are less likely to be promoted. Women's child-rearing obligations are one barrier to their advancement. As long as women have the primary (and often nearly total) responsibility for the care of children, even generous maternity leaves will not enable women to catch up to male colleagues who have been focusing all of their attention on their careers (De Angelis, 2000; Nonnemaker, 2000).

In athletics, women consistently fare worse than men. Since 2000, 90 percent of new head coaching jobs in women's athletics have gone to men (Acosta and Carpenter, 2002). Why? Some say that male athletic

addition, women do more of the tedious household chores, such as scrubbing the toilet, whereas men prefer to tend to their children and do "fun" things with them, like going to the movies or playing video games.

Fathers and Children   Many fathers think they're doing a better parenting job than their fathers did. In a *Newsweek* poll, for example, 55 percent of fathers said that being a parent is more important to them than it was to their own fathers, 61 percent said they understand their children better than their own fathers did, and 70 percent said they spend more time with their children than their fathers spent with them (Adler, 1996).

Fathers may feel very close to their children and be affectionate with them, but they are still less involved in child care than mothers. Despite their positive self-evaluations, most fathers still spend little time with children. When they do so, and as in previous years, most of the fathers' primary child-care activities are recreational (playing, reading) and not the "custodial" time that mothers mainly put in (feeding, dressing) (Robinson and Godbey, 1999).

Gender Roles in the Workplace

Although there has been progress in workplace equality, we still have a long way to go. In the United States, the average male employee still doesn't have options for flexible schedules, paternity leaves, or extended absences for

Kalpana Chawla, 41, immigrated to the United States from India in the 1980s and became an astronaut in 1994. She was one of seven astronauts who died on the space shuttle, Columbia, when it broke apart and burst into flames over Texas on February 1, 2003. Columbia was just 16 minutes away from a safe landing at NASA in Florida.

directors, who outnumber females five to one, often simply prefer to hire men (Steindorf, 2002).

In soccer, the bonus each player on the 1999 U.S. Women's World Cup team earned after coming in first was $65,000. The bonus for each player on the U.S. Men's World Cup (if the team had won) would have been $400,000. And in the prestigious Wimbledon tennis tournament, male champion Goran Ivanisec picked up $762,500, compared with $705,500 for female winner Venus Williams (Decker, 2002).

The proportion of women in top editor positions at major U.S. newspapers has declined from 25 percent in 2000 to 20 percent in 2002. Just one in five of the nation's top female editors say they definitely want to move up in the newspaper industry. Those who consider leaving say that the main obstacle to advancement is sexism, especially management's preference for men. Only 6 percent of male editors, in contrast, see sexism as a barrier to their promotion (Gibbons, 2002b; "The great divide . . .," 2002).

Sexual Harassment **Sexual harassment** is any unwelcome sexual advance, request for sexual favors, or other conduct of a sexual nature that makes a person uncomfortable and interferes with her or his work. Harassment includes touching, staring at, or making

jokes about a person's body, unreciprocated requests for sexual intercourse, and rape.

A landmark Supreme Court decision in 1986, *Meritor Savings Bank v. Vinson,* ruled that sexual harassment violates federal laws against discrimination and is unlawful. Sexual harassment in the workplace had a generally low profile, however, until the Senate confirmation hearings of Clarence Thomas, a candidate for the U.S. Supreme Court. In October 1991, sexual harassment got national coverage when Anita Hill, a law professor at the University of Oklahoma, testified that in the early 1980s Thomas had sexually harassed her while he was her supervisor and the director of the Equal Employment Opportunity Commission (EEOC).

Very few women complain about or sue for sexual harassment. In most cases, especially in lower-level positions, women just put up with the abuse because they don't want to lose their jobs. In other cases, even when women have some financial resources, they know that a lawsuit will take seven to eight years to settle and might cost them at least $300,000. Therefore, few women have the money or energy to pursue lawsuits.

The cases in which women have sued illustrate the types of sexual harassment that they've encountered. Here are a few examples:

- A California jury awarded six female employees $30 million because a manager at a Ralphs supermarket chain terrorized them for more than a year. The manager used foul language and racial slurs, threw telephones and 12-pack sodas at them, and touched female workers inappropriately.

- Lutheran Medical Center in Brooklyn, New York, agreed to pay more than $5.4 million to settle complaints by 51 current and past employees that a doctor sexually harassed them during pre-employment physical examinations. The suit accused the physician of touching the women's breasts and genitals needlessly and making lewd comments about their sexual and dating habits.

- The EEOC has sued Rent-A-Center in Illinois and Tennessee for destroying women's job applications. The lawsuit quotes a senior executive as saying, "Women should be home taking care of their husbands and children," and of smacking female employees' behinds.

- The EEOC has had more complaints about the fast-food industry than any other sector. Among other incidents, a store manager raped a 14-year-old employee, some of the young women were repeatedly called "bitch," some have had their breasts fondled or their buttocks towel-slapped, and others have encountered continuous obscene comments and gestures ("Harassment in the Supermarket," 2002; Zellner, 2002; Retsinas, 2003; Sanchez, 2003).

Some men say that they are confused about what sexual harassment is. They claim that they don't see the difference between flirting or complimenting someone and what is being called sexual harassment. This is nonsense. If someone says "stop it" and you don't, it's sexual harassment. We'll look at the prevalence, consequences, and legal ramifications of sexual harassment in more detail in Chapter 13.

Gender and the Consumer Marketplace

Consumer problems are typically more common and more serious for women than for men. Women are often overcharged for car and home repairs, even when they have some expertise in these areas.

Millions of women invest in stocks or bonds but experience unequal treatment. Stockbrokers are four to six times more likely to tell men about a wide range of investments (such as corporate bond funds, money market funds, and IRAs). They are twice as likely to explain investments to men and to urge men to open accounts (because they assume women will be confused by explanations and have less money to invest), and they ask men more probing questions about their finances (Wang, 1993).

According to stockbrokers, most women make three big mistakes in their investments. First, they don't know what's going on. Therefore, they trust financial managers who may be incompetent or dishonest. Second, they leave the finances in their husbands' hands instead of finding out where the household money goes. Third, women often take care of everyone else (such as setting up a grandchild's college trust) instead of providing for themselves, especially for retirement (Boss, 2002).

Two exceptions to women's paying more as consumers are in automotive and life insurance premiums. Young men pay more for car insurance because their driving records, on average, are worse than women's. At age 30, men and women pay the same life insurance premiums. At age 40, however, men's payments at a typical life insurance company may be $273 per year, compared with $235 per year for women (Wiener, 2003). Men pay a price, literally, for their shorter average life expectancy.

Gender and Communication

Language enables us to communicate, to interpret and organize our environment, and to give meaning to our everyday experiences. However, language can also limit our ideas and thought processes.

Sociolinguist Deborah Tannen (1990, 1994) proposes that women and men have distinctive communication styles that include different purposes, different rules, and different ways of interpreting communications.

For example, Tannen says, women are more likely than men to use "rapport-talk," a way of establishing connections and negotiating relationships. They are most concerned with how people feel and with making people feel comfortable.

In contrast, men are more likely to use "report-talk," a way of exhibiting knowledge and skill and holding center stage through storytelling, joking, or giving information. For example, if a man comes home and his wife asks, "How was your day?" she probably expects rapport-talk in response (such as office gossip). Often, however, she will get report-talk: "Fine. Had some problems but got 'em straightened out." Not hearing what she expects, the woman may be miffed, and her husband will probably not understand why she's upset. We'll examine other differences between women's and men's communication patterns in more detail in Chapter 10.

MAKING CONNECTIONS

■ Recently, the Augusta National Golf Club, which hosts the prestigious Masters golf tournament, stirred up controversy by refusing to admit women as members. Some people feel that private clubs have the right to do what they want. Others contend that such exclusion is demeaning and discriminatory. What do you think?

■ Some of my students maintain that instrumental and expressive roles no longer exist. Others argue that both roles are alive and well. Think about your parents, your spouse or partner, or your friends. Does their behavior reflect instrumental and expressive roles?

Current Gender Role Changes and Constraints

Most women and men, especially working parents, share the same concerns and want the same things in life. Both sexes worry about health care and retirement security, a lack of fairness and respect in the workplace, and limited family medical leave and child care (*Ask a Working Woman*, 2002).

Despite these similarities, there are still a number of differences in gender roles. Employed mothers, especially, consistently report more stress than men in their everyday lives. Some attribute such stress to role conflict. Others argue that our society—and feminists in particular—is creating strain by waging a war against boys and men.

Role Conflict

As gender roles change, most of us are bound to encounter **role conflict:** the frustration and uncertainties a person experiences when confronted with the requirements of two or more roles that are incompatible with each other. College students often experience role conflict because it is difficult to meet course requirements, especially if students register for a "full load" but also work 20 or more hours per week. The role conflict increases if the student also has young children or cares for an aging parent.

Faculty similarly grapple with role conflict. Many have evening classes and feel guilty because they must hire baby sitters to care for their young children. Women faculty often feel emotionally drained because it is difficult to keep up both with parental and academic roles such as teaching, grading exams, meeting with students, presenting talks at professional conferences, and meeting research deadlines.

Mothers who work full time report being exhausted by juggling jobs and family responsibilities ("Motherhood today . . .," 1997). Some men complain, however, that their wives' house cleaning standards are too high, that women add unnecessary "finishing touches" (such as rewiping the kitchen table after the husband has cleaned it), or that women grumble that the husbands "dressed the kids funny" (Coltrane, 1996).

As a result, men may feel unappreciated or inadequate and assume fewer housework and child-care responsibilities. Women, on the other hand, maintain that men should have higher standards and do domestic tasks "right." Such disagreements intensify some of the strain that characterizes changing gender roles.

Regardless of one's sex, role conflict is tiring. It can produce tension, hostility, aggression, and stress-related physical problems such as insomnia, headaches, ulcers, eating disorders, teeth grinding, anxiety attacks, chronic fatigue, nausea, weight loss or gain, and drug and alcohol abuse (Weber et al., 1997).

Are We Waging War against Boys and Men?

A recent *Business Week* cover, "The New Gender Gap," shows a picture of a young girl, arms crossed, and smiling smugly while a young boy looks sad and forlorn. The cover story then maintains that from kindergarten to graduate school, boys are now "the second sex"—far behind girls in education, less likely to participate in extracurricular activities, more likely to commit suicide, and so on. There have also been several well-publicized books claiming that girls (and women) are mean and vicious creatures (see Chesler, 2002; Simmons, 2002; Wiseman, 2002).

Is U.S. society neglecting boys? Or do these concerns signal a backlash against some of the gains that girls and women made in the 1980s and 1990s?

A Concern about Men's and Boys' Development In *Real Boys,* clinical psychologist William Pollack (1998: xxi) asserts that "boys today are in serious trouble, including many who seem 'normal' and to be doing just fine." Among other things, boys make up 67 percent of special education classes, are more likely than girls to suffer from attention deficit disorders, lag behind girls in reading scores, create more disciplinary problems in school, and are more likely than girls to be both perpetrators and victims of crime (Garbarino, 1999; Kindlon et al., 1999; Nikkah and Furman, 2000).

In a similar vein, Christina Hoff Sommers (2000) claims that U.S. culture ignores and dismisses boys. Sommers blames feminists, especially, for turning "masculinity into a politically incorrect idea" by spending too much time worrying about how girls are treated, in schools especially, and neglecting boys. According to Sommers, girls outshine boys in school: They get better grades, have higher educational aspirations, read more books, and are less likely than boys to be involved in crime, alcohol, and drugs.

Anthropologist Lionel Tiger (1999) contends, also, that "these are perilous times for men." He alleges that widespread use of the Pill by women has lessened men's virility, as evidenced by lower sperm production (a topic addressed in Chapter 11). Tiger is troubled by two-career couples who decide to be childless. He also worries that blue-collar workers can't find jobs in an "increasingly feminized workplace." He concludes that the rising confidence and power of women has eroded the confidence and power of men (see also Faludi, 1999).

A Backlash against Girls' and Women's Progress Critics respond that such accusations of antimale cultural biases are unwarranted and unsupported. The traditional gender gap in the national mathematics and science scores of 17-year-olds has narrowed, but males still outperform females (Campbell et al., 2000). And if girls are enjoying more success, perhaps they've earned it: "While the girls are busy working on sweeping the honor roll at graduation, a boy is more likely to be bulking up in the weight room . . . playing *Grand Theft Auto: Vice City* on his PlayStation2, or downloading rapper 50 Cent on his iPod" (Conlin, 2003: 76).

Although many girls are succeeding in school, they are twice as likely as boys to suffer from depression, they make up 90 percent of the teens with eating disorders, and they are catching up with boys in smoking, taking drugs, and drinking alcohol (see Chapter 14).

For girls, pressure to have sex begins at age 12 and comes from both boys and girls. White and Asian American girls, especially, report increasing pressure to fit in, do drugs, drink, and be popular and cool. In addition, one-fourth to one-third of girls are sexually victimized (ranging from sexual harassment to rape) by the time they finish high school (Haag, 1999; Phillips, 1999; see also Chapter 7).

Gender-role expectations are especially inconsistent in many ethnic families. As you saw in Chapter 4, recent immigrants try to maintain traditional values that often include a double standard regarding household duties, sexual behavior, and dating.

Instead of girl- and women-bashing, many researchers propose, we should look at the evidence, especially in adulthood. For example,

- 90 percent of the world's billionaires are men (Kroll and Goodman, 2002).

- Men dominate powerful positions in education, government, and the economy (see "Data Digest").

- Among full-time workers, women with bachelor's degrees earn $32,546 per year, compared with $30,414 for men with only a high school degree (U.S. Census Bureau, 2002; see also Chapter 13).

- 29 percent of women say that they experienced sexual assault in the military by their peers or officers. The percentage may be even higher in U.S. military academies (Schmitt and Moss, 2003; Tessier, 2003).

- Although women have had Ph.D.s for several decades, the percentage of female full professors in Western countries ranges from a low of 5 percent in Ireland to a high of only 21 percent in the United States (Bollag, 2002b).

Another way to look at women's progress is to note the number of "firsts" when you pick up the newspaper or turn on the news. In 2002 and 2003, for example, Brown University hired its first woman (and African American) as president; House Democrats elected the first congresswoman as a minority leader; and Atlanta, Georgia, and Cleveland, Ohio, elected their first female mayors, one of whom is black. When we stop reading about such "firsts," we can be more confident that there is greater equality between men and women.

Is Androgyny the Answer?

Some social scientists feel that androgyny may be the solution to sexist gender roles. In **androgyny**, both culturally defined masculine and feminine characteristics are blended in the same person.

According to Bem (1975), who did much of the pioneering work on androgyny, our complex society requires that people have both kinds of abilities. Adults must be assertive, independent, and self-reliant, but they must also relate to other people, be sensitive to their needs, and provide them with emotional support.

Androgyny allows people to play both roles. According to social psychologist Carol Tavris (2002: B8), both men and women demonstrate humanity's "graces and furies":

Both are equally likely to be empathic, kind, altruistic, and friendly and to be mean, hostile, aggressive, petty, conformist, and prejudiced. Both sexes can be competitive or cooperative, selfish or nurturant, loving parents or indifferent ones—and reveal all of those qualities on different occasions.

Androgyny might be especially beneficial for men. Many men might stop being workaholics, relax on weekends, refrain from engaging in risky sexual behavior (to demonstrate their sexual prowess), live longer, and stop worrying about being "real men." If we were more comfortable when children display nontraditional traits, assertive girls and nonaggressive boys would be happier and emotionally healthier (Martin, 1990).

There is still greater disapproval of boys than of girls who reject traditional gender roles. Do you think that androgyny might take some of the pressure off men, giving them more freedom to be and do whatever they want? Or do you think that androgynous men would be dismissed as wimps and sissies?

A Global View: Variations in Gender Roles

Because each culture has its own norms and values, the degree of equality between men and women differs widely across societies. Such cross-cultural variations constitute some of the best evidence that gender roles are learned rather than innate.

There is no easy way to compare the status of women around the world. Still, the Gender Development Index (GDI) is a measure that sheds some light on women's status and quality of life. The GDI is based on key indicators including life expectancy, educational attainment, and income. It also measures "intentional commitment to equality principles and policies" (Seager, 2003: 12). As *Figure 5.4* on page 136 shows, most of the world's women live in countries that rank from "medium" to the "bottom 10 countries." Let's begin with the "top 10 countries" that have the least disparity between women and men.

Top Ten Countries

The United States, Canada, Australia, Japan, Iceland, the Scandinavian countries, Netherlands, and Belgium rank the highest on the GDI (see *Figure 5.4*). Being in the "top ten" doesn't mean that women live in paradise, however. As you've seen throughout this chapter, there is great inequality between women and men in the United States in terms of power, income, and privilege.

There's also wide variation across the top ten countries on several indicators. In terms of the proportion of elected female government officials, for example, Sweden

FIGURE 5.4 **The State of Women around the World**

SOURCE: Seager, 2003: 12–13.

ranks at the top, with 55 percent women, compared with only 32 percent in the United States (Seager, 2003). Even then, Swedish women undergraduates report sexual harassment, and women faculty—only 11 percent of whom are tenured—complain about widespread discrimination in awarding of postdoctoral fellowships, hiring practices, and promotion criteria (Bollag, 2002a, 2002b).

In Japan, women represent 29 percent of the elected legislators and more than half of the work force. Yet women hold only 9 percent of all managerial positions, and full-time working women earn only 65 percent of what men earn. Some women quit work for marriage and motherhood. Those who stay on a job suffer wage inequality and few opportunities for career advancement (Gender Equality Bureau, 2000).

High-rank Countries

The countries that rank high in gender development include Greenland, most of the European countries, South Korea, Chile, Argentina, Uruguay, Greece, and several countries in the Middle East (Israel, Kuwait, and the United Arab Emirates). Again, women's equality is mixed. In South Korea, Ewha Woman's University ended its policy of banning married female undergraduates from attending only recently (Brender, 2003).

Some of the high-rank countries have such positive characteristics as high female literacy rates, low maternal mortality rates, and high percentages of female university students. Yet domestic violence is widespread. For example, 68 percent of the women in the United Kingdom and 53 percent of women in Portugal report having experienced physical abuse by a male partner. One woman every five days is killed by a male partner in Spain, and one woman is killed every nine days by a spouse in Israel (Seager, 2003).

Middle-rank Countries

The middle-rank countries are primarily those in Central and South America, northern and southern Africa, Russia, and much of the Middle East (see *Figure 5.4*). Especially in Islamic cultures, there is a great deal of variation in women's roles in the family, education, politics, and employment opportunities. Each country interprets women's rights under Islam somewhat differently, and within each country social class is a determining factor in women's privileges (Sabbagh, 1996; Gaouette, 2001).

In the Arab world, overall female literacy is more than 50 percent, but it ranges from a low of 30 percent in Iraq to a high of almost 100 percent in Jordan (Elson and Keklik, 2002). In some countries (including Kuwait, Indonesia, China, Thailand, and Saudi Arabia), thriving sex industries are fed by a steady supply of young women—mostly from Bangladesh, India, the Philippines, Sri Lanka, and other poor countries where the women cannot find employment. The unsuspecting women are told they are accepting overseas jobs as maids or domestic laborers. Instead, they are forced into prostitution (Seager, 2003).

In India, most women are under the authority of fathers, brothers, husbands, or husbands' families and are often considered property (epitomized by the dowry that the bride's family pays to the family of the groom). Despite laws, if a husband or his family is not satisfied with the bride's dowry, they may physically harass her, kill her, or drive her to suicide. Some regions still abort female fetuses in favor of sons. Only 54 percent of females are literate. Women with doctorate degrees report exclusion from the best jobs and are expected to be submissive in the workplace (Gupta and Sharma, 2001; Sharma, 2001).

Women's well-being and rights are mixed in other middle-rank countries as well. In South Africa, 84 percent of women are literate. Yet rapes of infants and very young children are widespread. According to one survey of rape victims, 38 percent of young girls said that a schoolteacher or principal had raped them. Fully one-third of children under age 18 have been victims of sexual abuse, and more than 700,000 children have been orphaned by AIDS. Child labor, child prostitution, and child pornography are pervasive (Singer, 2001; Human Rights Watch, 2003; *State of the World's Mothers*, 2003).

Low-rank Countries

The low-rank countries include Pakistan and several Middle Eastern countries as well as a number of African societies. In much of Africa, women's life expectancy rates are well under 55 years (see *Figure 5.4*). Early death results primarily from AIDS but also reflects high death rates during childbirth because of the scarcity of trained health personnel, poor nutrition, and murder by spouses (Seager, 2003).

In African countries, female literacy rates range from a low of 28 percent in Senegal to a high of 71 percent in Zambia. In Nigeria, women can be stoned to death for infidelity or, in the case of divorced women, having sexual relations without having remarried. In many African countries, forced marriage is common. In Nigeria, particularly in the north, an estimated 37 percent of girls aged 15 to 19 are forced to wed against their wishes ("Nigerian girl sues...," 2002; Robinson, 2002; Rosen, 2003; *State of the World's Mothers*, 2003).

In Pakistan, only 28 percent of the women are literate. In some regions, tribal councils decree that a young woman can be raped in revenge for a crime committed by a brother or other male family member. When a girl turns 15 or 16, she usually weds in an arranged marriage and leaves school to start having babies. In some poor regions, it's common for fathers to marry off 18-year-old girls to 80-year-old men to settle a "blood debt"—making amends for wronging someone (Addario, 2001; "Outrage over marriage . . .," 2002; Sarwar, 2002; *State of the World's Mothers*, 2003).

Many well-educated Pakistanis are trying to improve women's rights. They are fighting the rise of Islamic extremist groups, such as the Taliban, many of whom insist that women must wear full veils, quit school, marry at an early age, and accept the rule of men (Baldauf, 2003).

Bottom Ten Countries

The lowest-ranked countries in the status of women are 11 countries in Africa such as Ethiopia, Niger, and Sierra Leone (see *Figure 5.4*). Here, women have short life expectancies for the same reasons as the low-rank African societies.

In these countries, women's literacy rates range from a low of 8 percent in Niger to a high of only 47 percent in Malawi. Women's participation in government is negligible and as low as 1 percent in Niger. Women's sex trafficking to other countries is especially high in Ethiopia, Niger, and Burkina Faso. However, the rates are similar to those in such low-rank countries as the Democratic Republic of Congo, Angola, Zambia, and Tanzania (Seager, 2003; *State of the World's Mothers*, 2003).

Some of these and other countries are struggling to improve women's status. In Mozambique, for example, 70 percent of the country's schools were destroyed during 16 years of civil war. Although 80 to 90 percent of

the elementary-age children are now in school, there are numerous obstacles. In rural areas, most girls drop out by age 12 to marry. Some parents worry that if their daughters go to school, they might be lured into prostitution or be sexually abused by teachers. And in many regions, there are not enough teachers or classrooms. Even when there are teachers, there aren't enough desks or books and no blackboards (Itano, 2002a).

Conclusion

The past 25 years have seen the beginning of dramatic *changes* in some aspects of gender roles. More people today say they believe in gender equality, and unprecedented numbers of women have entered the labor force.

But do most people really have more *choices*? Women have become increasingly resentful of the burden of both domestic and economic jobs, especially in a society that devalues them and their labor. Men, although often freed from the sole-breadwinner role, feel that their range of choices is narrowing as women compete with them in more sectors of society.

Significant change in gender roles elicits *constraints* at every level: personal, group, and institutional. Those who benefit from gender-role inequality resist giving up their privileges and economic resources. Changes in attitudes, socialization, work, and family structures are ongoing. In the next chapter we examine how changes in gender-role attitudes and behavior affect love and intimate relationships.

SUMMARY

1. *Sex* and *gender* are not interchangeable terms. Sex refers to the biological characteristics we are born with. Gender refers to the attitudes and behavior society expects of each sex.

2. Scholars continue to debate how much of our behavior reflects nature (biology) and nurture (environment). Although biology is important, there is little evidence that women are naturally better parents, that men are naturally more aggressive, or that men and women are inherently different in other than anatomy and physiology.

3. Traditional gender roles are based on the beliefs that women should fulfill expressive functions and that men should play instrumental roles.

4. Traditional roles have both positive and negative consequences. On the positive side, men and women know what is expected of them. On the negative side,

traditional roles often create stress and anxiety and seriously limit choices.

5. Many theoretical perspectives try to explain how we learn gender roles. Social learning theory posits that we learn gender roles by reward and punishment, imitation, and role modeling. Cognitive development theory assumes that children learn gender identity by interacting with and interpreting the behavior of others. Feminist approaches argue that we learn gender roles through gender scripts that parents, especially, endorse.

6. We learn gender role expectations from many sources—parents, peers, teachers, and the media. Many of these socializing influences continue to reinforce traditional male and female gender roles.

7. During much of our adult life, our activities are sex-segregated. Typically, men and women play different roles in the home, in the workplace, and as consumers.

8. Many men and women communicate differently. These differences are often unintentional, but they may create misunderstandings.

9. Some writers contend that boys are ignored and devalued whereas girls are supported. Others argue that girls' and women's progress in closing gender gaps has been exaggerated.

10. There is wide variation across cultures in terms of gender roles. Many societies are male-dominated; others are much more progressive than the United States.

KEY TERMS

sex   *110*
gender   *110*
gender roles   *111*
gender identity   *111*
hormones   *112*

matriarchy   *114*
patriarchy   *114*
social learning theory   *117*
cognitive development theory   *117*
gender schema theory   *118*

gender-role stereotypes   *118*
sexual harassment   *132*
role conflict   *134*
androgyny   *135*

TAKING IT FURTHER

Gender Roles and Socialization Material Online

There are hundreds of gender-related Internet resources. Some of the most comprehensive and interesting Web sites include the following:

Women's Studies/Women's Issues WWW Sites offers hundreds of women-related e-mail lists, Websites around the world, and dozens of topical subsections on gender topics.

www.umbc.edu/wmst/links.html

The Men's Bibliography provides almost 13,000 references to material on men, gender roles, masculinities, and sexualities.

www.xyonline.net/mensbiblio

Women of Color Web focuses on issues related to feminisms, sexualities, and reproductive health and rights, as well as writing by and about women of color in the United States.

www.hsph.harvard.edu/grhf/WoC

International Gender Resources offers general and specific bibliographies and filmographies on issues pertaining to women and gender in Africa, Asia, Latin America, and the Middle East and Arab world and among minority cultures in North America and Europe.

globetrotter.berkeley.edu/GlobalGender

WWWomen! The Premier Search Directory for Women Online includes topics such as women in business, feminism, lesbians, publications, women's resources, science and technology, women's sports, and women throughout history.

www.wwwomen.com

Women's Resources on the Net includes dozens of links to women and politics, international women's agencies and global statistics, girls' education resources, and advocacy and academic organizations.

www.wic.org/misc/resource.htm

And more: www.prenhall.com/benokraitis offers resources on health and genetics, guidelines for nonsexist language, women's e-news sources, The Movie Mom's Guide to Family Movies, Girl Tech sites, men's centers, several international sites, information on dowry deaths, sexual harassment resources, and a gallery of the most negative ads about women and invites you to calculate how much unequal pay will cost you over your lifetime if you're a woman.

INVESTIGATE WITH RESEARCH NAVIGATOR

Research Navigator.com
RESOURCES FOR COLLEGE RESEARCH ASSIGNMENTS

Please go to www.researchnavigator.com and enter your LOGIN NAME and PASSWORD. For instructions on registering for the first time, please view the detailed instructions at the end of the Chapter 1. Please search the Research Navigator™ site using the following key search terms:

gender roles
role conflict
sexual harassment

Love and Loving Relationships

DATADIGEST

- **Love is great for business.** On Valentine's Day, Americans spend more than $400 million on roses, purchase more than $600 million worth of candy, and send more than 1 billion cards (compared with 150 million on Mother's Day). In 2003, men spent an average of $126 on Valentine's Day gifts, compared with only $38 for women.

- More than half of all American adults (52 percent) believe in love at first sight and **almost 75 percent believe in "one true love."**

- **Men are more likely than women to initiate romantic e-mail exchanges.** Of the people who engage in online chats, 64 percent—most of them men—say they experience "online chemistry."

- **Does love make life "richer or fuller"?** "Yes," say 37 percent of people born between 1965 and 1980, compared with only 9 percent of those born before 1930.

SOURCES: "Deck the box," 1999; Carlson, 2001; Yin, 2002; Alvear, 2003; "Homefront," 2003; Simon, 2003; White, 2003.

Many of the most popular movies have been about love: first love (*Titanic*), obsessive love (*Fatal Attraction*), self-sacrificing love (*The Bridges of Madison County*), love that survives obstacles (*My Big Fat Greek Wedding*), and falling in love with someone from the "wrong side of the tracks" (*Pretty Woman*). Love means different things to different people. As the box "On Love and Loving" on page 142 illustrates, love has been a source of inspiration, wry witticisms, and even political action for many centuries.

In this chapter we explore the meaning of love, why we love each other, the positive and negative aspects of love, and how love changes over time. We also look at some cross-cultural variations in people's attitudes about love. Let's begin with friendship, the root of love.

Loving and Liking

Love—as both an emotion and a behavior—is essential for human survival. The family is usually our earliest and most important source of love and emotional support (see Chapter 1). It is in families that we learn to love ourselves and, consequently, to love others.

Self-love

Love for oneself, or self-love, is essential for our social and emotional development. Actress Mae West once said, "I never loved another person the way I loved myself." Although such a statement may seem self-centered, it's actually quite insightful. Social philosopher Erich Fromm (1956) saw self-love as a prerequisite for loving others.

CHANGES

On Love and Loving

Throughout the centuries many writers have commented on the varieties, purposes, pleasures, and pain of love. Love is universal, a focus of concern in all societies.

- **Jesus (4 B.C.–A.D. 29):** "A new commandment I give unto you, that ye love one another."
- **I Corinthians 13:4–7:** "Love is patient and kind; love is not jealous or boastful; it is not arrogant or rude. Love does not insist on its own way; it is not irritable or resentful; it does not rejoice at wrong, but rejoices in the right. Love bears all things, believes all things, hopes all things, endures all things."
- **William Shakespeare (1564–1616):** "To say the truth, reason and love keep little company together nowadays" (from *A Midsummer Night's Dream*).
- **Hindustani proverb:** "Life is no longer one's own when the heart is fixed on another."

- **Abraham Cowley (1618–1667):** "I love you, not only for what you are, but for what I am when I am with you."
- **Ninon de Lenclos (1620–1705):** "Much more genius is needed to make love than to command armies."
- **Irish saying:** "If you live in my heart, you live rent-free."
- **Elizabeth Barrett Browning (1806–1861):** "How do I love thee? Let me count the ways. I love thee to the depth and breadth and height my soul can reach."
- **Henry Wadsworth Longfellow (1807–1882):** "Love gives itself; it is not bought."
- **Japanese saying:** "Who travels for love finds a thousand miles only one mile."
- **William Thackeray (1811–1863):** "It is best to love wisely, no doubt; but to love foolishly is better than not to be able to love at all."

- **Robert Browning (1812–1889):** "Take away love and our earth is a tomb."
- **Benjamin Disraeli (1804–1881):** "The magic of first love is our ignorance that it can ever end."
- **Marlene Dietrich (1901–1992):** "Grumbling is the death of love."
- **Turkish proverb:** "When two hearts are one, even the king cannot separate them."
- **Anonymous:** "Nobody is perfect until you fall in love with them."
- **Che Guevara (1928–1967):** "The true revolutionary is guided by a great feeling of love."
- **John Lennon (1940–1980):** "All you need is love."
- **Cher (1946–):** "The trouble with some women is that they get all excited about nothing—and then marry him."

Social scientists describe self-love as an important basis for self-esteem. Among other things, people who like themselves are more open to criticism and less demanding of others. People who don't like themselves may not be able to return friendship. Instead, they constantly seek love relationships to bolster their own poor self-images (Casler, 1974).

Love and Friendship

Do you like people that you don't love? Sure. Do you love people you don't like? No—at least not in a healthy relationship. According to his classic research on "the near and dear," Keith Davis (1985) found eight important qualities in friendship:

- **Enjoyment.** Friends enjoy being with each other most of time. They feel at ease with each other despite occasional disagreements.

- **Acceptance.** Friends accept each other as they are. They tolerate faults and shortcomings instead of trying to change each other.

- **Trust.** Friends trust and look out for each other. They lean on each other during difficult times.

- **Respect.** Friends respect each other's judgment. They may not agree with the choices that a person makes, but they honor their decisions.

- **Mutual support.** Friends help and support each other. They help each other out without expecting something in return.

- **Confiding.** Friends share experiences and feelings. They don't gossip about each other or backstab.

- **Understanding.** Friends are sympathetic about each other's feelings and thoughts. They can often read each other without saying very much.

■ **Honesty.** Friends are open and honest. They feel free to be "themselves" and say what they think.

Love includes all of these qualities and three more—sexual desire, priority over other relationships, and caring to the point of great self-sacrifice. A relationship can start off with friendship and develop into love. It's unlikely, however, that we can "really" love someone who isn't a friend. Love, like friendship, is a process that develops over time.

But just what is love? What attracts lovers to each other? And are lust and love similar?

What Is Love?

Love is an elusive concept. We have all experienced love and feel that we know what it is. When asked what love is, however, people give a variety of answers. According to a 9-year-old boy, for example, "Love is like an avalanche where you have to run for your life." And according to a 6-year-old girl, "Love is when mommy sees daddy on the toilet and she doesn't think it's gross." Before you read any further, test your general knowledge about love in the box "How Much Do You Know about Love?"

Some Characteristics of Love

People often make a distinction between "loving someone" (family members, relatives, and friends) and "being in love" (a romantic relationship). Both types of love, nonetheless, are multifaceted, based on respect, and often demanding.

Love Is Multifaceted Love has many dimensions. It can be romantic, exciting, obsessive, and irrational. It can also be platonic, calming, altruistic, and sensible. Love defies a single definition because it varies in degree and intensity and across social contexts. At the very least, and as you will see shortly, love includes caring, intimacy, and commitment.

Love Is Based on Respect Although love may involve passionate yearning, respect is a more important quality. If respect is missing, the relationship is not based on love. Instead, it is an unhealthy or possessive feeling or behavior that limits the lovers' social, emotional, and intellectual growth (Peele and Brodsky, 1976).

Love Is Often Demanding Long-term love, especially, has nothing in common with the images of infatuation

---

ASKYOURSELF

How Much Do You Know about Love?

The following statements are based on the material in this chapter.

	Fact	Myth
1. There is an ideal mate for every person; just keep looking.	☐	☑
2. Women are more romantic than men.	☐	☑
3. Love conquers all.	☑	☐
4. Men's and women's love needs are different.	☑	☐
5. Real love lasts forever.	☑	☐
6. Everybody falls in love sooner or later.	☐	☑
7. Love brings happiness and security.	☑	☐
8. Love endures and overcomes all problems.	☐	☑
9. Men are more interested in sex than in love.	☐	☑
10. I can change the person I love.	☐	☑

(The answers to these questions appear on page 145.)

or frenzied sex that we get from movies, television, and romance novels. These misconceptions often lead to unrealistic expectations, stereotypes, and disillusionment.

In fact, real love is closer to what one author calls "stirring-the-oatmeal" love (Johnson, 1985). This type of love is neither exciting nor thrilling but is usually mundane and unromantic. It means paying bills, putting out the garbage, scrubbing toilet bowls, being up all night with a sick baby, and performing myriad other tasks that aren't very sexy.

Some partners take turns stirring the oatmeal. Others don't and break up or get a divorce. Whether we decide to tie the knot or not, why are we attracted to some people and not others?

What Attracts People to Each Other?

Many people believe in "true love," that "there's one person out there that you're meant for," and that destiny will bring us together (see "Data Digest"). Such beliefs are romantic but unfounded. Cultural norms and values, not fate, bring people together. We will never meet millions of potential lovers because they are "filtered out" by formal or informal rules on partner eligibility due to factors such as age, race, social class, religion, sexual orientation, health, or physical appearance (see Chapter 8).

Beginning in childhood, parents indirectly encourage or limit future romantic liaisons by choosing to live in certain neighborhoods and selecting certain schools. In early adolescence, peer norms influence the adolescent's decisions about acceptable romantic involvements ("You want to go out with *whom*?!").

Even during the preteen years, romantic experiences are *cultured* in the sense that societal and group practices and expectations shape romantic experiences. Although romance may cross cultural or ethnic borders, criticism and approval teach us what is acceptable and with whom (Brown, 1999; Coates, 1999). As you saw in Chapters 1 and 4, all societies—including the United States—have "rules" about homogamy (dating and marrying within one's group) and exogamy (dating and marrying someone outside an "acceptable" group).

Even if we "fall in lust" with someone, our yearnings will not lead most of us to "fall in love" if there are strong cultural taboos. These taboos explain, in part, why we don't always marry our sexual partners.

Do Lust and Love Differ?

Lust and love differ quite a bit. Regan and Berscheid (1999) differentiate between sexual arousal (or lust), sexual desire, and love—especially romantic love. They describe *sexual arousal* as a physiological rather than an emotional response, one that may occur consciously or unconsciously (see Chapter 7). *Sexual desire,* in contrast, is a psychological state in which a person wants "to obtain a sexual object that one does not now have or to engage in a sexual activity in which one is not now engaging" (p. 17).

Sexual desire may or may not lead to *romantic love:* "If at any time sexual desire disappears, a person is no longer said to be in a state of romantic love" (Regan and Berscheid, 1999: 115). Once desire evaporates, disillusioned and disappointed lovers will wonder where the "spark" in their relationship has gone and may reminisce longingly about "the good old days."

This does not mean that sexual desire *always* culminates in sexual intercourse or that romantic love and love are synonymous. Married couples may love each other even though they rarely, or never, engage in sexual intercourse for health and other reasons. Regardless of the nature of love, healthy loving relationships reflect a balance of caring, intimacy, and commitment.

Caring, Intimacy, and Commitment

As you will see later in this chapter, people fall in love for many reasons—because they are physically attracted, have shared interests, seek companionship, or simply want to have fun. In any type of love, however, caring about the other person is essential.

Caring

Love includes *caring*, or wanting to help the other by providing aid and emotional support (Cutrona, 1996). People use such metaphors for love as "I'm crazy about you" or "I can't live without you." These terms of endearment, however, may not be translated into such ongoing, everyday behavior as valuing your partner's welfare as much as your own.

Caring means responding to the other person's needs. If a person sees no evidence of warmth or support over time, there will be serious doubts that a partner *really* loves her or him.

This doesn't mean that a partner should be submissive or docile. Instead, people who care about each other bolster each other's self-esteem and offer encouragement when there are problems. When a person is sensitive to a partner's needs, the relationship will become more intimate and flourish.

Intimacy

Although definitions of intimacy vary from writer to writer, all of them emphasize feelings of closeness. In his analysis of couples, for example, P. M. Brown (1995: 3) found people experience *intimacy* when they

- Share a mutual emotional interest
- Have some sort of history together
- Are mutually interdependent
- Have a distinct sense of identity as a couple
- Hold a reciprocal commitment to a continued relationship
- Share hopes and dreams for a common future

Still other writers distinguish among three kinds of intimacy—*physical* (sex, hugging, and touching), *affective* (feeling close), and *verbal* (self-disclosure). They also point out that physical intimacy is usually the least important (Piorkowski, 1994).

Self-disclosure refers to open communication in which one person reveals his or her honest thoughts and feelings to another person with the expectation that truly open communication will follow. In intimate relationships, people feel free to expose their weaknesses, idiosyncrasies, hopes, and insecurities without fear of ridicule or rejection (P. M. Brown, 1995). Lovers, for example, will reveal their innermost thoughts, and marital partners feel comfortable in venting their frustrations because their spouses are considered trustworthy, respectful, and their best friends or confidantes. Self-disclosure does *not* include nagging. Nagging decreases intimacy. If you nag your partner, you're saying "I'm better than you. Shape up." Most people resent nagging because it implies superiority.

Answers to "How Much Do You Know about Love?"

All ten statements are myths. Eight or more correct answers indicate that you know a myth when you hear one. Otherwise—watch out!

1. We can love many people, and we can love many times. This is why some people marry more than once.

2. Men fall in love more quickly, are more romantic, and suffer more intensely when their love is not returned.

3. Because almost one out of two marriages ends in divorce, love is not enough to overcome all problems and obstacles. Differences in race, ethnicity, religion, economic status, education, and age can often stifle romantic interest.

4. As in friendship, both men and women want trust, honesty, understanding, and respect.

5. A love can be genuine but not last eternally; good marriages do not always last a lifetime. People today live much longer, the world is more complex, and partners change as they mature and grow older.

6. Some people have deep-seated emotional scars that make them suspicious and unloving; others are too self-centered to give love.

7. Love guarantees neither happiness nor security. As you'll see shortly, love doesn't "fix" people who are generally insecure or anxious about themselves or their relationships.

8. People who love each other make sacrifices, but emotional or physical abuse should not be tolerated. Eventually, even "martyrs" become unhappy, angry, depressed, and resentful.

9. During the romantic stage, both women and men may be more interested in sex than in love. As love matures, both partners value such attributes as faithfulness, patience, and making the other person feel wanted.

10. You can only change yourself. Trying to change someone usually results in anger, resentment, frustration, and unhappiness.

Intimacy includes more than the relationship between two adults. It is also a relationship between children and parents, adult children and their parents, children and stepparents, children and grandparents, and so on. Even though much research has emphasized the role of the mother in intimate relationships with children, a father's love is just as important. If a father is close to his children, he can play a crucial role in their self-esteem, emotional stability, and avoidance of drugs and other risky behavior (Rohner and Veneziano, 2001).

In adult love relationships, intimacy increases as people let down their defenses, learn to relax in each other's company, and can expect reciprocal support during good and bad times (Josselson, 1992). Caring and intimacy, in turn, foster commitment.

Commitment

Commitment is a person's intention to remain in a relationship "through thick and thin." Mutual commitment can arise out of (1) a sense of loyalty and fidelity to one's partner; (2) a religious, legal, or moral belief in the sanctity of the marriage; (3) a continued optimism about future rewards—emotional, financial, sexual, or otherwise; and (4) strong emotional attachments, dependence, and love (P. M. Brown, 1995). Many people end their relationships, although they still love each other, if they feel that commitment is not increasing (Sprecher, 1999).

In a healthy relationship, commitment has many positive aspects such as affection, companionship, and trust. Each partner looks forward to staying together and is available to the other not only during times of stress but also day in and day out. Commitments generate responsibilities that support rather than threaten love. These responsibilities remain in the background but surface during rough times, temptations to be unfaithful, or mood fluctuations. In this sense, commitments reinforce, not replace, caring (Martin, 1993).

Commitment in a secure relationship is not "hearts and flowers." Instead, commitment is behavior that demonstrates—repeatedly and in a variety of situations—that "I'm here, I will be here, I'm interested in what you do and what you think and feel, I will actively support your independent actions, I trust you, and you can trust me to be here if you need me" (Crowell and Waters, 1994: 32).

In a dysfunctional or abusive relationship, in contrast, partners who define commitment as a lifelong tie can experience "a crushing burden of obligation, entrapment, and limited options" (P. M. Brown, 1995: 152). We'll examine unhealthy relationships more closely in Chapter 14.

MAKING CONNECTIONS

■ How are your friendships similar to and different from your love relationships? If you can have many friends, can you also be in love with several people at the same time?

■ How many times have you been in love? Were your feelings similar in all cases? Or did they change as you got older?

Some Theories about Love and Loving

Why and how do we love? Biological explanations tend to focus on why we love. Psychological, sociological, and anthropological approaches try to explain how as well as why.

The (Bio)Chemistry of Love

Biological perspectives maintain that love is grounded in evolution, biology, and chemistry. Biologists and some psychologists see romance as serving the evolutionary purpose of drawing men and women into long-term partnerships that are essential to child rearing. On open and often dangerous grasslands, for example, one parent could care for offspring while the other foraged for food.

When lovers claim that they feel "high" and as if they are being swept away, it's probably because they are flooded by chemicals. A meeting of eyes, a touch of hands, or a whiff of scent sets off a flood that starts in the brain and races along the nerves and through the bloodstream. The results are familiar: flushed skin, sweaty palms, and heavy breathing (Ackerman, 1994). Natural amphetamines such as dopamine, norepinephrine, and phenylethylamine (PEA) are responsible for these symptoms. PEA is especially effective; it revs up the brain, causing feelings of elation, exhilaration, and euphoria:

> No wonder lovers can stay awake all night talking and caressing. No wonder they become so absentminded, so giddy, so optimistic, so gregarious, so full of life. Naturally occurring amphetamines have pooled in the emotional centers of their brains; they are high on natural "speed" (Fisher, 1992: 53).

PEA highs don't last long, though, which may explain why passionate or romantic love is short-lived.

What about love that endures beyond the first few months? According to the biological perspective, another set of chemicals helps maintain relationships.

As infatuation wanes and attachment grows, another group of chemicals, called *endorphins,* which are chemically similar to morphine and reside in the brain, takes over. Unlike PEA, endorphins calm the mind, eliminate pain, and reduce anxiety. This, biologists say, explains why people in long-lasting relationships report feeling comfortable and secure (Walsh, 1991; Fisher, 1992).

Remember that there is no hard evidence for these biological theories. One observer has noted that these evolutionary perspectives are "exceeding the limits of knowledge, scientific method, and credulity" (Swedlund, 1993: 1053). Nonetheless, they provide food for thought.

Sociological perspectives—and some psychological theories—claim that culture, not PEA, is Cupid. The social science theories that help us understand the components and processes of love include attachment theory, Reiss's wheel theory of love, Sternberg's triangular theory of love, Lee's research on the styles of loving, and exchange theories.

Attachment Theory

Attachment theory posits that our primary motivation in life is to be connected with other people—because it is the only security we ever have. British psychiatrist John Bowlby (1969, 1984) asserted that attachment is an integral part of human behavior "from the cradle to the grave." Adults and children benefit by having someone look out for them—someone who cares about their welfare, provides for their basic emotional and physical needs, and is available when needed.

American psychologist Mary Ainsworth (Ainsworth et al., 1978), one of Bowlby's followers, assessed infant–mother attachment in her classic "strange situation" study. In both natural and laboratory settings, Ainsworth created mild stress for the infant by having the mother temporarily leave the baby with a friendly stranger in an unfamiliar room. When the mother returned, Ainsworth observed the infant's behavior toward the mother and the mother's reactions to the infant's behavior.

Ainsworth identified three infant–mother attachment styles. She characterized about 60 percent of the infants as *secure* in their attachment, with sensitive and responsive mothers. The babies showed some distress when left with a stranger, but when the mother returned, they clung to her for just a short time and then went back to exploring and playing.

About 19 percent of the infants displayed *anxious/ambivalent* attachment styles when mothers were inconsistent—sometimes affectionate, sometimes aloof. The infants showed distress at separation but rejected their mothers when they returned. The remaining 21 percent of the infants, most of whom had been reared by caregivers who ignored their physical and emotional

needs, displayed *avoidant* behavior when their mothers returned after an absence.

Some of the infant attachment research has been criticized for relying almost exclusively on laboratory settings instead of natural ones and for not capturing cross-cultural differences in child-rearing practices (see Feeney and Noller, 1996). Despite such criticisms some researchers propose that adult intimate relationships reflect these three attachment styles.

Using a "love quiz" based on Ainsworth's three attachment styles, Cindy Hazan and her associates questioned 108 college students and 620 adults who said they were in love (Hazan and Shaver, 1987; Shaver et al., 1988). The respondents were asked to describe themselves within their "most important romance" using three measures:

- *Secure style:* I find it easy to get close to others and am comfortable depending on them and having them depend on me. I don't often worry about being abandoned or about someone getting too close to me.

- *Avoidant style:* I am somewhat uncomfortable being close to others; I find it difficult to trust them completely and difficult to allow myself to depend on them. I am nervous when anyone gets too close, and lovers often want me to be more intimate than I feel comfortable being.

- *Anxious/ambivalent style:* I find that others are reluctant to get as close as I would like. I often worry that my partner doesn't really love me or won't want to stay with me. I want to merge completely with another person, and this desire sometimes scares people away.

In addition, the researchers asked the respondents whether their childhood relationships with their parents were warm or cold and rejecting. *Secure adults* (about 56 percent of the sample), who generally described their parents as having been warm and supportive, were more trusting of their romantic partners and more confident of a partner's love. They reported intimate, trusting, and happy relationships that lasted an average of ten years.

Anxious/ambivalent adults (about 20 percent) tended to fall in love easily and wanted a commitment almost immediately. *Avoidant adults* (24 percent of the sample) had little trust for others, had the most cynical beliefs about love, and couldn't handle intimacy or commitment.

Several studies have tracked attachment styles from toddlerhood to adulthood and have found that attachment styles can change over the life course regardless of a person's early childhood experiences. If, for example, we experience disturbing events such as parental

FIGURE 6.1 **The Wheel Theory of Love** Reiss likened his four stages of love to the spokes of a wheel. As the text describes, a love relationship begins with the stage of rapport and, in a lasting relationship, continues to build as the wheel turns, deepening rapport, fulfillment, and mutual dependence and increasing the honesty of self-revelation.

SOURCE: Based on Reiss, 1960: 139–45.

divorce, a relationship breakup, being dumped a few times in succession, or our own divorce, we may slip from a secure to an avoidant style. Alternatively, positive experiences can change a person from an avoidant to a secure attachment style (Kirkpatrick and Hazan, 1994; Lewis et al., 2000).

Therefore, "the view that children's experiences set attachment styles in concrete is a myth" (Fletcher, 2002: 158). Instead, critics point out, events such as divorce, disease, and financial problems are far more important in shaping a child's well-being by age 18 than any early bonding with his or her mother (Lewis, 1997; Hays, 1998; Birns, 1999).

Reiss's Wheel Theory of Love

Sociologist Ira Reiss and his associates proposed a "wheel theory" of love (*Figure 6.1*) that generated much research for several decades. Reiss describes four stages of love: rapport, self-revelation, mutual dependency, and personality need fulfillment (Reiss, 1960; Reiss and Lee, 1988).

In the first stage, partners establish *rapport* based on similar cultural backgrounds, such as upbringing, social class, religion, and education (see Chapter 1 on endogamy). Without this rapport, according to Reiss, would-be lovers would not have enough in common to establish an initial interest.

In the second stage, *self-revelation* brings the couple closer together. Because each person feels more at ease in the relationship, she or he is more likely to discuss hopes, desires, fears, and ambitions and to engage in sexual activities.

As the couple becomes more intimate, the partners' *mutual dependency* increases in the third stage, and they exchange ideas, jokes, and sexual desires. In the fourth and final stage, the couple experiences *personality need fulfillment*. The partners confide in each other, make mutual decisions, support each other's ambitions, and bolster each other's self-confidence.

Like spokes on a wheel, these stages can turn many times—that is, they can be repeated. For example, partners build some rapport, then reveal bits of themselves, then build more rapport, then begin to exchange ideas, and so on. The spokes may keep turning to produce a deep and lasting relationship. Or, during a fleeting romance, the wheel may stop after a few turns. The romantic wheel may "unwind"—even in one evening—if the relationship droops because of arguments, a lack of self-disclosure, or conflicting interests.

Sociologist Dolores Borland (1975) modified the wheel theory, proposing that love relationships be viewed as "clocksprings," like those in a watch. Like clocksprings, relationships can wind and unwind several times as love swells or ebbs. Tensions, caused by events like pregnancy and the birth of a child, may wind the spring tightly. If the partners communicate and work toward a common goal, such tensions may solidify rather than sap a relationship. On the other hand, relationships can end abruptly if they are so tightly overwound that the partners cannot grow or if one partner feels threatened by increasing or unwanted intimacy.

Others note that both the wheel theory and the clockspring theory ignore the variations in intensity between the stages of a relationship. People may love each other, but the intensity of their feelings may be high on one dimension and low on another. For example, when a couple stays together for the sake of their children, the intensity of personality need fulfillment might increase while the intensity of their rapport might decrease (Albas and Albas, 1987).

Sternberg's Triangular Theory of Love

Instead of focusing on stages of love, psychologist Robert Sternberg and his associates (1986, 1988) have proposed that there are three important components of love—intimacy, passion, and decision/commitment. *Intimacy* encompasses feelings of closeness, connectedness, and bonding. *Passion* leads to romance, physical attraction, and sexual consummation. *Decision/commitment* has a short- and a long-term dimension. In the short term, partners make a decision to love each other; in the long term, they make a commitment to maintain that love over time.

According to Sternberg, love can vary in its mix of intimacy, passion, and commitment. Relationships thus range from *nonlove,* where all three components are absent, to *consummate love,* where all the elements are present. Even when all components are present, they may vary in intensity and over time for each partner. Sternberg presents these three components as forming a triangle (*Figure 6.2*). In general, the greater the mismatching of dimensions, the greater the dissatisfaction in a relationship.

Let's use Jack and Jill to illustrate this model. If Jack and Jill are "perfectly matched" (*Figure 6.2A*), they will be equally passionate, intimate, and committed, and their love will be "perfect." Even if the degree to which they want intimacy and commitment varies a little, they may still be "closely matched" (*Figure 6.2B*). However, if both are about equally passionate, but Jack wants more intimacy than Jill does, and Jill is unwilling to make the long-term commitment that Jack wants, this couple will be "moderately mismatched" (*Figure 6.2C*). And if they want to marry each other (make a commitment), but Jill is neither as intimate nor as passionate as Jack, they will be "severely mismatched" (*Figure 6.2D*).

Some find this theory useful for counseling purposes. If, for instance, people recognized that love encompasses more than just passion—a fleeting component of love—there would be fewer unfulfilled expectations and disappointment. A decline of passion is normal and inevitable if a relationship moves from passion to commitment, a more stable union than just "being in love" (García, 1998).

Like the other perspectives we've discussed, the triangular theory of love has limitations. For example, "perfectly matched" love is found only in Disney movies. Also, love varies depending on one's marital status. Intimacy and passion are much stronger in casual dating, for example, than in marriage. Commitment, on the other hand, is much higher among married couples than among dating or engaged couples (Lemieux and Hale, 2002).

Lee's Styles of Loving

Canadian sociologist John A. Lee (1973, 1974) developed one of the most widely cited and studied approaches to love. Although not a full-fledged theory, Lee's approach was built on his collection of more than 4000 statements about love from hundreds of works of fiction and nonfiction.

The sources ranged from the literature of ancient Greece (which recognized *agape* and *eros* as two kinds of love), the Bible, and medieval, Victorian, and modern writers. Lee administered a 30-item questionnaire

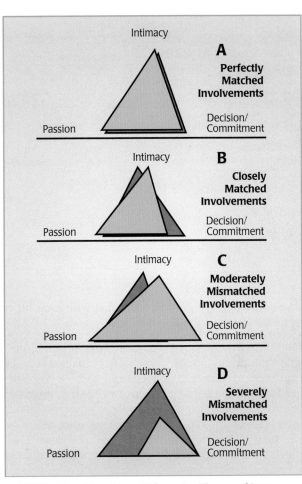

FIGURE 6.2 **Sternberg's Triangular Theory of Love**
This theory of love allows us to see how people can be very close on some dimensions but very far apart on others.

SOURCE: Adapted from Sternberg, 1988.

based on this research to people in Canada and Great Britain. From the responses he derived six basic styles of loving: eros, mania, ludus, storge, agape, and pragma (see *Table 6.1* on page 150), all of which overlap and vary in intensity in real life.

Eros Eros (root of the word *erotic*) is the love of beauty. Because it is also characterized by powerful physical attraction, eros epitomizes "love at first sight." This is the kind of love often described in romance novels, where the lovers are immediately love-struck and experience palpitating hearts, light-headedness, and intense emotional desire.

Erotic lovers want to know everything about the loved one—what she or he dreamed about last night and what happened on the way to work today. Erotic lovers often like to wear matching T-shirts, identical bracelets, and matching colors, to order the same foods

TABLE 6.1

Lee's Six Styles of Love

	Meaning	Major Characteristics
Eros	Love of beauty	Powerful physical attraction
Mania	Obsessive love	Jealousy, possessiveness, and intense love dependency
Ludus	Playful love	Carefree quality, casualness; fun-and-games approach
Storge	Companionate love	Peaceful and affectionate love based on mutual trust and respect
Agape	Altruistic love	Self-sacrificing, kind, and patient love
Pragma	Practical love	Sensible, realistic

SOURCES: Adapted from Lee, 1973 and 1974: 46–51.

when dining out, and to be identified with each other as totally as possible (Lasswell and Lasswell, 1976).

Mania Characterized by obsessiveness, jealousy, possessiveness, and intense dependency, **mania** may be expressed in anxiety, sleeplessness, loss of appetite, headaches, and even suicide because of real or imagined rejection. Manic lovers are consumed by thoughts of their beloved and have an insatiable need for attention and signs of affection (Lee, 1974). Mania is often associated with low self-esteem and a poor self-concept. As a result, manic people are typically not attractive to those who have a strong self-concept and high self-esteem (Lasswell and Lasswell, 1976).

Ludus Ludus is carefree and casual love that is considered "fun and games." Physical appearance is less important to ludic lovers than self-sufficiency and a nondemanding partner. They try to control their feelings and may have several lovers at one time. They are not possessive or jealous, primarily because they don't want lovers to become dependent on them. Ludic lovers have sex for fun, not emotional rapport. In their sexual encounters they are typically self-centered and may be exploitive because they do not want commitment, which they consider "scary."

Storge Storge (pronounced "STOR-gay") is a slow-burning, peaceful, and affectionate love that "just comes naturally" with the passage of time and the enjoyment of shared activities. Storgic relationships lack the ecstatic highs and lows that characterize some other styles; sex occurs late in this type of relationship, and the goals are usually marriage, home, and children. Even if they break up, storgic lovers are likely to remain good friends (Lee, 1974).

The storgic lover finds routine home activities relaxing and comfortable. Because there is mutual trust,

temporary separations are not a problem. In storgic love, affection develops over the years, as in many lasting marriages. Passion may be replaced by spirituality, respect, and contentment in the enjoyment of each other's company (Murstein, 1974).

Agape The classical Christian type of love, **agape** (pronounced "AH-gah-pay") is altruistic, self-sacrificing love that is directed toward all humankind. It is a self-giving love in which partners help each other develop their maximum potential without considering their own advantages or costs. Agape is always kind and patient, never jealous or demanding, and does not seek reciprocity. Lee points out, however, that he has not yet found an unqualified example of agape during his interviews.

Intense agape can border on masochism. For example, an agapic person might wait indefinitely for a lover to be released from prison, might tolerate an alcoholic or drug-addicted spouse, or might be willing to live with a partner who engages in illegal activities or infidelity (Lasswell and Lasswell, 1976).

Pragma According to Lee, **pragma** is rational love based on practical considerations, such as compatibility and perceived benefits. Indeed, it can be described as "love with a shopping list." A pragmatic person seeks compatibility in such things as background, education, religious views, and vocational and professional interests. If one person does not work out, the pragmatic person moves on, quite rationally, to search for someone else.

Pragmatic lovers look out for their partners, encouraging them, for example, to ask for a promotion or to finish college. They are also practical in divorce. For example, a couple might stay together until the youngest child finishes high school or until both partners find better jobs (Lasswell and Lasswell, 1976).

Researchers have developed dozens of scales to measure Lee's concepts of love (see Tzeng, 1993). *Table 6.2* on page 152 presents some items from the Love Attitudes Scale that was originally developed by the Lasswells and modified by later researchers.

Exchange Theory

Social scientists often describe love as a *social exchange process* (see Chapter 2). Romantic and long-term love relationships involve social exchanges in the sense that they provide rewards and costs to each person. If the initial interactions are reciprocal and mutually satisfying to both people, a relationship will continue. If, however, our needs are mismatched (see *Figure 6.2*) or change drastically over time, our love interests may wane or shift from adolescence to later life.

Love during Adolescence   Exchange theory is especially helpful in explaining why romantic love is short-lived among adolescents. Adolescent love is usually intense but also self-centered. Because adolescents are still "finding themselves," they often form relationships with peers who offer many benefits and few costs ("I can call him whenever I'm lonely" or "I'm hookin' up with a knockout cheerleader this weekend").

Love during Adulthood   As we mature, our perceptions of rewards and costs usually change. We might decide that nurturing a relationship with someone who's patient and confident, for example, outweighs the benefits of being with someone who's "a good catch" or "a knockout" but is controlling and self-centered.

Love during Later Life   We also weigh the costs and benefits of romance later in life. In a national survey of people age 60 and over, 90 percent said that they wanted a romantic partner who had moral values, a pleasant personality, a good sense of humor, and intelligence ("Half of older Americans . . .," 1998).

There were several distinct differences between men and women, however. More women (85 percent) than men (56 percent) sought financial security in a partner. More men (72 percent) than women (46 percent) wanted partners who were interested in sex. Men (67 percent) were more likely than women (48 percent) to want a partner with "a terrific body." Because women, especially older women, are less likely than men to be affluent, financial security may be a more important consideration than sex or physical appearance (see Chapters 8 and 17). In this sense, many women and men defined the "benefits" of a love relationship differently.

MAKING CONNECTIONS

▨ Return to *Figure 6.2* and think about your current love relationship. (If you are not currently involved with someone, reflect on a past relationship.) How well matched are you and your partner in terms of intimacy, passion, and commitment?

▨ Think about Lee's styles of loving (*Table 6.2*). Do you and your partner have similar or different love attitudes? If your styles of loving differ, does this create problems, or make the relationship more interesting? Did past relationships break up because the styles of loving differed? ◉◉

Agape, or altruistic love, includes kindness, self-sacrifice, compassion, and patience. Actor Christopher Reeve of the popular Superman films was confined to a wheelchair after a riding accident. Reeve's wife, Dana, has cared for him since the accident and has supported his lobbying Congress on such issues as raising the lifetime spending caps on catastrophic insurance policies.

Functions of Love and Loving

Love is the core of healthy and well-functioning relationships and families. Love fulfills many purposes that range from ensuring human survival to recreation.

Love Ensures Human Survival In a tongue-in-cheek article, one writer suggested that romantic love is a "nuisance" and "a nasty trick played upon us by nature to keep our species going," especially during the childbearing years (Chance, 1988: 23). In fact, love *does* keep our species going. Because children can be conceived outside of love and marriage, there is no guarantee that those engaging in sexual intercourse will feel an obligation to care for their offspring.

Unlike sex, love implies a commitment. Thus, by promoting interest in caring for helpless infants, love ensures the survival of the species.

Love Prolongs Life Babies and children deprived of love may develop a wide variety of problems—depression, headaches, physiological impairments, and neurotic and psychosomatic difficulties—that sometimes last a lifetime. In contrast, infants who are loved and cuddled typically gain more weight, cry less, and smile more. By age 5, they have significantly higher IQs and score higher on language tests (Klaus and Kennell, 1976).

Perhaps the most dramatic example of the impact of love, especially its absence, is suicide. People who commit suicide often feel socially isolated, rejected, unloved, or unworthy of love. Suicide is far more prevalent among divorced than married people. Divorced people also tend to suffer more serious illnesses and more chronic disabling conditions than do married couples (see Chapters 10 and 14).

Love doesn't guarantee that we'll live to be 100, of course. Instead, researchers suggest, there is a link between loving relationships and greater longevity.

TABLE 6.2

Some Items from the Love Attitudes Scale

Use this scale to examine your own and your partner's feelings. If you've never been in love or don't have a partner now, answer in terms of what you think your responses might be. There are no wrong answers to these statements; they're designed simply to increase your understanding of different types of love. For each item, mark "**1**" for "strongly agree," "**2**" for "moderately agree," "**3**" for "neutral," "**4**" for "moderately disagree," and "**5**" for "strongly disagree."

Eros

❑ **1.** My partner and I were attracted to each other immediately after we first met.

❑ **2.** Our lovemaking is very intense and satisfying.

❑ **3.** My partner fits my standards of physical beauty or handsomeness.

Ludus

❑ **4.** What my partner doesn't know about me won't hurt him or her.

❑ **5.** I sometimes have to keep my partner from finding out about other partners.

❑ **6.** I could get over my partner pretty easily and quickly.

Pragma

❑ **7.** In choosing my partner, I believed it was best to love someone with a similar background.

❑ **8.** An important factor in choosing my partner was whether or not he or she would be a good parent.

❑ **9.** One consideration in choosing my partner was how he or she would affect my career.

Agape

❑ **10.** I would rather suffer myself than let my partner suffer.

❑ **11.** My partner can use whatever I own as she or he chooses.

❑ **12.** I would endure all things for the sake of my partner.

Storge

❑ **13.** I expect to always be friends with the people I date.

❑ **14.** The best kind of love grows out of a long friendship.

❑ **15.** Love is a deep friendship, not a mysterious, passionate emotion.

SOURCES: Lasswell and Lasswell, 1976: 211–24; Hendrick and Hendrick, 1992a, 1992b; and Levesque, 1993: 219–50.

The family is usually our earliest and most important source of love and emotional support.

relationships, children acquire the confidence to face the world outside the family (Bodman and Peterson, 1995). Terminally ill patients, AIDS victims, and paraplegics report that they can accept death or cope with their disabilities when they are surrounded by supportive, caring, and loving family members and friends.

Not having a secure base of love, on the other hand, can lead to aggression, hostility, diminished self-confidence, and emotional problems. At least half of all teenage runaways are escaping a lack of love, as evidenced by violence, abuse, or incest. Battered wives become suspicious, fearful, and bitter (see Chapter 14).

Love Enhances Physical Health Numerous studies show a connection between emotions and physical well-being. According to one estimate, about 25 percent of people who visit the doctor have physical symptoms probably due to their emotional state (Roan, 2003).

Chronic stress, due to a demanding job or unloving home life, elevates blood pressure. Arguing or just thinking about a fight also raises blood pressure and produces stress. People who are lonely also tend to have higher blood pressure rates, especially in times of stress. Those in unhappy marriages may be less healthy because stress can change the levels of certain hormones in the blood and weaken the immune system. As a result, people who are stressed out face a higher risk of heart disease and other illnesses (Kiecolt-Glaser and Newton, 2001; Cacioppo et al., 2002; Glynn et al., 2002).

In contrast, positive feelings can contribute to overall better health. Friends, family, and positive relationships over a lifetime can help counteract the normal wear and tear of life as we age. People in their 70s who have had a lot of supportive friends, good relationships with their parents and spouses, and little criticism from their spouses and children suffer from fewer risk factors for diseases and death that include high blood pressure, high cholesterol levels, and abnormal blood sugar metabolism (Seeman et al., 2002).

Love Improves the Quality of Our Lives Love fosters self-esteem. From the solid basis of loving family

Love Invigorates and Uplifts

Love motivates us when life seems bleak. Some of the most popular love stories—*Romeo and Juliet, West Side Story, Camelot,* and *Love Story,* for example—are tragedies. Nevertheless, "they inspire a soaring hope within us that we will find the same magic power of love that has transformed the lives of tragic heroes and heroines" (Douglas and Atwell, 1988: 274). There are many examples of children, parents, and spouses who perform heroic feats or undergo enormous sacrifices because they are motivated by love.

Love Is Fun Without love, life is "a burden and a bore" (Safilios-Rothschild, 1977: 9). Even though love can be extremely painful, it is also enjoyable. Love can be pleasurable and exciting. It is both comforting and fun to plan to see a loved one, to travel together, to write and receive e-mail messages and exchange presents, to share personal activities, to have someone care for you when you are sick or grumpy, and to know that someone will pick you up if your car breaks down. Love is reassuring and comfortable, a diversion from mundane, day-to-day activities.

Overall, then, love and intimacy are critical for our emotional and physical well-being: "When you feel loved, nurtured, cared for, supported, and intimate, you are much more likely to be happier and healthier. You have a much lower risk of getting sick and, if you do, a much greater chance of survival" (Ornish, 1998: 24). In contrast, isolation, loneliness, hostility, anger, depression, and similar feelings often contribute to suffering, disease, and premature death.

Experiencing Love

For most people, caring, trust, respect, and honesty are central to love. There are some differences, however, in the ways men and women conceive of love and express it. In addition, although both heterosexuals and homosexuals share many of the same feelings and behaviors, there are also some differences in their experiences of love.

Are Women or Men More Romantic?

During a recent online discussion, Emily, one of my students, wrote:

> It's important to distinguish the truly romantic men from the "what-do-I-need-to-do-to-get-her-in-bed" romantic men. Truly romantic men do things for you that take a substantial amount of time and energy and involve some sacrifice on their part. For example, for Valentine's Day my boyfriend spent hours making me this absolutely beautiful Valentine's Day card. Now that meant more to me than dinner at a fancy restaurant (Author's files).

Many of the female students in class felt that Emily's boyfriend was an exception. Contrary to such popular opinion, however, many men seem to fall in love faster and are more likely than women to initiate romantic e-mail exchanges (see "Data Digest"). They are just as likely as women, for example, to believe that "To be truly in love is to be in love forever" and that there is only one person "out there" who's meant for them (Popenoe and Whitehead, 2003).

Men are more romantic than women in several other ways. According to a national poll, 17 percent of men compared to 14 percent of women think about a past love every day. And almost one in four men (24 percent), compared with one in ten women (11 percent), say that they have been in love five or more times since they turned 18 (Covel, 2003).

Both women and men link love and sex in their romantic relationships (Hendrick and Hendrick, 2002). Women are more likely to expect some of the trappings of romantic love, however. In recent surveys, for example, whereas 62 percent of men said that "just spending time together" would be an ideal Valentine's celebration, 53 percent of women said they'd probably break up with someone who didn't give them a gift. About 56 percent of the women wanted something sentimental, 15 percent wanted expensive jewelry, 13 percent hoped for a trip to an exotic location, and the rest said they'd be happy with lingerie, chocolates, and similar presents (Yin, 2002; Christenson, 2003).

One of women's biggest complaints is that the men who profess to love them are reluctant to marry. Women sometimes belittle men for being "commitment dodgers," "commitment phobics," "paranoid about commitment," and "afraid of the M word" (Crittenden, 1999; Millner and Chiles, 1999). Romance and commitment are different, however. Men can be very romantic but not necessarily see love as leading to marriage (see Chapter 9).

Are Women or Men More Intimate?

Some years ago, advice columnist Ann Landers sparked a nationwide controversy when she reported that many women prefer being touched, hugged, cuddled, and kissed over having sexual intercourse. When women complain about a lack of intimacy, they usually mean that the man doesn't communicate his thoughts or feelings. Many men believe that such expectations are unfair because they show their intimacy through sex. Whereas many women want to feel close emotionally before being sexual, many men use sex to stimulate emotional closeness (Piorkowski, 1994).

Love relationships and intimacy are complex. For wives, intimacy may mean talking things over. For husbands, as the box "Do I Love You? I Changed Your Oil, Didn't I?" shows, men may feel that *doing* things (such as taking care of the family cars) shows their love. According to one woman, Eddie, her husband, shows his love through "small, everyday courtesies":

> Eddie cleans the bugs off my windshield so I don't have to. He removes all his favorite cassettes from the tape deck in the car and puts mine in before I go to work. . . . At home, he makes sure I have my favorite bottled water in the fridge . . . (Ann Landers, 2001: 3D).

Although the sexes may show their affection differently, there are probably more similarities than differences between the love attitudes of women and men. In a study based on Lee's love typology (see *Table 6.1*), Montgomery and Sorell (1997) analyzed the love attitudes of people aged 17 to 70. The researchers found that the young singles were more likely than the married people to have manic (obsessive) and ludic (playful) attitudes and less likely to endorse agapic (self-sacrificing) attitudes.

Across all groups, however, *both* women and men valued passion (eros), friendship and companionship (storge), and self-sacrifice (agape). As a result, Montgomery and Sorell (1997: 60) question the shallowness of recent popular books (such as Gray's *Men Are from Mars, Women Are from Venus*), which have trumpeted "the radical differences in men's and women's approach to partnering relationships."

"Do I Love You? I Changed Your Oil, Didn't I?"

Are men less loving than women because they equate love with sex and never talk about their feelings? Not according to Francesca Cancian (1990: 171). She maintains that the fault lies not in men but in women's definitions of loving, which ignore masculine styles of showing affection:

We identify love with emotional expression and talking about feelings, aspects of love that women prefer and in which women tend to be more skilled than men. At the same time we often ignore the instrumental and physical aspects of love that men prefer, such as providing help, sharing activities, and sex.

Cancian calls excluding men's ways of showing affection the "feminization of love." Because of this bias, men rarely get credit for the kinds of loving actions that are more typical of them. According to Carol Tavris (1992: 255),

What about all the men . . . who reliably support their families, who put the wishes of other family members ahead of their own preferences, or who act in a moral and considerate way when conflicts arise? Such individuals are surely being mature and loving, even if they are not articulate or do not value "communication."

Thus, many social scientists contend, a man who is a good provider, who changes the oil in his wife's car, or who fixes his child's bike is showing just as much love as the wife who tells her husband she loves him and shares her innermost thoughts and feelings with him. Actions may not "speak louder than words," but they have an equal impact.

According to Cancian, there are several negative consequences of the feminization of love. First, it assumes that women need love more than men and are more dependent on men for emotional satisfaction.

Second, emphasizing only the expressive side of love ignores or diminishes the importance of women's instrumental activities, such as working inside and outside the home.

Finally, the feminization of love intensifies the conflicts over intimacy between women and men. As the woman demands more verbal contact, the man feels increased pressure and withdraws. The woman may then intensify her efforts to get closer.

This leads to a vicious cycle where neither partner gets what she or he wants. As the definition of love becomes more feminized, men and women move farther apart rather than closer together (Tucker, 1992). One way to break this vicious cycle is to give both men and women credit for the things they do to show their love for each other and for their families.

STOP AND THINK . . .

- *Do you agree or disagree with Cancian that women have "feminized" love?*
- *Consider your parents', friends', and your own relationships. Do women and men express their love differently?*

Same-sex Love

In the nineteenth century, friendships were almost exclusively same sex because women's and men's social spheres were rigidly defined (Swain, 1992). Although most of these friendships were not sexual, some were. They were called "romantic friendships" until the twentieth century, when health-care providers began to use such terms as "homosexual" and later "gay" or "lesbian."

Homophobia, the fear and hatred of homosexuals, has decreased in the last decade or so (see Chapter 7). One result is that lesbians and gay men are more likely to openly admit that they are lovers and to participate in commitment ceremonies (see Chapter 9).

Heterosexual and same-sex love are very similar. Regardless of sexual orientation, most partners want to be emotionally close, expect faithfulness, and often plan to grow old together (Clark, 1999). Breakups are generally as painful for same-sex partners as they are for most heterosexual couples. A few years ago, for example, one of my best students was devastated when his partner left. The student's grades plummeted because he was unable to concentrate on his courses. He became depressed and wanted to drop out of college. Because of counseling and supportive friends, he finished his senior year and graduated with honors.

One of the biggest differences between heterosexual and same-sex love is that lesbians and gay men are usually criticized for showing their affection in public. Otherwise, there are more similarities between men and women than between heterosexuals and gays in expressing sexual love (see Chapter 7).

Barriers to Experiencing Love

A number of obstacles can impede our road to love. Some barriers are *macro-level*—for example, the impersonality of mass society, demographic variables, our culture's double standard for men and women, and its emphasis on individualism. Other barriers are *micro-level*—for example, certain kinds of personality characteristics and family experiences.

Understanding some of these obstacles can give us more choices and more control over our decisions and our lives. Recognizing some of the macro-level hurdles, especially, can help us accept some constraints that we can't change.

Mass Society and Demographic Factors

Mass society's burgeoning technologies—such as answering machines, fax machines, electronic mail, and telemarketing services—decrease the opportunities for face-to-face interaction and tend to dehumanize interpersonal communication. In response, as you will see in Chapter 8, a "love industry" has mushroomed. Computerized matchmaking, Internet chat rooms, personal ads, singles bars, speed dating, and dozens of books promise singles that they can find love and counteract the isolation and impersonality of our society.

Demographic variables—such as age, income, and occupation—also shape our love experiences. Because older men tend to marry younger women, older women have a shortage of prospective partners. If women are financially independent, they are less likely to plunge into a relationship, including marriage, because they are unwilling to be burdened with the added housework. In addition, we are unlikely to bump into many prospective romantic relationships because of our jobs: We often work in sex-segregated workplaces or in occupations where people don't socialize across different socioeconomic levels.

The Double Standard

As you saw in Chapter 5, there is still a great deal of discrimination against women. The double standard is one of the most damaging forms of inequality because it often discourages the development of love. Many women feel angry and resentful of men because our society still condones men's having sex without love but labels women who "sleep around" as "sluts" and "tramps." This double standard creates a lack of mutual trust and often leads to playing power games. Men may perceive women as manipulative and demanding, and women may see men as sex-crazed, irresponsible, and domineering.

"Me-First" Individualism

Our cultural values encourage individualism and competition rather than community and cooperation. This emphasis on the individual leads to a preoccupation with self (Bellah et al., 1985; Kass, 1997). We still hear statements like "Look out for Number One" and "If it feels good, do it." Measuring love solely in terms of feeling good leaves us unequipped to handle its hard, painful, or demanding aspects, such as supporting a partner during unemployment or caring for a loved one who has a long-term illness.

Some observers maintain that we have been steeped in narcissistic messages that preach self-improvement, self-actualization, self-aggrandizement, and self-serving behavior, often at the expense of the couple or the family (Elshtain et al., 1993; Wilson, 2002). As a result, these writers argue, there has been an emphasis on fleeting sexual liaisons rather than long-term commitments.

Personality and Family Characteristics

Sometimes individual personality traits or family history get in the way of finding love. Many children, especially girls, whose parents have undergone hostile divorces, report that they are cynical about love or are afraid to fall in love (Rodberg, 1999).

As you saw earlier, some psychologists believe that attachment problems during childhood are replayed in adulthood. For example, children who grow up in a cold and unloving family may be initially suspicious, in adulthood, of potential partners who are warm and loving ("I wonder what she's after"). Or a child who was molested by a family member or relative may be distrustful of future relationships (see Chapter 14). In addition, some parents may be so suffocating that even adult children may never become independent enough to pursue love or marry people who don't meet parental approval.

When Love Goes Wrong

At the beginning of the chapter, I noted that some philosophers believe that self-love promotes love for others. Self-love can also lead to *narcissism*, an inflated love of self that derails romantic relationships. Jealousy and other controlling forms of behavior are also unhealthy and even hazardous to our emotional and physical well-being.

Narcissism: Playing with Love

Narcissists are people who have exaggerated feelings of power and self-importance. They believe that they are unique, smarter, and more attractive than others. Narcissists can be enjoyable dating partners because they can be charming and flattering. Don't expect them, however, to want long-term, committed relationships.

To maintain their dominance in romantic relationships, many narcissists resort to game-playing (ludic) love. Narcissists see themselves as superior to their partners and seek status—a spotlight on themselves—rather than meeting another's needs. As a result, they may be unfaithful, break confidences, and keep partners guessing about their commitment.

If a partner gets fed up with the "me, me, me" self-focus, narcissists aren't bothered by breaking up. Because they have already been cheating, narcissists link up right way with another "trophy" romance in the wings who admires the narcissist. In some cases, narcissists can be dangerous. If they feel social rejection—even outside of dating relationships—narcissists can become angry, aggressive, and even violent (Campbell et al., 2002; Twenge and Campbell, 2003).

Jealousy: Trying to Control Love

Typically, people experience *jealousy* when they believe that a rival is competing for a lover's affection. The jealous person feels threatened and is suspicious of his or her partner, often obsessive, and often angry and resentful. Some people are even jealous of their partner's spending time with family members, relatives, or hobbies (Brehm, 1992).

Why Are Lovers Jealous?

Love flourishes when it is based on trust and respect for the other's individuality. In contrast, jealousy is usually an unhealthy manifestation of insecurity, low self-confidence, and possessiveness (Douglas and Atwell, 1988; Farrell, 1997). Because all of us have some of these traits, why are some of us more jealous than others?

Jealous people tend to depend heavily on their partners for their own self-esteem, consider themselves inadequate as mates, and feel that they are more deeply involved in their relationship than their partners are. For example, college students who grew up in homes with continuous parental conflict or rejecting, overprotective parents are more likely than their counterparts to report jealousy and fears of abandonment in their love relationships (Hayashi and Strickland, 1998).

In some cases, people who are jealous often have been or are still unfaithful to their partners. They distrust a partner because of their own cheating. In other cases, rivalry triggers jealousy. A staple of sitcom romances is that a little bit of jealousy is good for a relationship: It reminds a partner not to take the loved one for granted. Often, however, the rivals already resent each other for other reasons (jobs, income, attractiveness, and the like). When a rival turns her or his attention to a romantic partner, jealousy becomes especially hostile and consuming (Solomon, 2002).

Are Women or Men More Jealous?

There is ongoing debate about this question. For *evolutionary psychologists*, jealousy is innately different in men and women. According to this perspective, jealousy evolved a million or so years ago. Men worried about sexual infidelity because if they were cuckolded, they might unknowingly end up raising someone else's child rather than passing down their own genes.

In contrast, women were more concerned about their partners' emotional—rather than sexual—entanglements. If a man became emotionally attached to other women, who would bring home the food and ensure their children's chances of survival? Thus, according to evolutionary psychologists, twice as many men as women report being more upset by imagining their partners' "enjoying passionate sexual intercourse" with other people than by imagining their partners' "forming a deep emotional attachment" (Buss et al., 1996; Buss, 2000).

Some psychologists have challenged evolutionary perspectives on methodological grounds (see Chapter 2). According to DeSteno and his colleagues (2002), for example, the "evolutionary chisel" has found differences between women and men because the research forced respondents into an "either/or" answer: "Do you feel more threatened with sexual *or* emotional infidelity?" In addition, evolutionary approaches have relied on samples of college students, whose responses are not representative of the larger population.

Some researchers also contend that evolutionary studies are limited because they ask only hypothetical questions ("How would you feel *if* your partner were unfaithful?"). When Harris (2003) asked people (other than college students) about their *actual* experiences, she found that men and women—heterosexual and gay—were more jealous of emotional rather than sexual infidelity. Harris speculates that people are more jealous about a mate's emotional affairs for two reasons. First, they blame themselves ("Maybe I don't satisfy her or him sexually"). Second, they see an emotional affair as more threatening because it could develop into a long-term relationship. And a long-term relationship may produce offspring who compete for the father's affection and resources.

Jealousy and Stalking

Some jealous lovers become obsessed. They constantly daydream about the person, make numerous phone calls, send flowers, cards, gifts, and love letters, or continuously check up on their partner's whereabouts.

Stalking is a serious problem. California passed the first antistalking law in 1990. By the mid-1990s, all 50 states had adopted similar legislation. Unfortunately, these laws rarely discourage suitors (almost always men) from threatening, harassing, or even killing those who reject them.

We often hear about people who stalk celebrities—like the man who scaled the 8-foot wall around pop star Madonna's property or the woman who broke into the home of talk show host David Letterman. However, most stalking involves formerly married (or romantically involved) average people. One in 12 women and one in 45 men have been stalked at some time in their life. According to the best available statistics, 70 to 80 percent of all stalking cases involve men who hound women ("Stalking," 2000).

Cyberstalking involves threatening behavior or unwanted advances toward someone using e-mail, instant messaging, and other electronic communications devices. Many chat rooms may evolve into offline stalking, including abusive or harassing phone calls, vandalism, threatening or obscene mail, trespassing, and physical assault ("Cyberstalking," 2000).

According to the U.S. Department of Justice (2001), the incidence of cyberstalking has been increasing. And, as in offline stalking, the majority of cases involve former intimates, most of the victims are women, and the stalkers are generally motivated by the desire to control the woman. Cyberstalking is sometimes more dangerous than offline stalking because the perpetrators can be anywhere in the country, a stalker can post inflammatory messages on bulletin boards and in chat rooms, and electronic communications are difficult to trace.

Is Jealousy Universal? Although it is widespread, jealousy is not universal. Surveying two centuries of anthropological reports, Hupka (1991) found two types of cultures: one in which jealousy was rare (for example, the Todas of southern India) and one in which jealousy was common (for example, the Apache Indians of North America).

Toda culture discouraged possessiveness of material objects or people. It placed few restrictions on sexual gratification, and it did not make marriage a condition for women's social recognition. In contrast, Apache society prized virginity, paternity, and fidelity. While an Apache man was away from home, for example, he had a close relative keep secret watch over his wife and report on her behavior when he returned. Based on the variations he found across cultures, Hupka concluded that jealousy is neither universal nor innate. Instead, jealousy is more common in societies where women are regarded as "property" and where expressing jealousy is culturally acceptable.

Other Types of Controlling Behavior

Jealousy is not the only type of unhealthy, controlling behavior in love relationships. Threatening the withdrawal of love or creating guilt feelings can be deeply distressing. Inflicting severe emotional and physical abuse can also be devastating.

"If You Loved Me . . ." One of the most common pressures for sex (especially by men) is to accuse someone of not loving them: "If you *really* loved me, you'd show it." People threaten to withdraw love to manipulate other behavior as well.

Faculty have many stories, for example, about students who choose majors they hate because they don't want to disappoint parents who insist that they become a doctor, a lawyer, an accountant, and so on. I've seen women drop out of college because their husbands or boyfriends accused them of placing more importance on earning their degrees than on maintaining their homes, preparing dinner, and being free on weekends instead of "always studying."

Essentially, controlling people want power over others. They use "love" to manipulate and exploit those who care about them. With pressure and ultimatums, they force partners to sacrifice their own interests. Whether such control is well intentioned or malicious, it ensures the controller's happiness, not the well-being of the person being manipulated.

Controllers are not all alike: "A wealthy executive may use money and influence, while an attractive person may use physical allure and sex" to manipulate another (Jones and Schechter, 1992: 11). Moreover, as the box "If This Is Love, Why Do I Feel So Bad?" shows, controllers use a variety of strategies in dominating a relationship. They may also switch strategies from time to time to keep the controlled person off balance.

The Guilt Trip People often use guilt to justify actions that have nothing to do with love. It is not uncommon for parents, especially, to rely on the love and guilt complex to influence children's behavior: "If you cared about me, you'd go to college. I've made a lot of sacrifices to save up for your education"; or "If you marry that Catholic [or Jew or Protestant], how can I face Rabbi Katz [or Mr. Beirne or Father Mulcahey] again!"

Such concerns may be well founded because a college education is a good investment, and marriage outside one's religious group often creates problems. The danger, however, is that the parents' attitudes may be driven by their own needs rather than their children's. At lower socioeconomic levels, especially, a parent can attain higher status in the community because of a child's educational or occupational achievements (see Chapter 4).

The guilt trip does not end when children become adults. Older parents and relatives sometimes use guilt to manipulate middle-aged children. One of the most disabling guilt trips is the "affection myth," in which children are taught that love is synonymous with caregiving. Children and grandchildren may feel that, regardless of their own circumstances, they must care for needy elderly family members at home. As a result, younger family members sometimes endure enormous stress, even though their elderly relatives would get much better medical care at a skilled nursing facility (see Chapter 17).

Emotional and Physical Abuse Love is sometimes used to justify severe emotional or physical neglect and abuse, but violence is *never* a manifestation of love (see Chapter 14). A partner who is sarcastic or controlling, a parent who severely spanks or verbally humiliates a child—such people are not expressing love for the child's "own good," as they often insist. They are simply being angry and brutal.

If This Is Love, Why Do I Feel So Bad?

If you feel bad, what you're experiencing may be *control*, not love (Clarke, 1990). Controllers use whatever tactics are necessary to maintain power over another person: nagging, cajoling, coaxing, flattery, charm, threats, self-pity, blame, insults, or humiliation.

In the worst cases, controllers may physically injure and even murder people who refuse to be controlled. As you read this brief list (based on Jones and Schechter, 1992: 16–22), check any items that seem familiar to you. Individually, the items may seem unimportant, but if you check off more than two or three, you may be dealing with a controller instead of forging your own choices in life.

❑ My partner calls me names: "dummy," "jackass," "whore," "creep," "bitch," "moron."

❑ My partner always criticizes me and makes even a compliment sound like

a criticism: "This is the first good dinner you've cooked in months."

❑ Always right, my partner continually corrects things I say or do. If I'm five minutes late, I'm scared my partner will be mad.

❑ My partner withdraws into silence, and I have to figure out what I've done wrong and apologize for it.

❑ My partner is jealous when I talk to new people.

❑ My partner often phones or unexpectedly comes by the place I work to see if I'm "okay."

❑ My partner acts very cruelly and then says I'm too sensitive and can't take a joke.

❑ When I try to express my opinion about something, my partner either doesn't respond, walks away, or makes fun of me.

❑ I have to account for every dime I spend, but my partner keeps me in the dark about our bank accounts.

❑ My partner says that if I ever leave he or she will commit suicide and I'll be responsible.

❑ When my partner has a temper tantrum, he or she says it's my fault or the children's.

❑ My partner makes fun of my body.

❑ Whether my partner is with us or not, he or she is jealous of every minute I spend with my family or other relatives or friends.

❑ My partner grills me about what happened whenever I go out.

❑ My partner makes sexual jokes about me in front of the children and other people.

❑ My partner throws things at me, hits, shoves, or pushes me.

According to Gelles and Cornell (1990: 20), "the most insidious aspect of family violence" is that children grow up unable to distinguish between love and violence and believe "that it is acceptable to hit the people you love." The film *What's Love Got to Do with It?*, based on singer Tina Turner's biography, dramatically portrays Turner's enduring many years of violence because she believed that doing so proved her love and commitment to her husband, Ike.

Other "Perverse" Reasons for Love Some people are in love for "dubious and downright perverse reasons" (Solomon, 2002). In many cases, we profess love even though we are really afraid of being alone or coping with changes (such as meeting new people after breaking up). Or we might stay in a bad relationship because we want to avoid a partner's hostility after breaking up.

In other cases, we don't want to hurt someone's feelings by telling them we don't love them. And if we promise to "love, honor, and obey" (although most couples have

deleted "obey" from their marital vows), we feel an obligation to love even though our love has dwindled over the years (or we never really loved the person to begin with). In addition, is it really realistic to "promise" to love someone for the next 40 to 50 years?

Unrequited Love

In unrequited love, one does not reciprocate another's romantic feelings. Why does this happen? There are several reasons. First, a person may "fall upward" in love. That is, someone who's "average" in appearance may fall in love with someone who's gorgeous. As you will see in Chapter 8, people tend to choose others of similar degrees of attractiveness to date and marry. Therefore, love for someone who is much more attractive may go unrequited.

The rebuff is especially painful if the person being rejected senses that physical appearance is the major reason for being cast aside (Baumeister and Wotman, 1992). We often hear both women and men complain that the object of their affections "never took the time to get to know me," implying that such things as personality, intelligence, and common interests should be more important than looks.

Second, unrequited love may be the outcome when only one of the partners wants to move from hooking up or casual dating to a serious romance. It can be very upsetting, even traumatic, to realize that the person one is dating, and perhaps having sexual relations with, is in it "just for the fun of it" (ludic lovers, including narcissists) and does not want to become more serious or exclusive.

Some people wait, sometimes for years, to have someone love them back. They assume that the situation "is bound to get better" (Duck, 1998). Forget about it. It's emotionally and physically healthier to let go of an unrequited love and develop relationships with people who care about you.

MAKING CONNECTIONS

■ Are you a narcissist? If not, have you gone out with a narcissist? If so, how long did the relationship last? Did you enjoy the relationship in some ways?

■ Have you ever dumped someone? Or has someone broken up with you? If you were dumped, how did you deal with the situation? If you were the "dumper," how did you cut the strings?

How Couples Change: Romantic and Long-term Love

Romantic love can be both exhilarating and disappointing. In contrast, long-term love provides security and constancy.

Some Characteristics of Romantic Love

According to Tennov (cited in Hatfield, 1983: 114), romantic love is usually a passionate and dizzying experience:

■ Lovers find it impossible to work, study, or do anything but think about the beloved.

■ Their moods fluctuate wildly; they are ecstatic when they hope they might be loved, despairing when they feel they're not.

■ They find it impossible to believe that they could ever love again.

■ They fantasize about how their partners will declare their love.

■ They care so desperately about the other that nothing else matters; they are willing to sacrifice anything for love.

■ Their love is "blind," and they idealize each other.

Thus, romantic love is idealized, emotional, passionate, and sometimes melodramatic. Romantic love might also be self-absorbed and self-serving. As you saw earlier, for example, narcissistic romantic love relies on enhancing one's self-esteem rather than expressing interest in one's partner ("Tell me what else you like about *me*" versus "How are *you* doing?").

People from other cultures often see romantic love as bizarre and frivolous, but Western countries take it very seriously (see "Data Digest"). Romantic love is considered the most legitimate reason for dating, living together, getting married, or getting a divorce ("the spark is gone"). Romantic love thrives on two beliefs—love at first sight and fate.

Love at First Sight Romantic love was less common in the United States in the 1800s than it is today for three reasons: Life expectancy was short, living in isolated towns and homes made it difficult to meet a variety of people, and most people did not live long enough

Reprinted by permission of Johnny Hart and Creators Syndicate, Inc.

Unique to Romantic Love	Common to Both	Unique to Long-term Love
• Romantic Walks • Obsession • Longing • Candlelit Trysts • Going Out For Dinner • Picnics and Sunsets • Playfulness • Fantasy • Physical Attraction • Loss of Sleep • Ecstasy	• Trust • Caring • Communication • Honesty • Friendship • Respect • Understanding • Having Fun Together • Passion (but More Intense in Romantic Love)	• Patience • Independence • Putting Other before Self • Possibility of Marriage • Making Other Feel Wanted

FIGURE 6.3 **Romantic Love and Long-term Love: Similar but Different** Try to rate your own relationship, if you are currently involved with someone, according to the characteristics shown here. Is your relationship one of romantic love? Or long-term love? Try to rate other relationships between people you know as well.

SOURCE: Based on Fehr, 1993, pp. 87–120.

to fall in love more than once. Today, with increased life spans, geographic mobility, and high divorce rates, we may fall in love with many people during our lifetime.

It's not surprising that more than half of Americans believe in love at first sight (see "Data Digest"). Unlike most of our everyday feelings, such love is fun and exciting and has an air of mystery. In addition, love at first sight typically overtakes people who not only are very lonely and starved for physical affection but who also have had little experience with love and sex (Douglas and Atwell, 1988).

Experience, however limited, may dampen beliefs about love at first sight. In a study of undergraduates, for example, Knox and his associates (1999) found that young college students (age 19 and under) were significantly more likely to believe in love at first sight and that "love conquers all" than older students (age 20 and over). This may also be one reason why people who are now in their 60s are less likely than those in their 20s to believe that love isn't everything it's cracked up to be (see "Data Digest").

Fate Some people see fate as an important component of romantic love. Songs tell us that "you were meant for me" and "that old black magic has me in its spell." In reality, fate has little to do with romantic love. Romantic love is typically ignited not by fate but by such factors as similar socioeconomic background, physical attractiveness, and a need for intimacy (Shea and Adams, 1984; Benassi, 1985).

Love in Long-term Relationships

Some characteristics of romantic and long-term love overlap. As *Figure 6.3* shows, both reflect such attributes as trust, understanding, and honesty. There are also some striking differences.

First, romantic love is simple, whereas lasting love is more complicated. It takes much less effort to plan a romantic evening than to be patient with a partner day after day, year after year. Thus, it's easier to fall in love than to stay in love.

Second, romantic love is self-centered, whereas long-term love is altruistic. For example, romantic lovers are often swept away by their own fantasies and obsessions, but lasting love often requires putting the other before oneself and making the partner feel cherished.

Third, romantic love is short-lived because love changes over time. Flaws that seemed "cute" during a whirlwind courtship may become unbearable a year after the wedding. For example, his dumpy furniture may have seemed quaint until she realized that he refuses to spend any money on home furnishings. And values, especially religious values, become increasingly important after the birth of the first child (Trotter, 1986).

Fourth, long-term love grows and develops, whereas romantic love is typically immature. For example, romantic lovers often feel insecure about themselves or the relationship. As a result, one of the partners may demand constant attention, a continuous display of affection, and daily "I love you" reassurances (Dilman, 1998). Most of us appreciate tokens of love, verbal or behavioral. However, never-ending and self-absorbed commands such as "prove to me that you love me" can become tedious, annoying, exasperating, and alienating.

Fifth, companionate (storgic) love is most characteristic of long-term relationships, compared with passion and game-playing in romantic love. Those who are the happiest describe their love as companionate (feeling of togetherness, of connectedness, sharing, and supporting each other) or committed. Committed lovers, ruled by the head as much as the heart, are faithful to each other and plan their future together (Hecht et al., 1994).

CHOICES

Helping Love Flourish

Several practitioners (Hendrix, 1988; Osherson, 1992) have suggested some "rules" for creating a loving environment. Although the rules do not guarantee everlasting love, they are worth considering:

- Relationships do not just happen; we create them. Good relationships are the result of conscious effort and work.

- One partner should be pleased, rather than threatened, by the other partner's successes or triumphs.

- A lover is not a solution to a problem. Love may be one of life's greatest experiences, but it is not life itself.

- Love is about acceptance: being sympathetic to another's flaws and cherishing the person's other characteristics that are special and lovable.

- Lovers are not mind readers. Open communication is critical.

- It is not what you say; it is what you do. Quite often, communication is used to manipulate, induce guilt, or place blame, even though it is presented as positive and loving. Communication can be, and very often is, a weapon.

- Stable relationships are always changing. We must learn to deal with both our own changes as individuals and the changes we see in our mates.

- Love is poisoned by infidelity. If a loved one is deceived, it may be impossible to reestablish trust and respect.

- Blame is irresponsible. It discourages communication, makes people feel angry, and damages self-esteem.

- Giving is contagious. People who feel loved, accepted, and valued are more likely to treat others in a similar manner.

- Love does not punish; it forgives. It may be difficult to forget cruel words or acts, but forgiveness is essential in continuing a healthy relationship.

- Even though partners are very close, they must respect the other person's independence and his or her right to develop personal interests and other friendships.

Finally, demographic variables play a role in sustaining love. In an analysis of two national polls, Smith (1994: 34) found an association between socioeconomic status and long-term relationships: "Having enough income to be out of poverty may alleviate financial problems enough to reduce stress and thereby facilitate feelings of love." So, although money may not buy love, its absence encourages falling out of love.

Piorkowski (1994: 286) describes healthy, long-term love as follows:

Happy couples have similar values, attitudes, interests, and to some degree, personality traits. They also share a philosophy of life, religion, vision, or passion that keeps them marching together in spite of minor differences. In addition, they are autonomous, fair-minded, emotionally responsive individuals who trust one another and love spending time together, especially in communication with one another. Because they are separate selves, they also enjoy spending time apart to *solidify their own individuality without feeling threatened by potential loss or abandonment.*

For more thoughts on how to achieve a satisfying, lasting relationship, see the box "Helping Love Flourish."

A Global View

Although people in all known societies have intimate and loving relationships, expressing love varies across countries and cultures. In Western societies that emphasize individualism, love is a self-choice that may or may not result in marriage. In cultures that stress the group and the community, arrangements between families are more important than romantic love.

Romantic Love

Anthropologists Jankowiak and Fischer (1992) found evidence of romantic love in 89 percent of the 166 cultures they studied. They concluded that romantic love is not a product of Western culture but constitutes "a human, universal, or at the least a near-universal" phenomenon.

Researchers have found variations of romantic love in a number of societies. In China, Hong Kong, and Taiwan, for example, love styles include passionate love, casual love, companionate love, and a belief in predestined love. Many Hawaiians, regardless of country of origin, are similar in feeling that companionate and passionate love are important (Doherty et al., 1994; Cho and Cross, 1995; Goodwin and Findlay, 1997).

Despite images of the French as being flirtatious and romantic, Murstein and his associates (1991) found that American college students were more likely to endorse emotional (manic) love, whereas French students emphasized agape, or compassionate and self-sacrificing love. The researchers suggested that the predominance of Catholics in the French sample might have accounted for their higher scores on agape.

Several studies suggest that romance is least important in societies where kin ties take precedence over conjugal relationships. In Burma, India, and Mexico, for example, college students said that storgic, agapic, and pragmatic love were more desirable than manic, erotic, and ludic love styles (Leon et al., 1994). In China, similarly, love is tempered by recognition that a match would need parental approval (Moore, 1998).

"Arranged Love"

In many countries, respect for parents' wishes, family traditions, and duty to the kin group are more important than romantic love. In much of India, Hindu children are taught that love should follow an arranged marriage. There are variations across regions and social class, however. Most middle- and upper-middle-class women can marry whomever they want. Many prefer arranged marriages and have veto power over undesirable candidates.

Arranged marriages are attractive because they offer stability. According to one highly educated woman in Calcutta, India, who has been happily married for three years to a man in an arranged marriage, love isn't essential for marital happiness: "I met a lot of people I liked, but no one was suitable for marriage, because I was looking for practicality also. Love is important, but it's not sufficient" (Lakshmanan, 1997: 2A).

In arranged marriages in Sri Lanka, men and women who fall in love usually let their parents know their choices in advance (de Munck, 1998). In Canada, some second-generation Muslim Pakistani women are "rebelling" against arranged marriages. Others participate willingly because they can't find a suitable partner on their own and feel that their parents know best (Zaidi and Shuraydi, 2002).

Romance can blossom even in cultures where marriages are strictly arranged. Many Arab states celebrate Valentine's Day "with much fanfare." In 2002, however, Saudi Arabia officially banned Valentine's Day, prohibiting shops from selling red roses and couples from displaying tokens of affection ("Valentine's a 'Worthless' Day?," 2002). A year later, Iranian police ordered shops in Tehran to remove heart-and-flower decorations, images of couples embracing, and other "corrupt" materials that symbolize "decadent" Western holidays ("Police in Iran . . .," 2003). In Saudi Arabia and some other Middle Eastern countries, public embracing between men and women is taboo, and the sexes cannot mix in public.

Love is important across societies. It may manifest itself differently across cultures and historical eras, but, "overall, people are more similar than different" (Hendrick and Hendrick, 2003: 1065).

MAKING CONNECTIONS

■ Have you ever experienced love at first sight? If so, was the person similar to you in physical appearance or very different? How long did the love last? Why do you think that some people are more likely to fall in love at first sight than others?

■ In arranged marriages, factors such as social class, religion, and ethnicity are seen as more important than romantic love or physical attraction. If Americans endorsed "arranged love," do you think that our divorce rates would decrease?

Conclusion

When love is healthy, it *changes* how we feel about others and ourselves. Love can inspire us and motivate us to care for family members, friends, and lovers. Love also creates *choices* in finding happiness during dating, marriage, and old age. There are *constraints,* however, because we sometimes confuse love with jealousy or controlling behavior.

Love is essential to human growth and development, but it is often shrouded in myths and surrounded by formidable barriers. For those who are willing to learn and to work at it, love is attainable and can be long-lasting. Do love and sex go together? Not always. We examine this and related issues in the next chapter.

SUMMARY

1. Love is a complex phenomenon that varies in degree and intensity between people and across social contexts. Minimally necessary for a loving relationship are a willingness to accommodate the other, to accept shortcomings, and to have as much concern about the other's well-being as about one's own.

2. Friendship is the root of love. Both share characteristics such as trust, respect, honesty, and mutual support.

3. Caring, intimacy (including self-disclosure), and commitment form the foundations of love. These characteristics strengthen relationships and help love flourish.

4. There are many approaches to understanding love and loving. Attachment theory posits that warm, secure, loving relationships in infancy are essential to forming loving relationships in adulthood. Reiss described four stages of love: rapport, self-revelation, mutual dependency, and personality need fulfillment. Sternberg focused on the relationships between passion, intimacy, and decision/commitment. Lee described six styles of loving, and exchange theorists see love as a process of mutually beneficial transactions.

5. Love serves many functions, and people fall in love for a variety of reasons. Availability of partners is one determining factor. Others include a wish to have children, survival, quality of life, inspiration, and just plain fun.

6. In contrast to popular beliefs, men are usually just as romantic as women and suffer more when a relationship ends. Women are more likely to express their love verbally and to work at a relationship, but they are also more pragmatic about moving on when love goes awry. There are more similarities than differences, however, in women's and men's love relationships.

7. There are many obstacles to love. Macro-level barriers include the depersonalization of mass society, demographic factors, a double standard, our society's emphasis on individual advancement, its negative view of gay and lesbian love, and family pressures. Micro-level obstacles include personality characteristics and childhood experiences.

8. Several kinds of negative and controlling behavior can kill love. Narcissism and jealousy are usually destructive and sometimes even dangerous. Other harmful forms of love include threatening people with the withdrawal of love, using guilt trips, and causing physical and emotional pain.

9. In our society, romantic love or its loss is generally the basis for cohabitation, marriage, and divorce. Although romantic love can be exhilarating, it is often short-lived and can be disappointing. In contrast to romantic love, long-term love is secure and constant and adapts over the life course.

10. There is a great deal of variation in expressing love attitudes across cultures. Some societies embrace love. Others view love as less important than marrying someone who meets with parental and kin approval.

KEY TERMS

TAKING IT FURTHER

Love and Romance in Cyberspace

Want to find out how romantic you are? Whether you and your partner are compatible? Here are a few self-assessment and other sites that you might enjoy:

Romance on the Air provides an *Interactive Romantic Survey* to see how romantic and sensitive you really are. It also includes *Romantic Stories for Some Inspiration,* a humor section, and an advice column.

members.aol.com/wakkarotti/romance.htm

Words of Love has a lovely array of Shakespeare's sonnets, songs, and witticisms about love.

www.randomhouse.com/wordsoflove

Valentines on the Web is "Dedicated to the One I Love." Netters can send Valentine cards that include both Websites and personal messages.

home.aristotle.net/valentines

Love Test, constructed by Betty Harris and Jim Glover, will remind you of Sternberg's and Lee's measures of love. You can take the *Concept of Love* quiz or the *Experience of Love* questionnaire and will receive an "analysis" of your (and your partner's) love styles after you submit the answers. It's fun!

dataguru.org/love/lovetest/findings

TheRomantic.com offers "1000s of Creative Ideas & Expert Advice on Love, Dating & Romance."

http://www.theromantic.com

And more: www.prenhall.com/benokraitis provides numerous other sites on the topics covered in this chapter. Some offer resources for stalking victims. Others are great diversions when you need a break from studying or writing papers: love quizzes, Valentine's Day and e-card sites, a collection of loving and nasty valentines that Victorian Americans sent their lovers and ex-lovers, and several anti–Valentine's Day URLs.

INVESTIGATE WITH RESEARCH NAVIGATOR

Research Navigator.com
RESOURCES FOR COLLEGE RESEARCH ASSIGNMENTS

Please go to www.researchnavigator.com and enter your LOGIN NAME and PASSWORD. For instructions on registering for the first time, please view the detailed instructions at the end of Chapter 1. Please search the Research Navigator™ site using the following key search terms:

intimacy
attachment theory
love

Sexuality
and Sexual Expression
throughout Life

DATADIGEST

- About 56 percent of adolescents ages 13 to 18 say that they want to **abstain from sex until they marry.**

- In the United States, **nearly one in five adolescents has had sexual intercourse before age 15.**

- Among people ages 15 to 24, **75 percent are misinformed about safer sex.** More than one-third, for example, don't know that they can get STDs and HIV through oral sex.

- More than 80 percent of adults are concerned about the **portrayal on television** of verbal references to sex, visual images of nudity or seminudity, premarital sex, and extramarital sex.

- Worldwide, **42 million people are estimated to be living with HIV/AIDS.** In 2002, more than 3 million died of AIDS, including 1.2 million women and 610,000 children under 15. The largest number of deaths was in sub-Saharan Africa (2.4 million).

SOURCES: Santelli et al., 2000; Morse, 2002; World Health Organization, 2002; Albert et al., 2003; Holt et al., 2003.

In the movie *Annie Hall,* a therapist asks two lovers how often they have sex. The character played by Woody Allen answers, "Hardly ever, maybe three times a week." The character played by Diane Keaton replies, "Constantly, three times a week."

As this anecdote illustrates, sex is more important for some people than others. Besides physical contact, sex provides an opportunity to express loyalty, passion, and affection. Culture shapes our sexual development, attitudes, and actions. Sexual behavior changes throughout life and varies over the years. In addition, cross-cultural research shows that there is great latitude in defining what is "normal" or "abnormal." Before you read any further, take the quiz in the "How Much Do You Know about Sex?" box on page 168.

Sexuality and Human Development

Our sexuality is much more complex than just physical contact. It is the product of our sexual identity, sexual orientation, and sexual scripts.

Sexual Identity

Our *sexual identity* is an awareness of ourselves as male or female and the way we express our sexual values, attitudes, feelings, and beliefs. It is part of how we define who we are and what roles we play. Sexual identity involves placing oneself in a category created by society (such as female and heterosexual) and learning, both consciously and unconsciously, how to act.

Sexuality is a multidimensional concept that incorporates psychological, biological, and sociological

167

ASKYOURSELF

How Much Do You Know about Sex?

After reading each question, choose the correct answer.

1. Birth-control pills offer protection from sexually transmitted diseases (STDs). ☐ True ☑ False

2. Out of every ten married American men, how many would you estimate have ever had an extramarital affair—that is, have been sexually unfaithful to their wives?
   - **a.** Fewer than one out of ten
   - **b.** One out of ten (10 percent)
   - →**c.** About two out of ten (20 percent)
   - **d.** About three out of ten (30 percent)
   - **e.** About four out of ten (40 percent)
   - **f.** About five out of ten (50 percent)
   - **g.** About six out of ten (60 percent)
   - **h.** More than six out of ten

3. If your partner is truly meant for you, sex is easy and wonderful. ☑ True ☐ False

4. Petroleum jelly, skin lotion, and baby oil are good lubricants to use with a condom or diaphragm. ☑ True ☐ False

5. About 10 percent of the U.S. population is exclusively homosexual. ☑ True ☐ False

6. A woman or teenage girl can get pregnant during her menstrual flow (her period). ☑ True ☐ False

7. A woman or teenage girl cannot get pregnant if the man withdraws his penis before he ejaculates. ☐ True ☑ False

8. Douching is an effective method of birth control. ☐ True ☑ False

9. A person can become infected with an STD only when a partner's symptoms are visible. ☐ True ☑ False

10. Menopause, or change of life, causes most women to lose interest in having sex. ☐ True ☑ False

11. What do you think is the length of the average man's erect penis?
    - **a.** 2–4 inches
    - **b.** 5–7 inches
    - **c.** 8–9 inches
    - **d.** 10–11 inches
    - **e.** 12 inches or longer

12. Which of the following STDs do experts call "the silent epidemic"?
    - **a.** scabies
    - **b.** genital herpes
    - **c.** syphilis
    - **d.** chlamydia

(Answers are on page 171.)

---

components such as sexual desire, sexual response, and gender roles (Bernhard, 1995). *Sexual desire* refers to the sexual drive that makes us receptive to sexual activity. *Sexual response* encompasses the biological aspects of sexuality that include experiencing pleasure or orgasm. <u>*Gender roles* reflect the behavior that women and men enact according to culturally prescribed expectations</u> (see Chapter 5).

In a typical situation, a man may be aroused by a woman's cleavage because our society considers breasts sexy (sexual desire), experience an erection (sexual response), and may take the initiative in having sexual intercourse with a woman he finds attractive (gender roles). However, what if the man is aroused by other men rather than women?

Sexual Orientation

Our sexual identity incorporates a **sexual orientation** or a preference for sexual partners of the same sex, of the opposite sex, or of both sexes. **Homosexuals** (from the Greek root *homo*, meaning "same") are sexually attracted to people of the same sex. **Heterosexuals**, often called *straight*, are attracted to partners of the opposite sex. Male homosexuals prefer to be called *gay*; female homosexuals are called *lesbians*. **Bisexuals**, sometimes called *bis*, are attracted to members of both sexes. *Coming out* is a person's public announcement of a gay or lesbian sexual orientation.

Sexual orientation is more complicated than simply identifying oneself as homosexual, heterosexual, or bisexual. Kinsey and his colleagues (1948) devised a 7-point rating scale to describe a person's overt sexual experiences and psychological reactions (such as fantasies). The continuum ranged from people who identified themselves as exclusively heterosexual to those who said they were exclusively homosexual. The five categories in between included people who viewed themselves as heterosexual but had had homosexual experiences, bisexuals, and gays who had had heterosexual experiences.

Although heterosexuality is the predominant sexual orientation, homosexuality exists in all known societies (see the box "Homosexuality in Non-Western Cultures"). Many gays and lesbians deny or try to suppress their sexual preference because our society is still characterized by heterosexism. *Heterosexism* is a belief that heterosexuality is superior to and more "natural" than homosexuality.

According to some estimates, about 2 percent of Americans are *transgendered* (Gorman, 1995). This term encompasses several groups:

- *Transsexuals*: people born one sex biologically but who choose to live their life as another sex—either by consistently cross-dressing or surgically altering their sex (see Chapter 5)

- *Intersexuals*: people whose medical diagnosis at birth is not clearly male or female

- *Transvestites*: people who cross-dress at times but don't necessarily consider themselves a member of the opposite sex

Transgendered people include gays, heterosexuals, bisexuals, and men and women who don't identify themselves with any specific gender category.

Homosexuality in Non-Western Cultures

In their classic studies, Ford and Beach (1972) examined data on 190 societies in Oceania, Eurasia, Africa, North America, and South America. They drew three conclusions about homosexuality: (1) social attitudes toward homosexuality diverge widely; (2) homosexuality occurs in all societies regardless of societal reactions; and (3) males seem more likely than females to engage in homosexual activity.

In the eighteenth and nineteenth centuries, missionaries, travelers, anthropologists, and colonists ignored same-sex relationships in many African countries or described them as "the foulest of crimes" among "savages." Despite many attempts to repress homosexuality and to "save the natives," homosexuality is common today in many parts of Africa. For example, woman-to-woman marriage has been documented in more than 30 African populations, including at least 9 groups in southern Africa (Carrier and Murray, 1998).

In China, both homosexuality and bisexuality date back to at least the Bronze Age (Hinsch, 1990). According to some estimates, 100 million Chinese, or 7 percent of the country's population, are gay ("*Reuters* highlights . . .," 2002). Although Chinese officials disapprove of homosexuality, Chinese psychiatrists have recently stopped classifying homosexuality as a mental disease (Chu, 2001). Several magazines are devoted to gay life, Internet chat rooms are burgeoning, and some gays and lesbians have celebrated "wedding ceremonies" although these marriages are not legally recognized (Pomfret, 2000).

Homosexuality is tolerated more in some countries than others:

- In Egypt, gays are arrested and may serve up to five years in prison for "habitual debauchery" and "contempt of religion" (Gauch, 2002: 7).
- In Afghanistan, homosexuality—including with young boys—has "long

been a clandestine feature of life" even though not practiced openly (Smith, 2002A: 4).

- Although gays aren't prosecuted, two-thirds of South Koreans believe that homosexuality is wrong and sinful. The most powerful force against homosexuality is Confucian beliefs, which stress ancestor worship and the continuity of families along bloodlines. Where even adoptions are unpopular, homosexuality, especially, threatens a family's permanence (Prusher, 2001).
- There is considerable variation in Latin America. Gay relationships are fairly open in some cities. In other cases, government and university officials define homosexuality as an illness that can and should be "cured" (Parker and Cáceres, 1999; Chauvin, 2002).

Like their heterosexual counterparts, most gay and lesbian parents are proud of their children and offer loving homes. In this Gay Pride Parade in New York City, fathers demonstrate their committed role as parents and affirm their identity as homosexuals.

Transgendered people are becoming increasingly more visible and accepted. A few years ago, for example, San Francisco approved health insurance to cover sex change operations, hormonal treatments, and any related costs. In higher education, Wesleyan University designated a "gender-blind" hall—the first transgender college housing in the nation—for students who don't want to categorize themselves as males or females. And Australia has become the first country in the world to issue a passport that lists a person's sex as "indeterminate" (Butler, 2003; Hoover, 2003).

What Determines Sexual Orientation? No one knows why we are heterosexual, gay, or bisexual. *Biological theories* maintain that sexual orientation has a strong genetic basis (Burr, 1996). Some studies of homosexuals with twin brothers and twin sisters have reported that a significantly greater proportion of identical than fraternal twins are gay or lesbian. These studies suggest that a particular region of the X chromosome may hold a "gay gene" (Bailey and Pillard, 1991; Bailey et al., 1993).

Others suggest that brain structure is associated with sexual orientation. According to some scientists, the size of the hypothalamus—an organ deep in the center of the brain that is believed to regulate the sex drive—differs between heterosexual and homosexual men (LeVay, 1993; Hamer et al., 1993). Most recently, however, Rice and his colleagues (1999) examined a sample of gay men and their brothers and found no evidence of a biological influence on homosexuality. The researchers concluded that the genes governing sexual orientation may

or may not exist somewhere on our chromosomes.

Social constructionist theories hold that sexual orientation is largely the result of social and environmental factors. According to this perspective, culture plays a large role in encouraging or discouraging heterosexual or homosexual behavior. In a study of adults who had been raised in lesbian families, for example, Golombok and Tasker (1996) found—and consistent with several previous studies—no evidence that parents' sexual orientation had a significant impact on their children's sexual orientation. The majority of the lesbian-raised adults identified themselves as heterosexual.

If there were a strong genetic predisposition, we'd expect gay children to come from gay households and straight children to come from straight households. This isn't the case, however. So far, no study has shown conclusively that there is a "gay gene" or that the environment "causes" sexual orientation. At this point, many researchers speculate that a combination of genetic and cultural factors probably shapes our sexual orientation.

The Politics of Sexual Orientation Many gays have mixed feelings about the scientific studies on sexual orientation. On the one hand, establishing that sexual orientation is genetic would mean that gays didn't *choose* their sexual identity, can't *change* it, and shouldn't be counseled to seek a "cure." Like eye or skin color, sexual orientation would be accepted as an innate characteristic. Such acceptance might decrease discrimination against gays for fear that they will "recruit" or molest heterosexual children. Proof of genetic factors might also rid parents of guilt feelings that, somehow, their child-rearing techniques produced gay offspring.

On the other hand, some lesbians and gay men worry that genetic proof of a person's homosexuality could lead to new forms of discrimination. Insurers, for example, might refuse health coverage to someone who is tested as gay because he might be seen as having a high risk for contracting AIDS. Others are concerned that antigay groups would encourage abortions after prenatal screening: "One can imagine a pregnant mother and father being told, 'Your baby is going to be queer. Do you want it?'" (Watson et al., 1996: 96).

Sexual Orientation and Gender Many researchers assert that gender is a more powerful factor than sexual orientation. That is, there are more similarities between straight and gay men than between lesbians and gays. For example,

- Lesbians and heterosexual women usually have monogamous relationships; gays and heterosexual men are more likely to have more than one lover at a time.

- For lesbians and heterosexual women, love and sex usually go hand in hand; many gays and heterosexual men often separate emotional intimacy and sex.

- Both lesbians and heterosexual women are much less interested in sex with strangers (or in public places) than are many gays and heterosexual men. Both groups of men are more likely than women to cruise for sexual partners.

- Many gays and heterosexual men want as much sexual variety as possible; most women seek long-term partners and less exotic experimentation.

- Heterosexual and homosexual men—not women—are the mainstay of such industries as prostitution, pornography, topless or gay bars, escort services, and adult bookstores (Brehm, 1985; Caldwell and Peplau, 1990; Goode, 1990).

Such findings may seem like "male bashing." These researchers are simply pointing out that gender roles may be much more important than sexual orientation in shaping our sexual scripts.

Sexual Scripts

Although we like to think that our sexual behavior is spontaneous, societal norms and practices shape even our erotic feelings. Sexual scripts influence our sexual behavior. A **sexual script** specifies the formal or informal norms for legitimate or unacceptable sexual activity, the eligibility of sexual partners, and the boundaries of sexual behavior in terms of time and place. Gender, race, and ethnicity, among other factors, shape our sexual scripts in important ways.

"And just what was that little window you clicked off when I came in?"

Gender and Sexual Scripts Although women are now more assertive in sexual encounters than in the past, most sexual behavior is still highly gendered. As you'll see throughout this chapter, men are more likely than women to masturbate, to engage in sex early, to have sex more frequently, and to have many partners over a lifetime. In contrast, many women have fewer sex partners, may go along with sex to avoid hurting a partner's feelings, equate sex with love, and dream of living happily ever after with a husband.

Some authors feel that male scripts still promote dominance rather than intimacy with sex partners. According to Brooks (1995), the "centerfold syndrome" is "one of the most malignant forces in contemporary relationships between men and women" because it objectifies women. Real women are bound to seem less appealing, and even ugly, compared to airbrushed, eternally youthful models: "Stretch marks, varicose veins, sagging breasts, and cellulite-marked legs, common phenomena for real female bodies, may be viewed as repugnant by men who see women as [sex] objects" (p. 5).

Women, too, can adopt this mindset. Plastic surgery and eating disorders are two ways in which women—especially white, middle-class women—surrender to and

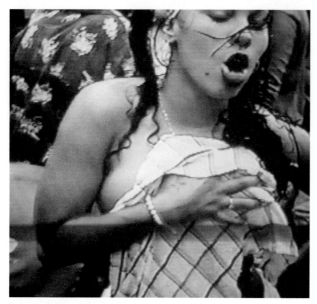

In June, 2000, at least 47 women reported that they were raped, their breasts grabbed, and their clothes ripped off by male participants in the National Puerto Rican Day Parade in New York City.

reinforce the notion that being sexy is synonymous with huge breasts, thinness, and youth (see Chapters 5 and 6).

Race, Ethnicity, and Sexual Scripts

Race and ethnicity also shape sexual scripts. Among many Latinos, for example, "good" women are not expected to be highly sexual or take the initiative. Men, on the other hand, are expected to be passionate and to use sexual conquest as proof of masculinity. For example, whereas 77 percent of black women say that they would have sex only if they were in love, only 43 percent of black men agree. White women and men have sex later in adolescence than African Americans and Latinos but engage in a greater variety of sexual practices, including oral sex (Mahay et al., 2001).

Among recent and even second-generation immigrants, sexual scripts differ for women and men. In many Middle Eastern, Latino, and Asian families, for example, parents monitor their daughters' sexual behavior but allow sons much more freedom (see Chapter 4).

The Double Standard Revisited

You will recall that the double standard emerged in the nineteenth century (see Chapter 3). Some believe that the *sexual double standard*—in which sexual intercourse outside marriage is acceptable for men but not women—has eroded. Others feel that the sexual revolution made only a small dent in the double standard.

The Sexual Revolution

In the late 1940s, social norms emphasized that love, sex, and marriage were deeply intertwined. By the early 1960s, the so-called sexual revolution created greater openness about sexuality. A growing acceptance of recreational sex replaced the emphasis on reproductive sex.

The invention of the birth-control pill ("the Pill") separated sex and childbearing for women. By the mid-1970s, the fear of pregnancy, the concepts of sin and guilt, and the value of virginity had changed, especially for teenagers (Bell and Coughey, 1980). According to journalist Loretta McLaughlin, "The Pill did more for the equality of women than any other single factor in the twentieth century" (cited in Potts, 2003). Is this really true?

The Sexual Revolution and the Double Standard

Some scholars believe that the sexual revolution broke down the old sexual double standard:

> *Women . . . express their sexuality more freely, they are rewriting our codes of sexual conduct and manners . . . with forays into sex earlier in adolescence, freer sex lives before wedding, and more sexual experimentation within marriage (Fisher, 1999: 219, 223).*

Others disagree. The sexual revolution encouraged more open communication about sex. There were also costs, however, especially for women. Women "were pressured more than ever [by men] to be sexually liberated . . . and then were accused of being uptight and puritanical if [they] didn't want sex" (Elshtain, 1988: 41). And as women became "free sexual agents," men were released from responsibility in marriage or parenthood (Ehrenreich et al., 1986; Crittenden, 1999).

Despite the sexual revolution, sexually active women who are unmarried are still labeled as "an easy lay," "sluts," or "whores," whereas their male counterparts are "a ladies' man." And "one-night stands" are still more acceptable for men than for women (Harvey and Weber, 2002). Even in committed relationships, such as love or engagement, women are expected to be more faithful than are men (Hatfield and Rapson, 1996; Hyde, 1996).

Sexual Assaults, Sexual Dysfunctions, and the Double Standard

One indicator of the double standard is the high rate of rape and other sexual assaults on women (see Chapter 8). Much sexual violence is still dismissed as masculine misbehavior rather than as a criminal assault.

Viagra, the male impotence pill, got front-page coverage when it came on the market in 1998. Insurance companies immediately covered the costs of Viagra, about $10 per pill, but still do not pay for female contraception methods such as birth-control pills, which typically cost around $30 per month. Nationwide, more women (43 percent) than men (31 percent) suffer from sexual difficulties that include an inability to achieve orgasm or pain during sexual intercourse (Laumann et al., 2001). Nonetheless, much pharmacological research focuses on erectile dysfunctions.

Patriarchy and the Double Standard The double standard is not limited to the United States and the Western world. The double standard allows much more sexual freedom to males than to females, especially in patriarchal societies (see Chapter 5).

Female genital mutilation, still practiced extensively in many parts of the world, reflects a double standard that allows men to mutilate women under the guise of making them more marriageable. Men have no comparable constraints. Female genital mutilation generally involves extensive damage to the sexual organs and causes lasting health problems for women.

In 1979, the World Health Organization denounced the practice as indefensible on medical and humane grounds. As the box on page 174 "Tradition or Torture? Female Genital Mutilation" shows, however, millions of girls are still subjected to these procedures.

Why We Have Sex

Sex, including the first experience of intercourse, doesn't "just happen." It typically progresses through such stages as approaching, flirting, touching, or asking directly for sex. Although it is usually a passionate act, first-time sex typically occurs after some planning and thought (Sprecher and McKinney, 1993). Even among adolescents, most sexual behavior is not irrational or impulsive but based on "reasoned action" that includes considerations about the consequences—both good and bad—and parents' values (Gillmore et al., 2002).

Sex the First Time

We have different reasons for having sex the first time. The reasons range from interpersonal decisions to structural factors.

Interpersonal Reasons For some, sex is an expression of affection and a means of communication. The majority of teens' first sexual relationships are with a romantic partner. Among teens aged 12 to 18, 79 percent of boys and 89 percent of girls said that they had sex the first time with someone they loved (Ryan et al., 2003).

Others experience physical arousal and allow themselves to be seduced. Curiosity about sex itself and about what it would be like to make love to a particular person is another reason. The reason may also be situational: People may take advantage of others who lose control after consuming alcohol or other drugs, for example.

Peer Pressure At least 10 percent of girls who first have sex before age 15 describe it as "unwanted." Some were coerced; others were pressured by their boyfriends or friends. Among adolescents ages 15 to 17, 36 percent of the males and 29 percent of females say that they were pressured to have sex—usually by males (Albert et al., 2003; Holt et al., 2003).

Why do many teens succumb to peer pressure? A teen boy might have sex to stop the teasing and harassment about being a virgin. According to a junior high school counselor, girls sometimes start rumors about a boy who wouldn't have sex that he is gay. Some boys have sex to disprove such gossip (Personal correspondence with Bill Meredith, Kansas State University, June 24, 2003).

If a boy is older, bigger, stronger, more popular, or more powerful than a girl, she may have trouble saying no, especially when drinking or using other drugs. In addition, one partner may feel obligated to have intercourse for fear of hurting the other's feelings or losing his or her interest (Abrahams and Ahlbrand, 2002).

Parental Inputs Parents, especially mothers, play a key role in promoting (although unintentionally) or discouraging first-time sex. The mothers who delay their teenage daughters' sexual debuts disapprove of adolescent sex, have close relationships with their daughters, and frequently talk with the parents of their daughters' friends. Although mothers have more influence on daughters than on sons, boys who have close relationships with their mothers are also more likely to delay sexual intercourse (Davis and Friel, 2001; McNeely et al., 2002; Albert et al., 2003).

Structural Factors Structural factors also affect early sexual activity. White teenage girls, for example, are more likely to engage in sex early when they experience family turbulence that includes parental conflict before a divorce, remarriage, and redivorce. Adolescents may disengage from their parents, looking to peer groups for emotional support, and thereby hasten their entry into sexual activity.

Black teenage girls may engage in sex at an early age if they reside with single parents who are sexually active, in cohabiting households where an adult does not have much authority, or in neighborhoods where adults who are role models don't have steady jobs and bear children out of wedlock. Latino adolescents who live with both biological parents and in neighborhoods with large numbers of foreign-born Latinos who share similar cultural values are likely to delay sex. In contrast, those from single-parent homes or low-density Latino communities that have assimilated to mainstream American values are more likely to engage in sex at an early age (Moore and Chase-Lansdale, 2001; Wu and Thompson, 2001; Upchurch et al., 2001).

CROSSCULTURAL

Tradition or Torture? Female Genital Mutilation

According to the World Health Organization, most of the girls and women who have undergone female genital mutilation (FGM) live in 28 African countries, although some live in Asia and the Middle East. FGM is also increasing in Europe, Australia, Canada, and the United States, primarily among immigrants. Each year, an estimated 2 million girls undergo FGM ("Female genital mutilation," 2000).

There are several types of FGM. The two most common, which remove all or part of the female's external genitalia, or vulva (see *Appendix A*), are excision and infibulation. In *excision*, part or all of the clitoris and the labia minora are removed. This operation often results in scar tissue that blocks the vaginal opening.

Infibulation combines removal of the clitoris and labia minora with excision of the inner layers of the labia majora. The raw edges of these inner layers are then sewn together with cat gut or acacia thorn. A sliver of wood or straw is inserted into the tiny opening that remains, allowing the slow, often painful passage of urine and menstrual flow.

When the woman marries, her husband may use his penis, razors, knives, or other instruments to penetrate the vagina during intercourse, and the opening must be further enlarged for childbirth. In many cases, the opening is re-closed in another excision or infibulation, and the cycle begins again.

FGM varies by a girl's age from one area to another. Among the Jewish Falashas in Ethiopia and the nomads of the Sudan, the girl may be only a few days old. In Egypt and many countries of central Africa, she may be anywhere from 3 to 9 years old.

The younger the girl, the less aware she is of what's going to happen to her and therefore the less she resists. During the circumcision, she is usually immobilized, with her arms tied behind her back, while women (sometimes including her mother) hold her thighs apart.

The "operator," an old village woman, cuts off the clitoris and then scrapes the labial flesh even though "the little girl howls and writhes in pain." The procedure lasts from 15 to 20 minutes, depending on the operator's competence and the child's struggling.

In rural areas, the instruments include razor blades, scissors, kitchen knives, or pieces of glass. Members of the elite and professional classes in urban areas use antiseptics and anesthesia during FGM.

FGM results in a number of immediate and long-term complications:

Sex in Committed Relationships

People who have committed to a relationship have a number of reasons for continuing to have sexual relations. As *Figure 7.1* on page 176 shows, sex serves many functions in both short-term and long-term relationships.

Short-Term Committed Relationships Sex can be an expression of *love* and *affection*. It can increase *intimacy*, a feeling of closeness that is emotional (expressing feelings), social (sharing friends), intellectual (sharing ideas), and recreational (sharing interests and hobbies). Sex can encourage *self-disclosure*: Telling a partner about one's hopes and insecurities (see Chapters 6 and 10).

Both love and sex provide an *exchange of resources* in an intimate relationship (see the discussion of social exchange theory in Chapter 2). A shy person, for example, may like a partner who is assertive during lovemaking. In other cases, however, an exchange may be manipulative. A sexually desirable person, for example, may use sex as a tool for acquiring power, status, or money (Flores, 1994).

Long-Term Committed Relationships All of the characteristics of short-term unions exist in long-term relationships as well, plus several others. Once a close bond continues, sexual and other physical expressions of intimacy are important in *maintaining the relationship*. There are many other ways (and even more important ones) such as communicating with one another, respecting each other, and making sacrifices for a partner.

Sex also fosters *interdependence* because the partners depend on each other for sexual satisfaction. Most importantly, many people have sex because they *want children* and plan to raise them together.

How Much Do We Know about Sex?

John Barrymore, the noted American actor, once said, "The thing that takes up the least amount of time and causes the most amount of trouble is sex." If sex causes a lot of trouble, it is probably because most of us know very little about it.

How did you do on the quiz on p. 168? According to some of my e-mail exchanges with faculty who use this textbook, their students—like mine—usually

- The girl can hemorrhage and die.
- The operator's poor eyesight or the child's resistance can cause cuts in other organs (such as the urethra or bladder).
- A rupture of the internal division between the vagina and the bladder or rectum may cause continual dribbling of urine or feces for the rest of the woman's life.
- The woman feels severe pain during intercourse or becomes sterile because of infections to the reproductive organs.
- During childbirth, even if the birth canal opening is enlarged, the woman may experience perineal tears or may even die because the baby cannot emerge through the mutilated vulva.

Cultures that practice FGM believe that women are highly sexual and by nature promiscuous. FGM curbs their presumably wild sexual desires, and a constricted vagina ensures virginity. Even disapproving mothers participate because if they refuse, their daughters would be ostracized, remain unmarried, and become financially destitute. The young girls who undergo FGM receive special clothes and food associated with the event and often feel proud of being like everyone else.

Disabling women makes them more marriageable, more economically dependent on their husbands, and, consequently, available for any sexual, emotional, or domestic demands made upon them.

Even though FGM has been banned in some African countries—like Burkina Faso and Kenya—some estimate that two-thirds of the young girls have been circumcised, often against their will. Although many African women have protested FGM, the practice continues.

SOURCES: Dorkenoo and Elworthy, 1992; Kamara, 1998; Abusharaf, 2001; Gruenbaum, 2001; "Burkina Faso . . .," 2002; "Kenyan girls flee mutilation," 2003; Lacey, 2003.

STOP AND THINK . . .

- *FGM is an important ritual in many countries. Should the United States and other countries interfere if they don't agree with the customs and rituals?*

- *Should male infants be circumcised? What if other countries denounce such U.S. practices as barbaric?*

- *Even though they are voluntary, do you think that breast implants, eating disorders, and liposuction are more "civilized" than FGM in making women's bodies more acceptable to men?*

"get" a C (especially if they're honest in reporting their scores). But even if you got a C, you know more about sex than most of your peers or even the average American adult (Reinisch and Beasley, 1990).

How Informed Are Adolescents about Sex? Many adolescents and young adults have little accurate information about reproductive anatomy or contraception (*Appendix D* discusses contraceptive methods). A health educator who visits eighth-graders says that although some of the children are sexually active, most don't know what sexually transmitted diseases are, how they can be prevented, when a girl can get pregnant, or how birth control works (Reimer, 1999). Some teenage girls in Texas, under the mistaken belief that they got pregnant through oral sex, call their children "spit babies" (Connolly, 2003).

On the national level, a survey of 13-year-olds found that less than a third were able to identify the most effective pregnancy prevention method (the Pill), only two-thirds knew the most effective STD prevention method (condoms), and only 8 percent correctly identified the point in the female fertility cycle when pregnancy is most likely to occur (about 14 days before the start of menstruation). Among 14-years-olds in this study,

- 50 percent believe that it is illegal for youth under 16 to buy condoms (it's legal).

- 20 percent believe (incorrectly) that "you could tell if a person has HIV/AIDS by looking at him/her."

- 39 percent of the boys and 51 percent of the girls agreed with the statement, "Most teens our age are having sex" (not true—see "Data Digest") (Albert et al., 2003).

And although 75 percent of teenagers aged 15 to 17 have engaged in oral sex, 20 percent didn't know that oral sex can result in an STD (Holt et al., 2003).

How Informed Are Young Adults about Sex? A number of college students also have information gaps about sex. Some believe, for example, that they cannot contract HIV if they are in monogamous relationships. In fact, being monogamous with an infected partner can be fatal.

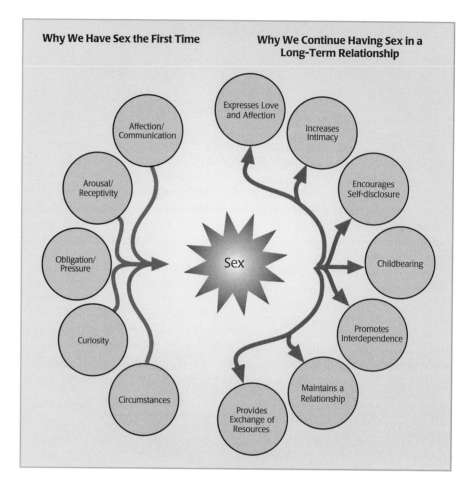

FIGURE 7.1 **Why We Have Sex**

At some colleges, including the Ivy Leagues, campus newspapers feature regular columns on sexuality where students can ask questions anonymously. Some have questions about "oral sex etiquette," some aren't sure about the safest sex methods, and others don't know whether they've experienced an orgasm (Rimer, 2002).

On the national level, young adults aged 18 to 24—especially those who are sexually active—have serious misconceptions about sex:

■ 71 percent believe that birth control methods that are not condoms provide "safe sex."

■ 60 percent don't know that STDs can cause some kinds of cancer.

■ 50 percent don't know that one in four sexually active people under 25 will get an STD during the year.

■ 36 percent believe that oral sex cannot transmit STDs.

■ 20 percent believe that pulling out a penis before ejaculation is a form of "safe sex."

■ 18 percent believe that "if someone I was dating had an STD, I would know it" (Holt et al., 2003).

As these studies show, young people (and probably older people as well) believe a lot of myths about sex and lack knowledge about core sexual issues and their impact on our health. Why are many of us so misinformed?

MAKING CONNECTIONS

■ How would you describe your sexual scripts? Have they remained constant or changed over time? Do your sexual scripts—or those of your friends, partners, and children—reflect a double standard?

■ Thinking about yourself, your friends, or children, why do people have sexual intercourse the first time? Or why have you or your friends remained virgins? ✺

How We Learn about Sex

What we see as normal sexual behavior is neither "normal" nor "natural" but is learned in a societal context. At least eight known societies, for example, view kissing as repulsive:

> When the Thonga first saw Europeans kissing they laughed. . . . "Look at them—they eat each other's saliva and dirt." The Siriono never kiss, although they have no regulation against such behavior. The Tinguian, instead of kissing, place the lips near the partner's face and suddenly inhale (Ford and Beach, 1972: 49).

We become sexual over time. Our main sources of information about anatomy, values, and sexual expression come primarily from parents, peers, the media and popular culture, and sex education programs in schools.

From Parents

When reporters asked Charles Barkley, the former National Basketball Association star, how he'd handle his 12-year-old daughter's future boyfriends, he said, "I figure if I kill the first one, the word will get out." Although humorous, Barkley's statement reflects a fairly typical but unrealistic parental stance: "I'll make sure my kid won't have sex."

Parents can be very influential in how children think and feel about sexuality. As you saw earlier, parents affect our sexual scripts by what they say (or don't say) about sex. Ideally, parents (or guardians) should be the first and best sex educators because they are experienced and have children's interests at heart. As *Figure 7.2* shows, however, many adolescents and young adults are more likely to get information about sex from friends, the media, and sex education classes than from parents.

Why? The reasons range from parents not knowing (or wanting to know, sometimes) that their kids are sexually active to simply not talking about sex. When parents talk about sex, however, they can be effective.

Do Parents Know Their Children Are Sexually Active?
Only about a third of parents of sexually active 14-year-olds know that their children have had or are having sex (Albert et al., 2003). The number of parents who are not aware that their older teens are sexually active may be just as high.

Teenagers may be reluctant to discuss sex with their parents because they don't want to disappoint, hurt, or shock them. Many teenagers feel that parents see them in an unrealistically innocent light, and they don't want to tarnish this idealized image:

> *16-year-old girl: "They have so much faith and trust in me. It would just kill them if they found out I had made love before. There's a lot of pressure on me to be good since I'm the most successful of my*

FIGURE 7.2 **How Do Young People Learn about Sex?**

SOURCE: Based on Holt et al., 2003, Table 30.

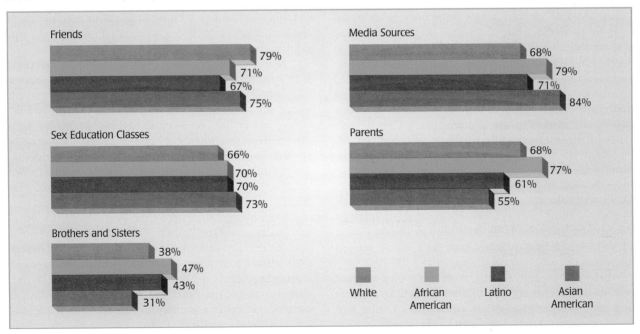

brothers and sisters. They feel I'm a reflection of all their efforts and their ideal child" (Hass, 1979: 168).

Even though the Hass research was published more than two decades ago, the reasons for parents' not knowing about their children's sexual activities are similar today. For example, 83 percent of teenagers in one survey said that their peers "fool around" during coed sleepovers. Yet many parents are confident that the teens obey such "clear rules" as no drinking, no drugs, separate sleeping bags, and no sex (McCarroll, 2002).

Do Parents Want to Talk about Sex?

Many parents feel uncomfortable talking about sex because they themselves have little knowledge about sexuality. Sex education programs were unavailable when they were youngsters, and sexuality was deemed an inappropriate topic of discussion in the home (Brock and Jennings, 1993; Kyman, 1995).

Parents may be uneasy in responding to what they view as gender-inappropriate sexual behavior. According to a mother of a 4-year-old, for example,

My son did that [played with his penis]. It was alright. I didn't have any problem with it. If he didn't want to let go, I'd just put him down on the floor without his diaper. But my daughter, I felt uncomfortable with her doing that. I just had to walk away from the situation because for some reason I was very uncomfortable with her exploring herself (Geeasler et al., 1995: 187).

Some parents may not want to talk about sex because they recognize that they don't practice what they preach and are poor role models. They themselves may "sleep around," initiate sexual intercourse with teens, have out-of-wedlock births, condone sleepovers that they suspect include sexual activity, and oversexualize 5 to 6-year-old girls by encouraging them to wear makeup and adultlike clothes (Haffner, 1999; Saltzman, 1999).

About 90 percent of parents and caregivers say that their 11 to 14-year-olds can be open with them in discussing sex, contraception, and pregnancy. Only 67 percent of these adolescents, however, feel that parents or caregivers would be comfortable with such discussions (Albert et al., 2003).

Do Parents Actually Talk about Sex?

Not as much as parents think they do. For example, 65 percent of the parents but only 41 percent of their children aged 11 to 14 say that parents have had conversations about sex or birth control (Albert et al., 2003).

Black youth rely slightly more on media sources than on parents for sex information. Parents are the second least likely sources of information for Latino and Asian American youth (see *Figure 7.2*). It may be that Asian American kids, especially recent immigrants, are expected to be more interested in family and academic issues than sex. In addition, the double standard probably prevents Asian American girls from discussing sex with their parents (see Chapters 4 and 5).

It's unclear why Latino youth are more likely to get information about sex from the media and from sex education classes than from parents. Some research shows that Latina mothers are more likely to discuss sex with daughters than with sons. Then again, mothers (and sometimes fathers) talk about relationships and values rather than "sexual facts," including contraceptives and STDs (Raffaelli and Green, 2003).

Are Parental Discussions about Sex Effective?

Many adolescents think their parents are old-fashioned and often lapse into "adultspeak," telling them "Don't do it" rather than discussing the implications of sex, such as the long-term responsibilities involved in raising a child. Nonetheless, communication between parents and children often postpones the first sexual experience. In addition, such discussions, as well as parental supervision of teenagers' activities, often result in safer sexual behaviors (such as using condoms) and fewer sexual partners across all racial and ethnic groups (Schreck, 1999; Lehr et al., 2000; Whitaker et al., 2000; Hutchinson, 2002).

From Peers

Peers are among the most common sources of knowledge about sex, especially for white adolescents and young adults (see *Figure 7.2*). Because peers typically are misinformed about sex, however, the instruction is similar to the blind leading the blind. As you saw earlier, many adolescents know little about such topics as the proper use of condoms, women's fertile periods, and contraceptives.

Many young people recognize that their information is limited. More than three-quarters of adolescents and young adults say that they want more information about sex and sexual health. They are especially concerned about how to recognize STDs, what HIV testing involves, and where they can get tested. One-quarter say they need more information on how to use condoms. Young adolescents (13- to 14-year-olds) who are not yet sexually active are also concerned about sexual violence in relationships (Holt et al., 2003).

Even though they aren't the best sources of information, peers can be helpful. Often they are more open than parents about discussing sexuality issues, offer support when a friend feels insecure about visible signs of maturing (such as the growth of breasts or facial hair), and encourage friends to seek information about birth control if parents are unwilling to talk about contraception (Gecas and Seff, 1991).

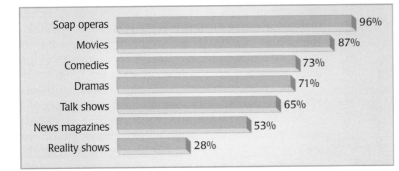

FIGURE 7.3 **Percentage of TV Shows with Sexual Content**

Note: *Sexual content* ranges from talk about sex to kissing to sexual intercourse.

SOURCE: Kunkel et al., 2003.

From the Media and Popular Culture

Many of us, especially young people, often get information from the media and popular culture (see *Figure 7.2*). Television, movies, music, magazines, romance novels, the Internet, and, sometimes, pornographic materials have become powerful sources of information—or misinformation—about sex.

Magazines You don't have to go to adult bookstores to find magazines that use sex to make sales. *Playboy, Penthouse, Hustler,* and other magazines for men are sold openly at drugstores, newsstands, and many discount stores. After continuous pressure from some Christian groups, Wal-Mart Stores (the nation's largest retailer) recently stopped selling *Maxim, Stuff,* and *FHM,* men's magazines that "feature a mix of scantily clad starlets and bawdy humor but go to some lengths to avoid being labeled as pornography" (Carr and Hays, 2003). According to one critic, magazines like *Men's Health* and *Men's Fitness* are more about sex than physical health (Kuczynski, 2001).

Many women's magazines also sell sex. Nearly every article and ad in *Cosmopolitan* is about sex. *Redbook* and *Mademoiselle* also have a heavy dose of articles about sex (e.g., "35 sexy new ways to touch your man"). Even magazines that target young teen and preteen girls, such as *YM,* often have sexually related articles ("Look summer sexy") (King, 2002; see also Chapter 5).

Movies Because rating systems are not strictly enforced (few moviegoers are stopped from seeing R-rated films, for example) and videos are accessible to most age groups, it is common for adolescents or even younger children to get much of their sex information from movies. As you saw in Chapter 5, sex permeates movies and videotapes and shapes our gender role scripts.

Television Sex is a staple in most television shows, ranging from 28 percent of reality shows to 96 percent of soap operas (*Figure 7.3*). *How* and *how much* sex is portrayed on television has increased between 1997

and 2002. Today, 64 percent of all shows contain some sexual content, up from 56 percent in 1997. Shows that depict sexual intercourse have doubled—from 7 percent to 14 percent—during the same period (Kunkel et al., 2003).

In the top 20 shows among teen viewers—such as *Friends, Titus, That 70s Show,* and *Boston Public*—83 percent contain some sexual content, and one in five involves sexual intercourse. Although the teen shows are more likely to include sex, 45 percent also contain references to safer sex, waiting to have sex, using protection, or the consequences of sex. This is a significant increase over 9 percent in 1997 (Kunkel et al., 1999, 2003).

The Internet We are deluged with *spam* (unsolicited commercial e-mail sent to a large number of addresses). Every day, it seems, spam urges us to enlarge our breasts or penises and to view pornography.

As access to the Internet expands, more and more young people are turning to the Web as a source of health information. Some of the most common topics searched include pregnancy, birth control, HIV/AIDS and other STDs. Many parents use some sort of filtering product at home. The Children's Internet Protection Act of 2000 requires that schools and libraries use Web-browsing filters to block pornographic content or risk losing federal funds. Each institution, however, can set the parameters it chooses.

How effective are these filters at institutions? According to a recent national study, the filters are blocking out important health information about sexuality. At the least restrictive level, the filters blocked only pornography. At the intermediate level, the filters also blocked sites with nudity and other material such as illicit drugs.

At the most restrictive level, the filters blocked 91 percent of the pornography sites (about the same as the least restrictive settings) but also 24 percent of health information sites. From 23 to 60 percent of the blocked sites included information about herpes, birth control, safer sex, and gay health. The barred sites also included women's health sites maintained by medical journals

At King Junior High School in Berkeley, California, the 9th grade "social living" class includes instruction in sexual anatomy. Do you think teachers should provide this information? Or should parents be responsible for educating their children about sexuality?

and U.S. government sites on STDs (Richardson et al., 2002; Rideout et al., 2002).

From Sex Education

As you just saw, many parents do *not* teach their children about sex. And the media and popular culture often bombard people with unrealistic portrayals of sexuality. Consequently, many schools and community groups have assumed responsibility for teaching children and adolescents about sex.

About 93 percent of U.S. adults approve of schools providing sex education, an increase from 65 percent in 1970. Despite such general approval, only 19 states mandate sexuality education (Squires, 1995; "Issues and answers . . .," 2001). And in some schools, athletic coaches rather than teachers teach sex education classes (Walker, 2003).

Some faith-based programs offer information on a variety of topics—besides abstinence—that include homosexuality, STDs, masturbation, and oral sex. A very vocal minority of parents, however, headed primarily by conservative religious groups, has opposed sex education in the schools. These groups, as well as organizations such as "Priests for Life," argue that sex education in the schools will put ideas into young children's heads, increase promiscuity, and result in abortions (Clarkson, 2002).

Such fears are unfounded. Several national studies report that teenagers at high schools that provide condoms and condom use instruction are less likely than their counterparts to engage in risky sex or to report lifetime or recent sexual intercourse (Blake et al., 2003; Johnson et al., 2003). It may be that teens who are informed about condoms (and the consequences of not using condoms) are less likely to have sex impulsively.

The Bush administration has funded primarily abstinence-only sex education programs. "Just say no" approaches rarely work, however. Many teens are already sexually active, and promises to abstain from sex are easily broken. It's also not clear why many of the abstinence-only groups oppose information about condoms and birth control. If teens are *really* going to abstain from sex until marriage, why should sex education change their behavior?

Which sex education programs are the most effective? Those that teach teens critical thinking skills by

- Including activities that tell young people how to resist peer pressure to engage in sex

- Focusing on specific issues such as delaying the initiation of intercourse or using protection

- Providing basic and accurate information about the risks of unprotected intercourse

- Involving students in small group discussions, games or simulations, role playing, and brainstorming and in real-world exercises such as locating contraceptives in local drugstores and visiting family planning clinics

- Addressing the problem of social and media pressure to have sex (such as advertising that uses sex to sell products or the "lines" men typically use to persuade someone to have sex)

- Including open discussions about homosexuality to address students who are struggling with their sexual orientation (Kirby et al., 1994; "Issues and answers . . .," 2001)

The most successful sex education programs train adolescents to serve as peer counselors. They also discuss sexual feelings and behavior as a normal part of human development rather than focusing only on danger and disease (Ehrhardt, 1996; Rust, 2000).

MAKING CONNECTIONS

- How did you learn about sex? Were the "facts" you got accurate?

- What kind of sex education classes, if any, did you have in middle school and high school? Did the classes influence your sexual behavior?

FIGURE 7.4 **Sex Survey Findings: Sex is Largely Monogamous and Very Satisfying** Although this nationwide U.S. survey of sexual behavior is now a decade old, the data are still considered the most authoritative available. These findings surprised many people. Why do you think this was the case?

SOURCE: Based on Laumann et al., 1994: 177–80; 369.

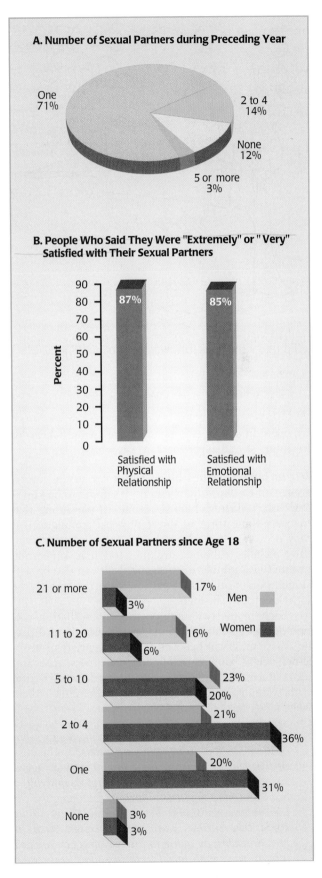

A. Number of Sexual Partners during Preceding Year

B. People Who Said They Were "Extremely" or "Very" Satisfied with Their Sexual Partners

C. Number of Sexual Partners since Age 18

Sexual Behaviors

Many of us have fairly conventional sex lives. Most U.S. adults have one or no sex partners during a year and more than 85 percent are happy with their sex lives. Men are much more likely than women, however, to have had 11 or more sexual partners since age 18 (*Figure 7.4*).

Keep in mind, too, that sex is not just sexual intercourse. Sexual expression encompasses many other behaviors, including autoeroticism, petting, and oral sex.

Autoeroticism

Autoeroticism is sexual gratification obtained solely by stimulating one's own body. Two of the most common forms of autoeroticism are sexual fantasies and masturbation.

Sexual Fantasies Most of us, regardless of our age or marital status, have sexual fantasies. Men are more likely than women to have sexual fantasies. We often fantasize differently, though, depending on whether we're male or female. Sexual fantasies often mirror differences in gender roles (see Chapter 5). Women's fantasies, for example, are typically romantic, passive, and submissive. Compared with women, men are more likely to fantasize about a number of partners and encounters that won't lead to a relationship (Battan, 1992; Geer and Manguno-Mire, 1996).

Even when women fantasize about "unusual" sex practices, they are less likely to act them out. In one national survey, for example, twice as many men as women said that they had acted out such fantasies as incest, sex with defecation, sadomasochism, or sex with an animal (Patterson and Kim, 1991).

Scientists maintain that sexual fantasies are emotionally and psychologically healthy. Fantasies can provide a safety valve for pent-up feelings or a harmless escape from boring, everyday routines: "to be covered in whipped cream and wrestle my lover, then the loser has to lick it off" or "having sex on the 50-yard line at a sold-out football game" (Patterson and Kim, 1991: 79).

Fantasies can also boost our self-image because we don't have to worry about penis size, breast size, height, or weight. Because we have total control in producing and directing the fantasy, we can change or stop it anytime

"I'd like a page 15 followed by a page 28 please!"

© www.CartoonStock.com

we want. In some cases, fantasies are mental rehearsals for future sexual experiences (Masters et al., 1992).

Masturbation When asked about sex in the future, comedian Robin Williams said: "It's going to be you—and you." **Masturbation** is sexual self-pleasuring that involves some form of direct physical stimulation. It may or may not result in orgasm. Masturbation typically includes rubbing, stroking, fondling, squeezing, or otherwise stimulating the genitals. It can also be self-stimulation of other body parts, such as the breasts, the inner thighs, or the anus.

Early in the twentieth century masturbation was branded as a source of damage to the brain and nervous system. It was believed to cause a variety of problems, such as bad breath, blindness, deafness, acne, and heart murmurs. Some physicians treated masturbation with recommendations for prayer or exercise. Others went much farther:

> *"Treatment" for boys included piercing the foreskin of the penis with wire, applying leeches to the base of the penis, or cutting the foreskin with a jagged scissors. "Treatment" for girls included applying a hot iron to the thighs or clitoris or removing the clitoris in an operation called a clitoridectomy. Adults could buy various commercial devices, such as metal mittens, an alarm that went off when the bed moved, rings with metal teeth or spikes to wear on*

the penis at night. . . . Some of these horrors were so popular that they were advertised in the Sears-Roebuck catalog (Wade and Cirese, 1991: 46).

Masturbation often begins in childhood and continues throughout the life cycle. Prepubertal children may stimulate themselves without realizing that what they are doing is sexual. For example, one girl learned when she was 8 years old that she could produce an "absolutely terrific feeling" by squeezing her thighs together (Nass et al., 1981). Thus, many children discover masturbation accidentally.

More than three times as many men as women report masturbating at least once a week. Black men (60 percent) are twice as likely as whites, Latinos, and Asians to say they never masturbated (Laumann et al., 1994). Women who frequently attend religious services are more likely to perceive masturbation as a sin and an unhealthy practice. This may be due to many religions' message that sex should not be used for self-pleasure (Davidson and Darling, 1995).

Like fantasies, masturbation fulfills several needs: It can relieve sexual tension, provide a safe means of sexual experimentation (avoiding disease and unwanted pregnancy), and may ultimately transfer valuable learning to two-person lovemaking. Masturbation can be as sexually satisfying as intercourse, and it does not hinder the development of social relationships during young adulthood or create problems in a marriage (Leitenberg et al., 1993; Kelly, 1994).

Petting

Petting includes touching, stroking, mutual masturbation, and fondling various parts of the body, especially the breasts and genitalia. Petting is generally more acceptable than intercourse because it is less intimate and does not result in pregnancy.

In the past, researchers sometimes differentiated between petting and necking. They defined petting as sexual touching below the waist and necking as any other sexual touching, including kissing. More recently, researchers have included oral sex in definitions of petting.

By the early 1950s (when, theoretically, at least, no one had sex until after marriage), 81 percent of boys and 84 percent of girls had had experience with petting by age 18. Approximately 23 percent of the men and 32 percent of the women between ages 16 and 20 had petted to orgasm (Kinsey et al., 1953).

More recently, a study of first-year college students found that 40 percent of the women and 50 percent of the men reported having experienced orgasm during petting (Masters et al., 1986). By age 18, more than 75 percent of teenagers have engaged in heavy petting (Roper Starch Worldwide, 1994).

Oral Sex

In January 1998, President Clinton wagged his finger at the television audience and proclaimed, his eyes glinting, that "I want to say one thing to the American people. I want you to listen to me. I'm going to say this again: I did not have sexual relations with that woman, Miss Lewinsky. . . . Never. These allegations are false." It turned out, however, that Monica Lewinsky (a White House intern) and former President Clinton routinely had oral sex.

Like many teenagers and college students, President Clinton apparently defined oral sex as not *really* sex. Some writers call this behavior "outercourse," a way of rationalizing sexual behavior because it's "almost sex" and an alternative to sexual intercourse (Harvey and Weber, 2002; Kamen, 2002).

Oral sex includes several types of stimulation. **Fellatio** (from the Latin word for "suck") is oral stimulation of a man's penis. **Cunnilingus** (from the Latin words for "vulva" and "tongue") is oral stimulation of a woman's genitals. Fellatio and cunnilingus can be performed singly or simultaneously. Simultaneous oral sex is sometimes called "69," indicating the physical positions of the partners.

One national survey found that 3 percent of youth aged 12 to 14 had experienced oral or anal sex (Albert et al., 2003). A survey of 15- to 17-year-olds found that 33 percent had engaged in oral sex with the opposite sex (Holt et al., 2003). Another national study of men between 20 and 39 years of age reported that almost 80 percent of those who were currently married had performed or received oral sex (presumably with their spouses). The same study found that 79 percent of white men had performed oral sex, compared with 73 percent of Latino men and only 43 percent of black men (Billy et al., 1993).

Some people find oral sex pleasurable or engage in it to please their partner. Others complain about the odors (although bathing solves the problem for both sexes), do not enjoy it, or find it revolting. When Wade and Cirese (1991: 334) asked their students what bothers them about oral sex, they got the following responses:

One woman wrote, "I can't swallow his semen! Choke! Choke!" Another wrote, "I always want to say 'Well, would you like me to blow my nose in your mouth?' That's how I feel about it."

Oral sex, like many other sexual behaviors, depends on personal preference. Many people don't realize, however, that sexual diseases can be transmitted orally.

Sexual Intercourse

Most people assume that sexual intercourse refers to heterosexual, vaginal-penile penetration. In fact, the term applies to any sort of sexual coupling, including oral and anal. *Coitus* specifically means penile-vaginal intercourse. Unless noted otherwise, we will use *sexual intercourse* to refer to coitus.

Some adolescents begin to be sexually active in their early teens (see "Data Digest"). On average, however, the first heterosexual intercourse takes place between ages 16 and 17 among both sexes. By age 65, men report that they've had sex with an average of 15 women; women have had sex with an average of 8 men (Clements, 1994). Average monthly sexual intercourse peaks between ages 25 and 34 and then declines over the years. Over time, as you'll see shortly, people develop other priorities in maintaining a family or a relationship.

Married couples and cohabitants have much higher rates of sexual intercourse than single people do (see *Figure 7.5* on page 184). Such figures challenge popular perceptions of "swinging singles." Having an easily accessible partner, such as in marriage or cohabitation, seems to have the largest impact on the frequency of sexual activity.

Married people are happier with their sex lives than either single people or cohabitants (Billy et al., 1993; Clements, 1994; Laumann et al., 1994). These findings support the notion, discussed in Chapter 6, that sexual intercourse is more than just the sexual act—it also involves intimacy, commitment, and love.

Sexual Response Fantasies, sounds, smells, touch, sexy pictures, dreams, hearing the person we love say "I love you," and a variety of other sources can arouse our sexual feelings. Our physiological reaction to sexual stimulation is sometimes called **sexual response**. Our sexual responses can vary greatly by age, gender, and health. Generally, however, the sexual response cycle consists of four phases: desire, excitement, climax, and resolution (Masters et al., 1992; Kaplan, 1979).

Desire usually triggers a physical response. Sexual fantasies or other stimuli can lead to sexual arousal so that a person is emotionally receptive to sexual intercourse. Because the brain sparks desire, there are cross-cultural variations in what people deem sexy or a turn-off. As noted earlier, some cultures see kissing as repulsive.

During the second phase, *excitement*, both sexes experience an increase in blood pressure, pulse rate, and breathing. In the male, the first responses to sexual stimulation are the swelling and erection of the penis and partial elevation of the testes. Female excitement results in vaginal lubrication and clitoral swelling, and the nipples may become erect and hard. During this phase, the penis may emit several drops of fluid that are not semen but may contain sperm cells. If this fluid is discharged while the penis is in the vagina, a woman can be impregnated. Thus, withdrawal before ejaculation, commonly used as a means of contraception, is typically ineffective in preventing conception.

Sexual tension reaches its peak, or *climax*, during orgasm and is suddenly discharged. This third stage of sexual response lasts only a few seconds. In the male, it is characterized by three or four major contractions of the entire length of the urethra and the spurting of semen during ejaculation. Women may feel contractions in the vagina, uterus, and rectum.

Ejaculation and orgasm can be experienced independently of each other because they are affected by different neurological and vascular systems. Penile erections, ejaculations, and orgasms do not occur simultaneously. Thus, men who argue that a penile erection must be followed by ejaculation during sexual intercourse lest they suffer dire consequences ("blue balls") are, quite simply, wrong. There is no scientific evidence that any man has ever died of a "terminal erection."

Do women and men experience orgasm differently? Read the box "How Do Orgasms Differ by Gender?" before continuing.

There are many individual variations in reaching orgasm. Some people may skip stages, experiencing excitement or arousal, for example, without or before desire (Basson, 2001). The major difference between male and female orgasms is that women can have several orgasms rapidly in succession, whereas most men cannot.

Women may also experience different kinds of orgasms: clitoral, vaginal, or a combination. An orgasm that comes from rubbing the clitoris can't be distinguished physiologically from one that results from breast stimulation alone or from intercourse. Many partners are fully satisfied with tender sexual activities that do not necessarily include orgasm.

After orgasm, in the *resolution phase*, the fourth and last stage of the sexual response cycle, the male's penis begins a rapid loss of swelling and erection. In the female, the clitoris returns to its normal position, followed by a reduction in the size and level of swelling. Breathing, heart rate, and blood pressure return to normal in both partners. Both partners may experience physical and mental relaxation and a sense of well-being.

Myths about Sexual Response One of some men's biggest concerns is that their penises aren't big enough to stimulate women during intercourse (Reinisch and Beasley, 1990). There is no association between clitoris, breast, or penis size and orgasm. Similarly, there is no evidence for the belief that, compared with white men, African American men have larger penises, a greater sexual capacity, or an insatiable sexual appetite (although some of my black male students would like to think so).

A second misconception about sexual response is that men can always tell if women have had an orgasm. To appease or please their partners, women sometimes fake orgasms (Hite, 1987). Except in the movies, women's orgasms are rarely accompanied by asthmatic breathing

FIGURE 7.5 **Cohabitants and Married Couples Have More Fun than Singles**
As the text points out, married couples and people who live together have sexual intercourse considerably more often than single people.

SOURCE: Based on Laumann et al., 1994: 88–89.

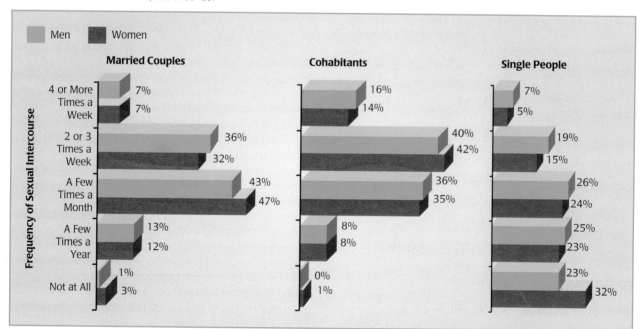

How Do Orgasms Differ by Gender?

Read each of the following descriptions of orgasm. Is the speaker a man or a woman?

	Man	Woman
1. For me, orgasm feels like a building wave of emotion. First I notice a pulsing sensation that is quite localized. Then it spreads through my whole body. Afterwards, I feel tired but also superrelaxed.	❏	❏
2. My anxiety about sex definitely inhibits my orgasm. There are times when I feel some intense sensations, but usually I am too inhibited to really let myself go. I have orgasms most easily when I masturbate.	❏	❏
3. Basically, I feel a glow which starts in my genitals and then spreads through my whole body. Sometimes one orgasm is enough, and other times it is not completely satisfying.	❏	❏
4. I think orgasm is overrated. I sometimes spend over an hour getting turned on, and then the orgasm takes only a few seconds.	❏	❏
5. I concentrate all my attention on the sensations in the genitals.	❏	❏
6. My body feels incredibly alive and seems to vibrate. Afterwards, I just want to hold my lover and be very still.	❏	❏

Answers

˙uǝɯ ʎq ǝɹɐ ɯsɐƃɹo ɟo suoᴉʇdᴉɹɔsǝp ǝɥʇ ɟo ll∀

SOURCE: Based on Vance and Wagner, 1976: 87–98.

and clutching the bedposts. Response can be explosive or mild, depending on a woman's emotional or physical state, stress, alcohol consumption, and a variety of other factors.

Finally, some marriage manuals promote a simultaneous orgasm (both partners experiencing orgasm at the same time) as the ultimate peak in sexual pleasure. Many people try to fine-tune the timing of their responses, but working so hard at sex becomes a job rather than a satisfying experience. Although simultaneous orgasm can be exhilarating, so can independent orgasms.

Sexuality throughout Life

We may love dozens of people over our lifetime. We'll have sex with very few of them, however. We might also have sex with people we don't love. There can be many sexual relationships during the life course and a diversity of sexual unions. There is also another option: abstinence.

Virginity and Abstinence

The terms "abstinence" and "virgin" have several meanings. One definition, which many religious groups endorse, refers to an absence of all types of sexual activity. Another definition, the standard one used in the scientific literature, pertains to people who have never had vaginal-penile intercourse.

As you saw earlier, large numbers of teenagers have engaged in heavy petting or oral sex. Are they virgins? And if they engage in everything except sexual intercourse, are they "abstainers" or not? There is no agreed-upon answer. Instead, definitions may vary from one study (or group) to another.

Although sexual activity is widespread, virginity is not a cultural dinosaur. About 12 percent of all women age 18 and older had their first sexual intercourse when they got married (comparable numbers are not available for men) (Abma et al., 1997). In 1990, 46 percent of teens in grades 9 to 12 said they had not had sexual

> ## TABLE 7.1
>
> ### Factors Related to Early Sexual Intercourse among Adolescents
>
> - Alcohol or other drug use
> - Delinquent behavior
> - Dating before age 16 or involvement in a committed relationship
> - Having a low grade point average or dropping out of school
> - Frequent geographic moves, which divert parental attention and decrease parental supervision; adolescents sometimes use sex to establish new friendships or combat loneliness
> - Parental divorce during adolescence
> - Poverty
> - Physical or sexual abuse at home or by relatives
> - Minimal parental monitoring of teens' activities and friends
> - Permissive parental values toward sex, including a parent who cohabits or entertains overnight guests
> - A lack of neighborhood monitoring of teens

intercourse. By 2001, the number had increased to 54 percent (Grunbaum et al., 2002).

There are numerous explanations for early sexual intercourse among adolescents (see *Table 7.1*). But why are some teens more likely to abstain than others? Also, why do many adults go without sex?

Why Teens Abstain from Sexual Intercourse There are several explanations for the decline of teen sexual intercourse. The reasons range from abstinence movements to family dynamics.

First, some credit the abstinence movement, especially religious and medical groups that advocate chastity for either moral or health reasons. Since 1993, numerous church groups have encouraged kids to publicly sign chastity-until-marriage pledges. The media have highly publicized such pledges with headlines such as "Abstinence Pledges Work." The headlines aren't entirely accurate, however. About 34 percent of the teens who signed pledges since 1993 were less likely to have sex than those who didn't. But the abstinence pledges postponed intercourse only for 14- and 15 year-olds, and for about 18 months. And when the pledgers broke their promise, they were less likely than nonpledgers to use contraceptives (Bearman and Brückner, 2001).

Second, some argue that sex education programs have decreased adolescents' sexual intercourse. When comprehensive education includes both abstinence and contraceptives, adolescents are more informed about their options and act more responsibly. The Bush administration, however, has pumped money into abstinence-only programs: $120 million in 2003 alone, compared with a total of $60 million between 1981 and 1996 (Cook, 2001; Wetzstein, 2003).

Critics point out, however, that teens in abstinence-only programs are more likely to get pregnant because they know little about contraception (Risman and Schwartz, 2002). In a study at Northern Kentucky University, researcher Angela Lipsitz found that more than half of the college students who vowed to abstain from sex until marriage broke the pledge. The students who broke their pledge were less likely to use a condom during their first sexual experience than students who did not promise chastity. According to Lipsitz, "If you're making a pledge to remain a virgin, it would be very inconsistent to carry a condom around with you. So when the desire to have intercourse comes up . . . people find themselves unprepared (cited in Mundell, 2003).

Third, and as you've already seen, many teenagers now engage in "outercourse," including oral sex, that they regard as less dangerous and less intimate than intercourse. In effect, then, adolescents are sexual, but their practices have been changing. Adolescents with high educational goals, especially, delay having intercourse—but not necessarily oral sex—because of the perceived risks (such as pregnancy and STDs) that may jeopardize their plans for the future (Halpern et al., 2000; Schvaneveldt et al., 2001).

Finally, family dynamics—such as child-parent "connectedness" and good communication—may delay sexual initiation (Miller et al., 1999; Rodgers, 1999; Kirby, 2001). Religious affiliation may also have an effect on early sexual activity. For example, teens—particularly girls—with strong religious views are less likely to have sex than are less religious teens. Dating, however, increases the likelihood of sexual intercourse regardless of the girls' religious views (Meier, 2003).

Why Adults Abstain from Sexual Intercourse A major reason for adult abstinence is not having a partner, bad luck in the dating game, divorce, or widowhood. Situational necessities can also encourage abstinence. Unlike food, sleep, and shelter, sex is not a prerequisite for physical survival. Sexual relationships can certainly be satisfying and rewarding, but neither virginity nor abstinence is fatal.

Sex and Adolescents

The first sexual experience can be happy and satisfying. It can also be a source of worry, disappointment, or guilt:

My first time was very unpleasant. The boy I was with rushed and fumbled around and then came so fast it was over before it started. I thought, "What's so great about this?" For weeks afterward, I was afraid I had V.D. and had bad dreams about it (Masters et al., 1992: 226).

Many males experience more anxiety than females about the first sexual experience, possibly because men are still more likely to be the planners or initiators. Still, many more men (79 percent) than women (7 percent) have an orgasm the first time. These differences may be due to men's greater freedom to enjoy sex because of sexual scripts or because early masturbation habits and prior petting experiences allow more men than women to be orgasmic. As a result, men are usually more pleased with their first intercourse experience (Sprecher et al., 1995).

The tasks adolescents face as they navigate through unknown sexual waters are formidable: They must forge an identity that includes culturally dictated gender-role expectations. They must learn about sexual and romantic relationships. They must also develop a personal set of sexual values.

Many adolescents have sexual intercourse before accomplishing these tasks. At age 15, 25 percent of girls and 30 percent of boys have had sexual intercourse (Holt et al., 2003). By the twelfth grade, almost half of all high school students have had sexual intercourse. The rates are higher for black and Latino students than for their white counterparts. About 14 percent of high school seniors have had four or more sex partners, and the highest rates are among African American and Latino males (see *Figure 7.6* on page 188).

Reasons for Adolescent Sex

"Raging hormones," the old explanation for adolescent sex, is more fiction than fact. Although adolescents who mature early are more likely to become sexually active at a younger age, the degree of interest in sex varies among young people. For young girls, sex still occurs most often in the context of close, romantic relationships, whereas many boys see sex as a goal. For example, 81 percent of girls who first had sex at age 14 or younger were dating that partner (Albert et al., 2003).

One reason for early premarital sex, you recall, and especially for boys, is *peer pressure*. One in three boys aged 15 to 17 say they feel pressure to have sex, compared with 23 percent of girls (Holt et al., 2003). Boys as young as 13 brag about their sexual prowess (although most are lying) and ridicule friends who have not "scored." Boys may even challenge a friend to "prove his manhood." Girls are more likely to have fewer partners and to engage in sex to keep or to please boyfriends (Sprecher and McKinney, 1993; Holt et al., 2003).

Adolescent sex sometimes results in unwanted pregnancy. This can be highly traumatic for a teenage girl and her partner. Boyfriends usually desert the mother and baby. The young mother typically drops out of school and lives in poverty.

Parental factors also play an important role in early premarital sex. As you've seen earlier, young teens (those between ages 14 and 16) are less likely to engage in sexual intercourse and with fewer partners if the mothers, in particular, monitor their teens' activities, maintain good communication, and have nonpermissive attitudes about adolescent sex. Middle-class children, especially, are likely to have demanding schedules that include music lessons, sports, summer camps, and family trips, all of which are supervised.

Parental monitoring doesn't guarantee abstinence, however. A third of 12-year-olds, for example, report that they had recently attended a party where no adults were in the house. By age 14, this percentage increased to 51 percent for boys and 42 percent for girls. In about half of the sexual encounters, an adult was "around" (Albert et al., 2003). Thus, teens are often having sex at home and just down the hall from a parent.

Environmental variables also influence early sexual intercourse. Teens who are more likely to engage in sexual activities are those who live in single-parent or remarried families, have more opportunity for sex (as in steady dating), associate with delinquent peers, use

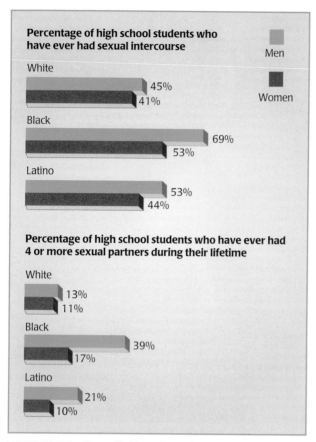

Percentage of high school students who have ever had sexual intercourse

Men
Women

White
45%
41%

Black
69%
53%

Latino
53%
44%

Percentage of high school students who have ever had 4 or more sexual partners during their lifetime

White
13%
11%

Black
39%
17%

Latino
21%
10%

FIGURE 7.6 **Sexually Experienced Teens, 2001**

SOURCE: Based on Grunbaum et al., 2002, Table 30.

alcohol and other drugs, or have been sexually abused (Perkins et al., 1998; Upchurch et al., 1999; Whitbeck et al., 1999; Lindberg et al., 2000).

Even <u>seasons</u> affect young peoples' sexual debuts. The first sexual intercourse of teens in grades 7 through 12 has two seasonal "peaks." One, in June (the "summer vacation effect"), occurs between people who are not in a romantic relationship but have proms, have a lot of free (and unsupervised) time at the end of the school year, and wear fewer and less restrictive clothes. The second peak, in December ("the holiday season effect"), occurs between adolescents in romantic relationships. The holidays seem to encourage lovemaking because they are bathed in romantic "trimmings" such as mistletoe and Christmas movies about people falling in love (Levin et al., 2002).

Cultural attitudes and expectations also influence early sexual experiences. Young Latino males, for instance, are much more likely than Latinas to report that they've had sexual intercourse and with more partners (see *Figure 7.6*). The double standard that we discussed earlier and in Chapters 5 and 6 probably explains some of the gender differences.

Two concepts common in Latin American culture promote female premarital abstinence: *verguenza* ("shame"), which connotes embarrassment about body parts and the notion that "good" girls should not know about sexuality, and *marianismo* (from the name of the Virgin Mary), which reflects values relating to chastity, purity, and virtue. If young Latinas endorse these cultural values, they are more likely to delay sexual activity (Liebowitz et al., 1999). As immigrants assimilate into U.S. culture, their children often internalize peer values and behaviors that encourage early sexual intercourse (see Chapter 4).

Forced Sexual Intercourse Nationwide, 10 percent of female and 5 percent of male high school students said they have had sex against their will. Black and Latino students (10 percent and 9 percent, respectively) were more likely than white students (7 percent) to have been forced to have sexual intercourse (Grunbaum et al., 2002).

The most common factors associated with a young girl's unwanted sex include her mother's having an abusive boyfriend, illicit drug use (by the parent, victim, or the nonparental abuser), lack of parental monitoring in the home, a history of sexual abuse in the victim's family, and the victim's living apart from parents before age 16 (Small and Kerns, 1993). Adolescent boys report unwanted sexual touching (kissing, petting, fondling) and a romantic partner's threatening a loss of love (for a review of this literature, see Christopher and Kisler, in press).

Sex and Singles

Since the mid-1960s, premarital intercourse has increased considerably among young adults in their early to mid-20s, especially women. High school graduates who take jobs, enroll in vocational training programs, or join the military services have more opportunity and money for recreational pursuits that may include sex.

Many young adults who go on to college find themselves free from parental monitoring for the first time. This first experience of independence among people of the same age and social class provides a fertile environment for courting and mating.

Who Initiates Sexual Contact? Traditional sexual scripts dictate that the man should initiate sexual contact because "nice girls don't." Many young women have become much more assertive, however. Instead of sitting around at home, they frequent singles bars or call men they're interested in. They also invite sexual contact in other ways, such as going to a man's apartment or dorm room. In steady dating relationships, women may touch or stroke a partner or make sensuous comments about his appearance to arouse him (O'Sullivan and Byers, 1993).

Women are still more likely than men to have sex only in a committed relationship. Many young women, however, such as these college students during a Spring Break, have more opportunities than in the past to initiate sexual activity.

Many young women rationalize intercourse in the same way that earlier generations justified petting ("It's O.K. if I love him"). The growing number of women who are having intercourse when "hookin' up," however, suggests that these traditional views are changing (see Chapter 8).

Will You Still Love Me Tomorrow?   Maybe. Young people view casual sex less favorably than they did a generation ago. In 1980, for example, 50 percent of first-year college students said that "if two people really like each other, it's all right for them to have sex even if they've known each other for a short time." In 2001, in contrast, 42 percent of the students (47 percent of the men and 70 percent of the women) agreed with this statement ("Attitudes and characteristics . . .," 2002).

And will you respect me tomorrow? Not if we're having casual sex, according to some researchers. Many men still have a double standard. They often judge sexually permissive women as terrific for casual dates or as regular sexual partners but unacceptable for long-term commitments or as marriage partners (see Chapter 8).

Sex in Marriage

Compared with premarital and extramarital sex, there is little information on marital sex. Perhaps marital sex is rarely a research focus because it is "generally not viewed as a social problem" (Christopher and Sprecher, 2001: 220). According to the available data, however, most married couples are happy with their sex lives.

Frequency of Sex   "I got married," says one guy to another, "so that I could have sex three or four times a week." That's funny," says his buddy. "That's exactly why I got divorced." There are many similar jokes about not enough sex in marriage. In fact, about 40 percent of married people have sex with their partner two or more times a week. This rate is much higher than for singles (see *Figure 7.5*).

In terms of such indirect measures of sexual frequency as condom sales, the highest sales are among married couples with children under age 12 and under age 6 (26 percent and 15 percent, respectively) (Fetto, 2003). This suggests that couples with young children are sexually active.

Among some couples, the frequency of sexual intercourse may remain constant or even increase over the years. Among others, sexual expression may change: Intercourse may decrease, but fondling and genital stimulation (with or without orgasm) may increase. Overall, however, marital sex typically decreases with partners' age and longevity of the marriage. As a marriage matures, concerns about earning a living, making a home, and raising a family become more pressing than lovemaking.

Quality of Sex   Although the frequency of sex decreases, the longer people are married the more likely they are to report that they are very satisfied with their current sex life (Mattox, 1994; Call et al., 1995). Sex is especially satisfying if both spouses feel—in terms of exchange theory—that their rewards and costs are similar and that they enjoy a mutually satisfying emotional relationship (Lawrance and Byers, 1995; Waite and Joyner, 2001).

The false notion that most married couples have unhappy sex lives has become big business. We have become so obsessed with this subject that sex manuals are constantly on best-seller lists. Most recently, for example, one writer insists that having sex about once a month is synonymous with a "sexless" or "sex starved" marriage (Weiner-Davis, 2003). Newsmagazines are fanning such opinions to increase sales. Less frequent marital sex is neither unusual nor abnormal, and it has nothing to do with the quality of a relationship. Even young married couples report that companionship is often more important than sexual passion. As one man stated,

> On my list [sex] would come fourth. Marriage, as far as I'm concerned, is friendship and companionship; that ranks first. Then there's consideration for one another, and then trust, and then fourth I'd say your physical relationship. And those three that come before hopefully enhance what you experience in your physical relationship (Greenblatt, 1983: 298).

Spouses in Middle Years

As we mature, our sexual interests, abilities, and responses change. Early in the twentieth century many women died, often in childbirth, long before they could experience **menopause,** the cessation of the menstrual cycle and the loss of reproductive capacity, or "the change of life," as it was once called.

Now gynecologists study not only all the stages of the menstrual cycle but also *perimenopause,* a normal phenomenon that precedes menopause. Whereas menopause typically begins in a woman's mid-40s to early 50s, perimenopause can begin in the early 40s and last 4 to 5 years.

The symptoms of both perimenopause and menopause include hormonally induced "hot flashes" (the sudden experience of overall bodily heat, sometimes accompanied by sweating), irregular menstrual cycles with uncharacteristically heavy or light bleeding, mood changes, fatigue, migraine headaches, backaches, insomnia, loss or increase of appetite, diarrhea or constipation, and urinary incontinence (Northrup, 2001). Because of these changes, one of my older students "defines" menopause as "Everyone around you suddenly has a bad attitude."

Not all women experience these symptoms, and some hardly notice that they are going through menopause. Hot flashes affect about 75 percent of all women, but they usually last only a few minutes. Most women do not consider menopause a crisis but a liberating time of life: Many enjoy sex more because they are no longer bothered by menstruation, the need for contraception, or the fear of pregnancy (Fisher, 1999).

It is unclear whether there is a **male climacteric,** or change of life analogous to female menopause. Although testosterone production declines with age, unlike women, men do not lose their reproductive capacity. Some men have fathered children in their late 70s.

Only a small percentage of men experience nervousness, depression, decreased sexual performance (which often can be treated medically), inability to concentrate, irritability, and similar problems. It may be that the male "change of life" is a more general "midlife crisis" in which men look back over their lives and feel distress at not having achieved all that they might have (Gould et al., 2000).

Although some spouses in their middle years are dissatisfied with their sexual lives, they represent a minority of all marriages (Edwards and Booth, 1994). Couples who have no children living at home and need not care for elderly parents are freed from time-consuming responsibilities. They have more time, energy, and privacy for talking, intimacy, and sex. Thus, "the empty nest may actually be a love nest" (Woodward and Springen, 1992: 71).

Sex and Later Life

An 80-year-old husband says, "Let's go upstairs and make love." His 75-year-old wife replies, "Pick one, sweetie. I can't do both." This is one of my elderly aunt's favorite jokes. Despite such jokes, many men and women remain sexually active into their 70s, 80s, and beyond.

Sexual Activity   Sexual activity among older people declines but doesn't evaporate. About half of 45- through 59-year-olds report having sex at least once a week. Among 60- through 74-year-olds, the proportion drops to 30 percent for men and 24 percent for women (Jacoby, 1999).

In the later years, sexuality encompasses a wide range of acts and feelings, from hugging and holding hands to sexual intercourse. In a study of the sexual practices of 202 men and women aged 80 to 102 (that's right, 102!), 47 percent of the respondents were having sexual intercourse and 34 percent engaged in oral sex. Also, 88 percent of the men and 71 percent of the women still fantasized or daydreamed about the opposite sex (Bretschneider and McCoy, 1988).

Sex and Emotional Satisfaction   Loving, committed relationships are much less problematic than situations where partners have little rapport (Marsiglio and Greer, 1994). Lowered activity—or inactivity—is not a problem if both partners are satisfied with their sex lives (Marsiglio and Donnelly, 1991; Matthias et al., 1997).

Among those aged 70 and over, the strongest predictors of a satisfying relationship are being sexually active (which may or may not include intercourse) and having good mental health, such as feeling happy, calm, and peaceful (Matthias et al., 1997). As a 71-year-old woman noted, sex can improve because partners are emotionally closer:

> My husband, Gerald, and I probably enjoy sex more now than we did in our 50s, because when you're younger, you worry about pleasing yourself. As you age, you're more knowledgeable and more aware of your partner's needs. When you're younger, I don't believe you really realize what sex is all about. It's not just about physical contact; it's about love and commitment. . . . There's laughter to sex, too. Some of those positions are pretty funny (Clements, 1996: 5–6).

Health and Sexuality   It's not until about age 70 that the frequency of sexual activity, in both men and women, begins to decline significantly. This generally results from poor health and habits. Smoking, alcoholism, heart disease, prostate problems, and vascular illnesses can decrease sexual desire and activity for both sexes.

For women, the drop in estrogen levels after menopause can decrease sexual desire and make sex painful because vaginal walls become thin and dry. In addition, especially for women, a mix of stress, anger, or a cooling relationship can dampen sexual desire. Some illnesses, such as diabetes and arteriosclerosis, as well as some medications for high blood pressure can cause impotence in older men (Butler and Lewis, 1993; McKinlay and Feldman, 1994).

Despite these difficulties, older men and women engage in and enjoy sex. A reporter asked a 90-year-old woman who married an 18-year-old man, "Aren't you afraid of what could happen on the honeymoon? Vigorous lovemaking might bring on injury or even a fatal heart attack!" She smiled and replied, "If he dies, he dies!"

More Double Standards and Sexual Scripts   Whereas gray-haired men in their 60s are considered "distinguished," their female counterparts are just "old." Men are not under the same pressure to remain young, trim, and attractive. When comparing her own public image with that of her actor husband, Paul Newman, actress Joanne Woodward remarked, "He gets prettier; I get older."

The aging process may enhance a man's desirability because he is seen as more distinguished and has more resources and power. In contrast, an older woman may be regarded as an asexual grandmother: "Because attractiveness is associated with feelings of well-being, a perceived decline in appearance can be particularly devastating for women" (Levy, 1994: 295–96). As in earlier stages of life, male sexual scripts usually focus on intercourse and orgasm. Older women are more interested in relational and nongenital activities (Johnson, 1996).

As people age, the biggest impediment to sex, especially for widows or divorcees, is a "partner gap." Because our culture frowns on liaisons and marriages between older women and younger men but approves of matches between older men and younger women, single older women have a small pool of eligible sexual partners (see Chapters 6, 9, and 17). In contrast, married women over age 70 report being both sexually active *and* sexually satisfied (Matthias et al., 1997).

MAKING CONNECTIONS

■ Have you ever been pressured to have sex? How did you react? What advice would you give younger people who would like to resist such pressure from their friends and girlfriends or boyfriends?

■ What kind of sex do you enjoy the most? The least? Why? If you haven't had sexual intercourse yet, do you fantasize about it? ✑

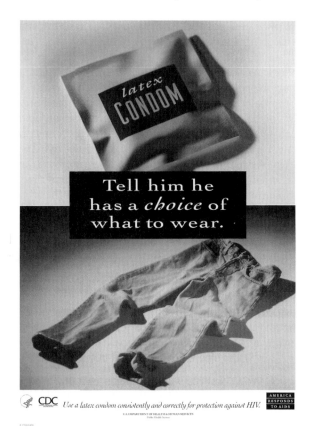

Tell him he has a *choice* of what to wear.

CDC *Use a latex condom consistently and correctly for protection against HIV.*
U.S. DEPARTMENT OF HEALTH & HUMAN SERVICES
Public Health Service

AMERICA RESPONDS TO AIDS

cases in black women and 40 percent of all cases in Latinas (Centers for Disease Control and Prevention, 2001; "HIV/AIDS among U.S. women . . .," 2002).

The most vulnerable groups are low-income women who use contaminated needles during drug use and engage in prostitution without using condoms. Prostitutes often exchange sex for drugs, such as cocaine. Cocaine lowers inhibitions, and unprotected sex is more likely. Being infected with HIV is largely a reflection of poverty or dependence for economic security on a male partner who is a drug user and has unprotected sex, often with another man. In addition, those who speak little or no English have less access to educational materials about HIV and AIDS (Jemmott et al., 1995; Centers for Disease Control and Prevention, 2001; Gilbert, 2003).

Older Women and AIDS One widespread misperception is that midlife women are immune to HIV infection. In Dade County, Florida, for instance, almost 20 percent of people with AIDS are seniors, mainly women (Marcus, 2003).

The life situations of midlife and older women increase their possible risk for infection. Because more older women than men are single, they may be sexually involved with men who don't admit that they are using drugs or having sexual relations with other women or men. In addition, older married women may be less assertive than younger women in insisting that a man use a condom. They may feel that they cannot refuse the sexual demands of their husbands, who may be infected, for unprotected sex (Center for Women Policy Studies, 1994).

Sexual Orientation and AIDS Even though the rate of HIV infection among intravenous drug users and heterosexuals has increased in the last decade, about 63 percent of all AIDS-infected people are MSM. Substantial numbers of young MSM are being infected with HIV. In 2000, for example, 59 percent of reported HIV infections were among adolescent males aged 13 to 19 and 53 percent of cases among men aged 20 to 24 ("Need for sustained . . .," 2002).

Men, Race-Ethnicity, and AIDS AIDS rates are disproportionately high among minorities (see *Figure 7.9*). Although African Americans make up about 12 percent of the U.S. population, they accounted for half of the new HIV cases in 2001. Half of these new cases occur among teenagers and young adults age 25 or younger. Although AIDS rates are lower for Latinos than blacks, they are more than three times the rate for whites (Centers for Disease Control and Prevention, 2001; "HIV/AIDS among Hispanics . . .," 2002).

Some Latino men avoid testing because they are migrant farm workers who can't afford medical attention.

drug use accounts for another 25 percent of cases (Centers for Disease Control and Prevention, 2001; "HIV/AIDS among U.S. women . . .," 2002).

Heterosexual women are more than twice as likely as men to become infected with HIV for several reasons. First, the genital surface exposed to the virus is much larger in women than in men. Second, vaginal secretions from an HIV-infected woman are believed to be less potent than an infected man's semen, which is capable of packing high concentrations of the virus. Third, a man's exposure to the virus is limited to the duration of sex, but semen remains in a woman's body after intercourse. Fourth, many women are not aware that their male partners are bisexual (Nicolosi et al., 1994; Stein, 2003). Finally, many women—especially those at low-income levels but 56 percent of college women as well—believe that they won't contract HIV or other STDs (though it's not clear why). As a result, they don't use condoms even when they have multiple sex partners (Yarnall et al., 2003).

Women, Race-Ethnicity, and AIDS Although African American women and Latinas represent less than one-fourth of all U.S. women, they account for 78 percent of AIDS cases among women. The leading cause of infection is heterosexual contact, followed by injection drug use, which accounts for about 25 percent of all

Even though all tests are confidential, many Latino men fear being deported if clinics or hospitals report their illegal status to immigration offices (Hernandez, 2003).

Sexual Orientation, Race-Ethnicity, and AIDS The largest number of HIV infections result from unprotected MSM: 76 percent among whites, 47 percent among African Americans, 57 percent among Latinos, 66 percent among Asians and Pacific Islanders, and 60 percent among American Indians and Alaska Natives. If we include injecting drugs among MSM, the percentages increase for all groups (for example, from 76 percent to 85 percent for white men) (Centers for Disease Control and Prevention, 2003).

African American and Latino MSM are less likely than their white counterparts to see themselves as gay or bisexual because of the enormous cultural stigma attached to homosexuality and injection drug use. Health experts believe that this view hinders discussions about HIV and AIDS and disease-prevention campaigns in many black and Latino communities (Brown, 2000; Johnson, 2003).

Preventing STDs and HIV

The drug cocktails that revolutionized AIDS treatment in the mid-1990s have not decreased the number of new infections. HIV diagnoses among MSM have increased by 18 percent since the lowest point in 1999. Health officials believe that the increase has resulted, in large part, from a return of risky sexual behavior. Even men who do not have HIV are less likely to use condoms than in the past because they're confident that drugs will prolong their lives or even prevent infections ("Number of new HIV cases . . .," 2003).

New drugs are *not* forthcoming. Experts say that a vaccine against HIV will not be ready until at least 2009. Even then, a successful vaccine may be only 30 or 40 percent effective in slowing the AIDS epidemic (Miles, 2003).

Many women are uninformed or silent about STDs and HIV/AIDS. In a recent survey of women aged 18 to 49, for example, 60 percent said they had never discussed STD or HIV testing with their current partner. One in six women withheld sexual health information from a health-care provider because they were embarrassed. In addition, most women did not know that STDs don't have immediate symptoms or that they can lead to certain cancers, and most thought (mistakenly) that a Pap smear tests for STDs ("National sexual health survey . . .," 2003).

You'll recall that many schools block Internet sites that include information about STDs, HIV/AIDS and that the federal government is funneling money into abstinence programs rather than sex education classes. This means that many adolescents have little information about STDs, HIV/AIDS. Therefore, "trusted adults"—such as parents, teachers, and other community members—must talk frankly with youth about how casual sex can lead to serious health consequences (Carter, 2003).

Conclusion

One of the biggest *changes* since the turn of the century is that we are better informed about human sexuality. Today we have more *choices* in our sexual expression, and most people recognize that sexuality is more than the sex act. Instead, sexuality comprises biological, emotional, intellectual, spiritual, and cultural components.

But there are also a number of *constraints*. We are often unwilling to provide young people with the information they need to make thoughtful decisions about sex. Gay men and lesbians still face discrimination and harassment because of their sexual practices. And our health and lives and the lives of our children are threatened by the rising incidence of STDs and HIV infection.

These changes have significant effects on both women and men in their search for suitable marriage partners and other long-term relationships. We will look at some of these issues in the next several chapters.

SUMMARY

1. Our sexual lives affect our families and marriages from birth to death. Regardless of age or marital status, sexual expression plays an important role throughout life.

2. Human sexuality is complex and incorporates components such as sexual identity, sexual orientation, and gender roles. Biological theories maintain that genes and sex hormones determine sexual preference, whereas social constructionist theories emphasize social and environmental factors.

3. Although we like to think that our sexual behavior is spontaneous, sexual scripts shape most of our sexual activities, attitudes, and relationships.

4.   Most of us do not learn about sex in the home. Much of our information, and misinformation, comes from peers and the media. Although there are variations across states, many sex education programs are being funded generously only if they provide abstinence-only approaches.

5.   Sexual activity encompasses many behaviors other than sexual intercourse, such as fantasies, masturbation, petting, and oral sex.

6.   Adolescent girls are more likely to romanticize sex, whereas adolescent boys typically see sex as an end in itself. The reasons for early premarital sex include early pubertal changes, peer pressure, environmental factors, and cultural expectations.

7.   Marital sex typically decreases over the course of a marriage, but married couples enjoy sexual intercourse and a variety of other sexual activities.

8.   Despite many stereotypes about sexuality and aging, people age 70 and older continue to engage in sexual activities, including intercourse, masturbation, and sexual fantasy.

9.   Gay and lesbian partners experience many of the same feelings as do heterosexuals and face some of the same problems in their relationships. Major factors that differentiate gay and lesbian couples from heterosexual couples are society's disapproval of homosexual practices and their consequent lack of legal rights in many areas.

10.   Although today more people are informed about STDs, HIV infection, and AIDS, many still engage in high-risk behavior, such as sharing drug needles, having sex with many partners, and not using condoms. The rates for new HIV infections are especially high among male-male couples, minorities, and heterosexual women.

KEY TERMS

sexual orientation   *168*
homosexual   *168*
heterosexual   *168*
bisexual   *168*
sexual script   *171*
autoeroticism   *181*
masturbation   *182*

petting   *182*
fellatio   *183*
cunnilingus   *183*
sexual response   *183*
menopause   *190*
male climacteric   *190*

sexually transmitted diseases (STDs)   *196*
human immunodeficiency virus (HIV)   *197*
acquired immunodeficiency syndrome (AIDS)   *197*

TAKING IT FURTHER

Everything You've Ever Wanted to Know about Sex

National Abstinence Clearinghouse offers resources and material that encourage premarital abstinence.

www.abstinence.net

Centers for Disease Control and Prevention provides health information, publications, international data, and links to numerous health-related sites on HIV, AIDS, and other STDs.

www.cdc.gov

SIECUS (Sexuality Information and Education Council of the United States) develops and disseminates information on sexuality education and responsible sexual behavior.

www.siecus.org

Kaiser Family Foundation is a wonderful source of information about sexuality, sex-related surveys, and sexual health. You can also get daily, weekly, or monthly e-mail alerts on a number of issues and recent news releases about sex and current research on sex.

www.kff.org

And more: www.prenhall.com/benokraitis includes numerous sites on safer sex, world statistics and maps on HIV and AIDS, decreasing teen pregnancy, menstruation, female genital mutilation, men's and women's sex-related health issues, and tips on reviving your sex life.

INVESTIGATE WITH RESEARCH NAVIGATOR

Research Navigator.com
RESOURCES FOR COLLEGE RESEARCH ASSIGNMENTS

Please go to www.researchnavigator.com and enter your LOGIN NAME and PASSWORD. For instructions on registering for the first time, please view the detailed instructions at the end of the Chapter 1. Please search the Research Navigator™ site using the following key search terms:

homosexuals
sexually transmitted diseases
double-standard

CHAPTER 8

Choosing Others:
Dating and Mate Selection

DATADIGEST

- In 2000, 25 percent of all **never-married adults** were between ages 30 and 44.

- By age 16, 83 percent of boys and 78 percent of girls **have been on at least one date.**

- Almost **60 percent of American adults are currently dating** or are interested in dating.

- About 63 percent of Americans say "I love you" to their pet every day; **90 percent would not consider dating someone who wasn't fond of their pet**.

- In mid-2003, **more than 45 million Americans visited online dating sites:** 46 percent were women, 54 percent were men, and 42 percent were ages 25 to 44.

- Some nations have a **shortage of marriageable women.** In India, for example, there are nearly 133 single men for every 100 single women. In China, 117 boys are born for every 100 girls and 140 boys for every 100 girls in some rural areas, well over the international norm of 105 to 100.

SOURCES: Michael and Bickert, 2001; "Come Here Often?", 2002; Fetto, 2002, 2003; U.S. Census Bureau, 2002; Harmon, 2003.

Someone once joked that dating is the process of spending lots of time and money to meet people you probably won't like. Yet some of the most popular television programs today include *The Bachelor, The Bachelorette, Cupid, Blind Date, Dismissed,* and *Change of Heart.* Why are these shows so popular?

Singlehood has its advantages (see Chapter 9). Most of us, however, seek intimacy with a lifelong partner. Regardless of what words we use—"dating," "going out," "hookin' up," "having a thing," or "seeing someone"—mate selection is a process that, most of us hope, will result in finding an intimate partner or marriage mate.

As the box "Courting throughout U. S. History" on page 204 shows, dating is a recent invention. It emerged in the United States in the twentieth century and became a well-established rite of passage in the 1950s. How we date has changed, but why and whom we date and why we break up have been fairly constant. Let's begin with the question of why we date.

Why Do We Date?

The reasons for **dating**—the process of meeting people socially for possible mate selection—seem self-evident. Dating is much more complicated than just having fun,

203

CHANGES

Courting throughout U. S. History

Contrary to what we might think, young people in colonial America often experienced and enjoyed premarital sex. As a young woman wrote passionately to her lover,

O! I do really want to kiss you. How I should like to be in that old parlor with you. I hope there will be a carpet on the floor for it seems you intend to act worse than you ever did before by your letter. But I shall humbly submit to my fate and willingly, too, to speak candidly (Rothman, 1983: 401).

There were also practical considerations. In colonial New England, the engaged woman's parents conducted economic negotiations, and most young men could not even think about courtship until they owned land. They were advised to "choose by ears, as well as eyes" and to select women who were industrious, hardworking, and sensible. Affection was expected to blossom into love after marriage.

Some women were also very down-to-earth about courtship. A New York woman wrote,

I am sick of all this choosing. If a man is healthy and does not drink and has a good little handful of stock and a good temper and is a good Christian, what difference can it make to a woman which man she takes? (Ryan, 1983: 40–41).

Before the Industrial Revolution, most courtship activities took place within the hustle and bustle of community life. Young people could meet after church services, during picnics, or at gatherings such as barn raisings and dances. The buggy ride was especially popular: There was no room for a chaperone, and "the horse might run away or lose a shoe so that one could be stranded on a lonely country road" (McPharlin, 1946: 10).

At the turn of the twentieth century, especially among the middle classes, gentlemen "called" on women. In calling, a woman or her mother invited a suitor to visit at the woman's home. Other family members would be present. If the relationship proceeded toward engagement, the couple enjoyed some privacy in the parlor (Bailey, 1988).

With the advent of bicycles and telephones, parlor sofas and front porch swings were quickly abandoned. People began to use the term *dating*, which referred to couples setting a specific date, time, and place to meet. When the automobile came into widespread use in the early 1920s, dating took a giant step. "The car provided more privacy and excitement than either the dance hall or the movie theater, and the result was the spread of petting" (Rothman, 1984: 295). Young people had the mobility to meet more frequently, informally, and casually.

Until the early 1970s, dating reflected a strict and gendered code of etiquette. Men initiated the dates and paid for all expenses. Women waited to be "asked out" and provided companionship (and sometimes sex) during a date.

STOP AND THINK . . .

- *Did the colonists have the right idea in being "practical" about courtship? Or should courtship always involve searching for a "soul mate"?*

- *Talk to your parents, grandparents, or other relatives about dating in the 1950s and 1960s. What were some of the advantages of these dating rituals? What about the disadvantages?*

however. Sociologists describe the dating process as a **marriage market** in which prospective spouses compare the assets and liabilities of eligible partners and choose the best available mate.

Everyone has a "market value," and whom a person "trades" with depends on one's resources. Like most other choices we make, dating involves taking risks with the resources we invest. The more valuable the "catch," the more likely we are to devote our time and money in looking attractive, accommodating the partner's personality or interests, or getting along with her or his family and friends, for example. In contrast, "one-night stands" entail taking few risks (assuming the partners don't contract STDs or the woman doesn't become pregnant) and investing few resources.

Also, people might use their resources differently depending on whether the relationship is new or "settling in." As one of my students observed, people may invest more time than money in a partner if they are no longer in the "trading" stage in the marriage marketplace:

It's very expensive to date. When two people are in a comfortable relationship, they tend not to go out as much. The quiet nights at home are considerably less expensive than extravagant nights on the town. The longer you date someone, the less need there is to impress that person with fancy dinners and costly dates (Author's files).

Dating fulfills a number of specific functions that enhance people's development and, ultimately, contribute to the needs of the larger society (see Chapter 1). These functions vary according to a person's age, social class, and gender. Dating functions can be either *manifest*—the purposes are visible, recognized, and intended—or *latent*—the purposes are unintended or not immediately recognized (see Chapter 2). Keep in mind that these functions often overlap.

Manifest Functions of Dating

Dating is an important activity because it signals adolescent *maturation*. Whether young people are interested in the opposite sex or the same sex, dating sends the message that a young person is reaching puberty. During puberty, adolescents learn development tasks that include emotional intimacy outside the family and, quite possibly, sexual expression (see Chapter 7).

Dating provides *fun* and *recreation*. Going out with people we like relieves boredom, stress, and loneliness. As more people postpone marriage (see Chapter 9), dating has become an important recreational activity. As one of my students said recently, "I can motivate myself to study during the week cuz I know I'll be seeing my girlfriend this weekend."

Another important manifest function of dating is *companionship*. Especially as people age, dating may be important for developing and maintaining long-term friendships. Dating can be a valuable source of companionship, especially after retirement, when leisure hours increase.

Dating also provides a socially accepted way of pursuing *love* and *affection*. Among college students, for example, both women and men say that they initiated a first date because they were in love and wanted a caring and serious relationship (Clark et al., 1999). The relationship may fizzle, but dating is an avenue for getting closer to another person.

Finally, whether people admit it or not, dating is usually a step in *mate selection*. Adolescents often become angry if their parents criticize their dates with such remarks as "We don't want you to marry this guy" or "She's not good enough for you." The teenager's impatient rebuttal is usually, "I'm not going to marry him (her). We're just going out!"

Parents are often judgmental because they recognize that dating *can* lead to marriage. Young people are "comparison shopping," acquiring knowledge of what sorts of people they are attracted to and may want to marry (Whyte, 1990). In contrast, there is little need for dating in cultures where parents influence their children's mate selection through arranged marriages, for instance. In many of these societies, values focus on the needs of the family rather than on those of the individual, and love is not the basis for marriage (see later sections of this chapter and Chapters 5 to 7).

Latent Functions of Dating

An important latent function of dating is *socialization*, in which people learn to adjust and adapt their own behavior to that of others (see Chapters 1, 5, and 7). Through dating, people learn about expected gender roles, about family structures that are different from their own, and about new attitudes, beliefs, and values. This kind of learning may be especially valuable for high school students, who can test and hone their self-confidence and their communication skills in one-on-one settings (Ramu, 1989; Berk, 1993).

Gaining social status is another important latent function of dating. Going out with an attractive or successful person enhances one's status and prestige. Being popular or going out with someone who's popular increases one's standing in a social group.

A related function of dating is *fulfilling ego needs*. Being asked out on a date or having one's invitation accepted boosts a person's self-esteem and self-image. Self-confidence rises if the date goes well or if the partner is understanding, flattering, or attentive.

Dating also provides *opportunities for sexual experimentation and intimacy*. Many teenagers learn about sex during dating. Females, especially, are likely to report that their first sexual intercourse occurred in a steady or serious dating relationship (see Chapter 7). As dating becomes more committed or the frequency of dating increases, there is an increase in wanting and experiencing sex (Michael and Bickert, 2001).

Finally, dating is *big business*. Dating activities provide a significant economic market for products and services that include clothing, grooming, food, and entertainment (Rouse, 2002).

Manifest and latent dating functions may change over time. As people mature, their expectations about dating change. Status may become less relevant and companionship more important, for example, if partners consider marriage.

The Dating Spectrum

Unlike a few generations ago, dating is now distinct from courtship and may or may not end in marriage. Is the date all but dead? Perhaps on many college campuses, but not nationally.

Between adolescence and the altar, speaking symbolically, most people initially get an overview of the marriage market by getting together in groups of prospective partners, then pairing off, and ultimately going off with one person. Although traditional dating is still widespread, there are a number of newer forms of getting together, as well as some combinations of traditional and contemporary dating.

Dating during the middle of the twentieth century was more structured than it is today. Although casual dates weren't unheard of, formal dates ruled by codes of dress and behavior were commonplace.

Traditional Dating

The *traditional date*, which predominated through the 1970s, is a fairly formal way of meeting potential spouses. In traditional dating, males and females follow culturally defined and clear gender role scripts, at least among the middle classes. The girl waits to be asked out, the boy picks her up at her home, and she is almost always late, giving Mom and Dad a chance to chat with the boy. The boy has specific plans for the evening, pays for everything, and brings her home by curfew.

Some older television programs such as *Happy Days* and *The Brady Bunch,* although idealized, portray this type of date. Men pay for the date, but what exactly are they buying? A good time, perhaps. Or female companionship. But there is always "an uncomfortable undercurrent of sexual favors lurking in the background" (Stone and McKee, 2002: 70). Although the expectation is unstated, the female is expected to show her gratitude in some way, usually through a goodnight kiss, petting, or intercourse.

Cultural Variations on Traditional Dating   The popularity of traditional dating is particularly evident in such formal events as *coming-out parties,* where young women, usually of the upper classes, are "introduced to society" at debutante balls (see Kendall, 2002). Other cultural rites of passage include the *bat mitzvah* for girls and the *bar mitzvah* for boys in the Jewish community. These rituals mark the end of childhood and readiness for adult responsibilities and such rights as dating.

In some Latino communities, the *quinceañera* (translated loosely as "fifteen years") is a coming-out party that celebrates a girl's entrance into adulthood. The *quince* (pronounced KEEN-say) is an elaborate and dignified religious and social affair given by the girl's parents. It begins with a Catholic Mass and is followed by a reception at which 14 couples (each couple represents one year in the girl's life before the *quince*) serve as her attendants.

The event includes a traditional waltz in which the young woman dances with her father, a champagne toast, and the tossing of a bouquet to the boys to determine who wins the first dance with the young woman. The girl may be allowed to date boys after her *quince* (Leff, 1994).

In Cuban American neighborhoods in Miami, middle-class and affluent parents pay between $30,000 and $50,000 for a *quince*. Parents of modest means pay as much as $10,000: "Factory workers, an auto body shop manager. . . . They save up for years for their daughters" (McLane, 1995: 42). There is no comparable rite of passage for Latino boys.

Going Steady   Going steady and "getting pinned" were common in the 1930s and became especially popular after World War II. A couple was "pinned" when a young man gave his fraternity pin to his girlfriend to show his affection and commitment. *Going steady,* which often meant that the partners were seeing only each other, usually came after a couple had had a number of dates, and it sometimes preceded engagement (Tuttle, 1993).

Typically, however, going steady was short-lived. As one teenage girl explained, "Going steady doesn't have to mean you're madly in love. . . . It just means you like one boy better than the rest" (quoted in Breines, 1992: 116). Going steady reduced many of the anxieties associated with traditional dating: It allowed emotional and sexual intimacy without a long-term commitment and gave a "hands-off" message to possible competitors.

A modern version of going steady is "going with" or "going together." For many middle school students, "goin' with" signals their transition from childhood to adolescence (Merten, 1996). Although the couples are not planning to get engaged, they are also not seeing others. "Goin' with" sometimes starts before puberty, even though the relationships of fourth-, fifth-, and sixth-graders usually break up after a few weeks (Albert et al., 2003). For older adolescents, such liaisons may last months or even years.

The advantage of "goin' with" is having a stable relationship when many other things are changing and unpredictable (such as physiological changes, divorcing parents, and preparation for college or a job). The disadvantage is that such relationships discourage meeting new people—especially when adolescents are experiencing many developmental changes in a short period of time (see Chapter 2).

Contemporary Dating

Contemporary dating falls into two general categories: *casual dating,* which includes hanging out, getting together, "pack dating," and "hooking up"; and *serious dating,* which can lead to cohabitation, engagement, and marriage.

Hanging Out

Parents and adolescents in many American homes engage in a familiar dialogue:

> Parent: Where are you going?
> Teenager: Out.
> Parent: What will you do?
> Teenager: Just hang out.
> Parent: Who will be there?
> Teenager: I don't know yet.
> Parent: When will you be back?
> Teenager: I'm not sure.
> Parent: Leave your cell phone on, please.

Whether *hanging out* occurs on a neighborhood street corner, at a fast-food place, or in a mall, it is a time-honored adolescent pastime. A customary meeting time and place may be set, with people coming and going. Or once a group gets together, the members decide what they want to do, and the information is quickly spread by phone or e-mail. Hanging out is possible both because many parents respect their teenagers' privacy and independence and because most 16- and 17-year-olds have access to cars.

Getting Together

Getting together is a more intimate and structured situation than hanging out. A group of friends meet at someone's house, a club, or a party. Either males or females can organize the initial effort, and the group often pools its resources, especially if alcohol or other drugs are part of the activities. Because participants are not dating, there is a lot of flexibility in meeting people.

Getting together typically involves "floating." The group may meet at someone's house for a few hours, decide to go to a party later, spend a few hours at a mall, and wind up at another party. Adolescents see getting together as normal and rational—"You get to meet a lot of people" or "We can go someplace else if the party is dead"—but it concerns parents. Even if teenagers call home from the various locations, parents worry that the gatherings can become unpredictable or dangerous because of drug abuse.

Getting together is a popular form of dating for several reasons. Because the activities are spontaneous, there is little anxiety about preparing for a formal date or initiating or rejecting sexual advances. The experience is less threatening emotionally because the participants don't have to worry about finding a date or getting "stuck" with someone (like a blind date) for the whole evening.

It also relieves females of sexual pressure because they may help organize the get-together, share in the expenses, and come alone or with friends (not as part of a couple). People may pair off, participate in the group as a couple, or gradually withdraw to spend more time together, but there is less pressure to have a date as a sign of popularity.

Finally, getting together decreases parental control over the choice of one's friends. Parents usually don't know many of the adolescents and are less likely to disapprove of the friendships or to compare notes with other parents.

"Pack Dating"

Whereas traditional dating and early marriages are common on some campuses, especially in the South and Midwest, many undergraduates socialize in unpartnered groups, or *pack dating:*

> *They go out to dinner in groups, attend movies in groups and at parties dance in a circle of five or six. The packs give students a sense of self-assurance and identity, but keep them from deeper, more committed relationships (Gabriel, 1997: 22).*

Pack dating may be popular for several reasons. If college students don't expect to marry until their 30s, socializing in small groups provides recreation without the pressure of making a commitment or getting romantically involved. Also, because increasing numbers of students hold down jobs while taking heavy course loads, many feel that they don't have the time and energy to find dates or maintain one-on-one relationships.

"Hooking Up"

Hooking up (or "hookin' up") refers to physical encounters, no strings attached. These encounters can mean anything from kissing to oral sex and sexual intercourse. In a recent national survey,

In one ritual of the Latino "quince", the young woman's father slips on her first pair of high heels. In the Miami Cuban community, some families spend as much as $50,000 on a daughter's quinceañera.

40 percent of college women said they had hooked up at least once, and 10 percent reported having done so more than six times (Glenn and Marquardt, 2001). Hooking up commonly, but not always, takes place when both people are drinking. People might also hook up with casual friends or a past girlfriend or boyfriend.

Hooking up has its advantages. It's cheaper than dating. Also, it's intentionally vague. Because no one knows for sure what, if anything, happened, women can avoid getting a bad reputation for being "loose" or "easy." Most importantly, there's an assumption that hooking up requires no commitment of time or emotion even though it may hurt to see a partner hook up with someone else.

Hooking up also has disadvantages. Because it's ambiguous, hooking up can create insecurity:

> If you can "hook up" with someone occasionally at a party but not be "hanging out" with them; or be "seeing" someone, but not "dating"; or "talking to" someone, but not really "having a conversation," how does a girl know when she's headed toward something serious, already there or, for that matter, when a relationship has ended? (Stepp, 2003: F1).

In addition, hookups aren't always as impersonal as people expect. In the survey of college women, many said that hookups made them feel sexy and desirable. However, between 18 and 64 percent also said that they later felt awkward, exploited, or disappointed. Others felt confused because they didn't know what to expect next or whether a guy would call back (Glenn and Marquardt, 2001).

Traditional–contemporary Combinations

Several dating patterns incorporate both traditional customs and contemporary trends. For example, 85 percent of adults feel it's okay for women to ask men out on dates, and 40 percent of women have done so ("Come here often?," 2002). Even though it is now more acceptable for either sex to initiate dates or to invite someone to a prom or dinner, many gender scripts remain remarkably traditional (see Chapter 5).

Proms and Homecoming Parties   *Proms* and *homecoming parties* are still among the most popular and traditional dating events (Best, 2000). As in the past, they are formal or semiformal. Women get corsages, men are typically responsible for transportation and other expenses, and females, especially, invest quite a bit of time and money in preparing for these events:

> She spends $196 for a dress; begins looking 12 weeks before the prom; shops at 11 different stores;

and tries on 36 different dresses before finding the perfect frock. He spends $162 on accessories and tuxedo rental or purchase and reserves his duds six weeks before the prom (Weissman, 1999b: 80).

Contemporary prom changes include "turnabout" invitations (those extended to men by women) and dining out beforehand with a large group of couples. Couples might prolong the event by holding a group sleepover (presumably chaperoned by parents), staying out all night and returning after breakfast, or continuing the festivities into the weekend at a nearby beach or other recreational area.

Dinner Dates   One of the most traditional forms of dating, the *dinner date*, is still popular today, particularly among adults. Dinner dates, and especially first dates of any kind, are still highly scripted. Men typically initiate the date, drive the car, open doors, and start sexual interaction (such as kissing good night or making out). Women spend a good deal of time on their appearance, depend on the men to make the plans, and often respond to a sexual overture rather than making the first move. Thus, making a "good impression" early in the dating relationship is still largely synonymous with playing traditional gender roles (Rose and Frieze, 1993). As in the past, men are much more likely than women to initiate a first date, including a dinner date, because they are more interested in sexual intimacy (Regan, 2003).

The rise of the women's movement in the 1970s led to the custom of *going Dutch*, or splitting the costs of a date. Sharing dating expenses frees women to initiate dates and relieves them from feeling they should "pay off" with sex.

When women ask men out, however, the rules aren't clear about who picks up the check. About half of Americans feel that the person who initiated the date should pay for it, but more than a third think that the man should *always* pay for the date. Thus, the "rules" are vague: "Some men tell tales of women who ask them out and then expect them to pick up the tab" (Campbell, 2002: 4).

Perhaps the least gender-typed dating, at least on first dates, is between same-sex partners. A study of lesbians and gay men found little gender typing compared with heterosexual dating: Both partners participated more equally in orchestrating the date, maintaining the conversation, and initiating physical contact. There was also less concern about appearance (Klinkenberg and Rose, 1994). Because there are no recent studies of same-sex dating, however, it's not clear whether these behaviors have changed.

Dating Later in Life   Dating after divorce and after being widowed can be both therapeutic and intimidating.

It can enhance one's self-esteem, decrease loneliness, and involve reassessing one's strengths and weaknesses in forging new relationships. Dating can also provide companionship while one is still grieving a spouse's death.

Dating can also be daunting. A recently divorced person may be bitter toward the opposite sex, or a parent may worry about a child's reactions to her or his dating. Widowed people may be nervous about reentering the marriage market, feel guilty about their romantic yearnings, and experience anxiety about their physical appearance or sex appeal.

Many, however, establish new and satisfying relationships through dating (see Chapters 15 and 17). Some seek out their teen heartthrobs online, rekindle the old flame, and marry. Not all reunions have a happy ending, of course. People change over the years, and our memories of our "first love" are highly romanticized. For example, the class Don Juan is still attentive, but now he's also bald and fat, has bad breath, and cheats on his wife. In other cases, however, sparks fly again and both partners see the same person they had loved, just older (Russo, 2002).

MAKING CONNECTIONS

■ What do *you* mean by "hookin' up"? If you or your friends' hookups included sex, what were the benefits and costs?

■ When women ask men out on dates, who should pick up the check?

Meeting Others

The quest for love involves a variety of creative strategies. At some new bars, singles can scope out other people using video monitors scattered around the room. Using a joystick, they can zoom in for a better look, send the "target" a message, and then meet at a private booth in the bar (Hamilton, 2002).

An especially determined, never-married, college-educated elderly woman contacted a research scientist at the University of Michigan to find states with "the highest concentration of retired, single gentlemen who are well-educated and healthy." At the time, the scientist suggested Nevada (Dortch, 1995: 15). And a growing number of cities have gay neighborhoods where men and women easily meet potential partners at the grocery store, the library, and church groups.

As you'll see shortly, many of us meet our dating partners through friends and family members. There are many other avenues for finding a mate, including clubs, college classes, matchmaking by your sister-in-law, and recreational activities such as hiking, bicycling, and bowling groups. Many people have also used online dating services (26 percent), personal ads (22 percent), and speed-dating services and professional matchmaking services (10 percent each) ("Come here often?," 2002). These and other sources provide options for meeting a prospective spouse.

Personal Classified Advertisements

Personal classified advertisements used to be published in the back pages of "smutty" magazines. Now mainstream newspapers include "personals" in their daily or weekend issues. Similarly, many suburban, religious, and local newspapers also carry personal ads.

Men are twice as likely as women to place personal ads. In addition, the ads seek companions with stereotypical gender characteristics. Male advertisers tend to emphasize appearance and attractiveness in women; women advertisers look for intelligence, a college degree, and financial status in men (Davis, 1990).

Ad placers are usually very "selective" in their self-descriptions because both sexes "are quite conscious of the cultural scripts" that females and males expect. Because women know that men want attractive partners, they emphasize their appearance and femininity. Men, aware of women's expectations, describe their success, professional status, or "caring" and "sensitive" nature (Raybeck et al., 2000).

In addition, single women rarely mention having children because the men might not be willing to support children from a previous marriage (Ahuvia and Adelman, 1992).

These findings suggest that most women and men barter with the qualities that they see as most important in the marriage market. Many men value youth and attractiveness. Therefore, women often describe themselves as "sexy" or "curvaceous." Women tend to rank the status and earning potential of a prospective mate higher than men do. As a result, many men emphasize being "college-educated," a "homeowner," or a "professional" (Dunbar, 1995).

The advantages of classified ads include anonymity, low cost and time savings, and numerous applicants. A major disadvantage is that advertisers often exaggerate their attributes. As one of my male students said, "I called her because she said she was devastatingly gorgeous and intelligent. She was neither."

Mail-Order Brides

Some American men seeking wives use mail-order services that publish photographs and descriptions of women, usually from Russia and poor countries in Asia or Latin America. Women's rights activists view men who seek mail-order brides as "losers" who want sock-sorters or live-in nurses. Although the men do not deny that they want housekeepers, they complain that American women are "too independent, too demanding, too critical" (Weir, 2002: 1).

Many American men are especially interested in Asian mail-order brides:

> The American men imagine the [Asian] woman as the epitome of the traditional wife: submissive, subservient, eager to please men and easy to please, erotic, exotic, a good housekeeper, contented with a nice home, faithful, loyal, and not inclined to divorce her husband (Ordoñez, 1997: 123).

Such stereotypes and expectations often clash with reality. In the case of Filipinas, for example, the brides come from a strong matriarchal culture, and the wife may not be submissive (see Chapter 5). If a husband doesn't allow his wife to send money back home, she may find a job to have her own income. Conflict arises if she neglects the housework or doesn't live up to the husband's idealized visions of marital happiness (Ordoñez, 1997).

Although there are no firm statistics, an estimated 6,000 Russian women marry U.S. citizens each year. Because the mail-order bride business is unregulated, there's no way of knowing how many of these marriages are successful. According to one official in a large Moscow matchmaking agency, "You can find out everything you need to know about a man in five e-mails" (Weir, 2002: 7). Such superficial attitudes are good for business, but not for the brides and grooms. Some Western men complain that they are "ripped off by wily Russian women, who write sweet e-mails, send sexy digital photos, hit them up for cash, and then disappear" (Weir, 2002: 7).

According to some social service agencies, the American Prince Charming often turns out to be abusive and controlling. Some have murdered their wives; some have beaten, choked, and raped their brides; and others control their spouses by threatening to deport them. Most mail-order wives don't know that they can leave abusive husbands without the danger of being deported. Whereas the women undergo rigorous background checks, their future husbands do not, even though some have criminal records (Loder, 2003).

Professional Matchmakers

In some countries, classified ads and especially "professional matchmakers" have replaced the old-fashioned, community-based matchmaker (see the box "Modern Arranged Marriages in India"). In the United States, prices, services, and personal attention vary according to the client's needs and finances. In Marina del Rey, California, for example, a "dating consultant" charges men $600 to attract a woman. The "advice" includes wearing a Rolex watch, buying black shoes, and not talking about his divorce (Jeffrey, 2001).

In Manhattan, New York, a "psychotherapist" charges women almost $10,000 for a talk with an interior designer on "how women's living spaces shut out men," a home visit by an image consultant who will make a woman's closet "man ready," and a trip to a bridal shop so that women can visualize themselves getting married. After spending thousands of dollars with the therapist, one woman said that she eventually met "her man" through an online dating service for $160 (Marder, 2002).

CROSSCULTURAL

Modern Arranged Marriages in India

In India, loyalty of the individual to the family is a cherished ideal. To preserve this ideal, marriages traditionally are carefully arranged so that young men and women will avoid selecting inappropriate mates. In some cities, however, traditional aspects of arranged marriages are combined with nontraditional methods of finding prospective spouses (Pasupathi, 2002).

Among the literate classes, newspaper advertisements and computer services are replacing traditional matchmakers. Every Sunday the newspapers are filled with classified ads inviting inquiries about "smart, well-educated, professional boys" and "really beautiful, homely, university graduate girls." ("Homely" in India means not that a woman is unattractive but that she would make a good homemaker.)

This style of mate selection is not confined to Indians living in India. For example, Sanjit, a 34-year-old engineer, has lived in the United States since he was 12.

Sanjit's family received 103 responses after placing the following ad in *The Times* of India: "Alliance invited for smart, Bengali Hindu engineer, 34, 185 cms [6 feet], settled in the United States, music addict, no encumbrances." Sanjit's family narrowed the list down to seven women and then started negotiations, writing or calling the women's families. Sanjit said he hoped his family would find the right woman so he could get married on his next trip to India ("Seek spouse . . .," 1989).

A 1976 study of upper-middle-class north Indian women found that 39 percent said love was essential for marital happiness. Two decades later, that figure had fallen to 11 percent. Among urban professionals polled in another survey, 81 percent said their marriages had been arranged, and 94 percent rated their marriages "very successful" (Lakshmanan, 1997).

Although educated, upper-middle-class women are allowed to marry whomever

they want, many opt for arranged marriages. One young woman explained, "Love is important, but it's not sufficient." She asked her parents to research and solicit proposals from parents of men with good earning potential and a higher education and who were refined, intellectual, and good human beings. She is reportedly happily married to a man she had met just three times before their engagement.

Arranged marriages persist, also, because of family ties. Even financially independent couples usually live with the husband's parents. As a result, similar backgrounds and compatibility with in-laws are more important than in the West. The advantage is that there tends to be much family support if a marriage runs into trouble. As one young woman noted, "In the United States, you go to your shrink. Here, we go to our family" (Lakshmanan, 1997: 2A).

Speed Dating

Recently, one of my friends participated in an 8-Minute Dating encounter at a local restaurant. He and 13 other guys attended an event to meet 14 women. The people went from one table to another and spent 8 minutes chatting with each person. At the end of an hour or so, the participants "graded" each other. If two people chose each other and wanted to meet, the event organizer e-mailed contact information to both parties.

This is an example of the fast-growing *speed dating* industry that emerged in 1999. Since then, speed dating has spawned a number of companies that serve heterosexuals, gays, and a variety of ethnic and age groups. The purpose of speed dating is to allow people to meet each other face to face, within a short period of time, to decide whether there is mutual interest in another date.

Speed dating has several advantages. It is inexpensive (about $30 per function), takes little time, guards against stalking because the participants use only their

first names, draws people from the same region, and avoids the awkwardness of blind dates. Some people initially feel embarrassed or uncomfortable about attending ("What if someone I know is there?"). According to the speed dating organizers, however, more than half of the participants meet someone with whom there is mutual interest in another date (Kurlantzick, 2001; Morris, 2003).

Cyberdating

Millions of people are turning to the Internet to find romance and dates (see "Data Digest"). According to one 34-year-old subscriber, "online dating is more convenient and comfortable than scouring dreary Manhattan bars and haranguing friends to set me up" (Stone, 2001: 48). People can subscribe to discussion groups and chat rooms, "meet" thousands of other people, and discuss anything from radishes to romance.

During this speed dating event in Indianapolis, Indiana, 17 women and 17 men spent four minutes with each "date." People who chose each other as matches received contact information through e-mail the following day.

There are large dating sites like Match.com, Yahoo! Personals, and Matchmaker.com that charge members from $20 to $25 a month to find compatible dates. Numerous dating sites—and many are free—now exist for almost every imaginable group. A few examples include Jdate.com (for Jewish singles), Singleswithscruples.com ("for people who have morals and a sense of honor"), PlanetOut.com (for gays, lesbians, and bisexuals), ThirdAge.com (for adults age 45 and over), TheSpark.com (for people with a weird sense of humor), GoodGenes.com (Ivy League graduates), CatholicSingles.com, AsianFriendFinder.com, and Black-PlanetLove.com. In addition, many online publications (such as *Salon* and *The Onion*) have added dating sites for their subscribers. Most sites offer the option of adding a photo to one's profile.

A major advantage of online dating is its accessibility and low cost. A $25 fee provides instant access to tens of thousands of eligible singles, and subscribers can then sift candidates based on height, age, income, mutual interests, and dozens of other traits. Singles who felt isolated now have up to three dates a week while corresponding with several dozen people at the same time (Stone, 2001).

Another advantage of electronic liaisons is that people use code names and remain anonymous for as long as they wish. Because physical appearance is in the background, verbal intimacy can lead to enduring relationships or even marriage. Match.com, for example claims credit for 1,300 marriages since it started in 1995 ("Romance on the Web," 2003).

Cyberdating also has its downside. Some complain that the dating sites have "this whole population of rebound people" who have not recovered from breakups. And some "hot" prospects simply disappear with no explanation after weeks of intensive e-mailing (Paulson, 2003).

Electronic romances can also be deceptive and superficial. As in classified personal ads, people may be dishonest or have a very high opinion of themselves. One critic notes that "you can learn more [about a person] from two minutes at a party than from months of e-mail communication" (Herbert and Hammel, 1999: 56).

Rejected suitors may start stalking or harassing their love interests (Catalfo, 1994; Plotnikoff, 1994). In addition, people who use the Internet to find real-life sex partners are much more likely to have engaged in risky behavior. As a result, people who seek sex using the Internet are at greater risk of STDs and HIV infection (McFarlane et al., 2000). Moreover, 30 percent of those using Internet dating sites are married (Gardner, 2003).

MAKING CONNECTIONS

■ How do *you* meet other eligible singles? Or are you waiting for Cupid to come to you?

■ Have you or your friends ever tried online dating? If so, were you happy with the results? If you've never cyberdated, why not?

Choosing Whom We Date: Choices and Constraints

Many people believe that "This is America. I can date anyone I want." This is a fiction. Most of us select dating partners and marry people like us because filtering processes shape and limit our choices.

Homogamy and Filter Theory: Narrowing the Marriage Market

Theoretically, we have a vast pool of eligible dating partners. In reality, our field of potential partners is limited by our culture. According to **filter theory**, we sift eligible people according to specific criteria and thus narrow the pool of potential partners to a small number of candidates (Kerckhoff and Davis, 1962). *Figure 8.1* depicts the filter theory of mate selection.

The major filtering mechanism is homogamy. Often used interchangeably with the term *endogamy* (see Chapters 1 and 4), **homogamy** refers to dating or marrying someone with similar social characteristics such as ethnicity and age. Some of the most important filtering variables include geographic proximity, physical appearance, and social characteristics such as race or ethnicity, religion, age, social class, and values.

Propinquity Geographic closeness, or **propinquity**, is one of the first filters that shapes whom we meet, get to know, interact with frequently, and subsequently date and marry. Despite the mushrooming business in personal ads, singles bars, and cyberdating, most singles meet potential dates through people they know. According to one recent survey (which allowed multiple responses), 67 percent of never-married singles said they met dates through friends, family, or co-workers. Other notable venues for dating were college classes (38 percent), work (34 percent), bars or coffee shops (28 percent), online dating (22 percent), churches (18 percent), bookstores or libraries (12 percent), or grocery stores, cleaners, and banks (6 percent) (Yin, 2002).

Thus, we typically meet sexual and marriage partners through physically close social networks of people who are very similar to us. And when we move or change jobs, we lose some critical matchmakers. Because a higher rate of blacks than whites meet other singles in church (28 percent vs. 16 percent), for example, moving to another area may decrease dating options (Fetto, 2001).

As more women enter the labor force, workplaces should offer many possibilities for meeting a prospective mate. This isn't always the case, however. Social contacts on the job are often superficial, impersonal, and with people who are of the wrong age or marital status (Glenn, 2002). Although 70 percent of employers say they have no policies or guidelines regarding office romances, liaisons between bosses (who are usually men) and subordinates (who are usually women) can decrease other employees' performance and morale if they believe the subordinate is getting special favors for example ("Taboo no more . . .," 2000).

Physical Appearance A number of classic studies show that men and women choose partners whose physical attractiveness is similar to their own (see

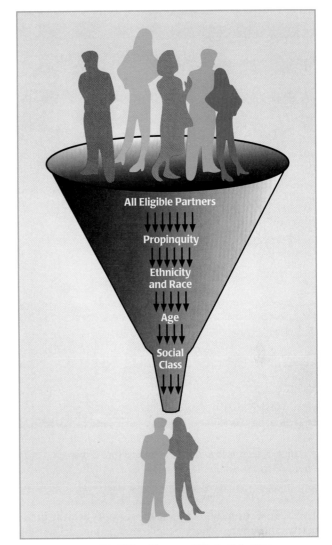

FIGURE 8.1 **The Filter Theory of Mate Selection**
According to filter theory, most of us narrow our pool of prospective partners by selecting people we see on a regular basis who are most similar to us in terms of variables such as age, race, values, social class, sexual orientation, and physical appearance.

Berscheid et al., 1982). Physically attractive people benefit from a "halo effect"; they are *assumed* to possess other desirable social characteristics as well, such as warmth, sexual responsiveness, kindness, strength, modesty, sensitivity, poise, sociability, and good character. They are also seen as likely to have more prestige, happier marriages, more social and professional success, and more fulfilling lives (Dion et al., 1972). In fact, life satisfaction is much the same for very attractive and less attractive people (Brehm, 1992).

Perceptions of beauty vary across cultures. Several Nigerian communities prize hefty women and "hail

Men assign more importance to physical attractiveness than women do, but both sexes tend to choose partners whose degree of attractiveness closely matches their own.

a woman's rotundity" as a sign of good health, prosperity, and allure. Many believe that a thin girl will be sickly and unable to bear children. Teenage girls spend several months in a "fattening room" eating starchy food such as yams, rice, and beans. The fattening room is a centuries-old rite of passage from girlhood to womanhood. The months are spent in gaining weight and supplemented by daily visits from elderly matrons who offer tips on how to cook and be a successful wife and mother (Simmons, 1998).

In the United States and many other Western countries, in contrast, and especially for women, attractiveness is synonymous with slimness and youth. The pressure to "look good" begins as early as middle school (see Chapters 5, 6, and 14).

Overweight girls ages 12 to 18 are less likely to date than are their thinner counterparts (Cawley, 2001). It's not surprising, then, that millions of teenage girls and women undergo cosmetic surgery to enlarge their breasts, reshape their noses and ears, and endure liposuction (Austin, 2000; see also Chapters 5 and 7). Even though models like Sudanese Alek Wek and Japanese American Devon Aoki are attractive because they are

"exotic," the number of Asian American women seeking cosmetic surgery to create creased eyelids and higher noses for a more "Western look" has more than quadrupled between 1999 and 2001 (Tan, 2002).

Businesses are delighted with women's obsession about their looks. According to one marketing analyst, "Anything with the words 'age defying' sells." As a result, we can be seduced into believing we've halted or slowed the aging process by using a variety of products, and most target women. A few of these products include Rembrandt Age Defying toothpaste, Age Defiance hosiery, Clairol's Revitalizing Age-Defying Color System, Oil of Olay Age Defying Daily Renewal Cream, Pond's Age Defying Lotion, Revlon's Age Defying eye color, and Clinique's Stop Signs Anti-Aging Serum (Mayer, 1999).

Although a pleasant appearance is desirable in both women and men, physical attractiveness may not always increase one's chances of finding a suitable partner. In a study of black women, for example, some of the respondents felt that being attractive sometimes had negative consequences. A good-looking woman might make a man feel so insecure that he will not approach her: "People assume you already have enough candidates." Many of the women also felt that "the guys want to show you off because an attractive woman increases a man's status in his friends' eyes" (Sterk-Elifson, 1994: 108). If some men treat attractive women as trophies instead of serious marriage candidates, the women may have a large pool of dating partners but few serious suitors.

Ethnicity and Race About 40 percent of Americans report having dated someone of another race or ethnic group. They are more likely to be men than women and Asian American or African American than Latino or white (*Figure 8.2*). As you saw in Chapter 4, relationships across racial and ethnic boundaries reflect a number of factors such as greater societal acceptance, acculturation, and the availability of eligible partners within one's own cultural group.

More than any other group, African American women face what one black journalist calls a "marriage crunch": "The better educated we are, the less likely we are to meet brothers who can match our credentials. The more successful we are, the less likely we are to meet brothers who can match our pocketbooks" (Chambers, 2003: 136).

About 12 percent of African American men in their twenties and early thirties are in prison or jail (Harrison and Karberg, 2003). Since 1976, nearly twice as many black women as black men have earned bachelor's, doctor's, and professional degrees (like medicine, law, and theology) (U.S. Department of Education, 2002). Well-educated and successful black women, then, find that they have "priced themselves out of the market" in finding a mate (Harris, 2003).

Unlike in the film *How Stella Got Her Grove Back,* most successful black women are unlikely to find happiness with a man 20 years younger or one who's not intimidated by their achievements (Offner, 2002; Cose, 2003). What are the woman's choices? Some are staying single; others are dating outside their ethnic or racial group. As the box "Why I Never Dated a White Girl" on page 216 shows, however, many African Americans endorse homogamy and disapprove of interracial dating. We'll return to interracial and interethnic dating later in this chapter.

Religion Religion can play a major role in dating and mate selection. All three of the major religions in the United States—Catholicism, Protestantism, and Judaism—have traditionally opposed interfaith marriages.

Most religions oppose interfaith marriage because of the belief that it weakens individual commitment to the faith. Church leaders, for example, often advise Mormon adolescents to date only within their own religion. One reason is that only Mormons are allowed to participate in the highly valued marriage ceremony in a Mormon temple (Markstrom-Adams, 1991).

In the Roman Catholic Church, interfaith couples must sign a premarital agreement promising to raise the children as Catholics. Some Jews consider intermarriage a serious threat to Jewish identity and culture (Wakin, 2002). As a result, many Jewish congregations do an "exemplary job of providing opportunities for unmarried people to get to know one another" to promote religious and ethnic endogamy (Glenn, 2002: 55).

Religion often sets clear standards regarding "respectable family styles." In black and other communities, religiously similar spouses typically share basic beliefs about child rearing and other family issues and hold compatible views of marriage and commitment to marital and familial roles (Ellison, 1997). If religions differ, especially in the case of interracial and interethnic marriages, a couple may be the brunt of gossip instead of being embraced by the clergy and church members.

Age In some African countries, girls under 15 are often married off to men who may be 30 or 40 years older (see Chapter 7). Americans are age-endogamous because they tend to marry within the same age group. The man is typically just a year or two older than the woman (see Chapter 10). If there are large age differences, and especially if the woman is the older dating partner, families and friends are likely to disapprove.

Large age differences may also lead to generation gaps in attitudes about lifestyle, such as music preferences, recreation, and family activities. Furthermore, a much older man may be unwilling to have children, especially if he has a family by a previous marriage or is expected to share in the child-rearing responsibilities. Even if he wants to raise a second family, he may not have the energy or patience to deal with high-spirited or rambunctious offspring (see Chapter 16).

Social Class Most people marry within their social class because they share similar attitudes, values, and lifestyles. Many of us face strong pressures to date people of similar (or preferably higher) social standing. Even when people from different ethnic groups intermarry, they usually belong to the same social class (Kalmijn, 1998).

Despite the popularity of films like *Pretty Woman,* in which a powerful business mogul marries a prostitute, very few of the rich and powerful marry outside their social class (Kendall, 2002). The *New York Times* wedding page provides a good example of our class consciousness. The *Times* emphasizes four things—college degrees, graduate degrees, career path, and parents' professions. Thus, couples from lower socioeconomic levels shouldn't expect to see their engagement or wedding

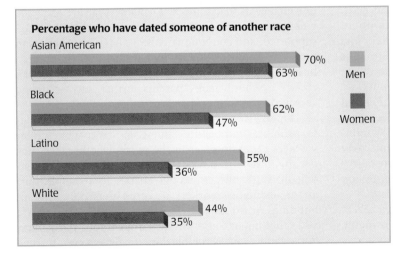

Percentage who have dated someone of another race

Asian American — 70% Men, 63% Women
Black — 62% Men, 47% Women
Latino — 55% Men, 36% Women
White — 44% Men, 35% Women

FIGURE 8.2 Dating People of Another Racial/Ethnic Group Overall, about 4 in 10 Americans report having dated someone of another race. A companion survey found that more than two-thirds of these relationships were "serious romantic relationships."

Source: *Washington Post*/Henry J. Kaiser Family Foundation/Harvard University survey, 2001; table presented in Fears and Deane, 2001, p. A4.

MULTICULTURAL

Why I Never Dated a White Girl

Although interracial dating is fairly common (see *Figure 8.2*), it is still controversial. Recently, for example, some white students at a Georgia high school voted to hold their own prom (Marbella, 2003).

Many African Americans, similarly, oppose interracial coupling. Lawrence Otis Graham (1996: 36–56) explains why he's never dated a white woman and, presumably, why other black men shouldn't, either:

- **Objection 1**: When black leaders or advocates marry outside the race, such decisions demonstrate less commitment to black people and our causes.
- **Objection 2**: We fear that intermarrying blacks are making a statement to black and white America that black spouses are less desirable partners and are therefore inferior.
- **Objection 3**: Interracial marriage undermines our ability to introduce our black children to black mentors and role models who accept their racial identity with confidence and pride.

- **Objection 4**: Because it diffuses our resources, interracial marriage makes it difficult to build a black America that has wealth, prestige, and power. This makes it harder to empower black America and to erase the stereotypes of a weak and impoverished black community.
- **Objection 5**: We worry that confused biracial children will turn their backs on the black race once they discover that it's easier to live as a white person.
- **Objection 6**: Today's interracial relationships are a painful reminder of a 250-year period in black American history when white people exploited our sexuality.

Interracial and interethnic couples encounter numerous obstacles on a fairly regular basis. One of the most common negative experiences is stares by others, particularly in public places. In the service sector, waiters or waitresses, gas station attendants, convenience store clerks, sales staff in retail outlets, or even other customers at these places are often

rude or hostile (McNamara et al., 1999; see also Chapter 4).

Other unpleasant, sometimes frightening expressions of disapproval come from passers-by:

We were in Sausalito a couple of years ago. . . . We were walking down the street, just sightseeing, and doing what tourists do. And this guy's coming up the street, and . . . as he approached us, he kind of said under his breath, "White girl, wake up" (Rosenblatt et al., 1995: 128).

STOP AND THINK . . .

- *Do you agree with Graham's reasons for not dating and marrying outside the African American community?*
- *Graham states why he feels that interracial dating and marriage are dysfunctional. Think back to the discussion of manifest and latent functions of dating at the beginning of the chapter. Are there ways in which interracial dating is functional?*

announcement in the *Times* or other national newspapers (Brooks, 2000).

Romance novels are probably popular, in part, because they reflect many women's fantasies about breaking out of our rigid mate-selection social class boundaries. In almost all of the novels, the heroine is a beautiful young virgin from the "wrong side of the tracks," and the hero is a rich and powerful hunk.

Some studies suggest that parents play a minimal role in whom adolescents date (Leslie et al., 1986; Longmore et al., 2001). However, parents have already influenced dating by choosing where to live. Parents may not have to exert pressure on their children to marry someone of "their own kind" because communities are typically organized by social class.

Schools, churches, and recreational facilities reflect the socioeconomic levels of neighborhoods. It is highly unlikely that children living in upper-class neighborhoods

will even meet those in middle-class, much less working-class, families. Eckland (1968) described colleges and universities as matrimonial agencies" that are arranged hierarchically; students at Ivy League, private, state-supported, and community colleges have few chances to meet one another. Because they influence their children by encouraging them to attend college and by helping them choose a school, many parents further narrow dating choices in terms of social class.

Finally, social class interacts with other variables to promote homogamy. Blue-collar and white-collar workers rarely interact in the workplace because they occupy different physical spaces and have different schedules. At colleges and universities, for example, staff and maintenance workers are often housed in different buildings or floors and rarely talk to each other. If we add religion, age, and physical appearance to the mix, homogamy reduces eligible dating partners even further.

Although endogamy continues to be a strong force in choosing a mate, interracial and interethnic marriages are becoming more common.

we've examined. Increasing numbers of people, however, are expanding their marriage markets through heterogamy.

Heterogamy and Permanent Availability: Expanding the Marriage Market

As U.S. society becomes more diverse and multicultural (see Chapters 1 and 4), many people are dating and marrying across traditionally acceptable religious, ethnic, racial, and social class confines. Whether we complain about the changes or accept them, mate-selection processes *are* changing because of heterogamy.

Values Mate-selection methods may have changed, but has there been a corresponding change in the values that shape our choices? College students' responses as to what they wanted in a future mate in three widely spaced studies—1939, 1956, and 1967—didn't change much (Hudson and Henze, 1969). Students wanted partners who were dependable, emotionally stable, intelligent, sociable, and good-looking. They sought pleasing dispositions, good health, similar religious background and social status, and evidence of mutual attraction.

The characteristics of the "ideal partner" changed only somewhat by the late 1990s. As *Table 8.1* on page 218 shows, both sexes are remarkably similar in valuing the same traits such as mutual attraction, good character, emotional maturity, and a pleasant disposition.

What has changed since 1939 is that chastity is now one of the least important characteristics for both sexes. And, in contrast to 1939, both sexes now rank "good financial prospect" higher. Another notable shift is the importance of good looks in a potential marriage partner. By the late 1990s, men ranked physical attractiveness as eighth, soaring from fourteenth in 1939. For women, good looks jumped from seventeenth in 1939 to thirteenth. The researchers attribute this change to some of the reasons we've discussed earlier, such as the media's emphasis on beauty—especially women's—and the greater availability of cosmetic surgery and gyms (Buss et al., 2001).

Homogamy thus narrows our pool of eligible partners in terms of values and the other characteristics

Heterogamy Often used interchangeably with the term *exogamy* (see Chapter 1), heterogamy refers to dating or marrying someone from a social, racial, ethnic, religious, or age group different from one's own. Most societies, for example, prohibit dating or marriage between siblings and between parents and children, aunts and uncles, or other relatives (see Chapters 1 and 4). In some countries, like India, exogamy rules forbid marriage between individuals of similarly named clans, even though the families have never met and live several hundred miles apart (Gupta, 1979).

In the United States, many states don't allow marriage between half-siblings. About half the states, however, allow marriage between in-laws and between stepchildren and stepparents. In this sense, some states are more heterogamous than others in terms of legal taboos about appropriate sex and marriage partners—depending on how a state defines "family" (see Chapter 1).

The Permanent Availability Model In the early 1960s, sociologist Bernard Farber (1964) challenged traditional explanations of mate selection and marriage with his *permanent availability model*. Farber argued, essentially, that adults are "permanently available" for marriage with anyone and at any time. Farber maintained that because people's needs and desires change over time, they "may not suffice to maintain the marriage." Because divorce and remarriage rates were increasing, and youth and glamour were becoming more important, Farber felt that "playing the field" would prepare people for marriage better than settling on a spouse at an early age.

TABLE 8.1

The Most Important Qualities in a Mate

Order of Priority	Men Want	Women Want
1	Mutual attraction and love	Mutual attraction and love
2	Dependable character	Dependable character
3	Emotional stability, maturity	Emotional stability, maturity
4	Pleasant disposition	Pleasant disposition
5	Education, intelligence	Education, intelligence
6	Good health	Desire for children, home
7	Sociability	Ambition, industriousness
8	Good looks	Sociability
9	Desire for home, children	Good health
10	Ambition, industriousness	Similar educational background
11	Refinement, neatness	Good financial prospects
12	Similar religious background	Refinement, neatness

SOURCE: Based on Buss et al., 2001.

The permanent-availability model is probably more applicable today than it was four decades ago. Although still bound by homogamy, mate-selection options are growing for many people, and they are increasing throughout the life cycle rather than just during early adulthood (see Chapter 16). These options are especially evident in same-sex, social class, interfaith, and interracial relationships.

Same-sex Relationships   Most societies still define a marriage as valid only between members of the opposite sex. Nonetheless, several countries now recognize same-sex civil unions as legitimate in the sense that partners can enjoy the same legal benefits as heterosexual couples.

In the United States, Vermont provides gay partners with many of the same rights as heterosexuals. And a Massachusetts court has recently ruled that gays can marry (see Chapter 7). Also, some Protestant denominations are allowing religious marriage ceremonies for gay and lesbian partners. We'll examine same-sex civil unions in Chapter 9. For now, suffice it to say that recognizing gay relationships increases heterogamy by not limiting dating to opposite-sex partners.

Social Class Relationships   Most of us marry within our social class, as you saw earlier. In open class societies like the United States, however, our dating and mate selection can move us up or down the social ladder.

Hypergamy involves "marrying up" to improve one's overall social standing. Because the United States is still a race-conscious society, minority women, especially, can improve their social status by marrying white men even though the men may have a lower educational level (Fu, 2001; Tsai et al., 2002).

Hypogamy, in contrast, involves "marrying down" in terms of social class. As women postpone marriage because of educations and jobs, they often find that "Mr. Right"—with similar credentials—just isn't on the horizon when they're ready to settle down (Whitehead, 2002).

Although hypergamy used to describe most women in the past, this is no longer the case. Increasing numbers of educated women make more money than their dating partners and spouses and do not have to rely on marriage for financial security or upward mobility. Since gender role scripts still dictate that women and not men should be hypergamous, many men feel intimidated by "high-powered" women and don't date them (Dowd, 2002).

Although interracial and interfaith marriages have grown over the past few decades, we rarely date or marry outside our social rank. According to a study of 728,000 Match.com members, 64 percent of the women who hold graduate degrees and 68 percent of those with a Ph.D. say they are looking for a man with at least a graduate degree (Gardyn, 2002).

As *Table 8.2* shows, 90 percent of the most highly educated singles say that finding a partner who is intelligent is extremely or very important, compared with only 66 percent of those with a high school degree. Intelligence and being a college graduate aren't synonymous, of course. Many singles, however, use formal education as a proxy for intelligence. Note also that wealth is much less important than intelligence.

Interfaith Relationships Historically, religion has been an important factor in dating and mate selection in the United States and many other countries. Now, however, interfaith marriages—and especially interfaith dating—are common in the United States. About 52 percent of Jewish-born U.S. adults, for example, had intermarried by 1990 (Van Biema, 1997).

Religion is less influential than race and ethnicity in determining whom we date and marry. As *Table 8.3* shows, for example, only 56 percent of long-term partnerships and 72 percent of marriages are between people with the same religious affiliations. And, compared with all relationships (from short-term partnerships to marriages), religion is less important than education, age, or race and ethnicity.

Happy couples respect each other's religious traditions. Some interfaith couples emphasize certain basic values in Judaism and Christianity: family, education, and taking care of the weak, the old, and the sick. Some Muslim-Christian marriages have also accommodated both religions. During the holiday season, for example, a family might celebrate Eid Al-fitr, a day of feasting and celebration that follows Ramadan, a month of

TABLE 8.2			
But Is He Smart?			
Percentage of single Americans who say that the following characteristics are "extremely important" or "very important" to them when looking for a mate.			
	High School or Less	**Some College**	**College Graduate**
Intelligent	66%	86%	90%
Funny	65	73	75
Attractive	32	36	37
Athletic	10	12	16
Wealthy	8	4	5

SOURCE: Adapted from Gardyn, 2002: 37.

fasting and reflection. The couple might also put up a Christmas tree and celebrate the holiday with family members (Lund, 2001).

Interracial and Interethnic Relationships One of my classes was recently discussing interracial dating and marriage on our online forum. I received a private message from a black female student, Tanya, who's usually

TABLE 8.3			
Sexual Relationships in Dating and Marriage			
Percentage of Relationships with People of Similar Background			
Characteristic	Marriages	Cohabitations	Long-Term Partnerships	Short-Term Partnerships
Racial/ethnic	93	88	89	91
Age	78	75	76	83
Education	82	87	83	87
Religion	72	53	56	60

Notes: Sexual relationships include both heterosexual and same-sex couples.

Marriages and *cohabitations* include only those that began within the past ten years.

Short-term partnerships are sexual relationships that lasted one month or less and involved no more than ten instances of sexual activity; all remaining partnerships are considered long-term.

Age similarity is defined as a difference of no more than five years between the partners' ages.

Educational similarity is defined as a difference of no more than one educational category (less than high school, high school graduate, vocational training, four-year college, and graduate degree).

SOURCE: Adapted from Laumann et al., 1994: 232, 255.

pretty talkative both in class and online. When I asked her to post her comments to the class, she refused:

I already get a lot of grief from my parents, brother, and friends for dating only white men. There is a HUGE double standard with the whole interracial dating/marriage thing. For instance, my brother and his friends all date white women, but they have a major issue with me dating white men. One person went so far as to say that a white man dating a black woman is only fulfilling a "slave-owner fantasy" (Author's files).

Tanya then referred me to an *Essence* magazine poll which reported that only a third of the female readers approved of interracial dating (see Johnson, 2002).

Why was Tanya so reluctant to post her message online? As she said, interracial dating still reflects a double standard. Black journalists such as Ellis Cose (1995), for example, have criticized black women but not black men for dating interracially.

Such criticism is unwarranted. The rate of interracial and interethnic marriage has increased slowly, from 3 percent in 1980 to just over 5 percent in 2000. As *Figure 8.3* shows, however, the percentage of black-white marriages is low (only 25 percent of all interracial marriages). The highest percentage of interracial marriages is between American Indians, Latino males, and Asian American women. Moreover, black men are three times more likely than black women to marry someone in another racial or ethnic group (see *Table 4.1* on p. 104). Black women, as a group, are more likely than their male counterparts to obtain college and graduate degrees. Thus, African American women have a smaller pool of educated black male partners.

MAKING CONNECTIONS

■ Return to *Table 8.1*. Are these the most important qualities that you expect from a date? What about a spouse?

■ *Figure 8.3* shows that the rate of white/black marriages is low. Why, then, do we hear so much about white/black relationships instead of other intermarriages?

■ Do you know anyone who criticizes interracial or interfaith dating? How do you react?

Why We Choose Each Other: Mate-selection Theories

Sociologists have offered various explanations of mate-selection processes (see Cate and Lloyd, 1992, for a summary of several theoretical perspectives). In the 1950s and 1960s, some theories proposed that people are drawn to each other because of *complementary needs*; in other words, opposites attract (Winch, 1958). This and other perspectives have fallen out of scientific favor because they were not supported by empirical data (Regan, 2003).

As you saw earlier, filter theory proposes that our social structure limits our opportunity to meet people who are very different from us. In this sense, the sifting process that narrows the pool of eligible candidates is largely unconscious and often beyond our control. What influences our decision to stay in a relationship

FIGURE 8.3 **Interracial Marriages Have Increased in the United States**

SOURCE: Based on U.S. Census Bureau, 2002, p. 47.

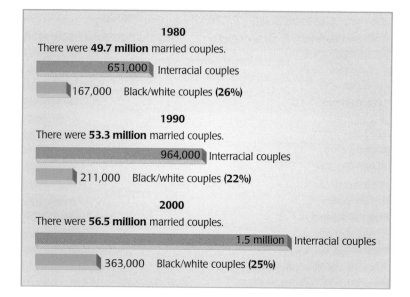

1980
There were **49.7 million** married couples.
651,000 Interracial couples
167,000 Black/white couples **(26%)**

1990
There were **53.3 million** married couples.
964,000 Interracial couples
211,000 Black/white couples **(22%)**

2000
There were **56.5 million** married couples.
1.5 million Interracial couples
363,000 Black/white couples **(25%)**

ASKYOURSELF

Am I Seeing the Wrong Person?

Because often "love is blind," many people overlook serious flaws and marry Mr. or Ms. Wrong. Here are some red flags that should alert you to possible problems.

- **Don Juans and other sexual predators.** Men admit using a variety of lines to persuade women to have sex. These Don Juans will *declare their love for you* ("I don't want to have sex with you—I want to make love to you"), *flatter you* ("You're one of the most beautiful women I've ever seen," "I've never met anyone like you before"), *make meaningless promises* ("Our relationship will grow stronger," "I swear I'll get a divorce"), *threaten you with rejection* ("Our relationship really needs to move on," "If you loved me, you would"), *put you down* if you refuse ("You're really old-fashioned"), or *challenge you* to prove you're "normal" ("Are you frigid?" "Are you gay?").
- **Incompatibility of basic values.** Initially, it may be exciting to be with someone who's very different. In the long run, however, serious differences in values may jeopardize a relationship. If your partner likes to curl up with a mystery novel but you want to go out with friends every weekend, you may be in for trouble.
- **Rigid sex roles.** If your partner wants you to be a full-time homemaker and parent, but you want a career, there may be strain.
- **Emotional baggage.** If your partner often talks about an ex-partner—comparing you with her "saintly" dead husband or talking about his past lovers—she or he is living in the past instead of getting to know you.
- **Extreme jealousy and violent tendencies.** Stay away from someone who is possessive, jealous, or violent. Such characteristics as a bad temper, frequent angry outbursts, constant criticism, and sudden mood swings will not decrease in the future.
- **Substance abuse.** The person addicted to alcohol or other drugs is the wrong choice for a mate. Watch for such things as slowed responses, slurred speech, glassy eyes, extreme mood swings, unexplained absences, or failure to keep dates.
- **Excessive time spent with others.** Does your partner spend several nights a week with others while you spend time alone? If your partner is always on the phone, or if family "emergencies" often come before your needs, there will probably be similar conflicts in the future.
- **Mr. Flirt and Ms. Tease.** If your partner is flirtatious or a sexual tease, watch out. Flirting may be entertaining at first, but not over the long run.
- **Lack of communication.** Good communication is critical for a good relationship. Feelings of boredom, evidence of your partner's disinterest, or finding that you have little to talk about may signal serious communication problems that will decrease intimacy.
- **Control freaks.** Does your partner always try to change or control you or the relationship? Do you constantly feel criticized, judged, scrutinized, and corrected, especially in public? If so, stay away.
- **Blaming others for problems.** It's always someone else's fault if something goes wrong ("My boss didn't appreciate me" instead of "I was fired because I always came in late").

SOURCES: Powell, 1991; Collison, 1993; Kenrick et al., 1993.

---

or to move on? Exchange theory and equity theory suggest that satisfaction is a key factor in weighing our mate-selection investments and our liabilities.

Dating as Give and Take: Social Exchange Theory

Recall from Chapters 2 and 6 that, according to social exchange theory, people are attracted to prospective partners who they believe will provide them with the best possible "deal" in a relationship. This may not sound very romantic, but social exchange theorists propose that it is the basis of most relationships.

Arguing that every relationship carries both rewards and costs, social exchange theory posits that people will begin (and remain in) a relationship if the rewards are high and the costs are low. *Rewards* may be intrinsic characteristics (intelligence, a sense of humor), directly rewarding behavior (sex, companionship), or access to desired resources (money, power). *Costs*, the "price" paid, may be unpleasant or destructive behavior (insults, violence) or literal losses (money, time). The box "Am I Seeing the Wrong Person?" offers advice from practitioners for filtering out undesirable candidates as you look for a long-term relationship.

Historically, because women were expected to bear children and be homemakers, physical attractiveness was one of the few assets they could offer in the marriage market. Men, on the other hand, had a variety of resources—including money, education, and power—and therefore had more dating options. Today, as more women earn college degrees and establish careers, they are increasing their assets and can be more selective in dating relationships. As a result, however, both sexes have a smaller pool of eligible partners.

As more women compete for jobs and as the economy worsens, women's values about desirable traits in men are changing. Although they are interested in men who are competent workers and high earners, women today are more concerned about a partner who will share housework and child-rearing responsibilities (see Chapters 5 and 10). Economic security may be less important than companionship and communication. Men who dismiss such characteristics as unimportant are less desirable partners; many women view such men as wanting one-sided relationships where they get all the rewards and have few or no costs.

Dating as a Search for Egalitarian Relationships: Equity Theory

According to **equity theory**, an extension of social exchange theory, an intimate relationship is satisfying and stable if both people see it as equitable and mutually beneficial (Walster et al., 1973). Equity theory advances several basic propositions:

- The greater the perceived equity, the happier the relationship.

- When people find themselves in an inequitable relationship, they become distressed. The greater the inequity, the greater the distress.

- People in an inequitable relationship will attempt to eliminate their distress by restoring equity.

Equity theory reflects the American sense of "fair play," the notion that one has a right to expect a reasonable balance between costs and benefits in life. If we give more than we receive, we usually get angry. If we receive more than our "fair share" of benefits, we might feel guilty. In each case, we experience dissatisfaction with the relationship. We try to decrease the distress and restore equity by changing our contributions, by persuading a partner to change his or her contribution, or by convincing ourselves that the inequity doesn't exist (Miell and Croghan, 1996).

Consider Mike and Michelle, who were initially happy with their dating relationship. Among other exchanges, she helped him with his calculus and he helped her write a paper for a sociology class. Mike and Michelle spent as much time as possible together and shared similar extracurricular interests. By the end of the semester, however, Michelle was still helping Mike with his calculus assignments, but Mike was no longer available to help Michelle with her sociology papers because he had joined the swim team. According to equity theory, Mike might feel guilty and increase his help, or Mike and Michelle will have to "renegotiate" their contributions. If the distress is too great, one or both will break up the relationship.

Judgments about equity can vary depending on the stage of the relationship. As two people get acquainted, severe inequity usually ends further involvement. Once a relationship enters a stage of long-term commitment, people tolerate inequality—especially if they plan to marry because they are optimistic about the future. Later in most long-term relationships, however, and especially as people face transitions (such as parenthood), perceived inequities can increase stress and dissatisfaction (Sprecher, 2001).

A Global View: Desirable Mate Characteristics and Selection

Most of us want prospective spouses who are dependable, mature, and loving (see *Table 8.1*). What about other countries? Do desirable mate traits and selection methods differ across societies? Or are they universal?

Preferred Mate Characteristics

To identify valued characteristics of potential mates worldwide, Buss (1990) and 59 other researchers interviewed almost 10,000 people in 37 cultures on six continents and five islands. The researchers drew several conclusions from this study. First, culture appears to have substantial effects on mate preferences. Second, the most pervasive difference between cultures appears to be a "traditional" versus a "modern" continuum about a prospective partner's characteristics. At one end of this continuum, China, India, Iran, and Nigeria placed a great value on chastity, good housekeeping, and a desire for home and children.

At the other end of the continuum, several countries emphasized different characteristics. Dutch respondents placed a higher value on political similarity, the British stressed education and political background, Finns valued creativity and artistry in potential mates, and Swedes desired mates who are politically similar, dependable, and healthy.

The researchers' third conclusion was that nearly all people, despite cultural differences, placed mutual attraction and long-term love (not romantic love) at the top of the list. Dependability, emotional stability/maturity, and kindness-understanding were the next most highly valued mate traits.

The researchers observed that such similarities imply that humans share "a degree of psychological unity" that transcends geographic, racial, political, and ethnic diversity. There was one significant difference, however:

An important sex difference appeared in nearly every sample in the study: More than females, males prefer mates who are physically attractive. More than males, females prefer mates who show ambition-industriousness and other signs of earning potential. These differences appear to be the most robust psychological sex differences of any kind to be documented across cultures (Buss et al., 1990: 37).

Why are there such "robust" sex differences between women and men in most cultures? Buss (1989) posits that different evolutionary selection pressures on females and males "signal" different valued mate characteristics. Women desire ambition and industriousness in men because it signals their financial capacity to provide for children, increased status and protection for the family unit, and even "good genes" that pass to the woman's offspring.

Men, in contrast, value physical attractiveness and relative youth (which signals a high reproductive capacity). To a great extent, then, according to sociobiological perspectives, mate-selection preferences reflect women's and men's efforts to maximize their personal benefits and minimize their personal costs in their social, cultural, and ecological settings (see Eagly and Wood, 1999).

Variations in Mate-selection Methods

Most countries do not have the "open" courtship systems common in Western nations. Many factors—including religion, rate of industrialization, the economic status of women, and family structure—promote traditional mate-selection arrangements. Some societies are trying to maintain their traditional mate-selection values; others are changing.

Traditional Societies In some Mediterranean, Middle Eastern, and Asian societies, the **dowry**—the money, goods, or property a woman brings to a marriage—is still an important basis for mate selection. Women with large dowries have a competitive edge in attracting suitors (Gaulin and Boster, 1990).

The minimum marriage age varies widely across countries. Only recently, for example, Iran passed a bill that permits girls to be married at age 13 (instead of 9) and boys at the age of 15 (instead of 14) without court permission. Female lawmakers saw the change as a major advance in protecting very young girls from an early marriage ("Iranian arbitrating board . . .," 2002).

"Mine was a marriage of convenience. I wanted desperately to get married and Hank was convenient."

As in India (see "Modern Arranged Marriages in India" on p. 211), in many countries parents arrange marriages for their children. In Saudi Arabia, Islamic (Muslim) society regulates the lives of its women strictly. Most women cover themselves in black, are forbidden to drive or drink, accept arranged marriages, and live with their parents, who act as chaperones. The box "Matchmaking in Muslim Societies" on page 224 provides a closer look at the criteria that many Muslim parents use in selecting partners for their children.

Small groups of Saudi and other Middle Eastern women are challenging some strict dating restrictions (see Chapter 5). Many Muslim women, however, including those living in the United States, believe in arranged marriages. Listen to a Muslim mother from Sierra Leone describe the arranged marriages of her sons and daughter:

We are saved from the evils of teen-age pregnancy that you see nowadays. We are saved from AIDS. We are saved from all sorts of different diseases, all sorts of evil vices being practiced, especially by the teenagers of America (Somerville, 1994: 4B).

Many young Asian Muslims who live in the United States agree with their parents about the benefits of arranged marriages. They feel that dating undermines girls' self-respect. As one Muslim teenager commented about her best friend, who is not Islamic, "She is always tortured about whether her boyfriend likes her or not, if she is fat, attractive, how many silly Valentine's cards she gets. I couldn't go through all of that. It's crazy." (Alibhai-Brown, 1993: 29).

Arranged marriages aren't paradise, however. In poor nations such as Afghanistan, parents arrange marriages between daughters and older men who are able to afford the $500 to $1,500 dowry. Thus, a 14-year-old girl may be given in marriage to a 60-year-old married man with

CROSSCULTURAL

Matchmaking in Muslim Societies

No matter where they live—North America, South Asia, or the Middle East—many Muslim families preserve family continuity through arranged marriages. Marriage in Islamic society is basically a family rather than an individual choice. Sons and daughters alike are raised to expect arranged marriages.

Although children do have veto power, typically parents and other kin initiate and decide the matter. Even college-educated youth in countries like Pakistan do not think it's necessary for them to meet their future spouses before they marry (Ba-Yunus, 1991).

What criteria do parents use in choosing a son- or daughter-in-law? Although priorities vary across families, there are two important criteria for a future son-in-law. One is education or training that will provide their daughter with economic and social assets equal to or better than those of her parents. A second important characteristic is close ties between the son-in-law and the daughter's family, regardless of where the young couple will live.

In addition, according to one mother, "We look for wisdom, patience, good sense, not qualities that may be more exciting, but which soon disappear" (Alibhai-Brown, 1993: 29).

For a prospective daughter-in-law, the major criterion is her ability to be integrated into the son's existing family, including, if possible, patrilocal residence for the young couple. Because the man is expected to be the provider, his wife's education is more of a social enhancement than an essential economic asset (Qureshi, 1991).

Islamic societies forbid dating and "other illicit meetings of the sexes" but allow polygyny. To reduce the number of unmarried middle-aged women, matchmakers in Saudi Arabia have set up services that provide wives for husbands who seek more than one wife.

These services have been flooded with telephone calls and faxes from devout Muslims in Sweden, the United States, and countries in the Middle East. Despite the protests of some Saudi housewives who

do not want their husbands to acquire additional wives, the matchmaking business is thriving (Boustany, 1994).

As in the semiarranged matches in India, most women are practical and religious: "I am a Saudi woman, 36, finished elementary school and have never been married. I wish to marry a man who fears God and heeds him and who will treat me to God's satisfaction, and who will also help me memorize the Koran and attend religion lessons, not younger than 40" (Boustany, 1994: A14).

STOP AND THINK . . .

- *Isn't love enough for a marriage? Do you think that arranged (or semiarranged) marriages in the United States would increase our marriage rates?*

- *In terms of the filter theory you read about earlier, do we already have some aspects of semiarranged marriages in the United States?*

grown children. To escape such arranged or unhappy marriages, girls and young women sometimes douse themselves with fuel and set themselves on fire. One regional hospital in Afghanistan has at least 100 such cases every year, and the numbers have been rising (Reitman, 2002).

Arranged marriages often involve marrying a first cousin as the "top choice." Across the Arab world, an average of 45 percent of married couples is related. Such "inbreeding" can increase the chances of passing down diseases (see Chapter 1). In some parts of Saudi Arabia, for example, where blood relatives range from 55 to 70 percent, inbreeding produces several genetic disorders that include thalassemia (a potentially fatal blood disease), sickle cell anemia, spinal muscular atrophy, diabetes, deafness, and muteness. Educated Saudis have begun to pull away from the practice, but the tradition of marrying first cousins "is still deeply embedded in Saudi culture" (Kershaw, 2003:).

In 2002 alone, 250 Pakistani girls born in Great Britain were lured home to visit but were then coerced into marrying first cousins or other men. If a father or uncle takes away the girl's passport and isolates her, she has little legal recourse or chance of escaping. Islam does *not* allow forced arranged marriages. Instead, these are social and cultural practices where men dominate and can force girls and women to marry against their will "to preserve culture and lineage" (Tohid, 2003: 7).

Societies in Transition Some countries in Asia are also experiencing changes in the way people meet and select mates. In some cases, these changes are the result of a shortage of women. In others, a rising number of women who pursue higher education and careers are postponing marriage.

India and China are experiencing a glut of single men and a scarcity of single women (see "Data Digest"). In both countries, the preference for boys has led to the killing of millions of female infants and to the deaths of many others as a result of neglect—poor nutrition, inadequate medical care, or desertion. Unmarried women have become scarce. Men in some poor rural regions of China often rely on a booming trade of kidnapped women in Vietnam and North Korea as a source of wives (see Chapter 5).

China has responded to the preponderance of males by implementing some Western-style mate-selection methods that include newspaper and magazine ads and Internet "singles" services ("Valentine's Day story," 2003). The classified advertisements differ quite a bit from those in the United States, however. According to Linlin (1993), there are some striking cultural differences in terms of desirable attributes:

- All the Chinese advertisers were marriage-minded and family-oriented, whereas many of their counterparts in the United States wanted someone to have fun with.

- Chinese advertisers emphasized health of both spouses because health is very important in a lasting marriage and implies good mental health.

- Because most male advertisers expect their future spouses to be virgins, marital status got close attention.

- Chinese women expect the husband to be the major decision maker. Therefore, signs of being resolute and career-minded were important.

- Chinese advertisers rarely asked about humor or communication because these qualities are seen as important in public life rather than in marriage and family life.

- Male suitors with apartments were seen as particularly attractive because there is a housing shortage in China.

Alarmed by the low rates of mating and procreation among its college-educated singles, Singapore is the only city in the world that has a government-run dating service. The matchmaking includes subsidized mixers, trips, "marriage awareness" seminars, and speed dating (Murphy, 2002).

In Japan and Korea the mating game has also changed, in part because more women are acquiring a college education, finding jobs, postponing marriage, or preferring to remain single. Japan has one of the highest average ages of marriage: 29 years for men and 26 years for women. To retain the loyalty of unmarried employees in the under-40 age bracket, several companies are including marriage in their benefit packages and have engaged matrimony brokerage firms to act as matchmakers. Matchmaking companies are thriving because they teach men how to date, court, and select a wife (Thornton, 1994).

In some countrysides in Spain, the Dominican Republic, Ecuador, and Colombia, women are scarce because they've left to work in cities. To help men find mates, some enterprising farmers have organized "Cupid crusades." Women who are disenchanted with cities board a bus and spend a day with bachelors: "Lonely hearts mingle over roasted lamb and a halting *pasodoble*, or two-step." An event usually lasts eight hours; the women pay $10 apiece and the men $30. Some of these encounters result in marriage (Fuchs, 2003).

Harmful Dating Relationships: Power, Control, and Sexual Aggression

A few years ago, one of my best students, Jennifer, a white woman, dropped by my office to apologize for missing an exam and a week of classes. I listened quietly as she fumbled with excuses: "I was sick. . . . Well, actually, my mom was sick. . . . I've been having car problems, too." She then burst into tears and showed me a bruise around her neck. Her boyfriend had been violent for some time but now had tried to strangle her.

So far we've focused on the positive side of dating: how people meet each other and what qualities they look for in marital partners. Dating also has a dark side. As in Jennifer's case, going together can be disappointing and even dangerous. Some major problems in dating, such as control and manipulation, may turn to violence. We can recognize risk factors for sexual aggression and date rape, however, and seek solutions.

Power and Control in Dating Relationships

Why do so many women still sit around waiting for their "boyfriends" to call even when they are in steady relationships or cohabiting? Sociologist Willard Waller's (1937) *principle of least interest* is useful in explaining the balance of power in many dating relationships.

Principle of Least Interest According to Waller, males have more power than females because they are usually the partner with the least interest. The person with more power is less dependent on others, is less interested in maintaining the relationship, and as a result, has more control (Lloyd, 1991). Conversely, the person with less power—usually the female—is more likely to be dependent, to try to maintain the relationship, and, often, to be exploited as a result (Sarch, 1993).

Gender Differences Men often maintain power and control during a dating relationship using direct strategies such as assertion, aggression, and discussion; women more often choose indirect strategies that include hinting,

CONSTRAINTS

How Abusers Control Dating Relationships

Both men and women try to control relationships. Although the following categories are based on the experiences of women who have been victims, men are also subject to abusive dating relationships.

- **Jealousy and blaming:** Blaming is often based on jealousy; almost anything the partner does is considered provocative. For example, a man may criticize his partner for not being at home when he calls or for talking to another man. He may say he loves her so much that he can't stand for her to be with others, including male friends.

- **Coercion, intimidation, and threats:** Abusers may coerce compliance with their demands by threatening to expose embarrassing secrets to family or friends. An abuser says things like "I'll break your neck" or "I'll kill you," and then dismisses them with "Everybody talks like that." Abusers also threaten to commit suicide or to attack a partner's family.

- **Isolation:** Typically, abusers spend a lot of time and energy watching their victims. They accuse family and friends of "causing trouble." Abusers may deprive the victim of a phone or car or even try to prevent them from holding a job. If these isolating techniques work, they break the partner's ties with other friends and increase dependence on the abuser.

- **Physical abuse:** Violent acts range from slaps and shoves to beatings, rape, and attacks with weapons. Many abusers manage to convince a partner, on each violent occasion, that "I really love you" and "This will never happen again," but it does. And in some cases, the last time the abuser strikes, he or she kills.

- **Emotional and verbal abuse:** Coming from a person the victim thinks she or he loves, emotional abuse is very powerful. Insults, which attack a person's feelings of independence and self-worth, are generally intended to get

a partner to accede to an abuser's demands ("Don't wear your skirt so short—it makes you look like a hooker"), denigrate the victim, and imply that she had better do what the partner wants or be left without anyone.

- **Sexual abuse:** Conflicts about sex often lead to violence. Often a male abuser decides whether to have sex, which sex acts are acceptable, and whether the couple should use condoms or other contraceptive devices to prevent AIDS and other STDs.

SOURCES: Gamache, 1990: Rosen and Stith, 1993.

STOP AND THINK . . .

- *Have you, your friends, or relatives experienced any of these forms of abuse? How did you react?*

- *Do you think that we can really love someone we're afraid of?*

---

withdrawing, or attempting to manipulate a partner's emotions (Christopher and Kisler, in press). A national study of single, never-married people between ages 18 and 30 found that women were more likely than men to keep tabs on their partners, to make their partners do what they wanted rather than what the partners wanted, and generally to set the rules in the relationship (Stets, 1993b).

Women's manipulation and control of men is the topic of a popular self-help book, *The Rules* (Fein and Schneider, 1996), that's still cited by many journalists and practitioners. The authors encourage women to scheme and maneuver men to get marriage proposals. Some of "the rules" include not calling the man, rarely returning his calls, and always ending phone calls first to maintain control of the relationship. Because *The Rules* was a best-seller, one might conclude that women are desperate to get married even if dating involves conniving and manipulating men. Tricks and dishonesty are

not a sound basis for marriage or a long-term relationship for either men or women, however (see Chapter 6). The box on "How Abusers Control Dating Relationships" examines some coercive tactics in more detail.

Aggression and Violence in Dating Relationships

Control often increases as a relationship progresses from casual to more serious dating. Men are much more likely than women to use physical force and sexual aggression to get their own way or to intimidate a partner (Stets, 1993a; Christopher and Kisler, in press). Women are also physically and emotionally abusive, however.

Dating Violence Dating violence is widespread. A study of adolescents in the sixth to eighth grades found that 42 percent had experienced dating violence, and 66 percent of these students reported that the violence was mutual (Gray and Foshee, 1997). Nationwide, 10 percent of high school students had been hit, slapped, or physically hurt on purpose by their boyfriend or girlfriend in the 12 months preceding the survey (Grunbaum et al., 2002). In another national study, one of every five high school girls had been abused physically or sexually by a dating partner (Silverman et al., 2001). The rates would be higher if girls interpreted such things as slapping and hair pulling as violence (Richard, 2002).

In a survey of college women, 27 percent reported having experienced physical abuse in a six-month period, and 77 percent reported some form of psychological abuse such as insults and intimidation (Neufeld et al., 1999). Among adults, women are six times more likely than men to experience dating violence ("Dating violence," 2000).

Dating violence is rarely a one-time event. Apparently, many women interpret the violence as evidence of love. According to a domestic violence counselor, "With so little real-life experience, girls tend to take jealousy and possessiveness to mean 'he loves me'" (L. Harris, 1996: 6). In some cases, couples who stay in abusive relationships seem to have accepted violence as a legitimate means of resolving conflict. It is almost as if they are testing the strength of their relationship, "If we can survive this, we can survive anything" (Lloyd, 1991).

Although gay and lesbian violence rates are similar to those of heterosexuals, they're highly underreported. In some cases, gays don't report dating or other violence for fear of increasing homophobia (Ristock, 2002). In other cases, and until recently, 13 states had sodomy laws. Therefore, gays could be prosecuted for same-sex intercourse rather than getting protection from an abusive partner (Hoffman, 2003; see also Chapter 9).

Acquaintance and Date Rape

Women are especially vulnerable to acquaintance and date rape. **Acquaintance rape** is the rape of a person who knows or is familiar with the rapist. Acquaintance rapists may include neighbors, friends of the family, co-workers, or people the victim meets at a party or get-together. In a highly publicized recent case, 54 female cadets had reported rape or sexual assaults by upperclassmen at the Air Force Academy in the past decade. The actual numbers may be twice as high. Most women don't report the assaults because they are afraid of being seen as weak or that their military careers would be over (Lorch and Tolme, 2003).

Date rape is unwanted, forced sexual intercourse in the context of a dating situation; the victim and the perpetrator may be on a first date or in a steady dating relationship. A number of research studies conducted on campuses show that 13 to 25 percent of the women reported being raped or had been taken advantage of when they were incapacitated by alcohol or other drugs

(Koss and Cook, 1993; Abbey et al., 1996). One of the reasons date rape is so common, and one of the reasons it comes as a great shock to the victim, is that, typically, the rapist seems to be "a nice guy"—polite, clean-cut, and even a leader in the community or on campus.

Factors Contributing to Date Violence and Date Rape

There are many reasons for dating violence and date rape. Some of the most important explanations include family violence and gender-role expectations, peer pressure, secrecy, and the use of alcohol and other drugs.

Family Violence and Gender-Role Expectations

A number of researchers have found an association between family violence and dating violence. Witnessing family violence, being hit by an adult, and seeing that aggression produces compliance increases the likelihood of being both an assailant and a victim during courtship (White and Humphrey, 1994; L. Harris, 1996; Foshee et al., 1999).

Some attribute violence to _misogyny, the hatred of women_. Dating violence and date rape are ways of striking out against women (especially independent and self-confident women) who challenge men's "right" to control women. Remember our discussion of narcissists—people who love themselves more than anyone else—in Chapter 6? Narcissistic men are especially likely to use sexual coercion during dating. They rationalize their behavior as having been encouraged by the woman's attention. They can become aggressive and even commit rape because they feel entitled to sexual gratification that they wanted and anticipated (Bushman et al., 2003).

Generally speaking, men who commit date rape hold traditional views of gender roles, seeing themselves as in charge and women as submissive. They initiate the date, pay the expenses, and feel that women lead them on by dressing suggestively (Hannon et al., 1995; Christopher, 2001). Traditional men can be sexually aggressive and not feel guilty because "She deserved it" or "Women enjoy rough sex" (Walker et al., 1993).

Women are more likely than men to blame themselves for dating violence because females are socialized to accept more responsibility for relationship conflict than males (Lloyd and Emery, 2000). Both male and female college students in one study, for example, saw the woman as encouraging or being responsible for acquaintance rape because women should "know better" than to visit men in their apartments or to "lead men on" through heavy petting (Szymanski et al., 1993).

Peer Pressure and Secrecy

Peer pressure is one of the major reasons why people are violent and why many

Parties provide a good avenue for meeting other singles. Drinking too much, however, may pave the way for trouble later in the evening, especially for women (see text).

partners stay in abusive dating relationships. "The pressure to date is fierce" and having any boyfriend is considered better than having none. Teens who date are seen as more popular than those who don't (L. Harris, 1996).

Peer pressure may be even more influential in college. According to a study of fraternity members, many of the men saw sexual behavior as a "hunt" in which the most successful hunter is the one who traps the largest number of "prey." To prove his masculinity, for example, one fraternity man decided to have intercourse with 13 new and different girls by the end of the semester (Sanday, 1990: 114).

Women are also sexually coercive. In a survey of 165 men and 131 women—all of them new members of fraternities or sororities—34 men and 36 women said they had experienced unwanted sexual contact. Most of the male victims reported giving in to sexual arousal or verbal pressure by women. The women were more likely to have been subjected to physical force or plied with alcohol or drugs (Larimer et al., 1999).

Secrecy protects abusers. Most teenagers remain silent about abusive relationships because they don't want to be pressured by their friends into breaking up. They rarely tell parents because they are afraid of losing the freedom they have, they don't want their parents to think they have poor judgment, or they are trying to figure out what to do on their own (M. Harris, 1996).

Racial-ethnic women may endure dating violence for several interrelated reasons. Young Asian/Pacific women, for instance, may be torn between duty to their values of virginity and family honor and accommodating the men they are dating. When violence occurs in a secret dating relationship, there is additional pressure to keep both the violence and the dating relationship itself from

parents. The secrecy intensifies the woman's feeling of being responsible for the violence (Yoshihama et al., 1991; Foo, 2002).

Use of Alcohol and Other Drugs Many college students deny any relationship between alcohol consumption and sexual aggression. Men say they can control themselves, and women feel they can resist attempts of unwanted sex (Cue et al., 1996; Nurius et al., 1996). However, alcohol lowers inhibitions against violence and also reduces a woman's ability to resist a sexual assault. In some cases, men admit that their strategies include getting women drunk to get them into bed (Martin and Hummer, 1993).

Since the mid-1990s, a growing number of college women have reported being raped after their drink was spiked with Rohypnol (also known as "roofies," "rope," and a variety of other street terms). Although Rohypnol is not marketed in the United States, it is widely available and inexpensive (less than $5 a tablet). When it is slipped into any beverage, Rohypnol's sedating effects begin within 20 minutes of ingestion and usually last more than 12 hours. Rohypnol has been called the "date-rape drug" and the "forget me pill" because women who have been knocked out with roofies have blacked out, been raped, and had no memory of what had happened. When mixed with alcohol or narcotics, Rohypnol can be fatal (Lloyd, 2002b).

A more recent "rape drug" is GHB, or gamma hydroxybutyrate, a liquid or powder made of lye or drain-cleaner that's mixed with GBL, gamma butyrolactone, an industrial solvent often used to strip floors. GHB is an odorless, colorless drug that knocks the victim out within 30 minutes. The coma-like effects of GHB last from 3 to 6 hours. As recently as 1994—when the drug was still new—there were only 56 GHB-related emergency room visits nationwide. By 2001, the number had jumped to 3,340 (Lloyd, 2002a).

Consequences of Dating Violence and Date Rape

Most dating violence and date rape occurs in situations that seem safe and familiar. This is why these behaviors often come as a great shock to victims, who cannot believe what is happening.

Violence and rape violate both body and spirit; they can affect every aspect of the victim's life. *Even though they are not responsible for the attack*, women often feel ashamed and blame themselves for the rape. Fear of men, of going out alone, and of being alone become part of their lives, as do anger, depression, and sometimes inability to relate to a caring sexual partner.

Table 8.4 lists other consequences of courtship violence and date rape.

Some Solutions

Because violent behavior and rape are learned behaviors, they can be unlearned. We need remedies on three levels: individual, organizational, and societal.

On the *individual level,* women should report assaults. When the offender is a current or former husband or boyfriend or a friend or acquaintance, 61 to 82 percent of completed rapes, attempted rapes, and sexual assaults are not reported to the police (Rennison, 2002). In addition, as the primary victims, women must become more "savvy" and avoid risky dating situations. One of these situations, drinking, can be prevented by both sexes.

Much can be done on the *organizational level* as well. The Student Right-to-Know and Campus Security Act of 1990 and the Higher Education Reauthorization Act of 1992 require colleges to report rape and other crimes. Only 37 percent of higher education institutions comply fully with these laws (Karjane et al., 2002; see also Hebel, 2003, and Fuller, 2003).

Some women are discouraged from reporting violence because they're told that they can be found guilty of drinking or having sex in the dorm. A number of schools, including the Ivy Leagues, are reluctant to investigate charges of sexual assaults. Even when assaults are reported, the perpetrators are not suspended or dismissed (Cook, 2003; Hoover, 2003). If colleges and law enforcement agencies prosecuted sexual violence, it would decrease.

Finally, to make a serious dent in the incidence of dating violence and date rape, we must change *societal attitudes and beliefs* about male and female roles in dating, about sexual behavior, and about violence. The traditional notion that it is the woman's job to maintain the tone of relationships often leads women to blame themselves when things go wrong and to overlook, forgive, or excuse sexual aggression by men.

Breaking Up

Social scientists have fancy terms for breaking up, including "uncoupling," "disengagement," and "relationship dissolution." In plain English, we dump someone or vice versa. According to one poll, nearly half of American adults have gotten the romantic heave-ho at least twice during their lifetime, and 22 percent say they have been dumped six to ten times by significant others (Mundell, 2002).

A classic song tells us that "breaking up is hard to do." It is, sometimes. According to college students in both the United States and Korea, for example, "relatedness" (feeling a sense of closeness with other people)

TABLE 8.4

Emotional and Behavioral Difficulties Experienced by Female and Male Victims of Courtship Violence or Date Rape

- General depression: Some signs are changes in eating and sleeping patterns and unexplained aches and pains. Depressive symptoms may prevent women from attending classes, completing course assignments, or functioning effectively on the job.

- A sense of powerlessness, helplessness, vulnerability, shame, and sadness.

- Loss of self-confidence and self-esteem, which may increase the likelihood of future sexual assaults.

- Changes in the victim's attitudes toward sexual relationships in general and in his or her behavior in an intimate relationship.

- Irritability with family, friends, or co-workers.

- Generalized anger, fear, anxiety, or suicidal thoughts.

- Inability to concentrate, even on routine tasks.

- Development of dependency on alcohol or drugs.

- Unwanted pregnancy.

SOURCES: Benokraitis and Feagin, 1995; Larimer et al., 1999; Silverman et al., 2001.

is more important than money, pleasure, and self-esteem (Sheldon et al., 2001). Why, then, do so many of us break up?

Why We Break Up   There are numerous reasons for breaking up dating and other intimate relationships that include both micro-level and macro-level reasons:

- *Individual (micro) reasons* include communication problems, different interests, emotional and physical abuse, obsessive "love" and controlling behavior, mismatched love and sexual needs, self-disclosure that reveals repulsive attitudes, disillusionment, lowered affectionate behavior, infidelity, and "freeloading" rather than making a commitment (Forward, 2002; Harley, 2002; Harvey and Weber, 2002; Regan, 2003).

- *Structural (macro) reasons* include moving away, economic recessions that trigger unemployment and arguments about finances, and societal reactions that disapprove of relationships between young partners, young men and older women, couples from different racial or ethnic and religious backgrounds, and same-sex partners (Martin, 1993; Regan, 2003).

How We React Breakups are usually very painful, but people respond in different ways. Women, for example, are usually more devastated by cheating than men—who feel that betraying a friend is a greater offense than sexual infidelity (Feldman et al., 2000). And, as you might expect, people who have fewer "chips" on the marriage market are more upset by dating breakups than those who have many options because they're sexy, successful, or attractive (Schmitt and Buss, 2001).

Getting upset is one of the most common reactions to breakups because we don't know why we were dumped. Discussing the reasons with an ex–dating partner would provide a sense of understanding and closure.

In addition, explaining the reasons for a breakup is "a cathartic purging of feeling guilt, anger, depression, loneliness, insecurity, and confusion", as well as pent-up wounded emotions that may last for a long time (Regan, 2003: 174).

Men seem to get over breakups more quickly than women. Shortly after a breakup, for example, 42 percent of men and 31 percent of women start dating someone else. In addition, 54 percent of women but only 31 percent of men call friends or family members for comfort (Fetto, 2003).

Is Breaking Up Healthy? Absolutely. Disagreements and conflict are part and parcel of any close relationship especially before marriage. Breaking up a dating or cohabiting relationship is much less complicated than breaking up a marriage (see Chapter 15).

Recall that Farber's permanent availability model suggests that we have no predestined partners. Instead, one of the important functions of dating and courtship is to filter out unsuitable prospective mates. It can also be a great relief to end a bad relationship. Thus, breaking up is a normal process (see Chapter 6). And, according to some sociologists, breakups are desirable because most of us don't "circulate" enough before getting married (Glenn, 2002).

If anything, breaking up should probably occur more often than it does. Ending dating relationships provides people with opportunities to find mates who may be more suitable for marriage. In addition, breaking up opens up a larger pool of eligible and interesting partners as we mature and become more self-confident before deciding to get married.

MAKING CONNECTIONS

▧ How long has it taken you to dump someone? What reasons did you give, if any? Or are you still with someone you'd like to dump?

▧ Some people feel that breaking up on e-mail (or Instant Messenger) is tacky. Others argue that this is a quick and painless way to end a relationship. What do you think? ⚭

Conclusion

We have more *choices* in mate selection today than ever before. A broad dating spectrum includes both traditional and contemporary ways to meet other people.

These choices emerge within culturally defined boundaries, or *constraints,* however. Factors that determine who selects whom for a partner come into play long before a couple marries and despite our romantic views that "I can date anyone I want." Besides the pressure to date and mate with people who are most similar to us, some partners must also deal with aggression and violence.

One response to today's array of choices and constraints in mate selection is to postpone marriage. In fact, a significant *change* today is the decision of many people to stay single longer, the subject of the next chapter.

SUMMARY

1. Sociologists describe the dating process as a marriage market where prospective spouses compare the assets and liabilities of eligible partners and choose the best available mate. In this sense, we "trade" with others depending on what resources we have.

2. Dating fulfills both manifest and latent functions. Manifest functions include recreation, companionship, fun, and mate selection. Latent functions include socialization, social status, sexual experimentation, and meeting intimacy and ego needs.

3. Dating forms have changed over the years. Many adolescents and young adults, especially, have forsaken traditional dating for more informal methods such as "getting together," "pack dating," and "hookin' up."

4. Adults use a variety of mate-selection methods to meet a potential spouse, including personal classified ads, marriage bureaus, computerized services, and the Internet.

5. Much of our dating and mate-selection behavior is shaped by homogamy—rules that define appropriate mates in terms of race, ethnicity, religion, age, social class, values, and other characteristics.

6. Our pool of eligible partners expands when we seek mates from dissimilar religious, racial, or ethnic groups.

7. Social exchange theory and equity theory suggest that partners seek a balance of costs and benefits in a relationship; the relationship is most satisfying when it is seen as egalitarian.

8. Unlike the United States and some other Western nations, most countries around the world do not have "open" courtship systems. Rather, marriages are often arranged by families and restricted to members of the same culture, religion, or race. The selection methods are changing in some traditional societies, however.

9. Although dating is typically fun, there are also many risks and problems. Women, especially, are often victims of sexual pressure and aggression, violence, and date rape. The reasons for such victimization include power differences between men and women, peer pressure and secrecy, and the use of alcohol and other drugs.

10. Ending a relationship may be painful, but it also provides opportunities for finding a better mate.

KEY TERMS

dating *203*
marriage market *204*
filter theory *213*
homogamy *213*

propinquity *213*
heterogamy *217*
hypergamy *218*
hypogamy *218*

equity theory *222*
dowry *223*
acquaintance rape *227*
date rape *227*

TAKING IT FURTHER

Meeting People Online and Avoiding Date Violence on Campus

Here are a few sites that are free, offer a free trial membership, or include interesting links to a variety of national, international, religious, and travel sites for "single and romance-minded individuals":

Meet Me Online: The 100% Free Single's Site

www.meetmeonline.com

Single Sites Directory of WWW sites, Chat, Forums, and Anonymous E-mail

www.singlesites.com

Yahoo Personals

personals.yahoo.com

The following sites provide valuable information on campus crime statistics and prevention of campus violence,

contain links to acquaintance and date rape sites, and offer a variety of resources to assist victims of violence:

Sexual Assault Resources

Sexual assault and rape:
http://www.ojp.usdoj.gov/ovc/help/rape.htm

Victims of sexual offenders:
http://www.ojp.usdoj.gov/ovc/assist/soo.html

Security on Campus, Inc.

www.campussafety.org

National Victim Center

www.nvc.org

And more: www.prenhall.com/benokraitis contains sites on interracial and intercultural relationships, the *quinceañera*, how to avoid marrying a jerk, speed dating, interfaith family resources, and several URLs on breaking up—politely or more bluntly—if she or he "just doesn't get it."

INVESTIGATE WITH RESEARCH NAVIGATOR

Please go to www.researchnavigator.com and enter your LOGIN NAME and PASSWORD. For instructions on registering for the first time, please view the detailed instructions at the end of the Chapter 1. Please search the Research Navigator™ site using the following key search terms:

date rape
homogamy
family violence

Singlehood, Cohabitation, and Other Nonmarital Options

DATADIGEST

- The number of **unmarried adults** (never married, divorced, and widowed) has increased from 37.5 million in 1970 to 81.7 million in 2000.

- The **never-married** make up the largest and fastest-growing segment of the unmarried population. The proportion of adults who have never been married rose from 15 percent in 1972 to 24 percent in 2000.

- In 2000, adults **lived alone** in 26 percent of the 105 million households.

- The number of **unmarried-couple households** has grown. Cohabitants represented only 1.1 percent of couples in 1960 compared with 9 percent in 2000.

- An estimated 594,000 households are made up of **same-sex** partners.

SOURCES: Saluter, 1996; Fields and Casper, 2001; U.S. Census Bureau, 2002; Simmons and O'Connell, 2003.

A couple who had been dating for several years went out to a Chinese restaurant for dinner one evening. After studying the menu, the man turned to the woman and asked, "How would you like your rice: fried or boiled?" She looked him straight in the eye and replied, "Thrown." Sound corny? Maybe not.

Most people eventually make that "love connection" and marry. Until then—or if relationships fizzle—there is more freedom today than ever before to pursue other alternatives. Traditional families have faded in the last century. This chapter examines four nontraditional living arrangements: singlehood, cohabitation, gay households, and communal residences. We will examine other nonmarital households, such as single parents and widowed people, in later chapters.

Before you read further, take the "A Quiz about Singles" on page 234. It asks how much you know about unmarried people and gives a preview of the chapter.

The Single Option

Many people are anxious about the family (see Chapter 1). They fear that marriage is disappearing, especially because of a growing singles population in the United States since 1970 (see "Data Digest").

Are Americans Opting Out of Marriage?

One social scientist maintains that we have "a marriage problem" in the United States. Among other things, he says, more people are not marrying, are living together, or are raising children alone (Wilson, 2002).

You can decide for yourself—after reading this chapter or by the end of the course—whether we have a marriage problem. It's certainly true, however, that more people feel that being single is a viable option. Between 1975 and 2002, for example, the share of Americans who had never married increased from about 24 percent to

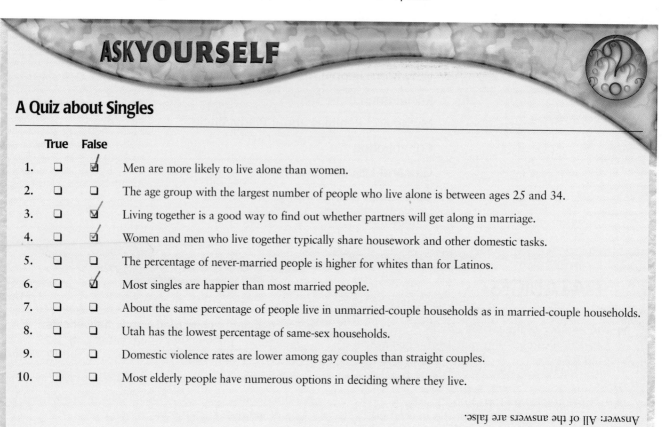

ASKYOURSELF

A Quiz about Singles

	True	False	
1.	☐	☑	Men are more likely to live alone than women.
2.	☐	☐	The age group with the largest number of people who live alone is between ages 25 and 34.
3.	☐	☑	Living together is a good way to find out whether partners will get along in marriage.
4.	☐	☑	Women and men who live together typically share housework and other domestic tasks.
5.	☐	☐	The percentage of never-married people is higher for whites than for Latinos.
6.	☐	☑	Most singles are happier than most married people.
7.	☐	☐	About the same percentage of people live in unmarried-couple households as in married-couple households.
8.	☐	☐	Utah has the lowest percentage of same-sex households.
9.	☐	☐	Domestic violence rates are lower among gay couples than straight couples.
10.	☐	☐	Most elderly people have numerous options in deciding where they live.

Answer: All of the answers are false.

29 percent ("Americans increasingly . . .," 2003). This doesn't mean that the singles will never marry, only that the percentages have grown when measured at different points in time. The never-married constitute only one cluster of a very diverse group of singles.

The Diversity of Singles

There are several kinds of singles: those postponing first marriages, the small percentage who will never marry, the currently unmarried who are divorced or widowed but may be looking for new partners, and lesbians and gay men, who are legally prohibited from marrying. In addition, people's living arrangements may vary greatly, from living alone during a part of one's adult life to singlehood in later life.

Single Adults in General   Singlehood reflects more dimensions than simply being not married. Being single can be freely chosen or unintentional as well as enduring or short-term:

■ *Voluntary temporary singles* are open to marriage but place a lower priority on searching for mates than on other activities, such as education, career, politics, and self-development. This group includes men and women who cohabit.

■ *Voluntary stable singles* include people who have never married and are satisfied with that choice, those who have been married but do not want to remarry, those who are living together but do not intend to marry, and those whose lifestyles preclude the possibility of marriage, such as priests and nuns. Also included are single parents—both never married and formerly married—who are not seeking mates and who are raising their children alone or with the help of relatives or friends.

■ *Involuntary temporary singles* are those who would like to be married and are actively seeking mates. This group includes people who are widowed or divorced and single parents who would like to get married.

■ *Involuntary stable singles* are primarily older divorced, widowed, and never-married people who wanted to marry or remarry but did not find a mate and now accept their single status. This group also includes singles who suffer from some physical or psychological impairment that limits their success in the marriage market (Stein, 1981).

A person's position in these categories can change over time. For example, voluntary temporary singles may marry, divorce, and then become involuntary stable singles because they are unable to find another suitable mate. In this sense, the boundaries between being single and married are fairly fluid for most people. For a much smaller number, singlehood is constant either because it's a choice or because some people have little to trade on the marriage market (see Chapter 8).

Single Adults in Later Life As one grows older, there is a greater tendency to become choosier. For older singles who date and want to marry or remarry, the double standard still favors men. Aging women are typically seen as "over the hill," whereas aging men are often described as "mature" and "distinguished." Older women are also more likely than older men to remain single after divorcing or being widowed because they have caretaker responsibilities for relatives, primarily aging parents (see Chapter 17).

There is little research on older people who have never married, probably because only 3 percent of men and women age 65 and over fall into this category (U.S. Census Bureau, 2002). Although few never-marrieds marry in later life, they are a diverse group: Some are isolated and others have many friends, some wish they were married, and others are glad they're single.

Some see the never-married elderly as lonely and unhappy. Marriage may be satisfying, but it also means making compromises and limiting one's freedom:

> *When I was a little girl and, later on, an adolescent, it never occurred to me that I would not meet the man of my dreams, get married, and live happily ever after. Now, at fifty-four, it seems unlikely, though not impossible, that this will happen. Not only do I live alone but I actually like it. I value my space, my solitude, and my independence enormously and cannot [imagine] the circumstances that would lead me to want to change it (Cassidy, 1993: 35).*

Never-marrieds don't have to deal with the desolation of widowhood or divorce. Many develop extensive social networks of friends and relatives. They work, date, and engage in a variety of hobbies, volunteer work, and church activities and often have lasting relationships.

As people age, however, the supportive social ties of never-married people aged 60 and older diminish compared with those of their married or divorced counterparts. Older never-married singles are likely to have the closest relationships with parents or older siblings. When these family members die or become physically impaired, the never-married lose confidants and caregivers and report lower life satisfaction (Barrett, 1999; Keith et al., 2000).

Some singles live with others. Some live alone. Let's take a brief look at who lives alone and why.

QUALITY TIME   Gail Machlis

The *Quality Time* cartoon by Gail Machlis is reprinted by permission of Chronicle Features, San Francisco, California.

Home Alone

Because more than 90 percent of all Americans marry at least once during their lifetimes, marriage is still the norm. Household size has been shrinking, however. In 1900, nearly half of the U.S. population lived in households of six or more people (Hobbs and Stoops, 2002). A century later, more than one of four Americans is living alone (see *Figure 9.1* on page 236). Who are the people living alone? And what explains the rise in solitary living?

Who Is Living Alone?

Singlehood is widespread. Nonetheless, there are some patterns in terms of geographic location, sex, age, and race and ethnicity.

Geographic Location There are substantial regional variations in the proportion living alone. Single-occupant households are most common in North Dakota (29 percent) and Rhode Island (29 percent). They are the least common in Utah (18 percent) and Idaho and Hawaii (22 percent each) (Simmons and O'Neill, 2001). In addition, suburbs outside large cities are

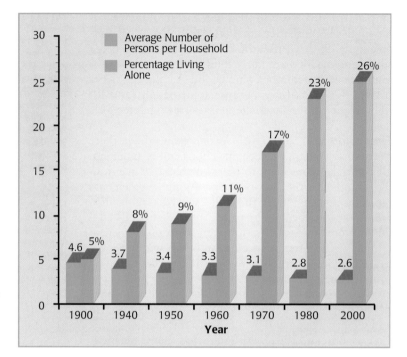

FIGURE 9.1   **The Shrinking Household** Both the decline in the average number of people per household and the rapidly rising numbers of people living alone have contributed to a smaller contemporary household.

Source: Hobbs and Stoops, 2002.

booming as singles follow jobs to sprawling office parks or try to escape high city rents (Cohn, 2002).

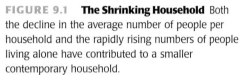 More women (15 percent) than men (11 percent) live alone. The proportion of 25- to 44-year-olds living alone increased from 3 percent in 1970 to 10 percent in 2002. Across all age groups, older Americans are the most likely to live alone: about 31 percent in 2002 (Fields and Casper, 2001; "Solitaire set . . .," 2003).

In their later years, women are more likely than men to live alone (see *Figure 9.2*). On average, women live about five years longer than men. If women enjoy good health and have enough income, they can care for themselves into their eighties and even nineties (see Chapter 17).

Race and Ethnicity   Of all those living alone, more than 80 percent are white (U.S. Census Bureau, 2002). Racial-ethnic families are more likely to live in extended households because of values that emphasize caring for family members and pooling financial resources (see Chapter 4).

Why Do People Live Alone?

Rachel, one of my graduate students, recently bought a townhouse in a nice neighborhood. Rachel is 32, has a good job as a bank manager, has no children, and hopes to marry. But, she says, "I'm not going to put off making this investment until Mr. Right comes along."

Rachel's reasons for living alone echo those of many other singles her age. Many Americans choose to live alone because *they can afford it*. In 2000, in fact, single women were second only to married couples in the number of homes they bought, and 30 percent of them were under age 35 (Paul, 2002).

A second and related reason is that *our values emphasize individualism* (see Chapters 1, 3, and 4). Most unmarried Americans across all ages are highly involved in their families but prefer to live alone if they can afford it. Living alone provides more privacy and freedom than living with parents or others (see Chapter 8).

Third, living alone varies at *different stages of life* (see Chapter 1). For example, those living alone include young adults, like Rachel, who are young but have decent-paying jobs. In addition, separated people, divorced people, and older people who are widowed and living apart from their children often live alone (Simmons and O'Neill, 2001).

A fourth reason for living alone is that Americans are *living longer and healthier lives*, allowing independent living after retirement (Belsie, 2001). Even before retirement, being healthy means that we can live alone instead of moving in with others.

Finally, and perhaps most importantly, many people are living alone because they are postponing marriage or deciding not to marry. That is, we have *more options that include singlehood*. As Rachel said, she doesn't want to put her life on hold "until Mr. Right comes along."

MAKING CONNECTIONS

■ There are several kinds of singles. Why are *you* single? Are you a voluntary or involuntary single, for example?

■ Do you or your friends live alone? Why? If you live with other people, do you enjoy it?

Why More People Are Single

Why has the number of singles increased? A major reason is that many people are postponing marriage.

Singles Are Postponing Marriage

Many people are pursuing college educations, preparing for jobs or careers, and spending more time in recreational or other activities before settling down. As a result, many of us are marrying later than our parents or grandparents.

In 1970, the median age at first marriage was 21 for women and 23 for men. By 2000, these ages had risen to 25 for women and 27 for men, the oldest ages at first marriage ever recorded by the U.S. Census Bureau (see *Figure 9.3* on page 238). (Remember that the *median* represents the midpoint of cases. Thus, half of all men were 27 or older and half of all women were 25 or older the first time they got married.)

From a historical perspective, our current tendency to delay marriage is the norm, especially for men. As *Figure 9.3* shows, men's median age at first marriage in 1890 was only slightly lower than in 2000 (26 and 27, respectively). The median for women has increased more noticeably, however, especially since 1960 (22 in 1890, 20 in 1960, and 25 in 2000) (Fields and Casper, 2001).

For both sexes, the younger age at first marriage in the 1950s and 1960s was a historical exception rather than the rule. As you saw in Chapter 3, World War II delayed many marriages. When the soldiers came back, there was a surge of weddings. Throughout the 1950s, the United States tried to regain "normalcy" by encouraging both women and men in their late teens or early twenties to marry and to have babies (see Chapters 3 and 5). Young couples themselves wanted to marry and to form families.

In the late 1960s, feminists, especially, began to question women's traditional roles within and outside the family (see Chapter 2). Over the last few generations, both women and men have thought more consciously and deliberately about when and whom to marry.

Many Americans will tell you they are single because they are not in love and, like Rachel, are still waiting for "the right person." Despite what people say, being single reflects a complex interplay of individual (micro-level), demographic, and macro-level variables.

Individual Choices and Constraints in Being Single

Although marriage offers many benefits, there are also parallel incentives for being single (see *Table 9.1* on page 238). Both choices and constraints shape our attitudes and behavior about getting married or staying single.

Waiting for a Soul Mate Many singles are delaying marriage because they are waiting for their "true love." In a study of never-married young singles aged 20 to 29, an overwhelming 94 percent agreed with the statement that "when you marry you want your spouse to be your soul mate, first and foremost" (Whitehead and Popenoe, 2001). Another national survey of never-married single adults aged 18 to 49 found that 79 percent of the women and men believed

FIGURE 9.2 Living Alone: 1990 and 2000 As these data show, older women are much more likely than men to be living alone in their midlife and later years, especially after age 74. How would you explain these differences?

SOURCE: Based on U.S. Census Bureau, 2002, Table 60.

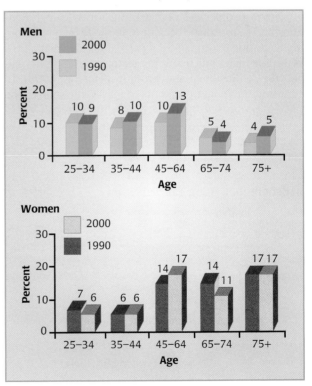

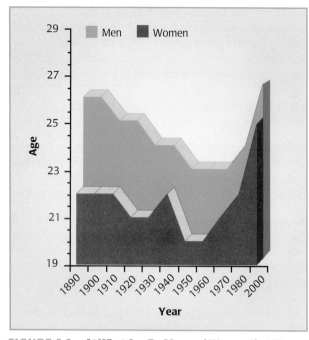

FIGURE 9.3 **At What Age Do Men and Women First Marry?**
As the text points out, the median age of first marriage for men was almost the same in 2000 as in 1890, but the median for women has risen since 1960.

SOURCE: Based on data from Saluter, 1994, Table B; Saluter, 1996, Table A-33; and Fields and Casper, 2001.

that they will eventually find and marry their "perfect mate" (Edwards, 2000).

Some people feel that waiting for a "super relationship" is unrealistic because a marriage involves more than emotional intimacy. If a partner decides that a love is no longer a soul mate, for example, she or he will become disillusioned and bail out (Peterson, 2003). In addition, the longer one waits to marry, the smaller the

pool of eligible partners, especially among the never-married (see Chapter 8).

Others contend that waiting for a soul mate isn't necessarily starry-eyed: "Perhaps more than ever before, young people have an opportunity to choose a partner on the basis of personal qualities and shared dreams, not economics or 'gender straitjackets'" (Rivers, 2001).

Being Independent One of the biggest advantages of being single is independence and autonomy. Both sexes can do pretty much what they please. According to a 32-year-old male newscaster, "You don't have to worry about commitments to your career [affecting] your commitment to a family. I'm not ruling out marriage. . . . There's just no rush" (Wilson, 2001: D1). When a 43-year-old freelance writer and yoga instructor decides to travel, she does so freely: "She packs her bags, gets on a plane, and goes hiking through Spain, mountain biking in Death Valley or touring the Caribbean" (Fallik, 2001). As one of my 27-year-old female students once said, "I don't plan to marry until my feet have touched six of the seven continents."

Having Fun Getting married doesn't end having fun or an active social life, of course. However, 58 percent of single adults in their late twenties and early thirties said that their social life and having fun were high priorities, compared with only 38 percent of their married friends (Phillips, 1999).

Enjoying Close Relationships A common reason for getting married is companionship (see *Table 9.1*). Singles who are delaying marriage rely on peers rather than a spouse for support and companionship. Single women have close friends with whom they socialize and spend time. According to a man, similarly, girlfriends, jobs,

TABLE 9.1

Benefits of Marriage and Singlehood

Benefits of Getting Married	Benefits of Being Single
Companionship	Privacy, few constraints, independence
Faithful sexual partner	Varied sexual experiences; cohabitation
Dependability, love	Exciting, changing lifestyle
Sharing mutual interests	Meeting new friends with different interests
Pooling economic resources	Economic autonomy
Social approval for "settling down" and producing children	Freedom from responsibility to care for spouse or children
Becoming a part of something larger than self	Basic need for independence

SOURCES: Based on Stein, 1981; Carter and Sokol, 1993.

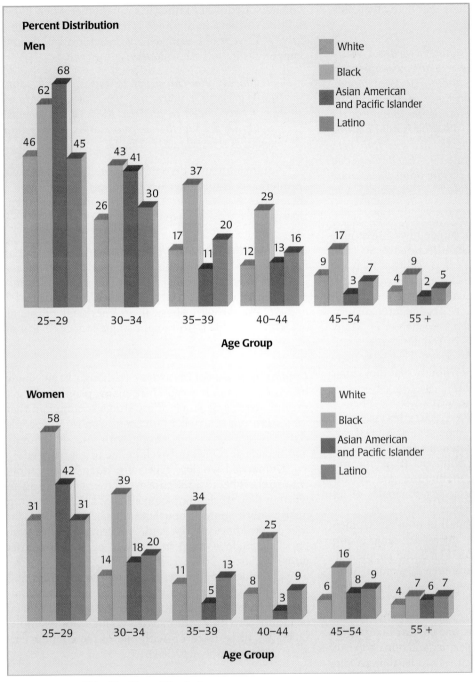

FIGURE 9.4   **Who Has Never Married**

SOURCE: Kreider and Fields, 2002: 8.

and apartments came and went but his group of male friends became an "urban tribe": "We met weekly for dinner at a neighborhood restaurant. We traveled together, moved one another's furniture, painted one another's apartments, and cheered one another on at sporting events" (Watters, 2001).

In addition, many singles are quite involved in family life. Some still live with their parents (see Chapter 12).

Others spend much time with nieces and nephews. Women, especially, devote much of their time and resources in supporting other family members (see Chapter 5).

Making a Commitment   There are more never-married men than women in most age groups (see *Figure 9.4*). Why, then, do so many women complain that "there's nothing out there"? One reason is that many men simply don't want to get married:

> Ed . . . is a charming, handsome, 48-year-old Washington, D.C., lobbyist who plans evenings that most women just fantasize about. His dates may involve box seats at a performance of Tosca, champagne served during the intermission, dinner at the best Italian restaurant. . . . What Ed is not planning is a long-term relationship: "I have had four very important relationships," he says. "Each one lasted about three years, but at a certain point the woman wanted marriage and I didn't" (Szegedy-Maszak, 1993: 88).

There's an old joke about single guys: "My girlfriend told me I should be more affectionate. So I got two girlfriends!" Some practitioners feel that men are the foot-draggers because there's little incentive for them to marry (Pittman, 1999). Because of the increase in premarital sex, most men can have sex and intimate relationships without getting married (see Chapter 7). Many men put off marriage because of stagnant wages and job losses in many employment sectors. They view marriage as a major economic responsibility that they don't want to undertake (Ooms, 2002).

Having Children Couples often marry because they plan to raise a family. Nearly 70 percent of Americans, however, disagree with the statement that "the main purpose of marriage is having children" (Popenoe and Whitehead, 2003). Because cohabitation and out-of-wedlock parenting are widely accepted, singles of all ages feel less pressure to get married.

Though still statistically small in number, women aged 35 and older are the fastest-growing group of unwed mothers (see Chapter 11). Some people call middle-class, professional, unmarried women who intentionally bear children "single mothers of choice" (Mattes, 1994).

Most of these women's *first* choice is to marry and *then* have children, however. As one 35-year-old mother said, "You can wait to have a partner and hope you can still have a baby. Or you can choose to let that go and have a baby on your own" (Orenstein, 2000: 149). Even if women find a soul mate, he may not want to participate in child care and other domestic activities that many women now expect men to share (see Chapter 5).

Fearing Divorce Divorce or prolonged years of conflict between parents can have a negative effect on young adults' perceptions of marriage. Many stay single as long as possible because they worry about divorce. If children have grown up in homes where parents divorced one or more times, they are wary of repeating the same mistake. As one 21-year-old

woman stated, "My father left my mother when I was 6. I don't believe in divorce" (Herrmann, 2003). Similarly, a 32-year-old man who works for a publishing company is in no rush to marry:

> I would say you can never be too choosy. I come from a generation where two-thirds or more of marriages have ended in divorce. Most of my friends' parents are not together anymore or on their second marriages (Hartill, 2001: 17).

Adult children of divorce are more likely than their counterparts from intact homes to experience divorce themselves (see Chapter 15). It's not surprising, then, that many singles are postponing marriage.

Being Healthy and Physically Attractive Emotional and physical health and physical appeal also affect singlehood. In the marriage market, most men are initially drawn only to attractive women (see Chapters 7 and 8). People with physical or emotional problems are also more likely to remain single longer or to not marry (Wilson, 2002).

Dealing with Social Pressure Although being single has become more acceptable, many people still get pressure to marry. Some of my students complain that "if you're not married by the time you're 30, people think there's something wrong with you. My family and friends are constantly telling me to get married."

Unmarried women, especially, often dread family get-togethers because they are asked over and over again whether they are dating "someone special." Parents drop not-so-subtle hints about grandkids. Invitations to friends' weddings pile up. And "bridesmaid dresses stare back at single women when they open their closet doors" (Hartill, 2001: 15).

The older singles are, the more often friends and relatives badger them about marriage plans. Others complain of feeling invisible and not being invited to social or family activities with married couples, for example, unless it's to be fixed up with one of the couple's single friends (Campbell, 2001).

Demographic Influences

As you've just seen, individual choices and constraints delay marriage. Demographic shifts, such as the sex ratio and the marriage squeeze, also help explain the large proportion of singles.

The Sex Ratio The **sex ratio,** expressed as a whole number, is the ratio of men to women in a country or group. A ratio of 100 means that there are equal numbers of men and women; a ratio of 110 means there are 110 men for every 100 women.

The biological norm is for about 95 girls to be born for every 100 boys. Male infants, however, have a naturally higher mortality rate (see Chapter 5). As a result, by early childhood the numbers are roughly equal. If not, other factors affect the ratio. In the United States, the sex ratio is around 100 until later in life. In the 75- to 84-year age group, for example, the ratio is 92 because women tend to live longer than men (see Chapters 17 and 18).

In some countries, the sex ratio is skewed from birth. For example, the sex ratio is 117 in China, 113 in the Caribbean and South Korea, 108 in India, and 105 in Latin America. On the other hand, the sex ratios of other countries are disproportionately female rather than male: 92 in sub-Saharan Africa, 94 in North Africa, and 96 in Central America (Brockerhoff, 2000; Sharma, 2001; Seager, 2003).

The uneven sex ratios result from a variety of factors. In countries such as China and India, there is a preference for boys who will carry on the family name, care for elderly parents, inherit property, and play a central role in family rituals. As a result, hundreds of thousands of female infants die yearly because of neglect, abandonment, murder, and starvation. Others are aborted after ultrasound scanners disclose the sex of the child (see Chapter 5).

In Africa, there are more women than men because of civil wars and AIDS deaths (see Chapter 7). In Central America, there are more men than women because women often migrate to other countries—like the United States—for jobs (see Chapter 4).

The Marriage Squeeze   A **marriage squeeze** is a sex imbalance in the ratio of available unmarried women and men. Because of this imbalance, members of one sex can be "squeezed" out of the marriage market. The squeeze may result from wealth, power, status, education level, age, or other factors that diminish the pool of eligible partners.

Is there a marriage squeeze in the United States? Yes. There are large numbers of never-married people, especially men, across almost all age categories and most racial-ethnic groups (see *Figure 9.4*). If we add to the pool another 156 million people who were unmarried because of divorce, separation, or being widowed during 2000, the marriage market appears very large. As you saw in Chapter 8, however, homogamy narrows the pool of eligibles. In addition, many "midlife" women experience a market squeeze because men their age are looking for much younger women (see Chapter 8).

Many countries are experiencing a much more severe marriage squeeze. Men in China, India, Korea, Taiwan, Africa, the Middle East, and other regions face a scarcity of young, single women because of skewed sex ratios. There are dozens of "bachelor villages" in

China's poorer regions that are inhabited primarily by men who can't find wives (Pomfret, 2001). As a result, there is a booming trade in kidnapped women who are brought to China as wives (see Chapter 8).

Some countries, such as China, are trying to change the sex ratio by changing the attitudes toward female infants and upgrading women's economic and social status. Population experts say, however, that cultural attitudes that devalue daughters and women will be hard to change despite marriage squeezes (Tefft, 1995).

Gender Roles   As gender roles change, so do attitudes about marriage. With the advent of washing machines, cleaning services, frozen foods, wrinkle-resistant fabrics, and 24-hour one-stop shopping, for example, "a man does not really need a woman to take care of cooking, cleaning, decorating, and making life comfortable" (Coontz, 1997: 81).

Women aren't rushing into marriage, either. Because the stigma once attached to "living in sin" has largely vanished, many women feel that they have more alternatives to cohabit and have babies outside marriage. Because it's difficult to juggle both a career and a family, many women have chosen to advance their professional lives before marrying and starting a family.

Macro-level Influences

A number of macro-level variables—over which we have no control—also affect our decisions about matrimony. A few examples include war, technology, social movements, and the economy.

War, Technology, and Social Movements   Marriage rates tend to drop during war. In Iraq, for example, decades of war have killed, handicapped, or psychologically traumatized many men, leading to a shortage of potential husbands. Newlyweds have been a rare sight in Baghdad since 2000 (Begos, 2003). In terms of technology, advances in contraceptive techniques have decreased unplanned pregnancies and "shotgun marriages."

Several social movements have also delayed marriage or shaped our definitions of "acceptable" relationships. The women's movement opened new educational and occupational opportunities for women, giving them career options outside marriage. The gay rights movement encouraged homosexuals to be more open about their sexual preferences and relieved the pressure some felt to marry.

Economic Factors   Economic realities also play an important role in delaying or promoting marriage. Economic depressions and unemployment tend to postpone marriage for men. The well-paid blue-collar jobs that once enabled high school graduates to support families

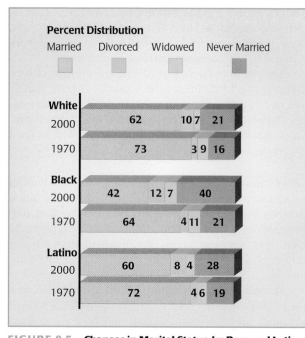

Percent Distribution

Married   Divorced   Widowed   Never Married

White
2000 — 62, 10 7, 21
1970 — 73, 3 9, 16

Black
2000 — 42, 12 7, 40
1970 — 64, 4 11, 21

Latino
2000 — 60, 8 4, 28
1970 — 72, 4 6, 19

FIGURE 9.5   Changes in Marital Status, by Race and Latino Origin, 1970 and 2000 The percentage of people who are married has decreased and the percentage of divorced and never-married people has increased, especially among blacks.

Source: Saluter, 1994: vi; U.S. Census Bureau, 2002, Table 46.

are mostly gone. Because of the continuing depressed economy, the job prospects for many college-educated men are also worsening rather than improving (see Chapter 13). In contrast, economic opportunities, as well as a belief that a person has access to those opportunities, encourage men to marry (Landale and Tolnay, 1991).

The effects of employment on women's tendency to marry are somewhat contradictory. On the one hand, being employed increases a woman's chances of meeting eligible men and may enhance her attractiveness as a potential contributor to a household's finances (see Chapter 8). On the other hand, if employed women want a spouse who earns more than they do, it will take longer to find a suitable mate (Raley and Bratter, 2000). Employed women with upscale salaries may decide not to marry at all if they don't find the right partner.

Racial and Ethnic Singles

The unmarried population among many racial and ethnic groups has increased, especially because of divorce (see *Figure 9.5*). Let's look at some of these racial and ethnic singles more closely, beginning with African Americans.

African Americans

Many African Americans are postponing marriage, but an even higher proportion may never marry. As *Figure 9.4* shows, 9 percent of black men and 7 percent of black women at age 55 and over have never married. Both structural factors and personal attitudes overlap in explaining this situation.

Structural Factors   A major reason for the high never-married rate among black women is the shortage of marriageable African American men (see Chapter 8). Some estimate that there are eight black men for every ten black women (Amott, 1993). This makes a marital commitment unnecessary in the eyes of some men.

The economy also plays a role. Deteriorating employment conditions often discourage young African American men from getting married (Ooms, 2002). Discrimination in employment also contributes to this problem, making many black men poor economic providers (see Chapter 4). Many black women age 55 and over are not interested in marrying or remarrying because they perceive an unemployed man as a potential "drain on their own finances" (Tucker et al., 1993).

Black men also have a lower life expectancy than their white counterparts. Occupational hazards in dangerous jobs have claimed many men's lives. Mortality rates for heart disease are almost three times higher for blue-collar workers—many of whom are black—than for managerial and professional groups, at least in part because of a lack of preventive medical care (Schulman et al., 1999).

Urban black men face a 10 percent chance of being killed in street crimes, compared with a 2 percent chance for white men. In 2002, 12 percent of black men, 4 percent of Latino men, and almost 2 percent of white men in their twenties and early thirties were in prison or jail (Harrison and Karberg, 2003).

As a group, black men earn more than black women in every occupation (see Chapter 13). There are more college-educated black women than black men, however (see Chapter 8). Many middle-class men are already married, and women are reluctant to "marry down." In a memorable scene in the movie *Waiting to Exhale*, the black women lament their marriage squeeze (though not in those words) and consider the merits and problems of marrying hardworking black men in lower socioeconomic levels.

Attitudes   Homogamy generally limits the pool of eligibles in terms of social class and regardless of race (see Chapter 8). Some of my black, "thirty-something," female students have stated emphatically, "I'm making a lot of sacrifices to be in college while working full time. I don't think a man will appreciate what I've accomplished unless he's gone through the same [expletive deleted]!"

Because of their advantage in numbers, some middle-class black men may simply screen out assertive, independent, or physically unappealing women because they enjoy a large pool of eligible romantic partners (Davis et al., 2000). And like many whites, blacks from divorced families tend to shun marriage (Bulcroft and Bulcroft, 1993).

Attitudes about social mobility also affect singlehood. Many middle-class black parents emphasize educational attainment over early marriage. As a result, black women who pursue higher education may place a higher priority on academic achievement than on developing personal relationships (Perry et al., 2003). Others have tight social schedules because they devote most of their time to successful businesses they own and to community activities (Jones, 1994).

Asian Americans

Asian Americans and Pacific Islanders have some of the lowest never-married rates. At ages 35–39, for example, only 11 percent of the men have never married, compared with 17 percent of white men, 20 percent of Latino men, and 37 percent of black men (see *Figure 9.5*).

As I've noted in previous chapters, it's important not to lump all Asian Americans into one group because doing so obscures important differences across subgroups (see, especially, Chapter 4). Although there is very little information about these singles, the available research suggests that there are some common characteristics across Asian American groups that explain the low number of singles.

Emphasis on Family　You might recall that many Asian American households see the family as the core of society. Among Chinese Americans, for example, divorce rates are much lower than in the general population. Divorced women find it difficult to survive economically and are not readily accepted in the community (Glenn and Yap, 2002). As a result, many women avoid divorce and becoming single again at almost all costs.

Acculturation　Despite the emphasis on family and marriage, many Asian Americans are experiencing higher divorce rates. Korean Americans born in the United States, for example, have a higher divorce rate than their immigrant counterparts. American-born Korean women, in particular, are more ready to accept divorce as an alternative to an unhappy marriage (Min, 2002). One of the results of acculturation, then, is a larger number of women and men who are single.

Intermarriage　Acculturation often results in marrying outside one's own group. Because Japanese Americans

have been in the United States for many generations and the pool of eligible partners is small, their intermarriage rates are high (Takaki, 2002). The high intermarriage rates suggest that Japanese Americans are less likely to be single because they decrease the marriage squeeze by choosing partners from a large pool.

Latinos

Singlehood is also increasing among Latinos (see *Figure 9.5*). The Latino population is much younger than the non-Latino population. As a result, a higher percentage of Latinos have not yet reached a marriageable age. In addition, the emphasis on familism, as you saw in previous chapters, encourages marriage and having children. There are some variations across Latino groups, however.

Cuban Americans　The Cuban community has a high number of middle-aged and elderly people who are married. Because of the emphasis on the importance of marriage and children, divorce rates are low. These rates have been increasing, however, as second and third generations have assimilated Americanized values and behaviors. Many Cuban American women remain single after divorce because the remarriage market is more favorable for men than for women. Men have higher educational levels, more wealth, and other resources that attract prospective mates (Pérez, 2002).

Mexican Americans　Large numbers of Mexicans who are migrating to the United States for economic reasons are postponing marriage until they can support a family. If people are undocumented (illegal) or are migrant workers, it's difficult to marry. In addition, low-paying jobs and high unemployment rates can delay marriage or increase singlehood through high divorce rates (Baca Zinn and Pok, 2002).

Puerto Rican Americans　Many Puerto Rican women and men have moved away from wholly familistic values because the relationships between families in Puerto Rico and the United States have weakened (Carrasquillo, 2002). Even though some familistic values have changed, many Puerto Rican women still have extensive kinship networks both in the United States and in Puerto Rico. As a result, Puerto Rican women are less dependent on having a husband to help raise out-of-wedlock children (Toro-Morn, 1998).

Whether people are committed to marrying their partner also depends on family reactions. In a study of Latinos and Anglos, Umaña-Taylor and Fine (2003) found that, among women, familial support (encouragement and approval) was related to a lower commitment to marrying among Latinas but a higher commitment to marrying among Anglo women. The authors suggest that Latino family members who support a dating relationship are more likely than their Anglo counterparts to dampen a daughter's romance by getting too involved (butting in). In contrast, familial support increased Latino and Anglo men's commitment to marry their partners. It's not clear why this is the case, however.

Other Racial/Ethnic Groups

American Indian women are more likely than men to be single because they are separated, widowed, or divorced. In addition, widowhood is more common among American Indian than among black and white women because American Indian men are more likely than their counterparts to die earlier because of poor health and alcohol-related deaths, such as car accidents and homicides (Yellowbird and Snipp, 2002; see also Chapter 4).

Some of the available data suggest that there are more singles among Indian Asian Americans and Middle Eastern Americans because of rising divorce rates. Outside of acculturation, however, it's not clear why this is the case. It bears repeating that we need much more research on both of these groups to understand how many singles there are and why some marry whereas others postpone marriage (see Chapter 4).

Single women and men often work long hours at their jobs, sometimes because they want to advance their careers but sometimes because they're perceived as being less burdened with home and family responsibilities.

Myths and Realities about Being Single

Being single has many advantages, but some of its benefits have been exaggerated or romanticized. Here are some of the most popular myths about singlehood (Cargan and Melko, 1982):

1. *Singles are tied to their mother's apron strings.* In reality, there are few differences between singles and marrieds in their perceptions of and relationships with parents or other relatives.

2. *Singles are selfish and self-centered.* In reality, singles often make more time for friends than married people do, and they tend to be more active in community service.

3. *Singles are well-off financially.* A number of single professionals and young college graduates in high-tech jobs are affluent, but more singles than marrieds live at or below the poverty level. In general, married couples are better off financially because both partners work. In fact, some people contend that our taxes support singles rather than married couples (see the box "The Marriage Penalty or a Singles Penalty?").

4. *Singles are happier.* Although singles spend more time in leisure activities such as attending movies, eating in restaurants, and going to clubs, they are also more likely to be lonely, to be depressed when they are alone, and to feel anxious and stressed.

5. *There is something wrong with people who don't marry.* There is nothing wrong with being or staying single. Many singles simply feel that the disadvantages of marriage outweigh the benefits.

In terms of personal well-being, single men have the *most* problems, married men the *fewest.* Compared with married men, single men have higher mortality rates and a higher incidence of alcoholism, suicide, and mental health problems (Coombs, 1991; Rowe and Kahn, 1997). This may be because married men have less time and money to engage in high-risk behavior (such as using alcohol

CONSTRAINTS

The Marriage Penalty or a Singles Penalty?

Using the logic that two can live more cheaply than one, the federal government has historically taxed married couples at a higher rate than single people. This "marriage penalty" affects more than 40 percent of married couples.

The marriage penalty varies depending on whether both spouses are employed and how much each partner earns. Consider a man with a taxable income of $50,000. As a single, he'd pay $10,712 in federal taxes. If he married and his wife didn't work, he'd pay $8502, a tax cut of 21 percent.

The marriage penalty is greatest for two-earner couples whose incomes are similar. They pay more as a couple than they would as two singles. Take two

people with taxable incomes of $30,000 and $20,000. As singles, their tax would total $7508. As a $50,000 couple, they'd pay $8502.

Some argue that singles generally pay taxes at a higher rate and are penalized for not marrying. On a $50,000 taxable income, for example, their tax comes to $10,712, which is $2210 more than many married couples have to pay.

In addition, unmarried couples don't have access to a partner's Social Security checks or retirement benefits. They also can't pass on a large amount of money, property, and other assets free of estate taxes after one of them dies.

President Bush signed a law that gradually decreases and eventually eliminates

the federal marriage tax penalty by 2004. However, 35 states also have marriage penalties; some are larger than others (Weston, 2001; Gardiner et al., 2002; www.savewealth.com; smartmoney.com).

STOP AND THINK . . .

- *Should married couples pay higher taxes than singles? Do they use public services differently, for example?*
- *Some singles feel that their taxes are especially unfair because they support other people's children. Do you agree with this position?*

or other drugs) due to greater family responsibilities. In addition, they often have wives who urge them to have annual physical checkups, who prepare more nutritious meals, and who may generally be more concerned about preventing illness (see Chapter 10).

On a day-to-day basis, however, single women encounter more problems than do single men. Single women, who often live alone, are more likely than their married counterparts to be mugged, burglarized, or raped. Professional women who travel must often take extra safety precautions because they are more vulnerable than single men.

Unmarried people of both sexes face a number of prejudices. They are often accused of being "immature" or "flighty" ("When are you going to put down roots?" "Are you ever going to settle down?"). In addition, they may be given more responsibilities at work because they are viewed as having more free time. For example, some single professional women complain that they are often expected to do "little extras" at work: "To serve on more committees, volunteer for more overtime, or to give up more holidays and weekends—because they are perceived as having nothing better to do" (Cejka, 1993: 10).

MAKING CONNECTIONS

■ Why are your classmates and friends single rather than married? Or married rather than single? Are there any racial/ethnic variations?

■ If you are single, why? What would you add to the discussion about the advantages and disadvantages of being single?

Cohabitation

When they moved in together, Susannah, 24, and James, 29, had been dating for more than a year. Then their daughter, Elizabeth, was born. But the Albuquerque, New Mexico, couple is not quite ready to take the big step into matrimony. "We want to make sure we're doing the right thing," says Susannah, who also has a 4-year-old daughter from a previous marriage (Kantrowitz and Wingert, 2001: 46).

Susannah and James illustrate **cohabitation**, a living arrangement in which two unrelated people are not married but live together and usually have a sexual relationship. The U.S. Census Bureau sometimes calls cohabitants **POSSLQs** (pronounced "possel-kews"), "persons of the opposite sex sharing living quarters" ("shacking up," in plain English). Unmarried couples also include same-sex relationships, a topic we'll cover later in this chapter.

Cohabitation Trends and Characteristics

The number of unmarried-couple households in the United States has increased tremendously, from an estimated 50,000 households in 1950 to almost 6 million in 2000 (Saluter, 1994; Simmons and O'Connell, 2003). Keep in mind, however, that only 9 percent of the population is cohabiting at any time. In contrast, married couples maintain 52 percent of all households.

Regional and State Variations Cohabitation is more common in the Northeast and the West than the South or Midwest. The highest cohabitation rates are in the District of Columbia (21 percent), Alaska and Nevada (13 percent each), and Maine (12 percent). The lowest are in Utah (5 percent), Alabama (6 percent), and Arkansas and Kansas (about 7 percent each) (Simmons and O'Connell, 2003).

Sexual Orientation Of all unmarried couples, about 1 in 9 (11 percent of all unmarried-partner households) are gay men or lesbians (Simmons and O'Connell, 2003). The highest same-sex cohabitation rates are in the District of Columbia (5 percent) and California (1.5 percent). The lowest—0.5 percent each—are in Iowa, North Dakota, and South Dakota (Simmons and O'Connell, 2003).

Why do cohabitation rates vary by region and by state? It could be that some states (such as Utah) and

some regions (such as the South and Midwest) are more conservative, more religious, and less supportive of family structures outside marriage (Newport, 1996). It might also be that cohabitants, especially same-sex partners, are drawn to cities and states that are more accepting of cohabitation, both socially and legally.

Duration Most cohabiting relationships are short-lived, with a median duration of 15 to 18 months. When these relationships end, about 50 percent result in marriage (Smock and Gupta, 2002). Whether a cohabiting relationship ends in marriage or a breakup depends, among other things, on *why* people are living together. Those with the lowest levels of commitment are the most likely to split up (see *Table 9.2*).

Types of Cohabitation

Sociologists have identified several types of cohabitation. The most common types are coresidential dating cohabitation, premarital cohabitation, and cohabitation that is a trial marriage or a substitute for a legal marriage.

Coresidential Dating Cohabitation Some people drift gradually into **coresidential dating cohabitation** when a couple that spends a great deal of time together eventually decides to move in together. The decision may be based on a combination of reasons, such as convenience, finances, companionship, and sexual accessibility. The couples are unsure about the quality of their relationship, and there is no long-term commitment.

Premarital Cohabitation For many people, premarital cohabitation is a step between dating and marriage (Gwartney-Gibbs, 1986). In **premarital cohabitation,** the couple is testing the relationship before making a final commitment. They may or may not be engaged, but they have definite plans to marry their partners. Just 19 percent of Americans in 1988 said they lived with their spouse before marriage, compared with 37 percent in 2002 (Jones, 2002). Thus, increasing numbers of Americans are cohabiting before marriage.

Trial Marriage In a **trial marriage,** the partners want to see what marriage might be like—to one another or someone else. This type of living together is similar to premarital cohabitation, but the people are less certain about their relationship. Such "almost married" cohabitation may be especially attractive to partners who doubt that they can deal successfully with problems that arise from differences in personalities, interests, age, ethnicity, religion, or other issues.

Substitute Marriage A **substitute marriage** is a long-term commitment between two people without a legal marriage. Motives for substitute marriages vary widely. For example, one or both partners may be separated but still legally married to someone else or may be divorced and reluctant to remarry. In some cases, one partner may be highly dependent or insecure and thus prefer any kind of relationship to being alone. In other cases, partners may feel that a legal ceremony is irrelevant to their commitment to each other (see Chapter 1).

Cohabitation is more complex than these classifications suggest. Especially where children are involved, cohabitation can include two biological parents, one biological parent, or an adoptive parent. In addition, one or both partners may be never married, divorced, or remarried. These variations can create very different relationship dynamics, a topic that researchers are just beginning to explore.

Who Cohabits and Why?

To the delight of some people and the dismay of others, cohabitation isn't a passing fad. Whether it's an alternative to marriage, an alternative to living alone, or a prelude to marriage, high cohabitation rates indicate that it's widespread and meaningful for millions of people in the United States and elsewhere (Hoelter and Stauffer, 2002).

Cohabitants are a diverse group. Even though many cohabitant characteristics overlap, there are some patterns in terms of age, gender, race and ethnicity, social class, and other traits.

Age Many people think that college-age students are the largest group of cohabitors. In fact, most cohabitors are in their mid-30s to mid-40s (Simmons and O'Connell, 2003). In this group, one or more partners may be divorced and involved romantically but not interested in remarriage.

Florida has a high number of opposite-sex cohabitation (more than 10 percent). It's not clear how many of these couples are retired. In many cases, however, seniors choose to cohabit rather than to marry because they don't want to lose access to their pension and health insurance or to complicate their inheritance plans. A 72-year-old woman who lives with her 78-year-old partner, for example, has no intention of getting married because she'd forfeit her late husband's pension: "My income would be cut by $500 a month if I got married, and we can't afford that" (Silverman, 2003: D1).

Gender By age 30, half of all U.S. women have cohabited outside marriage (Bramlett and Mosher, 2002). Women who plan to complete a four-year college degree or more are likely to delay marriage and cohabit instead (Barber and Axinn, 1998a).

Low-income women, especially, often cohabit rather than marry because of a "culture of gender distrust" (Coley, 2002: 97). Because of the shortage of marriageable men, many low-income black women don't want to marry because they feel that their live-in partners will be unemployed, unfaithful, or not responsible in caring for children (Jayakody and Cabrera, 2002).

TABLE 9.2				
Does Cohabitation Lead to Marriage?				
			After 5 to 7 Years	
Type of Cohabitation	**Percentage of Couples**	**Split Up**	**Cohabiting**	**Married**
Coresidential dating	29%	46%	21%	33%
Premarital cohabitation	46	31	17	52
Trial marriage	15	51	21	28
Substitute marriage	10	35	40	25
SOURCE: Adapted from Bianchi and Casper, 2000.				

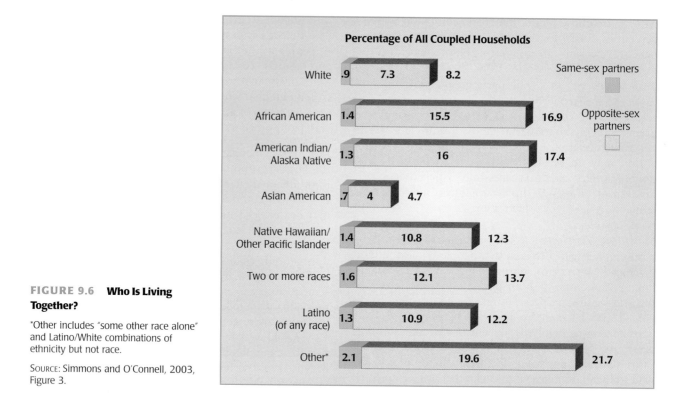

Percentage of All Coupled Households

FIGURE 9.6 **Who Is Living Together?**

*Other includes "some other race alone" and Latino/White combinations of ethnicity but not race.

Source: Simmons and O'Connell, 2003, Figure 3.

Race and Ethnicity The highest cohabitation rates are among American Indians and Native Alaskans and for African Americans (about 17 percent for each group), and the lowest rates are among Asian Americans (almost 5 percent) (see *Figure 9.6*). Latinos and blacks are more likely than whites to approve of cohabitation and to separate rather than marry their cohabiting partners (Brown, 2000).

Interracial cohabitation is fairly high—almost 14 percent of all unmarried couple households (see *Figure 9.6*). Interracial cohabitation is especially prevalent among Asian women aged 18 to 30 (Harris and Ono, 2000). Still, most people marry within their own ethnic group and social class (see Chapters 4 and 8).

Social Class Race, ethnicity, and gender intersect with social class in explaining cohabitation. Those who are less educated are more likely to cohabit. For example, 60 percent of women with no high school diploma or general equivalency diploma (GED) cohabit, compared with 38 percent of the women with a bachelor's degree or higher (Bumpass and Lu, 2000). Cohabitation may be more common at lower socioeconomic levels because partners can combine resources and avoid the legal costs of a possible future divorce.

Financial circumstances often weaken the odds of getting married. The probability of cohabitation breakups decreases when household earnings increase. Men who are employed full time, especially those in professional and semiprofessional occupations, are more likely to marry their live-in partners than are unemployed men (S. L. Brown, 2000; Gorman, 2000; Wu and Pollard, 2000).

Men—especially African American men—are more likely to cohabit than marry if their earnings and educational levels are low. They are also less likely to marry a cohabiting partner than men in other racial-ethnic groups (Smock and Gupta, 2002; Oppenheimer, 2003).

The men may want to marry but don't do so because they feel that they can't support a family. Many black women, as you saw earlier, are unwilling to marry men with erratic employment records and low earnings. Women in low-income groups yearn for "respectability and upward mobility" (including home ownership and financial stability). Many don't marry their current boyfriends, however, because they don't feel that the men will achieve economic stability (Ooms, 2002).

Religion Religious values also affect cohabitation rates. In the United States, the most religious Americans—those who attend church weekly—are more than twice as likely as those who seldom or never attend church to not cohabit because they believe that premarital cohabitation increases the odds of divorce (Jones, 2002).

Canadian women who reported not attending religious services in the past year were almost three times more likely than their counterparts to cohabit rather than to marry. In addition, women who attend church daily are much more likely to marry their cohabiting partner (Turcotte and Bélanger, 1997). Similarly, a study of 15 European countries found that women who attend church are more likely than those who don't to marry a partner rather than to cohabit (Kiernan, 2002).

Why Is Cohabitation So Common?   There are several reasons why cohabitation is widespread. First, as one social scientist notes, living together beats dating in terms of convenience and costs: "You can pay one rent rather than two, share all of your meals instead of just dinners together, get rid of unnecessary roommates, and have sex in your own bedroom instead of in a motel" (Wilson, 2002: 4).

Second, family experiences and values influence the decision to cohabit. Children whose parents divorced and whose mothers approve of cohabitation are more likely to cohabit as young adults than other children. In some cases, mothers who want their sons to have children encourage cohabitation indirectly because they don't care whether the offspring result from marriage or cohabitation (Barber and Axinn, 1998b).

Finally, as you've seen before, the stigma associated with cohabitation and out-of-wedlock births has declined. According to a recent Gallup poll, 62 percent of young people in their twenties thought that living together would avoid eventual divorce (Herrmann, 2003). More than a third of the Fortune 500 companies now offer benefits—from life insurance to rental cars—to the partners of unmarried couples (Belsie, 2003). In addition, as Bumpass and Lu (2000) observe, if children grow up in cohabiting households, parents are "unlikely to have much moral force" in arguing that their children should abstain from unmarried sex or cohabitation.

The Benefits and Costs of Cohabitation

As in any other relationship (including dating and marriage), cohabitation has advantages and disadvantages.

The Benefits of Cohabitation   Some of the benefits of cohabitation include the following:

- Couples have the emotional security of an intimate relationship but can also maintain their independence by having their own friends and by visiting family members alone (McRae, 1999).

- Couples can dissolve the relationship without legal problems, or they may marry with a feeling that they have laid a sound foundation.

- Couples who postpone a marriage have a lower likelihood of divorce because being older is one of the best predictors of a stable marriage (see Chapter 15).

- Cohabitation often encourages people to establish a meaningful relationship instead of playing superficial dating games.

- Intimate contact provides an opportunity for self-disclosure and may foster emotional growth and maturity. Living with someone can be annoying at

Many cohabitants, like this couple in Moscow, Russia, are 45-years-old or older and tend to live in large cities rather than rural areas.

times, but cohabitants may get a better understanding of their partners' needs, expectations, and weaknesses.

■ Cohabitation can help people find out how much they really care about each other when they have to cope with some unpleasant realities such as a partner who doesn't pay bills or has different hygiene standards.

■ A man or woman can freely exit an abusive relationship (DeMaris, 2001).

■ Among unmarried people age 65 and over, cohabitation may increase the chances of receiving caregiving that is usually provided by spouses (Chevan, 1996).

■ Cohabitants don't have to deal with in-laws (Silverman, 2003).

■ Children in cohabiting households—whether they are biological offspring or not—might enjoy some of the benefits associated with two-parent families. Even at lower socioeconomic levels, for example, children can reap some economic advantages by living with two adult earners instead of a single mother (Kalil, 2002).

The Costs of Cohabitation Cohabitation also has disadvantages. Some of the costs of cohabitation include the following:

■ Unlike married couples, cohabitants enjoy few legal rights. There's no automatic inheritance if a partners dies without a will, for example. In addition, a surviving partner receives no Social Security payments (Mahoney, 2002; Silverman, 2003).

■ Some partners experience a loss of identity or a feeling of being trapped. They may feel restricted from participating in activities with friends.

■ One or both partners may dislike being dependent on the other.

■ If cohabitants are sexually intimate (and most cohabiting couples are), they can experience the same kinds of difficulties married couples encounter, including a lack of sexual interest, failure to achieve orgasm, and a fear of pregnancy. Most important, if people are not honest about their sexual histories, partners can contract sexually transmitted diseases or HIV (see Chapter 7).

■ Women in cohabiting relationships do more of the cooking and other household tasks than in many married couples (Coley, 2002).

■ Cohabitants, compared with married couples, have a weaker level of commitment to their relationship, have lower levels of happiness and satisfaction,

report more alcohol problems, and are more likely to be unfaithful (Horwitz and White, 1998; Treas and Giesen, 2000; Waite, 2000).

■ Spouses who cohabit before marriage demonstrate more negative behaviors (such as trying to control a partner's thoughts or feelings, verbal aggression, and anger) than spouses who don't cohabit (Cohan and Kleinbaum, 2002).

■ Children who grow up in cohabiting households don't have role models for acquiring the skills necessary for marital success because cohabiting adults don't always respect each other or communicate effectively (Martin et al., 2001).

■ U.S. laws don't specify a cohabitant's responsibilities and rights. For example, it may be more difficult to collect child custody payments from a cohabiting than a married father (or mother) (see Chapter 11).

Even though cohabitation has both advantages and disadvantages, many cohabitors are convinced that cohabitation leads to better marriages. Is this true? Or wishful thinking?

Does Cohabitation Lead to Better Marriages?

No, it doesn't. The probability of a first marriage ending in separation or divorce within 5 years is 20 percent, but the probability of a premarital cohabitation breaking up within 5 years is 49 percent. After 10 years, the probability of a first marriage ending is 33 percent, compared with 62 percent for cohabitors (Bramlett and Mosher, 2002). Thus, divorce rates are higher for those who cohabit than people who don't live together before marriage.

Except for short-term premarital cohabitation, why is living together associated with a higher divorce risk? Sociologists feel that there may be either a *selection effect* or a *cohabitation experience effect*.

The Selection Effect Some cohabitors are poor marriage risks because of their higher incidence of drug problems, inability to handle money, trouble with the law, unemployment, sexual infidelity, and personality problems (Bumpass and Sweet, 1989; Teachman et al., 1991). These risk factors increase the likelihood of divorce after marriage. In addition, cohabitants are more likely than noncohabitants to have doubts about their partner or the institution of marriage as a sacred bond (Cunningham and Antill, 1995; McRae, 1999).

Cohabitants may make less effort to communicate with one another and to work out problems. There is also a difference between cohabitants who intend to marry their partners and those who do not. The latter put less effort into the relationship, are less likely to compromise, and tend to have poorer communication skills for solving interpersonal problems. Thus, "those who cohabit with no intention of marrying are ill equipped for a lasting relationship" (Stets, 1993b: 256; Cohan and Kleinbaum, 2002).

The Cohabitation Experience Effect The experience of cohabitation itself may lead to marital instability. Through cohabitation, people may come to accept the temporary nature of relationships and to view cohabitation as an alternative to marriage. Cohabitants who are independent and used to having their own way, for example, may be quick to leave a marriage (DeMaris and MacDonald, 1993).

Experiencing *serial cohabitation* (moving from one cohabiting relationship to another) may be especially harmful to marital stability. People who exit cohabiting relationships may also be more willing to dissolve other relationships, including marriage: "People's tolerance for unhappiness is diminished, and they will scrap a marriage that might otherwise be salvaged" (Popenoe and Whitehead, 2002: 5).

Cohabitation and troubled marriages often reflect both selection and cohabitation experience effects. In terms of selection, people choose "risky" partners (those who use drugs or are hard to live with, for example) because they think cohabitation will be easy to break up. Once a couple has lived together and shared possessions, pets, children, and have invested time in the relationship, they marry. Sharing time and possessions doesn't make a risky partner easier to live with, however. In terms of a cohabitation experience effect, the couples may also have poor communication and problem-solving skills that carry over into marriage (Dush et al., 2003).

How Does Cohabitation Affect Children?

Nearly half of all children today will spend some time in a cohabiting family before age 16 (Bumpass and Lu, 2000). What is the impact of cohabitation on children's well-being? There is no simple answer. Children of cohabitors often experience more violence than their counterparts in married households. Cohabiting women report two times more abuse than married women. Some of the reasons include many of the cohabiting men's lower investment in the relationship and many of the cohabiting women's willingness to tolerate the assaults (Cunningham and Antill, 1995).

Some researchers point out that how children are affected depends on the type of cohabiting union that partners form. In general, children living with two biological cohabiting parents fare better than those with "social fathers" (mothers' boyfriends). Social fathers are less involved in the children's emotional and physical well-being (Kalil, 2002).

Children living with cohabiting *partner families* (in which one partner is not a biological parent), not cohabiting *parent families* (in which both partners are biological partners), might be better off living with a single mother. Children in cohabiting partner families are more likely to be poor and food insecure (there is not enough to eat or children must skip meals) and to show more behavior problems such as depression, lying, and immaturity (Acs and Nelson, 2002). As in married families, cohabitation has a negative effect on children if the parents are poor, psychologically distressed, or unhappy (Brown, 2002; Manning, 2002).

Cohabiting couples (both partner and parent) spend a far greater share of their income on alcohol and tobacco—73 to 90 percent more—than married parents. The couples pay for the alcohol and tobacco by spending very little on the children's health care and education. The men are more interested in themselves than their children. Thus, it isn't cohabitation itself but "something about the men who are cohabitors" that leads to poor developmental outcomes for children. The parent's or partner's substance abuse decreases the quality of child-parent relationships, increases the likelihood of domestic violence, and increases children's behavior problems (DeLeire and Kalil, 2002).

Three-quarters of children born to cohabiting parents see their parents split up before they reach age 16, compared with 33 percent of children born to married parents (Bumpass and Lu, 2000). The breakups in cohabiting families "come on top of a plethora of already existing problems" (such as poverty) that "almost always entail a myriad of personal and social difficulties for children" that include more behavior problems and lower academic performance than children in intact families (Popenoe and Whitehead, 2002: 8).

Often, after my students read this section, they raise an important question: Should my girlfriend or boyfriend and I live together? Speaking sociologically, there's no simple "yes" or "no." Some of the research, however, suggests issues you should think about before or during cohabitation (see the box "Should We Live Together?" on page 252).

Cohabitation and the Law

Unmarried couples (and their children) have very little legal protection. Two of every five out-of-wedlock births are to parents who are cohabiting. A full 70 percent of the children living with a cohabiting couple are the offspring of only one partner (Scommegna, 2002). Unlike their counterparts with married parents, children in cohabiting homes and stepfamilies have few automatic rights and privileges (see Chapter 16).

Although the laws are not enforced, some states still forbid cohabitation. Recently, for example, North Dakota's Senate voted to keep a 113-year-old law that makes

CHOICES

Should We Live Together?

Most people live together because they're unwilling to make a long-term commitment or uncertain about wanting to marry. Such doubts are normal and should probably arise more often than they do (see Chapter 8, especially, on breaking up).

A few social scientists are adamantly opposed to living together. According to Popenoe and Whitehead (2002), for example,

- *You should not live together at all before marriage* because there is no evidence that cohabitation produces better or stronger marriages. People should not live together unless they've already set a wedding date, and the cohabitation should be as brief as possible.
- *Don't make a habit of cohabiting* because multiple experiences of living together decrease the chance of marriage and people's establishing a lifelong partnership.
- *Limit cohabitation to the shortest possible period of time.* The longer

you live together with a partner, the more likely it is that you, your partner, or both of you will break up and never marry.

- *Don't consider cohabitation if children are involved.* Children need parents over the long term. In addition, children are more likely to be abused by cohabitors than by biological parents.

On the other hand, people who live together give rational reasons for doing so:

- *Economic advantages:* "We can save money by sharing living expenses."
- *Time together:* "We are able to spend more time together."
- *Increased intimacy:* "We can share sexual and emotional intimacy without getting married."
- *Easy breakups:* "If the relationship doesn't work out, there's no messy divorce."
- *Compatibility:* "Living together is a good way to find out about each other's habits and character."

- *Trial marriage:* "We're living together because we'll be getting married soon" (Olson and Olson-Sigg, 2002; Solot and Miller, 2002).

So where does this leave you? You might use exchange theory (see Chapters 2 and 6) in making a decision. List the costs and benefits on a piece of paper and then decide what you want you do.

STOP AND THINK . . .

- *If you live with someone (or have done so in the past), why? What would you advise other people to do?*
- *Look at* Appendix F *("Premarital and Nonmarital Agreements"). Have you discussed any of these topics with someone you've lived with in the past or now?*

---

it a crime for unmarried couples to live together. Violations carry a maximum of 30 days in jail and a $1000 fine. One of the senators noted that, although not enforced, the law "stands as a reminder that there is right, and there is wrong" (Boldt, 2003: A3).

Many cohabitors are excellent parents. They have few legal rights, however. The probability of a first premarital cohabitation becoming a marriage is 58 percent after 3 years of cohabitation and 70 percent after 5 years of cohabitation (Bramlett and Mosher, 2002). Thus, the shorter the cohabitation duration, the lower the likelihood of marriage and the legal protections that marriage brings.

Because 20 percent of court cases that deal with family dissolution now involve cohabiting couples, a state must often intervene in deciding who has what rights and responsibilities (Hymowitz, 2003). Breakups are higher among black women than among white women and Latinas and in communities with high male unemployment, low median family income, and high

rates of poverty and welfare (Bramlett and Mosher, 2002). The women who are the most vulnerable, then, may not have the resources to go to court for child custody payments or other expenses.

According to many legal experts, cohabitants' best protection in financial matters is to maintain separate ownership of possessions. Partners should not have joint bank accounts or credit cards. They should prepare a written agreement about debts and how bills are to be paid. Shared leases should also be negotiated before moving in together. If partners buy real estate together they should spell out carefully, in writing, each person's share of any profit. Homeowners' and renters' insurance policies should carry both partners' names so that the possessions of both are clearly covered. Cars should not be registered in a woman's name just to escape the high insurance premiums commonly charged men under 25. If there is an accident, the woman will be liable even if the man was driving.

Health insurance plans that cover a spouse almost never extend to an unmarried partner. And if a partner dies and leaves no will, relatives—no matter how distant—can claim all of his or her possessions. The cohabiting partner has no claim at all. Cohabiting couples' best course is to put everything possible in writing. If a couple has children, both unmarried parents must acknowledge biological parenthood in writing to protect the children's future claims to financial support and inheritance (Mahoney, 2002).

Discussing legal matters may not seem very romantic when people love each other. But when a cohabiting relationship ends, the legal problems can be overwhelming. Many attorneys recommend that cohabitants draw up a contract similar to a premarital document. *Appendix F* describes some of the complex issues that cohabitants are likely to encounter.

A Global View: Cohabitation

Cohabitation has been around for a long time, but its prevalence and government benefits vary widely across countries.

Prevalence   Cohabitation is common in Latin America and the Caribbean—especially in Cuba, the Dominican Republic, Ecuador, Panama, and Venezuela—and less common in Africa and Asia. In China, an estimated one-third of all couples cohabit. About two-thirds of these unions occur in the countryside and constitute "early marriages" between adolescents who are below the legal minimum age for marriage—20 for women, 22 for men (Neft and Levine, 1997).

Although living together is still frowned upon in southern European countries such as Greece and Portugal, it has lost its social stigma elsewhere. In Britain, for example, 70 percent of first partnerships are cohabiting. Of all out-of-wedlock births, one-third are in cohabiting households (Berrington, 2001; Ford, 2002). In Australia, 71 percent of couples live together before marriage (Qu and Weston, 2001).

Cohabitation rates have risen dramatically in the last decade and are highest in industrialized countries. There is a great deal of variation across nations, however. Cohabitation is most common in the Nordic countries of Denmark, Sweden, and Finland, where up to one-third of the population has cohabited. Sweden is the only country with more first births born within cohabiting unions than marriages. The lowest cohabitation rates are in Northern Ireland (7 percent), Ireland and Italy (5 percent each) and Japan (3 percent) (Batalova and Cohen, 2002; Kiernan, 2002).

Government Benefits   As more and more couples live together before or instead of marrying, some countries have extended cohabitants many of the same rights as married couples. Argentina, for example, grants pension rights to spouses in common-law marriages. Canada provides insurance benefits to cohabiting partners. Other countries, including Australia, require a distribution of property when cohabiting relationships break up (Neft and Levine, 1997).

Many nations offer single women economic security regardless of marital status. In Sweden, for example, all parents, married or unmarried, receive a children's allowance from the state, and divorced and single mothers are entitled to cash advances on child-support payments if a child's father fails to pay. Norway's social policies are similar.

Many European countries give children born within and outside marriage the same inheritance and other rights. There is more ambivalence about the rights and responsibilities of cohabiting adults. After biological relationships have been established, Sweden, France, Norway, and Great Britain grant cohabiting parents the same obligations and rights as married couples. In Germany and Italy, in contrast, the father can gain some rights to guardianship but not necessarily to custody (Kiernan, 2002).

MAKING CONNECTIONS

■ Look back at *Table 9.2* on page 247. Are there other types of cohabiting couples that you can think of?

■ A few years ago, the prestigious American Law Institute (2002) created a stir when it proposed that cohabitation be legalized. Unmarried couples would have the same rights and responsibilities as married couples in terms of inheritance, child custody, paying debts, alimony, and health insurance, for example. Do you agree with this proposal?

Gay and Lesbian Couples

Regardless of sexual orientation, most of us seek an intimate relationship with one special person. Because homosexuals are denied marriage by law, they must turn to cohabitation.

Gay and Lesbian Relationships

Gay and lesbian couples come in "different sizes, shapes, ethnicities, races, religions, resources, creeds, and quirks, and even engage in diverse sexual practices" (Stacey, 2003: 145). An estimated 29 percent of gay men and

44 percent of lesbians currently have steady romantic partners (Black et al., 2000). In addition, many households are headed by same-sex partners (see "Data Digest").

Like heterosexuals, homosexual cohabitants must work out issues regarding communication, power, and household responsibilities. If there are children from previous marriages, gay and lesbian partners, like heterosexual parents, must deal with custody and child-rearing issues (see Chapter 12).

Love and Commitment Most lesbians and gay men want an enduring love relationship. Gender, however, seems to shape a couple's values and practices more powerfully than sexual identity. Lesbian and heterosexual women, for example, are less competitive and more relationship-oriented than gay or heterosexual men (Huston and Schwartz, 1995). In addition, both lesbian and straight women are more likely than either gay or straight men to value their relationships more than their jobs (Stacey, 2003).

Lesbian and gay couples are shattering some taboos by publishing their engagements and weddings in newspapers. In 2003, the *New York Times* announced that it would begin running same-sex commitment notices. It joined 70 other newspapers in the country that had already adopted the policy. The papers range from the one-million-circulation *New York Times* to the *Southern Utah News* of Kanab, Utah, with a circulation of about 4000. Having an engagement notice in a newspaper is a simple rite of passage that most heterosexuals don't think about twice. For lesbian and gay couples, it's a significant step in proclaiming their love and commitment publicly (Venema, 2003).

Power and Division of Labor A majority of gay and lesbian couples report having equal power in a relationship. When power is unequal, however, and as social exchange theory predicts, the older, wealthier, and better-educated partner usually has greater power. The "principle of least power" is also pertinent (see Chapter 8). As in heterosexual couples, the person in the gay couple who is less involved in the relationship and who is less dependent has more power (Patterson, 2001).

Gay life is not divided into "butch" and "femme" roles. One partner may usually perform most of the "feminine" activities such as cooking whereas the other performs most of the "masculine" tasks such as car repair. The specialization typically is based on individualistic factors, such as skills or interests, rather than traditional husband-wife or masculine-feminine roles (Peplau et al., 1996).

Problems and Conflict Like heterosexual cohabitants, gay and lesbian couples experience similar conflict in four areas. In terms of *power*, all couples are equally likely to argue about finances, lack of equality in the relationship, and possessiveness. They are also equally likely to complain about such *personal flaws* as smoking or drinking, driving style, and personal grooming. Couples are similar in being unhappy with some aspects of *intimacy*, especially sex and demonstrating affection. Both groups are also equally likely to criticize partners who are *physically absent*, usually because of job or education commitments. Suspicion may be more common among gay and lesbian cohabitants, however, because their previous lovers are likely to remain in their social support networks, increasing the possibility of jealousy and resentment (Kurdek, 1994, 1998).

According to a national survey, violence is more prevalent among gay male couples than either lesbian or heterosexual cohabitants. Compared with 8 percent of heterosexual couples, for example, almost 16 percent of gay cohabiting men reported being raped or physically assaulted by a male partner, and 11 percent reported such violence by a lesbian partner (Tjaden et al., 1999).

It's not clear why the violence rates among gay male cohabitants are so high. One explanation may be that gay men have internalized the notion that aggression is an acceptable "male" way of solving conflict in intimate relationships. Another reason may be that gay men are more likely than lesbians to be rejected by their family and friends and to strike out against intimate partners.

Racial-Ethnic Variations Gay and lesbian couples often get less social support from family members than do heterosexual couples. The greatest rejection may come from racial-ethnic families, whose traditional values about marriage and the family are often reinforced by religious beliefs. In some faiths, homosexual behavior is considered aberrant or a sin.

In African American, Asian American, Latino, and Middle Eastern groups, family members are expected to marry and to continue the traditional family structure (see Chapter 4). Many racial-ethnic groups also have strong extended family systems. A gay family member may be seen as jeopardizing not only the intrafamily relationships but also the extended family's continued strong association with the ethnic community (Morales, 1996; Liu and Chan, 1996; Mays et al., 1998).

Lesbian and gay couples might encounter additional problems because the partner is the "wrong" religion, racial-ethnic group, or social class. Even if both partners are out to their family and relatives, the family might exclude a partner in subtle ways such as inviting the heterosexual son-in-law of two years to be in the family picture but not the lesbian partner of fifteen years (Clunis and Green, 2000).

The War over Gay Marriage

In 1998, the Houston, Texas, police found two men in bed together and arrested them for sodomy because it was a crime for two people of the same sex to engage in sexual behaviors that were legal for heterosexual couples. The men were each fined $200 and spent the night in jail. They later went to court and appealed the ruling of a lower court.

In a landmark decision, *Lawrence v. Texas*, in June 2003, the Supreme Court struck down state laws against sodomy and stated that gays "are entitled to respect for their private lives." Some legal scholars feel that the *Lawrence* ruling "may be one of the two most important opinions of the last 100 years" (Thomas, 2003: 40). Although the decision did not address gay marriage, it called into question a host of other laws that gay rights advocates call discriminatory, including prohibitions against same-sex marriages.

Same-Sex Marriage One of the problems that gay and lesbian couples face is the lack of institutional recognition that heterosexuals enjoy through marriage. In 1996, President Bill Clinton signed the Defense of Marriage Act, which states that no U.S. state or territory has any legal duty to respect a marriage between homosexuals, even if such a marriage is valid in any other state. The act also bans any form of federal aid (such as Medicare) unless the couple is in "a legal union between one man and one woman as husband and wife."

Some 37 states have passed similar laws that prohibit same-sex marriages. This means that gays, unlike heterosexuals, don't have rights that include inheritance, child custody and visitation rights, adoption, and even the right to make funeral arrangements for a partner who has died.

In the United States, only Vermont recognizes civil unions between same-sex couples. (California and New Jersey are going in the same direction as this book goes to press.) According to Vermont's 1999 legislation, gay and lesbian couples can take advantage of more than 300 benefits previously available only to married couples, such as the ability to make medical decisions for their partners.

A Massachusetts court, you recall, has recently allowed gay marriage. It's still unclear, however, whether the legislators will pass an amendment to the state constitution to prohibit same-sex marriage (see Chapters 7 and 8).

In several countries, same-sex marriages are registered partnerships rather than official marriages. They were first legalized in Denmark in 1989, then in Norway in 1993, Sweden in 1994, France in 1998 as "civil solidarity pacts," and in the Canadian province of Ontario in 2003. Although the partners can't marry in

John Lawrence, left, and Tryon Garner were arrested for sodomy in Texas in 1998 and appealed the arrest. In 2003, the U.S. Supreme Court ruled that sodomy laws were unconstitutional. The decision might pave the way for legalizing same-sex marriages in the future (see text).

church, they have most of the same rights as heterosexual couples.

In mid-2003, Buenos Aires became the first city in Latin America to grant civil unions, even though 44 percent of the people opposed the legislation and the Catholic Church denounced it. The law extends health and insurance benefits as well as hospital visitation rights to the couples but does not allow them to adopt children or have inheritance rights (Byrnes, 2003).

The Pros and Cons of Same-Sex Marriage Many people, including gay men and lesbians, have mixed feelings about same-sex marriages. On the "against" side—and even though ministers, rabbis, and even priests have performed marriage ceremonies—many religious groups and individuals feel that same-sex marriage would legitimize "sinful" relationships that reflect a decline in family values (Calvert, 2003). As Justice Antonin Scalia warned in his dissent on the *Lawrence* ruling, most Americans "do not want persons who openly engage in homosexual conduct as partners in their business, as scoutmasters for their children, as teachers in their children's schools, or as boarders in their homes" (Thomas, 2003: 42).

Some gays also oppose same-sex marriages. If same-sex marriage were legalized, tax withholding forms might reveal information that could result in even greater discrimination for a gay or lesbian in the workplace, for example (Brownsworth, 1996). Others fear that defending same-sex marriages (both socially and legally) would sap the gay rights groups' limited resources in fighting persistent discrimination in employment and other sectors (Stacey, 2003).

For the most part, however, gay activists support marriage campaigns. If gay marriages were legal, for example, family members and relatives could not contest inheritance. Gay couples would be entitled to the hospitalization or bereavement leaves that married couples enjoy. Being able to marry would allow same-sex couples the same federal benefits and protections, such as Medicare, immigration laws, and joint filing of tax returns. Most important, legalizing same-sex marriages would provide the fundamental freedom of having "the equal right to choose whether and whom to marry" (Wolfson, 1996:89).

Currently, the biggest divide on the same-sex marriage issue is across generations. In a recent Gallup poll, for example, 72 percent of those aged 18 to 29 agreed that homosexual relations should be legal (up from a low of 32 percent in 1986), compared with 39 percent of those aged 65 and older (Paulson, 2003). Because younger generations are more accepting of same-sex marriage than their older counterparts, legislation might change in the future.

MAKING CONNECTIONS

■ Should your state (unless it's done so already) pass legislation to legitimate same-sex marriage?

■ What do you think are some of the advantages and disadvantages of same-sex marriages? Are the costs and benefits different for gays and straights?

Communal Living Arrangements

Communes are collective households where children and adults live together. The adults may be married or unmarried. Some communes permit individual ownership of private property; others do not. There is a great deal of historical variation in the amount of sharing of economic, sexual, and decision-making rights.

Communes in the Past

Communes are not a modern invention. They have existed since 100 B.C. The popularity of communal living has fluctuated in the United States, but its membership has never exceeded more than a tenth of 1 percent of the entire population (Kantor, 1970).

Both nineteenth-century and contemporary communes have differed widely in terms of structure, values, and ideology. In the nineteenth century, many such communities wrestled with the issue of monogamy and had very different solutions. One group, the Icarians, made marriage mandatory for all adult members. Others, such as the Shakers and Rappites, required everyone, including married couples, to live celibate lives. The Mormons, in emphasizing group rather than individual well-being, adopted polygyny. Others practiced free love, where sexual intercourse was permissible with all members, married or not (Muncy, 1988).

The Oneida Community, founded in New York State in the 1840s practiced "complex marriage," in which every adult was theoretically married to every other member. Much older men initiated girls into sexual intercourse shortly after their first menstruation. Mothers had the greatest difficulty with the idea that community adults, not biological parents, were responsible for raising children. In addition, women had to work on communal farms and do all the housework and communal child-rearing (Dalsimer, 1981).

Most communes have been short-lived (W. L. Smith, 1999). Often, the members are unwilling to give up their autonomy or private property. There may also be conflict and jealousy regarding sexual relationships. Furthermore, communes that practiced polygamy or free love "drew the wrath" of a culture that believed that sexual relations outside marriage and monogamy are evil (Muncy, 1988).

Other groups are dwindling because of a lack of new membership. For example, the Shakers have only a handful of elderly members left in one "family" in Maine. Most of the buildings and grounds in Maine and other states have been turned into tourist attractions (Kephart and Zellner, 1991).

Contemporary Communal Living

Communal living is common on many college campuses. For example, fraternities, sororities, and houses that are rented and shared by five or six students fulfill many of the social and economic functions that characterize all communes.

A new program, Co-Abode, matches low-income single mothers in subsidized housing. The mothers live together and split household bills, divvy up chores, cover for each other when they want to shop, and chat daily. Children often share a room. The housing is usually in safe neighborhoods with good school districts, and an "outreach program" provides the mothers with referrals "for everything from dentists to lawyers and credit counselors" (Wolcott, 2003: 14).

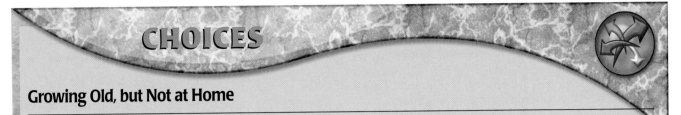

CHOICES

Growing Old, but Not at Home

Housing options have changed greatly in the last few years. Here are some of the most common alternatives for older people who can't or don't want to "age in place":

- *Retirement communities* offer apartments for residents who are mobile and can take care of themselves. These communities offer a variety of social and recreational activities, meals in a central dining room, and housekeeping service. There may be entrance fees (up to $40,000), and rents can vary widely (up to $4000 a month).

- *Homesharing* involves two or more people sharing a home or apartment. Each person has a private bedroom but shares the kitchen and other living spaces. Some homeowners seek this arrangement to avoid living alone or to supplement their income.

- *Elderly cottage housing opportunities (ECHOs)* are small, portable "cottages" that can be placed in the back or side yard of a single family home, usually

the home of an adult child. These units typically cost $25,000 and up.

- *Continuing care retirement communities (CCRCs)* offer several housing options and services depending on the resident's needs. Typically, people begin by living independently in their own apartment. Later they may move to an assisted living facility or nursing home on the same grounds. CCRCs are usually out of the financial range of many older people because they have large entrance fees and expensive monthly charges. The fees and rents can be as high as $400,000 a year.

- *Assisted living facilities* provide housing, group meals, personal care, recreation, social activities, and minimal nursing care (such as administering medications) in a residential setting. Residents often pay at least $3000 a month.

- *Board and care homes* are smaller in scale than assisted living facilities. They provide a room, meals, and help with daily activities. These homes

often are unlicensed, cost $350–$3000 a month, and might be supported by Supplemental Security Income (SSI), which helps people with low incomes.

STOP AND THINK . . .

- *Where do your elderly parents, grandparents, or other relatives live? What kinds of choices and constraints have they experienced in their living arrangements?*

- *When you look at some of these housing options, what do they tell you about social class and "aging comfortably"?*

At the other end of the age continuum, a growing proportion of older people is experimenting with communal living as an alternative to moving in with children or living in a nursing home. As you saw at the beginning of this chapter, about 10 percent of those living alone are people age 65 and over (see *Figure 9.2*). About 84 percent own their homes and "age in place" until they die (Lawler, 2001).

When older people can't live alone because of physical problems or dementia (see Chapter 17), there are increasing housing options. As the box "Growing Old, but Not at Home" illustrates, many elderly live in "communities" that provide medical, emotional, and physical care that have replaced many traditional family functions. The elderly have more options than before, but *only* if they have high incomes.

Conclusion

There have been a number of *changes* in relationships outside, before, and after marriage. Some of our *choices* include staying single longer, cohabiting, forming same-sex households, participating in communal living arrangements, or not marrying at all. Thus, larger numbers of people are single for a greater portion of their lives.

Our choices are not without *constraints*, however. For example, many U.S. laws do not encourage or protect most of these relationships. Despite the growing numbers of unmarried people, marriage is not going out of style; it is merely occupying less of the average adult's lifetime.

Although there is less pressure to marry, most of us will do so at least once in our lifetime. In the next chapter we examine the institution of marriage.

SUMMARY

1. Diverse lifestyles have always existed, but in the past 20 years, the numbers of alternative family forms have increased, including singlehood, cohabitation, gay households, and communal living arrangements.

2. Household size has been shrinking since the 1940s. A major reason for the decrease is the growing number of people who are postponing marriage and living alone.

3. People are postponing marriage more often because there is a greater acceptance of cohabitation and of children born out of wedlock.

4. Singles constitute an extremely diverse group. Some have been widowed, divorced, or separated; others have never been married. Some singles choose their status, whereas others are single involuntarily.

5. There are many reasons why the numbers of singles have increased since the 1970s. Some of the reasons are macro, some are demographic, and others reflect personal choices. African Americans, especially educated black women, are the most likely to postpone marriage or never marry.

6. Cohabitation has boomed since the 1970s. Although most cohabitation is short-lived, in some cases it is a long-term substitute for legal marriage. Like other living arrangements, cohabitation has both advantages and disadvantages.

7. There is no evidence that cohabitation leads to more stable or happier marriages. Cohabitants have higher divorce rates than noncohabitants, and men typically benefit more than women do from cohabitation.

8. Legal factors sometimes dictate living arrangements. Same-sex marriage is prohibited in all states although Vermont allows same-sex civil unions, and Massachusetts may be the first state to allow legal gay marriage in the future. Despite these recent changes, gay and lesbian partners still have fewer options than do heterosexuals.

9. Communal living arrangements have changed since the turn of the twentieth century and even since the 1970s. They are less numerous and less popular today, but they still fulfill the economic and social needs of many adults.

10. A growing number of elderly people are choosing to live in communal residences rather than move in with their children or live in nursing homes.

KEY TERMS

sex ratio 240
marriage squeeze 241
cohabitation 246

POSSLQ 246
coresidential dating cohabitation 246
premarital cohabitation 246

trial marriage 247
substitute marriage 247

TAKING IT FURTHER

Learn More about Nonmarried Living Arrangements

There are a number of informative Internet sites on heterosexual cohabitation, same-sex households, and communal living arrangements. Here are a few:

The Alternatives to Marriage Project has a wide variety of information, statistics, and legal guides about and for unmarried people.

www.unmarried.org

Cohabitation: Living Together offers numerous sites that include financial advice, national polls, and the pros and cons of living together before or instead of marriage.

http://dating.about.com/people/dating/msubcohab.htm

Queer Resources Directory contains almost 26,000 files that include links to "Queers and Their Families."

www.qrd.org

The Cohousing Network provides information on "collaborative housing that attempts to overcome the alienation of modern subdivisions."

www.cohousing.org

Law.com is a valuable source of information about cohabitation rights, prenuptial agreements, and many other nonmarital issues.

www.law.com/index.html

And more: www.prenhall.com/benokraitis includes links to sites of national organizations that lobby for singles' rights, information about the status of same-sex marriage legislation, collaborative housing options, and lists of government agencies, higher education institutions, and private sector employers that offer domestic partnership benefits.

INVESTIGATE WITH RESEARCH NAVIGATOR

Please go to www.researchnavigator.com and enter your LOGIN NAME and PASSWORD. For instructions on registering for the first time, please view the detailed instructions at the end of the Chapter 1. Please search the Research Navigator™ site using the following key search terms:

cohabitation
same-sex marriages
counseling

Marriage and Communication in Committed Relationships

DATADIGEST

- In a national study of first-year college students, 73 percent said that **raising a family was an "essential" or "very important"** objective.

- In 1984, **a typical American wedding cost $4000.** Today, it costs $22,000. The annual business of the bridal industry is about $70 billion.

- Nearly 2.4 million marriages are performed annually. By age 30, **three-quarters of U.S. adults have been married.**

- Almost 5 percent of **teens ages 15 to 19 married in 2000,** compared with 3 percent in 1990.

- On average, wives who work outside the home still do **more than 80 percent of the household work.**

SOURCES: "Mothers work," 2000; "Attitudes and characteristics . . .," 2002; U.S. Census Bureau, 2002; Gibbons, 2003.

On April 12, 1919, a young couple drove off (in a Model T Ford) to Jeffersonville, Indiana, because the bride-to-be, 14, was under the legal age to get married in Kentucky, their home state. In 2002, the same couple—William, 104, and Claudia Lillian Ritchie, 98—celebrated their 83rd wedding anniversary. Guinness World Records recognized the Ritchies as the world's oldest living married couple. When reporters asked about the secret to their long marriage, Mr. Ritchie said that they loved each other, there was a lot of give and take, and "We didn't have very many arguments" (Davis, 2002).

Enduring marriages are not born during the wedding ceremony. Instead, they are the fruits of years of mutual effort and cooperation, involving both enjoyment and sacrifice. Some people become disillusioned with matrimony because they have misconceptions about married life that are deeply ingrained in our culture. Before reading the rest of this chapter, take "A Marriage Quiz" in the box on page 262. It should encourage you to think more critically about some of our assumptions about wedded life.

In this chapter we discuss marital expectations and rituals, consider various types of marriages and how they change over the years, and examine communication processes that can strengthen or undermine intimate relationships within and outside of marriage. Let's begin by looking at why people tie the knot.

Why Do People Marry?

When someone announces, "I'm going to get married," we respond with "Congratulations" rather than "How come?" In Western societies, we assume that people marry because they love each other. We marry for a variety of reasons, however. Some are more conscious than others. In addition, some of our reasons are positive while others can be negative.

261

ASKYOURSELF

A Marriage Quiz

To respond to each statement, circle either True or False.

	Fact	Fiction
1. A husband's marital satisfaction is usually lower if his wife is employed outside the home full time than if she is a full-time homemaker.	True	False
2. In most marriages, having a child improves marital satisfaction for both spouses.	True	False
3. The best single predictor of overall marital satisfaction is the quality of the couple's sex life.	True	False
4. Overall, married women are physically healthier than married men.	True	False
5. African American women are happier in marriage than are African American men.	True	False
6. "If my spouse loves me, he/she should know what I want and need to make me happy."	True	False
7. In a marriage in which the wife is employed full time outside the home, the husband usually shares equally in housekeeping tasks.	True	False
8. "No matter how I behave, my partner should love me because he/she is my spouse."	True	False
9. Husbands usually make more lifestyle adjustments in marriage than do wives.	True	False
10. "I can change my spouse by pointing out his/her inadequacies and bad habits."	True	False
11. The more a spouse discloses positive and negative information to his/her partner, the greater the marital satisfaction of both partners.	True	False
12. For most couples, maintaining romantic love is the key to marital happiness over the life course.	True	False

Scoring the Marriage Quiz

All of the items are false. The more "true" responses you gave, the greater your belief in marital myths. The quiz is based on research presented in this chapter and on Larson (1988: 8–9).

Positive Reasons for Getting Married

Positive reasons are based on motives that have a high chance of ensuring a happy marital life. Although these reasons don't guarantee that a marriage will last, they're likely to encourage marital stability.

Love and Companionship   The single greatest attraction of marriage is continuous, intimate companionship with a loved one. Even though couples experience conflict, they have similar interests and enjoy each other's company (Bradbury et al., 2001). Romantic love changes over the years. If people are good friends, however, love and companionship will be steady anchors over time (see Chapter 6).

Desire for Children   A traditional reason for getting married is to have children. Some women have children outside of marriage, but they encounter more problems. Because marriage is a social institution (unlike singlehood and cohabitation), most societies have laws and customs that protect children within marriage but not outside of it (see Chapter 9).

Adult Identity Developmental theory, you recall, asserts that family members progress through various stages during the life course (see Chapter 2). Finding a job and being self-sufficient marks adulthood. So does marriage. Getting married says "I am an adult" to the community. A 32-year-old man who married at age 28 recalls,

> *You've made it to the next level, you've finally grown up. . . . Once I was married, it really suited me. I've found this with a lot of my married friends—you just feel more solid. You have this definite position in the world (Paul, 2002: 80).*

A woman who married in her late twenties said that she "was really excited about becoming a wife" because identifying herself as a wife was satisfying and reassuring (Paul, 2002: 79).

Connection and Personal Fulfillment Marriage connects people to each other. The happiest couples report that they help each other, spend time together, and feel emotionally close (Olson and Olson, 2000). Marriage also provides a dependable and caring sexual partner.

Continuity and Permanence Whereas much of life is unpredictable, marriage promises stability. We expect a spouse to be a constant source of support and understanding in a shifting and changeable world. As one man stated, "I wanted to know that there was someone I loved who also loved me and that we would be together for the rest of our lives" (Paul, 2002: 92).

Marriage also offers a sense of permanence and continuity by establishing one's own family. According to one of my students, "Whenever we look at our kids, my husband and I think about the wonderful things they might achieve someday. And I'm really looking forward to being a grandma."

However unintentionally, we might marry for one or more "wrong" reasons.

Negative Reasons for Getting Married

Negative reasons are based on motives that usually derail a marriage. They may be very functional in the sense that they fulfill a purpose (see Chapter 1). Often, however, our negative reasons for matrimony lead to misery and often end in divorce.

Social Legitimacy Some pregnancies end in wedlock. Some don't. Getting married to "legitimate" an out-of-wedlock baby is one of the worst reasons for getting married (even though many religious groups would probably disagree). Often, the partners are young, one or both may not want to marry, and the couple may have only sex in common.

Social Pressure Sometimes, parents are embarrassed that their children haven't married, and well-meaning (married) friends feel that marriage will bring happiness (see Chapter 8). Even if parents have been divorced, they project their own desires on their children by encouraging marriage. According to a 26-year-old media planner, for example,

> *My mother was in her sixties and single. Even after her own two divorces, she was by no means turned off by the idea of marriage; in fact, she wanted more than anything to marry again. . . . Even though she didn't say it outright, she worried that I would become one of those women—thirty-five, lonely, careerist, with a cat and a studio apartment, contemplating in-vitro fertilization (Paul, 2002: 58).*

Economic Security Marrying someone just for her or his money won't sustain a marriage. Among other things, a partner may be stingy and watch every penny after marriage. One or both partners may be laid off and use up their savings very quickly. Or, even if you marry someone who's rich and get a divorce, you'll have a difficult time getting any of the money—in most states—if you've been married less than ten years (see Chapter 15).

When we were in graduate school, one of my friends, Beth, married a successful businessman because he was wealthy. Within a few months, Beth was staying at the library longer and longer because she dreaded going home to be with her husband. Their marriage lasted two years.

Rebellion or Revenge Young people sometimes marry to get away from parents. They flee their families for a variety of reasons: physical, verbal, or sexual abuse; conflict between the parents or with a stepparent; and a yearning for independence. Whether the reasons for getting away from one's family are legitimate or not, rebellion is a feeble reason for marriage.

In other situations, people marry on the rebound: "I'll show Jeff that other guys love me even if he dumped me." Such marriages are bound to fail because revenge doesn't solve any problems. The ex-partner doesn't care, so an "I'll show him (or her)" attitude is meaningless. In addition, one-sided love is bound to topple a marriage.

Practical Solutions to Problems We sometimes marry for other "wrong" reasons because we're seeking practical solutions to a dilemma. Dating can be a disappointing series of experiences (see Chapter 8), and some people hope that marriage will be an "escape hatch" from their problems. It isn't, of course, because it is more complicated and demanding than singlehood.

In recent years, it's become more common for couples to break from tradition in planning their weddings. Here, the bubbling bride and groom have an underwater marriage at their favorite scuba diving spot.

Most of us have stories about people who marry because they want a "helpmate"—someone to put them through medical school, share expenses in a new business, care for kids after a divorce or widowhood, and so on. Such marriages typically are short-lived because they create more problems than they solve.

Positive reasons don't guarantee that a marriage will last. Negative motives, however, have a high chance of ensuring separation and divorce. Regardless of our reasons for tying the knot, what do most of us expect from marriage?

What Do We Expect from Marriage?

Marriages are very personal, but they don't occur or exist in a vacuum. Many wedding rituals and practices reinforce the idea that marriage is a fusion of lovers who make a lifelong commitment to each other. Some people are more guarded, however, and prepare prenuptial agreements. Let's begin with a look at the marriage rituals that presumably cement a marriage.

Our Marriage Rituals

Marriage is a critical rite of passage in almost every culture. The major events that mark the beginning of a marriage are engagement, showers and bachelor or bachelorette parties, and the wedding itself.

Engagement Traditionally, an **engagement** formalizes a couple's decision to marry. According to the *Guinness Book of Records*, the longest engagement was between Octavio Guillen and Adriana Martinez of Mexico, who took 67 years to make sure they were right for each other. Most engagements are at least 65 years shorter.

Whether or not a couple follows traditional customs, an engagement serves several functions:

- It sends a "hands-off" message to others.

- It gives both partners a chance to become better acquainted with their future in-laws and to strengthen their identity as a couple.

- It provides each partner with information about a prospective spouse's potential or current medical problems (through blood tests, for example).

- It legitimates secular or religious premarital counseling, especially if the partners are of different races, religions, or ethnic backgrounds.

- It signals the intent to make the union legal if the couple has been living together or has had a child out of wedlock.

At a *bridal shower*, female friends and relatives "shower" a bride with both personal and household gifts and commemorate the beginning of a new partnership. At a *bachelor party*, the groom's friends typically lament their friend's imminent loss of freedom and celebrate one "last fling." Some women also have *bachelorette parties* that include anything from dinner with female friends to male stripper shows.

Many men now participate in the wedding preparations. They attend bridal shows, voice their opinions about flowers, produce original wedding invitations on their computers, and make menu choices. Those who are remarrying often involve their children in the ceremony (Mathias, 1997).

The Wedding In 2001, in an annual ceremony in Seoul's Olympic Stadium, the Reverend Sun Myung Moon, founder of the Unification Church, married 30,000 couples from more than 100 countries, including the United States. Reverend Moon matched the couples—all of whom were strangers—by age and education. Although there are no accurate statistics, some estimate that the divorce rate of these couples is about 75 percent (Baker, 2000; Lampman, 2001).

Most weddings are more traditional. The wedding ceremony typically reinforces the idea that the marriage commitment is a sacred, permanent bond. The presence of family, friends, and witnesses affirms the acceptance and legitimacy of the union. Even when the partners are very young, a wedding marks the end of childhood and the acceptance of adult responsibilities. The box on "Some Cherished Wedding Rituals" on page 266 illustrates the historical origins of some of our current marriage conventions.

Many brides are often swept off their feet by the merchandising and spend at least a year planning a "perfect" and often extravagant wedding ceremony (see "Data Digest"). Increasingly, however, attorneys are advising both women and men to create prenuptial agreements just in case the marriage fizzles after a few years.

Love and Prenuptial Agreements

Prenuptial agreements are common among the very wealthy (such as Donald Trump and his second ex-wife, Marla Maples). Most people don't create prenuptial agreements because doing so seems unromantic and because little property is involved at the start of most marriages.

Unlike today, prenuptial agreements were common in the United States in the seventeenth and eighteenth centuries. In 1683, for example, John French and Eleanor Veazie signed a marriage contract in which John agreed "not to meddle with or take into his hand" any part of the estate that Eleanor had inherited from her former husband. He also promised to let her sell their apples and to give her a place for her garden plot (Scott and Wishy, 1982: 70–72).

As *Appendix F* shows, prenuptial agreements cover numerous topics—from how many times partners expect to have sexual intercourse to trusts and wills. These contracts also include agreements about disposing of premarital and marital property, whether the couple will have children (and how many), the children's religious upbringing, who buys and wraps presents for relatives, and whether there will be combined or "his" and "her" savings and checking accounts. Some of the arguments for and against prenuptial agreements are similar to those for cohabitation contracts (see Chapter 9).

Prenuptial Agreements Are a Good Idea Whether they are motivated by money or a concern for people's welfare, many attorneys recommend prenuptial agreements. If there are children from a first marriage, or if one partner has considerable assets, the contract makes ending a bad marriage less complicated. Because women usually are the ones who suffer financially after a divorce (see Chapter 15), a contract gives them some legal protection.

Attorneys recommend making a list of issues that could evolve into potential problems, including each partner's financial situation, medical status, and prior marriages. The contract might also include sections on the division of household chores and who pays for maintaining the home and automobiles.

Prenuptial Agreements Are a Bad Idea Those who oppose prenuptial agreements feel that such documents set

In 2000, in an annual single ceremony in Seoul's Olylmpic Stadium, the Reverend Sun Myung Moon, founder of the Unification Church, married 20,000 couples. Brides and grooms who could not be present were represented by photographs held by their future spouses. Reverend Moon conducts such mass marriages every year.

CHANGES

Some Cherished Wedding Rituals

Most of our time-honored customs associated with engagement and marriage, like rings and honeymoons, originally symbolized love and romance (Ackerman, 1994; Bulcroft et al., 1999). Many were designed to ensure the fertility of the couple and the prosperity of their household.

Some, however, also reflected the subordinate position of the woman in the union. For example, the Anglo-Saxon word *wedd*, from which "wedding" is derived, meant the groom's payment for the bride to her father. Thus, a wedding was literally the purchase of a woman. Here are some others:

- Before the twelfth century, the *best man* was a warrior friend who helped a man capture and kidnap a woman he desired (usually from another tribe).
- *Carrying the bride over the threshold* isn't simply a romantic gesture. Originally, it symbolized the abduction of the daughter who would not willingly leave her father's house.
- After a man captured (or bought) a bride, he disappeared with her for a while in a *honeymoon*, so that her family couldn't rescue her. By the time they found the couple, the bride would already be pregnant. In America, around 1850, the honeymoon was usually a wedding trip to visit relatives. The safety and comfort of the railroad popularized more distant honeymoons (Kern, 1992).

- The *engagement ring* symbolized eternity. The medieval Italians favored a diamond ring because they believed that diamonds were created from the flames of love.
- Soldiers of ancient Sparta first staged *stag parties*: "The groom feasted with his male friends on the night before the wedding, pledging his continued loyalty, friendship, or love. . . . The function of this rite of passage was to say goodbye to the frivolities of bachelorhood, while swearing continued allegiance to one's comrades despite being married" (Ackerman, 1994: 270).
- In the 1890s, the friend of a newly engaged woman held a party at which a Japanese parasol filled with little gifts was turned upside down over the bride-to-be's head, producing a shower of presents. Readers of fashion pages, learning of this event, then wanted *bridal showers* of their own.
- In medieval times the wedding party's *flower girl* carried wheat to symbolize fertility. Perhaps for symmetry, the male *ring bearer* also appeared in the Middle Ages.
- In biblical times, the color blue symbolized purity. In 1499, however, Anne of Brittany set the pattern for generations to come by wearing a white wedding gown for her marriage to Louis XII of France. The *white bridal gown* came to symbolize virginity and is still

worn by most first-time brides, even though they aren't virgins.
- The first *wedding ring* was probably made of iron so it wouldn't break. The Romans believed that a small artery or "vein of love" ran from the third finger to the heart and that wearing a ring on that finger joined the couple's hearts and destiny.
- The ancient Romans baked a special wheat or barley cake that they broke over the bride's head as a symbol of her hoped-for fertility. The English piled up small cakes as high as they could, and bride and groom tried to kiss over the cakes without knocking the tower over; success meant a lifetime of prosperity. The cakes evolved into a *wedding cake* during the reign of England's King Charles II, whose French chefs decided to turn the cakes into an edible "palace" iced with white sugar.
- *Tying shoes to the car bumper* probably came from ancient cultures. For example, the Egyptians exchanged sandals at a wedding ceremony to symbolize a transfer of property or authority. A father gave the groom his daughter's sandal to show that she was now in his care. In Anglo-Saxon marriage, the groom tapped the bride lightly on the head with the shoe to show his authority. Later, people began throwing shoes at the couple, and somehow this evolved into the current practice.

a pessimistic tone for the marriage. Disagreements about the contents might even end wedding plans. Prenuptial agreements are not always binding in court. If the contract is executed in a state other than where it was drawn up, for instance, the couple will experience legal problems. Furthermore, because people change over time, the contract may not reflect their future viewpoints.

Regardless of how people feel about prenuptial agreements, both scholars and practitioners maintain that most of us don't know very much about the people we marry (see Chapter 8). The box "Before You Say 'I Do'" suggests some questions couples should discuss before tying the knot, including whether to draw up a legal premarital contract.

MAKING CONNECTIONS

■ If you're single, do you want to get married? If so, why? If you're married, did you marry for the "right" reasons, the "wrong" reasons, or a combination?

■ Do you think that prenuptial agreements are a good idea? Read *Appendix F* before deciding.

Types of Marriages

When someone asked a happily married couple to what they owed their successful marriage of 40 years, the husband replied, "We dine out twice a week—candlelight, violins, champagne, the works! Her night is Tuesday; mine is Friday."

As this anecdote suggests, happily married couples aren't joined at the hip. Several well-known studies have examined different types of marriages. Although the research is not based on representative samples of couples, the studies offer insight into the broad range of existing marriages.

The Cuber and Haroff Perspective

Until the mid-1960s, social scientists proposed fairly simple descriptions of marriage. A happy marriage was one that did not end in divorce and in which the husband and wife fulfilled the traditional instrumental and expressive roles (see Chapters 2 and 5). Cuber and Haroff (1965) studied 400 "normal," upper-middle-class marriages (the partners ranged in age from 35 to 55) and identified five types of marriage: conflict-habituated, devitalized, passive-congenial, vital, and total. Some were happy and some were not, but all endured.

In a **conflict-habituated marriage,** the partners fight, both verbally and physically, but do not believe that fighting is a reason for divorce. They feel that feuding is an acceptable way to try to solve problems, and they thrive on the incompatibility. Usually the reason for the conflict is insignificant, and the partners seldom resolve their disputes.

The partners in a **devitalized marriage** are deeply in love when they marry, spend much of their time together, and have a strong, satisfying sex life. As time goes on, they continue to spend time together—raising the children, entertaining, and meeting community responsibilities—but begin to do so out of obligation, not joy. They get along, see no alternatives to the marriage and, as a result, do not consider a divorce. Although

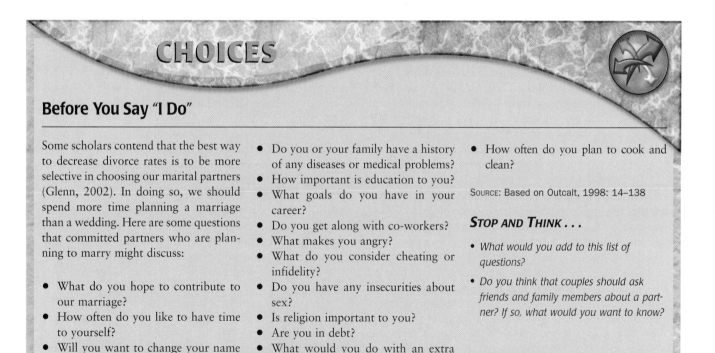

CHOICES

Before You Say "I Do"

Some scholars contend that the best way to decrease divorce rates is to be more selective in choosing our marital partners (Glenn, 2002). In doing so, we should spend more time planning a marriage than a wedding. Here are some questions that committed partners who are planning to marry might discuss:

- What do you hope to contribute to our marriage?
- How often do you like to have time to yourself?
- Will you want to change your name after marriage?
- Which holidays will we spend with which family?

- Do you or your family have a history of any diseases or medical problems?
- How important is education to you?
- What goals do you have in your career?
- Do you get along with co-workers?
- What makes you angry?
- What do you consider cheating or infidelity?
- Do you have any insecurities about sex?
- Is religion important to you?
- Are you in debt?
- What would you do with an extra $10,000?
- Do you have any child support or alimony payments?

- How often do you plan to cook and clean?

SOURCE: Based on Outcalt, 1998: 14–138

STOP AND THINK . . .

- *What would you add to this list of questions?*
- *Do you think that couples should ask friends and family members about a partner? If so, what would you want to know?*

When married couples work together on projects, they often learn better ways of communicating and of resolving difficulties. The seven years this couple spent building their California home may have helped them build their marriage as well.

one or both partners may be unhappy, they are both resigned to staying married.

In a **passive-congenial marriage,** the partners have a low emotional investment and minimal expectations that don't change. Fairly independent, the partners achieve satisfaction from other relationships, such as those with their children, friends, and co-workers. They often maintain separate spheres of activities and interests. Passive-congenial couples emphasize the practicality of the marriage over emotional intensity. The "Married Singles" box illustrates a more "modern" version of the passive-congenial marriage.

In the **vital marriage,** partners' lives are closely intertwined. They spend a great deal of time together, resolve conflict through compromise, and often make sacrifices for each other. They consider sex important and pleasurable. When a disagreement occurs, it is over a specific issue and is quickly resolved.

Finally, in the **total marriage,** which is similar to the vital marriage, the partners participate in each other's lives at all levels and have few areas of tension or unresolved hostility. Spouses share many facets of their lives; they may work together or have the same friends and outside interests. This type of marriage is more encompassing than the vital marriage.

Finding that approximately 80 percent of the marriages they studied fell into the first three categories, Cuber and Haroff characterized these as **utilitarian**

marriages because they appeared to be based on convenience. The researchers called the last two types **intrinsic marriages** because the relationships seemed to be inherently rewarding. In their sample, vital marriages made up 15 percent of the population, and total marriages accounted for only 5 percent.

Although the Cuber–Haroff typology has been widely cited, it has several limitations. The sample of upper-middle-class couples is hardly representative of most families. Also, couples who report minimal conflict are classified as "vital" and "total," whereas the more typical couples who admit having problems are labeled as "devitalized" and "conflict-habituated." These labels reinforce the idea that couples who argue or who have separate activities have inferior marriages. Such labels are not representative of many contemporary marriages.

The Lavee and Olson Perspective

In the early 1990s, Lavee and Olson (1993) collected data on nine dimensions of marriage from 8385 couples who participated in marital therapy or marital enrichment programs. The dimensions and the seven types of marital couples that the researchers identified are presented in *Figure 10.1* on page 270.

Although some of the types are similar to Cuber and Haroff's typology, Lavee and Olson reported more complexity and variety in marital relationship patterns. They found, for example, that traditional marriages (see Chapters 1 and 5) reflected problems in communication, conflict resolution, sexual relationships, and parenting issues. Even harmonious marriages experienced some problems related to parenting, family and friends, and religious beliefs.

The Lavee–Olson study was based on couples who *volunteered* for therapy. Therefore, they may be very different from couples who don't seek counseling or who are required to seek counseling during divorce mediation (see Chapter 15). Not surprisingly, then, the devitalized couples reported problems on *all* dimensions, from personality issues to conflicts over religious beliefs (see *Figure 10.1*). In contrast, couples who see some disagreements as normal or inevitable and who don't seek therapeutic intervention might present a different picture of married life.

As you've probably realized, neither of these perspectives—especially because they rely on nonrepresentative samples—tells us as much about "happy" or "successful" marriages as we'd like. Despite their limitations, these studies suggest that there are many types of marriages and that each type has both strengths and weaknesses. What, then, are the characteristics of stable and happy marriages?

Married Singles

An example of passive-congenial marriages might be characterized by what I call married singles. **Married singles** are married partners who, by choice or necessity, live under the same roof, may be good friends, and may or may not have sexual intercourse. They have drifted apart because of conflicting work schedules, interests, personality differences, or other reasons.

Married singles are companionable, but over time both partners may engage in sex less frequently or lose all interest in it. They may see other aspects of family life (such as raising children) as more important and time-consuming, and they may enjoy each other's company on a day-to-day basis (Avna and Waltz, 1992).

In other cases, marital partners' jobs may force them to live in different cities (see Chapter 13). Such commuter marriages require men and women to establish separate residences that prevent them

from getting together more than once a week or even once a month. Commuter partners often develop separate friendships and live as singles most of the time.

Some people purposely marry partners who will be absent. The wife has the advantage of having a husband who provides for the family while the wife is generally free to do as she pleases (Barreca, 1993).

Usually, however, it is the husband rather than the wife who leads a "married single" life. If he is often on the road or at the office, the husband is free to live his life as he pleases while the wife is at home or at work, or both, and caring for the children.

Finally, partners who live with alcoholics or other drug abusers must often function as married singles. They have no spouse to talk to, they may not want to discuss their problems with family members, and they may feel isolated if the

partner refuses to change his or her behavior or seek help.

The onset of a serious physical illness of one mate may also plunge the other into solitude:

Ellen and Roy had been married for ten years when he was diagnosed with multiple sclerosis. The disease took its slow and predictable course, transforming Roy from a vital and handsome artist into a sullen and degenerating invalid. . . . It was not merely that she sorely missed the healthy Roy, but she was overwhelmed by the huge amounts of time she was without him. When he slept, rested, or was in the hospital, Ellen found herself both lonesome for Roy and feeling very much alone in the world (Rosenzweig, 1992: 229–30).

Marital Success and Happiness

When a journalist interviewed couples celebrating their fiftieth or longer wedding anniversaries, she found some common characteristics: mutual respect, common goals, supportive spouses, and a focus on communication and problem solving rather than winning battles. Disagreements did occur, but they were toned down. As a 77-year-old woman said about her husband,

> *In all our 55 years, he has rarely gotten angry. If I get angry about something, we have a little argument, and he'll say something funny to me and I'll have to laugh and there goes the argument. Laughter has always been a big part of our life (Licht, 1995: 19).*

Researchers usually measure marital success according to marital "stability" and marital "satisfaction." *Marital stability* refers to whether a marriage is intact and whether the spouses have ever suggested divorce

to each other (Noller and Fitzpatrick, 1993; Holman et al., 1994).

Marital satisfaction refers to whether a husband or wife see their marriage as good. In assessing the quality of relationships, researchers have used such concepts as adjustment, lack of distress, contentment, happiness, and success. Often, these terms are used interchangeably (Fincham and Bradbury, 1987; Glenn, 1991).

Are Married Couples Happy?

Since 1973, the University of Chicago's National Opinion Research Center has asked representative samples of married Americans to rate their marriages as "very happy," "pretty happy" or "not too happy." As *Figure 10.2* on page 271 shows, the percentage saying "very happy" has fluctuated a bit since 1973 (67 percent) and declined only moderately by 1998 (63.5 percent). Because happiness is a self-reported and highly subjective measure, however, it's impossible to know how respondents define happiness. Do they mean a "vitalized marriage" that we just discussed? Acceptance of the status quo because "things could be worse"? Better than being alone? Or something else?

What's Important in a Successful Marriage?

Is there a recipe for an enduring and happy marriage? Researchers have been searching for an answer to this question for decades. Despite what marital advice manuals say, there are no 10, 12, or 20 steps for living happily ever after. Social scientists have uncovered some aspects of marital relations that describe satisfying and stable marriages, however.

Compatibility You recall that the dating and mating process screens out people who are very different from each other (see Chapter 8). Similar social backgrounds (in terms of ethnicity, religion, and education) decrease major interpersonal differences that can lead to conflict and disagreements. Couples are happier when they have similar personalities, emotional "wavelengths," and values about raising children (Whyte, 1990; Anderson et al., 2003).

Despite popular opinion, couples who play together don't necessarily stay together. The couples who participate together in leisure activities (such as watching television or going for a walk) that only one spouse likes become dissatisfied over time. Women, especially, are likely to engage in recreational activities that only their husbands enjoy. The more time women spend in those activities, the more likely they are to end up being unhappy with their marriages (Crawford et al., 2002; Gager and Sanchez, 2003).

Flexibility Our personalities are never 100 percent compatible. One spouse may be less organized, more tardy, or more outgoing than the other, for example. Happily married couples, however, are more likely than their unhappy counterparts to discuss how to handle and adjust to such differences (Olson and Olson, 2000).

FIGURE 10.1 **How Marriages Differ** Note that although the typologies offered by Lavee and Olson (shown here) and by Cuber and Haroff (see text) differ in category content and number of categories, their overall percentages paint a similar picture. That is, 75 to 80 percent of marriages are essentially based on convenience. Partners must also deal with such issues as personality differences, relationships with family and friends, and conflict resolution.

SOURCE: Based on data in Lavee and Olson, 1993, Figure 1, p. 332.

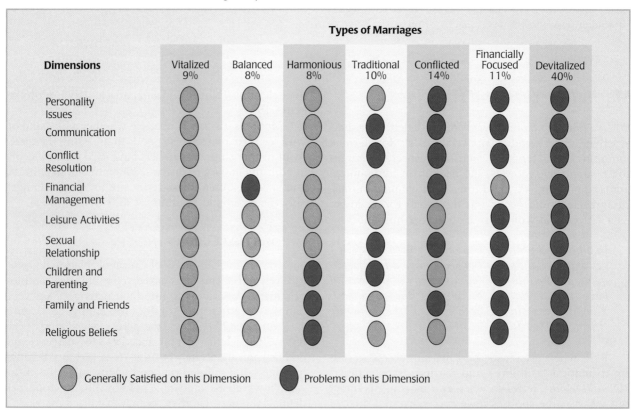

At the beginning of this chapter, the husband of the longest-married couple in the world said that their marriage had lasted so long because "It's a lot of give and take." That is, happily married people are flexible and compromise rather than control their spouses or always insist on doing everything their own way.

Positive Attitudes Spouses who like each other "as a person" and a good friend have happier marriages. Couples whose marriages begin in romantic bliss are especially prone to divorce because it's difficult to maintain such intensity. Couples in whirlwind courtships who marry are quickly disillusioned because they're saddled with fantasies and unrealistic expectations about married life (Pittman, 1999; Ted Huston, cited in Patz, 2000). The "How Close Is Our Relationship?" box on page 272 provides a quiz to determine whether you and your spouse (or other partner) have positive attitudes about each other.

Conflict Resolution Compared with unhappy couples, happy couples recognize and work at resolving problems and disagreements. Sometimes, conflict resolution means backing off because one or both partners are hurt or angry. For example, a salesperson who has been married 36 years advises,

> Discuss your problems in a normal voice. If a voice is raised, stop. Return after a short period of time. Start again. After a period of time both parties will be able to deal with their problems and not say things that they will be sorry about later (Lauer and Lauer, 1985).

Partners who see marriage as a long-term commitment or a sacred institution are more likely to manage conflict. Couples who stay together are much less likely to insult or put a partner down from the very beginning of marriage (Notarius and Markman, cited in Schrof, 1994). Moreover, those who believe that marital quality depends on determination and hard work are more likely to report having good marriages than couples who believe that relationships depend on fate, luck, or chance (Myers and Booth, 1999).

Emotional Support Happily married couples often say that providing emotional support is more important than romantic love (R. J. Erickson, 1993). A few years ago, the *Washington Post* conducted a survey of people who were happily married. Although the sample was self-selected, some of the comments about trust, privacy, and respect are instructive:

> There are times when each of us needs to be alone; we need to have our space. It is very important in our marriage, to know that if he buries himself in a book or I in an old movie, we respect each other's privacy (Married 9 years).

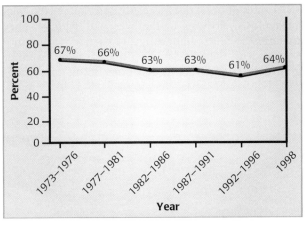

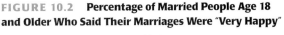

FIGURE 10.2 Percentage of Married People Age 18 and Older Who Said Their Marriages Were "Very Happy"

SOURCE: Based on Smith, 1999, Table 9.

> He makes me feel smart, pretty, capable and cherished (Married 21 years).

> I asked my husband why he thought our marriage was a success. He said it was because we don't "compete with each other" and because we "respect each other's independence." I agree (Married 33 years) (Mathias, 1992: B5).

In contrast, partners in unhappy marriages keep trying to change one another to fulfill their own needs. They often become frustrated and angry when their efforts fail (Quinn and Odell, 1998). Instead of cooling off and thinking a problem through, as the salesperson quoted earlier advises, the partners react when they are upset. For example, a 103-year-old man who recently celebrated an eightieth wedding anniversary advised, "When a woman is upset, keep quiet."

Such advice is equally effective for a wife whose husband is angry. Even when hostile and sarcastic comments don't lead to verbal or physical abuse, they are unhealthy in a marriage.

How Does Marriage Affect Health?

Actress Zsa Zsa Gabor once said, "Husbands are like fires: They go out when unattended." U.S. husbands must be forest fires because, according to most research, they are very well attended.

The Health Benefits of Marriage

Some writers describe marriage as having "medical power" (Waite and Gallagher, 2000). Overall, married people are generally healthier and happier than those who are single, divorced, or widowed. Married people have lower rates of heart disease, cancer, stroke, pneumonia, tuberculosis, cirrhosis of the liver, and syphilis. They attempt suicide less frequently and have fewer automobile accidents than singles. They are less likely to suffer from depression, anxiety, and other forms of psychological distress. Married people are also less likely to say they are sick, to be disabled, to visit the doctor, or to be hospitalized than unmarried people (Mastekaasa, 1994; Horwitz et al., 1996; Keith, 1997; Murphy et al., 1997; Wickrama et al., 1997).

Why is there a general positive relationship between marriage and physical and psychological well-being? The

ASKYOURSELF

How Close Is Our Relationship?

All marriages and other long-term relationships have difficult moments. When we feel valued by our partners, however, positive feelings overcome hurtful moments. This short quiz will give you an idea of whether you and your partner appreciate each other.

	True	False
1. We enjoy doing small things together, like folding laundry or watching TV.	❑	❑
2. I look forward to spending my free time with my partner.	❑	❑
3. At the end of the day, my partner is glad to see me.	❑	❑
4. My partner is usually interested in hearing my views.	❑	❑
5. I really enjoy discussing things with my partner.	❑	❑
6. My partner is one of my best friends.	❑	❑
7. I think my partner would consider me a very close friend.	❑	❑
8. We love talking to each other.	❑	❑
9. When we go out together, the time goes very quickly.	❑	❑
10. We always have a lot to say to each other.	❑	❑
11. We have a lot of fun together.	❑	❑
12. We are spiritually very compatible.	❑	❑
13. We tend to share the same basic values.	❑	❑
14. We tend to spend time together in similar ways.	❑	❑
15. We have a lot of common interests.	❑	❑
16. We have many of the same dreams and goals.	❑	❑
17. We like to do a lot of the same things.	❑	❑
18. Even though our interests are somewhat different, I enjoy my partner's interests.	❑	❑
19. Whatever we do together, we usually tend to have a good time.	❑	❑
20. My partner tells me when he or she has had a bad day.	❑	❑

Scoring: Give yourself one point for each true answer. If you score 10 or above, your marriage (or relationship) is strong. If you score below 10, your marriage (or relationship) could use some improvement.

Source: Gottman and Silver, 1999: 81–82.

Reprinted with special permission of King Features Syndicate.

two major sociological explanations have to do with selection and protection.

The "Selection Effect" Some researchers claim that married people are healthier than their unmarried counterparts because of a "selection effect." Healthy people are attracted to other healthy people and are more desirable marriage partners. Fit and healthy people are more likely to find and keep mates than those who have higher illness rates. In contrast, sick people tend to marry other sick people. This may be because healthy and less healthy people are attracted to each other because they share similar emotional stresses and lifestyles, including diets and alcohol usage (Booth and Johnson, 1994; Wilson, 2002).

The "Protection Effect" Marriage also contributes to one's health. Enjoying emotional, social, and physical support from a spouse improves one's general health and longevity. The feeling of security that such support brings may reduce anxiety and prevent or lessen depression (Collins et al., 1993; Murray, 2000).

The protection effect may also reduce risky activities and encourage healthy behaviors. For example, married people are more likely to quit smoking and to maintain low-cholesterol diets. They are less likely to drink heavily, get into fights, drive too fast, or take other risks that increase the likelihood of accidents and injuries (Kiecolt-Glaser and Newton, 2001).

And when one partner becomes ill, the physical and emotional support a spouse provides during recuperation after surgery or other medical treatment can help speed recovery (Ross et al., 1991). Such support, however, typically comes from wives rather than husbands and results in gender differences.

Gender and Health

A number of studies have found that married women are less healthy than married men. On average, women live longer than men. Still, unlike husbands, many wives experience depression and other health problems.

Why Husbands Are Healthy Many married men enjoy "emotional capital" because wives provide nurturing, companionship, and sustenance (Maushart, 2002). Wives tend to encourage behaviors that prolong life, such as their husbands' getting regular medical check-ups. Marriage introduces lifestyle changes that reduce some of men's bad habits:

> *Being married involves new sets of responsibilities, mutual caring, intimacy, and increased adult contacts, as well as less time spent in bars and at parties frequented by singles—the "singles scene," where a lot of smoking, drinking, and illicit drug use tend to take place (Bachman et al., 1997: 172).*

Men routinely report that their greatest (and sometimes only) confidantes are their wives while married women often talk to close friends and relatives (Steil, 1997). This suggests that husbands depend on their wives for emotional support, but wives often look outside the marriage for close personal relationships. Thus, husbands can depend on their wives for caring, but the same is not always true for women.

If husbands work long hours, there's no effect on the wives' health. If wives work more than 40 hours a week, however, the husbands are significantly less healthy than other married men because "they are impeded from managing their own health behavior, illness behavior, and social-emotional affairs" (Stolzenberg, 2001: 93). In plain English, husbands depend on wives (even those who work long hours) to take care of their health.

Why Wives Are Less Healthy Women typically are more attuned than men to the emotional quality of marriages. They work harder if the marriage is distressed, have many domestic responsibilities even if they work outside the home, have little time to "unwind," and neglect their own health while caring for family members, including husbands (Kiecolt-Glaser and Newton, 2001).

Employed wives—especially those with children—are at an especially high risk of depression. They often feel overwhelmed by the chronic strain of meeting the needs of their husbands and children while also working full time (Cross and Madson, 1997; Nolen-Hoeksema et al., 1999).

Social Class, Ethnicity, Age, and Health

Besides gender, other variables are associated with marriage and health. In married families, higher household incomes are correlated with good physical and mental health. Whether married or not, poor women—especially women of ethnic minorities or those living in rural communities—are often less healthy than their middle-class counterparts (Ross et al., 1991; Baezconde-Garbanti and Portillo, 1999). As a result, disparities in health and health care access can have a negative effect on the quality of a marriage.

Regardless of marital status, minority men—especially American Indians and African Americans at the lower end of the social class ladder—suffer from more health problems than their white counterparts. The negative health effects reflect economic problems, adverse working conditions, substance abuse, work in dangerous settings, high-risk behavior (such as fast driving or driving while intoxicated), and a lack of preventive health care plans (Rhoades, 2003; Williams, 2003).

In terms of age, a review of almost 35 years of research found that a stable marriage is only one of seven factors that affects men's longevity. The other factors are alcohol use, smoking, exercise, weight, coping mechanisms, and depression (Cole and Dendukuri, 2003). Thus, marriage alone does not work miracles in extending married men's lives.

Marital Quality and Health

Marriage isn't a magic potion that makes our lives healthier and happier. The *quality* of our marriages is much more important for our health than simply getting or being married.

Marriage and Life Satisfaction   Many of us feel that marriage will make us happier than we are. That's not the case, however. Married people are happier than unmarried people because marriage *improves* an already happy life. People who are very satisfied with life and have a rich social network of family members, friends, and co-workers have little to gain from marriage. On the other hand, people who are very lonely and dissatisfied with life can gain much by marrying because of the companionship (Lucas et al., 2003).

Troubled Marriages   The quality of the marriage is critical. Among other things, unhappy marriages increase rates of cardiovascular disease and elevate levels of stress hormones. Wives might "medicate" themselves with pills and husbands might turn to alcohol to decrease the stress (Kiecolt-Glaser and Newton, 2001). People who are unhappy in their marriages don't always end up in divorce court. Instead, they might experience marital burnout.

Marital Burnout

Marital burnout is the gradual deterioration of love and ultimate loss of an emotional attachment between marital partners. The process can go on for many years (Kayser, 1993). In marital burnout, even if spouses share housework and child care, one spouse may fail to provide the other with emotional support. A partner may complain that his or her partner is not confiding innermost thoughts and feelings, doesn't stick by the partner during bad times, or doesn't want to discuss problems (R. J. Erickson, 1993).

Marital burnout can develop so slowly and quietly that couples are often not aware of it. Sometimes one partner hides dissatisfaction for many years. At other times both partners may ignore the warning signs (see the box "Am I Heading toward Marital Burnout?"). Social exchange theory (see Chapter 2) suggests that when the costs in the relationship become much greater than the benefits, the couple will probably seek a divorce.

Marital Roles

When people marry, they have certain expectations about their marital roles. **Marital roles** are the specific ways in which married couples define their behavior and structure their time. Even if people have lived together before marriage, they experience changes. Who will do what housework? Who is responsible for paying the bills? Do you plan to have children? If you already have children, who is in charge of which child care tasks?

"His and Her Marriage"

More than 30 years ago, sociologist Jessie Bernard (1973) coined the phrase "his and her marriage." She argued that most men and women experience marriage differently. Because women make more adjustments to marriage than men, Bernard wrote, "his marriage is better than hers."

New Roles   Whether his marriage is better than hers is debatable. However, much research supports Bernard's observation that there are many gender differences in married life (Nock, 1998). Consider the process of

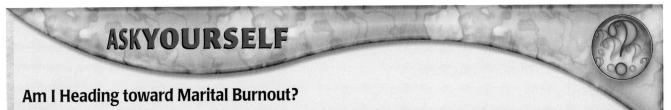

ASKYOURSELF

Am I Heading toward Marital Burnout?

All marriages have ups and downs, and checking off even as many as seven of the following items doesn't necessarily mean your marriage is in trouble. However, the more items you check, the wiser you may be to look further into these symptoms of burnout. The earlier you recognize symptoms, according to some practitioners, the better your chances of improving your marriage (based on Stinnett and DeFrain, 1985; Kayser, 1993).

If you've never been married, think about your parents or friends. Do you think that they have experienced marital burnout?

- You've lost interest in each other.
- You feel bored with each other.
- There's a lack of communication; neither of you listens to the other.
- You seem to have little in common.
- Deep down, you want a divorce.

- There's a lack of flexibility: you can no longer compromise with each other.
- Minor irritations become major issues.
- You no longer try to deal honestly with important issues.
- You find yourself making family decisions alone.
- You have no desire for physical touching of any kind.
- Your relationships with other people are more intimate than your relationship with your spouse.
- The children have begun to act up; they have frequent trouble at school, get into fights with friends, or withdraw.
- One of you controls the other through tantrums, violence, or threats of suicide or violence.
- You are both putting your own individual interests before the good of the marriage.

- You can't talk about money, politics, religion, sex, or other touchy subjects.
- You avoid each other.
- One or both of you subjects the other to public humiliation.
- You have increasing health problems, such as headaches, back pain, sleeplessness, high blood pressure, recurring colds, or emotional ups and downs.
- One or both of you is abusing alcohol or other drugs.
- Shared activities and attendance at family functions decrease.
- One or both of you is irritable and sarcastic.
- You are staying in the relationship because it is easier than being on your own.

identity bargaining, in which newly married partners readjust their idealized expectations to the realities of living together. In **identity bargaining,** partners negotiate adjustments to their new roles as husband and wife.

In these negotiations, gender—rather than age, personality, intelligence, or employment, for example—is generally the best predictor of marital roles. According to sociologist Susan Maushart (2002), wives contribute 100 percent of the husband care—the myriad tasks of physical and emotional nurture that she calls "wifework." Wifework includes

- Performing up to three-quarters of the unpaid household labor.

- Assuming total responsibility for the husband's emotional caretaking (from organizing his underwear drawer to arranging his social life).

- Taking full responsibility for child-care drudgework (laundry, meals, shopping) so that he can enjoy leisure time (games, sport, watching television with the kids).

- Monitoring his physical well-being (providing a healthful diet, making medical appointments).

- Preparing meals tailored to his taste, appetite, and schedule.

- Maintaining his extended family relationships (buying presents, sending thank-you notes, staging and catering family gatherings).

Maushart contends that there is no reciprocal "husbandwork" during marriage that maintains women's well-being.

More Roles   Marriage also increases the number of social roles each partner plays, thereby increasing the potential for role conflict (see Chapter 5). If both partners are employed, for example, they may feel strain in living up to extended family members' expectations to visit or spend time together. Or, in the case of one of our friends, the wife's father assumed that his new son-in-law would be "glad" to spend Saturdays helping the

CHANGES

Why I Want a Wife

The essay excerpted here has been reprinted more than 200 times in at least ten different countries (Brady, 1990). Written by Judy Brady [then Judy Seiters] in 1972, the article satirizes the traditional view of woman as wife and mother:

I am A Wife.... Why do I want a wife? ... I want a wife who will work and send me to school ... and take care of my children. I want a wife to keep track of the children's doctor and dentist appointments [and] ... mine, too. I want a wife to make sure my children eat properly and are kept clean.... I want a wife who takes care of the children when they are sick, a wife who arranges to be around when the children need special care because ... I cannot miss classes at school....

I want a wife who will take care of my physical needs. I want a wife who will keep my house clean ... pick up after me ... keep my clothes clean, ironed, mended, replaced when need be, and who will see to it that my personal things are kept in their proper place so that I can find what I need the minute I need it. I want a wife who cooks the meals, a wife who is a good cook. I want a wife who will plan the menus, do the necessary grocery shopping, prepare the meals, serve them pleasantly, and then do the cleaning up while I do my studying. I want a wife who will care for me when I am sick and sympathize with my pain....

I want a wife who ... makes love passionately and eagerly when I feel like it, a wife who makes sure that I am satisfied. And, of course, I want a wife who

will not demand sexual attention when I am not in the mood. ... I want a wife who assumes the complete responsibility for birth control, because I do not want more children....

When I am through with school and have a job, I want my wife to quit working and remain at home so that my wife can more fully and completely take care of a wife's duties.

My God, who wouldn't want a wife?

STOP AND THINK...

- Do you think that this excerpt is outdated or still describes many married women's roles today?

- Write a paragraph or two that would parallel this essay in terms of "Why I Want a Husband."

---

father-in-law with home improvement tasks. The son-in-law resented the intrusion on his weekend activities but felt that he couldn't refuse.

The couple will also add more roles if they associate with one (or both) of the partner's friends, attend her or his religious services, or join new community organizations. Some women must take on the most demanding role of all—that of mother—very quickly because as many as 13 percent of women are pregnant when they marry (Abma et al., 1997). A man also has to cope with the multiple roles of husband and father.

Variations in Domestic Roles

Domestic work includes two major activities: housekeeping (cooking, cleaning, laundering, outdoor work, repairs) and child rearing. Domestic work varies by a number of factors including age, life stage, employment (see Chapter 13), gender, presence of children, race and ethnicity, and social class.

Gender Although men's domestic work has increased since the 1960s, women still do two to three times as much as men (see Chapter 5). Being married usually means more housework for women and less for men.

Husbands typically create more housework than they perform (Coltrane, 2000). In time, women feel worn out and may become dissatisfied with the marriage (Piña and Bengston, 1993). In one case it resulted in an essay that has become a classic (see the box "Why I Want a Wife)."

Presence of Children Although child rearing is highly rewarding, it's also a 24-hour, 7-day job that's physically exhausting and emotionally draining. When couples have children, men tend to work more hours at paid jobs but rarely put in more hours of housework. Women, in contrast, tend to work fewer hours on the job and put in significantly more hours of domestic work. And as the number of children increases, so does women's share of child rearing and housework (Coltrane, 2000).

Race and Ethnicity Men's housework roles often vary by race and ethnicity. For example, employed Latino and African American men spend more time doing household tasks than employed white men, including such typically female tasks as meal preparation, dishwashing, and house cleaning (see Chapter 4).

Even so, men and women do not share household work equally. Although black, Asian, and Latino women have a long history of full-time work outside the home, they still bear a disproportionate share of housework and child care (Pessar, 1995; Repak, 1995; Kim and Kim, 1998; Kim, 1999). In two-earner households, for example, black men do only one-third as much household work as women (Kamo and Cohen, 1998).

Although their wives do the major share of child-care tasks, some Latino husbands report being much more involved in child rearing than their own fathers were (Coltrane and Valdez, 1993; López, 1999). While there is little sharing of family work in most Latino families, most men and women don't see the wife's much higher contributions as unfair because of cultural values about traditional gender roles (DeBiaggi, 2002).

Social Class The division of household labor also varies by social class. The higher a wife's socioeconomic status, the more likely it is that her husband will help with family tasks. Wives with high incomes get more help from their husbands than do wives who are employed at the lower end of the occupational scale (Moen, 1992; Perry-Jenkins and Folk, 1994).

One or more of a number of factors may be at work here: Educated, professional women may have more authority in the home, women with high-powered jobs may be required to spend longer hours at work, and successful self-employed women may feel more comfortable asking for help from their spouses. In addition, college-educated women tend to be married to college-educated men who are more likely to endorse gender equity and tend to do more of the domestic work (Coltrane, 2000).

In two-earner working-classe families in which both partners grew up in traditional homes where household tasks were sex-segregated, marital quality may be higher when the household labor is *not* collaborative. The woman may not want to give up control of traditionally female tasks that include housework. Men, who are often in low-paying jobs, may resent involvement in traditionally feminine household tasks, feeling that their time and energy should be focused on breadwinning (Helms-Erikson, 2001).

Domestic Roles and Marital Quality

Men are happy in their marriages when there's greater equality in decision making but not housework. Women are happier when there is greater equality in decision making *and* when both spouses share more equally in housework responsibilities (Amato et al., 2003).

A number of studies report that mothers, especially, are the least satisfied with their marriages when they have a disproportionate share of domestic responsibilities and child care, have little decision-making power, and do most of the "emotional work" to develop or maintain intimacy. The sense of carrying an unfair burden

(rather than the amount of work) creates anxiety, erodes the women's emotional and psychological well-being, and increases depression (Wilkie et al., 1998; Bird, 1999; Coltrane, 2000; Kiecolt-Glaser and Newton, 2001).

Doing an unfair share of housework is also costly to men:

> If men want the pleasure of living with women and children they are going to have to shape up. All work and no play may have made Jill too dull to understand a football game but all play and no work will make Jack that most vulnerable of creatures, a redundant male (Greer, 1999:136).

Although such words seem harsh, many women end marriages that they can't mend. Especially in the case of employed women, there's little motivation to stay in marriages where the costs are significantly and continuously greater than the rewards (see Chapter 5).

MAKING CONNECTIONS

■ One writer, you recall, contends that "wifework" characterizes most marriages. Do you agree that there are no comparable "husbandwork" roles?

■ Unequal housework increases men's marital satisfaction but decreases women's. How can people resolve this dilemma? Write premarital contracts? "Outsource" household work? Something else?

How Marriages Change throughout the Life Course

When I read the literature on marriage and think about my own marriage, the key word probably is "adjustment." From a developmental perspective, people fulfill different roles and learn new tasks as families establish their own structure and identity. Throughout the life course, we must adjust, adjust, adjust—to changing times, to specific goals, to marital changes, and to disagreements and conflict. The adjustments begin with the first year of marriage and continue until we die.

The Early Years of Marriage

The bridal media bombard women with merchandise. Many people spend more on a wedding than the cost of a four-year degree at an average-priced state college (see "Data Digest"). Because most couples don't attend premarital classes, what happens after the romantic wedding ceremonies are over?

After the Vows For every generation, the first year involves basic adjustments. After a tumultuous and exciting wedding, the groom takes on the new and unfamiliar role of husband. Brides, especially, often encounter a "marriage shock." Unlike their husbands, many women must take on such "wifely" roles as pleasing the husband's family and friends and being the "emotional guardians" of the marriage (Heyn, 1997). Many experience a "wedding postpartum":

> When . . . you find that your new husband blows his nose in the shower, few brides escape feeling some degree of disillusionment. You know then you're not at the champagne fountain anymore. Even though you weren't expecting perpetual bubbly from your marriage, the reality can be startling (Stark, 1998: 88).

It takes some women up to a year to feel comfortable with their new married name and the new identity of "wife" that it brings (Nissinen, 2000).

A second adjustment involves putting a mutual relationship before ties with others. Couples must strike a balance between their relationships with their in-laws and their own marital bond. Parents (especially mothers) who fear losing contact with their married children sometimes create conflict by calling and visiting frequently and "meddling" in the couple's life (Chadiha et al., 1998; Greider, 2000).

Settling In Many twenty-first-century newlyweds must adjust to three other changes after the marriage that their parents and grandparents rarely experienced. First, because many couples have lived together before saying "I do" (see Chapter 9), they must now address issues like where to spend the holidays.

Second, two-paycheck newlyweds—especially those who marry after a long period of independence—must make a transition from "my" money to "our" money. Adjusting to a joint bank account isn't always easy because individuals aren't used to pooling their money. In addition, the couple will have to reach consensus about paying off college loans, credit card debts, mortgage payments (if she just bought a house and he hasn't, for example) and saving for the future. And what if he's a spender and she's a saver?

Third, and as you saw earlier, many contemporary newlyweds are from divorced homes. They are simultaneously wary of marriage and more determined to make their marriage succeed. Because these couples haven't had role models for a successful marriage, they have to work especially hard at being married.

If both partners grew up in families where parents are responsive to each other's emotional needs, married couples have good role models. Women's experiences in their families of origin are more influential than men's, however (see chapter 5 on socialization). Thus, women wind up doing the lion's share of emotional work in their marriages (Sabatelli and Bartle-Haring, 2003).

Marriages with Children

One of the most important functions of the family is to socialize children to become responsible and contributing members of society (see Chapters 1, 4, and 5). In some societies, young teens marry and are considered adults. In Western societies, including the United States, however, adolescents have a prolonged dependence on parents (see Chapter 11). As a result, American parents enjoy (or suffer, depending on one's perspective) many years of socialization.

Young Children Socializing children takes enormous time and patience. Families with young children spend much of their time teaching rules, showing children how to live up to cultural expectations, and inculcating such values as doing well at school, following the rules, being kind, controlling one's temper, doing what one is asked, being responsible, and getting along with others (Acock and Demo, 1994).

Because women are socialized to "do everything," one of the biggest mistakes they make is to exclude the husband from an infant's everyday care. According to Joanne, one of my students who's now a mother of three teenagers, trusting a husband to care for an infant has benefits for both the baby and the couple:

> After I had my first baby, my sister-in-law (Susan) gave me some of the best advice I ever received. With a new baby, I was feeling very overwhelmed . . . bathing, feeding, changing the baby, packing the diaper bag, etc. I felt an incredible amount of responsibility when that baby was born. Although my husband helped with diaper changing and feedings, Susan suggested I let him bathe the baby. She told me to let him do it his way and to walk away if I didn't like how he was doing it. Although nervous, I did walk out of the room during that first bath. Afterward my husband was very proud of his clean bundle. I've enjoyed watching him bathe our babies over the years (Author's files).

In general, and as you'll see shortly, marital satisfaction tends to decrease once a couple has children. Most parents experience more frequent conflicts and disagreements after having children than childless spouses (Crohan, 1996). On the other hand, African American and white couples who wed before their out-of-wedlock child is born enjoy being married. Compared with their unmarried counterparts, after the first year of marriage they report greater financial security, a stable home life, and optimism about both spouses being good parents (Timmer and Orbuch, 2001).

Adolescents Raising adolescent children is difficult. Besides all the usual developmental tasks associated with the physical changes of puberty and emotional maturation, contemporary adolescents face more complicated lives than ever before. Both parents and children may have to cope with divorce, parental unemployment, and such dangers as violence and drugs in their schools and neighborhoods (Cotten, 1999). We'll return to the adolescent years in Chapter 12.

The potential for family conflict often increases as adolescents begin to press for autonomy and independence. Conflict is sometimes brought on not by the children but by a dip in the parents' marital happiness as a result of marital burnout or communication problems. Sometimes changes occur suddenly because of geographic moves. Depending on the breadwinner's (usually the father's) occupation and career stage, family members may have to adjust to new communities and build new friendships (see Chapter 13).

Marriages at Midlife

Like their younger counterparts, couples in the midlife years (between ages 45 and 65) undergo continuous adaptations. The most common adjustments include intergenerational experiences, relationships with in-laws, the empty nest syndrome, and the boomerang generation.

Intergenerational Ties Our family of origin, you recall, plays a significant role in shaping our values and behavior over the life course (see Chapter 1). Couples may be ambivalent about their intergenerational relationships, however. When families meet for holidays and celebrations, grandparents and other relatives might criticize the parents about how they discipline their children, especially teenagers. Married couples may be torn between pleasing their parents or their spouses (when parents want their adult children to visit more often, for example). Spouses might also experience strain about accepting help from their parents, especially money, because such assistance might obligate them in the future (Beaton et al., 2003).

Relationships with In-Laws There are tons of jokes about mothers-in-law (for example, "Hey guys, looking for a great gift for your mother-in-law on Mother's Day? Why not send her back her daughter!"). In contrast, we rarely, if ever, hear father-in-law jokes. Why is this the case?

First, women—not men—typically arrange family gatherings for both their own and their husband's family (Lee et al., 2003). If in-laws are unhappy with the get-togethers, they blame the wife and not the husband.

Second, most husbands are mute when their wives run into in-law problems. This "silent male syndrome" often reflects two male versions of staying out of in-law (especially mother-in-law) conflicts. In one response, husbands try to avoid the problem by maintaining that "We're all reasonable people." If the wife has problems, she must be the one who's "unreasonable." The second response by most husbands is that their wives are "making a mountain out of a mole hill." Thus, instead of supporting their wives, many husbands shrug off in-law problems as "hers" and not "mine" (Ehrlich, 2000).

Negative relations with in-laws can decrease marital success. Even after 20 years of marriage, in-laws can intrude on a couple's marriage and create problems by treating a daughter-in-law (or son-in-law) with disrespect, openly criticizing how a couple raises the children, and by making demands on the married couple, such as spending all holidays together (Bryant et al., 2001; Doherty, 2001).

The "Empty Nest Syndrome" Social scientists used to characterize middle-aged parents as experiencing the *empty-nest syndrome*—depression and a lessened sense of well-being, especially among women—when children leave home. But the children's departure gives many married couples a chance to relax and enjoy each other's company:

> Now that our . . . son is away [at college] we can talk about subjects that interest only us without having to consider whether he feels left out. We can talk about people he doesn't know without explaining who they are. . . . [Or we can] simply eat in companionable silence without the pressure to use mealtime for interacting with our kids (Rosenberg, 1993: 306–07).

Some parents, especially mothers who have devoted their lives to bringing up children, feel "empty" and "useless" when their kids fly from the nest. In many cases, however, both parents experience a sense of freedom and easing of responsibility (Antonucci et al., 2001). When our children established themselves by getting jobs and buying homes, for example, my husband and I breathed a deep sigh of relief. It didn't take us very long to turn their bedrooms into an office and a library.

Children who leave the nest sometimes return, however. In fact, many middle-aged parents have to live with a "boomerang generation" that keeps flying back to the nest.

The Boomerang Generation A recent phenomenon is the **boomerang generation,** young adults who move back into their parents' homes after living independently for a while. Because of a poor economy, low income, divorce, or the high cost of housing, many young adults don't leave their parents' home in the first place, or they move back. Parents try to launch their children, but, like boomerangs, some keep coming back.

Boomerang kids can have either a positive or negative impact on their parents' marital life. Co-residence, for example, has a more negative influence on remarried parents than on first-married parents because of unresolved tensions in the home. As one mother stated,

> *I did like it [living together] when she was in a good mood and she was playful. This was far and few between, though. The stress caused by her relationship with her stepfather—it was disruptive to the family (Mitchell and Gee, 1996: 446).*

Marital satisfaction also diminishes when a child returns home several times. The multiple returns prevent some parents from enjoying the expected greater intimacy, privacy, and freedom to pursue new interests. Marital satisfaction increases, however, if the children have a good relationship with their parents during co-residence. The children can provide assistance, emotional support, advice, and companionship. Thus, they can improve the overall quality of family relationships (Willis and Reid, 1999).

Marriages in Later Life

Many older couples describe their marriages as the best years of their lives. They have developed trust and intimacy over the years, enjoy each other's company, and are happier than their younger counterparts (Arp and Arp, 2001). Couples continue to make adjustments in later life, however, as evidenced by the U-shaped curve, retirement, and health issues.

The U-Shaped Curve A number of studies have found a U-shaped curve in marital satisfaction over the life cycle. Initially, romantic love produces a high degree of excitement and attraction in marriage. Marital satisfaction decreases because of the strain caused by family life-cycle events, especially those related to having and raising children. When the children grow up and leave home, marriage satisfaction usually increases (Glenn, 1991).

The U-shaped curve varies by ethnicity, gender, and age, however. In a longitudinal study of three generations of Mexican Americans, for example, Markides and his colleagues (1999) found that marital satisfaction declined for midlife women but remained about the same for midlife men. After children leave home, the researchers suggest, midlife Mexican American women may feel that something is missing in their motherhood roles and marriages. In addition, older Mexican American women often bear the burden of caring for extended family members. Thus, caretaking responsibilities may continue well past midlife and into old age.

Retirement Even before retirement, many older couples report an upturn in marital happiness. The U-shaped curve isn't the only explanation for this change, however. Older couples have few unresolved issues, settle conflicts more effectively than their younger and middle-aged counterparts, and savor the rewards of a long-term friendship.

Retirement typically brings more time to enjoy each other's company. Gender roles don't change very much. Husbands continue to do most of the "male" chores but may take on large-scale projects such as remodeling. Although men might do more shopping, women still invest much of their time in "female" chores such as food preparation, laundry, and cleaning the house (Charles and Carstensen, 2002). The biggest change in later life marriage for both sexes is physical decline.

Health and Well-Being The marital quality of older couples, whether one or both are retired, depends quite a bit on the partners' health. Sexual expression remains an important element in long-term marital relationships, although more so for men than for women (Vinick, 2000; see also Chapter 7). Older spouses who feel valued are happier and live longer than unhappy older couples (Tower et al., 2002).

A decline in health often impairs marital quality. Depression, for example, is the most common illness in aging populations. The depressed spouse may have problems communicating and making decisions and may get angry quickly. The nondepressed spouse may feel confused, frustrated, and helpless (Sandberg et al., 2002). If a spouse needs long-term care, whether at home or a nursing facility, the caregiver undergoes tremendous stress. And if a spouse is widowed, she or he may have to forge new relationships (see Chapter 17).

Power and communication issues affect marital quality throughout the life course. Most of these issues are similar whether people are married or single.

Communication: A Key to Successful Relationships

People who have been married a long time usually give very similar reasons for their long-term relationships: "We never yelled at each other," "We joked around a lot," "We treated each other with respect," "We tried to be patient," and "We accepted what we couldn't change about each other." Effective verbal and non-verbal communication is essential to any committed relationship, not just marriage.

What Is Good Communication?

Our most intimate relationships are in the family. Being able to express thoughts and feelings and to listen are critical components of all close relationships. Let's begin by looking at some of the major goals of effective communication in intimate relationships.

Communication Goals A major goal of effective communication is developing ways of interacting that are clear, nonjudgmental, and nonpunitive. A second important goal is resolving conflicts through problem solving rather than through coercion or manipulation. Very little can be gained "if someone tells us how we are *supposed* to feel, how we are *supposed* to behave, or what we are *supposed* to do with our lives" (Aronson, 1995: 404).

Good communication conveys *what* we and others feel. It incorporates different approaches that are equally valid (as when people agree to disagree). Effective communication also establishes an atmosphere of trust and honesty in resolving—or at least decreasing—conflict. An important first step in successful communication is self-disclosure.

Self-Disclosure Self-disclosure is telling another person about oneself and about one's thoughts and feelings with the expectation that truly open communication will follow (see also Chapter 6). *Reciprocity* is important if self-disclosure is to be effective in communication and conflict resolution. In terms of exchange theory, reciprocal self-disclosure increases partners' liking and trusting each other, eliminates a lot of guesswork in the relationship, and provides a balance of costs and benefits.

Women tend to disclose more than men do but hold back when they anticipate an uncaring, unemotional, or otherwise negative response. Men tend to disclose more to women than to men. Men withhold disclosure, however, when they feel they will get an emotional (rather than an objective and dispassionate) response (Arliss, 1991).

Disclosure can be either beneficial or harmful, depending on whether the reaction is supportive or worsens already negative feelings. Disclosure is beneficial under four conditions (Derlega et al., 1993):

- *Esteem support* can reduce a person's anxiety about troubling events. If the listener is attentive, sympathetic, and uncritical, disclosure can motivate people to change significant aspects of their lives.

Communication is a critical component in successful relationships. Body language conveys powerful messages about listening and being open to the other person's point of view.

- A listener may be able to offer *information support* through advice and guidance. For example, people under stress may benefit by knowing that their problems are not due to personal deficiencies.

- Disclosure can provide *instrumental support* if the listener offers concrete help, such as shopping for food or caring for the children if a partner is sick.

- Even if a problem is not easily solved, listeners can provide *motivational support*. For example, if a husband is distressed about losing a job, his wife can encourage him to keep "pounding the pavement" and assuring him that "we can get through this."

When is self-disclosure detrimental? If the feedback is negative, disclosure may intensify a person's already low self-esteem. (Disclosure: "I'm so mad at myself for not sticking to my diet." Response: "Yeah; if you had, you'd have something to wear to the party tonight.")

Where self-esteem is strong, even negative feedback will not be devastating. One of my students, in her mid-50s, said she was anxious about attending an honors' banquet for students with outstanding GPAs because "I'll look like everyone's grandmother." Expecting support, she asked her husband to attend the ceremony because she felt "out of place." He replied, "Well, just don't go. Everyone will wonder what an old lady is doing there and no one will hire you, anyway." (She attended alone, by the way, had a wonderful time, and accepted a job offer by the end of the summer. She also divorced her husband a year later.)

Self-disclosure is risky. People gain "information power" through self-revelation that they can then use against a partner ("Well, you had an affair, so you have

DILBERT reprinted by permission of United Feature Syndicate, Inc.

no right to complain about anything"). If the self-disclosure is one-sided, it sends the message that "I don't trust you enough to tell you about my flaws" (Galvin and Brommel, 2000). If this trust is violated, partners are unlikely to reveal intimate things about themselves in the future.

Do the sexes differ in self-disclosure and other communication patterns? And if they differ, is the interaction innate or learned socially?

Sex Differences in Communication

"Communication" has become a buzzword in recent years to summarize male–female relationship problems. This may explain why two of the best-selling books in the 1990s were Deborah Tannen's *You Just Don't Understand: Women and Men in Conversation* and John Gray's "borrowing" of Tannen's principles in the highly stereotypical but popular *Men Are from Mars, Women Are from Venus* (see Crawford, 1995).

We'll first consider some of the studies that suggest that men and women speak different languages. Then we'll examine some of the research showing that communication gaps reflect role and power disparities and social context rather than gender differences.

Women's Speech Because women tend to use communication to develop and maintain relationships, *talk is often an end in itself*. It is a way to foster closeness and understanding. A second important characteristic of women's speech is the *effort to establish equality between people*. Thus, women often encourage a speaker to continue by showing interest or concern ("Oh, really?" or "I feel the same way sometimes"). Or they may use affirmation, showing support for others ("You must have felt terrible" or "I think you're right").

Women often ask questions that *probe for a greater understanding* of feelings and perceptions ("Do you think it was deliberate?" or "Were you glad it happened?"). Women also do *conversational "maintenance*

work." They may ask a number of questions that encourage conversation ("Tell me what happened at the meeting").

Another quality of women's speech is a *personal, concrete style:* Women often use details, personal disclosures, and anecdotes. By using concrete rather than vague language, women's talk clarifies issues and feelings so that people are able to understand and identify with each other. *References to emotions* ("Wasn't it depressing when . . .?") personalize the communication but also make it more intimate.

A final feature of women's speech is tentativeness. This may be expressed in a number of ways. *Verbal hedges* ("I kind of feel you may be wrong") and qualifiers ("I may not be right, but . . .") modify, soften, or weaken other words or phrases. Men often give direct commands ("Let's go"), whereas women appear to show uncertainty by hedging ("I guess it's time to go").

Disclaimers weaken the message because they suggest that the speaker isn't serious, sincere, or very interested in the exchange. Women are more likely to use such disclaimers as "If you don't mind, could we . . ." or "Of course I don't know anything about politics, but I think. . . ."

Women also use more *verbal fillers*—words or phrases such as "okay," "well," "you know," and "like"—to fill silences. *Verbal fluencies*—sounds such as "mmh," "ahh," and "unhuh"—serve the same purpose. Women use fillers and fluencies much more frequently when they are talking to men than to other women (Pearson, 1985; Lakoff, 1990; Fitzpatrick and Mulac, 1995).

Men's Speech A prominent feature of men's speech is *instrumentality*; men tend to use speech to accomplish specific purposes ("Give me three reasons why I should . . ."). They often focus on problem solving: getting information, discovering facts, and suggesting courses of action or solutions. Thus, for men, speech is more often a *means to an end* than the end itself.

Masculine speech is also characterized by *exerting control* to establish, enhance, or defend their personal status and their ideas by asserting themselves and, often, challenging others ("I'll need more information to make a decision").

Men are much less likely than women to offer what women consider empathic remarks (such as "That must have been very difficult for you"). Men are also less likely to express sympathy or to divulge personal information about themselves.

Another feature of men's communication is *conversational dominance*. In most contexts, men tend to dominate the conversation, speaking more frequently and for longer periods of time. They also show dominance by interrupting others, reinterpreting the speaker's meaning, or rerouting the conversation. Men tend to express themselves in assertive, often absolutist, ways ("That approach won't work").

Compared with women, men's language is typically more forceful, direct, and authoritative; tentativeness is rare. Finally, men are apt to *communicate more often in abstract terms*, a reflection of their more impersonal, public style (Tannen, 1990, 1994).

Gender Roles and Communication

Some researchers consider the "female speech" and "male speech" dichotomy stereotypical and simplistic. The notion that women and men come from "two cultures" (or, worse yet, from two planets) ignores power dimensions (Crawford, 1995).

Both sexes tend to use "women's" powerless language when they feel they are in a subordinate position (interpersonally or in public), have little authority, and focus on connecting rather than competing for social status (Tannen, 1994). Many women are far from submissive or passive during marital conflict, for example. Even during the early years of marriage, husbands may withdraw or distance themselves in response to a wife who is hostile or critical or attacks her partner verbally (Roberts, 2000).

Gender roles also shape communication. Many men don't communicate in intimate relationships because they are accustomed to being "stress absorbers" and stoics. Although the noncommunicative male is missing an opportunity for intimacy, he is protecting his loved ones from "the disappointment, frustrations, and fears that are part and parcel of his daily work life" (Nowinski, 1993: 122). The expectation that unpleasant things are supposed to be "no big deal" is reflected in many men's not reporting personal troubles, such as posttraumatic stress disorders after returning from wars or sexual abuse during childhood. Instead of focusing on disturbing feelings, many men may turn to alcohol or drugs.

The Venus–Mars dichotomy also ignores communication variations in terms of social class, race, ethnicity, age, and sexual orientation. In terms of sexual orientation, for example, gay men and lesbians appear to be equally disclosing, equally "instrumental," and equally "expressive in their relationships" (Nardi and Sherrod, 1994). And in many cultures, languages use a formal "you" for adults and other elders and higher-status people and the informal "you" for children or intimate partners, regardless of one's sex (Eckert and McConnell-Ginet, 2003).

Social context is also important in understanding gender communication styles. Men are more likely to use "men's speech" when interacting with women in general than with their wives. Husbands decrease the interaction distance between themselves and their wives by adopting a more "feminine" style in conversations. Women, in contrast, tend to maintain the same "women's speech" both with husbands and with men in general (Fitzpatrick and Mulac (1995). This might reflect the power differences noted earlier.

Communication Problems

Despite our best intentions, many of us don't communicate effectively. Because communication involves *both*

partners, we can't control or change our partner's inter-action, but we can recognize and do something about our own communication style. Some of the most common communication problems include a variety of issues ranging from not listening to using silent treatments.

Not Listening Both partners may be so intent on making their point that they are simply waiting for their turn to speak rather than listening to the other person. Consider a nondiscussion with my husband while I was revising this textbook several years ago:

> Me: "I haven't had time to do any Christmas shopping yet."
>
> My husband: "Your computer needs more memory. That's probably why you get all those error messages."
>
> Me: "And I'll probably be writing Christmas cards in February."
>
> My husband: "We should get 64 MB. That'll bring you up to 128 MB."
>
> Me: "What I need is a clone."
>
> My husband: "We'd better increase your disk capacity, too."
>
> Me: "I'll never finish these revisions on time."
>
> My husband: "Will the kids be home for dinner tonight?"

This everyday exchange illustrates the common pattern of partners talking but not communicating. One of the most important components in communication is *really* listening to the other person instead of rehearsing what we plan to say when he or she pauses for a breath. Listening and responding are especially critical when partners discuss relationship problems.

Not Responding to the Issue at Hand If partners are not listening to each other, they will not be able to address a problem. There are three common miscommunication patterns in unhappy couples. In *cross-complaining*, partners present their own complaints without addressing the other person's point:

> Wife: "I'm tired of spending all my time on the housework. You're not doing your share."
>
> Husband: "If you used your time efficiently, you wouldn't be tired" (Gottman, 1982:111).

In *counterproposals*, a spouse ignores a partner's suggestions and presents his or her own ideas (Krokoff, 1987). In *stonewalling*, which is much more common among men than women, one of the partners may "Hmmmm" or "Uh-huh," but he or she really neither hears nor responds; it is as though the partner has turned into a stone wall (Gottman, 1994). If a partner is addicted to alcohol or drugs, for example, she or he might refuse to talk about the problem:

> *Whenever someone brings up the [alcohol] issue, he proclaims that they are making a big deal about nothing, are out to get him, or are just plain wrong. No matter how obvious it is to an outsider that the addict's life may be falling apart, he stubbornly refuses to discuss it. If that does not work, then he may just get up and walk out* (Nowinski, 1993: 137).

Blaming, Criticizing, and Nagging Instead of being listened to and understood, partners may feel they are neglected or unappreciated. They feel their spouse or partner magnifies their faults, belittles them, accuses them unjustly, and makes them feel worthless and stupid. The criticism may escalate from specific complaints ("The bank called today and I was embarrassed that your check bounced") to more global and judgmental derision ("Don't you know anything about managing money?").

The blamer is a faultfinder who criticizes relentlessly and generalizes: "You never do anything right," "You're just like your mother/father" (Gordon, 1993: 82). In blaming and criticizing, a partner uses sophisticated communication skills to emotionally manipulate a more vulnerable partner (Burleson and Denton, 1997). If I'm an effective blamer, for example, I can probably convince you that our family budget problems are due to *your* overspending rather than *my* low salary.

Scapegoating Scapegoating is another way of avoiding honest communication about a problem. By blaming others, we imply that our partner should change, not us. We may be uncomfortable about being expressive because we grew up in cool and aloof families. Or we might be suspicious about trusting people because a good friend took advantage of us. However, blaming parents, teachers, relatives, siblings, or friends for our problems is debilitating and counterproductive (Noller, 1984).

Coercion or Contempt Partners may be punitive and force their point of view on others. If this works, coercive behavior, which is related to scapegoating, can continue.

Contempt can be devastating. The most visible signs of contempt include insults and name-calling, sarcasm, hostile humor, mockery, and body language such as rolling your eyes, sneering, and curling your upper lip (Gottman, 1994). As you saw in the "Am I Heading toward Marital Burnout?" box, some of the red flags include a partner's or spouse's control through tantrums, violence, or threats of suicide or violence. In addition, a partner may subject the other to public humiliation.

The Silent Treatment People communicate even when they are silent. Silence in various contexts, and at particular points in a conversation, means different things to different people. Sometimes silence saves many of us from "foot-in-mouth" problems. Not talking to your spouse or partner, however, builds up anger and hostility. Initially, the "offender" may work very hard to make the silent partner feel loved and to talk about a problem. Eventually, however, the partner who is getting the silent treatment may get fed up, give up, or look for someone else (Rosenberg, 1993).

Power and Conflict in Relationships

Power and conflict are normal and inevitable in close relationships. Both shape communication patterns and decision making. The person who has the power to make decisions often influences many of the dynamics in marriage and in nonmarital relationships.

Sociologists define **power** as the ability to impose one's will on others. Whether we're talking about a dating relationship, a family, or a nation, some individuals and some groups have more power than others.

Theories of Power Some scholars use *resource theories* to explain marital power. Typically, the spouse with more resources has more power in decision making. Thus, a husband who earns more money than his wife or has more control over household finances has more power (Vogler and Pahl, 1994).

Resources are often interrelated. For example, people with high incomes often also have more education or higher occupational status. As women increase their resources through paid work, they become less dependent on their husbands and more powerful in demanding that household chores and child care be shared.

Sources of Power Power is not limited to tangible things such as money. Love, for example, is an important source of power. As you saw in Chapter 8, the *principle of least interest* explains why, in a dating relationship, the person who is less interested is more powerful than the committed partner. In marriage, similarly, if you are more committed to your marriage than your spouse is, you have less power. As a result, you may refrain from expressing negative feelings, defer to your partner's wishes, or do things you don't want to do.

Other nonmaterial sources of power include access to information or particular abilities or talents. For example, husbands often have more decision-making power about how to spend money on expensive things (such as houses or cars) because they are typically more knowledgeable about financial matters, investments, and negotiating contracts. In traditional households, wives may have more power than their husbands in furnishing a home or raising children. The wives usually devote more time to reading informational material, to shopping, or to becoming familiar with neighborhood professionals, like pediatricians and dentists, who provide important services.

Conflict and Communication *Conflict* refers to discrete, isolated disagreements as well as chronic relational problems (Canary et al., 1995). All partners and families, no matter how supportive and caring they are, experience conflict. A study of married couples found that the majority of participants reported an average of one or two "unpleasant disagreements" per month (McGonagle et al., 1993).

Comedian Phyllis Diller's quip, "Don't go to bed mad. Stay up and fight!" is actually insightful. Conflict is not in itself a bad thing. If families recognize conflict and actively attempt to resolve it, conflict can serve as a catalyst to strengthen relationships (Rosenzweig, 1992). Before considering coping techniques, let's look at some common reasons for conflict.

What Do Couples Fight About?

Couples fight about a variety of things. The most common disagreements are over gender roles, fidelity, sex, money, power, privacy, and children (see also Chapter 15 on divorce).

Gender Roles

Expectations about fulfilling gender roles can often cause disagreements. As you saw earlier, for example, spouses often have different attitudes about household work. If they cannot compromise, especially when both partners are employed, tension may rise and quarrels become more frequent (Lye and Biblarz, 1993).

Fidelity

Fidelity is another common source of friction. For unmarried couples, the most common violations include having sexual intercourse outside the relationship, wanting to date others, and deceiving the partner. As you saw in Chapter 7, extramarital affairs and cybersex are the most serious types of betrayal. Married and unmarried couples also argue about other violations of trust and commitment such as lying, betraying confidences, and gossiping (Jones and Burdette, 1994; Metts, 1994).

Sex

Sex can also be a source of marital and nonmarital conflict. Women are more likely to equate sex with emotional intimacy and to resent partners who are affectionate only when they want sex (Oggins et al., 1993; see also Chapter 7). Often, arguments over sex overlap with fidelity issues.

The most serious problem may be unwanted sex. In one national survey, 9 percent of the wives reported being forced to have sex against their will at least once during the marriage (Schrof and Wagner, 1994).

Money

Money is one of the major reasons for conflict. Arguments over money generally focus on how—or how not—to spend it. Although arguments typically erupt over specific expenditures, they are often really based on different values. For example, because Mary's family of origin is emotionally important to her, she spends a lot of money on long-distance telephone calls to them, which infuriates John because he thinks that he and the children should be enough emotional support for Mary. John, on the other hand, spends a lot of money on stereo equipment because listening to music helps him to relax. But Mary thinks turning on the radio can produce the same effect and thus sees this as a waste of money.

One reason married couples argue about money is because they don't know or even agree on how much they have. Disagreements arise because wives overstate debt and husbands overstate income. These dissimilar views of the family's finances increase disagreements about money (Zagorsky, 2003).

Power

Power struggles can create conflict on several levels. Some antagonism may arise over economic power. Even when wives work, husbands may feel that the man should be the one to decide how to spend the money, especially for expensive purchases like homes, cars, and large appliances.

Couples may disagree about specific household rules. Whether they are explicit or implicit, rules about dealing with in-laws, disciplining the children, or entertaining friends can provoke conflict.

There are also differences in the ways partners exercise power. The person with less power may use manipulation (such as flattery), supplication (crying or acting helpless), or disengagement (sulking, playing the martyr, or not speaking). The more powerful person is more likely to be autocratic (for example, by claiming to be better informed) or to bully (through threats, insults, ridicule, or violence).

Privacy

Most of us need and value privacy. No matter how close a couple is, partners can run into problems if they don't respect each other's needs for privacy, including having the physical space and time to be alone. A mother of young children, for example, may resent her husband's barging into the bathroom because it may be one of the few times during the day when she can be alone. Similarly, many men have workshops, not because they produce great furniture but because it gives them a chance for solitude.

Many couples fight about privacy because they equate it with secrecy, but privacy and secrecy are not synonymous. For example, some couples never open each other's mail, not because they are afraid a partner may get a letter from a lover but because they respect each other's privacy.

Children

Children are wonderful and sometimes strengthen a marriage (see Chapter 12). They also create stress, tension, and conflict. In addition to the demands children make on parents, partners may have different philosophies about such issues as discipline, the importance of teaching young children self-control, and the kinds of responsibilities a child should have.

As more spouses (and some partners) collaborate in child rearing, there is more opportunity for clashes between different child-rearing approaches. For example, although a wife may expect her husband to take on more child-care tasks, she may also resent his insistence on making decisions about playmates, bedtimes, or curfews. Children are especially likely to be a source of conflict in remarriages (see Chapter 16).

How Do Couples Deal with Conflict?

It bears repeating that conflict is a normal part of life. What may *not* be normal or healthy is the way a family handles the conflict.

Common Ways of Coping with Conflict Families typically use four techniques to end—although not necessarily resolve—conflict: submission, compromise, standoff, and withdrawal.

- *Submission.* One person submits to another; the conflict ends when one person agrees with or goes along with the other.

- *Compromise.* Partners find a middle ground between their opposing positions; each must give in a little to accept a compromise. The compromise can be suggested by a partner or by a third party.

- *Standoff.* The disputants drop the argument without resolving it; they agree to disagree and move on to other activities. No one wins or loses, and the conflict ends in a draw.

■ *Withdrawal.* When a disputant withdraws, he or she refuses to continue the argument, either by "clamming up" or by leaving the room. Among the four techniques, withdrawal is the most disruptive of family interaction because there is no resolution (Vuchinich, 1987).

Except for compromise, these aren't the best ways to resolve conflict.

Effective Ways of Handling Conflict One of the biggest myths about interpersonal relationships is that it's okay to "say what's on your mind" and "let it all hang out." Some spouses unleash "emotional napalm" at their partners because "if a man can't let down his hair at home and blow off some steam, he's likely to end up with stomach ulcers or have a heart attack" (Noller and Fitzpatrick, 1993: 178). Displaced rage, unbridled attacks, and physical aggression aren't normal ways of handling conflict.

On the other hand, denying conflict can destroy a relationship. Couples who confront their problems may be unhappy in the short term, but such confrontations may result in better relationships in the long run. Otherwise, the anger and bitterness fester.

Both researchers and practitioners have suggested effective ways of dealing with anger and strife, including guidelines for "fair fighting" (see the box "Ground Rules for Fair Fighting" on page 288). Fights that humiliate, embarrass, browbeat, or demoralize the other person will not clear the air. Rules for fair fighting do not guarantee a resolution. Because they are based on negotiation and compromise, however, they offer partners a better chance of developing more constructive ways of dealing with conflict.

MAKING CONNECTIONS

■ Think about the conflicts you've experienced with a partner or spouse during the last year or so. What were most of the disagreements about?

■ When you and your partner argue, how do you respond? How does your partner respond? Do you resolve the conflict? Or does it smolder until the next eruption? ◎

Productive Communication Patterns

Over time, communication problems can erode intimate relationships. It takes time to forge good communication networks.

Psychologist John Gottman interviewed and studied more than 200 couples during a 20-year period, finding that the difference between lasting marriages and those that split up was a "magic ratio" of 5 to 1; that is, five positive interactions between partners for every negative one:

> *As long as there was five times as much positive feeling and interaction between husband and wife as there is negative, the marriage was likely to be stable over time. In contrast, those couples who were heading for divorce were doing far too little on the positive side to compensate for the growing negativity between them (Gottman, 1994: 41).*

Improving Your Communication Style

Yelling is probably one of the most damaging ways of interacting. We rarely scream at guests, employers, or professors. Yet we do so quite often with partners, spouses, and family members, who are among our most important and longest-lasting relationships. "Hollering is just part of my personality" is no excuse for obnoxious behavior that injures other people.

According to researchers and practitioners, couples can increase positive communication and decrease negative interaction patterns in the following ways:

■ *Ask for information.* If your partner has a complaint ("I never get a chance to talk to you because you're always busy"), address the issue. Don't be defensive ("Well, if you were around more often, we could talk"); find out why your partner is upset.

■ *Get inside the other person's world.* See things from the other person's point of view. When we disagree on an issue, it is not always because "I'm right and you're wrong." It is more likely due to the fact that we have different perspectives.

■ *Keep the monsters in late-night movies.* Do not engage in "monster" behavior: Do not criticize, evaluate, or act superior. Being supportive, attentive, and nonjudgmental increases a partner's desire to talk about problems.

■ *Keep it honest.* Honesty not only means not lying, it means not manipulating others. Do not resort to bullying, outwitting, blaming, dominating, or controlling. Do not become a long-suffering martyr. Truthfulness and sincerity reinforce mutual trust and respect.

■ *Make it kind.* Some people use "brutal honesty" as an excuse for cruelty. Temper honesty with kindness.

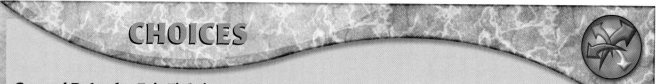

CHOICES

Ground Rules for Fair Fighting

Therapists, counselors, and researchers hold conflicting views as to whether and how marital partners and families should handle conflict. In general, however, many feel that arguing the issues is healthier than suffering in silence. Clinicians who deal with dissatisfied couples offer the following advice on changing some of our most destructive interaction patterns:

1. Don't attack your partner. He or she will only become defensive and will be too busy preparing a good rebuttal to hear what you have to say.
2. Avoid ultimatums; no one likes to be backed into a corner.
3. Say what you really mean and don't apologize for it. Lies are harmful, and apologetic people are rarely taken seriously.
4. Avoid accusations and attacks; do not belittle or threaten.
5. Start with your own feelings. "I feel" is better than "You said." Focus on the problem, not the other person.

6. State your wishes and requests clearly and directly; do not be manipulative, defensive, or sexually seductive.
7. Limit what you say to the present or near present. Avoid long lists of complaints from the past.
8. Refuse to fight dirty:
   - No *gunnysacking*, or keeping one's complaints secret and tossing them into an imaginary gunnysack that gets heavier and heavier over time.
   - No *passive-aggressive behavior*, or expressing anger indirectly in criticism, sarcasm, nagging, or nitpicking.
   - No *silent treatment*; keep the lines of communication open.
   - No *name-calling*.
9. Use humor and comic relief. Laugh at yourself and the situation—but not at your partner. Learning to take ourselves less seriously and to recognize our flaws without becoming so self-critical that we wallow in

shame or self-pity can have a healing effect during fights.
10. Strive for closure as soon as possible after a misunderstanding or disagreement by resolving the issue. This prevents dirty fighting and, more important, it holds the partners to their commitment to negotiate until the issue is resolved or defused (Crosby, 1991a; Rosenzweig, 1992).

STOP AND THINK . . .

- *According to Hendrickson (1994), "a good fight is an essential ingredient" in building a good marriage. Do you agree? Or does keeping silent and sidestepping conflict increase love and respect?*

- *Have you ever used the "rules for fair fighting" in your own relationships? If so, what were the results?*

- *Be specific.* A specific complaint is easier to deal with than a general criticism. "You never talk to me" is harder to manage than "I wish we could have 30 minutes each evening without television, the paper, or the kids."

- *Become allies.* Attack the problem rather than each other. If you treat each other as best friends and not as enemies, you have a better chance of resolving the problem.

- *Express appreciation.* Thanking your partner for something he or she has done will enhance the relationship.

- *Share your hopes.* Sharing hopes is integral to a strong relationship. Hopes can range from the mundane ("I hope you don't have to work this weekend") to ambitious goals ("What if we invest our money to buy a condo near the mountains for our retirement?").

- *Use nonverbal communication to express your feelings.* Nonverbal acts, such as hugging your partner, smiling, and holding his or her hand, can sometimes be more supportive than anything you might say.

- *Above all, just listen.* Sharpen your emotional communication skills by being really interested in what your partner is saying rather than always focusing on yourself (Stinnett and DeFrain, 1985; Gold, 1992; Knapp and Hall, 1992; Gordon, 1993; Gottman and DeClaire, 2001).

Family Therapy and Counseling

Because conflict is inevitable, and failing to deal with it can be destructive, family therapy and counseling have become a booming industry. Therapy and counseling are not always successful, however. In one survey, patients ranked marriage counseling at the bottom of the list of various psychotherapies. Part of the problem is that "almost anyone can hang out a shingle as a marriage counselor" (Kantrowitz and Wingert, 1999). And, as you saw in Chapter 2, the authors of some of the best-selling self-books include "therapists" who have been divorced at least twice, are estranged from their children, and know less about communication than you or I do.

Even some credentialed therapists use approaches that have no basis in empirical studies. According to some research, for example, the "active listening" models that many therapists promote are ineffective in resolving marital conflict. In active listening, people summarize each other's complaints and "validate" the other's feelings ("I'm hearing that you're angry"). Happily married couples don't use active listening exercises or validation. Instead, they try to prevent negativity from getting out of control, use humor as "repair attempts," and try to decrease anger through soothing (Gottman et al., 1998).

Many counselors have internalized cultural stereotypes about how women and men should behave according to traditional gender roles (Wright and Fish, 1997). In addition, instead of being neutral and objective, some therapists have strong feelings about keeping a couple together because of their religious or personal views even if the partners would be better off by leaving each other (see Doherty, 2001).

Furthermore, many people are not comfortable in seeking advice. They may be embarrassed, can't afford the cost, deny they have a problem, want to find their own solutions, or don't trust "shrinks."

Couple counseling can be very useful, however. Professional and experienced counselors can help couples identify their strengths and weaknesses, improve communication and conflict resolution skills, and develop a program that helps a couple or family achieve its goals for happier relationships (Olson and Olson, 2000).

Conclusion

Someone once said that marriages are made in heaven, but the details have to be worked out here on Earth. Working out those details is an ongoing process throughout a marriage or other committed relationships. The biggest sources of conflict and *change* are disagreements over household work and communication.

Different *choices* lead to different consequences. Deciding to have a more egalitarian division of domestic work and child-rearing responsibilities, for example, can diminish some of the *constraints* that many women (and some men) encounter as they juggle multiple roles.

In addition, deciding to interact more honestly can result in more effective communication and greater interpersonal satisfaction.

Despite the constraints, marriage is one of the most important rites of passage for almost all of us. Another is parenthood, our focus in the next two chapters.

SUMMARY

1. Marriage, an important rite of passage into adulthood, is associated with many traditions, rituals, and rules. Many of these rituals reflect historical customs.

2. There are several types of marriage. Most endure despite conflict over such issues as parenting, communication, finances, sex, and religious attitudes.

3. What people consider to be "very important" in marriage hasn't changed much over the years. Both men and women consider love, sexual fidelity, and the ability to discuss feelings the most important elements of a good marriage.

4. Marriage generally increases a person's physical and mental health. Married women, however, are less likely to enjoy good health than are married men.

5. Men and women often experience marriage differently. Some of these differences reflect differences in the status of men and women in society and the organization of household and child-care tasks.

6. Marriages change throughout the life cycle. In general, having children decreases marital satisfaction, but satisfaction increases again when grown children leave the home. Throughout the life cycle, families adjust to raising young children, communicating with adolescents, and enjoying the empty-nest and retirement stages.

7. Communication is a key to successful intimate relationships. Self-disclosure is important to effective communication, but couples should recognize that disclosing all their innermost thoughts might be detrimental rather than helpful over time.

8. Most marriages break down not because of conflict but because couples fail to cope adequately with conflict. Such negative coping strategies as complaining, criticizing, being defensive, and stonewalling may lead to a partner's isolation or withdrawal.

9. Resource theories are commonly used to explain how power is distributed and used within a family. Power resides not only in such tangible things as money and property but also in love, access to information, and abilities or talents.

10. Conflict is unavoidable and normal. It is unrealistic to expect communication to cure all marital problems. Nonetheless, effective communication can decrease power struggles and hostility that can lead to breakups in marriages and other committed relationships.

KEY TERMS

engagement *264*
conflict-habituated marriage *267*
devitalized marriage *267*
passive-congenial marriage *268*
vital marriage *268*

total marriage *268*
utilitarian marriage *268*
intrinsic marriage *268*
married singles *269*
marital burnout *274*

marital roles *274*
identity bargaining *275*
boomerang generation *280*
self-disclosure *281*
power *285*

TAKING IT FURTHER

Wedding Bells and Marriage Bytes

If you are planning to marry (or remarry), here are some informative sites.

Town and Country Wedding Registry has fashions, planning advice, and a free service that lets couples set up Web pages announcing their weddings and wedding registries.

tncweddings.com

Gay Wedding Planners offers same-sex couples complete wedding packages around the country for a civil union ceremony or "a grand wedding event."

www.gayweddingplanners.com

Indiebride, a site for the "independent-minded bride," explores "the highs, the lows, and the complexities" of weddings and marriage.

indiebride.com

Iowa State University Extension offers guidelines for communication about finances, worksheets, and other resources.

extension.iastate.edu/financial/management.html

Marriage Support provides information and encouragement to married and unmarried people who want to improve their relationship skills. The site includes bulletin boards, a relationship satisfaction quiz, and other resources.

www.couples-place.com

And more: www.prenhall.com/benokraitis offers numerous links on engagement and wedding sites (including those for same-sex marriages), honeymoon ideas, several sites that scramble family names and provide a list of suggestions for those who want a "new" surname after marriage that reflects both sides of the family, and the National Marriage Project at Rutgers University.

INVESTIGATE WITH RESEARCH NAVIGATOR

Please go to www.researchnavigator.com and enter your LOGIN NAME and PASSWORD. For instructions on registering for the first time, please view the detailed instructions at the end of the Chapter 1. Please search the Research Navigator™ site using the following key search terms:

marriage
communication
counseling

CHAPTER 11

To Be or Not to Be a Parent:
More Choices, More Constraints

DATADIGEST

- The **number of births** in the United States has decreased from 4.2 million in 1990 to 4 million in 2000.

- The **number of foreign-born adoptions** increased from 7000 in 1990 to 18,000 in 2000.

- Between 1986 and 1991, the **teen birth rate** rose by 25 percent, peaking at 62.1 births per 1000 females aged 15 to 19 in 1991. Since 1991, the rate has declined by 27 percent to 45.8 in 2001. The largest reductions occurred among teenagers aged 15 to 17 and African American teenagers.

- In 2000, there were 7325 **multiple births**, up from 1034 in 1971. These figures don't include twins. In 2000, 40 percent of all births to women aged 50 years and over were twins, triplets, or other multiple births.

SOURCES: Martin et al., 2002; Hamilton et al., 2003; Kreider, 2003.

A successful physician in his fifties took his 80-year-old mother to a performance of the Metropolitan Opera in New York City. They were making their way out the lobby doors to the physician's Mercedes when his mother turned to him and asked: "Do you have to go to the bathroom, dear?"

As this anecdote suggests, parenthood lasts forever. We may change colleges, buy and sell houses and cars, switch careers, and marry more than once, but when we become parents we create a lifelong commitment to our children. According to one author, "The way I bring up my children affects my grandchildren, too" (Ostrowiak, 2001: 18). That is, having a child also affects future generations.

Although today we are freer to decide whether to have children, our choices are more complicated than ever before. Most people can decide when to have children and how many. Women can postpone parenthood longer than ever before, sometimes even after menopause. We can become parents despite problems that prevent normal conception or birth. And we can decide to remain childless altogether. We cover all these possibilities in this chapter.

Parenthood is a process. *Having* children—through childbirth or adoption—is not the same as *raising* children. This chapter focuses primarily on the biological, economic, and social aspects of *becoming* a parent (or not). The next chapter examines the child-rearing roles, activities, and responsibilities in *being* a parent. Let's begin by looking at the choices that couples have.

Becoming a Parent

We sometimes hear about mothers, most often those in their teenage years, who abandon their newborn infants. Overwhelmingly, however, most couples have children because they really want them. A couple may

293

discuss family size before getting married, set up a savings account for their children's college education, enroll in a health insurance plan that will cover pregnancy costs, and even buy a house to accommodate the family they plan.

Almost half of all pregnancies in the United States are unintended (Santelli et al., 2003). Whether planned or not, a couple's first pregnancy is an important milestone. Pregnancies are "family affairs": Both parents typically worry about the developing fetus's health and look forward to the baby's birth with great anticipation. The reactions of both partners to the news of pregnancy can vary, however:

- *Planners* actively discuss the issue, having jointly decided to conceive a child. They are typically jubilant about becoming pregnant. As one wife said, "When the doctor called with the news that I was pregnant, I was so excited I wanted to run out in the street and tell everybody I met."

- *Acceptance-of-fate* couples are pleasantly surprised and quietly welcoming of a child, even though they have not planned the pregnancy. Often, such couples have unconsciously or intentionally engaged in an unspoken agreement to become pregnant by using contraceptive methods only sporadically or not at all.

- *Ambivalent couples* have mixed feelings before and after conception and even well into the pregnancy. As one wife noted, "I felt confused, a mixture of up and down, stunned, in a daze." Ambivalent couples decide to have the baby because one partner feels strongly about having a child and the other partner complies. Or the pregnancy might be unintended, but one or both partners don't believe in abortion.

- In *yes–no couples* one partner may not want children, even late in the pregnancy. Typically, the wife decides to go ahead with the pregnancy regardless of what her husband thinks, and the pregnancy sometimes causes a separation or divorce. Or, in the case of unmarried teenage couples, the father may simply stop seeing the woman once she becomes pregnant (Cowan and Cowan, 2000: 33–45).

It's not surprising that many couples are ambivalent about their prospective parenthood. After all, parenthood involves costs as well as benefits.

The Benefits and Costs of Having Children

Some people weigh the pros and cons of having a baby. Many don't. Emotions, after all, play a role in deciding to have a baby. Speaking both emotionally and practically, what are some of the benefits and costs in becoming a parent?

Benefits One of our thirty-something neighbors recently had their first baby. When I asked Matt how they were doing, he exclaimed, "There's nothing like it! She's the most gorgeous baby in the world!" Matt's reaction is fairly typical. For example, 96 percent of the first-time parents in a national survey said they were "in love" with their baby, and 91 percent reported being "happier than ever before" ("Bringing up baby," 1999). According to many parents, children bring love and affection; it is a pleasure to watch them grow; they bring joy, happiness, and fun; they create a sense of family; and they bring fulfillment and a sense of satisfaction (Gallup and Newport, 1990).

In the United States, unlike many countries, most parents don't expect their children to care for them in their old age (see Chapters 17 and 18). Instead, many parents say that having children brings a new dimension to their lives that is more fulfilling than their jobs, their relationships with friends, or their leisure activities. Most couples place a high priority on raising healthy and happy children. Even new parents who are struggling with a colicky infant (whose abdominal distress causes frequent crying) delight in the baby's social and physical growth.

Costs Parenthood isn't paradise. To begin with, having and raising children is expensive. *Figure 11.1* shows a typical year's expenses for a child 1 or 2 years old in husband–wife middle-income families. Middle-income ($39,700 to $66,900 per year) families spend about 25 percent of their earnings on a child every year from the child's birth to age 17.

Child-rearing costs are much higher, especially in low-income families, if a child is disabled or chronically ill or needs specialized care that welfare benefits don't cover (Lukemeyer et al., 2000). And if one or both parents are laid off, they usually lose any medical benefits that cover them or their children (see Chapter 13).

Becoming a parent has other economic and social costs. Many women pay a "mommy tax": Their unpaid work at home doesn't count toward Social Security pensions, they often forgo educational opportunities, and they are more likely to live in poverty in old age and after a divorce than men or childless women (Crittenden, 2001).

Women who combine work and motherhood also suffer. In higher education, for example, women faculty are much less likely than childless women or married fathers to be promoted or to get tenure because they fall behind in publishing or are perceived as mommies rather than colleagues even when they publish (Benokraitis, 1998; Mason and Goulden, 2002).

Contrary to what many people think, it is *not* selfish to consider economic costs before having a child (Folbre, 1994). In fact, it is selfish *not* to do so because a child raised in a poverty-stricken home may suffer lifelong disadvantages. One problem may be finding suitable housing. Large houses are expensive, some rental units exclude children or limit their number, and low-income families often have fewer housing options.

Children also carry emotional costs. While most parents report being "in love" with their baby, first-time parents, especially, experience anxiety or fatigue: 56 percent say they are stressed and worn out, 52 percent are afraid of doing something wrong, and 44 percent are unsure about what to do "a lot of the time" ("Bringing up baby," 1999).

As parents become more focused on the child, interpersonal relationships may deteriorate. Many mothers report strain in balancing employment and household responsibilities (Walzer, 1998). Others feel that their husbands become more distant emotionally—even though they're devoted fathers—because the wife spends most of her time caring for the infant.

Men also experience conflict with the birth of the first child. Although many men would like to be involved fathers, they are still expected to be full-time breadwinners (Lupton and Barclay, 1997). As a result, they may work long hours, rarely see the baby, and feel that they're missing out on parenting. New parents may take out their frustrations on each other: "For couples who thought that having a baby was going to bring them closer together, this is especially confusing and disappointing" (Cowan and Cowan, 2000: 18).

The Joys and Tribulations of Pregnancy

Pregnancy can be exciting and a time of joy, particularly when it is planned and welcomed. For both prospective parents, it can deepen feelings of love and intimacy, and it can draw them closer in planning for the family's future. At the same time, pregnancy—especially the first pregnancy—can arouse anxiety about caring for the baby properly and providing for the growing child economically.

The expectant mother may face numerous discomforts. In her first trimester (three-month period), she may experience frequent nausea, heartburn, insomnia, shortness of breath, painful swelling of the breasts, and fatigue. She may also be constantly concerned about the health of her *fetus* (the term for the unborn child from eight weeks until birth), especially if she or the baby's father has engaged in any of the high-risk behaviors described in the box "Having Healthier Babies" on page 296.

The second trimester can be very exciting because the mother begins to feel daily movements, or *quickenings*, as the fetus becomes more active. *Sonograms* (diagnostic imaging produced by high-frequency sound waves) can reveal an image of the baby and reveal its sex.

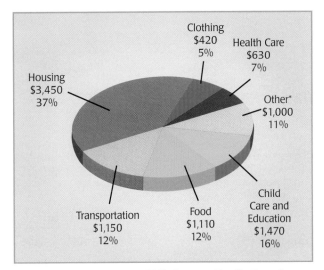

FIGURE 11.1 **What a Middle-Income Family Spends during the First Two Years of a Child's Life** In 2002, families earning $39,700 to $66,700 spent about $9,230 per year on each child under 2. This amount does not include the costs of prenatal care or delivery.

*Includes personal care items, entertainment, and reading materials.

SOURCE: Based on Lino, 2003.

On the down side, backaches may become a problem, and fatigue tends to set in more quickly. In her third trimester, a woman may start losing interest in sex, which becomes awkward and difficult because of her growing abdomen. She begins to retain water during this period and may feel physically unattractive and clumsy. Once-simple, automatic tasks, like tying shoelaces or retrieving something that has fallen on the floor, may require planning and assistance.

Vaginal births may be quick, or they may be long and exhausting. Sometimes they're not possible and a woman has a *cesarean section* (surgical removal of the baby from the womb through the abdominal wall), which afterwards is more painful for the mother and entails a longer recovery. Both vaginal births and cesarean sections involve bloody discharge for several weeks. Infections and fevers are also common.

Effects of Parenthood on Both Mother and Father

Parenthood is steeped in romantic misconceptions. And often we expect too much of mothers and ignore fathers. The infant responds to any person, mother or father, who is a consistent source of stimulation, love, attention, and comfort:

The father is usually larger than the mother, his voice is deeper, his clothes are not the same and he moves and reacts differently. Furthermore, parents

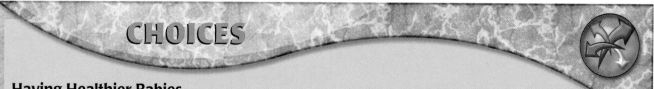

CHOICES

Having Healthier Babies

Most babies are born healthy. If parents engage in high-risk behaviors, however, the baby can be born with a variety of problems. Many are due to the parents' lifestyles rather than genetic diseases or other disorders.

Smoking

Smoking cuts off oxygen to the baby's brain, impairs the baby's growth, and is linked to the risk of spontaneous abortion, premature birth, low birth weight, and childhood illness. Researchers estimate that 2800 of annual infant deaths result from low birth weight caused by pregnant smokers (Aligne and Stoddard, 1997).

Low birth rate is conventionally defined as less than 2500 grams, or 5 pounds, 8 ounces. Low birth rate (which affects 7 percent of all newborns) increases the infant's chances of sickness, retarded growth, respiratory problems, infections, lower intelligence, learning problems, poor hearing and vision, and even death (Cornelius and Day, 2000).

Alcohol

Humans have a "brain growth spurt" that starts in the sixth month of gestation and continues for two years after birth. During this period, a single drinking binge—lasting four hours or more—can permanently damage the brain of the unborn child (Ikonomidou et al., 2000).

Birth defects associated with prenatal alcohol exposure can occur in the first three to eight weeks of pregnancy, before a woman even knows she's pregnant. One out of every 29 women who know they're pregnant reports "risk drinking" (seven or more drinks per week, or five or more drinks on any one occasion) ("Fetal alcohol syndrome," 2000).

Chronic drinking during pregnancy may lead to **fetal alcohol syndrome (FAS)**, a condition characterized by such physical abnormalities as congenital heart defects, defective joints, and often mental retardation (Baer et al., 2003). In the United States, about 8000 children are born with FAS each year.

Drugs

Mothers who use illicit drugs (heroin, cocaine, morphine, and opium) are likely to have infants who are addicted at birth. The baby may experience problems that include prenatal strokes, lasting brain damage, seizures, premature birth, retarded fetal growth, and malformations.

Even common prescription drugs or over-the-counter drugs can affect the fetus. These include antihistamines, some antibiotics, tranquilizers, barbiturates, and excessive amounts of vitamins A, D, B_6, and K (Boston Women's Health Book Collective, 1992).

Obesity and Eating Disorders

Women who are obese or overweight before pregnancy are at a much higher risk than women of normal weight of having infants with birth defects that include spina bifida, heart abnormalities, and other problems. Researchers suspect that obese women suffer from nutritional deficits—due to poor eating habits—that result in diabetes and health-related problems for infants (Watkins et al., 2003). Pregnant teenagers with poor diets can hurt their baby's bone growth because the fetus is not getting enough calcium (Chang et al., 2003).

Infectious Diseases

Problems from infectious diseases are numerous. A woman who contracts German measles during the first three months of pregnancy may give birth to a deformed or retarded child. Sexually transmitted diseases (STDs) are also dangerous or fatal to the unborn child. A woman with gonorrhea may give birth to a baby who becomes blind after passing through the infected birth canal. Herpes or syphilis can result in a spontaneous abortion, a stillborn birth, or a baby born brain-damaged, deformed, blind, or deaf. Finally, and perhaps most serious of all, a parent with AIDS can pass the deadly disease on to the fetus (see Chapter 7).

---

differ in odor and skin texture. The father and mother offer the child two different kinds of persons to learn about as well as providing separate but special sources of love and support. The infant also learns that different people can be expected to fulfill different needs. For example, the infant may prefer the mother when hungry or tired and the father when seeking stimulation or more active play (Biller, 1993: 12).

Mothers and Their Newborns There is a widespread myth that there is instant "bonding" between the mother and the newborn baby (see Chapter 6). In reality, it is not only mothers but also fathers, siblings, grandparents, and friends who have an effect on children.

Historically and in other cultures, children have been nurtured by many adults, not just mothers. Because responsibility for the baby's care tends to fall heavily on new mothers, however, they often feel frustrated or stressed out and experience a decline in marital satisfaction (Twenge et al., 2003).

Many women experience **postpartum depression**—"the blues" that appear after the birth of the baby. Some of this depression may be chemically caused. The sudden drop in estrogen and progesterone levels as the concentrations of these hormones in the placenta are expelled with other afterbirth tissue may have a depressive effect. And the high levels of the body's natural painkillers, called *beta-endorphins*, that the mother's body produces during labor also drop after birth. As a result, the mother may "crash," contributing to the postpartum depression. Newborn infants need frequent feeding and almost constant care, which may contribute to fatigue and depression. In addition, using alcohol or tobacco increases depression both during and after pregnancy (Marcus et al., 2003).

Despite the physical pain after childbirth, postpartum depression, and wondering whether they'll ever get two hours of uninterrupted sleep again, most mothers are elated with their infants. Many new mothers (and sometimes fathers) can spend hours describing the baby's eating schedule, every yawn and expression, and even the bowel movements of the "cutest and most intelligent baby you've ever seen."

Fathers and Their Newborns Our society tends to stress the importance of mothers over fathers, especially in caring for infants. Fathers, like mothers, are important for infants' emotional development. Fathers are just as effective in soothing crying babies, for example, and playing with them (Diener et al., 2002).

Like mothers, many fathers worry about being good parents. Even when they feel anxious, many men think that their task is to be calm, strong, and reassuring—a gender stereotype. Their tendency to keep their worries to themselves may increase the tension and distance between the partners. The couples who fare best are those who can listen sympathetically to each other without expecting immediate solutions (Cowan and Cowan, 1992).

Fatherhood often enhances maturity: "Being a father can change the ways that men think about themselves. Fathering often helps men to clarify their values and to set priorities" (Parke, 1996: 15). From a developmental perspective (see Chapter 2), fatherhood is an important transition in the man's life course.

Some men's transition to fatherhood is problematic. They may become abusive because of increased financial responsibilities, more emotional demands of new familial roles, and restrictions that parenthood brings (Schecter and Ganely, 1995; see also Chapter 14).

Most fathers forge stronger links with their own parents who are supportive grandparents. New fathers also have the opportunity to express loving and affectionate emotions to their children that "may be good for fathers as well as for babies" (Parke, 1996: 47). Although the mother may be more involved than the father in direct caregiving, a responsible father can get deep satisfaction by participating in child rearing (Johnson and Huston, 1998).

Becoming a parent seems to be an individual decision, but that's not entirely the case. Although most people have a choice about conception, childbearing also reflects what's going on in society and how it changes over time. Consider childbearing patterns in the last century.

Fertility Patterns in the United States

The United States is the world's third-largest country, though well behind China and India. Our population is growing faster than that of any other developed country because of high immigration rates (see Chapter 4). Fertility has been another important driving force in our population growth.

How Fertility Patterns Have Changed

Except for the baby boom "blip" of the 1950s, U.S. birthrates have been declining steadily since the turn of the twentieth century. As *Figure 11.2* on page 298 shows, the **birth rate**, or the number of live births annually per 1000 population, decreased from 30.1 in 1910 to 14.1 in 2001 (Ventura et al., 1997; Hamilton et al., 2003).

Demographers often use the **total fertility rate** (TFR) to measure the average number of children a woman would have given current birth rates. In the early 1900s, U.S.-born white women had an average TFR of 3.5 children compared with 1.9 children in 2001 (Kent and Mather, 2002).

A more specific measure is the **fertility rate**, or the number of births annually per 1000 women of childbearing age (aged 15 to 44). The U.S. fertility rate in 2001 was 65.3, compared with 118 in 1960 (Ventura, et al., 1997; Hamilton et al., 2003).

Why Fertility Patterns Have Changed

Much of the decrease in birth rates and fertility rates is due to macro-level societal changes. First, beginning with the Industrial Revolution in the mid-1800s, entry into paid employment allowed women to postpone marriage and, consequently, motherhood (see Chapter 3).

Second, improvements in contraceptive methods and greater opportunities in higher education since the 1960s have given women choices other than the traditional roles of wife and mother. Oral contraceptives, especially, allowed women to space their pregnancies and delay motherhood (Kent and Mather, 2002).

Third, advancements in medicine and hygiene have decreased infant mortality rates. Families no longer have to have six children because of the likelihood that three or four will die before their first birthday. As a result, family size has decreased. In 1900, for example, 45 percent of all households were made up of five or more people, compared with only 11 percent in 2000 (Hobbs and Stoops, 2002).

A fourth reason for the falling fertility rates reflects a combination of attitudes and economic factors, as reflected by relative income. **Relative income** is a person's earning potential compared with his or her desired standard of living. Couples need a higher income if they want to own a new BMW rather than an old Ford, for example.

As incomes for many American men under age 30 fell dramatically in the 1970s and 1980s, many wives joined the work force to be able to afford a lifestyle they had grown up with when they were children. As women joined the work force, their fertility levels declined. Postponing having children also means that women have fewer years to become pregnant (Macunovich, 2002). Thus, relative income, wages, and fertility trends are interrelated in explaining our lower fertility rates.

Variations by Racial and Ethnic Group

In 2001, racial and ethnic minorities contributed 42 percent of all births, although minorities accounted for just 31 percent of the U.S. population. During the same year, the fertility rate among whites was lower than that of other ethnic groups (see "Data Digest").

Fertility rates are higher among Latinas than other women across almost all age groups (see *Figure 11.3*). Within the Latino population, however, fertility rates range from a high of 106 for Mexican American women to a low of 57 for Cuban American women (Hamilton

et al., 2003). Most of the Mexicans who have recently immigrated from rural areas value large families. Children perform important economic functions, including contributing to the family income, often as migrant workers. In contrast, Cuban Americans are predominantly middle class, have low unemployment rates and higher education levels, and do not depend on children to augment family income (see Chapter 5).

Why are fertility rates higher among some racial and ethnic groups and subgroups? Two important factors are education and sexual practices.

Education One of the key factors in low fertility rates is education. Asian Americans and whites have the highest educational levels and the lowest fertility rates, for example. Better-educated couples tend to limit family size because of financial considerations (Kate, 1998; "Less is more," 1999).

A woman's educational level is especially important in explaining fertility rates. Women who seek a college or graduate education tend to use contraceptives more effectively, marry later, postpone childbearing, and usually have fewer children. Over a lifetime, for example, black women and Latinas with 13 to 15 years of education have an average of 1.6 children, compared with 4.1 and 4.5 children, respectively, for Latinas and black women with only a grade school education (Mathews and Ventura, 1997).

The highest fertility rates among Asian American and Pacific Islander women are for those aged 30 to 39 (see *Figure 11.3*). This may be because Asian American women—especially Japanese women and Filipinas—tend to postpone childbearing until they've completed college and attained professional degrees (see Chapter 5). Such findings suggest that young women—including teenagers—who expect to improve their lives through educational and vocational opportunities are

FIGURE 11.2 **Births in the United States, 1910-2001**

Sources: U.S. Census Bureau, 1999; Ventura, et al., 1997, Table 4; Hamilton et al., 2003.

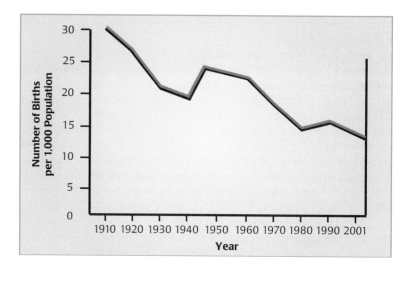

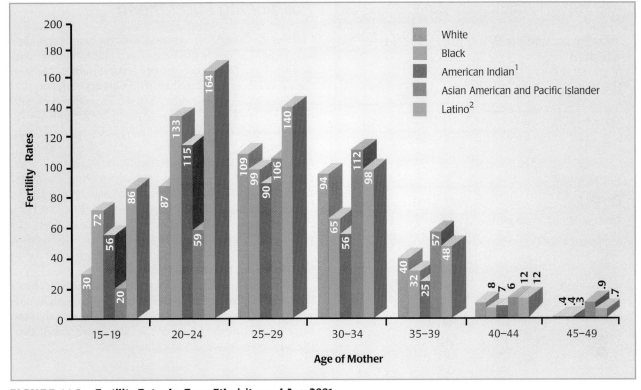

FIGURE 11.3 **Fertility Rates by Race, Ethnicity, and Age, 2001**

NOTE: [1]Includes births of Aleuts and Eskimos

[2]May be of any race

SOURCE: Based on Hamilton et al., 2003. Tables 1 and 2.

more likely to delay childbearing and to have few children over their lifetimes (Robinson and Frank, 1994; Trent, 1994).

Sexual Practices Young Latinos and African Americans typically begin sexual activities earlier than their white counterparts, and they have more partners (see Chapter 7). As you will see later in this chapter, some African American youth have babies purposely to fill emotional voids in their lives. Compared with white communities, black communities also tend to be more accepting of out-of-wedlock births and more likely to reject abortion.

Comparisons with Other Countries

In Milan, Italy, a 41-year-old fashion magazine consultant says that having children "has never been at the top of my list. It's never been in the top 200 things." Another Italian woman, 32, who is part of a two-career married couple, has a 3-year-old son and doesn't plan to have more children. She enjoys spending time with

her son, adding, "It doesn't make sense to have three children just to tuck them in at night" (Bruni, 2002).

These women are similar to many others around the world who are planning to have no children or very few. According to demographers, a country needs a 2.1 TFR to replenish the population by replacing those who die. Many countries are well below this rate, including some less developed countries such as the Ukraine, Russia, Poland, China, and Thailand (see *Table 11.1* on page 300).

As birth rates fall, some governments express concern about future labor pools. Some countries, such as Japan, are considering publicly funding fertility treatments and matchmaker services to increase the birth rate (Coeyman, 2002; "Japanese birth rate drops . . .," 2003). Other counties, such as Spain, are considering decreasing the cost of utility bills for large families, helping young couples buy homes, and creating hundreds of thousands of new preschools and nursery schools to accommodate working parents (Bruni, 2002).

In contrast, some countries have high TFRs: 6.4 in central Africa, 3.8 in the Middle East (which includes Israel and Arab countries), and 3.0 in Central America (which includes Mexico and Honduras) (Haub, 2003). The TFR

TABLE 11.1

Women around the World Are Having Fewer Children

Country	Children Born per Woman*
Ukraine	1.1
Greece, Spain	1.2
Germany, Italy, Japan, South Korea, Poland, Russia	1.3
Canada	1.5
Sweden, United Kingdom	1.6
Australia, China, Thailand	1.7
France	1.9
United States	2.0

*This is the total fertility rate (TFR), or the average total number of children born per woman given current birth rates.

SOURCE: Based on Haub, 2003.

of the United States is higher than in at least 70 other countries, however, and not just those in *Table 11.1*.

The reasons for the plunging birth rates in many countries are similar to those in the United States: More women are studying longer, working, and then marrying later, which doesn't necessarily include having a baby. Men are equally likely to postpone marriage and children because finding and keeping a job is unpredictable.

MAKING CONNECTIONS

■ If you don't have children, do you plan to have them in the future? If no, why not? If yes, at what age? And how many?

■ If you're a parent, what have been the major benefits and costs of having children?

■ Look back at *Figure 11.3*. How would you explain the high fertility rates of Latinas ages 20 to 24? Why do you think that the fertility rates of black women ages 30 and over are generally lower than those of most other groups? How might you explain the much higher fertility rates of Asian and Pacific Islander women after age 29?

Postponing Parenthood

"Babies vs. Career!" That was the cover of a recent *Time* magazine. The cover story expressed alarm that so many women have put careers before having babies. Most of the article discussed fertility problems and implied that childless women (not men) are selfish and too career-oriented (see Gibbs, 2002).

Although it is still typical for an American woman to have her first child before age 30, the numbers of first-time older mothers are rising. In the early 1970s, only 4 percent of American women having their first babies were 30 or older (Ventura, Martin, et al., 2000). In 2001, the numbers of women who had their first baby in their thirties and forties increased substantially: 25 percent for women aged 30 to 34, 36 percent for women aged 35 to 39, and 70 percent for women aged 40 to 44 (Hamilton et al., 2003).

Thus, despite *Time*'s sensationalistic coverage, most women are postponing parenthood rather than avoiding it. We'll look at childlessness later in the chapter. Here we'll consider some of the characteristics of people who postpone having children.

Reasons for Postponing Parenthood

Both micro-level and macro-level factors affect our decision to postpone parenthood. You'll notice as you read this section that women are usually much more likely than men to feel constrained in deciding whether and when to have children.

Micro-Level Factors Being single, you recall, has many attractions, including independence, the opportunity to develop a career, and more time for fun (see Chapter 9). There are similar individual-level reasons for postponing parenthood:

■ Daunting jobs and careers discourage meeting prospective mates (see Chapter 8).

■ Many single women don't want to conceive or adopt a child on their own. According to a 43-year-old woman whose mother raised her and her siblings, "The hardest thing you can be is a single, working mom" (Peterson, 2002: 2D).

■ Many couples don't want nannies or child-care centers to raise their children. Therefore, they delay having children until they feel that one of them (usually the wife) can afford to be a stay-at-home parent.

■ Both women and men want to build equity in homes, put some money aside, and save for retirement before having children (Poniewozik, 2002).

■ Women who feel valued at work, enjoy making a contribution, and need the money to boost their husbands' salaries are reluctant to give up their jobs for childbearing and child rearing or to struggle with balancing domestic and paid work (see Chapter 13).

Macro-level Factors

On the macro level, economic and reproductive factors seem to play the biggest role in postponing parenthood:

■ Because of economic recessions and high unemployment rates, many young men don't have the resources to start a family (see Chapter 10).

■ Young married couples living with their parents may postpone childbearing because they are reluctant to make already crowded living conditions even worse (see Chapter 10).

■ Disturbed by the current high rates of divorce, some young couples are apprehensive about their own chances of marital success and delay parenthood until they feel confident the marriage will work (see Chapter 15).

■ Many people believe that a woman today can conceive a child at almost any age. The advances in reproductive technology have reduced many women's concerns about biological clocks and finding mates.

■ Women and men are delaying childbearing because the United States—especially compared with many European countries—has abysmal family leave policies, no national child care programs, and rigid work schedules, particularly for women in middle- and low-level jobs (see Chapter 13).

One of the major reasons for many women's delaying having children is because the "best" years of childbearing (when women are young) also coincide with the best years for establishing careers. A woman who starts having babies at age 25, for example, will have a difficult time competing with younger men and women 10 or 20 years later. According to a fashion designer, 33, who dropped her X-Girl clothing line after having her son when she was 26, "How can you come back at 36 or 37 and say, 'I'm here, guys—snap, snap, let me start another line of hip-hop clothing'?" (Poniewozik, 2002: 58).

Many of the high-achieving women at age 40 and older may still bear their own children. Others will have to turn to adoption and reproductive technologies. Like most other options in life, being an older parent has both benefits and costs.

Chris Britt-Copley News Service © 1997

Characteristics of Older Parents

According to a recent national survey, 41 percent of Americans felt that fatherhood after age 60 was "inappropriate" ("Fatherhood after age 60?" 2002). There has been no comparable survey for motherhood after age 60, presumably because most people expect that by then women will be grandmothers, not mothers. Despite such sexist attitudes, both men and women experience advantages and disadvantages as older parents.

Advantages

Compared with younger mothers, older mothers are more likely to be white, married, and highly educated. Moreover, they tend to work in professional occupations and to have high family incomes (Bachu, 1993). Higher incomes decrease stress because the family has more resources in raising a child.

Older mothers tend to feel more self-assured, more ready for responsibility, and better prepared for parenthood than younger women. Younger mothers sometimes feel trapped by having a baby because they still want to party, go out with friends, and have a good time (Maynard, 1997).

Men who postpone parenthood usually enjoy more advantages and have fewer constraints than women. Most men do not face sex discrimination in the workplace, they earn higher salaries, and they have better health benefits. Therefore, they are less likely to worry about not having the resources to raise children later in life. With fewer economic concerns, men remarry more often and sometimes, after a divorce, support children from two families (see Chapter 16). Also, because their careers are more established, older fathers may have more flexibility to spend their nonwork hours and weekends with their families.

Disadvantages Although older parents may be more patient, mature, and financially secure, there are some distinct drawbacks to deferred parenthood. Pregnant women in their forties have a greater risk of having a baby with Down's syndrome than pregnant women in their thirties. Even beyond health risks, there are some practical liabilities in becoming a parent at age 49:

> *At 52, you'd be coming out of the "terrible twos" and hosting play groups for toddlers. As you turned 55, your child would start kindergarten and you'd qualify for dual memberships in the PTA and the American Association of Retired Persons (AARP). At 60, you and your spouse would be coaching soccer. . . . By the time you hit 70, you'd be buried under college tuition bills. And if your child delayed marriage and family like you did, you might be paying for a wedding when you were 80 and babysitting for your grandchildren at 90 (Wright, 1997: E5).*

A 16-year-old daughter of an almost 60-year-old mother feels that the "huge generation gap" has led to greater conflict because of their different attitudes and values ("How late is too late?" 2001). Furthermore, some women who have waited to have children find that it is too late to have as many children as they wanted.

Mature mothers, especially those who have risen to powerful but demanding executive positions, may feel especially guilty about splitting their time between their families and their employers and "cheating" both (see Chapter 13). Finally, postponing parenthood may mean that parents will never get to see their grandchildren.

You see, then, that there are many reasons for postponing childbearing—especially for women who seek more options in education and jobs. However, millions of Americans have fewer choices because they are infertile.

Infertility and Childlessness

Infertility is generally defined as the inability to conceive a baby after 12 months of unprotected sex. Infertility affects about 15 percent of all couples of reproductive age. Although infertility rates have been fairly stable since the mid-1960s, the likelihood of infertility increases as people delay childbearing. For example, the rate of infertility for couples between ages 30 and 34 years is more than 50 percent greater than for those between ages 25 and 29 (Mosher and Pratt, 1991).

There are many reasons for infertility, and the reactions are typically agonizing. First, let's look at some of the reasons for infertility.

Reasons for Infertility

Infertility is attributable about equally to problems in males and females; each sex independently accounts for about 40 percent of cases. Approximately 20 percent of infertile couples are diagnosed as having *idiopathic infertility*. In plain language, this means that doctors simply don't know what's wrong.

Until recently, most infertility research focused almost exclusively on women. For years people believed that the major reason for female infertility was aging. Although it is true that our reproductive organs age faster than other parts of our body, the notion that infertility is a "woman's curse" is both simplistic and uninformed. Either sex can be infertile.

Female Infertility The two major causes of female infertility are failure to ovulate and blockage of the fallopian tubes. A woman's failure to *ovulate*, or to produce a viable egg each month, may have a number of causes, among them poor nutrition, chronic illness, and drug abuse. Very occasionally, the lack of ovulation may be attributed to psychological stress (Masters et al., 1992).

The *fallopian tubes* carry the egg—whether or not it has been fertilized by sperm—from the ovaries to the uterus. The fallopian tubes can be blocked by scarring caused by **pelvic inflammatory disease (PID)**, an infection of the uterus that spreads to the tubes, the ovaries, and surrounding tissues. PID, in turn, is often caused by sexually transmitted diseases such as chlamydia.

Chlamydia, a bacterial infection often called "the silent epidemic" because it exhibits no symptoms in 75 percent of women and 33 percent of men, is a rapidly rising cause of PID. Once diagnosed, this infection is easily cured with antibiotics (see Chapter 7 and *Appendix E* for more information about sexually transmitted diseases).

Another major reason for women's infertility is **endometriosis,** a condition in which the tissue that forms in the endometrium (the lining of the uterus) spreads outside the womb and attaches itself to other pelvic organs, such as the ovaries or the fallopian tubes. Although the cause of endometriosis is still unknown, some researchers believe that women with endometriosis have certain malfunctioning genes that prevent an embryo from attaching to the uterine wall (Kao et al., 2003). Endometriosis can lead to PID, uterine tumors, and blockage of the opening to the uterus. *Table 11.2* summarizes the major reasons for women's infertility.

Male Infertility Male infertility often results from "sluggish" sperm or a low sperm count. Since 1938 sperm counts of men in the United States and 20 other countries have plunged by an average of 50 percent (Swan et al., 1997).

Chemical pollutants might play a major role in male infertility. For years men have been more likely than women to work in environments in which they come in contact with toxic chemicals or are exposed to other hazardous conditions.

Some scientists believe that the risks of infertility from these sources are high. *Table 11.3* on page 304 presents some known or suspected substances and conditions affecting male reproduction.

Other possible causes of low sperm counts include injury to the testicles or scrotum, infections such as mumps in adulthood, testicular varicose veins that impede sperm development, undescended testes (the testes in the male fetus normally descend from the abdominal cavity into the scrotum in about the eighth month of prenatal development), endocrine disorders, and excessive consumption of alcohol, tobacco, marijuana, narcotic drugs, or even some prescription medications.

There is also some evidence that long-distance bicycle riding or tight-fitting underwear can lower sperm counts. Spending hours on a bike saddle with a high "nose" can create enough pressure on the perineum (the area between the anus and the pubic bone) to damage the artery—sometimes permanently—that supplies blood to the penis. Although such evidence is still preliminary, physicians advise bicyclists who experience genital numbness to consult a doctor (Schrader et al., 2002).

Prolonged and frequent use of saunas, hot tubs, and steam baths may also have a negative effect because sperm production is sensitive to temperature. Male infertility can also result from such problems as an inability to ejaculate, ejaculation only outside the vagina, or inability to achieve or maintain an erection (Masters et al., 1992).

Sperm quality and the speed at which sperm travel toward an egg also decline in men over 50 (Marcus, 2003). In this sense, men may also have a "biological clock" that decreases their fertility as they age.

Reactions to Infertility

Although people respond to infertility in a number of ways, most couples are devastated by it. In most societies, including the United States, two procreative cultural norms dominate. One is that all married couples *should* reproduce; the other is that all married couples *should want to* reproduce (Veevers, 1980).

For many women, then, infertility becomes "an acute and unanticipated life crisis" that is characterized by stigma, grief, guilt, and a sense of violation. As one woman said, "It's a slap in the face. I feel like I'm isolated in a prison . . . no one understands how horrible this is" (Whiteford and Gonzalez, 1995: 29).

TABLE 11.2	
Possible Causes of Female Infertility	
Behavior or Clinical Sign	**Possible Causes**
Failure to ovulate	Poor nutrition, drug abuse, chronic illness, or (rarely) psychological stress
Blockage of fallopian tubes	Pelvic inflammatory disease (PID) resulting from infection with sexually transmitted bacteria or microorganisms
Endometriosis	Migration of uterine tissue outside the uterus, resulting in fallopian tube blockage
Scarring, adhesions, and cysts around ovaries and fallopian tubes	Sexually transmitted diseases (STDs) and PID
Impenetrable cervical mucus	Mucus from the lower portion of the uterus is too thick for sperm to penetrate or has an acid alkaline level that is harmful to sperm
Excessive exercise or rapid weight loss	Production of reproductive hormones may be compromised by loss of body fat
Regular use of vaginal douches and deodorants	Products may contain chemicals that kill sperm or inhibit their movement

SOURCES: Fogel and Woods, 1995; DeLisle, 1997.

Ending generational continuity may reinforce a woman's feelings of being a "failure" when she doesn't conceive:

> My husband is Italian and for the 10 years that we've been married, I have known that his having a son has been so important to him, and my not being able to deliver has been a real difficult thing for me to deal with. . . . My mother-in-law has been pushing for a grandchild since the day we got married (Whiteford and Gonzalez, 1995: 34).

Although well intentioned, potential grandparents' expectations exert pressure to carry on the family line. As the mother of one infertile woman asked, "Do you think that I will have a grandchild before I die?" (Daly, 1999: 18).

Many women, concerned that people will see them in a new and damaging light, engage in "information management" (Goffman, 1963). They may avoid the

TABLE 11.3	
Some Chemical and Environmental Factors Affecting Male Infertility	
Risk Factors	**Effects**
Lead, used in making storage batteries and paints	Fewer sperm, sperm that move more slowly than normal, and more abnormally shaped sperm
Ionizing radiation, found in nuclear plants and medical facilities, and nonionizing radiation in high-voltage switchyards and communication facilities	Possible damage to sperm cells and lowered fertility
Anesthetic gases	Unexposed female partners may have higher than normal number of miscarriages
Vinyl chloride, used in plastic manufacturing	Unexposed female partners may have more miscarriages and stillbirths
Pesticides like kepone and carbon disulfide, used in the manufacture of viscose rayon and as a fumigant	Possible loss of sex drive, impotence, abnormal sperm, lowered sperm count
Heat stress, found in foundries, smelters, bakeries, and farm work	Lowered sperm counts and sterility
Estrogen, used in the manufacture of oral contraceptives	Possible loss of sex drive, abnormal sperm, lowered sperm counts
Methylene chloride, used as a solvent in paint strippers	Possible very low sperm counts and shrunken testicles
Ethylene dibromide, used as an ingredient in leaded gasoline and as a fumigant of tropical fruit for export	Possible lower sperm count and decreased fertility in wives of workers

Source: Based on Kenen, 1993: 40–41.

topic whenever possible, or they may attribute the problem to a disease like diabetes or kidney trouble, taking the focus off specific reproductive disorders.

Because male infertility may be considered a defect in one's masculinity, women often accept the responsibility for infertility themselves:

> When I tell them we can't have children, I generally try to leave the impression that it's me. I may mutter "tubes you know" or "faulty plumbing" (Miall, 1986: 36).

Still other women disclose their infertility because they fear they will be considered self-centered for not having children:

> I know at one point I overheard someone saying, "Oh, they're too selfish, they're too interested in going on fancy holidays. Material things, that's why they're not having children." It was so untrue and it hurt (Miall, 1986: 37).

For many couples, infertility is socially isolating. As one woman remarked, "I feel sometimes like we're the only ones in the world who have this [problem]!" (Daly, 1999: 19).

Some infertile couples, however, enjoy vicarious parenthood through contact with the children of relatives and friends. Others become increasingly involved in work-related activities and even begin to regard their childlessness as advantageous.

Some couples accept infertility as a fact of life and remain childless. A much larger group tries to adopt.

MAKING CONNECTIONS

■ What are some of the advantages and disadvantages of having children when you're younger (during your twenties, for example) rather than when you're older?

■ Are people's reasons—especially women's—for postponing having children valid? Or are they being selfish and self-centered in delaying childbearing?

■ As *Table 11.1* shows, the United States has the highest fertility rate among developed countries. Why, then, do people often criticize married couples who don't have children?

Adoption: The Traditional Solution to Infertility

At one time, 80 percent of U.S. babies born out of wedlock were given up for adoption. This rate has dropped to about 2 or 3 percent. Being an unmarried parent no longer bears the stigma it used to (see Chapters 7 and 9). Therefore, many unwed mothers are keeping their babies instead of putting them up for adoption. How many children are adopted?

Prevalence of Adoption

An estimated 2.1 million children in the United States live with adoptive parents. Of these, nearly 18,000 are foreign-born children. The Census Bureau collected data on adopted children for the first time in 2000 but didn't differentiate between U.S.-born children who were adopted as stepchildren, informally by relatives (most common among Latinos), or through private or public adoptions (Kreider, 2003).

About 8 percent of all children in the United States live with adoptive parents (Kreider, 2003). However, adoption touches many more lives. A recent survey estimates that 65 percent of Americans have experience with adoption through their own family or friends (*National Adoption Attitudes Survey*, 2002; National Adoption Information Clearinghouse, 2002).

Furthermore, 4 in 10 Americans say they have considered adopting a child (Fetto, 2002). Those who want to adopt have several avenues for doing so.

Types of Adoption

There are several types of adoption in the United States:

- In *public adoptions*, government-operated agencies place children in the public child welfare system in permanent homes.

- In *private adoptions*, a private agency (nonprofit or profit) places children in nonrelatives' homes. In nonagency private adoptions, children are placed in nonrelatives' homes by birth parents or "facilitators" (such as medical doctors, members of the clergy, or attorneys).

- In *kinship adoptions*, children are placed in relatives' homes with or without services of a public agency.

- In *stepparent adoptions*, children are adopted by the spouse of one birth parent.

- In *transracial* or *transcultural adoption*, a child who is of one racial or ethnic group is placed with adoptive parents of another racial or ethnic group.

- In *international adoptions*, children who are citizens of another nation are adopted by U.S. families and brought to the United States.

Of the 560,000 foster children nationwide, at least 122,000 are eligible for adoption because the biological parents are dead or missing, have been found unfit, or have legally surrendered their rights to their children ("*Child welfare outcomes . . .,*" 2000). Many of these children are hard to place, however, because they are sick, physically handicapped, biracial, nonwhite, emotionally disturbed, or "too old."

The Adoption Triad

Adoption affects each member of a triad: The adoptee, the birth parents, and the adoptive parents. The adoptee, especially when not an infant, must adjust to a new environment and develop a personal identity. Birth parents may experience ambivalence about placing the child for adoption. Adoptive parents also face challenges that include ensuring the child's physical and emotional well-being and the possibility of maintaining contact with the birth parent throughout the child's life.

Whether we arrive by birth or adoption, none of us choose our families. Adoptive families, however, often experience "intrusions" that biological parents don't face (Melosh, 2002). Some of the most controversial issues include the rights of biological fathers, transracial adoptions, and open adoptions. There are also some misgivings about adoptions by same-sex partners and international adoptions.

The Rights of Biological Fathers

One controversial issue is the nature and extent of the rights of biological fathers. For years, fathers of out-of-wedlock children were rarely involved in adoptions. In 1994, however, in a highly publicized case, the Illinois Supreme Court ruled that a 3-year-old boy known as "Baby Richard" be returned to his biological parents. Three years later, the biological father moved out, leaving "Baby Richard" in the mother's care.

This case and others expanded the rights of biological fathers in contested adoptions and raised concerns among adoption advocates that such rulings may undermine the legitimacy of the adoption system. If biological parents change their minds after a child is adopted, adoptive parents must fight for the child in court.

Transracial Adoption

Another controversial issue is transracial adoptions. Advocates of transracial adoption claim that many African American or biracial children, especially those

The use of fertility drugs—especially among white, educated, middle-class women—has resulted in multiple births, including quintuplets.

Medical and High-Tech Solutions to Infertility

With the growth of genetic research, our ability to alter the course of nature has expanded greatly. These new technologies have generated some difficult questions. Some are medical, involving the health of mother and baby. Some are legal, involving issues of custody and inheritance. And others are ethical. Before examining these issues, let's look at the most common medical and high-tech treatments for infertility.

Medical Treatments for Infertility

Medical treatments include *artificial insemination* and *fertility drugs*. Artificial insemination is the most common treatment for men with low sperm counts. Fertility drugs improve the chance of conception in infertile women.

Artificial Insemination Artificial insemination, sometimes called *donor insemination (DI)*, is a medical procedure in which semen is introduced artificially into the vagina or uterus about the time of ovulation. The semen, taken from the woman's husband or from a donor, may be fresh or it may have been frozen. Artificial insemination was first performed successfully in the 1970s and was followed by a normal pregnancy and birth. The current success rate is close to 20 percent (King, 2002).

For single women, artificial insemination offers a means of having children without waiting for Mr. Right. Some single women turn to artificial insemination because their partner has a serious hereditary disease. Other women prefer the mutual anonymity between the recipient and the donor to avoid legal and emotional complications after the baby's birth. It also offers lesbians a way of conceiving a child without having to be sexually intimate with a man. Moreover, some couples prefer artificial insemination to adoption because the woman wants to experience a pregnancy and birth, or one or both parents want to contribute to the child's genetic makeup (Daniels, 1994).

Artificial insemination has its drawbacks. Sperm banks that freeze sperm for later use can make mistakes. In 1990, for example, a white couple sued a Manhattan sperm bank after giving birth to a black baby. In other cases, there have been accusations that one donor has been used for as many as 15 pregnancies. If the donor remains anonymous, two people might meet and mate not knowing that they share the same genetic father.

There are also emotional problems associated with artificial insemination. For example, although many lesbians purposely distance themselves from information about the donor fathers, the children may eventually seek information about their biological fathers. For instance, a young woman, age 19, who was conceived by donor insemination, feels frustrated because she has no idea of her father's biological roots: "With no records available, half my heritage is erased. I'll never know whose eyes I have inherited. I've searched family photo albums to no avail" (M. R. Brown, 1994:12).

Fertility Drugs If a woman is having problems becoming pregnant because she is not having regular menstrual cycles, and eggs are not being released, her physician will try **fertility drugs**, medications that stimulate ovaries to produce eggs. In 1997, a couple from Carlisle, Iowa, became the parents of the first septuplets ever born alive in the United States and the only known living ones in the world. The mother had been taking a fertility drug, Pergonal. For religious reasons, the couple refused to undergo a process known as *selective reduction*: aborting some of the fetuses to give the others a better chance to develop fully. An estimated two-thirds of triplets, quadruplets, and quintuplets are the result of increased use of fertility-enhancing drugs or a combination of drugs and other reproductive technologies (Ventura, Martin, et al., 2000).

Fertility drugs have a high success rate: 50 to 70 percent. A major concern, however, is that multiple births increase the chances of babies being born prematurely and of having low birth weight. As a result, the babies may end up with major health problems and lifelong learning disabilities (Elster et al., 2000).

High-Tech Treatments for Infertility

The infertile couple also has many more options for having a child than before through **assisted reproductive technology (ART)**, a general term that includes all treatments or procedures involving the handling of human eggs and sperm to establish a pregnancy. The Centers for Disease Control and Prevention (CDC) estimates that ART accounts for almost 1 percent of all U.S. births (*2000 Assisted Reproductive Technology . . .*, 2002).

Many ART techniques are risky, and success rates are modest at best. The most common is in vitro fertilization.

In Vitro Fertilization In vitro fertilization (IVF) involves surgically removing eggs from a woman's ovaries, fertilizing them in a petri dish (a specially shaped glass container) with sperm from her husband or another donor, and then transferring the resulting embryos into the woman's uterus. (An *embryo* is the developing organism up to the eighth week of pregnancy.)

Louise Brown, the first in vitro baby (*in vitro* is Latin for "in glass") was born in England in 1978 and celebrated her 25th birthday in 2003. IVF is an outpatient procedure conducted at nearly 400 clinics in the United States alone. More than 1 million children worldwide owe their births to this procedure (Mestel, 2003). *Table 11.5* describes three recent variations of IVF.

- **GIFT (gamete intrafallopian transfer)** involves using a fiber-optic instrument called a laparoscope to guide the transfer of unfertilized eggs and sperm (gametes) into the women's fallopian tubes through small incisions in her abdomen.

- **ZIFT (zygote intrafallopian transfer)** involves fertilizing a woman's eggs in the laboratory and then using a laparoscope to guide the transfer of the fertilized eggs (zygotes) into her fallopian tubes.

- **ICSI (intracytoplasmic sperm injection)** involves the injection of a single sperm directly into the egg using a needle.

ART is often categorized according to whether the procedure uses a woman's own eggs (nondonor) or eggs from another woman (donor) and according to whether

---

TABLE 11.5

Comparing Assisted Reproductive Technology Methods

Method	How It Works	First Successful in Humans	Cost per Cycle*	Success Rate
In vitro fertilization (IVF)	An egg and sperm are combined in a laboratory dish. If the egg is fertilized, the resulting embryo is transferred into the woman's uterus.	1978 (England)	$10,000	30%
Gamete intrafallopian transfer (GIFT)	Using a laparoscope, a doctor inserts eggs and sperm directly into a woman's fallopian tube through small incisions in her abdomen. Any resulting embryo floats into the uterus.	1984 (U.S.)	$6000 to $10,000	30%
Zygote intrafallopian transfer (ZIFT)	Eggs are fertilized in the laboratory, and resulting zygotes (fertilized eggs) are transferred to the woman's fallopian tubes.	1989 (Belgium)	$8000 to $10,000	28%
Intracytoplasmic sperm injection (ICSI)	Using a microscopic pipette, a doctor injects a single sperm into an egg.	1992 (Belgium)	$10,000 to $12,000	29%

*A cycle is the entire period of treatment, from the initial administration of ovulation-inducing drugs to harvesting eggs (or obtaining donor eggs), fertilizing them, and finally reimplanting them and monitoring the result. Typically, a complete cycle lasts about six weeks.

SOURCES: Centers for Disease Control and Prevention, 1997; Grady, 1996; *2000 Assisted Reproductive Technology . . .*, 2002; Mestel, 2003.

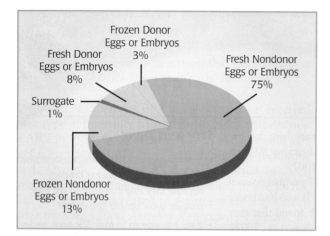

FIGURE 11.4 **Types of ART Procedures Used in the United States, 2000** In 2000, there were 99,639 ART cycles (see the definition of cycle in the text and *Table 11.5*). As this figure shows, most of the cycles (75 percent) used fresh embryos developed from a couple's own egg and sperm. In all of the fresh, nondonor cycles, .07 percent were GIFT, 1 percent were ZIFT, and 46 percent used ICSI.

SOURCE: *2000 Assisted reproductive technology success rates . . .,* 2002, Figures 2 and 25.

Two diagnostic procedures that have become fairly common are amniocentesis and chorionic villus sampling. In **amniocentesis**, performed in the twentieth week of pregnancy, a needle is inserted through the abdomen into the amniotic sac, and the fluid withdrawn is analyzed for such abnormalities as Down's syndrome and spina bifida (an abnormal opening along the spine).

The same information can be produced at ten weeks by **chorionic villus sampling (CVS)**, in which a catheter inserted through the vagina is used to remove some of the villi (fingerlike protrusions) from the chorion (the outer membrane that surrounds the amniotic sac). The chief advantage of detecting abnormalities early is that if parents decide on an abortion, they can use a simpler technique. Both of these tests have risks, although low (about 1 to 2 percent of all cases), of spontaneous abortions and possible deformities (Boodman, 1992).

Besides detecting prenatal abnormalities, genetic engineering produces children who are usually as healthy as children born naturally. Studies of IVF families have found that the mothers tend to be more protective of their children but that parents of children conceived by assisted reproduction "appear to have good relationships with their children, even in families in which one parent lacks a genetic link with the child" (Golombok, 2002: 355).

The Risks of Genetic Engineering As you saw earlier, medical treatments for infertility are limited to affluent couples because the procedures are expensive. In this sense, genetic engineering is a resource that only the rich can afford. In one case, for example, a low-income Washington, D.C., couple sold their new truck to pay for a round of in vitro fertilization (Mundy, 2003).

There is also concern about such issues as parents' and scientists' right to "manufacture" babies, creating "designer babies" by choosing genes for a child's hair color and height, parents' right to reject imperfect fetuses, and the rights of both parents and embryos. Suppose both parents of a fertilized egg that has been frozen and held for future use die. Who is responsible for the frozen embryo? Should it be destroyed because the parents are dead? Given to relatives? Placed for adoption? Turned over to doctors for medical research?

Since the birth of the Iowa septuplets in 1997, many fertility experts have become critical of physicians who don't limit the number of embryos implanted during IVF to three or four because "the human uterus is not meant to carry litters" (Cowley and Springen, 1997: 66). Triplets, quadruplets, and quintuplets are 12 times more likely than other babies to die within a year. Many suffer from respiratory and digestive problems. They're also prone to a range of neurological disorders, including blindness, cerebral palsy, and mental retardation. At age 2, three of the Iowa septuplets were suffering serious health problems that included several forms of cerebral palsy, digestive problems that necessitated feeding of high-calorie formula through tubes in the toddlers' stomachs, and an inability to walk or sit up without help ("McCaughey septuplets . . .," 1999). One reporter describes the children, at age 5, as "thriving," but all are developmentally delayed compared to other five-year-olds. Two have cerebral palsy and wear leg braces and one of these children has serious vision problems (Curry, 2002).

In 1999, in the first known birth of its kind in the United States, a California woman had a baby using sperm retrieved from her husband 30 hours after he died unexpectedly of an allergic reaction. The reproductive specialist who extracted the sperm cells did so to allay the family's stress and grief. Medical ethicists wondered whether it's appropriate to bring a child into this world whose father is dead ("Woman gives birth . . .," 1999).

Some parents conceive children primarily to use the tissue from the umbilical cord to provide life-saving cells for a sick sibling. They might certainly love the new baby as much as the other children. The question is whether it's ethical to bear babies primarily so that their tissue can be used to help other children in the family.

Finally, how many parents can a baby have? If lesbian moms split up, for example, who can establish parenthood rights: the sperm donor, the egg donor, the mother who bears the child, or all three people? And who are the parents of a child who has a sperm donor, an egg donor, a surrogate mother, and a stepparent who adopts the child?

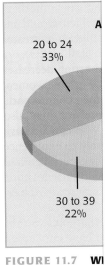

FIGURE 11.7 WI

*Other includes Asian/F

Source: Based on Finer

Incidence of A

In 2000, 1.3 millio
terminated pregna
or the number of
to 44, increased s
1980s and has dec
remained at 17 si
geographically, hc
trict of Columbia
et al., 2002; Finer

Characteristic Abortions

Abortion is mos
young (in their 2(
11.7). Proportio
women are almo
racial-ethnic grou
reflect socioeconc
example, women
$15,000 are four
women with fami
ner, 1998). Many
end an unintende
personal or religi
About 25
women who are c
up only about 1(
(Finer and Hensh
risk of unintende

MAKING CONNECTIONS

■ As you saw earlier in the chapter, there are thousands of U.S.-born children languishing in foster homes. Should our government forbid international adoptions until these children have been adopted?

■ Some scientists believe that all infertility problems can be treated within a decade, especially if researchers can use embryonic stem cells to reconstruct the equivalent of sperm and eggs. How do you feel about such research?

Having Children Outside Marriage

A few years ago, a Wisconsin Supreme Court judge "banned" a father of nine who owes child support from having more children unless he proves he will support all his offspring. The man has four sons and five daughters, ages 3 to 16, with four women. The judge said the man would go to prison if he had any more children

while on probation and refused to pay child support (Price, 2001).

It's not clear how the judge can enforce this ruling, especially if the man moves to another state. It was an unusual decision, however, because we typically associate having children outside marriage with women, not men. As a result, almost all of the research and data focus on female rather than male out-of-wedlock births and their consequences. We begin with a general description of nonmarital childbearing and then consider some differences between older single mothers and teens.

Characteristics of Nonmarital Childbearing

In 1950, about 3 percent of all births were to unmarried women. This percentage has increased steadily over the past 50 years. By 2001, there were 1.3 million births to unmarried women, accounting for a third of all births in the United States. Since 1991, the percentage of nonmarital births has increased, but at a slower pace than in earlier decades ("Births to unmarried women . . .," 2003). Thus, nonmarital childbearing shows little evidence of subsiding.

Why has the rate of out-of-wedlock births increased? The reasons encompass a multitude of decisions and complex processes that stretch across a person's lifetime.

So What's Next? Pregnant Men?

In the movie *Junior,* a scientist loses funding for his research and implants a fertilized egg in his own body to test a wonder drug that ensures healthy pregnancies.

In real life, there are some minor problems. Men don't produce the appropriate hormones. Men don't have ovaries and therefore don't produce eggs. And they don't have wombs.

However, hormones can be supplied by injection. And perhaps wombs may not be totally necessary. Abdominal pregnancies—those occurring outside the womb—are rare, but they do happen about once in every 10,000 pregnancies.

An abdominal pregnancy may occur when the placenta, which is produced partly by the fetus, attaches to something other than the womb. In August 1979, for

example, George Poretta attempted to perform an appendectomy on a Michigan woman suffering from stomach cramps. "I opened her up expecting to find an appendix," Poretta said, "and there was this tiny foot." The baby, a boy, weighed 3 pounds 5 ounces (Teresi, 1994: 55).

Both male and female abdomens offer a similar environment for impregnation, including a membrane, called the omentum, that encloses abdominal organs in which, theoretically, a fertilized egg could become implanted. Thus, fertilizing an egg in vitro and inserting the developing embryo through a small incision in the abdominal cavity could produce a male pregnancy (Peritz, 2003).

Scientists have recently turned stem cells from both female and male mice into

eggs (Hübner et al., 2003). This research suggests that even men might have the biological capacity to make eggs. If so, could a man become a child's biological mother, blurring the biological line between male and female reproduction?

STOP AND THINK . . .

• Should we continue to develop technology that will allow men to become pregnant and deliver babies? Or is such research a sci-fi nightmare?

• One of the advantages of creating human eggs, and using the same process that researchers use to create mouse eggs, is that there would be no need for donors. What are some possible disadvantages?

Unmarriec

Although tee
as you saw e
Digest"). Bet
birth rate for
by nearly 28
decreases var
ever. Birth ra
for white wor
significantly f
70), and incr
to 67) (Marti

**Why Has the
creased?** Tl
crease in nor
surveys indica
ally active, an
to use contrac

Some con
pro-abstinenc
seling, and can
some of the r
(Shatzkin, 19
Others feel th
traceptives and
is the preventi
ical, or chemi
most commor
effectiveness, a

Another fa
in the 1990s. A
able, some tee
(Ventura, Curt
cation researcl
tion program i
is providing te
believe that th
have opportun

Although i
many scholars
cerned. The nu
trialized natior
they are, most u
and maturity t

Adolescents a
tionally have
needs. "Babies
status, of pass
woman" (Ande
This pseudo-ac
sibilities and st
completely inc
parents often s

to another state, she has little choice except to bear an unwanted or unplanned baby. In addition, fewer hospitals offer abortion services or include such training during the obstetrics residency program for young physicians. As a result, fewer new physicians are skilled in performing abortions. Some seek such experience at local clinics, but many don't because they fear being picketed at home or even murdered by extreme antiabortion groups (Goldstein, 1998).

Laws and Policies Some states have cut or limited funds for clinics in low-income urban areas, and dozens of states have cut Medicaid funding for abortions. Teenagers in many states must get approval from a parent, judge, or counselor before seeking an abortion. In some cases, anti-abortion judges grill girls and their physicians for hours before granting permission for an abortion (Holmes, 2003).

You saw in Chapter 7 that the federal government and many states are pouring money into abstinence-only sex education rather than programs that provide information about contraception. The Bush administration is also funding crisis pregnancy centers (CPCs). The CPC staff—usually volunteers with no professional training—try to discourage girls and women from abortion by exaggerating the risks: "linking abortion to breast cancer and depression, playing gruesome videos depicting bloody fetuses, withholding pregnancy-test results, and even pressuring her to sign adoption papers" (Kashef, 2003: 18).

There are an estimated 4000 CPCs nationwide. Louisiana recently authorized $1.5 million for CPCs, Delaware granted $39,000 to a single center, and Florida has raised $1.3 million for CPCs through sales of "Choose Life" license plates. In other states, such as Pennsylvania, lawmakers gave $5 million to agencies that provide "alternatives to abortion" but withheld family-planning funds from facilities that provide abortion services (Kashef, 2003: 19).

MAKING CONNECTIONS

■ Do you consider yourself pro-choice or pro-life? What are the reasons for your position?

■ Do children have a right *not* to be born if the parents know the child will be severely disabled? Are parents irresponsible by not aborting a child who will always depend on others for care or die at an early age? ◯◯

Childless by Choice

Just as some couples make a conscious decision to have a child, others decide not to have children. The desire to have children is not universal. According to a 1990 nationwide survey, 4 percent of respondents said that they did not have children, did not want them, or were glad they had none (Gallup and Newport, 1990). The percentage of women still childless at ages 40 to 44 (most of whom subsequently remain childless) has increased in recent years, from 10 percent in 1980 to 19 percent in 2000 (Bachu and O'Connell, 2001).

Many couples without children prefer to call themselves "child free" because to them "childless" implies a lack or a loss. "Child free," in contrast, connotes freedom from the time, money, energy, and responsibility that parenting requires (Paul, 2001).

A few years ago, economist Sylvia Ann Hewlett (2002) created a stir when she contended that many professional women pay a huge price by pursuing careers: They end up childless. According to a recent survey, however, 72 percent of the women disagreed that being a mother is the key to a full life (Center for the Advancement of Women, 2003).

People have many reasons for being childless. Often, educated and successful men and women simply don't want kids. The couples remain intentionally child free because of the freedom to do what they want:

> *Non-parents never have to budget for diapers or college educations. They can make decisions about where to live without worrying about the quality of local schools or which pediatricians offer weekend hours. They can even experience parenthood vicariously through nieces, nephews, and friends' children—but only if they choose to (Crispell, 1993: 23–24).*

This freedom may well be one of the reasons childless couples say they're very happy. Women report enjoying stimulating discussions with their husbands, shared projects and outside interests, a more egalitarian division of household labor, more time and energy for work and volunteering, and the lack of troubling child–parent relationships that they themselves encountered (Somers, 1993; Safer, 1996; Casey, 1998).

Some couples remain childless because of inertia or indecision. When couples disagree about having a child, for instance, the partner who wants a child postpones further discussion, sometimes indefinitely (Thomson, 1997).

Others marry later in life and decide not to have children. As one husband said, "I didn't want to be 65 with a teenager in the house" (Fost, 1996: 16). Some are teachers or other professionals who work with children but like to "come home to peace and quiet and a relaxing night with my husband" (May, 1995: 205). For others, marriage is a precondition for parenthood:

> *A thirty-five-year-old divorced Black attorney who had grown up in a "secure two-parent family" wanted to have children as a part of a committed relationship with "two on-site, full-time loving parents." She had two abortions because the men involved "weren't ready for the responsibility of fatherhood," and she did not want to be a single mother (May, 1995: 193).*

Some feel it's irresponsible to bring more children into an already-crowded world. Some don't think they're suited for parenthood because they feel they'd be impatient with offspring. Others simply don't want to structure their lives around children's activities, school vacations, and worry about how a child will turn out (Paul, 2001).

Although today the general public is much more accepting of childless couples than in the past, some people are still suspicious of couples without children: "Throughout the culture, motherhood is celebrated while childlessness is promoted as a sorry state" (Morell, 1994: 1).

Childless couples are often seen as self-indulgent, selfish, self-absorbed, workaholics, less well adjusted emotionally, and less sensitive and loving, and have even been stereotyped as "weirdos," "child haters," or "barren, career-crazed boomers" (Arenofsky, 1993). In fact, people who don't marry are lonelier later in life than those who don't have children (Zhang and Hayward, 2001).

Why do these stereotypes about child free people exist? Perhaps couples with children resent the childless because the latter have (or seem to have) more freedom, time, money, and fun. As you will see in the next chapter, raising children is not an easy task, and parents sometimes feel unappreciated. A childless lifestyle can sometimes look very attractive.

Conclusion

Attitudes about becoming a parent have *changed* greatly, even during the last generation. There are more *choices* today than in the past in postponing parenthood, becoming pregnant despite infertility, and having children outside marriage.

These choices are bounded by *constraints*, however, and many expectations are contradictory. We encourage young adults to postpone parenthood but are still somewhat suspicious of people who decide to remain childless. We are developing reproductive technologies that help infertile couples become pregnant but have many hazardous work environments that increase people's chances of becoming infertile and of giving birth to infants with lifelong physical and mental disabilities.

In addition, the high costs of reproductive technologies limit their availability to couples who are at the higher end of the socioeconomic scale. Despite such contradictions, most people look forward to raising children, our focus of the next chapter.

SUMMARY

1. Parenthood is an important rite of passage. Unlike other major turning points in our lives, becoming a parent is permanent.

2. There are both benefits and costs in having children. The benefits include emotional fulfillment and personal satisfaction. The costs include a decline in marital satisfaction, problems in finding adequate housing, and generally high expenditures.

3. Fertility rates in the United States have fluctuated in the past 70 years but are still low worldwide. Fertility rates are higher for Latinas than other women, but there are intragroup variations.

4. Postponing parenthood is a common phenomenon. Remaining childless as long as possible has many attractive features, including independence and building a career, but there are costs, such as finding it difficult or impossible to have biological children later in life.

5. Approximately 15 percent of all couples are involuntarily childless. The reasons for infertility include physical and physiological difficulties, environmental hazards, and unhealthy lifestyles.

6. Couples have a variety of options if they are infertile, including adoption, artificial insemination, and a variety of high-tech procedures such as in vitro fertilization and surrogacy.

7. Some ongoing issues in the area of adoption include the rights of the biological father, transracial adoption, and open adoption.

8. Contrary to popular belief, women in their 20s have higher rates of nonmarital childbearing than do teenagers. The percentages of teenagers who are unmarried mothers have been decreasing but vary by race and ethnicity. There are both micro- and macro-level reasons for the surge of out-of-wedlock births.

9. Improved contraceptive techniques and the availability of abortion have resulted in fewer unwanted births. The incidence of abortion has declined since 1990, but abortion continues to be a hotly debated issue in the United States.

10. Couples who decide not to have children are still a minority, but remaining childless is becoming more acceptable.

KEY TERMS

fetal alcohol syndrome
   (FAS)   296
postpartum depression   297
birth rate   297
total fertility rate (TFR)   297
fertility rate   297
relative income   298
infertility   302
pelvic inflammatory disease
   (PID)   302
chlamydia   302
endometriosis   302

open adoption   306
closed adoption   306
semi-open adoption   306
artificial insemination   310
fertility drugs   310
assisted reproductive technology
   (ART)   311
in vitro fertilization (IVF)   311
gamete intrafallopian transfer
   (GIFT)   311
zygote intrafallopian transfer
   (ZIFT)   311

intracytoplasmic sperm injection
   (ICSI)   311
surrogacy   312
preimplantation genetic diagnosis
   (PGD)   313
amniocentesis   314
chorionic villus sampling
   (CVS)   314
contraception   318
abortion   318

TAKING IT FURTHER

Planning and Creating Families

There is a wealth of information about family planning issues on the Internet. Some of these sites include the following:

Child Trends, Inc. is a research organization that provides information on a variety of family-related issues including nonmarital birth.

www.childtrends.org

RESOLVE National Home Page provides information and support regarding infertility.

www.resolve.org

National Adoption Information Clearinghouse is a comprehensive resource for adoption statistics, a literature database, agency and support group lists, and dozens of links to specific areas of adoption such as open adoption, transracial adoption, and the costs of adopting.

www.calib.com/naic

Nature magazine offers online articles on the legal and ethical issues surrounding reproductive technology, among other topics.

www.nature.com

And more: www.prenhall.com/benokraitis provides sites on adoptions, sperm banks, planned parenthood, voluntary childlessness, information on "morning-after" contraception, and a guide to understanding depression during and after pregnancy.

INVESTIGATE WITH RESEARCH NAVIGATOR

Please go to www.researchnavigator.com and enter your LOGIN NAME and PASSWORD. For instructions on registering for the first time, please view the detailed instructions at the end of the Chapter 1. Please search the Research Navigator™ site using the following key search terms:

fertility patterns
infertility
parental rights

Raising Children:
Prospects and Pitfalls

DATADIGEST

- Congress recognized Mother's Day as a **national holiday** in 1914. Father's Day became official in 1972.

- According to 92 percent of U.S. children 10 to 17 years old, **parents are their most influential role models.**

- Almost **76 percent of U.S. adults favor spanking to discipline a child,** down from 84 percent in 1986. Views of spanking vary regionally: 67 percent of northeasterners support spanking, compared with 86 percent of southerners.

- About **60 percent of women return to work within six months of their child's birth,** and 46 percent return to work within three months after the first birth.

- The **most stressed people in the United States** are working mothers: 65 percent say they have little time to relax, compared with 55 percent of working dads and 27 percent of two-income couples with no children.

SOURCES: Fields et al., 2001; Martel, 2001; Jones, 2002a; Paul, 2002.

Want to practice some parenting skills? For the "mess exercise," smear peanut butter on the sofa and curtains or place a fish stick behind the couch and leave it there all summer. For the "grocery store exercise," borrow one or two small animals (goats are best) and take them with you as you shop. Always keep them in sight and pay for anything they eat or damage.

A Swahili proverb says that a child is both a precious stone and a heavy burden. Child rearing is both exhilarating and exhausting, a task that takes patience, sacrifice, and continuous adjustment. There are many rewards but no guarantees. The transition to motherhood or fatherhood is stressful, but parenthood is also one of the most satisfying, highly valued adult roles.

In this chapter we discuss some of the central issues relating to child rearing, such as parenting styles across a variety of families and social classes, raising biracial children, and nonparental child care. We begin by looking at contemporary parenting roles.

Contemporary Parenting Roles

Becoming a parent is a major life change. Even before they are born, children affect their parents. Most parents are emotionally and financially invested in planning a child's arrival. Months before the baby is born, prospective parents begin to alter their lifestyles. Many prospective parents shop for baby clothing and nursery furniture, and child-rearing manuals pile up on parents' nightstands.

The mother may eliminate Big Macs from her diet and increase her intake of calcium-rich dairy or soy products and fresh vegetables. "Parenthood effects" include

327

This 4-year-old girl seems as engrossed in filling her dump truck as she might be in dressing a doll. If parents and other caretakers don't steer children toward sex-stereotypical activities, little girls and little boys enjoy a variety of games and toys.

significant reductions in the use of cigarettes, alcohol, and other drugs by pregnant women and, often, by their spouses, that continue after childbirth (Bachman et al., 1997).

A Parent Is Born

Infants waste no time in teaching adults to meet their needs. Babies are not merely passive recipients of care; they are active participants in their own development:

> The infant modulates, tempers, regulates, and refines the caretaker's activities. . . . By such responses as fretting, sounds of impatience or satisfaction, by facial expressions of pleasure, contentment, or alertness he . . . "tells" the parents when he wants to eat, when he will sleep, when he wants to be played with, picked up, or have his position changed. . . . The caretakers, then, adapt to him and he appears content; they find whatever they do for him satisfying, and thus are reinforced (Rheingold, 1969: 785–86).

Rather than simply playing parental roles, people *internalize* them: "We absorb the roles we play to such a degree that our sense of who we are (our identities) and our sense of right and wrong (our consciences) are very much a product of our role-playing activities" (LaRossa, 1986: 14).

Internalizing the parental role also changes both partners. As people make the transition to parenthood, they help each other learn the role of parent, deal with the ambiguity of what constitutes a "good" parent, and share in the care of their child.

Parental socialization and internalization begin early in life: Young children play house, older siblings may help a parent feed or care for a younger brother or sister, and teenagers often baby-sit in or outside the home. All of these experiences prepare us for parenting roles.

Parenting does *not* come naturally. It is neither instinctive nor innate. Especially with the first child, most of us muddle through by trial and error or turn to "experts" for advice. Some of the advice can be valuable, especially on such topics as the baby's physical care and the stages of social development. Unfortunately, as you'll see later in this chapter, even some "experts" promote myths that have become widely accepted.

Parenting Rewards and Difficulties

Just as there are benefits and costs in having children (see Chapter 11), there are also benefits and costs in raising them:

> *Parenting can be an enormously satisfying, rewarding, enriching, and growth-promoting activity. It also can be frustrating, stress producing, isolating and lonely. For many (and perhaps most) parents, parenting varies, being enormously satisfying and seemingly easy at times as well as confounding, difficult, and burdensome at other times (Arendell, 1997: 22).*

Sociologists often use *role theory* to explain the interaction between family members. A *role*, you recall, is a set of expected behavior patterns, obligations, and privileges (see Chapter 1). Theoretically, every role has culturally defined rights and responsibilities. In practice, however, role strain may occur as norms or role expectations change.

Role Strain   Role strain involves conflicts that someone feels *within* a role. The role of student often reflects role strain. On the one hand, for example, professors encourage students to think creatively and critically. On the other hand, they also tell students to "concentrate on the study questions I gave you" or to "give me the facts, not your opinions."

Almost all people experience role strain because many inconsistencies are built into our roles. Four factors contribute to parents' role strain: unrealistic role expectations, decreased authority, increased responsibility, and high parenting standards.

Unrealistic Role Expectations   Many mothers and fathers experience problems because of unrealistic and one-sided expectations of parenting roles. Just as students accept the fact that some professors are better than others, most of us accept occasional mistakes from lawyers, ministers, social workers, and other professionals. Parents, however, expect and are expected to succeed with every child. Furthermore, because modern families typically are smaller than those in the past, parents may feel especially guilty if each child does not turn out "as expected" (LeMasters and DeFrain, 1989).

Decreased Authority A second problem associated with role strain is that parents find themselves with less authority. In recent court battles, parents have fought state laws to educate their children at home, to consent to a minor's abortion, or to take terminally ill children off life-support systems when there is no chance for recovery. Parents must also compete with television and movies in teaching children values about violence, sexual activity, and stereotypical images of gender roles, minorities, and elderly people (see Chapter 5).

Increased Responsibility Whereas parental authority has decreased, responsibility has increased. If parents raised several children and one ran away from home, relatives and friends would feel that these "good" parents had had one "bad apple". In contrast, many professionals (such as psychiatrists, lawyers, and social workers) often automatically assume that children do not run away from good homes. Therefore, they maintain, there must be something wrong with the parents. Such judgments increase role strain and make many parents feel insecure and guilty.

Some counties are passing "parental responsibility" statutes under which parents are liable and must pay for damage caused by their child, whether it's a minor offense such as graffiti or a serious offense such as homicide (Schrof, 1999). Thus, parents—rather than such influences as peers or the media—are held accountable for a child's misbehavior.

High Parenting Standards Finally, parents have no training for their difficult role but must live up to high standards. As many practitioners remind us, we receive more training to get a driver's license than to become parents. In contrast to previous generations, parents are now expected to be informed about the latest medical technologies, to watch their children closely for early signs of physical or mental abnormalities, and to consult with specialists immediately if they detect seeing or learning problems.

There's also a sense that the division of labor in families should be equal. But when we look at what is actually happening, we see that much less has changed in parenting roles than one expects. Both mothers and fathers experience contradictions in their child-rearing responsibilities.

Motherhood: Ideal versus Realistic Roles

New mothers often face enormous pressures and role strain. The expectation that mothering "comes naturally" creates three problems. First, it assumes that a good mother will be perfect if she simply follows her instincts. Second, it implies that there is something wrong with a mother who does not devote 100 percent of her life to child rearing. Third, it discourages the involvement of other adults, such as fathers or other caretakers.

Currently, almost 63 percent of children under age 18 live in families with two parents in the labor force (Fields, 2003). Nonetheless, mothers continue to do most of the work of raising children and maintaining the household (see Chapters 5, 10, and 13).

Mothers who are employed full time are still expected to play active community roles, such as fund-raising for Little League, organizing PTA activities, and providing a variety of services for religious organizations. Social scientists who emphasize the mother–child relationship often blame mothers for adolescent problems, preschool misbehavior, and difficulties in school (for example, see Wilson, 2002).

There's no evidence to support such claims. In fact, several recent national studies show that both working and stay-at-home mothers spend more time caring for their children than their own mothers did (see Chapter 10). Contemporary mothers do less housework but spend more time caring for children. Employed mothers report getting 5 to 6 fewer hours of sleep per week and have 12 fewer hours of free time per week than do nonemployed mothers (Bianchi, 2000).

The greater the participation by the father, the greater the mother's satisfaction with parenting and the marriage (Johnson and Huston, 1998; see also Chapters 5 and 10). How much do fathers contribute to child rearing?

Fatherhood: Ideal versus Realistic Roles

Fathers, like mothers, feel role strain. They may have very little opportunity to learn the necessary parenting skills, especially during the first year of a baby's life:

> *An old joke for musicians goes like this: A young man asks an older musician, "How do I get to Carnegie Hall?" To which the older man answers, "Practice, my son, practice." You can say the same for fatherhood. It takes practice to know how to handle a crying baby in the middle of the night and to diaper a squiggly baby on a changing table. . . . But first-time fathers who work outside of the home . . . [are expected] to know how to be dads instantaneously, and this unrealistic expectation causes problems (Marzollo, 1993: 10).*

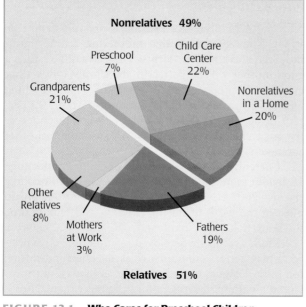

FIGURE 12.1 **Who Cares for Preschool Children of Employed Mothers?**

SOURCE: Based on U.S. Census Bureau, Current Population Reports, Historical Table, www.census.gov/population/socdemo/child/ppl-168/tabH-1.pdf (accessed August 28, 2003).

Gerson (1997) suggests that there are three types of contemporary fathers:

■ *Breadwinner fathers* see themselves as primary earners even if their wives work. They view fatherhood mainly in economic terms and prefer a wife who is responsible for domestic responsibilities and child care.

■ *Autonomous fathers* seek freedom from family commitments and distance themselves—usually after a marital breakup—from both their former spouses and their children (such as "deadbeat dads" who don't provide economic or emotional support after a marital breakup).

■ *Involved fathers* feel that "good fathering" includes extensive participation in the daily tasks of child rearing and nurturing. Although these fathers don't necessarily have equally shared or primary responsibility for their children's care, they forge satisfying relationships with their wives and children.

According to Gerson, the diversity of fatherhood patterns is the result of more women working outside the home. When mothers are employed, fathers are an important source of care for young children (see *Figure 12.1*). They are more likely to provide care if they work evening and weekend shifts or if they are unemployed. In addition, fathers in low-income families are more likely to take care of their children than fathers in middle-class families because child-care costs constitute a large proportion of a poor family's budget: 35 percent vs. 6 percent, respectively (Smith, 2000).

Parenting has positive consequences for most men. Compared with nonfathers, fathers are more satisfied with their lives, more involved in their communities, less caught up in work, and much more likely to have regular contact or exchanges with aging parents and siblings (Eggebeen and Knoester, 2001).

Many men want to be close to their children, but with long commutes and demanding employers, they have little time to do so. They often throw themselves into work to be good providers, but doing so shortens the amount of time they can spend with their children. Many men seek a "package deal" that includes fatherhood, marriage, employment, and home ownership. Such goals often conflict because it's typically impossible to be both a good father and a good employee or employer (Townsend, 2002).

What happens when fathers encounter such contradictions? They usually place a lower priority on parenting. More than 90 percent of mothers and fathers say that both parents should have equal involvement in a number of child-rearing tasks. In reality, only 17 percent of fathers discipline their children, 14 percent play with them, 24 percent provide children with emotional support, 27 percent monitor their children's play or friends, and 58 percent provide basic care that includes everything from changing diapers to making the children's meals (Bianchi, 2001).

Why are parenting roles so lopsided? Even when we have "modern" views about gender roles, sex-stereotypical attitudes linger. In a national survey, for example, 61 percent of men and 65 percent of women said that men are as competent as women in raising children. Despite the equality rhetoric, 27 percent of men and 20 percent of women said that they don't believe that men are as competent at parenthood as women (Fetto, 2002b).

Parents are the primary agents in children's socialization until the children become young adults (see Chapters 1 and 5). How do parents influence their children's development over time? Theorists have offered various answers to this question.

MAKING CONNECTIONS

■ Who did most of the child-rearing when you were growing up? Was mom or dad more influential during childhood? If you have children now, who does most of the parenting?

■ Do you feel that equal parenting is possible in most families if both parents are in the labor force?

Theories of Child Development

Social scientists have proposed a number of theories to explain child development. A few of these perspectives include learning theories, cognitive development theories, and feminist approaches (see Chapter 5). Others, which we won't cover here, include behaviorism, psychoanalytic theories, sociocultural theory, dynamic systems theory, and ecological theory (see Hetherington and Parke, 2002, for a discussion of these theories).

Three theorists have been especially influential in sociologists' thinking about child socialization and development. George Herbert Mead (1934, 1938, 1964) focused on the influence of social interactions on the developing human being. Jean Piaget (1932, 1954, 1960) was interested in the child's cognitive development: the ability to think, reason, analyze, and apply information (see Chapter 5). Erik Erikson (1963) combined elements of psychological and sociological theories that encompass adulthood. Refer to *Table 12.1* on page 332 as we look briefly at these major theories.

Mead's Theory of the Social Self

George Herbert Mead (1863–1931) saw the self as the basis of humanity and proposed that the *self* develops not out of biological urges but out of social interactions. For Mead, the infant was a blank slate (*tabula rasa*) with no predisposition to behave in any particular way. It is only as the infant interacts with other people in his or her environment, Mead said, that the infant begins to develop the attitudes, beliefs, and behaviors he or she needs to fit into society.

The child learns first by imitating the behavior of specific people, such as parents, sisters, and brothers. As the child matures, he or she learns to identify with the generalized roles that these people and many others fulfill. When the child has learned the significance of roles, according to Mead, she or he has learned to respond to the expectations of society (see Chapter 5).

Piaget's Cognitive Development Theory

Jean Piaget (1896–1980) was interested in the growing child's efforts to comprehend his or her world and to learn how to adapt to that world and develop an independent identity. In his four major developmental stages (see *Table 12.1*), Piaget traced the acquisition of such abilities as differentiating oneself from the external world and recognizing that objects in that world have an independent existence, learning to use such symbols as language to represent objects in the world, learning to take the perspective of another person, and learning to think and reason in abstract terms—as Piaget put it, to think "beyond the present and [to form] theories about everything" (Piaget, 1950: 48).

Piaget believed that children play an active role in learning, processing information, and seeking knowledge. He emphasized that although some children learn faster than others, they must pass through the same four stages, at a similar age and in the same order. Once children have mastered the tasks of one stage, they move on to the next one, which is more difficult.

Erikson's Psychosocial Theory of Development

Erik Erikson (1902–1994) is one of the few theorists whose explanation of human development encompassed the entire lifespan rather than just childhood and adolescence. In each of Erikson's eight stages of development, the growing person faces a specific challenge, a "crisis," that presents both tasks and risks.

The outcome of each "crisis" determines whether the person will move on successfully to the next stage. For example, the person may leave the first stage having learned to trust other people, such as parents or caregivers, or being unable to have confidence in anyone. For Erikson, resolving each of these "crises" is the responsibility of the individual, but successful resolution also reflects the person's social relationships with family members, peers, and others.

The developmental stages Erikson describes may occur in a different sequence or at different ages than those specified in *Table 12.1*. The stages can also vary across cultures. Societies that emphasize cooperation, for example, are more likely to emphasize shame and guilt than autonomy and initiative (see Chapter 4). In contrast, cultures like the United States reward autonomy and initiative rather than collaboration.

The important point in all three of these theories is that children grow and mature by learning to deal with new expectations and changes. The child who feels loved and secure has a good chance of developing into a reasonably happy and productive member of society, one of the family's major socialization functions (see Chapter 1).

These and other theories give us an insight into children's development but say nothing about parenting approaches. How do mothers and fathers parent? And what are the most effective parenting styles and forms of discipline?

Parenting Styles and Discipline

Parents differ greatly in the ways they approach parenting. These differences reflect social class, racial or ethnic heritage, religious beliefs, attitudes toward gender, and the parents' own childhood experiences. We'll look at parenting variations in racial-ethnic families and

TABLE 12.1

Some Theories of Development and Socialization

Theory of the Social Self (George Herbert Mead)	Cognitive Development Theory (Jean Piaget)	Psychosocial Theory of Human Development (Erik Erikson)
Preparatory stage (roughly birth to 1 year) The infant does not distinguish between the self and others. Gradually, as he or she interacts with objects and people and begins to perceive others' reactions, the infant builds the potential for a self.

Play stage (roughly 1½ to 5 years) As children begin to use language and continue to interact with significant others (parents, siblings, teachers, schoolmates) they learn that they have a self distinct from that of others, that others behave in many different ways, and that others expect the child to behave in certain ways. In other words, the child learns social norms.

Game stage (roughly 6 years and older) As children grow older and interact with a wider range of people, they learn to respond to and fulfill social roles. They learn to play different roles and participate in organized activities. | **Sensorimotor stage (birth to 2 years)** The child develops a physical understanding of her or his environment through touching, seeing, hearing, and moving around. The child learns the concept of object permanence, the fact that objects continue to exist even when they are out of sight.

Preoperational stage (2 to 7 years) Children learn to use symbols. For example, they learn to represent a car with a block, moving the block around. They learn to use language, putting words together to express increasingly complex ideas. But they have difficulty seeing things from the viewpoint of another.

Concrete operational stage (7 to 12 years) Children learn to discern cause and effect. They can anticipate possible causes of an action without having to try it out; they begin to understand the perceptions and views of others; they learn that quantities remain the same even when their shape or form changes (e.g., a fixed amount of liquid poured into a tall, thin glass and into a short, wide one is the same amount even though it looks different in differently shaped containers).

Formal operational stage (12 years and older) Children can reason using abstract concepts. They can think in terms of future consequences and evaluate the probable outcomes of several alternatives. They can evaluate their own thoughts. They can think about major philosophical issues such as why pain and suffering exist. | **I. Trust vs. mistrust (birth to 1 year)** *Task*: To develop basic trust in oneself and others. *Risk*: A sense of abandonment may lead to mistrust and a lack of self-confidence.

II. Autonomy vs. shame, doubt (2 to 3 years) *Task*: To learn self-control and independence. *Risk*: Parental shaming to control the child may lead to self-doubt.

III. Initiative vs. guilt (4 to 6 years) *Task*: To learn new tasks and pursue goals aggressively. *Risk*: Feeling guilty for having attempted forbidden activities or having been too aggressive.

IV. Industry vs. inferiority (7 to 12 years) *Task*: To develop an interest in productive work rather than just play. *Risk*: Failure or the fear of failure may result in feelings of inferiority.

V. Identity vs. identity confusion (13 to 19 years) *Task*: To achieve a sense of individuality and of one's place in society. *Risk*: Making important decisions may lead to confusion over who and what a person wants to be.

VI. Intimacy vs. isolation (20 to 30 years) *Task:* To achieve close ties with others and to fulfill commitments. *Risk*: The inability to take chances by sharing real intimacy may result in avoiding others and isolation.

VII. Generativity vs. self-absorption (31 to 65 years) *Task:* To establish and guide the next generation or to create and produce ideas and products. *Risk*: The inability to bear children or to create ideas or products may lead to stagnation.

VIII. Integrity vs. despair (66 years and older) *Task:* To feel a sense of satisfaction and dignity in what one has achieved. *Risk*: Disappointments and unrealized goals may lead to feelings of alienation and despair. |

social classes in more detail shortly. For now, suffice it to say that both ethnicity and social class affect parenting approaches and discipline.

Parenting Approaches

Parents use a variety of child-rearing techniques. Diana Baumrind (1968, 1989) has identified three broad approaches to interacting with and disciplining children: authoritarian, permissive, and authoritative (*see Table 12.2*).

Authoritarian Parenting   Parents who use the **authoritarian approach** are often very demanding, controlling, and punitive. They expect absolute obedience from their children and often use forceful measures to control behavior. Authoritarian parents, who tend to be working class, teach their children to respect authority, work, order, and traditional structure. Verbal give-and-take is rare because the child is expected to accept parental authority without question. Authoritarian parents are typically not responsive to their children and project little warmth and supportiveness.

Authoritarian parenting styles may reflect stress due to low income and other factors. For example, being poor, black, and an unmarried mother all bring added stress to the parenting experience because of discrimination and limited economic opportunity (Giles-Sims et al., 1995). In addition, psychological factors such as depression (for white as well as black mothers in working and middle classes) increase the likelihood of punitive parenting styles (Jackson et al., 1998; Bluestone and Tamis-LeMonda, 1999).

Permissive Parenting   In the **permissive approach** parents are warm, responsive, and nondemanding. They value a child's freedom of expression and autonomy. Permissive households' rules or regulations and the parents, who are usually middle class, make few demands on their children for orderly behavior or household tasks. The parents typically use reason rather than overt power to accomplish their ends.

Permissive parents don't set boundaries but are indulgent. Although permissive parents don't bully or tyrannize their children, they can be indifferent, even neglectful. Adolescents raised in indulgent households are often less mature, more irresponsible, and less able to assume positions of leadership (Steinberg and Silk, 2002).

Authoritative Parenting   Parents who use the **authoritative approach** are demanding and controlling because they impose rules and standards of behavior, but they are also responsive and supportive. These parents, usually middle- and upper-middle-class, encourage autonomy and self-reliance and tend to use positive reinforcement rather than punitive, repressive discipline.

Unlike authoritarian parents, authoritative parents encourage verbal give-and-take and believe that the child has rights. Although they expect disciplined conformity, the parents typically don't hem the child in with heavy-handed restrictions. Instead, they are open to discussing and changing rules in particular situations when the need arises.

Which Parenting Approach Is the Most Effective?
Although there are some exceptions, a number of studies show that healthy child development is most likely in authoritative family settings, where parents are consistent in combining warmth, monitoring, and discipline (Fletcher et al., 1999; Gray and Steinberg, 1999; Barnes et al., 2000). Children from authoritative households have better psychosocial development, higher school grades, greater self-reliance, and lower levels of delinquent behavior and are less swayed by antisocial peer pressure (to use drugs and alcohol, for example) than are adolescents whose parents are permissive or authoritarian (Mason et al., 1997; Collins et al., 2000). Among teenagers aged 12 to 17, those with hands-on, authoritative parents are one-fourth as likely as their

TABLE 12.2		
Three Approaches to Parenting		
Parenting Approach	**Attributes**	**Example**
Authoritarian	Highly demanding, controlling, and punitive	"You can't have the car on Saturday because I said so."
Permissive	Responsive but not demanding	"Sure; go ahead and borrow the car."
Authoritative	Highly demanding, controlling, supportive, and responsive	"You can borrow the car after you've picked your brother up from soccer practice. And remember to be home by curfew."

permissive counterparts to use drugs. In addition, only 24 percent of teenagers living in hands-off households have an excellent relationship with their parents, usually the mother, compared with 57 percent living in hands-on households (National Center on Addiction and Substance Abuse, 2001).

Some researchers note that the authoritarian–permissive–authoritative parenting styles overlap in real life. Immigrant Chinese mothers, for example, reflect a combination of parenting roles that might seem authoritarian because of high expectations about academic success but are also warm, nurturing, and supportive (Gorman, 1998; see also Chapter 4).

Authoritarian, permissive, and authoritative approaches describe some general parenting philosophies. There are also a number of specific parenting styles.

Some Parenting Styles

Parenting styles vary across families and may change over time. Moreover, they usually overlap; a particular family may use two or more styles at one time. Parental roles include the martyr, the pal, the police officer, the teacher, the booster, and, most recently, the snoop (LeMasters and DeFrain, 1989; Larson and Richards, 1994; Wood 2002):

■ *The martyr.* This parent sacrifices everything for the children, lets them do whatever they want, buys them everything they want, waits on them hand and foot, and tries to fulfill their every wish. If children don't revolt against the martyr model, they may never become self-sufficient.

■ *The pal or buddy.* Parents often let their children set their own rules because they want the children to like them. If there is disagreement, a parent who is a pal has little authority. The parent has little power in preventing the children's smoking, drinking, and using drugs. And, as someone once said, "What child needs a 40-year-old for a buddy?"

■ *The police officer or drill sergeant.* Parents who act as police officers or drill sergeants are usually authoritarian and punitive. They punish even minor offenses such as coming home ten minutes past a curfew. Although children may be submissive during the early years, they often rebel against this type of authority in adolescence and may demand more independence.

■ *The teacher.* Fathers, especially, relish playing the role of teacher. They enjoy helping children with their homework and are especially pleased when children ask for their advice or opinion.

■ *The booster and promoter.* Both mothers and fathers enjoy their children's accomplishments. They may be especially proud when their children do well in school, sports, or other activities. There may be conflict, however, if the children don't live up to the parents' expectations.

■ *The snoop.* Some parents spy on their children, especially teenagers, to find out about drug use and sexual relations. The surveillance techniques include reading diaries, conducting regular bedroom searches, taping phone conversations, accessing e-mail, hugging kids to smell for marijuana and alcohol, and even hiring private detectives to find out where their children go after school and on weekends.

Some people believe that parenting in the United States is difficult because our cultural values (such as competition, independence, and success) encourage individuality rather than conformity. In other cultures, parental values emphasize cooperation rather than independence (see the box on "Parenting in Japan").

Discipline

In 1994, a woman was shopping in a grocery store in Woodstock, Georgia, when her 9-year-old son, who reportedly was picking on his sister, talked back to his mother. The mother slapped him. Fifteen minutes later, in the parking lot, a police officer summoned by a store employee arrested the mother and charged her with cruelty to children, a felony that carries a jail sentence of 1 to 20 years.

Many parents were outraged by the arrest. Why should the police intrude in a private family matter? And what's wrong with slapping or spanking kids? The incident fueled a national debate over how Americans should discipline their children.

Children must learn discipline because self-control is not innate. Many parents feel that both verbal and corporal punishment are legitimate forms of discipline.

Verbal Punishment A national study found that almost all parents, across all socioeconomic groups, used verbal and psychological aggression to control or change their children's behavior (Straus and Field, 2000):

■ 50 percent yelled, screamed, and shouted at their infants and 1-year-old children, and 90 percent did the same with children aged 4 to 17.

■ 25 percent sometimes cursed at their children ages 18 and under, and 17 percent admitted calling a child a derogatory name (such as "dumb" or "lazy").

Parenting in Japan

Japan's approach to parenting is considerably, different from that in the United States. Most Americans value individualism, independence, and initiative and raise their children to be self-reliant. From the Japanese viewpoint, these attitudes and behaviors are too narrowly goal-oriented. The Japanese value loyalty to the family and community over personal success. Respect for authority and obedience are taught early in the home, and they are reinforced in nursery school (Downs, 1994).

Japanese child rearing is based on a concept called *amae*, which is a sense of complete dependence based on the desire for love and caring. Mothers, who give them 24-hour love, instill *amae* in Japanese children. Many Japanese mothers spend every waking hour with their babies. They often sleep with the babies, pick them up whenever they cry, and cater to their every whim.

Most American parents think this kind of behavior will spoil a child and discourage independence and self-reliance. In contrast, the Japanese feel that keeping children happy will motivate them to be cooperative later in life. *Amae*-based care and guidance are continued in the school system, where children are rewarded for cooperative behavior and teamwork.

Although Japanese fathers are often absent from home, the father's authority is reinforced in daily mother–child interaction:

"Since my husband is gone most of the time, my son really needs a role model to be a strong and responsible man. That's why I remind him constantly of what a diligent, dedicated, responsible, and great father he has.

I also tell my daughter that it is important for her to find a hard-working man like her father who earns a comfortable living for the family." This is from a homemaker–mother whose 9-year-old daughter and 6-year-old son see their father on the average of 4 minutes a day (Ishii-Kuntz, 1993: 59).

Because provider and father roles are synonymous, co-workers or family members may criticize Japanese men who reduce work hours to be at home with their children. Because many fathers devote themselves to their jobs, mothers have complete authority in the home: "It's motherhood, not wifehood, which gives a woman a sense of accomplishment and it's the children around which the family revolves" (Diggs, 1998: 49).

STOP AND THINK . . .

- *Violence rates, such as homicide, are much higher in the United States than in Japan (see Chapters 1 and 5). Do you think that* amae *can explain these differences?*

- *What advantages and disadvantages do you see with American versus Japanese parenting approaches?*

■ 33 percent swore at their teens and called them names.

■ 20 percent threatened, at least once, to kick the child out of the house.

All of these percentages are probably low because many parents don't want to admit that they attack their children verbally or because the incidents have become so common and "normal" that parents have forgotten them.

The researchers noted that such psychological and verbal aggression is associated with higher rates of delinquency and psychological problems because parents criticize the child rather than the child's misbehavior. The researchers observed that the high prevalence of psychological aggression between adult partners shouldn't be surprising because almost all American children experience such violence from their parents and see it as normal.

Corporal Punishment   Surveys indicate that 94 percent of American parents spank their children by the time they are 3 or 4 years old. About 35 percent of parents discipline their infants by slapping their hand or leg, spanking their buttocks, pinching, shaking, hitting on the buttocks with a belt or paddle, or slapping the infant's face. More than half of the parents hit their children at age 12, a third at age 14, and 13 percent at age 17. Parents who hit teenage children do so an average of about six times a year. Hitting the child with a belt or paddle is most common for children aged 5 to 12 (28 percent of such children) (Straus and Stewart, 1999).

Corporal punishment is more prevalent among low-income parents, in the South, for boys, and by mothers, especially younger white mothers (those under age 33). Overall, older parents are less likely to use corporal punishment than younger parents (Day et al., 1998; Straus and Stewart, 1999; Walsh, 2002).

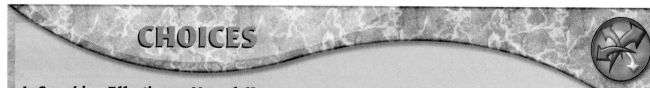

CHOICES

Is Spanking Effective or Harmful?

Eleven countries have made it illegal for parents to spank their children: Austria, Croatia, Cyprus, Denmark, Finland, Germany, Israel, Italy, Latvia, Norway, and Sweden. In contrast, many adults in the United States support spanking (see "Data Digest").

Advocates feel that spanking is effective, prepares children for life's hardships, and prevents misbehavior. Proponents maintain that spanking is acceptable if it is age-appropriate, used selectively, and done for the purpose of teaching and correcting, not for revenge or out of rage (Davis, 1994; Trumbull and Ravenel, 1999; Larzelere, 2000; Baumrind et al., 2002).

Some pediatricians feel that a "mild" spanking (one or two spanks on the buttocks) is acceptable when all other discipline fails but that slapping a child's face is abusive. Others argue that spanking and all other types of physical punishment are unacceptable. They maintain that children who are spanked regularly, from as early as 1 year old, face a higher risk of developing low self-esteem,

depression, alcoholism, and aggressive and violent behavior and of physically abusing their own spouses and children (Straus and Yodanis, 1996; Whipple and Richey, 1997; Swinford et al., 2000).

Some researchers have offered a variety of reasons for not spanking or hitting children:

- *Physical punishment sends the message that it is okay to hurt someone you love or someone who is smaller and less powerful.* A parent who spanks often says, "I'm doing this because I love you." Thus, children learn that violence and love can go hand in hand and that hitting is an appropriate way to express one's feelings.
- *No human being feels loving toward someone who hits her or him.* A strong relationship is based on kindness and cooperation. Hitting may produce only temporary and superficially "good" behavior based on fear.
- *Unexpressed anger is stored inside and may explode later.* Anger that

has accumulated for many years may erupt during adolescence and adulthood, when the person feels strong enough to show this rage.
- *Spanking can be physically damaging.* It can injure the spinal column and nerves and even cause paralysis. Some children have died after mild paddlings because of undiagnosed medical problems.
- *Physical punishment deprives the child of opportunities to learn effective problem solving.* Physical punishment teaches a child nothing about how to handle conflict or disagreements (Hunt, 1991; Segal and Segal, 1991; Straus, 2001).

STOP AND THINK . . .

- *When you were a child, did your parents spank you? If so, how did you feel?*
- *Some people feel that spanking is synonymous with hitting. Do you agree?*

Does Corporal Punishment Work? Spanking vents a parent's anger and frustration, but does physical punishment change a child's behavior? Several studies of 2- and 3-year-olds found that parents who use reasoning and back it up with physical and nonphysical punishment have well-behaved children (Larzelere et al., 1998; Holden et al., 1999).

However, most research shows that corporal punishment increases a child's aggression and misbehavior. In a study of preschool-age children, for example, children whose mothers threatened, insulted, spanked, or yelled at them were more likely to remain defiant and disruptive as they entered school (Spieker et al., 1999). An analysis of 88 studies over 62 years concluded that spanking children can make them temporarily more compliant but raises the risk that children will become aggressive, antisocial, and chronically defiant (Gershoff, 2002a).

Many researchers, pediatricians, and practitioners maintain that physical punishment is a futile disciplinary

method (see the box "Is Spanking Effective or Harmful?"). Increasingly, child experts recommend nonphysical methods of punishment that have better long-term results, such as removing temptation for misbehavior, making rules simple, being consistent, setting a good example, praising good behavior, and disciplining with love and patience instead of anger (Gibson, 1991; Simons et al., 1994).

Variations by Race and Ethnicity Does parents' ethnicity or race affect corporal punishment? The data are inconclusive. Some studies report that African American and Latino parents use corporal punishment more than white parents, some studies show that white parents spank the most, and other studies have found that the frequency of spanking is about the same for all three groups but that Asian American and American Indian parents report the lowest spanking rates (McDade, 1995; Ellison et al., 1995; Loeber et al., 2000; Pinderhughes et al., 2000; Wissow, 2001).

When parents spank, how does corporal punishment affect children across racial and ethnic groups? Several studies have found that corporal punishment has few negative psychological effects on white, black, and Latino children if the children perceive the punishment as just, not harsh. Even if parents (who are usually mothers) yell and spank, black children especially interpret such parental discipline as an expression of concern rather than hostility if the mothers are also affectionate and warm (Rohner et al., 1996; Spieker et al., 1999; Mosby and Rawls, 1999; Hill and Bush, 2001; McLoyd and Smith, 2002).

Minority parents often discipline their children by emphasizing self-control and doing well in school rather than by corporal or verbal punishment. Ethnic parents may be stricter, placing greater demands and expectations on their children, because they feel that their children will face discrimination (Julian et al., 1994; Ng, 1998).

It appears, then, that effective disciplinary measures are associated with a number of factors, such as cultural attitudes, the harshness of the punishment, and a child's perception of a parent as loving or rejecting.

What's a Parent to Do? According to many family educators, it's important not to discipline too early. Children under 6 years old are curious and eager to learn (see *Table 12.1*). Parents can often avoid problems by guiding children's exploration and interest in new activities instead of yelling "Stop that!" or "Don't go there!"

Effective discipline involves more than rewards and punishments. Children need three types of inner resources if they are to become responsible adults: good feelings about themselves and others, an understanding of right and wrong, and alternatives for solving problems. *Table 12.3* lists 12 building blocks that parents can use to establish these inner resources in their children.

TABLE 12.3

Some Building Blocks of Discipline for Parents

- **Show your love**. You can express your love not only through a warm facial expression, a kind tone, and a hug but also through doing things with your children such as playing, working on a craft together, letting them help with grocery shopping, and reading their favorite books. When children feel loved, they want to please their parents and are less likely to engage in undesirable behavior.

- **Be consistent**. Predictable parents are just as important as routines and schedules. A child who is allowed to do something one day and not the next can become confused and start testing the rules.

- **Communicate clearly**. Ask children about their interests and feelings. Whenever possible, encourage them. Constant nagging, reminding, criticizing, threatening, lecturing, questioning, advising, evaluating, and demanding make a child feel dumb or bad.

- **Understand problem behavior**. Observe a problem behavior for several days and look for a pattern that may explain why; for example, a child may become unusually cranky when tired or hungry.

- **Be positive**. Sometimes children act up because they want us to notice them. Because children usually repeat attention-getting acts, approval of good conduct encourages them to repeat the positive behavior.

- **Set up a safe environment**. Children are doers and explorers. Removing hazards shortens the lists of "no's," and changing play locations relieves boredom and prevents destructive behavior.

- **Have realistic rules**. Set few rules, state them simply, and supervise closely. (Rules can become more extensive and abstract as toddlers become preschoolers.) Don't expect more than your child can handle; for instance, don't expect a toddler to sit quietly during long meetings.

- **Defuse explosions**. Try to avert temper tantrums and highly charged confrontations (for example, guide feuding preschoolers into other activities).

- **Teach good problem-solving skills**. Children under 4 years of age need very specific guidance in solving a problem and positive reinforcement for following suggestions.

- **Give children reasonable choices**. Don't force them to do things that even you wouldn't want to do (such as sharing a favorite toy). Removing children from the play area when they misbehave and giving them a choice of other activities is often more effective than scolding or punishing.

- **Seek professional help when needed**. Although most children outgrow common behavioral problems, some may need professional guidance, particularly if the parents themselves are experiencing a stressful time, such as divorce.

- **Be patient with your child and yourself**. Parents may have little control over their lives, but patience, love, and understanding are important for handling problems of all sizes (Harms, 1989; Goddard, 1994).

TABLE 12.4

How Often Do Parents Read to Their Kids?

Percentage of Children Never Read to Last Week

Race or Ethnicity of Child	Children 1 or 2 Years Old	Children 3 to 5 Years Old
White	5	4
Black	11	13
Asian and Pacific Islander	19	11
Latino (of any race)	24	17

SOURCE: Based on Lugaila, 2003, Table 3.

We've touched on some racial-ethnic variations in parents' disciplinary approaches. How do race, ethnicity, and social class affect other parenting aspects?

Parenting, Ethnicity, and Social Class

Ethnicity, race, and social class play powerful roles in the United States. It's not surprising, then, that there are some racial, ethnic, and class variations in child rearing. We'll examine racial-ethnic families first and then look at social class differences. You'll notice as you read this section that ethnicity and social class are highly interrelated.

Parenting across Racial-Ethnic Families

We looked at socialization practices across a number of racial-ethnic families in Chapter 4. Other child-rearing tasks include spending time with children and monitoring their activities.

Spending Time with Children   One important characteristic of a child's well-being is the type and amount of interaction that occurs between children and their parents. Interactions include reading to a child and taking children on outings.

Reading is an important activity not only because it stimulates a child's cognitive and intellectual abilities but also because it's a way for parents to spend time with their youngsters. Latino parents are less likely to read to their young children than African American, Asian American, and white parents (see *Table 12.4*).

Another way to spend time with children is to take them on outings to a park, a church, a playground, or a zoo or to visit with friends or relatives. Such trips provide an opportunity for parents to talk to their

children and to get to know them. White children under 12 years old experience more outings than either black or Latino children, regardless of social class. For example, even in high-income families, white children have an average of 14 outings with a parent during a month, compared with 12 outings for black children and 10 outings for Latino children (Lugaila, 2003).

There may be several explanations for these racial and ethnic variations in parental reading and outings. One is marital status. Many single parents who work have less time and energy to interact with their children. In multigenerational homes, mothers may be caring for older family members and also depend on their children for the caregiving. As a result, these parents may be less aware of their children's needs and can devote less time to activities such as reading and outings (Jambunathan et al., 2000). Furthermore, recent immigrants who don't speak English well may be uncomfortable with or unaware of recreational opportunities outside the home.

Monitoring Children's Activities   African American and Latino fathers typically supervise their children's activities more closely than do white fathers. Recent immigrants are also more likely to monitor their children than U.S.-born parents. As children acculturate, parental supervision and control decrease because many adolescents conform to the values of their peer groups rather than their families (see Chapter 4).

In terms of monitoring television, a major source of recreation for children, parents often impose three rules: the type of program, times of day, and the number of hours that a child may watch television. Families across racial-ethnic groups are similar in setting up all three rules. For example, about 70 percent of white, black, Asian American, and Latino parents report having such rules for children ages 6 to 11 (Lugaila, 2003).

These rules vary by a parent's social class, however. As a parent's educational level increases, so do restrictions about watching television. For example, 67 percent of parents with a high school degree or less compared with 78 percent of parents with an advanced degree restrict television watching for children ages 6 to 11 (Fields et al., 2001; Lugaila, 2003).

Parents in racial and ethnic groups spend more time teaching their children to deal with the realities of prejudice and discrimination than white parents do. Such racial socialization creates stress that white parents don't have to deal with (see Chapter 4).

Parenting Biracial Children

In 1997, professional golfer Tiger Woods sparked a controversy when he told talk show host Oprah Winfrey that he objected to being called an African American. He said he was "Cablinasian," a word he'd made up as a boy, because he was one-eighth Caucasian, one-fourth black, one-eighth American Indian, one-fourth Thai, and one-fourth Chinese. Many blacks were upset that Woods seemed to reject his African American roots, but Woods felt that he was embracing all parts of his multicultural heritage.

There are no national data comparing the development of single-race and biracial children. However, several qualitative studies suggest that most biracial adolescents have positive self-concepts, high self-esteem, and about the same percentage of behavioral problems as their single-race peers (Gibbs and Hines, 1992; Field, 1996). Some researchers attribute the children's strong, positive, and confident sense of identity to parents who provide strong support, give the child identity-bolstering books and toys, instruct the child about what to say when his or her racial identity is questioned, and build connections to their racial and ethnic communities (Rosenblatt et al., 1995).

Some biracial children struggle with their multicultural and biracial identity as they grow up. Children with black and white parents or black and Asian parents, for example, may feel ambiguous loyalties to each heritage or a marginal status in both groups, or they may be accused of "talking like a honky" if they're raised in middle-class families (Maxwell, 1998; Williams and Thornton, 1998; Berry, 2000).

American Indian children who have interracial or interethnic roots report that they're often rejected by both groups, don't look "Indian enough," or have been raised by parents who teach only a white worldview rather than a mixed-heritage perspective (D. D. Jackson, 1998; Mihesuah, 1998; Herring, 1999).

Junior high and high school may be especially challenging because friends start dividing up along racial lines, most visibly at lunch in the cafeteria. On many college campuses, however, mixed-race students are increasingly forming their own student groups. As young adults, many appreciate their biracial heritage. According to a young woman who is now an executive at a film-producing company in Los Angeles, "Because of my multiracial background, I can connect with and make relationships with so many different types of people. It's something extra that I have that others don't have" (Nakazawa, 2003: 5).

Parenting and Social Class

As you've just seen, many racial and ethnic parenting differences often reflect social class variations. That is, middle-class parents, regardless of race and ethnicity, are more similar to each other than to low-income and high-income parents. Even though not every parent in a given social class raises children the same way, social class influences child rearing.

Sociologists and other social scientists typically measure social class using **socioeconomic status (SES)**, an overall rank of one's position based on income, education, and occupation. Although sociologists delineate as many as nine social classes in America, for our purposes, low-SES families are those living just above or below the poverty level, middle-SES families are those in blue-collar and white-collar occupations, and high-SES families are professionals and higher.

Low-SES Families Most low-SES families raise responsible and hard-working children, but parents must grapple with numerous obstacles. Macro-level stressors such as poverty, unemployment, and racism often create interpersonal conflict (Galvin and Brommel, 2000). Besides living in violent neighborhoods, children have little physical space at home and usually attend schools that are overcrowded and underfunded.

Low-SES parents, compared with middle-SES parents, typically give infants fewer opportunities for daily stimulation and appropriate play materials (Bornstein, 2002). Although many school-related activities are free, parents must have the time, energy, health, and economic resources to encourage children to participate in extracurricular activities.

Children are especially vulnerable in low-income families where the parents also have mental health problems, are unemployed, or experience psychological distress. These children are less likely to be successful in school (in terms of basic language, math, and reading skills) by age 7 and 8. They are also more likely to experience cognitive problems if the family's household income drops even lower and resources become more meager (Votruba-Drzal, 2003).

Despite such dire circumstances, many low-SES parents raise happy and healthy kids. In terms of family activities, for example, almost 25 percent of parents living at or below the poverty level read to their children at least once a week. Almost 86 percent of Latino children, 91 percent of black children, and 95 percent of white children in poverty-level homes have an average of ten outings per month with a parent (Lugaila, 2003).

The same proportion of parents (59 percent) in low-SES and high-SES families would like their children to get a college education and believe they will do so (Lugaila, 2003). Despite poverty, then, low-income parents have similar values and aspirations for their children as do higher-income parents.

Middle-SES Families Middle-SES parents have more resources (money, time, education) to enhance their children's emotional, social, and cognitive development. Many working-class and middle-class men feel that they show their commitment to parenthood by staying in their jobs—even jobs they hate—because doing so provides for their families (Cohen, 1993). Such fathers furnish the resources for children to pursue educational or cultural opportunities (and also counteract the detrimental influences of peers) by sending children away to camp or enrolling them in music lessons or sports (Ambert, 1997). Economically disadvantaged parents aren't able to provide such alternatives.

Middle-SES mothers talk to their infants more, and in more sophisticated ways, than do low-SES mothers. Such conversing facilitates children's self-expression. Middle-SES parents, more than lower-SES parents, also seek professional advice about child development (Bornstein, 2002).

High-SES Families The more money parents have, the more they can spend on their children's education, health care, reading materials, and other expenses that enhance their children's life chances. From a child's birth to age 17, a high-income family ($100,000 income a year) spends $250,000 on a child, compared with $170,000 for a middle-income family ($53,000 income a year) and $125,000 for a low-income family ($25,000) a year (Lino, 2003). Thus, a child from a high-income family enjoys much more material resources from birth until late adolescence than a child in a middle- or low-income family.

Parents in high-SES families read more often to their children and provide more outings. Their children are involved in more extracurricular activities that broaden a child's self-confidence, knowledge base, and physical and intellectual abilities. For example, 20 percent of children ages 6 to 17 in low-SES homes participate in sports, compared with 41 percent of children in high-SES households. Similarly, only 23 percent of children in low-income families belong to school clubs, compared with 40 percent of children in high-income families (Lugaila, 2003).

Most of us associate child rearing with childhood and adolescence. In fact, parenting continues until both parents die. Because there are more multigenerational families, numerous economic hard times, and closer relationships between parents and children, parenting often spans the entire life course.

Parenting across the Life Course

Good parenting influences the next generation more than socioeconomic status or family structure (Chen and Kaplan, 2001). Raising children from infancy to adulthood entails a variety of adjustments and changes over time.

Parenting Infants and Babies

Expecting a baby is very different from *having* a baby. The first year of a child's life can be very demanding.

Infants need what LaRossa (1986: 88) calls "continuous coverage": "They need to be talked to, listened to, cuddled, fed, cleaned, carried, rocked, burped, soothed, put to sleep, taken to the doctor, and so on."

Infancy, sometimes called babyhood, is the period of life between birth and about 1½ years. Infancy encompasses only a small fraction of the average person's lifespan but is a period of both enormous helplessness and physical and cognitive development. Parents spend twice as much time with their infants as they do with their children who are in elementary school (Bornstein, 2002).

Because there is always something parents have to do for their dependent charges, they are on call 24 hours a day, which often results in a lack of privacy, minimal time to oneself, stress, and fatigue.

The Demands of Irritable Infants Infants communicate hunger or discomfort by crying and being "fussy." Both mothers and fathers experience frustration when they can't soothe a crying infant. Mothers, especially, may feel they're inadequate and experience stress and a decline in marital satisfaction (Crnic and Low, 2002).

Parents should recognize that crying is the most powerful way a baby can get attention. Babies cry during the first few months for a variety of reasons. They may be unable to digest cow's milk if they are bottle-fed, if they are breast-fed they may want to suckle even if they are not hungry, they may be in pain from ear or urinary tract infections, they may be uncomfortable because of an allergy or other condition, they may be wet or soiled, or they may simply want some company (Kitzinger, 1989).

Sometimes parents bring colicky babies to bed with them because "bed sharing" quiets the infant and promotes family companionship. Breast-feeding mothers find bed sharing more convenient. Although bed sharing is common in much of the world, it's a new trend in the United States. The percentage of babies sleeping with a parent or another caregiver at least part of the night rose from 6 percent in 1993 to 13 percent in 2000. Bed sharing is more common among Asian Americans (32 percent) and African Americans (31 percent) than among Latinos (13 percent) and whites (10 percent) (Willinger et al., 2003).

Should parents sleep with their infants and babies? Although most pediatricians are neutral, others feel that bed sharing can increase risks for the infant: falling out of bed, suffocating, and being injured or killed by a parent (especially one who's been drinking) who rolls over on the baby (Springen, 2003; Stein, 2003).

Fatigue and Stress Babies are demanding. As a father of a newborn commented, "Going out for a quick beer, staying late at work, being spontaneous—all that stuff is history" (Blanchard, 1999–2000: 20). As the workload increases, parents have less time for each other.

Mothers, in particular, are often exhausted by child care. Those who are employed outside the home are tired and may temporarily lose interest in sex. Even though many wives accommodate their husbands' sexual overtures, they experience a loss of desire. Part of the disinterest results from fatigue and always being "on call." Some women don't enjoy sex because the baby may be crying in the next room (Walzer, 1998).

Parental characteristics often affect a parent's stress levels. Mothers who are more withdrawn, anxious, or depressed generally experience greater stress during their children's infancy. Mothers are often insecure about their parenting and need support from their partners such as positive statements and discussions about the difficulties of parenting (Mulsow et al., 2002).

Some of the parenting insecurity comes from "experts" who give contradictory advice or reinforce misconceptions about babies. Parents can protect themselves by recognizing some of the myths about babies.

Myths about Babies and Infants Most of us learn about child rearing from parents, friends, relatives, self-help books, and even television talk shows. Some of the advice can be more harmful than helpful, especially that of self-help books and talk shows. According to Segal (1989), some of the ideas parents have about child development are myths that reflect common misperceptions about the baby's early years:

1. *Myth 1: You can tell in infancy how bright a child is likely to be later on.* On the contrary, a baby's early achievements, such as reaching, sitting, crawling, or talking, are not always good indicators of intelligence or predictors of later intellectual ability. For example, early agility in building with blocks or imitating words has almost no relationship to later performance in school.

2. *Myth 2: The more stimulation a baby gets, the better.* A stimulating environment has a positive effect on babies' intellectual capacities by influencing the brain's rate of growth. But babies can be overstimulated, agitated, or even frightened into withdrawal by the constant assault on their senses by an intrusive rattle, toy, or talking face.

   Millions of parents buy "enrichment" products such as flash cards and educational software for children as young as 6 months ("Your baby will learn the numbers 1–20!" according to some ads). Others play classical music all day or play cassette tapes in the crib that teach a baby hour after hour to speak French or German (Marcus et al., 1999; MacDonald, 2003).

Such products do little more than ease parents' fears about raising a child in a success-oriented world. Classical music and language tapes don't make babies more intelligent or intellectually superior. Although positive stimuli are better than none, parents can have an equally positive effect by just talking to their infants.

3. *Myth 3: Parents who pick up crying babies will spoil them.* It's impossible to spoil a child who is under 1 year old. Crying is the only way a baby can tell parents that he or she is hungry, uncomfortable, in pain, or ill. Parents should pick up their baby as much as they want and not worry about discipline at such a young age. Ignoring a newborn's cries sets off a vicious cycle that leads to more crying, which further discourages the parents from responding, which makes the baby even more irritable, and so on (Kohn, 1991; Bornstein, 2002).

4. *Myth 4: If a baby cries every time a parent leaves, it is an early sign of emotional insecurity.* Not at all. It is normal for babies aged 8 to 15 months to become agitated, to cry, or to show anxiety when separated from their mother or other steady caretaker.

5. *Myth 5: Special talents surface early or not at all.* This is not true. Many gifted children do not recognize or develop their skills until adolescence or even later. Innate talents may never surface if there are no opportunities for their expression. For example, jazz musician Louis Armstrong was a neglected and abandoned child. It was only years later, when Armstrong was living in the New Orleans Colored Waifs Home for Boys, that he was taught to play an instrument, and his talent was ignited.

6. *Myth 6: Parental conflicts don't affect babies.* Wrong. Infants recognize expressions of suspicion, anger, or contempt. Babies as young as 12 months old understand the facial expressions and voice tones of people around them and react, accordingly, in positive or negative ways (Mumme and Fernald, 2003). Children as young as 18 to 24 months become sufficiently upset to try to break up their parents' fights, and they may act more aggressively toward their playmates. Thus, parents are mistaken if they think that their yelling or arguing doesn't affect a baby.

Parenting is harder when adults believe these and other myths. Such fictions create unnecessary anxiety and guilt for many parents because they set up false expectations or unrealistic goals.

Although many parents experience strain, relationships can become richer. As the baby starts sleeping

These kindergarteners seem very attentive to their teacher's instruction on how to use a computer. If they're loved and supported by their parents and families, children are more likely to meet this and other challenges successfully.

through the night and parents develop a schedule, life (including sex) usually returns to normal. It just takes time.

Parenting Children

The nature and quality of relationships with adults and other adult caregivers have a profound impact on a child's development. Most parents realize this and spend a lot of physical and emotional energy, as well as financial resources, to encourage their child's healthy development.

Daily Interaction   The majority of children under 6 years old interact with their parents quite a bit. About 75 percent have dinner with one or both parents every day, and 70 percent receive parental praise three or more times a day ("Good for you" or "Way to go") (Lugaila, 2003). Children aged 3 to 12 spent an average of 31 hours per week with mothers and 23 hours with fathers in 2001, compared with 25 and 19 hours, respectively, in 1981 (Sandberg and Hofferth, 2001).

Although both parents still view childrearing as primarily the mother's responsibility, fathers in intact families spend 67 percent as much time with children as mothers on weekdays and 87 percent as much on weekends. Fathers' child-rearing involvement increases for school-aged children, especially in sports, outdoor activities, hobbies, and television or video viewing (Yeung et al., 2001).

Parental and Children's Inputs   Child rearing reflects both parental inputs and children's temperaments. In terms of parents' inputs, children as young as 3 and 4 years old who are routinely exposed to "complex language" (rather than baby talk) are more likely to develop important language skills (Huttenlocher et al., 2002). Parents who encourage their 3-year-old children's curiosity and verbalization (such as physical exploration and active social play) improve their children's cognitive abilities (Raine et al., 2002). And children age 13 and younger who spend time in family activities and have regular bedtime schedules have fewer behavior problems than their counterparts (Hofferth and Sandberg, 2001).

Although parents shape a baby's environment, each baby arrives in the world with its own genes, physical appearance, temperament, and personality (Ambert, 2001). Even children in the same family can vary greatly. Some children are born easier to satisfy and soothe and have a happy demeanor. Others are more cautious and shy. Still others are difficult to please and seem constantly unsatisfied.

There can be considerable differences even between same-sex twins in their personalities and behavior (Lytton and Gallagher, 2002). One of my colleagues tells the story of his twin girls who received exactly the same dolls when they were 3 years old. When the parents asked the girls what they would name the dolls, one twin chattered that the doll's name was Lori, that she loved Lori, and she would take good care of her. The second twin muttered, "Her name is Stupid," and flung the doll into a corner. By adolescence, identical twins can be very different emotionally even though they are the same age, gender, ethnicity, and social class, have the same parents, live in the same community, attend the same school, and share genetically based traits (Crosnoe and Elder, 2002).

Despite children's different temperaments, parents have similarly high expectations of their children. Some fall for marketing gimmicks. Others overmedicalize and overprogram their offspring.

The Marketing of Childhood   Many parents and educators believe that the first three years of a child's life are the critical learning period. As a result, there are "Ivy League" preschools—with an average tuition of $14,000 a year—where 3-year-olds are given French lessons and the lunch menu consists of "salmon patties, garlic mashed potatoes, and legumes" (Barney, 1999). Many researchers contend that such obsession with "early child development" is little more than expensive marketing. Instead of organized activities and commercial gimmicks, what toddlers need most is adult attention and an opportunity to explore their environment (Gopnik et al., 1999).

The Medicalization of Childhood Medical researchers are also concerned that, increasingly, physicians and parents are overmedicating children aged 2 to 4. In a study of 200,000 children, Zito and her colleagues (2000) found that almost 2 percent of children were receiving stimulants (like Ritalin), antidepressants (like Prozac), or tranquilizers. Overall, about 4 percent of children aged 5 to 14 receive Ritalin (Cox et al., 2003). By age 20, children might be taking a range of potent drugs that have been tested only on adults (Zito et al., 2003).

Antipsychotic drugs like Zyprexa and Risperdal are given as "quick fixes" to kids who "act out," and clonidine, a blood pressure medication, is now being given to children with attention deficit hyperactivity disorder (ADHD) and even to "sleep resistant" babies. Since 1997, prescription spending for children has risen faster than spending for any other group, including seniors and baby boomers.

Many of the drugs have had adverse side effects that include an increase in suicidal thoughts, reduced bowel control, heart problems, and even the death of 769 children in 2000 (Cordes, 2003). It could be that "unruly" preschoolers are reacting to stressors such as divorce, neglect, or poor child care rather than ADHD (Diller, 1998).

The Overprogramming of Childhood Many children 12 and under lead very structured lives. Children today have 6 hours a week of free play time, compared with almost 10 hours in 1981 (Karasik, 2000). As a result, many children have much more hectic schedules than in the past.

Structured activities increase children's self-confidence and provide valuable interpersonal interaction. On the other hand, they can also interfere with play time and sleep. Many parents have no idea that their children are overbooked: Kids are three times as likely to feel time-deprived as their parents believe (Weiss, 2001). Some children don't mind. Others complain that their days are filled with "a mad scramble of sports, music lessons, prep courses, and then hours of homework" (Kantrowitz and Wingert, 2001).

Parenting Teenagers

Adolescence is a time of tremendous change. Like younger children, teenagers are active agents in the family. Adolescents are establishing their own identity and are testing their autonomy as they mature and break away from parental supervision, a healthy process in human development (see Erikson's stages in *Table 12.1* on page 332). Teenagers often complain that parents treat them like little children: "Have you done your homework?" "Did you brush your teeth?"

A good parent–child relationship may change suddenly during adolescence. As children enter the seventh and eighth grades, there may be conflict over such issues as relationships, money, and spending time with friends.

As teenagers become more independent, parents may feel rejected and suspicious. The most difficult part of parenting adolescents, according to some mothers, is dealing with adolescents' changing moods and behavior:

By 14 she didn't hang around the kitchen after school anymore and tell you everything that happened. She endlessly told her friends on the phone instead. [Now] if you try to broach personal subjects, she leaves the room. . . . She slams the door

The dinner-hour myth in which family members relax with each other and share their day's experiences is often exploded when children—especially adolescents—and parents disagree over such things as where and with whom they have been, when they're going to clean up their rooms, or why they miss curfews.

TABLE 12.5

Teens at High Risk for Substance Abuse

According to the National Center on Addiction and Substance Abuse (2003), almost one in four U.S. teens is at "high risk" for substance abuse:

- 25 percent smoke.

- 94 percent have tried alcohol, and 43 percent drink alcohol in a typical week.

- 42 percent get drunk at least once a month.

- 79 percent have friends who use marijuana.

- 69 percent know a friend or classmate using acid, cocaine, or heroin.

- 71 percent have tried marijuana.

- 57 percent could buy marijuana in one hour or less.

to her room and stays there. . . . She used to chatter incessantly on car rides; now . . . "What's new in school today?" you ask. "Nothing," she answers. Now she's 15 and 16, and a boy comes over. They go up to her room and close the door. You start to worry: If you set limits on them, won't they just find somewhere else to go? (Patner, 1990: C5).

Normal adolescent development can put stress on a marriage. In most cases, the husband and wife are also experiencing their own pressures in their relationship, at work, and with extended family members. Parenting teenagers adds to marital role strain but doesn't necessarily cause it. Instead, "the seeds of parents' individual and marital problems are sown long before their first baby arrives" and continue through a child's adolescence (Cowan and Cowan, 2000: ix; see also Grych, 2002).

The parenting sections of bookstores are stocked with books "advising parents on how to enjoy and promote the development of their cuddly infants alongside volumes on how to discipline their spiteful and problem-ridden teenagers" (Steinberg and Silk, 2002: 103). Why are many parents so anxious about raising adolescents?

Are Teenagers Getting a Raw Deal? Yes and no. One of the reasons parents worry about their teenagers or see them as moody, rebellious, and difficult is because such stereotypes pervade popular culture and self-help books. When was the last time you opened a newspaper or watched the news to see a positive story about a teenager?

A study of 59 self-help books for parents of adolescents found that 20 percent characterized adolescence as a period of "storm and stress or turmoil," and 42 percent projected negative stereotypes about adolescence as "turbulent," "a struggle," and in "conflict" and that parents need to "survive." Even worse, some of the books, written by parents with no professional training, have "a confessional tone and consist of anecdotes about parent-adolescent conflicts. . . . Anecdotal books about parenting teenagers are likely to be little better than good fiction about family life" (Smith et al., 2003: 178).

Some parental nervousness about teenagers is warranted, however. Teens have high rates of sexually transmitted diseases because many engage in sex by the time they're 15 or 16, have many partners, and don't use condoms (see Chapter 7). Parents are also concerned about substance abuse. According to a recent national survey, 21 percent of teens ages 12 to 17 are at a "high risk" and another 34 percent are at a "moderate risk" for substance abuse (see *Table 12.5*).

Teenagers' substance abuse is influenced by many factors that include peers who smoke or drink, parents who smoke or abuse drugs, who are unmarried, and ongoing family conflict (Bray et al., 2001; Gritz et al., 2003; National Center on Addiction and Substance Abuse, 2003). Simply telling teens "to do" or "not to do" something is much less effective than being a good role model. Parents who let teenage children know they care about them and who share activities with adolescents play an important role in steering them away from trouble and into productive pursuits (Klein, 1997).

Instead of giving teens undeserved praise, parents can boost adolescents' psychological and emotional well-being by teaching them good social skills that include prosocial behaviors (such as being considerate to others), self-control, taking an initiative in developing social relationships, empathy (experiencing other peoples' feelings), and using constructive strategies (such as discussion) to resolve conflict (Hair et al., 2002; Moore and Zaff, 2002; Zaff et al., 2002).

Gender Differences in Parenting Teenagers Parents differ in their relationships with their children. Some children get along better with their mother, some with their father, and others report no difference.

Although many studies find that adolescents generally feel closeness (feelings of warmth, acceptance, and affection) with both parents, many adolescents feel closer to their mothers than to their fathers. According to a recent survey, when asked which parent deserves the most thanks for all that they do, 44 percent of teens said "Mom," 50 percent said "both parents are equally deserving," and only 4 percent said "Dad" (Fetto, 2003). Mothers probably get higher ratings because they are more likely than fathers to express love in terms of compliments, praise, and support (Hosley and Montemayor, 1997).

Employed parents often experience **role overload,** a feeling of being overwhelmed by multiple commitments and not having enough time for themselves. Because men are more likely than women to work longer hours, many fathers spend little time with their adolescents (Crouter et al., 2001). Despite spending little time with their children, fathers seem to have a stronger influence on adolescent self-esteem than do mothers (Ellis and Garber, 2000). This may be because of the father's greater power and authority in family and social relations. Because fathers are less likely than mothers to yield their authority as adolescents get older, fathers play an important leadership role, even though they may be less likely than mothers to understand their teenagers (Larson and Richards, 1994).

Only Children and Birth Order

Parenting also differs for only children and for children who are born first, second, or later. Although in the latter case parents insist that they treat all children alike, this isn't true, nor should it be because birth order brings different advantages and disadvantages.

Only Children

Being an only child is not unusual; 20 percent of children today are "onlies." The general public's attitude toward only children hasn't changed much, however. Many people believe that only children are spoiled, selfish, and self-centered (Boodman, 1995).

Only children sometimes wish they had had siblings. One grandmother remembers,

Even though I loved being an only child, there was always this moment of loneliness when I walked home from school with my best friend and her sister. At the last corner they walked down one street to their house, and I had to walk down the other alone. I always wished I had a sibling to walk the rest of the way (McCoy, 1986: 119).

Only children feel overprotected and think that routine family problems are sometimes magnified because they are always the center of attention or because parents have unrealistically high expectations. Parents of only children also see some disadvantages. They think that only children do not learn important lessons in sharing, caring, and getting along, that they can't handle teasing from peers, and that they don't learn how to stand up for themselves (McCoy, 1986).

For the most part, however, "onlies" aren't very different from children who grow up with siblings. They are no more selfish or maladjusted and are as likely to be successful in college and careers, to have happy marriages, and to be good parents. They do well in school,

have higher IQs, and tend to be more self-confident and popular among their peers. They are also more likely to have better verbal skills and to finish high school and go to college (Polit and Falbo, 1987; Blake, 1989).

Some famous onlies who have excelled in various fields include Hans Christian Andersen (writer), Leonardo da Vinci (artist and scientist), Albert Einstein (scientist), Clark Gable (actor), Elvis Presley (singer), and Jean-Paul Sartre (philosopher and writer). One of the reasons why only children may be more successful than children with siblings is the availability of financial assets. In larger families parental resources must be divided among a larger number of siblings. As a result, these children often have lower levels of educational attainment and achievement (Travis and Kohli, 1995; Baydar et al., 1997).

Birth Order

Many children are onlies until another baby is born. How does a sibling affect parenting? Generally, parents experience less conflict with the second-born than the first-born, mainly because the parents are more experienced, know more about the second-born's everyday activities, and are still focusing on the first child's transition to adolescence (Whiteman et al., 2003). Later-born children probably get away with more because they continue to get less parental attention than the first-born (Ambert, 2001).

According to a study of medical students and undergraduates, parents tend to encourage first-born children to pursue interests that could lead to a prestigious career such as lawyer or doctor. Parents are more relaxed and open with younger children and allow them to develop their interests that are artistic or oriented to the outdoors (Leong et al., 2001).

Even though many parents enjoy their teenagers, they look forward to the end of child rearing. Often, however, children bounce back to the parental nest in young adulthood and later.

Parenting in the Crowded "Empty Nest"

In prior centuries, women often died a few years after the birth of their last child. Now, as people live much longer, only about a third of the adult lifespan is spent raising children. Therefore, there may be a long stretch of time to enjoy life without the responsibilities of child rearing.

In the 1960s and 1970s, sociologists almost always included the "empty-nest" stage in describing the family life cycle (see Chapter 2). This is the stage when parents, typically in their 50s, find themselves alone at home after their children have married, gone to college, or found jobs and moved out.

The pendulum has swung back, especially for middle-class, white families. More young adults are living at home longer. And there is a new group of young adults, called the *boomerang generation*, who move back with their parents after having lived independently (see Chapter 10).

The Kids Are Back, with Their Kids

The younger you are when you leave home, the more likely you are to return. Although most young adults leave the parental nest by age 23, the proportion of adults aged 25 to 34 who are living with parents increased from 9 percent in 1960 to nearly 17 percent in 2000. More than twice as many men (12 percent) as women (5 percent) in this age group are living with their parents (Fields and Casper, 2001). Some journalists have called these people "adultolescents" because they're still "mooching off their parents" instead of living on their own (Large, 2002).

Among the middle classes, some of these boomerangers, especially men, are not moving out or are returning home because they are delaying marriage or because they enjoy the comforts of the parental nest: "Some parents find they have an adult on their hands who still wants Mom to cook his meals and do his laundry . . . but may resent being asked to account for his comings and goings" (Large, 2002: 4N).

Women who leave their parents' home early in young adulthood see employment and privacy as more important than maintaining family bonds and obligations to kin. In contrast, remaining home until marriage or moving back later has little effect in changing sons'

sense of commitment to caring for others or participating in the increased housework (Goldscheider and Lawton, 1998).

Macro-level factors also encourage a larger number of young adults to stay or move home. Many young adults have found it difficult to find well-paid employment or any employment. Marital dissolution and unmarried motherhood have increased in the past decade, bringing single mothers and divorced sons and daughters back home. Living with parents is both economical and convenient.

About 14 percent of all children under age 15 lived in extended families with a relative and at least one parent. African American children are twice as likely as white children and as likely as Latino, Asian American, and American Indian children to be living in such households (see *Figure 12.2*). Most of these children are in one-parent families. They are more likely to move in with grandparents than with any other relatives (see Chapter 17). Many Asian American and Latino parents live in extended families because older Latino and Asian American parents rely on their adult children for financial support (Glick and Van Hook, 2002).

Relationships between Parents and Adult Children

How do adult children and parents get along, especially when they're living under the same roof? Some parents report that they are tolerant of but unhappy with the return of their children. There is often conflict

FIGURE 12.2 **Children under Age 15 Living in Extended Families**

SOURCE: Based on Fields, 2001, Table 7.

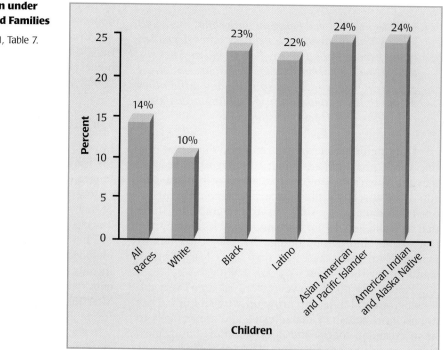

about clothes, helping out, the use of the family car, and the adult child's lifestyle (Wolcott, 2001). Parents whose adult children suffer from mental, physical, or stress-related problems or who are unemployed or unwilling to help out with household expenses experience greater depression than do parents whose children don't have these difficulties (Pillemer and Suitor, 1991; Mogelonsky, 1996).

The biggest problems arise if the adult children are unemployed or if grandchildren live in the home. College-educated fathers, especially, are hostile toward children who move back home instead of living on their own. This may result in part from the fathers' higher expectations for their children's success (Aquilino, 1997). Single mothers who move back to their parents' homes are often unhappy because grandparents are likely to interfere with the mother's child-rearing practices (Stolba and Amato, 1993).

Other research shows that co-residence brings mutual benefits. For example, adult children and their parents under age 75 often benefit, reciprocally, by sharing expenses and child care. Much of the conflict can be avoided if both sides agree to set up and follow such ground rules as not engaging in activities parents don't approve of (such as bringing in sexual partners) and respecting each side's privacy (Estess, 1994).

Parenting in Later Life

The majority of parents (62 percent) provide some form of help to at least one of their adult children. Parents are most likely to give advice (46 percent), and about one-third of parents assist with child care and household tasks. Although monetary help is the least common, such assistance varies. For example, low-income adult children are significantly more likely to receive financial help from a parent than their better-off siblings. Parents with the most resources are more likely to help at least one of their children, to assist children who live close, and to help children with whom they have a good relationship (Zarit and Eggebeen, 2002). The helping roles switch as parents become old and their adult children provide caregiving (see Chapter 17).

Although they don't expect to do so, a number of grandparents find themselves raising grandchildren in their later years, especially if the parents are on drugs, are in prison, or have mental health problems. Many American Indian children are likely to live with grandparents, usually grandmothers, when the parents move to urban areas to search for jobs (see Chapter 4).

Grandparents pitch in, but they're not always happy to do so. Most grandparents would prefer to spend their time reading, gardening, or visiting friends rather than raising grandchildren or great-grandchildren (see Chapter 17).

You see, then, that whether people are married, unmarried, partnered, or single, they parent their children throughout the life course. What about same-sex parents? Are their child-rearing practices similar to or different from those of heterosexual parents?

MAKING CONNECTIONS

■ Think about how your parents or guardians raised you. Did the parenting differ in terms of your parents' gender or your siblings' birth order? If you're an only child, are you glad you had no brothers or sisters?

■ Is it "fair" for adults to move back home (or never move out) when their parents have looked forward to the "empty nest"? ◯◯

Parenting in Lesbian and Gay Families

An estimated 1 to 5 million children in the United States have at least one gay parent (Patterson, 2002). In most respects, lesbian and gay families are like heterosexual families: The parents must make a living, family members may disagree about the use of space or money, and they must all develop problem-solving strategies (Laird, 1993; see also Chapters 6, 7, and 8).

Gay and lesbian parents face the added burden of raising children who will often experience discrimination because of their parents' sexual orientation. For this reason and for fear of alienating their children, not all homosexual parents reveal their sexual orientation to their children, even though they may want to do so.

Disclosure to Children

Despite the anxiety of some homosexual parents, many children are accepting of gay or lesbian parents. If there is a strong parent–child bond, disclosure rarely undermines this relationship. Furthermore, disclosure may help to relieve family tensions. For example, parents may have been arguing about a partner's sexual orientation or may divorce because of it. Children who are told the truth at an earlier age tend to have fewer problems with acceptance than do children who are told later (Bozett, 1987).

Although most children are accepting, they may be ambivalent about disclosing to their friends that a parent is gay. Some try to hide the information from their peers or try to prevent them from seeing how their own home life differs from that of their friends:

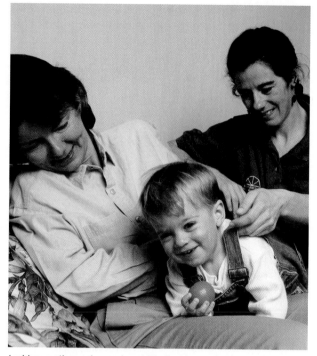

Lesbian mothers who work outside the home often have to struggle, just as heterosexual parents do, for quality time with their children.

High school was the hardest. I was into all kinds of clubs, but I was afraid everything I had gained socially would disappear if anyone ever found out that while they went home after volleyball practice to their Brady Bunch dinners with Mom and Dad, I went home to two moms. My brother and I would never allow Mom and Barb to walk together or sit next to each other in a restaurant. We wouldn't have people spend the night; if we did have friends over, we would hide the gay literature and family pictures (McGuire, 1996: 53).

Children with Lesbian and Gay Parents

Despite the particular difficulties children in gay families face, their peer and other social relationships do not differ very much from those of children raised in heterosexual families. In a summary of gay parenting studies, for example, Stacey and Biblarz (2001) concluded that the effects of gender "trump those of sexual orientation." For example, lesbians—like straight mothers—have better parenting skills than gay or heterosexual fathers and are more involved with their children. In fact, children raised by gay and lesbian parents may have some advantages. For example, teachers see the children as more responsive, and gay and lesbian parents tend to report fewer behavioral problems with their children than do heterosexual parents (Laird, 1993).

Lesbian and gay parents often do a better job of managing their anger than heterosexual couples. Lesbian and gay parents are more likely than heterosexual parents to use discussion instead of physical punishment to discipline their children. Only 15 percent of gay and lesbian parents use corporal punishment, compared with 60 percent of heterosexual parents. One of the reasons may be that lesbian and gay parents tend to be highly educated: Almost half have graduate degrees (Nanette Silverman, cited in Schorr, 2001). As you saw earlier, high-SES parents are less likely than low-SES parents to hit or spank their children.

Sometimes gay and lesbian parents are stricter in setting limits on their children's behavior (Bigner and Jacobsen, 1989). This may reflect the additional pressures that homosexual parents experience as a result of their guilt over their sexuality or their fear that accusations of bad parenting can limit visitation or custody rights. Such fears are often justified. In some cases gay and lesbian parents have succeeded in getting visitation rights or have regained custody of their children only after appealing their cases to higher courts (Paulson, 2003).

Parents with Gay and Lesbian Children

When children come out, many heterosexual parents are initially negative because they think that their children could be heterosexual if they wanted. Most Asian parents, for example, view homosexuality as a chosen lifestyle, "an undesirable indulgence of individual freedom in the United States" (Leonard, 1997: 148). A child who once was familiar now appears to be a stranger. Parents may also be concerned about becoming stigmatized themselves.

Negative feelings are frequently followed by strong feelings of guilt and personal failure in their parenting roles. A common question is "Where did we fail?" Some parents may break off contact with their children, try to convince them to change their sexual preference, or ignore the issue. Over time, others accept the child's homosexuality (Barret and Robinson, 1990; Savin-Williams and Dubé, 1998).

Regardless of sexual orientation, mothers and fathers who are consistently and positively involved in their children's lives help them to grow up with a strong sense of self, a feeling of security, and a host of other positive characteristics. Parents can also stunt their children's development.

Parents' Impact on Child Development

Recently, a school superintendent in Lebanon, Pennsylvania, proposed that teachers grade parents on how involved they are in the children's education. Some parents were furious because they felt that being judged by their children's teachers would be demeaning. Others thought it was a good idea because many parents aren't on top of their children's academic progress ("Report cards for parents . . .," 2003). Whether it's education or other areas, parents can have either positive or negative effects on their children.

Parents' Positive Impact

By around age 11 or 12, children start withholding private thoughts and feelings from their parents because they fear rejection through sarcasm, putdowns, or scorn. Parents and children have many similar rights. For example, both should be treated with respect, forgiven when they make mistakes, and safe from physical, sexual, and emotional abuse ("Parenting skills . . .," 2000). The biggest difference is that parental rights also include adult responsibilities.

An important adult responsibility is to set guidelines or rules that teach children the difference between right and wrong and what kind of behavior is considered acceptable. Much research supports the idea that limit-setting is a critical element in shaping children's judgment and developing a conscience (Brown et al., 2001).

Setting guidelines includes establishing routines and rituals. Especially during times of stress and transition, family routines and rituals improve family relationships and well-being. Routines get things done and promote a sense of order and reciprocal expectations. Rituals, such as dinnertimes and birthday celebrations, enhance family members' sense of stability and belonging to the group (Fiese et al., 2002).

As you saw earlier, parents who spend time with their children (reading, going on outings, performing household tasks) experience greater warmth and closeness. Parents who are involved with their children are more likely to report that their teenagers have fewer mental health problems, greater academic motivation, and fewer emotional difficulties (McElhaney and Allen, 2001; Flouri and Buchanan, 2003). In addition, many parents who participate in religious activities with their children have more cohesive family relationships, lower levels of conflict, and fewer behavioral problems among children (Brown et al., 2001).

The majority of parents are responsible and have a beneficial effect on their children. In other cases, parenting styles or the lack of parenting can jeopardize children's well-being.

Parents' Negative Impact

Parents aren't always good role models. A few years ago, a father became enraged when his son took an elbow to the face during a 9- and 10-year-old hockey game. An argument erupted between the fathers, and

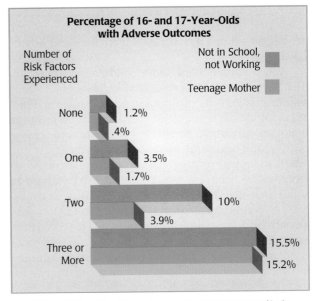

FIGURE 12.3 **The More Risk Factors, the More Likely Adverse Outcomes** As the text discusses, the six risk factors for children and adolescents include the following: 1) poverty, 2) welfare dependence, 3) both parents are absent, 4) one-parent families, 5) unwed mothers, and 6) a parent who has not graduated from high school.

SOURCE: U.S. Census Bureau, *America's Children at Risk,* Census Brief (97-2), September 1997, p. 2.

one (in front of his three sons) beat the other to death (Wingert and Lauerman, 2000).

Researchers have identified many factors that put children at risk of problems ranging from hyperactivity to criminal involvement. Six of the most important risk factors are poverty, welfare dependence, absent parents, single parents, unwed mothers, and parents who did not graduate from high school. Children exposed to three or more risk factors are much more likely at ages 16 and 17 to be out of school and unemployed and, in the case of girls, to be teenage mothers (see *Figure 12.3*).

Poor parenting often has negative effects on children that are apparent in early childhood and later. By 18 months, for example, the children of alcohol-abusing fathers have more symptoms of anxiety, depression, and temper tantrums than their counterparts (Olson et al., 2001; McKelvey et al., 2002). Even if fathers aren't alcoholics, by age 5 the children of fathers who are aggressive and engage in other antisocial behavior are more likely than their peers to have behavioral problems such as cheating, swearing, and physically attacking other children (Jaffee et al., 2003).

By age 3, the children of depressed mothers, especially those who are poor, show delayed cognitive and motor development compared with their peers. By age 9, children of depressed mothers have a number of behavioral problems that include aggressiveness and delinquency (Luoma et al., 2001; Petterson and Albers, 2001).

When parents fight about children, or when children blame themselves for the conflict, children as young as fifth-graders have problems in school and experience stress (Rudolph et al., 2001). Children who grow up in households where parents fight and are cold, unsupportive, and neglectful are more likely as teenagers and adults to engage in drug and alcohol abuse, smoking, risky sexual behavior, and antisocial behavior and to suffer lifelong health problems such as cancer, heart disease, hypertension, diabetes, obesity, depression, and anxiety disorders (Briggs-Gowan et al., 2001; Repetti et al., 2002; Cartwright et al., 2003).

Parenting, then, can be harmful to many children's health. Is nonparental child care a better alternative for these and other families?

MAKING CONNECTIONS

■ Much research shows that sexual orientation has little effect on children's child rearing. Why, then, are many people opposed to gay and lesbian parenting?

■ Think about your own parents. What positive impacts did they have on you? What about negative influences?

Nonparental Child Care

The Reverend Jesse Jackson reportedly said, "Your children need your presence more than your presents." In 1993, a 15-year-old British boy went to court to force his mother to spend more time with him. Such cases are rare, but many parents, especially absentee fathers, spend little time with their children. Some latchkey kids must fend for themselves after school until a parent comes home from work. In many other cases, employed parents must rely on child care outside the family.

Absentee Fathers

Some people believe (see Chapter 1) that one of the most serious problems facing contemporary families is that the United States is becoming an increasingly fatherless society:

> Tonight, about 40 percent of American children will go to sleep in homes in which their fathers do not live. Before they reach the age of eighteen,

> more than half of our nation's children are likely to spend at least a significant portion of their childhoods living apart from their fathers. . . . Never before have so many children grown up without knowing what it means to have a father. (Blankenhorn, 1995: 1)

We discuss the effects on children who do not see their nonresident fathers after a divorce or separation in Chapters 15 and 16. There are millions of children born outside marriage who also don't see their fathers. Among unmarried fathers, 20 percent never see their children, and another 21 percent see them only a few times a year (Jacobsen and Edmondson, 1994; McLanahan, 2002).

Absentee fathers can have a highly negative impact on their children, from birth to young adulthood. Three disadvantages associated with father absence are economic deprivation, poor parenting, and a lack of social support (McLanahan, 2002).

Economic Deprivation Half of families headed by single mothers live below the poverty line, compared with 10 percent of two-parent families (see Chapter 13). Although many single-mother families were poor even before the father left, the father's departure reduces a child's economic resources even further. Economic problems, in turn, affect the quality of a neighborhood and its schools, the ability of a mother to pay for child care, and the child's access to enriching after-school and summer programs.

Poor Parenting A father's absence may also affect the quality of the mother–child relationship. As you've seen, poverty-related stress can bring on depression, health problems, and substance abuse for both mothers and children.

Compared with children living with both biological parents, children with an absentee father are twice as likely to drop out of high school, more likely to spend time in juvenile correctional facilities, 20 to 42 percent more likely to suffer health problems, and more likely to have lower earnings in young adulthood. They are also more likely to be poor, to experience a marital disruption themselves, or to have a child out of wedlock, thereby repeating the cycle of single parenthood (Goulter and Minninger, 1993; Lino, 1994; Ellis et al., 2003).

Lack of Social Support The negative outcomes of poor parenting don't result only from the father's absence. Compared with children raised in single-mother households, for example, those raised in single-father homes are less well behaved at school, are less successful at getting along with others, and put forth less effort in class. Thus, teenagers who have behavioral problems in school and in the community reflect the problems that arise from the absence of a second parent, male or female (Downey et al., 1998).

Single mothers sometimes get important financial and other support from "social fathers," male relatives and mothers' boyfriends who are like fathers to the children. Male relatives, especially, can enhance a child's cognitive abilities by providing books, reading to children, and spending time with them (Jayakody and Kalil, 2002). If social fathers leave or move away, however, children lose access to the support and resources.

Latchkey Kids

The traditional family is changing to a family in which both parents are employed full time outside the home, creating a family type that has been called **DEWKS**, or **dual-employed with kids**. The proportion of DEWK families in the United States has increased from 33 percent of all families in 1976 to 63 percent in 2001 (U.S. Census Bureau, 2002). As a result, latchkey kids have become a growing concern.

There's nothing new about children being on their own at home. The phrase *latchkey children* originated in the early 1800s, when youngsters who were responsible for their own care wore the key to their home tied to a string around their necks. Today **latchkey kids** are children who return home after school and let themselves in, with their own keys, to an empty house or apartment, where they are alone and unsupervised until their parents or another adult comes home.

The number of latchkey kids has almost doubled since the 1970s. Almost 7 million children 5 to 14 years old (18 percent of children in this age group) care for themselves on a regular basis before or after school. About one in four children is completely alone after school. On average, children spend six hours per week in self-care (Hofferth et al., 2000; Smith, 2000).

Who are the children who are home alone? The older children are, the more likely they are to be latchkey kids. For example, 2 percent of those in self-care are 5 years old compared to 48 percent of 14-year-olds. There are also dramatic differences by the parent's sex. Grade-school age children living with a single father are more likely to be in self-care than children living with a single mother, 31 percent and 17 percent, respectively (Smith, 2000). White 10- to 12-year-olds are nearly twice as likely as their African American and Latino peers to spend time in self-care regularly but there are few differences among racial and ethnic groups in the use of self-care for younger children (Capizanno et al., 2000; Smith, 2000).

Many children enjoy being home alone, savoring the independence. They watch television, play, do homework, read, and do some housework (Hofferth et al., 2000).

Millions of "latchkey kids" return from school every day to empty houses for two to four hours until an adult or other caretaker arrives. Most schools don't provide after-school care. In other cases, parents—especially single mothers—can't afford expensive after-school programs.

Others, however, are frightened about being by themselves, don't structure their time, don't do their homework or chores, or invite friends against house rules (Belle, 1999). Some researchers believe that most 6- to 9-year-olds are not ready developmentally to care for themselves regularly, and certainly less able than older children to deal with household emergencies (Vandivere et al., 2003).

Child Care

As the number of divorces and working single parents grows, parents must make child-care arrangements. Mothers who work unusual hours or on weekends must often stitch together multiple arrangements. About 65 percent of parents juggle multiple child-care arrangements that include day-care centers, Head Start programs, relatives, friends, and baby-sitters (Capizzano and Adams, 2000b; Capizzano et al., 2000).

Some companies, such as Stride-Rite (a shoe manufacturer) in Cambridge, Massachusetts, have implemented innovative programs that combine elder care and child care.

Child-Care Patterns and Characteristics About 76 percent of children under age 5 with employed parents are in some form of nonparental care each week. Nationwide, 62 percent of children are in only one child-care arrangement. Almost two out of five children (38 percent) in nonparental care have two or more child-care arrangements. The arrangements vary with such factors as availability of suitable care, costs of care, ability of parents to pay, and differences between work schedules and the hours of the child-care programs

(Uttal, 1999; Capizzano and Adams, 2000b). Of the children under age 5 in child care, 41 percent are in nonparental care for 35 or more hours per week (see *Figure 12.4*).

Almost a third of children 3 to 5 years old start child care by the time they are 3 months old. About equal percentages of children under 5 are cared for by relatives and nonrelatives (see *Figure 12.1*). Before- and after-school programs and baby-sitting by relatives are the most common child-care arrangements for 21 percent of 6- to 9-year-old children, and 17 percent of 10- to 12-year-old children rely on relatives as their primary care provider (Capizzano et al., 2000; Fields et al., 2001).

Higher-income families are more likely to use child care arrangements than their lower-income counterparts. These families can better afford to pay for child-care services, can afford higher-quality services, and live in neighborhoods that parents consider safe for child care at early ages (Capizzano et al., 2000; Fields et al., 2001). In terms of racial and ethnic backgrounds, Latinos are less likely (18 percent) to rely on nonrelatives than white (23 percent) or African American parents (22 percent) (Smith, 2000).

Effects of Child Care on Children Day care is a controversial issue. One study found that more than six in ten parents were concerned about abuse and neglect in day-care centers, even though children are more likely to be abused by relatives than by day-care workers ("Necessary compromises . . .," 2000).

A national study rated only 10 percent of day-care facilities for children aged 3 and under as "excellent." Nearly one-third were rated "good," 53 percent were ranked "fair," and 8 percent were deemed "poor" (Russell, 1999). Such studies reinforce parental concerns about unsafe and low-quality child-care centers, even though preschool children are almost twice as likely to be injured on playground equipment at home as in other locations, including child-care centers (U.S. Consumer Product Safety Commission, 2001).

On the other hand, a number of studies show that a well-run day-care center has positive effects on children's social and cognitive development (Harvey, 1999; NICHD . . ., 1999a, 2000). In high-quality day care, even children from low-income families outscore more

FIGURE 12.4 **Hours Spent in Nonparental Care by Children under Age Five**

SOURCE: Based on Capizzano and Adams, 2000a, Figure 1.

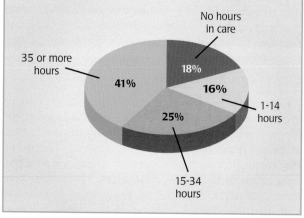

ASKYOURSELF

How Can I Find a Good Day-Care Program?

Following are some questions that will help you to evaluate the day-care programs you visit. Some are questions to ask of the administrators, teachers, and other staff, as well as of other parents. Others are questions to ask yourself as you mull over the information you've gathered.

1. **What is the staff–child ratio?** The best programs have enough staff members on hand so that children get plenty of attention. Suggested staff–child ratios are 1 to 3 for infants, 1 to 10 for 5- and 6-year-olds, and 1 to 12 for children over 6.

2. **What is the staff turnover rate?** If half of the staff leaves every year it probably means that they are paid extremely low wages or feel that the program is not run well. Another warning signal is a high attrition rate, reflecting the probability that parents have arranged for care elsewhere.

3. **How do the staff and children look when you visit?** If the children seem unhappy, have runny noses, and seem passive, the center is probably ignoring such things as colds (which are easily spread) and is not providing meaningful activities for the children. If the staff seems distant or lackadaisical, they are probably not engaging kids in interesting projects.

4. **How well equipped is the facility?** There should be interesting indoor activities that give children a choice of projects and ample playground space with swings, jungle gyms, and other exercise equipment. If there is no adjacent outdoor area, do the children go regularly to a park or playground where they can run, jump, and swing? In addition, is the day-care facility clean and organized, and does it have a range of toys, books, materials, and activities?

5. **What are the safety regulations and hygienic practices?** Are children always accounted for when they arrive and leave? Are staff trained in first-aid? Do they use latex gloves when they change diapers or attend to a sick or bleeding child? What are the policies about children who take medications (for allergies, for example)?

6. **Is the director of the center willing to have you talk to other parents who use the child-care center?** Better yet, does the center have video cameras so you can log on from work or home? The "Taking It Further" section at the end of this chapter provides Internet sites for accessing a wealth of information about day-care facilities.

---

advantaged children on IQ tests by the time they enter kindergarten (Posner and Vandell, 1994; NICHD . . ., 1999b). The higher the quality of child care in the first three years of life, the greater the child's language abilities at 15, 24, and 36 months and the more school readiness—such as counting and knowing the alphabet—a child shows at age 3 (NICHD . . ., 2003).

The effect of high-quality educational child care in infancy may persist into adulthood. Early intervention programs such as Head Start provide low-income children with many benefits. Throughout their school years, children in high-quality day care are less likely to get into trouble or to drop out of school. They also have better language and mathematical skills and higher academic achievement than their counterparts from a "regular" day-care group and are also more likely to attend college (Campbell and Ramey, 1999; Reynolds et al., 2001).

The day-care centers with the best results are small and have high adult-to-child ratios (see the box "How Can I Find a Good Day-Care Program?"). Good child-care providers often quit, however, because they earn among the lowest wages: about $17,000 a year, less than pet groomers. Few receive health insurance, and almost none receive retirement benefits. Consequently, 30 percent of day-care workers leave their jobs within a year (Zuckerman, 2000). Top-notch day-care service that includes competent staff, high adult-to-child ratios, and staff stability is expensive: at least $200 a week. Because this is more than many families can afford, the lack of high-quality day care remains a serious problem.

Current Social Issues and Children's Well-being

Despite absentee fathers and societal limitations such as inadequate child care, most people reach adulthood without serious damage. Millions of children face tough

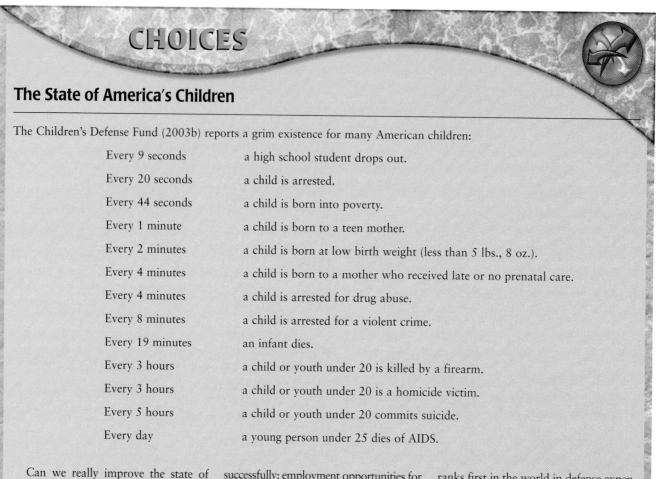

CHOICES

The State of America's Children

The Children's Defense Fund (2003b) reports a grim existence for many American children:

Every 9 seconds	a high school student drops out.
Every 20 seconds	a child is arrested.
Every 44 seconds	a child is born into poverty.
Every 1 minute	a child is born to a teen mother.
Every 2 minutes	a child is born at low birth weight (less than 5 lbs., 8 oz.).
Every 4 minutes	a child is born to a mother who received late or no prenatal care.
Every 4 minutes	a child is arrested for drug abuse.
Every 8 minutes	a child is arrested for a violent crime.
Every 19 minutes	an infant dies.
Every 3 hours	a child or youth under 20 is killed by a firearm.
Every 3 hours	a child or youth under 20 is a homicide victim.
Every 5 hours	a child or youth under 20 commits suicide.
Every day	a young person under 25 dies of AIDS.

Can we really improve the state of America's children? Certainly, according to many social analysts. There can be greater support for all families to rear kids successfully: employment opportunities for parents, high-quality health care, organized recreation, and safe streets (*Kids Count Data Book*, 2003). A nation that ranks first in the world in defense expenditures should allocate more than 0.7 percent of the nation's budget for children's needs (Children's Defense Fund, 2002).

odds of surviving or thriving, however. In this final section we examine some of the risks that children face, and we discuss foster care, one of the responses for at-risk infants and children.

Children at Risk

Life is improving for many American children. They are living longer, smoking less, and taking more honors courses, and the portion of children with health insurance is at an all-time high of 88 percent.

In addition, teen pregnancy and gun violence have fallen, and mainstream banks and credit unions are devising alternatives to high-cost financial services for low-income families (*Federal Interagency Forum . . .*, 2003; *Kids Count Data Book*, 2003).

Compared with other industrialized countries, however, the United States ranks fairly low in children's

health and well-being (see the box "The State of America's Children"). The proportion of kids ages 6 to 18 who are overweight increased from 6 percent in the late 1970s to 15 percent in 2000. The number of black children under 18 years old who live in extreme poverty has risen sharply since 2000 and is at one of the highest levels since the government began collecting extreme poverty figures in 1980.

In addition, housing for more than one in three U.S. households with kids is physically inadequate, is crowded, or costs more than 20 percent of the household income (Children's Defense Fund, 2003a; *Federal Interagency Forum . . .*, 2003).

Foster Care

The growth of poverty, child abuse, and parental neglect has increased children's out-of-home placements. These placements include foster care, care by relatives, hospitalization, residential treatment facilities, group homes (which house a number of children under the auspices of a charitable organization), and shelters for runaways. The most common out-of-home placement for children is the **foster home**, where parents raise children who are not on their own for a period of time but do not formally adopt them.

Prevalence and Characteristics of Foster Homes

Currently, more than 580,000 children are in foster care in the United States, twice as many as in 1987. In contrast, there are only 144,000 foster families. This means that hundreds of thousands of children end up in group homes, temporary detention, and psychiatric wards awaiting placement, a wait that can last months or even years (Marks, 2003).

An estimated 40 to 80 percent of the families who become child protective service cases have problems with alcohol or drugs. Of the children in foster care, two-thirds are African American or Latino, nearly 45 percent enter care as babies or toddlers, and nearly all have been neglected rather than abused (Pascual, 1999/2000). About 72,000 to 125,000 of the children are in foster homes because they have lost their parents to AIDS (Children's Defense Fund, 2000a).

Recent years have seen a dramatic growth in kinship care, sometimes called relative foster care. In 1986, 18 percent of the children in foster care lived with relatives; the number had increased to 25 percent by 2000. Some states limit kinship care to biological relatives; others extend the definition of kin to include neighbors, godparents, and other adults with a close relationship but no biological ties to the child (Barbell and Freundlich, 2001).

Problems of Foster Homes

In theory, foster homes are supposed to provide short-term care until the children can be adopted or returned to their biological parents. In reality, many children go through multiple placements and remain in foster care until late adolescence. Approximately 25 to 30 percent of the children returned to their biological parents are soon back in foster care. Children who are older or have behavioral or emotional problems are the most likely to bounce from home to home. In this sense, the foster care system may sometimes worsen children's already significant physical and mental health problems (Barbell and Freundlich, 2001).

The typical foster parent, usually a woman, is paid little to care for a child (about $400 a month for a child age 2). Although this might sound like a hefty sum to some people, foster parents typically use their own income to pay for many expenses (Barbell and Freundlich, 2001).

Some children are closer to their foster families than their biological parents and prefer to live with their foster parents (Gardner, 1996). Others never adjust to a foster home (Fanshel et al., 1989). The children are often confused about why they were taken from their homes and don't know what will happen in the future. Many experience fear, anger, and a sense of loss about not seeing their family and relatives (Whiting and Lee, 2003).

If children have gone through more than two placements and have been in foster care for more than a few years, their self-esteem, self-confidence, and ability to forge satisfying relationships with peers may erode (Kools, 1997). The solution, some propose, is to move children as quickly as possible from foster care to adoption (Bartholet, 1999).

Benefits of Foster Homes

The obvious benefit of foster homes is that many children experience physical and emotional safety: "We had some parents that we could trust [and] . . . they care about me" or "You don't get beat, they teach you the right way to do stuff, they teach you not to lie, stuff like that" (Whiting and Lee, 2003: 292).

Foster parents often make sure that the kids get the medical and mental health services they need. Instead of being in a group home where many kids with severe behavioral problems live together, a child in a foster home is with "healthy" adults (Wiltenburg, 2003).

Conclusion

As this chapter shows, there have been many *changes* in raising children in the last decade. On one hand, many fathers are more interested in helping raise their children; on the other hand, there are more at-risk children and a widespread need for high-quality day care.

Parents face many micro- and macro-level *constraints*. The most severe problems are generated by political and economic conditions. Even though the United States is one of the wealthiest countries in the world, the number of American children who live in poverty and are deprived of basic health care and other services has been increasing since 1980.

Socioeconomic status, race, ethnicity, and other factors shape parental *choices*. Gay and lesbian, minority, and working-class parents, for example, have to struggle to raise healthy children. In the next chapter we address the economic constraints and choices that many families confront.

SUMMARY

1. Infants are not merely passive recipients of care; they play an active role in their own development and socialization. Parenting is not a "natural" process but a long-term, time-consuming task that must be learned through trial and error rather than by means of formal training.

2. Among the major theories of child development and socialization are Mead's theory of the social self, Piaget's theory of cognitive development, and Erikson's psychosocial theory of development over the life cycle.

3. Many parents experience problems in raising children because they have unrealistic expectations and believe many well-entrenched myths about child development and child rearing.

4. Parenting stretches across the life course. Largely for economic reasons, adult children are staying in the home longer and are returning to their parents' homes, sometimes with their own children.

5. Social scientists have identified three broad approaches to child rearing: authoritarian, permissive, and authoritative. Parenting styles vary across racial-ethnic families and social classes, however.

6. Corporal punishment is a controversial issue. Although many parents maintain that physical punishment is necessary, most educators argue that there are more effective discipline methods than spanking, slapping, or verbal putdowns.

7. Parents are usually the most important people in their children's lives, and most children see their parents as loving and supportive. Parenting can be stressful, however, if fathers are not involved in a constructive manner, if very young children are latchkey kids, and if child care is expensive, low quality, or otherwise inaccessible.

8. In general, gay and lesbian parenting is not different from heterosexual parenting. Some gay and lesbian parents fear disclosure of their sexual orientation and feel more pressure to be successful as parents because they risk losing visitation or custody rights.

9. Many children face adverse outcomes such as not finishing high school, not working, and becoming teen parents. Many of these negative outcomes result from macro-level factors such as poverty and parental unemployment.

10. One response to at-risk families is to place children in out-of-home care, especially foster homes. Although many foster homes are beneficial, some create more problems than they solve.

KEY TERMS

role strain   *328*
authoritarian approach   *333*
permissive approach   *333*
authoritative approach   *333*

socioeconomic status (SES)   *339*
role overload   *345*
DEWK   *351*

latchkey kids   *351*
foster home   *355*

TAKING IT FURTHER

Parenting Resources

There are many great parenting Web sites.

Preparing for Parenthood offers humorous and serious information on anticipating and coping with parenthood.

www.sowashco.k12.mn.us/lake/pk/html/pfp.html

Zero to Three offers excellent material on promoting young children's social, emotional, and intellectual development.

www.zerotothree.org

Family provides a unique directory of regional activities for kids and families.

www.family.go.com

CYFERNet provides practical, research-based information on children, youth, and families from the Cooperative Extension Services of universities in all 50 states.

http://www.cyfernet.org

The National Fatherhood Initiative encourages more effective fathering. The "tips from fathers" section is especially interesting.

www.fatherhood.org

The National Child Care Information Center offers a wealth of information, including a link to Child Care Resources on the Internet, which provides links to at least 100 sites on child-care issues.

www.nccic.org

And more: www.prenhall.com/benokraitis provides numerous links to parenting newsletters from professional and government organizations, single-parenting sites, online journals, discussion groups about pregnancy and expectant parents, national parent information centers, sites targeted at fathers and at children with disabilities, resources for families of various racial and ethnic groups with young children, and foster care.

INVESTIGATE WITH RESEARCH NAVIGATOR

Please go to www.researchnavigator.com and enter your LOGIN NAME and PASSWORD. For instructions on registering for the first time, please view the detailed instructions at the end of the Chapter 1. Please search the Research Navigator™ site using the following key search terms:

child care
parenting
Erik Erikson

Families and Work:
Facing the Economic Squeeze

DATADIGEST

- The **percentage of Americans who described the economy as "poor"** increased from 58 percent in 2002 to 78 percent in 2003.

- In 2002, **the median income for all U.S. households** was $42,409: $52,606 for Asian Americans and Pacific Islanders, $46,900 for white households, $33,103 for Latinos, and $29,026 for African Americans.

- In 2000, 55 percent of **mothers of children 1 year of age or younger were in the labor force,** down from 58 percent in 1998 but up from 31 percent in 1976.

- In 2002, only 7 percent of **households conformed to the traditional model** of a wage-earning father, a stay-at-home mother, and one or more children.

- The **average number of vacation days a worker receives** after being on the job for one year varies widely, from 30 to 31 days in Denmark and Finland to 6 in Mexico. The average number of vacation days for employees in Canada, Japan, and the United States is 10 days.

SOURCES: "Who gets the most time off," 2000; Bachu and O'Connell, 2001; DeNavas-Walt et al., 2003; "Economy: Limping along," 2003; "Traditional families . . .," 2003.

In July 2003, the U.S. unemployment rate hit a record nine-year high of 6.4 percent. The corporate downsizing, stock market slump, and low interest rates have had a big impact on families at most socioeconomic levels, including this one:

James Kennedy, a machinist for 25 years, said he earned $20 to $25 an hour, plus benefits, working for Victaulic Corp., a company that makes mechanical pipes in Easton, Pa. But last fall he and 200 other workers at the plant were laid off, and he has been looking for a permanent job ever since. What work he's found pays less than $10 an hour, with few benefits—not enough, he said, to support his wife and two teenage children and provide them with health coverage. "It's real scary," Kennedy, 44, said. He is making ends meet with $388-a-week unemployment insurance payments that end in a few weeks (Downey, 2003: E3).

As James Kennedy's experience illustrates, macroeconomic conditions affect individual families. You'll see in this chapter that many mothers have entered the labor force, family roles are changing as parents juggle domestic and job responsibilities, and many of our social programs are hurting families rather than helping them.

359

Macroeconomic Changes Affecting the Family

Many contemporary parents feel that they are working harder than their own parents did, just to maintain a modest standard of living. Many researchers agree: "Families seem to be in a situation where they have to run as fast as they can just to remain in the same place" (Zill and Nord, 1994: 11). Because of an increase in income inequality, poverty, and homelessness in the past 30 years, some families fell out of the race no matter how fast they tried to run, whereas a growing number of families are watching the race from their penthouses.

Unequal Income Distribution

The expansion in the U.S. economy in the past 25 years has not benefited all families. Instead, income inequality has increased since the late 1960s (Karoly, 1993). The rich have gotten richer and the poor have gotten poorer. Income inequality in the United States is greater than in any other Western, industrialized nation (Galbraith, 1998; Bernstein, McNichol et al., 2000).

The Census Bureau uses several methods to measure income inequality. One of the most common methods is the share of combined household income, by which households are ranked from lowest to highest on the basis of income and then divided into quintiles, or fifths. Census Bureau data and other studies on household incomes show that the rich are getting richer, the middle class is shrinking, and the working class is barely surviving. A *social class* is a category of people who have a similar standing or rank based on wealth, education, power, prestige, and other valued resources.

The Rich Are Getting Richer The degree of wealth inequality in the United States is staggering. (Wealth, or net worth, includes income, savings, the value of real estate, stocks and bonds, and other assets minus outstanding debts.) The top 1 percent of households has nearly a third of all wealth, as does the next-highest 9 percent. The lowest 50 percent of families hold only 3 percent of all wealth (Kennickell, 2003). The net worth of families with incomes under $25,000, which had been rising since 1989, turned downward after 1995 (Kennickell et al., 2000; Aizcorbe et al., 2003).

The proportion of families both in the highest 20 percent quintile and, within that group, in the top 5 percent, has increased since 1976. The richest 20 percent of American households have more than half of the nation's total family income, up from 44 percent in 1967 (see *Figure 13.1*). The mean household incomes represent quite a range: lowest quintile, $10,136; second quintile, $25,468; third quintile, $42,629; fourth quintile, $66,839; and highest quintile, $145,970 (DeNavas-Walt and Cleveland, 2002).

The stock market decline over much of 2000 and 2001 reversed gains posted earlier, and by the end of 2001 it had brought most major indexes (such as the NASDAQ index) close to their 1998 levels (Aizcorbe et al., 2003). Wealthy families didn't notice much difference. In 2002, for example, the average chief executive officer's salary alone (excluding stock, bonuses, and so on) was almost $7 million a year—282 times the average worker's pay of $26,267 (Francis, 2003).

The Middle Class Is Shrinking The U.S. public's definition of "rich" means an annual median income of about $120,000 or financial assets of about $1 million (Moore, 2003). According to two national polls, 61 percent of Americans identified themselves as "middle income" and 45 percent said they were "middle class" ("A middle-class nation," 1999).

Although there is no across-the-board definition of "middle class," there's some consensus that the income of the average middle-class person or household is $46,000 to $80,000 a year (O'Hare, 2002; Gilbert, 2003; Wellner,

FIGURE 13.1 **Distribution of Household Income, 1976-2001**

SOURCES: U.S. Census Bureau, Current Population Reports, p60-209, 1999; DeNavas-Walt and Cleveland, 2002, Table A-2.

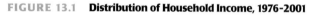
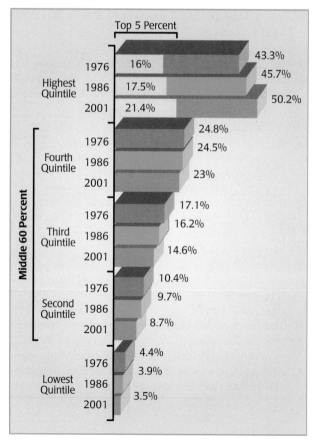

Top 5 Percent

	1976	16%	43.3%
Highest Quintile	1986	17.5%	45.7%
	2001	21.4%	50.2%
	1976		24.8%
Fourth Quintile	1986		24.5%
	2001		23%
	1976		17.1%
Third Quintile	1986		16.2%
	2001		14.6%
	1976		10.4%
Second Quintile	1986		9.7%
	2001		8.7%
	1976		4.4%
Lowest Quintile	1986		3.9%
	2001		3.5%

Middle 60 Percent

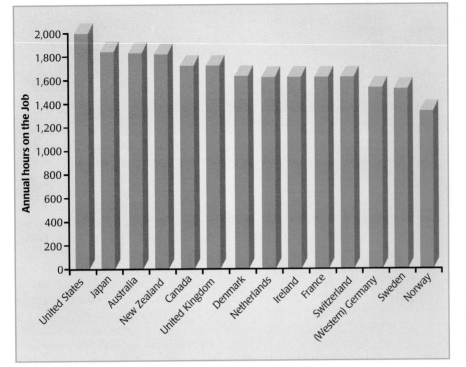

FIGURE 13.2 **On-the-Job Hours in Industrialized Countries**

SOURCE: Based on "Working longer, working better?," International Labor Organization, 1999.

2003). Even within this income range, a middle class isn't easy to define because it encompasses a wide range of people who may differ quite a bit on such variables as occupation, education, prestige, and lifestyle. For example, an experienced elementary school teacher may earn $46,000 a year, whereas a young chemical engineer may have an entry salary of about $70,000 a year. Both are considered middle class because they have college degrees and hold professional jobs. However, the difference in their lifetime salaries means considerably less access to better housing, recreation, retirement benefits, and other goods and services for the lower-paid worker.

The middle class works very hard for what it has. Americans spend more time on the job than workers anywhere else in the industrialized world (see *Figure 13.2*). Although hours spent working have decreased in almost all industrialized countries since 1980, those for U.S. workers *increased* by 4 percent between 1980 and 1997. Americans now spend the equivalent of two more 40-hour workweeks a year on the job than the Japanese, who have long been viewed as a nation of "workaholics." U.S. workers also have fewer vacation days than their counterparts in many countries (see "Data Digest").

In 1999, nearly nine in ten (89 percent) of workers said they were satisfied with their jobs (Harrison and Dautrich, 1999). By 2003, 44 percent said that a family member or friend had lost a job, and 53 percent were concerned about losing their own jobs or taking a pay cut ("Economy: Limping along," 2003).

American workers, especially those in the middle class and below, are justified in feeling scared. The share of American workers with company pension plans has slipped from almost 40 percent in 1980 to 20 percent in 2003 (Revell, 2003). Because of a sharp drop in income due to the steep decline in savings interest rates, many people who had retired are going back to work:

When he worked as a wholesaler in New York, Jack Baum was known for his strong work ethic. But when he retired 20 years ago to south Florida, he expected to enjoy the relaxing coastal life with his wife. Now in his 80s, he claims to be the oldest employee at the Hallandale Beach Wal-Mart. "We've had to scrimp and save and work, work, work," he says while stocking needles and threads in the sewing aisle (Scherer, 2003: 1).

Although many already affluent middle-class families are reaping financial benefits, those in the third and second quintiles, such as Jack Baum, have stagnating or declining incomes.

The Working Class Is Barely Surviving

Whereas many middle-class households are managing to stay afloat, numerous working-class families are clinging to a sinking ship:

CONSTRAINTS

Does Corporate Welfare Help Working-Class Families?

Business incentives take many forms: tax discounts, payroll rebates, cash grants, training funds, low-cost loans and leases, free buildings, and free land. A number of states, counties, and cities offer generous business incentives to companies with the understanding or promise that the incentives will create new jobs, especially among low-wage earners. Instead, corporations and high-income families have benefited from such largesse. For example,

- Between 1994 and 1996, the state of Maryland gave London Fog Industries Inc. funds to train workers and subsidized their monthly rent. In addition, union employees agreed to cut the base hourly rate from $7.90 to $6.90 and to increase production quotas. In 1997, however, London Fog closed the plant and moved its production overseas, where labor is cheaper.
- BMW, a German company that assembles luxury cars in Greer, South Carolina, has never paid the state's 5 percent tax on corporate profits. BMW pays $1 a year to lease its $36-million piece of land. In addition, South Carolina taxpayers spent $40 million on a runway for BMW's planes and furnished millions more for BMW worker "training," including whitewater rafting trips for executives. More than 200 other companies in South Carolina have received property tax discounts since 1997. To support crumbling schools and improve roads, the state has increased homeowner taxes and the taxes of established businesses.
- Sunlite Casual Furniture Company negotiated more than $8 million in state incentives for promising to create 900 jobs in Paragould, Arkansas. The jobs never materialized.
- Fruit of the Loom, a clothing manufacturer, obtained more than $10 million in tax breaks from the state of Louisiana before it closed several plants there and laid off more than 4000 employees over a three-year period.
- Rite Aid Corporation laid off 600 employees and closed a West Virginia distribution center that received more than $2 million in low-cost loans.
- Fulcrum Direct, owner of a children's playclothes industry, shut down in New Mexico and laid off 700 workers after costing the state $1 million in training funds.

Who profits from the corporate welfare packages that many states offer? Three groups: companies that can increase their profits, well-paid consultants who represent businesses in negotiations, and politicians who are elected for promising to bring jobs into poor and working-class neighborhoods (Hetrick, 1994; Henry, 1999; Hancock, 1999a, 1999b).

Most recently, American Airlines received concessions from its machinists, flight attendants, and pilots to take at least 25 percent pay cuts to keep the airline flying. However, American Airlines executives quietly gave themselves pensions worth millions, even if the airlines become bankrupt (Kadlec, 2003).

STOP AND THINK . . .

- *Would you be willing to pay about twice as much for clothes, food, and other products if they were produced in the United States?*
- *Should U.S. legislators put a cap on how much profit a company can make to discourage moving jobs overseas?*

When Howard Hagen took early retirement from a steel mill 10 years ago, he was making $23 an hour. Today, his daughter, Nancy, makes $5.25 an hour selling advertising. On that, she supports her four children. . . . Her ex-husband, a plumber, works only sporadically and hasn't kept up his child support payments. Even with public help—Medicaid for the children, subsidies for her heating bills—her budget, like an old car, is constantly breaking down. . . . She buys clothes at thrift shops, and even a simple purchase like new tennis shoes requires a juggling act. "Every Friday night we went out for dinner," she remembers. "Now, when I take the kids to McDonald's, it's a big deal!" (Roberts, 1994: 32).

Most of the reasons for the dire financial predicament of working-class families, whose members range from skilled blue-collar workers (for example, auto mechanics and construction workers) to those who make barely the minimum wage, are macro-level. First, technological changes have replaced many manual workers with machines. The number of so-called smokestack industries and assembly lines that used to employ many production workers has declined, or they have upgraded jobs that use robots or computerization.

Ten years ago, U.S. manufacturers flocked to Mexico because of the low labor costs. Most recently, many of these companies have relocated to China because manufacturing workers earn an average of only $1182 per year (Fleeson, 2003). The United States accounts for 70 percent of India's software exports, which increases the savings of U.S. companies by more than 60 percent (Kripalani et al., 2003).

Second, the entire industrial structure of the economy has changed. Many high-paying, goods-producing industries have been replaced by service industries that pay only a minimum wage. Between 1981 and 1989, the minimum wage of $3.35 an hour remained unchanged. It was raised to $3.80 an hour in 1990, to $4.25 in 1991, and to $5.15 in 1996. Currently almost 12 million Americans work for the minimum wage: 75 percent are adults, and 40 percent are sole providers for their families ("Universal living wage," 2002). Yet the hourly wage necessary to support a family of four on two incomes is close to $18 in many parts of the country with high housing costs (Economic Policy Institute, 2003).

Third, many working-class families are barely surviving because a number of states place a higher priority on corporate welfare than family welfare. To attract new businesses and expand employment possibilities among low-wage earners, a number of counties and states have offered enticing tax incentives to corporations. According to some observers, however, the tax incentives have benefited big business rather than working-class families. The box "Does Corporate Welfare Help Working-Class Families?" examines this issue more closely.

Many working-class families are a paycheck away from plunging into poverty. Millions of other families move in and out of poverty or are chronically poor, even if they are employed.

Poverty

In January 2002, Linda Lay, wife of former Enron CEO Ken Lay, appeared on NBC's *Today* show and wailed, tearfully, that her family was in financial ruin: "There's nothing left. Everything we had mostly was in Enron stock" and lamented that all their property "other than the home we live in" was for sale (Eisenberg, 2002: 38). The home the Lays lived in was a five-bedroom high-rise condo in Houston that's worth at least $8 million.

In one national survey, 21 percent of respondents with annual household incomes of less than $20,000 described themselves as "haves," whereas 6 percent of those making more than $75,000 a year saw themselves as "have-nots" (Parmelee, 2002). How is it that someone with an $8 million condo sees herself as poor while people with an income of less than $20,000 a year view themselves as "haves"?

There are two ways to define poverty: absolute and relative. **Absolute poverty** is not having enough money to afford the most basic necessities of life, such as food, clothing, and shelter. A person or family that can't get enough to eat, lives in inadequate housing, or suffers poor health faces a life-threatening existence.

Relative poverty is the inability to maintain an average standard of living. People in relative poverty may feel poor compared with a majority of others in society, but they have the basic necessities to survive. Clearly, the Lays live in neither absolute nor relative poverty.

The Poverty Line In 1965, the U.S. government adopted an official poverty line to designate people who live in

David Sadat of New York works full time at the Broadway 99 Cent Store in Harlem. After paying rent, he has little left to live on (see text). The number of full-time workers who live in poverty has climbed in the past 20 years.

absolute poverty. The **poverty line** is the minimum level of income that the government considers necessary for individuals' and families' basic subsistence.

To determine the poverty line, the Department of Agriculture (DOA) estimates the annual cost of food that has the minimum nutrients. Assuming—based on a 1955 DOA study—that a family spends about one-third of its income on food, the government multiplies this figure by three to cover the minimum cost of clothing, housing, care, and other necessities. Below this line, one is considered officially poor and is eligible for government assistance (such as food stamps and health care). The poverty line also measures the extent of poverty in the United States: more than 12 percent of the population, or nearly 35 million people, in 2002 (see *Figure 13.3*).

The poverty level doesn't include the value of non-cash benefits such as food stamps, medical services (Medicare and Medicaid, for example), and public housing subsidies. The poverty line, which was $18,244 in 2002 for a family of four, changes every year. It reflects changes in the *Consumer Price Index*, an index of prices that measures the change in the cost of basic goods and services in comparison to a fixed base period.

Policy analysts disagree on the validity of official poverty statistics. Some feel that poverty rates are inflated because the amount of money needed for subsistence varies drastically by region. They also argue that revising poverty definitions to include more families would place greater demands on government programs.

Others claim that the poverty level is unrealistically low. For example, a single mother with two children needs only $14,494 to avoid being counted as poor. To afford basics (food, clothing, shelter, utilities, and a small amount for other necessities) such families need between $20,000 and $40,000, depending on the region where they live (Bernstein, Brocht, and Spade-Aguilar, 2000).

There's quite a gap, then, between the official poverty line and what a family needs for basic necessities.

More than half of unemployed husbands in poor married-couple families are ill or disabled; the remainder are unable to find work, are going to school, or are retired (Lamison-White, 1997). Those who are disproportionately poor are children, the elderly, women, and racial-ethnic minorities.

Children and the Elderly   Children make up only 26 percent of the U.S. population but represent 35 percent of the poor. Nearly one out of every five children under age 18 lives in poverty. In contrast, people 65 and over account for 12 percent of the total population and 9 percent of the poor (American Community Survey, 2003). The poverty rate for older Americans has never been lower. Although government programs for the elderly have kept up with the rate of inflation, since 1980 many welfare programs for children have been reduced or eliminated. About 40 percent of *all* children will experience poverty at some point in their lives because families move in and out of poverty over time (Kacapyr, 1998).

Children's economic well-being varies substantially by race-ethnicity and by type of family. Most children living in poverty, 4.2 million, are white. However, in terms of proportions, 9 percent of white children are poor, compared with 31 percent of black children, 28 percent of Latino children, and 11 percent of Asian American and Pacific Islander children (Proctor and Dalaker, 2003). Children who fare worst are those who face multiple risks, such as being born to young, never-married mothers, living in economically depressed areas, and being on public assistance (Acs and Gallagher, 2000; see also Chapter 12).

FIGURE 13.3   Poverty in the United States, 1959–2002

Note: The data points represent the midpoints of the respective years.

SOURCES: Proctor and Dalaker, 2003, Figure 1.

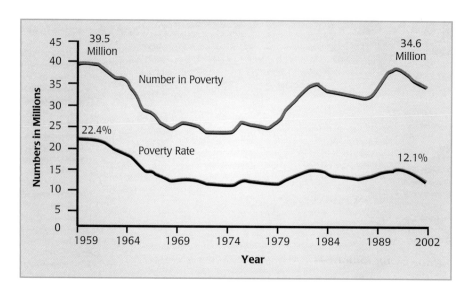

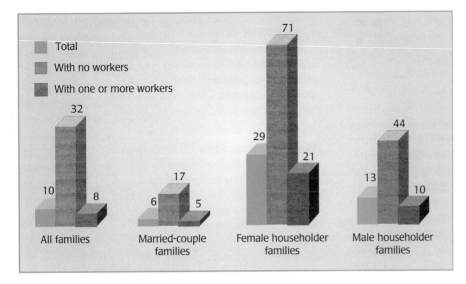

FIGURE 13.4 **Poverty Rates by Family Type and Presence of Workers, 2002**

SOURCE: Proctor and Dalaker, 2003, Figure 4.

Women Single mothers and their children make up a large segment of the poor. As *Figure 13.4* shows, poverty rates are higher for people who live in single-female households (29 percent) than in single-male households (13 percent) or in married-couple families (6 percent). Even with one or more workers, female-headed households are twice as likely to be poor as male-headed households.

Almost 50 percent of children under age 6 who are poor are living with only a mother, more than five times the rate of their counterparts in married-couple families (9 percent) (Proctor and Dalaker, 2003). As you saw in Chapter 12, children raised in poor households often suffer such long-term negative effects as lower educational achievement, at-risk behavior, and cognitive developmental problems.

Researcher Diana Pearce (1978) coined the term **feminization of poverty** to describe the growing proportion of women and their children who are poor. There are several reasons for the feminization of poverty. Unmarried teen mothers have little *human capital*, or work-related assets such as education, job training, experience, and specialized skills (Becker, 1964). Others, as you'll see later, work in low-paying jobs, are laid off, and experience job and wage discrimination.

Some men desert their children and their mothers, whether wives or girlfriends (see Chapters 9 and 12). Divorce also pushes many mothers into poverty. Ex-husbands and absent fathers typically offer very little support to women and their children (see Chapter 15). The poorer the family is to begin with, the less likely it is that the father will provide support after a divorce (Amott, 1993; Lino, 1995).

Racial-Ethnic Minorities About half of the poor people in the United States are white (45 percent). Most

white people are not poor, however. As *Figure 13.5* shows, proportionately more racial-ethnic minorities are poor given their numbers in the general population (see Chapter 1).

During economic recessions, African Americans and Latinos are particularly vulnerable to layoffs because they often fall victim to "last hired, first fired" policies. (See Chapter 4 for a discussion of poverty across Latino subgroups.) Because many racial-ethnic minorities have a smaller cushion of wealth than whites do on average, extended unemployment takes a bigger toll. In some cases, accepting a job for only half of the previous salary can thrust many families to just above the poverty level (Cauthen and Lu, 2003).

FIGURE 13.5 **Percentage of Families Living in Poverty, 2002**

*Based on 1999–2001 average.
SOURCE: Proctor and Dalaker, 2003.

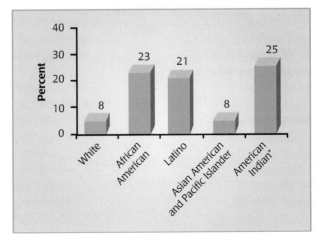

According to a 19-year-old young adult from Chicago's South Side, "I don't think I can take it much longer. I get up in the morning. I take a bath. I put on my clothes. I'll do any kind of work if they'll just hire me. It doesn't matter, as long as it's a job" (Herbert, 2003b: A35). Such jobs are rarely available however.

Young people ages 16 to 24 are likely to live in poverty if they have little human capital. The racial-ethnic minorities in this age group are especially vulnerable. Their population is growing faster than that of whites, but the labor market pool has increased very little since the late 1980s. Recessions are expected to take a substantial toll on job opportunities for out-of-school youth, especially those without four-year college degrees. Even new college graduates are getting jobs that went to young high school graduates in the past (Sum et al., 2002).

Many families are poor even when both parents work full time, year-round. Parental employment may reduce poverty but not eliminate it.

The Working Poor Almost 40 percent of all workers now fall into the category of the working poor (Proctor and Dalaker, 2003). The U.S. Department of Labor defines the **working poor** as people who spend at least 27 weeks in the labor force (working or looking for work) but whose family or personal incomes fall below the official poverty level (Beers, 2000). For example,

Donna Chambers works at a job that sounds decent enough: assistant manager at the Broadway 99 Cent store in Harlem, N.Y. She puts in long hours—often six days a week. Yet the mother of two doesn't earn enough that she can always put food on the table: She frequently gets free groceries from food pantries. She has no health insurance. She's struggling to pay an outstanding medical bill . . . Another obstacle is the cost of living. Housing alone consumes most of Chambers's income, which averages $1,000 a month. "The rent is horrendous," she says. Her boss, David Sadat, says he, too, has barely enough to live on after paying rent. "It doesn't matter if you work full time. It's still not enough" (Francis, 2000a: 1, 9).

Although many people think that the working poor are simply looking for government handouts,

- 12 percent are full-time, year-round workers.

- 12 percent are single mothers who work full-time and year-round.

- 27 percent are employed during part of the year.

- 50 percent of all children, most of whom are white, live with two parents in working-poor families (Barrington, 2000; Beers, 2000; Proctor and Dalaker, 2002).

As these statistics indicate, the poor are not "a bunch of loafers and parasites," but working does not guarantee staying out of poverty. The greatest hardships are faced by two-parent working-poor families in rural areas where job opportunities are minimal, the poor are isolated socially, and social services and benefits are less available than in urban areas (Duncan, 1999).

Why Are People Poor? Why does the United States, one of the wealthiest countries in the world, have such high poverty rates? According to several polls, more than half of all Americans feel that the poor don't believe in hard work, lack motivation, and are lazy (Lichter and Crowley, 2002). Such attitudes ignore the millions of poor who are desperately looking for jobs. Recently, for example, there were rumors that job applications for a Ford assembly plant would be accepted on Chicago's North Side:

Chicagoans by the thousands responded, turning out in bitterly cold weather for a shot at gainful employment. The first arrivals showed up well before dawn. By 7 A.M. more than 2,000 people had lined up, and the hopefuls kept coming throughout the morning. They shivered, and tears from the cold ran down some of their faces. It was like a scene out of the Depression (Herbert, 2003a: A23).

The rumors turned out to be false. Instead of job applications, there was an "orientation" session to identify candidates who might be qualified for low-paying jobs that might materialize in the distant future at a supplier of parts for Ford.

In a classic article on poverty, sociologist Herbert Gans (1971) maintained that poverty and inequality have many functions: (1) The poor ensure that society's dirty work gets done; (2) they subsidize the middle and upper classes by working for low wages; (3) they buy goods and services (such as day-old bread, used cars, and the services of old, retired, or incompetent "professionals") that otherwise would be rejected; and (4) they absorb the costs of societal change and community growth (e.g., by providing the backbreaking work that built railroads and cities in the nineteenth century and by being pushed out of their homes by urban renewal construction projects).

Many employers profit from poverty. Latino day laborers work for almost nothing while agencies collect hefty fees (see Chapter 4). Corporations like Labor Ready, the nation's top employer of temporary manual labor, makes $1 billion in annual revenues by recruiting homeless workers and then paying them below-minimum-wage salaries, illegally charging workers for safety gear (such as gloves and goggles), and charging 5 percent for cash payments (Cook, 2002).

TABLE 13.1

Where Can Low-Income Families Afford Decent Housing?

These are the hourly wages (the "housing wage") a person working full time must earn to rent a modest but "decent" two-bedroom unit at the area's fair market rent (FMR) and using no more than 30 percent of one's gross income. If you live in Massachusetts, for example, you must earn $21.14/hour to rent a humble but livable two-bedroom apartment—excluding utility costs. You can explore the FMR values in your state by clicking on www.nlihc.org/oor2003 and then searching by county, metropolitan area, or rural area.

Least Affordable States	Housing Wage for Two-Bedroom FMR
Massachusetts and California	More than $21.00
New Jersey, New York, Connecticut, and Maryland	Between $18.00 and $19.74
Alaska, Colorado, and Hawaii	Between $16.00 and $17.02
Most Affordable States	
Kansas, South Carolina, South Dakota, Tennessee, Louisiana, Nebraska, Wyoming, Montana, and Idaho	Between $10.01 and $10.74
Oklahoma, North Dakota, Kentucky, Alabama, Mississippi, and Arkansas	Between $9.04 and $9.98
West Virginia and Puerto Rico	Between $8.59 and $8.78

SOURCE: Based on National Low Income Housing Coalition, 2003.

One of the most devastating consequences of poverty is homelessness. The rate of homelessness is increasing among people who work.

Homeless Families

There are no accurate statistics on homelessness because many people are "hidden" homeless who are not counted by researchers. The uncounted include people who live in automobiles, have makeshift housing (such as boxes and boxcars), or stay with relatives for short periods. According to the best estimates, however, about 3.5 million people, a third of whom are children, are likely to experience homelessness in a given year. This translates to approximately 1 percent of the U.S. population (National Coalition for the Homeless, 2002).

Characteristics of Homeless Families Families have been the fastest-growing group of homeless people. Families with children account for 34 percent of the homeless population; 84 percent are single-mother families. In terms of race and ethnicity, 43 percent are black, 39 percent are white, 15 percent are Latino, 3 percent are American Indian, and 1 percent are of another race (Burt et al., 1999).

Homelessness is creeping into rural areas instead of being confined to cities. In 2003, for example, a community center called Love Inc. in Burlington, Wisconsin (with a population of 25,000), got four calls a day, instead of one, from homeless families with urgent pleas to "find us a place to sleep." In parts of rural Illinois,

similarly, women with children and men with families make up more than half of the 180,000 homeless people in the state (Gardner, 2003b).

Why Families Are Homeless In general, homelessness results from a combination of factors, some of which are beyond individuals' or families' control, such as mental illness or physical disability. Other factors include poverty, lack of education, lack of marketable skills, unemployment, domestic violence, substance abuse, and the inability of relatives and friends to provide social and economic support during crises (National Coalition for the Homeless, 2002).

The homeless also include teenage runaways escaping from family violence or incest (Whitbeck and Hoyt, 1999; see also chapter 14). About half of the teens at shelters are "throwaways": those whose parents forced them out of the house or simply don't care whether the teenagers leave (Flowers, 2001).

One of the biggest reasons for homelessness is the lack of affordable housing. Between 1973 and 1993, for example, 2.2 million low-rent units disappeared from the market. These units were abandoned, were converted into condominiums or expensive apartments, or became too expensive because of cost increases (National Coalition for the Homeless, 2002).

Because rents are high and housing assistance is in short supply, the most vulnerable renters are the working poor. The average American must earn $15.21 an hour—about three times the $5.15/hour minimum wage—to rent a small apartment. *Table 13.1* ranks some states in terms of affordability and the hourly wage a worker must earn to afford a modest two-bedroom apartment.

Reactions to Homelessness Although many community groups offer food, clothing, and temporary housing to homeless families, many shelters and the general public are becoming less sympathetic to the plight of the homeless. In Minneapolis, for example, it's a crime to create an odor (by urinating in public places, for example). Santa Monica, California, long known for its generosity in providing a haven for the homeless, has passed laws making it illegal to occupy downtown doorways between 11 P.M. and 7 A.M. if business owners post a sign to that effect (Wood, 2002). In 147 communities in 42 states, Puerto Rico, and the District of Columbia, homeless people can be arrested for violations that include panhandling, loitering, camping, obstructing the sidewalk, spitting, street performing, and lying in doorways or on park benches (National Coalition for the Homeless, 2003).

We've discussed the macroeconomic changes affecting American families. How do families cope with these ongoing constraints?

MAKING CONNECTIONS

▨ What role does race or ethnicity play in the feminization of poverty? What about age?

▨ What do you think can be done about reducing the numbers of children living in poverty? Or do you feel that it's impossible to do anything at all? ◎

Families' Adaptations to Changing Economic Trends

Across the country, many families are struggling to survive. They have adopted a variety of techniques, including taking low-paying jobs, moonlighting, working shifts, doing part-time work, and working overtime. If these tactics fail, they join the ranks of the unemployed.

Low-Wage Jobs, Moonlighting, and Shift Work

One researcher (Levine, 1994) has described the United States as "a nation of hamburger flippers" because of the growing number of low-wage jobs. Measured in terms of buying power, hourly wages have declined 15 percent since 1973 and are now at mid-1960s levels.

Especially for low-income workers, a changing economy has meant layoffs, a loss of job security, lower wages, and no health benefits. When corporations merge, workers in lower-end jobs are the first to be laid off.

Low-Wage Jobs An explosion of jobs in the information technology sector in the late 1990s resulted in well-paid jobs for highly educated employees. The bubble burst in 2001, however, when many dot-com companies collapsed. Since then, most young adults in their twenties and thirties have seen their six-figure incomes plummet to less than $50,000 a year. Others are still unemployed. Many are clipping coupons, making only partial payments on the interest on their credit cards, and taking lower-wage jobs such as working for Pottery Barn as a temp for $18 an hour. Some have even sold their compact discs to pay for food (Conlin, 2003a).

Moonlighting Almost 6 percent of all employed people hold two or more jobs (U.S. Census Bureau, 2002). Most are moonlighting to meet regular household expenses or to pay off debts (see *Figure 13.6*). The multiple jobholders are about equally likely to be married or single, and women and men are similar in moonlighting rates (about 5 percent for each).

Not all moonlighting can be blamed on low wages, of course. Some middle-class professionals moonlight to pay off credit-card debt, buy a vacation home, or increase their annual income. In many cases, however, especially in remote midwestern rural areas, holding down a second job is often a matter of economic survival (Wilkinson, 2000).

Shift Work Parenting is especially difficult if mothers and fathers have unconventional work schedules. According to an AFL-CIO study, 40 percent of all women who are married or cohabiting say they work a different schedule than their spouse or domestic partner ("Ask a working woman," 2002). The share of split-shift workers is higher among couples with preschool-age children than among other types of families. Single mothers with only a high school diploma are especially likely to be locked into evening and night-shift jobs because they work as cashiers, nursing home aides, waitresses, and janitors—positions most likely to require nonstandard work hours (Presser and Cox, 1997).

The globalization of industries means that workers are needed almost around the clock because business is being conducted somewhere almost every hour of the day. Because day care is so expensive, many two-income families are working split shifts so that parents can save money by taking turns at child-care tasks (see Chapter 12).

Husbands who work rotating evening shifts (six days on, three days off, for example) often feel guilty and angry because they rarely see their kids. One father saw himself reliving a situation he had resented as a child:

> *I always remember my father as sleeping during the day. Never seeing him because he'd be in bed. Then I'd hear him get up and go to work at night. I didn't see much of my father. I missed that. Now I feel guilty if I can't have time with my family (Hertz and Charlton, 1989: 501).*

When both parents work shifts, husbands and wives may rarely see each other or participate as a family with their children:

> *My husband works a 9-to-5 shift, and I work from 6 P.M. until 2:30 A.M. We have done this for 12 years because with three kids, it helps save the cost of child care. I average four hours of sleep a night. My husband comes home after an eight-hour day of work, has dinner with the kids, helps with their homework, takes care of baths and reads them stories at bedtime. I wake up, get the kids off to school, clean the house, do the laundry, start dinner and prepare for another night of work. Since I also have a 3-year-old at home, going back to bed is out of the question. I barely see my older kids, and my husband and I have no social life. . . . I have no time for myself, and neither does my husband. As soon as he walks in the door from work, I walk out ("Night shift . . .," 1996: 3D).*

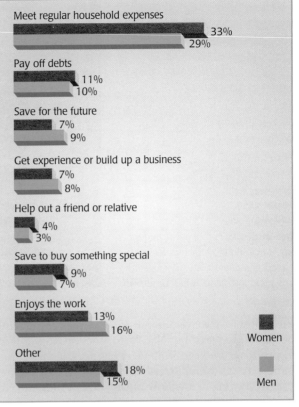

FIGURE 13.6 **Why Women and Men Have Multiple Jobs**
SOURCE: Based on data in U.S. Census Bureau, 1999, Table 669.

Too Little Work or Too Much

Many families face an economic dilemma: On the one hand, an increasing proportion of available jobs are only part time. On the other hand, some employees are required to work unwanted overtime.

Part-Time Jobs About 19 percent of all employed people work part time (defined as working less than 35 hours a week). Of these part-timers, 38 percent are men and 62 percent are women. Although 75 percent of part-timers are "voluntary" because they don't want to work more hours, 25 percent are involuntary because they want full-time employment (U.S. Department of Labor, 2000).

The percentage of part-time employees, voluntary or not, is likely to increase because many employers can save money by not providing health care or other benefits. Currently, only 70 percent of employers offer their full-time workers some health insurance (Bhandari, 2002). Part-time employees, many of whom are women, are especially attractive to employers because health benefits are not included in the job.

Overtime Demands At the other extreme is the demand by some employers that experienced workers, especially those in production, work more overtime. For employers, paying overtime is less expensive than hiring and training new employees. The most common violation of this practice is failing to pay hourly wage earners time-and-a-half when they work more than 40 hours a week—or failing to pay anything at all for the extra hours (Shatzkin, 2000).

Skilled and highly educated salaried employees are especially likely to work long hours. Among those with professional, technical, or managerial jobs, more than 33 percent of men and 17 percent of women now put in 50-hour-plus weeks, compared with 20 percent of men and 7 percent of women in other occupations. College graduates are four times more likely to work long hours than those with a high school degree or less. Some are compensated for their overtime, and some are not (Jacobs and Gerson, 1998).

During weak economic times, many employers squeeze their full-time workers instead of hiring additional employees. Because many people are afraid of losing their jobs, they don't protest. In Wal-Mart stores,

There are many husband-wife businesses where both partners, such as these owners of a photo store, work together to support themselves and their families.

for example, the average full-time worker earns barely $18,000 a year, but Wal-Mart pockets $6.6 billion in profits every year. Wal-Mart has such large profits, in part, because employees work overtime for no extra pay. According to a widow raising three children, "My kids have this bad habit of eating. . . . Working unpaid overtime equaled saving your job" (Olsson, 2003: 58).

In other cases, executive-level employees don't complain when secretaries are laid off and they must do the work themselves. Many workers are silent, even when they make only $40,000 a year after being laid off from a $130,000-a-year job (Kadlec, 2003). Companies can squeeze more out of employees than ever before with grueling schedules because they know that workers fear being laid off (Conlin, 2002).

Unemployment

According to some economists, the job losses since 2001—especially in the private sector—are the worst since the Great Depression (Bernstein and Mishel, 2003; see also Chapter 3). The unemployed include such diverse groups as people who have been laid off or fired, who have quit their job, or who are about to begin a new job. Overall, more than half of the unemployed are those who have been laid off.

People have lost jobs across all sectors in the last few years. However, unemployment hits some people and sectors harder than others. Historically, and in 2003, unemployment rates among African Americans were twice as high as among whites. One of the reasons, as you saw earlier, is that black youth are less likely than other groups to have the human capital to compete for jobs. In addition, nearly 90 percent of those who lost

jobs were in manufacturing. Because African Americans have been employed in manufacturing more than in other sectors, unemployment hits blacks harder than whites (Altman, 2003; Uchitelle, 2003).

Unemployment figures are low, however, because they don't count discouraged and underemployed workers. Families across all racial-ethnic groups include both types of workers.

Discouraged Workers Unemployment figures are misleading because they ignore the **discouraged worker**, or what some call the "hidden unemployed." The discouraged worker wants a job and has looked for work in the preceding year but has not searched recently because she or he believes that job-hunting efforts are futile. Millions of discouraged workers include retirees, mothers who have been taking care of their kids but can't find a job after entering the job market, and teenagers who have dropped out of high school (Davey and Leonhardt, 2003).

Why do people give up? Usually because they've found no work available in their area of expertise; they lack necessary schooling, training, or experience; they believe employers have rejected them as too young or too old; or they have experienced other types of discrimination. Many young discouraged workers, including African American and Latino males, may turn to illegal ways of making a living because they lack the skills and education that many employers seek (Soltero, 1996).

Underemployed Workers Unemployment rates are also misleading because they ignore the **underemployed worker.** The underemployed include people who have part-time jobs but would rather be working full time and those who accept jobs below their level of job experience and educational credentials. Women, particularly those with children, are more likely than men to suffer from underemployment because of problems in finding and affording good child-care services.

Another large group of underemployed workers are professionals (engineers, physicists, and chemists)—especially men in their fifties—who are laid off when corporations want to increase their profits. Companies can hire two young college graduates for the price of a senior-level employee, and they often do so.

Effects of Unemployment Regardless of social class, unemployment is often overwhelming. Unemployment can start a vicious "chain of adversity" of financial strain, depression, loss of personal control, decreased emotional functioning, and poorer physical health. Even two years after finding a new job, people still report negative effects such as insecurity and lowered self-esteem. Those who are less educated experience more financial hardship, a loss of control, and lower self-esteem than their counterparts with higher educational levels (Broman et al., 2001; Price et al., 2002).

People who lose their jobs also lose health coverage. An average family can't afford $270 a month for a child's health insurance (Broder, 2002). In many cases banks repossess houses because the couple can no longer afford the monthly mortgage payments. In 2002, for example, banks foreclosed 4 in every 1000 mortgaged homes, the highest rate since 1970 (Kilborn, 2002). About 56 percent of families cut back on food spending, 33 percent cut off or delay their educations, and 26 percent move in with relatives or friends (National Employment Law Project, 2003).

Sometimes, unemployment is so stressful that couples divorce. In other cases, they hang in there. As one wife said, unemployment "is a phase. This isn't permanent. This, too, shall pass" (Gardner, 2003a: 21). The situation would be much worse for many families if women weren't employed.

Women's Increasing Participation in the Labor Force

Surveys of adolescents and college students suggest that many young people expect to have a career and raise children simultaneously. In a nationwide study of college students, for example, 73 percent of college freshmen said that being very well off financially was "very important" or "essential." And 74 percent felt the same way about raising a family. However, almost 28 percent of the men and 17 percent of the women said that "the activities of married women are best confined to the home and family" ("Attitudes and characteristics . . .," 2003). Unless

they have very high-paying jobs and expect equally high job security in the future, it's not clear how one-earner families can expect to be well off financially.

Juggling Family and Work Roles

The high proportions of high school and college women who say they expect to marry, have children, and work are right on target, for many will find it necessary to work to support themselves and their families. In fact, the widespread employment of mothers is often cited as one of the most dramatic changes in family roles in the twentieth century. Except for a brief period after the end of World War II, the numbers of working women have been increasing steadily since the turn of the century (see *Table 13.2*).

Women's labor force rates are expected to grow more rapidly than those of men in the future. By 2005, for example, the Bureau of Labor Statistics predicts that about 63 percent of women will be in the labor force, compared with 74 percent of men. One reason is that female baby boomers are far more likely than their predecessors to have gone to college and to have more and better-paying work opportunities.

TABLE 13.2

Women and Men in the Labor Force in the Twentieth Century

Year	Percentage of all Men and Women in the Labor Force		Women as a Percentage of All Workers
	Men	Women	
1890	84	18	17
1900	86	20	18
1920	85	23	20
1930	82	24	22
1940	83	28	25
1945	88	36	29
1947	87	32	27
1950	87	34	29
1960	84	38	33
1970	80	43	37
1980	78	52	42
1990	76	58	45
2001	74	60	47

SOURCE: U.S. Census Bureau, 1997, 2002.

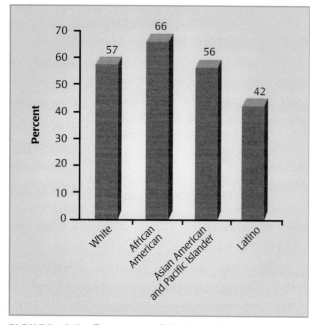

FIGURE 13.7 **Percentage of Mothers with Infants in the Labor Force, 2000**

SOURCE: Based on Bachu and O'Connell, 2001: Table 4.

An even more dramatic change has been the increase of mothers in the labor force who have an infant at home (see "Data Digest"). Historically, African American mothers with infants were more likely than any other group to be employed, but the gap has narrowed. As *Figure 13.7* shows, except for Latinas, the majority of women with babies are going back to work within the child's first year of life.

Labor force participation rates are appreciably higher for women with graduate or professional degrees (65 percent) and for women with college degrees (63 percent) than for women who are high school graduates (55 percent) or who are not high school graduates (39 percent). Women who have invested more time in their education return to work more rapidly because they have a greater career commitment, can command higher salaries, and have more work experience than do women with fewer years of schooling. In addition, they have the resources to purchase child care services, especially if a husband is also employed (Bachu and O'Connell, 2001).

Why Do Women Work?

The two principal reasons that women work outside the home are the same reasons that men do so: personal satisfaction and to support themselves and their dependents. Work usually adds meaning to life. The opportunity to succeed at tasks and to be rewarded for competence enhances self-esteem, which, in turn, increases overall well-being. This is especially true for people who enjoy their work or who are employed in stimulating, rewarding jobs.

As you saw earlier, the purchasing power of families with a median income has declined since the mid-1980s. It is not surprising, then, that seven out of ten mothers are in the labor force (U.S. Census Bureau, 2002). Although the need for a creative outlet motivates some women to work, in most cases women are employed because of economic necessity. The box "Variations in the Working Mother Role" examines motherhood and employment more closely.

The labor force participation rate for women with infants dropped slightly between 1998 and 2000 (see "Data Digest"). Reporters published dozens of articles with headlines like "Mommy is really home from work" or "Mothers who choose to stay home." The articles focused on white, married, middle-class, and professional mothers rather than minority, unmarried, or working-class mothers (see, for example, Clark, 2002). The message seems to be that these stay-at-home moms are less interesting or important than those from higher socioeconomic levels.

In fact, most mothers can't afford to stay home. They are single parents, can't take unpaid maternity leaves for financial reasons, or are married to men who don't have high-paying jobs (Landry, 2000). Only 27 percent of women now quit their job around the time of their first birth, compared with 63 percent between 1961 and 1965 (Smith et al., 2001). The biggest recent increase in stay-at-home moms of young children has been in families earning at least $50,000 a year and by women who are college-educated and "who have racked up considerable track records, making them more confident about re-entering the workforce" (Conlin et al., 2002: 102).

Employed mothers and stay-at-home moms aren't the only possibilities. There are several other alternatives in marital roles that reflect a couple's economic resources and choices.

MAKING CONNECTIONS

■ In a recent national survey, 48 percent of Americans said that mothers with preschoolers shouldn't work outside the home (Gerson, 2003). Do you agree?

■ Do you think that the stresses for working mothers are similar to or different from those of working fathers?

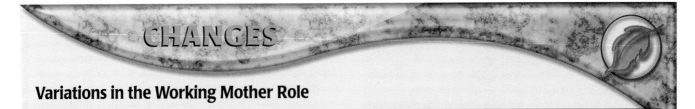

Variations in the Working Mother Role

Because economic realities have changed, fewer women than in the past have a choice between being full-time homemakers and working outside the home. Of Moen's (1992: 42–44) four categories of working mothers—captives, the conflicted, copers, and the committed—only members of the last group have fully chosen their roles.

- *Captives* would prefer to be full-time homemakers. These mothers may be single parents who are sole breadwinners, wives of blue-collar workers whose own incomes are insufficient to support the family, or middle-class wives who find two salaries necessary for a desired standard of living. Captives find their multiple responsibilities

overwhelming and remain in the labor force reluctantly.

- *Conflicted* mothers feel that their employment is harmful to their children. They are likely to leave the labor force while their children are young, and many quit work when they can afford to do so. Conflicted mothers include many Latinas whose husbands support their wives' employment as long as the mothers continue to fulfill all housework and child-care duties despite their outside work, and who quit their jobs as soon as their husbands secure better-paying work (Segura, 1994).
- *Copers* are women with young children who choose jobs with enough flexibility to accommodate family needs.

Some manage to reduce their daily or weekly working hours or leave the labor force for brief periods. As a result, they often must settle for minimally demanding jobs that offer lower wages and fewer benefits and, in the long run, forgo promotions, seniority advantages, and pay increases.

- *Committed* mothers have both high occupational aspirations and a strong commitment to marriage and family life. As the section on dual-earner families shows, however, mothers who can afford good child care and who are free to pursue career goals are still a minority.

New Economic Roles within Marriage

In Chapter 5 we examined the traditional male breadwinner–female homemaker roles. There are currently two variations on the traditional division of labor within marriage: the two-person single career and the stay-at-home dad.

The Two-Person Single Career

In the **two-person single career**, one spouse, typically the wife, participates in the partner's career behind the scenes without pay or direct recognition (Papanek, 1979). The wives of many college and university professors, for example, support their husbands' careers by entertaining faculty and students, doing library research, helping to write and edit journal articles or books, and grading exams.

The best public example of the two-person single career is presidential first ladies, who have often enjoyed power and influence behind the scenes. Most recently, Nancy Reagan influenced her husband's staffing decisions, Barbara Bush criticized her husband's opponents, Hillary Rodham Clinton promoted her husband's domestic policies and defended him during his sexual indiscretions,

and Laura Bush endorsed improvements in teaching. First ladies are expected to pursue issues for the good of the country but not to be co-presidents (Allgor, 2002).

Many middle-class homemakers are proud of their husbands' accomplishments and experience a sense of fulfillment by helping them. Some wives, however, complain that a two-person career is very stressful and that they experience burnout as commonly as their high-powered husbands do. They are constantly involved in activities such as entertaining and organizing fund-raising events besides running a household and raising their children.

Stay-at-Home-Dads

In the movie *Daddy Day Care*, Eddie Murphy is as an unemployed father who starts a "guy run" day-care center with a buddy. Stay-at-home dads (or *househusbands*, as they were called in the 1990s) are the rare men who stay home to care for the family and do the housework while their wives are the wage earners.

Prevalence   An estimated 105,000 stay-at-home dads cared for 189,000 children in 2002. These are married fathers with children under 15 who are not in the labor force primarily so they can care for the family while their wives work outside the home. In all two-parent families,

Ernestina Galindo owns and operates a factory in Austin, Texas, that makes Mexican foods such as tortillas.

only 0.8 percent of all fathers were stay-at-home dads compared with 28 percent of all mothers. That is, children under age 15 were 56 times as likely to have a stay-at-home mom than a stay-at-home dad (Fields, 2003).

Reasons Being a stay-at-home dad is usually a temporary role. Some get the role by default; they are unemployed or are not working because of poor health or a disability. Others are retired, remarried much younger women who are employed, and want a "second chance" in watching a child grow up (Gutner, 2001). Sometimes graduate students who are supported by their wives take on a modified housekeeping role, doing household chores between classes and studying at the library.

Many of these men have wives who earn more than they do, have greater job security, better health care benefits, and high-powered jobs. Of the 187 participants at *Fortune* magazine's Most Powerful Women in Business Summit, for example, a third had househusbands. A number of the stay-at-home dads took early retirements from high-level executive positions, are wealthy, and sometimes hire nannies to assist in the child care (Morris, 2002).

Staying home with the kids is harder for men who don't feel they have a choice. After being laid off, for instance, a systems engineer, 43, is caring for their 3-year-old son, but it's a jolt to his ego because "I've been programmed all my life to be a provider" (Morris, 2002: 94).

Benefits and Costs Recent experiential accounts suggest that being a full-time father is a mixed blessing. On the one hand, the fathers enjoy seeing a child crawl and take a first step. Some fathers find childrearing a joy because they are more intimately involved with their kids: "I know my son's and daughter's friends. I know everything they like and dislike. I have the chance to be there to help answer questions" (Barovick, 2002: B10). They also don't have to worry about the quality of day-care or afterschool facilities.

On the other hand, some stay-at-home-dads are concerned about losing skills and their "professional place in line." Some feel unappreciated by their working wives, who may complain that the house is a mess or that people view them as "nonachievers" professionally (Baldauf, 2000).

In most families, parents don't have the choice of staying home with their children. Instead, both work part-time, full-time, and sometimes both.

Dual-Earner Families

After 61 years of being a traditional housewife and mother, in the late 1990s the comic-strip character Blondie opened up a catering business and went to work for herself. Blondie and Dagwood's shift to a dual-earner marriage reflects what has been happening in many U.S. families. There are several types of dual-earner families: dual-career marriages, trailing spouses, commuter marriages, and marriages in which wives earn more than their husbands.

Dual-Earner versus Dual-Career Families

In the past 50 years, the proportion of married women in the work force has almost tripled. Families with a working wife have seen their incomes nearly triple, too. As *Figure 13.8* shows, 2001 median family incomes when wives were in the labor force, part-time or full-time, were 85 percent higher than when wives stayed at home. The labor force figures include both dual-earner and dual-career families.

Dual-Earner Couples In **dual-earner couples,** both partners are employed outside the home. They are also called *dual-income, two-income, two-earner,* or *dual-worker* couples. These employed couples make up 62 percent of all married couples (U.S. Census Bureau, 2002).

Despite their two incomes, dual-earner families are seldom affluent. Only a small fraction of such households has a significant amount of **discretionary income,** or income remaining for other purposes after such basic necessities as food, rent, utilities, and transportation have been paid.

Even though the modern two-earner family brings in 75 percent more inflation-adjusted income than the

FIGURE 13.8   Median Family Income, 1949-2001

Source: U.S. Census Bureau, 2002, "Historical Income Tables—Families," Table F-13, www.census.gov/hhes/income/histinc/f13.html (accessed September 11, 2003.)

one-earner family of a generation ago, it still has less discretionary income. The primary reason is that the decline of public education has dramatically raised the price of housing in good school districts, prompting parents to overstretch on mortgages (Warren and Tyagi, 2003). Besides paying mortgages, many dual-earner families consist of middle-aged people who are paying for their children's college education, saving for their own retirement, and sometimes helping low-income aging parents.

Having two wage earners raises the family's standard of living, however. And if a husband's income is low or he is laid off, a wife's financial support relieves some of the pressure on the man to be a successful provider. In many ethnic groups that rely on unpaid family members' participation to create a small business, much of the discretionary income may be invested in the entrepreneurship (Wong, 1998; see also Chapter 4).

Dual-Career Couples   In **dual-career couples**, both partners work in professional or managerial positions that require extensive training, a long-term commitment, and ongoing professional growth. Usually, but not always, dual-career partners earn incomes well above average. Only about 5 percent of dual-earner families are dual-career couples. Married women in such professions as law, medicine, high-level management, or college teaching remain a small group among dual-earner couples as a whole. Because such women are less likely to have children, dual-career families with children make up a tiny percentage of all dual-earner families. Although no hard data are available, perhaps only 1 to 2 percent of dual-career couples include children.

Both dual-career and dual-earner families experience stress, role strain, and role overload (see Chapter 12). A common source of stress for dual-earner families is finding affordable child care. Ironically, many dual-earner mothers work as child-care providers or baby sitters for dual-career mothers who are able to pay for such services.

The most common source of stress for dual-career couples is the pressure of role overload , especially when children are young. To achieve their career goals, both partners often feel driven to work intensely and competitively. As a result, they may experience guilt and frustration when they neglect their spouse and children.

Role overload due to multiple work and family responsibilities can lead to increased health risks; decreased productivity; increased tardiness, absenteeism, and turnover; and poor morale at work (see Chapter 12). On the positive side, dual-earner parents feel that they provide responsible adult role models for their children and that their children are more independent and less "needy" than they would be if both parents didn't work (Silberstein, 1992; Barnett and Rivers, 1996).

Besides dual-earner and dual-career couples, some couples opt for a one-earner family. Some, as you saw earlier, are stay-at-home moms who leave the labor force to raise their children. Others are trailing spouses who hope to find work after moving to a new city or state.

Trailing Spouses

By 1996, about 30 percent of U.S. companies provided employment assistance for the **trailing spouse**: the partner who gives up his or her work and searches for another position in the location where a spouse has taken a job.

Who's the Trailing Spouse? Male trailing spouses—only 10 to 15 percent of cases—fall into five categories: (1) men who can't find suitable employment in their present location; (2) men with portable professions, such as photographers, computer programmers, and engineers; (3) men who take pride in and accommodate their wives' relocation because of job offers; (4) men with blue-collar skills, such as construction workers, who are used to changing jobs; and (5) laid-off managers and executives whose wives are climbing the corporate ladder (Cohen, 1994; "The big picture," 2000).

In many cases, the wife is the trailing spouse because of traditional gender roles to accommodate (see Chapter 5). According to a faculty member, for example, about 90 percent of male Ph.D. students apply for almost every job that "remotely matches their qualifications," compared with only 50 percent of their female counterparts:

> *Many intelligent and talented women substantially reduce their chances for career success, prestige, and financial security by being unwilling to participate in a national job search—usually because the men in their lives don't want to move. We rarely see male graduate students severely limiting their job searches because of their partners' desires (Williams, 2001: B20).*

Often, income is the best predictor of who the trailing spouse will be. As a wife's income increases, both in absolute terms and relative to that of her husband, she tends to play a greater role in deciding whether the family will move. Typically, however, the husband has more influence because his income is usually higher than his wife's (Bielby and Bielby, 1992).

What Are the Costs for Trailing Spouses? There are drawbacks to being the trailing spouse. Frame and Shehan (1994) found that moving was much harder on wives than husbands. Most husbands continued to perform similar tasks in new locations and maintained their contacts with colleagues through meetings and conferences. Wives lost contact with friends, were concerned about the children's adjustment to a new environment, and felt lonely and isolated. In addition, nearly 60 percent of the wives had been employed, and many felt anxiety over the loss of their jobs.

Many female instructors who are adjunct faculty are trailing spouses. They often move with their spouses hoping to find a full-time teaching position. Instead, they must often piece together a string of part-time teaching jobs: "After nearly two years of driving 65 miles each way to teach for less than $10,000 a semester, the truth was apparent: My car was going the distance, but my career and my spirits were in neutral" (Carroll, 2003: C4).

In other cases, highly educated couples might find similar academic jobs in the same region. If they have children, however, one of them will have to make more sacrifices. Often, the wife will accept a less-demanding job (and with a lower salary) to juggle childrearing and employment (Watanabe, 2002).

Relocating can be especially stressful because it is often a lateral job shift rather than a step up the career ladder. Sometimes an employee must choose between relocating—even if it is only a lateral career move—and losing her or his job. If there's a choice, however, 1 in 12 prospective transferees reject relocation offers because moving may be too disruptive and stressful for all family members, especially children who must change schools (Capell, 1995).

The most recent wrinkle in the relocation and trailing spouse issue involves divorce and remarriage. If a divorced parent who has custody of a child (or children) remarries and decides to relocate as a trailing spouse, state laws may bar her or him from doing so. In Illinois, for example, the parent who wants to leave the state has to prove that the move won't damage the noncustodial parent–child relationship. In Missouri, it's illegal for a divorced parent to move, "even across the street," over an ex's objection (Downey, 2000).

Because of such difficulties, many couples don't or can't relocate. Instead, they try to pursue their independent careers in commuter marriages.

Commuter Marriages

In a **commuter marriage**, married partners live and work in different geographic areas and get together intermittently, such as over weekends. An estimated 2 million American couples have such long-distance marriages (U.S. Census Bureau, 1999).

Why Do They Do It? There are several reasons why a couple may have a commuter marriage. First, if one partner (usually the wife) sees that relocation will have negative effects on her employment prospects, she may decide not to move. Second, if both partners have well-established careers in different cities, neither may be willing to make major sacrifices after marriage. Third, a commuter marriage may create less stress on the family because it avoids uprooting teenage children or elderly parents. Fourth, if jobs become less secure, financial security is an increasingly important factor in maintaining commuter marriages. As you saw earlier, many professional and high-skilled workers are working multiple jobs to save for the future (see *Figure 13.6*). Some of these jobs may involve living apart during part of the week or on weekends.

Finally, racial-ethnic couples may feel that commuter marriages are the only possible route to occupational success. According to Jackson and her associates (2000), black dual-career commuter marriages have risen in response to exclusionary employment practices. Although black commuter marriages increase career options and social mobility, they also take a toll (very similar to those of their white counterparts) on the couple's interpersonal relationships, child–parent interactions, community life, and friendship networks.

Benefits What are the advantages of commuter marriages? Long-distance couples feel that they can devote more attention to their work during the week and that they learn to appreciate and make the most of the time they have together. Each person is more independent and can take advantage of time alone to pursue hobbies or recreational interests that the other partner might not enjoy. As one writer noted, "She can watch all the foreign movies she wants and eat sushi for lunch and dinner. I can play Wiffle ball in the living room and clean the bathtub with a mop" (Justice, 1999: 12).

Costs Commuter marriages also have several costs, one of which is financial. The costs of long-distance telephone bills, frequent airplane flights, and two homes can be very high. In addition, the commuting partner may feel isolated from community and social relationships, potentially resulting in extramarital relationships on the part of either partner. Furthermore, the stay-at-home parent may resent that the weekend parent is not shouldering his or her parenting responsibility. And if the couple has no children, deciding whether and when to have children—and with whom they will live—may prove stressful (Belkin, 1985; Justice, 1999).

Not surprisingly, physical exhaustion is a common problem in commuter marriages. Many commuting partners work 14- to 18-hour days during the week, live in hotel rooms or small apartments, and subsist on TV dinners or deli sandwiches. Their spouses, on the other hand, often work equally long hours and have the added burden of child care. Besides feeling lonely, parents also report feeling helpless if something goes wrong at home. For example, one father said that the worst moment of the year was when he was paged—800 miles from home—with the message that his 6-year-old daughter had stitches in her forehead after an accident at school (Stiehm, 1997).

Whether a two-income marriage involves long-distance commuting or not, women continue to earn less than their male counterparts. There is also an increasing number of families in which wives earn more than their husbands.

When Wives Earn More

In 2002, 28 percent of women earned more than their husbands, up from 22 percent in 1990 (DeNavas-Walt and Cleveland, 2002). Wives who earn more than their

Although the numbers are low, stay-at-home dads care for the children and do housework while their wives work full time and are the family's "breadwinners."

husbands typically work full time year-round as professionals or managers. The majority have no children at home, and many have a college degree. In other cases, as profits in farming and ranching communities have decreased, wives who work as county treasurers, as tax assessors, or in other public offices earn more than their husbands (Belsie, 2003).

In some cases, women's reported higher incomes may be short term. For example, a wife's income may be higher only for a year or so because her husband has been laid off on disability leave or is pursuing a degree in higher education (Roberts, 1994).

Effect on Marital Happiness According to a *Newsweek* poll, 41 percent of Americans agreed that "it is much better for everyone involved if the man is the achiever outside the home and the woman takes care of the home and family." One in four said it was "generally not acceptable" for a woman to be the major wage earner in a marriage (Tyre and McGinn, 2003: 49).

Are husbands happy when their wives make bigger contributions to the family income? Not always. If a husband holds traditional views about being the primary provider, an increasing salary gap tends to decrease the husband's marital satisfaction (Brennan et al., 2001).

In contrast, increases in women's income generally boost their own marital happiness and psychological well-being.

Men are usually pleased when their wives' income increases—up to a point. Even husbands with egalitarian attitudes about women tend to become gloomier, suffer more headaches, and generally feel more pressured and stressed if their wives' income increases by a larger percentage. For example, men don't feel glum if their wives get a 10 percent raise as long as they also get a raise of 10 percent or more (Rogers and DeBoer, 2001).

Effect on Marital Roles In contrast to exchange and resource theories (see Chapters 2 and 10), there is little impact on marital power when wives earn more than their husbands do. Couples typically ignore the income differences or minimize them by having joint bank accounts and contributing equally to joint expenses. They often stick to traditional roles in public: Husbands pick up the tab at restaurants and pay for the groceries, for example (Hales, 2002).

To compensate for not meeting cultural expectations of being the primary breadwinner, the husband may avoid "feminine" activities or not do them well. If the wife is sympathetic and doesn't want to threaten his masculinity further, she may do more of the housework to support his self-esteem (Brines, 1994). Greenstein (2000) describes such situations as "deviance neutralization." That is, couples violate traditional gender-role expectations if the wife's earnings are higher and the husband is economically more dependent on his wife. To neutralize such deviant identities, husbands may do less housework and wives may do more than their share.

High-earning wives enjoy a more equitable division of labor in the home than their lower-income counterparts, but they often still bear the larger burden of domestic labor. They don't see this as unfair because they tend to judge their success as wives and mothers by how much they do around the house rather than how much they earn. Fathers who contribute a smaller proportion of the family income are still seen as providers both because wives don't want to challenge such perceptions and because "providing is not just about money." Thus, gender, rather than the women's income or status, reinforces the husband's marital power (Tichenor, 1999).

MAKING CONNECTIONS

◼ If you, your friends, or parents are two-income couples, are there more benefits or stresses?

◼ If women earn more than their husbands, should husbands do more of the housework and child care than their wives?

The Effect of Work on Family Dynamics

Employment—whether in dual-earner families, dual-career marriages, or commuter marriages—affects the family in many ways. Most importantly, of course, work keeps most families out of poverty. Work roles also have an impact on the quality of a marriage, the division of household labor, and children's well-being.

Marital Quality and Family Life

The workplace affects the family and vice versa. Work and family have positive and negative "spillover effects" in the sense that one affects the other (Grzywacz et al., 2002). Marital quality, however, is more influential than work. If people are happily married, their job satisfaction increases, and strong marital ties can "buffer" job stress. If there is marital discord, job satisfaction decreases for both sexes (Grzywacz and Marks, 2000; Rogers and May, 2003).

Overall, most two-income parents find the home, and not work, a haven from life's stresses. In an examination of data spanning several decades (1973–1994), Kiecolt (2003) found that men and women who found home a haven increased from 32 percent to 40 percent, and those who found work to be a sanctuary decreased from 16 percent to 11 percent. Those with children under age 6 were especially likely to prefer home to work: The children made family life more satisfying and enhanced their parents' sense of meaning and purpose.

Women's employment and income do *not* undermine marriage. On the contrary, marital discord significantly increases the likelihood that wives who are not employed will enter the labor force, work more hours per week, or seek more training (Rogers, 1999). If wives are unhappy in their marriages, the increased income may also increase their likelihood of initiating a divorce at a later time (see Chapter 15).

Division of Household Labor

As you saw in Chapters 5 and 10, many married mothers have decreased their hours of housework as married fathers have increased their involvement in such work. Disparities in the domestic roles of employed men and women persist, however.

Social Class and Household Labor In some cases, middle-class employed mothers report feeling closer to their children and being "good" mothers when they do more of the daily child-care chores than fathers (for example, taking children to the park and to and from day care) (Ehrenberg et al., 2001). In most cases, however, dissatisfaction with time spent on housework and child care decreases women's marital satisfaction, but not men's (Stevens et al., 2001).

Much of the dissatisfaction may reflect the types of housework tasks that women and men do. According to Barnett and Shen (1997), mothers in dual-earner families, regardless of social class, are more likely to experience anxiety and depression because they spend more time on "low-schedule-control" housework, or tasks that must be done immediately to keep the household running smoothly, such as meal preparation, cleaning up after meals, buying the groceries, and doing the laundry. Although there are times when the plumbing needs immediate attention, most tasks labeled "male" (such as looking after the car and making repairs around the home) don't have to be performed on a regular schedule and permit high control in terms of whether, how, and when they need to be done. Barnett and Shen found that when men have many low-schedule-control tasks, they feel just as anxious and distressed as their wives do.

Working-class families, especially those in which spouses are over age 40, may experience greater conflict over family work than their middle-class counterparts. Worn out from working one shift at home and one at work, wives may feel entitled to their husbands' full participation in domestic labor:

"Sure, he helps me out. . . . He'll give the kids a bath or help with the dishes. But when I ask him. He doesn't have to ask me to go to work every day, does he? Why should I have to ask him?" (Rubin, 1994: 87).

Some men, on the other hand, feel that their wives' complaints are unreasonable and unfair:

The men, battered by economic uncertainty and by the escalating demands of their wives, feel embattled and victimized on two fronts—one outside the home, the other inside. Consequently, when their wives . . . fail to appreciate them, the men feel violated and betrayed. "You come home and you want to be appreciated a little. But it doesn't work that way, leastwise not here anymore," complains a twenty-nine-year-old drill press operator (Rubin, 1994: 87–88).

If men have jobs that are tedious or unrewarding, being expected to do low-schedule-control housework may create marital conflict. Moreover, because employed married men tend to work longer hours than their full-time employed wives, their wives' demands to do more family work may seem especially oppressive (Perry-Jenkins and Folk, 1994).

Occupational and Racial-Ethnic Differences The division of household labor varies not only by social class but also by occupational level and racial and ethnic origin. As you saw in Chapter 4, African American men are more likely than men of other races to cook, clean, and care for children. The greater participation in family work might reflect the historical exclusion of African American men from many jobs:

"My mother worked six days a week cleaning other people's houses, and my father was an ordinary laborer, when he could find work, which wasn't very often," explains thirty-two-year-old Troy Payne, a black waiter and father of two children. "So he was home a lot more than she was, and he'd do what he had to do around the house. The kids all had to do their share, too. It seemed only fair, I guess" (Rubin, 1994: 92).

The more resources a wife has, such as job status and income, the more likely it is that family work will be divided more equitably between marriage partners. In a study of Latino families, for example, Valdez and Coltrane (1993) found that wives who earned less money, worked fewer hours, held less prestigious jobs, had less education, or were much younger than their husbands were the most likely to feel responsible for all of the housework and child care. Asian and Latino men who are least likely to share in family work are those who live in ethnic neighborhoods where there is strong support for traditional gender roles, even when the wife works outside the home (see Chapters 4 and 12).

Children's Well-being

Managing parent–child relationships in the dual-earner family can be stressful:

In an all too familiar scenario, Mother comes home exhausted, wanting support from Father; Father comes home irritable and . . . wanting to be left alone; neither can give the other the support he or she needs, and their interactions are tense and brief. Meanwhile, the children are demanding attention—the little one needs diapering, while the older one is watching television instead of doing his homework. . . . And dinner still needs to be prepared (Piokowski and Hughes, 1993: 198).

Time and energy are precious commodities in many dual-earner families. Young families, especially, spend many years accommodating their child-rearing tasks to the demands of the workplace. Both dual-earner parents try to balance work and family life by making trade-offs, such as taking on additional work when it's economically necessary to do so and sometimes missing family occasions or holidays. Others scale back in meeting the demands of high-powered jobs to maintain a sense of family (Becker and Moen, 1999; Milkie and Peltola, 1999).

CHOICES

Juggling Competing Demands in Dual-Earner Families

The strains of juggling work and family life are bound to affect a marriage. Following are several strategies for maintaining one's sanity and the well-being of all family members (Beck, 1988; Crosby, 1991b):

- **Emphasize the positive.** Concentrate on the benefits you get from having a job: personal fulfillment, a higher standard of living, an ability to provide more cultural and educational opportunities for your children, and greater equality between you and your spouse.
- **Set priorities.** Because conflicts between family and job demands are inevitable, establish guiding principles for resolving clashes. For example, parents might take turns meeting such emergencies as staying at home with sick children.
- **Be ready to compromise.** Keep in mind that striving for perfection in family and job responsibilities is unrealistic. Instead, aim for the best possible balance between your various activities, making compromises when

necessary. For example, you may have to spend a little less time with your children than you would like, or you may have to sacrifice an opportunity for advancement at work.
- **Separate family and work roles.** Many mothers, especially, feel guilty while at work because they are not with their children; and when they are with their children, they feel guilty about not working on assignments from the office. If you must work at home, set time limits for the work and spend the rest of the time fully with your family.
- **Have realistic standards.** Some people believe that their homes should be just as immaculate after they have children as before, or when both spouses work instead of just one. You may need to adjust your standards and accept some disorder.
- **Organize domestic duties.** Resolve domestic overload by dividing family work more equitably between spouses and children. Many families find it

useful to prepare a weekly or monthly job chart in which everyone's assignments are clearly written down. It's also useful to rotate assignments so that everyone gets to do both the "better" and the "worse" jobs.
- **Cultivate a sharing attitude.** Sit down with your spouse periodically and discuss what you can do to help each other in your respective jobs at home and at work. Home problems deserve as much respect and attention as do work problems. Many husbands and wives are relieved when their partners offer a sounding board or give advice or encouragement.
- **Maintain a balance between responsibilities and recreation.** If you are both working to improve your standard of living, use some of your extra income to enjoy life. If you invest all your vitality in job and home responsibilities, you will have little energy left for activities that will make your life more enjoyable.

Although parents may feel stressed, most children see their parents as loving and responsive. In a national study of children in the third through twelfth grades, for example, Galinsky (1999) asked the children to "grade" both their mothers and fathers on "making me feel important and loved." Most children (72 percent) gave their mothers an A and 67 percent gave their fathers an A. There was no difference in the grades the children gave to employed mothers and to those who stayed at home or between mothers who worked part time and those who worked full time.

Perhaps the greatest stressors for the dual-earner family are those created by work-related tensions. For example, when parents experience job stress and role overload, they are more restrictive, they withdraw more, and they are less positive when interacting with their children. Parental job stress may also be associated with a child's poor academic achievement or behavioral problems in school, and it can also lead to child abuse

(Piokowski and Hughes, 1993; Parcel and Menaghan, 1994). Suggestions for problems that families encounter are offered in the box "Juggling Competing Demands in Dual-Earner Families."

Inequality in the Workplace

Employed women are often romanticized by the media, who present images of perfectly groomed women, briefcases in hand, chairing important meetings or flying across the country, cell phone in hand and laptop in action. In fact, the majority of working women have much less exciting jobs than men.

Like men, women encounter a lack of advancement opportunities, wage discrimination, and layoffs as well as sexual harassment. All of these difficulties affect the family's interpersonal and economic well-being.

The Mommy Track and the Daddy Penalty

In a work that has become a classic, Felice Schwartz (1989) divided women managers into two groups: the career-primary track and the career-and-family track. According to Schwartz, *career-primary women*, who sacrifice family and children for upward mobility, should be identified early and groomed for top-level positions alongside ambitious men. In contrast, *career-and-family women*, who are also valuable assets to a company, should be allowed to work part time and to spend more time at home. The latter option, quickly dubbed the **mommy track** by the media, was defined as a slower track or even a sidetrack for women who wanted to combine careers with child rearing.

Many feminists argued that the mommy track concept perpetuated gender-role stereotypes and gave employers reasons not to hire or promote talented women to high-level positions. Critics also pointed out that the concept could well legitimize the actions of employers who were not yielding to pressures for paid parental leave, flextime, and child care (Ehrenreich and English, 1989).

These concerns are justified. Although women make up 47 percent of the work force (see *Table 13.2*), men still hold more than 95 percent of the top management jobs in America's largest corporations (see Chapter 5). Although there are some very successful women in business (such as Meg Whitman, who built eBay into a multimillion-dollar online flea market), women receive only 4 percent of the estimated $20 billion that venture capitalists invest in funding start-up companies (McDonald, 2000).

Men's and women's wages differ, in general, because there is a "hidden" negative effect for women but not men. Because women do most of the housework and child care, they have less time and energy to pursue and invest in higher-paying jobs that demand more hours. Most men don't have such constraints because they do few domestic tasks and invest most of their time in their jobs (Noonan, 2001).

Furthermore, in what some see as a backhanded attempt to keep women out of the workplace, some corporations are penalizing the husbands of women who work outside the home, a phenomenon that the media call the **daddy penalty**.

According to some economists, married men whose wives aren't employed earn about 31 percent more per hour than never-married men, but men married to women with a full-time job earn only 3 percent more. Thus, having a wife who devotes most of her time to raising the kids and other housework frees men up to work longer and harder (Chun and Lee, 2001). In effect, corporate prejudice in favor of traditional families produces a "double whammy": "The dual-career wife earns less than she would if she were her husband, and her husband earns less than he would if she were not working" (Harris, 1995: 27).

The Gender Gap in Wages

In 2001, women who worked full time year-round had a median income of $29,215, compared with $38,275 for men. Women earn 76 cents for every male dollar (DeNavas-Walt and Cleveland, 2002). Compared with 1969, when women earned 59 cents for every dollar a man made, women have "made economic progress at roughly the rate of half a cent a year" (Goodman, 1999: 15A). Even if the snail-like increase continues, women won't achieve income parity until 2042 ("Women in red . . .," 2003).

For many ethnic minorities, the situation is even worse. Although Asian American and Pacific Island women earn 80 cents for every dollar that men earn, African American women earn only 69 cents and Latinas earn only 56 cents for every dollar that men earn. Over a lifetime of work, the average 25-year-old working woman will lose more than $523,000 in unequal pay. Families of working women lose $200 billion every year to the gender wage gap ("It's time for working women . . .," 1998; Business and Professional Women, 2003).

In some cases a woman's income is lower than a man's, *even when the man doesn't work*, because many unemployed men still have income from unemployment, disability, pensions, and investments (Krafft, 1994). As *Figure 13.9* on page 382 shows, men earn more than do women in *every* occupational category, and the earning gap *increases* at the higher-paying managerial and professional levels.

If we think about earnings as a ladder, men are on top: first white men, then black men, followed by Latinos. At the bottom of the ladder are women, with Latinas faring worse than any of the other groups. We see, then, that sex *and* race or ethnicity intersect in the workplace.

Many conservatives have an explanation for the gender wage gap:

> *Women have made enormous workplace gains, but they earn less because of their own choices, not because of discrimination. They choose to be teachers, or child-care providers, or mothers, even though they earn less. Then they compound the pay-gap by opting out of the labor force at times or by scaling back their career ambitions—and sometimes work schedules—for personal reasons (Grimsley, 2000: E3).*

According to numerous studies, however, gender, and not "choices," explains much of the earnings difference between women and men. That is, a wage gap

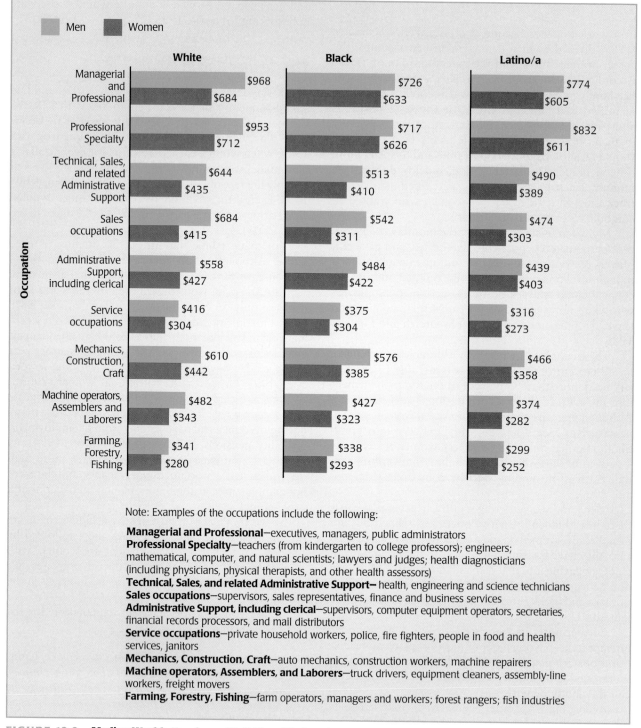

FIGURE 13.9 **Median Weekly Earnings of Full-Time Workers by Occupation, Sex, and Race/Ethnicity**

SOURCE: Based on unpublished data, Bureau of Labor Statistics, Division of Labor Force Studies, 2000.

remains even when women and men have the same education, number of years in a job, seniority, marital status, and number of children and are similar in numerous other factors (Hughes and Dodge, 1997; Goyette and Xie, 1999; Evans, 2000; "Summary of recent studies . . .," 2000; Holden, 2001; Fogg, 2003).

As you can see from *Figure 13.10*, for example, male nurses, who make up only 7 percent of the profession, are earning more than the women who far outnumber them. The same is true in other traditionally female jobs, such as social work and elementary school teaching. Because all of these occupations have been traditionally "female" for decades, it can't be argued that men earn more because of seniority, higher educational levels, or more work experience.

Some women have tried to remedy the pay inequality. They have filed *class action suits*, or legal proceedings brought by one or more people but representing the interests of a larger group. In many of these lawsuits, the courts have ordered back pay, promotions, or job reinstatement in higher education institutions and businesses such as Lucky Stores (a grocery store chain), Merrill Lynch and Salomon Smith Barney (financial institutions), and Home Depot USA Inc. (a large hardware retail corporation). Most recently, 700,000 women are suing Wal-Mart for employment discrimination (Greenhouse, 2003).

There is no country in the world where women's average earnings are equal to those of men. However, the size of the wage gap varies enormously from one country to the next. As the box "Women as Cheap Labor around the World" on page 384 shows, the United States is not the only nation that exploits women in the workplace.

Persistent employment inequality hurts all families. In addition, many women and some men must also endure work-related abuses such as sexual harassment.

Sexual Harassment

Sexual harassment was designated an illegal form of sex discrimination as early as 1964, in Title VII of the Civil Rights Act of 1964, and again in the 1980 Equal Employment Opportunity Commission (EEOC) guidelines. According to the EEOC, the fastest-growing area of employment discrimination complaints is sexual harassment, with more than 150,000 complaints filed with the EEOC between 1992 and 2002. Take the quiz in the box on page 385 "Do You Recognize Sexual Harassment?" to see how attuned you are to what sexual harassment really is.

As you saw in Chapter 5, sexual harassment includes

■ *Verbal behavior* (such as pressures for dates or demands for sexual favors in return for hiring, promotion, or tenure as well as the threat of rape)

■ *Nonverbal behavior* (such as indecent gestures and displaying posters, photos, or drawings of a sexual nature)

■ *Physical contact* (such as pinching, touching, and rape)

Sexual or nonsexual harassment in the workplace is a display of power that usually is perpetrated by a boss and directed at a subordinate. Because men dominate positions of power in business and industry, it is far more likely that a harasser will be a man than a woman. The superior–subordinate relationship of

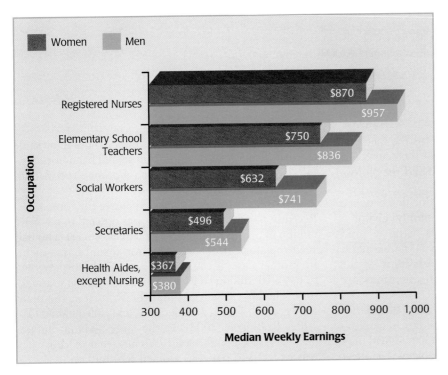

FIGURE 13.10 **Median Weekly Earnings in Traditionally Female Occupations, 2002**

Percentage of women in each occupation: secretaries (98 percent), registered nurses (93 percent), elementary school teachers (83 percent), health aides (79 percent) and social workers (73 percent).

Source: U.S. Department of Labor, 2002, Table 39, Household data annual averages, http://stats.bls.gov/cps/cpsaat39.pdf (accessed September 12, 2003).

CROSSCULTURAL

Women as Cheap Labor around the World

Occupational sex segregation and wage disparities between men and women are the norm in most countries. U.S. corporations with plants in unindustrialized countries and other nations where labor is cheap are among the worst offenders, but national governments also practice much of this discrimination.

Countries with the biggest wage disparities in manufacturing, where many women work, include Bangladesh (where women earn 50 percent of what men earn), Brazil (54 percent), Japan (56 percent), Malaysia (58 percent), and Jordan (62 percent) (Seager, 2003).

In Kuwait, one of the wealthiest countries in the Middle East, Filipino maids normally put in exhausting 14-hour days as domestic servants and earn a monthly salary of about $150 (Prusher, 2000). Hundreds of thousands of poor women are sent to work as domestic servants in middle- and upper-class homes in Europe, Japan, the Middle East, the United Kingdom, and the United States. Both the Philippine government and recruiting agencies reap tremendous profits from providing employers in these "host" countries with extremely cheap service workers who are often

mistreated and are required to work in appalling conditions (Chang, 2000; Gordy, 2000).

Although Maoist political slogans proclaimed that "women hold up half the sky" and the constitution of the People's Republic of China grants women a high status, Chinese women earn only 61 percent of what men earn (Seager, 2003). A delegate to the local National People's Congress who has spoken out against bias toward women noted that "women are always in the low-paying, dead-end jobs, like nurses, grade school teachers, nursery school teachers, and street sweepers" ("A great leap back," 1993: A24).

Even countries that promote women's rights in many areas still lag in the workplace. In Norway, for example, where women have political clout, even though the Prime Minister is a woman who supports equal rights, and although women hold almost half the seats in the Cabinet and Parliament, "Norwegian women remain second-class citizens in the job market. They are hired last, fired first, denied equal pay for the same work as men and held back from promotions to top executive jobs" (Coleman, 1994: 58).

In Norway, women who are full-time workers earn 71 percent of what men earn. The pay gap is also wide in several other counties such as Ireland (65 percent), Russia (70 percent), Canada (73 percent), and Germany (76 percent) (Seager, 2003).

Multinational corporations that move their production units into countries with abundant and cheap labor reap huge profits. In China, for example, 3 million young women work for wages as low as 12 cents an hour to make sporting goods and toys sold in the United States and Canada. Nike's $5-billion empire has been built by exploiting labor in poor countries such as China, Indonesia, and Vietnam. Workers receive less than three dollars a day, child labor is common, people aren't paid for overtime, and many women suffer sexual and verbal abuse (Dixon, 1996; MacAdam, 2003).

perpetrator and victim also accounts for the fact that women often fail to report harassment incidents. The women feel that nothing will be done and they'll lose their jobs if they complain.

Some people claim that there is a fine line between sexual harassment and flirting or simply giving a compliment. Wrong. If someone says "stop it" and the perpetrator does not stop, it is sexual harassment. Most people know—instinctively and because of the other person's reaction—when sexual attentions are unwelcome.

Sexual harassment can be very costly, both emotionally and financially, to victims, perpetrators, employers, and corporations. Victims of sexual harassment may experience emotional and behavioral problems that affect

their families, including depression; changes in attitude toward sexual relationships or in sexual behaviors; irritability with family, friends, or co-workers; and alcohol and drug abuse (see Chapter 5).

Sexual harassment is also expensive for companies. Recently, Salomon Smith Barney was ordered to pay $3.2 million in punitive damages to a female worker who had sued the stock brokerage firm for sexual harassment. In another case, a class action suit, Dial Corp. agreed to pay $10 million to 91 women at its Illinois soap factory. The lawsuit alleged that the women at the plant were groped, shown pornography, and called names (Yu, 2002; Robinson, 2003). In the largest sexual harassment case so far, in the late 1990s auto maker Mitsubishi was ordered to pay 486 women $34 million.

MAKING CONNECTIONS

■ Why does the gender wage gap persist? Are women too accepting of the inequality between their and men's income?

■ Have you, your friends, or family members ever observed or experienced sexual harassment? If so, what did you or they do about it?

Social Policy: Is the Workplace Family-Friendly?

The mommy track, the daddy penalty, gender-related wage gaps, and sexual harassment can be devastating to workers and, consequently, to their families. Is there anything in the workplace that supports the family? Absolutely.

Pregnancy discrimination laws protect pregnant workers and their jobs, and family leave policies have made it easier to care for newborns and sick family members. On the other hand, child and elder care provisions and welfare reform still leave a great deal to be desired (see Chapters 17 and 18).

Pregnancy Discrimination Laws

Pregnancy discrimination cuts across many types of jobs. For example,

■ A driver for a valet service in Mesa, Arizona, was fired because "pregnant women are susceptible to cramps and nausea while driving customers around, which might result in accidents and lawsuits."

■ A supervisor at a restaurant chain in New York was fired after getting pregnant because, according to her (male) manager, "it was going to be a challenge to be a single parent and to continue the job."

ASKYOURSELF

Do You Recognize Sexual Harassment?

Is it sexual harassment if:

	Yes	No
1. An employee uses e-mail to send sexual jokes to co-workers.	❑	❑
2. An employee continues to ask a co-worker to go out despite the person's repeated refusals.	❑	❑
3. Employees tell bawdy jokes to co-workers who enjoy them in social, non-workplace settings.	❑	❑
4. A male employee frequently brushes up against female employees "accidentally."	❑	❑
5. Male and female co-workers repeatedly talk about their respective sexual affairs and relationships during breaks around the office coffeepot.	❑	❑
6. A cashier in an eatery in the building greets each customer by calling him or her "Honey" or "Dearie."	❑	❑
7. A male supervisor tells a female employee, "You look very nice today."	❑	❑
8. Employees put up pornographic material on company bulletin boards or in lockers.	❑	❑
9. Employees or supervisors make frequent comments to co-workers on sexually explicit material in the media (films, television, magazines).	❑	❑
10. At the end of a staff meeting, a male manager says to two female secretaries, "Why don't you two girls clean up this room?"	❑	❑

(The answers to these questions are on page 386.)

Answers to "Do You Recognize Sexual Harassment?"

1. Repeated instances could meet the legal definition of sexual harassment if they create an offensive and hostile work environment.

2. Yes.

3. No.

4. Yes.

5. No, if no one else is around and the talk is consensual. It could be if a passerby finds such talk offensive.

6. No, if the comments are directed at both sexes and aren't intentionally derogatory or degrading.

7. No.

8. Yes; this creates a hostile work environment.

9. Yes.

10. No, but it's a sexist comment.

SOURCES: Based on Langelan, 1993; Coolidge, 1998.

■ A district manager at Mothers Work, Inc., a maternity-wear chain, sued the company for belittling her pregnancy, making her feel ugly, and later firing her.

■ A Boston lawyer filed a complaint against her employer, the city's second-largest law firm, for not promoting her after two pregnancies despite an excellent track record. According to a law professor, when women attorneys get pregnant or return from a maternity leave, they are perceived as low-competence caregivers rather than as high-competence businesswomen ("Boston lawyer . . .," 2003; Estes, 2003, Donnelly, 2003).

Five former Krispy Kreme employees sued the doughnut corporation in 2003. The employees alleged sexual harassment and racial discrimination at the company's store in Issaquah, Washington, and at a distribution center in Seattle, Washington.

The federal Pregnancy Discrimination Act of 1978 makes it illegal for employers with more than 15 workers to fire, demote, or penalize a pregnant employee. Some state laws extend this protection to companies with as few as four employees. In addition, many pregnant workers are entitled to up to 12 weeks of unpaid, job-protected parental leave under the Family and Medical Leave Act (which we discuss shortly).

Despite all these protections, the EEOC reports that charges of pregnancy discrimination are increasing. Charges reached a ten-year high in 2002 (a 181 percent increase) when nearly 4800 women filed complaints that they were fired, demoted, or had some of their responsibilities taken away when their employers learned they were pregnant ("Pregnancy discrimination charges," 2003).

This is just the tip of the iceberg. The EEOC figures don't reflect the complaints filed with state human rights commissions or lawsuits settled out of court. Furthermore, only a fraction of the women victimized by pregnancy-related job discrimination ever take action because many aren't aware of their rights.

Family and Medical Leave Policies: Benefits and Limitations

One of the most important pieces of legislation for many families is the Family and Medical Leave Act (FMLA),

CHOICES

A Tour of the Family and Medical Leave Act

Employees who know their rights under the Family and Medical Leave Act (FMLA) are more likely to take advantage of its benefits.

Who is covered? Any employee is eligible for 12 weeks of leave if she or he has worked at least 1250 hours during a 12-month period—roughly the equivalent of 25 hours a week—at a company or work site employing at least 50 people.

The highest-paid 10 percent of employees must be granted a leave like all others. However, this group is not guaranteed a job on return if their absences cause "substantial and grievous economic injury" to their employers.

What are the purposes of family and medical leave? An employee may take family or medical leave for the birth or adoption of a child and to care for a newborn; to care for a spouse, child,

or parent with a serious illness; and to recuperate from a serious illness that prevents an employee from working.

Who pays for the leave? The employee pays for the leave. A company may require or allow employees to apply paid vacation and sick leave to the 12 weeks of family leave but does not have to pay workers who take leave. On their return employees must be given the same health benefits that they received before going on leave.

When should the employer be notified? In foreseeable cases, such as a birth, adoption, or planned medical treatment, 30 days' verbal or written notice is required. When that's impossible (for example, if a baby is born early), the employer must be notified as soon as possible, generally within one or two business days. Employers may ask for medical proof that a leave is needed.

Must the leave be taken all at once? Leave need not be taken all at once. For example, it can be used to shorten the workweek when an employee wants to cut back after the birth of a child. Medical leave can also be taken piecemeal (for example, to accommodate weekly appointments for chemotherapy treatments).

What if you feel your rights have been violated? Any local or regional office of the U.S. Department of Labor's Wage and Hour Division, Employment Standards Administration, will accept complaints, which must be filed within two years of the alleged violation. Private lawsuits must also be filed within two years of the violation.

According to a recent Supreme Court ruling (*Nevada Department of Human Resources v. Hibbs*), state employees can now sue agencies that violate the FMLA.

which was introduced in Congress in 1985 and finally signed into law by President Clinton in 1993. This law allows eligible employees to take up to 12 weeks of unpaid, job-protected annual leave, with continuation of health benefits, after the birth or adoption of a child, to care for a seriously sick family member, or to recover from their own illnesses. The box "A Tour of the Family and Medical Leave Act" provides a closer look at these rights.

Benefits of the FMLA   The most obvious benefit of family leave policies is that many employees no longer lose their jobs because of sickness, childbirth, or parental leave. Furthermore, most employees, except for the top 10 percent, are guaranteed their jobs or equivalent jobs when they return. The FMLA defines an "equivalent" position as one with the same pay, benefits, and working conditions and "substantially similar" duties and responsibilities. Most important, because the act is law, employees don't have to depend on the supervisor's good will.

Limitations of the FMLA   The FMLA and other leave policies have several weaknesses. The biggest problem is that the 60 percent of U.S. employees who work in companies with fewer than 50 employees are not covered by the FMLA. Such small companies are much less likely than larger ones to provide employee benefits such as health insurance, paid sick leave, and disability insurance. Thus, the FMLA ignores millions of employees who already have limited benefits. In addition, the many workers in part-time, temporary positions (most of whom are women) are excluded from family leave policies.

In addition, the FMLA is of little help to many parents because it involves unpaid time off and covers only major illnesses that typically necessitate a hospital stay. In most cases, children don't need hospitalization but instead have frequent routine illnesses. And as we discussed at the beginning of this chapter, because the number of low-paid service jobs is increasing while the number of higher-paid jobs is decreasing, many employees can't afford to take unpaid leave.

Sales representatives, like this mother, can often work from home, which enables them to interact more frequently with their children.

What's more, employees and employers may disagree about what constitutes an "equivalent" job or "substantially similar" responsibilities. Does a person have an "equivalent" job if it involves driving an extra 30 minutes to work to an unfamiliar office and a less desirable location?

Finally, employers may label men who use flextime or paternity leave as not fully dedicated to their jobs or careers. And, with downsizing, "few male employees want to send a signal that they are less than 100 percent devoted to their jobs" (Saltzman, 1993: 66). In response, many men refuse paternity leave and instead use vacation days, sick days, or compensatory time off to spend time with their wives and newborns (Pleck, 1993). Yet according to a recent survey, 90 percent of businesses report no additional costs by providing unpaid leave or actually increase their profits through better employee morale and higher productivity (Smith et al., 2001).

California is the only state that provides up to six weeks of paid leave for employees to care for a new child or an ailing relative (Broder, 2002). In contrast to the rest of the United States, 17 other industrialized countries have provided 12 to 72 weeks of *paid* parental leave since 1989 (Ruhm and Teague, 1997). "From Germany to Gabon, from Belgium to Brazil, from Switzerland to Senegal, women receive paid maternity leave" (Heymann, 2002: 12).

Day Care for Dependents

One of the most serious problems facing families today is inadequate day care for young children. And, increasingly, families are confronting the need for day-care services for elderly parents. What, if anything, are businesses and government doing to help families?

Child Care As you saw in Chapter 12, high costs, poor quality, and long waiting lists are just some of the obstacles that confront working parents who seek safe and reliable care for their children. "The search for quality nonparental care for young children is daunting at best and can reach crisis proportions at worst, because our nation currently lacks a policy that ensures reliable, affordable, developmentally appropriate care for all children who need it" (Piokowski and Hughes, 1993: 193).

Unlike many other industrialized countries, we have no national child-care program. Some companies that tout child-care assistance actually do little more than provide a list of potential child-care providers in the area. Moreover, most companies charge for day-care services, and many low-wage workers are unable to pay even these reduced costs. Chapter 18 describes some innovative child-care facilities that some companies have implemented.

Only a few companies, recognizing that offering family benefits is good for business, provide some form of child-care assistance. The assistance includes a company-run, on-site child-care center, access to a reputable child-care center near the company's facilities, and summer camps.

One of the most popular issues of *Working Mother* magazine is its annual ranking of the 100 companies that offer the best working conditions and benefits for working mothers. Major criteria in these rankings include competitive wages, opportunities for advancement, support for child care, and such family-friendly benefits as leave for childbirth, flextime, and job sharing. *Table 13.3* lists *Working Mother's* top ten companies for 2003.

Working at home, or *telecommuting*, is one of the newest modes of more flexible work styles. As the box "Working at Home: Still Not a Paradise" on page 390 shows, telecommuting has both benefits and costs.

Elder Care Most businesses rarely provide or subsidize elder-care services for their employees. Some companies, however, offer seminars on a variety of elder-care topics, such as how to choose a nursing home or help elderly family members with financial matters. A Canadian company, Microchip Human Services in suburban Toronto, maintains a 24-hour database service that employees from client companies can call toll free for detailed information on elder-care services anywhere in the country (Mergenbagen, 1994). In the United States, and as you'll see in Chapter 17, family members—especially women—provide most of the elder care.

TABLE 13.3

Ten Best U.S. Companies for Working Mothers

Name of Company	Years Ranked in Top 100*	Business
Abbott Laboratories	3	Pharmaceutical products
Booz Allen Hamilton	5	Financial services
Bristol-Myers Squibb Company	6	Pharmaceutical products
Eli Lilly and Company	9	Pharmaceutical products
Fannie Mae	10	Financial services
General Mills	8	Packaged consumer foods
IBM	18	Computer hardware and business consulting
Prudential Financial Inc.	14	Financial services
S.C. Johnson & Son, Inc.	15	Manufactures household products
Wachovia Corporation	8	Financial services

*Working Mother has been compiling this list since 1985.

SOURCE: Based on Working Mother, "100 Best Companies for Working Mothers" (October 2003): 56–63.

Welfare Programs for Poor Families

The United States is the only one among 19 wealthy nations with a double-digit poverty rate (Smeeding et al., 2000). Unlike the United States, countries such as Germany, Italy, and the Netherlands have less poverty because they have higher minimum wages, guaranteeing that full-time workers' children will not be poor.

What help is available for the poor? Not much. In 1996 Congress passed the Personal Responsibility and Work Opportunity Reconciliation Act (PRWORA), which reformed the welfare system. PRWORA was targeted almost entirely at poor, mother-only families. The central feature of PRWORA was the replacement of Aid to Families with Dependent Children (AFDC) with block grants. The states set their own eligibility criteria and benefit levels. Three other important changes included the following: (1) Federal money cannot be used to provide cash assistance to unmarried women under age 18 or to children born to mothers who are already receiving assistance; (2) adults are expected to work after receiving welfare for two years; and (3) a family cannot receive cash assistance for more than five years over its lifetime.

PRWORA advocates are delighted that some families have left the welfare rolls. Critics argue, however, that PRWORA has scapegoated poor, unmarried mothers and their children instead of focusing on macro-level problems such as widespread economic inequality, jobs that don't provide decent wages and benefits, and a growing poverty among young two-parent families (Sidel, 1998).

In 2001, when unemployment increased, many of the "welfare leavers" lost their low-paying jobs. Others have jobs in the low end of the labor market that don't lift working parents out of poverty. The median hourly wage for former welfare recipients is $7.15. Only about a third of the employers offer any health insurance or paid sick leave (Weil, 2002; Wertheimer, 2003).

Welfare reform has pushed at least a million preschoolers into mostly low-quality day care because mothers who participate in the required welfare-to-work programs can't afford high-quality child care. In a study of child care in three states, researchers found that many of the 2- to 4-year-olds were in home-based care with few educational materials, little reading or storytelling, dirty facilities, and lots of television viewing. The researchers concluded that children in low-quality facilities are behind in social and language development and will be unlikely to break out of poverty (Fuller and Kagan, 2000).

Conclusion

Because many families lack sufficient economic resources, they have very few *choices* in the workplace. Macro-level economic *changes* have created numerous *constraints* that often present dilemmas. Incomes have not kept up with the rate of inflation, so more household members have to work. This cuts into family time and creates stress that can contribute to illness, absenteeism, and layoffs. The more successful employed women and men are, the more

CHANGES

Working at Home: Still Not a Paradise

Many analysts predicted that personal computers would help decrease the conflict between work and family roles. People could work at home, or *telecommute*, that is, work from home through computer hookups to a company office.

In 2001 about 21 million people did some work at home as part of their primary job:

- 80 percent were in managerial, professional, and sales jobs.
- 80 percent were white.
- 50 percent were women.
- 17 percent were parents with children under 18 ("Work at home . . .," 2002).

On the *positive side*, many telecommuters spend less money on clothes, have a more flexible work schedule, and have reduced the cost of child care by working at home (Koncius, 1995). Some report that working at home brings the family closer together. A parent is available when a child returns after school, and family members often become involved in the business tasks (Schafer, 1999).

On the *negative side*, some telecommuters miss their work friends, and others feel that nothing replaces face-to-face communication. Some telecommuters resent having to maintain or fix complicated office equipment like computers or fax machines. Others worry that telecommuting might make them less visible to managers who award promotions and raises (Allen and Moorman, 1997; Tanaka, 1997).

Telecommuting can decrease instead of increase the quality of family time. Some parents resent interruptions or distractions because of household chores, worry that they can't leave job stress at the office, or find that it's hard to separate their family and business lives (Garland, 2000).

Noise from children, pets, and appliances may also decrease productivity and create stress. Some people are also concerned that the expenses for telecommuting may be screened more carefully by the Internal Revenue Service and increase the risks of audits (Allen and Moorman, 1997). Finally, there are numerous work-at-home scams that lie about the potential earnings and profits and require workers to purchase software and other products that never pay off (Learner, 2002).

STOP AND THINK . . .

- *Telecommuting in the United States has decreased from almost 23 million people in 1997 to 21 million in 2001. Why do you think this is the case?*
- *Have you ever telecommuted or done paid work at home? If so, what were the advantages and disadvantages?*

difficult it is for them to find time for family activities.

If men and women are not successful, they and their families have fewer choices in maintaining a decent standard of living. Many parents, especially single mothers, can't afford child care because it is too expensive, but without child care, they can't get the training for jobs that will pull them out of poverty. Many of the same economic and political structures also have an impact on whether interpersonal relationships within the family are healthy or destructive, a topic we examine in the next chapter.

SUMMARY

1. Social class and economic resources play a major role in what happens to families. A small proportion of affluent families is getting richer, an increasing number of middle-class families is experiencing lower income and unemployment, and the number of poor families is growing.

2. Some scholars feel that poverty rates are exaggerated because they ignore noncash benefits from the government, such as food stamps, housing subsidies, and medical services. Most scholars, however, maintain that the proportion of the poor is underestimated because the amount of money needed for subsistence varies drastically by region and because the U.S. Census Bureau undercounts the poor.

3. Although there are no exact figures, about 3.5 million people are homeless in a given year. About a third of the homeless are children.

4. Economic recessions and stagnant incomes have resulted in more dual-earner families. There is a great deal of variation in dual-earner families, however, in terms of social class and willingness to relocate or to have a commuter marriage.

5. The widespread employment of mothers was one of the most dramatic changes in family roles in the twentieth century.

6. Employment impacts the family in many ways. Regardless of whether the results are positive or negative, work roles affect the duration and quality of a marriage, household labor, and children's well-being.

7. Because of economic changes and the increasing number of mothers with young children who must work, many families face serious child-care problems.

8. One of the biggest problems employed women face is the gender gap in wages and salaries. Some women have filed class action suits to remedy the situation. Other problems include pregnancy discrimination and sexual harassment.

9. A landmark piece of legislation is the Family and Medical Leave Act. Although the law protects an employee's job during illness and maternity and paternity leave, the bill provides little or limited coverage to most families.

10. Welfare reforms have done little to lift families out of poverty. In fact, many families are worse off than ever before.

KEY TERMS

absolute poverty *363*
relative poverty *363*
poverty line *364*
feminization of poverty *365*
working poor *366*

discouraged worker *370*
underemployed worker *370*
two-person single career *373*
dual-earner couple *374*
discretionary income *374*

dual-career couple *375*
trailing spouse *375*
commuter marriage *376*
mommy track *381*
daddy penalty *381*

TAKING IT FURTHER

Combining Family and Work More Effectively

The Internet offers a wide range of information on improving our working conditions and family life. Sites include the following:

U.S. Department of Labor Home Page provides a cornucopia of data and practical information on employment, workplace illnesses, and employee benefits.

www.bls.gov

U.S. Department of Labor Women's Bureau Home Page offers statistics, advice on hiring someone to work in your home, and much data on women in the workplace.

www.dol.gov/dol/wb

The Families and Work Institute conducts research on the changing work force and examines policy in family and personal lives.

www.familiesandwork.org

The Center on Budget and Policy Priorities conducts research and analysis on a range of government work policies and programs, with an emphasis on those affecting low- and moderate-income families.

www.cbpp.org

Home Business Network provides networking tips and a newsletter for home-based businesses.

www.home-careers.com

And more: www.prenhall.com/benokraitis includes sites on the economic situation worldwide, reports on U.S. workers, homelessness, family finances, how to calculate your personal gender wage gap online, FMLA research, at-home-dad resources, stay-at-home moms, and more.

INVESTIGATE WITH RESEARCH NAVIGATOR

Please go to www.researchnavigator.com and enter your LOGIN NAME and PASSWORD. For instructions on registering for the first time, please view the detailed instructions at the end of the Chapter 1. Please search the Research Navigator™ site using the following key search terms:

underemployment
family leave
household labor

Family Violence and Other Crises

DATADIGEST

- Between 1993 and 2001 the **rate of reported child abuse or neglect decreased** from 15.3 to 12.4 per 1000 children.

- In 2001, **an intimate partner killed 33 percent of female murder victims,** compared with only 4 percent of male murder victims.

- In 2001, 42 percent of the women who were physically assaulted by an intimate partner **were injured during their most recent assault,** compared with 20 percent of men.

- **The cost of child abuse is almost $95 billion a year.** The costs are direct (such as hospitalization and law enforcement) and indirect (such as juvenile delinquency and adult criminality).

- Each year, on average, a spouse, adult child, or close acquaintance **injures about 36,000 people age 65 or older and kills about 500.**

SOURCES: Klaus, 2000; Fromm, 2001; U.S. Department of Health and Human Services, 2003a; Rennison, 2003.

Recently the Newark, New Jersey, police were horrified by what they saw. Two little boys, ages 4 and 7, were locked in the basement:

The children were starving and filthy, their bodies covered with excrement and burn marks. A day after finding the boys in the basement, police discovered the body of a third child, stuffed inside a plastic container. . . . The 7-year-old boy, a twin, had been dead for more than a month. Investigators described the body as so withered and stiff it was "mummified" (Smalley and Braiker, 2003: 32).

According to the police, the boys had also been sexually assaulted over a number of years by relatives and their mother's boyfriends.

Families can be warm, loving, and nurturing, but they can also be cruel and abusive. Family members are more likely than outsiders to assault or kill other family members. As Gelles (1997:12) observes, "That violence and love can coexist in a household is perhaps the most insidious aspect of family violence, because we grow up learning that it is acceptable to hit the people we love."

This chapter examines the different forms of domestic violence, describes its prevalence, and discusses why people who say they love each other are so abusive. We then turn to other family crises such as drug abuse, depression and suicide, eating disorders, and some successful prevention and intervention strategies.

Marital and Intimate Partner Violence

Marital and intimate partner violence is pervasive in U.S. society. According to a recent national survey, 20 percent of women and 3 percent of men said they had been physically assaulted by a current or former spouse, cohabiting partner, or date at some time in their

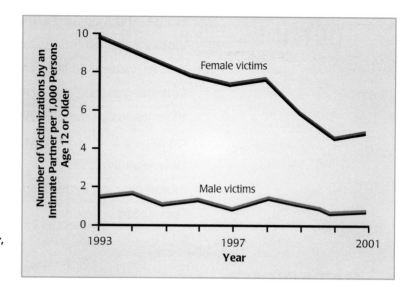

FIGURE 14.1 **Rate of Violence by an Intimate Partner, by Gender, 1993-2001**

SOURCE: Rennison, 2003.

lifetime (Rennison, 2003). These numbers are probably conservative because people are often too ashamed or afraid to report the victimization.

Types of Domestic Violence

Violence in marriages may be physical or emotional. *Physical violence* includes such behaviors as throwing objects, pushing, grabbing, shoving, slapping, kicking, biting, hitting, beating, choking, threatening with a knife or gun, or using a knife or gun.

Emotional abuse (which includes psychological and verbal abuse), equally damaging, is more insidious. Scorn, criticism, ridicule, or neglect by loved ones can be emotionally crippling. Listen to a 33-year-old mother of two children: "He rarely says a kind word to me. The food is too cold or . . . too hot. The kids are too noisy. . . . I am too fat or too skinny. No matter what I do he says it isn't any good. He tells me I am lucky he married me 'cause no one else would have me" (Gelles and Straus, 1988: 68).

Prevalence and Severity of Domestic Violence

Female victimization by intimate partners decreased slightly between 1993 and 2001, but the numbers are still high and considerably higher than those for men (see *Figure 14.1*). During this period, women were five times more likely than men to experience violence by an intimate partner. In fact, almost 85 percent of all attacks by intimate partners are against women (Rennison, 2001).

Men are more likely than women to engage in repeated violence against their partners (Tjaden and Thoennes, 2000b). Women are also more likely to sustain serious

and chronic physical injuries because they are usually smaller than their partners or because they are attacked when they are pregnant and especially physically vulnerable (Wiist and McFarlane, 1998; Tjaden and Thoennes, 2000b).

Most victims of intimate homicide are killed by their spouses (see *Figure 14.2*). Although homicide rates for husbands decreased by 75 percent, those for wives almost tripled between 1976 and 1995 (Puzone, 2000).

We'll examine why women's victimization rates are much higher than men's shortly. First, however, let's look at some of the traits of domestic violence.

Characteristics of the Violent Household

Who batters? There is no "typical" batterer profile. *Table 14.1* on page 396 lists some characteristics that are common to abusers. Some reflect macro-level influences, such as unemployment and poverty. Others reflect micro-level factors, such as drug abuse. The more risk factors, the more likely the violence.

In general, both male and female abusers tend to be young, poor, unemployed, and divorced or separated, may use alcohol and other drugs, and may have seen a father use violence to resolve conflict. Typically, however, abusive relationships reflect a combination of these and other factors. They also vary across groups in terms of gender, age, marital status, race and ethnicity, and social class.

Gender As you saw earlier, women are much more likely than men to be victims rather than offenders in domestic violence (see *Figure 14.1*). In terms of homicide rates, for example, and across all racial-ethnic groups, women are almost twice as likely as men to be murdered by an intimate partner (Paulozzi et al., 2001).

Age   In general, younger rather than older people are more likely to be the victims and perpetrators of domestic violence. Younger women generally have higher rates of intimate partner violence than older women. For example, women aged 16 to 24 are the most likely to be abused by their intimate partners. In every age category, women are more likely than men to be murdered by an intimate partner. For people aged 35 to 49, for example, 38 percent of the homicide victims are women, compared with 6 percent of men (Rennison, 2001).

Teen mothers are especially likely to experience domestic violence for several years after a child's birth. Much of the violence probably results from financial responsibilities that the couple can't manage. As a result, there may be stress, conflict, and violence (Harrykissoon et al., 2002).

Marital Status   Women who are separated from their husbands—especially women aged 20 to 34—experience higher violence rates than married, divorced, widowed, or never-married women. The next highest rate is for divorced women (Rennison, 2001).

Many separated and divorced women have high rates of partner abuse because the husbands or ex-husbands are determined to control their past partners. According to Websdale (1999), men are considerably more likely than women to commit what he calls "familicide." That is, men murder their wife and children before committing suicide. Although women may kill their children, they rarely commit familicide.

Race and Ethnicity   Since 1980, the homicide rates for white females killed by intimate partners have increased whereas those for white males and for African Americans of both sexes have decreased (Fox and Zawitz, 2003).

In terms of abuse generally, there is wide variation across racial-ethnic groups (see *Figure 14.3* on page 397). For example, American Indian women report the highest abuse rates (38 percent), and Asian American women report the lowest (15 percent). African American and American Indian men report the highest and most similar domestic violence rates (12 percent each). Women who are mixed race also have high victimization rates, similar to those of black women (30 percent and 29 percent, respectively).

National data on intimate partner violence should be interpreted cautiously for several reasons. First, there are still no data *within* ethnic-racial groups, such as possible variations within Latino and Asian American subgroups and American Indian tribes (Tjaden and Thoennes, 2000a).

Second, recent immigrants probably don't report most domestic abuse. For example, Asian American women, especially those who don't speak English well, may not report marital violence because they fear being deported or ostracized by their community, or they don't know about or trust social service organizations that provide help (Lira and Koss, 1999; Foo, 2002; Raj and Silverman, 2002).

Social Class   Contrary to popular opinion, violence does not occur *only* in low-income families. For example, Melzer (2002) found that men in some middle-class occupations (such as police, correction officers, and emergency workers) are especially likely to lash out at home. These men work in dangerous or violent surroundings. Because they have control and authority at work, however, the men in these occupations often become violent when their intimate partners disagree with them.

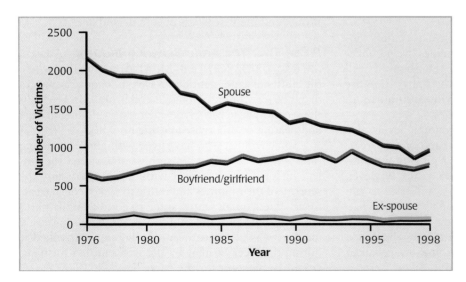

FIGURE 14.2   Homicides of Intimates by Relationship of Victim to the Offender

SOURCE: Rennison and Welchans, 2000: Figure 2.

TABLE 14.1

Risk Factors Associated with Domestic Violence

- There are social class differences, especially if the woman's educational level is higher than the man's.

- The couple is cohabiting rather than married.

- The male partner is more likely to be the victim if his race or ethnicity differs from the woman's.

- The man is sadistic, aggressive, or obsessively jealous.

- The man has threatened, injured, or killed a family pet.

- One or both partners grew up seeing a parent hit the other parent.

- One or both partners is divorced and remarried or their current marriage is common-law.

- The man is unemployed and the woman is employed.

- The man is a high school dropout.

- The family income is below the poverty line.

- The man is under age 30.

- Either or both partners abuse alcohol and other drugs.

- The man has assaulted someone outside the family or has committed some other violent crime.

- The family is socially isolated from neighbors, relatives, and the community.

Sources: Leonard and Senchak, 1993; Straus, 1993; Bachman, 1994; Gelles, 1995; Tjaden and Thoennes, 2000a; Hutchison, 1999; MacMillan and Gartner, 1999.

Regardless of occupation, middle-class family violence is less visible because such families are less likely to live in crowded housing where the neighbors call the police during fights. Moreover, their physicians are often reluctant to report domestic violence injuries to the police or to social service agencies.

Husbands from higher socioeconomic levels also abuse their wives. The attorney-husband of a 50-year-old Colorado woman appeared to be a pillar of the community. According to his wife of 28 years, however, he hit her, threw her down the stairs, and tried to run over her. "One night in Vail," she said, "when he had one of his insane fits, the police came and put him in handcuffs. . . . My arms were still red from where he'd trapped them in the car window, but somehow, he talked his way out of it" (Ingrassia and Beck, 1994: 29).

Although domestic violence cuts across all social classes, it is most common in low-income households. The most likely abusers are those who marry at a young age or cohabit. Violence escalates if one or both partners abuse drugs, are unemployed, and have more children than they can afford to raise (DeMaris et al., 2003).

The Cycle of Domestic Violence

In 1991, the governors of Maryland, Ohio, and Washington pardoned a group of women imprisoned for killing or assaulting partners who had abused them physically. The women were pardoned based on the defense of the **battered-woman syndrome**, a condition that describes a woman who has experienced many years of physical abuse and who feels incapable of leaving. In a desperate effort to defend themselves, such women sometimes kill the abusers.

A "cycle theory of battering incidents" supports the battered-woman syndrome claim. According to this theory, a tension-building phase leads to an acute battering incident. The cycle ends with a period of calm that lasts until the cycle starts again (Walker, 1978, 2000).

Phase One: The Tension-Building Phase In the first phase of the cycle, when minor battering incidents occur, the wife tries to prevent her husband's anger from escalating by catering to him or staying out of his way. At the same time, the battered wife often feels that her husband's abuse is justified: "When he throws the dinner she prepared for him across the kitchen floor she reasons that maybe she did overcook it, accidentally. As she cleans up his mess, she may think that he was a bit extreme in his reaction, but she is usually so grateful that it was a relatively minor incident that she resolves not to be angry with him" (Walker, 1978: 147). Although the wife hopes the situation will change, the tension typically escalates, the husband becomes more brutal, and the wife is less able to defend herself.

Phase Two: The Acute Battering Incident Abusers often have a Dr. Jekyll and Mr. Hyde personality where the rational and gentle Dr. Jekyll changes, unpredictably, into an unreasonable and brutal Mr. Hyde. In the second phase Mr. Hyde emerges, exploding in rage and beating or otherwise abusing his wife.

Some women who have lived with abuse for a long time actually anticipate this phase and trigger the violent incident to get it over with. They often deny the severity of their injuries and refuse to seek medical treatment. One woman who wanted to go to a family party with her husband and sensed that an acute battering incident was about to occur deliberately provoked it during the week so that by the weekend her husband would be pleasant for the party (Walker, 1978).

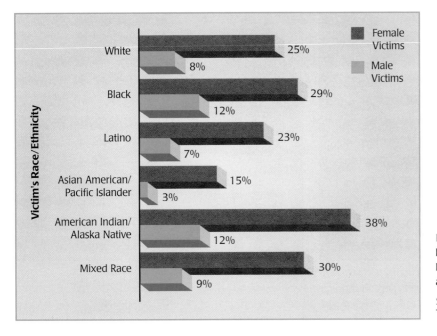

FIGURE 14.3 **Percentage of People Victimized by an Intimate Partner in Lifetime, by Victim's Sex and Race/Ethnicity**

SOURCE: Based on data in Tjaden and Thoennes, 2000a: Exhibits 6 and 7.

Phase Three: Calm Mr. Hyde becomes the kindly Dr. Jekyll in the third phase, begging his wife's forgiveness and promising that he will never beat her again: "He manages to convince all concerned that this time he means it; he will give up drinking, dating other women, visiting his mother, or whatever else affects his internal anxiety state. His sincerity is believable" (Walker, 1978: 152). If his wife has been hospitalized because of her physical injuries, the husband often deluges her with flowers, candy, cards, and gifts. He may also get his mother, father, sisters, brothers, and other relatives to plead his case to his wife.

They all build up her guilt by telling her that her husband would be destroyed if she left him and that a father should not be separated from his children. Because most battered women hold traditional values about love and marriage, the wife convinces herself that *this* time he will *really* change.

Because he is now loving and kind, she identifies this "good man" as the one she loves. After a while, though, the calm, loving behavior gives way to battering incidents, and the cycle starts all over again. The cycle of violence often includes marital rape.

Marital Rape

Marital rape (sometimes also called *spousal rape* or *wife rape*) is a violent act in which a man forces his wife to have sexual intercourse. Raping a wife has been a crime in all states since 1993. However, 32 states and the District of Columbia grant a *marital rape exemption*. That is, they do not prosecute a rape case if the man is actually living with the woman, married or not, or if the wife is mentally or physically impaired, unconscious, or asleep during the act (Bergen, 1999).

Some states permit prosecution of a husband-rapist only if the rape occurred after one spouse filed for divorce or if the parties were not living together at the time of the rape (Russell, 1990). Even in states where a husband can be charged for marital rape, a wife may have difficulty proving rape if she shows no visible signs of having been forced, such as bruises or broken bones.

Although an estimated 15 percent of married women nationwide are raped by their spouses, very few report these crimes. A traditional wife, believing that she has no choice but to perform her "wifely duty," may accept the situation as normal, especially if her husband does not use a weapon or threaten her with physical harm (Michael et al., 1994).

Among South Asian immigrants, women subjected to marital rape rarely reveal the abuse. Consenting to marriage generally assumes the woman's availability for sexual intercourse, even when it's unwanted, because a man controls the marriage (Abraham, 2000). Latino wives may also be silent about marital rape because of cultural values to remain loyal and protect the man's honor and reputation. Such loyalty is not seen as weakness "but as a sign of warmth and goodness" (Vandello and Cohen, 2003: 1008).

Why Do Women Stay?

Battered wives are often dependent women who suffer from low self-esteem and feelings of inadequacy and

Hedda Nussbaum was the live-in lover of criminal attorney Joel Steinberg when he "adopted" infant Lisa (left). Six years later, battered beyond recognition by her "lover" (center), Hedda witnessed his arraignment for the murder of Lisa, whom he had begun to abuse as well. Doctors, teachers, and neighbors had noticed Lisa's bruises but did nothing. Late in 1987 Steinberg hit Lisa and left her lying on the floor, comatose. Lisa died three days later. Steinberg was convicted and jailed. Nussbaum, judged incapable of either harming or helping Lisa, began slowly to rebuild her life. She now spends much of her time on lecture circuits to help battered women (right).

helplessness. It's not clear whether these characteristics reflect personality traits battered women possessed before they met the abusers, whether they are the result of the abuse, or a combination of both (Rathus and O'Leary, 1997).

Still, the obvious question is "Why do these women stay?" Despite the common tendency to think of abused women as passive punching bags, 87 percent of abused wives and female partners seek help at various medical facilities that include hospital emergency rooms (Tjaden and Thoennes, 2000a). Many rely on family, friends, and shelters to leave batterers safely and permanently (Goetting, 1999). Some women, like one of my students, find the courage to leave only when they suddenly realize that the abusive relationship is harming their children:

> *John never laid a finger on our daughter but struck me in front of her. . . . I cringe to remember but at the time I chose to believe that what Sheri saw wasn't affecting her. One afternoon when I heard Sheri banging and yelling, I rushed to her room. . . . Sheri was hitting her doll and screaming four-letter words she often heard her father yell at me. She was just starting to talk, and that was what she was learning. That moment changed our lives forever. . . . I left John that night and . . . never went back (Author's files).*

There is no single reason why some women don't leave violent relationships. Instead, there are multiple and overlapping explanations for a victim's staying with an abusive partner:

1. **Negative self-concept and low self-esteem.** Many battered women feel they have nothing to offer another person. Most batterers convince their partners that they are worthless, stupid and disgusting: "Behind a closed door, a man calls a woman a 'slut' and a 'whore.' He tells her that she is too fat, too sexy or too frumpy, that she is 'a poor excuse for a mother,' a worthless piece of dirt" (Goode et al., 1994: 24).

   Such tyranny is effective because in many cultures a woman's self-worth still hinges on having a man. Women are often willing to pay any price to hold on to the relationship because they believe no one else could love them.

2. **Belief that the abuser will change.** One woman with a cheek still raw from her husband's beating said, "I'm still in love with him, and I know he's going to change as soon as he gets past these things that are troubling him."

   Our society has long nurtured the myth that women are responsible for changing men into kind and loving beings. Consider the message in the popular Walt Disney film *Beauty and the Beast*. The Beast turns into a prince only after Beauty stays with him and says she loves him despite his cruelty, threats, and breaking furniture—in a word, acting like a beast.

Many women stay in violent relationships because they are seduced by the Cinderella fantasy. The Cinderella fantasy is the illusion that "a man can transform a woman's life, erase her insecurities, protect her from her fears, or save her from her problems or all four" (Rosen, 1996: 159). The woman believes that, sooner or later, the abuser will change and that she and Prince Charming will live "happily ever after." Millions of women stay in the relationship because they would rather "rehabilitate" the man than break up the family (Sontag, 2002).

3. **Economic hardship and homelessness.** Because many abused women do not work outside the home and have few marketable skills, they see no way to survive economically if they leave the abusive relationship (Choice and Lamke, 1997). A social worker who works with welfare recipients points out that many men do not want their partners to become employed and independent. Some men resort to violence to prevent women from completing employment training programs or from entering the work force (Raphael, 1995).

A few years ago, an award-winning high school coach in Baltimore stabbed his wife ten times with a screwdriver, leaving her partially paralyzed. The wife pleaded with the judge not to send the husband to jail. Ironically, she wanted him to keep working so his health insurance could pay for treating her injuries; she had worked part time and had no medical benefits (Shatzkin, 1996).

Many batterers keep their wives in economic chains. Nothing is in the woman's name—not checking or savings account, automobile, or home. Because most abusers keep their victims isolated from friends and relatives, the women have no one to turn to. Moreover, those who might give battered women a place to stay fear endangering their own families. Without resources, some abused women who do leave become homeless (Browne, 1993).

4. **Need for child support.** Leaving a husband or filing charges against him may push a wife and children into poverty. Many women believe that even an abusive husband (and father) is better than none. As one of my students, a former abused wife, once said in class, "This man brings in most of the family's income. Without him, you can't pay the rent, buy the groceries, or pay the electric bills. If he goes to jail, he'll probably lose his job. And then what will you and the kids do?"

5. **Sense of shame or guilt.** Strong cultural factors may also keep a woman from moving out of an abusive relationship. Among some Asian American communities, especially, there is strong pressure not to bring shame or disgrace to the family by exposing such problems as domestic violence.

Even when women are employed, they rarely have the resources to survive economically. Women in rural areas are especially isolated: There are no shelters, their wages range from $5.15 to $6.95 an hour, and the women are afraid that disclosing abuse to co-workers or supervisors will bring gossip and shame to the family (Swanberg and Logan, 2003).

6. **Blaming themselves.** Battered women often feel that somehow they have brought the violence on themselves. Men who batter may be well-respected ball players, community leaders, or attorneys. The women start thinking that because the men have a "good" reputation, it must be their fault when the men are abusive at home (Parameswaran, 2003).

This is particularly likely if women have seen their mothers or grandmothers suffer similar treatment: "One woman whose bruises from her husband's beatings were clearly visible was told by her grandmother, 'You have to stop provoking him. You have two children, and the bottom line is you have nowhere to go. If he tells you to shut up, shut up'" (Goode et al., 1994: 27).

Thus a tradition is passed on. Women feel they are responsible for preventing male violence, and if they don't succeed, they believe that they must accept the consequences (Jones, 1993). Moreover, because some priests, ministers, and rabbis remind a woman that she is married "for better or for worse," religious women may feel guilty and sinful for wanting to leave. Many abused spouses don't realize that they have the same rights as anyone else (see *Table 14.2* on page 400).

7. **Fear of the husband.** Fear is a *major* reason why women stay in abusive marriages. Husbands have threatened to kill their wives, their wives' relatives, and even the children if the wives try to run away. Several directors of battered women's shelters have told me that it is not unusual for husbands to track down their families from as far away as 1000 miles and threaten violence to get them to return.

Women often have no place to go. Hundreds of women and children are turned away from domestic violence shelters every day because of overcrowding and underfunding.

Even when women go to court to protect themselves, they may find that a judge does not take domestic violence seriously. Consider this courtroom experience:

[The judge] took a few minutes to decide on the matter. . . . He said, "I don't believe anything that you're saying . . . because I don't believe that anything like this could happen to me. If I was you and someone had threatened me with a gun, there is no way that I would continue to stay with them.

TABLE 14.2

The Rights of a Battered Spouse or Intimate Partner

I have the right to be angry over emotional or physical abuse.

I have the right to be free from fear or humiliation.

I have the right to have friends.

I have the right to privacy.

I have the right to express my thoughts and feelings.

I have the right to develop my talents and abilities.

I have the right to provide my children with a peaceful home.

I have the right to seek help.

I have the right to leave an abuser.

I have the right to prosecute an abuser.

I have the right to be happy.

SOURCES: Based on Fedders, 1990; A. Jones, 1994.

. . . Therefore, since I would not let that happen to me, I can't believe that it happened to you." When I left the courtroom that day, I felt very defeated, very defenseless, and very powerless and very hopeless (Maryland Special Joint Committee, 1989: 3).

Such reactions by judges are not as dated as you might think. Some judges take domestic violence seriously, but others still view it as little more than "marital spats" (Ptacek, 1999).

8. **The home becomes a prison.** Both emotional and physical abuse trap the battered woman in her home, which becomes a jail, with little chance of escape. The battered wife is very much like a prisoner. Her husband is the ultimate authority, and she is punished if she disagrees with him. She must follow his "house rules" about not leaving the house or even making phone calls without his permission. In some cases, he takes the phone with him when he leaves for work. She has no control over her body, is isolated from her friends and relatives, and is watched constantly (Avni, 1991; Cottle, 1994).

All these factors help explain why most women stay in abusive relationships: "Staying may mean abuse and violence, but leaving may mean death. A bureaucracy may promise safety, but cannot ensure it. For many battered women, this is a risk they cannot take" (Englander, 1997: 149–50). The battered woman's inability to leave the abusive spouse has serious consequences not only for her own welfare but also for the welfare of her children. We will return to this issue later.

Women Who Abuse Men

In 2003, a highly publicized case brought attention to women's violence toward men. A jury in Houston, Texas, sentenced a 45-year-old dentist to 20 years in prison for killing her husband, an orthodontist. The wife ran over her husband several times with her Mercedes-Benz after finding him with his mistress, a former receptionist. The case got prominent national attention because the couple was upper middle class.

Some researchers and journalists have argued that women hit men as often as men hit women and that husband abuse is the most underreported form of marital violence (Steinmetz, 1978; Pearson, 1997). Why don't men defend themselves? Many men believe that only a bully would hit a woman. Others fear they might hurt their wives if they fight back. Finally, some husbands feel they can punish their wives through guilt by showing them the injuries the wives inflicted.

According to some (usually male) advocates, many men fail to report spousal assaults because "society simply doesn't take the issue seriously . . . and men who claim such abuse are deemed wimps and laughed at" (Hastings, 1994: 1D; see also Brooks, 1994).

Although many wives strike their husbands, Gelles (1997: 92) maintains that there has been considerable rhetoric but "precious little scientific data" that women are as abusive as their husbands. He notes that data from studies of households where the police intervene in domestic violence "clearly indicate" that men are rarely the victims of assault and battery and that women are ten times more likely than men to be injured in domestic violence cases. In addition, battered men are less physically injured than battered women, are less trapped than women because of greater economic resources, and can walk out of an abusive situation because, typically, women—not men—feel responsible for the children.

Even when the abuse is mutual, the outcomes are different. Although intimate partner violence is associated with negative health consequences among both women and men, women are much more likely than men to experience depression and substance abuse (Anderson, 2002). Moreover, partner violence often spills over into violence against one's children.

Violence against Infants and Children

A few years ago, Andrea Yates, a suburban homemaker in Houston, Texas, filled the bathtub and drowned each of her five children, who ranged in age from 6 months to 7 years: "It took a bit of work for her to chase down the last of the children; toward the end, she had a scuffle in the family room, sliding round on wet tile" (Roche, 2002: 44).

Abusing and killing children is not a recent phenomenon. Among the Puritans, women were instructed to protect children "if a man is dangerously cruel with his children in that he would harm either body or spirit" (Andelin, 1974: 52). And men were not the only offenders: In 1638, Dorothy Talbie "was hanged at Boston for murdering her own daughter, a child of 3 years old" (Demos, 1986: 79).

In 1946, after observing unexplained fractures in children he had seen over the years, pediatric radiologist John Caffey suggested the possibility that the children had been abused. And in what may have been the first formal paper on the subject, in 1962 physician C. Henry Kempe and his colleagues published an article on the battered-child syndrome in the *Journal of the American Medical Association*. Nevertheless, only in recent years has child abuse become a major public issue.

What Is Child Abuse?

Although I will use the older and more familiar term *child abuse* frequently throughout this section, I will also use a newer term, *child maltreatment*. These terms are often used interchangeably. Their definitions are similar, but the newer term puts more emphasis on emotional abuse and the failure of caretakers to provide a child with proper care. (For a comprehensive overview of child maltreatment, see Miller-Perrin and Perrin, 1999.)

Child abuse, as defined by the National Center on Child Abuse and Neglect and codified in Public Law 93-237 in 1974, is "the physical or mental injury, sexual abuse, negligent treatment, or maltreatment of a child under the age of 18 by a person who is responsible for the child's welfare under circumstances that indicate that the child's health or welfare is harmed or threatened thereby."

Child maltreatment characterizes a broad range of behaviors that place the child at serious risk, including physical abuse, sexual abuse, neglect, and emotional maltreatment.

Physical Abuse *Physical abuse*, which refers to an ongoing pattern of bodily injurious actions, includes beating with the hands or an object, scalding, and severe physical punishments.

In a rare form of abuse called *Munchausen syndrome by proxy*, an adult (usually a white, middle-class mother who is knowledgeable about medicine or nursing) feigns or induces illness in a child to attract medical attention and support for herself and her child. The motives for the illness include wanting to be the center of attention; tangible rewards such as money, charitable donations, or life insurance; and getting a husband's attention.

The mother may be needy and lonely or may have a psychiatric problem (Rosenberg, 1997; Parnell and Day, 1998).

Sexual Abuse *Sexual abuse* includes making a child watch sexual acts, fondling a child's genitals, forcing a child to engage in sexual acts for photographic or filmed pornography, and incest. This category also includes sexual assault on a child by a relative or a stranger.

Child Neglect *Child neglect* is the failure to provide basic caretaking obligations. Most recently, some clinicians have included stimulation neglect and language neglect under the child neglect umbrella. In *stimulation neglect*, Cantwell (1997) includes parents who don't cuddle and talk to babies, who don't take their children to the park (or other recreational spots), and who don't play with or engage in activities that nourish a child's development.

Language neglect includes discouraging the child's communication skills, such as ignoring an infant's babbling, not reading to a child, and commanding young children ("Put this here" or "Don't do that") instead of conversing with the child and eliciting a response ("Where do you think we should hang this picture?") (Oates and Kempe, 1997). Neglectful caretakers are usually the child's parents but may also include people in residential centers for children or foster-care homes.

Emotional Maltreatment *Emotional maltreatment*, sometimes referred to as psychological maltreatment, conveys to children that they are inferior, worthless, flawed, unloved, or unwanted. Verbal abusers devalue and reject their children with constant criticism, putdowns, and sarcasm (Briere, 1992; Brassard and Hardy, 1997).

More specifically, emotional maltreatment includes *spurning* (rejecting a child verbally and nonverbally), *terrorizing* (threatening to hurt, kill, or abandon a child), *isolating* (denying a child opportunities to interact with peers or adults inside or outside the home), and *exploiting* or *corrupting* (modeling, permitting, or encouraging a child's antisocial behavior) (Hart et al., 2003).

Other forms of emotional maltreatment include neglect by parents who focus on their own problems and ignore those of their children, who use guilt and other manipulations to control children's lives, who subject children to unpredictable mood swings due to alcoholism and other drug abuse, and who frequently demand that children assume adult caretaking responsibilities (Forward, 1990).

How Prevalent Is Child Abuse?

A few years ago, the Tampa, Florida, police arrested a mother and her boyfriend for locking up the woman's

7-year-old daughter in a room for four nights. They gave the girl so little food that she looked like a "walking skeleton." She weighed just 25 pounds, less than half the normal weight for a child her age ("Florida couple . . .," 2002).

This little girl is just one of approximately 903,000 children who are victims of child maltreatment (U.S. Department of Health and Human Services, 2003a). Nearly four children die every day because of child abuse or neglect (Peddle et al., 2002). A number of these deaths include infants.

Infant Homicide Homicide is the leading cause of death among infants. Between 1970 and 2001, infant homicide rates nearly doubled from 4.3 to 7.7 per 100,000 children under age 1 ("Infant homicide," 2003). The first and eighth weeks of an infant's life are the most deadly:

- Among homicides on the first day of life, 95 percent of the infants are not born in a hospital.

- During the first week of life, 89 percent of the murderers are female, usually the mother.

- The second peak of death, around week 8, probably reflects a mother's inability to cope with the constant crying of normal infants (Paulozzi and Sells, 2002).

Black infants are substantially more likely to be killed during the first year of life (26 infants per 100,000

children) than white or Latino babies (6 and 7 per 100,000, respectively). Most mothers who kill their infants are unmarried teenagers, are high school dropouts, already have one or more children, have had little or no prenatal care, may not know who the baby's father is, and may have a history of mental illness ("Infant homicide," 2003).

Some infants whose deaths are attributed to sudden infant death syndrome (SIDS), also called crib or cot death, might actually have been murdered. According to some pediatricians, many hospital emergency wards don't examine the dead infant for maltreatment, don't conduct postmortem examinations, and know little about the baby's medical history. As a result, many physicians attribute infant deaths to SIDS rather than homicide (Kairys et al., 2001.)

Other Child Abuse Between ages 4 and 17, most abused children experience neglect, although 29 percent of the maltreatment involves physical abuse (see *Figure 14.4*). Victimization rates by race and ethnicity range from a low of 3.8 per 1000 children for Asian Americans and Pacific Islanders to 20.7 for African Americans (see *Figure 14.5*).

Although the differences in rates across groups appear large, there is some evidence that reporting child abuse may be more common in poor and black families (Ards et al., 1998). In contrast, white, middle-class child abuse often is underreported. According to a study of children under age 3, for example, doctors were twice

FIGURE 14.4 **Child Maltreatment: 2001** These figures represent 903,000 confirmed child maltreatment cases. "Neglect" includes medical neglect (about 2 percent of these cases). "Other" includes abandonment, threats of harm to the child, and babies who are born drug-addicted. The percentage for "type of abuse" total more than 100 percent because some children were victims of more than one type of maltreatment.

Source: U.S. Department of Health and Human Services, 2003.

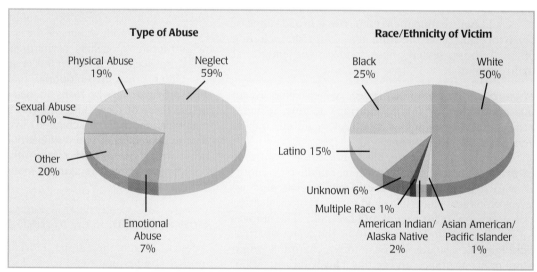

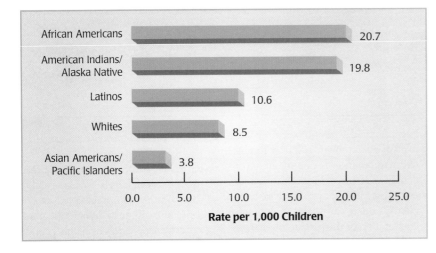

FIGURE 14.5 **Child Victimization Rates by Race/Ethnicity**

Note: Latinos are counted both by race and by ethnicity. The rates are based on 673,372 cases reported by 40 states.

SOURCE: U.S. Department of Health and Human Services, 2000, Figure 4-5.

as likely to miss abuse in white, two-parent families as in minority, single-parent families. The researchers attributed the misdiagnoses to physicians' lack of training (such as recognizing head traumas) and especially to discomfort about casting suspicion on the parents (Jenny et al., 1999).

The maltreatment of young children can result in murder. As *Figure 14.6* shows, only 17 percent of child fatalities in 2001 were caused by people who were not parents (such as relatives or boyfriends and girlfriends). Mothers often kill children during infancy, whereas fathers are more likely to murder children age 8 and older (Greenfeld and Snell, 1999). Although there are no hard data, the higher rates of fathers' murdering children who are older may result from men's greater likelihood, as discussed earlier, of killing the entire family—including a wife, ex-wife, or girlfriend—before committing suicide or fleeing from prosecution.

Some social scientists think that "official" child victimization rates are too low. For example, a study of homicide records of children age 10 and younger in North Carolina found that the number of children who died at the hands of parents or other caregivers was underreported by nearly 60 percent (Herman-Giddens et al., 1999). Other analysts believe that the number of child deaths from maltreatment may be four times higher than those reported every year ("Child fatalities fact sheet," 2000).

Sexual Abuse and Incest

In the most conservative estimates based on reports to child protective agencies, 10 percent of abuse cases involved sexual abuse (see *Figure 14.4*). Sexual abuse rates are probably much higher than those reported to law enforcement agencies and child protective services. For example, in a study of southwestern American Indian

tribal members, investigators found that 49 percent of females and 14 percent of males had experienced childhood sexual abuse, most by family members and relatives (Robin et al., 1997).

In a study of Latinas in Los Angeles County, 33 percent of respondents reported sexual abuse before age 18. Of the alleged perpetrators, 96 percent were male, and more than 50 percent were family members (Romero and Wyatt, 1999). Nationally, an estimated 21 percent of adolescents who run away from home do so to escape physical or sexual abuse (Hammer et al., 2002).

Forcible sodomy, sexual assaults with objects, forcible fondling, and incest affect up to 8 percent of children age 12 and younger. Most of these crimes are committed by parents or adult family members (Finkelhor and Ormrod, 2000).

FIGURE 14.6 **Who Kills Children?**

SOURCE: U.S. Department of Health and Human Services, 2003: Figure 5-2.

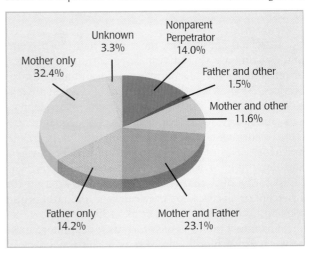

CONSTRAINTS

Myths and Facts about Incest

Forcing, coercing, or cajoling a child into an incestuous relationship is one of the most devastating things an adult can do to a child. Even when family members are aware of incestuous behavior in the family, most neither report nor try to stop it. Why? Because they believe in myths such as the following:

- *Myth: Children lie about incest.*
  Fact: Children rarely lie about incest. Most are too young to know about the sexually explicit acts they describe.
- *Myth: Children fantasize about incest. Every daughter fantasizes a romantic relationship with her father; every son imagines a romantic relationship with his mother.*
  Fact: A child wants and needs love and caring from a parent, not sexual intimacy.
- *Myth: If a child is not coerced, it is not incest.*
  Fact: Regardless of whether a child has been verbally seduced or violently raped, the act of intercourse between blood relatives is incest, and in most states incest is a punishable crime.
- *Myth: If a child experiences pleasurable feelings during the encounter, the incest isn't harmful.*

Fact: A child's physiological excitement as an automatic response to sexual manipulation is one of the most damaging effects of incest. It can cause confusion and feelings of guilt or complicity, and it can make it difficult, later in life, for the person to separate satisfying sexual experiences from the original incestuous one.

- *Myth: The younger the victim, the less traumatic the incest.*
  Fact: Incest is traumatic at any age. People who are asked to recall incestuous experiences vividly describe feelings of pain and humiliation.
- *Myth: Incest happens only in poor, disorganized, or unstable families.*
  Fact: Incest is more likely to be discovered in poor, disorganized, or unstable families because these families often come to the attention of social services. Incest occurs in many seemingly "normal" middle-class families.
- *Myth: Fathers turn to their daughters for warmth and nurturance denied them by their wives.*
  Fact: The majority of men who are guilty of incest have gotten plenty of nurturance from their mothers, wives, and other women.

- *Myth: Incest is usually punished by incarceration.*
  Fact: Perpetrators are rarely charged or imprisoned, largely because a child's testimony is seldom accepted as evidence of incest. In addition, solid physical evidence is rarely available because the event is not reported and investigated quickly enough.
- *Myth: An overprotective father is simply concerned about his daughter(s).*
  Fact: A sexually abusive father who isolates a daughter as much as possible is concerned that the child might reveal the abuse to friends or relatives.
- *Myth: A child can be seductive and thus is often responsible for the adult's sexual arousal.*
  Fact: Children are never responsible for adults' sexual arousal or for their physical advances.

SOURCES: Tamarack, 1986; Faller, 1990; Adams et al., 1994.

In sexual abuse cases, more than half (56 percent) of the victims are abused by male parents, male relatives, or other males (U.S. Department of Health and Human Services, 2000). More than 25 percent of children are sexually abused by a birth parent, 25 percent by stepparents, and nearly 50 percent by relatives or acquaintances (U.S. Department of Health and Human Services, 1996).

Most cases of reported incest are between fathers and daughters or stepfathers and stepdaughters. The rarest forms of sexual abuse, estimated to account for 1 percent of all cases, are between sons and fathers and sons and mothers (Masters et al., 1992).

The incest taboo, which forbids sexual intercourse between close blood relatives, is a cultural norm in almost all known societies (see Chapter 1). In the United States, **incest** is defined by law as sexual intercourse or marriage between nuclear family members, as well as between uncles and nieces, aunts and nephews, grandparents and grandchildren, and, often, first cousins and half-siblings.

There are strong social sanctions against any sexual activity between such relatives. Nevertheless, a national survey found that 15 percent of adults said they had been victims of unwanted sexual touching and intercourse as children. About 75 percent of those who had been sexually abused were women, and nearly 50 percent said they had never told anyone about the experience (Patterson and Kim, 1991). One of the effects of underreporting is that many people refuse to believe that incest is a serious problem (see the box "Myths and Facts about Incest").

Characteristics and Behaviors of Incestuous Adults

Although the personality traits of people who commit incest vary greatly, they have some common traits. Sexual offenders often have low self-esteem and lack self-control. Incest offenders are usually "narcissistic, uninhibited men who believe that their own sexual impulses must be fulfilled" (Hanson et al., 1994: 197).

Typically, a man who abuses his child or children starts when a child is between 8 and 12 years of age, although in some cases the child is still in diapers. The father may select only one child (usually the oldest daughter) as his victim, but it is common for several siblings to be victimized, either sequentially or simultaneously over the years.

According to some researchers, as long as children are nurtured almost exclusively by women, men are going to be likely to view their children—especially daughters—as sexual objects rather than as their flesh and blood to be cared for and nurtured (M. T. Erickson, 1993). They often intimidate victims with promises of physical retaliation against the victim and other family members. They threaten that they will be arrested or the family will break up if the incest is reported. Children remain silent out of fear and guilt because they feel they are somehow responsible for the abuse.

Is Incest the Mother's Fault?

Many people blame mothers for the incest that occurs between fathers and daughters or between stepfathers and stepdaughters: "Why didn't her mother do something about it? She must have known that something was going on" or "She probably wasn't giving her husband enough sex." Such accusations are usually (but not always) unfounded.

In some cases the mother may be a *colluder*—selfish, irresponsible, or dysfunctional who sacrifices her daughter either intentionally or inadvertently (Jacobs, 1990). In other cases, a mother may lose interest in sex, withdraw from her husband, and ignore the incestuous relationship that may develop between the husband and the daughter.

Sometimes the mother is a *dependent*—a helpless person who is suffering from a disabling condition like depression or a physical infirmity. She may have extremely low self-esteem and few problem-solving skills, and she may be mentally ill. As a result, and rather than dealing with marital problems, the husband may distance himself from

Oprah Winfrey is one of the world's richest and most influential women. Here, Winfrey launches O: The Oprah Magazine, *one of her many successful enterprises. When she was nine years old, Winfrey's 19-year-old cousin started to molest her sexually. At age 14, she gave birth to a premature baby who died shortly after birth. Winfrey says that she was too confused and afraid to report the sexual abuse.*

his wife and turn to his daughter for emotional and sexual gratification. The daughter may become a surrogate wife to her father and assume the mother's responsibilities in both homemaking and sex (Reis and Heppner, 1993).

Finally, the mother may be a *victim* who fails to intervene in the father–daughter relationship because of her own victimization as a child. Such mothers are accustomed to a situation in which the dominant male does whatever he wants (Jacobs, 1990).

Still, you might ask, how can a mother fail to protect her child from her husband's sexual attacks? One reason may be that the public has not been taught to recognize the symptoms of incest. Some mothers may not realize that incest is occurring. If a child shows unusual interest in sex, becomes rebellious, or withdraws, a mother may interpret such behavior as part of a developmental stage.

The mother may blame the onset of adolescence or a response to other difficulties, such as school problems or peer interactions. One mother, for example, interpreted her 4-year-old daughter's resistance to her going to work as resentment rather than as fear of being left alone with the sexually abusive father (Elbow and Mayfield, 1991). Many women lack the resources they need to protect their children. Some mothers, such as the colluders just described, ignore the problem.

Why Do Parents Abuse Children?

There are many reasons for child maltreatment. Some of the most important factors are substance abuse, family size, poverty, wife abuse, and divorce.

Substance Abuse A number of studies have linked child abuse with the parents' substance abuse. Children whose parents abuse alcohol and other drugs are three times more likely to be abused and more than four times more likely to be neglected than children from nonabusing families ("Child welfare and chemical dependency . . .," 2001).

Alcohol-abusing parents usually have poor parenting skills: They typically don't provide children with emotional support and don't monitor them. As a result, children in these families haven't learned social control, lack social skills, and often use alcohol themselves at an early age ("Alcohol and health," 2000).

Family Size Children from larger families (with four or more children) often experience more abuse and neglect than children from smaller families. For parents, additional children, especially closely spaced children in large families, means additional tasks and responsibilities and more worry about finances (Belsky, 1993).

Poverty Most abusive homes are experiencing economic stress and poverty. Children from families with annual incomes under $15,000 are 26 times more likely than children from families with annual incomes above $30,000 to be abused or neglected (U.S. Department of Health and Human Services, 1996). Moreover, low-income teen mothers may be more abusive than older mothers because of a variety of factors such as substance abuse and inadequate information about a child's developmental needs (Gaudin et al., 1996; Zuravin and DiBlasio, 1996).

Wife Abuse Child maltreatment is also highly likely in homes where the wife is abused. The greater the amount of violence toward a spouse, the greater the probability of child abuse, especially by the husband (Ross, 1996). Noting that 70 percent of wife beaters also physically abuse their children, Kurz (1993) posits

that family violence, including child maltreatment, is a direct outcome of men's attempts to maintain control over the powerless members of the family—women and children.

Divorce The period just after divorce may make child maltreatment more likely because parental conflict and family tension are high. For example, the custodial parent may be changing residences, working longer hours, and experiencing more turmoil. Parents who are already stressed may react abusively to infants who, also affected by the parents' emotional state, become more irritable and harder to soothe (see Chapters 12 and 15).

Thus, even if parents insist that they love their children, love isn't enough. Whether the reasons are micro, macro, or a combination, child abuse has a very negative effect on most children's lives.

How Violence Affects Children

Some children manage to survive and do well despite growing up in abusive homes. Most, however, suffer the costs of domestic violence over the course of a lifetime.

Children who survive severe violence are often left with brain injuries. Infants who are shaken violently may suffer intracranial (within the brain) bleeding. Abused infants may have feeding and sleeping disorders, fail to thrive or show persistent lethargy, hyperactivity, or irritability. And children who are neglected may have poor physical growth, including underdevelopment of the brain and consequent problems in intellectual and speech development (Kernic et al., 2002).

Whether abuse is physical, emotional, or sexual, children often suffer from a variety of physiological, social, and emotional problems, including headaches, bed-wetting, chronic constipation, difficulty in communicating, learning disabilities, poor performance in school, and a variety of mental disorders. Children from violent families are often more aggressive than children from nonviolent families. Being abused or neglected as a child increases the likelihood of arrest as a juvenile by 59 percent, as an adult by 28 percent, and for a violent crime by 30 percent (Widom and Maxfield, 2001).

Parental conflict and violence in both married and divorced families place the children at risk for problem behaviors. The behaviors include cheating, running away from home, bullying classmates, and feeling worthless, depressed, angry, and sad (Hyman, 2000; Buehler and Gerard, 2002; Brown and Bzostek 2003).

Adolescents who experience maltreatment are more likely than their nonabused counterparts to engage in early sexual activity, have unintended pregnancies, suffer emotional and eating disorders, abuse alcohol and other drugs, engage in delinquent behavior, and attempt suicide. They are also more likely to be violent with intimate partners as adults (Anda et al., 2001; Heyman and Slep, 2002; Ehrensaft et al., 2003).

A history of child abuse increases the likelihood of problems during adolescence that include engaging in violent delinquency, using drugs, performing poorly in school, displaying symptoms of mental illness, and (for girls) becoming pregnant. Childhood abuse is associated with an increased risk of at least 25 percent for each of these outcomes (Kelley et al., 1997).

Incestuous relationships in childhood often lead to lack of trust, fear of intimacy, and sexual dysfunctions in adulthood. *Table 14.3* on page 408 summarizes some of the physical and behavioral signs that a child is being abused and needs protection.

MAKING CONNECTIONS

- Do you think that the battered-woman syndrome is a valid defense in killing an abuser?

- Some people argue that emotional maltreatment is less serious in its consequences than physical abuse. Do you agree?

Hidden Victims: Siblings and Adolescents

Violence between siblings and the abuse of adolescents may be less common than the other forms of domestic abuse we've discussed, but they are equally devastating. They are less visible primarily because the authorities are rarely notified.

Sibling Abuse

Siblings' abuse of each other is so common it is almost normative. Physical, emotional, and sexual abuse between siblings is widespread (Wallace, 1996; Underwood and Patch, 1999).

Physical and Emotional Abuse Almost all young children hit a sibling occasionally. More than 80 percent of parents in one survey said that their children had engaged in at least one incident of sibling violence (such as kicking or punching) in the preceding year. Furthermore, whereas in the late 1970s only .3 percent of siblings used a knife or gun, by the late 1980s this number had increased to 3 percent. Thus every year in

the United States more than 100,000 children may face brothers or sisters with lethal weapons (Gelles and Straus, 1988).

Although most sibling abuse does not involve weapons, it is highly traumatic. Wiehe and Herring (1991) describe various forms of sibling abuse:

- **Name-calling and ridicule.** Name-calling is the most common form of emotional abuse among siblings, and ridicule is closely linked to it. Victims still remember being belittled about things like their height, weight, looks, intelligence, or athletic ability. One woman is still bitter because her brothers called her "fatso" and "roly-poly" during most of her childhood. Another woman said, "My sister would get her friends to sing songs about how ugly I was" (p. 29).

- **Degradation.** Degrading people, or depriving them of a sense of dignity and value, can take many forms: "The worst kind of emotional abuse I experienced was if I walked into a room, my brother would pretend he was throwing up at the sight of me. As I got older, he most often would pretend I wasn't there and would speak as if I didn't exist, even in front of my father and my mother" (p. 35).

- **Promoting fear.** Siblings may often use fear to control or terrorize their brothers or sisters. A woman in her forties said that her siblings would take her sister and her "out into the field to pick berries. When we would hear dogs barking, they would tell us they were wild dogs, and then they'd run away and make us find our own way home. We were only five or six, and we didn't know our way home" (p. 37).

- **Torturing or killing a pet.** The emotional impact on the child who loves, and is loved by, an animal that a sibling tortures or destroys can last for many years: "My second-oldest brother shot my little dog that I loved dearly. It loved me—only me. I cried by its grave for several days. Twenty years passed before I could care for another dog" (p. 39).

- **Destroying personal possessions.** Childhood treasures, such as favorite toys, can become instruments of emotional abuse: "My brother would cut out the eyes, ears, mouth, and fingers of my dolls and hand them to me" (p. 38).

Many children report that parents rarely take physical or emotional abuse by siblings seriously: "'You must have done something to deserve it,' parents might say. My parents seemed to think it was cute when my brother ridiculed me. Everything was always a joke to them. They laughed at me. Usually their reply was for me to quit complaining—'You'll get over it'" (Wiehe and Herring, 1991: 22, 73).

TABLE 14.3

Signs of Child Abuse

	Physical Signs	Behavioral Signs
Physical Abuse	• Unexplained bruises (in various stages of healing), welts, human bite marks, bald spots • Unexplained burns, especially cigarette burns or immersion burns (glovelike) • Unexplained fractures, lacerations, or abrasions	• Acts self-destructively • Withdrawn and aggressive, displays behavioral extremes • Arrives at school early or stays late, as if afraid to be at home • Is uncomfortable with physical contact • Displays chronic runaway behavior (adolescents) • Complains of soreness or moves uncomfortably • Wears inappropriate clothing to cover bruises
Physical Neglect	• Abandonment • Unattended medical needs • Lack of parental supervision • Consistent hunger, inappropriate dress, poor hygiene • Lice, distended stomach, emaciation	• Fatigue, listlessness, falling asleep • Steals food, begs from classmates • Reports that no caretaker is at home • Frequently absent or tardy • School dropout (adolescents)
Sexual Abuse	• Torn, stained, or bloody underclothing • Pain or itching in genital area • Difficulty walking or sitting • Bruises or bleeding from external genitalia • Sexually transmitted disease • Frequent urinary or yeast infections	• Withdraws or is chronically depressed • Is excessively seductive • Role reversal; is overly concerned for siblings • Displays lack of self-esteem • Experiences drastic weight gain or loss • Displays hysteria or lack of emotional control • Has sudden school difficulties • Exhibits sex play or premature understanding of sex • Threatened by closeness, problems with peers • Is promiscuous • Attempts suicide (especially adolescents)
Emotional Maltreatment	• Speech disorders • Delayed physical development • Substance abuse • Ulcers, asthma, severe allergies	• Exhibits habit disorders (sucking, rocking) • Antisocial; is responsible for destructive acts • Displays neurotic traits (sleep disorders, inhibition of play) • Swings between passive and aggressive behaviors • Exhibits delinquent behavior (especially adolescents) • Exhibits developmental delay

SOURCE: Based on American Humane Association, 2001.

Parents often promote sibling violence by treating children differently or having favorites. They may describe one child as the "smart one" or the "lazy one." Such labeling often inhibits sibling respect for each other and creates resentment. The preferred child may target a "less preferred" sibling for maltreatment, especially when parents aren't present.

Also, a favored child may become abusive toward siblings because of his or her power and status in the family. A child's perception that she or he is less loved damages not only sibling relationships but also the child's self-image (Caffaro and Conn-Caffaro, 1998).

Most parents view sibling violence as a normal part of growing up and may unwittingly encourage competition rather than cooperation. However, statistics on family homicides reveal that about 10 percent of all murders in families are *siblicides*, killing one's sibling, and account for almost 2 percent of all murders (Dawson and Langan, 1994).

The mean age of siblicide victims is 33 years, and the murder occurs during early and middle adulthood rather than adolescence, as one might expect. Men are much more likely to be both the offenders (88 percent) and the victims (84 percent) in siblicide cases. The most common circumstance preceding a sibling homicide is an argument between the perpetrator and the victim (Underwood and Patch, 1999).

By not discouraging sibling violence, parents send the message that it's okay to resolve conflict through fighting. Children raised in such violent environments learn that aggression is acceptable not only between brothers and sisters but also later with their own spouses and children (Gelles, 1997).

Siblings, like parents, are an important influence on a child's development. When siblings are violent, the child learns that violence is a normal or acceptable way of dealing with others. Such perceptions increase the likelihood of aggression with friends, in dating relationships in adolescence, and young adulthood (Simonelli et al., 2002).

Sexual Abuse Sexual abuse by a sibling is rarely a one-time event. In most instances the episodes continue over time. They are often accompanied by physical and emotional abuse and may escalate. According to one woman,

> I can't remember exactly how the sexual abuse started but when I was smaller there was a lot of experimenting. My brother would do things to me like putting his finger in my vagina. Then, as I got older, he would perform oral sex on me (Wiehe, 1997:72).

Many respondents said they were sexually abused by brothers who were baby-sitting. Some used trickery:

"At about age ten my brother approached me to engage in 'research' with him. He told me he was studying breast-feeding in school and needed to see mine. He proceeded to undress me and fondle my breasts" (Wiehe and Herring, 1991:52).

Others threatened violence: "I was about twelve years old. My brother told me if I didn't take my clothes off, he would take his baseball bat and hit me in the head and I would die. I knew he would do it because he had already put me in the hospital. Then he raped me" (Wiehe and Herring, 1991:55). Most children say nothing about sexual abuse, either because they are afraid of reprisal or because they think their parents won't believe them.

In most cases of sibling incest, older brothers molest younger sisters. Male and female roles in sibling incest families are often shaped by rigid gender stereotypes. Girls generally perceive themselves as less powerful than their brothers. As a result of gender-based power differences in offender and victim roles, an older brother and a younger sister are most at risk for sibling incest. As one woman explained,

> My brother was the hero of the family. He was the firstborn, and there was a great deal of importance placed on his being a male. My father tended to talk to him about the family business and ignore us girls. My mother would hang on every word my brother said. . . . If he ever messed up or did something wrong, my parents would soon forgive and forget. When I finally confronted them about Shawn molesting me as a teenager, at first they didn't believe me. Later, they suggested that I just get over it (Caffaro and Conn-Caffaro, 1998: 53).

It's not a coincidence that boys are the perpetrators in most sibling-abuse cases. Although girls and sisters are also abusive, our society is more likely to condone violence by boys as normal or masculine (Miedzian, 1991; see also Chapter 5).

Adolescent Abuse

Although family violence and child homicide decrease as children get older, a staggering number of parents (or stepparents) abuse teenagers. Victimization in early childhood and adolescence is the root of many problems later in life.

Prevalence of Adolescent Abuse Many parents are physically and verbally abusive with their children throughout the teen years (see Chapter 12). When adolescents fail to live up to their parents' expectations, parents sometimes use physical force to assert control (Gelles, 1997).

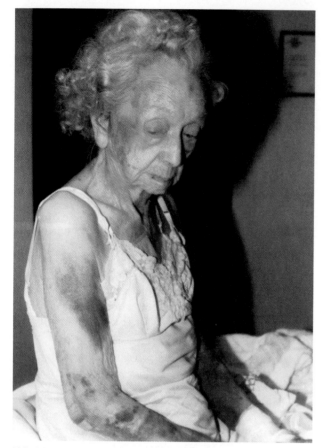

This 84-year-old woman suffered continuous physical abuse by a caregiver in the older woman's home. When arrested, the caregiver claimed that the woman had fallen out of bed.

About 20 percent of teenagers are abused by their parents (U.S. Department of Health and Human Services, 1997). Almost 22 percent of adolescents aged 12 to 17 have been sexually assaulted by a family member, including adult relatives. The highest rates are among African American and American Indian youth (Kilpatrick et al., 2003).

Consequences of Adolescent Victimization Some teenagers strike back physically and verbally. Others rebel, run away from home, withdraw, use alcohol and other drugs, become involved in juvenile prostitution and pornography, or even commit suicide (Estes and Weiner, 2002).

Being abused *and* witnessing domestic violence has twice the negative effect on children's development (Wasserman et al., 2003). Compared with nonvictims, adolescent victims of other violence are 50 percent more likely to be victims of other violent crimes and domestic violence, perpetrators of domestic violence, and problem drug users as adults. They are also more than 2.5 times as likely to be serious property offenders and 3 times as likely to be serious violent offenders (Menard, 2002).

Compared with 17 percent of nonvictim boys, 48 percent of boys who have been sexually assaulted engage in delinquent acts. About 20 percent of sexually assaulted girls engage in delinquency, compared with 5 percent of their nonvictim counterparts (Kilpatrick et al., 2003).

In addition, children who have experienced physically abusive punishment are five times more likely to experience *posttraumatic stress disorder* (PTSD) during their lifetimes. PTSD is a mental disorder, following exposure to extreme stress, that is characterized by intense fear, helplessness, horror, or disorganized and agitated behavior (Kilpatrick et al., 2003).

Another aspect of family violence that receives little attention is mistreatment of the elderly. Although elder abuse is less common than other forms of domestic violence, it is a serious problem.

Violence against Elderly Family Members

Baby boomers, now in their early forties to late fifties, are often referred to as the **sandwich generation** because they care not only for their own children but also for their aging parents. The percentage of younger workers who can support the elderly is expected to shrink. As a result, there is increasing pressure on these children to care for aging parents who are living longer but who are in frail health and who often have minimal financial resources (Zal, 1992).

Most people in the sandwich generation are remarkably adept at meeting the needs of both the young and the old. Those who are not as capable may abuse their children, their elderly parents and relatives, or both.

What Is Elder Abuse?

Elder abuse, sometimes also called *elder mistreatment,* includes physical abuse (such as hitting or slapping), negligence (such as inadequate care), financial exploitation (such as borrowing money and not repaying it), psychological abuse (such as swearing at or blaming the elderly for one's problems), deprivation of such basic necessities as food and heat, isolation from friends and family, and failing to administer needed medications (Decalmer and Glendenning, 1993; Carp, 2000).

Police officers who are guest lecturers in my classes describe some horrific cases of elder abuse or neglect. Some elderly people die of starvation, and their bodies aren't discovered for a year or more. A 71-year-old woman was left in bed for so long that her bedsores became infested with maggots.

Family members and acquaintances mistreat an estimated 5 percent of the elderly every year (see "Data

Digest"). Some researchers call elder abuse "the hidden iceberg" because about 84 percent of cases are not reported to police or other protective agencies (Tatara, 1998).

Cultural variations also shape family members' definitions of elder abuse. Some aging Asian Americans might see their children's behavior as neglectful if sons don't fulfill their filial responsibilities to provide for parents' unmet medical, transportational, financial, or emotional needs. Similarly, if daughters-in-law don't live up to cultural expectations to perform filial services for parents-in-law, they might be seen as emotionally or psychologically abusive (Chang and Moon, 1997).

Characteristics of the Abused

Although most elder abuse is hidden, researchers estimate that 1 to 2 million Americans age 65 or older have been injured, exploited, or otherwise mistreated by a family member or caretaker (Bonnie and Wallace, 2003). The rates for different types of maltreatment include physical abuse, 62 percent; abandonment, 56 percent; emotional or psychological abuse, 54 percent; financial or material abuse, 45 percent; and neglect, 41 percent (Tatara, 1998).

Older women experience abuse at higher rates than men in all categories except abandonment. Although they made up about 58 percent of the total national elderly population in 1996, women were the victims in 76 percent of emotional or psychological abuse cases, 72 percent of physical abuse cases, 63 percent of financial or material exploitation cases, and 60 percent of neglect cases, the most common type of maltreatment. A majority of the abandoned victims were men (62 percent) (Tatara, 1998).

Elderly women are probably more likely than men to be abused because they live longer than men, are more dependent on caretakers because they have fewer economic resources, and may command less authority and power with family members (see Chapters 5 and 17).

Who Are the Abusers?

Adult children are the largest group of perpetrators (53 percent), followed by the victim's spouse (19 percent) (see *Figure 14.7*). Overall, men are the perpetrators of abuse and neglect in 53 percent of the cases. Only in cases of neglect are women slightly more frequent perpetrators than men (52 percent).

Those aged 41 to 59 are the most likely offenders (38 percent), followed by those age 40 and under (27 percent). About one-third of perpetrators are elderly themselves. In terms of race and ethnicity, 84 percent of the victims are white, 8 percent black, 5 percent Latino, 2 percent Asian, and 0.4 percent American Indian (Tatara, 1998).

Why Do They Do It?

Why do family members mistreat the elderly? A number of risk factors increase the likelihood of elder abuse. You'll notice as you read this section that the risk factors include experiences, behaviors, lifestyle and environmental factors, and personal characteristics.

Living Arrangements A shared living situation is a major risk factor for elder mistreatment. Sharing a residence increases the opportunities for contact, tensions that can't be decreased simply by leaving, and conflict that arises in everyday situations (Bonnie and Wallace, 2003).

Social Isolation Elder abuse is more likely in living arrangements where the family members don't have a strong social network of kin, friends, and neighbors. Care providers who don't have supportive networks to provide occasional relief from their caretaking activities experience strain and may become violent toward their elderly parents or relatives (Kilburn, 1996).

Alcohol Abuse Alcohol use and abuse are common among perpetrators of elder abuse. Daily alcohol consumption is more than twice as likely among those who abuse elders as among those who do not (Reay and Browne, 2001; Bonnie and Wallace, 2003).

Impairment of the Caregiver or the Care Recipient A 70-year-old "child" who cares for a 90-year-old parent—not uncommon today—may be frail, ill, or mentally disabled and thus unaware that he or she is being abusive or neglectful (Harris, 1990; Pillemer and Suitor, 1991).

FIGURE 14.7 Relationship of Perpetrators to Victims of Domestic Elder Abuse

SOURCE: Based on Tatara, 1998: Figure 4-9.

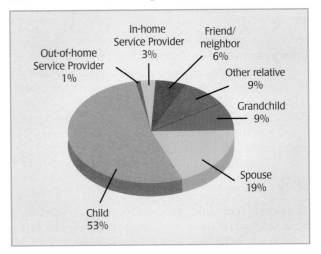

Some elderly people suffer from dementia (deteriorated mental condition) after a stroke or the onset of Alzheimer's disease (see Chapter 17). They may pinch, shove, bite, kick, or strike their caregivers. Children or spouses, especially when they know little about debilitating diseases, are likely to hit back during such assaults (Coyne et al., 1993; Bonnie and Wallace, 2003).

Dependency of the Older Person or Caregiver   Elderly people who live with their children because they are too poor to live on their own may also be impaired by incontinence, serious illness, or mental disabilities. They become physically as well as economically dependent on their caretakers. If the elderly are demanding, caregivers may feel angry or resentful.

The dependency between the abuser and the victim is often mutual. Spouses, for example, may depend on each other for companionship (Wolf, 1996). In the case of children and parents, although the abuser may need the older person for money or housing, the older parent needs the abuser for help with chores or to alleviate loneliness (Baron and Welty, 1996). If the adult child is still dependent on an elderly parent for housing or finances, she or he may strike out or maltreat the parent to compensate for the lack or loss of power (Gelles, 1997; Payne, 2000).

Medical Costs and Stress   Having to pay medical costs for an elderly relative may trigger abuse. Unlike low-income people, middle-class families are not eligible for admission to public institutions, yet few can afford the in-home nursing care and service that upper-class families can access. As a result, cramped quarters and high expenses increase the caretakers' stress.

Personality Characteristics   Sometimes personality traits of elderly people increase their risk of abuse. Chronic verbal aggression and hostility can spark a caretaker's physical and verbal maltreatment (Comijs et al., 1998).

Intergenerational Transmission of Violence   According to social learning theory (see Chapters 2 and 5), victims of child abuse may grow up to be abusers themselves, a pattern often described as *the cycle of violence.* Children who have learned to deal with conflict through abuse may do so themselves with their elderly parents or relatives (Bonnie and Wallace, 2003).

Why Do the Elderly Tolerate Abuse?

The elderly often tolerate abuse from family caretakers because they love the abusers, because they see no viable alternatives, or because they are lonely. According to one

of my elderly relatives who's housebound, for example, "I do everything he [the son] says and keep my mouth shut. What else can I do?"

Others are afraid of depriving their grandchildren or of being deprived of contact with them, or they have decided (unconsciously) to exchange submissiveness and passivity for the care they need (see Chapter 2 on exchange theory). Women who had abusive parents or who have been married to an abusive spouse are especially likely to accept assaults from caregivers as normal (Simons et al., 1993).

MAKING CONNECTIONS

■ Think about your or your friends' relationships with brothers and sisters. Are the relationships abusive? Do parents take sibling mistreatment seriously?

■ There's an old saying: "Be nice to your children because they may be taking care of you someday." How does the saying illustrate the cycle of violence? ◎

Violence in Gay and Lesbian Households

Another overlooked form of violence is abuse in gay and lesbian households. Researchers estimate that the incidence of battering in lesbian and gay couples is about the same as it is for heterosexual couples, occurring in approximately 25 to 33 percent of all couples (Brand and Kidd, 1986; Lundy, 1993). About 10 percent of men and 2 percent of women are violent with their same-sex partners (Rennison, 2001).

Much of the abuse tends to recur. Renzetti (1992), for example, found that 54 of the 100 respondents in her study of lesbian couples said that they experienced more than ten abusive incidents during the course of the relationship. In almost 35 percent of cases, the birth mother's partner abused the children.

A study of 288 gay and lesbian batterers referred for treatment reported that all of the men and women had been psychologically abused as children. About 93 percent of men and 88 percent of women said they had experienced physical abuse during childhood (Farley, 1996). Because treatment and support services for violent gay and lesbian households are practically nonexistent, children living in these families may be an especially high-risk group for future violence (Leventhal and Lundy, 1999).

Explaining Family Violence

Why are families violent? Why is violence among family members so widespread? As we look at the explanations offered by patriarchy or male dominance theory, psychological theories, social learning theory, resource theory, conflict theory, and exchange theory, you will also see how societal institutions—religion, the law, government, and politics—support family violence.

Patriarchy or Male Dominance Theory

Family violence is found in societies around the world. The *patriarchy or male dominance theory* maintains that in societies in which men hold authority (see Chapter 1) and in which women and children are defined as the property of men, male violence against women and children is common, particularly against female children. In such a society, men hold power, resources, and privilege and feel free to use women and children as sexual objects and as targets of physical abuse. Because of societal values, neither women nor children are likely to challenge the abusive male (Ollenburger and Moore, 1992):

> Kate was involved in an incestuous relationship until she was 16. When she was 9, her father crept into her bedroom one night and "began fondling my genitals. I woke up because it was uncomfortable. I told him it hurt, so he stopped and explained my body to me. That was the first time anyone told me I had a vagina. My father was the household god—the absolute authority. All decisions went through him, and it didn't occur to me to question him" (Kinkead, 1977: 172).

Men may demonstrate their masculinity by showing contempt for anything feminine or for females in general. According to a number of scholars, as long as our culture encourages men to be controlling, dominant, competitive, and aggressive rather than nurturing, caring, and concerned for the welfare of others, men will continue to express their anger and frustration through violent and abusive behavior (see, for example, Birns et al., 1994). And, as you can see from the box "Worldwide Male Violence against Women and Children" on page 414, other cultures face similar problems.

Psychological Theories

Some researchers rely on psychological models to explain family violence. A *personality theory* of abuse maintains that the abuser's personality characteristics are the major determinants of family abuse. Some psychologists believe that abusers have deep-seated feelings of powerlessness because they grew up with emotionally rejecting or absent fathers and only intermittently available mothers (Dutton and Golant, 1995). Presumably, such men never recover from these traumas and engage in wife battering to claim some of the power they never experienced.

Some psychologists attribute male domestic violence to insecure attachments to parents, especially mothers, during childhood (see Chapter 2). If men with insecure attachment histories have unrealistic expectations about their partners' (especially wives') ability to fulfill their needs, the men may be unusually aggressive (Kesner et al., 1997).

When women are stressed, they often express their emotions through crying, depression, or sadness. Men are more likely than women to repress their emotions in response to stress. Violence occurs among some men when they lose control of their suppressed emotions. They often rationalize their violence by claiming that their partners provoked them ("It wasn't my fault") (Umberson et al., 2003).

Other researchers have found that the most abusive men are also violent outside of marriage. They have antisocial and controlling personalities, have high rates of depression in response to stress, are substance abusers, and condone violence against women (Delsol et al., 2003). In this sense, it's not just stress and suppressed emotions that lead to violent outbursts.

Some psychiatrists and psychologists note that a child's characteristics may also contribute to parental abuse. For example, if a child is demanding, hyperactive, or moody, the child's personality may add to a parent's stress and increase the likelihood of a parent's abuse (Ammerman and Patz, 1996).

Social Learning Theory

Recall from Chapter 2 that, according to social learning theory, we learn by observing the behavior of others. For most people the family is the first "school" of behavior, so to speak. Some people try to avoid the kind of violence that they've experienced. However, continuous exposure to abuse and violence during childhood increases the likelihood that a person will be violent as an adult (McKay, 1994).

Moreover, people learn and internalize social and moral justifications for abusive behavior. A child may grow up believing that the explanation "it's for your own good" is a legitimate reason for abusive behavior (Gelles and Cornell, 1990; see also Chapter 12).

So far, no one really knows whether or how much family violence is transmitted intergenerationally through modeling or imitation (see National Research Council, 1998, for a review of some of this literature). Modeling probably plays an important role in learning abusive behavior, but macro-level stressors such as

CROSSCULTURAL

Worldwide Male Violence against Women and Children

Many cultures have beliefs, norms, and social institutions that legitimize and therefore perpetuate violence against women. Violence by men against women and girls includes physical, sexual, psychological, and economic abuse. It is often known as gender-based violence because it arises from women's subordinate status in society (see Chapter 5).

Worldwide, at least one of every three women has been beaten, coerced into sex, or otherwise abused in her lifetime. According to the World Health Organization, up to 70 percent of female murder victims worldwide are killed by their male companions, and as many as 33 percent of girls are forced into their first sexual experience (Lite, 2002).

In many areas of the developing world, both laws and customs work against women who are victims of violent male assaults. For example,

- In Vietnam, 80 percent of women have experienced some form of violence. Men blame alcohol or temper for their violence, and the women, in the tradition of stoic Vietnamese womanhood, accept it as normal.
- In the Islamabad, Pakistan region more than 4000 women in the last eight years have been doused in kerosene and burned by family members, predominantly in-laws or spouses. These "stove deaths" may be inflicted because the woman failed to give birth to a son, the husband wants to marry a second wife and can no longer support the first wife, there is long-running hostility with mothers-in-law or almost any other

disagreement. Police usually call such attacks suicides.

- In Bolivia and Puerto Rico, 59 percent of battered women have been sexually assaulted by their partners; in Colombia the figure is 46 percent.
- In Australia, Aboriginal women and children are 45 times more likely to be victims of domestic violence than non-Aboriginal women and 8 times more likely to be murdered. Some judges view such murders and rapes as "traditional culture that whites do well to ignore."
- In Zambia, Africa, sexual attacks on girls, some as young as 8 years old, are common. As a result, HIV is spreading quickly among Zambian girls. Police and authorities rarely enforce anti–sexual abuse laws.
- In Tanzania, Africa, about 500 elderly women are killed each year as witches.
- In Alexandria, Egypt, nearly half of all murder victims are women who have been raped and are then killed by family members as an act of "cleansing."
- A survey of nine Caribbean countries found that 48 percent of girls reported their first intercourse as "forced or somewhat forced."
- In Japan, 10 percent of reported serious crimes are rapes. Japanese laws are usually lenient on rapists and batterers because such crimes are seen as domestic matters.
- Studies from Australia, Canada, Israel, and the United States show that 40 to 70 percent of female murder victims are killed by husbands or boyfriends,

compared with about 5 percent of men killed by current or former female partners (Arthurs, 2002; Chelala, 2002; Krug et al., 2002; Terzieff, 2002; "Abuse spreads HIV . . .," 2003; Kakuchi, 2003).

Even though India has legally abolished the institution of dowry, dowry-related violence is on the rise. More than 5000 women are killed annually by their husbands and in-laws, who burn them in "accidental" kitchen fires if their ongoing demands for dowry before and after marriage are not met.

Sulfuric acid has emerged as a cheap and easily accessible weapon to disfigure and sometimes kill women and girls for reasons as varied as family feuds, inability to meet dowry demands, and rejection of marriage proposals. In Bangladesh, it is estimated that there are more than 200 acid attacks each year ("Domestic violence . . .," 2000).

In several countries, including Bangladesh, Egypt, Iraq, Jordan, Lebanon, Pakistan, and Turkey, women are killed to uphold the "honor" of the family. Any reason—alleged adultery, premarital relationships (with or without sexual relations), rape, or falling in love with a person of whom the family disapproves—is enough reason for a male member of the family to kill a woman ("Domestic violence . . .," 2000; Sandler, 2003). And from 1991 to 1996, Chinese police freed 88,000 kidnapped women and children who had been sold into slavery (Elliott, 1998).

---

unemployment increase the probability of family violence. Furthermore, as you've seen in Chapter 5, cultural values—including television programs and movies—that demean, debase, and devalue women and children promote and reinforce abusive behavior.

Resource Theory

From the perspective of resource theory (see Chapter 2), men usually command greater financial, educational, personal, and social resources than women do, so they have more power. In general, people who don't have these resources feel powerless and resort to force and violence. For example, a husband who wants to play the dominant role in the family but has little education, holds a job low in prestige and income, and has poor communication skills may use violence to maintain his dominant position (Babcock et al., 1993). Many women cannot assert themselves against men simply because they have even fewer resources than their partners.

A decline of resources and the resulting stress can also provoke violence. If a man's contribution to earnings decreases relative to the wife's or the man experiences spells of unemployment, the woman is more likely to experience abuse. The situation can be aggravated by living in a disadvantaged neighborhood, having a large number of children, and the wife's refusing to work even more hours (Fox et al., 2002).

Resource theory also helps explain premarital violence. Violence, you recall, is common in dating relationships (see Chapter 8). If a woman feels she has few resources to offer, she may be willing to date an abusive man just to have *someone*. Or, as you saw earlier, she may convince herself that she can reform the batterer. On the other hand, a woman who has more resources (such as money, a good job, or a college education) is often less willing to put up with the abuse (see Chapter 13).

A few years ago, heavy metal rocker, Tommy Lee, was arrested and convicted after his wife, actress Pamela Anderson (of the Baywatch *television series), accused him of spousal abuse and drug addiction. Anderson also maintained that she contracted hepatitis C, a liver infection, after sharing a tattoo needle with her then husband. They were married after knowing each other for three days and had two children.*

Conflict Theory

Conflict theory, like resource theory and patriarchy or male dominance theory, posits that groups with such resources as wealth, power, and prestige can impose their rules or their will over groups who lack these resources. Conflict theorists argue that women and children are victimized in the family not only because they have few individual resources but also because societal institutions such as the legal system, religious organizations, and medical institutions rarely take violence against women and children seriously (see Chapter 5). As you will see shortly, conflict theorists often support their positions by documenting minimal institutionwide commitment to preventing or treating domestic violence.

Exchange Theory

According to exchange theory, both victimizers and victims tolerate or engage in violent behavior because they believe it offers them more benefits than costs. As you saw earlier, victims may stay in an abusive relationship because of economic benefits. Rewards for perpetrators include the release of anger and frustration and the accumulation of power and control.

From an exchange perspective, unemployed and unmarried men become more violent because they have

little to lose: They don't care about being identified as a wife beater, they spend little time in jail, they don't have to worry about losing a job while in jail because they're already unemployed, and the women they abuse often take them back (Sherman, 1992). Thus, abusive men are in control.

Violence also has costs. First, it's possible that the victim will hit back. Second, a violent assault could lead to arrest or imprisonment and a loss of status among family and friends. Finally, the abuser may break up the family (Gelles and Cornell, 1990). However, if a patriarchal society condones violence against women and children and defines violence as an important resource, the costs will be minimal.

Using Several Theories

When researchers try to explain family violence, they rarely rely on only one theory because the reasons for human behavior, including violence, are complex. For example, resource theory suggests that men who have few assets in fulfilling a provider role are more likely to be violent toward their wives than men who earn a high income. However, men who have average incomes but lower educational and income levels than their employed wives may also resort to violence. Patriarchy or male dominance theory suggests that these men have less egalitarian expectations about decision making or explode when the wives pressure them to share more of the housework (Anderson, 1997). If we also consider personality variables and exchange factors, explaining family violence becomes even more complicated.

Other Family Crises

Although abuse and violence can destroy a family, other health-related problems can also become crises. For example, many families must deal with such long-term problems as the inappropriate use of steroids or other drug abuse, depression and suicide, and eating disorders such as anorexia and bulimia. The family may also have to cope with the death—sometimes sudden and unexpected—of young family members.

Drug Abuse

Recently, Baltimore Orioles pitcher Steve Bechler, 23, collapsed and died during a workout in Florida. According to the medical examiner, the death was related to taking weight loss stimulants containing ephedra, a dietary supplement (Carmichael, 2003). Although millions of people have been taking ephedra with no ill effects, the incident sparked national discussions about curtailing the drug. A number of drugs—whether legal or illegal—can create problems during both adolescence and adulthood.

Illicit Drugs In 2002, an estimated 8 percent of the U.S. population age 12 and older were illicit drug users. Those with the lowest usage rates were college graduates, employed adults, people living in rural areas, and women. In terms of race-ethnicity, American Indian youth had the highest rates and Asian Americans the lowest (see *Figure 14.8*).

Marijuana is the most commonly used illicit drug (6 percent of the U.S. population). Short-term effects of marijuana use include problems with memory and learning, distorted perception, difficulty in thinking and problem solving, loss of coordination, increased heart rate, and anxiety ("Drug facts: Marijuana," 2003).

Although many users maintain that marijuana is less harmful than tobacco or alcohol, some researchers describe it as a "gateway" drug that leads to harder drugs. According to a study of fraternal and identical twins, for example, the twin who used marijuana before age 17 was five times more likely to later use cocaine, heroin, hallucinogens, sedatives, or alcohol (Lynskey et al., 2003).

About 1 percent of Americans (2 million people) use cocaine, 567,000 of whom use crack (U.S. Department of Health and Human Services, 2003b). An estimated 20 percent of women use illicit drugs while pregnant, including cocaine, exposing half a million fetuses to potentially damaging substances every year (Lewis and

FIGURE 14.8 **Illicit Drug Use, by Race/Ethnicity and Age, 2002**

SOURCE: U.S. Department of Health and Human Services, 2003b: Figures 2.8 and 2.9.

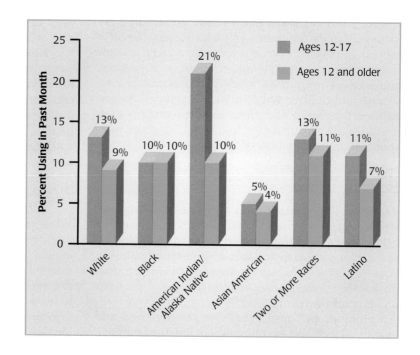

Bendersky, 1995). Exposure to cocaine has a negative effect on a child's cognitive development. At 2 years old, cocaine-exposed babies have lower memory scores, less language and problem-solving ability, and less motor control and coordination (Singer et al., 2002).

Alcohol   Alcohol use increases with age: 2 percent at age 12, 20 percent at age 15, 36 percent at age 17, and 71 percent for people 21 years old. Among young adults aged 18 to 25, 26 percent reported driving under the influence of alcohol at least once during the year (U.S. Department of Health and Human Services, 2003b).

Alcohol can cause greater damage to the brain development of those under 21 than to any other age group. The prefrontal region of the brain plays a role in forming adult personality, planning, and monitoring behaviors. Because this part of the brain develops until late adolescence, adolescents need to drink only half as much as adults to suffer the same negative effects, such as learning and memory impairments ("Underage drinkers . . .," 2002).

Adolescent drug use also leads to health problems in adulthood. Twenty years later, for example, people who had used drugs as teens report more health problems that include a higher incidence of respiratory problems such as colds and sinus infections; cognitive problems such as difficulty in concentrating, remembering, and learning; and headaches, dizziness, and vision problems (Brook et al., 2002). Besides other problems, alcoholics are five to ten times more likely than the general population to experience depression and to commit suicide (Preuss et al., 2003).

Steroids   An estimated 12 to 17 percent of adolescent males and 3 percent of adolescent females take **steroids**, which are synthetic hormones—most often testosterone—used to improve their performance in sports but often just to improve their appearance (Yesalis et al., 1997). When taken orally or injected, steroids increase the size and strength of muscles in just a few months.

Boys as young as 10, and high school students who do not play sports, are "bulking up simply because they want to look good" (Egan, 2002: A1). By 2002, 4 percent of twelfth-grade boys had used steroids, up from 2 percent in 1991 (Johnston et al., 2003).

Steroids can be dangerous. Many people who use them are unfamiliar with the side effects of inappropriate use, which include a decrease in testosterone production, a possibly irreversible shrinkage of the testicles, disinterest in sex, acne, increased facial and body hair, early balding, strokes and heart attacks, reduced sperm counts, liver disorders, kidney disease, a sharp increase in aggression, and, with heavy usage, the possible development of psychosis. Teenagers run the particular risk of

permanent damage to their reproductive and skeletal systems. Steroids may prevent one from reaching full height; for example, one 13-year-old who had taken steroids for two years stopped growing at five feet (Fultz, 1991).

Why Are Drug Rates So High?   Although there are many reasons, such as poverty and peer pressure, parents play an important role in their children's drug use. Many middle-class parents, especially, rely on Ritalin and other drugs to control young children's behavior (see Chapter 12). And, as you saw earlier in this chapter, children who experience domestic violence—including physical and sexual abuse—are more likely to use drugs and alcohol in adolescence and adulthood than their nonabused counterparts.

Although even the best parents can't prevent their children from trying drugs, many parents don't discuss drug use with their children or do not do so adequately. According to one national survey, for example, 35 percent of parents but only 14 percent of teenagers age 14 to 17 said that parents talk to teenagers about drugs "a lot" (Schultz, 2000).

What's more, in a study of drug addicts in drug treatment centers in four states, 20 percent of the respondents said that their parents had introduced them to drugs. The parent–teen drug sharing cut across racial lines (22 percent white, 18 percent black, 22 percent Latino) and was almost as pervasive in the suburbs (17 percent) as in the inner city (22 percent) (Baldauf, 2000). Parents increase children's chances of using alcohol by insisting that other kids—not theirs—drink or drink and drive instead of monitoring their children and discouraging adolescent drinking (Bogenschneider et al., 1998).

Depression and Suicide

Two major problems for families, especially those with adolescents, are depression and suicide. Depressed youngsters often have the same symptoms as depressed adults, but young children may not be able to articulate their problems. Children are likely to be agitated, sleep poorly, and have phobias. Adolescents are more likely to feel hopeless, sleep excessively, be irritable and angry, withdraw socially, have a weight loss or gain, and use alcohol and other drugs (Marbella, 1990; Obeidallah and Earls, 1999).

College counseling centers report that more students are seeking help for depression and suicidal thoughts. Since 1988, some of problems have remained constant, including substance abuse, eating disorders, and chronic mental illness. Other difficulties, especially depression and academic problems, have increased since 1996 (Benton et al., 2003).

Depression may lead to suicide, a major cause of teenage deaths. The suicide rate among young people between 15 and 24 years of age has increased to 11 per 100,000 in that age group, three times the rate of the mid-1950s (U.S. Census Bureau, 2002).

Teenagers often exhibit problematic behaviors during normal maturation. Experts feel, however, that when some of these behaviors form a consistent pattern, parents, friends, teachers, and relatives should seriously consider the possibility that the adolescent is planning suicide and should intervene. According to the Youth Suicide National Center, the most common suicide warning signs are the following:

- Withdrawal from family or friends
- Verbal expression of suicidal thoughts or threats, even as a joke
- Major personality changes
- Changes in sleeping or eating habits
- Drug or alcohol abuse
- Difficulty concentrating
- Violent or rebellious outbursts
- Running away
- Recent suicide of a relative or friend
- Rejection by a boyfriend or girlfriend
- Unexplained, sudden drop in quality of schoolwork or athletic endeavors
- Giving or throwing away prized possessions
- Showing a sudden lack of interest in one's friends or activities
- Extreme and sudden neglect of appearance
- Anorexia

Suicide rates for American Indians are almost twice as high as the national rates. Young men aged 15 to 24 account for 64 percent of all suicides among American Indians and Native Alaskans ("Suicide and suicidal behavior," 2000).

Some attribute such self-destructive behavior to acculturation. Instead of being moored in American Indian values that emphasize health and well-being, acculturation often results in feelings of marginalization, a loss of self-respect, and alienation from both Anglo and American Indian cultures (Angell et al., 1997). Other researchers suggest that the use of alcohol and marijuana—rather than the degree of acculturation—increases the likelihood that American Indian adolescents will commit suicide and engage in truancy, interpersonal violence, and gang activity (Potthoff et al., 1998).

Suicide attempts and completions are also rising for young teenage Latinas. As they become more Americanized, Latinas (much more than young Latinos) have a host of insecurities about appearance, academic success, peer popularity, family expectations, and sex. Especially in low-income families where the parents don't speak English, teens may have the added burden of acting as translators. The teens also worry about the health of parents who may be struggling to make ends meet and often find themselves in a push-and-pull match between meeting their parents' traditional expectations and fitting in with friends (Flores et al., 2002; see also Chapter 5).

A family environment that includes violence in the form of physical or sexual abuse also contributes to the risk of suicide, regardless of ethnicity. In addition, and especially among young people, there may be such triggering events as the sudden death of a friend or interpersonal rejection (Moscicki, 1994).

Sometimes if they are already depressed, teenagers may overreact to problems like being dumped by a boyfriend or girlfriend. Men age 19 and younger account for eight of ten adolescent suicides ("Kids and guns," 2000). Many men, including adolescents, seem to have a harder time accepting breakups with their girlfriends (see Chapter 8). Therefore, they may react violently against the women or commit suicide in a final desperate act.

Eating Disorders: Anorexia and Bulimia

In 1994, former gymnast Christy Henrich died of multiple-organ system failure that resulted from a history of anorexia nervosa and bulimia. She was 22 and weighed 60 pounds. Henrich, who missed making the 1988 U.S. Olympic team by 0.118 points, became concerned about her weight later that year when, at a meet in Hungary, she overheard a judge say that she was too fat to make the Olympic team. At that time, she was 4 feet 11 and weighed 93 pounds (Lonkhuyzen, 1994).

Anorexia nervosa, often an intractable and dangerous eating disorder, is characterized by fear of obesity coupled with a distorted body image and the conviction that one is "fat," significant weight loss (in people over 18, at least 25 percent of original body weight), and a refusal to maintain weight within the normal limits for one's age and height. **Bulimia**, another eating disorder, is characterized by a cyclical pattern of eating binges followed by self-induced vomiting, fasting, excessive exercise, or the use of diuretics or laxatives.

According to the American Anorexia Bulimia Association, 7 million women and 1 million men between age 10 and the early 20s suffer from eating disorders. The association estimates that 15 percent of young women have "substantially disordered eating attitudes and behaviors" and that 1000 women die of anorexia every year.

Girls who participate in competitive sports in which body shape and size are a factor (for example, ice skating, gymnastics, crew, and dance) are three times more at risk for eating disorders than their peers ("Facts about eating disorders," 2000; Messner, 2002). Anorexic men include models, actors, gymnasts, and jockeys, as well as young men in nonprofessional sports training who are trying to keep their weight down during competitions (Seligmann and Rogers, 1994; Morgan, 2002).

Both disorders can result in death. Anorexia may cause a slowing of the heartbeat, a loss of normal blood pressure, cardiac arrest, dehydration, skin abnormalities, hypothermia, lethargy, potassium deficiency, kidney malfunction, constipation, and the growth of fine, silky body hair, or *lanugo*, in an effort to conserve heat.

Bulimia's binge-purge cycle can be devastating to health in many ways. It can cause fatigue, seizures, muscle cramps, an irregular heartbeat, and decreased bone density, which can lead to osteoporosis. Repeated vomiting can damage the esophagus and stomach, cause the salivary glands to swell, make the gums recede, and erode tooth enamel.

Most anorexics and bulimics are young white women of high socioeconomic status who suffer from low self-esteem and a negative body image. These young women also tend to be perfectionistic in whatever they undertake (Szabò and Blanche, 1997). Their family histories often include eating disorders in other family members and abuse of such substances as alcohol, marijuana, amphetamines, diet pills, and barbiturates. Girls who have experienced sexual abuse are also more likely to have severe eating disorders (DeGroot et al., 1992; Laws and Golding, 1996).

Although the numbers are low, some researchers are finding that the number of Latinas and African American women with eating disorders is increasing, especially for binge eating (Striegel-Moore et al., 2003). And in a study of college students, Tsai and Gray (2000) found that 5 percent of the Asian American women were bulimic.

Although women and girls are beginning to discard some of the worst stereotypical images associated with their traditional gender roles, dieting is widespread. Up to 50 percent of 9-year-olds and up to 80 percent of 10-year-olds fear being fat or are already dieting, even though only 15 percent are actually overweight (Pertig, 1994).

Kilbourne (1994: 402) notes that women are conditioned to be terrified of fat: "Prejudice against fat people, especially against fat women, is one of the few remaining prejudices that are socially acceptable." Consequently, the most common explanation of anorexia and bulimia is that women are trying to live up to a cultural fixation that equates thinness with beauty and success:

U.S. gymnast Christy Henrich performing during the 1988 Olympic trials, six years before her death from the effects of anorexia and bulimia.

If I'm thin, I'll be popular. If I'm thin, I'll turn people on. If I'm thin, I'll have great sex. If I'm thin, I'll be rich. If I'm thin, I'll be admired. If I'm thin, I'll be sexually free. If I'm thin, I'll be tall. If I'm thin, I'll have power. If I'm thin, I'll be loved. If I'm thin, I'll be envied (Munter, 1984: 230).

Some researchers believe that specific genes may account for eating disorders (Bulik et al., 2003). So far, however, the sample sizes of the studies are small, and the results are inconclusive (see Chapter 2).

Death and the Family

A death in the family typically distresses family members, but the death of a child can be shattering. It often results in what Knapp (1987) calls *shadow grief*—grief that is never totally resolved. Shadow grief involves depression, a dull ache that never goes away, ongoing sadness, and a mild sense of anxiety. Many parents who have lost a child say that they have never since feared their own death. They often become much less involved in worldly achievements and much more concerned with cultivating and strengthening family relationships (Goodman et al., 1996).

Although the death of a child can strengthen a conjugal bond, it can also lead to separation or divorce. The grieving mother and father blame themselves or each other for not saving the child or they cannot find solace through each other (Schwab, 1998; Gottlieb et al., 1996). As the box "Coping with a Child's Death" on page 420 illustrates, family members and friends can be supportive and understanding, rather than intrusive, in helping people cope with a child's death.

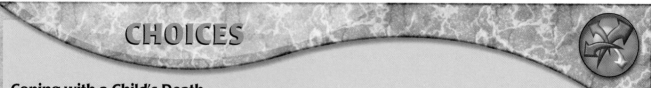

CHOICES

Coping with a Child's Death

When children die, they do not stop being their parents' children or their siblings' brothers or sisters. Most of us feel awkward and uncomfortable in helping family members and friends survive the death of a child. We don't know what to say or how to express our sympathy and personal sense of loss (James and Friedman, 1998; Silverman, 2000).

According to Zunin and Zunin (1991: 43–44), there are four key components in writing a thoughtful note. You can change some of the wording if you didn't know the person who died:

1. **Acknowledge the loss.** "Our family was deeply saddened when we heard that your son died."
2. **Express your sympathy.** "We are all thinking of you and send our heartfelt sympathy."
3. **Note special qualities of the deceased or the bereaved, or recount a memory about the deceased.** "In the

years we lived next door, your daughter was delightful! We feel fortunate to have known her."
4. **Close with a thoughtful word or phrase.** "With affection and deepest condolences." Or, if you know the family is religious, you may want to offer a spiritual message.

MAKING CONNECTIONS

■ In your experience, why do adolescents and young adults use drugs? Do the reasons differ from those of adults?

■ The number of men with eating disorders is increasing. Is this because men are becoming more concerned about their appearance? Because they are more likely to seek help? Or other reasons?

Most of my students feel pretty depressed after reading this chapter. It's also depressing, as an author, to read the research and summarize the results. However, many groups (and individuals) have been successful in implementing a variety of programs that decrease family violence and other crises.

Intervening in Domestic Violence and Other Family Crises

One of the major reasons why we have such high family violence rates is that many people don't realize the extent of domestic abuse. Once people are more informed, prevention and intervention strategies can reduce domestic violence and other family crises.

Raising Awareness about Domestic Violence

Most of us are simply not aware of the prevalence of family violence and other family crises. Public education efforts to raise awareness about domestic violence, for example, have typically been addressed to women. If such efforts leave men—especially young men—out of the conversation, there'll be little change. How do you stop a 30-year-old man from beating his wife? "Talk to him when he's 12," writes a journalism professor, and as often as possible about not abusing girls (Voss, 2003).

Women can and should also encourage men to participate in antiviolence efforts. On the personal level, for example, I've convinced one of my brothers to make an annual donation to a women's abuse shelter in his town. On campuses, women should encourage their boyfriends and male friends to attend antiviolence meetings and lectures to raise men's awareness of the problem.

Preventing Domestic Violence and Other Crises

Numerous organizations offer programs and strategies to prevent domestic violence and other family crises. In terms of substance abuse, for example, many schools and communities have implemented "keeping kids clean" programs that teach youth how to avoid risky behavior and instruct parents how to talk to their children more effectively about the dangers of drugs (Atkin, 2002).

Children model their parents. Thus, as you saw earlier, if parents abuse drugs or are violent, children get the message that both behaviors are okay. As much of this chapter has shown, what's wrong with kids is usually not kids, but their parents, caregivers, and other adults (see also Chapter 12).

Preschool programs can reduce child abuse. For example, children of low-income parents who are involved in their children's preschool programs have a 52 percent lower rate of maltreatment by age 17 than children whose parents don't participate in such programs (Reynolds and Robertson, 2003).

The Watchful Shepherd (www.watchful.org), a nonprofit organization founded in Pennsylvania, protects at-risk children with electronic devices that children can use to contact hospital emergency personnel when they feel threatened or fear abuse. An unexpected outcome has been use of the device by parents who feared that they were losing control and might hurt their child unless someone intervened.

Intervening in Domestic Violence and Other Crises

There are thousands of programs and laws that intervene in family crises. Some are ineffective because the staff is overworked, the agency is underfunded, or the police and judges don't enforce domestic violence laws. There have also been many successful programs. For example,

- Abused women who obtain permanent (rather than temporary) court orders of protection are 80 percent less likely to be assaulted again.

- Teen substance abuse programs that involve the entire family have a higher success rate than those that simply treat the adolescent.

- Women who are treated for substance abuse are much more likely to have healthy babies than those who don't have prenatal care.

- Nurses and trained volunteers who visit teenage mothers and reinforce their parenting skills can decrease child abuse (Barnet et al., 2002; Mendel, 2002; Tanner, 2002).

Although many programs have decreased violence and other family crises, there are still numerous gaps. A father who served four years in prison for raping his 5-year-old daughter still has visitation rights, for example ("Man who raped . . .," 2002). And 70 percent of men who have battered their wives have convinced judges that the mother shouldn't have sole custody of a child (Waller, 2001).

There are few services for Latinas and American Indian and Asian American women who are trapped in abuse because wife battering is sometimes culturally acceptable (Nesmith, 2001). Also, few programs monitor batterers who are under restraining orders or are released from prison (Jackson, 2003).

Conclusion

Millions of U.S. families are experiencing many negative *changes*, such as more domestic violence, more child abuse and neglect, more abuse of the elderly, and high drug abuse among middle school children and teenagers. This does not mean that the situation is hopeless, however. As people become more informed about these and other problems, they have more *choices* in accessing supportive community resources and legal intervention agencies.

These choices are sometimes eclipsed by a number of *constraints*. Laws are not always enforced, our society still condones violence—especially male violence—and policy discussions of poverty and drug abuse rarely include the problem of family violence.

SUMMARY

1. People are more likely to be killed or assaulted by family members than by outsiders.

2. Although both men and women can be violent, abuse of wives and other intimate female partners results in much more serious physical and emotional damage than does husband or other intimate male partner abuse.

3. Battered wives are often dependent women who suffer from low self-esteem and feelings of inadequacy and helplessness. It's not clear whether these characteristics reflect personality traits or are the result of battering and abuse.

4. Women don't leave abusive relationships for a number of reasons: poor self-concept, a belief that the men they love will reform, economic hardship, a need for child support, doubt that they can get along alone, fear, shame and guilt, and being imprisoned in their homes.

5. There are four major categories of child abuse: physical abuse, sexual abuse, neglect, and emotional maltreatment.

6. Whether or not the abuse is sexual, many studies show that abused children suffer from a variety of physiological, social, and emotional problems.

7. Much more physical and sexual abuse is perpetrated by siblings on each other and by family members on elderly relatives than is reported.

8. The most influential theories that try to explain the reasons for family violence and female victimization include patriarchy or male dominance theory, psychological theories, social learning theory, resource theory, conflict theory, and exchange theory.

9. Besides violence, families must grapple with other health-related issues, such as drug abuse. Parental drug abuse, the inappropriate use of steroids, depression and suicide, anorexia and bulimia, and a child's death also affect families.

10. To decrease domestic violence and other family crises, we must do a better job of informing people about the problems, provide successful prevention programs, and implement better intervention strategies.

KEY TERMS

battered-woman syndrome *396*
marital rape *397*
child abuse *401*
child maltreatment *401*

incest *404*
sandwich generation *410*
elder abuse *410*
steroids *417*

anorexia nervosa *418*
bulimia *418*

TAKING IT FURTHER

Family Violence: Resources and Remedies

The National Coalition against Domestic Violence provides dozens of sites on women's shelters, counseling, legal aid, and other domestic violence resources.

www.ncadv.org

The National Clearinghouse on Child Abuse and Neglect Information focuses on the prevention, identification, and treatment of child abuse and neglect.

www.calib.com/nccanch

The National Center on Elder Abuse defines and illustrates the various types of abuse of the elderly and also suggests agencies and hotline phone numbers established by federal, state, and local governments for seeking assistance.

www.elderabusecenter.org

The Bureau of Justice Statistics provides statistics, data, and numerous reports related to domestic violence, child abuse, and runaways.

www.ojp.usdoj.gov

American Anorexia Bulimia Association, Inc., provides many services, including information, referrals, and prevention programs.

www.aabainc.org

Women's Law Initiative is an online resource that provides legal information to women and girls living with or escaping domestic violence. This site offers step-by-step instructions on filing for and obtaining restraining orders in all 50 US states and Washington, DC.

Also, the site contains "plain language translations" of domestic violence statutes, as well as online links to counseling services, shelters, legal assistance, downloadable court documents, locations of courthouses and sheriffs' offices for filing forms and serving court papers, and legislation news regarding domestic violence.

www.womenslaw.org/index.htm

And more: www.prenhall.com/benokraitis provides links to abuse prevention centers, men's domestic violence home pages, state domestic violence laws, a "Wheel Gallery" of abuse, a test to evaluate whether you or someone you know has eating disorders, and much more.

INVESTIGATE WITH RESEARCH NAVIGATOR

Research Navigator.com
RESOURCES FOR COLLEGE RESEARCH ASSIGNMENTS

Please go to www.researchnavigator.com and enter your LOGIN NAME and PASSWORD. For instructions on registering for the first time, please view the detailed instructions at the end of the Chapter 1. Please search the Research Navigator™ site using the following key search terms:

child abuse
elder abuse
eating disorders

Separation and Divorce

DATADIGEST

- About 50 percent of all U.S. **first marriages are projected to end in divorce,** compared with two out of five marriages in Britain, Denmark, and Sweden and one in ten in France and other European countries.

- After five years, **20 percent of all first marriages have undergone either separation or divorce.** After ten years, 33 percent of all marriages have broken up.

- **Among men who have ever been divorced,** 22 percent are white, 19 percent are African Americans, 13 percent are Latinos, and 9 percent are Asian Americans. The respective rates for women are 23 percent, 21 percent, 17 percent, and 11 percent.

- In 2002, almost 17 million children were **living with only a mother:** 48 percent of black children, 25 percent of Latino children, 16 percent of white children, and 13 percent of Asian American children.

- Of the **13.5 million custodial parents** in 2000, 7.9 million (59 percent) had some type of support agreement or award for their children.

SOURCES: Bramlett and Mosher, 2002; Grall, 2002; Kreider and Fields, 2002; U.S. Census Bureau, 2002; Fields, 2003.

When I was in college in the mid-1960s, divorce was rare. In hushed tones, adults often described the few friends whose parents were divorced as "unfortunate children" and "poor dears" and their parents as "disgraceful" and "selfish." As divorce rates climbed in the 1970s, however, marital dissolution became more common. Statistically, nearly one out of every two students reading this chapter probably comes from a divorced home.

In the 1950s and 1960s, marriage and family textbooks typically described divorce as deviant behavior. Today, in contrast, many people view divorce as a normal event that may occur in a person's life. Thus, both divorce rates and our reactions to divorce have changed dramatically within just one generation.

Just as divorce rates have increased, so have those of remarriage and redivorce (see Chapter 16). This means that family structures and relationships are more complex today than they were in the past. Whether these changes produce costs, benefits, or both, separation and divorce involve long-term processes and consequences.

Separation: Process and Outcome

Separation can mean several things. It may be a temporary time-out in a highly stressful marriage, in which the partners decide whether to continue their marriage. One person may move out of the home in a trial separation, enabling partners to see what living apart feels like.

Physical separation can also be a permanent arrangement because some religious beliefs don't allow divorce. Or partners may seek a legal separation, that is, a temporary period of living apart required by most states before a divorce is granted.

425

The Phases of Separation

Separation is usually a long and painful process that encompasses four phases: preseparation, early separation, midseparation, and late separation (Ahrons and Rodgers, 1987). Regardless of the duration of a particular phase and whether or not the partners go through all four phases, the process rarely happens quickly. Typically people agonize for months or years before making a final break.

Preseparation   During the *preseparation* phase, partners may fantasize about what it would be like to live alone, to escape from family responsibilities, or to form new sexual liaisons. Although the fantasies rarely become reality, they can make separation or divorce seem appealing.

In the later stages of the preseparation phase, the couple splits up after a gradual emotional alienation. The partner who feels that a separation can end the unhappiness of one or both partners usually initiates the separation.

Even when couples are contemplating separation (or have already made the decision), they often maintain a public pretense that nothing is wrong. The couple may attend family and social functions together, continuing rituals like holding hands right up until the actual separation.

Despite such outward appearances of tranquility, separation usually is traumatic, especially for the person who is left. He or she may feel guilty for causing the separation and may also experience anxiety, fear of being alone, and panic about the future.

Early Separation   The *early separation* phase is beset with problems because our society doesn't have clear-cut rules for this process. Many questions, both serious and trivial, plague the newly separated couple: Who should move out? What should the partners tell their family and friends? Should the child's teacher be notified? Who gets the baseball season tickets?

In addition, the partners may have very ambivalent feelings about the impending dissolution. They are confused and upset when their feelings vacillate—as they usually do—between love and hate, anger and sadness, euphoria and depression, and relief and guilt.

Partners also must confront economic issues such as paying bills, buying the children's clothing, and splitting old and new expenses. Particularly problematic may be the question of the wife's economic survival. Even when employed outside the home, she typically earns much less than her spouse (see Chapter 13). As a result, she faces a lower standard of living. This is especially likely if the children live with her. Some partners get support from family and friends, but most must cope on their own.

Midseparation   In the *midseparation* phase, the harsh realities of everyday living set in. The pressures of maintaining two separate households and meeting the daily emotional and physical needs of the children mount, and stress intensifies. If family or friends don't help or if their help diminishes, the partners may feel overwhelmed, especially if there are additional stressors such as illness, unexpected expenses, a dependent elderly parent, or difficulties at school or work.

Because of these problems, and especially when couples have been married at least ten years, people may experience "pseudo-reconciliation." That is, the earlier preseparation expectations or fantasies may be followed by a sense of loss when partners don't see their children, by guilt over abandoning the family, and by disapproval from parents, relatives, or friends. As a result, partners may move back in.

This second honeymoon, when partners feel less loneliness, fear, and guilt, rarely lasts. Soon the underlying problems that led to the separation in the first place surface again, conflicts reemerge, and the partners may separate once again (Everett and Everett, 1994).

Late Separation   In the *late separation* phase, partners must learn how to survive as singles again. This phase may be especially stressful for men who have been raised with traditional gender-role expectations. For example, many men report frustration and anger when they can't perform such routine tasks as ironing their shirts or preparing a favorite dish.

Both partners must often deal with mutual friends who have a hard time with the separation. Some friends may avoid both partners because it threatens their perceptions of their own marriages. Others may take sides, which forces separating partners to develop new friendships.

Finally, and perhaps most important, partners must help their children deal with anxiety, anger, confusion, and sadness. We return to this topic later in the chapter.

On the positive side, separating partners may experience what Nelson (1994) calls "growth-oriented coping." That is, many separating women become more autonomous, further their education, and experience an increase in confidence and a greater feeling of self-control.

Some Outcomes of Marital Separation

Not all separations end in divorce. Sometimes people reconcile and try to give their marriage a second chance.

Separation and Reconciliation   Data on reconciliation are rare. According to the most recent study, however, approximately 10 percent of all currently married U.S. couples (9 percent of white women and 14 percent of black women) have separated and reconciled (Wineberg and McCarthy, 1993).

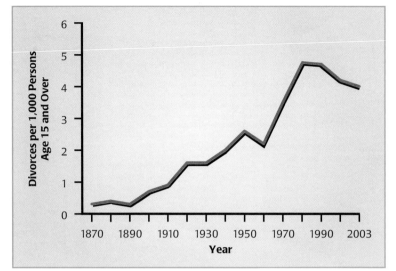

FIGURE 15.1 **Divorce in the United States, 1870–2003**

Sources: Plateris, 1973; U.S. Census Bureau, 2002; Sutton, 2003.

In a national study of black women who had a successful reconciliation in their first marriage, Wineberg (1996) found that the reconciliation varied by age. Women separating after age 23 were substantially more likely to reconcile than their younger counterparts. Wineberg attributed this difference to older women being more mature and more willing to make the sacrifices necessary to reconcile.

Additionally, older women have a greater incentive to reconcile because they have invested more in the marriage than women who separate before age 23. If there are children, both spouses may attempt reconciliation because they have a strong commitment to the institution of marriage and "may exhaust all options to save the marriage (Wineberg, 1996: 84). Although some couples reconcile, many others separate but don't get a divorce.

Separation but No Divorce Although many people separate and even file the necessary paperwork for a divorce, they never make the divorce official. Within five years, 97 percent of white women have moved from a separation to a divorce, compared with 77 percent of Latinas and only 67 percent of African American women (Bramlett and Mosher, 2002).

Why the variation between racial-ethnic groups? There's an old saying that people marry for love and divorce for money. If women (or their husbands) don't have the money to get a divorce, the separation might go on for many years. Long-term separations are most likely among women without a high school degree, women with a low income and who are not employed, and women who have one or more out-of-wedlock children (Bramlett and Mosher, 2002).

Although there are no hard data, it could be that low-income women with low educational levels have no incentive to pay the costs of a divorce because their husbands may be unemployed and unable to pay for child support. In other cases, a wife can't afford hiring a detective agency to track down a deserter. In most cases, however, separations end in divorce.

Separation and Divorce Divorce, the legal and formal dissolution of a marriage, is not a new phenomenon. The Code of Hammurabi, written almost 4000 years ago in ancient Mesopotamia, allowed the termination of a marriage. Among the nobility, especially, divorce was apparently as easy for women as for men:

> *If she was careful and was not at fault, even though her husband has been going out and disparaging her greatly, that woman, without incurring any blame at all, may take her dowry and go off to her father's house (J. Monk, cited in Esler, 1994).*

Writing about the family in 1887, Thwing and Thwing expressed alarm that divorce had been increasing since 1830 rather than marriage being "a permanent and lifelong state" (cited in Reiss, 1971: 317). And in the early twentieth century, a number of marriages ended by desertion, even though there was no legal divorce. Thus, the rising divorce rate reflects not only more dissolution of marriages but more legal dissolutions.

According to Brehm (1985), this change is an improvement: When a wife was deserted, she often had no idea whether her husband (deserters were more often male than female) would return. Moreover, a deserting husband rarely left his spouse any money or sent money later, which often put the wife and children in serious financial straits.

In the United States, the divorce rate has risen gradually throughout the twentieth century (*Figure 15.1*). The small peak in the early 1950s, after the end of World

Divorced men, particularly if they've been married to traditional wives, often find it difficult to do mundane household chores.

War II, has been attributed to divorces among people who had married impulsively before the men left for war. When the men returned, the couples found that they had nothing in common. War-related family stress also increased divorce rates (Riley, 1991; Tuttle, 1993; see also Chapter 3).

In the mid-1960s, divorce rates began to climb steadily. Since 1980, the divorce rate has plateaued, with a slight drop since 1995. In effect, divorce rates are lower today than between 1975 and 1990. It's not clear why this is the case. It may be that the lower divorce rates are due to more people working harder to save their marriages. On the other hand, the lower divorce rates may reflect the growing number of couples who cohabit, instead of marry, and break up (Glenn, 2001). That is, many cohabiting couples in "trial marriages" break up instead of getting married and then divorcing (see Chapter 9).

Most people want to marry and to stay married. In a recent nationwide survey, for example, 79 percent of the adults said that one of life's major goals was "having one marriage partner for life" (Rapaport, 2000). Despite such goals, divorce is a painful milestone in many people's lives.

The Process of Divorce

Few divorces are spontaneous, spur-of-the-moment acts. The divorce process is usually spread over a long period during which two people gradually redefine, reorganize, and sometimes rebuild their relationship and their expectations of one another. In navigating this transition, many people go through a number of stages. One widely cited conceptualization is Bohannon's (1971) six "stations"

of divorce: emotional, legal, economic, coparental, community, and psychic.

Emotional Divorce

The *emotional divorce* begins before any legal steps are taken. One or both partners may feel disillusioned, unhappy, or rejected. The person who eventually initiates the divorce may feel that the marriage was never "right" to begin with, that she or he was mismatched, or that they were living a lie because there had never been a marital bond:

> *I came to realize after all this time that there had been a very long time when we really had no life together. We just sort of shared a house, and sort of took care of the kids together. But mostly I did that with the kids and he went and did his thing, and we were sort of this phony family for friends and neighbors and the relatives (Hopper, 2001: 436).*

Although they may irritate one another, couples remain in the marriage because they don't want to be alone, because they believe that divorce would hurt their children, or because they feel bound by their marriage vows "for better or for worse." Partners may be aloof or polite, despite their anger, or they may become overtly hostile, making sarcastic remarks or hurling accusations at each other.

The emotional divorce often progresses through stages, from a beginning phase to an ending phase. In the *beginning phase* of the emotional divorce, partners feel disappointment in each other but hope that the marriage will improve (Kersten, 1990).

During the *middle phase*, their feelings of hurt and anger increase as efforts to correct the situation seem unsuccessful. The partner who is less happy begins evaluating the rewards and costs of leaving the marriage.

In the *end phase*, one of the partners stops caring and detaches emotionally from the other. Apathy and indifference replace loving, intimate feelings. Even when partners don't hate each other, it may be too late to rekindle the marriage:

> *I knew I was going to die if I didn't get out of this marriage. We couldn't talk. We buried our feelings until there was nothing between us except the shell of a life. I was depressed for a long time before I got the courage to leave. I think I must have been grieving for years. It was so sad. He is not a bad person* (Gold, 1992: 45).

Some couples try to prolong the marriage: "They go to great lengths to set up roadblocks to ending the marriage, refusing to settle anything, including plans for their children" (P. M. Brown, 1995: 211). Others, as we discuss later in this chapter, may use mediation and counseling to ward off the impending loss. Most seek legal advice to end the marriage.

Legal Divorce

The *legal divorce* is the formal dissolution of the marriage. During this stage, partners come to agreements on such issues as child custody and the division of property and other economic assets.

In part because divorce is an adversarial procedure during which each partner's attorney tries to maintain the upper hand, the process is rarely trouble-free. For example, the partner who does not want the divorce may try to forestall the inevitable end of the marriage or to get revenge by making demands that the other spouse will find hard to accept, such as getting custody of the family dog.

Other issues may include **alimony** (sometimes called *spousal maintenance*), monetary payments made by one ex-spouse to the other to support the latter's basic needs for survival, and especially **child support**, monetary payments by the noncustodial parent to the custodial parent to help pay child-rearing expenses. Because spouses often disagree on what is fair and equitable, they may use money to manipulate each other into making more concessions ("I'm willing to pay child support if you agree to sell the house and split the proceeds").

Even after a divorce is legal, couples may experience ambivalence: "Did I really do the right thing in getting a divorce?" or "Should I have been satisfied with

what I had?" Such doubts are normal, but some clinicians caution divorcing parents not to reveal their ambivalence to their children, who may become confused or anxious or deny the reality of divorce and fantasize about reconciliation (Everett and Everett, 1994).

Economic Divorce

During the *economic divorce*, the couple may argue about who should pay past debts, property taxes, and expenses for the children such as braces. Thus, discussions and conflict over economic issues may continue even after the legal issues have been settled. In addition, partners may try to change child-support agreements or not make the required payments.

Most recently, directors of retirement funds are advising couples who are contemplating divorce to think about their finances because retirement funds are among the largest assets to be divided. According to one reporter, a downturn in the economy, especially, "has injected an extra dose of venom into the already poisonous process of divorce" (Tyre, 2003: 49). As a result, many financial planners urge prospective divorcees to go to court and renegotiate payments, especially for child support. In doing so, couples may be involved in an economic divorce for several decades if their children are very young at the time of the divorce.

Coparental Divorce

The *coparental divorce* involves the agreements between the partners regarding legal responsibility for financial support of the children, the day-to-day care of the children, and the rights of the custodial and noncustodial parents in spending time with the children. As you'll see shortly, the amount of conflict in this period may be short-lived or long term, depending on how well the parents get along and whether the children are caught in the middle of parental hostility.

Community Divorce

Partners also go through a *community divorce*, when they inform friends, family, teachers, and others that they are no longer married. Relationships between grandparents and grandchildren often continue, but in-laws may sever ties. The partners may also replace old friendships with new ones, and they typically start dating again.

Psychic Divorce

In this final stage, the couple goes through a *psychic divorce,* in which the partners separate from each other emotionally and establish separate lives. One or both people may undergo a process of mourning. Some people

CHOICES

How You Relate Can Make All the Difference

Because divorcing partners are often angry, hurt, or bitter, many divorces are hostile and painful. As the following five styles of relating to each other suggest, the more civility partners can maintain in their post-divorce relationship, the more productive their relationships will be with each other and with their children (Ahrons and Rodgers, 1987; Gold, 1992).

Perfect Pals Some partners remain friends even after they have decided to divorce. A small group of divorced spouses share decision making and child rearing much as they did in marriage, and many feel that they are better parents after the divorce. These former spouses may even spend holidays together and maintain relationships with each other's extended families.

Cooperative Colleagues Although a sizable number of divorced spouses do not consider themselves good friends, they are able to cooperate. Working together often takes effort, but they accept their roles as parents and believe it is their duty to make responsible decisions about their children.

Cooperative parents want to minimize the trauma of divorce for their children and try to protect them from conflict. Such parents are willing to negotiate and compromise on some of their differences. They may also consult counselors and mediators to resolve impasses before going to court.

Angry Associates Anger is still an integral part of many relationships between divorced partners. These couples harbor bitter resentments about events in their past marriages as well as the divorce process. Some have long and heated battles over such things as custody, visitation rights, and financial matters. These battles may continue years after the divorce.

Fiery Foes Some divorced spouses are completely unable to coparent. Such partners are incapable of remembering any good times in the marriage, and each clings to the wrongs done by the other. Children are caught in the middle of the bitter conflict and are expected to side with one parent and regard the other as the enemy.

One parent, usually the father, sees the children less and less frequently over the years, and both parents blame each other for this declining contact. The divorces tend to be highly litigious; legal battles sometimes continue for years after the divorce, and the power struggle pervades the entire family.

Dissolved Duos Unlike the battling "fiery foes," the partners break off entirely with each other. Noncustodial parents may "kidnap" the children, or a partner may leave the geographic area where the family has lived.

In some cases one partner, usually the man, actually disappears, leaving the other partner with the entire burden of reorganizing the family. The children have only memories and fantasies of the vanished parent.

never complete this stage because they can't let go of the pain, anger, and resentment, even after they remarry. Recently, some couples have had "divorce ceremonies" to help them finalize the divorce symbolically and publicly. Although still rare, such ceremonies "ask the partners to offer apologies to each other and seek forgiveness for the hurt they have inflicted" (Tesoriero, 2002: F11).

Not all couples go through all six of Bohannon's stages. Also, some couples may experience some stages, such as emotional and economic divorce, simultaneously. The important point is that divorce is a *process* that involves many people, not just the divorcing couple, and may take time to complete. Moreover, because people differ, divorcing couples may respond to each other in varying ways, as the box "How You Relate Can Make All the Difference" illustrates.

Why Do People Divorce?

Researchers explain the rise in divorce rates on three levels: macro, or societal; demographic; and interpersonal. As you read this section, keep in mind that these various factors often overlap. As *Figure 15.2* shows, macro variables influence demographic variables, which in turn may cause specific marital problems, including divorce.

Macro-level Reasons for Divorce

There are many macro-level reasons for the increase in divorce rates. Four important sources of change are social institutions, social integration, gender roles, and cultural values.

Social Institutions Changes in legal, religious, and family institutions have affected divorce rates. The increasing number of people entering the legal profession and the growth of free legal clinics have made divorce more accessible and less expensive.

Some Americans feel that divorce laws are too lax. In 1974, for example, 33 percent thought that laws should be changed to make it easier to get a divorce. This number declined to 25 percent in 1998. Still, 75 percent of people feel that unhappy couples shouldn't be trapped in a marriage (T. W. Smith, 1999).

All states have **no-fault divorce** laws so that neither partner need establish the guilt or wrongdoing of the other. Before no-fault divorce laws, the partner who initiated the divorce had to prove that the other was "to blame" for the collapse of the marriage because of adultery, desertion, or physical and mental cruelty, for example. Courts took fault into account in dividing up the property and assigning custody if the couple had children.

No-fault laws did away with blame and proving that a partner was at fault. Couples can now simply give "irreconcilable differences" or "incompatibility" as a valid reason for divorce. Judges then try to divide the property as fairly as possible, decide which partner should have custody of the children, and determine child-support payments.

Some researchers claim that the switch from fault divorce law to no-fault divorce law have led to an increase in the divorce rate in the United States and other countries (Nakonezny et al., 1995; Rodgers et al., 1997). Others point out that divorce rates started increasing in some states years before those states adopted no-fault legislation in the 1970s. In addition, there's little evidence that passage of no-fault laws increased divorce rates overall. Instead, no-fault laws simply ratified, symbolically, changes in values about marriage and divorce that had already occurred (Glenn, 1997).

Regardless of how people feel about divorce, it's a thriving industry. Because domestic relations cases account for one-third of all civil lawsuits, divorce cases provide jobs for many lawyers, judges, and other employees of the legal system. If a divorcing couple has had a long-term marriage, accountants may spend several years disentangling property rights, accumulated marital property, and the rights of children still living at home. "Forensic accountants" may be asked to track down hidden assets in a contested divorce, and attorneys may hire appraisers, who can charge up to $50,000, to determine the value of jewelry, cars, boats, antiques, and businesses.

In child-custody disputes, attorneys may hire marriage counselors, psychologists, education specialists, medical personnel, clergy, social workers, and mediators (De Witt, 1994). Although not everyone who wants a divorce can afford all these services, their very availability sends

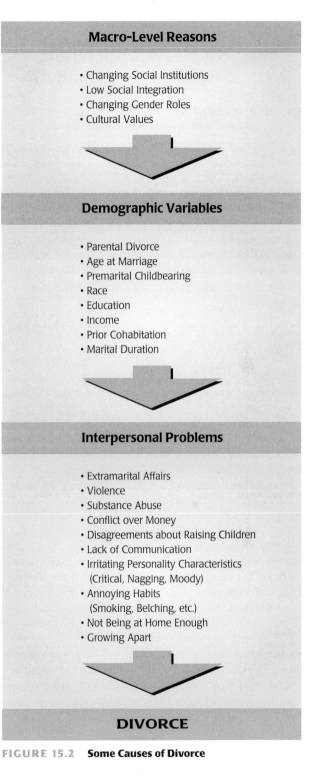

FIGURE 15.2   Some Causes of Divorce

the message that divorce is acceptable and that many professionals are ready to help.

Technological advances, such as the Internet, have also made marital dissolution more accessible than in the past. Many people now go online to save money and

CROSSCULTURAL

Divorce around the World

In a study of 27 nations, researchers found that divorce rates rose in 25 countries between 1950 and 1985, whereas marriage rates declined in 22 (Lester, 1996b). Divorce rates in the United States are two to three times as high as those in such other industrialized countries as Sweden, Canada, France, and the United Kingdom. Among developed countries, Russia has the highest divorce rate.

Some of the lowest divorce rates (about 20 percent of all marriages) are in Greece, Portugal, Italy, and Spain. In Eastern Europe, similarly, low divorce rates characterize Bulgaria, Croatia, Poland, and Slovenia (*The World's Women*, 2000). Religious and traditional values, in part, may account for these low rates.

One of the reasons divorce rates are rising around the world is that, since the 1970s, many countries—including Argentina, Australia, Canada, India, and Japan—have liberalized their divorce laws. Divorce is increasingly easy to obtain, men are less often required to provide their ex-wives with economic support, and parents are often encouraged to have joint child custody (Fine and Fine, 1994).

In 1997, Ireland became the last major European country to legalize divorce. The Philippines, a predominantly Roman Catholic country, is one of the few nations where divorce is still prohibited, even though a marriage can be easily annulled on psychological grounds. Similarly, Chile permits legal separation and annulment

but not divorce. Because an annulled marriage never legally existed, however, the wives in these situations are not legally entitled to alimony or child support from their husbands (Neft and Levine, 1997; Rohter, 2003).

Divorce is rare in the Muslim world, but the husband may obtain one unilaterally merely by repeating the phrase, "I divorce thee" to his wife three times in front of witnesses. In contrast, the wife who wants to divorce her husband must usually take the matter to a religious court and prove that her husband has had a harmful moral effect on the family or that he has failed to support her (Neft and Levine, 1997).

In 2000, however, Egypt passed a law that allows women to seek a unilateral, no-questions-asked divorce. The woman must return the husband's dowry (which can often be as modest as $30) and relinquish all financial claims, including alimony. Some argue that the new changes do not go far enough and that it will be difficult for poor women to return their dowries and renounce financial rights (Eltahawy, 2000). Others feel that the new law is a vast improvement in providing women even limited divorce rights (Schneider, 2000).

Divorce has become much simpler in China since the 1980 passage of a law that allowed couples who had fallen out of love to separate formally. The divorce rate has increased most sharply in urban

centers like Beijing, where it rose from 2 percent of marriages in 1981 to 18 percent in 1992 (Walker, 1993).

Some factors contributing to the rising divorce rate in China include Western television programs that depict extramarital sex, growing numbers of well-educated urban women who are more likely to leave an unhappy marriage, and the growth of prostitution (Linlin, 1993).

STOP AND THINK...

- *Is there too much divorce going on in the world? Should many countries eliminate their no-fault divorce laws?*

- *What are the advantages and disadvantages, especially for women and children, in having greater access to divorce?*

time and avoid the emotional clashes that can play out in lawyers' offices. Some online do-it-yourself divorces cost as little as $50 for all the necessary court forms and documents. According to the owners of two Internet national sites that were launched in 2001, there have been more than 50,000 divorce customers so far (Campbell, 2003).

Some critics contend that the online services invite impulsiveness. People who have used the services,

however, say that the decision to divorce is always agonizing but that the online accessibility saves money on legal fees. According to one proponent of online services, "You're not going to get divorced because it's on special offer" (O'Donnell et al., 1999: 8).

Religion also affects divorce rates. Women who say that religion is important to them experience lower separation and divorce rates (Bramlett and Mosher, 2002). Having the same religion is also highly associated with marital stability (Lehrer and Chiswick, 1993). Spouses who follow the same religion or who convert to a spouse's religion at marriage are more likely to reconcile after a separation. Religious similarity may be important in marital stability because it increases the commonality between partners' traditions, values, and sense of community (Wineberg, 1994).

Changes in the family institution have also had an effect on divorce. As you saw in Chapter 1, as the United States shifted from a preindustrial to an industrial society, family members became less dependent on one another. Institutions outside the family emerged that met people's economic, recreational, and other needs. As more people moonlight or work evening and weekend shifts, for example, many family members spend less time together, especially in recreational activities (see Chapter 13).

Nonstandard work schedules, as when parents have night and rotating shifts, increase physiological stress because parents don't get enough sleep when there are children to care for. Fatigue, combined with demanding child-rearing responsibilities, may take a toll on the marriages (Presser, 2000). As the box "Divorce around the World" shows, nonindustrial societies are also experiencing increasing levels of marital dissolution.

Social Integration At the turn of the twentieth century, Émile Durkheim argued that people who are integrated into a community are less likely to divorce, to commit suicide, or to engage in other self-destructive behavior. A number of contemporary social scientists contend, similarly, that **social integration**—the social bonds that people have with others and with the community at large—discourages divorce. For example, communities in which people hold similar values about marital roles and in which people stay in the same neighborhoods for long periods tend to have high integration and low divorce rates (Glenn and Shelton, 1985; Shelton, 1987). Similarly, low divorce rates characterize religious groups, such as Orthodox Jews, in which members feel a strong commitment to the group (Brodnar-Nemzer, 1986).

Social integration helps explain the high divorce rates in the United States: The great diversity of subcultures, languages, religious practices, and political organizations decreases social integration. Moreover, as workers are laid off and move to find other jobs or accept lateral career moves instead of being fired, relocation disrupts existing bonds between family, friends, and neighbors (see Chapter 13).

Divorces of first marriages are more likely in communities with high unemployment, low median family income, and high poverty levels (Bramlett and Mosher, 2002). Stress often leads to conflict, disagreements, and splitting up. In contrast, more affluent neighborhoods

"It's National We're History Month."

can strengthen shaky marital bonds by providing a variety of services for adults and children that connect people to each other and to the community during stressful periods.

Remember, however, that none of these studies is claiming that all couples who stay married are happy. They are saying only that people who live in communities and societies that are more socially integrated are more likely to stay married.

Gender Roles Contemporary U.S. women are twice as likely as men to initiate a divorce. Some are escaping abusive marriages (see Chapter 14). For others, getting a divorce can increase the likelihood that a father who has abandoned his family can be tracked down for child-support payments. Women are also more likely to initiate a divorce in states where they feel that they have a good chance of getting sole custody instead of shared custody (Brinig and Allen, 2000).

Changing gender roles, especially employed women's growing economic independence, might be associated with an increase in divorce rates (Hiedemann et al., 1998). Increasingly, women expect their spouses to communicate with them and to share domestic tasks (see Chapters 5 and 13). If women are employed, they are more likely to leave unhappy relationships when these expectations are not met.

Women with more resources—those with college degrees, for example—are filing for divorce instead of living with a husband who isn't emotionally satisfying or is adulterous (Hacker, 2003). Men are more likely than women to have problems with drinking, drug abuse, or infidelity and to be physically abusive (see Chapters 7 and 14). If women are economically self-sufficient, they don't have to tolerate such behavior.

A wife's employment can also have a stabilizing effect on a marriage. Her income increases the family's financial security, which makes remaining married a more attractive alternative for both partners than becoming single again (Ono, 1998).

Cultural Values   American attitudes and beliefs about divorce have been changing. Some scholars feel that Americans are emphasizing individual happiness rather than family commitments (see Chapter 1). According to one family therapist, for example, a "narcissistic greed for personal happiness" is at the root of many divorces. As people pursue self-fulfillment, he contends, they betray the spouses who love them (Pittman, 1999).

The women's movement of the late 1960s challenged traditional beliefs that women should stay in unhappy or abusive marriages. Throughout the 1970s and 1980s, many therapists and attorneys not only sent messages that "divorce is okay" but flooded the market with self-help books on how to get a divorce, how to cope with loneliness and guilt after a divorce, how to deal with child-custody disputes, and other legal issues.

Television programs such as *Divorce Court* (and its many recent variations) show viewers that divorce is not an anomaly but an everyday occurrence. Although there is still some stigma attached to divorce, for the most part, U.S. society now accepts it as normal.

Some scholars echo these shifting values. They feel that we should "normalize" divorce by supporting couples and their children. In the last half of the twentieth century, writes one psychologist, divorce replaced death as the primary terminator of marriage. Because divorce has become a "normal marital endpoint," social policies should support all couples and children, married, divorced, or living together (Pinsof, 2002).

Demographic Variables in Divorce

Many demographic variables help explain the divorce-prone couple. The most important factors are having divorced parents, the presence of children, age at marriage, premarital childbearing, race and ethnicity, and education.

Parental Divorce   If the parents of one or both partners in a marriage were divorced during childhood, the partners themselves are more likely to divorce (McLanahan and Bumpass, 1988; Wolfinger, 1999, 2000). One reason for this may be that children of divorced parents tend to have lower educational attainment and to marry at younger ages, as you'll see shortly. Because children of divorced parents are less able to afford college, they are more likely to marry early, and the younger partners are when they marry, the more likely they are to divorce (Saluter, 1994).

The effect of parental divorce varies by gender and social class. When parents from lower social classes divorce, they may be less likely to encourage their

daughters than their sons to continue their education after high school. They may also become more lax about checking out their daughters' dating partners. As a result, daughters may choose high-risk mates at a young age (Keith and Finlay, 1988). Because parents still tend to encourage higher education more often for sons than for daughters, many young men from middle-class families continue to enjoy the parents' economic resources, allowing them to go to college, to postpone marriage, and to be older and more mature in handling marital relationships (Feng et al., 1999).

Presence of Children   Several studies have found that the presence of preschool children, especially firstborn children, increases marital stability. This may reflect the fact that some couples stay together for the sake of the children (White, 1991; Previti and Amato, 2003). In addition, the presence of young children may make the divorce process more costly emotionally and financially.

Marital disruption is significantly more likely in families where children are 13 or older (Rankin and Maneker, 1985; Waite and Lillard, 1991). The risk of separation is low when the youngest child is less than 3; it reaches a plateau as the youngest child passes through ages 7 to 12, peaks at the midteens, and drops sharply after age 17 (Heaton, 1990).

Whereas the presence of younger children appears to help hold marriages together, when children are older couples may have fewer incentives to stay together. Or they may postpone divorce until their children are older. In some cases, problems with adolescent children exacerbate already strained marital relationships, and the marriage may fall apart (see Chapter 12).

Marital disruption is less likely when children are male rather than female. Because fathers play a more active role in raising sons than daughters—in such areas as rule setting and discipline—they are more involved in the family that has sons and are less likely to seek a divorce when problems arise. Because boys continue to be valued more than girls in U.S. society, mothers with sons feel more satisfied in their marriages and are less likely to consider separation from their spouses (Morgan et al., 1988; Katzev et al., 1994).

Age at Marriage   Several studies have found that early age at marriage increases the chance of divorce (Thornton and Rodgers, 1987; Greenstein, 1990; Kurdek, 1993). In fact, early marriage may be the strongest predictor of divorce in the first five years of marriage (Martin and Bumpass, 1989).

Couples who marry under age 18 are especially prone to divorce. After ten years of marriage, for example, 48 percent of first marriages of women under age 18 have dissolved, compared with only 24 percent of those to women at least age 25 at marriage (Bramlett and Mosher, 2002).

Why do young spouses have high divorce rates? Sometimes if young couples are experiencing problems, parents and relatives who disapproved of the marriage may encourage divorce.

In most cases, however, young couples are not prepared to handle marital responsibilities. They are less happy than older spouses about their partners in terms of love, affection, sex, earnings, companionship, and faithfulness. They also complain that their spouses become angry easily, are jealous or moody, spend money foolishly, drink or use drugs, and get into trouble with the law (Booth and Edwards, 1985).

Premarital Pregnancy and Childbearing Women who conceive or give birth to a child *before* marriage have higher divorce rates after the first marriage than women who conceive or have a child *after* marriage. Divorce is especially likely among adolescents, who generally lack the education or income to maintain a stable family life (Norton and Miller, 1992; Garfinkel et al., 1994; Teachman, 2002).

The effects may be especially negative for Latinas and African American women. In terms of premarital pregnancy, the probability that the first marriage will break up when the first birth is within seven months of marriage is 23 percent for white women, 26 percent for Latinas, and 36 percent for black women (Bramlett and Mosher, 2002).

Other variables also interact with premarital pregnancy and childbirth and divorce. For example, low educational attainment, high unemployment rates, and poverty increase separation and divorce rates (see Chapters 5 and 13).

Race and Ethnicity In a national survey, 66 percent of the general population felt that divorce was acceptable, compared with 57 percent of Latinos (Deane et al., 2000). Even though many Latinos feel that divorce is wrong, their divorce rates have been only slightly lower than those of white couples (see *Figure 15.3*).

Divorce is most likely in the early years of marriage. After five years, for example, about 10 percent of all marriages end in divorce (Kreider and Fields, 2002).

Divorce rates vary quite a bit by race and ethnicity, however. While 40 percent of ever-married white women and Latinas had divorced from their first marriage by 1996, 24 percent of Asian American women and 48 percent of black women had done so (see *Figure 15.3*). After ten years of marriage, only 20 percent of Asian American women's first marriages have dissolved, compared with 32 percent for white women, 34 percent for Latinas, and 47 percent for black women (Bramlett and Mosher, 2002).

One of the most consistent research findings is that blacks are more likely to divorce than any other racial-ethnic group. Divorce rates among African Americans have been more than 75 percent higher than those among whites and Latinos since 1960, and since 1980 they have been nearly twice as high (Saluter, 1994). These differences persist at all income, age, educational, and occupational levels (Rank, 1987; White, 1991).

Being African American does not, of course, cause one to divorce. Other demographic, macro, and interpersonal factors are at work. One of the reasons for higher black marital dissolution rates is the higher rate of black teenage and premarital pregnancies. As you've just seen, women whose first birth is out of wedlock

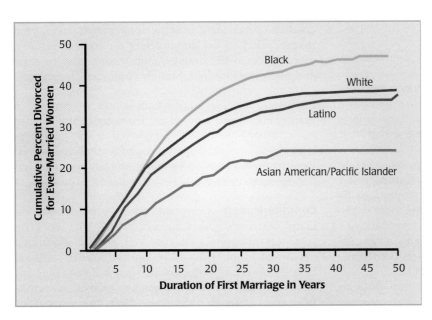

FIGURE 15.3 **Divorce among Racial–Ethnic Groups**

Source: Kreider and Fields, 2002: Figure 5.

or within seven months of a marriage have a higher risk of separation or divorce.

Another reason for the high divorce rate among blacks is poverty. Because African Americans are disproportionately poor, they are more likely to face the many poverty-related stresses and strains that lead to divorce (Blackwell, 1991; see also Chapters 4 and 13).

Finally, some researchers suggest that divorce may be more acceptable among African Americans. Divorce may be less strained because the community offers divorcing partners more social support (Cherlin, 1998). During such stressful life events, African American families provide its members with love, services, money, and other resources (Blake and Darling, 2000).

Education and Income   In a study of 11 nations, Lester (1996a) found an association between unemployment and high divorce rates in nine countries. Such an association is not surprising because unemployment and poverty increase family stress, violence, and disruption (see Chapters 13 and 14).

Nevada has the highest U.S. divorce rate: 6.8 per 1000 people, compared with the national average of 4.0. Aside from Nevada, which some call the "quickie divorce capital" of the United States, four so-called Bible belt states also have much higher divorce rates than the national average: 5.2 in Tennessee and West Virginia, 5.3 in Alabama, 5.4 in Mississippi, and 6.6 in Arkansas (U.S. Census Bureau, 2002; data for California, Colorado, Indiana, and Louisiana are not available.)

Why are the divorce rates so high in fundamentalist states that promote marriage and family values? Low household incomes (Arkansas ranks 48th, West Virginia ranks 49th, and Mississippi 50th) and the tendency for couples to marry at younger ages than in other states help explain the high divorce rates. In addition, many southern states have large numbers of Protestants, whose churches allow divorce, unlike Roman Catholics, who populate the northeastern states ("Bible belt wrestles . . .," 1999).

In general, low educational attainment and low income (especially the father's) increase the possibility of divorce (Kurdek, 1993). People with a bachelor's degree are less likely to divorce than those with a high school education (Kreider and Fields, 2002).

Do people with college degrees have more stable marriages because they're smarter? No. Rather, going to college postpones marriage for many couples, with the result that they are often more mature, more experienced, and more capable of dealing with personal crises when they marry. They also have higher incomes and better health care, which lessen marital stress over financial problems (Kreider and Fields, 2002).

The more education a man has, the less likely he is to divorce. The effects of educational attainment on women's likelihood of divorce are more complex. Even though a wife's higher education decreases the probability of divorce early in a marriage, it may increase her risk of divorce later in the marriage (Hiedemann et al., 1998). As you saw earlier, a college-educated woman may get a divorce if her income increases and she is increasingly dejected about a husband who doesn't share domestic and child-rearing tasks (see also Chapters 5 and 13).

Interpersonal Reasons for Divorce

Macro and demographic variables often affect interpersonal reasons for divorce. Some feel that the divorce rate has climbed because of greater longevity. Because we live longer than people did in the past, a married couple may spend a significantly longer period of time together, and there is a greater chance that over the years some partners may grate on each other's nerves. Four common stressors are high expectations, children, income, and communication.

High Expectations   Because people have fewer children, they have more time to focus on their relationship as a couple, both while the children are living at home and after they move out. And because they have more time to focus on the marital relationships, there is a greater chance that some marital partners will become disillusioned. They may expect to be comforted, to be told that they are loved, or to be shown in other ways that they are appreciated and valued. Or couples may compare themselves with unrealistic models portrayed in films and on television and feel that they *should* have higher expectations about marriage (see Chapter 1).

Children   One of the top reasons for arguments is children. Regardless of how long people have been married, they report that much of the conflict before a divorce was over disagreements about how to raise and discipline children (Stanley et al., 2002).

Income   Money is a common source of conflict in marital breakups. Wives grow disillusioned if husbands can't find or hold a job. Unemployed or low-paid men, who already feel inadequate, complain that their wives' nagging makes them feel even more incompetent (Hetherington and Kelly, 2002).

Communication   Communication problems derail many marriages (see Chapters 5 and 10). Some researchers maintain that they can predict whether a newlywed couple will still be married four to six years later by observing not *what* they say but *how* they say it. Couples that stay together listen to each other respectfully even when they disagree, don't start discussions with accusatory statements ("You're lazy and never do anything around the house"), and have more positive than negative interaction (Gottman et al., 1998; Carrere and Gottman, 1999; Patz, 2000). Although lasting relationships may not be blissful, the communication may be peaceful or passionate, but it's not venomous.

Often, however, such interpersonal factors as communication reflect demographic or macro-level factors (see *Figure 15.2*). In their study of black divorced men, for example, Lawson and Thompson (1999) found that financial strain created or aggravated existing communication problems. As one divorced father explained, "I worked too much and spent little time at home. . . . It is ironic that my efforts to provide for my family made me vulnerable to charges of being distant and uncaring" (p. 65).

Because divorce is a process rather than an overnight event, many of the stressors that lead to divorce begin years before a couple breaks up. Besides arguments over children and income, there may be conflict over extramarital affairs, substance abuse, spending too many evenings with friends, and other problems for many years before the separation (Stewart et al., 1997; Amato and Rogers, 1997).

Although trashing wedding memorabilia may release some anger and hurt, it also suggests that the person has not come to terms with divorce and needs some physical sign to make it real.

MAKING CONNECTIONS

■ Some people send humorous greeting cards to proclaim their divorce. A smaller number hold divorce ceremonies announcing their marital breakup. Are these effective ways of getting some closure on divorce?

■ Think about the people you know who have experienced a divorce. Were the reasons macro, demographic, interpersonal, or a combination?

How Divorce Affects Adults

In the popular film *The First Wives Club*, three middle-aged women get revenge on their ex-husbands for dumping them for younger girlfriends. Among other stereotypes, the husbands are portrayed as cads, the wives are presented as innocent victims, and getting even is fun.

In real life, marital dissolution is usually an agonizing process both for women and for men, across socioeconomic levels, and regardless of race or ethnicity. Divorce has a significant effect in at least three areas of a couple's or family's life: physical, emotional, and psychological well-being; economic and financial changes; and child-custody and child-support arrangements.

Physical, Emotional, and Psychological Effects

Unhappily married people, especially women, experience numerous health problems, including high blood pressure, cardiovascular diseases, and depression. Compared with women, men have a higher risk of substance abuse and earlier death (Gallo et al., 2003; see also Chapter 10).

A number of studies also show that the divorced are worse off than the married in many ways. They report more social isolation and less satisfying sex lives and are often as unhappy as they were before the divorce (Mastekaasa, 1997; Waite et al., 2002; see also Chapter 7). Despite our modern acceptance of divorce, separated and divorced people sometimes feel stigmatized by family, friends, and co-workers (Gasser and Taylor, 1990; Kitson and Morgan, 1991). Some people feel anxious about "disgracing" their families and being objects of gossip or criticism.

People age 40 and older reenter the dating scene with a mixed sense of dread and eager anticipation.

Do You Know Someone with Divorce Hangover?

In a "healthy" divorce, ex-spouses must accomplish three tasks: letting go, developing new social ties, and, when children are involved, redefining parental roles (Everett and Everett, 1994). Often, however, divorced partners suffer from what Walther (1991) describes as "divorce hangover." They are unable to let go, develop new friendships, or reorient themselves as single parents.

In each of the following statements, put the name of someone you know who has just gone through a divorce in the blanks and decide whether the statement is true of that person. There is no scoring on this quiz, but if you agree that many of these statements describe your friend or acquaintance, you know someone with divorce hangover.

Sarcasm When someone mentions the ex-spouse, _____ is sarcastic or takes potshots at the former partner. The sarcasm may be focused on the marriage in particular or applied to all relationships: "All men leave the minute their wives turn forty" or "All women are just after their husbands' money."

Using the children _____ tries to convince the children that the divorce was entirely the other person's fault and may grill the children for information about the other parent.

Lashing out _____ may try to assert control in such ways as making unreasonable demands (for example, refusing joint custody) or blowing up at a friend because the ex-spouse was invited to a party.

Paralysis _____ can't seem to get back on track, going back to school, getting a new job, becoming involved in new relationships, or finding new friends. Sometimes it's even hard for _____ to get up in the morning and go to work, clean the house, or return phone calls.

Holding on The ex-spouse's photograph still sits on _____'s piano, and clothing or other former possessions remain in view, keeping the ex-spouse's presence alive in _____'s daily life.

Throwing out everything Or _____ may throw away things of value—even jewelry, art, or priceless collections—that are reminders of the ex-spouse. This may suggest just as much attachment as holding on.

Blaming and finding fault Everything that went wrong in the marriage or the divorce was someone else's fault, _____ maintains. The ex-spouse was responsible—or his or her family or friends, his or her lover, his or her kids, his or her job, his or her golf game, and so on.

Excessive guilt _____ feels guilty about the divorce regardless of which partner left the other. _____ buys the children whatever they want and gives in to the children's or the ex-spouse's demands, however unreasonable.

Living vicariously _____ may try to live through the children by pressuring them to succeed at things in which they have no interest or particular talent and may also latch on to friends who are more successful at work than _____ or more outgoing and at ease in social functions.

Dependency To fill the void left by the ex-spouse, _____ leans heavily on other people, particularly new romantic involvements.

Divorce can be devastating when it means a loss of emotional and sexual intimacy, identity as part of a couple, financial security, self-esteem, friends, possessions, predictability, and even a home. Confronting these symptoms of divorce hangover can help a divorced person recognize and begin to overcome these losses.

Women, especially, may feel initially self-conscious about dating again. But, as a 59-year-old woman admitted, "I want the passion and excitement of a relationship" (Boss, 2001: 16).

The psychic divorce that we described earlier may continue for many years. Even when both partners know their marriage cannot be salvaged, they are often ambivalent. They may fluctuate between a sense of loss and a feeling of emancipation; they may have periods of depression punctuated with spurts of euphoria. The box "Do You Know Someone with Divorce Hangover?"

examines some of the psychological adjustments the newly divorced face.

It's not clear whether divorce lowers people's well-being, whether poorly functioning people are especially likely to divorce, or whether there's a combination of both factors. Some people are prone to psychological or interpersonal problems before divorce but exhibit additional problems after a marital breakup. For example, an aggressive husband may become physically abusive with new partners after a divorce. In other cases, long-standing problems such as infidelity and substance abuse play a major role in dissolving a marriage (Amato, 2002).

Economic and Financial Changes

Although both men and women undergo psychological adjustments after a divorce, one's sex has a dramatic impact on economic status. As one accountant noted, "The man usually walks out with the most valuable asset, earning ability, while the woman walks out with the biggest cash drain, the kids and house" (Gutner, 2000).

Most often this change reflects low educational attainment, which may limit a woman to low-paying jobs in the service sector. Also, having a young child makes it difficult for a woman to find full-time employment and may limit her to part-time jobs that have more flexible hours (Smock, 1993). On the other hand, although many men are financially able to support their children, they don't do so, especially if they disagree with the child-custody arrangements (Finkel and Roberts, 1994).

In 1997, Lorna Wendt, the wife of a wealthy General Electric corporate executive, rejected a $10 million settlement after her husband of 32 years sought a divorce. Ms. Wendt went to court, arguing that she was worth more as a full-time homemaker because she had raised their children single-handedly, entertained her husband's business associates, and made numerous business-related trips in 40 countries to support her husband's career. The judge awarded her half of the marital estate—worth about $100 million. In 1998, Wendt founded the Institute for Equality in Marriage (www.equalityinmarriage.org) to help women in similar circumstances.

Property Settlements and Alimony   As you saw earlier, in the past the law assumed that one partner was responsible for a marital breakup because of a transgression, such as adultery, desertion, or cruelty. No-fault divorce statutes have changed the adversarial nature of divorce and have reduced the long court battles and emotional trauma associated with establishing fault as grounds for divorce.

Alimony is less common than in the past, but it still exists. In some states, and even if the wife is employed and the couple is childless, the higher earner, usually the man, may pay up to a third of his salary to his ex-wife for several years if they've been married longer than ten years or if a spouse is deemed physically or emotionally unhealthy.

Family Income   According to some observers, no-fault divorce has done more harm than good to many women. Because both partners are now treated as equals, each, theoretically at least, receives half of the family assets, and the ex-wife is expected to support

herself regardless of whether she has any job experience or work-related skills. Typically, the economic well-being of mothers declines by 36 percent and the financial status of fathers improves by 28 percent (Bianchi et al., 1999). Whether a couple has children or not, the woman must often fight for a portion of an ex-husband's retirement income that was earned during the marriage (Tergeson, 2001).

Although young men, particularly minority men, may not be faring well economically themselves, women's post-divorce financial welfare is significantly lower than men's for all racial-ethnic groups (Smock, 1994). For example, Stroup and Pollock (1999) found that the average incomes for Latino married and divorced men were essentially the same. In contrast, Latinas experienced a loss of about 24 percent of their income after a divorce. Those who were the most economically vulnerable included mothers with responsibilities for young children and who were employed in low-wage jobs.

Many women's incomes plunge because in 85 percent of all divorce cases, the children live with the mother (Grall, 2002). Even if both parents have child custody rights, child support payments rarely meet the mothers' and children's living expenses. Let's look at child custody first and then examine child support issues.

Custody Issues

Children often are caught in the middle of custody battles:

> **Mark, age eight:** *"I don't think either one of them should get me. All they ever do is fight and yell at each other. I'd rather live with my grandma."*
>
> **David, age five:** *"Dad says he wants me there but every time we go over all he does is watch football and drink beer. I don't think he really wants us. I think he just says that to make Mommy mad."*
>
> **Mary, age ten:** *"I hate going to my dad's because every time I come back I get the third degree from Mom about what we did and who was there and whether Dad did anything wrong or anything that made us mad. I feel like a snitch."*
>
> **Robin, age seven:** *"Mom wants me to live with her and Dad wants me to live with him. But I want to live with both of them. Why do I have to choose? I just want us to be happy again."*
> (Everett and Everett, 1994: 84–85)

Custody is a court-mandated ruling as to which parent will have primary responsibility for the welfare and upbringing of a couple's children. Children live with a custodial parent, whereas they see the noncustodial parent according to specific visitation schedules worked out in the custody agreement. Approximately 90 percent of all divorces are not contested but are settled out of court through negotiations (Clarke, 1995a).

When men sue, they win either sole or joint custody in 40 to 70 percent of cases (Burke, 2002). This is why divorce attorneys sometimes advise their male clients to wage an all-out battle for custody, even when they don't want it, simply as a bargaining chip in negotiations over child support.

Mothers, afraid of losing custody, often agree to a modest alimony or child-support arrangement (Winner, 1996). Some mothers relinquish custody at the time of divorce or shortly thereafter for a variety of reasons: They feel they can't support the children financially, they experience emotional problems because life becomes tumultuous and mothers feel they're "falling apart," they want to avoid the threat of a legal custody fight, or they're in an abusive relationship with a mate who threatens to harm the children if the mother fights for custody (Herrerías, 1995).

Types of Custody   There are three types of custody: sole custody, split custody, and joint custody. In **sole** custody (about 81 percent of cases), one parent has sole responsibility for raising the child; the other parent has specified visitation rights. Parents may negotiate informally over such things as schedules or holidays, but if they disagree, the legal custodian has the right to make the final decisions.

In **split custody** (about 2 percent of cases), the children are divided between the parents either by gender (the mother gets the daughters and the father gets the sons) or by choice (the children are allowed to choose the parent with whom they want to live).

In **joint custody**, sometimes called *dual residence* (about 16 percent of cases), the children divide their time between parents, who share in the decisions about their upbringing. In another 1 percent of cases, custody is awarded to someone other than the husband or wife, such as a relative (Clarke, 1995a).

There are two types of joint custody. In *joint legal custody*, both parents share decision making on such issues as the child's education, health care, and religious training. In *joint physical custody*, the court specifies how much time children will spend in each parent's home.

Pros and Cons of Joint Custody   Joint custody is a heated issue—a "politically charged minefield," according to one author (Mason, 1999)—because fathers' rights groups and many women are on opposite sides of the battlefield. In addition, and as you'll see shortly, studies show mixed effects in the outcomes of joint custody.

Proponents advance several arguments. First, they maintain that men and women should have equal child-rearing responsibilities, both during marriage and after divorce. Second, many men say they want to care for their children and have formed organizations such as Fathers United for Equal Justice to lobby in almost every state for joint-custody laws. Third, much research indicates that the relationship between a noncustodial father and his children is critical in the children's development (Hetherington and Stanley-Hagan, 1997). Finally, a joint-custody arrangement lightens the responsibility of each parent and eases the economic burdens of parenting, particularly for mothers (Irving and Benjamin, 1991).

Opponents of joint custody argue that it creates loyalty conflicts for children and worsens postdivorce conflicts between ex-spouses, who may disagree on child-rearing practices (Ferreiro, 1990). Parents who argued frequently before they divorced are likely to continue. Therefore, children may still have to deal with parental conflict (Maccoby et al., 1991). Critics of joint custody also maintain that this arrangement makes it possible for men who abused their wives or children before the divorce to continue the same behavior (Fineman, 1991).

Some argue that joint custody does more harm than good. School attendance may be disrupted as children are shuttled between two homes and a school. In addition, even when fathers don't show up for scheduled visits or totally ignore their children, mothers who move out of state may lose custody of their children if they don't have the fathers' permission to move (Hoffman, 1995).

The residential parent may feel that the nonresidential parent spoils the child, uses "bad" language during the child's visitation, or does not provide an acceptable religious upbringing. The nonresidential parent, on the other hand, may feel that the residential parent argues about visitation times or changes plans on short notice. It is difficult, then, for many parents to assume coparenting outside of marriage (Wolchik et al., 1996).

Finally, some observers feel that there is a gender bias in the court system. When custody is contested, for example, courts sometimes apply a double standard: "Often, men are judged by the availability of other child care, from a second wife to a girlfriend, while women are evaluated based on their own, personal ability to be with a child, ignoring the presence of a grandmother or a babysitter" (Feldmann and Goodale, 1995: 18).

Some mothers claim that they must choose between their child and their job. In Mississippi, for example, a flight attendant whose work took her away two nights a week had to let her daughter live with her ex-husband. The judge ruled that the ex-husband's job as a Federal Express courier provided him a more regular work schedule (Steinbach, 1995). Thus, some contend, judges give fathers credit for doing even a minimal amount of parenting while criticizing mothers if they take any time at all for themselves or work outside the home (Burke, 2002).

What Should Courts Do?

Research doesn't provide a clear-cut answer to this question. Some researchers find that noncustodial fathers often are "Disneyland dads" who are more likely to engage in leisure activities with their children (picnics, movies, sports) than to participate in school events or supervise homework. Talking to kids about things at school provides a "safe way" for nonresident fathers and children to communicate, giving fathers a window on the children's daily activities and concerns, and children a chance to vent. Participating in leisure activities in contrast, does little to enhance a child's well-being (Stewart, 2003).

Other research shows that joint custody works well if both parents act like adults. If there is little interparental conflict and both parents manage the separate households, set rules, and supervise their children, most adolescents adjust to joint legal custody with few problems (Buchanan et al., 1996; Braver and O'Connell, 1998). The key is minimal parental conflict. If former spouses continue to have frequent disagreements, children often are troubled and exhibit more behavior problems (Lee, 2002).

Joint legal custody also seems to work well if the custodial mother encourages coparental interaction and supports the father–child relationship after divorce. In these situations, joint legal custody facilitates divorced fathers' parenting role in two ways. It increases a father's sense of control and influence as a parent. In addition, it allows fathers to maintain their legal authority as parents. These benefits increase a father's satisfaction with his parenting performance and coparental interaction (Madden-Derdich and Leonard, 2000; Bauserman, 2002).

In some cases, fathers get child custody by "default:" A biological mother doesn't want to raise the children, child protective agencies seek the father's involvement, or a child wants to live with the father. Even in impoverished communities, fathers often enjoy raising their children: "It's the best part of who I am," according to one father. However, they must often rely on fictive and biological kin for childrearing support because of inflexible work schedules and low wages (Hamer and Marchioro, 2002: 126).

Custody among Gay Parents

Gay parents face ongoing problems in custody and visitation rights. In many cases, judges still assume that gay and lesbian households don't constitute a family, even when the mother or father provides evidence of good parenting. Judges may deem gay and lesbian parents unfit because of their sexual orientation and despite a child's preference to live with a gay rather than a heterosexual parent (Duran-Aydintug and Causey, 1996; Stein, 1996).

Recently, courts in Maryland, Massachusetts, and New Jersey have ruled that ex-partners in gay and lesbian relationships can have visitation rights similar to those of divorced couples. In Maryland, the appeals court allowed visitation with a 5-year-old girl because it viewed the lesbian ex-partner as having a similar legal standing to a stepparent (Siegel, 2000). In many states, however, gay parents must still fight for custody or visitation.

Child Abduction

When parents don't get custody, they might abduct their children. **Child abduction** is the taking or keeping of a child by a family member in violation of a custody order, a decree, or other legitimate custodial right. The estimated 203,900 children who were victims of a family abduction in 1999 (the most recent year for these statistics) "represent a large group of children caught up in divisive and potentially disturbing family dynamics" (Hammer et al., 2002: 9).

Of all "missing" children, 1.3 million (9 percent) were family abductions (Sedlak et al., 2002). In family abduction cases, 44 percent of the children are younger than age 6, 53 percent are snatched by their biological fathers, and 46 percent are gone less than a week. In most cases, the custodial parent knows the ex-spouse's and the children's whereabouts. In 6 percent of cases, however, the parent who abducts the child or children "disappears" (Hammer et al., 2002).

Child custody is a prickly issue. Child support is even more volatile and has very negative outcomes over the life course.

Child Support

Nearly 50 percent of all men neither see nor support their children after a divorce (Sorensen and Zibman, 2000). In fact, two-thirds of noncustodial fathers spend more on car payments than they do for child support (Kitson and Holmes, 1992). Others ignore their children entirely, including not buying birthday presents (Garfinkel et al., 1994).

Demographic Characteristics of Custodial Parents

In 2000, an estimated 14 million parents had custody of 22 million children under age 21 whose other parent lived elsewhere. Women made up 85 percent of all custodial parents. Among all custodial mothers, 54 percent were white, 28 percent black, and 15 percent Latinas. The proportion of custodial parents and their children living below the poverty level decreased between 1993 and 1999 (Grall, 2002). Custodial mothers are still almost three times as likely as custodial fathers to be poor (see *Figure 15.4*).

Only 59 percent of custodial parents had child-support agreements in 2000. The average amount of child support that custodial parents received was $3787 a year: $3800 by custodial mothers and $3200 by custodial fathers.

Besides financial payment, many noncustodial parents also provide noncash support. More than half of all custodial parents receive such noncash support as birthday, holiday, or other gifts (57 percent), clothes for the children (39 percent), food and groceries (27 percent),

medical assistance other than health insurance (19 percent), or partial or full payments for child care or summer camp (9 percent) (Grall, 2002).

Even when child support is awarded, the payments vary. As *Figure 15.5* shows, custodial mothers with the highest child-support payments tend to be white or Latinas, are divorced, and have some college education. In contrast, those with the lowest payments are black, have never been married, and are high school dropouts. These figures suggest that women with greater resources, such as a college degree, are able to collect more financial support, may have ex-husbands who can provide more support, or are more aggressive about getting court-ordered awards.

Child Support and Visitation Noncustodial parents (who are typically men) are more likely to pay full or partial child support when they have joint custody and visitation rights. About 85 percent of custodial parents with these arrangements received full or partial support payments in 1999, compared with only 46 percent of those without shared custody or visitation rights (Grall, 2002).

Both interpersonal and other micro variables help explain why noncustodial parents, especially the majority of fathers, don't comply with child-support orders. According to Nuta (1986), for example, nonpaying fathers fall into four major categories:

- The *parent in pain* may feel shut out of the family and distance himself physically or emotionally from his children. He may even rationalize his distancing ("She turned them against me"). Other fathers are angry if they feel that visitation rights are unfair.

- The *overextended parent* is overburdened with financial obligations. Anxious to get out of his marriage as soon as possible, he may agree to pay more support than he can afford. He may remarry and, unable to support two families, fail to provide for the children of his first marriage (Manning et al., 2003). Or he may become ill and unemployed and thus unable to make the child-support payments.

- The *vengeful parent* uses child support as a form of control. He may use nonpayment to change a visitation agreement or to punish his wife for initiating the divorce.

- The *irresponsible parent*, representing the greatest number of child-support dodgers, simply does not take his parental duties seriously. He may expect others to take care of his family ("Welfare will pay" or "Her family has more money than I do"), or he may think that taking care of himself is more important than providing for his children. The irresponsible parent includes noncustodial

FIGURE 15.4 **Poverty of Custodial Parents: 1993–2000**

SOURCE: Grall, 2002: Figure 1.

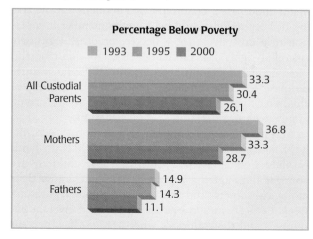

Percentage Below Poverty

■ 1993 ■ 1995 ■ 2000

All Custodial Parents: 33.3, 30.4, 26.1

Mothers: 36.8, 33.3, 28.7

Fathers: 14.9, 14.3, 11.1

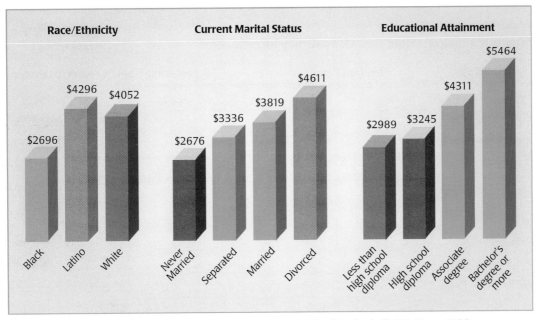

FIGURE 15.5 **Average Yearly Child Support Payments Received by Custodial Mothers: 1999**

SOURCE: Based on Grall, 2002: Table 5.

parents with psychological and drug abuse problems who do not seek employment or cannot keep a job (Dion et al., 1997).

Child Support Enforcement In 1984, Congress passed the Child Support Enforcement Amendments that require states to deduct delinquent support from fathers' paychecks and tax returns. The Family Support Act of 1988 authorizes judges to use their discretion when support agreements cannot be met as, for example, when a father is unemployed and cannot pay child support. This act also mandates periodic reviews of award levels to keep up with the rate of inflation. Because many divorced fathers rarely provide for their children through means other than child support, court-ordered awards often are the only monetary contributions that many fathers make (Paasch and Teachman, 1991).

Court-ordered child support has several problems, however. Sometimes attorneys advise their clients to trade child-support payments for property settlements. For example, a mother may agree to minimal monthly child-support payments in exchange for ownership of the house. Before long the custodial parent may realize that the child support is inadequate because she is having difficulty meeting the monthly mortgage payments. Going back to court to increase payments or to collect delinquent payments may be time-consuming and very expensive.

Another problem arises from the discretionary nature of the judicial system. Custodial parents in similar economic circumstances may find themselves with very different support payments depending on how capable their attorneys are in presenting the case and whether a judge is sympathetic to the custodial parent's financial situation (Wong, 1993; Chisholm and Driedger, 1994).

States also vary a great deal in enforcing child-support laws. Never-married low-income fathers with less than a high school education are the least likely to have support agreements or to fulfill them. In a study of noncustodial fathers, Folse (1997) found that compared with their white and black counterparts, many Latino fathers want to maintain ties with their children. Their good intentions, however, are often stymied by child enforcement systems that penalize fathers who don't have steady employment. The divorced fathers in Folse's study also complained that child-support bureaucracies are sympathetic to mothers but ignore fathers. As a result, Folse suggests, even well-intentioned fathers may lose contact with their children after a divorce.

As you might expect, ex-spouses who have good relationships with their former partners are more likely to receive court-ordered child-support awards than are those who are not on good terms. In Folse's study, noncustodial Latino fathers who had hostile relationships with their ex-wives accused them of sabotaging the fathers' efforts to see their children. Thus, good parental relationships appear critical in determining whether the children of divorced parents get economic and emotional assistance from their fathers (Garfinkel et al., 1994).

Some observers suggest that enforcing child-support payment laws will alleviate but not end poverty in single-mother homes. According to Amott (1993), for example, poverty in divorced-mother households will

TABLE 15.1

Living Arrangements of Children under Age 18, by Family Income, 1995

Race and Living Arrangement	Median Family Income	Percentage below Poverty Level
White families		
Living with both parents	$47,048	10%
Living with divorced mother	18,633	36
Living with divorced father	29,894	17
Black families		
Living with both parents	39,355	15
Living with divorced mother	15,662	47
Living with divorced father	16,784	38
Latino families		
Living with both parents	26,934	31
Living with divorced mother	11,926	58
Living with divorced father	30,111	35

SOURCE: Based on Saluter, 1996, Table 6.

diminish only when women's earnings are comparable to those of men.

Are Men Deadbeat Dads? As you saw earlier, children living in never-married mother-only homes are more economically disadvantaged than those living with divorced mothers (see *Figure 15.5*). As *Table 15.1* shows, 38 percent of all children living in divorced-mother households live below the poverty level, compared with 19 percent of children living in divorced-father households and 11 percent of those living in two-parent families.

In white homes, especially, children living with divorced fathers fare much better economically than children living with divorced mothers. In black families, the median family income is less than 50 percent as much as when children live with a divorced mother or a divorced father rather than with both parents. The percentage of children living below the poverty level increases dramatically in both divorced-father and divorced-mother homes.

Many middle-class parents, especially fathers, avoid child-support payments because they don't agree with the visitation rights or feel that their ex-wives are squeezing them for money. Among low-income fathers, however, many fathers are "dead broke" rather than "deadbeat dads." For example, a typical unmarried father earns about $17,000 a year. With such low earnings, it's difficult for fathers to meet court-ordered child support payments that might consume 65 percent of their wages (Talvi, 2002).

Many mothers feel that such child-support payments are fair because they and their children are living at or below the poverty level (see Chapter 13). However, many analysts argue that the United States doesn't provide job training, placement, or employment opportunities for low-income fathers who could then support their children (Primus and Daugirdas, 2000).

MAKING CONNECTIONS

■ Judges have vast discretion in divorce proceedings, which vary from state to state and from case to case. The American Law Institute has proposed, instead, that a court should grant child custody to parents in proportion to the amount of time they spent caring for a child before divorce. Do you agree with this proposal?

■ Some states have passed laws to include college expenses in setting child-support payments in divorce cases (Morgan, 2002). Do such laws give an unfair advantage to children from divorced families compared with intact families?

How Divorce Affects Children

Divorce is beneficial for some children but harmful for most. The harmful effects often decrease within two to

CONSTRAINTS

Children of Divorce

The way a couple deals with divorce may have long-term effects on their children. After interviewing adult children of divorce about their memories of their parents' divorce and their current behaviors and lifestyles, Fassel (1991) proposed five types of divorce and their subsequent effects on children:

The Disappearing Parent Suddenly, one parent leaves the home, and the children receive little explanation beyond "Your mother and I were divorced today." Adult children who recalled this situation often grew up suspicious of people, fearing that they too, would leave them. Some tried to be perfect parents to avoid hurting their own children in the ways they had been hurt.

The Surprise Divorce In this situation, parents often seemed close and open with each other, but without any warning, one filed for divorce. Adult children recalled feeling shock, bewilderment, and anger that the parent who left disrupted what they had thought was a happy family. As they grow up, children may erect walls to protect themselves, becoming distant from friends and avoiding intimate relationships because they expect a partner, like the parent who left, to be unpredictable or undependable.

The Violent Divorce Spouse abuse and, sometimes, child abuse causes many divorces. Children in such a setting don't learn how to handle anger because their role models could not handle it. The children often repress conflict for fear of violence, or they grow up believing that fighting is a way to test intimacy and to get a partner's attention.

The Late Divorce When parents stay together "for the children's sake," they often create an environment of veiled criticism and threats, unspoken anger, and even hatred. Many children in such homes learn to deny feelings just to survive, and some equate love with suffering in silence. Many are wary of commitment, which they equate with loss of freedom, and become cynical about the possibility of having a good relationship with anyone.

Protect-the-Kids Divorce Some well-intentioned parents may decide to protect their children by withholding information about the real reasons for their divorce. They don't accuse one another, they communicate well, and each listens respectfully as the other tells the children about the divorce.

Sounds good? Not necessarily. In one case, a couple told their children that their father felt the need to explore,

to be free, and to see the world. When, many years later, the children learned that their father was gay, they felt betrayed and angry.

How can divorcing couples avoid these negative outcomes for their children? Gold (1992) recommends "CPR" (a play on the abbreviation for cardiopulmonary resuscitation, an emergency procedure used to keep the heart and lungs going in case of cardiac arrest):

Continuity Introduce all changes gradually; maintain regular routines and child-rearing responsibilities as consistently as possible.

Protection Be civil with one another; don't put your children in the middle of your conflicts. Preserve your relationships with your children.

Reassurance Assure your children that you love them, that the divorce is not their fault, and that you will not abandon them. Explain your plans for them to spend time with each of you, discuss the possibility that they may have to move or change schools, and give them advance warning of any impending financial changes.

---

six years if children have "protective" factors that help their adjustment. One of the most important adjustment factors is the way parents interact and handle the divorce (see the box "Children of Divorce"). The more civilized and mature the divorce, the easier it is on children.

Absent Fathers

About 15 percent of fathers get custody of their children (Grall, 2002). In the other cases, the mothers have custody and the fathers get visitation rights. One national

study found that more than 60 percent of fathers either did not visit their children or did not visit them *and* had no telephone or mail contact with them over a one-year period (Bianchi, 1990). In a study of 1400 families, Hetherington and Kelly (2002) found that only a third of noncustodial fathers saw their children at least once a week. Nonresident mothers are more likely than nonresident fathers to maintain contact with their children by letters, telephone calls, and extended visitations (Stewart, 1999).

How important is a noncustodial father's involvement to his children's well-being? The findings are mixed.

Divorced fathers can maintain close relationships with their children by seeing them as often as posssible, setting rules, discussing problems, and providing guidance.

There is much evidence that the father's payment of child support benefits the children's educational achievement. For example, children supported by such payments are more likely to finish high school and to enter college (Graham et al., 1994; Knox and Bane, 1994). Regular payments may also increase children's academic well-being because mothers, feeling more financially secure, are able to deal better with school-related problems (McLanahan et al., 1994).

When child-support payments are voluntary, fathers have better relationships with their children and ex-spouses. The lack of parental conflict, which is ordinarily distressing and distracting, helps children focus on academic pursuits (Baydar and Brooks-Gunn, 1994).

There is less evidence that visits from a noncustodial father have beneficial effects on the child's emotional and behavioral well-being. Within a few years, children adapt to a father's absence, and some behavioral problems, especially among boys, decrease (Mott et al., 1997).

Children (and mothers) are better off having minimal contact with nonresident fathers if the fathers are abusive, fight with their ex-wives, or have other problems (King, 1994). For example, some fathers may abuse alcohol, some may be too depressed after a divorce to maintain meaningful ties with their children, some may feel that they are losing control over their children, and some may have developed closer relationships with new

partners and their children (Aseltine and Kessler, 1993; Umberson and Williams, 1993).

Divorced fathers can also enhance their children's development. For example, fathers who maintain close ties with their offspring can reestablish the children's trust in the fathers and other adults (King, 2002). Maintaining ties with one's children takes time and effort, however. Practitioners suggest that fathers can take specific steps to ensure the continuity of their relationship with their children:

■ A father should be guided by his child's developmental needs. For example, because toddlers' sense of time is different from that of adults and because their memories are shorter, it's better for a father to make frequent brief visits than long visits with less frequency. On the other hand, older children who are settled comfortably in social and school activities need more visitation flexibility.

■ A father should live close to his children if possible, especially when they are young. Furthermore, regardless of whether he and his former wife are friendly, he should not stop seeing his children. He should be with his children whenever he can, whether he is changing their diapers or helping them with their homework.

■ A father should pay child support regularly. Skipping payments not only deprives the child of material things but also lowers the father's self-respect. At the same time, a father should not overindulge his children; children of *all* ages expect a parent to establish limits for them.

■ A father should not cross-examine his children or dwell on the divorce. His job is to figure out how he and the children can fit into one another's lives and then make that happen (Pruett, 1987).

Crisis need *not* spawn failure. Although divorce often is sad and difficult for all concerned, the rewards are immeasurable when a father perseveres in maintaining close ties with his children.

Parents as Peers

A 23-year-old daughter recently complained to "Dear Ann," the advice columnist, that her divorced mother had started to treat her less like a daughter and more like a girlfriend: "She has told me some hair-raising stories about her sexual escapades, and now she keeps pressing me for details about my sex life. . . . I don't want to hear all the personal stuff she tells me" (Dear Ann, 2001: C7).

As this example illustrates, divorced parents sometimes make the mistake of treating their children like peers. Particularly if the children are bright and verbal, a parent may see them as being more mature than they really are. Mothers, who usually have custody, often share their feelings on a wide range of personal issues. They may express bitterness toward their ex-husbands, anger at men in general, or frustration over financial concerns or social isolation.

In response, children may console the parent and appear concerned and caring, but they may also feel anger, resentment, sadness, or guilt. According to a 15-year-old girl, for example,

> *Don't look to kids for emotional support. I was going through so much of my own emotional hell that my mom leaning on me was the last thing that I wanted, and it made me very, very resentful of her. My mom tried to use me as her confidant for all the bad stuff my dad did to her, but she refused to see that he was still my dad, and I still loved him (S. Evans, 2000: C4).*

Children might manifest their anger and resentment through psychosomatic problems such as stomach pains, sleeping or eating problems, sexual or other aggression, or drug use. They may be truant from school, exhibit a decline in academic performance, or run away. They may appear overcompliant with parental requests or simply withdraw (Devall et al., 1986; Glenwick and Mowrey, 1986).

Despite these findings, some researchers maintain that the mother–child "lean on me" relationship sometimes works well. For example, in a study of 58 first-year college students, Arditti (1999) concluded that mothers' leaning on children for emotional support and advice during and after a divorce contributed to a sense of equality, closeness, and friendliness. And in a study of adolescents from divorced families, Buchanan et al. (1996) found that parents' confiding in their adolescents had no negative effect unless the parent conveyed weakness, vulnerability, and a need for the adolescent to be strong—to be the caretaker.

Regardless of the message parents think they're conveying to children, an especially sensitive or responsible child (often a girl) who is "parentified" during a divorce may find it difficult to focus on her (or his) own individual growth:

> *Many a time the only time Mom talked to Dad, and vice-versa, was through messages sent through me. Even my brother and sister saw the advantages in using me as a courier in getting the things they wanted. . . . I would feel an overwhelming sense of loneliness and desperation, as if no one understood me or would sympathize with my struggles to keep the peace and save the family. . . . I believe I went far away to college unconsciously, but once I was here, I suffered from guilt in abandoning my family duties. . . . Now after three years I still feel anger and sadness and loneliness when I see that it is once again my duty to restore the harmony in the family (Brown and Amatea, 2000: 180).*

What Hurts Children during and after Divorce?

Although divorce increases the risk of problems such as worrying and feeling unhappy, many children of divorce don't experience these difficulties (Cherlin, 1999). Still, a large number of studies have found that children from divorced families, compared with their counterparts in married families, experience a variety of difficulties that include lower academic success, behavioral problems, a lower self-concept, and some long-term health problems (Thornberry et al., 1999; Furstenberg and Kiernan, 2001; see also Amato, 2002, for a summary of some of this research).

The differences are usually small, but they exist. Several major stressors decrease children's development and adjustment to the divorce.

Long-Term Parental Problems Typically, divorce crystallizes long-standing family problems rather than creates them. Especially for boys, achievement and behavioral problems exist well before the separation and divorce occur (Cherlin et al., 1991). Some of the processes that end in divorce begin long before marital disruption occurs. That is, partners who divorce are more likely to have poor parenting skills and high levels of marital conflict or to suffer from persistent economic stress (Furstenberg and Teitler, 1994).

Parents in these predivorce families are less involved in their children's education, have lower expectations for their children, little discussion of school-related issues, and low attendance at school events. Besides poor academic progress, the children in these families have behavior problems and low self-concepts at least three years before and after the divorce (Sun, 2001).

Quality of Parenting Poor parenting usually increases after a divorce. The problems include a lack of parental supervision, poor parent–child relationships, and open disagreements between custodial mothers and adolescents on such issues as clothes, friends, girlfriends or boyfriends, sexual behavior, and helping around the house (Buchanan et al., 1996; Demo and Acock, 1996a).

If noncustodial fathers don't play the role of parent, mere contact or even sharing good times together may not contribute to children's development (Amato, 1996). However, if nonresident fathers play an authoritative role (such as listening to children's problems, giving advice, and working together on projects), fathers and children report a close relationship (Amato and Gilbreth, 1999).

According to many studies (see text), it is not the divorce itself but parental conflict during and after a divorce that is most damaging to children.

Parental Conflict and Hostility Several studies show that interparental conflict is high before a divorce and increases after the breakup. Such conflict has negative effects on offspring that reveal themselves in behavior problems in school and the community (Vandewater and Lasford, 1998; Hetherington, 1999).

Often, it is not the divorce itself but parental attitudes during and after the divorce that affect children's behavior and their perceptions about family life. Divorcing or divorced parents may communicate negative attitudes to their children about marriage and may view cohabitation (and, consequently, premarital sex) as an attractive alternative to marriage (Axinn and Thornton, 1996). Some divorced parents may communicate sexually permissive values by expressing negative feelings about marriage and by engaging in sexual relations outside of marriage.

Economic Hardship Financial difficulties also create problems, especially after the divorce. As you saw earlier, the mother's income usually drops by about a third after the divorce. Boys may respond to income-related stress behaviorally (arguments or anger), whereas girls manifest distress in less observable ways, such as becoming more anxious or depressed (Morrison and Cherlin, 1995; Simons et al., 1999). Although the divorce may reduce domestic conflict, the financial disadvantages and related strain persist (Sun and Li, 2002).

Other Negative Life Events Divorce usually disrupts a child's life and increases the chances of developmental problems. Children may have to move (often to a poorer and more dangerous neighborhood), change schools, and become accustomed to a new community (South et al., 1998). In addition, children may have to live with a parent with whom they don't get along and lose access to a parent with whom they've had a good relationship (Videon, 2002).

Cumulative Effects of Divorce Children do not develop difficulties simply because their parents get a divorce (Simons's Associates, 1996). Divorce is disruptive and increases the chances of negative consequences for parents and children when it affects the life course in other ways. That is, if divorce interferes with continued schooling, this disadvantage cumulates through life, affecting occupational status, income, and economic well-being. People with low levels of educational attainment and high levels of economic hardship are more likely to have high levels of depression as adults and to experience unhappy or unstable interpersonal relationships (Chase-Lansdale et al., 1995; Ross and Mirowsky, 1999).

Similarly, marital dissolution increases the probability that a woman will experience economic pressures and psychological depression. This strain and emotional distress tend to reduce the quality of her parenting. Reductions in the quality of parenting, in turn, increase a child's risk of emotional and behavioral problems and poor developmental outcomes.

Despite all these stressors, 80 percent of children from divorced homes navigate through troubled waters and "eventually are able to adapt to their new life and become reasonably well adjusted" (Hetherington and Kelly, 2002: 228). Among other things, children fare well if they have protective factors during and after the divorce.

What Helps Children during and after Divorce?

The biggest advantage of divorce is that it decreases the amount of stress that children experience in a high-conflict, quarrelsome home (Booth and Amato, 2001; Videon, 2002). Although counseling helps many children, a minority of young adults develops psychiatric problems such as depression or anxiety as a result of parental divorce and needs clinical intervention.

Children who experience the least negative effects are those who get support from friends, neighbors, and schools, especially when parents are self-absorbed or depressed (Rodgers and Rose, 2002). Even if a nonresident parent isn't around, the most effective custodial parents provide many protective factors that include warmth, responsiveness, monitoring, involvement in the children's activities, and distance from the parental battleground (Leon, 2003).

Helping Children Adjust during Divorce

It bears repeating that children experience the greatest stress when they are put in the middle of their parents' conflicts. Parents do this by trying to get children to side with them, using the children to get information about the other parent, or bad mouthing a former spouse (Massey, 1992; Cummings and Davies, 1994; Schaefer and DiGeronimo, 1999). According to researchers and clinicians, parents can lessen some of these negative effects in the following ways:

■ Parents can help prepare children for the physical separation by giving them advance notice and by being around to answer their questions. They should clearly explain what divorce is to the children, including expected changes in their day-to-day experience, and they should be prepared to repeat this information several times for younger children.

■ Each parent should contribute to the explanation given the children, speaking for himself or herself, and the couple should agree ahead of time on what they will and will not reveal. The mother and the father should speak about their own feelings and perspective without criticizing the other spouse.

■ Partners should reassure children that both parents will continue to love and care for them, emphasizing that they will remain actively involved with them and that the children will always be free to love both parents.

■ Partners should not be afraid to talk about their feelings. Talking sets the stage for open communication between parents and their children. Partners can discuss their unhappiness and even their anger, but they should not blame the other parent because this will force the children to take sides.

■ Parents should modify what they say based on the children's ages. For example, younger children need more concrete examples to help them understand the nature of divorce.

■ The mother and father should emphasize that the children are not responsible for problems between the parents, pointing out that each adult is divorcing the other but not the children.

■ Parents should give the children news when they are together so that siblings can lean on one another for support. Parents should encourage children to ask questions that occur to them at any time.

■ Partners should make it clear that they have made the decision to divorce carefully, rationally, but regretfully. Expressing your own sadness encourages children to cry and mourn without having to hide their feelings of loss from you or from themselves.

■ Parents should reassure their children that they will continue to see their grandparents on both sides of the family.

■ Each parent should recognize the cries of help in their children's behavior during and after the divorce. For example, preschool children may regress to an earlier stage of their development and suck their thumbs or be afraid of the dark. They may lose their appetites and wake frequently during the night crying anxiously.

Elementary school children may suddenly show a disinterest in school or get poor grades in courses in which they previously excelled.

Adolescents may "tell" you that you need to work on your relationship with them if they suddenly begin to cut class, become verbally abusive or sexually irresponsible, defy curfew rules, or start using alcohol, cocaine, or other drugs.

■ Parents must understand that the children's fundamental need for security has not changed. The children need to feel, above all else, that Mom and Dad will always provide them with the emotional and physical security to develop into confident, mature people.

The children's security does not depend on your income or where you live but on whether you and your ex-spouse demonstrate by your behavior that both of you are fully competent to weather the storms of change that divorce entails and to shelter them from these storms (Lansky, 1989; Greif, 1990).

■ The noncustodial parent, usually the father, must maintain an ongoing relationship with the children. When noncustodial fathers maintain stable, frequent visitation, they give more advice to their children, and their adolescent children are more satisfied with their support and less likely to experience depression (Barber, 1994).

MAKING CONNECTIONS

■ What long-term effects of divorce, if any, have you experienced in your own life or observed in someone close to you?

■ Should divorced parents treat their children as peers or as children?

■ In what specific ways can parents help their children deal with divorce so it's less destructive?

Should It Be Harder to Get a Divorce?

In a recent *Time*/CNN poll, 61 percent of the respondents said it should be harder for married couples with young children to get a divorce (Kirn, 1997). High U.S. divorce rates and research show, as you've seen, that children of divorced parents have a greater likelihood of dropping out of school, getting into trouble with the law, and having children out of wedlock.

As a result, many religious and political groups are considering eliminating "revolving-door marriages" by reforming no-fault divorce laws. In 1997, for example, Louisiana passed a law that couples could sign a license for a "covenant marriage" that includes the line, "We understand that a covenant marriage is for life" (Banisky, 1997).

Those who sign the license give up the right to no-fault divorce. A couple promises to have counseling if the marriage falters and can divorce only for a limited number of reasons (including adultery, a felony conviction, abuse, and abandonment) or after a two-year separation. The purpose of the covenant marriage license

is to discourage divorce by making it more difficult to get.

Here are a few arguments from both sides of this issue:

Make Getting a Divorce More Difficult

- Simply discussing the covenant marriage option will force couples to consider their vows more seriously and to seek counseling.
- It's too easy to get a divorce.
- Couples break up over little things because a divorce is "no big deal."
- No-fault divorces disregard the interests of children.
- Ending no-fault divorce would give more rights to the partner who doesn't want a divorce.

Leave Current Divorce Laws Alone

- Covenant marriages could trap people whose spouses suffer from alcoholism or hurt low-income families with little means for counseling.

- Getting a divorce is already difficult, complicated, expensive, and stressful.
- Many couples seek therapy to keep the marriage together and stay in destructive relationships for many years.
- Children fare worse in high-conflict two-parent families than in loving single-parent families.
- Ending no-fault divorce could keep children in high-conflict homes longer and make divorce even more adversarial (Galston, 1996; Leland, 1996; Shipley, 1997; Trafford, 1997).

STOP AND THINK . . .

- *What are other advantages in making divorce harder to get? What about the disadvantages?*

- *Should we make it harder to get a divorce? Harder to get married? Both? Leave things alone?*

Some Positive Outcomes of Divorce

Much of this chapter has addressed the debilitating effects of divorce on adults and children. In response to such negative outcomes, some groups are proposing that no-fault divorce be eliminated and that divorce laws be tougher (see the box "Should It Be Harder to Get a Divorce?"). Does divorce have any positive effects?

In a highly publicized book, *The Unexpected Legacy of Divorce*, Wallerstein and her colleagues (2000) advise parents to stay in unhappy marriages to avoid hurting their children. However, such well-intentioned advice is based on a clinical study of a small group of highly dysfunctional divorced families. In contrast, most divorced couples and their children adjust and function well over time.

The major positive outcome of divorce is that it provides options for people in miserable marriages. If a divorce eliminates an unhappy, frustrating, and stressful

situation, it may improve the mental and emotional health of both ex-spouses and their children. Divorced parents who take joint-custody arrangements seriously, maintain good communication with their children and with each other, and receive support from family, friends, and the community report being physically and mentally healthier (Golby and Bretherton, 1998).

In addition, parental separation is better for children, at least in the long run, than remaining in an intact family where there is continuous conflict (Booth and Amato, 2001). Divorce can offer parents and children opportunities for personal growth, more gratifying relationships, and a more harmonious family situation (Hetherington and Kelly, 2002).

Both men and women cite gains after a divorce. Women enjoy their new-found freedom from overbearing husbands, have less money but control what they have, take pride in learning to fix things around the house, and develop self-confidence as they take on economic roles or go back to school. According to one woman, "Divorce is a happy word: I've found things that I truly love to do instead of doing things that my husband or my family thought I should like to do. I have hobbies and interests and things; I have great joy in the ways I spend my time" (Orenstein, 2001: 233).

Men have also reported benefits such as spending more money on themselves or their hobbies, learning to manage a household, having more leisure time, and dating numerous partners (Riessman, 1990). As one African American author advises black men, "While the break-up may mean broken dreams, it doesn't have to mean broken homes. It may present fresh opportunities for men to reassess their lives and learn from their mistakes. And, perhaps, they won't stumble over the same rocks" (Hutchinson, 1994: 113).

Although most adult children of divorce value marriage, they are more aware of its limitations and more accepting of alternatives to traditional family forms. Moreover, children who grow up in father-absent homes may be less pressured to conform to traditional gender roles and may instead learn more androgynous roles that will help them be better parents in adulthood (Gately and Schwebel, 1992; see also Chapter 5).

Gold (1992) and other clinicians have suggested that the positive effects of divorce can be increased if adults act like adults. For example, divorcing parents can make "divorce vows" that reinforce their commitment to their children:

- I vow to continue to provide for our children's financial and emotional welfare.

- I vow to place our children's emotional needs above my personal feelings about my former spouse.

- I vow to be fair and honest about the divorce settlement.

- I vow to support the children's relationships with my former spouse and never to do anything that might compromise that relationship.

- I vow to deal with the issues in this divorce as constructively as I know how so that we can all go forward.

Such vows may seem hokey. On the other hand, they might remind divorcing parents that continuous parental conflict is unhealthy for their children. According to one counselor,

> The kids are hearing way too much about finances and child support payments and not getting enough care. They're so tuned into their parents' conflict and the financial situation that they lose the sense that they're valued and cared for. . . . Some children are so preoccupied with parental conflict that they become incapacitated, unable to focus on any task. . . . I've seen kids in the schools

> that are so worried about their mothers or fathers that they sit in the classroom and do nothing. All their energy goes into worrying (Suro, 1997: 12).

Counseling and Divorce Mediation

Marital counseling and mediation can help some families get through divorce. Counseling and mediation are most effective for couples who aren't abusive, are not hiding assets, and are not intent on "punishing" a partner.

Counseling

Counseling can be useful for a number of reasons. Most importantly, therapists typically serve as impartial observers rather than favoring one side or the other (as attorneys do). Counselors can help parents recognize that a child is having a problem by being preoccupied with the parents' discord. Thus therapists can help divorcing parents build stronger relationships with their children.

Family practitioners assist divorcing couples and families in a number of ways: They individualize treatment programs, assist parents in learning to coparent as effectively as possible, help children cope with fears such as losing the nonresidential parent permanently, provide information on remarriage and its potential impact on the children and ex-spouse, and organize a variety of support networks (Leite and McKenry, 1996).

Women who divorced at age 40 or older report that counselors helped them to understand why they were "dumped," to get rid of the guilt, and to learn to cope with the new situation. In other cases, therapy gives some women the strength to leave abusive or alcoholic husbands (Hayes et al., 1993).

Increasingly, many jurisdictions are ordering divorcing parents to attend educational seminars with professional counselors before going to court. The purpose of the sessions is not to convince parents to stay together but to teach them about their children's emotional and developmental needs during the divorce. In other cases, counseling is a preliminary step before meeting with a mediator.

Divorce Mediation

Divorce mediation is a technique and practice in which a trained arbitrator helps the divorcing couple to come to an agreement. Some of the resolutions include custody arrangements, child support and future college expenses, and the division of marital property (which might include a house, furniture, stocks, savings accounts, retirement accounts, pension plans, cars, and computers, and even other assets such as rental property and vacation homes, debts, medical expenses, and self-employment income). Although most mediators are attorneys or mental health professionals, accountants and others are now seeking training in mediation to facilitate divorce settlements (De Witt, 1994).

Advantages Mediation will not eliminate the hurt caused by separation and divorce, but it has several advantages (see Hahn and Kleist, 2000, for a review of the conditions under which mediation is the most effective). First, mediation increases communication between spouses. It decreases the anger and does not force the children to choose sides in the divorce.

Second, mediation reduces the conflict between spouses. When parents can resolve a dispute—whether it is over a weekend visitation schedule or the division of the proceeds of an employee stock plan—without screaming at each other or exchanging bitter looks, children benefit, and parents see that they are capable of reaching an agreement.

Third, mediation creates a more cooperative attitude between parents, sparing the child from the difficult role of a go-between (Kelly, 2000).

Fourth, mediation generally reduces the time needed to negotiate the divorce settlement. A mediation settlement typically takes two to three months; a divorce obtained through a court proceeding may take two to three years.

Fifth, mediated agreements generally make it easier to accommodate changes as the children grow. For example, as a child's activities and schedule change from a Saturday morning ballet lesson at age 8 to Wednesday night driving lessons at age 15, parents can negotiate schedule changes without resorting to costly and time-consuming requests for changes in court-imposed arrangements.

Finally, mediation prevents children from being pawns or trophies in a divorce contest. The mediator's approach is "What arrangements are best for you, your spouse, and your children?" There is no room for the adversarial stance, "Which of you will win the children?" Mediation assumes that divorcing parents can work together to benefit both themselves and their children.

Mediation is more likely than litigation to make men feel satisfied with the settlement. Noncustodial fathers who used mediation were more likely than the fathers who had opted for litigation to communicate about the children with the ex-spouses frequently, to see their children more often, and to be more involved in child-related decisions (Dillon and Emery, 1996).

Disadvantages Mediation doesn't work for everyone. If one partner is savvier about finances than the other, for example, the less informed spouse may be at a disadvantage. In addition, an aggressive or more powerful spouse can be intimidating.

Another problem is that mediators may be unschooled in issues pertaining to children. Because the parent, not the child, is the client, mediation may not always serve the child's best interests (Wallerstein, 2003).

Conclusion

The greater acceptance of divorce in the late twentieth and early twenty-first centuries has created *change* in family structures. Indeed, separation and divorce now seem to have become "an intrinsic feature of modern family life rather than a temporary aberration" (Martin and Bumpass, 1989: 49). As this chapter shows, a large segment of the adult population flows in and out of marriage during the life course.

This means that people have more *choices* in leaving an unhappy marriage. Often, however, parents don't realize that what are choices for them may be *constraints* for their children, who often feel at fault, guilty, and torn between warring parents.

If parents handled divorces in more rational and civilized ways, many children would be spared the emotional pain and economic deprivation that they now suffer. Some of the pain that both parents and children experience may become even greater after parents remarry, the topic of the next chapter.

SUMMARY

1. A separation can be temporary or a permanent arrangement that precedes a divorce. In most cases, separation is a lengthy process involving four phases: preseparation, early separation, midseparation, and late separation.

2. Marital separation leads to one of three outcomes: divorce, long-term unresolved separation, or reconciliation. The outcomes of marital separation often vary by race and socioeconomic status.

3. Divorce rates increased rapidly in the 1970s, reached a plateau in the 1980s, and have decreased slightly since the mid-1990s. Whereas in the past many marriages ended because of death or desertion, in the early 2000s divorce is the most common reason for marital dissolution.

4. Women file for divorce nearly twice as often as men do. Some want to legalize men's emotional or physical absence. Others are more independent economically and

thus less inclined to tolerate husbands' extramarital affairs or other unacceptable behavior.

5. Divorce is often a long, drawn-out process. In most divorces, people go through one or more of six stages: the emotional divorce, the legal divorce, the economic divorce, the coparental divorce, the community divorce, and the psychic divorce.

6. The many reasons for divorce include such macrolevel causes as changing gender roles, such demographic variables as marriage at a young age, and such interpersonal factors as conflict over children and money.

7. Divorce has psychological, economic, and legal consequences. Because child-support awards typically are very low, many women and children plunge into poverty after a divorce.

8. There are several types of child custody: sole, split, and joint. Although most mothers receive sole custody, joint custody is becoming more common.

9. Divorce is harmful to most children. Many of the problems that lead to marital disruption begin many years before the legal breakup.

10. Counseling and divorce mediation are alternatives to the traditional adversarial approach common to the legal process. Mediated divorces tend to be less bitter and less expensive and offer each partner more input in child-custody decisions.

KEY TERMS

separation *425*	no-fault divorce *431*	split custody *440*
divorce *427*	social integration *433*	joint custody *440*
alimony *429*	custody *440*	child abduction *441*
child support *429*	sole custody *440*	divorce mediation *451*

TAKING IT FURTHER

Divorce Help and Information on the Internet

The Divorce Support Page contains links to many divorce, custody, and mediation sites, as well as divorce laws and professionals for each state.

www.divorcesupport.com

The **Association for Conflict Resolution** can refer you to a divorce mediator in your area.

www.mediators.org

The **Human Development and Family Life Education Resource Center** of the Ohio State University provides online bulletins on topics such as divorce and noncustodial fathers, guides for parents helping children with divorce, and a Web site for adolescents whose parents are divorcing.

www.hec.ohio-state.edu/famlife/bulletin/bullmain.htm

Dads at a Distance suggests ideas and activities on how to strengthen long-distance relationships with children.

www.daads.com

Divorce Helpline is aimed at helping couples reduce conflict and stay out of court and includes materials to minimize the need for a lawyer.

www.divorcehelp.com

And more: www.prenhall.com/benokraitis provides links to bulletin boards to post divorce-related questions, lobby groups to reform divorce laws, state-by-state information on divorce, chat rooms, academic resources, and online do-it-yourself divorce sites.

INVESTIGATE WITH RESEARCH NAVIGATOR

Please go to www.researchnavigator.com and enter your LOGIN NAME and PASSWORD. For instructions on registering for the first time, please view the detailed instructions at the end of the Chapter 1. Please search the Research Navigator™ site using the following key search terms:

child custody
divorce
separation

Remarriage and Stepfamilies:
Life after Divorce

DATADIGEST

- The U.S. Census Bureau estimates that **stepfamilies will outnumber traditional nuclear families by the year 2007.**

- **One out of three Americans** is now a stepparent, a stepchild, a stepsibling, or some other member of a stepfamily.

- Within three years of divorce, **50 percent of people remarry.** Remarriage rates are highest among white women and lowest among black women.

- About 3 percent of Americans have been **married three or more times.**

- **Fewer than 5 percent of all remarried couples have three sets of children:** yours, mine, and ours.

SOURCES: Larson, 1992; Clarke, 1995a; Herbert, 1999; Bramlett and Mosher, 2002; Kreider and Fields, 2002.

Even with rising divorce rates, most people aren't disillusioned about marriage. Indeed, many divorced people remarry, some more than once. When this happens, new family relationships can become intricate. Listen to a woman who married a widower describe her multifaceted family relationships shortly before the marriage of her stepdaughter. Both had children from previous marriages:

> Ed will be my stepson-in-law, but there's no simple way to state the relationships between his daughter, Amy, and me. . . . Amy becomes my husband's stepgranddaughter, his daughter's stepdaughter, his granddaughters' stepsister or his son-in-law's daughter. But to me, the linguistic link is truly unwieldy: my husband's stepgranddaughter, my stepdaughter's stepdaughter, my stepgrandchildren's stepsister! (Borst, 1996, p. 16).

Because not all remarried couples have children from previous marriages, we'll discuss remarriage and stepfamilies separately. Quite clearly, though, the two family forms overlap.

This chapter examines the prevalence and characteristics of remarriages and stepfamilies, their varied structures, stepfamily development, key relationships in stepfamilies, and some characteristics of happy stepfamilies. Let's begin with courtship after divorce, the step before remarriage and forming a stepfamily.

Courtship after Divorce

Often partners start dating again even before the divorce is legally final. To insulate themselves from the pain of divorce, many people rush into another relationship: "It's not unusual to see women and men frantically dating in the first year after their separation, trying to fill

Reprinted with permission. All rights reserved.

the void with an intense new love or even with just another warm body" (Ahrons, 1994: 65).

If the partners are young and have not been married very long, reentering the "dating scene" is fairly easy. Dating and courtship may be more awkward for older people or for those who have been married a long time because they may feel uneasy about the marriage market (see Chapter 8). For example, one of my friends, a woman who divorced after 12 years of marriage, wanted to pursue new relationships but was very anxious about dating: "Am I supposed to pay for myself when we go to dinner? Should I just meet him at the restaurant, or do men still pick women up? What if he wants to jump into bed after the first date?"

As people age, they may become more concerned about their physical appearance. Feeling nervous about intimacy is a big reason for staying on the dating sidelines. According to a 53-year-old recently divorced man, for example, "I don't like even like looking at me naked anymore" (Mahoney, 2003).

Although all dating couples—whether or not they have been married previously—often express similar concerns, people who have not been dating for many years are often more apprehensive. They tend to feel that their dating skills are "rusty." They are often less self-confident in approaching new relationships because they believe they "failed" in their marriages. They may even avoid dating altogether or marry on the rebound. Some parents who date frequently may feel guilty about being unavailable to their children.

Custodial mothers sometimes rush into a new marriage because they want their children to have a father figure and a male role model. Men may see mothers as less attractive dating partners, however, because they don't want parental responsibilities.

Although some custodial parents delay dating because they believe it will further disrupt their children's

lives, postponing dating may increase future problems. According to one study, for example, the more time children spend in a single-parent household, the more likely it is that a stepfather and his stepchildren will experience difficulties in their relationships (Montgomery et al., 1992).

Why does this happen? Daily family routines become more entrenched as time goes by, and changing the rules may be especially stressful for young adolescents. It may be less disruptive for children to move into a remarriage household quickly after a divorce than to establish a stable single-parent household, only to have that stability disrupted by another transition. In addition, divorced mothers often rely on their children—especially their daughters—for emotional support. The stronger this dependency becomes, the more difficult it may be for a daughter to accept the loss of her role as her mother's confidante and supporter (see Chapter 15).

Some people may rush through the courtship process because they feel they are running out of time or are desperate for financial or child-rearing help. Others may feel that they don't need as much time to get to know each other because they have learned from past mistakes. As you'll see later in this chapter, high redivorce rates show that such assumptions are often wrong.

Not all courtship ends in a remarriage. Some stepfamilies are formed through remarriage, but others are cohabiting stepfamily households. What, then, is a stepfamily? And how common is remarriage?

What Is a Stepfamily? How Common Is Remarriage?

In the past, sociologists defined a *stepfamily* as a household in which at least one of the spouses had a child from a previous marriage (Visher and Visher, 1988). Increasingly, however, sociologists are including cohabitants and their children in both gay and heterosexual unions in a definition of a stepfamily (Coleman et al., 2001).

What is a Stepfamily?

A **stepfamily** is a household in which two adults are married or cohabiting and at least one of the adults has a child. As in the case of defining *family* (see Chapter 1), not everyone, including some social scientists, would agree with this definition because it includes cohabitors. Nonetheless, this definition is more inclusive because it incorporates many low-income households where one or both adults have never been married but the family functions very much like a "traditional" stepfamily (Bumpass et al., 1995).

Sometimes reporters use terms such as *blended family*, *reconstituted family*, and *binuclear family* interchangeably with *stepfamily*. However, *reconstituted* and *binuclear* are awkward, and family sociologists rarely use these terms (Kelley, 1996).

Some researchers (including those at the U.S. Census Bureau) use *blended family*, but the leaders of some stepfamily organizations disagree. For example, according to Margorie Engel (2000), the founder and president of the Stepfamily Association of America, stepfamilies don't "blend." Instead, families expand, there are several parents and divided loyalties, and families must deal, realistically, in adjusting to a new family structure.

Some stepfamilies are formed through cohabitation, but many are the result of remarriage. How often do couples remarry?

How Common Is Remarriage?

Remarriage has spawned an industry of services, magazines and books. *Bride Again* magazine, for example, aimed at "encore brides" who marry again and again, is booming.

The U.S. remarriage rate, the highest in the world, has been erratic. It peaked in the mid-1940s, continued in the 1950s and 1960s, and has declined steadily since about 1967 (see *Figure 16.1*). The rate is still high, however. More than 40 percent of all marriages are remarriages for one or both partners (Coleman and Ganong, 1991). About 13 percent of women and men have been married twice, and 3 percent have married three or more times (Kreider and Fields, 2002).

The increase in divorce and remarriage rates has important implications for family structure and family roles in the future. For example, whereas 70- to 85-year-olds today have 2.4 biological children on average, by 2030 that group will average only 1.6 biological children. Since 1980, the ratio of biological children to stepchildren for people 70 to 85 has doubled and is expected to rise by another 50 percent by 2030 (Wachter, 1997).

This means that the baby-boom generation (see Chapters 1, 3, and 13) will have to rely more on stepchildren and stepgrandchildren rather than biological children and biological grandchildren for caregiving when the boomers reach 70 to 85 and experience incapacitation. So, be nice to your steprelatives. (We'll examine aging and caregiving in Chapter 17.)

Cohabitation, divorce, remarriage, and stepfamilies have created a variety of family structures. Despite the variations, researchers have uncovered some common characteristics of remarried couples and stepfamilies. We'll look at remarriages first and then examine stepfamilies.

Characteristics of Remarried Couples

Many factors affect people's decision to remarry. They include age, sex, race and ethnicity, social class, and the

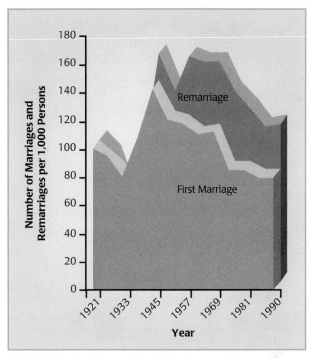

FIGURE 16.1 **Rates of First Marriage and Remarriage, 1921–1990** These data are based on numbers of first marriages per 1,000 single women between ages 15 and 44 and the numbers of remarriages per 1,000 widowed or divorced women between ages 15 and 54.

SOURCE: Norton and Miller, 1992, p. 2.

marital status of potential partners. These variables usually interact to explain remarriage rates.

Age and Sex

The average age of a divorced woman who remarries for the first time is 32; the average age of a divorced man is 34 (Kreider and Fields, 2002). Typically, both men and women have been divorced for about three years before remarrying the first time, but men remarry more quickly than women.

Because divorced men rarely have custody of their children, they are usually freer to socialize and to date. As you saw in Chapter 8, they also have a larger pool of eligible partners. The older a woman is, the harder it is for her to attract a man to marry (see Chapters 5, 7, and 10).

The women most likely to remarry are those who married at a young age the first time, who have few marketable skills, and who want children (Wu, 1994). These women are especially attractive to older divorced (or widowed) men who want a traditional wife who "sparks" their lives. For example, Antonio, a 40-year-old divorced man who married Marisa, 22, says that

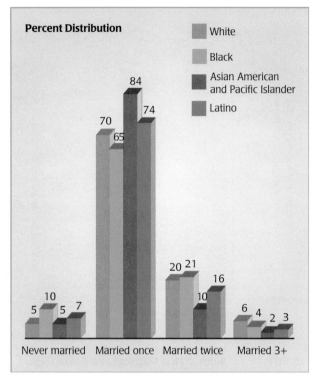

FIGURE 16.2   **How Often Do We Marry?**

Note: These figures show the number of times people age 45 and over have married.

Source: Kreider and Fields, 2002: Figure 3.

he loves it despite the family complexity that the marriage and having a child have created:

> *"She was like a Barbie to me," recalls Antonio, a department manager at a Target store. . . . Marisa's attentions made him "feel young again," he said. . . . One of his daughters from his first marriage is two years younger than his second wife. Another daughter has married his wife's brother—making her both his daughter and sister-in-law. "We're all one happy family," he says, bouncing his toddler son on his lap (Herrmann, 2003: 6).*

Remarriage rates decline with age for both men and women. Some people find lasting happiness with new partners. Other remarried couples have fewer marital conflicts because they don't have young children who refuse to accept a stepparent or because the couple marries when the children are out of the house and on their own. Still others, especially women, may stay with a husband because they feel that they have few prospective partners and don't want to be alone in their aging years (see Chapter 17).

Race and Ethnicity

As *Figure 16.2* shows, 21 percent of African Americans have married twice, compared with 20 percent of whites, 16 percent of Latinos, and only 10 percent of Asian Americans. In terms of actual numbers, however, African Americans and Latinos remarry less frequently than whites (Coleman et al., 2002). African Americans are also more likely than other groups to separate without divorcing and to stay single longer after a divorce (Ganong and Coleman, 1994; see also Chapter 15).

One of the most significant trends of the last few decades is that women are less likely to remarry than in the past. For example, only 50 percent of divorced women remarry within five years, compared with 67 percent in the 1950s. African American women, especially, are less likely to remarry after a divorce than women in other racial-ethnic groups. Five years after divorce, for example, the probability of remarriage is 58 percent for white women, 44 percent for Latinas, and only 32 percent for black women (Bramlett and Mosher, 2002).

Why do African American women have lower remarriage rates? The reasons are similar to those for high divorce rates (see Chapter 15). That is, college-educated black women have a small pool of eligible partners because many college-educated black men are marrying women with lower educational levels and some are marrying and remarrying across racial-ethnic boundaries.

Because of the large pool of eligible partners, many black men marry younger and less educated women, who exchange their youth and attractiveness for an older man's economic security (see Chapter 9). In addition, black women with low socioeconomic status have little to gain if they remarry men who are unemployed or have few economic prospects for the future (see Chapter 10).

Social Class

In general, the more wealth a divorced man has, the more likely he is to remarry. In the marriage market, men tend to be "worth more" than women of the same age because they are usually financially better off (see Chapters 10 and 11). Divorced women, on the other hand, often have severe financial problems (see Chapter 15).

For many women, then, the surest way to escape poverty is to remarry (Folk et al., 1992). Not surprisingly, less-educated, low-income divorcees are more likely to remarry than divorced women who are older, highly educated, and financially independent (Ganong and Coleman, 1994).

In his Canadian study, Wu (1994) found that men with high educational attainment were more likely to remarry than their female counterparts. Wu notes that although women with higher socioeconomic standing are more eligible remarriage candidates and are likely to attract more desirable marriage partners, they have less to gain from remarriage because they are often economically independent. Moreover, highly educated women have a smaller pool of eligible mates because they may be unwilling to marry someone from a lower socioeconomic level.

Marital Status

The majority of divorced men and women (61 percent) remarry other divorced people, 35 percent marry single men and women, and 4 percent marry widowed people. Widowers tend to remarry sooner than divorced men, probably because they have a more positive attitude toward married life, are economically secure, and have a large pool of marriage partners (Wilson and Clarke, 1992).

In contrast, widows are slower to remarry. This may be due to the strong emotional attachment many widows have to their deceased husbands. It may also reflect the fact that because widows are generally older than divorced women, they may be seen as less desirable by eligible men (Wu, 1994). Among middle-aged widows, African Americans and those with dependent children are less likely to remarry than whites or women who have no children (Smith et al., 1991). Some women, whether divorced or widowed, don't remarry because they don't want to take care of a man (see Chapter 10).

Like divorce, remarriage is a process rather than a one-time act. And, like divorce, remarriage involves a series of stages.

MAKING CONNECTIONS

■ Do you agree that the definition of stepfamilies should include cohabitors and people who have never married?

■ Besides variables such as age and social class, what else affects remarriage rates? Think about religion, family-of-origin attitudes, and peer pressure, for example.

Remarriage as a Process

Remarriage is generally much more complicated than divorce. If the remarried couple didn't draw up a prenuptial agreement or a will and is killed in a car accident,

for example, should all of the children share in the estate, even though most of the assets came from one partner (Manners, 1993)?

The remarriage process may involve as many as six stages, similar to Bohannon's six stations of divorce (Goetting, 1982; see also Chapter 15). Like the stages of divorce, the stages of remarriage aren't necessarily sequential, and not every couple goes through all of them or with the same intensity. If partners can deal successfully with each stage, however, they are more likely to emerge with a new identity as a couple.

Emotional Remarriage

The emotional remarriage stage is often a slow process in which a divorced person reestablishes a bond of attraction, commitment, and trust. Because many people feel inadequate after a divorce, this stage often involves a fear that the new emotional investment will also lead to loss and rejection. These feelings may make the remarriage painful or volatile.

Some people get remarried to get even with a former spouse. Others feel like failures and think that family members look down on them because of a divorce. If parents have married for life, especially, some people remarry to prove that they're not "losers" and can succeed in a new marriage (Herrmann, 2003).

In addition, remarriages are emotionally complicated because the roles aren't clear. What are a spouse's responsibilities to new relatives? If the husband's ailing mother wants to move in with her son, for example, should the second wife be willing to care for her?

Psychic Remarriage

People's identities change from individuals to couples after they remarry. Because social status and personal identity are independent of marital status for many men, a shift in marital status does not require an extreme change in personal identity.

The identify shift may be more difficult for women. For a traditional woman, the psychic remarriage represents the recovery of a valued identity as a wife. A nontraditional woman may worry about the loss of her highly valued independence and freedom.

Community Remarriage

People often change their community of friends when they remarry. Remarriage may be a turbulent process because unmarried friends, especially those of the opposite sex, are typically lost and replaced by married or remarried couples who are friends with both members of the new couple. During the community remarriage

Filling the role of the stepparent may be easier when stepchildren are grown than when they are very young.

stage, close personal ties that were established after a divorce may be severed and result in a loss of valuable friendships.

In addition, people may move to another community after a remarriage. Such moves include meeting new neighbors, going to a different church, and sometimes changing the children's schools. These transitions often loosen ties with previous communities and social networks.

Parental Remarriage

The parental remarriage involves developing relationships between one partner and the children of the new spouse. If the children's other biological parent still plays an active role in their lives, the stepparent may have to overcome many hurdles. He or she cannot assume the role of father or mother but must behave as a nonparent, deferring to the biological parent's rights.

The stepparent and the biological parent generally share in making decisions that affect the children. Because there are no guidelines for this cooperation, however, the parental remarriage stage can lead to confusion and frustration for biological parents, stepparents, and children.

In some families, biological nonresidential fathers may step aside as stepfathers move in. If divorced fathers live close to their biological children, however, they maintain ties through telephone calls or visits. The higher the father's educational level, the more likely he is to maintain close relationships with his children (Cooksey and Craig, 1998).

Especially when one or both partners have children from previous marriages, there may be little time to develop workable and comfortable marital relationships and to establish a primary husband–wife bond. Instead, both marital and parental roles must be assumed simultaneously, and this may lead to conflict between the couples and the children.

Parental roles are often fuzzy. When problems arise that involve children from former marriages, for example, who should handle these issues? The children's biological parent or stepparents? Both biological and remarried partners?

Economic Remarriage

Remarriage reestablishes a marital household as an economically productive unit. The main problems during this stage may stem from the existence of children from a former marriage. The economic behavior of the remarried couple and that of the ex-spouses are often interrelated. For example, a biological father's child-support payments may become sporadic once a custodial mother has remarried. Many stepfamilies can't predict how much money will be available from month to month because of the uncertainty of such payments.

Another source of economic instability is the unpredictable nature of the needs of the husband's children, who typically live with their biological mother. The possibility of unexpected expenses, such as dentists' and doctors' fees, can cast a financial shadow over the biological father's remarriage.

There may also be disagreements about the distribution of resources: If his daughter is taking ballet lessons, should the stepfather also pay for his stepson's tennis lessons? If the noncustodial parent is not honoring child-custody payments, should the stepparent provide the money for recreational, educational, and social expenses for the children?

Legal Remarriage

Remarriage does not mean that a person exchanges one family for another. Instead, she or he takes on an additional family. Because the legal system does not delineate responsibilities, people are left to struggle with many problems on their own (Skinner and Kohler, 2002; Hans, 2002). For example, the remarriage raises such questions as which wife deserves a man's life and accident insurance, medical coverage, retirement benefits, pension rights, and property: the former wife, who played a major role in building the estate, or the current wife? Which children should a remarried father or remarried mother support, especially in such high-priced bills as a college education: his, hers, or theirs?

State laws rarely recognize the rights or responsibilities of stepparents in providing for the stepchildren. If the marriage ends, the stepparent has no legal standing to ask for custody or visitation. Instead, the courts rule on such petitions one by one.

Most schools and other public institutions typically don't recognize the stepparent as a legitimate parent. Usually, school registration forms, field trip permission slips, and health emergency information are requested of biological parents, not stepparents. "The message, whether intended or not, has been that only biological parents count" (Herbert, 1999: 67).

Even when there is a will, many state inheritance laws do not recognize the existence of stepchildren. In most states, stepchildren may have to go to court and battle biological children even when a stepparent has left the estate or other assets to a stepchild (Mason and Mauldon, 1996).

Each remarriage stage may be further complicated if one or both partners is still adjusting to his or her divorce. Some people begin the stages of remarriage without having completed the stages of divorce. That is, remarrying partners may bring anger and pain into a new relationship that can baffle and annoy a current partner ("Why is he always complaining about his ex-wife?" "Why can't she just get over her ex-husband's infidelity?").

Some couples cope with the remarriage stages and move on. Others don't. Whether remarried couples succeed or fail, they must deal with new issues that people in first marriages don't confront.

MAKING CONNECTIONS

■ If you, your parents, or friends have remarried, which of the remarriage stages were the most problematic? Why?

■ Numerous gay and lesbian parents are stepparents. What kinds of social and legal obstacles do you think they encounter as "second parents" (see also Chapter 12)?

How Do First Marriages and Remarriages Differ?

First marriages and remarriages differ in several important ways. Family composition tends to vary more in remarriages, role expectations are less defined, family members in remarriages may be at different points in their life cycles, and stress factors pile up as the stepfamily tries to readjust to its expanded family relationships. In addition, people who remarry may look specifically for spouses who offer more than their first partners did in terms of communication, income, or companionship.

Family Composition

Children's membership in two households is becoming increasingly common because of joint legal and physical custody (see Chapter 15). A stepparent and stepchild need not live together all or part of the time to have a relationship and to share stepfamily membership. And, as you saw in the quote at the beginning of this chapter, both the remarried couple and their children may have several combinations of household membership and kinship.

Remarriages often result in myriad new relationships and a dramatic change in family composition. Children may suddenly find themselves with **half-siblings**—brothers or sisters who share only one biological parent—as well as stepsiblings, stepgrandparents, and a host of other relatives. As a result, the children's experiences may change radically. For example, they may have to share their biological parent's time, as well as their physical space, with stepsiblings. Listen to one 8-year-old:

We feel like guests in Jim's house. We are careful of what we do. It is like we are the intruders. And I feel very bad that we took Tommy's room. They

CHANGES

Trophy Wives and Trophy Husbands in Remarriages

In the late 1980s, *Fortune* magazine ran a cover story on the "trophy wives" for whom, the story said, chief executive officers (CEOs) were trading their loyal, self-sacrificing, matronly, child-rearing wives. The newer, younger, and flashier trophy wives were sexier and more socially skilled. They pampered their husbands and never criticized them, spent money on these men rather than hoarding it for the children's education, and generally made the CEOs feel like kings of the castle (Connelly, 1989).

According to the *Fortune* article, second wives were enticing for a number of reasons. They were younger and thinner than the first wife and bolstered the man's corporate image of being successful both professionally and sexually.

Because many of these women were successful in their own right (many were well educated and had thriving small businesses of their own), they enhanced the man's status without overshadowing his success. The trophy wives also spent a lot of time on looking good. Nancy Brinker, 42, the third wife of Norman Brinker, 58, who founded the Steak and Ale and Bennigan's restaurant chains and who was the CEO of Chili's restaurant chain, said, "I work out one hour a day

at aerobics, I diet rigorously, and I play polo with my husband. . . . Norman likes me to look good" (Connelly, 1989: 54).

Unlike the first wife, who is busy caring for the children, the trophy wife has the time and connections to improve her husband's reputation: "She totes him to small dinner parties, opera galas, museum benefits, and auctions for worthy causes, having secured the invitations by serving on various committees and getting her husband to cough up something suitable in the way of a donation" (Connelly, 1989: 54).

Most important, the trophy wife has the advantage of being glamorous, independent, and available because she is not saddled with the husband's children: "The CEO now wants a playmate, someone who is free to travel with him and have fun" (Connelly, 1989: 61). The husband can play father when he wants to rather than when he must. His children need not interfere in his or his trophy wife's economic or romantic life: "Having pots of money may ease the burden of not being there because the CEO can afford to fly the kids out to see him and go on exciting vacations with them" (Connelly, 1989: 61).

More recently, Finke (1994) has suggested that a handful of successful women are now seeking trophy husbands

in their second or third marriage: "The basic criterion is this: No matter how successful a woman is in her profession, he is at least her equal, and maybe her better. He has three or more of the five attributes that tend to accompany achievement: fame, prestige, power, brains, and money" (Finke, 1994: 37, 39).

For example, when television's Diane Sawyer married Academy Award–winning director Mike Nichols, the media claimed that "they hadn't so much wed as 'acquired' each other." Furthermore, "Kennedy cousin Maria Shriver brought home perhaps the only thing she could find bigger than her famous family—Arnold Schwarzenegger" (Finke, 1994: 40).

STOP AND THINK . . .

- *Do only wealthy people and celebrities have trophy wives and trophy husbands? Or have such remarriages occurred among people you know?*

- *If a partner has children, what are the advantages of marrying a trophy husband or wife? What are the disadvantages?*

---

fixed up a room for him in the basement, with posters and all, but he's still mad at us for taking his room (Fishman and Hamel, 1981: 185).

Remarriage creates a unique set of issues because it combines people from at least two families. Imagine the transition involved when a custodial mother marries a custodial father and the couple then decides to have their own children. Each partner's children from the former marriage may fear that new children will be loved more or receive more attention because they belong to both partners rather than to just one or the other.

A child who travels between two houses may feel left out of some everyday activities and treats. According to

a 12-year-old, for example, "I get jealous when I come back to my mom's and see candy wrappers laying around and I didn't get any" (Hamilton, 2002: J2).

For their part, the parents may worry about dividing their attention between three sets of children so that none feels left out. To complicate matters further, ex-spouses and ex-grandparents may want to have input to the new family system, input that may not be welcomed by the remarried spouses.

Remarriage partners sometimes seek someone who is more successful, more supportive, or more attractive than the ex-spouse. The box "Trophy Wives and Trophy Husbands in Remarriages" examines this phenomenon at the higher socioeconomic levels of American society.

Role Expectations

The absence of normative role expectations for stepfamilies creates perplexing questions. For example, should stepparents have as much authority over children as the children's biological parents do? Should a noncustodial parent who has visitation rights have the same decision-making rights regarding his or her children as a custodial parent does? Should a child born to a remarriage have more legal rights than the stepchildren? And does the fact that few states have specific laws against marriage between stepchildren mean that such relationships are acceptable?

Life-cycle Stages

People who remarry sometimes find that they and their children are at different stages of the family life cycle. As a result, their goals may conflict. For example, a man with young adult children from his first marriage who is planning for his retirement may marry a younger woman who is looking forward to starting a family. Or his new wife may be an older woman who has already raised her family and now looks forward to a career:

> Claire and Sydney had been married for 4 years. Sydney had two adult children, ages 25 and 27, who had never lived with the couple, and Claire had a daughter who was 18 and in college. Sydney was a computer expert who had risen from working in the field as a technician to heading the marketing department for a large and successful electronics firm. He now had a month's vacation each year and looked forward to retirement in 10 years. Sydney wished to purchase a vacation home on a lake, as he had spent a number of years "dreaming about retiring there and fishing to his heart's content."

> Claire, on the other hand, had gone to work at the telephone company to support herself and her daughter after her divorce. Now that she and Sydney were married, she had been able to return to school and study to be a nurse. She was employed at a local hospital, loved her work, and hoped to become a supervisor before long. She worked various shifts and had little time off. Claire's favorite way to relax was to read or knit. . . . [but she also] liked to go dancing or to the movies in the evenings. Claire and Sydney worked out many of the stresses of their relationship arising from the joining of their two family groups, but they began to argue over weekend plans and future arrangements (Visher and Visher, 1988: 161–62).

On the other hand, an older man may look forward to remarriage and a new set of biological children. If he's at the top of his career ladder and economically secure, for example, he has time to enjoy watching his "new" children grow up and to participate in their upbringing. Also, his much younger second (or third) wife might encourage him to pursue recreational activities (such as skiing or socializing with friends) that he missed during his first marriage because of the struggle to pay bills and raise children.

Stress and Resources

Remarriage creates stresses that traditional first-marriage families rarely face. Among other things, as you'll see shortly, remarriage involves trying to combine several families, jealousy when biological parents or stepparents seem to favor some children over others, children having to move and leave their friends when a parent remarries, and half-siblings who don't get along.

Remarriage also provides resources. Children have more adults who care about them, less conflict between biological parents who were always fighting, and step-grandparents who might be delighted to add more grandkids to the fold (Crosbie-Burnett and McClintic, 2000). According to one adolescent, for example, the bright side of stepfamilies is having two Christmases, two vacations, and two birthday celebrations every year (Hamilton, 2002).

Remarriage Relationships

A popular song tells us that "love is better the second time around." Often, however, people have fantasies about the second marriage that have little to do with reality.

Myths about Remarriage

Some couples are more realistic than others in their expectations of a second marriage. Here are the most common myths that "can promote dangerous stepfamily expectations" (Hetherington and Kelly, 2002: 174):

- **The Nuclear Family Myth:** Believers of this fantasy expect family members to love and feel close to one another, children to show deference to parents, and "discomforting appendages" such as a nonresidential parent to disappear. Even in long-lasting stepfamilies, tight-knit relationships are not the norm.

- **The Compensation Myth:** The new mate is expected to be everything the problematic old mate wasn't: kind, sensitive, responsible, and true. People prefer to be who they are; when pushed to be someone else, they often become angry and resistant.

■ *The Instant Love Myth:* Believing marriage to be a form of parental entitlement, new stepparents presume an intimacy and authority they have yet to earn. The instant love myth often produces disillusionment even faster than the nuclear family myth.

■ *The Rescue Fantasy:* Stepparents think they will "shape those kids up" and rescue the children from the negative, lenient, or ineffectual discipline of a custodial parent. Custodial fathers expect the stepmother to take over responsibility for the care and nurturing of a stepchild, something a stepmother may be unable or unwilling to do because of employment, personality, or other factors.

Some couples continue to nurture these myths and fantasies and eventually break up. Others become more realistic and work on building satisfying relationships between themselves and the stepchildren.

Marital Dynamics

In reviewing the studies published in the 1990s, Coleman et al. (2002) found that remarried couples reported sharing decision-making equally. The researchers suggest that power in remarriages is more equitable than in first marriages for several reasons: Women demand more power, women who bring more resources into the marriage have more authority, remarried women and men have more egalitarian attitudes about marital roles, and men are more likely to back off during conflict than they did in their first marriages.

Shared decision making doesn't always mean that couples perform household tasks equally. Although remarried husbands do more housework than husbands in first marriages, domestic work is based on traditional gender roles, and remarried women do most of the housework (Deal et al., 1992; Pyke, 1994; Pyke and Coltrane, 1996).

Remarriage Quality

The data on marital satisfaction are mixed. Although people in first marriages report greater satisfaction than do remarried spouses, the differences are small (Vemer et al., 1989). Some studies have found few differences between people in first marriages and remarriages. Especially if the remarried parents have a stable relationship and the mother feels that the children's life is going well, remarried mothers benefit psychologically from remarriage and are happier than divorced mothers (Demo and Acock, 1996b).

Other researchers report that remarried spouses are more likely to express criticism, anger, and irritation. The disagreements generally center on issues related to stepchildren, such as discipline, rules, and distribution of resources (Coleman et al., 2002).

The negative interactions in remarried couples probably result from the strain and change associated with the new marriage and stepfamily formation. In the first few years of marriage, stress could reflect the same poor communication and problem-solving skills that led to a previous divorce. Remarriages may also suffer from the increased stress of the behavior problems of young adolescents (Bray, 1999).

Remarriage Stability

Remarriages end in divorce around 60 percent of the time. The average duration of first marriages is approximately eight years, compared with about seven years for second marriages (Kreider and Fields, 2002). Third marriages end about two years sooner than second marriages (Clarke, 1995a).

When age is factored in, however, second marriages may be more stable than first ones. According to a national study, for example, the most stable marriages are remarriages between people age 45 or older in which both partners have been married previously. Older couples may choose their second mates more carefully, may have more resources to make the marriage work, or may be reluctant to divorce again (Clarke and Wilson, 1994).

Why do remarried people divorce? There are several reasons. First, those who marry as teenagers are more likely to divorce after a second marriage (Wilson and Clarke, 1992). This may reflect a lack of problem-solving skills or immaturity in dealing with marital conflict.

Second, people most likely to divorce again see divorce as a solution for marital dissatisfaction. Remarriages are more fragile because people don't have clear rules, they have dissimilar values and interests, and there may be greater conflict in remarriages. Disagreements over stepchildren also increase redivorce rates (Booth and Edwards, 1992; Pyke, 1994).

Third, if a woman has a child between marriages, she is more likely to divorce. Intermarital birth (giving birth between marriages) may force a newly married couple to cope with an infant rather than devote time to their relationship (Wineberg, 1991).

Finally, the instability of a remarriage may reflect failure in one of four main areas: commitment, cohesion, communication, and maintenance of the family's boundaries (Ihinger-Tallman and Pasley, 1987).

People may fail to make a *commitment* to a remarriage for a number of reasons. Having survived one divorce, they may feel that another divorce is a ready remedy for an unhappy marriage; therefore, they may exert less effort to make the remarriage work. They may be unwilling to invest the time and energy necessary to try to resolve problems. Or one or both partners may have personal or emotional problems. For example, alcoholics, drug users, those who are physically violent, or those who are emotionally unstable are more likely to move in and out of marriage repeatedly.

Achieving *cohesion*, or the development of ties that hold the family together, takes time and effort. Merging two families is difficult because the members have no shared family history. To reduce conflict, family members may have to develop new rules (pertaining to the number of phone calls per evening or to teens' curfew, for example) and redistribute resources regarding such matters as who may use the family car and the timing or amount of children's allowance.

Communication is also important. If poor communication was a problem in one or both partner's previous marriages, couples may have to break old habits and learn to interact with each other differently. Effective interaction may be especially difficult if children from a former marriage are part of the new family, in part because the couple has less time and privacy to cultivate new communication patterns.

Remarried couples must also deal with more *boundary maintenance* issues than people in first marriages. For example, people in remarriages often have to insulate themselves against interference from ex-spouses and ex–in-laws. Remarried couples must also devote more effort to establishing boundaries with new family members and new relatives, especially if one of the partners is a custodial parent.

Remarriage Effects on Children

About 7 percent of all children live in stepfamilies (Fields, 2001). African American and American Indian children are more likely to live in stepfamilies and Asian American children the least likely (*Figure 16.3*).

How Children Fare Although the results are mixed, many studies show that children in remarried families don't do as well as children in nondivorced households. They tend to have more problems academically in terms of grades, scores on achievement tests, school attendance, and high school graduation rates (Teachman et al., 1996; Bogenscheider, 1997; Pong, 1997).

Compared with children in first-marriage families, stepchildren on average also show more internalizing behavior problems, such as depression, and have a higher risk of emotional problems. Adolescent stepchildren also generally show more externalizing behavioral problems such as using drugs and alcohol, engaging in sexual intercourse, and nonmarital childbearing (see Coleman et al., 2002, for a summary of some of this literature).

Negative effects vary by ethnic groups, however. According to McLanahan and Sandefur (1994), for example, black teenage boys who live with stepfathers are significantly less likely to drop out of school, and black teenage girls with stepfathers are significantly less likely to become teen mothers than those in single-parent

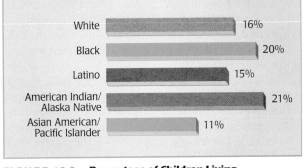

FIGURE 16.3 **Percentage of Children Living in Stepfamilies**

SOURCES: Based on Fields, 2001: Table 4.

households. The researchers suggest that the income and role models African American stepfathers provide may be critical in communities with few resources or minimal adolescent supervision.

Another study found that married stepfamilies, but not cohabiting ones, protect adolescent daughters living in high-poverty neighborhoods. According to Moore and Chase-Lansdale (2001), daughters in stepfamilies were 92 percent less likely to have had sexual intercourse than daughters of single mothers. They were also less likely to become pregnant. The researchers suggest that a mother's marriage increases the family's economic and social stability, support, and household maintenance and decreases risky sexual behavior.

Theoretical Explanations for the Effect on Children
Studies that find differences in the effects of remarriage on children propose several explanations for the variations. Although there are about a dozen theoretical perspectives, three of the most common are the cumulative effects hypothesis, risk and resilience theories, and social capital models.

In the *cumulative effects hypothesis*, children whose parents had several partners over time had more internalizing and externalizing problems than children who lived with a parent who had remarried only once (Capaldi and Patterson, 1991; Kurdek and Fine, 1993). That is, children who undergo multiple transitions experience more emotional and behavioral difficulties because the problems snowball.

Risk and resilience theories suggest that the effects of remarriage on children reflect both costs (risks) and benefits (resources that increase resilience). Remarriage can help single mothers escape from poverty. If children have a good relationship with stepfathers and noncustodial fathers, they experience about the same number of problems as children from nondivorced families. In addition, supportive schools and peers decrease the likelihood of adjustment problems (Lansford et al., 2001;

White and Gilbreth, 2001; Rodgers and Rose, 2002). Children are less resilient, however, if the ex-spouses' "anger and acrimony undermine the happiness, health, and adjustment of family members" (Hetherington and Stanley-Hagan, 2000: 177).

Social capital models maintain that children in stepfamily households have more problems than children in nondivorced families if the parenting is inadequate, if the parents are not involved in the children's school activities and homework, and if there is tension between the adults (Leung, 1995; Pong, 1997; Kim et al., 1999).

Relationships between stepchildren and stepparents, as you see, are diverse. This diversity is also evident in the structure of stepfamilies.

Stepfamily Diversity and Complexity

Stepfamilies come in many forms and sizes. We'll look at the various types of stepfamilies first, consider the unique challenges of gay and lesbian families, and then examine some of ways that stepfamilies differ from nondivorced families.

Types of Stepfamilies

When a stepfamily is formed, new family networks emerge. These new networks are often traced through a **genogram,** a diagram showing the biological relationships between family members. The genogram in *Figure 16.4* depicts the possible family systems when two previously married people with children from previous marriages marry each other.

Although stepfamilies vary in terms of parent–child relationships, there are three basic types:

- In the **biological mother–stepfather family,** all the children are biological children of the mother and stepchildren of the father.

- In the **biological father–stepmother family,** all the children are biological children of the father and stepchildren of the mother.

- In the **joint biological–stepfamily,** at least one child is the biological child of both parents, at least one child is the biological child of only one parent and the stepchild of the other parent, and no other type of child is present.

Stepfamilies can be even more complicated. In a *complex stepfamily,* both adults have children from previous marriages. And in *joint step–adoptive families* and *joint biological–step–adoptive families,* at least one child is a biological child of one parent and a stepchild of the other parent and one or both parents have adopted at

FIGURE 16.4 **Stepfamily Networks** Each set of parents of our target couple, Bill and Maria, are grandparents to at least two sets of children. For example, Maria's parents are the grandparents of her children with her former husband, Bob (Billy, Mario, and Linda) and of her child with Bill (Joy). Depending on the closeness of the relationship Bill maintains with his former wife, Althea, however, Maria's parents might play a grandparental role to Peter and Julian, Bill and Althea's boys, as well.

Source: Based on Everett and Everett, 1994: p. 132.

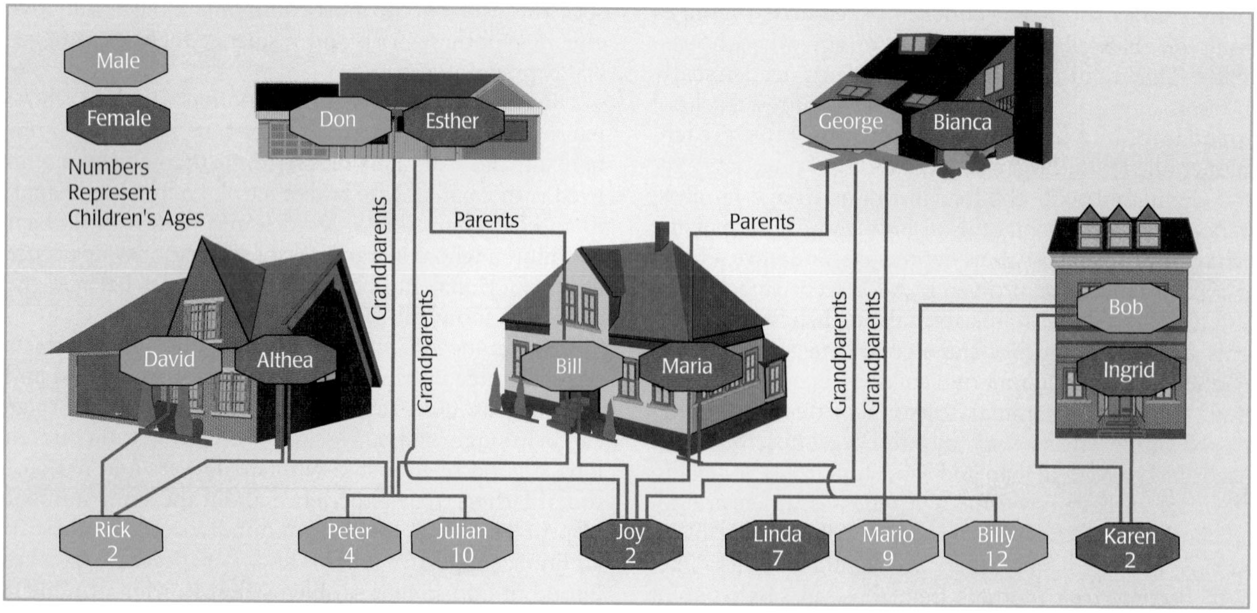

least one child. Nor does *complex stepfamily* take account of relationships between cohabitants, one or both of whom may have been married and have children from previous unions.

The concept of stepfamily could also be expanded to include the increasingly common situation in which an unmarried mother and her child move in with a man who is not the child's biological father. Thus, families can be fairly simple, composed of only a biological parent and his or her children and a stepparent. They can also be intricate and include stepparents, stepsiblings, half-siblings, and a combination of stepparents, stepsiblings, and half-siblings. The latter combination makes up over 2 percent of all stepfamilies (Fields, 2001).

It is important in stepfamilies to make sure that all the children receive love and attention. If signs of jealousy appear, both parents should listen to their children's concerns and try to understand.

Gay and Lesbian Stepfamilies

Gay and lesbian stepfamilies share the problems of all other stepfamilies, but these problems often are exacerbated by the parent's and stepparent's sexual orientation. Berger (1998) posits that lesbian and gay stepfamilies encounter triple stigmatization. First, they are stigmatized for their homosexuality, which many people view as immoral. Second, gay and lesbian stepfamilies are still seen as deficient compared with nuclear families. Last, gay parenthood is often stigmatized by the nonparental homosexual community, especially by gay men, because "the gay culture tends to emphasize primacy of the couple relationship" rather than parenting (Berger, 1998: 153).

Despite these obstacles, there is evidence that lesbian stepfamilies are resilient and as diverse as heterosexual stepfamilies. According to Wright (1998), for example, lesbian stepfamilies reflect three distinct stepparent roles:

- In the *co-parent family*, the nonbiological mother is a supporter of and helper and consultant to the biological mother, an active parent of the children, and a dedicated and committed family member.

- The *stepmother family* parallels heterosexual stepmother families. That is, the lesbian stepmother does most of the traditional mothering kinds of tasks, but the biological mother (like the biological father in heterosexual families) retains most of the decision-making power.

- In the *co-mother family*, both mothers have equal rights and responsibilities in everyday decisions and child-rearing tasks.

Characteristics of Stepfamilies

Most children under age 18 live with their biological mothers and fathers (see *Table 16.1* on page 468). Among stepfamilies, the most common form is biological mothers and stepfathers. Across racial-ethnic groups, African American children and American Indian children are the most likely to live with a biological mother and stepfather.

Stepfamilies may look like intact nuclear families because they are composed of married adults and children living in the same household. However, they differ from nondivorced families in many ways that make stepparenting more difficult.

1. **The structure of stepfamilies is complex.**

   It bears repeating that stepfamilies create new roles: stepparents, stepsiblings, half-siblings, and step-grandparents. Note that this structure does not make stepfamilies better or worse than nuclear families; they are simply different.

   Stepfamilies offer the possibility for many different kinds of ties, including relationships with uncles, aunts, and cousins. Ties between step-grandparents and their stepgrandchildren range from no contact to close relationships, depending largely on the investment that stepgrandparents make (Cherlin and Furstenberg, 1994).

TABLE 16.1

Children Living with Two Parents in Biological, Step, and Adoptive Families, by Race/Ethnicity

	White	African American	Latino	American Indian and Alaska Native	Asian American and Pacific Islander
Children living with two parents[1]	36.8 million	4.4 million	7.1 million	667,000	2.2 million
Percentage living with					
Biological mother and father	88	83	91	81	92
Biological mother and stepfather	7	12	6	9	3
Biological father and stepmother	2	2	2	4	1
Adoptive mother and father	1	1	—[2]	5	4
Other combinations[3]	1	1	1	1	—

[1]Includes unmarried mothers and fathers.

[2]A dash represents less than 1 percent.

[3]These combinations include adoptive parents, biological parents, and stepparents.

SOURCE: Based on Fields, 2001: Table 2.

2. A stepfamily must cope with unique tasks.

The stepparent may struggle to overcome rejection because the children may still be grieving over the breakup of the biological family, or the stepparent may disagree with the biological parent about discipline and rules (Hetherington and Kelly, 2002).

One of the most common tasks is redefining and renegotiating family boundaries. This may include making "visiting" children feel welcome and working out "turf" problems:

Consider the stepfamily in which the husband's three children rejoined the household every 3–4 days for a few days' time. The house was small, and the mother's three children who lived in the household had to shift where they slept, where they put their clothes, and where they could go to relax or to be alone in order to make the available space accommodate the extra family members. Bedrooms became dormitories, and the continual chaos created tension and instability for everyone (Visher and Visher, 1993: 241).

In such situations, it is difficult to develop clear and consistent rules about property rights and private spaces for each family member.

3. Stepfamilies often experience more stress and conflict than nuclear families.

As the previous example illustrates, much of the stress in stepfamilies is caused by ambiguity and the "lack of fit" with cultural norms that, however unrealistic, define the "ideal" family. Ambiguity may decrease as family members adjust to new roles and lifestyles, and the sense that the family doesn't fit the ideal model may decrease as family functioning improves.

A major source of tension is the fact that family members must adjust to each other all at once rather than gradually, as in a nuclear family. Stress may come from several sources. More people make more demands, parents may differ on how to discipline children, one partner may feel excluded from the relationship between her or his spouse and the spouse's biological children, or there may not be enough resources to meet the larger family's needs (Whitsett and Land, 1992).

4. Stepfamily integration typically takes years rather than months.

The age and sex of the children and the type of stepfamily (whether there is a stepmother or stepfather and whether there are children from both previous marriages) can affect adjustment. As the box "The Stepfamily Cycle" on page 470 suggests, it may take as long as eight years for a couple to consolidate their family and to work as a team. And if they have a new baby or if there are unexpected problems such as unemployment or a death in the family, the process may take even longer.

5. **Important relationships may be cut off or end abruptly and others spring up overnight.**

As you saw in Chapter 15, many fathers have no contact with their children after a divorce. Furthermore, siblings sometimes are split between parents and may rarely see one another. Children are especially distressed if a biological parent's wedding announcement comes as a surprise:

One divorced father awakened his children one morning, asked them to get dressed, and drove them to the courthouse where he married a woman they had only recently met. The children were shocked and felt betrayed that they were not allowed to know that their father was serious about this woman and wanted to marry her. The woman also had a child, so that by 10 P.M. these children went to bed in a house that now included a new stepmother and a new stepsister. The children were not happy about it (Knox and Leggett, 1998: 184).

According to both researchers and clinicians, children should be given plenty of notice about an impending marriage. The new partner and the children should get to know each other over the course of a year or two, go on vacations and have meals together, and just "hang around the house," getting to know each other (Bray and Kelly, 1998; Knox and Leggett, 1998).

6. **There are continuous transitions and adjustments instead of stability.**

In a stepfamily, the people living in a household can change continuously. The boundaries between who is a member of a stepfamily and who is not are sometimes fuzzy. For example, is the new spouse of a child's noncustodial parent a part of the child's family? And who decides the answer to this question?

Many families agree to flexible boundaries so that at any age, including during adulthood, children have access to both of their biological parents and can move easily between households. If each adult child has parents who are divorced or remarried, there may be some difficulty in juggling individual needs, family traditions, and emotional ties between as many as four families.

7. **Stepfamilies are less cohesive than nuclear or single-parent households.**

Stepchildren often feel closer to biological parents than to stepparents. As children grow up, they may also feel alienated because of differential economic support, as when only certain children in a stepfamily are supported during college. Or they may resent unequal favors and inheritance inequities bestowed by grandparents.

Children in stepfamilies may often feel divided loyalties between their biological fathers, with whom they spend time periodically, their mothers, and their stepfathers.

8. **Stepfamilies need great flexibility in terms of their everyday behavior.**

Varying custody and residential arrangements necessitate different daily or weekly routines. Moreover, within the household, the "expected" ways a family operates may not apply. For example, is the clarinet at Mom's house or Dad's? It's Amy's day to live at Mom's house, but over at Dad's they're going to play miniature golf (Hamilton, 2002).

The need for creativity and flexibility may decrease over time, but situations often arise (such as weddings, births, deaths, and holidays) that may necessitate unusual solutions and arrangements. Should a noncustodial father who rarely visits his children pay for his daughter's wedding, or should her stepfather pay for it? Or if both the biological father and stepfather are important in a young woman's life, who should walk down the aisle at her wedding? Both of them?

9. **Stepfamily members often have unrealistic expectations.**

Many couples have unrealistic expectations of their new families. In 41 percent of stepfamilies in one

CHANGES

The Stepfamily Cycle

Clinician Patricia Papernow (1993: 70–231) divides the process of becoming a stepfamily into three major stages. The early stage is characterized by fantasies, confusion, and slowly getting to know the others; in the middle stage the family begins to restructure; and in the late stage the family achieves its own identity.

The Early Stages: Getting Started without Getting Stuck

Stage 1: Fantasy. Most remarrying couples start out with the fantasy that they will love the children of the person they love and be loved by them and that they will be welcomed into a ready-made family. They see themselves as filling voids for the children, their spouses, and themselves.

Children in new stepfamilies also have fantasies encompassing a mixture of hope and fear. Some children still hope that their biological parents will reunite. Or they may fear losing or hurting one of their own parents if they come to love a stepparent.

Stage 2: Immersion. Chaos and confusion often characterize this stage. Familiarity and strangeness continually clash, with problems seen differently by biological parents, children, and stepparents. Stepparents may feel left out of the biological parent–child unit and may experience jealousy, resentment, and inadequacy.

Biological parents often are caught in the middle. Some exhaust themselves trying to meet everyone's needs and make the

stepfamily work; others try to deny the difficulties. Particularly in the latter case, the children may feel lost and ignored. Some children respond with tears and angry outbursts; others withdraw.

Stage 3: Awareness. Members of the stepfamily get to know each other and map the territory of each family member. Stepparents can learn about the children's likes and dislikes, their friends, and their memories without trying to influence the children.

Biological parents can try to find the right balance between overprotecting children and asking too much of them. Children should be encouraged to look at the positive aspects of the stepfamily, such as the parents' love.

The Middle Stages: Restructuring the Family

Stage 4: Mobilization. Many stepfamilies fall apart at this critical stage. The stepparent's task is to identify a few essential strategies for change (such as establishing family meetings to deal with difficult issues) and to make a sustained effort to communicate them to other family members while respecting the biological unit.

The biological parent's task is to voice the needs of her or his children and exspouse while supporting and addressing the stepparent's concerns. Children should voice their own needs to ease the pressures of their conflicting loyalties.

Stage 5: Action. In this stage, the stepfamily can begin to make larger moves to reorganize its structure by making some joint decisions about how the family will operate. The stepparent begins to play a more active role in the family, and the biological parent doesn't feel the pressure to be all things to all people. Both parents work together as a team in making decisions and carving time out for themselves.

The Later Stages: Solidifying the Stepfamily

Stage 6: Contact. In this stage, family members begin to interact more easily. There is less withdrawal and more recognition of each other's fruitful efforts. The stepparent has become a firm insider in the adult couple relationship and has begun to forge a more intimate, authentic relationship with at least some of the stepchildren.

Stage 7: Resolution. Relationships begin to feel comfortable. The stepparent role is well defined and solid. Stepparents become mentors to some of their stepchildren. Other stepparent–stepchild relationships have reached a mutually suitable distance.

In this stage, the adult stepcouple has become a sanctuary, a place to turn for empathy, support, and cooperative problem solving. The stepfamily finally has a sense of character and its own identity.

---

study, one or both partners said that they had entered remarried life expecting that their stepfamily would become as close as a nuclear family. Many of the couples reported disappointment and astonishment when the everyday realities of stepfamily life were fraught with problems (Pill, 1990).

Stepfamilies often compare themselves with biological families and have idealized or naive

expectations. There is no reason why members of the stepfamily—aside from the newly married adults—should automatically feel any sort of familial relation or affection. It is physically and emotionally impossible for a stepfamily to try to mirror a biological family; there are simply too many players and too many new relationships. As you saw in the box on "The Stepfamily Cycle," stepfamilies must forge their own rules and identities.

10. **There is no shared family history.**

The new stepfamily is a group of individuals who must develop meaningful, shared experiences. To do this, they must learn one another's patterns of communication (verbal and nonverbal) and interaction. New stepfamily members often speak of culture shock: When their own behavioral patterns and those of others in the household are different, they sometimes feel as if they are in an alien environment. For example, mealtimes and the meals themselves may be different from the past.

One way to ease some of the strangeness is to mesh rituals. In one remarried family, when a major holiday was approaching, family members were asked to suggest favorite foods. By preparing and serving these dishes, the new family honors the traditions of the previous families (Imber-Black and Roberts, 1993).

11. **There may be many loyalty conflicts that occur.**

Although questions of loyalty arise in all families, loyalty conflicts in stepfamilies are intensified. For example, suppose a child in the stepfamily feels closer to the noncustodial parent or to that parent's new spouse than to the biological and custodial parent or that parent's new spouse. Should these relationships be nurtured despite the resentment of the custodial parent or stepparent?

Furthermore, a newly remarried adult must make a sustained effort to maintain loyalty to a new spouse despite loyalty to biological children. For example, when Gwen, who had lived with her mother and stepfather for nine years and then lived on her own while attending college, came back home for a time, her mother felt conflicted:

Hugh [Gwen's stepfather] wants her to pay rent. I don't want her to. I feel that at this point in her life I would be a little more lenient than Hugh is. A lot of the difficulty is that she's been away for five years and now she's back in the fold. Hugh's a very rigid person—everything is preplanned and set up that way and that's the way you do it. I'm a little more loose (Beer, 1992: 133).

Gwen's mother's task was to find ways to help her daughter that did not diminish her loyalty to her husband. Had her husband been as "loose" as she was, adjustment might have been easier for this stepfamily.

12. **Stepfamily roles are often ambiguous.**

A positive aspect of role ambiguity is that it provides freedom of choice: One may be able to choose from among a variety of roles played with different children and adults. For example, a stepparent who is willing to be a friend to the children rather than a parent can serve as a mediator when there is conflict between the children and the biological, custodial parent.

However, ambiguity creates problems because people don't always know what's expected of them or what to expect from others. A partner may want a spouse who offers support, not mediation, when there are disagreements with the children.

When adults have problems, so do children. If adults are resilient and adjust, so do children. What, more specifically, are the everyday processes of living in stepfamilies?

MAKING CONNECTIONS

■ Have you been raised in a stepfamily? Looking at the list of 12 characteristics, which ones were most difficult for you or someone you know?

■ What are some advantages of growing up in a stepfamily compared with a nondivorced family?

Living in a Stepfamily

Stepparents don't have complete control in building happy relationships. They must often overcome stereotypes and work very hard to merge several households.

Stereotypes about Stepfamilies

The *myth of the evil stepmother*, perpetuated in Western culture by such classic tales as "Cinderella" and "Snow White," still exists (Ganong and Coleman, 1997; Kheshgi-Genovese and Genovese, 1997). This myth, which depicts stepmothers as cruel, unloving, and abusive, has had a ripple effect over time, and many people still view the stepfamily with disapproval. In two studies, college students had more negative evaluations of stepparents than of biological, adoptive, or widowed parents (Bryan et al., 1986; Schwebel et al., 1991). The harmful image persists even though many stepmothers neither wish nor expect to replace the stepchild's mother (Orchard and Solberg, 1999).

To satisfy their husband's expectations, stepmothers often impose some kind of order on the household. Many stepchildren become angry, resenting and resisting the rules:

In our most contentious stepfamilies, a real demonizing of the stepmother often occurred. We heard stepmothers described by some stepchildren as "evil," "malevolent," "wicked," or as "monsters,"

"You're right, I should spend more time with the kids. Which ones are ours?"
Medical Economics, January 25, 1993.

and nicknamed "Dog Face" or "The Dragon." Stepfathers rarely encountered this level of vitriol. Many well-intentioned but angry, discouraged, and defeated stepmothers gradually gave up and pulled out of the marriage (Hetherington and Kelly, 2002: 193).

In contrast, the more recent *myth of instant love,* as you saw earlier, maintains not only that remarriage creates an instant family but that stepmothers will automatically love their stepchildren. In the *Sound of Music,* for example, Julie Andrews wins the affections of the von Trapp children within a few months. Remarried parents, especially women, expect instant love because—according to another myth, discussed in Chapter 5—mothering comes easily and naturally to all women (see Quick et al., 1994, for a summary of the research on negative images of stepmothers).

Members of a newly constituted family who believe both of these myths may experience stress as they try to adapt to new personalities, new lifestyles, and new schedules and routines (Dainton, 1993). And considering the unrealistic views that people hold of the intact nuclear family (see Chapter 1), it is not surprising that the stepfamily suffers by comparison (Gamache, 1997).

A woman who grew up believing that a stepmother is inevitably bad may try to become a "super stepmom." She may be especially frustrated if her stepchildren rebel despite all her efforts and mothering. By the same token, a child who grew up with the same ideas about stepmothers may have negative expectations and resist developing a positive relationship. Thus, a self-perpetuating

cycle is set in motion. The children expect the stepmother to be nasty and will stay aloof. Their unpleasant behavior may cause the stepmother to become more demanding and critical (Berger, 1998).

Parenting in Stepfamilies

Most stepfamilies encounter a number of tasks in merging two households after a remarriage. Some of the most common issues include unclear terminology, sexual boundaries, legal issues, integrating the children into the family, establishing discipline and authority, helping children adjust to the new family form, and developing intergenerational relationships.

Unclear Terminology
The English language has fairly clear terms for relationships in intact families, such as "father," "mother," "brother," and "daughter." There are no words for many stepfamily relationships, however. For example, such designations as "my spouse's ex-spouse's new spouse" or "my stepsister's stepbrother" require most of us to stop and think to understand what is meant (Beer, 1992).

Why is the lack of stepfamily terminology problematic? Suppose, for example, that a new wife's own children want to call their stepfather "Dad," but the stepfather's biological children, their security threatened, refuse to permit this? One of my friends admits that she feels pangs of anger and envy when her son calls his stepmother "Mom." Thus, bad feelings may result all around.

Moreover, "it may be difficult to think clearly about a relationship when the words to describe it are inaccurate or when there is no word at all. Being unable to think clearly may make it more difficult to decide how to behave" (Beer, 1992: 11).

In contrast to English, many other languages have specific terms for stepfamily members. In Spanish, for example, there's *padrastro* (stepfather), *madrastra* (stepmother), *hermanastro* (stepbrother), *hermanastra* (stepsister), *hijastra* (stepdaughter), and *hijastro* (stepson).

One stepmother was uncomfortable with her three young stepchildren's calling her by her first name (as her husband does) because it seemed impersonal and disrespectful. Here's her solution:

I did not want to confuse the children by asking them to call me "Mom," since they already have a mother. So, I came up with a name that worked— "Smom." It's now a year later, and the kids are completely comfortable calling me Smom. Even my husband's ex-wife calls me that. Sometimes, the kids have variations, like "Smommy" or "Smama." I'm happy, they're happy (Ann Landers, 2000: C11).

CHOICES

Dealing with Sexual Boundaries in the Stepfamily

Only some states prohibit romantic relationships between non–biologically related members of a stepfamily. The weakened incest taboo in the stepfamily makes rules less clear, and sexual liaisons can create confusion, anger, and a sense of betrayal.

Practitioners Emily and John Visher (1982: 162–66) offer the following suggestions to remarried partners for dealing with sexuality in the stepfamily:

- Be affectionate and tender but not passionate with each other when the children are with you. Teenagers are particularly sensitive to open displays of affection because of their own emerging sexuality. Be aware of this sensitivity and forgo the stolen kisses and embraces in the kitchen.
- Don't be sexually provocative. Walking around in undershorts or a bra and underparts will counteract efforts to keep sexuality under control in your household, even when only younger children are around. Set a limit on teenagers' behaving in provocative ways. The first time a teenager parades

around the house scantily or inappropriately clad, for example, he or she should be told firmly to go back to his or her room and to dress properly. Be firm in setting limits for appropriate dress and behavior.

- Avoid roughhousing with children after they are 10 or 11 years old. This kind of behavior may become a physical turn-on between stepsiblings or between children and stepparents.
- Relinquish some forms of intimate behavior with children after they turn 10 or 11 years of age. For example, sitting on a stepfather's lap and showering him with kisses is inappropriate behavior for a teenage stepdaughter.
- If a teenager develops a crush on a stepparent, talk to him or her openly. Discuss the nature of crushes. Point out that the teen's affections are misplaced (for example, you're married to his or her parent). Suggest alternatives, such as schoolmates. Finally, make it clear that there is a big difference between feelings and behavior. Just because people are attracted to

others does not mean that they should act on their impulses.

- When you and your partner are having an argument or there is some emotional distance between you, don't turn for emotional support to a younger person in the household. You may open the door to feelings of intimacy that should not be encouraged. Instead, keep the lines of communication open between you and your partner.
- Rearrange the living space to cool off a sexual situation between stepsiblings. For example, avoid adjoining bedrooms and rearrange the bathroom sharing so that older children have privacy and less temptation.
- Do not tolerate sexual involvement in your home. In one family, the adults asked the college-aged son to move out of the house because they were unwilling to accept his sexual relationship with his stepsister. Although stepparents can't control sexual attractions between stepsiblings, they can control what happens in their home.

Sexual Boundaries   The law is inadequate in regulating or guiding families after remarriage. For example, most states prohibit sexual relations between siblings and between parents and children in nuclear biological families but have no restrictions about sexual relations between stepfamily members, either between stepchildren or between a stepparent and a stepchild.

There is much evidence that some stepfathers and male cohabitants abuse children sexually (see Chapter 14). An estimated 30 percent of all cases of adult–child sexual abuse involve a stepfather (Levine, 1990). Also, stepsiblings may drift into romantic relationships, which can lead to serious problems in the stepfamily. As the box "Dealing with Sexual Boundaries in the Stepfamily" suggests, one way to cope with such sexual problems is to prevent them in the first place.

Legal Issues   Financial matters are more complicated in stepfamilies than in first marriages. Financial planners and marriage experts are nearly unanimous in urging people who are planning a second marriage to spell out their financial obligations to each other in a legally binding prenuptial agreement. The issues to be resolved include whether to share financial responsibility for children from previous marriages, how to divide up estates, whether to merge assets and liabilities, and how to divide property acquired before and after the marriage in case of divorce (Rowland, 1994; see also *Appendix F*).

The rules that control disposition of an estate vary from state to state, but almost everywhere, the spouse is entitled to a major share, from 25 to 50 percent. And no matter where you live, federal law says the spouse is the sole beneficiary of your company pension or profit-sharing plan, both of which may be the major portion of an estate.

Unless there is a prenuptial agreement that allows a future spouse to waive his or her rights to a share of an estate, children from a previous marriage may be practically disinherited even though this was not the intention of the parent. Moreover, biological children may resent their inheritance being divided with step-siblings (Cleaver, 1999).

Legal experts also advise setting up a trust fund to safeguard the biological children's or grandchildren's inheritance. Trusts allow parents to transmit gifts and inheritances to whomever they choose while they are alive or after their death. In addition, to minimize family friction, attorneys advise people to discuss their estate plans with those who are affected by them (Spears, 1994).

Distributing Economic Resources

The children of remarried fathers typically are at a financial disadvantage if they live with their biological mothers. The stepchildren living with their remarried father may receive more support, such as loans, gifts, and health coverage (White, 1992; Aquilino, 1994). The loss of economic support can impoverish biological children and create hostility.

The partners must decide whether to pool their resources and how to do so. They may experience stress and resentment if there are financial obligations to a former family (such as custody awards, mortgage payments, or outstanding debts).

There may also be conflict about whose children should be supported at college or how wills should be written (e.g., whether the common property should be divided equally between the two families or between the children). Disagreements may range from seemingly petty issues such as how much should be spent for relatives' birthday and wedding presents to drastically different attitudes about whether money should be saved or spent.

Because men typically have more economic resources than women do, stepfathers may have more decision-making power in the new family. Sometimes men use money to control the children's and spouse's behavior ("If you don't shape up, you can pay for your own car insurance next time"). This kind of manipulation creates hostility.

Distributing Emotional Resources

Resources such as time, space, and affection must also be allocated and distributed equitably so that all family members feel content with the new living arrangements. Mothers sometimes are angry about spending much of their time and energy on live-in stepchildren but receiving few rewards:

My husband's kids don't see me as their mother. They shouldn't because I'm not. But I've gone out of my way to hold my tongue and do special things for them. It's as if whatever I do can be sloughed off, because I really don't count. I can do things for the kids and my husband gets the credit, not me. I resent them at those moments, and I resent him. It's really hard (Vissing, 2002: 193–194).

Although such difficulties are common, stepmothers are often "carpenters for damaged relationships" (Vinick, 1997). They might reestablish estranged ties between their husbands and his biological children by urging their husbands to make phone calls or by calling themselves, sending invitations for visits and family get-togethers, and writing letters. Biological mothers can strengthen ties between their children and stepfathers by nudging them to spend time together. As one mother said, "I'd send them off to the movies or to a park. They had to form a relationship without me intervening" (Wolcott, 2000: 16).

Developing Parent–Child Relationships

Children from stepfamilies show less emotional, social, and familial adjustment than children from intact nuclear families (see Hetherington and Stanley-Hagan, 2002, for a summary and review of some of this research). As you saw earlier, children in single-mother and remarried households are more likely than children in nondivorced families to have emotional and behavioral problems.

Even if biological children have close family ties, they may be at greater risk for problem behavior if stepfathers are not supportive and do not monitor the child's behavior (Marsiglio, 1995; Mekos et al., 1996). Some of the problems may reflect stepfamily-related characteristics rather than the stepfamily structure itself. Even though the family's economic resources increase after a remarriage, alternating residences during the school year increases a child's risk of dropping out of school or having problems with school authorities. This is more likely for children in stepfamilies than for those who live with both biological parents (Astone and McLanahan, 1994).

Relationships with stepchildren are often more difficult for stepmothers than stepfathers (Lee et al., 1994; MacDonald and DeMaris, 1996). Although stepfathers who don't monitor their stepchildren may have a long-term negative effect on children's behavior, stepmothers may be less likely to have good relationships with their stepchildren because the stepmother is more often the disciplinarian (Kurdek and Fine, 1993).

If the stepmother is at home more than her husband, she may be expected to be more actively involved in domestic duties, including raising the stepchildren.

Regardless of the parent's gender, relations between children and parents in both intact and remarried homes are more positive when the parents include the children in decision making and are supportive rather than critical (Barber and Lyons, 1994; Crosbie-Burnett and Giles-Sims, 1994).

Establishing Discipline and Closeness   Even though many stepfathers are more permissive than stepmothers, two of the biggest problems in stepfamilies concern discipline and authority, especially in relationships between a stepfather and adolescents. Teenagers complain, "He's not my father, and I don't have to listen to him." Stepfathers resent not being obeyed both because they consider themselves authority figures and because they may be working hard to support the family.

Mothers may feel caught in the middle. Although they love their husbands, they may feel guilty for having married someone the children don't like, or they may disagree with the stepfather's disciplinary measures (Hetherington and Stanley-Hagan, 2002).

Whether they intend it or not, when parents find themselves forming strong relationships with the children of a new partner, they may feel that they are betraying their biological children. Similarly, children may feel guilty if they find themselves liking a stepparent better than a biological parent because the stepparent is more fun, more understanding, or easier to get along with (Papernow, 1993).

Integrating a stepfamily that includes teenagers can be particularly difficult because adolescents begin to move away from their parents during puberty. If adolescent children have supportive relationships with friends, neighbors, and other relatives, their adjustment after a remarriage will be smoother (Quick et al., 1994).

Regardless of age, visiting (nonresidential) children may feel awkward and uncomfortable. If their visits are intermittent, they may not develop a sense of belonging or fitting in. As mentioned earlier, however, ensuring that each family member has a private physical space can lessen the alienation of visitors.

Friendship is probably the best way to enhance steprelationships. If stepparents go slowly in approaching stepchildren, especially adolescents, they have a better chance of establishing discipline or setting rules. Some stepparents act as *quasikin*, a role between parent and friend, by assuming some of the functions of parents but letting biological parents make final decisions about children. Maintaining a quasikin relationship can be tricky, however:

> *Stepparents must balance engaging in daily parenting activities such as getting children ready for school, giving allowances, and supervising household chores while taking a more distant, interested-friendly stance when the stepchildren's parents are*

Children may feel anger and hostility when a parent or stepparent must go to court over such things as support payments owed by a child's biological father.

Reprinted with permission of the *Daily Breeze* ©2002.

> *making major decisions about the children (Coleman et al., 2001: 263).*

Taking a quasikin role is easier with nonresidential (visiting) than custodial children and with older than younger children. It is also more likely for stepfathers than stepmothers, who are often responsible for everyday monitoring and discipline.

Gender Differences in Children's Adjustment   Several studies have found that stepdaughter–stepfather relationships are more negative than are those between stepsons and stepparents of either sex. Even when stepfathers make friendly overtures, stepdaughters may withdraw (Vuchinich et al., 1991). One explanation for this distancing behavior is that daughters, who once had a privileged status in the family because they shared much of the authority in helping to raise younger children, may resent being replaced with someone with more power in the family (see Chapter 15). The stepdaughter–stepfather relationship may also be more distant because the stepfather has made sexual overtures or behaved in other inappropriate ways toward the stepdaughter (see Chapter 14).

Whatever the reasons for the problems girls experience in remarried families, they are serious enough to cause adolescent girls to leave stepfamily households at an earlier age than do girls in single-parent or intact homes. Stepdaughters also leave earlier to establish independent or cohabiting households (Goldscheider and Goldscheider, 1993). In a longitudinal British study, for example, the girls who had lived in stepfamily households were much more likely than those who had lived in intact households to report that they left because of friction at home (Kiernan, 1992).

CHOICES

The Ten Commandments of Stepparenting

All families, including stepfamilies, have to work at peaceful coexistence. Practitioners (Turnbull and Turnbull, 1983; Visher and Visher, 1996) offer the following advice to stepparents who want to increase family harmony.

1. **Provide neutral territory.** Most people have a strong sense of territoriality. Stepchildren may have an especially strong sense of ownership because some of their privacy may be invaded. If it is impossible to move to a new house where each child has a bedroom, provide a special, inviolate place that belongs to each child individually.

2. **Do not try to fit a preconceived role.** Be honest right from the start. Each parent has faults, peculiarities, and emotions, and the children will have to get used to these weaknesses. Children detect phoniness and will lose respect for any adult who is insincere or too willing to please.

3. **Set limits and enforce them.** One of the most difficult issues is discipline. Parents should work out the rules in advance and support each other in enforcing them. Rules can change as the children grow, but there should be agreement in the beginning on such issues as mealtimes,

bedtimes, resolving disagreements, and household responsibilities.

4. **Allow an outlet for the children's feelings for the biological parent.** The stepparent should not feel rejected if a child wants to maintain a relationship with a noncustodial biological parent. Children's affections for their biological parents should be supported so that the children do not feel disloyal.

5. **Expect ambivalence.** Children's feelings can fluctuate between love and hate, sometimes within a few hours. Ambivalence is normal in human relationships.

6. **Avoid mealtime misery.** Many families still idealize the family dinner hour as a time when family members have intelligent discussions and resolve problems. Although both parents should reinforce table manners, an unpleasant family mealtime should be ignored or avoided. Some suggested strategies include letting the children fix their own meals, eating out once in a while, and letting the father do some of the cooking.

7. **Do not expect instant love.** It takes time for emotional bonds to be forged; sometimes this never occurs. Most children under 3 years of age

adapt easily. Children over age 5 may have more difficulty. Some children are initially excited at having a new mother or father but later find that the words "I hate you" are potent weapons. This discovery often coincides with puberty. A thick skin helps during this potentially hurtful time.

8. **Do not accept all the responsibility; the child has some, too.** Children, like adults, come in all types and sizes. Some are simply more lovable than others. Like it or not, the stepparent has to take what he or she gets. This does not mean assuming all the guilt for a troubled relationship, however.

9. **Be patient.** Good relationships take time. The first few months, and often years, are difficult. The support and encouragement of other parents who have had similar experiences can be invaluable.

10. **Maintain the primacy of the marital relationship.** The couple must remember that the marital relationship is primary in the family. The children need to see that the parents get along together, can settle disputes, and, most of all, will not be divided by the children.

In many cases, the negative reactions of children (especially young children) are fairly short-lived. According to several national studies, stepmothers and stepchildren establish more positive relationships within a few years (Baydar, 1988; Hetherington and Clingempeel, 1992).

Stepfathers, especially, need to be patient in establishing new relationships after a remarriage. In describing the gradual process of developing a relationship with the stepchild, one stepfather commented, "Brian is different now. At first he was reclusive and jealous and he saw me as infringing. It was a slow progression"

(Santrock et al., 1988: 159). The box on "The Ten Commandments of Stepparenting" suggests guidelines for stepparents.

Intergenerational Relationships Ties across generations, especially with grandparents and stepgrandparents, can be close and loving or disruptive and intrusive. After a divorce or during a remarriage, grandparents can provide an important sense of continuity to children when many other things are changing. Although many children typically do not become as attached to their new stepgrandparents as to their biological grandparents, they can resent new grandparents who seem to neglect or reject them:

> One twelve-year-old girl in our practice became angry and aggressive toward her two new and younger stepsiblings following their first Christmas holiday together, even though she had been very loving with them before that. Several weeks later she revealed to her father that she was hurt and disappointed because the stepsiblings received twice as many gifts from their grandparents as she received in total from everyone in the family (Everett and Everett, 1994: 140).

Relations with paternal grandparents tend to decrease when a child lives with his or her mother after divorce and remarriage. When parents remarry, they tend to live further away, have fewer visits with grandparents, and make fewer telephone calls (Lawton et al., 1994).

Such distanced behavior can decrease grandparent–stepgrandchild contact and closeness. Even maternal grandparents may visit less often, call less often, and offer less baby-sitting time to remarried daughters than to married or divorced daughters (Spitze et al., 1994). Intergenerational relationships, then, depend on how much effort the remarried partners and steprelatives put into maintaining or forging close family ties (see Chapter 17).

MAKING CONNECTIONS

■ Should stepparents be parents, friends, quasikin, or some combination of these roles?

■ What kinds of traditions, rituals, and celebrations might stepfamilies implement to build a new identity for both stepchildren and stepparents?

Successful Remarriages and Stepfamilies

Many stepfamilies, as you've seen, encounter difficulties such as boundary issues, cohesiveness, and conflicting loyalties that biological families rarely face. Yet we rarely hear about well-adjusted and happy stepfamilies that don't need or seek therapeutic interventions (Ihinger-Tallman and Pasley, 1997). Although forging a civil relationship with an ex-spouse or new spouse and raising stepchildren is a daunting task, it can be done.

Some Characteristics of Successful Stepfamilies

In a review of the literature, Visher and Visher (1993) suggest that seven characteristics are common to remarried families in which children and adults experience warm interpersonal relationships and satisfaction with their lives. Some of these characteristics are the opposite of the problems we've discussed earlier. The major point to remember is that these traits can be achieved.

First, successful stepfamilies have developed *realistic expectations*. They have rejected the myth of instant love because they realize that trying to force a friendship or love simply doesn't work. In addition, they don't try to replicate the biological family because they accept the fact that the stepfamily structure is "under construction." Teenagers who are beginning to rebel against authority generally are particularly sensitive to adult supervision. As one teenager in a stepfamily put it, "Two parents are more than enough. I don't need another one telling me what to do" (Visher and Visher, 1993: 245).

Second, adults in successful stepfamilies let *children mourn their losses*. These adults are sensitive to children's feelings of sadness and depression. They also support their children's expressing fear, confusion, and anger, neither punishing the children nor taking these reactions as personal rejection.

Third, the adults in well-functioning stepfamilies forge a *strong couple relationship*. This provides an atmosphere of stability because it reduces the children's anxiety about another parental breakup. It also provides children with a model of a couple who can work together effectively as a team and solve problems rationally (Kheshgi-Genovese and Genovese, 1997).

Fourth, the *stepparenting role proceeds slowly*. A stepparent is catapulted into a parenting role, whereas a biological parent's relationship with a child develops over many years (see the discussion of achieved and ascribed status in Chapter 1). One of the biggest mistakes that stepfathers make, usually with a wife's encouragement, is assuming an active parenting role too early in the marriage and presuming an intimacy and authority that have not been earned.

Although many stepfathers are caring, attentive, and loving, the children often reflect a spectrum of behaviors that include surliness, door slamming, loud shouting, and painful insults. The children are often unprepared to accept both intimacy and authority from a stepfather during the first year or two of stepfamily life (Bray and Kelly, 1998). Children might still be feeling the effects of "emotional divorce" even if their biological parent has recovered (see Chapter 15).

Fifth, except when young children are present, the *stepparent should take on a disciplinary role gradually*. As one teenage girl stated, "My stepfather wasn't ever in my face, which was good, because I would have been mad if he had tried to discipline me" (Minton, 1995: 25).

With teenagers, the biological parent should be the disciplinarian while the stepparent supports his or her rules ("What did your mom say about going to the movies tonight?"). In successful stepfamilies, adults realize that the relations between a stepparent and stepchildren can be quite varied: the stepparent may be a parent to some of the children, a companion to others, or just a good friend to all. And even if there are no warm, interpersonal ties, it is enough that family members are tolerant and respectful of individual differences.

Here white stepfamilies can learn from the experiences of many African American families. In black families, "living in two cultures simultaneously [one white and one black] means that situations arise in which role expectations and definitions of self and family are ambiguous, or even in conflict" (Crosbie-Burnett and Lewis, 1993: 245). Thus, black adults are more likely to teach their children that there are several possible sets of behaviors, expectations, and roles.

Sixth, successful *stepfamilies develop their own rituals.* They recognize that there is more than one way to do the laundry, cook a turkey, or celebrate a birthday. It is not a matter of a right or a wrong way. Instead, successful remarried households may combine previous ways of sharing household tasks, develop new schedules of what to do together on the weekends, or try out several ways of sharing household tasks. The most important criteria are flexibility and cooperation.

Finally, well-functioning stepfamilies work out *satisfactory arrangements between the children's households.* Adults don't have to like each other to be able to get along. In fact, it is useful for many adults to have a "business relationship" in working together during such family events as holidays, graduations, and weddings. Many black families have flexible familial boundaries so that children feel welcome in several households regardless of biological "ownership" (Crosbie-Burnett and Lewis, 1993). In addition, many African American families, including fictive kin, share material and emotional resources in raising children (Blake and Darling, 2000; see also Chapter 2).

The most successful stepfamilies have two sets of parents but one set of rules. They collaborate at school functions, parent–teacher meetings, and after-school activities. For example, if each child has a list in his or her backpack, both sets of parents can check off items (such as homework, musical instruments, and gym shorts) when children move back and forth from house to house.

Communication is critical in successful stepfamilies. If adult relationships are strained, relying on e-mail, especially, can "take the 'feelings' out of communication. You can simply put the facts down, and you don't have to talk to the person" (Cohn, 2003: 13). Most importantly, adults should never criticize the children's biological parents or stepparents.

The Rewards of Remarriage and Stepparenting

Couples often describe their remarriage as offering more benefits than their first marriage. Many feel they learned valuable lessons in their first marriage and that they have matured as a result of the experience. They feel they know each other better than they knew their former spouses, talk more openly and more freely about issues that concern them, and are less likely to suppress their real feelings to avoid causing pain.

Successful remarried couples say they try harder, are more tolerant of minor irritations, and tend to be more considerate of each other's feelings than they were in the first marriage. They also report enjoying the new interests and new friends a remarriage brings (Westoff, 1977).

Reactions from stepparents are more mixed. When Rosin (1987) asked stepfathers about the rewards they experienced, the responses ranged from one stepfather who felt that the rewards are "the same as the rewards of biological fathering" to another who said "none." In another study of 29 stepfamilies, nearly 33 percent of the couples said that living in a stepfamily took a continual and deliberate effort. One father wearily commented, "Stepfamily life is intense, and weekends feel like a workout!" (Pill, 1990: 190). Most were unprepared for the unrelenting nature of the demands placed on them.

The quality of stepfamily relationships depends in part on the stepparents' role identity and those of their stepchildren. In one study, for example, 52 percent of the stepparents felt that "parent" was the ideal stepparent role, but only 29 percent of the stepchildren felt this way. Instead, 40 percent of the stepchildren said the ideal stepparent role was "friend" (Fine et al., 1999). Such dissimilar perceptions and subsequent expectations might explain why stepparents' relationships with their stepchildren are tense.

Despite the ups and downs, a stepfamily provides members with opportunities that may be missing in an unhappy intact family. Because children see loving adults, they have positive models of marriage (Rutter, 1994).

When remarried partners are happy, children benefit from being in a satisfying household. A well-functioning stepfamily increases the self-esteem and well-being of divorced parents and provides children who have minimal contact with noncustodial parents with a caring and supportive adult (Pill, 1990). In addition, the children's economic situation often improves after a parent, especially a mother, remarries (see Chapter 15).

One of the greatest benefits of remarriage and step-parenting is that family members learn flexibility and more open attitudes about family issues and boundaries. Gender roles, for example, are less likely to be stereotypical because in well-functioning stepfamilies, both parents typically earn money, write checks, do housework, and take care of the children (Kelley, 1992).

In many stepfamilies, the children benefit by having a more objective sounding board to discuss problems, and they may be introduced to new ideas, different perspectives, and a new appreciation for art, music, literature, sports, or other leisure activities (Ihinger-Tallman and Pasley, 1987). Finally, if stepsiblings live together, they get more experience in interacting, cooperating, and learning to negotiate with peers.

In some cases, children don't recognize the contributions of stepparents until they themselves are adults. One of my students, who admitted to being very rebellious and "a real pain" after her mother remarried, is now grateful that her stepfather didn't give up:

> *The best solution to mine and my stepfather's problems was age. As I am getting older and supporting myself more and more, I realize just how much my stepfather has done for me. Even though he is not my "real" dad, he is the only father I have known. He has provided me with food, clothes, an education, and a home. Growing up, I thought I had it so rough. I now realize that he's my friend. It's funny, but now I actually enjoy watching TV or a movie with my stepfather (Author's files).*

Conclusion

As this chapter shows, there is life after divorce. Of all the different marriage and family forms discussed in this textbook, stepfamilies are the most varied and complex.

Sometimes a new baby creates stress in a stepfamily, but when the children from former marriages are adolescents or young adults, family members often adapt well to the new relationships.

Thus, both children and adults must make many *changes* as the family adapt and work together.

Despite high redivorce rates, remarriage and stepparenting give people more *choices* in establishing a well-functioning and satisfying family life. Although stepfamilies must deal with many *constraints* after a remarriage, there are also numerous rewards in establishing a new household.

SUMMARY

1. After a divorce, dating and courtship patterns vary by age and gender. Most divorced people marry within four years after a divorce.

2. The most dramatic changes in family structure and composition result from remarriage and the formation of stepfamilies. More than 40 percent of marriages are remarriages for one or both partners.

3. Remarriage rates vary by sex, race, age, socioeconomic status, and marital status. Men remarry more quickly than do women, remarriage rates are much higher for white women than for black women and Latinas, and women with low incomes and lower educational levels are the most likely to remarry.

4. Remarriage is a process that involves emotional, economic, psychic, community, parental, and legal aspects. Some of these stages involve children, whereas others don't.

5. There are several important differences between first marriages and remarriages. Some of these differences include the composition of the family, the children's experiences, stepfamily roles, life-cycle events, family goals and objectives, and family structure.

6. Stepfamilies are very diverse in terms of parent–child relationships and their ties to biological families. Stepfamilies can have three "sets" of children under the same roof, which may result in strained living arrangements.

7. Stepfamilies still suffer from negative perceptions and stereotypes, even though much research shows that stepfamilies are similar to nondivorced families in fulfilling basic family functions.

8. Although stepfamilies share many of the same functions as do intact nuclear families, there are a number of unique tasks in merging two households after a remarriage. The most common issues include legal issues, the integration of children into the family, and intergenerational relationships.

9. Two major stepfamily tasks include establishing discipline and closeness. Although the data are mixed, stepfather–stepdaughter relationships are more strained than those between stepsons and stepparents.

10. Many couples who have remarried say they know each other better, communicate more openly, and are more considerate of each other's feelings than they were in their first marriage. Thus, although there are problems in remarriages, there are also many rewards.

KEY TERMS

stepfamily 456
half-sibling 461
genogram 466

biological mother–stepfather family 466
biological father–stepmother family 466

joint biological–stepfamily 466

TAKING IT FURTHER

Getting Information and Support on the Internet

Remarriage at iVillage.com offers "pop psychology" articles on remarriage, message boards, newsletters, and several quizzes, including "How Realistic are Your Expectations of Marriage?"
www.ivillage.com/topics/relation/0,166909,00.html

The **Stepfamily Association of America** provides information, support, and articles on stepparenting.
www.saafamilies.org

The **Children of Separation and Divorce Center, Inc.,** describes itself as "an advocate and liaison for families in transition" and offers publications, parent seminars, newsletters, and suggestions for dealing with changes in family relationships.
www.divorceabc.com

The **Second Wives Club** serves stepmoms and second wives and offers resources that include articles, legal and practical advice, and information on finalizing custody arrangements.
www.secondwivesclub.com

CoMamas Association hopes to teach stepwives and their families how to develop cooperative and respectful relationships so they can end their war and get along for the sake of the children.

www.comamas.com

The **Stepfamily Foundation** offers information on stepfamily research, counseling, and other resources.

www.stepfamily.org

The **American College of Trust and Estate Counsel** provides referrals for local lawyers who draw up prenuptial agreements, trusts, and wills.

www.actec.org

And more: www.prenhall.com/benokraitis offers resource directories, sites for legal referrals, online information about stepparent adoptions, Websites that offer support and solutions for stepfamilies, and a map of states where gay and lesbian stepfamilies are legally recognized.

INVESTIGATE WITH RESEARCH NAVIGATOR

Please go to www.researchnavigator.com and enter your LOGIN NAME and PASSWORD. For instructions on registering for the first time, please view the detailed instructions at the end of the Chapter 1. Please search the Research Navigator™ site using the following key search terms:

stepfamilies
remarriage

Aging and Family Life:
Grandparents, the Widowed, and Caregivers

DATADIGEST

- The **percentage of the U. S. population over age 65 has been increasing steadily:** 4 percent in 1900, 5 percent in 1920, 7 percent in 1940, 9 percent in 1960, and 13 percent in 2000. It is expected to grow to 20 percent by 2030.

- The **oldest old** (people age 85 and over) are a small but growing group. In 2000, this group made up 1.6 percent of the U.S. population, compared with 0.6 percent in 1900.

- The **average U. S. life expectancy** was 47 years in 1900, 68 years in 1950, and 77 years in 2001 (79.8 years for women and 74.4 years for men).

- The **percentage of racial and ethnic minorities age 65 and older** in the U.S. population will increase from 16 percent in 2000 to 25 percent in 2030 and to 32 percent by 2050.

- **Grandparents' Day,** instituted by presidential proclamation in 1978, is the first Sunday after Labor Day.

- More than 4 million American **children are being raised by grandparents,** increasing 30 percent in 10 years.

SOURCES: Arias and Smith, 2003; Fields, 2003; Smith, 2003.

On a sweltering June weekend in 1994, more than 600 over-age-50 athletes from 11 states competed in 20 events—ranging from basketball to the pole vault—in the U.S. National Senior Sports Classic in Springfield, Massachusetts. The 73-year-old woman who jumped 8 feet to win the gold medal in the long jump also won golds in the high jump, the shot put, and the hammer throw. Another contender, 84 years old, had collected 205 gold and 23 silver medals in such events as discus, shot put, javelin, and the 1500-meter run since the Senior Games began in 1992 (Rohde, 1994).

What's more, the contestants in the Senior Games were youngsters compared with many other active older people. For example,

- Marta Aurenes, 91, is a bouncer at her favorite pub in Stavanger, Norway.

- Mieczyslaw Horszowski, the classical pianist, recorded a new album at age 99.

- At age 99, twin sisters Kin Narita and Gin Kanie recorded a hit single in Japan and starred in a TV ad.

- At 97, Martin Miller of Indiana was working full time as a lobbyist for older citizens.

- At 91, Hulda Crooks climbed Mount Whitney, the highest mountain in the continental United States.

- Renowned chef Julia Child tasted French food for the first time at the age of 37 and was in her fifties when she became famous for her televised expertise in French cuisine. In her eighties, she embarked on a new show in which she played host to famous chefs from around the world.

- In 1997, 94-year-old former South Carolina Senator Strom Thurmond, who had served in Congress more than 41 years, decided not to run for reelection in 2002 because he wasn't sure how his health would be at age 100.

- Before France's Jeanne Calment, the world's oldest living person, died at age 122, she took up fencing at 85, still rode a bicycle at 100, and released a rap CD at age 121.

- Millie Benson, author of the Nancy Drew mystery books, learned to fly at age 59. She wrote a weekly column about everyday life and older people for *The Blade* newspaper in Toledo, Ohio, until she died at age 96.

- George Dawson, the grandson of slaves, learned to read at age 99 and co-authored a book at age 102 (see Dawson and Glaubman, 2000).

Are these people unusual? Probably. But as we continue into the twenty-first century, more older people are and will be similarly active and productive. As the numbers of older people continue to grow (see "Data Digest"), the later years can become increasingly more interesting and enjoyable.

At the same time, we must recognize that older family members must often deal with the death of loved ones, with their own health problems, and with both giving and receiving care. As this chapter shows, aging forges changes for older people and for their family and friends. Among other things, a long life generates multi-generational families.

The Rise of Multigenerational Families

Until the last 50 years, life expectancy increased as a result of decreasing child mortality: Fewer children died and grew up to adulthood. Most of us will live past age 65, largely because of medical advances. In 1800, your chance of living to 100 would have been roughly 1 in 20 million; today it's 1 in 50 (Jeune and Vaupel, 1995).

Despite the high incidence of illnesses such as cancer and heart disease, more people are reaching age 65 than ever before, and American children born in 1990 have an average life expectancy of almost 76 years. Because many racial and ethnic groups in America have higher birth rates than whites, the numbers of *elderly*, those 65 or older, in these groups are expected to grow at an even greater rate. As *Figure 17.1* shows, the ethnic population age 65 and over is expected to grow from 16 percent in 2000 to 36 percent in 2050.

Gerontologists— scientists who study the biological, psychological, and social aspects of aging—emphasize that the aging population should not be lumped into one group. Instead, there are significant differences between the *young-old* (ages 65 to 74), the *old-old* (ages 75 to 84), and the *oldest-old* (ages 85 and older) in terms of living independently, working, and health service needs.

One of the fastest-growing groups is the oldest-old, a population that increased from 100,000 in 1900 to 4.3 million in 2000. By 2030, this group is expected to constitute almost 3 percent of the country's population ("Older Americans 2000 . . .," 2000).

By 2010, about 129,000 people will be centenarians, or people who are 100 years old or older: white, 74 percent; African Americans, 12 percent; Latinos,

FIGURE 17.1 **Population Age 65 and Older by Race and Ethnicity, 2000 and 2050**

Note: Latino may be of any race.

Source: "Older Americans 2000 . . .," 2000: 4.

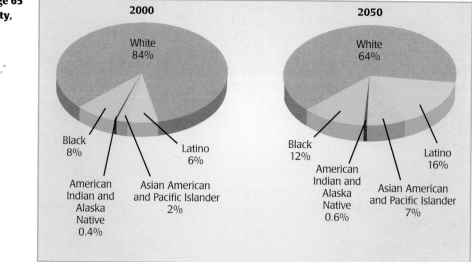

9 percent; Asian Americans, 3 percent; and American Indians, 2 percent ("Projections of the resident population . . .," 2000). As you saw at the beginning of the chapter, some centenarians are releasing rap CDs and writing books. Others, as you'll see shortly, suffer from numerous health problems.

Because many of the elderly are healthy, their longevity has increased the number of multigenerational families. In 2002, for example, 5.6 million children (8 percent of all children) were living in households with a grandparent present (Fields, 2003). Even when children, parents, and grandparents don't live under the same roof, families are more likely than ever before to have several generations of kin.

As you recall, some sociologists and other social scientists argue that the family is declining in importance because of the increase in divorces, cohabitation, single-mother households, and out-of-wedlock births (see Chapter 1). In contrast, other sociologists maintain that multigenerational bonds are becoming more important than the nuclear family for well-being and support over the life course (Bengston, 2001). Although some multigenerational ties create conflict, many provide affection, help, and emotional as well as financial support.

As the number of older Americans increases, the proportion of young people is decreasing. As *Figure 17.2* shows, by 2030 there will be more elderly people than young people in the United States. As a result, the years of parent–child relationships will be prolonged. Many adult children will care for frail and elderly parents, and many young children will have not only great-grandparents but also great-great-grandparents (Dellmann-Jenkins et al., 2000).

Multigenerational families have created a great deal of diversity among **later-life families**, that is, families that are beyond the child-rearing years who have launched their children or childless families who are beginning to plan for retirement. As later-life families age, they experience a variety of changes physically and socially.

Aging: Changes in Physical, Mental, and Social Status

Orroli, a small town on the Italian island of Sardinia, has the world's highest documented percentage of centenarians. The inhabitants debate the secret to their long life: the air, the pure groundwater, homegrown vegetables, genes, moderation in all things, little intermarrying with outsiders, and a daily glass or two of red wine (Israely, 2002).

Although gerontologists and other social scientists define the elderly as people who are 65 years and older, people in this age group don't agree. Instead, 45 percent

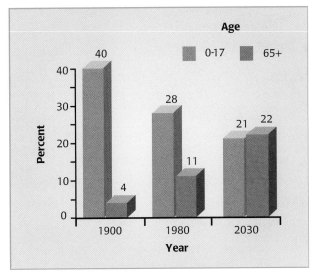

FIGURE 17.2 **The Young and the Old, 1900 to 2030**
SOURCE: U.S. Senate Special Committee on Aging et al., 1991: 9.

of 65- to 69-year-olds consider themselves "middle-aged," as do 33 percent of Americans in their 70s (Gardyn, 2001).

Whether people feel middle-aged or old depends on a number of factors, including personality, social status, and, perhaps most important, the quality of one's health. Let's look first at the issue of health, then at the social status of the elderly and the societal stereotypes that many older people must often endure.

Is Deterioration in Health Inevitable?

In a recent survey, 72 percent of those age 65 and over reported being in good, very good, or excellent health. Even among those 85 or older, about half of the people reported good to excellent health ("Older Americans 2000 . . .," 2000).

Several national studies report that older Americans are healthier and better able to live independently than recent generations. Because disability rates among older people have declined substantially, nursing home use rates have also decreased, especially among people aged 75 and older (Korczyk, 2002; Redfoot and Pandya, 2002).

Physical Decline Is Normal According to a 90-year-old retired diplomatic correspondent, a long life comes down to "keeping your heart pumping, your noodle active, and your mood cheery" (Roberts, 2001: 16). Researchers would agree that this is good advice. Nevertheless, some physical decline across all age groups is normal and inevitable.

TABLE 17.1

Aging and Health

	Age			
	25	**45**	**65**	**85**
Maximum heart rate	100%	94%	87%	81%
Lung capacity	100%	82%	62%	50%
Muscle strength	100%	90%	75%	55%
Kidney function	100%	88%	78%	69%
Cholesterol level	198	221	224	206

SOURCE: Based on Begley et al., 1990: 44–48.

Compared with 40 percent of adults between ages 18 and 64, approximately 80 percent of those 65 years of age and over experience one or more chronic diseases such as heart disorders, arthritis, and respiratory and digestive problems (Adams and Marano, 1995). As *Table 17.1* shows, people over 85 typically experience the most severe failure of lung capacity and muscle strength. Some older people are healthier than others, of course. During and after his flight in space in 2000, for instance, 77-year-old John Glenn's heart rate was better than those of astronauts half his age ("Glenn's health . . .," 2000).

A gradual process of physical deterioration begins early in life, affecting all body systems: Reflexes slow, hearing and eyesight dim, and stamina decreases. No matter how well tuned we keep our bodies, the parts eventually wear down.

People age differently, depending on lifestyle, genetic predisposition, and their attitude toward life. A healthful diet and regular exercise can help many older people preserve their good health. According to exercise physiologists, at least half of the physical decline during aging is due to a sedentary lifestyle (Krucoff, 1999).

Variations by Race and Ethnicity Race and ethnicity also affect our health. According to the most comprehensive study of its kind of Medicare beneficiaries, researchers found that elderly African Americans receive worse health care than older white people even when they have the same health insurance and comparable incomes. For example, blacks are 21 percent less likely than whites to receive follow-up help after hospitalizations for mental illnesses, 9 percent less likely to get heart medications, 8 percent less likely to be screened for breast cancer, and 7 percent less likely to get eye exams to prevent blindness from glaucoma resulting from diabetes (Schneider et al., 2002).

Many health differences result from socioeconomic differences rather than race or ethnicity. As the Medicare study found, however, there are considerable racial disparities in health care delivery.

Mental Health

In some illnesses, physical changes can lead to emotional and behavioral changes. Two of the most common mental health problems for older people are depression and dementia.

Depression Depression is a mental disorder characterized by pervasive sadness and other negative emotions that interfere with the ability to work, study, sleep, eat, and enjoy once pleasurable activities. Depression affects 15 percent of Americans age 65 or older.

It's not clear whether depressive disorders are inherited. Whether inherited or not, depression is often associated with changes in brain structures or brain function. In recent years, researchers have found that physical changes in the body can be accompanied by mental changes. Medical illnesses such as a stroke, a heart attack, cancer, Parkinson's disease, and hormonal disorders can cause depression (Strock, 2002).

Depression is often characterized by pervasive sadness and other negative feelings such as a sense of worthlessness. Among elderly people, depression often accompanies such physical symptoms as diarrhea, chest discomfort, nausea, or loss of appetite which have no apparent physiological causes.

Scientists believe that depression has roots in a combination of genetic, personal history, and environmental

TABLE 17.2

Symptoms of Depression

1. Changes in appetite and weight
2. Disturbed sleep (such as insomnia or oversleeping)
3. Persistent sadness, anxiety, or an "empty" feeling
4. Fatigue and loss of energy
5. Depressed or irritable mood
6. Loss of interest or pleasure in usual activities
7. Difficulty thinking or concentrating
8. Feelings of worthlessness, self-reproach, excessive guilt
9. Suicidal thoughts or attempts
10. Chronic pain, headaches, and digestive disorders that don't respond to treatment

SOURCES: Kaplan and Strawbridge, 1994; Strock, 2002.

ASKYOURSELF

What Do You Know about Alzheimer's Disease?

	True	False	Don't Know
1. Anyone who lives long enough will almost certainly get Alzheimer's disease.	❑	❑	❑
2. At present there is no cure for Alzheimer's disease.	❑	❑	❑
3. A person with Alzheimer's experiences both mental and physical decline.	❑	❑	❑
4. The primary symptom of Alzheimer's disease is memory loss.	❑	❑	❑
5. If you are over 75, memory loss probably indicates the beginning of Alzheimer's.	❑	❑	❑
6. Depression in an older person can sometimes look like Alzheimer's.	❑	❑	❑
7. Men are more likely to develop Alzheimer's than women.	❑	❑	❑
8. Alzheimer's disease is fatal.	❑	❑	❑
9. The majority of people with Alzheimer's live in nursing homes.	❑	❑	❑
10. Alzheimer's is hereditary.	❑	❑	❑
11. Alzheimer's disease can be diagnosed by a blood test.	❑	❑	❑
12. Alzheimer's patients become passive and withdrawn.	❑	❑	❑
13. Medicare covers nursing home costs for Alzheimer's patients.	❑	❑	❑
14. Medicines taken for high blood pressure can cause symptoms that look like Alzheimer's disease.	❑	❑	❑

(Answers are on page 488.)

factors. Researchers speculate that 20 to 100 genes, most of them still unknown, might be causing depression (Monastersky, 2003). People who weather multiple stressful life experiences or crises (such as divorce, losing a job, or financial problems), for example, are more likely to develop depression because the protein in their genes does not protect them from multiple emotionally difficult incidents (Caspi et al., 2003).

Because family members tend to interpret the "down" mood they see in an older relative as a reaction to the death of loved ones or to the loss of a job or good health, they may not recognize the signs of depression. Seven of the ten symptoms of depression listed in *Table 17.2*, including numbers 5 and 6 (depressed mood and loss of interest), must be present for at least a two-week period for a physician to diagnose major depression that should be treated. Among the elderly, about 85 percent of those diagnosed can be treated successfully with antidepressant medications (Henry, 1995).

Dementia Dementia is the loss of mental abilities that most commonly occurs late in life. Dementia increases with age, from about 8 percent of all people over age 65 to as many as 50 percent over age 85 (Brynes, 2001).

The most common form of dementia is **Alzheimer's disease**, a progressive, degenerative disorder that attacks the brain and impairs memory, thinking, and behavior. Before you continue reading, take the quiz "What Do You Know about Alzheimer's Disease?"

Medical researchers have linked Alzheimer's to genes that cause a dense deposit of protein and debris called "plaques," along with twisted protein "tangles" that kill nerve cells in the brain (Scinto et al., 1994; Reilly, 2000). According to neuroscientists, Alzheimer's spreads "like a wild fire," destroying more and more brain cells as it progresses. After two years, the disease engulfs almost the entire brain in some patients (Thompson et al., 2003).

The disease afflicts about 4.5 million U.S. elderly—about 10 percent of those age 65 and older and 40 percent

Answers to "What Do You Know about Alzheimer's Disease"?

1. **False.** Alzheimer's occurs most often in the elderly, but it is a disease and not the inevitable consequence of aging.

2. **True.** There is no known cure for Alzheimer's. However, research suggests that some currently experimental drugs may be successful in slowing the disease (Scinto et al., 1994).

3. **True.** Memory and cognitive decline are characteristic of the earlier stages of Alzheimer's disease; physical decline follows in the later stages.

4. **True.** This is the earliest sign of Alzheimer's disease.

5. **False.** Although Alzheimer's does produce memory loss, memory loss can be due to other factors.

6. **True.** Depression can cause disorientation that looks like Alzheimer's.

7. **False.** Both sexes are equally likely to get Alzheimer's.

8. **True.** Alzheimer's produces mental and physical decline that is eventually fatal, but the course of the disease may run from a few years to as many as 20. On average, death occurs within eight years (DiBacco, 1994).

9. **False.** The early and middle stages of the disease usually do not necessitate institutional care. Only a small percentage of those with the disease live in nursing homes, most of whom are over age 85 (Havemann, 1997b).

10. **False.** Your risk of developing Alzheimer's is higher if you have a close blood relative with the disease. According to most researchers, however, the disease is probably caused by several factors.

11. **False.** At present there is no blood test that can determine with certainty that a patient has Alzheimer's disease. Some recent studies suggest that certain psychological tests may predict Alzheimer's disease among the healthy elderly (Masur et al., 1994).

12. **False.** Some Alzheimer's patients become aggressive, physically violent, and combative with caretakers and others (Lyman, 1993).

13. **False.** Medicare generally pays only for short-term nursing home care after hospitalization, not for long-term care. Medicaid can pay for long-term nursing home care, but because it is a state-directed program for the medically indigent, coverage for Alzheimer's patients depends on state regulations and on the income of the patient and family.

14. **True.** Some antihypertensive medications can cause symptoms that resemble Alzheimer's.

of those over 85. Unless a cure is found, medical researchers predict a future epidemic. According to some estimates, Alzheimer's will increase by 27 percent in 2020 and 300 percent by 2050, affecting about 14 million people (Hebert et al., 2003). According to Sheldon Goldberg, president and CEO of the Alzheimer's Association, "If left unchecked, it is no exaggeration to say that Alzheimer's disease will destroy the health care system and bankrupt Medicare and Medicaid" ("New Alzheimer's projections . . .," 2003).

Patients with Alzheimer's need round-the-clock care, costing about $50 billion yearly in medical expenses, absenteeism, the time of unpaid caregivers, and the patients' earning losses (Himes, 2001). Although Alzheimer's is incurable and irreversible, researchers are experimenting with a variety of medications and therapies to delay or prevent its onset or slow its progression (Cowley, 2000; Morris et al., 2002; Reisberg et al., 2003).

Memory Lapse or Alzheimer's? All of us experience slips of memory such as misplacing car keys (or locking them in the car), forgetting which floor of the parking garage we left our car, being unable to recall the name of the movie we saw a few weeks ago, or forgetting someone's name. As *Table 17.3* shows, the signs of Alzheimer's are much more severe.

Until breakthroughs emerge from the labs, researchers suggest that the best way to prevent dementia is to exercise your mind as well as your body. In a well-known study of 678 elderly Catholic nuns, epidemiologist David Snowdon (2001) attributed their longevity and avoidance of Alzheimer's to lives "well lived" that were filled with mental and social activities, healthful eating, exercise, and a variety of interests that included reading, knitting, and playing cards and a positive outlook early in life.

Slower recall is normal as we age, but we can delay the speed of aging if we exercise our brains and bodies. A team of researchers found support for the "use it or lose it" claims in a recent study of subjects age 75 and older. Purely physical activities like walking or doing housework have health benefits, but they don't lower the risk of Alzheimer's.

In contrast, activities that stimulate the brain seem to reduce the risk of dementia. Such activities include reading, crossword puzzles, board games (chess or checkers),

TABLE 17.3

Ten Warning Signs of Alzheimer's Disease

The Alzheimer's Association (www.alz.org) provides a widely circulated list of symptoms that warrant medical evaluation:

1. **Memory loss:** Although it's normal to forget names or telephone numbers, those with dementia forget such things more often and do not remember them later (for example, "I never made that doctor's appointment").

2. **Difficulty performing familiar tasks:** Not knowing the steps for preparing a meal, using a household appliance, or participating in a lifelong hobby.

3. **Problems with language:** Forgetting simple words. If a person with Alzheimer's is unable to find his or her toothbrush, for example, the person may ask for "that thing for my mouth."

4. **Disorientation to time and place:** Becoming lost on your own street, forgetting where you are and how you got there, and not knowing how to get back home.

5. **Poor or decreased judgment:** Dressing without regard to the weather, wearing several shirts or blouses on a hot day or very little clothing in cold weather. People with dementia often show poor judgment about money, giving away large amounts of money to telemarketers or paying for home repairs or products they don't need.

6. **Problems with abstract thinking:** In balancing a checkbook, for example, someone with Alzheimer's could forget completely what the numbers are and what should be done with them.

7. **Misplacing things:** Putting things in unusual places, such as an iron in the freezer or a wristwatch in the sugar bowl.

8. **Changes in mood or behavior:** Showing rapid mood swings—from calm to tears to anger—for no apparent reason.

9. **Changes in personality:** Changing a lot, becoming extremely confused, suspicious, fearful, or dependent on a family member.

10. **Loss of initiative:** Becoming very passive, such as sitting in front of the television for hours, sleeping more than usual, or not wanting to do usual activities.

playing a musical instrument, taking classes, dancing, gardening, and any other pursuit that involves mental effort (Verghese et al., 2003). Don't spend all of your time in front of video games just yet, however. Although the researchers did their utmost to screen out people who already had dementia, their sample might have included subjects who were not participating in various activities because they were suffering from undiagnosed dementia.

According to brain researchers, the neurons that store and process information are incredibly flexible and, unless interrupted by disease or injury, constantly replace and rearrange themselves, even into old age. Therefore, most healthy elderly people do not experience cognitive decline with advancing age. Those who tend to deteriorate have high levels of cardiovascular disease and diabetes, both of which are linked to obesity (Haan et al., 1999). In addition, mental and cognitive health are often associated with one's socioeconomic and social status.

Social Status of the Elderly

We often hear that elderly people no longer have the respect they enjoyed in "the good old days." Historians point out, however, that the elderly did not necessarily enjoy respect and deferential treatment in the past. In colonial America, for example, treatment of the elderly depended very much on the person's wealth and social class. Church fathers gave wealthy and successful men in their thirties seats in the front row, but poor men in their seventies occupied seats near the back (Demos, 1986). Elderly women were rarely treated with respect, primarily because many were poor and thus powerless.

Still, the status of the elderly has generally declined since the turn of the twentieth century. Grandparents' influence on their children and grandchildren has diminished because families often live far apart. And because divorce and remarriage rates are high, familial ties in many cases have loosened. At family gatherings, for example, biological grandparents may have to compete with stepgrandparents (see Chapters 15 and 16).

Perhaps most important, whereas in many societies the elderly were once the source of all wisdom, contemporary advances in science, technology, and other areas have made some of the ideas of the elderly seem old-fashioned and outdated. According to some of my students, for example, their grandparents are appalled when their grandchildren highlight passages (and in a variety of colors) in textbooks because "I never did that when I was in school."

In some cultures the elderly still maintain an influential position. Societies that do not emphasize self-reliance and independence are likely to bestow older people with more power and privilege because the young depend on the old for approval and other rewards (Ishii-Kuntz and Lee, 1987).

In addition, preindustrial societies that endorse *familism* and filial piety, characterized by absolute obedience to the elderly and a sacred duty to support one's parents in their old age, may be more likely to honor and respect the elderly (Cowgill, 1986). In these and many developing societies, older women enjoy more leisure because they delegate most of the work of the family to daughters or daughters-in-law, who defer to their knowledge and experience (Brown, 1992).

Stereotypes and Ageism

In 2001, 70-year-old Viktor Korchnoi won the elite Biel International Chess Festival in Switzerland, defeating another Russian champion, Peter Svidler, age 25. Korchnoi's victory surprised many chess fans because they assumed that younger contenders are smarter (Restak, 2002). They were wrong.

In our youth-oriented society, many people dread growing old. Writer Betty Friedan admits that her reaction to turning 60 was anything but jubilant:

> "When my friends threw a surprise [birthday] party . . . I could have killed them all. Their toasts seemed [to be] . . . pushing me out of life . . . out of the race. Professionally, politically, personally, sexually . . . I was depressed for weeks" (Friedan, 1993: 13).

Some women, such as actress Jane Fonda and Cher, try to resist aging through technological "fixes" such as plastic surgery, cosmetic "disguises," and obsessive exercising. Others, such as former First Lady Barbara Bush, have accepted their aging bodies and remain resolutely natural. Although Mrs. Bush admitted always wearing three strands of pearls to cover her "sagging neck," she refused to dye her hair because "people who worry about their hair all the time are boring." Mrs. Bush considers women who are slaves to the latest fashions to be frivolous and narcissistic (Dinnerstein and Weitz, 1994).

Ageism In his classic book *Why Survive? Being Old in America*, physician Robert Butler (1975) coined the term **ageism** to refer to discrimination against people on the basis of age, particularly those who are old. Among other things, Butler pointed out the persistence of the "myth of senility," the notion that if old people

show forgetfulness, confusion, and inattention, they are senile.

If a 16-year-old boy can't remember why he went to the refrigerator, we say he's "off in the clouds" somewhere or in love, but if his 79-year-old grandfather forgets why he went to the refrigerator, we're likely to call him senile (Slade, 1985; see also Palmore, 1999, for examples of historical and current ageist humor). Our language is full of ageist words and phrases that malign, stereotype, and generally disparage elderly people: "senior citizen," "old bat," "old bag," "old fart," "old fogey," "fossil," "old goat," "old hag," "deadwood," "old maid," "dirty old man," "crotchety," and "over the hill" (Saporta, 1991). In contrast, how many negative words do we have that demean young people?

Although the data collected by gerontologists show otherwise, many people continue to believe that older Americans are less intelligent, less competent, and less active than younger people (Levin, 1988). This view of the elderly is well illustrated by the experiment conducted by Patricia Moore, who wanted to know what it's like to be an older person in our society. As you can see from the box "Being Old in America," Moore found a strong and pervasive negative attitude toward the elderly.

Stereotypes When you turn on the TV, what kinds of images do you see of older people? Usually those complaining about their health, bladder problems, dentures, and diabetes. Children as young as 5 years old have negative stereotypes of older people. According to a recent study, for example, many children see older people as incompetent compared with younger people (Kwong See and Rasmussen, 2003).

However unintentionally, educators sometimes reinforce stereotypical attitudes. In a study of 27 undergraduate textbooks on marriage and family published between 1988 and 1993, for example, Stolley and Hill (1996) found that the aged received little coverage and were generally associated with specific "elderly" topics such as retirement and widowhood. According to the researchers, the elderly are rarely mentioned in chapters on gender, race, ethnicity, or sexuality.

The media also create and perpetuate negative images of aging. For instance, researchers examined 100 top-grossing motion pictures spanning the 1940s through the 1980s. They concluded that ageist stereotypes were prevalent across the five decades in their portrayal of older people as unattractive, unfriendly, and having few positive characteristics compared with younger characters.

The films were sexist as well as ageist in two ways: (1) They underrepresented older women (only 8 percent of the central characters were women over age 35), and (2) they consistently depicted more negative images of older women than of older men. Compared with older men, for example, older women were portrayed as less

CONSTRAINTS

Being Old in America

With the help of a professional makeup artist, industrial designer Patricia Moore put on latex wrinkles and a gray wig, wore splints under her clothes to stiffen her joints, and put plugs in her ears to dull her hearing. Putting baby oil in her eyes irritated them and blurred her vision. "The look was that of eyes with cataracts, as the baby oil would float on the surface of the eyeball" (Moore and Conn, 1985: 56). She used a special type of crayon, mixed with oil paint, to stain and discolor her teeth, and she gargled with salt to make her voice raspy (Ryan, 1993). Then she shuffled out into the world to find out what it's really like to be old in America.

Over a three-year period, Moore found dramatic differences between the way people reacted to "Young" and "Old" Pat Moore. For example, as Old Pat she went into a store to buy a typewriter ribbon. Ignoring her at first, the salesman finally approached her and was irritated when she was not sure what kind of ribbon she wanted and impatient when she fumbled with the clasp on her handbag. Wordlessly, he gave her the change and dropped the package on the counter instead of handing it to her.

The next day, Young Pat, "sandy-blonde hair curled and falling on my shoulders, sunglasses and sandals," but wearing the same dress she had worn the day before, went to the same store to buy typewriter ribbon. This time the salesman smiled and immediately offered his assistance. When Pat pretended not to know what kind of ribbon she wanted, he was solicitous ("As long as you know it when you see it, you're all right"), and when

she fumbled with the clasp of the purse, saying, "Darn thing always gives me trouble," he was amiable ("Well, better for it . . . to take a little longer to open than to make it easy for the muggers and the pickpockets"). He chatted as he counted out her change and opened the door because "it sticks sometimes."

What impressed Pat Moore almost as much as the negative attitudes and behavior she continued to encounter as Old Pat was the way she accepted and internalized those negative responses. When she appeared to be 85 and people were more likely to push ahead of her in line, she didn't protest this behavior: "It seemed somehow . . . that it was okay for them to do this to the Old Pat Moore, since they were undoubtedly busier than I was anyway. . . . After all, little old ladies have plenty of time, don't they?"

"Old Pat Moore."

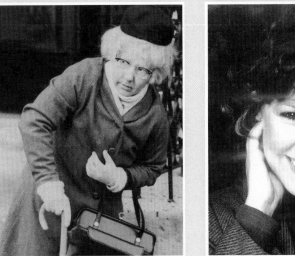

Moore found that clerks assumed she was hard of hearing, that she would be slow in paying for purchases, or that she would "somehow become confused about the transaction. What it all added up to was that people feared I would be trouble, so they tried to have as little to do with me as possible. And the amazing thing is that. . . I absorbed some of their tacitly negative judgment about people of my age. It was as if, unconsciously, I was saying . . . 'You're right. I'm just a lot of trouble. I'm really not as valuable as all these other people, so I'll just get out of your way as soon as possible so you won't be angry with me.' . . . I think perhaps the worst thing about aging may be the overwhelming sense that everything around you is letting you know that you are not terribly important any more" (Moore and Conn, 1985: 75–76).

Patricia Moore as herself.

friendly, less intelligent, sleazy, poor, and unattractive (Bazzini et al., 1997). Think about the films produced since this study was done. How many motion pictures use a double standard in the images of older women and older men?

Aging and Personality   One of the most common stereotypes is that older people become nasty as they age. Some research shows that people's personalities are stable over a lifetime (McCrea and Costa, cited in Belsky, 1988). If you're grumpy or unpleasant at 75, you were probably grumpy and unpleasant at 15, 35, and 55. Although work, marriage, and other life experiences do affect people, in general those who are depressed, hostile, anxious, and poorly adjusted in their twenties are likely to be depressed, hostile, anxious, and poorly adjusted in old age.

Other studies report that our personalities aren't "set in plaster" and can change after age 30. As people mature, they become more conscientious (organized and disciplined), more agreeable (warm and helpful), and less neurotic (constant worry and emotional instability) (Srivastava et al., 2003).

And when older people (ages 65 to 80) seem to forget things, it may reflect emphasizing positive images rather than physiological changes. As people get older and become more aware of the limited time left in life, they tend to focus more on positive thoughts, activities, and memories than people ages 18 to 53 (Charles et al., 2003).

Contrary to the popular notion that people become more stubborn as they age, Tyler and Schuller (1991) found that older people are more flexible than their younger counterparts. Older people have a larger repertoire of experiences, these researchers say, and they've developed ways of dealing with bureaucratic red tape and other daily problems. As a result, many older people realize that with a little patience they can often get what they want.

Some researchers suggest that as people age, they lose their cognitive ability to be more tolerant. As a result, they might think and express prejudicial or stereotypical thoughts (Von Hippel et al., 2000). As British statesman Benjamin Disraeli once said, "My idea of an agreeable person is someone who agrees with me."

On the other hand, some people become less docile and subservient as they age. When older people "suddenly" seem stubborn and defiant, they may simply be shedding some long-term inhibitions:

> One of the greatest thrills of being a woman of 70 is having the luxury to be open about what I really think. When I was younger, I was so afraid of hurting people or worried about what they would think of me that I . . . kept my mouth shut. Now when I don't like something, I speak up.
>
> It's gotten me into trouble with my daughter and sister, but I don't care. It's not that I try to be mean. . . . It's just that age has made me more truthful. And that's one of the reasons that I feel better about myself now than I have at any other time in life (Belsky, 1988: 65–66).

As people age, their family roles change. Retirement is a major transition during adulthood. In U.S. society, it usually marks the end of the midlife years and entry into life as a "senior citizen." Even though older people may reenter the labor force (out of choice or necessity), retiring affects family life.

MAKING CONNECTIONS

■ Some widely read publications such as *Parents* magazine have questioned the effectiveness of "grandma" as a child-care provider. One article, for example, maintained that many professional caretakers have more training in child rearing than grandparents do and they take the job more seriously because the profession is regulated by a state's licensing system (Ogintz, 1994). What do you think of this claim?

■ Although dementia, including Alzheimer's disease, is incurable, many researchers are developing drugs to slow down the disease's progression. Should we let nature take its course? Or delay death using drugs even though it decreases the quality of life?

Retirement and Family Life

Retirement, the exit from the paid labor force, is a recent phenomenon. Historians point out that many people who reached old age in colonial America worked well past the age of 65. Men in their seventies hauled grain, transported rugs, and tanned leather. One man still worked in the coal mines at age 102. Men over age 65 who were in government positions (such as governors and their assistants) or who were ministers typically retained their offices until death, and some women worked as midwives well into their seventies (Demos, 1986).

Social Security, a public retirement pension system administered by the federal government, provides income support to more than 90 percent of the elderly, but the benefits depend on how long people have been in the labor force and how much they have earned. Those who saw their retirement portfolios decrease by a third or more during the stock market decline in the early 2000s, for example, reentered the labor force (Lim, 2003).

Who Retires?

Anthropologist Margaret Mead once said, "Sooner or later I'm going to die, but I'm not going to retire." True to her word, Mead authored and co-authored several books before she died at age 77. Like Mead, some people work until they die because they want to do so.

Others retire from full-time work but continue to work part-time to supplement pension and Social Security income.

In 2002, 18 percent of men and 10 percent of women age 65 and over were in the labor force (Smith, 2003). People who continue to work past age 65 are more likely to be self-employed. Because they don't have pension benefits and because Social Security payments are usually low, they work out of economic necessity (Himes, 2001).

Health also affects retirement decisions. Husbands and wives often coordinate retirement plans and withdraw from the labor force at about the same time. They are less likely to retire before age 65, however, if one of the spouses has a health problem and especially if the spouses aren't yet eligible for Social Security benefits. In other cases, people continue to work if they have family responsibilities that include financially supporting adult children or frail parents (Johnson and Favreault, 2001).

Retirement Lasts Longer

Because we have greater life expectancy today, we may well spend a third of our adult life in retirement. We often hear that retirement is particularly difficult for men because the traditional male role calls for breadwinning and productivity. Researchers have found, however, that health and financial security are the major determinants of retirees' satisfaction with life. When people are unhappy in retirement, it is usually because of health or income problems rather than the loss of the worker role (Gradman, 1994; Solomon and Szwabo, 1994). If retirement benefits do not keep up with inflation or if the retiree is not covered by a pension plan, poverty can be just a few years away.

Variations in the Financial Impact

The overall poverty rate for Americans age 65 and older has dropped from 35 percent in 1959 to 10 percent in 2002 (Proctor and Dalaker, 2003). The aged are an economically diverse group. The national median income for people 65 and over is $18,965, but there are wide differences: 21 percent have an income under $10,000 per year, and 15 percent have an income of $50,000 or more (Koenig and Mulpuru, 2003). There are also large differences by age, marital status, sex, and race and ethnicity.

Age Median income decreases as people age: almost $26,000 at ages 65 to 69, $21,000 at ages 70 to 74, $18,000 at ages 75 to 79, and $15,000 at age 80 and older. The longer people live, the more likely they are to be poor: 9 percent of people ages 65 to 69 are poor, compared with 12 percent of those age 80 or older (Koenig and Mulpuru, 2003).

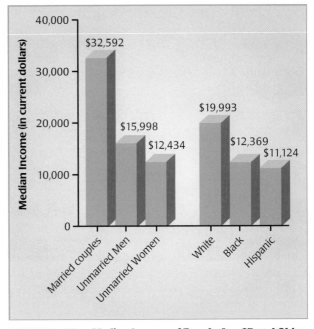

FIGURE 17.3 **Median Income of People Age 65 and Older, by Marital Status, Sex, and Ethnicity, 2001**

SOURCE: Koenig and Mulpuru, 2003: 16.

Marital Status As *Figure 17.3* shows, married couples have twice the median income as single men and more than twice that of single women. This difference characterizes every age group. Even at age 80 and older, for example, when many people have depleted most of their savings, married couples have an annual income of almost $28,000, compared with about $16,000 for single men and $12,000 for single women (Koenig and Mulpuru, 2003).

Sex Marriage protects many older women from poverty (see *Figure 17.3*). Nonetheless, retirement presents more financial problems for women than men.

At every age group, older women have a lower median income than men. About 23 percent of single men are poor or just above the poverty line, compared with 28 percent of single women (Koenig and Mulpuru, 2003). Many women live in poverty for more than half of their old-age years. Divorced, never married, and separated women are as likely to experience poverty in old age as widows (Vartanian and McNamara, 2002).

Many women have had an uneven employment history because they have spent many years as homemakers and mothers or because they have left jobs periodically to raise children. Therefore, many women must continue to work at least part time after age 65 because their Social Security benefits are very low. (Chapter 18 examines the Social Security system more closely.)

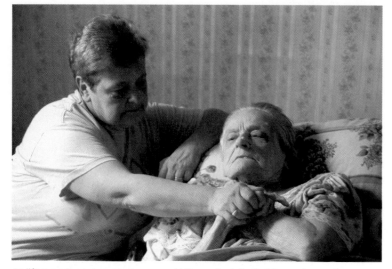

As life expectancy increases, many middle-aged adults find themselves caring for their aging parents. Most of the elder care is provided in the children's or the older person's home rather than in institutions, such as nursing homes.

Older women are poorer than their male counterparts in every racial group. Elderly African Americans are poorer than whites or Latinos, and elderly African American women are the most likely to be poor ("Older Americans 2000 . . .," 2000).

Nationally, at least 90 percent of older Americans receive most of their income from Social Security or Supplemental Security Income (SSI) (Koenig and Mulpuru, 2003). Across all groups, women have lower retirement benefits than men (see *Table 17.4*). Some women, such as Latinas and Asian American women, are less likely to have been in the labor force than white and black women and consequently have lower Social Security benefits (see Chapter 4). For the most part, however, women's benefits are lower because they tend to work in lower-paying jobs and get paid less in comparable jobs (see Chapter 13). In addition, racial-ethnic women are more likely to remain in poverty because they have little in personal savings and have worked in jobs that don't offer pension plans (Hounsell and Humphlett, 2002).

Retirement has an especially devastating impact on black women. Many have worked in low-paying clerical or service positions lacking adequate pensions. If their husbands had low-paying jobs or a sporadic employment history because of recessions and discrimination, the husbands' benefits may also be inadequate.

Retirement is an important role transition. Well before retirement, however, many adults take on another important role—that of a grandparent.

Widows may receive Social Security benefits based on their husband's earnings, but these benefits are only two-thirds of the benefit the couple received. In addition, most women do not receive benefits from a partner's pension. Divorced women for example, are often unable to receive any assets from their ex-husband's pension (Himes, 2001).

Even women who have worked full time often have been confined to low-paying jobs, and their earnings have been lower than those of men, even in comparable jobs. In 2001, for example, the average Social Security benefit was $756 per month for retired women workers, compared with $985 for their male counterparts ("Women and Social Security," 2003). There have been more women in higher-paid jobs in the last few decades. Many who are ages 65 to 74, however, were primarily in low-paying jobs and must continue to work (Francese, 2003).

Such payments may seem adequate. Remember, however, that Medicare doesn't cover such expenses as dental care and dentures, over-the-counter drugs and most prescribed medicine, eyeglasses and eye examinations, hearing aids and hearing examinations, immunization shots, custodial care in the home, or long-term care in nursing homes. As a result, many older people spend at least 33 percent of their income on health care.

Race and Ethnicity   Elderly whites have almost twice the median income as African Americans and Latinos (see *Figure 17.3*). About 9 percent of elderly whites live in poverty, compared with 22 percent of blacks and Latinos (Koenig and Mulpuru, 2003).

TABLE 17.4

Monthly Social Security Payments, by Sex and Ethnicity, 2000

	Women	Men
All groups	$696	$928
African Americans	$640	$794
American Indians	$575	$739
Asian Americans	$510	$818
Latinos	$543	$804

Note: Data for whites only are not available.

Source: Based on several reports on Social Security Online, *Fact Sheets for Demographic Groups*, www.socialsecurity.gov (accessed October 11, 2003).

Grandparenting

According to many gerontologists, grandparents are the glue that keeps the family close. In many families, grandparents represent stability and the continuity of family rituals and values. They often help their adult children with parenting by providing emotional support, encouragement, help with day-to-day parental needs (such as baby-sitting), and support in times of emergency or crisis, including illness and divorce (see Szinovacz, 1998, and Smith and Drew, 2002, for good summaries of grandparenting across racial-ethnic groups). No matter how strict they were with their own children, many grandparents often serve as family mediators, advocates for their grandchildren's point of view, and shoulders to cry on.

In general, today's grandparents are more affluent than grandparents of just a decade ago. About 30 percent have incomes of $50,000 or more per year. Therefore, many are able to buy their grandchildren gifts that range from small toys and items of clothing to expensive computers, sporting goods, and financial investments such as stocks, bonds, and trust funds (Paul, 2002).

More than 25 percent of grandparents buy costly gifts, averaging more than $500 each, for their grandchildren. In addition, many grandparents give their adult children (who can't afford such expensive items) cameras and video cameras to capture their grandchildren's growing years (Brazil, 1998; Davies and Williams, 2002). With more money, more energy, and more leisure time than ever before, growing numbers of grandparents are taking advantage of tour packages designed specifically for grandparents and grandchildren.

African Americans and Latinos become grandparents earlier than other groups. By age 65, however, 84 percent of all men and 80 percent of all women are grandparents (Himes, 2001). Like aging, grandparenting styles are diverse.

Grandparenting Styles

Grandparents usually take great pleasure in their grandchildren. Their new grandparenting role gives their lives stability and provides them with new experiences. Not all grandparents feel the same about this role, however. There are a number of different styles of grandparenting. In this section we look at five: remote or detached, companionate and supportive, involved and influential, advisory and authoritative, and cultural transmitters.

Remote or Detached   In the *remote or detached* relationship, the grandparents and grandchildren live far apart and see each other infrequently, maintaining a largely ritualistic, symbolic relationship. For example, grandparents who are "distant figures" may see their

Love, intimacy, and companionship are just as important to older couples as to younger people.

grandchildren only on holidays or special occasions. Such relationships may be cordial but are also uninvolved and fleeting (Thompson and Walker, 1991).

Only about 3 percent of grandparents are remote or detached from their grandchildren because they never see their grandchildren and never write them (Davies and Williams, 2002). About 33 percent of grandparents live less than 25 miles away and are able to see their grandchildren several times a week (Baker, 2001). In other cases, grandparents are remote or detached because they're experiencing health problems or their grandchildren's busy schedule discourages getting together (Davies and Williams, 2002).

Grandparents may be close to one grandchild but detached from others. Sometimes, grandparents see a grandchild as "special" because of the child's personality, accomplishments, or respect for grandparents. Not surprisingly, then, grandparents sometimes spend more time with these grandchildren than those whom a grandparent finds irritating (Smith and Drew, 2002; Mueller and Elder, 2003).

Although they report feeling close to their great-grandchildren, great-grandparents often have remote relationships because they are in frail health, live far away, or feel that grandparents should play a more authoritative role.

Great-grandparents may also have difficulty adapting to new situations such as divorce and remarriage and often feel embarrassed, uncomfortable, or confused about great-grandchildren produced in cohabiting relationships.

This 5-year-old and her grandmother are attending the 1998 groundbreaking ceremonies for the Grandfamilies House in Dorchester, Massachusetts. This was the nation's first housing center designed for grandparents raising their grandchildren. For example, there are grab-bars in the bathrooms, safety covers on the electrical outlets, and a playground in the rear within easy view of caregivers. A live-in manager is available for emergencies and other needs. A coordinator organizes meetings, transportation, and services ranging from preschool and after-school child care to exercise and parenting classes for the grandparents. A funded van is also available for trips and errands.

As one great-grandparent said, "I guess I have two or three great-grandchildren, depending on how you look at it. My grandson is living with someone and they have a child" (Doka and Mertz, 1988: 196).

Companionate and Supportive   The *companionate and supportive* style of grandparenting is the most common pattern. According to an AARP survey, more than eight out of ten grandparents had seen a grandchild or chatted on the phone in the previous month. About 54 percent of the grandmothers and 42 percent of the grandfathers saw their role as companion or friend (Straw et al., 1999).

Supportive grandparents see their grandchildren often, frequently do things with them, and offer them emotional and instrumental support (such as providing money), but they have absolutely no role of authority in the grandchild's life. These grandparents are typically on the maternal side of the family, are younger, and have more income than other grandparents—characteristics that might encourage meddling—but stay away from parental child-rearing decisions (Mueller and Elder, 2003).

Companionate grandparents often say that they love having their grandchildren with them and then remark, "And the best thing is that they go home!" According to satirist Erma Bombeck (1994: 8E), "Grandparenting is great. You can look at your grandchild with a diaper dragging on the floor and say to his mother, 'That kid is carrying a load! Change him!'"

Companionate grandparents generally don't want to share parenting and tend to emphasize loving, playing, and having fun. Most often, when visiting, grandparents and grandchildren eat together, watch TV comedy shows, shop for clothes, play sports, and attend church (Straw et al., 1999).

Involved and Influential   In a *Newsweek* poll of parents with children age 3 and under, 59 percent said the grandparents were very involved in their children's lives. About half of the parents reported that grandparents were also involved with grandchildren aged 6 to 17 (Hugick, 1999).

In the *involved and influential* grandparenting style, grandparents play an active role in influencing their grandchildren's lives. They may be spontaneous and playful, but they also exert substantial authority over their grandchildren, imposing definite—and sometimes tough—rules. According to a study of white and African American working-class grandparents, grandmothers were more involved in teaching their grandchildren than were grandfathers. Black grandmothers, especially, said that they were concerned with teaching grandchildren sensitivity to others' feelings and the value of lifelong education (Watson and Koblinsky, 1997).

Involved grandparents are often younger than other types of grandparent. They typically welcome their daughters and grandchildren back home after a divorce. In other cases, grandparents, usually the grandmother, care for the grandchildren while the mother works. Involved grandparents include those who step in occasionally or daily to help manage a family crisis because the parent—usually a single mother—is young, poor, immature, or irresponsible in caring for the children (Oysterman et al., 1993).

Black grandparents, especially those who live in inner cities, often see themselves as family protectors against separation, divorce, drugs, and crime (Poe, 1992). Even when children are doing well, African

American grandparents, especially grandfathers, report being close to their grandchildren because they "hold the key to the future" (Kivett, 1991).

In general, grandparents are more likely to be involved if their grandchildren are struggling in school. They are also twice as likely to be involved and influential in their grandchildren's lives if they had close relationships with their own grandparents who were involved in their lives (Mueller and Elder, 2003).

Advisory and Authoritative In the fourth type of grandparenting, *advisory and authoritative*, the grandparent serves as an adviser, or what Neugarten and Weinstein (1964) call a "reservoir of family wisdom." The grandfather, who may be the family patriarch, may act also as a financial provider, and the grandmother often plays a crucial advisory role in the grandchildren's lives.

Especially when the mother is very young, the maternal grandmother may help the "apprentice mother" make the transition to parenthood by supporting and mentoring—but not replacing—her in the parenting role. The grandmother provides emotional, financial, and child-care support until the "apprentice" shows that she is responsive to and responsible for the baby (Apfel and Seitz, 1991).

The relationships between advisory and authoritative grandparents and their own children can be tense if the grandparents disagree about how a grandchild is being raised. However, "the picture is not of a meddling, domineering grandparent, but rather one of a grandparent who plays an important role in the family, shaped by both love and conflict" (Mueller and Elder, 2003: 415).

Many teenagers begin to break away from their families, including their grandparents. Sometimes the roles reverse at this stage, with teenage grandchildren helping their grandparents with errands or chores. Many adolescents, however, turn to their grandparents for advice or understanding. For example, a 17-year-old boy said, "With my grandpa we discuss usually technical problems. But sometimes some other problems, too. He told me how to refuse to drink alcohol with other boys." A 16-year-old girl said that she and her grandmother go for walks and added, "I can tell her about everything" (Tyszkowa, 1993: 136).

Cultural Transmitters Advisory grandparenting often overlaps with a fifth role in which grandparents are *cultural transmitters* of values and norms. Among American Indian families, grandmothers may provide active parenting in the teaching and instruction of domestic chores, responsibility, and discipline that reflect tribal tradition. Grandfathers may transmit knowledge of tribal history and cultural practices through storytelling (Woods, 1996).

Except for Japanese Americans, many of whom have lived in the United States for five generations (see Chapter 4), many recently arrived Asian immigrants live in extended families and are more likely to do so than Latinos. Between 20 percent (Chinese) and 39 percent (Asian Indians) of Asian Americans 55 years or older live with their grandchildren (Kamo, 1998).

Such coresidence facilitates grandparents being "historians" who transmit values, ethnic heritage, and cultural traditions to their grandchildren even if there are language barriers (Kamo, 1998). Chinese American grandparents, for example, help to develop their grandchildren's ethnic identity by teaching them Chinese, passing on traditional practices and customs during holidays, and reinforcing cultural values. One mother commented, "My father taught [my children] well. Since he lived with us and had time to look after the children at home, he often told them to show filial piety towards their parents because parents worked very hard outside the home" (Tam and Detzner, 1998: 257).

Grandparents as Surrogate Parents

An emerging grandparenting role is that of *surrogate*, in which the grandparent provides regular care or replaces the parents in raising the grandchildren. In 2002, 5.6 million children were living in a household run by a grandparent. Of the 1.3 million children being raised entirely by grandparents, many are white (see *Figure 17.4*). Contrary to the stereotype of the inner-city welfare mother who is raising her teenage daughter's baby,

FIGURE 17.4 **Grandparents Raising Grandchildren, 2002**

SOURCE: Based on Fields, 2003: Table 3.

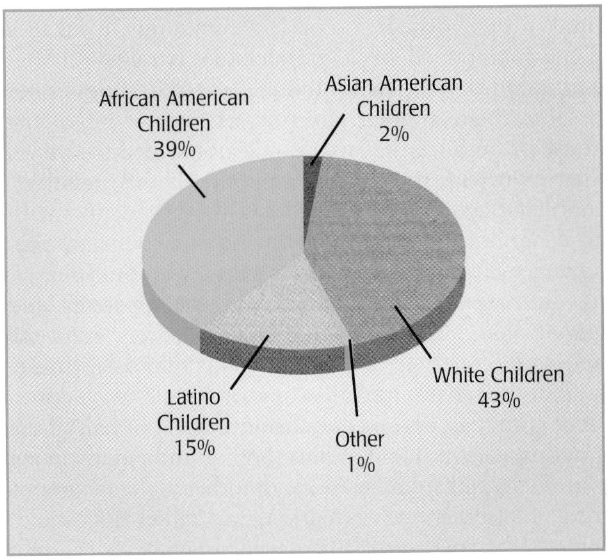

African American Children 39%
Asian American Children 2%
White Children 43%
Other 1%
Latino Children 15%

the majority of grandparent caregivers are white, own their own homes, and live in the suburbs (Fields, 2003).

The increase in grandchildren living with grandparents in these "skipped generation" homes results from many factors: the growth in drug use among parents, teen pregnancy, divorce, the rapid rise of single-parent households, disability due to mental and physical illness (including AIDS, child abuse and neglect), and the death or incarceration of parents (Carten and Fennoy, 1997; Bryson and Casper, 1999).

According to Jendrek (1994), there are at least three categories of surrogate grandparents: custodial, living-with, and day-care grandparents.

Custodial Grandparents

The *custodial* grandparents Jendrek interviewed had a legal relationship with their grandchildren through adoption, guardianship, or custody. Most did not view themselves as taking the grandchild away from the parent but believed they had taken legal action only when the situation became intolerable, such as when the parent—usually the daughter—became an alcoholic or a drug addict and neglected or abandoned the grandchild. At age 75, actor George Kennedy and his wife, 68, adopted their 5-year-old granddaughter because the little girl's mother could not kick her drug habit. In other cases, grandparents might adopt a grandchild after the death of one or both parents.

Many grandparents aren't eager to accept responsibility for their grandchildren. They do so, however, as a result of pressure from other family members, the decisions of the judicial system, or a sense of loyalty and duty. For many grandparents, the new responsibility may mean that they must give up work to provide care, whereas others find they have little or no time for their usual activities or friends (Cox, 2000).

Living-with Grandparents

Living-with grandparents, according to Jendrek, typically had the grandchild in their own home or, less commonly, lived in a home maintained by a grandchild's parents. Living-with grandparents took on these responsibilities either because their children had not yet moved out of the house or because the latter could not afford to live on their own with their young children. These grandparents felt that they could provide the grandchild with an economically stable and loving environment, preferring such an arrangement to care by an outsider.

In 75 percent of families with grandparents and grandchildren living together, a grandparent runs the household. A parent of the children maintains the household in the remaining 25 percent of families with coresident grandparents and grandchildren. About half of the grandparent-run families have both grandparents living with the grandchildren. A grandmother alone maintains most of the others (42 percent). A grandfather alone maintains only 7 percent of the grandparent–grandchildren

families (Fields, 2003). Grandparent-run households are more common among African Americans than other groups (see "Data Digest").

With the recent deployment of thousands of young parents to the war in Iraq, grandparents have taken on the care of grandchildren full or part time. The grandparents experience a "double whammy" by looking after their grandchildren and worrying about their children's safety in Iraq (Greider, 2003).

Day-Care Grandparents

The *day-care grandparents* in Jendrek's study had assumed responsibility for the physical care of their grandchildren, usually those of their daughter, until the parents came home from work because of the high cost of day care. These grandparents were not casual baby-sitters, however. Some of the grandmothers even quit their part-time jobs to care for their grandchildren.

Some of the children in surrogate grandparent families are among the most needy and most emotionally damaged children in the United States (Sands and Goldberg-Glen, 2000). In low-income areas, very few grandparents have reliable sources of support for their parenting roles. Although white, black, and Latino custodial parents often seek help from family members and formal services, becoming a primary caregiver often worsens already difficult economic circumstances (Roe and Minkler, 1998; Burnette, 1999).

Grandparents provide a variety of child care. African American grandmothers are more likely than their Latina and white counterparts to provide full-time care from the child's birth to 3 years. In all ethnic groups, grandparents are the most likely to provide care for these young grandchildren if the mothers are 28 years old and younger, have full-time employment, and work nonstandard hours such as evenings and weekends (Vandell et al., 2003).

Although many grandmothers enjoy caring for grandchildren, they also experience stress and isolation, financial difficulties, and multiple roles that they hadn't anticipated in their later years (Rodgers and Jones, 1999). These "nanny-grannies" often combine caregiving with careers and express emotions ranging from joy and satisfaction to fatigue and resentment. As one grandmother said, "It's very sad that after a lifetime of working full time, grandparents should have a second full-time job of caring for their grandchildren unpaid. . . . Something's wrong here" (Gardner, 2002: 16). Some grandmothers are especially resentful because they are part of a sandwich generation that takes care of young grandchildren and elderly parents (Ingersoll-Dayton et al., 2001).

Providing care is especially stressful if the grandchildren have emotional or behavioral problems and if the grandparent, usually a grandmother, is a full-time surrogate and has few resources to meet the grandchild's needs (Bowers and Myers, 1999; Gattai and Musatti,

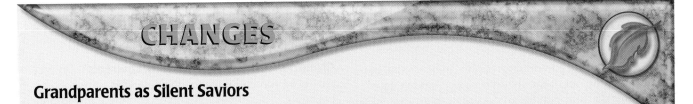

CHANGES

Grandparents as Silent Saviors

Many grandparents have become the "silent saviors" (or "martyrs," according to some of my students) of grandchildren whose parents have abandoned them because of poverty, drug abuse, or other problems (Clemetson, 2000). Creighton describes one such family (1991: 85–86):

When the Richmond weather turns cold and bitter, 59-year-old May Toman and her two granddaughters pile blankets onto the worn living-room couch and chairs in their rundown row house. There, around an ancient gas burner, they sleep at night. The upstairs is without heat or electricity, and the leaky kitchen ceiling has already fallen in once. But May is afraid to complain for fear the landlord will raise her $110-a-month rent, a development that could leave them homeless. The girls—Shelly, 8, and Tabatha, 9—make do with thrift-shop clothing, and a steak dinner is a treat remembered for weeks.

Shelly's mother was only 17 when Shelly was born, and soon afterward she and Shelly's father began leaving the baby with friends or near friends, sometimes for long periods without contact. For May, the final straw came when Shelly was 2.

May found her alone in the yard one evening. She took Shelly home and called the Richmond Department of Social Services. After an investigation, May got legal custody.

Several years later, May's son, Wayne, ran into marriage problems. When his wife left, he gave his daughter Tabatha, then 7, to his mother and his infant son to his mother-in-law. Tabatha's health had been neglected; her teeth were abscessed. May applied for custody and got it.

May, whom the girls call "Nanny," became their mother. May makes ends meet by taking in sewing and cutting corners. Up at 7, she walks the girls to school, then cleans house and grocery shops with food stamps. At 3, she meets the girls outside their brick school eight blocks away "so they know there's someone waiting."

One of Shelly's favorite pastimes is studying her baby album of herself and her mother smiling from behind plastic pages. The album ends abruptly when she is 2, and Shelly turns back to the first page to begin again. "I want to live with my mama in a big house," says Shelly, "but I don't really think I'll ever get that."

Shelly's mother lives across town and sees Shelly fairly often. But she has another child now, a year old, and says she does not have plans to take Shelly back soon.

Tabatha says, "Well, my daddy lives in the neighborhood, but he can't take me right now. My mama used to call, which made me cry terribly, but she hasn't called now in a long time. She said she was going to send me a birthday card but she never did." Her father, Wayne, lives next door with two new children and their mother, and though in many ways he and Tabatha are close, he says, "I feel like Tabatha's better off with Nanny."

Although she loves her grandchildren, May is representative of many grandparents who had not anticipated raising their grandchildren. Even when a parent assumes some of the child-care responsibilities, many grandparents provide physical and emotional care but have little decision-making power. As one grandmother summed it up, "I've been feeling very hurt and self-pitying. . . . This is not what we had planned . . . and it's just not fair for this to happen to us."

1999; Smith and Drew, 2002). The box "Grandparents as Silent Saviors" provides a closer look at grandparents who are surrogate parents.

Grandparents and Divorce

Traditionally, divorce meant that a grandparent would have to establish new relationships with the ex-spouse or stepparent. More recently, the family ties might shift because grandparents themselves are getting a divorce.

Grandparents and Their Children's Divorce   Divorce creates both opportunities and dilemmas for grandparents. Grandparents on the custodial side often deepen their relationships with children and grandchildren, especially when they provide financial assistance, a place to live, and help in child rearing, guidance, or advice. In contrast, grandparents on the noncustodial side typically have less access to the grandchildren.

Many custodial parents move after the breakup, increasing the visiting distance. And troubled postdivorce relationships often result in a loss of contact between grandchildren and some of their grandparents because the mother feels a closer relationship to her biological kin than to in-laws (Ganong and Coleman, 1999).

In other cases, because of estrangement or poor relationships with their child's ex-spouse, grandparents aren't allowed to see their grandchildren. Grandchildren are sometimes used as pawns to punish grandparents for real or imagined misunderstandings and slights. As one 76-year-old grandmother complained, "Why do daughters-in-law act this way without any provocation?" (Baker, 2001: 31).

If a custodial parent remarries, the noncustodial parent may drop out of the children's lives, making it awkward for the noncustodial grandparents to arrange visits with the grandchildren. However, if the custodial parent tries to maintain a relationship with the noncustodial grandparents so the children do not lose half of their family, and if the ex-spouses do not "bad-mouth" each other, children can have strong relationships with noncustodial grandparents (Bray and Berger, 1990).

Many grandparent–grandchild relationships become closer after the parents divorce or remarry (Thomas, 1994). For example, if the mother gets custody of the children but has little or no child support, she may move in with her parents. Baby-sitting while the mother works and generally being in close proximity to the grandchildren can foster a close emotional relationship between grandparent and grandchild.

Often, grandparents can provide a safe haven for grandchildren whose divorcing parents are often so emotionally distraught that they do not recognize the children's fears and worries about the breakdown of their parents' marriage:

> *Last night I was reading and Penny came out of the bedroom and she was crying a bit and I said "come sit on gramma's lap" and we cuddled. She was upset because she had wet her bed, so I changed her. Her father had gone away and she is afraid her mother will be going away, too. So I talked to her and reassured her that her mother wouldn't go away. Then I asked her if she'd like to get into bed with gramma and she said "yes" and then went to sleep (Gladstone, 1989: 71).*

The close relationship between grandchildren and grandparents often continues into the grandchildren's young adulthood. In one study, for example, college students from stepfamilies and single-parent families saw grandparents playing a more active role in their families than did students from intact families. The former said that grandparents had important decision-making authority in the family, provided gifts or financial assistance, acted more like friends than authoritative elders, facilitated communication between the grandchildren and the parents, and helped parents in child rearing (Kennedy, 1990).

A divorce can create unexpected financial burdens for the grandparents, however. If grandparents anticipate being cut off from their grandchildren after the divorce, they may have to petition for visitation rights, thus incurring legal expenses. In other cases, parents may provide financial help to children, especially daughters, in their efforts to obtain a divorce. One father noted, "I'm at the age where a lot of my friends are retiring, and I'm spending all my retirement savings on attorneys" (Chion-Kenney, 1991: B5).

Grandchildren and Their Grandparents' Divorce

About 33 percent of married people who were born between 1935 and 1944 have divorced by age 50 (Kreider and Fields, 2002). Because divorce rates among older people are increasing, many grandchildren will experience their grandparents' breakup (Uhlenberg and Kirby, 1998).

When grandparents split up, both they and their grandchildren may suffer. Grandparents who divorce don't have as much contact with their grandkids, feel less close to them, and consider the role of grandparent less important in their lives. Grandfathers seem particularly affected by divorce. They have less contact, fewer shared activities, and higher levels of conflict with their grandchildren than grandmothers who have divorced. However, grandparents who can maintain a good relationship with adult children despite a divorce will be able to establish strong ties to grandchildren (King, 2003).

Grandparents' Visitation Rights

Whether an adult child is divorced or not, do grandparents have the right to visit a grandchild when the child's parents object? As divorce, out-of-wedlock birth, and drug use rates increased, states began passing laws bolstering grandparent rights when parents died, divorced, separated, or were jobless or disabled.

Now the pendulum is swinging back. Because of a perception that parents' rights have eroded, more than a third of the states have narrowed their visitation laws. In some states, for example, grandparents must show a close relationship with grandchildren to get visitation rights. Many parents welcome the changes because they have more control over grandparents' visitation and deciding what's best for their children. However, the American Association of Retired Persons (AARP) and other groups argue that grandparents are part of an extended family and have a right to visitation despite parents' objections, especially when high divorce rates fragment a nuclear family (Gearon, 2003).

MAKING CONNECTIONS

■ What are the grandparenting styles in your family? Do they differ in terms of the grandparent's age and gender, for example?

■ Should grandparents sue for visitation rights with their grandchildren? Or respect a parent's decision even if they disagree?

Relationships between Aging Parents and Adult Children

In many cases, adult children and aging parents live close enough to stay in touch on a daily basis. For example, 60 percent of parents age 60 and older have at least one child within ten miles (Lin and Rogerson, 1995). Geographic closeness is not the most critical factor that shapes intergenerational relationships, however. Intergenerational relationships also vary by a child's gender and marital status, residence, and older people's decisions about living independently or with their children.

Gender and Marital Status

Adult daughters provide about the same amount of help to their parents regardless of the parents' health, but sons tend to provide financial assistance only when parental health fails (Hamon, 1992). Another critical variable is the quality of family relationships. Regardless of their own marital status, both black and white adults are more likely to provide emotional and instrumental support (such as transportation and health care when parents are ill) if early family relationships were caring and loving. These strong and helpful relationships continue into the parents' seventies and eighties (Chatters and Taylor, 1993; Johnson, 1993).

Divorced daughters with child custody have more contact than married daughters and often receive more help from parents. Sons, on the other hand, receive more baby-sitting help from their parents when they are married than in other situations (Spitze et al., 1994). Married sons probably get more help because the grandparents are involved with their grandchildren. If sons are divorced or cohabiting, however, grandparents may see their grandchildren less often because the mother gets custody of the children or the father remarries, starts a new family, and the grandparents split their time between their son's "old" and "new" families (see Chapters 15 and 16).

Urban and Rural Residence

Rural elderly parents generally depend on their children for financial and emotional support more than do urban elderly parents. This is probably because the urban elderly typically have more resources and more access to social service organizations, which makes them less dependent on their children. Even when formal support systems outside the family are available, the rural elderly still depend more on kinship networks. The older urban parents are, the more likely they are to rely on their children for assistance (Dorfman and Mertens, 1990).

Living Together

Elderly parents generally try to avoid moving in with their children, primarily because they don't want to give up control of their own lives. In addition, they don't want to cause or to endure crowding and are reluctant to do the extra housework in a packed home. For many women, the "empty nest" is a relief. Some older parents feel that there would be a clash over different lifestyles or child-rearing ideas and higher household expenses (Mancini and Blieszner, 1991). Finally, both younger and older generations value independence, and aging parents prefer to be both financially and emotionally self-sufficient.

There are advantages to multigenerational households, however. Such families exchange services and support on a regular basis: caring for family members during illness; giving money; providing gifts; running errands; preparing meals; taking care of children; giving advice on home management; cleaning the house and making repairs; giving advice on jobs, business matters, and expensive purchases; helping with transportation; counseling about life problems; and giving emotional support and affection (Mancini and Blieszner, 1991).

Contrary to what many of us might expect, it is often the needs and circumstances of adult children—rather than those of their elderly parents—that trigger dependent relationships (see Chapter 14). That is, coresidency is most likely among adult children who are unmarried and whose parents are in good health, are under age 65, contribute to the family income, and often provide child care for their grandchildren while the parents work (Casper and Bryson, 1998; Bryson and Casper, 1999).

Whether they have children and grandchildren or not, aging couples can enjoy many years together because of our greater life expectancy (see "Data Digest"). Sooner or later, however, family members must cope with another important life course event—the death of a spouse, a parent, or a grandparent.

Dying, Death, and Bereavement

Woody Allen once said, "It's not that I'm afraid to die. I just don't want to be there when it happens." Although people who are very old and in poor health sometimes welcome death, most of us have difficulty facing it, no matter what our age and physical condition.

In this section we look first at several theories of how people deal with imminent death. Then we examine the kind of care available to the dying. Finally, we explore the ways survivors deal with their own loss and grief and console each other.

Family members in Chiba Prefecture, Japan, follow a Buddhist priest in a funeral procession. The daughter carries her father's photograph, the son his cremated remains.

Dealing with Death and Dying

The way we deal with death depends on whether we are the medical personnel treating the ill patient, the relatives and friends of the patient, or the patient. Each has a different perspective on death and dying.

Health-Care Professionals Physicians and other health-care professionals often use the term *dying trajectory* to describe how a very ill person is expected to die. In a *lingering trajectory*—for example, death from a terminal illness such as cancer—medical personnel do everything possible to treat the patient, but ultimately custodial care predominates. In contrast, the *quick trajectory* is an acute crisis caused by cardiac arrest or a serious accident. Staff typically work feverishly to preserve the patient's life and well-being, sometimes with success.

When an elderly patient suffers from a terminal illness such as advanced cancer, health-care professionals and family members often perceive the course of dying and its treatment differently. For example, it is especially likely that overworked hospital staff who expect an elderly patient to have a lingering death will respond to the patient's requests more slowly, will place the patient in more remote wards, or even bathe and feed him or her less frequently.

Family members, in contrast, typically expect their elderly relatives to be treated as painstakingly as any other patient. Moreover, a patient's perceived social worth can influence care. For example, elderly patients in private hospitals or those with high socioeconomic status often receive better care than poor elderly patients or those in public hospitals (Hooyman and Kiyak, 2002).

Patients, Families, Friends Among the several perspectives of the dying process from the point of view of those most deeply concerned, probably the most well known is that of Elizabeth Kübler-Ross (1969). Based on work with 200 primarily middle-aged cancer patients, Kübler-Ross proposed five stages of dying: denial, anger, bargaining, depression, and acceptance.

Many have criticized this stage-based theory. Some claim that the stages are not experienced by everyone or in the same order. Others point out that the stages do not apply to the elderly. However, many practitioners believe that Kübler-Ross's model offers some useful ideas in understanding the psychology of most patients and families, regardless of age or specific illness:

- **Denial.** In an effort to cope with the dreaded news that a loved one will die, many people simply refuse to believe it. Patients and their families may ask for more tests, change physicians, or try in other ways to stave off the inevitable.

- **Anger.** When denial is no longer possible, people may become angry and sometimes project their anger onto medical staff or one another.

- **Bargaining.** The dying person sometimes tries to forestall death by making a deal with God: "If I can just live until my daughter's college graduation, I'll make a large contribution to my church."

- **Depression.** When the dying person recognizes that death is imminent, depression may set in. In *reactive depression*, patients experience sadness as a result of the various other losses that accompany illness and dying, such as the loss of hair during radiation therapy or the loss of functions such as the ability to walk unaided. *Preparatory depression* anticipates the loss of cherished objects; patients may give away prized belongings or spend extra time with family members.

■ **Acceptance.** When patients finally come to accept their approaching death, they may reflect on their lives and anticipate dying with quiet resignation.

In another model of dying among the elderly, Retsinas (1988) emphasizes the gradual acceptance of illness and dying. Whereas the middle-aged person facing death usually has one defined catastrophic illness, such as heart disease or cancer, the illness and disabilities suffered by an elderly person may include such ailments as increasing visual and auditory problems, stroke, diabetes, and crippling arthritis. More accustomed to the sick role, many elderly have had to confront the possibility of death for many years.

In addition, says Retsinas, the process of aging involves a series of role redefinitions. For example, even before the onset of illness, elderly people may have to give up such activities as driving, gardening, or climbing stairs. Unlike the middle-aged person, the dying elderly person does not suddenly confront the loss of an active social role and related worries like the effects on the family of the loss of a person's earning power.

Moreover, rather than deny death, some elderly may actually welcome it. Many have seen their spouses and friends die over the years, and unlike middle-aged people, the elderly may have already outlived most of the people who mattered to them.

Elderly patients often view death as a natural part of the life course, and they may even await death as an end to pain, sorrow, social isolation, dependency, and loneliness. In sum, Retsinas suggests that the elderly may not experience Kübler-Ross's stages of denial, anger, bargaining, and depression because they have been experiencing a "social death" over the course of many years.

Hospice Care for the Dying

Taken from the medieval term that meant a place of shelter and rest for weary or sick travelers, a **hospice** is a place for the care of dying patients that stresses pain control, gives patients a sense of security and companionship, and tries to make them comfortable. Hospice care is implemented in a variety of settings: in patients' homes, in hospitals, or in other inpatient facilities.

In the hospice approach, both professional and lay workers work as a team in assessing and meeting the physical, psychosocial, and spiritual needs of the patient and family and in giving dying people full and accurate information about their condition.

Another important function is to develop supportive environments in which people can talk about their lives with sympathetic listeners. Hospice staff members work directly with family and friends to help them deal with their feelings and relate compassionately to the dying patient. Although some people prefer to care for a dying person at home, some practitioners warn that the in-home approach can be stressful for both family and friends and may severely strain a family's physical and emotional resources.

Coping with Death

The state of having been deprived by death of a loved person is called **bereavement**, and those close to the dead person are known as the *bereaved*. Bereavement takes on different expressions in different people, but grief and mourning are common reactions to the death of someone close.

Grief and Mourning The emotional response to loss, **grief** is seen by some as an entire process in which a variety of feelings—sadness, longing, bewilderment, anger, and loneliness—combine. The grieving process may extend several years after the death of a loved one.

Mourning is the customary outward expression of grief that varies between different social and cultural groups. Mourning ranges from normal grief to pathological melancholy that may include physical or mental illness. Whether it's the death of a child, a parent, or grandparent, most people don't "recover" and end mourning. Instead, they adapt, accommodate, and change (Silverman, 2000).

By the time they turn 50, 25 percent of the population typically lose their mothers and 50 percent lose their fathers. A parental death can be a serious trauma, often leading to depression, family conflict, or a midlife crisis because adult children realize that they're "next in line." Parents' death may be especially tough for baby boomers. They often live thousands of miles away from their families and have to commute for a parent's final moments or plan burials by long distance (McGinn and Halpert, 1998). In addition, many funeral homes inflate their prices wildly because they know that grief-stricken customers, especially those living far away, are unlikely to shop around (Carlson, 1998).

Coping with death also varies between and within racial-ethnic groups. Although many ethnic groups are acculturating to the values of mainstream society, traditional ceremonies reinforce family ties among many groups (see the box "Death: A Family Event for Mexican Americans" on page 504).

Phases of Grief There are clusters or phases of grief (Hooyman and Kiyak, 2002). When a loved one dies, people generally respond *initially* with shock, numbness,

MULTICULTURAL

Death: A Family Event for Mexican Americans

Despite acculturation, there are cultural, religious, and ethnic differences in families' coping with death that include rituals, display of emotion, the appropriate length of mourning, celebrating anniversary events, and beliefs about the afterlife (Murray, 2000). For example, many African American families give the deceased a "good sendoff" that includes buying the best casket the family can afford and a funeral in the home church with stirring songs and eulogies (Willis, 1997).

Among many Middle Eastern families, traditional Muslim women display extreme emotions—crying, screaming and pulling their hair—to express grief. Wearing black, Muslims usually mourn the death of a loved one for at least one year by organizing big gatherings of relatives and friends on the third day, the fortieth day, and the one-year anniversary of the death of a loved one (Sharifzadeh, 1997).

Among many Mexican Americans, death reintegrates family members and reunites them despite any geographic or psychological distances. Despite their heterogeneity, Mexican American and other Latino families are consistent in their ideology and rituals regarding death. Attitudes toward death may vary among the highly educated and more acculturated family members. Nevertheless, *familism* (see Chapters 3 and 4) brings family members together and reinforces cultural traditions.

According to Estella Martinez (2001), the death of a loved one strengthens familist values and ties in several ways:

- There is a common belief that it is more important to attend a funeral than any other family event. The family and the community rally for the funeral and offer emotional support.
- The funeral reflects traditional family values of respect for elders, tradition, and the importance of the family. Even if family members are not religious, they attend religious funeral events.

- Socialization to death begins at a young age. Children attend wakes and funerals regularly, for example, and participate in memorial masses and family gatherings after the funeral.
- Many Mexican Americans cope with death through ritualistic acts such as a rosary, a mass, a graveside service, and the annual observance of All Souls' Day on November 2, which is more commonly known as the Day of the Dead (Día de los Difunios).

STOP AND THINK . . .

- *How do the rituals that Martinez describes differ from your family's? How are they similar?*
- *Talk to some of the international students on your campus or in class. How do their families cope with death? What kinds of rituals do the students practice?*

and disbelief, followed by an all-encompassing feeling of sorrow. Recently bereaved elderly report more illnesses and an increased use of new medications and usually rate their overall health more poorly.

In the *intermediate stage* of grief, people often idealize loved ones who have died and may even actively search for them. For example, a widow may see her husband's face in a crowd. Recent widows or widowers may also feel guilty, regretting every lapse: "Why wasn't I more understanding?" "Why did we argue that morning?" Survivors may also become angry, blowing up at children and friends in a seemingly irrational way. Even the dead person may not escape their rage: "Why didn't he prepare me better for life on my own?" "Why didn't she take better care of her health?"

When people are hurt, they tend to lash out and to try to find a source of blame. Some people may displace their anger onto doctors and medical science for having failed to preserve life, even when they know that the death was inevitable (Belsky, 1988). When the grieving person finally accepts the loss and stops yearning for the deceased person, disorganization, anguish, and despair often follow. The person may feel aimless, without interest, purpose, or motivation, incapable of making decisions, and lacking in self-confidence.

The *final stage* of grief, recovery and reorganization, may not occur for several years after the death, although many people begin to readjust and to reorganize their lives after about six months. For the elderly, grieving may be more complex than it is for younger people. Over a brief period, and at a time when their coping capacities and resources may be diminished, they often experience the deaths of many people who were important to them.

Intensity of Grief The intensity of a person's grief depends on a number of factors, including the quality of the lost relationship, the age of the deceased person, and the suddenness of the death. For many people, no matter how private they may be in their grief, holidays

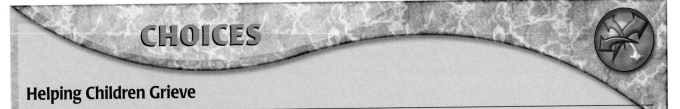

CHOICES

Helping Children Grieve

Because families are becoming increasingly complex and multigenerational, many children will experience the death not only of grandparents but also of great-grandparents, stepgrandparents, and other relatives. The following are some ways that Huntley (1991: 38–42) suggests for helping children grieve:

- **Recognize that each child will grieve differently.** How children will grieve is influenced both by the responses of those close to them and by their relationship with the deceased. Moreover, children may have mixed emotions if the deceased was sometimes unloving or uncaring.
- **Encourage questions.** When someone dies, children usually want to know what has happened and what will follow next. Tell them honestly what has occurred and explain what the word "dead" means. Don't be afraid to say "I don't know" when you don't know.

  If at any time you cannot deal with the children's questions (because you may be physically or emotionally exhausted, for example), tell them why you can't explain now and specify when you will be able to talk with them about the death.
- **Encourage the expression of feelings.** Encourage children to show their emotions (Nolen-Hoeksema and Larson, 1999). Talk about other people's feelings as well. For example, if Grandma

seems to be angry, explain that it is not because the children did anything wrong but because Grandma is upset that the doctors couldn't save Grandpa's life.

Because children, like adults, vary in the degree to which they are comfortable expressing feelings, some may prefer to write down their thoughts, make an album of photos of the loved one, draw or paint pictures, or do some other kind of activity.

- **Encourage participation in events after the death.** Tell the children about the events that will be taking place (wake, memorial service or funeral, and burial). Explain that these rituals provide us with a way to say goodbye to the deceased, but don't force children to participate in these events if they are uncomfortable or are frightened by them.

  Instead, a child may prefer to commemorate the life of the deceased in his or her own way. For example, "If . . . Erin and her grandmother used to play under a particular tree at Grandma's house, then maybe Erin would like to plant a similar tree at home in her own backyard" (Huntley, 1991: 41).
- **Try to maintain a sense of normalcy.** To restore some semblance of security, try to follow the children's normal routine as closely as possible. During the first few months after the death, try to avoid

making any drastic changes, such as moving, unless it is absolutely necessary.
- **Take advantage of available resources.** Schools, churches, or local hospitals sometimes have children's support groups. When grieving children get together with other bereaved children, they become aware that they are not alone in their grief.

Books written for children can be helpful, whether they are read by an adult to children or by the children themselves. When necessary, counselors who specialize in the area of grief and bereavement can help both you and your child. Increasingly, the Internet is providing a new way for people to seek solace after the death of a loved one (see "Taking It Further" at the end of the chapter).

STOP AND THINK . . .

- *How has an aged person's death affected you and your family members? Did you or your family seek support services? If so, did the services help cope with the death?*
- *If you were dying, what kind of care would you prefer to receive and where: at home, a hospital, or a hospice, for example? Would you refuse life-prolonging treatments?*

are especially difficult because they are so connected to family customs and rituals.

People who are grieving may dread the normal festivities because everything—from cards and decorations to special meals and traditional music—may remind them of the loved one who has died. Counselors and therapists suggest that survivors not force themselves to participate in special family traditions if doing so is too painful (Thomas-Lester, 1994).

Adults sometimes don't realize that children may be confused or experience grief over a death. Parents may be so involved in their own loss that they overlook a child's attachment to the person who has died. Some *thanatologists*—social scientists who study death and grief—encourage parents and educators to talk about death with children openly and honestly (see the box "Helping Children Grieve") and to teach children how to deal with loss, especially the death of someone they love.

Being Widowed

The death of a spouse often means not just the loss of a life companion but the end of a whole way of life. Unfamiliar tasks—managing the finances, cooking meals, fixing the faucet—suddenly fall on the surviving spouse. Friendships may change or even end because many close relationships during marriage are based on being a couple.

Some ties, such as relationships with in-laws, may weaken or erode. In other cases, the widowed forge new relationships through dating and remarriage.

Who Are the Widowed?

In the last few years, several of our older friends and relatives have died. In all cases, those who died were women. Despite our personal experiences, widows, not widowers, are the norm because women have a longer life expectancy (see "Data Digest").

As *Figure 17.5* shows, there are more widows than widowers in all categories age 65 and over. At age 75 and over, over 66 percent of men are married (or remarried) and living with a spouse, compared with only 27 percent of women. Furthermore, African American widows age 85 and older outnumber their counterparts compared to other racial-ethnic groups (Lugaila, 1998).

The numbers of elderly people living alone are expected to increase from 9 percent in 1990 to more than 15 percent in 2020. Most of those living alone will be women. Why? First, the life expectancy of a woman now exceeds that of a man by almost five years (see "Data Digest"). Second, the death rate of married men is two to three times higher than that of same-age married women. Third, a wife typically is three or four years younger than her husband, which increases the likelihood that she will survive him. Fourth, widowers over age 65 are eight times as likely to remarry as are widows.

As you saw in Chapter 8, social norms encourage the marriage of older men to younger women but discourage marriage between older women and younger men. Given the large pool of eligible women (those who are younger, widowed, divorced, or never married) and the shortage of men, it is easier for older men to remarry.

Facing Widowhood

Many recently widowed men and women exhibit such depressive symptoms as sadness, insomnia, appetite loss, weight loss, tearfulness, and self-dissatisfaction. Some longitudinal studies report that men and women experience similar physical and emotional difficulties initially and, with time, do not differ much in their ability to

FIGURE 17.5 **Widowhood Is More Common for Older Women Than for Older Men, 2002**

SOURCE: Adapted from Smith, 2003: Figure 5.

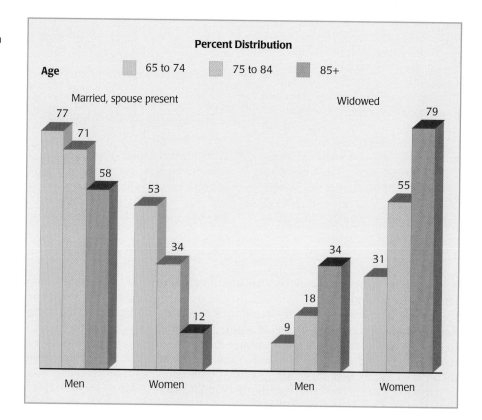

By permission of Johnny Hart and Creators Syndicate, Inc.

cope with the loss of a spouse (Brubaker, 1991; Van Baarsen and Van Groenou, 2001).

Although widows experience depression for the first year after a spouse's death, they usually bounce back within three years. Some widows also have better mental health because they no longer experience the stress of caring for an ill spouse (Wilcox et al., 2003).

Women who have been economically dependent on their husbands often find their incomes drastically reduced. If they are under age 60 and have never worked outside the home, they may experience the "widow's gap": Under present law, unless she is disabled, a widow is not eligible for Social Security benefits until she is 60. Moreover, some private pension plans provide no coverage for the spouse after the husband's death.

Insurance benefits, when they exist, tend to be exhausted within a few years of the husband's death. Financial hardships may be especially great for a woman who cared for a spouse during a long illness or for the widow who depleted their joint resources during the spouse's institutionalization. Furthermore, many older widows have few opportunities to increase their income through paid employment.

Social Isolation and Loneliness

Many men have depended on their wives not only for emotional support and household maintenance but also for arranging a social life. Consequently, men appear to "need" remarriage more than women do to restructure their lives. By age 85, only 34 percent of men are unmarried compared with 79 percent of women this age (see *Figure 17.5*). This is primarily because many older men have remarried: They want a wife and usually have the resources to attract a woman (see Chapters 8 to 10).

Although widows often have fewer resources than married women, they often have more time and more freedom to help friends and relatives (Gallagher and Gerstel, 1993; Bradsher, 1997). Thus, their ties with family and friends may grow stronger in widowhood.

Forging New Relationships

Some widows and many widowers begin to date again within a few years after losing a mate. In fact, as a "Dear Ann Landers" letter shows, a family may be unhappy even when in-laws date:

> My brother died a year ago. He left behind his wife of 30 years and two grown children. Two months after his death, my sister-in-law removed all his clothes from the closet, as well as the wall photos of him and the trophies he had won. Eight months later, she began to date.
>
> This has been quite painful for the rest of his family. We don't understand why she is dating so soon ("Ann Landers," 2001: 3E).

Ann Landers told the writer to stop being "petty and mean-spirited" because the sister-in-law had grieved for nearly a year (and this was enough), and that she should be able to enjoy male companionship and continue with her life.

Friendship is the most important reason for dating. Like younger people, older people enjoy having friends and companions to share interests and on whom they can call in emergencies. As you saw in Chapter 8, dating also decreases loneliness and isolation. In some cases, older people meet, date, and marry while they're in retirement communities ("Honeymoon in a retirement community?" 2002).

Having a confidant is especially important for men who grew up in an era when it was considered unmasculine to have intimate relationships with one's children, other men, or female friends. Lovers play a crucial role

Besides being healthy exercise, dancing is one way to be with people and, sometimes, to meet possible companions or mates. Square dancing and related forms of "country" dancing have become increasingly popular, especially among older adults.

because love, intimacy, and sexual activity continue to be an important part of life for the older person. Caregivers are also important providers of emotional and physical help in the event of accidents or illness.

Family Caregiving in Later Life

We often hear that adult children ignore their elderly parents and place them in institutions instead of caring for them themselves. In 1992, the media publicized the notion of "granny dumping": abandoning an elderly person with Alzheimer's disease or some other form of psychiatric disorder in a public place such as a shopping mall. Such cases are the exception, however.

Children today actually provide more care (and more difficult care) to more parents over much longer periods of time than they did in the so-called good old days. For example, only 7 percent of people age 65 and older rely exclusively on paid caregivers (Tilly et al., 2001). If people who take care of ill or disabled family members were paid for their work, the bill would come to nearly $188 billion a year (Family Caregiver Alliance, 2003).

Who Becomes a Caregiver?

The *sandwich generation*, you recall, is composed of midlife men and women who feel caught between meeting responsibilities to their own children and to their aging parents (Putney and Bengston, 2001; see also Chapter 13). "They find themselves tightly sandwiched between the needs and problems of their adolescent and young adult children, as they push toward independence,

and their aging parents as they slowly slide into a more dependent role" (Zal, 1992: 1).

About 57 percent of older people rely exclusively on family members for care. About 75 percent of caregivers are women. The typical caregiver is a married woman in her mid-forties who works full time, is a high school graduate, and has an annual household income of $35,000 (Tilly et al., 2001; Family Caregiver Alliance, 2003).

In terms of ethnicity, Asian American (32 percent) and African American households (30 percent) are more likely to include a caregiver than Latino households (27 percent) or white families (24 percent). Unlike other groups, Asian American caregivers are as likely to be male as female. And Asian American and black caregivers are more likely than white and Latino caregivers to be involved in caring for more than one person ("Family caregiving . . .," 1997).

There are several reasons for the racial-ethnic differences in caretaking. Most Latinos are young compared with the national population and have fewer aging family members (see Chapters 1 and 4). Many elderly Asian Americans may rely on family members for assistance because there is a strong sense of filial responsibility. In addition, some immigrants depend on family members rather than formal agencies because of a lack of knowledge of services, language difficulties, and a lack of transportation to organizations that provide assistance (Tsai and Lopez, 1997; see also Chapters 4 and 14).

For many black families, caregiving is a fact of life. It may be that they are better able to cope in this labor-intensive and time-consuming caregiving work because of more effective lifelong adaptive skills. Elderly African Americans may also value and expect support from children more than do their white counterparts, even though the former are more likely to receive assistance from formal agencies. In addition, many black families have developed informal support systems through churches and other organizations that encourage caregiving to aging parents (Lee et al., 1998; Mui et al., 1998; Shuey and Hardy, 2003).

Midlife adults are not the only caregivers, however. In 1996, for example, 40 percent of women and 26 percent of men in their fifties and early sixties provided at least 100 hours of care for aging parents (Johnson and Lo Sasso, 2000).

Spouses are most likely to care for aging or infirm partners, and one-third of the caregivers of the frail elderly are themselves over 65. As parents age, however, adult children provide more care, and daughters outnumber sons as caretakers by more than three to one (Cox, 1993; Tilly et al., 2001).

Family and Other Support Systems

The family is an important caregiving unit for frail elderly people. The fact that only 5 percent are institutionalized—typically in nursing homes—shows that families are the primary source of assistance. Some formal support services exist, but they are often expensive or limited to those who are ambulatory, who can take care of their own physical needs, and who do not suffer from depression or dementia.

Day Care for the Elderly
One formal support service is the day-care center for the elderly. This type of program is in the vanguard of efforts to keep elderly people out of nursing homes and in their own homes and communities as long as possible. Most centers are run by nonprofit organizations, such as churches or government-funded senior centers. Increasingly, hospitals and nursing homes are also instituting day-care programs. In 1975 there were only 15 adult day-care centers, but by 1999 there were more than 4000 (Field, 1999). Program providers estimate that 10,000 are needed.

Many centers provide transportation, and some have medical personnel on staff. Some even offer overnight and weekend services. These centers provide needed respite for family caregivers, allowing them to work, run errands, or spend time with their children. For the aging participants, the centers offer structure, stimulation, social life, and a chance for renewed self-esteem.

Alzheimer's experts say the extra stimulation of a day-care center seems to help stave off some mental deterioration in these patients. Often the lighting, color schemes, furniture, and background music in the centers are chosen to have a calming effect, and many include fenced paths for patients who tend to wander. Some have exercise programs, showers, and beauty parlors.

The day-care center's biggest problem is a financial one. In some states, Medicaid covers fees for elderly people who meet income requirements. The middle-income group is the one that can't afford to participate. Attending five days a week can cost $700 or more per month, far more than the average Social Security check pays. Many long-term care insurance providers now cover adult day-care expenses (Field, 1999).

Retirement Communities
Older people have more options today than previously in finding appropriate living arrangements. As you saw in Chapter 9, the range of available amenities and services includes home health care, housekeeping, meals, property maintenance, recreational facilities, and transportation.

A growing number of retirement villages that serve African American elderly are sprouting nationwide. Many are rooted in the black church (Chambers and Clemetson, 1999). Increasingly, moreover, Asian Americans are establishing assisted living facilities where the nurses speak fluent Korean, for example, and caregivers prepare traditional meals and celebrate cultural holidays (Song, 2002).

Some retired educators are drawn to retirement communities that are located near colleges or universities. Such "academic villages," which feature libraries and computer facilities, provide residents with lectures and seminars "on everything from humanities to international economics" (Vanderpool, 1999).

Caregiving Styles

Families care for their elderly members in different ways. According to Matthews and Rosner (1988), there are five primary types of family caregiving in later life.

Routine Help
The style that forms the backbone of the caregiving system is *routine help*. The adult child incorporates regular assistance to the elderly parent into his or her ongoing activities. For this system to work, a family member—generally one of the elderly person's children—is regularly available to do whatever needs to be done. Routine involvement may include a wide range of activities: household chores, checking to see whether the person is all right, providing outings, running errands, managing finances, and visiting.

Backups
In a second style, relatives serve as *backups*. Although one person may provide routine care to an aging parent, a brother or sister may step in when needed. For example, one sister explained, "I do what my sisters instruct me to do." She responded to her sisters' requests but did not initiate involvement. Another sibling was described as the "favorite child" and was called in primarily when a parent needed to be

convinced to do something that the routine caregivers thought was necessary.

Circumscribed

The *circumscribed* style of participation is highly predictable and carefully delineated. For example, one respondent said of her brother, "He gives a routine, once-a-week call." This call was important to the parent. The brother was not expected to increase his participation in providing parental care, however.

Siblings who adopt this style can be counted on to help but make clear the limits to their availability. For example, in one family, a son who was a physician was relied on for medical advice or assistance but was not expected to assume any other responsibility.

Sporadic

In contrast to the first three types of caregiving, the *sporadic* style describes adult children who provide services to parents at their own convenience. For example, one daughter said, "We invite Mom to go along when we take trips." Another said, "My brother comes when he feels like it to take Mother out on Sunday, but it's not a scheduled thing." Some siblings don't mind this behavior, but others resent brothers and sisters who avoid the most demanding tasks:

> [My sister and I] were always very close, and we're not now. I don't think she comes down often enough. . . . She calls, big deal: that's very different from spending three to four hours a day. . . . She does not wheel my mother to the doctor, she does not carry her to the car, she does not oversee the help (Abel, 1991: 154).

Disassociation

The last style is *disassociation* from responsibility altogether. This behavior is quite predictable: Other sisters and brothers know that they cannot count on a sibling at all. In one family of three daughters, for example, the two younger sisters are routinely involved in helping their mother, whereas their older sister "is not included in our discussions or dealing with mother. . . . She doesn't do anything" (Matthews and Rosner, 1988: 188).

Such children do not always disassociate themselves entirely from the family. In one case, the brother had broken off contact with his mother early in his life and, consequently, from parental care but not from contact with his siblings. His sister explained, "My brother has no interest at all and does not care about mother to any extent. The few times he comes into town, we deliberately don't discuss Mother with him" (Matthews and Rosner, 1988: 188–89).

Siblings might use personality, geographic proximity, employment, and other family responsibilities as excuses for not assuming caregiving responsibilities. Such justifications, however, may increase resentment among those who provide care (Ingersoll-Dayton et al., 2003).

The Satisfaction and Strain of Caregiving

Caregivers are a diverse group. Some enjoy caregiving, believing that family relationships can be renewed or strengthened by helping elderly members. They see caregiving as a "labor of love" because of strong ties of affection that have always existed in the family (Saldana and Dassori, 1999).

For others, caregiving provides a feeling of being useful and needed. As one daughter said, "For me, that's what life's all about!" (Guberman et al., 1992: 601).

Caring for parents may be especially gratifying when the work does not conflict with employment and when the provider is not caring for other family members or relatives. Even when there are responsibilities to one's own family, however, women often report that the caregiving enhanced their sense of self-worth and well-being, especially when family members helped out (Martire et al., 1997).

Often, however, caretaking creates stress and strain in families (Aranda and Knight, 1997; Dilworth-Anderson et al., 1999). Older people often need support at a time when their children's lives are complicated with many varied responsibilities. Families are often unprepared for the problems involved in caring for an elderly person. In general, daily routines are disrupted, caregivers are confined to the home, and parent–child conflict may increase. Parents who are cognitively impaired, who can't accomplish basic daily tasks of self-care, or who engage in disruptive behavior are clearly the most difficult to care for ("Family caregiving . . .," 1997).

Financial burdens include not only the direct costs of medical care but also such indirect costs as lost income or missed promotions. Funds for services to reduce caregivers' strains are limited. Women are more likely than men to quit their jobs or to decrease their work hours to provide care (Family Caregiver Alliance, 2003). Those who interrupt employment to be parental caregivers generally receive fewer retirement benefits for themselves.

Caregivers bear the emotional burdens of feeling alone, isolated, and without time for themselves. Rates of depression increase, especially among female caregivers, and distress may intensify because of little information about and access to potential helping services. Even when support is available, the caregiver of the disabled, frail, or mentally ill elderly person often faces many years of increasing dependence, decline, and demanding physical care tasks (Wilson, 1990).

It takes caregivers a while to recover after the death of a loved one. People who have cared for a partner with dementia, for example, feel depressed and lonely up to three years after the spouse's death. Those who reported the greatest psychological difficulties included caregivers who sometimes felt angry or guilty about their caregiving experiences or who had received little support from family and friends (Robinson-Whelen et al., 2001).

Particularly when formal support services are unavailable or unknown, caregivers' feelings of isolation and strain may increase. In some cases, stress may become severe enough to lead to family breakdown, neglect, or even abuse of the older person (see Chapter 14).

In addition, an adult child may have to forgo important social events and activities to meet caregiving needs. This may create additional strain and role conflict (Mui and Morrow-Howell, 1993; Saldana and Dassori, 1999).

Most often, it is a daughter or daughter-in-law who is responsible for organizing and providing care to an elderly family member. Married female caretakers get more financial and emotional support from their spouses and children than do never-married, divorced, or remarried female caregivers. Nonetheless, they often experience strain because of the competing demands from their spouses and children, on the one hand, and their elderly relative on the other (Brody et al., 1992).

A troubled marital relationship may become more problematic with such added stress. Or if female caretakers do not get support from their immediate family, they can fall into the "martyrdom trap" by making unreasonable demands on themselves (Couper and Sheehan, 1987).

For many women, caring for elderly relatives is not a single episode but continues throughout their life course, and dependence and independence issues may be replayed many times. The caregiving may be necessary for multiple elderly relatives and may be multilayered as a person's parents, in-laws, grandparents, and other elderly relatives need help sequentially or simultaneously. Given our longer life expectancy, inevitably many of these women will also care for dependent husbands in the future.

Conclusion

As this chapter has shown, there are many similarities in later-life families. Women tend to live longer, and men are more likely to remarry after being widowed.

On the one hand, because of an increased life expectancy, many of us will have more *choices* in later life as to how we will spend our "golden years" and how we will play grandparenting roles. On the other hand, we will also face *constraints*, the most serious of which is how we will care for aging family members as longevity increases and health-related costs rise.

Another critical issue is how we will respond to the *changes* of an aging population that has diverse social, health, and financial needs. As you've seen in earlier chapters, contemporary lifestyles vary greatly. Some people remain single, some marry but have no children, and some marry several times. These variations will probably continue as the population ages. Conner (1992: 203) notes that "perhaps the biggest challenge for the future is to successfully meet the needs of our increasingly diverse population of senior citizens." Meeting family needs in the future is the focus of Chapter 18.

SUMMARY

1. The aging of our society is occurring at an exceedingly rapid pace for several reasons, including a decrease in fertility rates and an increase in life expectancy.

2. Although there is great diversity in the aged population, people age 65 and over must confront such similar aging issues as accepting changes in health, dealing with stereotypes, and coping with mandatory retirement.

3. One of the biggest changes in the last two or three decades has been the rapid growth of the multigenerational family. Because families now often span three or four generations, the importance of the grandparent role has increased.

4. There are at least five styles of grandparenting: remote, companionate, involved, advisory, and cultural transmitters. These styles, and grandparents who act as surrogate parents, often reflect such factors as the grandparents' age, physical proximity, and relationships with their own children, especially daughters.

5. Adult children's divorce creates both opportunities and dilemmas for grandparents. In some cases, relationships with grandchildren grow stronger; in other cases, especially for in-laws, the ties become weaker.

6. All families must deal with the death of elderly parents. Physicians and other health-care professionals often view death in terms of the dying trajectory.

Alternatively, the dying process can be understood from the point of view of the dying person or those who will survive the person.

7. Although many elderly parents and relatives die in hospitals and nursing homes, hospice care provides an alternative by making the patient more comfortable and

by providing companionship, a sense of security, and pain control.

8. On average, women live about five years longer than men. Although most women outlive their husbands, both widows' and widowers' coping strategies typically involve adapting to a change in income and dealing with loneliness and the emotional pain of losing a spouse.

9. Children today provide more care (and more difficult types of care) to more parents over much longer periods of time than ever before. As our population ages, more disabled and frail Americans will need long-term care.

10. Caregiving includes both family support systems and formal services such as day care for the elderly. There are several caregiving styles, all of which involve the expression of love and some degree of stress. For the most part, the primary caregivers are women.

KEY TERMS

gerontologist *484*
later-life family *485*
depression *486*
dementia *487*

Alzheimer's disease *487*
ageism *490*
Society Security *492*
hospice *503*

bereavement *503*
grief *503*
mourning *503*

TAKING IT FURTHER

Aging on the Internet

There is an overwhelming number of aging-related resources on the Net. Here are a few URLs to whet your appetite:

Administration on Aging provides information on older people and services for the elderly, numerous links, fact sheets, and other resources.

www.aoa.gov

National Institute on Aging offers publications on health and aging topics and many links to caregiving sites.

www.nih.gov/nia

SeniorLaw Home Page includes materials on elder law, Medicare, Medicaid, estate planning, trusts, and the rights of the elderly and disabled.

www.seniorlaw.com

Senior Women.com offers many useful resources on grandparenting, politics, health, computers, a "letters from readers" column, and many links.

www.seniorwomen.com

Seniors-Site.com is fun. It provides a "unique, informative, interesting, and entertaining" Web site for adults over 50 and others. A site map includes links to information on advisers, pets, fitness, sex, and many other topics.

seniors-site.com

And more: www.prenhall.com/benokraitis gives dozens of URLs on national organizations for seniors, grandparents' organizations, caregiver associations, home-care directories, health-related topics (such as Alzheimer's and vision loss), grief resources, health-care financing, locating reputable funeral organizations, e-mailing letters to loved ones after death, and much more.

INVESTIGATE WITH RESEARCH NAVIGATOR

Please go to www.researchnavigator.com and enter your LOGIN NAME and PASSWORD. For instructions on registering for the first time, please view the detailed instructions at the end of the Chapter 1. Please search the Research Navigator™ site using the following key search terms:

caregiving
Alzheimer's disease
ageism

The Family
in the Twenty-first Century

DATADIGEST

- By 2010, **couples with children under age 18** are expected to make up 38 percent of all married-couple households, down from 47 percent in 1990.

- The **number of households headed by single mothers under age 25** is expected to increase by 44 percent, from 831,000 in 1995 to 1.2 million in 2010.

- The **number of single fathers** will grow an estimated 44 percent between 1990 and 2010, to 1.7 million, but it will remain less than 2 percent of all households.

- **One-person households,** 24 percent of all households in 1995, are expected to rise to 27 percent of all households in 2010.

- Between 1995 and 2010, the number of **middle-aged householders** is expected to increase greatly. The number of householders aged 45 to 54 is expected to rise from 17 million to 25 million, a 45 percent increase; and the number of households headed by people between 55 and 64 is expected to rise from 12 million to 20 million, a 62 percent increase.

- The number of **elderly householders** grew 5 percent between 1995 and 2000, from 21.7 million to 22.8 million. This group is expected to increase another 14 percent during this decade, to 26.1 million in 2010.

SOURCES: Miller, 1995; Simpson, 1995; U.S. Census Bureau, 2002.

When studying the family of the twenty-first century, many observers assume that the dynamic processes that have shaped it in the past two decades will continue to influence it in the future. The family's importance has been a major theme throughout this book. In this chapter we briefly consider the future of this institution, discussing its outlook in six areas: family structure, racial-ethnic diversity, children's rights, health-related issues, economic concerns, and global aging.

Family Structure

In the future, it's likely that the current variations in family structures will increase in number and form. We will probably see more households that are multigenerational and composed of unrelated adults and more stepfamilies with his, her, and their children. The high number of divorces and remarriages may mean that senior citizens will depend as much (or more) on "stepkin" as on biological kin to provide care (see Chapter 16).

In 2030, the oldest baby boomers will be in their eighties. Whether or not stepkin will support their elderly relatives will depend on geographic mobility and the degree to which stepparents form close relationships with their children. If society's attitude toward homosexuals becomes more positive and domestic partners acquire more legal rights, we may also see greater numbers of families headed by lesbian and gay parents.

Despite these changes, there is no evidence that the institution of marriage will become extinct. As you saw in earlier chapters, although many people are cohabiting

515

and remaining single longer, about 93 percent of Americans marry at least once.

Although many family functions have changed since the turn of the century (see Chapter 1), the family is still the primary group that provides the nurturance, love, and emotional sustenance that people need to be happy, healthy, and productive. Commuter marriages, increased work responsibilities, divorce, and other stressors aside, many Americans report that the family is one of the most important aspects of their lives (see Chapters 10 and 11).

Racial-Ethnic Diversity

One of the most striking changes in American society today, the growth of racially and ethnically diverse families, is expected to continue in the future. Such factors as immigration from abroad and higher fertility rates among African Americans and some Asian American and Latino groups contribute to this change. Minorities account for 24 percent of the U.S. population, with an increase to 30 percent expected by 2020 (Population Reference Bureau, 1990).

One analyst has observed, "The question isn't really whether non-Hispanic whites will become a minority; it's a question of when" (Kate, 1997: 42). As minorities make up a larger share of the population and the labor force, they will have a greater impact on political, educational, and economic institutions. By 2025, for example, Latinos are expected to make up 48 percent of the population in New Mexico, 43 percent in California, 38 percent in Texas, and about 25 percent in Nevada and Florida.

Some expect that as the Latino population increases, its political power will grow proportionately as well (Morgenthau, 1997). In the twenty-first century we may find that minority youth are working to support a largely older, white population. If older, white men continue to control the government and economy, such dominance, especially if current discrimination persists (see Chapter 4), may increase racial-ethnic tension across generational lines.

Racial-ethnic communities will continue to grow and change in the twenty-first century. For example, whereas the most recent Asian Indian, Cambodian, and South American immigrants often live and work in interethnic areas of many large cities, Filipino and Korean American families have been moving to the suburbs and establishing communities where they have their own houses of worship and programs to teach their native languages to their children.

Children's Rights

In an unprecedented 1992 lawsuit, an 11-year-old Florida boy asked a judge to "divorce" him from his parents.

To protect the boy and his two younger brothers from their abusive, alcoholic father and neglectful mother, authorities had placed the children in the care of social service agencies for nearly two and a half years.

During that time, the 11-year-old had lived in three foster homes and a boys' home. He chose to stay with the last foster family, a couple with eight children who wanted to adopt him. The boy's mother and father, who were separated, tried to regain custody of their son. The mother's attorney argued that parents have the constitutional right to control the custody of their children. The boy's foster father, also an attorney, maintained that children have a right to pursue happiness. The judge ruled that his foster parents could adopt the boy. Some people would undoubtedly cite this case as another example of the American family in decline. Others might argue that the case illustrates the right of children to be part of a healthy, responsible, and loving household.

A national study of U.S. families concluded that the United States, the most prosperous nation on Earth, is failing many of its children:

Although many children grow up healthy and happy in strong, stable families, far too many do not. They are children whose parents are too stressed and busy to provide caring attention and guidance. They are children who grow up without the material support and personal involvement of their mothers and fathers. They are children who are poor, whose families cannot adequately feed and clothe them and provide safe, secure homes. They are children who are victims of abuse and neglect at the hands of adults they love and trust, as well as those they do not even know. They are children who are born too early and too small, who face a lifetime of chronic illness and disability. They are children who enter school ill prepared for the rigors of learning, who fail to develop the skills and attitudes needed to get good jobs and become responsible members of adult society. They are children who lack hope for what their lives can become, who believe they have little to lose by dropping out of school, having a baby as an unmarried teenager, committing violent crimes, or taking their own lives (National Commission on Children, 1991: vii–viii).

Such conclusions are well founded. Much of the research has shown not only that the United States has abandoned many of its children but that the situation has been deteriorating since 1980 (see Chapters 12 and 13). Moreover, some scholars argue that our children are being ignored because adults are investing more in themselves and their personal pursuits than in raising their children (see Chapter 1).

Almost 12 percent of children living below the poverty level experience "moderate" or "severe" hunger

("America's children . . .," 2000). Scientific research indicates that hunger and malnutrition rob children of their potential. Biologists and neurologists have found that physical nourishment determines how many brain cells children develop. In addition, researchers believe that stress activates hormones that can impair learning and memory and lead to intellectual and behavioral developmental problems (see Chapter 12).

Family Policy

About 17 million children in this country have absent fathers; each year 1 million children are born to unwed parents and another million are newly affected by divorce (see Chapters 11, 12, and 13). **Family policy**—the measures taken by government bodies to achieve specific objectives relating to the family's well-being—has improved many of these children's lives.

One bright spot is the future of child support. The first federal legislation to enforce child-support payment was enacted in 1950, and additional bills were passed in 1965 and 1967, but the 1975 Office of Child Support Enforcement law was the first really significant piece of legislation in this area.

A new law, enacted in 1984, not only requires all states to establish state offices of child-support enforcement but also provides federal reimbursement for nearly 75 percent of each state's enforcement costs. Whereas the 1975 act created the bureaucracy to enforce the private child-support obligation, the 1984 Child Support Enforcement Amendments require states to adopt formulas and guidelines that the courts can use to determine child-support obligations. These amendments also require the states to withhold pay equal to child-support obligations from wages and other income of noncustodial parents who are delinquent in their payments (Garfinkel et al., 1994).

In 1988, the Family Support Act strengthened the 1984 guidelines, requiring that judges provide a written justification for review by a higher court if they want to depart from the state guidelines in any way. The act also requires that states review and update the child-support awards handled by the Office of Child Support Enforcement at least every three years. In addition, the legislation requires that by 1994 the states withhold funds for child-support payment in all cases, not just those that are delinquent. States have varied quite a bit in enforcing the latter requirement, however (see Chapter 15).

Courts are also becoming more likely to recognize children's rights. In 35 states, for example, statutes specifically mandate that trial judges consider the presence of domestic violence in child-custody disputes (Lehrman, 1996). Many divorcing women are afraid to testify against a batterer because they fear retaliation (see Chapter 14).

In 1992, Gregory Kingsley won the right to "divorce" his biological mother and to stay with his foster parents, who later adopted him.

However, trial judges who take domestic violence seriously are more likely to protect children from emotional and physical harm by not requiring joint physical and legal custody (see Chapter 15) and not awarding visitation rights to the violent parent.

Child Care and Parental Leave

Very few U.S. families, especially those on welfare, can afford high-quality child-care services (see Chapter 13). Moreover, because mothers are much more likely than fathers to take time off from work to care for their children, female workers, as a group, fall permanently behind male workers in terms of pay, benefits, and seniority.

Women who are heads of households are even more disadvantaged. In a national study, researchers found that nearly 23 percent of mothers between 21 and 29 years of age are out of the labor force because they can't afford child care. Because many of these mothers lack high school diplomas, they have difficulty competing in the labor market. And even for two employed parents, paying an average of $8540 per year per child for high-quality child care is more than most working-class or middle-class parents can afford (Gardner, 1995b).

Child Care Provisions   Compared with those of other industrialized countries, the United States' record of child-care provisions has been abysmal. Congresswoman Pat Schroeder of Colorado once remarked, "Under our tax laws, a businesswoman can deduct a new Persian rug for her office but can't deduct most of her costs for child care. The deduction for a thoroughbred horse is greater than that for children" (Gibbs et al., 1990: 42).

A child-care center in Denmark, where more than three quarters of children between ages 3 and 5 are in state-funded programs.

In contrast to the U.S. system, 60 percent of child care in Japan is provided by the government, and both the government and most companies offer monthly subsidies to parents with children (Shimomura, 1990). One of the most successful programs is in France, where parents can enroll their children in a variety of child-care centers, preschools, and special day-care homes run by the government. Tuition is free or minimal, adjusted according to the family income. Similar systems have been established in Denmark, Sweden, and other European countries (Neft and Levine, 1997).

For example, in Belgium, Italy, and Denmark, at least 75 percent of children age 3 to 5 are in some form of state-funded preschool program, and in Germany, parents may deduct the cost of child care from their taxes. In Sweden, parents receive the equivalent of $1667 for each child in the form of a child-care subsidy, and local communities organize and maintain child-care centers, for which parents pay about 10 percent of the actual cost (Herrstrom, 1990).

Parental Leave Provisions Many countries try to ensure children's rights by giving parents time for parenting, especially in families where both parents are employed. In more than 30 developing countries, such as Angola and Ghana, parents have a paid infant-care leave (Frank and Zigler, 1996). Two major industrialized countries that do not mandate paid maternity leave are New Zealand and the United States (Neft and Levine, 1997). In the United States, the Family and Medical Leave Act passed in 1993 provides only unpaid leave and only to some employees (see Chapter 13).

Unlike the United States, a number of developed nations provide generous parental leave benefits. The minimum childbirth-related leave among European countries is three months in the Netherlands and a few other countries, sixteen weeks in France, six months in Canada, nine months to one year in Italy, one year in Denmark, one and one-half years in Sweden, and three years in Austria, Finland, France (with third and subsequent children), Germany, and Hungary (Kamerman, 1996).

In Sweden, the parental leave can be shared equally by both parents. Sweden also is unique in providing an 18-month job-protected leave and a cash benefit that covers 80 percent of wages for one year, three additional months at a minimum flat rate, and three more months as an unpaid leave. The benefit is available to either parent and can be prorated so that parents may use it to cover full-time, half-time, or three-quarter-time work while children are young. This enables parents to share child-care responsibilities during the first two years of the child's life (Kamerman, 1996).

In Austria, Canada, Denmark, Germany, Hungary, and Norway, fathers can share in some portion of the leave. In most of these countries the extended parental leave carries with it the right to a wage-related benefit, or a benefit is provided at a flat rate. In Finland, parents have a choice after the end of a one-year, fully paid parental leave. They can choose between a guaranteed, heavily subsidized place in a child-care center, a subsidy to help pay for in-home child care, or a cash benefit to provide support for an extended two-year parental leave at home to care for a child until her or his third birthday (Kamerman, 1996).

Because of the archaic parental leave policies in the United States, the lack of good child-care facilities, and the increased numbers of women entering the labor force or higher education institutions, battles over who should care for children will probably escalate. According to some researchers, such conflicts will decrease only when family policies take children and working parents seriously (Leach, 1994).

Health-related Issues

In some ways, many Americans are healthier now than in the past. Smoking and alcohol consumption among youth have decreased. In 1974, for example, about half of those 12 to 17 years of age said they had tried cigarettes and alcohol. In 1999, 8 percent of eighth-graders, 16 percent of tenth-graders and 23 percent of twelfth-graders reported smoking cigarettes daily in the previous 30 days. In the same year, 31 percent of twelfth-graders, 26 percent of tenth-graders, and 15 percent of eighth-graders reported having had at least five drinks in a row in the previous two weeks ("America's children . . .," 2000). Thus, although smoking and drinking have decreased among young people since the 1970s, the rates are still high and may increase as children reach adulthood.

Among older Americans, consumption of red meat and eggs, two foods purportedly associated with stroke and heart disease, decreased greatly between 1970 and 1992 (Holmes, 1994; see also Bachman et al., 1997). Although a number of Americans are adopting healthier lifestyles, two health-related issues will probably have a greater impact on marriages and families in the coming years: HIV and AIDS and the growing concern over the lack of a national health-care system.

Some observers urge that laboratories like this one that freeze and store human sperm be regulated to screen out and dispose of samples that contain the genetic codes for diseases like AIDS or cystic fibrosis.

HIV and AIDS

We might reasonably expect that, knowing that there is no cure for AIDS, people would engage in casual sexual intercourse less often and with fewer partners and that they would use condoms. However, although some gay men have changed their patterns of sexual activity, there is little evidence that the threat of HIV and AIDS has changed sexual behavior among many heterosexuals. Adolescent males and females are unlikely to protect themselves, and a number of college students and others who are aware of the risks of contracting AIDS are still not using condoms, including during casual sex (see Chapter 7).

According to a study of HIV-infected people seeking treatment at hospitals, about 40 percent of the men and women didn't tell their partners they were infected because doing so would be "too stressful," or they expressed fear of being rejected by their partners. The majority also didn't insist on the use of condoms (Stein, 1998).

In the future, HIV and AIDS will also affect multigenerational families. As the AIDS virus spreads, increasing numbers of children are being orphaned and will probably be cared for by foster parents, grandparents, or even great-grandparents (see Chapter 17).

National Health Care

The United States is one of the few industrialized countries that lacks national health insurance or a system that makes health care a right of all citizens. In 1999, 16 percent of the population had no private or employer-sponsored health insurance. Despite the existence of such government programs as Medicaid and Medicare, almost 33 percent of the poor had no health insurance of any kind. Among the poor, more than 40 percent of Latinos and Asian Americans had no health insurance (see *Figure 18.1* on page 520).

Our chances of not having health insurance or having lapsing coverage depend on gender, age, and employment status. Women are slightly more likely than men to have health insurance because more of them live in families below the poverty line and thus qualify for Medicaid. Young adults aged 18 to 24 are more likely than

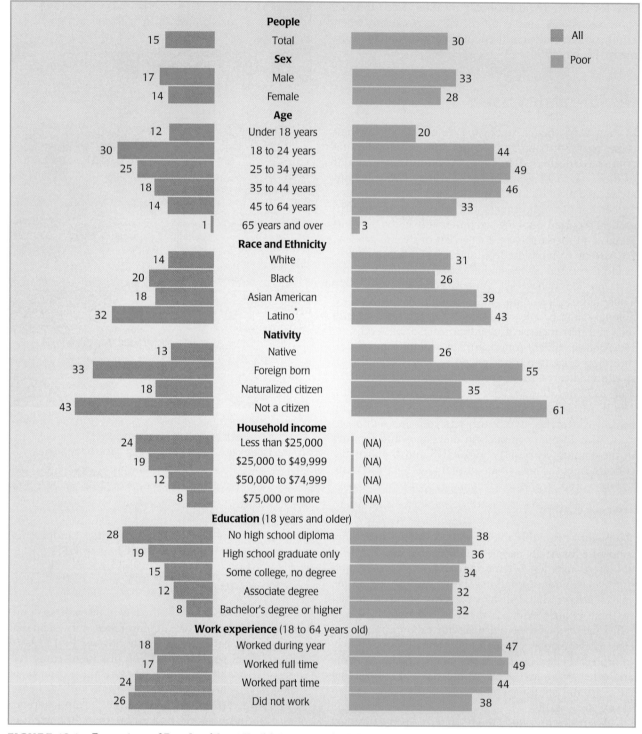

People

	All	Poor
Total	15	30

Sex
Male	17	33
Female	14	28

Age
Under 18 years	12	20
18 to 24 years	30	44
25 to 34 years	25	49
35 to 44 years	18	46
45 to 64 years	14	33
65 years and over	1	3

Race and Ethnicity
White	14	31
Black	20	26
Asian American	18	39
Latino*	32	43

Nativity
Native	13	26
Foreign born	33	55
Naturalized citizen	18	35
Not a citizen	43	61

Household income
Less than $25,000	24	(NA)
$25,000 to $49,999	19	(NA)
$50,000 to $74,999	12	(NA)
$75,000 or more	8	(NA)

Education (18 years and older)
No high school diploma	28	38
High school graduate only	19	36
Some college, no degree	15	34
Associate degree	12	32
Bachelor's degree or higher	8	32

Work experience (18 to 64 years old)
Worked during year	18	47
Worked full time	17	49
Worked part time	24	44
Did not work	26	38

FIGURE 18.1   Percentage of People without Health Insurance by Selected Characteristics, 2002

*Latino may be of any race. NA = Not Applicable.

SOURCE: Mills and Bhandari, 2003: Figure 2.

any other group to have no health insurance because they have part-time jobs or low-paying jobs that offer no health benefits. Stable, full-time employment improves the chances that workers will have continuous coverage (Bennefield, 1995). According to one study (cited in Lief, 1997), about 12 percent of parents of uninsured children restrict their children's play because of fears of injuries.

The Canadian health-care system has received much attention from the U.S. news media. Among other appealing characteristics, there is little paperwork when seeing a doctor:

> *Several years ago I moved from the United States to Canada, and a few months later I had my first experience with a nationalized health-care system. After making my appointment with a physician who had been recommended to me by friends, I waited only a brief time to see the doctor and when we were finished I asked the receptionist whether there was anything I needed to do—I expected to pay a bill or fill out some forms or sign something. The receptionist seemed puzzled by my question and when I explained she said that there was nothing for me to do and that I could leave (Klein, 1993).*

Although often applauded as a model that the United States should adopt, the Canadian health-care system is not without its problems. Some observers point out that socialized medicine, as practiced in Canada and England, is most effective when health problems are minor and people are able to wait for services. Also, high-tech resources such as sophisticated medical equipment are often scarce in these countries. Hundreds of physicians have reportedly left Canada, most for the United States, because increased government interventions cut their incomes and put restrictions on where and how doctors practice (Krauss, 2003).

You probably have seen print or broadcast media coverage of older Americans traveling to Canada (or placing Internet orders with Canadian firms) for less expensive prescription drugs. What is less widely known, however, is that while many U.S. citizens go to Canada for lower-cost pharmaceuticals, thousands of Canadians come to the United States—especially the Northeast—for treatment of cancer and other life-threatening diseases. Because of financial problems, the Canadian government has closed 44 hospitals since 1995, and some hospitals have turned away ambulances, citing overcrowding in the hospital wards. The Canadian government pays for treatment in the United States, including hotel and related costs (Walker, 1999). These problems suggest that the Canadian national health-care system isn't working as well as many people maintain.

Many Americans are ambivalent about national health-care coverage. About 88 percent, who already have health insurance, worry that a national plan might erode some of their existing benefits. According to a Gallup poll, for example, 54 percent of respondents feared they could end up with worse coverage than they have at present, and 38 percent believed that national reform would hurt the middle class more than any other income group (Saad, 1994). Ambivalence about helping the poor at the expense of the middle and working classes may increase in the future.

Economic Concerns

Most Americans' income comes from employment (rather than investments or inherited wealth, for example). However, the traditional assumption that holding a job will keep a person out of poverty or off welfare rolls is becoming increasingly shaky (see Chapters 4 and 13).

Many families that don't have health care coverage must spend long hours in crowded waiting rooms of public clinics to receive medical treatment.

Since the passage of the "Welfare Reform Act" in 1996 (see text), eligibility for food stamps was made stricter for some recipients, including able-bodied beneficiaries who are expected to work.

Poverty

Much research suggests that poverty, especially child poverty, is not treated as a compelling social issue in the United States. National reports have documented a high incidence of child poverty since 1909 (Jacobs and Davies, 1991).

Moreover, the United States has higher child-poverty rates than many other industrialized countries: 1 out of 5 U.S. children lives in poverty, compared with 1 out of 10 in Canada and Australia, 1 out of 25 in France, 1 out of 50 in Germany, and 1 out of 100 in Sweden (Danziger and Danziger, 1993).

According to some researchers, one of the reasons that U.S. poverty rates are high is that the government has never developed a comprehensive antipoverty agenda. Danziger and Danziger (1993), for example, suggest that an integrated set of policies would include many components: improved education and training, subsidies to working-poor families, greater access to health care and child care, expanded support services for children and their parents (such as youth development programs and decent housing), elimination of labor-market practices that discriminate against minorities and women, and provision of employment opportunities for those unable to find jobs (see Chapters 4 and 13).

Most important, child and family poverty could be alleviated if parents had jobs that paid a living wage. For example, a head of household would have to earn $8.50 per hour (well above the $5.15 per hour minimum wage) and work full time, 52 weeks a year to have an annual gross salary (before taxes) of $17,600, barely above the $17,029 income level defined by the federal government as the poverty level for a family of four (in 1999). How many full-time jobs pay $8.50 an hour to people with a high school education or less? Very few.

Welfare

Most Americans are direct or indirect recipients of some form of **welfare**: government aid to those who can't support themselves, generally because they are poor or unemployed. There are many nonwelfare programs that help the middle class, the upper class, and corporations. For example, the middle class can take advantage of student loans, expensive farm subsidies that pay farmers not to raise crops, and loans to veterans (see Chapter 13).

The Welfare Reform Act In 1996, former President Clinton signed the Personal Responsibility and Work Opportunity Reconciliation Act (PRWORA, also called the "Welfare Reform Act"), which transferred control of federally financed welfare programs to the states. The law converts AFDC (Aid to Families with Dependent Children) to a block grant—a set amount of dollars—called Temporary Assistance to Needy Families (TANF), with a five-year lifetime limit on benefits for welfare recipients.

Under the terms of the law, cash assistance cannot exceed a period of five years regardless of whether a family moves from state to state or goes off welfare and returns later. In addition, after receiving two years of benefits welfare recipients are legally required to work, to enroll in on-the-job or vocational training, or to do community service. Unmarried mothers under age 18 are required to live with an adult and to attend school as a condition of receiving welfare. And while employed in any three-year period, poor, unemployed people aged 18 to 50 who are not raising children are limited to three months of food stamps.

Proponents of this law have argued that the best way to get people off welfare is to require them to work. Even if the work is low-paid, proponents maintain, job participation will give welfare recipients work experience and a job history and require them to contribute to their own support (Mead, 1996). Supporters of the new law also contend that eliminating entitlements, restricting cash assistance, and requiring work will fundamentally alter the employment and family patterns of current AFDC recipients (Meyer and Cancian, 1997). The underlying assumption here is that welfare causes illegitimacy and single parenthood. A mother who doesn't receive AFDC benefits, many believe, will stop having babies out of wedlock or will marry the biological father because he will be the mother's primary (or only) source of financial support.

Critical Assessment The welfare rolls have declined by 43 percent since enactment of the law in 1996, and some states have spent much of the TANF money on job training and child care. Other states, however, have allegedly stashed the money away or have punished welfare recipients harshly for both minor and serious infractions. That is, many states have cut off checks to poor families not only when they refuse to work but also when they miss scheduled appointments with social workers or fail to provide complete information on welfare forms ("Strict new rules . . .," 1999; Kuttner, 2000).

Opponents of PRWORA maintain that the law increases child poverty and punishes children for their parents' economic mistakes (Stevens, 1997). Others feel that the law is misguided. According to Harris (1996), for example, eliminating welfare without improving pay and benefits for employed welfare recipients keeps welfare families poor.

There is also no evidence that welfare causes out-of-wedlock births and single parenthood, opponents argue. The Netherlands, Germany, France, Sweden, and Denmark all have generous welfare programs for single mothers but lower proportions of families headed by single mothers than does the United States (Sandefur, 1996). In 1993, New Jersey was the first state in the nation to deny cash payments to mothers who had additional out-of-wedlock babies. These "family caps" have not reduced out-of-wedlock birth rates ("N.J. finds . . .," 1997). Because many births to unmarried teenagers are unintended, there is no evidence that cutting welfare benefits will lower out-of-wedlock birth rates.

Although millions of people have depended on welfare for survival, the median period of time over which a person has received welfare benefits throughout his or her lifetime is less than four years. About 30 percent of people have been on welfare for less than a year, and 70 percent have left the system within two years. About 20 percent have been welfare recipients for five or more years (Waldman et al., 1994). Furthermore, most children growing up in "welfare homes" have not themselves become dependent on welfare. If critics of the welfare system are successful in decreasing the aid to current welfare recipients without increasing the number of jobs that provide a living, poverty levels will, in all likelihood, increase.

In conclusion, although many states have cut their welfare rolls, there's no evidence that welfare leavers have lifted themselves out of poverty. According to some policy analysts, most welfare leavers have entered the low end of the labor market, where they are working in much the same circumstances as the near-poor and low-income mothers who have not recently been on welfare. Nearly a third of those who left welfare because of PRWORA had returned to welfare and were receiving benefits in 1997. And a sizable proportion (about 25 percent) of leavers is not working and has no partner working (Loprest, 1999).

Corporate Welfare Corporate welfare is even greater. The federal government has directly subsidized the shipping, railroad, and airline industries, along with exporters of iron, steel, textiles, paper, and other products. Since the late 1970s, the federal government has bailed out such companies as Chrysler Corporation, Penn Central, Lockheed, a number of petroleum companies, and hundreds of savings and loan banks when they declared bankruptcy because of fraud, bad investments, or widespread embezzlement (Eitzen and Baca Zinn, 1994).

Why should we be concerned about corporate welfare? Corporate welfare programs cost taxpayers about $10 billion in 1997. Some of the most egregious examples of corporate welfare include the Market Access Program. This program gives such companies as Campbell Soup, Ralston Purina, and Gallo Winery millions of dollars to promote their goods overseas instead of borrowing from banks for investments abroad. Critics of such "corporate welfare queens" note that corporate welfare programs are supported by both U.S. presidents and Congress because the companies make large contributions to fund-raising by both Democrats and Republicans—up to $345 million for former President Bill Clinton from major technology companies alone, for example (Glassman, 1997). Because taxpayer dollars fund corporate welfare, there's less money available for financial assistance for poor, working-poor, and middle-class families.

Comparable Worth

A chronic problem that contributes to women's and children's economic vulnerability is the wage gap between women and men (see Chapter 13). The sex gap in pay stems from many factors, one of which is employment discrimination. Whatever their source, pay inequities have a negative impact on the family.

According to the concept of **comparable worth**, men and women should receive equal pay for doing work that involves comparable skill, effort, and responsibility and is performed under similar working conditions. Proponents argue that jobs can be measured in terms of such variables as required education, skills, experience, mental demands, and working conditions, and that the inherent worth of a job—for example, in terms of its importance to the society—can also be assessed.

Assigning point values in these and other categories, investigators have demonstrated that in several

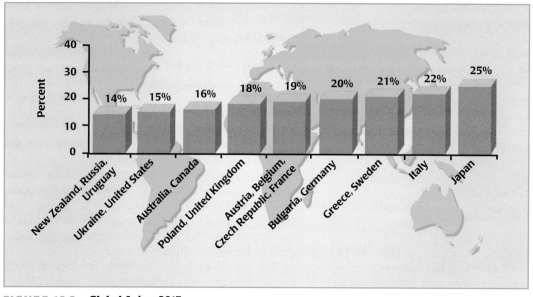

FIGURE 18.2 **Global Aging, 2015**

SOURCE: Based on Kinsella and Velkoff, 2001, Table 1.

communities, women were receiving much lower salaries than men even though their jobs had comparable points. For example, a legal secretary was paid $375 a month less than a carpenter, but both received the same number of job evaluation points (U.S. Commission on Civil Rights, 1984).

Since 1984, a few states (such as Minnesota, South Dakota, New Mexico, and Iowa) have raised women's wages after conducting comparable-worth studies. Although conservatives argue that these kinds of adjustments are too costly, proponents point out that the cost of implementing pay equity in Minnesota came to less than 4 percent of the state's payroll budget. In a mid-1990s study, investigators found that the Minnesota law had improved women's wages in government by more than 10 percent, and a half dozen states now have similar pay equity laws (Kleiman, 1993).

Such pay adjustments have affected only public sector workers, however, because no U.S. law requires comparable worth in wages. In contrast, comparable-worth legislation has been enacted in half of the jurisdictions in Canada, a majority of which require that employers in both public and private sectors set pay levels in accordance with comparable-worth standards (Aman and England, 1997).

Global Aging

Our global population is aging at an unprecedented rate. By 2000, almost 7 percent of the world's population was 65 years old or older. As *Figure 18.2* shows, in some countries, such as Greece, Italy, Japan, and Sweden, more than 20 percent of the people are age 65 years and older. Such "world graying" is likely to affect both the young and the old. In the United States, for example, two emerging issues include the right to die and competition for scarce resources.

Right-to-Die Issues

In 1994, the Netherlands legalized physician-assisted suicide under certain conditions. In that country, a dying patient must have made voluntary, deliberate, and repeated requests to die; the patient must be suffering with no prospect of relief; and the doctor must consult with colleagues before acting. Government figures estimate that in 1995 about 19 percent of all deaths in the Netherlands were assisted suicides. Most requests came from patients with AIDS or terminal cancer (Shapiro, 1997).

In the United States, legal, religious, and medical groups historically have taken a strong stand against assisted suicide. In 1994, however, voters supported a referendum in Oregon to legalize assisted suicide. The provisions of the Oregon proposal were as follows:

- Right-to-die decisions were limited to competent adults who were terminally ill; children were not eligible.

- The patient was required to make at least three requests to the physician—two verbally and one in writing—over the course of at least 15 days.

- A second physician had to make an independent diagnosis of both terminal illness and mental competence.

■ If either physician felt the patient was not emotionally stable, the process was to be stopped and the patient was to be referred to a psychiatrist or clinical psychologist.

■ If the two physicians concurred that the patient was both terminally ill and mentally stable, the patient was to have the prescription filled and was to self-administer the drug. Patients not physically able to do this were not to be eligible for the "physician-aid-in-dying" process (Pridonoff, 1994).

The referendum passed but was appealed. In 1997, the Supreme Court left it up to the states to decide the legality of doctor-aided suicide. Later that year, 60 percent of Oregon voters decided, a second time, to keep their Death with Dignity law. In the five months after voters approved the law, only two Oregonians were known to have used drugs prescribed under the law to commit suicide (Knickerbocker, 1998).

There is no evidence that the legalization of Oregon's 1997 Death with Dignity Act has triggered numerous physician-assisted suicides. According to Oregon health officials, 16 patients ingested lethal medications in 1998 and 27 did so in 1999. In 1999, the median age of those patients was 71 years, half were college graduates, all had health insurance, 21 were receiving hospice care, and 17 were dying of cancer. According to both physicians and family members, the patients requested assistance with suicide for several reasons, including loss of autonomy, loss of control of bodily functions, and a determination to control the manner of their death (Sullivan et al., 2000; see also Ganzini et al., 2000).

The right-to-die debate was triggered in 1990 when Dr. Jack Kevorkian built a "suicide machine" to help people who suffered from chronic pain or terminal illnesses to kill themselves. He had been acquitted of second-degree murder several times because he had merely provided lethal drugs to patients rather than administering them.

In 1999, however, a Michigan judge sentenced Kevorkian to 10 to 25 years in prison because he had actually injected the drugs into the arm of a 52-year-old man suffering with amyotrophic lateral sclerosis (Lou Gehrig's disease). Kevorkian will be eligible for parole in 2007.

Those opposed to the right-to-die movement argue, among other things, that elderly people may be pressured by caregivers to end their lives, that their acts may result from feelings of guilt about being a burden, that they should be persuaded that much of their pain is treatable, and that physicians are responsible for extending rather than ending life (Veatch, 1995).

Despite such opposition, many elderly and their families are becoming more vocal about a person's right to die with dignity, at home, and on his or her own terms. In 1992, Derek Humphry's *Final Exit*, describing how the elderly and terminally ill can commit suicide, became a best-seller. Since then, several authors have addressed the right-to-die issue (for example, see Kramer, 1993; Quill, 1993; Humphry and Clement, 2000).

Such organizations as Choice in Dying, End of Life Choices, and Concern for Dying have reported widespread interest in information on living wills. A **living will** is a legal document in which people can specify which, if any, life-support measures they want in the case of serious illness and whether or when they want to have such measures discontinued.

Preparing such a document does not guarantee compliance, however. Physicians or hospitals may refuse to honor living wills if their policies support prolonging life at any cost, if family members contest the living will, or if there is any question about the patient's mental competence when the will was drawn up (Veatch, 1995). For these reasons and because state laws and policies vary widely, people who want living wills to be enforced should consult attorneys to minimize legal problems and to make sure their wishes are carried out.

Such expressions of individual rights are bound to increase in the future. Because of their large numbers, baby boomers will undoubtedly be instrumental in challenging or promoting right-to-die laws.

Competition for Scarce Resources

When the Social Security Act was passed in 1935, life expectancy in the United States was just below 62 years, compared with around 78 years today (see Chapter 17). In the years ahead, the increasing numbers of older Americans will put a significant strain on the nation's health-care services and retirement income programs.

According to Crenshaw (1992: 4), older people "are one of the largest and politically best organized groups in the nation." They vote in large numbers, follow issues carefully, and usually come well prepared to defend their positions during congressional hearings. The American Association of Retired Persons (AARP) is one of the most powerful advocates for the elderly. AARP has over 33 million members, more than $300 million in revenues, and more than 400,000 volunteers. Many other groups also lobby for older people, including the American Association of Homes for the Aging, the Gray Panthers, the National Association of Retired Federal Employees, the National Council of Senior Citizens, the National Council on the Aging, the Older Women's League, and the National Committee to Preserve Social Security and Medicare. It is not surprising, then, that the elderly have been successful in safeguarding and even increasing many of their benefits.

This 70-year-old stonemason is laying the foundation for a fountain in a public park.

Although the elderly once had the highest poverty rates in the United States, they now have the lowest. In part because of the growth of Social Security and Medicare (which claim about one-third of the federal budget), in 1998 about 11 percent of the elderly had incomes below the poverty line, compared with more than a third in 1959 (see Chapter 17).

Some observers have charged that during a time of fiscal austerity older people have benefited at the expense of others, primarily children, because AFDC support has been cut while programs for the elderly have maintained their funding. There is an increasing chasm between the young and the old that also reflects racial and ethnic differences. For example, projections for 2030 indicate that 41 percent of the children but only 24 percent of the old will be minorities. In the future, some speculate, the growing number of middle-aged minorities and parents with large numbers of children may resist increasing federal expenditures for a predominantly white elderly population.

Remember, however, that although today's senior citizens, as a group, are better off financially than previous generations, there are specific pockets of poverty. For example, the poverty rate for minority elderly is two to three times higher than for the white elderly (see Chapter 17).

Poverty rates in the older population also increase dramatically with age. In 2002, about 11 percent of people age 65 and over were living in poverty, but nearly 20 percent of those age 85 or older were poor (see

Chapter 17). Furthermore, the number of people who will be 85 or older is expected to triple by the year 2030, and much of the elderly population will have chronic health conditions that will increase the need for long-term care (Light, 1988).

Some Possible Solutions

Some feel that the competition for scarce resources between the young and the old can be lessened. For example, increasing the eligibility for old-age benefits from age 65 to age 70 can reduce the size of the elderly dependent population. Because people reaching age 65 now and in the future generally will be better educated and have more work-related skills than earlier cohorts, they are more likely to be productive employees. They may also offer an employer more skills than some young people, whose academic performance, as measured on standardized exams and college graduation, appears to have diminished.

Moreover, because the rates of adolescent criminal behavior, drug and alcohol use, out-of-wedlock births, and children living in poverty have increased, large numbers of retirees in the year 2010 will be depending on a small group of people in the labor force to support their Social Security and health-care benefits. Thus, some observers suggest, redefining "old age" would be beneficial to both the young and the old. If the definition of old age and the time of mandatory retirement were pushed up to age 70 or higher, many productive older Americans could continue to work and contribute to Social Security. As a result, the burden of supporting an aging population would not fall wholly on younger workers.

Others have suggested combining the needs of the elderly and those of children. For example, a few companies have built day-care facilities at or near workplaces for the young and the old, where both generations can visit, talk, and forge friendships. Such programs can help fulfill reciprocal needs for the elderly to help children and for children to understand an older generation.

Conclusion

The family in the twenty-first century will be much more diverse in terms of racial and ethnic characteristics. It is difficult to predict whether this *change* will lead to greater cooperation or to conflict. Because the United States is the only country in the world with such a heterogeneous mix of cultural groups, there are no models for comparison. Optimists argue that cultural diversity is healthy and will strengthen communities.

Another expected but unprecedented change is the growth of an older population that will have to rely on a generally less educated young population for its resources and health care. Given the increased health-care and economic problems of recent years, this new century may see more multigenerational households and greater numbers of adult children providing care to their aging parents.

The family in the twenty-first century will probably incorporate a wide variety of work roles and family roles. Because women's participation in the labor force is expected to increase, work and family functions will continue to overlap. The *constraints* posed by the need to balance domestic and work responsibilities are not expected to diminish, however. Consequently, women (and some men) may become more vocal in demanding family policies that put a higher priority on children, parenting, and the family.

Overall, families in the twenty-first century will continue to have more *choices* than they did in the past. Because divorce and remarriage are no longer uncommon, these options will probably become even more widespread in the future. In addition, as the technology improves eyeglasses, hearing aids, wheelchairs, and biomedical devices to strengthen or replace legs, arms, hearing, and eyesight, many older Americans will be able to live independently instead of depending on care from others (Longino, 1994).

The *Quality Time* cartoon by Gail Machlis is reprinted by permission of Chronicle Features, San Francisco, California.

SUMMARY

1. In the twenty-first century, some of the greatest changes will probably be in six areas: family structure, racial and ethnic diversity, children's rights, health-related issues, economics, and the needs of an aging population.

2. Family structures will continue to be diverse. Demographers predict that racial-ethnic diversity will increase because of increased immigration and higher fertility rates among African Americans and some Asian American and Latino families.

3. Children have few rights today. Except for an increase in child-support payments, there is little evidence that the economic and emotional well-being of most U.S. children will improve very much in the future. Our child-care and parental leave policies, for example, are backward compared with those of all other developed countries. They are also paltry compared with those of some developing countries.

4. Health-care issues will probably be a major constraint on family life in the twenty-first century. Two of the dominant issues will be caring for patients with

HIV and AIDS and developing a national program that provides families with minimal health care.

5. There is little evidence that the economic problems of many families will decrease in the future. The United States has generous corporate welfare policies, whereas programs for the poor typically provide access to low-paying jobs that don't include health benefits and little opportunity for better wages.

6. As the world's population ages, right-to-die issues are becoming more prominent. In the United States, living wills are becoming more common, and some states are considering legalizing physician-assisted suicide.

7. In the future, there will probably be greater competition over resources between the young and the old. Because the elderly population is growing, is well organized, and has political clout, elderly issues may well be a higher priority than children's issues.

8. Overall, families in the twenty-first century will continue to have more choices than they did in the past, but there will also be many constraints.

KEY TERMS

family policy   *517*   comparable worth   *523*   living will   *525*
welfare   *522*

TAKING IT FURTHER

Families and the Future

IDB Population Pyramids, Census Bureau, allows you to obtain population pyramids by age and sex for a variety of countries for 1997, 2025, and 2050.

www.census.gov/ipc/www/idbpyr.html

Futurework, Department of Labor, provides information on technology and globalization and the role of the twenty-first-century workplace.

www.dol.gov/dol/asp/public/futurework/report.htm

The **National Committee on Pay Equity** offers information on pay equity facts and activities throughout the United States and the world.

www.feminist.com/fairpay.htm

National Center for Policy Research on Women & Children examines policies and programs that address women's and children's economic and physical health.

www.cpr4womenandfamilies.org

The **Compassion in Dying Federation** provides legal advocacy and public education to improve pain and symptom management, increase patient empowerment and self-determination, and expand end-of-life choices to include aid-in-dying for terminally ill, mentally competent adults.

http://www.compassionindying.org

Several sites explain the **Personal Responsibility and Work Opportunity Reconciliation Act of 1996,** including the following:

www.urban.org
www.acf.dhhs.gov/news/welfare/wr/wr.htm

And more: www.prenhall.com/benokraitis provides sites on the future of children's health, analyses of welfare reform, aging around the world, and prospective changes in retirement.

INVESTIGATE WITH RESEARCH NAVIGATOR

Research Navigator.com
RESOURCES FOR COLLEGE RESEARCH ASSIGNMENTS

Please go to www.researchnavigator.com and enter your LOGIN NAME and PASSWORD. For instructions on registering for the first time, please view the detailed instructions at the end of the Chapter 1. Please search the Research Navigator™ site using the following key search terms:

poverty
children's rights
family structure

APPENDIX A

Sexual Anatomy

The better you understand your own body, the more comfortable you may become with your sexuality. Also, remember that the word *intercourse* means "communication"; sexual intercourse is an activity in which two people communicate with each other through mutual bodily stimulation.

Female Anatomy

Collectively known as the **vulva** (Latin for "covering"), the external female genitalia consist of the mons veneris, labia majora, labia minora, clitoris, and vaginal and urethral openings. *Figure A.1* shows these structures and the internal female reproductive organs.

The **mons veneris** (Latin for "mount of Venus," referring to the Roman goddess of love) is the soft layer of fatty tissue overlaying the area where the pubic bones come together. Because of the many nerve endings in the mons area, most women find gentle stimulation of the mons pleasurable. Below the mons are the **labia majora** (major, or larger, lips) and **labia minora** (minor, or smaller, lips), outer and inner elongated folds of skin that, in the sexually unstimulated state, cover and protect the *vaginal* and *urethral* openings. The labia majora extend from the mons to the hairless bit of skin between the vaginal opening and anus, called the **perineum**. Located at the base of the labia minora are **Bartholin's glands**, which, during prolonged stimulation, secrete a few drops of an alkaline fluid that help neutralize the normal acidity of the outer vagina (sperm cannot survive in an acidic environment).

The **clitoris** (Greek for "hill" or "slope") develops from the same embryonic tissue as the penis and is extremely sensitive to touch. In fact, it is the only structure in either females or males whose only known function is to focus sexual sensations. Also highly sensitive are the labia minora, which meet at their upper end to form the **clitoral hood**, analogous to the male **foreskin** (or *prepuce*), hiding all but the tip, or **glans**, of the clitoris.

The area between the two labia minora is sometimes called the **vestibular area** (Latin for "entrance hall") because it contains the entrance to the vagina. In sexually inexperienced females, or "virgins," a thin membrane called the **hymen** may partially cover the opening to the vagina. The urethral opening, also located in this area between the clitoris and the vaginal opening, is the outlet of the **urethra**, which carries urine from the bladder out of the body.

The internal female reproductive system consists of the vagina, uterus, fallopian tubes, and ovaries. The **vagina** (Latin for "sheath") is an internal structure located behind the bladder and in front of the rectum. It serves not only to receive sperm during sexual intercourse but as the passageway for a fully developed fetus at the time of birth.

The **uterus**, or womb, which holds and protects a developing fetus (see *Appendix C*), is connected to the vagina through its narrow end, called the **cervix**. The uterus has three layers: the innermost **endometrium**, in which a fertilized egg implants; a middle layer of muscles called the **myometrium**, which contract during labor; and an external cover called the **perimetrium**. Each month, after ovulation (see next paragraph), the endometrium

FIGURE A.1   **Side View of the Female Reproductive System**

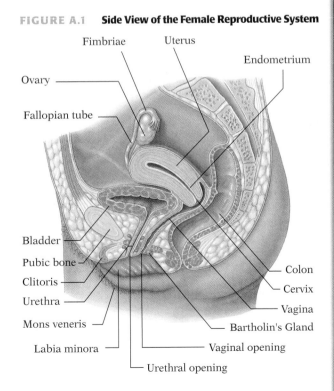

Appendix A is adapted from Bruce M. King, Human Sexuality Today, 4th ed. (Upper Saddle River, NJ: Prentice Hall, 2002), pp. 31–52. Adapted by permission of Prentice Hall, Upper Saddle River, New Jersey.

thickens and becomes rich in blood vessels in preparation for the implantation of a fertilized egg. If fertilization does not occur, this tissue is sloughed off and discharged from the body as the menstrual flow.

Extending from each side of the uterus are the two fallopian tubes. The *fimbriae*, fingerlike structures at the end of each tube, brush against the **ovary**, which is the female sex gland. The ovaries, or gonads, are supported by ligaments on each side of the uterus and have two functions: to produce eggs (*ova*) and female hormones (*estrogen* and *progesterone*). Each month, in the process called *ovulation*, an egg is expelled from an ovary and picked up by the fimbriae, pulling it into one of the fallopian tubes. Fertilization, if it occurs, usually happens in the tube.

Male Anatomy

The external male genitalia are the penis and the scrotum. (The external and internal male reproductive organs are spongelike shown in *Figure A.2*.) The **penis**, which has both reproductive and excretory functions, consists of three parts: the body or shaft, the glans, and the root. Only the first two parts are visible. The *shaft* contains three parallel cylinders of spongelike tissue: two *corpora cavernosa*, or cavernous bodies, on top; and a *corpus spongiosum*, or "spongy body," on the bottom. The **glans** is the smooth, rounded end of the penis. The raised rim between the shaft and glans is the **corona**, the most sensitive to touch of any part of the penis. The **urethra**, which serves as a passageway for both urine and sperm, runs through the corpus spongiosum, and the urethral opening (*meatus*) is located at the tip of the glans.

The root of the penis is surrounded by two muscles (*bulbocavernous* and *ischiocavernosus*) that aid in both urination and ejaculation. (*Sphincter* muscles, which surround the urethra as it emerges from the bladder, contract during erection to prevent urine from mixing with semen.) The skin of the penis is very loose, to allow expansion during erection; unstimulated, the penis is about 3.75 inches long and 1.2 inches in diameter, but when erect it is about 6 inches long and 1.5 inches in diameter.

The sac located beneath the penis is called the **scrotum**. It holds the testicles outside the body cavity to protect the sperm, which can be produced only at a temperature about 5° F lower than normal body temperature. For this reason the skin of the scrotum has many sweat glands that aid in temperature regulation.

The male internal reproductive system consists of the testicles, a duct system that transports sperm out of the body, the prostate gland, the seminal vesicles that produce the fluid in which the sperm are mixed, and Cowper's glands.

The **testes**, or testicles (the male gonads), have two functions: The testes produce sperm (*spermatozoa*) and male hormones (*testosterone* and other *androgens*). Millions of new sperm are produced each day in several hundred *seminiferous tubules*.

Once produced, sperm pass through a four-part duct system (*epididymus, vas deferens, ejaculatory duct,* and *urethra*) before being expelled from the penis during ejaculation. Although an average ejaculation of semen contains about 300 million sperm, most of the volume of the ejaculate is fluid from the prostate gland and seminal vesicles. Among other substances, the **seminal vesicles** secrete fructose, prostaglandins, and substances. The **prostate gland** also secretes these substances, as well as a substance (fibrinogenase) that causes semen to coagulate temporarily after ejaculation, thus helping to keep it in the vagina. **Cowper's glands** are two pea-sized structures located beneath the prostate. They secrete a few drops of alkaline fluid that may appear at the tip of the penis before orgasm. Cowper's secretion neutralizes the normal acidity of the urethra, protecting sperm as they pass through the penis during ejaculation. Because Cowper's secretion often contains sperm, withdrawal of the penis just before ejaculation is a very unreliable method of birth control.

FIGURE A.2   **Side View of the Male Reproductive System**

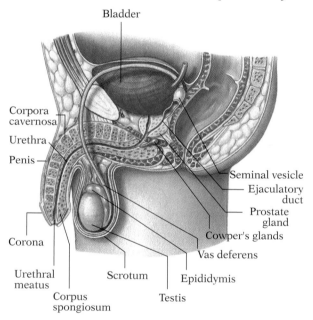

Bladder

Corpora cavernosa

Urethra

Penis

Corona

Urethral meatus

Corpus spongiosum

Scrotum

Seminal vesicle

Ejaculatory duct

Prostate gland

Cowper's glands

Vas deferens

Epididymis

Testis

APPENDIX B

Sexual Problems, Dysfunctions, and Treatment

There are many reasons for dissatisfaction with sex: poor general health, unhappiness with available sex partners, and not feeling loved by a partner. Most couples, at some time or other, may experience **sexual dysfunctions**, or conditions in which the ordinary physical responses of sexual function are impaired. Sometimes these problems are physiological, sometimes they are interpersonal, and sometimes they reflect a combination of both physiological and interpersonal factors. In general, serious sexual dysfunctions affect small numbers of people.

Male Sexual Dysfunctions

Erectile dysfunction, or **impotence**, is the inability to attain or maintain an erection. It is a rare man who does not experience this problem at least once in his lifetime. Impotence can occur at any age and can assume many different forms. Typically, the male with erectile dysfunction has partial erections that are too weak to permit insertion in the vagina. Sometimes firm erections quickly disappear when intercourse is attempted.

Impotence can have a negative effect on the female partner's self-esteem if she feels that she is not sexually desirable or is doing something wrong. Most continuing erectile dysfunctions—some estimates are as high as 86 percent—have an organic basis, such as circulatory problems, neurological disorders (due to multiple sclerosis or spinal cord injury, for example), hormone imbalances, and infections or injuries of the penis, testes, urethra, or prostate gland. Diabetes, alcoholism, prescription medications (such as drugs for high blood pressure), and amphetamines, barbiturates, and narcotics can also cause erectile dysfunction.

Several other male dysfunctions are related to ejaculation. The most common of these dysfunctions is **premature ejaculation**: unintentional ejaculation before or while the male tries to enter his partner or soon after intercourse begins. An estimated 15 to 20 percent of all American men ejaculate prematurely on a regular basis. Whereas many female partners are understanding and accepting of the problem, others may feel angry, avoid sex, or seek another lover. Some men are not bothered, but others may question their masculinity. Some may experience heightened anxiety about performance, which in turn exacerbates the condition.

Many therapists believe that premature ejaculation is due to psychological factors. Others suggest that men who view women as sex objects are more likely to ejaculate prematurely, regardless of the woman's readiness. Other ejaculatory problems, such as the backward spurting of the semen into the bladder during orgasm, known as *retrograde ejaculation*, and ejaculation in the vagina only after a lengthy period and strenuous efforts (*retarded ejaculation*), or failure to ejaculate or achieve orgasm at all, may be caused by drug use, alcoholism, neurological disorders, or prescription medicines.

Female Sexual Dysfunctions

Approximately 2 to 3 percent of adult women are affected by **vaginismus**, or pain during penetration because of involuntary spasms of the muscles surrounding the outer third of the vagina. Vaginismus can be so severe that it prevents not only intercourse but even insertion of a finger or tampon. A woman's partner may deliberately avoid intercourse because vaginismus can be painful. Some men may become passive about sex, whereas others become impatient or openly hostile and may seek other sexual partners.

Vaginismus may have organic causes, such as poor vaginal lubrication, drugs that have a drying effect on the vagina (such as antihistamines, tranquilizers, or marijuana), diabetes, vaginal infections, or pelvic disorders. It can also reflect psychological difficulties, such as anxieties about intercourse, a fear of injury or harm to the internal organs, trauma (due to rape or abortion, for example), a strict religious upbringing in which sex was equated with sin, or fear of or hostility toward men. Such psychological problems are often treated by relaxation exercises followed by a gradual dilation of the vagina.

Another female sexual dysfunction is **anorgasmia**: the inability to reach orgasm. Anorgasmia, which used to be called frigidity, has several variations. In *primary anorgasmia*, a woman has never had an orgasm. In *secondary anorgasmia*, a woman who was regularly orgasmic at one time is no longer. And in *situational anorgasmia*, a woman is able to achieve orgasm only under certain circumstances, such as through masturbation.

Some anorgasmic women find that sex is satisfying and stimulating even though they have never experienced an orgasm. For others, the condition can lead to lowered self-esteem, a sense of futility, and depression. About 5 percent of cases of anorgasmia are attributed to organic causes. Orgasm can be blocked by severe chronic illness, diabetes, alcoholism, neurological problems, hormone deficiencies, pelvic disorders (due to infections, trauma, or scarring from surgery), or drugs (including narcotics, tranquilizers, and blood pressure medications). Other reasons for anorgasmia have an interpersonal basis. For example, women's most common sexual complaints include not getting enough sex because the partner gets tired too fast, intercourse does not last long enough, the partner is unskilled, the woman cannot readily lubricate because there is not enough foreplay, sex is boring ("same place, same time, same channel," according to one woman), or the timing is bad.

Finally, approximately 15 percent of adult women experience **dyspareunia**, or painful intercourse, several times a year. Another 1 to 2 percent are believed to have painful intercourse on a regular basis. Men, too, can experience dyspareunia (it is sometimes associated with problems of the prostate gland), but this disorder is believed to be much more common in women than in men. Like anorgasmia, female dyspareunia may be caused by any of a number of physical conditions, including poor vaginal lubrication, drugs, infections, diseases, and pelvic disorders.

Inhibited Sexual Desire

Both men and women can experience another common sexual problem, **inhibited sexual desire (ISD)**, or a low interest in sex. Although the exact incidence of ISD is unknown, approximately 33 percent of the people who consult sex therapists do so because of ISD problems. It is important to remember that a low level of interest in sex is not uncommon. It creates a problem only when it becomes a source of personal distress. An extreme example of ISD is **sexual aversion**, in which people experience persistent or intense feelings of anxiety or panic in sexual situations and avoid sexual contact altogether. The causes of ISD are both organic and nonorganic. Organic factors include hormone deficiencies, alcoholism, kidney failure, drug abuse, and severe chronic illness. Nonorganic factors include fatigue, overwork, depression, and poor lovemaking skills.

Relationship Factors and Sexual Dysfunction

Personal and cultural factors play an important role in sexual expression. Many people do not realize that sex is not just a physiological response. Good or bad sex reflects the quality of our interpersonal relationships, especially in long-term situations. According to Wade and Cirese (1991), therapists typically encounter four interpersonal problems that are destructive to sexual relationships. The first is *anger and hostility*. Dissension and conflict are inevitable in any close relationship, but long-term resentments can sour erotic feelings and behavior.

A second destructive problem in interpersonal relationships is *boredom*. Boredom may be related specifically to sexual activity—it always takes place at the same time and in the same way—or it may reflect a general disinterest in the partner. Some people like sexual relations that are predictable; others become bored with predictability.

Third, *conflicting sexual expectations* can also be harmful to the relationship. One partner may demand oral sex, for example, but the other may find this activity repulsive.

Finally, *poor communication* is a constant problem in interpersonal relationships. Instead of saying what they want in sex, most people are reluctant to say anything, fearing to seem critical of the partner or to demand something they think the partner may not want to give. Suppressing their own needs may lead them to become angry and to strike out verbally at the partner ("You don't love me anymore"). Because many people find communicating about sex so difficult, they often deny the problem and allow it to fester.

Treating Sexual Problems

Because many sexual dysfunctions are caused by *organic* (physical or physiological) problems, a person experiencing such a dysfunction should first see a physician. If a thorough examination reveals no organic abnormalities, the physician may recommend that the person consult a psychiatrist or a psychotherapist. Be careful, however. Because sex therapy is largely an unregulated profession, people can offer their services with little more preparation than having attended a few workshops or reading a book. People seeking help should contact sex therapy centers that are affiliated with universities, medical schools, or hospitals. They can also seek advice about qualified therapists from local medical societies, psychological associations, or family physicians. Even when a clinician is trained and competent, people should feel free to change to a therapist who may be better suited to their temperament and personality.

APPENDIX C

Conception, Pregnancy, and Childbirth

About midway through a woman's menstrual cycle, an *ovum*, or egg, is released into the abdominal cavity, where it is picked up by the *fimbriae* at the end of one of the fallopian tubes. The ovum takes three to seven days to move through the fallopian tube to the uterus, and it is only during the first 24 hours after the egg leaves an ovary that it can be fertilized.

Conception

At orgasm during sexual intercourse, a man ejaculates into a woman's vagina 200 million to 400 million sperm, all of which attempt to pass through the cervix and uterus into the fallopian tubes. However, only a few thousand live long enough to complete the journey, and fewer than 50 reach the egg itself during its own journey through the tube. Because sperm can live for only 72 hours inside a woman's reproductive tract, the period during which conception can normally occur is extremely limited.

Conception takes place when one of the sperm penetrates the egg's surface. Within hours, spermatozoon (a single sperm cell) and ovum fuse to form a one-celled organism called a **zygote**, which contains the complete genetic code, or blueprint, for the new human life that has just begun. Shortly afterward, the zygote splits into two separate cells, then four, then eight, and so on. While this cell division continues, the organism journeys through the tube toward the uterus, a trip that transforms it into a hollow ball of cells called a **blastocyst**. At about 11 to 12 days after conception, the blastocyst, whose inner cell mass will become an embryo and whose outer layers will form structures to nourish and protect the growing fetus, burrows into the wall of the uterus in a process called **implantation**.

By about 14 days after conception, implantation is usually complete (see *Figure C.1*), and a series of connections between the mother and the **embryo**—the term for the developing organism after implantation—begins to form. The outer layers of the blastocyst begin to form the **placenta**, the organ that serves as a connection, or interface, between the infant's various systems and the mother's. One layer forms the **umbilical cord**, which connects the developing baby with the placenta. The **amnion**, a thick-skinned sac filled with fluid that surrounds and protects the baby from sudden movements and changes in temperature, and the **chorion**, which develops into the lining of the placenta, begin to form.

Pregnancy

Pregnancy lasts an average of 260 to 270 days, or nine months. This time is divided into three-month periods called *trimesters*.

The First Trimester Women exhibit a varying number of symptoms during the first three months of pregnancy. Breasts may begin to enlarge and become tender. Veins may begin to show on the breasts, and the *areolas* (the darker rings surrounding the nipples) may turn dark. Nipples may also become larger. Urination may increase in frequency, and bowel movements may no longer be regular. Many women feel tired and run-down. One of the more common symptoms of pregnancy is nausea. Although it is called "morning sickness," it can occur at any time of the day.

In the first trimester, the developing baby undergoes a great deal of change (see *Figure C.1*). After implantation, cell division continues, and portions of the organism begin to differentiate in an orderly fashion. Growth in the unborn child occurs from the head downward and from the center outward. In the embryo, three inner cell layers form specific parts of the body. The **ectoderm** forms the nervous system, skin, and teeth. The **mesoderm** forms the muscles, skeleton, and blood vessels. The **endoderm** forms the internal organs (such as lungs, liver, and digestive system).

In the third week of pregnancy, a central structure—the *neural tube*—becomes a dominant feature. This will become the central nervous system. By the end of the fourth week, the umbilical cord, heart, and digestive system begin to form. By eight weeks, all organs have begun to develop. The heart is pumping, and the stomach has begun to produce some digestive juices. From eight weeks until birth, the developing organism is called a **fetus**.

The Second Trimester In the fourth or fifth month of pregnancy, the movements of the fetus can be felt by its mother. The first experience of movement is called **quickening**. As her abdomen expands, red lines, or "stretch marks," may develop on the mother-to-be. The breasts begin to swell and may start to leak *colostrum*, a thick, sticky liquid that is produced before milk starts to flow.

Appendix C is adapted from Bruce M. King, Human Sexuality Today, 4th edition (Upper Saddle River, NJ: Prentice Hall, 2002), Chapter 7. Adapted by permission of Prentice Hall, Upper Saddle River, New Jersey.

Water retention may cause swelling in the ankles, feet, and hands. Women may develop varicose veins or hemorrhoids. Morning sickness begins to diminish, which often brings an increase in appetite, and some women may experience heightened sexuality.

At this time, the fetus begins to make sucking motions with its mouth. In the fifth month, the fetus has a detectable heartbeat and will respond to sound. It also begins to show definite periods of sleep and wakefulness. In the sixth month, the fetus can open its eyes and will suck its thumb and respond to light. At the end of the second trimester, the fetus is almost a foot long and weighs well over a pound and a half.

The Third Trimester   In the third trimester, walking, sitting, and rising become more difficult for the expectant mother, who may experience back pain as a result of the increasing burden she carries in her abdomen. The rapidly growing fetus puts pressure on the mother's bladder and stomach, often making urination more frequent. Indigestion, heartburn, gas, and constipation are also common complaints, and the active movements of the fetus may prevent restful sleep.

In the eighth month, the fetus's weight begins to increase dramatically. At the end of the eighth month, the fetus will weigh about 4 pounds and will be 16 to 17 inches long. From this point on, the fetus will gain about 0.5 pounds per week. In the ninth month, the fetus will grow to about 20 inches in length and weigh 7 to 7.5 pounds, but these measurements vary widely. Shortly before birth (weeks or even hours before birth), the fetus will rotate its position so that its head is downward. This is called **lightening** because once the fetus's head has lowered in the uterus, pressure on the mother's abdomen and diaphragm is greatly reduced.

Complications of Pregnancy

Teratogens are agents that can cross the placental barrier and harm a fetus, such as diseases, drugs, or environmental pollutants. Until recently the placenta was thought to be a perfect filter that kept out all harmful substances, but now we know that hundreds of teratogens can invade the fetus's small world. Three things determine the harm that can be caused by teratogens: the amount of the agent, the duration of time of exposure of the fetus, and the fetus's age. Each part of the fetus's body has a time, or *critical period*, when it is most susceptible to damage. Although teratogens should be avoided at all times, most body parts are maximally susceptible to damage during the first eight weeks of development.

Diseases   Even the "weakened" disease organisms of certain vaccines can be harmful to a fetus if taken by the mother just before or during early pregnancy. Some strains of the flu, mumps, chicken pox, and other common diseases can also harm the fetus. One of the first teratogens to be discovered was the *rubella* virus, or German measles. A fetus exposed to rubella may be born blind, deaf, or intellectually impaired. A woman can be safely inoculated against rubella any time up to three months before becoming pregnant. Most types of *sexually transmitted diseases* can also affect a fetus or newborn baby.

Preeclampsia   A pregnant woman can also have a disease called **preeclampsia** (formerly called *toxemia*), whose symptoms include high blood pressure, excessive water retention, and protein in the urine. In about 5 percent of cases, the disease advances to *eclampsia*, which is characterized by convulsions and coma. Preeclampsia and eclampsia are among the leading causes of maternal and fetal death. The cause of preeclampsia is unknown. A low-salt diet, bedrest, and blood pressure medications are the usual treatments, but delivering the baby is the only cure.

Rh Factor   Most people's blood contains a protein called the **Rh factor**. If they do, they are "Rh positive"; if they don't, they are "Rh negative." The presence or absence of the Rh factor is determined genetically. In about 8 percent of pregnancies in the United States, the mother is negative and her baby is positive. Although this is not usually a dangerous situation in a first birth, antibodies may build up in the mother's blood and attack a

FIGURE C.1   **Prenatal Development**

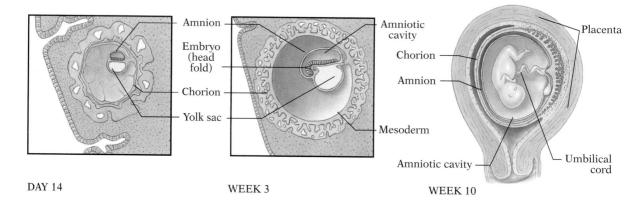

Amnion — Embryo (head fold) — Chorion — Yolk sac

Amniotic cavity — Chorion — Amnion — Mesoderm — Amniotic cavity

Placenta — Umbilical cord

DAY 14   WEEK 3   WEEK 10

second fetus who is also Rh positive. To prevent this, an injection should be given an Rh negative mother immediately after her first delivery to prevent the buildup of antibodies.

Smoking   Cigarette smoking is associated with an increased risk of miscarriage, complications of pregnancy and labor, preterm birth, lower birth weight, and higher rates of infant mortality. It has also been associated with an increased risk that the placenta will separate from the uterus too soon and with malformation of fetal organs such as the heart.

Alcohol   The mother's use of alcohol during pregnancy can lead to physical deformities or mental retardation in the infant, a condition known as **fetal alcohol syndrome,** or **FAS** (see also Chapter 11). Alcohol can also cause the umbilical cord to collapse temporarily, cutting off oxygen to the fetus and causing a condition known as **minimal brain damage,** which has been associated with hyperactivity and learning disabilities. Even if a woman consumes only moderate amounts of alcohol, her baby still may develop health or emotional problems.

Other Drugs   Many drugs—whether illegal, prescription, or over-the-counter—can cross the placental barrier. Women who are addicted to heroin (or methadone) while pregnant will give birth to infants who are addicted as well. These infants must go through withdrawal and typically show such symptoms as fevers, tremors, convulsions, and difficulty in breathing. Even moderate cocaine use by a mother can result in her baby exhibiting low birth weight. "Crack babies" have a variety of sensorimotor and behavioral deficits, including irritability and disorientation. In addition, commonly used drugs such as antihistamines and megadoses of certain vitamins have proven to have harmful effects; for example, over-the-counter aspirin products taken in the last trimester can affect fetal circulation and cause complications during delivery.

Environmental Pollutants   Substances such as heavy metals (lead and cadmium, for example) in drinking water can cause damage to the fetus. Physical deformities and mental retardation have been found in children whose mothers ate mercury-contaminated fish. Radiation and x-rays are also powerful teratogens, especially in the first trimester. Exposure to x-rays has been linked to increased risk of leukemia.

Detecting Problems in Pregnancy   The safest technique of examining the fetus in the womb for possible abnormalities is *ultrasound,* a "noninvasive" method in which sound waves are bounced off the fetus and the uterus. This technique is useful primarily in detecting structural problems. Other "invasive" techniques, those in which instruments are inserted into the womb or even the amniotic sac that holds the fetus, include *amniocentesis* and *chorionic villus sampling* (see Chapter 11), *celocentesis,* and *fetoscopy.* These methods can detect chromosomal problems, such as Down's syndrome, and certain diseases.

Childbirth

Labor is divided into three stages (see *Figure C.2*). In the initial, start-up stage, the woman's body prepares to expel the fetus from the uterus and into the outside world. This stage usually lasts from 6 to 13 hours. At this time, uterine contractions begin to push the baby downward toward the cervix, which undergoes **dilation**—widening—and **effacement**—thinning out. At first, contractions are far apart (one every 10 to 20 minutes) and last no more than 15 to 20 seconds, but eventually they begin to come closer together (1 to 2 minutes) and last longer (45 to 60 seconds or longer).

During labor, the thick layer of mucus that has plugged the cervix during pregnancy (to protect the developing baby from infection) is discharged, either as a bloody plug that pops out like a cork or a little at a time. In 10 percent of cases, the amniotic sac will also break before labor begins, and the fluid gushes out (the "water breaks"). Labor usually begins within a day after this happens. If not, most physicians will induce labor with drugs in order to prevent contact with the outside world from causing infection in the fetus. Physicians sometimes break the amniotic sac on purpose to speed up labor.

The last part of the first stage of labor is called the *transition phase*. It takes place when the cervix is almost fully dilated (8 to 10 centimeters). Contractions are severe, and the woman may feel nauseous, chilled, and very uncomfortable. The transition phase usually lasts 40 minutes or less, and it marks the end of the initial stage of labor and the beginning of the next.

The second stage of labor, which concludes with the actual birth, begins when the cervix is fully dilated and the fetus begins moving through the birth canal. Contractions during this stage of labor are accompanied by an intense desire to push or "bear down," and they cause the opening of the vagina to expand. This stage lasts from 30 to 80 minutes, on average. Just before delivery, physicians often use a surgical procedure called an **episiotomy,** in which they make an incision from the lower portion of the vagina through the perineum to avoid tearing.

Crowning usually gives the first sight of the fetus. In most cases, the crown of its head appears at the opening of the vagina. In 2 to 4 percent of cases, a fetus will try to come through the birth canal feet or buttocks first, called a *breech birth*. Sometimes it is possible to turn the fetus, but often this situation necessitates a cesarean section (see next section). As the head is delivered, it is crucial to make sure the umbilical cord is not wrapped around the baby's neck. Suction is immediately applied to the baby's mouth and nose with a small rubber bulb to remove mucus so that the baby can breathe more easily. The head then turns, and the shoulders and the rest of the body come out rather quickly. A newborn will usually cry at birth. If not, the baby's back will be rubbed to start the

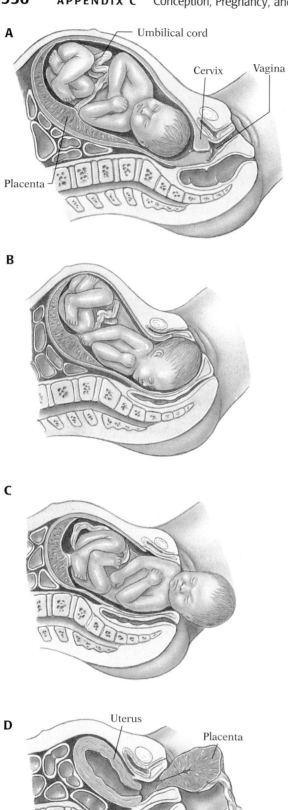

A
Umbilical cord
Cervix   Vagina
Placenta

B

C

D
Uterus
Placenta

FIGURE C.2   **The Stages of Labor**
(A) The fetus is fully developed. (B) The first stage, dilation and effacement. (C) The second stage, expulsion. (D) The last stage, placenta detachment.

baby breathing. The umbilical cord is clamped and cut about 1.5 inches from the baby's body; this stub will fall off in a few days, leaving what we call a *navel.*

In the third stage of labor the placenta detaches from the uterus and leaves the mother's body (along with other matter). Called the **afterbirth**, this stage usually lasts only 10 to 12 minutes. If even small pieces of the placenta stay in the uterus, infection and bleeding can occur. In this case, physicians use a procedure called *dilation* and *curettage,* or *D and C,* in which the cervix is dilated to allow access to the uterus, which is scraped clean. After the third stage of labor, the uterus normally contracts, returning eventually to its usual size.

Cesarean Section   A cesarean section, or *C-section,* involves the surgical delivery of a baby. In the past cesarean sections involved making a long vertical cut high on the abdomen through which the baby was delivered. Abdominal muscles run horizontally, however, so after these muscles have been cut, they are too weak to withstand the stress of labor in future pregnancies. Now physicians typically use a new type of incision that is horizontal and low on the abdomen (the "bikini cut"), which makes it possible to have normal (vaginal) deliveries in later pregnancies.

Prepared Childbirth   **Prepared childbirth** is the modern term for what was long called "natural childbirth": techniques first used in the 1930s by a British physician, Grantly Dick-Read, and later expanded by the French physician Fernand Lamaze. On the theory that much of the pain and fear experienced by women during childbirth was the result of being in a strange environment, surrounded by strangers, and not knowing what was going to happen next, these and other medical professionals began to teach expectant mothers—and ultimately their partners as well—about pregnancy, labor, and birth. In addition, such physical methods as relaxation training and breathing techniques can help make labor easier.

APPENDIX **D**

Birth Control and Disease Prevention Techniques

There are three primary questions to ask yourself when you choose a contraceptive, or birth control, technique. First, do you wish to prevent both pregnancy and the transmission of AIDS and other sexually transmitted diseases? As you will see, the methods that are most effective in preventing pregnancy are not always those that are most effective in protecting against disease. If you are single and dating different people, your need to protect yourself against disease is very great. If you are married and certain of your and your spouse's faithfulness, your concern about pregnancy may take priority. Second, if you wish to prevent pregnancy, do you want only to postpone it or to rule it out permanently? The most effective method of contraception—other than abstinence—is sterilization by surgical means, and in most cases this is irreversible. Therefore, it is suitable only for those who are quite certain that they do not want (more) children. Third, do you need to consider such factors as religious restrictions? For example, the Catholic Church forbids artificial means of contraception. Your answers to these questions will help you sort through the various alternatives we discuss.

Appendix D is adapted from Bruce M. King, Human Sexuality Today, 4th ed. (Upper Saddle River, NJ: Prentice Hall, 2002), Chapter 6. Adapted by permission of Prentice Hall, Upper Saddle River, New Jersey.

Preventing Disease

Although spermicides that contain nonoxynol-9 not only kill sperm but have been shown to be effective against the bacteria and viruses that cause some STDs, spermicides reduce the risk of disease by only about 50 percent. The safest method of protection against disease is the latex rubber male condom used with a nonoxynol-9 spermicide.

Preventing Pregnancy

The chart that follows provides information on the most common contraceptive methods, giving a general description and data on the effectiveness of each method, its particular advantages, and its possible side effects. Note that two figures are given for effectiveness. The first, labeled "With Perfect Use," is the rate at which pregnancy will occur if the method is used precisely as prescribed. The second, labeled "With Typical Use," allows for the fact that people often do *not* use these products as they are instructed to do; a woman may forget to take a pill, or a man may wait too long to put on a condom. In general, the chart moves from the most effective to the least effective methods; slight discrepancies in the progression of effectiveness rates reflect the desire to keep male and female methods (for example, male and female condoms) or related methods (the three different "fertility awareness" methods) together.

PREGNANCIES PER 100 WOMEN IN FIRST YEAR OF CONTINUOUS USE

Method	With Perfect Use	With Typical Use	Advantages	Problems
Voluntary Sterilization: A **vasectomy** is a male sterilization technique in which the vas deferens is tied off and cut, preventing passage of sperm through the male's reproductive tract. A **tubal ligation** is the procedure by which a woman's fallopian tubes are tied off or, more often, cut and tied. The procedure prevents passage of the egg, which simply disintegrates and is discharged during menstruation. The procedure is performed by **laparoscopy,** in which a long, tubelike instrument that transmits video pictures is inserted through a small incision; once the tubes are located, they are cauterized. Some doctors approach the fallopian tubes through the vagina (called a *culpotomy*).	0.1 for vasectomy; 0.2 for tubal ligation	0.2 for vasectomy; 0.4 for tubal ligation	Once done, many people report an increase in sexual desire because they no longer have to worry about pregnancy or contraceptive side effects; sexual relations can be completely spontaneous.	Surgical procedures always involve some risk, in part from the use of general anesthesia. Although it is sometimes possible to reverse vasectomy and, less often, a tubal ligation, sterilization should be considered permanent. Therefore, it should be used only by those who are quite sure they do not want any (or more) children.
Norplant: Norplant is a hormonal implant that offers contraceptive protection for up to 5 years. Six flexible silicone rubber tubes (or two rods), each about the size of a match, are inserted under the skin of the inside of a woman's arm, in a fanlike pattern. The tubes or rods contain levonorgestrel, a synthetic form of progesterone, that is slowly released over time and prevents pregnancy by inhibiting ovulation and thickening cervical mucus.	0.2	0.2	Believed by World Health Organization to be safer than the Pill because it contains no estrogen. Tubes can be removed at any time if a woman wants to conceive.	Spotting or irregular bleeding, weight gain, and headaches; less often, nervousness, dizziness, nausea, breast tenderness, and acne. However, more than 2/3 of users are very satisfied with this method.
Depo-Provera: Known as "the Shot," this injectable drug contains progestin. **Depo-Provera** works by preventing ovulation and lasts for 3 months. After discontinuation of the injections, it may take a woman from several months to a year to regain her fertility.	0.3	0.3	Avoids problem of pregnancy resulting from missing a daily dose, as with the Pill.	Initially thought to increase risk of several cancers, the drug is now approved by the World Health Organization. Some side effects are menstrual irregularities, fatigue and weakness, dizziness, and headaches.
The Pill: The most popular **Pill** combines synthetic estrogen and progesterone (progestins). It works by preventing ovulation, by inhibiting the buildup of the uterine lining necessary for implantation, and by keeping the cervical mucus thick and thus impeding the passage of sperm. A *minipill*, containing only progestin, has only the second and third of these actions and is for women who are breast-feeding or who cannot tolerate the side effects of the Pill's estrogen. Some combination pills try to adjust the levels of progestins to mimic "natural" hormonal phases of the menstrual cycle, but manufacturers don't agree on what is "natural." The Pill is taken for 21 days and then discontinued for 7 to permit menstrual bleeding.	0.1 (Pill); 0.5 (minipill)	0.3	May reduce risk of cancer of endometrium, benign breast tumors, ovarian cysts, rheumatoid arthritis, and pelvic inflammatory disease. Alleviates premenstrual syndrome and menstrual pain and reduces menstrual bleeding.	Cardiovascular problems, particularly in women who smoke, are over 35, or have diseases such as diabetes or hypertension. May be less effective if antibiotics, analgesics, or tranquilizers are used at the same time. Backup methods must be used during the first month and whenever a woman forgets to take a pill.

PREGNANCIES PER 100 WOMEN IN FIRST YEAR OF CONTINUOUS USE (CONT.)

Method	With Perfect Use	With Typical Use	Advantages	Problems
Intrauterine Device (IUD): The **intrauterine device,** or **IUD,** is a small, plastic or metal device (of various shapes and sizes) that is placed in the uterus by a doctor. IUDs work primarily by impeding the transit of sperm, and a copper or progesterone coating further impairs this passage. The copper-coated IUD is effective for up to 10 years. Insertion of an IUD requires dilation of the cervical opening, which may be uncomfortable or painful. Doctors must be certain that a woman is not pregnant and does not have a sexually transmitted disease at the time of insertion, and they must use proper sterilization procedures to avoid infection.	0.8 (copper); 1.5 (progesterone)	1.0 (copper); 2.0 (progesterone)	97% of women who use the IUD have a favorable opinion of it. Progesterone coating decreases menstrual blood loss and pain. The IUD permits spontaneity in sexual relations.	Today's IUDS are generally regarded as safe, although they may cause spotting, bleeding, and infection and are sometimes expelled. Some earlier IUDs—the Dalkon Shield in particular—were associated with serious cases of pelvic inflammatory disease.
Condom: The best **condom** is a thin sheath made of latex rubber or polyurethane[a] that fits over the penis and thus traps sperm. It also prevents contact between the man's and woman's skin and membranes, thus preventing the spread of sexually transmitted diseases. The condom should be put on *as soon as the penis is erect.* If the condom does not have a nipple tip, the man should leave a little extra space at the tip of the penis to catch the ejaculate. He should also hold the base of the condom as he withdraws after intercourse. Condoms can be used only once and should not be stored for long periods of time in a warm place (such as a wallet) or where they are exposed to light. For greatest effectiveness, condoms should be used with a spermicide.	Less than 1.0 with spermicide; 3.0 without spermicide	12.0	**Highly effective in reducing the spread of sexually transmitted diseases, including AIDS.** Putting on a condom takes less time than inserting any female device, and spermicide application is less messy.	Some men will not use condoms because they say they are allergic to rubber or that condoms reduce their sensitivity. Others complain about lack of spontaneity. These disadvantages are far outweighed by the high rate of effectiveness of this method in preventing both conception and disease.
Diaphragm: A **diaphragm** is a shallow rubber cup with a flexible rim that fits snugly between the pubic bone and the back of the cervix, sealing the entrance to the uterus and preventing the passage of sperm. The diaphragm must be fitted by a doctor or health-care worker, and refitting may be needed after pregnancy or weight changes of 10 pounds or more. For maximum effectiveness, it must be used with a spermicide and inserted no more than 2 hours before intercourse (lest the spermicide dissipate). More spermicide should be added (with an applicator) if intercourse is repeated. A diaphragm should be left in for 6 to 8 hours after intercourse to make sure no live sperm remain.	6.0	15.0	Offers some protection against gonorrhea and chlamydia. Is inexpensive, lasting for several years (but should be checked regularly for defects). Is associated with very few serious risks to fertility or general health.	Possible infection if left in for a prolonged period of time. Some couples feel that insertion (if not done until sex play has begun) takes away from the spontaneity of sexual activity.
Female Condom: The **female condom** is a 7-inch-long polyurethane pouch that is closed at one end, which is surrounded by a flexible metal rim, and open at the other, which is surrounded by a similar ring. The inner ring fits over the cervix, like a diaphragm, thus closing the entrance to the uterus; the outer ring covers part of the vulva. At present, the Reality Female condom is the only one on the U.S. market.	5.0–6.0	15.0	Thinner than male condoms, feels softer than rubber, and transfers heat. Some feel that it simulates bare-skin intercourse.	Much more expensive than male condom and, like it, can be used only once.

PREGNANCIES PER 100 WOMEN IN FIRST YEAR OF CONTINUOUS USE (CONT.)

Method	With Perfect Use	With Typical Use	Advantages	Problems
Cervical Cap: The **cervical cap** is another barrier device designed to prevent passage of sperm from the vagina into the uterus. Made of latex rubber, it is smaller and more compact than a diaphragm and resembles a large rubber thimble. It should be used with spermicide, and it fits over the cervix by suction. It is especially useful for women whose vaginal muscles have been relaxed by childbearing. Insertion and removal of the cap are more difficult than for the diaphragm, but it is more comfortable and can be left in for 48 hours. Women should make sure after intercourse that the cap has not dislodged.	8.0–10.0[b]	18.0	May offer some protection against gonorrhea and chlamydia.	Possible infection with prolonged use due to long exposure to secretions trapped by the cap. Currently recommended only for women who have normal Pap smears lest it adversely affect cervical tissues.
Spermicides: Spermicides are chemicals that kill sperm (nonoxynol-9 or octoxinol-9). Used alone, spermicidal foams and suppositories are more effective than jellies and creams, but for maximum effectiveness any of these should be used with a physical barrier method (e.g., condom, diaphragm). Spermicides must be placed in the vagina shortly before intercourse begins. They lose their effectiveness over time, so new spermicide must be inserted before each time a woman has intercourse.	6.0	26.0	Spermicides reduce the risk of some STDs, including AIDS, by killing bacteria and viruses. They may also reduce the risk of cervical cancer.	Several studies have found that nonoxynol-9–containing spermicides–increase the risk of urinary tract infection. Some complain that they irritate the vagina or penis, detract from oral-genital sex, and interfere with spontaneity.
Withdrawal: In **withdrawal,** or *coitus interruptus,* the male withdraws his penis just before reaching orgasm and ejaculates outside his partner's vagina. However, because sperm are found in the fluid secreted by the Cowper's glands just before a man ejaculates, this method is highly unreliable.	4.0	18.0	The withdrawal method is better than no method at all.	Highly ineffective compared with other methods. Also, withdrawal may not be very physically or emotionally satisfying for either partner.
Fertility Awareness: Fertility awareness (*natural planning* or *rhythm*) is based on predicting ovulation and identifying "safe days" in a woman's menstrual cycle. A woman can become pregnant only in the first 24 hours or so after ovulation; after that, the egg is overly ripe, and a sperm can't fertilize it. There are three variations of this method. The **calendar method** uses a formula to calculate the unsafe period based on the length of a woman's menstrual cycles. According to the **basal body temperature method,** or **BBT,** a couple should abstain from having sexual intercourse from the end of menstruation until 2 to 4 days after a temperature rise is noted (a woman's basal body temperature rises 24 to 72 hours after ovulation by a few tenths of a degree Fahrenheit). The **Billings method** attempts to pinpoint the time of ovulation by noting changes in the consistency of a woman's cervical mucus, which changes from white (or cloudy) and sticky to clear and slippery (like that of an egg white) 1 or 2 days before ovulation. The *symptothermal* method combines the BBT and Billings methods.	9.0 for calendar method; 3.2 for BBT; 3.2 for Billings	25.0+ for calendar method; 25.0+ for BBT; 20.0+ for Billings	Rhythm methods are usually considered to be safer than other contraception techniques and are acceptable to most religious groups.	All rhythm methods may be frustrating because they involve fairly long periods of abstinence from sex. However, chemical testing kits that will pinpoint the time of ovulation accurately enough to serve as contraceptives may soon be available for home use. To be effective, a method will have to predict ovulation at least 4 days in advance. Current products available, which predict 12 to 36 hours in advance, are useful only for couples who *want* to conceive.

[a]Do *not* buy condoms made of lamb intestine. These "skins" are porous, and HIV and other viruses and bacteria may easily penetrate through the tiny holes.
[b]In those who have not yet given birth.

HIV, AIDS, and Other Sexually Transmitted Diseases

Sexually transmitted diseases (once called *venereal diseases*, after the Roman goddess of love, Venus) are diseases that are spread either exclusively through sexual contact, such as chlamydia, gonorrhea, herpes, and human papillomavirus infection (genital warts), or primarily through sexual activity but by other means as well, such as HIV, hepatitis B, syphilis, and trichomoniasis. The chart on the following pages provides information on the symptoms, causes, and means of transmission of these diseases and their current forms of treatment and progress if left untreated. (STDs, with an emphasis on HIV and AIDS, are also discussed in Chapter 7.) Although there are probably more than 20 known STDs, these 8 have the highest incidence and the most serious effects.

In the United States, there have been major outbreaks of STDs from time to time. The present epidemic situation can probably be attributed to several factors. First, the discovery of penicillin and other antibiotics about the time of World War II may have given some people a false sense of confidence, leading them to engage in sexual intercourse when previously they might have feared to do so. Second, the new feeling of sexual freedom given people by the arrival of the Pill and other reliable means of birth control may have lessened their attention to disease prevention. And third, because recent drug treatments have slowed the progression of HIV and AIDS, many people have become lax about using condoms (see Chapter 7).

Appendix E is adapted from Bruce M. King, *Human Sexuality Today,* 4th ed., (Upper Saddle River, NJ: Prentice Hall, 2002), Chapter 5. Adapted by permission of Prentice Hall, Upper Saddle River, New Jersey.

Disease and Symptoms	Incidence[a]	Cause	How Transmitted	Progress of Disease if Untreated	Current Treatments
Acquired Immunodeficiency Syndrome (AIDS): HIV may remain dormant for a time and then cause such flulike symptoms as diarrhea, fever, and other infections that linger on. In full-blown AIDS, diseases such as lymphoma, Kaposi's sarcoma, and pneumocystis carinii pneumonia appear.	50,000+	*Human immuno-deficiency virus,* resident in semen, vaginal fluids, and blood.	Intimate sexual contact (anal or vaginal intercourse, occasionally oral sex), exposure to infected blood (sharing of needles among HIV drug users), mother-to-fetus transmission through blood.	AIDS is terminal, but death can be postponed and the quality of life improved with treatment.	Four *antiretroviral drugs* slow progression of HIV infection: zidovudine (AZT), di-danosine (DDI), zalcitabine (DDC), and stavudine (D4T). Since 1996, new drugs known as protease inhibitors, used in combination with AZT and DDI, have been found to slow or reduce HIV in the bloodstream.
Chlamydia: In both men and women, irritation and burning of the urethra and a thin, clear discharge. However, many people have no symptoms in the initial stage.	4,000,000	*Chlamydia trachomatis* bacterium.	Sexual activity, contact between mucous membranes of infected person and those of another person.	In men, infection of prostate and epididymis and possible sterility. In women, *pelvic inflammatory disease,* leading to increased risk of tubal pregnancy and sterility. Babies born to infected women may have eye, nose, or throat infections.	Tetracycline, doxycycline, or an erythromycin. Some doctors are using newer drugs such as azithromycin.
Gonorrhea: Inflammation of urethra or vulva; discharge from penis or vagina; irritation during urination. Some men and many women show no initial symptoms.	800,000	*Neisseria gonorrhoeae* bacterium (often called *gonococcus*).	Almost exclusively through intimate sexual contact.	In men, inflammation of prostate, seminal vesicles, bladder, and epididymis; severe pain and fever; possible sterility. In women, pelvic inflammatory disease with severe abdominal pain and fever; possible sterility. Baby born to infected mother may become blind.	Ceftriaxone followed by tetracycline or an erythromycin. The bacterium is becoming resistant to many drugs.
Hepatitis B: Poor appetite, diarrhea, fever, vomiting, pain, fatigue, jaundiced or yellow tinge of skin and eyes, dark urine.	50,000–1,000,000	HBC virus.	By infected blood or body fluids such as saliva, semen, and vaginal secretions. About half of U.S. cases are contracted sexually (commonest through anal sex); also by sharing drug-use needles, by blood transfusions, and by blood exchange between mother and fetus.	Serious, sometimes fatal liver disease.	Interferon is effective in about a third of patients; 90% of patients recover, but up to 10% remain infected and become carriers, infecting others.
Herpes: *Prodrome stage*—tingling, burning, itching of skin that contacted	200,000–500,000	Herpes simplex virus types I and II. I is thought to cause oral herpes,	Direct contact between infected site on one person and skin of another. One	Herpes is a leading cause of infectious blindness today. *Herpes encephalitis* is a rare disease of the brain	No cure. Once you have herpes, the potential for another attack is

Disease and Symptoms	Incidence[a]	Cause	How Transmitted	Progress of Disease if Untreated	Current Treatments
virus; *vesicle stage*—fluid-filled blisters, flulike symptoms, painful urination; *crusting-over stage*—sores develop scales and form scabs.		II to cause genital herpes, but the symptoms and outcome of both types are the same.	can get genital herpes from contact with a blister on a partner's lip or oral herpes from a genital sore. People can spread their own herpes from one site to another (such as the eyes) by touch.	that is often fatal. *Herpes meningitis* (inflammation of membranes covering brain and spinal cord) is also possible. In women, risks cancer of cervix. A baby may be infected during childbirth, suffering neurological, eye, skin, and internal organ damage.	always there. Acyclovir relieves symptoms and speeds healing during primary attack. Researchers are working on a herpes vaccine.
Human Papilloma Virus Infection (also *genital warts*): Some people have symptoms that only a doctor can detect; others develop cauliflower-like warts that cause itching, irritation, or bleeding. In males, warts usually appear on penis, scrotum, or anus and sometimes in the urethra; in females, on the cervix and vaginal wall, vulva, and anus.	200,000–500,000	Human papilloma virus (HPV) causes nongenital warts and other skin conditions; two types of HPV cause genital warts.	By sexual intercourse or sometimes oral–genital sex; highly contagious, and most common STD caused by viruses in the United States.	In women, HPV infection increases risk of cervical cancer. Cancer of penis occurs but is rare. Recurrence of symptoms of HPV infection is common.	No cure. External treatment with podophyllin; large warts may be removed surgically, internal ones by laser surgery. Cervical HPV infection is treated with cryotherapy (freezing). Vaccine to prevent HPV infection may be developed in the near future.
Syphilis: *Primary stage* begins with ulcerlike sore called *chancre,* usually on penis, cervix, lips, tongue, or anus, that is highly infectious but usually painless. Sore may disappear, but spirochete enters bloodstream and infection spreads throughout the body. In *secondary stage,* an itchless, painless rash spreads over the body; sores appear in moist areas around the genitals; other flu- and cold-like symptoms.	113,000	*Treponema pallidum* bacterium (called the *spirochete*).	Majority of cases are transmitted by sexual contact. Spirochete can also pass directly into the bloodstream through a cut or scrape; thus one can get syphilis by merely touching the sores of an infected person.	If initial chancre is ignored it will disappear, but the person remains infected. In the third, *latent stage,* there are usually no symptoms although in about a third of victims large ulcers develop on skin and bones. In all cases bacteria continue their attack on the body's internal organs, particularly the heart, blood vessels, and brain and spinal cord. Deafness, paralysis, insanity, and death often result.	Spirochetes are easily eradicated with antibiotics; penicillin is still the most effective, although there are some indications that the bacterium may be becoming resistant to this agent.
Trichomoniasis: In women a heavy vaginal discharge with a foul odor accompanied by severe vaginal itching.	3,000,000+	One-celled protozoan, *Trichomonas vaginalis.*	Majority of cases are transmitted by sexual intercourse, but disease can be contracted from a wet toilet seat or by sharing towels (protozoan survives in urine and tap water for hours to days).	Can lead to adhesions in the fallopian tubes and sterility.	Metronidazole is the treatment of choice. However, this drug is under study as a possible carcinogen.

[a]Estimated new cases per year in the United States; based on 1999 data.

APPENDIX **F**

Premarital and Nonmarital Agreements

A premarital (also called a prenuptial or antenuptial) agreement is a contract between potential spouses that spells out the rights and expectations of the partners and determines how their property will be divided if they divorce. It specifies what is "yours, mine, and ours."

Most lawyers agree that never-before-married young people with few assets don't need a premarital agreement, but such contracts are recommended for couples marrying for the first time later in life, especially if they have pursued careers and have accumulated assets or remarry. Although some lawyers think that preparing a premarital agreement creates distrust and may damage the marriage, many others believe such pacts help ensure a successful marriage because both partners (and their children, if any) know what to expect in case there is a divorce or death.

I begin with some of the standard issues, especially property rights, covered by legal contracts and lawyers (see, for example, Winer and Becker, 1993; Dorf et al., 1996). I also include some items that would not be legally enforceable but that might be useful for couples who are planning to marry, as well as those living together, that "how-to" books written by lawyers often omit.

Premarital Property

- Do the partners plan to keep or dispose of premarital property (such as houses and land)?
- If the premarital property is kept or sold, how will the real estate profits be divided between the partners?
- If the premarital property increases in value over time, will both partners share the income that is generated when the property is sold?

Assets, Liabilities, and Income

- What is the income of both partners? What about savings, stocks, and other assets?
- Have both partners seen each other's tax returns?
- Who will be responsible for filing tax returns? Who will pay the taxes? How will refunds be distributed?
- Who is responsible for paying a partner's debts (such as college loans, credit card balances, and bank loans)?
- Should both partners hold all property jointly? Or should income, rents, profits, interest, dividends, stock splits, bank accounts, and other assets also be held separately by each partner?

Business or Investment Partnerships

- Should a spouse be a business partner, especially in a family-owned business?
- In a privately held corporation, should a spouse inherit stock or receive stock as part of a divorce settlement?

Disposition of Marital Property

- In case of death or divorce, will marital property go to the partner or the deceased partner's children?
- Will the property be sold? If so, how will the partners share the profits?
- What happens to such personal property as clothing, jewelry, collections (art, coins, stamps, etc.), recreation or sports equipment, expensive tools, or home maintenance equipment (such as lawn tractors)?

Life Insurance

- Do both partners have life insurance?
- What is the life insurance coverage? How much does each partner pay?
- Who is the beneficiary of the life insurance?
- Do both partners have documentation from the insurance company about the beneficiary?

Spousal Maintenance (Alimony)

- Will either partner receive alimony in case of divorce? If so, how much?
- Will alimony be paid in cash or through the disposition of property?
- Will alimony payments increase to keep up with inflation?
- How much should a spouse (typically a wife) be compensated if she has sacrificed her own career to support her husband's career or business?

Child Custody and Support

- If there is a divorce, who will have custody of the children?
- Will the custody be joint, split, or sole (see Chapter 15)?
- Who will be responsible for child support?
- What percentage of one's earnings is "reasonable" or "fair" for child support?
- Would both partners have the right to move to another state or country?

- Is either partner responsible for supporting children who attend college or trade schools after age 18?

Trusts and Wills

- If there are trust funds (such as leaving money or property to biological children), are these funds consistent with the terms of the will?
- Have all assets been listed in the will?
- Does the will list the beneficiaries of stock, bonds, and other income?
- Does the surviving partner have a right to live in the home even though she or he doesn't inherit the property?
- Does the surviving spouse have a right to choose a cemetery and burial decisions for the deceased partner?
- If the surviving spouse doesn't inherit the property, is there a monthly or annual allowance from the estate?

Although "lifestyle clauses" are not legally enforceable, they give partners a tool to disclose, examine, and specify expectations about their own and their partner's behavior. If people realize they cannot resolve major disagreements, they are preventing a future divorce by not getting married. Here are some topics that might be included in an informal nonmarital or premarital agreement:

Sex and Contraception

- What birth control methods will be used? Are both partners willing to abort an unwanted fetus?
- How does each partner define "sex" (sexual intercourse, cuddling, fondling)?
- How often do partners expect to have sexual intercourse?
- Are there any sexual acts that one partner considers demeaning or offensive?
- What happens if a partner loses interest in sexual intercourse?
- How serious is infidelity? How does each partner define "infidelity"?

Having and Raising Children

- Do both partners want children? If so, how many and at what intervals?
- Is attending religious services important? If so, how often? Should current or future children have a religious upbringing?

- If the woman keeps her surname, will the children have the father's or the mother's surname?
- Who is responsible for disciplining children? Does discipline include spanking, slapping, or hitting?
- Who will do the housework? What chores will each person perform?

Relatives and Friends

- How important is it to maintain contact with one's parents, siblings, or other relatives? If they live far away, is there a limit on long-distance phone calls?
- Which partner's parents should the couple visit, especially during the holidays?
- Is it important to celebrate relatives' birthdays, anniversaries, and other occasions? If so, who buys the cards and presents? Should there be a limit on gift-giving for births, birthdays, graduations, weddings, and other milestones?
- Can parents or other relatives live in the couple's home? Under what conditions and for how long?
- Who is responsible for caretaking an elderly or disabled parent or other relative?
- How important is socializing with friends? Is it acceptable for each partner to socialize with friends on her or his own? Can partners discuss their personal problems with friends or family members?

Financial Issues

- Should there be joint or separate savings and checking accounts? A combination?
- Can a partner do anything she or he wants with "his" or "her" separate checking or savings account?
- Who is responsible for paying the monthly bills?
- Who is responsible for preparing state and federal taxes?
- Do both partners agree that credit card debts are acceptable? If so, is there a limit on the amount of debt?
- Who decides whether and how much life insurance to buy? Who will be the beneficiaries?
- Who decides whether and when to invest in the stock market?
- If partners disagree about financial issues, how will the conflict be resolved?

GLOSSARY

abortion The artificially induced or natural expulsion of an embryo or fetus from the uterus.

absolute poverty Not having enough money to afford the most basic necessities of life such as food, clothing, or shelter.

acculturation The process of adapting to the language, values, beliefs, roles, and other characteristics of a host culture.

acquaintance rape Unwanted, forced sexual intercourse, often in a social context such as a party; the rapist may be a neighbor, a friend of the family, a co-worker, or a person the victim has just met.

acquired immunodeficiency syndrome (AIDS) A degenerative disease caused by a virus that attacks the body's immune system and makes it susceptible to a number of diseases such as pneumonia and cancer.

agape Love that is altruistic, self-sacrificing, and directed toward all humankind.

ageism Discrimination against people on the basis of age, particularly against those who are old.

alimony Monetary payments made by one ex-spouse to the other after a divorce to support the latter's basic needs.

Alzheimer's disease A progressive, degenerative disorder that attacks the brain and impairs memory, thinking, and behavior.

amniocentesis A procedure performed in the twentieth week of pregnancy, in which a sample of the amniotic fluid is withdrawn by a needle inserted into the abdomen. The fluid is analyzed for possible genetic disorders and biochemical abnormalities in the fetus.

androgyny A blend of culturally defined male and female characteristics.

anorexia nervosa An often intractable and dangerous eating disorder characterized by fear of obesity, the conviction that one is fat, and significant weight loss.

artificial insemination An assisted reproductive technique in which semen is introduced artificially into the vagina or uterus about the time of ovulation.

assimilation The conformity of ethnic group members to the culture of the dominant group, including intermarriage.

assisted reproductive technology (ART) A general term that includes all treatments and procedures that involve the handling of human eggs and sperm to produce a pregnancy.

attachment theory The notion that a warm, secure, and loving relationship is essential to human emotional growth and development.

authoritarian approach A parenting style that is demanding, controlling, and punitive; emphasizes respect for authority, work, order, and traditional family structure; often

uses punitive, forceful measures to control behavior.

authoritative approach A parenting style that is demanding and controlling but supportive and responsive; encourages autonomy and self-reliance; generally uses positive reinforcement instead of punitive, repressive discipline.

autoeroticism Sexual gratification obtained solely by stimulating one's own body.

baby boomer A person born in the post–World War II generation between 1946 and 1964.

battered–woman syndrome A condition in which women who have experienced many years of physical abuse come to feel incapable of making any satisfactory change in their lives; recently used as a defense in cases in which such women have killed their abusive husbands.

bereavement The state of having been deprived, by death, of the presence of a loved one.

bigamy The act of marrying one person while still legally married to another.

biological father–stepmother family A family in which all the children are biological children of the father and stepchildren of the mother.

biological mother–stepfather family A family in which all the children are biological children of the mother and stepchildren of the father.

birth rate The number of live births per 1000 people.

bisexual A person who is sexually attracted to members of both sexes.

boomerang generation Young adults who move back into their parents' homes after living independently for a while.

bulimia An eating disorder characterized by a cyclical pattern of eating binges followed by self-induced vomiting, fasting, excessive exercise, or the use of diuretics or laxatives.

bundling A courting custom in American colonial times in which a young man and woman, both fully dressed, spent the night in bed together, separated by a wooden board.

child abduction Taking or keeping of a child by a family member in violation of a custody order, decree, or other legitimate custodial right.

child abuse According to Public Law 93-237, the physical or mental injury, sexual abuse, negligent treatment, or maltreatment of a child under the age of 18 by a person responsible for the child's welfare.

child maltreatment A wide range of behaviors that place the child at serious risk, including physical abuse, sexual abuse, neglect, and emotional mistreatment.

child support Monetary payments by the noncustodial parent to the parent who has custody of children to help pay the expenses of raising the children.

chlamydia A sexually transmitted bacterial infection that can contribute to infertility by triggering pelvic inflammatory disease. The symptoms of chlamydia often go unnoticed.

chorionic villus sampling A procedure in which some of the villi, or protrusions, of the membrane that surrounds the amniotic sac are removed by a catheter through the vagina and analyzed for abnormalities in the fetus.

clinical research The study of individuals or small groups of people who seek help for physical or social problems from mental health professionals.

closed adoption Adoption in which all information is confidential and the triad of birth parents, adoptive parents, and adopted children have no contact and do not exchange any identifying information.

cognitive development theory A theory positing that children learn by interacting with their environment and, using the processes of thinking, understanding, and reasoning, by interpreting and applying the information they gather.

cohabitation A living arrangement in which two people who are not related and not married share living quarters and usually have a sexual relationship.

common-law marriage A nonceremonial form of marriage, established by cohabitation or evidence of consummation (sexual intercourse).

commuter marriage A marriage in which partners live and work in separate geographic areas and get together intermittently.

compadrazgo A Mexican American family system in which close family friends are formally designated as godparents of a newborn, participate in the child's important rites of passage, and maintain continuing strong ties with their godchild.

comparable worth A concept that calls for equal pay for men and women who are doing work that involves similar skill, effort, responsibility, and work conditions.

conflict-habituated marriage A marriage in which the partners fight both verbally and physically but do not believe that fighting is a reason for divorce.

conflict theory A macro-level sociological theory that examines the ways in which groups disagree and struggle over power and compete for scarce resources and that views conflict and its consequences as natural, inevitable, and often desirable.

contraception The prevention of pregnancy by behavioral, mechanical, or chemical means.

coresidential dating cohabitation A living arrangement into which people "drift" gradually.

cultural pluralism The degree to which immigrants maintain aspects of their original cultures while living peacefully with the host culture.

cunnilingus Oral stimulation of a woman's genitals.

custody A court-mandated ruling as to which parent will have the primary responsibility for the welfare and upbringing of a child. The custodial parent cares for the child in her or his home, whereas the noncustodial parent may have specified visitation rights. *See also* joint custody.

daddy penalty A phenomenon in which men whose wives are employed outside the home are paid lower salaries than their counterparts whose wives are full-time homemakers.

date rape Unwanted, forced sexual intercourse in the context of a dating situation.

dating The process of meeting people socially for possible mate selection.

dementia The loss of mental abilities that most commonly occurs late in life.

depression A mental disorder characterized by pervasive sadness and other negative emotions that interfere with the ability to work, study, sleep, eat, and enjoy once pleasurable activities.

developmental tasks Specific role expectations and responsibilities that must be fulfilled as people move through the family life course.

devitalized marriage A marriage in which the partners are initially in love, spend time together, and have a satisfying sex life but in time find they are staying together out of duty. Because they see no alternatives, they do not consider divorce.

DEWKS (dual-employed with kids) A term that describes a family in which both parents are employed full time outside the home.

discouraged worker An unemployed person who wants to work but who has recently given up the search for a position because of the belief that the job hunt is futile.

discretionary income Income remaining after essentials, such as rent or mortgage, food, utilities, and transportation costs, have been paid and that people can spend as they please.

discrimination An *act* that treats people unequally or unfairly.

divorce The legal and formal dissolution of a marriage.

divorce mediation The technique and practice in which a trained arbitrator helps a divorcing couple come to an agreement and resolve such issues as support, child custody, and the division of property.

dowry The money, goods, or property a woman in traditional societies brings to a marriage.

dual-career couple Both partners work in professional or managerial positions.

dual-earner couple Both partners work outside the home.

ecological theory A theoretical perspective that examines the relationship between individuals, family roles, and the social environment.

elder abuse Physical abuse, negligence, financial exploitation, psychological abuse, deprivation of necessities such as food and heat, isolation from friends and relatives, and failure to administer needed medications to people age 65 or older.

endogamy A cultural rule requiring that people marry or have sexual relations only within their own particular group.

endometriosis A condition in which endometrial tissue spreads outside the womb and attaches itself to other pelvic organs, such as the ovaries or the fallopian tubes.

engagement The formalization of a couple's decision to marry and the last step in courtship.

equity theory A theoretical perspective that proposes that an intimate relationship is satisfying and stable if both people see it as equitable and mutually beneficial.

eros Love based on beauty and physical attractiveness.

ethnic group A set of people who identify with a common national origin or cultural heritage.

evaluation research Research that assesses the effectiveness of social programs in both the public and private sectors.

exogamy A cultural rule requiring people to marry outside of their particular group.

experiment A data collection method where researcher investigates presumed cause-and-effect relationships under srictly controlled conditions.

expressive role In structural-functional theory, the supportive and nurturing role of the wife or mother, who must sustain and support the husband or father and children.

extended family A family in which two or more generations live together or in close proximity.

familism The notion that family relationships take precedence over the concerns of individual family members.

family Defined in this book as an intimate environment in which two or more people live together in a committed relationship, see their identity as importantly attached to the group, and share close emotional ties and functions.

family life course development theory A micro-level theory that examines the changes that families experience over the lifespan.

family life cycle A series of stages, each focusing on a different set of events, that the family goes through from the early days of a marriage to the death of one or both partners.

family of orientation The family into which a person is born.

family of procreation The family a person forms by marrying and having or adopting children.

family policy The measures taken by governmental bodies to achieve specific objectives regarding the family's well-being.

family systems theory A theoretical perspective that examines the daily functioning and interactions of family members with each other and the larger society.

fellatio Oral stimulation of a man's penis.

feminist theories Theoretical perspectives that analyze socially constructed expectations based on variables such as gender roles, social class, race, ethnicity, and sexual orientation.

feminization of poverty The growing proportion of women and their children who are poor.

fertility drugs Drugs that stimulate ovaries to produce eggs.

fertility rate The number of births per year per 1000 women of childbearing age (15 to 44).

fetal alcohol syndrome (FAS) Physical deformities or mental retardation in an infant caused by the mother's excessive use of alcohol during pregnancy.

fictive kin Nonrelatives who are accepted as part of a family.

field research A data-collection method in which researchers collect information by systematically observing people in their natural surroundings.

filter theory The theory that people in search of potential mates screen out eligible partners according to certain criteria to reduce the pool of eligibles to a small number of candidates.

foster home A home in which a family raises a child or children who are not their own for a period of time but does not formally adopt them.

gamete intrafallopian transfer (GIFT) A variation of in vitro fertilization in which eggs and sperm are artificially inserted into a woman's fallopian tube.

gender The socially learned attitudes and behaviors that characterize a person of one sex or the other, based on differing social and cultural expectations of the sexes.

gender identity A person's emotional and intellectual awareness of being either masculine or feminine.

gender roles Distinctive patterns of attitudes, behaviors, and activities that society prescribes for females and males.

gender-role stereotype The belief and expectation that women and men display rigid, traditional gender-related characteristics.

gender schema theory The theory that children develop schemas, or information-processing categories, that organize and guide their perceptions of cultural stimuli to develop a gender identity.

genogram A diagram of the biological relationships between family members.

gerontologist A scientist who studies the biological, psychological, and social aspects of aging.

grief The emotional response to loss.

half-sibling A brother or sister with whom one shares only one biological parent.

heterogamy Dating or marrying someone from a social, racial, ethnic, religious, or age group different from one's own.

heterosexual A person who is sexually attracted to members of the opposite sex.

homogamy Dating or marrying someone with similar social characteristics such as ethnicity, race, religion, age, and social class.

homophobia Fear and hatred of homosexuality.

homosexual A person who is sexually attracted to people of the same sex.

hormones Chemical substances secreted into the bloodstream by glands of the endocrine system.

hospice A place for the care of the dying that stresses relieving pain, providing a sense of security and companionship to dying patients, and making such patients comfortable.

human immunodeficiency virus (HIV) The virus that causes AIDS.

hypergamy Dating or marrying someone who is in a higher socioeconomic group than one's own.

hypogamy Dating or marrying someone who is in a lower socioeconomic group than one's own.

identity bargaining A stage in the evolution of a marriage in which partners readjust their idealized expectations to the realities of their life together.

incest Sexual intercourse between family members who are closely related. *See also* incest taboo.

incest taboo Cultural norms and laws that forbid sexual intercourse between close blood relatives, such as brother and sister, father and daughter, or mother and son.

infertility The inability to conceive a baby after 12 months of unprotected sex.

instrumental role In structural-functional theory, the "breadwinner" role of the husband or father, who must be hardworking, tough, and competitive.

intracytoplasmic sperm injection (ICSD) A procedure that involves injecting sperm directly into an egg in a laboratory dish to produce a pregnancy.

intrinsic marriage A marriage that is inherently rewarding.

in vitro fertilization (IVF) An assisted reproduction technique in which eggs are surgically removed from a woman's ovaries, fertilized with sperm from the woman's husband or a donor, and then transferred into the woman's uterus.

joint biological–stepfamily A family in which at least one child is a biological child of both parents, at least one child is the biological child of one parent and the stepchild of the other parent, and no other "type" of child is present.

joint custody A custody arrangement in which the children divide their time between both parents. In *joint legal custody* parents share decision making about the children's upbringing. In *joint physical custody*, the children live alternately and for specified periods in each parent's home.

kinship system A network of people who are related by blood, marriage, or adoption.

latchkey kids Children who return after school to an empty home and are alone and unsupervised until their parents or another adult arrives.

latent functions Functions that are not recognized or intended, present but not immediately visible.

later-life family A family that is beyond the years of child rearing and has launched the children or a childless family beginning to plan for retirement.

living will A legal document in which a person specifies what, if any, life-support measures she or he wants in the case of serious illness and whether or when such measures should be discontinued.

ludus Love that is carefree and casual, "fun and games."

machismo A concept of masculinity that stresses such attributes as dominance, assertiveness, pride, and sexual prowess.

macro-level perspective A sociological perspective that focuses on large-scale patterns that characterize society as a whole.

male climacteric A "change of life" in men proposed by some as analogous to female menopause.

mania Love that is obsessive, jealous, and possessive.

manifest functions Functions that are recognized or intended and are clearly present.

marital burnout The gradual deterioration of love and, ultimately, the loss of an emotional attachment between marital partners.

marital rape A violent act in which a husband forces his wife to engage in sexual intercourse.

marital roles The specific ways in which married couples define their behavior and structure their time.

marriage A socially approved mating relationship that is expected to be stable and enduring.

marriage market Courtship seen as a process in which prospective spouses compare the assets and liabilities of eligible partners and choose the best available mate.

marriage squeeze An imbalance in the number of available women and men.

married singles Married partners who continue to live together, may be good friends, and may be sexually intimate but who, in many ways, have drifted apart.

masturbation Sexual self-pleasuring that involves some form of direct physical stimulation.

matriarchy A familial relationship in which the authority is held by the oldest female, usually the mother. Women control cultural, political, and economic resources and, consequently, have power over men.

matrilineal A kinship system in which children trace their family descent through their mother's line and property is passed on to female heirs.

menopause The cessation of the menstrual cycle.

micro-level perspective A sociological perspective that focuses on small-scale patterns of social interaction in specific settings.

minority group A group of people who may be treated differently or unequally because of their physical or cultural characteristics, such as gender, sexual orientation, religion, or skin color.

mommy track A slower or even a side track in business along which women managers who want to combine career and child rearing are expected to move.

monogamy The practice of having only one husband or wife.

mourning The customary outward expression of grief over the loss of a loved one that varies between different social and cultural groups.

no-fault divorce A divorce process in which neither partner has to establish the guilt or wrongdoing of the other.

norm A culturally defined rule for behavior.

nuclear family A family made up of a wife, a husband, and their biological or adopted children.

open adoption An adoption process that encourages the sharing of information and contact between biological and adoptive parents throughout the adopted child's life.

passive-congenial marriage A marriage in which partners with minimal emotional investment and expectations of their union maintain independent spheres of interests and activities and derive satisfaction from relationships with others rather than from each other.

patriarchy A society or familial relationship in which the positions of power and authority—political, economic, legal, religious, educational, military, and domestic—are generally held by men.

patrilineal A kinship system in which children trace their family descent through their father's line and property is passed on to male heirs.

pelvic inflammatory disease (PID) An infection of the uterus that spreads to the fallopian tubes, ovaries, and surrounding tissues and produces scarring that blocks the fallopian tubes.

permissive approach A parenting style that encourages freedom of expression, autonomy, and internal control and allows the children to do mostly what they want.

petting Physical contact that produces erotic arousal without necessarily leading to sexual intercourse.

polygamy A form of marriage in which one woman or one man has two or more spouses.

POSSLQs "Persons of the opposite sex sharing living quarters," a U.S. Census Bureau household category.

postpartum depression Depression experienced by some women soon after childbirth, thought to be at least partially caused by chemical imbalances.

poverty line The minimum income level determined by the federal government to be necessary for individuals' and families' basic subsistence.

power The ability to impose one's will on others.

pragma Love that is rational and based on practical considerations, such as compatibility and perceived benefits.

preimplantation genetic diagnosis (PGD) An assisted reproductive technology that enables physicians to identify genetic diseases in the embryo, before implantation.

prejudice An *attitude* that prejudges people, usually in a negative way.

premarital cohabitation A living arrangement in which a couple tests its relationship before making a final commitment to get married.

primary group Important people, such as family members and close friends, characterized by close, long-lasting, intimate, and face-to-face interaction.

propinquity Geographic closeness.

qualitative research A data–collection process in which researchers rely on observation and interviews and report their findings from the respondent's point of view.

quantitative research A data–collection process in which researchers assign numbers to qualitative (i.e., nonnumeric) observations by counting and measuring attitudes or behavior.

racial-ethnic group A group of people with distinctive racial and cultural characteristics.

racial group a category of people who share physical characteristics, such as skin color, that members of a society consider socially important.

racial socialization a process in which parents teach their children to negotiate race-related barriers and experiences in a racially stratified society and to take pride in their ancestry.

racism A belief that people of one race are superior or inferior to others.

relative income A person's earning potential compared with his or her desired standard of living.

relative poverty Not having enough money to afford an average standard of living.

role Pattern of behavior attached to a particular status, or position, in society.

role conflict Frustration and uncertainty experienced by a person who is confronted with incompatible role requirements or expectations.

role overload A feeling of being overwhelmed by multiple commitments and not having enough time for oneself.

role strain Conflicts that someone feels *within* a role.

sandwich generation Midlife men and women who feel caught between the need to care for both their own children and their aging parents.

secondary analysis Analysis of data that have been collected by other researchers.

secondary group Groups characterized by impersonal and short-term relationships in which people work together on common tasks or activities.

self-disclosure Open communication in which one person offers his or her honest thoughts and feelings to another person in the hope that truly open communication will follow.

semi-open adoption Sometimes called a *mediated adoption*, in which there is communication between the adoptive parents, birth parents, and adopted children but through a third party (e.g., an agency caseworker or attorney) rather than directly.

separation Parting from one's spouse but not getting a divorce.

serial monogamy Marrying several people, one at a time; that is, marrying, divorcing, remarrying, divorcing again, and so on.

sex The biological—chromosomal, anatomical, hormonal, and other physical and physiological—characteristics with which we are born and that determine whether we are male or female.

sex ratio The proportion of men to women in a country or group.

sexual harassment Any unwelcome sexual advance, request for sexual favors, or other conduct of a sexual nature that makes a person uncomfortable and interferes with her or his work.

sexually transmitted diseases (STDs) Diseases that are spread by contact with body parts or fluids that harbor what are usually bacterial or viral microorganisms.

sexual orientation Refers to a preference for sexual partners of the same sex (homosexual), of the opposite sex (heterosexual), or of either sex (bisexual).

sexual response A person's physiological reaction to sexual stimulation.

sexual script Norms that specify what is acceptable and what is unacceptable sexual activity, identify eligible sexual partners, and define the boundaries of sexual behavior in time and place.

significant others People who play an important emotional role in a person's socialization.

social class A category of people who have a similar standing or rank based on wealth, education, power, prestige, and other valued resources.

social exchange theory A micro-level theory that proposes that the interaction between two or more people is based on the efforts of each to maximize rewards and minimize costs.

social integration The social bonds that people have with others and the community at large.

socialization The process of acquiring the language, accumulated knowledge, attitudes, beliefs, and values of one's society and culture and learning the social and interpersonal skills needed to function effectively in society.

social learning theory The notion that people learn attitudes and behaviors through interaction with the environment. Learning may occur through reward and punishment or through imitation or role modeling.

Social Security A public retirement pension system administered by the federal government.

socioeconomic status (SES) An overall rank of one's position based on income, education, and occupation.

sole custody A type of custody in which one parent has exclusive responsibility for raising a child and the other parent has specified visitation rights.

split custody A custody arrangement in which children are divided between the parents, usually girls going to the mother, boys to the father.

stepfamily A household in which two adults are married or cohabiting and at least one of the adults has a child.

steroid A synthetic hormone, most often testosterone, that is taken to increase the size and strength of muscles.

storge Love that is slow-burning, peaceful, and affectionate.

structural-functional theory A macro-level theoretical perspective that examines the relationship between the family and the larger society as well as the internal relationships between family members.

substitute marriage A long-term commitment between two people without a legal marriage.

surrogacy An assisted reproduction technique in which a woman carries a pregnancy to term and serves as a substitute for a woman who cannot bear children.

surveys Data–collection methods that systematically collect information from respondents by a mailed or self-administered questionnaire or by a face–to–face or telephone interview.

symbolic interaction theory A micro-level theory that views everyday human interaction as governed by a society's or group's communication of knowledge, ideas, beliefs, and attitudes.

theory A set of logically related statements that explain why a phenomenon occurs.

total fertility rate The average number of children a woman would have given current birth rates.

total marriage A marriage in which the partners participate in each other's lives at all levels and have few areas of tension or unresolved hostility.

trailing spouse A partner who resigns from a position to search for another job in the location where her or his spouse has taken a position.

trial marriage People living together to find out what marriage might be like, with each other or someone else.

two-person single career An arrangement in which one spouse participates in the other's career behind the scenes without pay or direct recognition.

underemployed worker A worker who holds part-time jobs but would rather work full time or who accepts jobs below his or her level of expertise.

utilitarian marriage A marriage based on convenience.

vital marriage A marriage in which partners maintain a close relationship, resolve conflicts quickly through compromise, and often make sacrifices for each other.

welfare Government aid to people who can't support themselves, generally because they are poor or unemployed.

working poor People who spend at least 27 weeks in the labor force but whose family or personal incomes falls below the official poverty level.

zygote intrafallopian transfer (ZIFT) A variation of in vitro fertilization in which a woman's eggs are fertilized by her husband's or a donor's sperm in vitro and are then transferred to the fallopian tube.

REFERENCES

A first, N.H. Episcopalians elect openly gay bishop as new leader. 2003. *Baltimore Sun,* June 8, 10A.

A great leap back. 1993. *Baltimore Sun,* Mar. 31, A24.

A middle-class nation. 1999. *Public Perspective* 10 (Apr./May): 13.

ABALOS, D. T. 1993. *The Latino family and the politics of transformation.* Westport, CT: Praeger.

ABBEY, A., L. ROSS, D. McDUFFIE, AND P. McAUSTIN. 1996. Alcohol and dating risk factors for sexual assault among college women. *Psychology of Women Quarterly* 20 (Mar.): 147–69.

ABEL, E. K. 1991. *Who cares for the elderly? Public policy and the experiences of adult daughters.* Philadelphia: Temple University Press.

ABMA, J., A. CHANDRA, W. MOSHER, L. PETERSON, AND L. PICCINO. 1997. *Fertility, family planning, and women's health: New data from the 1995 National Survey of Family Growth.* Washington, DC: National Center for Health Statistics. *Vital Health Statistics* 23 (19).

ABRAHAM, M. 2000. *Speaking the unspeakable: Marital violence among South Asian immigrants in the United States.* New Brunswick, NJ: Rutgers University Press.

ABRAHAMS, G., AND S. AHLBRAND. 2002. *Boy v. girl? How gender shapes who we are, what we want, and how we get along.* Minneapolis: Free Spirit.

ABU-LABAN, S. M., AND B. ABU-LABAN. 1999. Teens between: The public and private spheres of Arab-Canadian adolescents. In *Arabs in America: Building a new future,* ed. M. W. Suleiman, 113–28. Philadelphia: Temple University Press.

ABUDABBEH, N. 1996. Arab families. In *Ethnicity and family therapy,* 2nd ed., ed. M. McGoldrick, J. Giordano, and J. K. Pearce, 333–46. New York: Guilford.

Abuse spreads HIV among Zambian girls. 2003. BBC, Jan. 28. http://news.bbc.co.uk/2/hi/africa/2700771.stm (accessed Feb. 4, 2003).

ABUSHARAF, R. M. 2001. Virtuous cuts: Female genital circumcision in an African ontology. *Differences: A Journal of Feminist Cultural Studies* 12 (Spring): 112–40.

ACKERMAN, D. 1994. *A natural history of love.* New York: Random House.

ACOCK, A. C., AND D. H. DEMO. 1994. *Family diversity and well-being.* Thousand Oaks, CA: Sage.

ACOSTA, R. V., AND L. J. CARPENTER. 2002. Women in intercollegiate sport. http://bailiwick.lib.uiowa.edu/ge/Acosta/womensp.html (accessed May 19, 2003).

ACS, G., AND M. GALLAGHER. 2000. Income inequality among America's children. Series B, no. B-6. Urban Institute, Washington, DC, newfederalism. urban.org/pdf/anf_b6.pdf (accessed Oct. 12, 2000).

ACS, G., AND S. NELSON. 2002. The kids are alright? Children's well-being and the rise in cohabitation. The Urban Institute. www.urban.org/UploadedPDF/310544_B48.pdf (accessed July 12, 2003).

ACUNA, R. 1988. *Occupied America: A history of Chicanos,* 3rd ed. New York: Harper & Row.

ADAMS, B. 1980. *The family.* Chicago: Rand McNally.

ADAMS, B. N., AND R. A. SYDIE. 2002. *Contemporary sociological theory.* Thousand Oaks, CA: Pine Forge.

ADAMS, J. A., K. HARPER, S. KNUDSON, AND J. REVILLA. 1994. Examination findings in legally confirmed child sexual abuse: It's normal to be normal. *Pediatrics* 94 (Sep.): 310–17.

ADAMS, P. F., AND M. A. MARANO. 1995. *Current estimates from the National Health Interview Survey, 1994.* Vital Health Statistics Series 10, no. 193, Dec. Washington, DC: National Center for Health Statistics.

ADAMS, S., J. KUEBLI, P. A. BOYLE, AND R. FIVUSH. 1995. Gender differences in parent–child conversation about past emotions: A longitudinal investigation. *Sex Roles* 33 (Sep.): 309–23.

ADDARIO, L. 2001. Jihad's women. *New York Times,* Oct. 21. www.nytimes.com/2001/10/21/magazine/21WOMEN.html (accessed Oct. 22, 2001).

ADLER, J. 1996. Building a better dad. *Newsweek,* June 17, 58–64.

ADLER, N. E., ET AL. 1990. Psychological responses after abortion. *Science* 248: 41–44.

ADLER, P. A., AND P. ADLER. 1994. Observational techniques. In *Handbook of qualitative research,* ed. N. K. Denzin and Y. S. Lincoln, 377–92. Thousand Oaks, CA: Sage.

ADLER, S. M. 2003. Asian-American families. In *International encyclopedia of marriage and family,* 2nd ed., Vol. 2, ed. J. J. Ponzetti, Jr., 82–91. New York: Macmillan.

AHRONS, C. 1994. *The good divorce: Keeping your family together when your marriage comes apart.* New York: HarperCollins.

AHRONS, C. R., AND R. H. RODGERS. 1987. *Divorced families: A multidisciplinary developmental view.* New York: Norton.

AHUVIA, A. C., AND M. B. ADELMAN. 1992. Formal intermediaries in the marriage market: A typology and review. *Journal of Marriage and the Family* 54 (May): 452–63.

AINSWORTH, M., ET AL. 1978. *Patterns of attachment: A psychological study of the strange situation.* Hillsdale, NJ: Erlbaum.

AIZCORBE, A. M., A. B. KENNICKELL, AND K. B. MOORE. 2003. Recent changes in U.S. family finances: Evidence from the 1998 and 2001 survey of consumer finances. *Federal Reserve Bulletin* 89 (Jan.): 1–32.

AJROUCH, K. 1999. Family and ethnic identity in an Arab-American community. In *Arabs in America: Building a new future,* ed. M. W. Suleiman, 129–39. Philadelphia: Temple University Press.

ALBAS, D., AND C. ALBAS. 1987. The pulley alternative for the wheel theory of the development of love. *International Journal of Comparative Sociology* 28 (3–4): 223–27.

ALBERT, B., S. BROWN, AND C. M. FLANNIGAN, EDS. 2003. *14 and younger: The sexual behavior of young adolescents.* The National Campaign to Prevent Teen Pregnancy. www.teenpregnancy.org/resources/reading/pdf/14summary.pdf (accessed June 10, 2003).

Alcohol and health. 2000. U.S. Department of Health and Human Services. www.niaaa.nih.gov/publications/10report/intro.pdf (accessed Sep. 19, 2003).

ALDOUS, J. 1996. *Family careers: Rethinking the developmental perspective.* Thousand Oaks, CA: Sage.

ALIBHAI-BROWN, Y. 1993. Marriage of minds not hearts. *New Statesman & Society,* Feb. 12, 28–29.

ALIGNE, C. A., AND J. J. STODDARD. 1997. Tobacco and children: An economic evaluation of the medical effects of parental smoking. *Archives of Pediatrics & Adolescent Medicine* 151 (July): 648–744.

ALLEN, K. S., AND G. F. MOORMAN. 1997. Leaving home: The emigration of home-office workers. *American Demographics* 19 (Oct.): 57–61.

ALLEN, W. R., AND A. D. JAMES. 1998. Comparative perspectives on black family life: Uncommon explorations of a common subject. *Journal of Comparative Family Studies* 29 (Spring): 1–10.

ALLGOR, C. 2002. *Parlor politics: In which the ladies of Washington help build a city and a government.* Charlottesville: University of Virginia Press.

ALMEIDA, R. V., ED. 1994. *Expansions of feminist family theory through diversity.* New York: Haworth.

ALTMAN, D. 2003. Jobless rate hits 6.4%, highest level in 9 years. *New York Times,* July 4, A1.

ALTON, B. G. 2001. You think being a dad is a good deal? *Business Week,* Apr. 2, 20.

ALTORKI, S. 1988. At home in the field. In *Arab women in the field: Studying your own society,* eds. S. Altorki and C. F. El-Solh, 51–59. New York: Syracuse University Press.

ALVEAR, M. 2003. The annual rite: Dumbing down love. *Christian Science Monitor,* Feb. 14, 11.

AMAN, C. J., AND P. ENGLAND. 1997. Comparable worth: When do two jobs deserve the same pay? In *Subtle sexism: Current practices and prospects for change,* ed. N. V. Benokraitis, 297–314. Thousand Oaks, CA: Sage.

AMATO, P. R. 1996. More than money? Men's contributions to their children's lives. Paper presented at the Men in Families Symposium, Pennsylvania State University.

AMATO, P. R. 2002. The consequences of divorce for adults and children. In *Understanding families into the new millennium: A decade in review,* ed. R. M. Milardo, 488–506. Minneapolis: National Council on Family Relations.

AMATO, P. R., AND J. G. GILBRETH. 1999. Nonresident fathers and children's well-being: A meta-analysis. *Journal of Marriage and the Family* 61 (Aug.): 557–73.

AMATO, P. R., D. R. JOHNSON, A. BOOTH, AND S. J. ROGERS. 2003. Continuity and change in marital quality between 1980 and 2000. *Journal of Marriage and Family* 65 (Feb.): 1–22.

AMATO, P. R., AND F. RIVERA. 1999. Paternal involvement and children's behavior problems. *Journal of Marriage and the Family* 61 (May): 374–84.

AMATO, P. R., AND S. J. ROGERS. 1997. A longitudinal study of marital problems and subsequent divorce. *Journal of Marriage and the Family* 59 (Aug.): 612–24.

AMBERT, A.-M. 1997. *Parents, children, and adolescents: Interactive relationships and development in context.* New York: Haworth.

AMBERT, A.-M. 2001. *The effect of children on parents,* 2nd ed. New York: Haworth.

AMBROSE, M. W., AND A. M. COBURN. 2001. Report on intercountry adoption in Romania. http://cb1.acf.dhhs.gov/programs/cb/publications/romanadopt.pdf (accessed Aug. 8, 2002).

American Community Survey. 2003. U.S. Census Bureau, selected tables. www.census.gov/acs/www/Products/Profiles/Chg/2002/0002/Tabular/010/01000US3.htm and www.census.gov/acs/www/Products/Profiles/Chg/2002/0002/Tabular/010/01000US2.htm (accessed Sep. 9, 2003).

AMERICAN HUMANE ASSOCIATION. 2001. Answers to common questions about child abuse and neglect. www.americanhumane.org/site/PageServer?pagename=nr_fact_sheets_childfaqs (accessed Oct. 3, 2003).

AMERICAN LAW INSTITUTE. 2002. *Principles of the law of family dissolution: Analysis and recommendations.* New York: Matthew Bender & Company.

Americans consider infidelity wrong, but acknowledge its prevalence in society. 2001. Gallup Poll Analysis, July 9. www.gallup.com/subscription/?m=f&c_id=10743 (accessed July 10, 2001).

Americans increasingly opting out of marriage. 2003. Population Reference Bureau. www.prb.org/optoutmarriage (accessed July 11, 2003).

Americans' lifestyles: Homemakers. 2002. Gallup Organization, June 3–9. www.gallup.com/poll/pollInsights/#GPV (accessed July 1, 2002).

America's children: Key national indicators of well-being 2000. 2000. Washington, DC: Federal Interagency Forum on Child and Family Statistics.

AMMERMAN, R. T., AND R. J. PATZ. 1996. Determinants of child abuse potential: Contribution of parent and child factors. *Journal of Clinical Child Psychology* 25 (Sep.): 300–307.

AMOTT, T. 1993. *Caught in the crisis: Women and the U.S. economy today.* New York: Monthly Review Press.

ANCHETA, A. N. 1998. *Race, rights, and the Asian American experience.* New Brunswick, NJ: Rutgers University Press.

ANDA, R. F., ET AL. 2001. Abused boys, battered mothers, and male involvement in teen pregnancy. *Pediatrics* 107 (Feb.): E19.

ANDELIN, H. 1974. *Fascinating womanhood: A guide to a happy marriage.* Santa Barbara, CA: Pacific.

ANDERS, G. 1994. The search for love goes on. *Washington Post,* Sep. 19, D5.

ANDERSEN, M. L. 2000. *Thinking about women,* 4th ed. New York: Macmillan.

ANDERSON, C. A., N. L. CARNAGEY, AND J. EUBANKS. 2003. Exposure to violent media: The effects of songs with violent lyrics on aggressive thoughts and feelings. *Journal of Personality and Social Psychology* 84 (May): 960–71.

ANDERSON, C. A., AND K. E. DILL. 2000. Video games and aggressive thoughts, feelings, and behavior in the laboratory and in life. *Journal of Personality and Social Psychology* 78 (Apr.): 772–90.

ANDERSON, C., D. KELTNER, AND O. P. JOHN. 2003. Emotional convergence between people over time. *Journal of Personality and Social Psychology* 84 (May): 1054–68.

ANDERSON, E. 1999. *Code of the street: Decency, violence, and the moral life of the inner city.* New York: Norton.

ANDERSON, E. R., S. M. GREENE, E. M. HETHERINGTON, AND W. G. CLINGEMPEL. 1999. The dynamics of parental remarriage: Adolescent, parent, and sibling influences. In *Coping with divorce, single parenting, and remarriage: A risk and resiliency perspective,* ed. E. M. Hetherington, 295–319. Mahwah, NJ: Erlbaum.

ANDERSON, J. 1990. *The single mother's book: A practical guide to managing your children, career, home, finances, and everything else.* Atlanta: Peachtree.

ANDERSON, K. L. 1997. Gender, status, and domestic violence: An integration of feminist and family violence approaches. *Journal of Marriage and the Family* 59 (Aug.): 655–69.

ANDERSON, K. L. 2002. Perpetrator or victim? Relationships between intimate partner violence and well-being. *Journal of Marriage and Family* 64 (Nov.): 851–63.

ANGELL, G. B., B. J. KURZ, AND G. M. GOTTFRIED. 1997. Suicide and North American Indians: A social constructivist perspective. *Journal of Multicultural Social Work* 6 (3/4): 1–26.

ANGELL, M., R. D. UTIGER, AND A. J. J. WOOD. 2000. Disclosure of authors' conflicts of interest: A follow-up. *New England Journal of Medicine* 342 (Feb. 24): 586–87.

Ann Landers. 2000. *Washington Post,* May 9, C11.

Ann Landers. 2001. *Baltimore Sun,* Aug. 10, 3E.

ANTONUCCI, T. C., H. AKIYAMA, AND A. MERLINE. 2001. Dynamics of social relationships in midlife. In *Handbook of midlife development,* ed. M. E. Lachman, 571–98. New York: Wiley.

APFEL, N. H., AND V. SEITZ. 1991. Four models of adolescent mother–grandmother relationships in black inner-city families. *Family Relations* 40 (Oct.): 421–29.

AQUILINO, W. S. 1994. Impact of childhood family disruption on young adults' relationships with parents. *Journal of Marriage and the Family* 56 (May): 295–313.

AQUILINO, W. S. 1997. From adolescent to young adult: A prospective study of parent–child relations during the transition to adulthood. *Journal of Marriage and the Family* 59 (Aug.): 670–86.

ARANDA, M. P., AND B. G. KNIGHT. 1997. The influence of ethnicity and culture on the caregiver stress and coping process: A sociocultural review and analysis. *The Gerontologist* 37 (3): 342–54.

ARDITTI, J. A. 1999. Rethinking relationships between divorced mothers and their children: Capitalizing on family strengths. *Family Relations* 48 (Apr.): 109–19.

ARDS, S., C. CHUNG, AND S. L. MYERS, JR. 1998. The effects of sample selection bias on racial differences in child abuse reporting. *Child Abuse & Neglect* 22 (Feb.): 103–16.

ARENDELL, T. 1997. A social constructionist approach to parenting. In *Contemporary parenting: Challenges and issues,* ed. T. Arendell, 1–44. Thousand Oaks, CA: Sage.

ARENOFSKY, J. 1993. Childless and proud of it. *Newsweek,* Feb. 8, 12.

ARIAS, E., AND B. L. SMITH. 2003. Deaths: Preliminary data for 2001. *National Vital Statistics Reports* 51 (Mar.): 1–45. www.cdc.gov/nchs/data/ nvsr/nvsr51/nvsr51_05.pdf (accessed Oct. 11, 2003).

ARIES, P. 1962. *Centuries of childhood.* New York: Vintage.

ARLISS, L. P. 1991. *Gender communication.* Upper Saddle River, NJ: Prentice Hall.

ARONSON, E. 1995. *The social animal,* 7th ed. New York: W. H. Freeman.

ARP, C., AND D. ARP. 2001. The magic of older love: Stoking your marital fires through the years. In *Why do fools fall in love? Experiencing the magic, mystery, and meaning of successful relationships,* eds. J. R. Levine and H. J. Markman, 117–22. San Francisco: Jossey-Bass.

ARTHURS, C. 2002. Most Vietnamese women abused. BBC, Oct. 22. http://news.bbc.co.uk/2/hi/world/ asia-pacific/2349059.stm (accessed Oct. 8, 2002).

ASELTINE, R. H., JR., AND R. C. KESSLER. 1993. Marital disruption and depression in a community sample. *Journal of Health and Social Behavior* 34 (Sep.): 237–51.

Ask a working woman. 2002. Findings from the Ask a Working Woman Survey 2002: Respect, work, strengthen family, AFL-CIO. afl-cio.org (accessed May 23, 2003).

ASTONE, N. M., AND S. S. McLANAHAN. 1994. Family structure, residential mobility, and school dropout: A research note. *Demography* 31 (Nov.): 575–84.

ASWAD, B. C. 1994. Attitudes of immigrant women and men in the Dearborn area toward women's employment and welfare. In *Muslim communities in North America,* eds. Y. Haddad and J. Smith, 501–20. Albany: State University of New York Press.

ASWAD, B. C. 1997. Arab American families. In *Families in cultural context: Strengths and challenges in diversity,* ed. M. K. DeGenova, 213–47. Mountain View, CA: Mayfield.

ASWAD, B. C. 1999. Attitudes of Arab immigrants toward welfare. In *Arabs in America: Building a new future,* ed. M. W. Suleiman, 177–91. Philadelphia: Temple University Press.

ATKIN, R. 2002. Keeping kids "clean." *Christian Science Monitor,* Dec. 4, 11–13.

Attitudes and characteristics of freshmen. 2002. *Almanac 2002–3. Chronicle of Higher Education* 49 (Aug.): 26.

Attitudes and characteristics of freshmen. 2003. *Almanac 2003–4. Chronicle of Higher Education* 50 (Aug. 29): 12.

AUSTIN, A. 1999. Favorite toys of the 20th century. *Christian Science Monitor,* Dec. 8, 13.

AUSTIN, A. 2000. More teens opt for plastic surgery. *Christian Science Monitor,* Aug. 30, 14.

AVNA, J., AND D. WALTZ. 1992. *Celibate wives: Breaking the silence.* Los Angeles: Lowell House.

AVNI, N. 1991. Battered wives: The home as a total institution. *Violence and Victims* 6 (2): 137–49.

AXINN, W. G., AND A. THORNTON. 1996. The influence of parents' mutual dissolutions on children's attitudes toward family formation. *Demography* 33 (Feb.): 66–81.

BABCOCK, J. C., J. WALTZ, N. S. JACOBSON, AND J. M. GOTTMAN. 1993. Power and violence: The relation between communication patterns, power discrepancies, and domestic violence. *Journal of Consulting and Clinical Psychology* 61 (1): 40–50.

BACA ZINN, M., AND A. Y. H. POK. 2002. Tradition and transition in Mexican-origin families. In *Minority families in the United States: A multicultural perspective,* 3rd ed., ed. R. L. Taylor, 79–100. Upper Saddle River, NJ: Prentice Hall.

BACA ZINN, M., AND B. WELLS. 2000. Diversity within Latino families: New lessons for family social science. In *Handbook of family diversity,* eds. D. H. Demo, K. R. Allen, and M. A. Fine, 252–73. New York: Oxford University Press.

BACHMAN, J. G., K. N. WADSWORTH, P. M. O'MALLEY, L. D. JOHNSTON, AND J. E. SCHULENBERG. 1997. *Smoking, drinking, and drug use in young adulthood: The impacts of new freedoms and new responsibilities.* Hillsdale, NJ: Erlbaum.

BACHMAN, R. 1994. *Violence against women: A national crime victimization survey report.* U.S. Department of Justice, Office of Justice Programs, Bureau of Justice Statistics. Fall.

BACHRACH, C. A., P. F. ADAMS, S. SAMBRANO, AND K. A. LONDON. 1990. Adoption in the 1980s. *Vital Health Statistics,* no. 181, Jan. 5, advance data. Hyattsville, MD: National Center for Health Statistics.

BACHU, A. 1993. Fertility of American women: June 1992. U.S. Census Bureau, Current Population Reports P20–470. Washington, DC: U.S. Government Printing Office.

BACHU, A., AND M. O'CONNELL. 2001. Fertility of American women: June 2000. U.S. Census Bureau, Current Population Reports, P20-543RV. www.census.gov/prod/2001pubs/p20-543rv.pdf (accessed Feb. 27, 2003).

BADEN, A. 2001. *Psychological adjustment of transracial adoptees: Applying the cultural–racial identity model.* Paper presented at the American Psychological Association, San Francisco, Aug. 2001.

BAER, J. S., P. D. SAMPSON, H. M. BARR, P. D. CONNOR, AND A. P. STREISSGUTH. 2003. A 21-year longitudinal analysis of the effects of prenatal alcohol exposure on young adult drinking. *Archives of General Psychiatry* 60 (Apr.): 377–86.

BAEZCONDE-GARBANTI, L., AND C. J. PORTILLO. 1999. Disparities in health indicators for Latinas in California. *Hispanic Journal of Behavioral Sciences* 21 (Aug.): 302–29.

BAGLEY, C. 1993. Transracial adoption in Britain: A follow-up study, with policy considerations. *Child Welfare* 72 (May/June): 285–300.

BAHR, K. S., AND H. M. BAHR. 1995. Autonomy, community, and the mediation of value: Comments on Apachean grandmothering, cultural change, and the media. In *American families: Issues in race and ethnicity,* ed. C. K. Jacobson, 229–60. New York: Garland.

BAILEY, B. 1988. *From front porch to back seat: Courtship in twentieth-century America.* Baltimore: Johns Hopkins University Press.

BAILEY, J. M., AND R. C. PILLARD. 1991. A genetic study of male sexual orientation. *Archives of General Psychiatry* 48 (Dec.): 1089–96.

BAILEY, J. M., R. C. PILLARD, M. C. NEALE, AND Y. AGYEI. 1993. Heritable factors influence sexual orientation in women. *Archives of General Psychiatry* 50 (Mar.): 217–23.

BAILEY, M. 2003. *The man who would be queen: The science of gender-bending and transsexualism.* Washington, DC: Joseph Henry.

BAILEY, W., M. YOUNG, C. KNICKERBOCKER, AND T. DOAN. 2002. A cautionary tale about conducting research on abstinence education: How do state abstinence coordinators define "sexual activity"? *American Journal of Health Education* 33 (Sep./Oct.): 290–96.

BAKER, B. 2001. Grandparents speak out. *AARP Bulletin,* Apr., 32–33.

BAKER, L., T. H. WAGNER, S. SINGER, AND M. K. BUNDORF. 2003. Use of the Internet and e-mail for health care information. *Journal of the American Medical Association* 289 (May 14): 2400–2406.

BAKER, M. 2003. Adolphus gets married; soon he'll meet his wife. *Christian Science Monitor,* Feb. 15, 7.

BAKER, S. 2002. The coming battle for immigrants. *Business Week,* Aug. 26, 138, 140.

BALDAUF, S. 2000. More men forsake jobs to be fulltime fathers. *Christian Science Monitor,* May 10, 1, 5.

BALDAUF, S. 2003. A bold move on women's rights. *Christian Science Monitor,* Feb. 5, 6.

BANDURA, A., AND R. H. WALTERS. 1963. *Social learning and personality development.* New York: Holt, Rinehart & Winston.

BANG, H.-K., AND B. B. REECE. 2003. Minorities in children's television commercials: New, improved, and stereotyped. *Journal of Consumer Affairs* 37 (Summer): 42–67.

BANISKY, S. 1997. Altering the way to the altar. *Baltimore Sun*, Oct. 20, 1A, 7A.

BANNER, L. W. 1984. *Women in modern America: A brief history*, 2nd ed. New York: Harcourt Brace Jovanovich.

Baptist missionaries must affirm doctrine. 2003. *The Guardian*, Apr. 16. www.guardian.co.uk/uslatest/story/0,1282,-2572751,00.html (accessed Apr. 17, 2003).

BARBARIN, O. A., AND T. McCANDIES. 2003. African-American families. In *International encyclopedia of marriage and family*, 2nd ed., Vol. 1, ed. J. J. Ponzetti, Jr., 50–56. New York: Macmillan.

BARBELL, K., AND M. FREUNDLICH. 2001. *Foster care today*. Washington, DC: Casey Family Programs.

BARBER, B. K. 1994. Cultural, family, and personal contexts of parent–adolescent conflict. *Journal of Marriage and the Family* 56 (May): 375–86.

BARBER, B. L. 1994. Support and advice from married and divorced fathers: Linkages to adolescent adjustment. *Family Relations* 43 (Oct.): 433–38.

BARBER, B. L., AND J. M. LYONS. 1994. Family processes and adolescent adjustment in intact and remarried families. *Journal of Youth and Adolescence* 23 (Aug.): 421–36.

BARBER, J. S., AND W. G. AXINN. 1998a. Gender role attitudes and marriage among young women. *Sociological Quarterly* 39 (Winter): 11–31.

BARBER, J. S., AND W. G. AXINN. 1998b. The impact of parental pressure for grandchildren on young people's entry into cohabitation and marriage. *Population Studies* 52 (July): 129–44.

BARLETT, D. L., AND J. B. STEELE. 2002a. Playing the political slots. *Time*, Dec. 23, 52–63.

BARLETT, D. L., AND J. B. STEELE. 2002b. Wheel of misfortune. *Time*, Dec. 16, 42–58.

BARNES, A. S. 2000. *Everyday racism: A book for all Americans*. Naperville, IL: Sourcebooks.

BARNES, G. M., A. S. REIFMAN, M. P. FARRELL, AND B. A. DINTCHEFF. 2000. The effects of parenting on the development of adolescent alcohol misuse: A six-wave latent growth model. *Journal of Marriage and the Family* 62 (Feb.): 175–86.

BARNES, J. S., AND C. E. BENNETT. 2002. The Asian population: 2000. U.S. Census Bureau. www.census.gov/prod/2002pubs/c2kbr01-16.pdf (accessed Apr. 18, 2003).

BARNET, B., A. K. DUGGAN, M. DEVOE, AND L. BURRELL. 2002. The effect of volunteer home visitation for adolescent mothers on parenting and mental health outcomes. *Archives of Pediatrics & Adolescent Medicine* 156 (Dec.): 1216–22.

BARNETT, R. C., AND C. RIVERS. 1996. *She works, he works: How two-income families are happy, healthy, and thriving*. Cambridge, MA: Harvard University Press.

BARNETT, R. C., AND Y.-C. SHEN. 1997. Gender, high- and low-schedule-control housework tasks, and psychological distress: A study of dual-earner couples. *Journal of Family Issues* 18 (July): 403–28.

BARNEY, B. 1999. A preschool with snob appeal. *U.S. News & World Report*, Sep. 13, 48.

BARON, S., AND A. WELTY. 1996. Elder abuse. *Journal of Gerontological Social Work* 25 (1–2): 33–57.

BAROVICK, H. 2002. Domestic dads. *Time*, Aug. 15, B4–B10.

BARRECA, R. 1993. *Perfect husband (& other fairy tales): Demystifying marriage, men, and romance*. New York: Harmony.

BARRET, R. L., AND B. E. ROBINSON. 1990. *Gay fathers*. Lexington, MA: Lexington Books.

BARRET-DUCROCQ, F. 1991. *Love in the time of Victoria: Sexuality, class and gender in nineteenth-century London*. New York: Verso.

BARRETT, A. E. 1999. Social support and life satisfaction among the never married. *Research on Aging* 21 (Jan.): 46–72.

BARRINGER, H. R., R. W. GARDNER, AND M. J. LEVIN. 1993. *Asians and Pacific Islanders in the United States*. New York: Russell Sage Foundation.

BARRINGTON, L. 2000. Does a rising tide lift all boats? The Conference Board. www.conference-board.org/expertise/frames.cfm?main=about.cfm (accessed Oct. 13, 2000).

BARTFELD, J., AND D. R. MEYER. 2001. The changing role of child support among never-married mothers. In *Out of wedlock: Causes and consequences of nonmarital fertility*, eds. L. L. Wu and B. Wolfe, 229–55. New York: Russell Sage Foundation.

BARTHOLET, E. 1999. *Nobody's children: Abuse and neglect, foster drift, and the adoption alternative*. Boston: Beacon.

BASSON, R. 2001. Using a different model for female sexual response to address women's problematic low sexual desire. *Journal of Sex and Marital Therapy* 27 (Dec.): 395–403.

BATALOVA, J. A., AND P. N. COHEN. 2002. Premarital cohabitation and housework: Couples in cross-national perspective. *Journal of Marriage and Family* 64 (Aug.): 743–55.

BATTAN, M. 1992. *Sexual strategies*. New York: Putnam.

BAUMEISTER, R. F., AND S. R. WOTMAN. 1992. *Breaking hearts: The two sides of unrequited love*. New York: Guilford.

BAUMRIND, D. 1968. Authoritarian versus authoritative parental control. *Adolescence* 3, 255–72.

BAUMRIND, D. 1989. Rearing competent children. In *Child development today and tomorrow*, ed. W. Damon, 349–78. San Francisco: Jossey-Bass.

BAUMRIND, D., R. E. LARZELERE, AND P. A. COWAN. 2002. Ordinary physical punishment: Is it harmful? Comment on Gershoff (2002). *Psychological Bulletin* 128 (July): 580–89.

BAUSERMAN, R. 2002. Child adjustment in joint-custody versus sole-custody arrangements: A meta-analytic review. *Journal of Family Psychology* 16 (Mar.): 91–102.

BAYDAR, N. 1988. Effects of parental separation and reentry into union on the emotional well-being of children. *Journal of Marriage and the Family* 50 (Nov.): 967–81.

BAYDAR, N., AND J. BROOKS-GUNN. 1994. The dynamics of child support and its consequences for children. In *Child support and child well-being*, ed. I. Garfinkel, S. S. McLanahan, and P. K. Robins, 257–84. Washington, DC: Urban Institute.

BAYDAR, N., A. GREEK, AND J. BROOKS-GUNN. 1997. A longitudinal study of the effects of the birth of a sibling during the first 6 years of life. *Journal of Marriage and the Family* 59 (Nov.): 939–56.

BA-YUNUS, I. 1991. Muslims in North America: Mate selection as an indicator of change. In *Muslim families in North America*, eds. E. H. Waugh, S. M. Abu-Laban, and R. B. Qureshi, 232–55. Edmonton: University of Alberta Press.

BAZZINI, D. G., W. D. McINTOSH, S. M. SMITH, S. COOK, AND C. HARRIS. 1997. The aging woman in popular film: Underrepresented, unattractive, unfriendly, and unintelligent. *Sex Roles* 36 (7/8): 531–43.

BEAN, R. A., D. R. CRANE, AND T. L. LEWIS. 2002. Basic research and implications for practice in family science: A content analysis and status report for U.S. ethnic groups. *Family Relations* 51 (Jan.): 15–21.

BEARMAN, P. S., AND H. BRÜCKNER. 2001. Promising the future: Virginity pledges and first intercourse. *American Journal of Sociology* 106 (Jan.): 859–912.

BEATON, J. M., J. E. NORRIS, AND M. W. PRATT. 2003. Unresolved issues in adult children's marital relationships involving intergenerational problems. *Family Relations* 52 (Apr.): 143–53.

BECK, A. T. 1988. *Love is never enough: How couples can overcome misunderstandings, resolve conflicts, and solve relationship problems through cognitive therapy*. New York: Harper & Row.

BECKER, G. S. 1964. *Human capital*. New York: Columbia University Press.

BECKER, P. E., AND P. MOEN. 1999. Scaling back: Dual-earner couples' work–family strategies. *Journal of Marriage and the Family* 61 (Nov.): 995–1007.

BEER, W. R. 1992. *American stepfamilies*. New Brunswick, NJ: Transaction.

BEERS, T. M. 2000. *A profile of the working poor, 1998*. U.S. Department of Labor, Bureau of Labor Statistics, stats.bls.gov/pdf/cpswp98.pdf (accessed Oct. 12, 2000).

BEGLEY, S., WITH M. HAGER AND A. MUIR. 1990. The search for the fountain of youth. *Newsweek*, Mar. 5, 44–48.

BEGOS, K. 2003. War, terror, and poverty rob Iraq of bridegrooms. *Christian Science Monitor*, July 25, 1, 9.

BELKIN, L. 1985. Affording a child: Parents worry as costs keep rising. *New York Times*, May 23, C1, C6.

BELL, R. R., AND K. COUGHEY. 1980. Premarital sexual experience among college females, 1958, 1968, and 1978. *Family Relations* 29, 353–57.

BELLAH, R. N., R. MADSEN, W. M. SULLIVAN, A. SWIDLER, AND S. M. TIPTON. 1985. *Habits of the heart: Individualism and commitment in American life*. Berkeley: University of California Press.

BELLE, D. 1999. *The after-school lives of children: Alone and with others while parents work*. Mahwah, NJ: Erlbaum.

BELLIS, D. D., AND B. P. PFEIFFER. 2001. Intercollegiate athletics: Four-year colleges' experiences adding and discontinuing teams. U.S. Government Accounting Office, GAO-01-297. www.gao.gov (accessed May 24, 2003).

BELSIE, L. 2001. An Iowa debate over newcomers. *Christian Science Monitor*, July 27, 1, 4.

BELSIE, L. 2001. Rise of "home alone" crowd may alter US civic life. *Christian Science Monitor*, May 24, 1–3.

BELSIE, L. 2003. More couples live together, roiling debate on family. *Christian Science Monitor*, Mar. 13, 1, 4.

BELSIE, L. 2003. Where do women out-earn men? Hint: not a city. *Christian Science Monitor*, Aug. 1, 12.

BELSKY, J. 1993. Etiology of child maltreatment: A developmental–ecological analysis. *Psychological Bulletin* 114 (Nov.): 413–34.

BELSKY, J. K. 1988. *Here tomorrow: Making the most of life after fifty*. Baltimore: Johns Hopkins University Press.

BEM, S. L. 1975. Androgyny vs. the tight little lives of fluffy women and chesty men. *Psychology Today*, Sep., 58–62.

BEM, S. L. 1983. Gender schema theory and its implications for child development: Raising gender-schematic children in a gender-schematic society. *Signs* 8: 598–616.

BEM, S. L. 1993. *The lenses on gender: Transforming the debate on sexual inequality*. New Haven, CT: Yale University Press.

BENASSI, M. A. 1985. Effects of romantic love on perception of strangers' physical attractiveness. *Psychological Reports* 56 (Apr.): 355–58.

BENET, S. 2001. Muslim, Asian women target of insults, harassment. *Women's E-News*, Sep. 21. www.womensenews.org/article.cfm?aid=660 (accessed Sep. 21, 2001).

BENGSTON, V. L. 2001. Beyond the nuclear family: The increasing importance of multigenerational bonds. *Journal of Marriage and Family* 63 (Feb.): 1–16.

BENNEFIELD, R. 1995. Health insurance coverage: Who had a lapse between 1991 and 1993? *Statistical Brief SB/95-21*, Aug. U.S. Census Bureau, Washington, DC: U.S. Government Printing Office.

BENNETT, L., JR. 1989. The 10 biggest myths about the black family. *Ebony* (Nov.): 114–16.

BENNETT, L. 2002. Watch out, listen up! 2002 feminist primetime report. National Organization for Women Foundation. www.nowfoundation.org/watchout3/reportA.pdf (accessed May 23, 2003).

BENNETT, R. L., A. G. MOTULSKY, A. BITTLES, L. HUDGINS, S. UHRICH, D. LOCHNER DOYLE, K. SILVEY, C. R. SCOTT, E. CHENG, B. McGILLIVRAY, R. D. STEINER, AND D. OLSON. 2002. Genetic counseling and screening of consanguineous couples and their offspring: Recommendations of the National Society of Genetic Counselors. *Journal of Genetic Counseling* 11 (Apr.): 97–119.

BENOKRAITIS, N. V. 1998. Working in the ivory basement: Subtle sex discrimination in higher education. In *Career strategies for women in academe: Arming Athena*, eds. L. H. Collins, J. C. Chrisler, and K. Quina, 3–36. Thousand Oaks, CA: Sage.

BENOKRAITIS, N. V., ED. 2000. *Feuds about families: Conservative, centrist, liberal, and feminist perspectives*. Upper Saddle River, NJ: Prentice Hall.

BENOKRAITIS, N. V. 2002. The changing ethnic profile of U.S. families in the twenty-first century. In

Contemporary ethnic families in the United States: Characteristics, variations, and dynamics, ed. N. V. Benokraitis, 1–14. Upper Saddle River, NJ: Prentice Hall.

BENOKRAITIS, N. V., AND J. R. FEAGIN. 1995. *Modern sexism: Blatant, subtle, and covert discrimination*, 2nd ed. Upper Saddle River, NJ: Prentice Hall.

BENSON, J. M., AND M. J. HERRMANN. 1999. Right to die or right to life? *Public Perspective* 10 (June/July): 15–19.

BENTON, S. A., J. M. ROBERTSON, W.-C. TSENG, F. B. NEWTON, AND S. L. BENTON. 2003. Changes in counseling center client problems across 13 years. *Professional Psychology: Research & Practice* 34 (Feb.): 66–72.

BERGEN, R. K. 1999. Marital rape. Violence against Women Online Resources. www.vaw.umn.edu/ documents/vawnet/mrape/mrape.pdf (accessed Sep. 18, 2003).

BERGER, R. 1998. *Stepfamilies: A multi-dimensional perspective*. New York: Haworth.

BERGMAN, P. M. 1969. *The chronological history of the Negro in America*. New York: Harper & Row.

BERK, B. R. 1993. The dating game. *Good Housekeeping* (September.): 192, 220–21.

BERLAND, G. K., ET AL. 2001a. Health information on the Internet: Accessibility, quality, and readability in English and Spanish. *Journal of the American Medical Association* 285 (May 23/30): 2612–21.

BERLAND, G. K., ET AL. 2001b. Evaluation of English and Spanish health information on the Internet. www.rand.org/publications/documents/internet eval/index.html (accessed Aug. 8, 2001).

BERLIN, I. 1998. *Many thousands gone: The first two centuries of slavery in North America*. Cambridge, MA: Belknap Press of Harvard University.

BERNARD, J. 1973. *The future of marriage*. New York: Bantam.

BERNHARD, L. A. 1995. Sexuality in women's lives. In *Women's health care: A comprehensive handbook*, eds. C. I. Fogel and N. F. Woods, 475–95. Thousand Oaks, CA: Sage.

BERNIER, J. C., AND D. H. SIEGEL. 1994. Attention-deficit hyperactivity disorder: A family and ecological systems perspective. *Families in Society: The Journal of Contemporary Human Services* (Mar.): 142–50.

BERNSTEIN, J., C. BROCHT, AND M. SPADE-AGUILAR. 2000. *How much is enough? Basic budgets for working families*. Washington, DC: Economic Policy Institute.

BERNSTEIN, J., E. C. MCNICHOL, L. MISHEL, AND R. ZAHRADNIK. 2000. Pulling apart: A state-by-state analysis of income trends. Center on Budget and Policy Priorities, Washington, DC. www.cbpp.org/1-18-00sfp.pdf (accessed Oct. 12, 2000).

BERNSTEIN, J., AND L. MISHEL. 2003. Labor market left behind. Economic Policy Institute, Washington, DC. www.epinet.org/briefingpapers/142/ bp142.pdf (accessed Sep. 13, 2003).

BERNSTEIN, R. 2002. 1-in-5 U.S. residents either foreign-born or first generation. U.S. Census Bureau. www.census.gov/Press-Release/www/2002/ cb02-18.html (accessed Mar. 3, 2003).

BERNSTEIN, R. 2003. Census bureau releases population estimates by age, sex, race and Hispanic origin. U.S. Census Bureau. www.census.gov/ Press-Release/www/2003/cb03-16.html (accessed Mar. 2, 2003).

BERRINGTON, A. 2001. Entry into parenthood and the outcome of cohabiting partnerships in Britain. *Journal of Marriage and Family* 63 (Feb.): 80–96.

BERRY, C. 2000. It's time we rejected the racial litmus test. *Newsweek*, Feb. 7, 13.

BERRY, J. M. 1997. Gap between pay of men, women may have expanded since 1993. *Washington Post*, Sep. 16, C3.

BERSCHEID, E., K. DION, E. WALSTER, AND G. W. WALSTER. 1982. Physical attractiveness and dating choice: A test of the matching hypothesis. *Journal of Experimental Social Psychology* 1, 173–89.

BEST, A. L. 2000. *Prom night: Youth, schools, and popular culture*. New York: Routledge.

BETCHER, W., AND W. POLLACK. 1993. *In a time of fallen heroes: The re-creation of masculinity*. New York: Atheneum.

BHANDARI, S. 2002. Employment-based health insurance: 1997. U.S. Census Bureau, Current Population Reports, P70-81. www.census.gov/prod/ 2003pubs/p70-81.pdf (accessed Sep. 14, 2003).

BIANCHI, S. 1990. America's children: Mixed prospects. *Population Bulletin* 45 (June): 3–41.

BIANCHI, S. M. 2000. Maternal employment and time with children: Dramatic change or surprising continuity? Presidential address to the Population Association of America, Los Angeles, Mar. 24.

BIANCHI, S. M. 2001. *American families resilient after 50 years of change*. Washington, DC: Population Reference Bureau.

BIANCHI, S. M., AND L. M. CASPER. 2000. *American families*. Population Bulletin 55 (Dec.). Washington, DC: Population Reference Bureau.

BIANCHI, S. M., M. A. MILKIE, L. C. SAYER, AND J. P. ROBINSON. 2000. Is anyone doing the housework? Trends in the gender division of household labor. *Social Forces* 79 (Sep.): 191–227.

BIANCHI, S. M., L. SUBAIYA, AND J. R. KAHN. 1999. The gender gap in the economic well-being of nonresident fathers and custodial mothers. *Demography* 36 (May): 195–203.

Bible belt wrestles with high divorce rate. 1999. *Baltimore Sun*, Nov. 14, 19A.

BIELBY, W. T., AND D. D. BIELBY. 1992. I will follow him: Family ties, gender-role beliefs, and reluctance to relocate for a better job. *American Journal of Sociology* 97 (Mar.): 1241–67.

BIGNER, J., AND R. B. JACOBSEN. 1989. Parenting behaviors of homosexual and heterosexual fathers. *Journal of Homosexuality* 18 (1–2): 173–86.

BILLER, H. B. 1993. *Fathers and families: Paternal factors in child development*. Westport, CT: Auburn House.

BILLINGSLEY, A. 1992. *Climbing Jacob's ladder: The enduring legacy of African-American families*. New York: Simon & Schuster.

BILLY, J. O. G., K. TANFER, W. R. GRADY, AND D. H. KLEPINGER. 1993. The sexual behavior of men in the United States. *Family Planning Perspectives* 25 (Mar.): 52–60.

BINSON, D. 1995. Prevalence and social distribution of men who have sex with men. *Journal of Sex Research* 32 (3): 245–54.

BIRD, C. E. 1999. Gender, household labor, and psychological distress: The impact of the amount and division of housework. *Journal of Health & Social Behavior* 40 (Mar.): 32–45.

BIRNS, B. 1999. Attachment theory revisited: Challenging conceptual and methodological sacred cows. *Feminism & Psychology* 9 (Feb.): 10–21.

BIRNS, B., M. CASCARDI, AND S.-L. MEYER. 1994. Sex-role socialization: Developmental influences on wife abuse. *American Journal of Orthopsychiatry* 64 (Jan.): 50–59.

Births to unmarried women: end of the increase? 2003. Ameristat, Population Reference Bureau, Jan.. www.prb.org (accessed Aug. 3, 2003).

BISHOP, G. F., R. W. OLDENDICK, A. J. TUCHFARBER, AND S. E. BENNETT. 1980. Pseudo-opinions on public affairs. *Public Opinion Quarterly* 44 (Summer): 198–209.

BISKUPIC, J. 2003. Same-sex couples redefining family law in USA. *USA Today*, Feb. 18. www. usatoday.com/news/nation/2003-02-17-cover-samesex_x.htm (accessed Feb. 20, 2003).

BLACK, D., G. GATES, S. SANDERS, AND L. TAYLOR. 2000. Demographics of the gay and lesbian population in the United States: Evidence from available systematic data sources. *Demography* 37 (May): 139–54.

Black volunteers for AIDS studies may be hard to find. 2003. *Baltimore Sun*, Feb. 26, 5A.

BLACKWELL, J. E. 1991. *The black community: Diversity and unity*, 3rd ed. New York: HarperCollins.

BLAKE, J. 1989. *Family size and achievement*. Berkeley: University of California Press.

BLAKE, S. M., R. LEDSKY, C. GOODENOW, R. SAWYER, D. LOHRMANN, AND R. WINDSOR. 2003. Condom availability programs in Massachusetts high schools: Relationships with condom use and sexual behavior. *American Journal of Public Health* 93 (June): 955–62.

BLAKE, W. M., AND C. A. DARLING. 2000. Quality of life: Perceptions of African Americans. *Journal of Black Studies* 30 (Jan.): 411–27.

BLANCHARD, K. 1999–2000. Guy anxiety: What he's really nervous about. *Parents Expecting* 33 (Winter): 20–21.

BLANKENHORN, D. 1995. *Fatherless America: Confronting our most urgent social problem*. New York: HarperPerennial.

BLASKO, L. 2000. Blood and guts fly faster as video games get gorier. *Baltimore Sun*, June 19, 1C–2C.

BLAU, F. D., AND R. G. EHRENBERG, EDS. 1997. *Gender and family issues in the workplace*. New York: Russell Sage Foundation.

BLUESTONE, C., AND C. S. TAMIS-LEMONDA. 1999. Correlates of parenting styles in predominantly working- and middle-class African American mothers. *Journal of Marriage and the Family* 61 (Nov.): 881–93.

BOBO, L. D., M. C. DAWSON, AND D. JOHNSON. 2001. Enduring two-ness. *Public Perspective* 12 (May/ June): 12–16.

BODMAN, D. A., AND G. W. PETERSON. 1995. Parenting processes. In *Research and theory in family science*, eds. R. D. Day, K. R. Gilbert, B. H. Settles, and W. R. Burr, 205–25. Pacific Grove, CA: Brooks/Cole.

BODMAN, J. 1985. *The transplanted: A history of immigrants in urban America*. Bloomington: Indiana University Press.

BOGENSCHNEIDER, K. 1996. An ecological risk/protective theory for building prevention programs, policies, and community capacity to support youth. *Family Relations* 45 (Apr.): 127–38.

BOGENSCHNEIDER, K. 1997. Parental involvement in adolescent schooling: A proximal process with transcontextual validity. *Journal of Marriage and the Family* 59 (Aug.): 718–33.

BOGENSCHNEIDER, K., M.-Y. WU, M. RAFFAELLI, AND J. C. TSAY. 1998. "Other teens drink, but not my kid": Does parental awareness of adolescent alcohol use protect adolescents from risky consequences? *Journal of Marriage and the Family* 60 (May): 356–73.

BOHANNON, P. 1971. *Divorce and after*. New York: Doubleday.

BOLDT, M. 2003. North Dakota law forbids unmarried cohabitation. *Washington Post*, Apr. 3, A3.

BOLLAG, B. 2002a. Incident raises issue of harassment of women in Swedish universities. *Chronicle of Higher Education*, Sep. 20, A41.

BOLLAG, B. 2002b. Wanted in Sweden: Female professors. *Chronicle of Higher Education*, Sep. 20, A40–A42.

BOMBECK, E. 1994. The art of grandmothering isn't lost. *Baltimore Sun*, Feb. 24, 8E.

BONNER, R. 2003. A challenge in India snarls foreign adoptions. *New York Times*, June 23, A3.

BONNETTE, R. 1995a. Housing of American Indians on reservations: Equipment and fuels. *Statistical Brief SB/95–11*. U.S. Census Bureau. Washington, DC: U.S. Government Printing Office.

BONNETTE, R. 1995b. Housing of American Indians on reservations: Plumbing. *Statistical Brief SB/95–9*. U.S. Census Bureau. Washington, DC: U.S. Government Printing Office.

BONNIE, R. J., AND R. B. WALLACE, EDS. 2003. *Elder mistreatment: Abuse, neglect, and exploitation in an aging America*. Washington, DC: The National Academies Press.

BOODMAN, S. G. 1992. Questions about a popular prenatal test. *Washington Post Health Supplement*, Nov. 3, 10–13.

BOODMAN, S. G. 1995. The only child: Lonely or lucky? *Washington Post Health Supplement*, Oct. 24, 10–13.

BOOTH, A., AND P. R. AMATO. 2001. Parental predivorce relations and offspring postdivorce well-being. *Journal of Marriage and Family* 63 (Feb.): 197–212.

BOOTH, A., AND J. N. EDWARDS. 1985. Age at marriage and marital instability. *Journal of Marriage and the Family* 47 (Feb.): 67–75.

BOOTH, A., AND J. N. EDWARDS. 1992. Starting over: Why remarriages are more unstable. *Journal of Family Issues* 13 (June): 179–94.

BOOTH, A., AND D. R. JOHNSON. 1994. Declining health and marital quality. *Journal of Marriage and the Family* 56 (Feb.): 218–23.

BOR, J. 1995. Rise in multiple births a concern to physicians. *Baltimore Sun,* Feb. 1, 1A, 10A.

BORDERS, L. D., D. L. K. BLACK, AND B. K. PASLEY. 1998. Are adopted children and their parents at greater risk for negative outcomes? *Family Relations* 47 (July): 237–41.

BORGMAN, A. 1995. Adoptions abroad mix highs, lows. *Washington Post,* Jan. 8, B3.

BORLAND, D. M. 1975. An alternative model of the wheel theory. *Family Coordinator* 24 (July): 289–92.

BORNSTEIN, M. H. 2002. Parenting infants. In *Handbook of parenting,* 2nd ed., Vol. 1: *Children and parenting,* ed. M. H. Bornstein, 3–43. Mahwah, NJ: Erlbaum.

BORST, J. 1996. Relatively speaking. *Newsweek,* July 29, 16.

BOSS, S. J. 2001. Loving & learning. *Christian Science Monitor,* Feb. 14, 15–17.

BOSS, S. J. 2002. Women step up hunt for financial advice. *Christian Science Monitor,* Mar. 18, 17.

Boston lawyer files complaint against law firm for alleged pregnancy bias. 2003. Kaiser Network, Mar. 14. www.kaisernetwork.org/daily_reports/rep_index.cfm?DR_ID=16584 (accessed Mar. 16, 2003).

BOSTON WOMEN'S HEALTH BOOK COLLECTIVE. 1992. *The new our bodies, ourselves: A book by and for women.* New York: Touchstone.

BOUSTANY, N. 1994. Matchmaker, matchmaker, find me some wives. *Washington Post,* Sept. 5, A14.

BOWERS, B. F., AND B. J. MYERS. 1999. Grandmothers providing care for grandchildren: Consequences of various levels of caregiving. *Family Relations* 48 (July): 303–11.

BOWLBY, J. 1969. *Attachment and loss,* Vol. 1: *Attachment.* New York: Basic Books.

BOWLBY, J. 1984. *Attachment and loss,* Vol. 1, 2nd ed. Harmondsworth, UK: Penguin.

Boys to men: Entertainment media, messages about masculinity. 1999. Children Now. www.childrennow.org/media/boystomen/index.html (accessed Aug. 24, 2000).

BOZETT, F. W. 1987. *Gay and lesbian parents.* New York: Praeger.

BRADBURY, T., R. ROGGE, AND E. LAWRENCE. 2001. Reconsidering the role of conflict in marriage. In *Couples in conflict,* eds. A. Booth, A. C. Crouter, and M. Clements, 59–81. Mahwah, NJ: Erlbaum.

BRADLEY-DOPPES, P. 2002. Men still have more opportunities. *Chronicle of Higher Education,* Dec. 6, B8.

BRADSHER, J. E. 1997. Older women and widowhood. In *Handbook on women and aging,* ed. J. M. Coyle, 418–29. Westport, CT: Greenwood.

BRADY, J. 1990. Why I still want a wife. *Ms.* (July/Aug.): 17.

BRAMLETT, M. D., AND W. D. MOSHER. 2002. Cohabitation, marriage, divorce, and remarriage in the United States. Centers for Disease Control and Prevention, Vital and Health Statistics. www.cdc.gov/nchs/data/series/sr_23/sr23_022.pdf (accessed July 3, 2003).

BRAND, P. A., AND A. H. KIDD. 1986. Frequency of physical aggression in heterosexual and female homosexual dyads. *Psychological Reports* 59 (Dec.): 1307–13.

BRASSARD, M. R., AND D. B. HARDY. 1997. Psychological maltreatment. In *The battered child,* 5th ed., ed. M. E. Helfer, R. S. Kempe, and R. D. Krugman, 392–412. Chicago: University of Chicago Press.

BRAUND, K. E. H. 1990. Guardians of tradition and handmaidens to change: Women's roles in Creek economic and social life during the eighteenth century. *American Indian Quarterly* 14 (Summer): 239–58.

BRAVER, S. L., with D. O'CONNELL. 1998. *Divorced dads: Shattering the myths.* New York: Penguin Putnam.

BRAY, J. H. 1999. From marriage to remarriage and beyond: Findings from the developmental issues in Stepfamilies Research Project. In *Coping with divorce, single parenting, and remarriage: A risk and resiliency perspective,* ed. E. M. Hetherington, 253–71. Mahwah, NJ: Erlbaum.

BRAY, J., G. J. ADAMS, G. J. GETZ, AND T. STOVALL. 2001. Interactive effects of individuation, family factors, and stress on adolescent alcohol use.

American Journal of Orthopsychiatry 71 (Oct.): 436–49.

BRAY, J. H., AND S. H. BERGER. 1990. Noncustodial father and paternal grandparent relationships in stepfamilies. *Family Relations* 39 (Oct.): 414–19.

BRAY, J. H., AND J. KELLY. 1998. *Stepfamilies: Love, marriage, and parenting in the first decade.* New York: Broadway.

BRAZIL, J. 1998. You talkin' to me? *American Demographics* 20 (Dec.): 55–59.

Breast implants. 2002. U.S. Food and Drug Administration. www.fda.gov/cdrh/breastimplants/breast_implant_risks_brochure.html (accessed May 15, 2003).

BREHM, S. S. 1985. *Intimate relationships.* New York: Random House.

BREHM, S. S. 1992. *Intimate relationships,* 2nd ed. New York: McGraw-Hill.

BREINES, W. 1992. *Young, white, and miserable: Growing up female in the fifties.* Boston: Beacon.

BRENDER, A. 2003. Women's university in South Korea drop ban on married students. *Chronicle of Higher Education,* Feb. 3. http://chronicle.com/daily/2003/02/2003020306n.htm (accessed Feb. 4, 2003).

BRENNAN, R. T., R. C. BARNETT, AND K. C. GAREIS. 2001. When she earns more than he does: A longitudinal study of dual-earner couples. *Journal of Marriage and Family* 63 (Feb.): 168–82.

BRENNEMAN, G. R., A. O. HANDLER, S. F. KAUFMAN, AND E. R. RHOADES. 2000. Health status and clinical indicators. In *American Indian health: Innovations in health care, promotion, and policy,* ed. E. R. Rhoades, 103–21. Baltimore: Johns Hopkins University Press.

BRESLAU, K. 2001. Hate crime: He wasn't afraid. *Newsweek,* Oct. 15, 8.

BRETSCHNEIDER, J. G., AND N. L. McCOY. 1988. Sexual interest and behavior in healthy 80- to 102-year olds. *Archives of Sexual Behavior* 17 (2): 109–29.

BREWER, C. A., AND T. A. SUCHAN. 2001. Mapping census 2000: The geography of U.S. diversity. CENSR/01-1, Census Bureau. www.census.gov/population/cen2000/atlas/censr01-1.pdf (accessed Feb. 26, 2003).

BRIERE, J. N. 1992. *Child abuse trauma: Theory and treatment of the lasting effects.* Thousand Oaks, CA: Sage.

BRIGGS-GOWAN, M. J., A. S. CARTER, E. M. SKUBAN, AND S. M. HORWITZ. 2001. Prevalence of social-emotional and behavioral problems in a community sample of 1- and 2-year-old children. *Journal of the American Academy of Child & Adolescent Psychiatry* 40 (July): 811–19.

BRINES, J. 1994. Economic dependency, gender, and the division of labor at home. *American Journal of Sociology* 100 (Nov.): 652–88.

Bringing up baby. 1999. *Public Perspective* 10 (Oct./Nov.): 19.

BRINIG, M. F., AND D. A. ALLEN. 2000. "These boots are made for walking": Why most divorce filers are women. *American Law and Economic Review* 2 (1): 126–69.

BRINK, S. 1994. Too sick to be adopted? *U.S. News & World Report,* May 2, 66–69.

BRISSETT-CHAPMAN, S., AND M. ISSACS-SHOCKLEY. 1997. *Children in social peril: A community vision for preserving family care of African American children and youths.* Washington, DC: Child Welfare League of America.

BROADHURST, S. C. 2003. Joe sitcom. *Christian Science Monitor,* Mar. 7, 13, 17.

BROCK, L. J., AND G. H. JENNINGS. 1993. Sexuality education: What daughters in their 30s wish their mothers had told them. *Family Relations* 42 (Jan.): 61–65.

BROCKERHOFF, M. P. 2000. An urbanizing world. *Population Bulletin,* 55 (Sep.), Washington, DC: Population Reference Bureau.

BRODER, J. M. 2002. Family leave in California now includes pay benefit. *New York Times,* Sep. 23, A20.

BRODER, J. M. 2002. In a first, a lesbian is elected district attorney in San Diego. *New York Times,* Nov. 13, A16.

BRODER, J. M. 2002. Problem of lost health benefits is reaching into the middle class. *New York Times,* Nov. 25, A1.

BRODERICK, C. B. 1988. To arrive where we started: The field of family studies in the 1930s. *Journal of Marriage and the Family* 50 (Aug.): 569–84.

BRODERICK, C. B. 1993. *Understanding family process: Basics of family systems theory.* Thousand Oaks, CA: Sage.

BRODIE, M., A. STEFFENSON, J. VALDEZ, AND R. LEVIN. 2002. 2002 national survey of Latinos. Pew Hispanic Center/The Henry Kaiser Family Foundation. www.pewhispanic.org/site/docs/pdf/LatinoReportExecSumandSectionOne.pdf (accessed Apr. 16, 2003).

BRODNAR-NEMZER, J. Y. 1986. Divorce and group commitment: The case of the Jews. *Journal of Marriage and the Family* 48 (May): 329–40.

BRODY, E. M., S. J. LITVIN, C. HOFFMAN, AND N. H. KLEBAN. 1992. Differential effects of daughters' marital status on their parent care experiences. *The Gerontologist* 32 (1): 58–67.

BRODY, L. R. 2000. The socialization of gender differences in emotional expression: Display rules, infant temperament, and differentiation. In *Gender and emotion: Social psychological perspectives,* ed. A. H. Fischer, 24–47. New York: Cambridge University Press.

BROMAN, C. L., V. L. HAMILTON, AND W. S. HOFFMAN. 2001. *Stress and distress among the unemployed: Hard times and vulnerable people.* New York: Kluwer Academic/Plenum.

BRONFENBRENNER, U. 1979. *The ecology of human development: Experiments by nature and design.* Cambridge, MA: Harvard University Press.

BRONFENBRENNER, U. 1986. Ecology of the family as a context for human development: Research perspectives. *Developmental Psychology* 22: 723–42.

BROOK, J. S., C. M. CONNELL, C. M. MITCHELL, AND S. M. MASON. 2002. Drug use and neurobehavioral, respiratory, and cognitive problems: Precursors and mediators. *Journal of Adolescent Health* 30 (June): 433–41.

BROOKS, A. 1994. Sexism's bitterest trick. *New Scientist,* Mar. 12, 48–49.

BROOKS, D. 2000. *Bobos in paradise: The new upper class and how they got there.* New York: Simon & Schuster.

BROOKS, G. R. 1995. *The centerfold syndrome: How men can overcome objectification and achieve intimacy with women.* San Francisco: Jossey-Bass.

BROOKS-GUNN, J., P. K. KLEBANOV, AND G. J. DUNCAN. 1996. Ethnic differences in children's intelligence test scores: Role of economic deprivation, home environment, and material characteristics. *Child Development* 67 (Apr.): 396–408.

BROWN, B. B. 1999. "You're going out with *who?*" Peer group influences on adolescent romantic relationships. In *The development of romantic relationships in adolescence,* eds. W. Furman, B. B. Bradford, and C. Feiring, 291–329. New York: Cambridge University Press.

BROWN, B. V., AND S. BZOSTEK. 2003. Violence in the lives of children. Washington, DC: Child Trends Data Bank. www.childtrendsdatabank.org/PDF/Violence.pdf (accessed Sep. 17, 2003).

BROWN, B. V., E. A. MICHELSEN, T. G. HALLE, AND K. A. MOORE. 2001. Fathers' activities with their kids. Washington, DC: Child Trends. www.childtrends.org/PDF/June_2001.pdf (accessed Aug. 23, 2003).

BROWN, D. 2000. Demographic shift noted in new cases of AIDS. *Washington Post,* Jan. 14, A1, A15.

BROWN, J. K. 1992. Lives of middle-aged women. In *In her prime: New views of middle-aged women,* 2nd ed., eds. V. Kerns and J. K. Brown, 17–30. Urbana: University of Illinois Press.

BROWN, L. S. 1995. Lesbian identities: Concepts and issues. In *Lesbian, gay, and bisexual identities over the lifespan: Psychological perspectives,* eds. A. R. D'Augelli and C. J. Patterson, 3–23. New York: Oxford University Press.

BROWN, M. R. 1994. Whose eyes are these, whose nose? *Newsweek,* Mar. 7, 12.

BROWN, N. M., AND E. S. AMATEA. 2000. *Love and intimate relationships: Journeys of the heart.* Philadelphia: Brunner/Mazel.

BROWN, P. M. 1995. *The death of intimacy: Barriers to meaningful interpersonal relationships.* New York: Haworth.

BROWN, R. A. 1994. Romantic love and the spouse selection criteria of male and female Korean college students. *Journal of Social Psychology* 134 (2): 183–89.

BROWN, S. 2002. Child well-being in cohabiting families. In *Just living together: Implications of cohabitation on families, children, and social policy*, eds. A. Booth and A. C. Crouter, 173–88. Mahwah, NJ: Erlbaum.

BROWN, S. L. 2000. Union transitions among cohabitors: The significance of relationship assessments and expectations. *Journal of Marriage and the Family* 62 (Aug.): 833–46.

BROWNE, A. 1993. Family violence and homelessness: The relevance of trauma histories in the lives of homeless women. *American Journal of Orthopsychiatry* 63 (July): 370–84.

BROWNSWORTH, V. A. 1996. Tying the knot or the hangman's noose: The case against marriage. *Journal of Gay, Lesbian, and Bisexual Identity* 1 (Jan.): 91–98.

BRUBAKER, T. H. 1991. Families in later life: A burgeoning research area. In *Contemporary families: Looking forward, looking back*, ed. A. Booth, 226–48. Minneapolis: National Council on Family Relations.

BRUNI, F. 2002. Persistent drop in fertility reshapes Europe's future. *New York Times*, Dec. 26, A1.

BRYAN, L. R., M. COLEMAN, AND L. H. GANONG. 1986. Person perception: Family structure as a cue for stereotyping. *Journal of Marriage and the Family* 48 (Feb.): 169–74.

BRYANT, C. M., R. D. CONGER, AND J. M. MEEHAN. 2001. The influence of in-laws on change in marital success. *Journal of Marriage and Family* 63 (Aug.): 614–26.

BRYNES, G. 2001. Dealing with dementia. Northern County Psychiatric Associates, Baltimore. www.ncpamd.com/dementia.htm (accessed Oct. 9, 2003).

BRYSON, K., AND L. M. CASPER. 1999. Coresident grandparents and grandchildren. Current Population Reports, P23-128, U.S. Census Bureau. www.census.gov/prod/99pubs/p23-198.pdf (accessed Oct. 28, 2000).

BUCHANAN, C. M., E. E. MACCOBY, AND S. M. DORNBUSCH. 1996. *Adolescents after divorce*. Cambridge, MA: Harvard University Press.

BUDD, K. 2002. Egg beaters. *AARP Magazine*, May/June, 15.

BUEHLER, C., and J. M. GERARD. 2002. Marital conflict, ineffective parenting, and children's and adolescents' maladjustment. *Journal of Marriage and Family* 64 (Feb.): 78–92.

BUEHLER, C., and B. B. TROTTER. 1990. Nonresidential and residential parents' perceptions of the former spouse relationships and children's social competence following marital separation: Theory and programmed intervention. *Family Relations* 39 (Oct.): 395–404.

BULCROFT, K., L. SMEINS, AND R. BULCROFT. 1999. *Romancing the honeymoon: Consummating marriage in modern society*. Thousand Oaks, CA: Sage.

BULCROFT, R. A., AND K. A. BULCROFT. 1993. Race differences in attitudinal and motivational factors in the decision to marry. *Journal of Marriage and the Family* 55 (May): 338–55.

BULIK, C. M., ET AL. 2003. Significant linkage on chromosome 10p in families with bulimia nervosa. *American Journal of Human Genetics* 72 (Jan.): 200–207.

BUMPASS, L., AND H.-H. LU. 2000. Trends in cohabitation and implications for children's family contexts in the United States. *Population Studies* 54 (Mar.): 29–41.

BUMPASS, L. L., R. K. RALEY, AND J. A. SWEET. 1995. The changing character of stepfamilies: Implications of cohabitation and nonmarital childbearing. *Demography* 32 (Aug.): 425–36.

BUMPASS, L. L., AND J. A. SWEET. 1989. National estimates of cohabitation. *Demography* 26 (Nov.): 615–25.

BURGESS, E. W., H. J. LOCKE, AND M. M. THOMES. 1963. *The family from institution to companionship*. New York: American Book Co.

BURKE, P. 2002. Fit Calif. moms losing custody to abusive dads. *Women's E-News*, Oct. 22. www.womensenews.org/article.cfm/dyn/aid/1080 (accessed Oct. 24, 2002).

Burkina Faso: Female circumciser sentenced to prison. 2002. *Africa Online*. www.africaonline.com/site/Articles/1,3,47251.jsp (accessed Apr. 26, 2002).

BURLESON, B. R., AND W. H. DENTON. 1997. The relationships between communication skill and marital satisfaction: Some moderating effects. *Journal of Marriage and the Family* 59 (Nov.): 884–902.

BURNETTE, D. 1999. Social relationships of Latino grandparent caregivers: A role theory perspective. *The Gerontologist* 39 (Feb.): 49–58.

BURR, C. 1996. *A separate creation: The search for the biological origins of sexual orientation*. New York: Hyperion.

BURR, W. R. 1995. Using theories in family science. In *Research and theory in family science*, eds. R. D. Day, K. R. Gilbert, B. H. Settles, and W. R. Burr, 73–90. Pacific Grove, CA: Brooks/Cole.

BURT, M. R., L. Y. ARON, T. DOUGLAS, J. VALENTE, E. LEE, AND B. IWEN. 1999. Homelessness: Programs and the people they serve. Urban Institute, Washington, DC. www.urban.org/housing/homeless/homelessness.pdf (accessed Oct. 11, 2000).

BURTON, L. M., AND C. B. STACK. 1993. Conscripting kin: Reflections on family, generation, and culture. In *Family, self, and society: Toward a new agenda for family research*, eds. P. A. Cowan, D. Field, D. A. Hansen, A. Skolnick, and G. E. Swanson, 115–42. Hillsdale, NJ: Erlbaum.

BUSHMAN, B. J., A. M. BONACCI, M. VAN DIJK, AND R. F. BAUMEISTER. 2003. Narcissism, sexual refusal, and aggression: Testing a narcissistic reactance model of sexual coercion. *Journal of Personality and Social Psychology* 84 (May): 1027–40.

BUSINESS AND PROFESSIONAL WOMEN. 2003. 101 facts on the status of working women. www.bpwusa.org/Content/Workplace/FactsandFigures/101Facts.pdf (Sep. 11, 2003).

BUSS, D. M. 1989. Sex differences in human mate preferences: Evolutionary hypotheses tested in 37 cultures. *Behavioral and Brain Sciences* 12 (Mar.): 1–49.

BUSS, D. M. 2000. *The dangerous passion: Why jealousy is as necessary as love and sex*. New York: Free Press.

BUSS, D. M., ET AL. 1990. International preferences in selecting mates: A study of 37 cultures. *Journal of Cross-Cultural Psychology* 21 (Mar.): 5–47.

BUSS, D. M., R. J. LARSEN, AND D. WESTEN. 1996. Commentary: Sex differences in jealousy: Not gone, not forgotten, and not explained by alternative hypotheses. *Psychological Science* 7 (Nov.): 373–75.

BUSS, D. M., T. K. SHACKELFORD, L. A. KIRKPATRICK, and R. J. LARSEN. 2001. A half century of mate preferences: The cultural evolution of values. *Journal of Marriage and Family* 63 (May): 491–503.

BUSSEY, K., AND A. BANDURA. 1992. Self-regulatory mechanisms governing gender development. *Child Development* 63 (Oct.): 1236–50.

BUTLER, J. 2003. XXY marks the spot "X." FTM Australia, Jan. 21. www.ftmaustralia.org/media/03/0121.html (accessed June 11, 2003).

BUTLER, R. N. 1975. *Why survive? Being old in America*. New York: Harper & Row.

BUTLER, R. N., AND M. I. LEWIS. 1993. *Love and sex after 60*. New York: Ballantine.

BYRNES, B. 2003. Wary of past abuses, Argentine capital approves gay rights. *Christian Science Monitor*, July 14, 7.

CACIOPPO, J. T., ET AL. 2002. Loneliness and health: Potential mechanisms. *Psychosomatic Medicine* 64 (May/June): 407–17.

CAFFARO, J. V., AND A. CONN-CAFFARO. 1998. *Sibling abuse trauma: Assessment and intervention strategies for children, families, and adults*. New York: Haworth.

CAIAZZA, A. B., ED. 2002–2003. The status of women in the states. Institute for Women's Policy Research. www.iwpr.org/states (accessed May 23, 2003).

CALDWELL, M. A., AND L. A. PEPLAU. 1990. The balance of power in lesbian relationships. In *Perspectives on the family: History, class, and feminism*, ed., C. Carlton, 204–15. Belmont, CA: Wadsworth.

CALL, V., S. SPRECHER, AND P. SCHWARTZ. 1995. The incidence and frequency of marital sex in a national sample. *Journal of Marriage and the Family* 57: 639–50.

CALVERT, S. 2003. Ruling on gays stirs up emotions. *Baltimore Sun*, June 28, 1A, 5A.

CAMARILLO, A. 1979. *Chicanos in a changing society: From Mexican pueblos to American barrios in Santa Barbara and southern California, 1848–1930*. Cambridge, MA: Harvard University Press.

CAMPBELL, F., AND C. RAMEY. 1999. *The Carolina abecedarian project*. www.fpg.unc.edu/~abc (accessed Sep. 24, 2000).

CAMPBELL, J. R., C. M. HOMBO, AND J. MAZZEO. 2000. NAEP 1999 trends in academic progress: Three decades of student performance. nces.ed.gov/nationsreportcard/pubs/main1999/2000469.shtml (accessed Aug. 27, 2000).

CAMPBELL, K. 2001. A "woman shortage"? Reports shift men's views on dating. *Christian Science Monitor*, Dec. 27, 3.

CAMPBELL, K. 2002. Today's courtship: White teeth, root beer, and e-mail? *Christian Science Monitor*, Feb. 14, 1, 4.

CAMPBELL, K. 2003. Divorce online: Faster, cheaper, and lawyer-free. *Christian Science Monitor*, June 18, 1, 4.

CAMPBELL, P. W. 1999. Researcher found guilty of misconduct. *Chronicle of Higher Education*, Jan. 15, A34.

CAMPBELL, W. K. 1999. Narcissism and romantic attraction. *Journal of Personality and Social Psychology* 77 (Dec.): 1254–70.

CAMPBELL, W. K., C. A. FOSTER, AND E. J. FINKEL. 2002. Does self-love lead to love for others? A study of narcissistic game playing. *Journal of Personality and Social Psychology* 83 (Aug.): 340–54.

CANARY, D. J., W. R. CUPACH, AND S. J. MESSMAN. 1995. *Relationship conflict: Conflict in parent–child, friendship, and romantic relationships*. Thousand Oaks, CA: Sage.

CANCIAN, F. M. 1990. The feminization of love. In *Perspectives on the family: History, class, and feminism*, ed. C. Carlson, 171–85. Belmont, CA: Wadsworth.

CANEDY, D. 2002. Hospitals feeling strain from illegal immigrants. *New York Times*, Aug. 25. www.nytimes.com/2002/08/25/health/25IMMI.html?todaysheadlines (accessed Aug. 25, 2002).

CANTWELL, H. B. 1997. The neglect of child neglect. In *The battered child*, 5th ed., eds. M. E. Helfer, R. S. Kempe, and R. D. Krugman, 347–73. Chicago: University of Chicago Press.

CAPALDI, D. M., AND G. R. PATTERSON. 1991. Relation of parental transitions to boys' adjustment problems: I. A linear hypotheses. II. Mothers at risk for transitions and unskilled parenting. *Developmental Psychology* 66 (May): 489–504.

CAPELL, P. 1995. The stress of relocating. *American Demographics* 17 (Nov.): 15–16.

CAPIZZANO, J., AND G. ADAMS. 2000a. The hours that children under five spend in child care: Variations across states. Urban Institute. newfederalism.urban.org/pdf/anf_b8.pdf (accessed Sep. 27, 2000).

CAPIZZANO, J., AND G. ADAMS. 2000b. The number of child care arrangements used by children under five: Variation across states. Urban Institute. newfederalism.urban.org/pdf/anf_b12.pdf (accessed Sep. 27, 2000).

CAPIZZANO, J., K. TOUT, AND G. ADAMS. 2000. Child care patterns of school-age children with employed mothers. Occasional Paper no. 41. Urban Institute. newfederalism.urbanorg/pdf/occa41.pdf (accessed Sep. 27, 2000).

CARGAN, L., AND M. MELKO. 1982. *Singles: Myths and realities*. Beverly Hills, CA: Sage.

CARLSON, D. K. 2001. Over half of Americans believe in love at first sight. Gallup News Service, Feb. 14. www.gallup.com/poll/releases/pr010214d.asp (accessed May 19, 2003).

CARLSON, L. 1998. *Caring for the dead: Your final act of love*. New York: Upper Access.

CARLSON, L. H., AND G. A. COLBURN, EDS. 1972. *In their place: White America defines her minorities, 1850–1950*. New York: Wiley.

CARMICHAEL, M. 2003. Are we dying to be thin? *Newsweek*, Mar. 3, 62–63.

CARP, F. M. 2000. *Elder abuse in the family: An interdisciplinary model for research.* New York: Springer.

CARR, D., AND C. L. HAYS. 2003. 3 racy men's magazines banned by Wal-Mart. *New York Times,* May 5. www.nytimes.com/2003/05/06/business/media/06MAG.html?th (accessed May 6, 2003).

CARRASQUILLO, A. L. 1991. *Hispanic children and youth in the United States: A resource guide.* New York: Garland.

CARRASQUILLO, H. 2002. The Puerto Rican family. In *Minority families in the United States: A multicultural perspective,* 3rd ed., ed. R. L. Taylor, 101–13. Upper Saddle River, NJ: Prentice Hall.

CARRERE, W., AND J. M. GOTTMAN. 1999. Predicting divorce among newlyweds from the first three minutes of a marital conflict discussion. *Family Process* 38 (Fall): 293–302.

CARRIER, J. M., AND S. O. MURRAY. 1998. Woman–woman marriage in Africa. In *Boy-wives and female husbands: Studies of African homosexualities,* eds. S. O. Murray and W. Roscoe, 255–66. New York: St. Martin's.

CARROLL, B. T. 2003. Salvaging a career. *Chronicle of Higher Education,* May 16, C4.

CART, J. 2002. Activists aim to end "dirty little secret." *Miami Herald,* Aug. 19. www.miami.com/mld/miamiherald/3891719.htm (accessed Aug. 20, 2002).

CARTEN, A. J., AND I. FENNOY. 1997. African American families and HIV/AIDS: Caring for surviving children. *Child Welfare* 76 (Jan./Feb.): 107–25.

CARTER, L. D. 2003. Trusted adults prevent HIV. *Democrat and Chronicle,* June 18. www.democratandchronicle.com/news/0618story18_news.shtml (accessed June 20, 2003).

CARTER, S., AND J. SOKOL. 1993. *He's scared, she's scared: Understanding the hidden fears that sabotage your relationships.* New York: Delacorte.

CARTWRIGHT, M., ET AL. 2003. Stress and dietary practices in adolescents. *Health Psychology* 22 (July): 362–69.

CASEY, T. 1998. *Pride and joy: The lives and passions of women without children.* Hillsboro, OR: Beyond Words.

CASLER, L. 1974. *Is marriage necessary?* New York: Human Sciences Press.

CASPER, L. M., AND K. R. BRYSON. 1998. *Co-resident grandparents and their grandchildren: Grandparent maintained families.* Population Division Working Paper no. 26. U.S. Census Bureau. www.census.gov/population/www/documentation/twps0026/twps0026.html (accessed Oct. 28, 2000).

CASPI, A., ET AL. 2003. Influence of life stress on depression: Moderation by a polymorphism in the 5-HTT gene. *Science* 301 (July 18): 386–89.

CASSIDY, J., AND S. R. ASHER. 1992. Loneliness and peer relations in young children. *Child Development* 63 (Apr.): 350–65.

CASSIDY, M. L., AND G. R. LEE. 1989. The study of polyandry: A critique and synthesis. *Journal of Comparative Family Studies* 20 (Spring): 1–11.

CASSIDY, S. 1993. A single woman: The fabric of my life. In *Single women: Affirming our spiritual journeys,* eds. M. O'Brien and C. Christie, 35–48. Westport, CT: Bergin & Garvey.

CATALFO, P. 1994. Love at first link-up. *New Woman* 24 (Mar.): 56, 58.

CATE, R. M., AND S. A. LLOYD. 1992. *Courtship.* Thousand Oaks, CA: Sage.

Catholic archdiocese withdraws award from lesbian. 2003. *Women's E-News,* May 24. www.womensenews.org/article.cfm/dyn/aid/1341/context/outrage (accessed June 15, 2003).

CAUTHEN, N. K., AND H.-H. LU. 2003. Living at the edge. National Center for Children in Poverty. www.nccp.org/media/lat03a-text.pdf (accessed Sept. 16, 2003).

CAVAN, R. S., AND K. H. RANCK. 1938. *The family and the Depression: A study of one hundred Chicago families.* Chicago: University of Chicago Press.

CAWLEY, J. 2001. Body weight and the dating and sexual behaviors of young adolescents. In *Social awakening: Adolescent behavior as adulthood approaches,* ed. R. T. Michael, 174–98. New York: Russell Sage Foundation.

CEBALLO, R., T. A. DAHL, M. T. ARETAKIS, AND C. RAMIREZ. 2001. Inner-city children's exposure to community violence: How much do parents know? *Journal of Marriage and the Family* 63 (Nov.): 927–40.

CEJKA, M. A. 1993. A demon with no name: Prejudice against single women. In *Single women: Affirming our spiritual journeys,* eds. M. O'Brien and C. Christie, 3–11. Westport, CT: Bergin & Garvey.

CENTER FOR THE ADVANCEMENT OF WOMEN. 2003. *Progress and perils: New agenda for women.* www.advancewomen.org/womens_research/Progress&Perils.pdf (accessed Aug. 21, 2003).

CENTER FOR DISEASE CONTROL AND PREVENTION. 2003. HIV/AIDS Surveillance Report, 2002, 14: 1–48. www.cdc.gov/hiv/stats/hasr1402/2002SurvellianceReport.pdf (accessed November 26, 2003).

CENTER FOR WOMEN POLICY STUDIES. 1994. *Midlife & older women & HIV/AIDS.* Washington, DC: American Association of Retired Persons.

CENTERS FOR DISEASE CONTROL AND PREVENTION. 1997. *1995 Assisted reproductive technology success rates: National summary and fertility clinic reports.* National Center for Chronic Disease Prevention and Health Promotion, Division of Reproductive Health, Atlanta. www.cdc.gov/nccdphp/drh/arts/index.htm (accessed Jan. 15, 1998).

CENTERS FOR DISEASE CONTROL AND PREVENTION. 2001. *HIV/AIDS surveillance report* 13 (2). www.cdc.gov/hiv/stats/hasr1302.pdf (accessed June 18, 2003).

CHADDOCK, G. R. 2003. For Hispanics, cultural heft and new tensions. *Christian Science Monitor,* Jan. 23, 1, 3.

CHADIHA, L. A., J. VEROFF, AND D. LEBER. 1998. Newlyweds' narrative themes: Meaning in the first year of marriage for African American and white couples. *Journal of Comparative Family Studies* 29 (Spring): 116–30.

CHAFE, W. H. 1972. *The American woman: Her changing social, economic, and political roles, 1920–1970.* New York: Oxford University Press.

CHAMBERS, V. 2003. *Having it all? Black women and success.* New York: Doubleday.

CHAMBERS, V., AND L. CLEMETSON. 1999. A place they can call home. *Newsweek,* Apr. 19, 58–59.

CHAN, S. 1997. Families with Asian roots. In *Developing cross-cultural competence: A guide for working with children and families,* 2nd ed., eds. E. W. Lynch and M. J. Hanson, 251–353. Baltimore: Paul H. Brookes.

CHAN, S. 1999. Families with Asian roots. In *Developing cross-cultural competence: A guide for working with children and their families,* 2nd ed., eds. E. W. Lynch and M. J. Hanson, 251–344. Baltimore: Paul H. Brookes.

CHANCE, P. 1988. The trouble with love. *Psychology Today* (Feb.): 22–23.

CHANG, G. 2000. *Disposable domestics: Immigrant women workers in the global economy.* Cambridge, MA: South End.

CHANG, J., L. D. ELAM-EVANS, C. J. BERG, J. HERNDON, L. FLOWERS, K. A. SEED, AND C. J. SYVERSON. 2003. Pregnancy-related mortality surveillance: United States, 1991–1999. *Morbidity and Mortality Weekly Report* 52 (Feb. 21): 1–8. www.cdc.gov/mmwr/PDF/SS/SS5202.pdf (accessed Aug. 2, 2003).

CHANG, J., AND A. MOON. 1997. Korean American elderly's knowledge and perceptions of elder abuse: A qualitative analysis of cultural factors. *Journal of Multicultural Social Work* 6 (1/2): 139–54.

CHANG, S.-C., K. O. O'BRIEN, M. S. NATHANSON, L. E. CULFIELD, J. MANCINI, AND F. R. WITTER. 2003. Fetal femur length is influenced by maternal dairy intake in pregnant African American adolescents. *American Journal of Clinical Nutrition* 77 (May): 1248–54.

CHAO, R., AND V. TSENG. 2002. Parenting of Asians. In *Handbook of parenting,* 2nd ed., Vol. 4: *Social conditions and applied parenting,* ed. M. H. Bornstein, 59–93. Mahwah, NJ: Erlbaum.

CHARLES, S. T., AND L. L. CARSTENSEN. 2002. Marriage in old age. In *Inside the American couple: New thinking/new challenges,* eds. M. Yalom

and L. L. Carstensen, 236–54. Berkeley: University of California Press.

CHARLES, S. T., M. MATHER, AND L. L. CARSTENSEN. 2003. Aging and emotional memory: The forgettable nature of negative images for older adults. *Journal of Experimental Psychology* 132 (June): 310–24.

CHASE-LANSDALE, P. L., A. J. CHERLIN, AND K. E. KIERNAN. 1995. The long-term effects of parental divorce on the mental health of young adults: A developmental perspective. *Child Development* 66 (Dec.): 1614–34.

CHATTERS, L. M., AND R. J. TAYLOR. 1993. Intergenerational support: The provision of assistance to parents by adult children. In *Aging in black America,* eds. S. Jackson, L. M. Chatters, and R. J. Taylor, 60–83. Thousand Oaks, CA: Sage.

CHAUVIN, L. 2002. Catholic U. in Peru angers students by handing out pamphlet calling homosexuality an illness. *Chronicle of Higher Education,* Sep. 19. http://chronicle.com/daily/2002/09/2002091906n.htm (accessed Sept. 20, 2002).

CHEKKI, D. A. 1996. Family values and family change. *Journal of Comparative Family Studies* 27 (Summer): 409–13.

CHELALA, C. 2002. World violence against women a great unspoken pandemic. *Philadelphia Inquirer,* Nov. 4. www.commondreams.org/views02/1104-02.htm (accessed Nov. 7, 2002).

CHEN, A. S. 1999. Lives at the center of the periphery, lives at the periphery of the center: Chinese American masculinities and bargaining with hegemony. *Gender & Society* 13 (Oct.): 584–607.

CHEN, Z.-Y., AND H. B. KAPLAN. 2001. Intergenerational transmission of constructive parenting. *Journal of Marriage and Family* 63 (Feb.): 17–31.

CHENG, T. L., R. A. G. RENNER, J. L. WRIGHT, H. C. SACHS, P. MOYER, AND M. RAO. 2003. Community norms on toy guns. *Pediatrics* 111 (Jan.): 75–79.

CHERLIN, A. J. 1998. Marriage and marital dissolution among black Americans. *Journal of Comparative Family Studies* 29 (Spring): 147–58.

CHERLIN, A. J. 1999. Going to extremes: Family structure, children's well-being, and social science. *Demography* 36 (Nov.): 421–28.

CHERLIN, A. J., AND F. F. FURSTENBERG, JR. 1994. Stepfamilies in the United States: A reconsideration. *Annual Review of Sociology* 20, 359–81.

CHERLIN, A. J., F. F. FURSTENBERG, JR., P. L. CHASE-LANSDALE, K. E. KIERNAN, P. K. ROBINS, D. R. MORRISON, AND J. O. TEITLER. 1991. Longitudinal studies of effects of divorce on children in Great Britain and the United States. *Science,* June 7, 1386–89.

CHESHIRE, T. C. 2001. Cultural transmission in urban American Indian families. *American Behavioral Scientist* 44 (May): 1528–35.

CHESLER, P. 2002. *Woman's inhumanity to woman.* New York: Thunder's Mouth/Nation.

CHEVAN, A. 1996. As cheaply as one: Cohabitation in the older population. *Journal of Marriage and the Family* 58 (Aug.): 656–67.

CHICAGO COUNCIL ON FOREIGN RELATIONS. 2002. Worldviews 2002: American public opinion and foreign policy. www.worldviews.org/detailreports/usreport/html/ch5s5.html (accessed Aug. 15, 2003).

Child fatalities fact sheet. 2000. National Clearinghouse on Child Abuse and Neglect Information, Washington, DC. www.calib.com/nccanch/pubs/factsheets/fatality.htm (accessed Oct. 18, 2000).

Child welfare and chemical dependency fact sheet. 2001. Child Welfare League of America. www.cwla.org/programs/chemical/aodcwfactsheet.htm (accessed Sept. 19, 2003).

Child welfare outcomes: 1998 annual report. 2000. Washington, DC: Department of Health and Human Services.

CHILDREN NOW. 1998. A different world: Children's perceptions of race and class in the media, 1998. www.childrennow.org/redesigns/media/mc98/MC98page6.html (accessed Aug. 24, 2000).

CHILDREN'S DEFENSE FUND. 2000a. *The state of America's children yearbook 2000.* Washington, DC: Children's Defense Fund.

CHILDREN'S DEFENSE FUND. 2000b. Where America stands. www.childrensdefense.org/facts_america98.html (accessed Aug. 12, 2000).

CHILDREN'S DEFENSE FUND. 2002. *The state of children in America's union.* www.childrensdefense.org/pdf/minigreenbook.pdf (accessed Aug. 25, 2003).

CHILDREN'S DEFENSE FUND. 2003a. Analysis: Number of black children in extreme poverty hits record high. www.childrensdefense.org/pdf/extreme_poverty.pdf (accessed Aug. 25, 2003).

CHILDREN'S DEFENSE FUND. 2003b. Moments in America for children. www.childrensdefense.org/factsfigures_moments.htm (accessed Aug. 29, 2003).

CHION-KENNEY, L. 1991. Parents of divorce. *Washington Post*, May 6, B5.

CHISHOLM, P., AND S. D. DRIEDGER. 1994. Paying for the children of divorce. *Maclean's*, Jan. 10, 36–37.

CHO, D. 2003. For Koreans, changes in store; N. Va. grocery, churches reflect shifts in community. *Washington Post*, Jan. 13, A1. www.washingtonpost.com/wp-dyn/articles/A47604-2003Jan12.html?referer=email (accessed Jan. 13, 2003).

CHO, W., AND S. E. CROSS. 1995. Taiwanese love styles and their association with self-esteem and relationship quality. *Genetic, Social, and General Psychology Monographs* 121: 283–309.

CHOI, N. G. 1992. Correlates of the economic status of widowed and divorced elderly women. *Journal of Family Issues* 12 (Mar.): 38–54.

CHOICE, P., AND L. K. LAMKE. 1997. A conceptual approach to understanding abused women's stay/leave decisions. *Journal of Family Issues* 18 (May): 290–314.

Choices. 2000. *Public Perspective* 11 (July/Aug.): 22.

CHRISTENSON, E. 2003. What women want. *Newsweek*, Feb. 17, 11.

CHRISTOPHER, F. S. 2001. *To dance the dance: A symbolic interactional exploration of premarital sexuality.* Mahwah, NJ: Erlbaum.

CHRISTOPHER, F. S., AND T. S. KISLER. In press. Sexual aggression in romantic relationships. In *The handbook of sexuality in close relationships*, eds. J. Harvey, A. Wenzel, and S. Sprecher. Mahwah, NJ: Erlbaum.

CHRISTOPHER, F. S., AND S. SPRECHER. 2001. Sexuality in marriage, dating, and other relationships: A decade review. In *Understanding families into the new millennium: A decade in review*, ed. R. M. Milardo, 218–36. Minneapolis: National Council on Family Relations.

CHU, H. 2001. Chinese psychiatrists decide homosexuality isn't abnormal: New guidelines are hailed as a "leap forward" bringing nation more in line with the West. *Los Angeles Times*, Mar. 6, A1.

CHUN, H., AND I. LEE. 2001. Why do married men earn more: Productivity or marriage selection? *Economic Inquiry* 39 (Apr.): 307–19.

CLARK, C. L., P. R. SHAVER, AND M. F. ABRAHAMS. 1999. Strategic behaviors in romantic relationship initiation. *Personality and Social Psychology Bulletin* 25: 707–20.

CLARK, J. M. 1999. *Doing the work of love: Men & commitment in same-sex couples.* Harriman, TN: Men's Studies Press.

CLARK, K. 2002. Mommy's home. *U.S. News & World Report*, Nov. 25, 32–38.

CLARKE, J. W. 1990. *On being mad or merely angry: John W. Hinckley, Jr., and other dangerous people.* Princeton, NJ: Princeton University Press.

CLARKE, S. C. 1995a. Advance report of final divorce statistics, 1989 and 1990. *Monthly Vital Statistics Report* 43 (9(S)), Mar. 22. Centers for Disease Control and Prevention.

CLARKE, S. C., AND B. F. WILSON. 1994. The relative stability of remarriages: A cohort approach using vital statistics. *Family Relations* 43 (July): 305–10.

CLARKSON, F. 2002. Priest group launches anti-sex-ed campaign. *Women's E-News*, Nov. 14. www.womensnews.org/article.cfm/dyn/aid/1105 (accessed Nov. 15, 2002).

CLAYTON, M. 2002. Has equality in sports gone too far? *Christian Science Monitor*, Dec. 27, 1, 4.

CLEAVER, J. Y. 1999. Good old dad. *American Demographics* 20 (June): 59–63.

CLEMENTS, M. 1994. Sex in America today. *Parade Magazine*, Aug. 7, 4–7.

CLEMENTS, M. 1996. Sex after 65. *Parade Magazine*, Mar. 17, 4–6.

CLEMETSON, L. 1999. Haunted by a painful history. *Newsweek*, Feb. 22, 46–47.

CLEMETSON, L. 2000. Grandma knows best. *Newsweek*, June 12, 60–61.

CLUNIS, D. M., AND G. D. GREEN. 2000. *Lesbian couples: A guide to creating healthy relationships.* Seattle: Seal.

CLYMER, A. 2002. Critics say government deleted Web site material to push abstinence. *New York Times.* www.nytimes.com/2002/11/26/national/26ABST.html?tntemail0 (accessed Nov. 27, 2002).

COATES, D. L. 1999. The cultured and culturing aspects of romantic experience in adolescence. In *The development of romantic relationships in adolescence*, eds. W. Furman, B. B. Bradford, and C. Feiring, 330–63. New York: Cambridge University Press.

COEYMAN, M. 2002. In Japan, life without children is savored with guilt. *Christian Science Monitor*, Mar. 27, 8.

COHAN, C. I., AND S. KLEINBAUM. 2002. Toward a greater understanding of the cohabitation effect: Premarital cohabitation and marital communication. *Journal of Marriage and Family* 64 (Feb.): 180–92.

COHEN, C. E. 1994. The trailing-spouse dilemma. *Working Woman* (Mar.): 69–70.

COHEN, T. F. 1993. What do fathers provide? Reconsidering the economic and nurturant dimensions of men as parents. In *Men, work, and family*, ed. J. C. Hood, 1–22. Thousand Oaks, CA: Sage.

COHN, D. 2000. Census complaints hit home. *Washington Post*, May 4, A9.

COHN, D. 2002. Cities and suburbs are trading paces: Young singles, other "non-families" taking over outer areas, study shows. *Washington Post*, Feb. 6, A3.

COHN, L. 2003. One child, four parents. *Christian Science Monitor*, Feb. 19, 11–13.

COLAPINTO, J. 1997. The true story of John/Joan. *Rolling Stone* (Dec. 11): 54–73, 92–97.

COLE, A. 1996. Yours, mine and ours. *Modern Maturity* (Sep./Oct.): 12, 14–15.

COLE, M. G., AND N. DENDUKURI. 2003. Risk factors for depression among elderly community subjects: A systematic review and meta-analysis. *American Journal of Psychiatry* 160 (June): 1147–56.

COLEMAN, F. 1994. Political power is only half the battle. *U.S. News & World Report*, June 13, 58.

COLEMAN, M., AND L. H. GANONG. 1991. Remarriage and stepfamily research in the 1980s. In *Contemporary families: Looking forward, looking back*, ed. A. Booth, 192–207. Minneapolis: National Council on Family Relations.

COLEMAN, M., L. H. GANONG, AND M. FINE. 2002. Reinvestigating remarriage: Another decade of progress. In *Understanding families into the new millennium: A decade in review*, ed. R. M. Milardo, 507–26. Minneapolis: National Council on Family Relations.

COLEMAN, M., L. H. GANONG, AND C. GOODWIN. 1994. The presentation of stepfamilies in marriage and family textbooks: A reexamination. *Family Relations* 43 (July): 289–97.

COLEMAN, M., L. H. GANONG, AND S. WEAVER. 2001. Relationship maintenance and enhancement in remarried families. In *Close romantic relationships: Maintenance and enhancement*, eds. J. H. Harvey and A. Wenzel, 255–76. Mahwah, NJ: Erlbaum.

COLEY, R. L. 2002. What mothers teach, what daughters learn: Gender mistrust and self-sufficiency among low-income women. In *Just living together: Implications of cohabitation on families, children, and social policy*, eds. A. Booth and A. C. Crouter, 97–106. Mahwah, NJ: Erlbaum.

COLLIER, J. 1947. *The Indians of the Americas.* New York: Norton.

COLLINS, N. L., C. DUNKEL-SCHETTER, M. LOBEL, AND S. C. SCRIMSHAW. 1993. Social support in pregnancy: Psychosocial correlates of birth outcomes and postpartum depression. *Journal of Personality and Social Psychology* 65: 1243–58.

COLLINS, W. A., E. E. MACCOBY, L. STEINBERG, E. M. HETHERINGTON, AND M. H. BORNSTEIN. 2000. Contemporary research on parenting: The case for nature and nurture. *American Psychologist* 55 (Feb.): 218–32.

COLLISON, M. N.-K. 1993. A sure-fire winner is to tell her you love her; women fall for it all the time. In *Women's studies: Thinking women*, eds. J. Wetzel, M. L. Espenlaub, M. A. Hagen, A. B. McElhiney, and C. B. Williams, 228–30. Dubuque, IA: Kendall/Hunt.

COLTRANE, S. 1996. *Family man: Fatherhood, housework, and gender equality.* New York: Oxford University Press.

COLTRANE, S. 1998. *Gender and families.* Thousand Oaks, CA: Pine Forge.

COLTRANE, S. 2000. Research on household labor: Modeling and measuring the social embeddedness of routine family work. *Journal of Marriage and the Family* 62 (Nov.): 1208–33.

COLTRANE, S., AND E. O. VALDEZ. 1993. Reluctant compliance: Work–family role allocation in dual-earner Chicano families. In *Men, work, and family*, ed. J. C. Hood, 151–75. Beverly Hills, CA: Sage.

Come here often? 2002. *Public Perspective* 13 (Sep./Oct.): 52.

COMIJS, H. C., A. M. POT, H. H. SMIT, AND C. JONKER. 1998. Elder abuse in the community: Prevalence and consequences. *Journal of American Geriatrics Society* 46 (7): 885–88.

CONGER, R. D., AND K. J. CONGER. 2002. Resilience in Midwestern families: Selected findings from the first decade of a prospective, longitudinal study. *Journal of Marriage and the Family* 64 (May): 361–73.

CONLEY, D. 1999. *Being black, living in the red: Race, wealth, and social policy in America.* Berkeley: University of California Press.

CONLIN, M. 2001. Taking precautions—or harassing workers? *Business Week*, Dec. 3, 84.

CONLIN, M. 2002. The big squeeze on workers. *Business Week*, May 13, 96–97.

CONLIN, M. 2003a. For gen X, it's paradise lost. *Business Week*, June 30, 72–74.

CONLIN, M. 2003b. The new gender gap. *Business Week*, May 26, 75–78.

CONLIN, M., J. MERRITT, AND L. HIMELSTEIN. 2002. Mommy is really home from work. *Business Week*, Nov. 25, 101–3.

CONNELLY, J. 1989. The CEO's second wife. *Fortune*, Aug. 28, 53–62.

CONNER, K. A. 1992. *Aging America: Issues facing an aging society.* Upper Saddle River, NJ: Prentice Hall.

CONNOLLY, C. 2003. Texas teaches abstinence, with mixed grades. *Washington Post*, Jan. 21, A1.

COOK, C. D. 2002. Street corner, incorporated. *Mother Jones* (Mar./Apr.): 65–69.

COOK, G. 2003. Campuses may be developing tactics to hide rapes. *Women's E-News*, May 25. www.womensenews.com/article.cfm/dyn/aid/1342/context/cover/ (accessed May 26, 2003).

COOK, S. 2001. Deciding it's ok to wait. *Christian Science Monitor*, Feb. 28, 15, 18–19.

COOKSEY, E. C., AND P. H. CRAIG. 1998. Parenting from a distance: The effects of paternal characteristics on contact between nonresidential fathers and their children. *Demography* 35 (May): 187–200.

COOLIDGE, S. D. 1998. Harassment hits higher profile. *Christian Science Monitor*, Mar. 2, B4–B5.

COOMBS, R. H. 1991. Marital status and personal well-being: A literature review. *Family Relations* 40 (Jan.): 97–102.

COONTZ, S. 1992. *The way we never were: American families and the nostalgia trap.* New York: Basic Books.

COONTZ, S. 1997. *The way we really are: Coming to terms with America's changing families.* New York: Basic Books.

COOPER, R. S., J. S. KAUFMAN, AND R. WARD. 2003. Race and genomics. *New England Journal of Medicine* 348 (Mar. 20): 1166–70.

CORDES, H. 2003. Doping kids. *Mother Jones* (Sep./Oct.): 17–18.

CORNELIUS, M. D., AND N. L. DAY. 2000. The effects of tobacco use during and after pregnancy on exposed children: Relevance of findings for alcohol research. *Alcohol Research & Health* 24 (4): 242–49.

COSE, E. 1995. Black men & black women. *Newsweek*, June 5, 66–69.

COSE, E. 1999. Deciphering the code of the street. *Newsweek*, Aug. 30, 33.

COSE, E. 2003. The black gender gap. *Newsweek*, Mar. 3, 46–51.

COTT, N. F. 1976. Eighteenth century family and social life revealed in Massachusetts divorce records. *Journal of Social History* 10 (Fall): 20–43.

COTT, N. F. 1977. *The bonds of womanhood.* New Haven, CT: Yale University Press.

COTT, N. F., AND E. H. PLECK, EDS. 1979. *A heritage of her own: Toward a new social history of American women.* New York: Simon & Schuster.

COTTEN, S. R. 1999. Marital status and mental health revisited: Examining the importance of risk factors and resources. *Family Relations* 48 (July): 225–33.

COTTLE, T. J. 1994. Women who kill. *North American Review* 279 (May): 4–9.

COUGLE, J. R., D. C. REARDON, AND P. K. COLEMAN. 2003. Depression associated with abortion and childbirth: A long-term analysis of the NLSY cohort. *Medical Science Monitor* 9 (4): CR105–12.

COUNCIL ON SCIENTIFIC AFFAIRS. 1993. Adolescents as victims of family violence. *Journal of the American Medical Association*, Oct. 20, 1850–56.

COUPER, D. P., AND N. W. SHEEHAN. 1987. Family dynamics for caregivers: An educational model. *Family Relations* 36: 181–86.

COVEL, S. 2003. Cheating hearts. *American Demographics* 25 (June): 16.

COVEL, S. 2003. The heart never forgets. *American Demographics* 25 (July/Aug.): 15.

COWAN, C. P., AND P. A. COWAN. 1992. *When partners become parents: The big life change for couples.* New York: HarperCollins.

COWAN, C. P., AND P. A. COWAN. 2000. *When partners become parents: The big life change for couples.* Mahwah, NJ: Erlbaum.

COWGILL, D. O. 1986. *Aging around the world.* Belmont, CA: Wadsworth.

COWLEY, G. 2000. Alzheimer's: Unlocking the mystery. *Newsweek*, Jan. 31, 46–51.

COWLEY, G., WITH M. HAGER AND J. C. RAMO. 1993. The view from the womb. *Newsweek*, Nov. 8, 64.

COWLEY, G., AND K. SPRINGEN. 1997. Multiplying the risks. *Newsweek*, Dec. 1, 66.

COX, C. 1993. *The frail elderly: Problems, needs, and community responses.* Westport, CT: Auburn House.

COX, C. B., ED. 2000. *To grandmother's house we go and stay: Perspectives on custodial grandparents.* New York: Springer.

COX, E. R., B. R. MOTHERAL, R. R. HENDERSON, AND D. MAGER. 2003. Geographic variation in the prevalence of stimulant medication use among children 5 to 14 years old: Results from a commercially insured US sample. *Pediatrics* 111 (Feb.): 237–43.

COY, P., AND L. COHN. 2003. Stats: Now you see 'em. . . . *Business Week*, Feb. 10, 10.

COYNE, A. C., W. E. REICHMAN, AND L. J. BERBIG. 1993. The relationship between dementia and elder abuse. *American Journal of Psychiatry* 150 (Apr.): 643–46.

CRABB, P. B., AND D. BIELAWSKI. 1994. The social representation of material culture and gender in children's books. *Sex Roles* 30 (1/2): 69–79.

CRAMER, J. C., AND K. B. MCDONALD. 1996. Kin support and family stress: Two sides to early childbearing and support networks. *Human Organization* 55 (Summer): 160–69.

CRAWFORD, D. W., R. M. HOUTS, T. L. HUSTON, AND L. J. GEORGE. 2002. Compatibility, leisure, and satisfaction in marital relationships. *Journal of Marriage and Family* 64 (May): 433–49.

CRAWFORD, M. 1995. *Talking difference: On gender and language.* Thousand Oaks, CA: Sage.

CREIGHTON, L. L. 1991. Silent saviors. *U.S. News & World Report*, Dec. 16, 80–89.

CRENSHAW, A. R. 1992. Assessing the political power of seniors. *Washington Post Family and Retirement Supplement*, Apr. 29, 4–7.

CRISPELL, D. 1992. Myths of the 1950s. *American Demographics* (Aug.): 38–43.

CRISPELL, D. 1993. Planning no family, now or ever. *American Demographics*, 6 (Oct.): 23–24.

CRITTENDEN, A. 2001. *The price of motherhood: Why the most important job in the world is still the least valued.* New York: Metropolitan.

CRITTENDEN, D. 1999. *What our mothers didn't tell us: Why happiness eludes the modern woman.* New York: Simon & Schuster.

CRNIC, K., AND C. LOW. 2002. Everyday stresses and parenting. In *Handbook of parenting*, 2nd ed., Vol. 5: *Practical issues in parenting*, ed. M. H. Bornstein, 243–68. Mahwah, NJ: Erlbaum.

CROHAN, S. E. 1996. Marital quality and conflict across the transition to parenthood in African American and white couples. *Journal of Marriage and the Family* 58 (Nov.): 933–44.

CROSBIE-BURNETT, M., AND J. GILES-SIMS. 1994. Adolescent adjustment and stepparenting styles. *Family Relations* 43 (Oct.): 394–99.

CROSBIE-BURNETT, M., AND E. A. LEWIS. 1993. Use of African-American family structures and functioning to address the challenges of European-American postdivorce families. *Family Relations* 42 (July): 243–48.

CROSBIE-BURNETT, M., AND K. M. MCCLINTIC. 2000. Remarriage and recoupling: A stress perspective. In *Families & change: Coping with stressful events and transitions*, 2nd ed., eds. P. C. McKenry and S. J. Price, 303–32. Thousand Oaks, CA: Sage.

CROSBY, F. J. 1991a. *Illusion and disillusion: The self in love and marriage*, 5th ed. Belmont, CA: Wadsworth.

CROSBY, F. J. 1991b. *Juggling: The unexpected advantages of balancing career and home for women and their families.* New York: Free Press.

CROSNOE, R., AND G. H. ELDER. 2002. Adolescent twins and emotional distress: The interrelated influence of nonshared environment and social structure. *Child Development* 73 (Nov./Dec.): 1761–74.

CROSS, S. E., AND L. MADSON. 1997. Models of the self: Self-construals and gender. *Psychological Bulletin*, 122: 5–37.

CROSS, T. L. 1998. Understanding family resiliency from a relational world view. In *Resiliency in Native American and immigrant families*, eds. H. I. McCubbin, E. A. Thompson, A. I. Thompson, and J. E. Fromer, 143–57. Thousand Oaks, CA: Sage.

CROSSEN, C. 1994. *Tainted truth: The manipulation of fact in America.* New York: Simon & Schuster.

CROUTER, A. C., M. F. BUMPUS, M. R. HEAD, AND S. M. MCHALE. 2001. Implications of overwork and overload for the quality of men's family relationships. *Journal of Marriage and Family* 63 (May): 404–16.

CROWELL, J. A., AND E. WATERS. 1994. Bowlby's theory grown up: The role of attachment in adult love relationships. *Psychological Inquiry* 5 (1): 31–34.

CROWLEY, K., M. A. CALLANAN, H. R. TENENBAUM, AND E. ALLEN. 2001. Parents explain more often to boys than to girls during shared scientific thinking. *Psychological Science* 49 (May): 258–61.

CRUZ, S. 2003. Home health care exec hit with $1 million verdict in sex discrimination case. *Star Tribune*, Mar. 12. www.startribune.com/stories/535/3749479.html (accessed Mar. 13, 2003).

CUBER, J., AND P. HAROFF. 1965. *Sex and the significant Americans.* Baltimore: Penguin.

CUE, K. L., W. H. GEORGE, AND J. NORRIS. 1996. Women's appraisals of sexual-assault risk in dating situations. *Psychology of Women Quarterly* 20 (Dec.): 487–504.

CUMMINGS, E. M., AND P. DAVIES. 1994. *Children and marital conflict: The impact of family dispute and resolution.* New York: Guilford.

CUNNINGHAM, J. D., AND J. K. ANTILL. 1995. Current trends in nonmarital cohabitation: In search of the POSSLQ. In *Under-studied relationships: Off the beaten track*, eds. J. T. Wood and S. Duck, 148–72. Thousand Oaks, CA: Sage.

CURRY, A. 2002. McCaughey septuplets turn five. MSNBC News, Nov. 19. www.msnbc.com/news/836810.asp#BODY (accessed Sep. 25, 2003).

CURTIS, C. M., AND R. ALEXANDER, JR. 1996. The Multiethnic Placement Act: Implications for social work practice. *Child and Adolescent Social Work Journal* 13 (Oct.): 401–10.

CURTIS, J. 1998. *Making and breaking families: The way ahead for parents and their children.* New York: Free Association Press.

CUTRONA, C. E. 1996. *Social support in couples: Marriage as a resource in times of stress.* Thousand Oaks, CA: Sage.

Cyberstalking. 2000. www.ncvc.org/special/cyber_stk.htm (accessed Aug. 30, 2000).

Daily reproductive health report. 2002. The Henry Kaiser Family Foundation. www.kaisernetwork.org/daily_reports/rep_index.cfm?DR_ID=14169 (accessed Mar. 16, 2003).

DAINTON, M. 1993. The myths and misconceptions of the stepmother identity: Descriptions and prescriptions for identity management. *Family Relations* 42 (Jan.): 93–98.

DALLA, R. L., AND W. C. GAMBLE. 1997. Exploring factors related to parenting competence among Navajo teenage mothers: Dual techniques of inquiry. *Family Relations* 46 (Apr.): 113–21.

DALSIMER, M. 1981. Bible communists: Female socialization and family life in the Oneida Community. In *Family life in America: 1620–2000*, eds. M. Albin and D. Cavallo, 30–46. New York: Revisionary Press.

DALY, K. J. 1999. Crisis of genealogy: Facing the challenges of infertility. In *The dynamics of resilient families*, eds. H. I. McCubbin, E. A. Thompson, A. I. Thompson, and J. A. Futrell, 1–40. Thousand Oaks, CA: Sage.

DALY, K. J. 2001. Deconstructing family time: From ideology to lived experience. *Journal of Marriage and the Family* 63 (May): 283–94.

DANIEL, J. L., AND J. E. DANIEL. 1999. African-American childrearing: The context of a hot stove. In *Communication, race, and family: Exploring communication in black, white, and biracial families*, eds. T. J. Socha and R. C. Diggs, 25–43. Mahwah, NJ: Erlbaum.

DANIELS, K. R. 1994. Adoption and donor insemination: Factors influencing couples' choices. *Child Welfare* 73 (Jan./Feb.): 5–14.

DANZIGER, S. K., AND S. DANZIGER. 1993. Child poverty and public policy: Toward a comprehensive antipoverty agenda. *Daedalus* 122 (Winter): 57–84.

Dating violence. 2000. Centers for Disease Control and Prevention. www.cdc.gov/ncipc/factsheets/datviol.htm (accessed July 3, 2003).

DAUER, S. 2002. Pakistan: Violence against women continues. *Interact* (Summer): 1, 5.

DAVEY, M., AND D. LEONHARDT. 2003. Jobless and hopeless, many quit the labor force. *New York Times*, Apr. 27. www.nytimes.com/2003/04/27/national/27JOBS.html?th (accessed Apr. 28, 2003).

DAVIDSON, J. K., SR., AND C. A. DARLING. 1995. Religiosity and the sexuality of women: Sexual behavior and sexual satisfaction revisited. *Journal of Sex Research* 32: 235–43.

DAVIES, C., AND D. WILLIAMS. 2002. *The grandparent study 2002 report.* AARP. http://research.aarp.org/general/gp_2002.pdf (accessed Oct. 10, 2003).

DAVIS, E. C., AND L. V. FRIEL. 2001. Adolescent sexuality: Disentangling the effects of family structure and family context. *Journal of Marriage and Family* 63 (Aug.): 669–81.

DAVIS, K. E. 1985. Near and dear: Friendship and love compared. *Psychology Today* 19: 22–30.

DAVIS, L. E., J. H. WILLIAMS, S. EMERSON, AND M. HOURD-BRYANT. 2000. Factors contributing to partner commitment among unmarried African Americans. *Social Work Research* 24 (Mar.): 4–15.

DAVIS, M. 2002. Champion lovers share 83 years of marriage. *Lexington Herald-Leader*, Apr. 9. www.kri.com/papers/greatcolumns/davis2.html (accessed July 23, 2003).

DAVIS, P. W. 1994. The changing meanings of spanking. In *Troubling children*, ed. J. Best, 133–53. New York: Aldine de Gruyter.

DAVIS, P. W. 1996. Threats of corporal punishment as verbal aggression: A naturalistic study. *Child Abuse & Neglect* 20 (4): 289–304.

DAVIS, S. 1990. Men as success objects and women as sex objects: A study of personal advertisements. *Sex Roles* 23 (1/2): 43–50.

DAVIS-KIMBALL, J. 1997. Warrior women of the Eurasian steppes. *Archaeology* 50 (Jan.): 44–48.

DAVIS-PACKARD, K. 2000. Why the number of teen mothers is falling. *Christian Science Monitor,* Aug. 15, 1, 11.

DAWSEY, D. 1996. *Living to tell about it: Young black men in America speak their piece.* New York: Anchor.

DAWSON, G., AND R. GLAUBMAN. 2000. *Life is so good.* New York: Random House.

DAWSON, J. M., AND P. A. LANGAN. 1994. *Murder in families.* Washington, DC: Bureau of Justice Statistics.

DAY, R. D. 1995. Family-systems theory. In *Research and theory in family science,* eds. R. D. Day, K. R. Gilbert, B. H. Settles, and W. R. Burr, 91–101. Pacific Grove, CA: Brooks/Cole.

DAY, R. D. 2002. *Introduction to family processes.* Mahwah, NJ: Erlbaum.

DAY, R. D., G. W. PETERSON, AND C. MCCRACKEN. 1998. Predicting spanking of younger and older children by mothers and fathers. *Journal of Marriage and the Family* 60 (Feb.): 79–94.

DAY, S. 2003. Prosecutors call Tyson smuggling trial a case of "corporate greed." *New York Times,* Feb. 6. www.nytimes.com/2003/02/06/national/06TYSO.html?th (accessed Feb. 6, 2003).

DE ANGELIS, C. D. 2000. Women in academic medicine: New insights, same sad news. *New England Journal of Medicine* 342 (Feb. 10): 426–27.

DE LA CANCELA, V. 1994. "Coolin": The psychosocial communication of African and Latino men. In *African American males: A critical link in the African American family,* ed. D. J. Jones, 33–44. New Brunswick, NJ: Transaction.

DE MORAES, L. 1999. TV's open closet. *Washington Post,* Mar. 3, C1, C3.

DE MUNCK, V. C. 1998. Lust, love, and arranged marriages in Sri Lanka. In *Romantic love and sexual behavior: Perspectives from the social sciences,* ed. V. C. de Munck, 295–300. Westport, CT: Praeger.

DE WITT, P. M. 1994. Breaking up is hard to do. *American Demographics,* reprint package 8–12.

DEAL, J. E., M. STANLEY-HAGAN, AND J. C. ANDERSON. 1992. The marital relationships in remarried families. *Monographs of the Society for Research in Child Development* 57: 2–3, serial no. 227.

DEANE, C., ET AL. 2000. Leaving tradition behind: Latinos in the great American melting pot. *Public Perspective* 11 (May/June): 5–7, 10.

Dear Ann. 2001. *Washington Post,* Apr. 13, C7.

DEBIAGGI, S. D. 2002. *Changing gender roles: Brazilian immigrant families in the U.S.* New York: LFB Scholarly Publishing.

DEBORD, K. B., and J. T. R. DE ATILES. 1999. Latino parents: Unique preferences for learning about parenting. *Forum for Family and Consumer Issues* 4 (Spring): 1–10. www.ces.ncsu.edu/depts/fcs/pub/1999/latino.html (accessed Mar. 14, 2000).

DECALMER, P., AND F. GLENDENNING, EDS. 1993. *The mistreatment of elderly people.* Thousand Oaks, CA: Sage.

Deck the box. 1999. *American Demographics* 21 (Nov.): 72.

DECKER, J. D. 2002. Women are the show, men get the dough. *Christian Science Monitor,* June 28, 12.

DEGLER, C. 1981. *At odds: Women and the family in America from the Revolution to the present.* New York: Oxford University Press.

DEGLER, C. N. 1983. The emergence of the modern American family. In *The American family in social-historical perspective,* 3rd ed., ed. M. Gordon, 61–79. New York: St. Martin's.

DEGROOT, J. M., S. KENNEDY, G. RODIN, AND G. MCVEY. 1992. Correlates of sexual abuse in women with anorexia nervosa and bulimia nervosa. *Canadian Journal of Psychiatry* 37 (Sept.): 516–18.

DEL CASTILLO, R. G. 1984. *La familia: Chicano families in the urban Southwest, 1848 to the present.* Notre Dame, IN: University of Notre Dame Press.

DEL PINAL, J., AND A. SINGER. 1997. Generations of diversity: Latinos in the United States. *Population Bulletin* 52 (Oct.). Washington, DC: Population Reference Bureau.

DELAIRE, T., AND A. KALIL. 2002. *How do cohabiting couples with children spend their money?* University of Chicago, Harris Graduate School of Public Policy Studies. http://harrisschool.uchicago.edu/wp/02-04.html (accessed July 14, 2003).

DELISLE, S. 1997. Preserving reproductive choice: Preventing STD-related infertility in women. *Siecus Report* 25 (Mar.): 18–21.

DELLMANN-JENKINS, M., M. BLANKEMEYER, AND O. PINKARD. 2000. Young adult children and grandchildren in primary caregiver roles to older relatives and their service needs. *Family Relations* 49 (Apr.): 177–86.

DELSOL, C., G. MARGOLIN, AND R. S. JOHN. 2003. A typology of maritally violent men and correlates of violence in a community sample. *Journal of Marriage and Family* 65 (Aug.): 635–51.

DEMARIS, A. 2001. The influence of intimate violence on transitions out of cohabitation. *Journal of Marriage and Family* 63 (Feb.): 235–46.

DEMARIS, A., M. L. BENSON, G. L. FOX, T. HILL, AND J. VAN WYK. 2003. Distal and proximal factors in domestic violence: A test of an integrated model. *Journal of Marriage and Family* 65 (Aug.): 652–67.

DEMARIS, A., AND W. MACDONALD. 1993. Premarital cohabitation and marital instability: A test of the unconventionality hypothesis. *Journal of Marriage and the Family* 55 (May): 399–407.

DEMO, D. H., AND A. C. ACOCK. 1996a. Family structure, family process, and adolescent well-being. *Journal of Research on Adolescence* 6 (4): 457–88.

DEMO, D. H., AND A. C. ACOCK. 1996b. Singlehood, marriage, and remarriage. *Journal of Family Issues* 17 (May): 388–407.

DEMOS, J. 1970. *A little commonwealth: Family life in Plymouth colony.* New York: Oxford University Press.

DEMOS, J. 1986. *Past, present, and personal: The family and the life course in American history.* New York: Oxford University Press.

DENAVAS-WALT, C., R. CLEVELAND, AND B. H. WEBSTER, JR. 2003. *Income in the United States: 2002.* U.S. Census Bureau, Current Population Reports, P60-221. Washington, DC: U.S. Government Printing Office.

DENAVAS-WALT, C., AND R. CLEVELAND. 2002. *Money income in the United States: 2001.* U.S. Census Bureau, Current Population Reports, P60-218. http://landview.census.gov/prod/2002pubs/p60-218.pdf (accessed Apr. 10, 2003).

DERLEGA, V. J., S. METTS, S. PETRONIO, AND S. T. MARGULIS. 1993. *Self-disclosure.* Thousand Oaks, CA: Sage.

DESTENO, D., M. Y. BARTLETT, J. BRAVERMAN, AND P. SALOVEY. 2002. Sex differences in jealousy: Evolutionary mechanism or artifact of measurement? *Journal of Personality and Social Psychology* 83 (Nov.): 1103–16.

DEVALL, E., Z. STONEMAN, AND G. BRODY. 1986. The impact of divorce and maternal employment on pre-adolescent children. *Family Relations* 35 (Jan.): 153–60.

DEVOR, H. 1997. *FTM: Female-to-male transsexuals in society.* Bloomington: Indiana University Press.

DIAMOND, M., AND K. SIGMUNDSON. 1997. Sex reassignment at birth: Long-term review and clinical implications. *Archives of Pediatrics & Adolescent Medicine* 15 (Mar.): 298–304.

DIBACCO, T. V. 1994. Tracing the trail of Alzheimer's. *Washington Post Health Supplement,* Nov. 29, 9.

DICKERSON, B. J. 1995. Introduction. In *African American single mothers: Understanding their lives and families,* ed. B. J. Dickerson, ix–xxx. Thousand Oaks, CA: Sage.

DICKEY, C., AND D. MCGINN. 2001. Meet the bin Ladens. *Newsweek,* Oct. 15, 55–56.

DIENER, M. L., S. C. MANGELSDORF, J. L. MCHALE, AND C. A. FROSCH. 2002. Infants' behavioral strategies for emotion regulation with fathers and mothers: Associations with emotional expressions and attachment quality. *Infancy* 3 (May): 153–74.

DIETZ, T. L. 1998. An examination of violence and gender role portrayals in video games: Implications for gender socialization and aggressive behavior. *Sex Roles* 38 (Mar.): 425–42.

Differences within. 2000. *Public Perspective* 11 (May/June): 12.

DIGGS, N. B. 1998. *Steel butterflies: Japanese women and the American experience.* Albany: State University of New York Press.

DILLER, L. H. 1998. *Running on Ritalin: A physician reflects on children, society, and performance in a pill.* New York: Bantam.

DILLIN, J. 2001. Immigration proposals get mixed reviews. *Christian Science Monitor,* Mar. 20, 3.

DILLON, P. A., AND R. E. EMERY. 1996. Divorce mediation and resolution of child custody disputes: Long-term effects. *American Journal of Orthopsychiatry* 66 (Jan.): 131–40.

DILMAN, I. 1998. *Love: Its forms, dimensions, and paradoxes.* New York: St. Martin's.

DILWORTH-ANDERSON, P., L. M. BURTON, AND W. L. TURNER. 1993. The importance of values in the study of culturally diverse families. *Family Relations* 42 (July): 238–42.

DILWORTH-ANDERSON, P., S. W. WILLIAMS, AND T. COOPER. 1999. The contexts of experiencing emotional distress among family caregivers to elderly African Americans. *Family Relations* 48 (Oct.): 391–96.

Dinky families on the rise in China, survey shows. 2002. Xinhua News Agency. www.humanrights-china.org/news/2002-8-20/200282091021.htm (accessed Aug. 20, 2003).

DINNERSTEIN, M., AND R. WEITZ. 1994. Jane Fonda, Barbara Bush and other aging bodies: Femininity and the limits of resistance. *Feminist Issues* 14 (Fall): 3–24.

DION, K., E. BERSCHEID, AND E. WALSTER. 1972. What is beautiful is good. *Journal of Personality and Social Psychology* 24, 285–90.

DION, M. R., S. L. BRAVER, S. A. WOLCHIK, AND I. N. SANDLER. 1997. Alcohol abuse and psychopathic deviance in noncustodial parents as predictors of child-support payment and visitation. *American Journal of Orthopsychiatry* 67 (Jan.): 70–79.

DIVOKY, D. 2002. Utah women to highlight hazards of polygamy. *Women's E-News.* www.womensenews.org/article.cfm?aid=776 (accessed Jan. 8, 2002).

DIXON, N. 1996. Nike: How cool is exploitation? *Green Left Weekly.* www.greenleft.org.au/back/1996/244/244p28.htm (accessed Sept. 14, 2003).

DO, D. D. 1999. *The Vietnamese Americans.* Westport, CT: Greenwood.

DOHERTY, R. W., E. HATFIELD, K. THOMPSON, AND P. CHOO. 1994. Cultural and ethnic influences on love and attachment. *Personal Relationships* 1: 391–98.

DOHERTY, W. J. 2001. *Take back your marriage: Sticking together in a world that pulls us apart.* New York: Guilford.

DOKA, K. J., AND M. E. MERTZ. 1988. The meaning and significance of great-grandparenthood. *The Gerontologist* 28 (2): 192–96.

Domestic violence against women and girls. 2000. United Nations Children's Fund. www.unicef-icdc.org/pdf/domestic.pdf (accessed Sep. 22, 2000).

DONNELLY, M. 2003. EEOC files suit against LI eatery. *Newsday,* Aug. 6. www.newsday.com/business/printedition/ny-bzeeoc063403968aug06,0,5421168.story?coll=ny-business-print (accessed Aug. 18, 2003).

Donor-egg pregnancies called safe after age 50. 2002. *New York Times,* Nov. 13, A27.

DORF, P. A., J. E. LANDAU, AND M. R. SANDERS. 1996. *Effective family law practice in Maryland.* Eau Claire, WI: National Business Institute.

DORFMAN, L. T., AND C. E. MERTENS. 1990. Kinship relations in retired rural men and women. *Family Relations* 39 (Apr.): 166–73.

DORKENOO, E., AND S. ELWORTHY. 1992. *Female genital mutilation: Proposals for change.* London: Minority Rights Group.

DORRINGTON, C. 1995. Central American refugees in Los Angeles: Adjustment of children and families. In *Understanding Latino families: Scholarship, policy, and practice,* ed. R. E. Zambrana, 107–29. Thousand Oaks, CA: Sage.

DORTCH, S. 1995. Mature, active woman seeks educated, healthy man. *American Demographics* 17 (Feb.): 11–12.

DORTCH, S. 1997. Chinese Yellow Pages. *American Demographics* 19 (Oct.): 39.

DOUGLAS, J. D., AND F. C. ATWELL. 1988. *Love, intimacy, and sex.* Beverly Hills, CA: Sage.

DOWD, M. 2002. Men. Listen up. This one's for you. *New York Times,* Apr. 17. www.nytimes.com/2002/04/17/opinion/17DOWD.html?todaysheadlines (accessed Apr. 18, 2002).

DOWNEY, D. B., J. W. AINSWORTH-DARNELL, AND M. J. DUFUR. 1998. Sex of parent and children's well-being in single-parent households. *Journal of Marriage and the Family* 60 (Nov.): 878–93.

DOWNEY, K. 2003. More settle in for a slow job hunt. *Washington Post,* May 8, E3.

DOWNEY, S. 2000. The moving-van wars. *Newsweek,* Feb. 28, 53.

DOWNS, L. 1994. In Japan where mom knows best. *Washington Post Education Review,* Apr. 3, 16.

DOYLE, L. 2001. *The surrendered wife.* New York: Fireside.

Drug facts: Marijuana. 2003. Executive Office of the President, Office of National Drug Control Policy. www.whitehousedrugpolicy.gov/drugfact/marijuana/index.html (accessed Sep. 18, 2003).

DUCK, S. 1998. *Human relationships,* 3rd ed. Thousand Oaks, CA: Sage.

DUNBAR, R. 1995. Are you lonesome tonight? *New Scientist* 145, Feb. 11, 26–31.

DUNCAN, C. M. 1999. *Worlds apart: Why poverty persists in rural America.* New Haven, CT: Yale University Press.

DUNCAN, G., AND K. A. MAGNUSON. 2002. Economics and parenting. *Parenting Science and Practice* 2 (Oct./Nov.): 437–50.

DURAN-AYDINTUG, C., AND K. A. CAUSEY. 1996. Child custody determination: Implications for lesbian mothers. *Journal of Divorce & Remarriage* 25 (1/2): 55–74.

DUSH, K., C. COHAN, AND P. AMATO. 2003. The relationship between cohabitation and marital quality and stability: Change across cohorts? *Journal of Marriage and Family* (Aug.): 539–49.

DUSTER, T. 2001. Buried alive: The concept of race in science. *Chronicle of Higher Education,* Sept. 14, B11.

DUTTON, D. G., AND S. K. GOLANT. 1995. *The batterer: A psychological profile.* New York: Basic Books.

DUTTON, S. 2001. School colors. *Public Perspective* 12 (May/June): 19–21.

DUVALL, E. M. 1957. *Family development.* Philadelphia: Lippincott.

EAGLY, A. H., AND W. WOOD. 1999. The origins of sex differences in human behavior. *American Psychologist* 54 (June): 408–23.

EARLE, A. M. 1899. *Child life in colonial days.* New York: Macmillan.

EAST, P. L., AND M. E. FELICE. 1996. *Adolescent pregnancy and parenting: Findings from a racially diverse sample.* Mahwah, NJ: Erlbaum.

EBLING, R., AND R. W. LEVENSON. 2003. Who are the marital experts? *Journal of Marriage and Family* 65 (Feb.): 130–42.

ECCLES, J. S., C. FREEDMAN-DOAN, P. FROME, J. JACOBS, and K. S. YOON. 2000. Gender-role socialization in the family: A longitudinal approach. In *The developmental social psychology of gender,* eds. T. Eckes and H. M. Trautner, 333–60. Mahwah, NJ: Erlbaum.

ECKEL, S. 1999. Single mothers, many faces. *American Demographics* 21 (May): 63–66.

ECKERT, P., AND S. MCCONNELL-GINET. 2003. *Language and gender.* New York: Cambridge University Press.

ECKLAND, B. K. 1968. Theories of mate selection. *Eugenics Quarterly* 15 (1): 71–84.

ECONOMIC POLICY INSTITUTE. 2003. Living wage: Frequently asked questions. www.epinet.org/content.cfm/issueguides_livingwage_livingwagefaq (accessed Sep. 9, 2003).

Economy: Limping along. 2003. *Public Perspective* 14 (May/June): 44–45.

EDIN, K., AND L. LEIN. 1997. *Making ends meet: How single mothers survive welfare and low-wage work.* New York: Russell Sage Foundation.

EDMONSTON, B. 1999. The 2000 census challenge. *Population Reference Bureau* 1 (Feb.): 1.

EDMONSTON, B., S. M. LEE, AND J. S. PASSEL. 2002. Recent trends in intermarriage and immigration and their effects on the future racial composition of the U.S. population. In *The new race question: How the census counts multiracial individuals,* eds. J. Perlmann and M. Waters, 227–55. New York: Russell Sage Foundation.

EDWARDS, J. N., AND A. BOOTH. 1994. Sexuality, marriage, and well-being: The middle years. In *Sexuality across the life course,* ed. A. S. Rossi, 233–59. Chicago: University of Chicago Press.

EDWARDS, T. M. 2000. Flying solo. *Time,* Aug. 28, 47–51.

EGAN, T. 2002. Body-conscious boys adopt athletes' taste for steroids. *New York Times,* Nov. 22, A1, A22.

EGGEBEEN, D. J., AND C. KNOESTER. 2001. Does fatherhood matter for men? *Journal of Marriage and Family* 63 (May): 381–93.

EHRENBERG, M. F., M. GEARING-SMALL, M. A. HUNTER, AND B. J. SMALL. 2001. Childcare task division and shared parenting attitudes in dual-earner families with young children. *Family Relations* 50 (Apr.): 143–53.

EHRENREICH, B., AND D. ENGLISH. 1989. Blowing the whistle on the "mommy track." *Ms.* (July/Aug.): 56–58.

EHRENREICH, B., E. HESS, AND G. JACOBS. 1986. *Re-making love: The feminization of sex.* Garden City, NY: Anchor.

EHRENSAFT, M. K., ET AL. 2003. Intergenerational transmission of partner violence: A 20-year prospective study. *Journal of Consulting and Clinical Psychology* 71 (Aug.): 741–53.

EHRHARDT, A. A. 1996. Editorial: Our view of adolescent sexuality—a focus on risk behavior without the developmental context. *American Journal of Public Health* 86 (Nov.): 1523–25.

EHRLICH, A. S. 2000. Power, control, and the mother-in-law problem: Face-offs in the American nuclear family. In *New directions in anthropological kinship,* ed. L. Stone, 175–84. Lanham, MD: Rowman & Littlefield.

EISENBERG, D. 2002. "Ignorant & poor?" *Time* (Feb. 11): 37–39.

EITZEN, D. S., AND M. BACA ZINN. 1994. *Social problems,* 6th ed. Boston: Allyn & Bacon.

ELAM-EVANS, L. D., L. T. STRAUSS, J. HERNDON, W. Y. PARKER, S. WHITEHEAD, AND C. J. BERG. 2002. Abortion surveillance: United States, 1999. *Morbidity and Mortality Weekly Report* 51 (Nov. 29): SS-9. www.cdc.gov/mmwr/PDF/SS/SS5109.pdf (accessed July 25, 2003).

ELBOW, M., AND J. MAYFIELD. 1991. Mothers of incest victims: Villains, victims, or protectors? *Families in Society* 72 (Feb.): 78–86.

ELDER, R. K. 2002. In "Lilo & Stitch," Disney reshapes its female characters. *Baltimore Sun,* June 26, 3E.

ELLIOT, P., AND N. MANDELL. 1995. Feminist theories. In *Feminist issues: Race, class, and sexuality,* ed. N. Mandell, 3–31. Scarborough, Ont.: Prentice Hall Canada.

ELLIOTT, D. 1998. Trying to stand on two feet. *Newsweek,* June 29, 48–49.

ELLIS, A. 1963. *The origins and the development of the incest taboo.* New York: Lyle Stuart.

ELLIS, B., ET AL. 2003. Does father absence place daughters at special risk for early sexual activity and teenage pregnancy? *Child Development* 74 (May): 801–21.

ELLIS, B. J., AND J. GARBER. 2000. Psychosocial antecedents of variation in girls' pubertal timing: Maternal depression, stepfather presence, and marital and family stress. *Child Development* 71 (Mar.): 485–501.

ELLIS, L., P. E. GAY, AND E. PAIGE. 2001. Daily hassles and pleasures across the lifespan. Paper presented at the Annual American Psychological Association meetings, San Francisco.

ELLISON, C. G. 1997. Religious involvement and the subjective quality of family life among African Americans. In *Family life in black America,* eds. R. J. Taylor, J. S. Jackson, and L. M. Chatters, 117–31. Thousand Oaks, CA: Sage.

ELLISON, C. G., T. E. THOMPSON, AND M. L. SEGAL. 1995. Race differences in the parental use of corporal punishment. Unpublished manuscript, University of Texas at Austin.

ELSHTAIN, J. B. 1988. What's the matter with sex today? *Tikkun: A Bimonthly Jewish Critique of Politics, Culture and Society* 3 (3): 42–43.

ELSHTAIN, J. B., E. AIRD, A. ETZIONI, W. GALSTON, M. GLENDON, M. MINOW, AND A. ROSSI. 1993. *A communitarian position paper on the family.* Washington, DC: Communitarian Network.

ELSON, D., AND H. KEKLIK. 2002. *Progress of the world's women: 2002.* www.undp.org/unifem/resources/progressv2 (accessed May 28, 2003).

ELSTER, N., ET AL. 2000. Less is more: The risks of multiple births. *Fertility and Sterility* 74: 617–23.

ELTAHAWY, M. 2000. Giving wives a way out. *U.S. News & World Report,* Mar. 6, 35.

ENGEL, M. 2000. Stepfamilies are not blended. Stepfamily Association of America. www.saafamilies.org/faqs/faqs.htm (accessed Sept. 29, 2003).

ENGLANDER, E. K. 1997. *Understanding violence.* Hillsdale, NJ: Erlbaum.

ERICKSON, M. T. 1993. Rethinking Oedipus: An evolutionary perspective of incest avoidance. *American Journal of Psychiatry* 150 (Mar.): 411–16.

ERICKSON, R. J. 1993. Reconceptualizing family work: The effect of emotion work on perceptions of marital quality. *Journal of Marriage and the Family* 55 (Nov.): 888–900.

ERIKSON, E. 1963. *Childhood and society.* New York: Norton.

ESLER, A. 1994. *The Western world: Prehistory to the present,* 3rd ed. Upper Saddle River, NJ: Prentice Hall.

ESPELAGE, D. L., M. K. HOLT, AND R. R. HENKEL. 2003. Examination of peer-group contextual effects on aggression during early adolescence. *Child Development* 74 (Feb.): 205–20.

ESPINO, R., AND M. M. FRANZ. 2002. Latino phenotypic discrimination revisited: The impact of skin color on occupational status. *Social Science Quarterly* 83 (June): 612–23.

ESPIRITU, Y. L. 1995. *Filipino American lives.* Philadelphia: Temple University Press.

ESTES, A. 2003. Maternity-wear chain is sued over firing. *Boston Globe,* June 26.

ESTES, R. J., AND N. A. WEINER. 2002. The commercial sexual exploitation of children in the U.S., Canada, and Mexico. University of Pennsylvania, School of Social Work. http://caster.ssw.upenn.edu/~restes/CSEC_Files/Abstract_010918.pdf (accessed Sep. 17, 2003).

ESTESS, P. S. 1994. When kids don't leave. *Modern Maturity* (Nov./Dec.): 56, 58, 90.

ETAUGH, C. E., AND M. B. LISS. 1992. Home, school, and playroom: Training grounds for adult gender roles. *Sex Roles* 26 (3/4): 129–47.

EVANS, C. 2000. *Facts about female faculty: 1999–2000 AAUP faculty compensation survey.* www.aaup.org/wsalrep.htm (accessed Oct. 15, 2000).

EVANS, K. 2000. *The lost daughters of China: Abandoned girls, their journey to America, and the search for a missing past.* New York: Tarcher/Putnam.

EVANS, S. 2000. The children of divorce. *Washington Post,* May 9, C4.

EVERETT, C., AND S. V. EVERETT. 1994. *Healthy divorce.* San Francisco: Jossey-Bass.

Facts about eating disorders. 2000. Harvard Eating Disorders Center. www.hedc.org/info.html (accessed Oct. 20, 2000).

Facts for features. 2003. Father's day: June 15, U.S. Census Bureau. www.census.gov/Press-Release/www/2003/cb03-ff08.html (accessed Sept. 12, 2003).

FALLER, K. C. 1990. *Understanding child sexual maltreatment.* Beverly Hills, CA: Sage.

FALLIK, D. 2001. Women booking rooms of their own—and more. *Women's E-News,* Aug. 28. www.womensenews.org/article.cfm/dyn/aid/635 (accessed Aug. 31, 2001).

FALUDI, S. 1999. *Stiffed: The betrayal of the American man.* New York: Morrow.

FAMILY CAREGIVER ALLIANCE. 2003. Fact sheet: New women and caregiving, facts and figures. www.caregiver.org/caregiver/jsp/content_node.jsp?nodeid=892 (accessed Oct. 11, 2003).

Family caregiving in the U.S.: Findings from a national survey. 1997. National Alliance for Caregiving and American Association of Retired Persons. www.hedc.org/info.html (accessed Oct. 20, 2000).

FANSHEL, D., S. J. FINCH, AND J. F. GRUNDY. 1989. Modes of exit from foster family care and adjustment at time of departure of children with unstable life histories. *Child Welfare* 68 (July/Aug.): 391–402.

FARAGHER, J. M. 1986. *Sugar Creek: Life on the Illinois prairie*. New Haven, CT: Yale University Press.

FARBER, B. 1964. *Family: Organization and interaction*. San Francisco: Chandler.

FARBER, B. 1972. *Guardians of virtue: Salem families in 1800*. New York: Basic Books.

FARLEY, J. 2002. Just a Hollywood ending. *Time*, Apr. 8, 90.

FARLEY, N. 1996. A survey of factors contributing to gay and lesbian domestic violence. In *Violence in gay and lesbian domestic partnerships*, eds. C. M. Renzetti and C. H. Miley, 35–42. New York: Harrington Park Press.

FARLEY, R. 2002. Racial identities in 2000: The response to the multiple-race response option. In *The new race question: How the census counts multiracial individuals*, eds. J. Perlmann and M. C. Waters, 33–61. New York: Russell Sage.

FARRELL, D. M. 1997. Jealousy and desire. In *Love analyzed*, ed. Roger E. Lamb, 165–88. Boulder, CO: Westview.

FASSEL, D. 1991. *Growing up divorced: A road to healing for adult children of divorce*. New York: Pocket Books.

Fatherhood after age 60? 2002. Gallup News Service. www.gallup.com/poll/pollInsights/#RD (accessed June 29, 2002).

FEARS, D. 2001. Mixed-race question defies easy answers. *Washington Post*, Apr. 16, A1, A8.

FEARS, D., AND C. DEANE. 2001. Biracial couples report tolerance. *Washington Post*, July 5, A1, A4.

FEDDERS, C. 1990. In their own words. *Washington Post*, Oct. 6, E5.

FEDERAL INTERAGENCY FORUM ON CHILD AND FAMILY STUDIES. 2003. *America's children: Key national indicators of well-being: 2003*. Washington, DC. www.childstats.gov/ac2003/pdf/ac2003.pdf (accessed Aug. 15, 2003).

FEENEY, J., AND P. NOLLER. 1996. *Adult attachment*. Thousand Oaks, CA: Sage.

FEHR, B. 1993. How do I love thee? Let me consult my prototype. In *Individuals in relationships*, ed. S. Duck, 87–120. Thousand Oaks, CA: Sage.

FEIN, E., AND S. SCHNEIDER. 1996. *The rules: Time tested secrets for capturing the heart of Mr. Right*. New York: Warner.

FELDMAN, H. 1931. *Racial factors in American industry*. New York: Harper & Row.

FELDMAN, S. S., E. CAUFFMAN, AND J. J. ARNETT. 2000. The (un)acceptability of betrayal: A study of college students' evaluations of sexual betrayal by a romantic partner and betrayal of a friend's confidence. *Journal of Youth and Adolescence* 29 (Aug.): 499–523.

FELDMANN, L., AND G. GOODALE. 1995. Custody cases test attitudes of judges. *Christian Science Monitor*, Mar. 3, 1, 18.

Female genital mutilation. 2000. World Health Organization. www.who.int/inf-fs/en/fact241.html (accessed June 12, 2003).

FENG, D., R. GIARRUSSO, V. L. BENGSTON, AND N. FRYE. 1999. Intergenerational transmission of marital quality and marital instability. *Journal of Marriage and the Family* 61 (May): 451–63.

FERREIRO, B. W. 1990. Presumption of joint custody: A family policy dilemma. *Family Relations* 39 (Oct.): 420–25.

FESTINGER, T. 2002. After adoption: Dissolution or permanence. *Child Welfare* 81: 515–33.

Fetal alcohol syndrome. 2000. Centers for Disease Control and Prevention. www.cdc.gov/nceh/cddh/fas/fasfact.htm (accessed Sept. 22, 2000).

FETTO, J. 2001. Gather 'round. *American Demographics* 23 (June): 11–12.

FETTO, J. 2001. What a girl (and boy) wants. *American Demographics* 23 (Apr.): 10–11.

FETTO, J. 2002. "Woof, woof" means "I love you." *American Demographics*, 24 (Feb.): 11.

FETTO, J. 2002a. Bringing up baby. *American Demographics* 24 (Oct.): 15.

FETTO, J. 2002b. Does father really know best? *American Demographics* 24 (June): 10–11.

FETTO, J. 2002c. Guys who shop. *American Demographics* 24 (Nov.): 16.

FETTO, J. 2003. Don't forget your rubbers. *American Demographics* 25 (Mar.): 16.

FETTO, J. 2003. First comes love. *American Demographics* 25 (June): 13.

FETTO, J. 2003. Love stinks. *American Demographics* 25 (Feb.): 10–11.

FETTO, J. 2003. Moms make the grade. *American Demographics* 25 (May): 12–13.

FIELD, A. 1999. The best old-age home may be at home. *Business Week*, Nov. 22, 180–1.

FIELD, L. D. 1996. Piecing together the puzzle: Self-concept and group identity in biracial black/white youth. In *The multiracial experience: Racial borders as the new frontier*, ed. M. P. P. Root, 211–26. Thousand Oaks, CA: Sage.

FIELDS, J. 2001. Living arrangements of children: 1996. U.S. Census Bureau, Current Population Reports, p70-74. www.census.gov/prod/2001pubs/p70-74.pdf (accessed Feb. 15, 2003).

FIELDS, J. 2003. *Children's living arrangements and characteristics: March 2002*. Current Population Reports, P20-547. Washington, DC: U.S. Census Bureau.

FIELDS, J., AND L. M. CASPER. 2001. *America's families and living arrangements: 2000*. U.S. Census Bureau, Current Population Reports, P20-537. www.census.gov/prod/2001pubs/p20-537.pdf (accessed Feb. 25, 2003).

FIELDS, J., K. SMITH, L. E. BASS, AND T. LUGAILA. 2001. *A child's day: Home, school, and play (selected indicators of child well-being): 1994*. Current Population Reports, P70-68. Washington, DC: U.S. Census Bureau. www.census.gov/prod/2001pubs/p70-68.pdf (accessed Aug. 24, 2003).

FIESE, B. H., ET AL. 2002. A review of 50 years of research on naturally occurring family routines and rituals: Cause for celebration? *Journal of Family Psychology* 16 (Dec.): 381–90.

FIESTER, L. 1993. Teen survey sparks concern. *Washington Post*, Feb. 2, 1, 3.

FINCHAM, F. D., AND T. N. BRADBURY. 1987. The assessment of marital quality: A reevaluation. *Journal of Marriage and the Family* 49 (Nov.): 797–809.

FINE, G. A. 1993. Ten lies of ethnography: Moral dilemmas of field research. *Journal of Contemporary Ethnography* 22 (Oct.): 267–94.

FINE, M. A., M. COLEMAN, AND L. H. GANONG. 1999. A social constructionist multi-method approach to understanding the stepparent role. In *Coping with divorce, single parenting, and remarriage: A risk and resiliency perspective*, ed. E. M. Hetherington, 273–94. Mahwah, NJ: Erlbaum.

FINE, M. A., AND D. A. FINE. 1994. An examination and evaluation of recent changes in divorce laws in five western countries: The critical role of values. *Journal of Marriage and the Family* 56 (May): 249–63.

FINEMAN, M. 1991. *The illusion of equality: The rhetoric and reality of divorce reform*. Chicago: University of Chicago Press.

FINER, L. B., AND S. K. HENSHAW. 2003. Abortion incidence and services in the United States in 2000. *Perspectives on Sexual and Reproductive Health* 35 (Jan./Feb.): 6–15.

FINER, L. B., S. K. HENSHAW, AND R. K. JONES. 2003. An overview of abortion in the United States. Physicians for Reproductive Choice and Health and the Alan Guttmacher Institute. www.agi-usa.org/pubs/abslides/abort_slides.pdf (accessed Aug. 5, 2003).

FINK, D. 1992. *Agrarian women: Wives and mothers in rural Nebraska, 1880–1940*. Chapel Hill: University of North Carolina Press.

FINKE, N. 1994. Trophy husbands. *Working Woman* (Apr.): 37, 39, 41, 88, 90–91.

FINKEL, J., AND P. ROBERTS. 1994. *The incomes of noncustodial fathers*. Washington, DC: Center for Law and Social Policy.

FINKELHOR, D., AND R. ORMROD. 2000. *Characteristics of crimes against juveniles*. Washington, DC: U.S. Department of Justice, Office of Justice Programs, Office of Juvenile Justice and Delinquency Prevention.

FISHER, A. P. 2003. A critique of the portrayal of adoption in college textbooks and readers on families, 1998–2001. *Family Relations* 52 (Apr.): 154–60.

FISHER, B. S., F. T. CULLEN, AND M. G. TURNER. 2000. The sexual victimization of college women. U.S. Department of Justice. www.ncjrs.org/pdffiles1/nij/182369.pdf (accessed July 3, 2003).

FISHER, H. 1992. *Anatomy of love: The natural history of monogamy, adultery, and divorce*. New York: Norton.

FISHER, H. 1999. *The first sex: The natural talents of women and how they are changing the world*. New York: Ballantine.

FISHMAN, B., AND B. HAMEL. 1981. From nuclear to stepfamily ideology: A stressful change. *Alternative Lifestyles* 4: 181–204.

FITZPATRICK, M. A., AND A. MULAC. 1995. Relating to spouse and stranger: Gender-preferential language use. In *Gender, power, and communication in human relationships*, eds. P. J. Kalbfleisch and M. J. Cody, 213–31. Hillsdale, NJ: Erlbaum.

FIVUSH, R., AND J. P. BUCKNER. 2000. Gender, sadness, and depression: The development of emotional focus through gendered discourse. In *Gender and emotion: Social psychological perspectives*, ed. A. H. Fischer, 232–53. New York: Cambridge University Press.

FIX, M. E., AND R. CAPPS. 2002. The dispersal of immigrants in the 1990s. Urban Institute. www.urban.org/UploadedPDF/410589_DispersalofImmigrants.pdf (accessed Apr. 4, 2003).

FIXICO, D. L. 2001. Myths and realities of Indian gaming. *Journal of the West* 40 (Spring): 2–3.

FLANDERS, S. 1996. The benefits of marriage. *The Public Interest* 124 (Summer): 80–86.

FLANNAGAN, D., AND S. PERESE. 1998. Emotional references in mother–daughter and mother–son dyads' conversations about school. *Sex Roles* 39 (Sep.): 353–67.

FLEESON, L. 2003. Leaving Laredo. *Mother Jones* (Sep./Oct.): 24–27.

FLETCHER, A. C., C. L. STEINBERG, AND E. B. SELLERS. 1999. Adolescents' well-being as a function of perceived interparental consistency. *Journal of Marriage and the Family* 61 (Aug.): 599–610.

FLETCHER, G. 2002. *The new science of intimate relationships*. Malden, MA: Blackwell.

FLETCHER, M. A. 1997. Latinos see signs of hope as middle class expands. *Washington Post*, July 22, A8.

FLORES, B. R. 1994. *Chiquita's cocoon*. New York: Villard.

FLORES, C. 2002. Wrestling coaches sue education department over Title IX enforcement. *Chronicle of Higher Education*, Feb. 1, A39.

FLORES, G., ET AL. 2002. The health of Latino children. *Journal of the American Medical Association* 288 (July 3): 82–90.

Florida couple accused of starving 7-year-old girl. 2002. *Baltimore Sun*, Sep. 23, 2A.

FLOURI, E., AND A. BUCHANAN. 2003. The role of father involvement and mother involvement in adolescents' psychological well-being. *British Journal of Social Work* 33 (Apr.): 399–406.

FLOWERS, R. B. 2001. *Runaway kids and teenage prostitution: America's lost, abandoned, and sexually exploited children*. Westport, CT: Praeger.

FOGEL, C. I., AND N. F. WOODS. 1995. Midlife women's health. In *Women's health care: A comprehensive handbook*, eds. C. I. Fogel and N. F. Woods, 79–100. Thousand Oaks, CA: Sage.

FOGG, P. 2003. The gap that won't go away. *Chronicle of Higher Education*, Apr. 18, A12-A15.

FOLBRE, N. 1994. *Who pays for the kids? Gender and the structures of constraint*. New York: Routledge.

FOLK, K. F., J. W. GRAHAM, AND A. H. BELLER. 1992. Child support and remarriage: Implications for the economic well-being of children. *Journal of Family Issues* 13, 142–57.

FOLSE, K. A. 1997. Hispanic fathers and the child support enforcement experience. *Journal of Multicultural Social Work* 6 (3/4): 139–58.

FONG, T. P. 2002. *The contemporary Asian American experience: Beyond the model minority*, 2nd ed. Upper Saddle River, NJ: Prentice Hall.

FOO, L. J. 2002. *Asian American women: Issues, concerns, and responsive human and civil rights advocacy.* New York: Ford Foundation.

FORD, C., AND E. BEACH. 1972. *Patterns of sexual behavior.* New York: Harper & Row. (Originally published 1951.)

FORD, P. 1999. Europe puts mute on kid ads. *Christian Science Monitor,* Dec. 16, 1, 10.

FORD, P. 2002. In Europe, marriage is back. *Christian Science Monitor,* Apr. 10, 1–2.

FOREMAN, A. K., AND T. NANCE. 1999. From miscegenation to multiculturalism: Perceptions and stages of interracial relationship development. *Journal of Black Studies* 29: 540–57.

FORWARD, S. 1990. *Toxic parents: Overcoming their hurtful legacy and reclaiming your life.* New York: Bantam.

FORWARD, S. 2002. *Obsessive love: When it hurts too much to let go.* New York: Bantam.

FOSHEE, V. A., K. E. BAUMAN, AND G. F. LINDER. 1999. Family violence and the perpetuation of adolescent dating violence: Examining social learning and social control processes. *Journal of Marriage and the Family* 61 (May): 331–42.

FOST, D. 1996. Child-free with an attitude. *American Demographics* 18 (Apr.): 15–16.

FOUST, D., B. GROW, AND A. M. PASCUAL. 2002. The changing heartland. *Business Week,* Sep. 9, 80–84.

FOX, G. L., M. L. BENSON, A. A. DEMARIS, AND J. VAN WYK. 2002. Economic distress and intimate violence: Testing family stress and resources theories. *Journal of Marriage and Family* 64 (Aug.): 793–807.

FOX, G. L., AND V. M. MURRY. 2001. Gender and families: Feminist perspectives and family research. In *Understanding families into the new millennium: A decade of review,* ed. R. M. Milardo, 379–91. Lawrence, KS: National Council on Family Relations.

FOX, J. A., AND M. W. ZAWITZ. 2003. *Homicide trends in the United States: 2000 update.* Washington, DC: U.S. Department of Justice.

FRAME, M. W., AND C. L. SHEHAN. 1994. Work and well-being in the two-person career: Relocation stress and coping among clergy husbands and wives. *Family Relations* 43 (Apr.): 196–205.

FRANCESE, P. 2003. Working women. *American Demographics* 25 (Mar.):40–41.

FRANCIS, D. R. 2000a. The unsolved mystery of the gilded economy. *Christian Science Monitor,* June 30, 1, 9.

FRANCIS, D. R. 2003. Grass looks greener, but welcome cools. *Christian Science Monitor,* Mar. 20, 13, 16.

FRANCIS, D. R. 2003. Moves afoot to curb CEO salaries. *Christian Science Monitor,* July 8, 2, 4.

FRANK, M., AND E. F. ZIGLER. 1996. Family leave: A developmental perspective. In *Children, families, and government: Preparing for the twenty-first century,* eds. E. F. Zigler, S. L. Kagan, and N. W. Hall, 117–31. New York: Cambridge University Press.

FRAZIER, E. F. 1937. The impact of urban civilization upon Negro family life. *American Sociological Review* 2 (Oct.): 609–18.

FRAZIER, E. F. 1939. *The Negro family in the United States.* Chicago: University of Chicago Press.

FRIEDAN, B. 1993. *The fountain of age.* New York: Simon & Schuster.

FROMM, E. 1956. *The art of loving.* New York: Bantam.

FROMM, S. 2001. Total estimated cost of child abuse and neglect in the United States: Statistical evidence. Prevent Child Abuse America. www.preventchildabuse.org/learn_more/research_docs/cost_analysis.pdf (accessed Sep. 20, 2003).

FU, V. K. 2001. Racial intermarriage pairings. *Demography* 38 (May): 147–59.

FUCHS, D. 2003. In Spain's lonely country side, a Cupid crusade. *Christian Science Monitor,* June 10, 1, 14.

FULIGNI, A. J., V. TSENG, AND M. LAM. 1999. Attitudes towards family obligations among American adolescents with Asian, Latin American, and European backgrounds. *Child Development* 70: 1030–44.

FULLER, B., AND S. L. KAGAN. 2000. *Remember the children: Mothers balance work and child care under welfare reform.* www.gse.berkeley.edu/research/PACE/PDF/GUPExSum.pdf (accessed Sep. 28, 2000).

FULLER, N. 2003. University officials are accused of failing to report a student's alleged rape. *Chronicle of Higher Education,* Feb. 28. http://chronicle.com/daily/2003/02/2003022802n.htm (accessed Feb. 28, 2003).

FULTZ, O. 1991. 'Roid rage. *American Health,* May, 60–64.

FURGATCH, V. 1995. It's time to remove all barriers to adoption across racial lines. *Christian Science Monitor,* Sep. 12, 19.

FURSTENBERG, F. F., AND K. E. KIERNAN. 2001. Delayed parental divorce: How much do children benefit? *Journal of Marriage and Family* 63 (May): 446–57.

FURSTENBERG, F. F., JR., AND J. O. TEITLER. 1994. Reconsidering the effects of marital disruption: What happens to children of divorce in early adulthood? *Journal of Family Issues* 15 (June): 173–90.

GABRIEL, T. 1997. Pack dating: For a good time, call a crowd. *New York Times,* Jan. 5, 22.

GAGER, C. T., AND L. SANCHEZ. 2003. Two as one?: Couples' perceptions of time spent together, marital quality, and the risk of divorce. *Journal of Family Issues* 24 (Jan.): 21–50.

GAITER, L. 1994. The revolt of the black bourgeoisie. *New York Times Magazine,* June 26, 42–43.

GALBRAITH, J. K. 1998. *Created unequal: The crisis in American pay.* New York: Free Press.

GALINSKY, E. 1999. *Ask the children: What American children really think about working parents.* New York: Morrow.

GALL, C. 2003. The women of Kabul are going back to work. *Working Mother* (Apr.): 49–53.

GALLAGHER, M. 1996. *The abolition of marriage: How we destroy lasting love.* Washington, DC: Regnery.

GALLAGHER, S. K., AND N. GERSTEL. 1993. Kinkeeping and friend keeping among older women: The effect of marriage. *The Gerontologist* 33 (5): 675–81.

GALLO, L. C., W. M. TROXEL, K. A. MATTHEWS, AND L. H. KULLER. 2003. Marital status and quality in middle-aged women: Associations with levels and trajectories of cardiovascular risk factors. *Health Psychology* 22 (5): 1–11.

GALLUP, G., JR., AND F. NEWPORT. 1990. Virtually all adults want children, but many of the reasons are intangible. *Gallup Poll Monthly* (June): 8–22.

GALSTON, W. A. 1996. Divorce American style. *The Public Interest* (Summer): 12–26.

GALVIN, K. M., AND B. J. BROMMEL. 2000. *Family communication: Cohesion and change,* 5th ed. New York: Addison-Wesley-Longman.

GAMACHE, D. 1990. Domination and control: The social context of dating violence. In *Dating Violence: Young women in danger,* ed. B. Levy, 69–118. Seattle: Seal.

GAMACHE, S. J. 1997. Confronting nuclear family bias in stepfamily research. *Marriage & Family Review* 26 (1/2): 41–69.

GANONG, L. H., AND M. COLEMAN. 1994. *Remarried family relationships.* Thousand Oaks, CA: Sage.

GANONG, L. H., AND M. COLEMAN. 1997. How society views stepfamilies. *Marriage & Family Review* 26 (1/2): 85–106.

GANONG, L. H., AND M. COLEMAN. 1999. *Changing families, changing responsibilities: Family obligations following divorce and remarriage.* Mahwah, NJ: Erlbaum.

GANONG, L., M. COLEMAN, AND M. FINE. 1995. Remarriage and stepfamilies. In *Research and theory in family science,* eds. R. D. Day, K. R. Gilbert, B. H. Settles, and W. R. Burr, 287–303. Pacific Grove, CA: Brooks/Cole.

GANS, H. J. 1971. The uses of poverty: The poor pay all. *Social Policy* (July/Aug.): 78–81.

GANS, H. J. 1979. *Deciding what's news: A study of CBS Evening News, NBC Nightly News, Newsweek and Time.* New York: Pantheon.

GANZINI, L. H. D. NELSON, T. A. SCHMIDT, D. F. KRAEMER, M. A. DELORIT, AND M. A. LEE. 2000. Physicians' experiences with the Oregon Death with Dignity Act. *New England Journal of Medicine* 342 (Feb.): 557–63.

GAOUETTE, N. 2001. Voices from behind the veil. *Christian Science Monitor,* Dec. 19, 1, 10–12.

GARBARINO, J. 1982. Sociocultural risk: Dangers to competence. In *The child: Development in a social context,* eds. Claire B. Kopp and Joanne B. Krakow, 630–87. Reading, MA: Addison-Wesley.

GARBARINO, J. 1999. *Lost boys: Why our sons turn violent and how we can save them.* New York: Free Press.

GARCIA, A. M. 2002. *The Mexican Americans.* Westport, CT: Greenwood.

GARCÍA, C. Y. 1998. Temporal course of the basic components of love throughout relationships. *Psychology in Spain* 2 (1): 76–86. www.psychologyinspain.com/content/full/1998/9bis.htm (accessed Mar. 30, 2003).

GARCIA, M. T. 1980. La familia: The Mexican immigrant family, 1900–1930. In *Work, family, sex roles, language,* eds. M. Barrera, A. Camarillo, and F. Hernandez, 117–40. Berkeley, CA: Tonatiua-Quinto Sol International.

GARDINER, K. N., M. E. FISHMAN, P. NIKOLOV, A. GLOSSER, AND S. LAUD. 2002. State policies to promote marriage: Final report. The Lewin Group. http://aspe.hhs.gov/hsp/marriage02f/ (accessed July 17, 2003).

GARDNER, H. 1996. The concept of family: Perceptions of children in family foster care. *Child Welfare* 75 (Mar./Apr.): 161–82.

GARDNER, M. 1995a. Full-time dads launch nationwide group. *Christian Science Monitor,* Aug. 29, 1, 12.

GARDNER, M. 1995b. Parents who work shifts seek off-hours care. *Christian Science Monitor,* June 22, 6, 12.

GARDNER, M. 2002. Avalanche of advice. *Christian Science Monitor,* Nov. 20, 15, 18–19.

GARDNER, M. 2002. Grandmothers weigh in on providing child care. *Christian Science Monitor,* Aug. 14, 16.

GARDNER, M. 2003. When Cupid keeps missing. *Christian Science Monitor,* Feb. 12, 15–17.

GARDNER, M. 2003a. For better or worse: Couples confront unemployment. *Christian Science Monitor,* May 28, 19–20.

GARDNER, M. 2003b. Small towns confront an urban problem: A rise in homelessness. *Christian Science Monitor,* Mar. 7, 1, 4.

GARDNER, R. 2001. A league of their own. *American Demographics* 23 (Mar.): 12–13.

GARDYN, R. 2002. The mating game. *American Demographics* 24 (July/Aug.): 33–37.

GARFINKEL, I., S. S. MCLANAHAN, AND P. K. ROBINS, EDS. 1994. *Child support and child well-being.* Washington, DC: Urban Institute.

GARLAND, E. 1999. An anthropologist learns the value of fear. *Chronicle of Higher Education,* May 7, B4–B5.

GARLAND, S. B. 2000. Work at home? First, get real. *Business Week,* Sept. 18, 112, 116.

GARROD, A., AND C. LARIMORE, EDS. 1997. *First person, first peoples: Native American college graduates tell their life stories.* Ithaca, NY: Cornell University Press.

GASSER, R. D., AND C. M. TAYLOR. 1990. Role adjustment of single parent fathers with dependent children. *Family Relations* 40 (July): 397–400.

GATELY, D., AND A. I. SCHWEBEL. 1992. Favorable outcomes in children after parental divorce. In *Divorce and the next generation: Effects on young adults' patterns of intimacy and expectations for marriage,* ed. C. Everett, 57–78. New York: Haworth.

GATTAI, F. B., AND T. MUSATTI. 1999. Grandmothers' involvement in grandchildren's care: Attitudes, feelings, and emotions. *Family Relations* 48 (Jan.): 35–42.

GAUCH, S. 2002. Egypt cracks down on gays, trumping Islamists. *Christian Science Monitor,* Mar. 2, 7.

GAUDIN, J. M., JR., N. A. POLANSKY, A. C. KILPATRICK, AND P. SHILTON. 1996. Family functioning in neglectful families. *Child Abuse & Neglect* 20 (Apr.): 363–77.

GAULIN, S. J. C., AND J. S. BOSTER. 1990. Dowry as female competition. *American Anthropologist* 92 (Dec.): 994–1005.

GAYLIN, W. 1992. *The male ego.* New York: Viking.

GEARON, C. J. 2003. Visiting the "kids" gets harder. *AARP Bulletin,* Feb., 6–7.

GECAS, V., AND M. A. SEFF. 1991. Families and adolescents: A review of the 1980s. In *Contemporary families: Looking forward, looking back,* ed.

A. Booth, 208–25. Minneapolis: National Council on Family Relations.

GEEASLER, M. J., L. L. DANNISON, AND C. J. EDLUND. 1995. Sexuality education of young children: Parental concerns. *Family Relations* 44 (Apr.): 184–88.

GEER, J. H., AND G. M. MANGUNO-MIRE. 1996. Gender differences in cognitive processes in sexuality. *Annual Review of Sex Research* 7: 90–124.

GELLES, R. J. 1995. *Contemporary families: A sociological view*. Thousand Oaks, CA: Sage.

GELLES, R. J. 1997. *Intimate violence in families*, 3rd ed. Thousand Oaks, CA: Sage.

GELLES, R. J., AND C. P. CORNELL. 1990. *Intimate violence in families*, 2nd ed. Thousand Oaks, CA: Sage.

GELLES, R. J., AND M. A. STRAUS. 1988. *Intimate violence*. New York: Simon & Schuster.

GENDER EQUALITY BUREAU. 2000. www.gender.go.jp/danjyo/english/plan2000/1999/index.html.

GENOVESE, E. D. 1981. Husbands and fathers, wives and mothers, during slavery. In *Family life in America: 1620–2000*, eds. M. Albin and D. Cavallo, 237–51. St. James, NY: Revisionary Press.

GERAGHTY, M. 1997. Hazing incidents at sororities alarm colleges. *Chronicle of Higher Education*, June 20, A37–A38.

GERBER, R. 2002. Girls need not apply. *Christian Science Monitor*, June 24, 11.

GERDES, K., M. NAPOLI, C. PATTEA, AND E. SEGAL. 1998. The impact of Indian gaming on economic development. *Journal of Poverty* 4 (2): 17–30.

GERSHOFF, E. T. 2002a. Corporal punishment by parents and associated child behaviors and experiences: A meta-analytic and theoretical review. *Psychological Bulletin* 128 (July): 539–79.

GERSHOFF, E. T. 2002b. Corporal punishment, physical abuse, and the burden of proof: Reply to Baumrind, Larzelere, and Cowan (2002), Holden (2002), and Parke (2002). *Psychological Bulletin* 128 (July): 602–11.

GERSON, K. 1997. The social construction of fatherhood. In *Contemporary parenting: Challenges and issues*, ed. T. Arendell, 119–53. Thousand Oaks, CA: Sage.

GERSON, K. 2003. Work without worry. *New York Times*, May 11. www.nytimes.com/2003/05/11/opinion/11GERS.html?th (accessed May 12, 2003).

GERSTEL, N., AND S. K. GALLAGHER. 1993. Kinkeeping and distress: Gender, recipients of care, and work-family conflict. *Journal of Marriage and the Family* 55 (Aug.): 598–607.

GIBBONS, S. 2002a. Biased newsrooms risk losing female staff, readers. *Women's E-News*, Nov. 22. www.womensenews.org/article.cfm/dyn/aid/1115 (accessed Nov. 23, 2002).

GIBBONS, S. 2002b. Top jobs elude women in broadcast news. *Women's E-News*, Oct. 4. www.womensenews.org/article.cfm/dyn/aid/1051/context/uncoveringgender (accessed Oct. 5, 2002).

GIBBONS, S. 2003. Bridal media promote merchandise, not marriage. *Women's E-News*, June 7. www.womensenews.org/article.cfm/dyn/aid/1353 (accessed June 9, 2003).

GIBBS, J., AND A. HINES. 1992. Negotiating ethnic identity: Issues for black-white biracial adolescents. In *Racially mixed people in America*, ed. M. P. P. Root, 223–38. Thousand Oaks, CA: Sage.

GIBBS, N. 2002. Making time for a baby. *Time*, Apr. 15, 48–53.

GIBBS, N., J. JOHNSON, M. LUDTKE, AND M. RILEY. 1990. Shameful bequests to the next generation. *Time*, Oct. 8, 42–46.

GIBSON, J. T. 1991. Disciplining toddlers. *Parents* (May): 190.

GILBERT, D. 2003. *The American class structure in an age of growing inequality*, 6th ed. Belmont, CA: Wadsworth.

GILBERT, D. J. 2003. The sociocultural construction of AIDS among African American women. In *African American women and HIV/AIDS: Critical responses*, eds. D. J. Gilbert and E. W. Wright, 1–26. Westport, CT: Praeger.

GILES-SIMS, J., M. A. STRAUS, AND D. B. SUGARMAN. 1995. Child, maternal, and family characteristics associated with spanking. *Family Relations* 44 (Apr.): 170–76.

GILLIS, J. R. 1996. *A world of their own making: Myth, ritual, and the quest for family values*. New York: Basic Books.

GILLMORE, M. R. ET AL. 2002. Teen sexual behavior: Applicability of the theory of reasoned action. *Journal of Marriage and Family* 64 (Nov.): 885–97.

GLADSTONE, J. W. 1989. Perceived changes in grandmother–grandchild relations following a child's separation or divorce. *The Gerontologist* 28 (1): 66–72.

GLASS, S. 2002. *Not "just friends": Protect your relationship from infidelity and heal the trauma of betrayal*. New York: Free Press.

GLASSMAN, J. E. 1997. The corporate welfare queens. *U.S. News & World Report*, May 19, 53.

GLAZER, N., AND D. P. MOYNIHAN. 1963. *Beyond the melting pot*. Cambridge, MA: MIT Press and Harvard University Press.

GLENN, E. N., WITH S. G. H. YAP. 1994. Chinese American families. In *Minority families in the United States: A multicultural perspective*, ed. R. L. Taylor, 115–45. Upper Saddle River, NJ: Prentice Hall.

GLENN, E. N., AND S. G. H. YAP. 2002. Chinese American families. In *Minority families in the United States: A multicultural perspective*, 3rd ed., ed. R. L. Taylor, 134–63. Upper Saddle River, NJ: Prentice Hall.

GLENN, N. D. 1991. Quantitative research on marital quality in the 1980s. In *Contemporary families: Looking forward, looking back*, ed. A. Booth, 28–41. Minneapolis: National Council on Family Relations.

GLENN, N. D. 1996. Values, attitudes, and the state of American marriage. In *Promises to keep: Decline and renewal of marriage in America*, eds. D. Popenoe, J. B. Elshtain, and D. Blankenhorn, 15–33. Lanham, MD: Rowman & Littlefield.

GLENN, N. D. 1997. A reconsideration of the effect of no-fault divorce on divorce rates. *Journal of Marriage and Family* 59 (Nov.): 1023–30.

GLENN, N. D. 2001. Is the current concern about American marriage warranted? *Virginia Journal of Social Policy & the Law* 9 (Fall): 5–47.

GLENN, N. D. 2002. A plea for greater concern about the quality of marital matching. In *Revitalizing the institution of marriage in the twenty-first century*, eds. L. D. Wardle and D. O. Coolidge, 45–58. Westport, CT: Praeger.

GLENN, N., AND E. MARQUARDT. 2001. *Hooking up, hanging out, and hoping for Mr. Right: College women on dating and mating today*. Institute for American Values. www.americanvalues.org/Hooking_Up.pdf (accessed July 5, 2003).

GLENN, N. D., AND B. A. SHELTON. 1985. Regional differences in divorce in the United States. *Journal of Marriage and the Family* 47: 641–52.

GLENN, N. D., AND J. M. WHITE. 2003. Marital interaction. In *International encyclopedia of marriage and family*, 2nd ed., Vol. 3, ed. J. J. Ponzetti, Jr., 1069–78. New York: Macmillan.

Glenn's health in space in line with colleagues'. 2000. *Baltimore Sun*, Jan. 29, 3A.

GLENWICK, D. S., AND J. D. MOWREY. 1986. When parent becomes peer: Loss of intergenerational boundaries in single parent families. *Family Relations* 35 (Jan.): 57–62.

GLICK, J. E., AND J. VAN HOOK. 2002. Parents' coresidence with adult children: Can immigration explain racial and ethnic variation? *Journal of Marriage and Family* 64 (Feb.): 240–53.

GLYNN, L. M., N. CHRISTENFELD, AND W. GERIN. 2002. The role of rumination in recovery from reactivity: Cardiovascular consequences of emotional states. *Psychosomatic Medicine* 64 (Sep./Oct.): 714–26.

GODDARD, H. W. 1994. *Principles of parenting*. Auburn, AL: Auburn University, Department of Family and Child Development.

GOETTING, A. 1982. The six stations of remarriage: Developmental tasks of remarriage after divorce. *Family Relations* 31 (Apr.): 231–22.

GOETTING, A. 1999. *Getting out: Life stories of women who left abusive men*. New York: Columbia University Press.

GOFFMAN, E. 1963. *Stigma: Notes on the management of spoiled identity*. Upper Saddle River, NJ: Prentice Hall.

GOLBY, B. J., AND I. BRETHERTON. 1998. Resilience in postdivorce mother–child relationships. In *The dynamics of resilient families*, eds. H. I. McCubbin, E. A. Thompson, A. I. Thompson, and J. A. Futrell, 237–65. Thousand Oaks, CA: Sage.

GOLD, L. 1992. *Between love and hate: A guide to civilized divorce*. New York: Plenum.

GOLDSCHEIDER, F. K., AND C. GOLDSCHEIDER. 1993. *Leaving home before marriage: Ethnicity, familism, and generational relationships*. Madison: University of Wisconsin Press.

GOLDSCHEIDER, F. K., AND L. LAWTON. 1998. Family experiences and the erosion of support for intergenerational coresidence. *Journal of Marriage and the Family* 60 (Aug.): 623–32.

GOLDSTEIN, A. 1998. Legal procedure, hostile climate. *Washington Post*, Jan. 22, A1, A8.

GOLOMBOK, S. 2002. Parenting and contemporary reproductive technologies. In *Handbook of parenting*, 3rd ed., Vol. 3: *Social conditions and applied parenting*, ed. M. H. Bornstein, 339–60. Mahwah, NJ: Erlbaum.

GOLOMBOK, S., AND F. TASKER. 1996. Do parents influence the sexual orientation of their children? Findings from a longitudinal study of lesbian families. *Developmental Psychology* 32 (1): 3–11.

GONZÁLEZ, R. 1996. *Muy macho: Latino men confront their manhood*. New York: Anchor.

GOODE, E. 1990. *Deviant behavior*, 3rd ed. Upper Saddle River, NJ: Prentice Hall.

GOODE, E. 2002. Group backs gays who seek to adopt a partner's child. *New York Times*, Feb. 4. www.nytimes.com/2002/02/04/national/04ADOP.html?todaysheadlines (accessed Feb. 5, 2002).

GOODE, E., ET AL. 1994. Till death do them part? *U.S. News & World Report*, July 4, 24–28.

GOODE, W. J. 1963. *World revolution and family patterns*. New York: Free Press.

GOODMAN, E. 1999. Equal pay an issue, again. *Baltimore Sun*, Mar. 18, 15A.

GOODMAN, E. 2003. Here's a marriage proposal we should reject. *Baltimore Sun*, Feb. 24, 11A.

GOODMAN, M., H. K. BLACK, AND R. L. RUBINSTEIN. 1996. Paternal bereavement in older men. *Omega* 33 (4): 303–22.

GOODSMITH, L. 2000. Taliban's yoke crushes women. *Baltimore Sun*, June 11, 1C, 4C.

GOODWIN, R., AND C. FINDLAY. 1997. "We were just fated together." Chinese love and the concept of *yuan* in England and Hong Kong. *Personal Relationships* 4: 85–92.

GOPNIK, A. A., N. MELTZOFF, AND P. K. KUHL. 1999. *The scientist in the crib: Minds, brains, and how children learn*. New York: Morrow.

GORDON, L. H. 1993. Intimacy: The art of working out your relationships. *Psychology Today* 26 (Sep./Oct.): 40–43, 79–82.

GORDY, M. 2000. A call to fight forced labor. *Parade Magazine*, Feb. 20, 4–5.

GORMAN, C. 1995. Trapped in the body of a man? *Time*, Nov. 13, 94–95.

GORMAN, E. H. 2000. Marriage and money. *Work & Occupations* 27 (Feb.): 64–88.

GORMAN, J. C. 1998. Parenting attitudes and practices of immigrant Chinese mothers of adolescents. *Family Relations* 47 (Jan.): 73–80.

GOSE, B. 1994. Spending time on the reservation. *Chronicle of Higher Education*, Aug. 10, A30–A31.

GOTTLIEB, L. N., A. LANG, AND R. AMSEL. 1996. The long-term effects of grief on marital intimacy following an infant's death. *Omega* 33 (1): 1–19.

GOTTMAN, J. M. 1982. Emotional responsiveness in marital conversations. *Journal of Communication* 32, 108–20.

GOTTMAN, J. M. 1994. *What predicts divorce? The relationships between marital processes and marital outcome*. Hillsdale, NJ: Erlbaum.

GOTTMAN, J. M., J. COAN, S. CARRERE, AND C. SWANSON. 1998. Predicting marital happiness and stability from newlywed interactions. *Journal of Marriage and the Family* 60 (Feb.): 5–22.

GOTTMAN, J. M., AND J. DECLAIRE. 2001. *The relationship cure: A five-step guide for building better connections with family, friends, and lovers*. New York: Crown.

GOTTMAN, J. M., AND N. SILVER. 1999. *The seven principles for making marriage work*. New York: Crown.

GOULD, D. C., R. PETTY, AND H. S. JACOBS. 2000. For and against: The male menopause—does it exist? *British Medical Journal* 320 (Mar.): 858–60.

GOULTER, B., AND J. MINNINGER. 1993. *The father–daughter dance: Insight, inspiration, and understanding for every woman and her father.* New York: Putnam's.

GOYETTE, K., AND Y. XIE. 1999. The intersection of immigration and gender: Labor force outcomes of immigrant women scientists. *Social Science Quarterly* 80 (June): 395–408.

GRADMAN, T. J. 1994. Masculine identity from work to retirement. In *Older men's lives,* ed. E. H. Thompson, Jr., 104–21. Thousand Oaks, CA: Sage.

GRADY, D. 1996. How to coax new life. *Time* Special Issue (Fall): 37–39.

GRAHAM, E. 1996. Craving closer ties, strangers come together as family. *Wall Street Journal,* Mar. 4, B1, B5.

GRAHAM, J. W., A. H. BELLER, AND P. M. HERNANDEZ. 1994. The effects of child support on educational attainment. In *Child support and child well-being,* eds. I. Garfinkel, S. S. McLanahan, and P. K. Robins, 317–54. Washington, DC: Urban Institute.

GRAHAM, L. O. 1996. *Member of the club: Reflections on life in a racially polarized world.* New York: HarperCollins.

GRALL, T. 2002. *Custodial mothers and fathers and their child support: 1999.* U.S. Census Bureau, Current Population Reports, P60-217. Washington, DC: Government Printing Office.

GRAVES, J. L., JR. 2001. *The emperor's new clothes: Biological theories of race at the millennium.* New Brunswick, NJ: Rutgers University Press.

GRAY, H. M., AND V. FOSHEE. 1997. Adolescent dating violence: Differences between one-sided and mutually violent profiles. *Journal of Interpersonal Violence* 12 (Feb.): 126–41.

GRAY, M. R., AND L. STEINBERG. 1999. Unpacking authoritative parenting: Reassessing a multidimensional construct. *Journal of Marriage and the Family* 61 (Aug.): 574–87.

GREENBERG, J., AND M. RUHLEN. 1992. Linguistic origins of Native Americans. *Scientific American* 267: 94.

GREENBLATT, C. S. 1983. The salience of sexuality in the early years of marriage. *Journal of Marriage and the Family* 45 (May): 289–99.

GREENE, D. L. 2000. Tribe at war against alcohol. *Baltimore Sun,* Apr. 17, 1A, 4A.

GREENFELD, L. A., AND S. K. SMITH. 1999. *American Indians and crime.* Washington, DC: U.S. Department of Justice, Office of Justice Programs.

GREENFELD, L. A., AND T. L. SNELL. 1999. *Women offenders.* Washington, DC: U.S. Department of Justice, Office of Justice Programs, Bureau of Justice Statistics.

GREENHOUSE, S. 2003. Wal-Mart faces lawsuit over sex discrimination. *New York Times,* Feb. 16. www.nytimes.com/2003/02/16/national/16WALM.html (accessed Feb. 17, 2003).

GREENSTEIN, T. N. 1990. Marital disruption and the employment of married women. *Journal of Marriage and the Family* 52 (Aug.): 657–76.

GREENSTEIN, T. N. 2000. Economic dependence, gender, and the division of labor in the home: A replication and extension. *Journal of Marriage and the Family* 62 (May): 322–35.

GREENSTEIN, T. N. 2001. *Methods of family research.* Thousand Oaks, CA: Sage.

GREENWALD, J. 1996. Barbie boots up. *Time,* Nov. 11, 48–50.

GREER, G. 1999. *The whole woman.* New York: Knopf.

GREIDER, L. 2000. How not to be a monster-in-law. *Modern Maturity* (Mar./Apr.): 57–59.

GREIDER, L. 2003. "The old skills kick in." *AARP Bulletin,* May, 12.

GREIF, G. L. 1990. *The daddy track and the single father.* Lexington, MA: Lexington.

GRIMSLEY, K. D. 2000. Panel asks why women still earn less. *Washington Post,* June 9, E3.

GRIMSLEY, K. D. 2001. More Arabs, Muslims allege bias on the job. *Washington Post,* Dec. 12, E1, E4.

GRISWOLD, R. L. 1993. *Fatherhood in America: A history.* New York: Basic Books.

GRITZ, E. R., ET AL. 2003. Predictors of susceptibility to smoking and ever smoking: A longitudinal study in a triethnic sample of adolescents. *Nicotine & Tobacco Research* 5 (July): 493–506.

GROTEVANT, H. D. 2001. Adoptive families: Longitudinal outcomes for adolescents. Report to the William T. Grant Foundation. http://fsos.che.umn.edu/mtarp/Final%20Report%202%20convert.htm (accessed Aug. 17, 2003).

GROVES, E. R. 1928. *The marriage crisis.* New York: Longmans, Green.

GROW, B. 2003. Skilled workers—or indentured servants? *Business Week,* June 16, 54–55.

GROW, B., AND M. KRIPALANI. 2003. A loophole as big as a mainframe. *Business Week,* Mar. 10, 82–83.

GRUENBAUM, E. 2001. *The female circumcision controversy: An anthropological perspective.* Philadelphia: University of Pennsylvania Press.

GRUNBAUM, J. A., ET AL. 2002. Youth risk behavior surveillance: United States, 2001. Centers for Disease Control and Prevention, *Morbidity and Mortality Weekly Report,* June 28. www.cdc.gov/mmwr/preview/mmwrhtml/ss5104a1.htm#tab8 (accessed June 13, 2003).

GRYCH, J. H. 2002. Marital relationships and parenting. In *Handbook of parenting,* 2nd ed., Vol. 4: *Social conditions and applied parenting,* ed. M. H. Bornstein, 203–25. Mahwah, NJ: Erlbaum.

GRZYWACZ, J. G., D. M. ALMEIDA, AND D. A. MCDONALD. 2002. Work–family spillover and daily reports of work and family stress in the adult labor force. *Family Relations* 51 (Jan.): 28–36.

GRZYWACZ, J. G., AND N. F. MARKS. 2000. Family, work, work–family spillover, and problem drinking during midlife. *Journal of Marriage and the Family* 62 (May): 336–48.

GUBERMAN, N., P. MAHEU, AND C. MAILLÉ. 1992. Women as family caregivers: Why do they care? *The Gerontologist* 32 (5): 607–17.

GUEST, J. 1988. *The mythic family.* Minneapolis: Milkweed.

GUIDO, M. 2003. Women lose ground in the tech field. *Mercury News,* Feb. 14. www.bayarea.com/mld/mercurynews/5184984.htm (accessed Feb. 15, 2003).

GUPTA, G. R. 1979. Love, arranged marriage and the Indian social structure. In *Cross-cultural perspectives of mate-selection and marriage,* ed. G. Kurian, 169–79. Westport, CT: Greenwood.

GUPTA, N., AND A. K. SHARMA. 2001. Triple burden among women scientists in India: A sociological study of women faculty at some reputed centres of higher learning and research. *Social Action* 51 (Oct./Dec.): 395–416.

GUPTA, S. 2003. Those fragile hearts. *Time,* Feb. 10, 84.

GURIAN, M. 2002. *The wonder girls: Understanding the hidden nature of our daughters.* New York: Pocket Books.

GUTMAN, H. 1976. *The black family in slavery and freedom, 1750–1925.* New York: Pantheon.

GUTMAN, H. G. 1983. Persistent myths about the Afro-American family. In *The American family in socio-historical perspective,* 3rd ed., ed. M. Gordon, 459–81. New York: St. Martin's.

GUTMAN, L. M., AND J. S. ECCLES. 1999. Financial strain, parenting behaviors, and adolescents' achievement: Testing model equivalence between African and American and European American single- and two-parent families. *Child Development* 70 (Nov./Dec.): 1464–76.

GUTNER, T. 2000. Getting your fair share in a divorce. *Business Week,* May 29, 250.

GUTNER, T. 2001. Househusbands unite! *Business Week,* Jan. 22, 106.

GWARTNEY-GIBBS, P. A. 1986. The institutionalization of premarital cohabitation: Estimates from marriage license applications, 1970 and 1980. *Journal of Marriage and the Family* 48 (May): 423–34.

HAAG, P. S. 1999. *Voices of a generation: Teenage girls on sex, school, and self.* Washington, DC: American Association of University Women.

HAAN, M. N., L. SHEMANSKI, W. J. JAGUST, T. A. MANOLIO, AND L. KULLER. 1999. The role of APOE E4 in modulating effects of other risk factors for cognitive decline in elderly persons. *Journal of the American Medical Association* 282 (July 7): 40–46.

HACKER, A. 2003. *Mismatch: The growing gulf between women and men.* New York: Scribner.

HAFFNER, D. W. 1999. Facing facts: Sexual health for American adolescents. *Human Development & Family Life Bulletin* 4 (Winter): 1–3.

HAHN, R. A., AND D. M. KLEIST. 2000. Divorce mediation: Research and implications for family and couples counseling. *Family Journal* 8 (Apr.): 165–71.

HAIR, E., J. JAGER, AND S. B. GARRETT. 2002. *Helping teens develop healthy social skills and relationships: What the research shows about navigating adolescence.* Washington, DC: Child Trends. www.childtrends.org/PDF/K3Brief.pdf (accessed Aug. 23, 2003).

HALES, D. 2002. When *she* earns more. *Parade,* Mar. 17, 6.

HALEY, A. 1976. *Roots: The saga of an American family.* Garden City, NY: Doubleday.

Half of older Americans report they are sexually active; 4 in 10 want more sex, says new survey. 1998. National Council on Aging. www.ncoa.org/news/archives/sexsurvey.htm (accessed Aug. 30, 2003).

HALL, C. C. I., AND M. J. CRUM. 1994. Women and "body-isms" in television beer commercials. *Sex Roles* 31 (Sep.): 329–37.

HALPERN, C. T., K. JOYNER, AND C. SUCHINDRAN. 2000. Smart teens don't have sex (or kiss much either). *Journal of Adolescent Health* 26 (Mar.): 213–25.

HAMER, D. H., S. HU, V. MAGNUSON, N. HU, AND A. M. L. PATTATUCCI. 1993. A linkage between DNA markers on the X chromosome and male sexual orientation. *Science,* July 16, 321–27.

HAMER, J., AND K. MARCHIORO. 2002. Becoming custodial dads: Exploring parenting among low-income and working-class African American fathers. *Journal of Marriage and Family* 64 (Feb.): 115–29.

HAMILTON, A. 2002. Sex, drinks and videotape. *Time,* Mar. 25, 8.

HAMILTON, B. E., P. D. SUTTON, AND S. J. VENTURA. 2003. Revised birth and fertility rates for the 1990s and new rates for Hispanic populations, 2000 and 2001: United States. *National Vital Statistics Reports,* 51, Aug. 4. www.cdc.gov/nchs/data/nvsr/nvsr51/nvsr51_12.pdf (accessed Aug. 25, 2003).

HAMILTON, T. F. 2002. Caitlin's families: Two families overcome their differences for the sake of a 12-year-old girl. *Grand Rapids Press,* Sep. 15, J1.

HAMMER, H., D. FINKELHOR, AND A. J. SEDLAK. 2002. *Children abducted by family members: National estimates and characteristics.* Washington, DC: U.S. Department of Justice.

HAMMER, H., D. FINKELHOR, AND A. J. SEDLACK. 2002. *Runaway/thrownaway children: National estimates and characteristics.* Washington, DC: U.S. Department of Justice.

HAMON, R. R. 1992. Filial role enactment by adult children. *Family Relations* 41 (Jan.): 91–96.

HANCOCK, J. 1999a. A business bonanza paid by taxpayers. *Baltimore Sun,* Oct. 10, 1A, 16A–17A.

HANCOCK, J. 1999b. S.C. pays dearly for added jobs. *Baltimore Sun,* Oct. 12, 1A, 8A–9A.

HANNON, R., D. S. HALL, T. KUNTZ, S. VAN LAAR, AND J. WILLIAMS. 1995. Dating characteristics leading to unwanted vs. wanted sexual behavior. *Sex Roles* 33 (11/12): 767–83.

HANS, J. D. 2002. Stepparenting after divorce: Stepparents' legal position regarding custody, access, and support. *Family Relations* 51 (Oct.): 301–7.

HANSON, M. J. 1998. Ethnic, cultural, and language diversity in intervention settings. In *Developing cross-cultural competence: A guide for working with children and their families,* 2nd ed., eds. E. W. Lynch and M. J. Hanson, 3–22. Baltimore: Paul H. Brookes.

HANSON, R. K., R. GIZZARELLI, AND H. SCOTT. 1994. The attitudes of incest offenders: Sexual entitlement and acceptance of sex with children. *Criminal Justice and Behavior* 21 (June): 187–202.

HANSON, S. L. 1996. *Lost talent: Women in the sciences.* Philadelphia: Temple University Press.

HARARI, S. E., AND M. A. VINOVSKIS. 1993. Adolescent sexuality, pregnancy, and childbearing in the past. In *The politics of pregnancy: Adolescent sexuality and public policy,* eds. A. Lawson and D. I. Rhode, 23–45. New Haven, CT: Yale University Press.

Harassment in the supermarket. 2002. ABC News. www.abcnews.go.com/sections/primetime/Daily News/primetime_ralphs_020620.html (accessed June 25, 2002).

HAREVEN, T. K. 1984. Themes in the historical development of the family. In *Review of child development research*, Vol. 7: *The family*, ed. R. D. Parke, 137–78. Chicago: University of Chicago Press.

HARLEY, W. F. JR. 2002. *Buyers, renters & freeloaders: Turning revolving-door romance into lasting love.* Grand Rapids, MI: Fleming H. Revell.

HARMON, A. 2003. Online dating sheds its stigma as losers.com. *New York Times.* www.nytimes.com/2003/06/29/national/29DATE.html?th (accessed June 29, 2003).

HARMS, T. 1989. The 12 building blocks of discipline. *Parents* (Aug.): 76–78, 81–82.

HARRIS, C. R. 2002. Sexual and romantic jealousy in heterosexual and homosexual adults. *Psychological Science* 13 (Jan.): 7–12.

HARRIS, C. R. 2003. A review of sex differences in sexual jealousy, including self-report data, psychophysiological responses, interpersonal violence, and morbid jealousy. *Personality & Social Psychology Review* 7 (May): 102–28.

HARRIS, D. 1995. Salary survey: 1995. *Working Woman* (Jan.): 25–34.

HARRIS, D. K. 1990. *Sociology of aging,* 2nd ed. New York: Harper & Row.

HARRIS, D. R., AND H. ONO. 2000. Intimate relationships between races more common than thought. www.umich.edu/~newsinfo/Releases/2000/Mar00/r032300a.html (accessed Sep. 16, 2000).

HARRIS, L. 1996. The hidden world of dating violence. *Parade Magazine,* Sep. 22, 4–6.

HARRIS, M. 1994. *Down from the pedestal: Moving beyond idealized images of womanhood.* New York: Doubleday.

HARRIS, M. 1996. Aggressive experiences and aggressiveness: Relationship to ethnicity, gender, and age. *Journal of Applied Social Psychology* 26: 843–70.

HARRIS, T. 2003. Mind work: How a Ph.D. affects black women. *Chronicle of Higher Education,* Apr. 11, B14–B15.

HARRISON, C., AND K. DAUTRICH. 1999. The modern American worker. *Public Perspective* 10 (Aug./Sept.): 38–41.

HARRISON, P. M., AND J. C. KARBERG. 2003. *Prison and jail inmates at midyear 2002.* Washington, DC: U.S. Department of Justice.

HARRYKISSOON, S. D., V. I. RICKERT, AND C. M. WIEMAN. 2002. Prevalence and patterns of intimate partner violence during the postpartum period. *Archives of Pediatrics & Adolescent Medicine* 156 (Apr.): 325–30.

HART, S. N., M. R. BRASSARD, N. J. BINGGELI, AND H. A. DAVIDSON. 2003. Psychological maltreatment. In *International encyclopedia of marriage and family,* 2nd ed., Vol. 1, ed. J. J. Ponzetti, Jr., 221–27. New York: Macmillan.

HARTILL, L. 2001. Vow or never. *Christian Science Monitor,* July 18, 15–17.

HARVEY, E. 1999. Short-term and long-term effects of early parental employment on children of the National Longitudinal Survey of Youth. *Developmental Psychology* 35 (Mar.): 445–59.

HARVEY, J. H., AND A. L. WEBER. 2002. *Odyssey of the heart: Close relationships in the 21st century,* 2nd ed. Mahwah, NJ: Erlbaum.

HARWOOD, R., B. LEYENDECKER, V. CARLSON, M. ASENCIO, AND A. MILLER. 2002. Parenting among Latino Families in the U.S. In *Handbook of parenting,* 2nd ed., Vol. 4: *Social conditions and applied parenting,* ed. M. H. Bornstein, 21–46. Mahwah, NJ: Erlbaum.

HASS, A. 1979. *Teenage sexuality: A survey of teenage sexual behavior.* New York: Macmillan.

HASTINGS, D. 1994. Battered men continue to have no place to go. *Baltimore Sun,* Aug. 1, 1D, 5D.

HATCHER, R. A., ET AL. 1990. *Contraceptive technology 1990–1992,* 15th ed. New York: Irvington.

HATCHETT, S. J. 1991. Women and men. In *Life in black America,* ed. J. S. Jackson, 84–104. Thousand Oaks, CA: Sage.

HATCHETT, S. J., AND J. S. JACKSON. 1993. African American extended kin systems: An assessment. In *Family ethnicity: Strength in diversity,* ed. H. P. McAdoo, 90–108. Thousand Oaks, CA: Sage.

HATCHETT, S., J. VEROFF, AND E. DOUVAN. 1995. Marital instability among black and white couples in early marriage. In *The decline in marriage among African Americans,* eds. M. B. Tucker and C. Mitchell-Kernan, 177–218. New York: Russell Sage Foundation.

HATFIELD, E. 1983. What do women and men want from love and sex? In *Changing boundaries: Gender roles and sexual behavior,* eds. E. R. Allgeier and N. B. McCormick, 106–34. Mountain View, CA: Mayfield.

HATFIELD, E., AND R. L. RAPSON. 1996. *Love and sex: Cross-cultural perspectives.* Boston: Allyn & Bacon.

HAUB, C. 2003. *2003 World population data sheet.* Washington, DC: Population Reference Bureau.

HAURIN, D. R., T. L. PARCEL, AND R. J. HAURIN. 2002. Does homeownership affect child outcomes? *Real Estate Economics* 30 (Winter): 635–66.

HAVEMAN, R., B. WOLFE, AND K. PENCE. 2001. Intergenerational effects of nonmarital and early childbearing. In *Out of wedlock: Causes and consequences of nonmarital fertility,* eds. L. L. Wu and B. Wolfe, 287–316. New York: Russell Sage Foundation.

HAVEMANN, J. 1997a. N.J. allows gays to adopt jointly. *Washington Post,* Dec. 18, A1, A24.

HAVEMANN, J. 1997b. Nursing home alternatives gaining in popularity. *Washington Post,* Jan. 24, A6.

HAWKE, D. F. 1988. *Everyday life in early America.* New York: Harper & Row.

HAYANI, I. 1999. Arabs in Canada: Assimilation or integration? In *Arabs in America: Building a new future,* ed. M. W. Suleiman, 284–303. Philadelphia: Temple University Press.

HAYASHI, G. M., AND B. R. STRICKLAND. 1998. Longterm effects of parental divorce on love relationships: Divorce as attachment disruption. *Journal of Social & Personal Relationships* 15 (Feb.): 23–38.

HAYES, C. L., D. ANDERSON, AND M. BLAU. 1993. *Our turn: The good news about women and divorce.* New York: Pocket Books.

HAYS, S. 1998. The fallacious assumptions and unrealistic prescriptions of attachment theory: A comment on parents' socioemotional investment in children. *Journal of Marriage and the Family* 60 (Aug.): 782–95.

HAZAN, C., AND P. R. SHAVER. 1987. Conceptualizing romantic love as an attachment process. *Journal of Personality and Social Psychology* 52: 511–24.

HEADDEN, S. 1997. The Hispanic dropout mystery. *U.S. News & World Report,* Oct. 20, 64–65.

HEALY, M. 2003. Fertility's new frontier. *Los Angeles Times,* July 21. www.latimes.com/features/health/la-he-pgd21jul21,1,2585793.story (accessed July 22, 2003).

HEATON, T. B. 1990. Marital stability throughout the child-rearing years. *Demography* 27 (Feb.): 55–63.

HEBEL, S. 2003. U. of California system failed to report many campus crimes, U.S. Education Dept. finds. *Chronicle of Higher Education,* Apr. 8. http://chronicle.com/daily/2003/04/2003040301n.htm (accessed Apr. 8, 2003).

HEBERT, L. E., P. A. SCHERR, J. L. BIENIAS, D. A. BENNETT, AND D. A. EVANS. 2003. Alzheimer disease in the US population. *Archives of Neurology* 60 (Aug.):1119–22.

HECHT, M. L., P. J. MARSTON, AND L. K. LARKEY. 1994. Love ways and relationship quality in heterosexual relationships. *Journal of Social and Personal Relationships* 11 (1): 25–43.

HELLER, D. E., AND P. MARIN. 2002. *Who should we help? The negative social consequences of merit aid scholarships.* Civil Rights Project. www.civilrightsproject.harvard.edu/research/meritaid/call_merit02.php (accessed Jan. 14, 2003).

HELLERSTEDT, W. 2002. Health and environmental risks associated with early childbearing. *Healthy Generations* 3 (May): 1–5.

HELMS-ERIKSON, H. 2001. Marital quality ten years after the transition to parenthood: Implications of the timing of parenthood and the division of housework. *Journal of Marriage and Family* 63 (Nov.): 1099–1110.

HENDRICK, C., AND S. HENDRICK. 1992a. *Liking, loving, and relating,* 2nd ed. Monterey, CA: Brooks/Cole.

HENDRICK, C., AND S. S. HENDRICK. 2003. Love. In *International encyclopedia of marriage and family,* 2nd ed., Vol. 3, ed. J. J. Ponzetti, Jr., 1059–65. New York: Macmillan.

HENDRICK, S., AND C. HENDRICK. 1992b. *Romantic love.* Thousand Oaks, CA: Sage.

HENDRICK, S. S., AND C. HENDRICK. 2002. Linking romantic love with sex: Development of the perceptions of love and sex scale. *Journal of Social and Personal Relationships* 19 (June): 361–78.

HENDRICKSON, M. L. 1994. Couples should fight for a good marriage. *U.S. Catholic* 59 (Apr.): 20–25.

HENDRIX, H. 1988. *Getting the love you want: A guide for couples.* New York: Henry Holt.

HENRY, K. 1999. Chapter 11 for London Fog. *Baltimore Sun,* Sep. 28, 1A, 7A.

HENRY, S. 1995. America's hidden disease. *Parade Magazine,* Feb. 12, 4–6.

HERBERT, B. 2002. The gift of mayhem. *New York Times,* Nov. 28. www.nytimes.com/2002/11/28/opinion/28HERB.html?todaysheadlines (accessed Nov. 29, 2002).

HERBERT, B. 2003a. A crush of applicants. *New York Times,* Feb. 10, A23.

HERBERT, B. 2003b. Young, jobless, hopeless. *New York Times,* Feb 6, A35.

HERBERT, W. 1999. When strangers become family. *U.S. News & World Report,* Nov. 29, 58–67.

HERBERT, W., AND S. HAMMEL. 1999. Getting close, but not too close. *U.S. News & World Report,* Mar. 22, 56–57.

HERDT, G. 1997. *Same sex, different cultures.* Boulder, CO: Westview.

HERMAN-GIDDENS, M., G. BROWN, S. VERBIEST, P. J. CARLSON, E. G. HOOTEN, E. HOWELL, AND J. D. BUTTS. 1999. Underascertainment of child abuse mortality in the United States. *Journal of the American Medical Association* 282 (Aug.): 463–67.

HERN, W. M. 1992. Shipibo polygyny and patrilocality. *American Ethnologist* 19 (Aug.): 501–22.

HERNANDEZ, S. 2003. Study: Diverse Hispanic groups must be included in broader AIDS battle. *South Florida Sun-Sentinel,* July 25. www.sun-sentinel.com/news/local/florida/sfl-caids25jul25.story (accessed Aug. 4, 2003).

HERRERÍAS, C. 1995. Noncustodial mothers following divorce. *Marriage & Family Review* 20 (1/2): 233–55.

HERRING, R. D. 1999. Experiencing a lack of money and appropriate skin color: A personal narrative. *Journal of Counseling & Development* 77 (Winter): 25–27.

HERRMAN, A. 2003. An American way of life. *Chicago Sun Times,* June 9, 6.

HERRMANN, A. 2003. Children of divorce in no rush to repeat error. *Chicago Sun Times,* June 10. www.suntimes.com/output/news/cst-nws-fam10.html (accessed June 12, 2003).

HERRSTROM, S. 1990. Sweden: Pro-choice on child care. *New Perspectives Quarterly* 7 (Winter): 27–30.

HERTZ, R., AND J. CHARLTON. 1989. Making family under a shiftwork schedule: Air force security guards and their wives. *Social Problems* 36 (Dec.): 491–507.

HETHERINGTON, E. M. 1999. Should we stay together for the sake of the children? In *Coping with divorce, single parenting, and remarriage: A risk and resiliency perspective,* ed. E. M. Hetherington, 93–116. Mahwah, NJ: Erlbaum.

HETHERINGTON, E. M., AND W. G. CLINGEMPEEL. 1992. Coping with marital transitions: A family systems perspective. *Monographs of the Society for Research in Child Development* 57, 2–3, serial no. 227.

HETHERINGTON, E. M., S. H. HENDERSON, AND D. REISS. 1999. *Adolescent siblings in stepfamilies: Family functioning and adolescent adjustment.* Malden, MA: Society for Research in Child Development.

HETHERINGTON, E. M., AND J. KELLY. 2002. *For better or for worse: Divorce reconsidered.* New York: W.W. Norton.

HETHERINGTON, E. M., AND R. D. PARKE. 2002. *Child psychology: A contemporary viewpoint,* 5th ed. Boston: McGraw Hill.

HETHERINGTON, E. M., AND M. M. STANLEY-HAGAN. 1997. The effects of divorce on fathers and their children. In *The role of the father in child development*, ed. M. E. Lamb, 191–211. New York: Wiley.

HETHERINGTON, E. M., AND M. M. STANLEY-HAGAN. 2000. Diversity among stepfamilies. In *Handbook of family diversity*, eds. D. H. Demo, K. R. Allen, and M. A. Fine, 173–96. New York: Oxford University Press.

HETHERINGTON, E. M., AND M. M. STANLEY-HAGAN. 2002. Parenting in divorced and remarried families. In *Handbook of parenting*, 2nd ed., Vol. 3: *Being and becoming a parent*, ed. M. H. Bornstein, 287–315. Mahwah, NJ: Erlbaum.

HETRICK, R. 1994. London Fog workers swallow pride, cuts. *Baltimore Sun*, Sep. 27, A1, A14.

HEWLETT, S. A. 2002. *Creating a life: Professional women and the quest for children*. New York: Miramax.

HEYMAN, R. E., AND A. M. S. SLEP. 2002. Do child abuse and interparental violence lead to adulthood family violence? *Journal of Marriage and Family* 64 (Nov.): 864–70.

HEYMANN, J. 2002. Can working families ever win? *Boston Review* 27 (Feb./Mar.): 4–13.

HEYN, D. 1997. *Marriage shock: The transformation of women into wives*. New York: Villard.

HICKMAN, J. 2002. America's 50 best companies for minorities. *Fortune*, July 8, 110–18.

HIEDEMANN, B., O. SUHOMLINOVA, AND A. M. O'RAND. 1998. Economic independence, economic status, and empty nest in midlife marital disruption. *Journal of Marriage and the Family* 60 (Feb.): 219–31.

HILL, N. E., AND K. R. BUSH. 2001. Relationships between parenting environment and children's mental health among African American and European American mothers and children. *Journal of Marriage and Family* 63 (Nov.): 954–66.

HILL, R. B. 1998. Understanding black family functioning: A holistic perspective. *Journal of Comparative Family Studies* 29 (Spring): 15–25.

HILL, R. B., ET AL. 1993. *Research on the African-American family: A holistic perspective*. Westport, CT: Auburn House.

HIMES, C. L. 2001. *Elderly Americans. Population Bulletin* 56 (Dec.): 1–40. Washington, DC: Population Reference Bureau.

HINSCH, B. 1990. *Passions of the cut sleeve: The male homosexual tradition in China*. Berkeley: University of California Press.

HITE, S. 1987. *Women and love: A cultural revolution in progress*. New York: Knopf.

HIV/AIDS among Hispanics in the United States. 2002. Centers for Disease Control and Prevention. www.cdc.gov/hiv/pubs/facts/hispanic.pdf (accessed June 20, 2003).

HIV/AIDS among U.S. women: Minority and young women at continuing risk. 2002. Centers for Disease Control and Prevention. www.cdc.gov/hiv/pubs/facts/women.pdf (accessed June 18, 2003).

HIV/AIDS update: A glance at the HIV epidemic. 2002. Centers for Disease Control and Prevention. www.cdc.gov/nchstp/od/news/At-a-Glance.pdf (accessed June 16, 2003).

HOBBS, F., AND N. STOOPS. 2002. *Demographic trends in the 20th century*. U.S. Census Bureau, 2000 Special Reports, Series CENSR-4. www.census.gov/prod/2002pubs/censr-4.pdf (accessed May 25, 2003).

HOCHSCHILD, A., WITH A. MACHUNG. 1989. *The second shift: Working parents and the revolution at home*. New York: Penguin.

HOELTER, L. F., AND D. E. STAUFFER. 2002. What does it mean to be "just living together" in the new millennium? An overview. In *Just living together: Implications of cohabitation on families, children, and social policy*, eds. A. Booth and A. C. Crouter, 255–71. Mahwah, NJ: Erlbaum.

HOERLYCK, A. 2003. Racial disparity still haunts housing market. *Baltimore Sun*, July 3, 21A.

HOFFERTH, S. L., Z. JANKUNIENE, AND P. D. BRANDON. 2000. *Self-care among school-age children*. University of Michigan, Institute for Social Research, unpublished paper.

HOFFERTH, S. L., AND J. F. SANDBURG. 2001. How American children spend their time. *Journal of Marriage and Family* 63 (May): 295–308.

HOFFMAN, B. A. 2003. Gay rights as source of strength. *Baltimore Sun*, July 5, 11A.

HOFFMAN, J. 1995. Divorced fathers make gains in battles to increase rights. *New York Times*, Apr. 26, B1, B5.

HOGAN, D. P., L.-X. HAO, AND W. L. PARISH. 1990. Race, kin networks, and assistance to mother-headed families. *Social Forces* 68: 797–812.

HOJAT, M., R. SHAPURIAN, D. FOROUGHI, H. NAYERAHMADI, M. FARZANEH, M. SHAFIEYAN, AND M. PARSI. 2000. Gender differences in traditional attitudes toward marriage and the family: An empirical study of Iranian immigrants in the United States. *Journal of Family Issues* 21 (May): 419–34.

HOLDEN, C. 2001. General contentment masks gender gap in first AAAS salary and job survey. American Association for the Advancement of Science. http://recruit.sciencemag.org/feature/salsurvey/v294i5541p396.pdf (accessed Oct. 15, 2001).

HOLDEN, G. W., P. C. MILLER, AND S. D. HARRIS. 1999. The instrumental side of corporal punishment: Parents' reported practices and outcome expectancies. *Journal of Marriage and the Family* 61 (Nov.): 908–19.

HOLLINGSWORTH, L. D. 2003. When an adoption disrupts: A study of public attitudes. *Family Relations* 52 (Apr.): 161–66.

HOLMAN, T. B., AND W. R. BURR. 1980. Beyond the beyond: The growth of family theories in the 1970s. *Journal of Marriage and the Family* 42 (Nov.): 729–41.

HOLMAN, T. B., J. H. LARSON, AND S. L. HARMER. 1994. The development and predictive validity of a new premarital assessment instrument: The preparation for marriage questionnaire. *Family Relations* 43 (Jan.): 46–52.

HOLMES, S. A. 1994. A generally healthy America emerges in a census report. *New York Times*, Oct. 13, B13.

HOLMES, S. A. 2003. Courts put girls on the stand in Alabama. *New York Times*, January 20. www.nytimes.com/2003/01/20/national/20ALAB.html (accessed Jan. 21, 2003).

HOLT, T., L. GREENE, AND J. DAVIS. 2003. *National survey of adolescents and young adults: Sexual health knowledge, attitudes and experiences*. The Henry Kaiser Family Foundation. www.kff.org/content/2003/3218/kff_youth_survey_Final_04_03.pdf (accessed June 12, 2003).

HOLZER, H. J. 2001. Racial differences in labor market outcomes among men. In *America becoming: Racial trends and their consequences*, Vol. 2, eds. N. J. Smelser, W. J. Wilson, and F. Mitchell, 98–123. Washington, DC: National Academy Press.

HOMEFRONT. 2003. Everything but the kitchen sink. *Christian Science Monitor*, Feb. 12, 14.

Homosexuality remark draws fire for senator. 2003. *Baltimore Sun*, Apr. 23, 10A.

HONEY, M. 1984. *Creating Rosie the Riveter: Class, gender, and propaganda*. Amherst: University of Massachusetts Press.

Honeymoon in a retirement community? 2002. *Guide to Retirement Living* (Fall): 23, 29, 33.

HOOVER, E. 2003. Drug and alcohol. Arrests increased on campuses in 2001. *Chronicle of Higher Education*, May 16, A38–A39.

HOOVER, E. 2003. Wesleyan U. will offer "gender-blind" housing, a first for transgender students. *Chronicle of Higher Education*, May 22. http://chronicle.com/daily/2003/05/2003052205n.htm (accessed May 23, 2003).

HOOYMAN, N. R., AND H. A. KIYAK. 2002. *Social gerontology: A multidisciplinary perspective*, 6th ed. Boston, MA: Allyn & Bacon.

HOPE, T. L., AND C. K. JACOBSON. 1995. Japanese American families: Assimilation over time. In *American families: Issues in race and ethnicity*, ed. C. K. Jacobson, 145–75. New York: Garland.

HOPPER, J. 2001. The symbolic origins of conflict in divorce. *Journal of Marriage and Family* 63 (May): 430–45.

HORWITZ, A. V., AND H. R. WHITE. 1998. The relationship of cohabitation and mental health: A study of a young adult cohort. *Journal of Marriage and the Family* 60 (May): 505–14.

HORWITZ, A. V., H. R. WHITE, AND S. HOWELL-WHITE. 1996. Becoming married and mental health: A longitudinal study of a cohort of young

adults. *Journal of Marriage and the Family* 58 (Nov.): 895–907.

HOSLEY, C. A., AND R. MONTEMAYOR. 1997. Fathers and adolescents. In *The role of the father in child development*, ed. M. E. Lamb, 162–78. New York: Wiley.

HOSSAIN, Z. 2001. Division of household labor and family functioning in off-reservation Navajo Indian families. *Family Relations* 50 (July): 255–61.

HOUNSELL, C., AND P. HUMPHLETT. 2002. Minority women and retirement income. Women's Institute for a Secure Retirement. www.wiser.heinz.org/wiseryfpminrpt.pdf (accessed Oct. 9, 2003).

HOUNSELL, C., AND P. HUMPHLETT. 2003. Older minority women need retirement help now. *Women's E-News*, May 24. www.womensenews.org/article.cfm/dyn/aid/1335 (accessed May 25, 2003).

How late is too late? 2001. Letter to the editor. *Newsweek*, Sep. 3, 14.

HOWARD, J. A., AND J. A. HOLLANDER. 1997. *Gendered situations, gendered selves: A gender lens on social psychology*. Thousand Oaks, CA: Sage.

HÜBNER, K., ET AL. 2003. Derivation of oocytes from mouse embryonic stem cells. *Science* 300 (May): 1251–56.

HUDAK, M. A. 1993. Gender schema theory revisited: Men's stereotypes of American women. *Sex Roles* 28 (5/6): 279–92.

HUDSON, J. W., AND L. F. HENZE. 1969. Campus values in mate selection: A replication. *Journal of Marriage and the Family* 31 (Nov.): 772–75.

HUGHES, D., AND M. A. DODGE. 1997. African American women in the workplace: Relationships between job conditions, racial bias at work, and perceived job quality. *American Journal of Community Psychology* 25 (Oct.): 581–99.

HUGICK, L. 1999. Taking credit where it's due. *Public Perspective* 10 (Oct./Nov.): 10–14.

HUMAN RIGHTS WATCH. 2003. World report 2003: South Africa. www.hrw.org/wr2k3/africa11.html (accessed May 15, 2003).

HUMPHRY, D., AND M. CLEMENT. 2000. *Freedom to die: People, politics, and the right-to-die movement*. New York: St. Martin's/Griffin.

HUNT, J. 1991. Ten reasons not to hit your kids. In *Breaking down the wall of silence: The liberating experience of facing painful trust*, ed. A. Miller, 168–71. Meridian, NY: Dutton.

HUNTLEY, T., ED. 1991. *Helping children grieve: When someone they love dies*. Minneapolis: Augsburg.

HUPKA, R. B. 1991. The motive for the arousal of romantic jealousy: Its cultural origin. In *The psychology of jealousy and envy*, ed. P. Salovey, 252–70. New York: Guilford.

HURH, W. M. 1998. *The Korean Americans*. Westport, CT: Greenwood.

HURTADO, A. 1995. Variations, combinations, and evolutions: Latino families in the United States. In *Understanding Latino families: Scholarship, policy, and practice*, ed. R. E. Zambrana, 40–61. Thousand Oaks, CA: Sage.

HUSTON, M., AND P. SCHWARTZ. 1995. The relationships of lesbians and of gay men. In *Understudied relationships: Off the beaten track*, eds. J. T. Wood and S. Duck, 89–121. Thousand Oaks, CA: Sage.

HUTCHINSON, E. O. 1994. *Black fatherhood. II: Black women talk about their men*. Los Angeles: Middle Passage.

HUTCHINSON, M. K. 2002. The influence of sexual risk communication between parents and daughters on sexual risk behaviors. *Family Relations* 51 (July): 238–47.

HUTCHISON, I. W. 1999. The effect of children's presence on alcohol use by spouse abusers and their victims. *Family Relations* 48 (Jan.): 57–65.

HUTTENLOCHER, J., M. VASILYEVA, E. CYMERMAN, AND S. LEVINE. 2002. Language input and child syntax. *Cognitive Psychology* 45 (Nov.): 337–74.

HUTTER, M. 1998. *The changing family*, 3rd ed. Boston: Allyn & Bacon.

HWANG, S.-S., R. SAENZ, AND B. F. AGUIRRE. 1994. Structural and individual determinants of outmarriage among Chinese-, Filipino-, and Japanese-Americans in California. *Sociological Inquiry* 64 (Nov.): 396–414.

HWANG, S.-S., R. SAENZ, AND B. E. AGUIRRE. 1997. Structural and assimilationist explanations of Asian American intermarriage. *Journal of Marriage and the Family* 59 (Aug.): 758–72.

HYDE, J. S. 1996. Where are the gender differences? Where are the gender similarities? In *Sex, power, conflict: Evolutionary and feminist perspectives*, eds. D. M. Buss and N. M. Malamuth, 107–18. New York: Oxford University Press.

HYMAN, B. 2000. The economic consequences of child sexual abuse for adult lesbian women. *Journal of Marriage and the Family* 62 (Feb.): 199–211.

HYMOWITZ, K. S. 2003. The cohabitation blues. *Commentary* 116 (Mar.): 66–69.

IHINGER-TALLMAN, M., AND K. PASLEY. 1987. *Remarriage*. Beverly Hills, CA: Sage.

IHINGER-TALLMAN, M., AND K. PASLEY. 1997. Stepfamilies in 1984 and today: A scholarly perspective. *Marriage & Family Review* 26 (1/2): 19–40.

IKONOMIDOU, C., P. ET AL., 2000. Ethanol-induced apoptotic neurodegeneration and fetal alcohol syndrome. *Science* 287, Feb. 11, 1056–60.

IMBER-BLACK, E., AND J. ROBERTS. 1993. Family change: Don't cancel holidays! *Psychology Today* 26 (Mar./Apr.): 62, 64, 92–93.

Infant homicide. 2003. Child Trends Data Bank. www.cdc.gov/mmwr/PDF/SS/SS5003.pdf (accessed Sep. 20, 2003).

INGERSOLL-DAYTON, B., M. B. NEAL, J.-H. HA, AND L. B. HAMMER. 2003. Redressing inequity in parent care among siblings. *Journal of Marriage and Family* 65 (Feb.): 201–12.

INGERSOLL-DAYTON, B., M. B. NEAL, AND L. B. HAMMER. 2001. Aging parents helping adult children: The experience of the sandwiched generation. *Family Relations* 50 (July): 262–71.

INGRASSIA, M., AND M. BECK. 1994. Patterns of abuse. *Newsweek*, July 4, 26–33.

Inside-OUT: A report on the experiences of lesbians, gays and bisexuals in American and the public's views on issues and policies related to sexual orientation. The Henry Kaiser Family Foundation. www.kff.org/content/2001/3193/LGBSurvey Report.pdf (accessed June 18, 2003).

International migration report. 2002. United Nations. www.un.org/esa/population/publications/ittmig2002/2002ITTMIGTEXT22-11.pdf (accessed Apr. 15, 2003).

Interracial marriages rising, study of census data says. 1997. *Baltimore Sun*, Mar. 26, 3A.

Interracial wedding barred in Ohio. 2000. *Baltimore Sun*, July 11, 3A.

Iranian arbitrating body approves marriage age increase. 2002. Yahoo News, June 23. http://story.news.yahoo.com/news?tmpl=story&u=/ap/20020623/ap_wo_en_po/iran_marriage_2 (accessed June 24, 2002).

IRVING, H. H., AND M. BENJAMIN. 1991. Shared and sole-custody parents: A comparative analysis. In *Joint custody and shared parenting*, 2nd ed., ed. J. Folberg, 114–31. New York: Guilford.

ISHII-KUNTZ, M. 1993. Japanese fathers: Work demands and family roles. In *Men, work and family*, ed. J. C. Hood, 45–67. Thousand Oaks, CA: Sage.

ISHII-KUNTZ, M. 1997. Intergenerational relationships among Chinese, Japanese, and Korean Americans. *Family Relations* 46 (Oct.): 23–32.

ISHII-KUNTZ, M., AND G. R. LEE. 1987. Status of the elderly: An extension of the theory. *Journal of Marriage and the Family* 49 (May): 413–20.

ISRAELY, J. 2002. Something in the air. *Time*, Dec. 9, 28.

Issues and answers: Fact sheet on sexuality education. 2001. *SIECUS Report* 29 (Aug./Sep.). www.siecus.org/pubs/fact/fact0007.html (accessed June 12, 2003).

Italy promises pensions for housewives. 1996. *Baltimore Sun*, Aug. 11, 18A.

ITANO, N. 2002a. Fighting tradition, girls yearn to learn. *Christian Science Monitor*, Mar. 18, 12.

ITANO, N. 2002b. How Rwanda's genocide lingers on for women. *Christian Science Monitor*, Nov. 27, 8.

It's time for new voices for new choices which truly leave no child behind. 2002. Children's Defense Organization. www.childrensdefense.org/pdf/budget_analysis_022603.pdf#xml=http://childrensdefense.org.master.com/texis/master/

search/mysite.txt?q=under151mortality&order=dd&id=28406abb10b46050&cmd=xml (accessed Mar. 1, 2003).

It's time for working women to earn equal pay. 1998. AFL-CIO. www.aflcio.org/women/equalpay.htm (accessed Oct. 16, 2000).

JACKSON, A. P., R. P. BROWN, AND K. E. PATTERSON-STEWART. 2000. African Americans in dual-career commuter marriages: An investigation of their experiences. *Family Journal: Counseling and Therapy for Couples and Families* 8 (Jan.): 22–36.

JACKSON, A. P., P. GYAMFI, J. BROOKS-GUNN, AND M. BLAKE. 1998. Employment status, psychological well-being, social support, and physical discipline practices of single black mothers. *Journal of Marriage and the Family* 60 (Nov.): 894–902.

JACKSON, D. D. 1998. "This hole in our heart": Urban Indian identity and the power of silence. *American Indian Culture and Research Journal* 22 (4): 227–54.

JACKSON, S. 2003. Analyzing the studies. In *Batterer intervention programs: Where do we go from here?* ed. S. Jackson et al., 23–29. Washington, DC: U.S. Department of Justice.

JACKSON, S. A. 1998. "Something about the word": African American women and feminism. In *No middle ground: Women and radical protest*, ed. K. M. Blee, 38–50. New York: New York University Press.

JACOBS, F. H., AND M. W. DAVIES. 1991. Rhetoric or reality? Child and family policy in the United States. *Social Policy Report* 5 (4): 1–25.

JACOBS, J. A., AND K. GERSON. 1998. Who are the overworked Americans? *Review of Social Economy* 56 (Winter): 442–59.

JACOBS, J. L. 1990. Reassessing mother blame in incest. *Signs* 15 (Spring): 500–14.

JACOBSEN, L., AND B. EDMONDSON. 1994. Father figures. *American Demographics*, Parenting Reprint Package, 31–37.

JACOBY, S. 1999. Great sex. *Modern Maturity* (Sep./Oct.): 41–45, 91.

JAFFEE, S. R., T. E. MOFFITT, A. CASPI, AND A. TAYLOR. 2003. Life with (or without) father: The benefits of living with two biological parents depend on the father's antisocial behavior. *Child Development* 74 (Jan./Feb.): 109–26.

JAIMES, M. A., WITH T. HALSEY. 1992. American Indian women: At the center of indigenous resistance in contemporary North America. In *The state of Native America: Genocide, colonization, and resistance*, ed. M. A. Jaimes, 311–44. Boston: South End.

JALALI, B. 1996. Iranian families. In *Ethnicity and family therapy*, 2nd ed., eds. M. McGoldrick, J. Giordano, and J. K. Pearce, 347–63. New York: Guilford.

JAMBUNATHAN, S., D. C. BURTS, AND S. PIERCE. 2000. Comparisons of parenting attitudes among five ethnic groups in the United States. *Journal of Comparative Family Studies* 31 (Autumn): 395–406.

JAMES, A. D. 1998. What's love got to do with it? Economic viability and the likelihood of marriage among African American men. *Journal of Comparative Family Studies* 29 (Summer): 373–86.

JAMES, J. W., AND R. FRIEDMAN. 1998. *The grief recovery handbook: The action program for moving beyond death, divorce, and other losses*. New York: HarperPerennial.

JANKOWIAK, W. R., AND E. F. FISCHER. 1992. A cross-cultural perspective on romantic love. *Ethnology* 31 (Apr.): 149–55.

JANOFSKY, M. 2003. Young brides stir new outcry on Utah polygamy. *New York Times*. www.nytimes.com/2003/02/28/national/28POLY.html?tntemail0 (accessed Feb. 28, 2003).

Japanese birth rate drops to lowest level since World War II. 2003. Kaiser Network, June 9. www.kaisernetwork.org/daily_reports/rep_index.cfm?DR_ID=18148 (accessed June 10, 2003).

JARRETT, R. L. 1994. Living poor: Family life among single parent, African-American women. *Social Problems* 41 (Feb.): 30–49.

JAYAKODY, R., AND N. CABRERA. 2002. What are the choices for low-income families? Cohabitation, marriage, and remaining single. In *Just living together: Implications of cohabitation on families, children, and social policy*, eds. A. Booth and A. C. Crouter, 85–96. Mahwah, NJ: Erlbaum.

JAYAKODY, R., AND A. KALIL. 2002. Social fathering in low-income, African American families with preschool children. *Journal of Marriage and Family* 64 (May): 504–16.

JEFFREY, N. A. 2001. Bachelors begin to lose upper hand. *Wall Street Journal*, Dec. 8. www.richbaker.com/articles/social/bachelorslose.htm (accessed July 2, 2003).

JEMMOTT, L. S., V. CATAN, A. NYAMAATHI, AND J. ANASTASIA. 1995. African American women and HIV risk-reduction issues. In *Women at risk: Issues in the primary prevention of AIDS*, eds. A. O'Leary and L. S. Jemmott, 131–57. New York: Plenum.

JENDREK, M. P. 1994. Grandparents who parent their grandchildren: Circumstances and decisions. *The Gerontologist* 34 (2): 206–16.

JENNY, C., K. P. HYMEL, A. RITZEN, S. E. REINERT, AND T. C. HAY. 1999. Analysis of missed cases of abusive head trauma. *Journal of the American Medical Association* 281 (Feb.): 621–26.

JERROME, D. 1994. Time, change and continuity in family life. *Aging and Society* 14 (Mar.): 1–27.

JEUNE, B., AND J. W. VAUPEL, EDS. 1995. *Exceptional longevity: From prehistory to the present*. Odense, Denmark: Odense University Press.

JO, M. H. 1999. *Korean immigrants and the challenge of adjustment*. Westport, CT: Greenwood.

JOHN, D., AND B. A. SHELTON. 1997. The production of gender among black and white women and men: The case of household labor. *Sex Roles* 36 (Feb.): 171–93.

JOHN, R. 1988. The Native American family. In *Ethnic families in America: Patterns and variations*, 3rd ed., eds. C. H. Mindel, R. W. Habenstein, and R. Wright, Jr., 325–66. New York: Elsevier.

JOHNSON, B. K. 1996. Older adults and sexuality: A multidimensional perspective. *Journal of Gerontological Nursing* 22 (Feb.): 6–15.

JOHNSON, B. T., M. P. CAREY, K. L. MARCH, K. D. LEVIN, AND L. A. J. SCOTT-SHELDON. 2003. Interventions to reduce sexual risk for the human immunodeficiency virus in adolescents, 1985–2000. *Archives of Pediatrics and Adolescent Medicine* 157 (Apr.): 381–88.

JOHNSON, C. 2003. AIDS still taboo for many blacks: Secrecy hampers effort to fight disease. *San Francisco Chronicle*, June 16. www.sfgate.com/cgi-bin/article.cgi?file=/chronicle/archive/2003/06/16/BA251474.DTL (accessed June 20, 2003).

JOHNSON, C. L. 1993. The prolongation of life and the extension of family relationships: The families of the oldest old. In *Family, self, and society: Toward a new agenda for family research*, eds. P. A. Cowan, D. Field, D. A. Hansen, A. Skolnick, and G. E. Swanson, 317–30. Hillsdale, NJ: Erlbaum.

JOHNSON, E. M., AND T. L. HUSTON. 1998. The perils of love, or why wives adapt to husbands during the transition to parenthood. *Journal of Marriage and the Family* 60 (Feb.): 195–204.

JOHNSON, L. 1996. Some rural Chinese women seek greater role in society. *Baltimore Sun*, Oct. 12, 10A.

JOHNSON, P. 2002. The color of love. *Essence*, July 17. www.essence.com/essence/bodyandsoul/relationships/0,16109,334861,00.html (accessed June 25, 2003).

JOHNSON, R. 1985. Stirring the oatmeal. In *Challenge of the heart: Love, sex, and intimacy in changing times*, ed. J. Welwood. Boston: Shambhala.

JOHNSON, R. W., AND M. M. FAVREAULT. 2001. Retiring together or working alone: The impact of spousal employment and disability on retirement decisions. Center for Retirement Research at Boston College, Mar. www.bc.edu/centers/crr/papers/wp_2001-01.pdf (accessed Oct. 9, 2003).

JOHNSON, R. W., AND A. T. LO SASSO. 2000. Parental care at midlife: Balancing work and family responsibilities near retirement. The Retirement Project no. 9, Urban Institute. www.urban.org/retirement/briefs/9/BRIEF9.PDF (accessed Oct. 28, 2000).

JOHNSTON, L. D., P. M. O'MALLEY, AND J. G. BACHMAN. 2003. *Monitoring the future: National results on adolescent drug use: Overview of key findings, 2002.* University of Michigan Institute for Social Research. http://monitoringthefuture. org/pubs/monographs/overview2002.pdf (accessed Sep. 25, 2003).

JONES, A. 1994. *Next time, she'll be dead: Battering and how to stop it.* Boston: Beacon.

JONES, A., AND S. SCHECHTER. 1992. *When love goes wrong: What to do when you can't do anything right.* New York: HarperCollins.

JONES, C. 1994. Living single. *Essence* (May): 138–40.

JONES, D. 2003. Few women hold top executive jobs, even when CEOs are female. *USA Today,* Jan. 27. www.usatoday.com/money/jobcenter/2003-01-26-womenceos_x.htm (accessed Jan. 28, 2003).

JONES, J. 1985. *Labor of love, labor of sorrow: Black women, work and the family from slavery to the present.* New York: Basic Books.

JONES, J. M. 2002a. Parents of young children are most stressed Americans. Gallup News Service, Nov. 8. www.gallup.com/poll/releases/pr021108.asp (accessed Nov. 10, 2002).

JONES, J. M. 2002b. Public divided on benefits of living together before marriage. Gallup News Service, Aug. 16. www.gallup.com/poll/releases/pr020816.asp (accessed Aug. 18, 2002).

JONES, M. 2003. The mystery of my eggs. *New York Times,* Mar. 16, 44.

JONES, N. A., AND A. S. SMITH. 2001. *The two or more races population: 2000.* U.S. Census. www.census.gov/prod/2001pubs/c2kbr01-6.pdf (accessed Apr. 16, 2003).

JONES, R. K. 1993. Female victim perceptions of the causes of male spouse abuse. *Sociological Inquiry* 63 (Aug.): 351–61.

JONES, R. K., J. E. DARROCH, AND S. K. HENSHAW. 2002. Contraceptive use among U.S. women having abortions in 2000–2001. *Perspectives on Sexual and Reproductive Health* 34 (Nov./Dec.): 294–303.

JONES, W. H., AND M. P. BURDETTE. 1994. Betrayal in relationships. In *Perspectives on close relationships,* eds. A. L. Weber and J. H. Harvey, 243–62. Boston: Allyn & Bacon.

JOSEPH, S, ED. 1999. *Intimate selving in Arab families: Gender, self, and identity.* New York: Syracuse University Press.

JOSSELSON, R. 1992. *The space between us: Exploring the dimensions of human relationships.* San Francisco: Jossey-Bass.

JOYCE, R. 2001. Sexual superpower U.S. leads world in love-making, survey reports. Reuters, Nov. 27. www.boston.com/news/daily/27/sexual_superpower.htm (accessed June 15, 2003).

JUDGE, S. 2003. Determinants of parental stress in families adopting children from Eastern Europe. *Family Relations* 52 (July): 241–48.

JULIAN, T. W., P. C. MCKENRY, AND M. W. MCKELVEY. 1994. Cultural variations in parenting: Perceptions of Caucasian, African-American, Hispanic, and Asian-American parents. *Family Relations* 43 (Jan.): 30–37.

JUSTICE, G. 1999. We're happily married and living apart. *Newsweek,* Oct. 18, 12.

KACAPYR, E. 1998. How hard are hard times? *American Demographics* 20 (Feb.): 30–32.

KADLEC, D. 2003. Where did my raise go? *Time,* May 26, 44–54.

KAIRYS, S. W., ET AL. 2001. Distinguishing sudden infant death syndrome from child abuse fatalities. *American Academy of Pediatrics* 107 (Feb.): 437–41.

KAKUCHI, S. 2003. Japan's battlers of sex abuse confront culture, law. *Women's E-News,* Apr. 21. www.womensenews.org/article.cfm/dyn/aid/1295 (accessed Apr. 23, 2003).

KALB, M. 2001. *One scandalous story: Clinton, Lewinsky, and thirteen days that tarnished American journalism.* New York: Free Press.

KALIL, A. 2002. Cohabitation and child development. In *Just living together: Implications of cohabitation on families, children, and social policy,* eds. A. Booth and A. C. Crouter, 153–60. Mahwah, NJ: Erlbaum.

KALMIJN, M. 1993. Trends in black/white intermarriage. *Social Forces* 72 (Sep.): 119–46.

KALMIJN, M. 1998. Intermarriage and homogamy: Causes, patterns, trends. *Annual Review of Sociology* 24: 395–421.

KAMARA, C. H. 1998. *Guinea means woman: Guinea's national efforts in the fight against female genital mutilation.* London: Rainbow.

KAMEN, P. 2002. *Her way: Women remake the sexual revolution.* New York: Broadway.

KAMERMAN, S. B. 1996. Child and family policies: An international overview. In *Children, families, and government: Preparing for the twenty-first century,* eds. E. F. Zigler, S. L. Kagan, and N. W. Hall, 31–48. New York: Cambridge University Press.

KAMO, Y. 1998. Asian grandparents. In *Handbook on grandparenthood,* ed. M. E. Szinovacz, 97–112. Westport, CT: Greenwood.

KAMO, Y., AND E. L. COHEN. 1998. Division of household work between partners: A comparison of black and white couples. *Journal of Comparative Family Studies* 29 (Spring): 131–45.

KANALEY, R. 2000. Women closing gap in Net use, report finds. *Baltimore Sun,* May 15, 1C–2C.

KANTOR, R. M. 1970. Communes. *Psychology Today* (July): 53–57, 78.

KANTROWITZ, B., AND P. WINGERT. 1999. The science of a good marriage. *Newsweek,* Apr. 19, 52–57.

KANTROWITZ, B., AND P. WINGERT. 2001. The parent trap. *Newsweek,* Jan. 29, 49–53.

KANTROWITZ, B., AND P. WINGERT. 2001. Unmarried with children. *Newsweek,* May 28, 46–54.

KAO, L. C., ET AL. 2003. Expression profiling of endometrium from women with endometriosis reveals candidate genes for disease-based implantation failure and infertility. *Endocrinology* 144 (Apr. 10): 2870–81.

KAPLAN, G. A., AND W. J. STRAWBRIDGE. 1994. Behavioral and social factors in healthy aging. In *Aging and quality of life,* eds. R. P. Abeles, H. C. Gift, and M. G. Ory, 57–78. New York: Springer.

KAPLAN, H. S. 1979. *Disorders of sexual desire.* New York: Brunner/Mazel.

KAR, S. B., A. JIMENEZ, K. CAMPBELL, AND F. SZE. 1998. Acculturation and quality of life: A comparative study of Japanese-Americans and Indo-Americans. *Amerasia Journal* 24 (Spring): 129–42.

KARANJA, W. W. 1987. "Outside wives" and "inside wives" in Nigeria: A study of changing perceptions of marriage. In *Transformations of African marriage,* eds. D. Parkin and D. Nyamwaya, 247–61. Manchester, UK: Manchester University Press.

KARASIK, S. 2000. More latchkey kids means more trouble: High-risk behavior increases when parents are gone. www.apbnews.com/safetycenter/family/2000/04/14/sitter0414_01.html (accessed Sep. 28, 2000).

KARJANE, H. M., B. S. FISHER, AND F. T CULLEN. 2002. Campus sexual assault: How America's institutions of higher education respond (Report to Congress). Education Development Center, Inc. http://secure.edc.org/publications/prodView.asp?1522 (accessed July 6, 2003).

KAROLY, L. A. 1993. The trend in inequality among families, individuals, and workers in the United States: A twenty-five year perspective. In *Uneven tides: Rising inequality in America,* eds. S. Danziger and P. Gottschalk, 19–97. New York: Russell Sage Foundation.

KASHEF, Z. 2003. The fetal position. *Mother Jones* (Jan./Feb.): 18–19.

KASS, L. R. 1997. The end of courtship. *The Public Interest* 126 (Winter): 39–63.

KATE, N. T. 1997. What if whites become a minority? *American Demographics* 19 (Dec.): 42.

KATE, N. T. 1998. How many children? *American Demographics* 20 (Mar.): 35.

KATZEV, A. R., R. L. WARNER, AND A. C. ACOCK. 1994. Girls or boys? Relationship of child gender to marital instability. *Journal of Marriage and the Family* 56 (Feb.): 89–100.

KAUFMAN, M. 1993. *Cracking the armour: Power, pain and the lives of men.* New York: Viking/Penguin.

KAUFMAN, M. 2002. Popularity of breast implants rising. *Washington Post,* Sep. 22, A1.

KAWAMOTO, W. T. 2001. Introduction. *American Behavioral Scientist* 44 (May): 1445–46.

KAWAMOTO, W. T., AND T. C. CHESHIRE. 1997. American Indian families. In *Families in cultural context: Strengths and challenges in diversity,* ed.

M. K. DeGenova, 15–34. Mountain View, CA: Mayfield.

KAYE, K. 2001. Differences in nonmarital childbearing across states. In *Out of wedlock: Causes and consequences of nonmarital fertility,* eds. L. L. Wu and B. Wolfe, 49–76. New York: Russell Sage Foundation.

KAYSER, K. 1993. *When love dies: The process of marital disaffection.* New York: Guilford.

KEITH, P. M., S. KIM, AND R. B. SCHAFER. 2000. Informal ties of the unmarried in middle and later life: Who has them and who does not? *Sociological Spectrum* 20 (Apr.–June): 221–38.

KEITH, V. M. 1997. Life stress and psychological well-being among married and unmarried blacks. In *Family life in black America,* eds. R. J. Taylor, J. S. Jackson, and L. M. Chatters, 95–116. Thousand Oaks, CA: Sage.

KEITH, V. M., AND B. FINLAY. 1988. The impact of parental divorce on children's educational attainment, marital timings, and likelihood of divorce. *Journal of Marriage and Family* 50 (Aug.): 797–809.

KELLEY, B. T., T. P. THORNBERRY, AND C. A. SMITH. 1997. *In the wake of childhood maltreatment.* Washington, DC: U.S. Department of Justice, Office of Justice Programs, Office of Juvenile Justice and Delinquency Prevention.

KELLEY, P. 1992. Healthy stepfamily functioning. *Families in Society: The Journal of Contemporary Human Services* 73 (Dec.): 579–87.

KELLEY, P. 1996. Family-centered practice with stepfamilies. *Families in Society: The Journal of Contemporary Human Services* 77 (Nov.): 535–44.

KELLY, G. F. 1994. *Sexuality today: The human perspective,* 4th ed. Guilford, CT: Dushkin.

KELLY, J. B. 2000. Children's adjustment in conflicted marriage and divorce: A decade review of research. *Journal of the American Academy of Child & Adolescent Psychiatry* 39 (Aug.): 963–73.

KEMP, S., AND J. SQUIRES, EDS. 1997. *Feminisms.* New York: Oxford University Press.

KENDALL, D. 1999. *Sociology in our times,* 2nd ed. Belmont, CA: Wadsworth.

KENDALL, D. 2002. *The power of good deeds: Privileged women and the social reproduction of the upper class.* Lanham, MD: Rowman & Littlefield.

KENEN, R. H. 1993. *Reproductive hazards in the workplace: Mending jobs, managing pregnancies.* New York: Haworth.

KENNEDY, G. E. 1990. College students' expectations of grandparent and grandchild role behaviors. *The Gerontologist* 30 (1): 43–48.

KENNEDY, R. 2002. *Nigger: The strange career of a troublesome word.* New York: Pantheon.

KENNICKELL, A. B. 2003. A rolling tide: Changes in the distribution of wealth in the U.S., 1989–2001. *Federal Reserve Bulletin,* June. www.federalreserve.gov/pubs/oss/oss2/papers/concentration.2001.pdf (accessed Sep. 14, 2003).

KENNICKELL, A. B., M. STARR-MCCLUER, AND B. J. SURETTE. 2000. Recent changes in U.S. family finances: Results from the 1998 survey of consumer finances. *Federal Reserve Bulletin* 40 (Jan.): 1–29.

KENRICK, D. T., G. E. GROTH, M. R. TROST, AND E. K. SADALLA. 1993. Integrating evolutionary and social exchange perspectives on relationships: Effects of gender, self-appraisal, and involvement level on mate selection criteria. *Journal of Personality and Social Psychology* 64 (6): 951–69.

KENT, M. M., AND M. MATHER. 2002. What drives U.S. population growth? *Population Bulletin* 57 (Dec.): 1–40. Washington, DC: Population Reference Bureau.

KENT, M. M., K. M. POLLARD, J. HAAGA, AND M. MATHER. 2001. First glimpses from the 2000 U.S. Census. *Population Bulletin* 56 (June). Washington, DC: Population Reference Bureau.

Kenyan girls flee mutilation. 2003. BBC. http://news.bbc.co.uk/1/hi/world/africa/2736317.stm (accessed Feb. 8, 2003).

KEPHART, W. M., AND W. W. ZELLNER. 1991. *Extraordinary groups: An examination of unconventional lifestyles,* 4th ed. New York: St. Martin's.

KERCKHOFF, A. C., AND K. E. DAVIS. 1962. Value consensus and need complementarity in mate selection. *American Sociological Review* 27 (June): 295–303.

KERN, S. 1992. *The culture of love: Victorians to moderns.* Cambridge, MA: Harvard University Press.

KERNIC, M. A., ET AL. 2002. Academic and school health issues among children exposed to maternal intimate partner abuse. *Archives of Pediatrics & Adolescent Medicine* 156 (June): 549–55.

KERSHAW, S. 2003. Saudi Arabia awakes to the perils of inbreeding. *New York Times,* May 1. www.nytimes.com/2003/05/01/international/middleeast/01GENE.html?tntemail0 (accessed May 2, 2003).

KERSTEN, K. K. 1990. The process of marital disaffection: Interventions at various stages. *Family Relations* 39 (July): 257–65.

KESNER, J. E., T. JULIAN, AND P. C. MCKENRY. 1997. Application of attachment theory to male violence toward female intimates. *Journal of Family Violence* 12 (June): 211–28.

KETTNER, P. M., R. M. MORONEY, AND L. L. MARTIN. 1999. *Designing and managing programs: An effectiveness-based approach,* 2nd ed. Thousand Oaks, CA: Sage.

Key facts: TV violence. 2003. The Henry Kaiser Family Foundation. www.kff.org/content/2003/3335/TV_Violence.pdf (accessed June 20, 2003).

KHESHGI-GENOVESE, Z., AND T. A. GENOVESE. 1997. Developing the spousal relationship within stepfamilies. *Families in Society: The Journal of Contemporary Human Services* 78 (May/June): 255–64.

KIBRIA, N. 1994. Vietnamese families in the United States. In *Minority families in the United States: A multicultural perspective,* ed. R. L. Taylor, 164–76. Upper Saddle River, NJ: Prentice Hall.

KIBRIA, N. 1997. The construction of "Asian American": Reflections on intermarriage and ethnic identity among second-generation Chinese and Korean Americans. *Ethnic and Racial Studies* 20 (July): 523–44.

KIBRIA, N. 2002a. College and notions of "Asian Americans": Second-generation Chinese Americans and Korean Americans. In *Minority families in the United States: A multicultural perspective,* 3rd ed., ed. R. L. Taylor, 183–207. Upper Saddle River, NJ: Prentice Hall.

KIBRIA, N. 2002b. Vietnamese American families. In *Minority families in the United States: A multicultural perspective,* 3rd ed., ed. R. L. Taylor, 181–92. Upper Saddle River, NJ: Prentice Hall.

Kids and guns. 2000. Washington, DC: U.S. Department of Justice, Office of Justice Programs, Office of Juvenile Justice and Delinquency Prevention.

Kids count data book. 2003. Baltimore: Annie E. Casey Foundation.

KIECOLT, K. J. 2003. Satisfaction with work and family life: No evidence of a cultural reversal. *Journal of Marriage and Family* 65 (Feb.): 23–35.

KIECOLT-GLASER, J. K., AND T. L. NEWTON. 2001. Marriage and health: His and hers. *Psychological Bulletin* 127 (July): 472–503.

KIERNAN, K. E. 1992. The impact of family disruption in childhood on transitions made in young adult life. *Population Studies* 46: 213–34.

KIERNAN, K. 2001. European perspective on nonmarital childbearing. In *Out of wedlock: Causes and consequences of nonmarital fertility,* eds. L. L. Wu and B. Wolfe, 77–108. New York: Russell Sage Foundation.

KIERNAN, K. 2002. Cohabitation in Western Europe: Trends, issues, and implications. In *Just living together: Implications of cohabitation on families, children, and social policy,* eds. A. Booth and A. C. Crouter, 3–32. Mahwah, NJ: Erlbaum.

KIERNAN, V. 2002. Boston U. chancellor orders gay support group at university's prep school to disband. *Chronicle of Higher Education.* http://chronicle.com/daily/2002/09/2002090905n.htm (accessed Sep/ 10, 2002).

KILBORN, P. T. 2002. Easy credit and hard times bring a flood of foreclosures. *New York Times,* Nov. 23. www.nytimes.com/2002/11/24/national/24FORE.html?todaysheadlines (accessed Nov. 24, 2002).

KILBOURNE, J. 1994. Still killing us softly: Advertising and the obsession with thinness. In *Feminist perspectives on eating disorders,* eds. P. Fallon, M. A. Katzman, and S. C. Wooley, 395–418. New York: Guilford.

KILBOURNE, J. 1999. *Deadly persuasion: Why women and girls must fight the addictive power of advertising.* New York: Free Press.

KILBURN, J. C., JR. 1996. Network effects in caregiver to care-recipient violence: A study of caregivers to those diagnosed with Alzheimer's disease. *Journal of Elder Abuse & Neglect* 8 (1): 69–80.

KILPATRICK, D. G., B. E. SAUNDERS, AND D. W. SMITH. 2003. *Youth victimization: Prevalence and implications.* Washington, DC: U.S. Department of Justice.

KIM, E. 1999. Sexual division of labor in the Korean American family. Paper presented at the annual National Council on Family Relations meetings, Washington, DC.

KIM, H. K., AND P. C. MCKENRY. 1998. Social networks and support: A comparison of African Americans, Asian Americans, Caucasians, and Hispanics. *Journal of Comparative Family Studies* 29 (Summer): 313–36.

KIM, J. E., E. M. HETHERINGTON, AND D. ROSS. 1999. Associations among family relationships, antisocial peers, and adolescents' externalizing behaviors. *Child Development* 70 (Sep./Oct.): 1209–30.

KIM, K. C, AND S. KIM. 1998. Family and work roles of Korean immigrants in the United States. In *Resiliency in Native American and immigrant families,* eds. H. I. McCubbin, E. A. Thompson, A. I. Thompson, and J. E. Fromer, 225–42. Thousand Oaks, CA: Sage.

KINDLON, D. J., WITH T. BARKER AND M. THOMPSON. 1999. *Raising Cain: Protecting the emotional life of boys.* New York: Random House.

KING, B. 2002. *Human sexuality today,* 4th ed. Upper Saddle River, NJ: Prentice Hall.

KING, V. 1994. Nonresident father involvement and child well-being: Can dads make a difference? *Journal of Family Issues* 55 (Mar.): 78–96.

KING, V. 2002. Parental divorce and interpersonal trust in adult offspring. *Journal of Marriage and Family* 64 (Aug.): 642–56.

KING, V. 2003. The legacy of a grandparent's divorce: Consequences for ties between grandparents and grandchildren. *Journal of Marriage and Family* 65 (Feb.): 170–83.

KING, W. 1996. "Suffer with them till death": Slave women and their children in nineteenth-century America. In *More than chattel: Black women and slavery in the Americas,* eds. D. B. Caspar and D. C. Hine, 147–68. Bloomington: Indiana University Press.

KINGTON, R. S., AND H. W. NICKENS. 2001. Racial and ethnic differences in health: Recent trends, current patterns, future directions. In *America becoming: Racial trends and their consequences,* Vol. 2, eds. N. J. Smelser, W. J. Wilson, and F. Mitchell, 253–310. Washington, DC: National Academy Press.

KINKEAD, G. 1977. The family secret. *Boston Magazine* (Oct.): 100.

KINSELLA, K., AND V. A. VELKOFF. 2001. An aging world: 2001. U.S. Department of Health and Human Services, National Institute on Aging. www.census.gov/prod/2001pubs/p95-01-1.pdf (accessed Mar. 5, 2003).

KINSEY, A. C., W. B. POMEROY, AND C. E. MARTIN. 1948. *Sexual behavior in the human male.* Philadelphia: Saunders.

KINSEY, A. C., W. B. POMEROY, C. E. MARTIN, AND P. H. GEBHARD. 1953. *Sexual behavior in the human female.* Philadelphia: Saunders.

KIRBY, D. 2001. Understanding what works and what doesn't in reducing adolescent sexual risk-taking. *Family Planning Perspectives* 33 (Nov./Dec.): 276–81.

KIRBY, D. 2002. Effective approaches to reducing adolescent unprotected sex, pregnancy, and childbearing. *Journal of Sex Research* 39 (Feb.): 51–57.

KIRBY, D., ET AL. 1994. School-based programs to reduce sexual risk behaviors: A review of effectiveness. *Public Health Reports* 109 (May/June): 339–60.

KIRKPATRICK, L. A., AND C. HAZAN. 1994. Attachment styles and close relationships: A four-year prospective study. *Personal Relationships* 1 (June): 123–42.

KIRN, W. 1997. The ties that bind. *Time,* Aug. 18, 48–50.

KISSMAN, K., AND J. A. ALLEN. 1993. *Single-parent families.* Beverly Hills, CA: Sage.

KITSON, G. C., WITH W. M. HOLMES. 1992. *Portrait of divorce: Adjustment to marital breakdown.* New York: Guilford.

KITSON, G. C., AND L. A. MORGAN. 1991. The multiple consequences of divorce. In *Contemporary families: Looking forward, looking back,* ed. A. Booth, 150–61. Minneapolis: National Council on Family Relations.

KITZINGER, S. 1989. *The crying baby.* New York: Penguin.

KIVETT, V. R. 1991. Centrality of the grandfather role among older rural black and white men. *Journal of Gerontology: Social Sciences* 46 (5): S250–58.

KLADKO, B. 2002. At computer camp, the gender gap is obvious. www.bergen.com/page.php?level_3_id=7&page=4401776 (accessed July 29, 2002).

KLAUS, M., AND J. KENNELL. 1976. *Maternal-infant bonding.* St. Louis, MO: Mosby.

KLAUS, P. A. 2000. *Crimes against persons age 65 or older, 1992–97.* Washington, DC: U.S. Department of Justice, Office of Justice Programs.

KLEIMAN, C. 1993. Comparable pay could create jobs. *Orlando Sentinel,* Oct. 13, C5.

KLEIN, J. D. 1997. The national longitudinal study on adolescent health: Preliminary results, great expectations. *Journal of the American Medical Association* 278 (Sep. 10): 864–66.

KLEIN, R. 1993. Personal correspondence.

KLINKENBERG, D., AND S. ROSE. 1994. Dating scripts of gay men and lesbians. *Journal of Homosexuality* 26 (4): 23–35.

KNAPP, L. G., ET AL. 2002. Enrollment in postsecondary institutions, Fall 200 and financial statistics, fiscal year 2000. National Center for Education Statistics. http://nces.ed.gov/pubs2002/2002212.pdf (accessed May 18, 2003).

KNAPP, M. L., AND J. A. HALL. 1992. *Nonverbal communication in human interaction,* 3rd ed. New York: Holt, Rinehart & Winston.

KNAPP, R. J. 1987. When a child dies. *Psychology Today,* July, 60–65.

KNICKERBOCKER, B. 1998. Oregon escalates its heated right-to-die debate. *Christian Science Monitor,* Apr. 8, 4.

KNICKERBOCKER, B. 2000. Forget crime—but please fix the traffic. *Christian Science Monitor,* Feb. 16, 3.

KNOX, D., WITH K. LEGGETT. 1998. *The divorced dad's survival book: How to stay connected with your kids.* New York: Insight.

KNOX, D., C. SCHACHT, AND M. E. ZUSSMAN. 1999. Love relationships among college students. *College Student Journal* 33 (Mar.): 149–51.

KNOX, D., M. E. ZUSMAN, C. BUFFINGTON, AND G. HEMPHILL. 2000. Interracial dating attitudes among college students. *College Student Journal* 34 (Mar.): 69–71.

KNOX, V. W., AND M. J. BANE. 1994. Child support and schooling. In *Child support and child well-being,* eds. I. Garfinkel, S. S. McLanahan, and P. K. Robins, 285–316. Washington, DC: Urban Institute.

KOENIG, M., AND S. MULPURU. 2003. *Income of the aged chartbook, 2001.* Social Security Administration. www.ssa.gov/policy/docs/chartbooks/income_aged/2001/iac01.pdf (accessed Oct. 10, 2003).

KOHLBERG, L. 1969. Stage and sequence: The cognitive-developmental approach to socialization. In *Handbook of socialization theory and research,* ed. D. A. Goslin, 347–480. Chicago: Rand McNally.

KOHN, A. 1991. The spoiled child. *Ladies Home Journal* (May): 78.

KONCIUS, J. 1995. At home, at work. *Washington Post Home Supplement,* Oct. 19, 9, 20–21.

KOOLS, S. M. 1997. Adolescent identity development in foster care. *Family Relations* 46 (July): 263–71.

KOOP, C. 1989. *Letter to President Ronald Reagan concerning the health effects of abortion: Medical and psychological impact of abortion.* Washington, DC: U.S. Government Printing Office.

KORCZYK, S. M. 2002. Back to which future: The U.S. aging crisis revisited. Public Policy Institute, Washington, DC. http://research.aarp.org/econ/inb65_aging.html (accessed Oct. 10, 2003).

KORENMAN, S., R. KAESTNER, AND T. J. JOYCE. 2001. Unintended pregnancy and the consequences of nonmarital childbearing. In *Out of wedlock: Causes and consequences of nonmarital fertility,* eds. L. L. Wu and B. Wolfe, 259–86. New York: Russell Sage Foundation.

KOSS, M. P. AND S. I. COOK. 1993. Facing the facts: Date and acquaintance rape are significant problems for women. In *Current controversies on family violence,* eds. R. J. Gelles and D. R. Losede, 104–19. Thousand Oaks, CA: Sage.

KRAFFT, S. 1994. Why wives earn less than husbands. *American Demographics* 16 (Jan.): 16–17.

KRAMER, H. 1993. *Conversations at midnight: Coming to terms with dying and death.* New York: Morrow.

KRANCE, M. 1993. Conquest. In *Reinventing love: Six women talk about lust, sex, and romance,* eds. L. Abraham, L. Green, M. Krance, J. Rosenberg, J. Somerville, and C. Stoner, 159–61. New York: Plume.

KRAUSS, C. 2003. Long lines mar Canada's low-cost health care. *New York Times,* Feb. 13, C1.

KREEGER, K. Y. 2002a. Sex-based differences continue to mount. *The Scientist* 16 (Feb. 18). www.the-scientist.com/yr2002/feb/research_020218.html (accessed July 14, 2002).

KREEGER, K. Y. 2002b. X and Y chromosomes concern more than reproduction. *The Scientist* 16 (Feb. 4). www.the-scientist.com/yr2002/feb/research_020204.html (accessed July 14, 2002).

KREIDER, R. M. 2003. *Adopted children and stepchildren: 2000.* U.S. Census Bureau, Census 2000 Special Reports. www.census.gov/prod/2003pubs/censr-6.pdf (accessed Sep. 3, 2003).

KREIDER, R. M., AND J. M. FIELDS. 2002. *Number, timing, and duration of marriages and divorces: 1996.* U.S. Census Bureau, Current Population Reports, p70-80. www.census.gov/prod/2002pubs/p70-80.pdf (accessed Mar. 1, 2003).

KRIPILANI, M., B. EINHORN, AND P. MAGNUSSON. 2003. India: A tempest over tech outsourcing. *Business Week,* June 16, 55.

KROKOFF, L. J. 1987. The correlates of negative affect in marriage: An exploratory study of gender differences. *Journal of Family Issues* 8 (Mar.): 111–35.

KROLL, L., AND L. GOLDMAN. 2002. The world's billionaires. *Forbes.* www.forbes.com/2002/02/28/billionaires.html (accessed Jan. 20, 2003).

KRUCOFF, C. 1999. Setting standards for seniors. *Washington Post,* July 20, 28.

KRUEGER, R. A. 1994. *Focus groups: A practical guide for applied research,* 2nd ed. Thousand Oaks, CA: Sage.

KRUG, E. G., L. L. DAHLBERG, J. A. MERCY, A. B. ZWI, AND R. LOZANO, EDS. 2002. World report on violence and health. World Health Organization. www5.who.int/violence_injury_prevention/download.cfm?id=0000000582 (accessed May 15, 2003).

KÜBLER-ROSS, E. 1969. *On death and dying.* New York: Macmillan.

KUCZYNSKI, A. 2001. Men's magazines: How much substance behind the covers? *New York Times,* June 24. www.nytimes.com/2001/06/24/health/24ALEX-MH.html (accessed June 25, 2001).

KULCZYCKI, A., AND A. P. LOBO. 2001. Deepening the melting pot: Arab-Americans at the turn of the century. *Middle East Journal* 3 (Summer): 459–73.

KULCZYCKI, A., AND A. P. LOBO. 2002. Patterns, determinants, and implications of intermarriage among Arab Americans. *Journal of Marriage and Family* 64 (Feb.): 202–10.

KUNJUFU, J. 1987. *Lessons from history: A celebration in blackness.* Chicago: African American Images.

KUNKEL, D., E. BIELY, K. EYAL, K. COPE-FERRAR, E. DONNERSTEIN, AND R. FANDRICH. 2003. Sex on TV3. Kaiser Family Foundation. www.kff.org/content/2003/20030204/Sex_on_TV_3_Full.pdf (accessed June 15, 2003).

KUNKEL, D., K. M. COPE, W. J. M. FARINOLA, E. BIELY, E. ROLLIN, AND E. D. DONNERSTEIN. 1999. Sex on TV: A biennial report to the Henry Kaiser Family Foundation. Washington, DC: Henry J. Kaiser Family Foundation. www.kff.org (accessed Sep. 3, 2000).

KURDEK, L. A. 1993. Predicting marital dissolution: A 5-year prospective longitudinal study of newlywed couples. *Journal of Personality and Social Psychology* 64 (2): 221–42.

KURDEK, L. A. 1994. Areas of conflict for gay, lesbian, and heterosexual couples: What couples argue about influences relationship satisfaction. *Journal of Marriage and the Family* 56 (Nov.): 923–34.

KURDEK, L. A. 1998. Relationship outcomes and their predictors: Longitudinal evidence from heterosexual married, gay cohabiting, and lesbian cohabiting couples. *Journal of Marriage and the Family* 60 (Aug.): 553–68.

KURDEK, L. A., AND M. A. FINE. 1993. The relation between family structure and young adolescents' appraisals of family climate and parenting behavior. *Journal of Family Issues* 14: 279–90.

KURLANTZICK, J. 2001. Hello, goodbye, hey maybe I love you? *U.S. News & World Report,* June 4, 43.

KURZ, D. 1993. Physical assaults by husbands: A major social problem. In *Current controversies on family violence,* eds. R. J. Gelles and D. R. Loseke, 88–103. Thousand Oaks, CA: Sage.

KUSHNER, E. 1997. *Experiencing abortion: A weaving of women's words.* New York: Haworth.

KUTTNER, R. 2000. The states are ending welfare as we know it—but not poverty. *Business Week,* June 12, 36.

KWONG SEE, S. T, AND C. RASMUSSEN. 2003. An early start to age stereotyping: Children's beliefs about an older experimenter. Cited in *University of Alberta News.* www.expressnews.ualberta.ca/expressnews/articles/news.cfm?p_ID=116&s=a.

KYMAN, W. 1995. The first step: Sexuality education for parents. *Journal of Sex Education and Therapy* 21 (3): 153–57.

LACEY, M. 2003. African women gather to denounce genital cutting. *New York Times,* Feb. 6, A3.

LACHMAN, M. E. 2001. *Handbook of midlife development.* New York: Wiley.

LADD, E. C. 1999. Everyday life: How are we doing? *Public Perspective* 10 (Apr./May): 1, 7.

LAFFERTY, E. 1999. Ruling against anti-abortion Website raises storm in US over rights. *Irish Times.* courses.cs.vt.edu/~cs3604/lib/Freedom.of.Speech/Nuremburg.Irish.Times.html (accessed Sep. 24, 2000).

LAFRANCE, M., M. A. HECHT, AND E. L. PALUCK. 2003. The contingent smile: A meta-analysis of sex differences in smiling. *Psychological Bulletin* 129 (Mar.): 305–35.

LAIRD, J. 1993. Lesbian and gay families. In *Normal family processes,* 2nd ed., ed. F. Walsh, 282–330. New York: Guilford.

LAKOFF, R. T. 1990. *Talking power: The politics of language.* New York: Basic Books.

LAKSHMANAN, I. A. R. 1997. Marriage? Think logic, not love. *Baltimore Sun,* Sep. 22, 2A.

LAMISON-WHITE, L. 1997. *Poverty in the United States: 1996.* U.S. Census Bureau, Current Population Reports, Series P60–198. Washington, DC: U.S. Government Printing Office.

LAMPMAN, J. 2001. The new American dream. *Christian Science Monitor,* Sep. 24, 13–15.

LAMPMAN, J. 2001. Rev Moon raising his profile. *Christian Science Monitor,* Apr. 19, 18–19.

LAMPMAN, J. 2003. Deflating the fear. *Christian Science Monitor,* Mar. 20, 13–14.

LANDALE, N. S., AND S. E. TOLNAY. 1991. Group differences in economic opportunity and the timing of marriage. *American Sociological Review* 56 (Feb.): 33–45.

LANDERS, A. 2001. Husband shows his love in small ways every day. *Baltimore Sun,* June 16, 3D.

LANDRY, B. 2000. *Black working wives.* Berkeley: University of California Press.

LANGELAN, M. J. 1993. *Back off! How to confront and stop sexual harassment and harassers.* New York: Simon & Schuster.

Language spoken at home. 2000. U.S. Census Bureau. http://factfinder.census.gov/servlet/QTTable?ds_name=D&geo_id=D&qr_name=

DEC_2000_SF3_U_QTP16&_lang=en (accessed Mar. 2, 2003).

LANSFORD, J. E., R. CEBALLO, A. ABBEY, AND A. J. STEWART. 2001. Does family structure matter? A comparison of adoptive, two-parent biological, single-mother, stepfather, and stepmother households. *Journal of Marriage and Family* 63 (Aug.): 840–51.

LANSKY, V. 1989. *Vicki Lansky's divorce book for parents.* New York: New American Library.

LANTZ, H. R. 1976. *Marital incompatibility and social change in early America.* Beverly Hills, CA: Sage.

LAPCHICK, R. 2003. Racial and gender report card. University of Central Florida. www.bus.ucf.edu/sport/public/downloads/media/ides/2003_racial_gender_report_card.pdf (accessed May 15, 2003).

LARGE, E. 2002. Homeward bound. *Baltimore Sun,* June 9, 1N, 4N.

LARIMER, M. E., A. R. LYDUM, AND A. P. TURNER. 1999. Male and female recipients of unwanted sexual contact in a college student sample: Prevalence rates, alcohol use, and depression symptoms. *Sex Roles* 40 (Feb.): 295–308.

LAROSSA, R. ED. 1984. *Family case studies: A sociological perspective.* New York: Free Press.

LAROSSA, R. 1986. *Becoming a parent.* Thousand Oaks, CA: Sage.

LAROSSA, R., AND D. C. REITZES. 1993. Symbolic interactionism and family studies. In *Sourcebook of family theories and methods: A contextual approach,* eds. P. G. Boss, W. J. Doherty, R. LaRossa, W. R. Schumm, and S. K. Steinmetz, 135–63. New York: Plenum.

LARSON, J. 1992. Understanding stepfamilies. *American Demographics* 14 (July): 36–40.

LARSON, J. H. 1988. The marriage quiz: College students' beliefs in selected myths about marriage. *Family Relations* 37 (Jan.): 3–11.

LARSON, R., AND M. H. RICHARDS. 1994. *Divergent realities: The emotional lives of mothers, fathers, and adolescents.* New York: Basic Books.

LARZELERE, R. E. 2000. Child outcomes of nonabusive and customary physical punishment by parents: An updated literature review. Unpublished manuscript, University of Nebraska Medical Center, Omaha, and Father Flanagan's Boys' Town, NE.

LARZELERE, R. E., P. R. SATHER, W. N. SCHNEIDER, D. B. LARSON, AND P. L. PIKE. 1998. Punishment enhances reasoning's effectiveness as a disciplinary response to toddlers. *Journal of Marriage and the Family* 60 (May): 388–403.

LASCH, C. 1977. *Haven in a heartless world: The family besieged.* New York: Basic Books.

LASLETT, P. 1971. *The world we have lost,* 2nd ed. Reading, MA: Addison-Wesley.

LASSWELL, T. E., AND M. E. LASSWELL. 1976. I love you but I'm not in love with you. *Journal of Marriage and Family Counseling* 2 (July): 211–24.

LASZLOFFY, T. A. 2002. Rethinking family development theory: Teaching with the systemic family development (SFD) model. *Family Relations* 51 (July): 206–14.

LAUER, J., AND R. LAUER. 1985. Marriages made to last. *Psychology Today* (June): 22–26.

LAUMANN, E. O., J. H. GAGNON, R. T. MICHAEL, AND S. MICHAELS. 1994. *The social organization of sexuality: Sexual practices in the United States.* Chicago: University of Chicago Press.

LAUMANN, E. O., A. PAIK, AND R. C. ROSEN. 2001. Sexual dysfunction in the United States: Prevalence and predictions. In *Sex, love, and health in America,* eds. E. O. Laumann and R. T. Michael, 352–76. Chicago: University of Chicago Press.

LAVEE, Y., AND D. H. OLSON. 1993. Seven types of marriage: Empirical typology based on research. *Journal of Marital and Family Therapy* 19 (Oct.): 325–40.

LAWLER, K. 2001. Aging in place: Coordinating housing and health care provision for America's growing elderly population. Joint Center for Housing Studies, Harvard University. www.jchs.harvard.edu/publications/seniors/lawler_w01-13.pdf (accessed Sep. 10, 2003).

LAWRANCE, K., AND E. S. BYERS. 1995. Sexual satisfaction in long-term heterosexual relationships: The interpersonal exchange model of social satisfaction. *Personal Relationships* 2: 267–85.

LAWS, A., AND J. M. GOLDING. 1996. Sexual assault history and eating disorder symptoms among white, Hispanic, and African-American women and men. *American Journal of Public Health* 86 (Apr.): 579–82.

LAWSON, A. 1988. *Adultery: An analysis of love and betrayal.* New York: Basic Books.

LAWSON, E. J., AND A. THOMPSON. 1999. *Black men and divorce.* Thousand Oaks, CA: Sage.

LAWTON, L., M. SILVERSTEIN, AND V. BENGSTON. 1994. Affection, social contact, and geographic distance between adult children and their parents. *Journal of Marriage and the Family* 56 (Feb.): 57–68.

LEACH, P. 1994. *Children first: What our society must do—and is not doing—for our children today.* New York: Knopf.

LEAPER, C. 2002. Parenting girls and boys. In *Handbook of parenting,* 2nd ed., Vol. 1, ed. M. H. Bornstein, 189–215. Mahwah, NJ: Erlbaum.

LEARNER, N. 2002. A not-so-simple plan. *Christian Science Monitor,* Sep. 30, 11, 14–16.

LEDERER, W. J., AND D. D. JACKSON. 1968. *The mirages of marriage.* New York: Norton.

LEDUFF, C. 2002. Attacks on gays upset Los Angeles suburb. *New York Times,* Nov. 25, A14.

LEE, E., G. SPITZE, AND J. R. LOGAN. 2003. Social support to parents-in-law: The interplay of gender and kin hierarchies. *Journal of Marriage and Family* 65 (May): 396–403.

LEE, G. R., C. W. PEEK, AND R. T. COWARD. 1998. Race differences in filial responsibility expectations among older parents. *Journal of Marriage and the Family* 60 (May): 404–12.

LEE, J. A. 1973. *The colors of love.* Upper Saddle River, NJ: Prentice Hall.

LEE, J. A. 1974. The styles of loving. *Psychology Today* (Oct.): 46–51.

LEE, M.-Y. 2002. A model of children's postdivorce behavioral adjustment in maternal- and dual-residence arrangements. *Journal of Family Issues* 23 (July): 672–730.

LEE, V. E., D. T. BURKAN, H. ZIMILES, AND B. LADEWSKI. 1994. Family structure and its effects on behavioral and emotional problems in young adolescents. *Journal of Research on Adolescence* 4: 405–37.

LEFF, L. 1994. Becoming woman: At 15, Hispanic girls celebrate rite of passage. *Washington Post,* Feb. 6, B1, B8.

LEHR, S. T., C. DiLORIO, W. N. DUDLEY, AND J. A. LIPANA. 2000. The relationship between parent–adolescent communication and safer sex behaviors in college students. *Journal of Family Nursing* 6 (May): 180–96.

LEHRER, E. L., AND C. U. CHISWICK. 1993. Religion as a determinant of marital stability. *Demography* 30 (Aug.): 385–404.

LEHRMAN, F. 1996. Factoring domestic violence into custody cases. *Trial* 32 (Feb.): 32–39.

LEITE, R., AND P. C. MCKENRY. 1996. Putting nonresidential fathers back into the family portrait. *Human Development and Family Life Bulletin* 2 (Autumn). www.hec.ohio-state.edu/famlife/index.htm (accessed Feb. 3, 1998).

LEITENBERG, H., M. J. DETZER, AND D. SREBNIK. 1993. Gender differences in masturbation and the relation of masturbation experience in preadolescence and/or early adolescence to sexual behavior and sexual adjustment in young adulthood. *Journal of Social Behavior* 22 (Apr.): 87–98.

LELAND, J. 1996. Tightening the knot. *Newsweek,* Feb. 19, 72–73.

LELAND, J. 2000. Shades of gay. *Newsweek,* Mar. 20, 45–9.

LEMASTERS, E. E., AND J. DEFRAIN. 1989. *Parents in contemporary America: A sympathetic view,* 5th ed. Belmont, CA: Wadsworth.

LEMIEUX, R., AND J. L. HALE. 2002. Cross-sectional analysis of intimacy, passion, and commitment: Testing the assumptions of the triangular theory of love. *Psychological Reports* 90 (June): 1009–14.

LEON, J. J., J. L. PHILBRICK, F. PARRA, E. ESCOBEDO, AND F. MALGESINI. 1994. Love-styles among university students in Mexico. *Psychological Reports* 74: 307–10.

LEON, K. 2003. Risk and protective factors in young children's adjustment to parental divorce: A review of the research. *Family Relations* 52 (July): 258–70.

LEONARD, K. E., AND M. SENCHAK. 1993. Alcohol and premarital aggression among newlywed couples. *Journal of Studies on Alcohol* Suppl. 11: 96–108.

LEONARD, K. I. 1997. *The South Asian Americans.* Westport, CT: Greenwood.

LEONG, F., AND P. J. HARTUNG. 2001. Appraising birth order in career assessment: Linkages to Holland's and Super's models. *Journal of Career Assessment* 9 (Winter): 25–39.

LESLIE, L. A., T. L. HUSTON, AND M. P. JOHNSON. 1986. Parental reactions to dating relationships: Do they make a difference? *Journal of Marriage and the Family* 48 (Feb.): 57–66.

Less is more. 1999. *Public Perspective* 10 (Oct./Nov.): 19.

LESTER, D. 1996a. The impact of unemployment on marriage and divorce. *Journal of Divorce & Remarriage* 25 (3/4): 151–53.

LESTER, D. 1996b. Trends in divorce and marriage around the world. *Journal of Divorce & Remarriage* 25 (1/2): 169–71.

LEUNG, J. J. 1995. Family configuration and students' perceptions of parental support for schoolwork. *Sociological Imagination* 32: 185–96.

LEVAY, S. 1993. *The sexual brain.* La Jolla, CA: MIP.

LEVENTHAL, B., AND S. E. LUNDY, EDS. 1999. *Same-sex domestic violence: Strategies for change.* Thousand Oaks, CA: Sage.

LEVESQUE, R. J. R. 1993. The romantic experience of adolescents in satisfying love relationships. *Journal of Youth and Adolescence* 11 (3): 219–50.

LEVIN, M. L., X. XU, AND J. P. BARTKOWSKI. 2002. Seasonality of sexual debut. *Journal of Marriage and Family* 64 (Nov.): 871–84.

LEVIN, W. C. 1988. Age stereotyping. *Research on Aging* 10 (Mar.): 134–48.

LEVINE, A. 1990. The second time around: Realities of remarriage. *U.S. News & World Report,* Jan. 29, 50–51.

LEVINE, M. V. 1994. A nation of hamburger flippers? *Baltimore Sun,* July 31, 1E, 4E.

LEVY, J. A. 1994. Sex and sexuality in later life stages. In *Sexuality across the life course,* ed. A. S. Rossi, 287–309. Chicago: University of Chicago Press.

LEWIN, T. 2003. Arkansas school is accused of harassing a gay student. *New York Times,* Mar. 25, A10.

LEWIS, M. 1997. *Altering fate: Why the past does not predict the future.* New York: Guilford.

LEWIS, M., AND M. BENDERSKY, EDS. 1995. *Mothers, babies, and cocaine: The role of toxins in development.* Hillsdale, NJ: Erlbaum.

LEWIS, M., C. FEIRING, AND S. ROSENTHAL. 2000. Attachment over time. *Child Development* 71 (May/June): 707–20.

LIBBON, R. P. 2000. MediaChannels. *American Demographics* 21 (May): 29.

LICHT, J. 1995. Marriages that endure. *Washington Post Health Supplement,* Oct. 31, 18–20.

LICHTER, D. T., AND M. L. CROWLEY. 2002. Poverty in America: Beyond welfare reform. *Population Bulletin* 57 (June). Washington, DC: Population Reference Bureau.

LICHTER, D. T., AND D. R. GRAEFE. 2001. Finding a mate? The marital and cohabitation histories of unwed mothers. In *Out of wedlock: Causes and consequences of nonmarital fertility,* eds. L. L. Wu and B. Wolfe, 317–43. New York: Russell Sage Foundation.

LIEBOWITZ, S. W., D. C. CASTELLANO, AND I. CUELLAR. 1999. Factors that predict sexual behavior among young Mexican American adolescents: An exploratory study. *Hispanic Journal of Behavioral Sciences* 21 (Nov.): 470–79.

LIEF, L. 1997. Kids at risk. *U.S. News & World Report,* Apr. 28, 66–70.

LIGHT, P. C. 1988. *Baby boomers.* New York: Norton.

LIM, P. J. 2003. The new retirement journey. *U.S. News & World Report,* June 2, 49–58.

LIN, G., AND P. A. ROGERSON. 1995. Elderly parents and the geographic availability of their adult children. *Research on Aging* 17 (Sep.): 303–09.

LINDBERG, L. D., S. BOGGESS, L. PORTER, AND S. WILLIAMS. 2000. *Teen risk-taking: A statistical portrait.* Washington, DC: Urban Institute.

www.urban.org/family/TeenRiskTaking.pdf (accessed Sep. 4, 2000).

LINDSEY, L. L. 1997. *Gender roles: A sociological perspective,* 3rd ed. Upper Saddle River, NJ: Prentice Hall.

LINLIN, P. 1993. Matchmaking via the personal advertisements in China versus in the United States. *Journal of Popular Culture* 27 (Summer): 163–70.

LINO, M. 1994. Income and spending patterns of single-mother families. *Monthly Labor Review* (May): 29–37.

LINO, M. 1995. The economics of single parenthood: Past research and future directions. *Marriage & Family Review* 20 (1/2): 99–114.

LINO, M. 2003. *Expenditures on children by families, 2002.* U.S. Department of Agriculture, Publication no. 1528–2002. www.cnpp.usda.gov/Crc/crc2002.pdf (accessed Aug. 13, 2003).

LIPPA, R. A. 2002. *Gender, nature, and nurture.* Mahwah, NJ: Erlbaum.

LIRA, L. R., AND M. P. KOSS. 1999. Mexican American women's definitions of rape and sexual abuse. *Hispanic Journal of Behavioral Sciences* 21 (Aug.): 236–65.

LITE, J. 2002. Report indicates gender-related violence is global. *Women's E-News,* Oct. 4. www.womensenews.org/article.cfm/dyn/aid/1059 (accessed Oct. 6, 2002).

LIU, P., AND C. S. CHAN. 1996. Lesbian, gay, and bisexual Asian Americans and their families. In *Lesbians and gays in couples and families: A handbook for therapists,* eds. J. Laird and R.-J. Green, 137–54. San Francisco: Jossey-Bass.

LIU, W. M. 2002. The social class–related experiences of men: Integrating theory and practice. *Professional Psychology: Research & Practice* (Aug.): 355–60.

Living humbled, unhappy lives. 1996. *Baltimore Sun,* May 23, 2A.

LLOYD, J. 2002a. *Gamma hydroxybutyrate (GHB).* Washington, DC: Office of National Drug Control Policy.

LLOYD, J. 2002b. *Rohypnol.* Washington, DC: Office of National Drug Control Policy.

LLOYD, S. A. 1991. The dark side of courtship: Violence and sexual exploitation. *Family Relations* 40 (Jan.): 14–20.

LLOYD, S. A., AND B. C. EMERY. 2000. *The dark side of courtship: Physical and sexual aggression.* Thousand Oaks, CA: Sage.

LODER, A. 2003. Mail order brides find U.S. land of milk, battery. *Women's E-News,* June 27. www.womensenews.org/article.cfm/dyn/aid/1390/context/cover/ (accessed June 28, 2003).

LOEBER, R., M. DRINKWATER, Y. YIN, S. J. ANDERSON, L. C. SCHMIDT, AND A. CRAWFORD. 2000. Stability of family interaction from ages 6 to 18. *Journal of Abnormal Child Psychology* 28 (Aug.): 353–69.

LONGINO, C. F., JR. 1994. Myths of an aging America. *American Demographics* (Aug.): 36–42.

LONGMORE, M. A., W. D. MANNING, AND P. C. GIORDANO. 2001. Preadolescent parenting strategies and teens' dating and sexual initiation: A longitudinal analysis. *Journal of Marriage and Family* 63 (May): 322–35.

LONKHUYZEN, L. V. 1994. Female gymnasts prone to eating disorders. *Baltimore Sun,* July 29, C1, C3.

LÓPEZ, R. A. 1999. *Las comadres* as a social support system. *Affilia* 14 (Spring): 24–41.

LOPREST, P. 1999. Families who left welfare: Who are they and how are they doing? Washington, DC: Urban Institute. newfederalism.urban.org/pdf/discussion99-02.pdf (accessed Oct. 14, 2000).

LORCH, D., AND P. TOLME. 2003. Ghosts of Tailhook. *Newsweek,* Mar. 17, 43.

LORD, M. G. 1994. *Forever Barbie: The unauthorized biography of a real doll.* New York: Morrow.

LOWELL, B. L. 2002. Recession pounds U.S. Hispanics. *Population Today* 30 (Apr.): 1, 4.

LUCAS, R. E., A. E. CLARK, Y. GEORGELLIS, AND E. DIENER. 2003. Reexamining adaptation and the set point model of happiness: Reactions to changes in marital status. *Journal of Personality and Social Psychology* 84 (Mar.): 527–39.

LUGAILA, T. A. 1998. Marital status and living arrangements: March 1998 (update). Current Population Reports, P20-514, U.S. Census

Bureau. www.census.gov/prod/99pubs/p20514. pdf (accessed Aug. 8, 2000).

LUGAILA, T. A. 2003. *A child's day: 2000 (selected indicators of child well-being).* Current Population Reports, P70-89. Washington, DC: U.S. Census Bureau. www.census.gov/prod/ 2003pubs/p70-89.pdf (accessed Aug. 24, 2003).

LUKEMEYER, A., M. K. MEYERS, AND T. SMEEDING. 2000. Expensive children in poor families: Out-of-pocket expenditures for the care of disabled and chronically ill children in welfare families. *Journal of Marriage and the Family* 62 (May): 399–415.

LUND, E. 2001. The search for common ground. *Christian Science Monitor,* Dec. 19, 15–17.

LUNDBERG, S. 2001. Nonmarital fertility: Lessons for family economics. In *Out of wedlock: Causes and consequences of nonmarital fertility,* eds. L. L. Wu and B. Wolfe, 383–89. New York: Russell Sage Foundation.

LUNDY, S. E. 1993. Abuse that dare not speak its name: Assisting victims of lesbian and gay domestic violence in Massachusetts. *New England Law Review* 28 (Winter): 272–311.

LUOMA, I., ET AL. 2001. Longitudinal study of maternal depressive symptoms and child well-being. *Journal of the American Academy of Child & Adolescent Psychiatry* 40 (Dec.): 1367–74.

LUPTON, D., AND L. BARCLAY. 1997. *Constructing fatherhood: Discourses and experiences.* Thousand Oaks, CA: Sage.

LYE, D. N., AND T. J. BIBLARZ. 1993. The effects of attitudes toward family life and gender roles on marital satisfaction. *Journal of Family Issues* 14 (June): 157–88.

LYMAN, K. A. 1993. *Day in, day out with Alzheimer's: Stress in caregiving relationships.* Philadelphia: Temple University Press.

LYNN, D. B. 1969. *Parental and sex role identification: A theoretical formulation.* Berkeley, CA: McCutchen.

LYNN, M., AND M. TODOROFF. 1995. Women's work and family lives. In *Feminist issues: Race, class, and sexuality,* ed. N. Mandell, 244–71. Scarborough, Ont.: Prentice Hall Canada.

LYNSKEY, M. T., ET AL. 2003. Escalation of drug use in early-onset cannabis users vs. co-twin controls. *Journal of the American Medical Association* 289 (Jan. 22): 427–33.

LYTTON, H., AND L. GALLAGHER. 2002. Parenting twins and the genetics of parenting. In *Handbook of parenting,* 2nd ed., Vol. 1: *Children and parenting,* ed. M. H. Bornstein, 227–53. Mahwah, NJ: Erlbaum.

MACADAM, M. 2003. Sweatshop struggle strengthens solidarity: Campaign against exploitation of foreign workers unites activists. Policy Alternatives. www.policyalternatives.ca/publications/ articles/article361.html (accessed Sep. 13, 2003).

MACCALLUM, F., AND S. GOLOMBOK. 2002. *Families through surrogacy: Psychological implications.* London: Family and Child Psychology Research Centre, City University. http://conf.eshre.com/ PDF/O-012.pdf (accessed Aug. 18, 2003).

MACCOBY, E. E. 1990. Gender and relationships: A developmental account. *American Psychologist* 45 (4): 513–20.

MACCOBY, E. E., C. E. DEPNER, AND R. H. MNOOKIN. 1991. Co-parenting in the second year after divorce. In *Joint custody and shared parenting,* 2nd ed., ed. J. Folberg, 132–52. New York: Guilford.

MACDONALD, G. J. 2003. Smarter toys, smarter tots? *Christian Science Monitor,* Aug. 20, 12–13.

MACDONALD, W. L., AND A. DEMARIS. 1996. The effects of stepparents' gender and new biological children. *Journal of Family Issues* 17 (1): 5–25.

MACHAMER, A. M., AND E. GRUBER. 1998. Secondary school, family, and educational risk: Comparing American Indian adolescents and their peers. *Journal of Educational Research* 91 (July/Aug.): 357–69.

MACKENZIE, J. 2002. Britain toughens immigration stance. *Christian Science Monitor,* Aug. 16, 7, 9.

MACMILLAN, R., AND R. GARTNER. 1999. When she brings home the bacon: Labor-force participation and the risk of spousal violence against women. *Journal of Marriage and the Family* 61 (Nov.): 947–58.

MACPHEE, D., J. FRITZ, AND J. MILLER-HEYL. 1996. Ethnic variations in personal social networks and parenting. *Child Development* 67 (6): 3278–95.

MACUNOVICH, D. J. 2002. Using economics to explain U.S. fertility trends. *Population Bulletin* 57 (Dec.): 8–9. Washington, DC: Population Reference Bureau.

MADDEN-DERDICH, D. A., AND S. A. LEONARD. 2000. Parental role identity and fathers' involvement in coparental interaction after divorce: Fathers' perspectives. *Family Relations* 49 (July): 311–18.

MADIGAN, N. 2003. Suspect's wife is said to cite polygamy plan. *New York Times.* www. nytimes.com/2003/03/15/national/15UTAH. html?th (accessed Mar. 16, 2003).

MAHAY, J., E. O. LAUMANN, AND S. MICHAELS. 2001. Race, gender, and class in sexual scripts. In *Sex, love, and health in America,* eds. E. O. Laumann and R. T. Michael, 197–238. Chicago: University of Chicago Press.

MAHONEY, M. 2002. The economic rights and responsibilities of unmarried cohabitants. In *Just living together: Implications of cohabitation on families, children, and social policy,* eds. A. Booth and A. C. Crouter, 247–54. Mahwah, NJ: Erlbaum.

MAHONEY, S. 2003. Seeking love. *AARP Magazine,* Nov./Dec.. www.aarpmagazine.org/lifestyle/ Articles/a2003-09-23-seekinglove.html (accessed Sep. 28, 2003).

MAIER, T. 1998. *Dr. Spock: An American life.* New York: Harcourt Brace.

MAJOR, B., AND C. COZZARELLI. 1992. Psychological predictors of adjustment to abortion. *Journal of Social Issues* 48: 121–42.

Male latex condoms and sexually transmitted diseases. 2002. Centers for Disease Control and Prevention. www.cdc.gov/nchstp/od/condoms.pdf (accessed Mar. 16, 2003).

Man who raped child retains visitation rights. 2002. *Women's E-News,* Apr. 22. www. womensenews.org/article.cfm/dyn/aid/884/ context/outrage (accessed Apr. 24, 2002).

MANCINI, J. A., AND R. BLIESZNER. 1991. Aging parents and adult children: Research themes in intergenerational relations. In *Contemporary families: Looking forward, looking back,* ed. A. Booth, 249–64. Minneapolis: National Council on Family Relations.

MANNERS, J. 1993. The perils of a second marriage. *Money,* Jan., 108–20.

MANNING, C. 1970. *The immigrant woman and her job.* New York: Ayer.

MANNING, W. D. 2002. The implications of cohabitation for children's well-being. In *Just living together: Implications of cohabitation on families, children, and social policy,* eds. A. Booth and A. C. Crouter, 121–52. Mahwah, NJ: Erlbaum.

MANNING, W. D., S. D. STEWART, AND P. J. SMOCK. 2003. The complexity of fathers' parenting responsibilities and involvement with nonresident children. *Journal of Family Issues* 24 (July): 645–67.

MANNIS, V. S. 1999. Single mothers by choice. *Family Relations* 48 (Apr.): 121–28.

MARBELLA, J. 1990. A chorus of opinions on what love's got to do with it. *Baltimore Sun,* Feb. 14, 1F, 5F.

MARBELLA, J. 2003. Ga. high school returns to racially divided proms. *Baltimore Sun,* May 3, 3A.

MARCUS, A. D. 2003. Guys, your clock is ticking, too: doctors now say male fertility falls as early as age 35; the case for banking your sperm. *Wall Street Journal,* Apr. 1, D1.

MARCUS, D. L., A. MULRINE, AND K. WONG. 1999. How kids learn. *U.S. News & World Report,* Sep. 13, 44–52.

MARCUS, M. B. 2002. Aging of AIDS. *U.S. News & World Report,* Aug. 12, 40–41.

MARCUS, S. M., H. A. FLYNN, F. C. BLOW, AND K. L. BARRY. 2003. Depressive symptoms among pregnant women screened in obstetrics settings. *Journal of Women's Health* 12 (May): 373–80.

MARDER, D. 2002. For $9,600, women taught how to find a mate. Knight Ridder News Service, Jan. 13. archives.his.com/smartmarriages/msg01731. html (accessed Jan. 15, 2002).

MARGOLIS, J., AND A. FISHER. 2002. *Unlocking the clubhouse: Women in computing.* Cambridge, MA: MIT Press.

MARKIDES, K. S., J. ROBERTS-JOLLY, L. A. RAY, S. K. HOPPE, AND L. RUDKIN. 1999. Changes in marital satisfaction in three generations of Mexican Americans. *Research on Aging* 21 (Jan.): 36–45.

MARKS, A. 2000. Vermont launches revolution by allowing same-sex unions. *Christian Science Monitor,* Apr. 27, 2.

MARKS, A. 2002. As teens' prospects rise, pregnancies fall. *Christian Science Monitor,* Oct. 22, 3.

MARKS, A. 2003. Fewer foster homes and a rising need. *Christian Science Monitor,* July 8, 1, 4.

MARKSTROM-ADAMS, C. 1991. Attitudes on dating, courtship, and marriage: Perspectives on in-group relationships by religious minority and majority adolescents. *Family Relations* 40 (Jan.): 91–98.

Marriage between blacks and whites. 2002. Gallup Poll Vault. www.gallup.com/poll/pollInsights/ #GPV (accessed Dec. 15, 2002).

MARSIGLIO, W., ED. 1995. *Fatherhood: Contemporary theory, research, and social policy.* Thousand Oaks, CA: Sage.

MARSIGLIO, W., AND D. DONNELLY. 1991. Sexual relations in later life: A national study of married persons. *Journal of Gerontology* 46 (Nov.): S338–S344.

MARSIGLIO, W., AND R. A. GREER. 1994. A gender analysis of older men's sexuality. In *Older men's lives,* ed. E. H. Thompson, 122–40. Thousand Oaks, CA: Sage.

MARTEL, D. W. 2001. Kids thirst for knowledge. *Public Perspective* 12 (Jan./Feb.): 7.

MARTEL, D. W., ED. 2001. Protective instincts. *Public Perspective* 12 (Mar./Apr.): 5.

MARTIN, A. 1993. *The lesbian and gay parenting handbook: Creating and raising our families.* New York: HarperPerennial.

MARTIN, C. L. 1990. Attitudes and expectations about children with nontraditional and traditional gender roles. *Sex Roles* 22 (Feb.): 151–65.

MARTIN, C. L., AND R. A. FABES. 2001. The stability and consequences of young children's same-sex peer interactions. *Developmental Psychology* 37 (May): 431–66.

MARTIN, J. A., B. E. HAMILTON, S. J. VENTURA, F. MENACKER, AND M. M. PARK. 2002. Births: Final data for 2000. *National Vital Statistics Reports* 50 (Feb.). www.cdc.gov/nchs/data/nvsr/ nvsr50/nvsr50_05.pdf (accessed Aug. 6, 2003).

MARTIN, K. A. 1998. Becoming a gendered body: Practices of preschools. *American Sociological Review* 63 (Aug.): 494–511.

MARTIN, P., AND E. MIDGLEY. 1999. Immigration to the United States. *Population Bulletin* 54 (June): 1–44.

MARTIN, P., AND E. MIDGLEY. 2003. Immigration: Shaping and reshaping America. *Population Bulletin* 58 (June). Washington, DC: Population Reference Bureau.

MARTIN, P. D., D. MARTIN, AND M. MARTIN. 2001. Adolescent premarital sexual activity, cohabitation, and attitudes toward marriage. *Adolescence* 36 (Fall): 601–9.

MARTIN, P. Y., AND R. A. HUMMER. 1993. Fraternities and rape on campus. In *Violence against women,* eds. P. B. Bart and E. G. Moran, 114–31. Thousand Oaks, CA: Sage.

MARTIN, T. C., AND L. L. BUMPASS. 1989. Recent trends in marital disruption. *Demography* 26 (Feb.): 37–51.

MARTINEZ, E. A. 2001. Death: A family event for Mexican Americans. *Family Focus,* National Council on Family Relations, Dec., F4.

MARTIRE, L. M., M. P. STEPHENS, AND M. M. FRANKS. 1997. Multiple roles of women caregivers: Feelings of mastery and self-esteem as predictors of psychosocial well-being. *Journal of Women & Aging* 9 (1/2): 117–31.

MARYLAND SPECIAL JOINT COMMITTEE. 1989. *Gender bias in the courts.* Annapolis, MD: Administrative Office of the Courts.

MARZOLLO, J. 1993. *Fathers & babies: How babies grow and what they need from you from birth to 18 months.* New York: HarperCollins.

MASON, C. A., A. M. CAUCE, AND N. GONZALES. 1997. Parents and peers in the lives of African-American adolescents: An interactive approach to the study of problem behavior. In *Social and emotional adjustment and family relations in ethnic minority families,* eds. R. D. Taylor and M. C. Wang, 85–98. Mahwah, NJ: Erlbaum.

MASON, M. A. 1999. *Custody wars: Why children are losing the legal battle and what we can do about it.* New York: Basic Books.

MASON, M. A., AND M. GOULDEN. 2002. Do babies matter? The effect of family formation on the lifelong careers of academic men and women. *Academe.* www.aaup.org/publications/Academe/02nd/02ndmas.htm (accessed Aug. 5, 2003).

MASON, M. A., AND J. MAULDON. 1996. The new stepfamily requires a new public policy. *Journal of Social Issues* 52 (3): 11–27.

MASSEY, L. 1992. What is really the best interest of the child? *Legal Assistant Today* (Nov./Dec.): 140–41.

MASTEKAASA, A. 1994. Marital status, distress, and well-being: An international comparison. *Journal of Comparative Family Studies* 25 (Summer): 183–205.

MASTEKAASA, A. 1997. Marital dissolution as a stressor: Some evidence on psychological, physical, and behavioral changes during the preseparation period. *Journal of Divorce and Remarriage* 26: 155–83.

MASTERS, W. H., V. E. JOHNSON, AND R. C. KOLODNY. 1986. *On sex and human loving.* Boston: Little, Brown.

MASTERS, W. H., V. E. JOHNSON, AND R. C. KOLODNY. 1992. *Human sexuality,* 4th ed. New York: HarperCollins.

MASUR, D. M., M. SLIWINSKI, AND H. A. CRYSTAL. 1994. Neuropsychological prediction of dementia and the absence of dementia in healthy elderly persons. *Neurology* 44 (Aug.): 1427–33.

MATHER, M. 2002. Homeownership rates divide U.S. racial and ethnic groups. *Population Today* 30 (Nov./Dec.): 2.

MATHES, V. S. 1981. A new look at the role of women in Indian society. In *The American Indian: Past and present,* 2nd ed., ed. R. L. Nichols, 27–33. New York: Wiley.

MATHEWS, T. J., F. MACDORMAN, AND F. MENACKER. 2002. Infant mortality statistics from the 1999 period linked birth/infant death data set. Centers for Disease Control and Prevention, *National Vital Statistics Reports* 50 (Jan. 30). www.cdc.gov/nchs/data/nvsr50/nvsr50_04.pdf (accessed May 10, 2003).

MATHEWS, T. J., AND S. J. VENTURA. 1997. Birth and fertility rates by educational attainment: United States, 1994. *Monthly Vital Statistics Report* 45 (10), suppl. Hyattsville, MD: National Center for Health Statistics.

MATHIAS, B. 1992. Yes, Va. (Md. & D.C.), there are happy marriages. *Washington Post,* Sep. 22, B5.

MATHIAS, B. 1997. No longer just a member of the wedding. *Washington Post,* Mar. 18, C5.

MATTES, J. 1994. *Single mothers by choice.* New York: Times Books.

MATTHAEI, J. A. 1982. *An economic history of women in America: Women's work, the sexual division of labor, and the development of capitalism.* New York: Schocken.

MATTHEWS, S. H., AND T. T. ROSNER. 1988. Shared filial responsibility: The family as the primary caregiver. *Journal of Marriage and the Family* 50 (Feb.): 185–95.

MATTHIAS, R. E., J. E. LUBBEN, K. A. ATCHISON, AND S. O. SCHWEITZER. 1997. Sexual activity and satisfaction among very old adults: Results from a community-dwelling Medicare population survey. *The Gerontologist* 17 (1): 6–14.

MATTOX, W. 1994. The hottest valentines. *Washington Post,* Feb. 13, C5.

MAULDON, J. 2003. Families started by teenagers. In *All our families: New policies for a new century,* 2nd ed., eds. M. A. Mason, A. Skolnick, and S. D. Sugarman, 40–65. New York: Oxford University Press.

MAUSHART, S. 2002. *Wifework: What marriage really means for women.* New York: Bloomsbury.

MAXWELL, A. 1998. Not all issues are black or white: Some voices from the offspring of cross-cultural marriages. In *Cross-Cultural marriage: Identity*

and choice, eds. R. Breger and R. Rosanna, 209–26. New York: Berg.

MAY, E. T. 1995. *Barren in the promised land: Childless Americans and the pursuit of happiness.* New York: Basic Books.

MAY, P. A. 1999. The epidemiology of alcohol abuse among American Indians: The mythical and real properties. In *Contemporary Native American cultural issues,* ed. D. Champagne, 227–44. Walnut Creek, CA: AltaMira.

MAYER, C. E. 1999. For a generation in denial, a fountain of youth products. *Washington Post,* May 6, A1, A16.

MAYNARD, M. 1994. Methods, practice and epistemology: The debate about feminism and research. In *Researching women's lives from a feminist perspective,* eds. M. Maynard and J. Purvis, 10–26. London: Taylor & Francis.

MAYNARD, R. A., ED. 1997. *Kids having kids: Economic costs and social consequences of teen pregnancy.* Washington, DC: Urban Institute.

MAYO, Y. 1997. Machismo, fatherhood, and the Latino family: Understanding the concept. *Journal of Multicultural Social Work* 5 (1/2): 49–61.

MAYS, V. M., L. M. CHATTERS, AND S. D. COCHRAN. 1998. African American families in diversity: Gay men and lesbians in family networks. *Journal of Comparative Family Studies* 29 (Spring): 73–88.

MCADOO, H. P. 2002. African American parenting. In *Handbook of parenting,* 2nd ed., Vol. 4: *Social conditions and applied parenting,* ed. M. H. Bornstein, 47–58. Mahwah, NJ: Erlbaum.

MCADOO, J. L. 1986. Black fathers' relationships with their preschool children and the children's development of ethnic identity. In *Men in families,* eds. R. A. Lewis and R. E. Salt, 159–68. Thousand Oaks, CA: Sage.

MCCARROLL, C. 2002. Coed sleepovers: Platonic or premature? *Christian Science Monitor,* Dec. 4, 1, 4.

MCCAUGHEY septuplets celebrate their second birthday. 1999. *Baltimore Sun,* Nov. 19, 23A.

MCCOY, E. 1986. Your one and only. *Parents,* Oct., 118–21, 236.

MCDADE, K. 1995. How we parent: Race and ethnic differences. In *American families: Issues in race and ethnicity,* ed. C. K. Jacobson, 283–300. New York: Garland.

MCDONALD, K. A. 1999. Studies of women's health produce a wealth of knowledge on the biology of gender differences. *Chronicle of Higher Education,* June 25, A19, A22.

MCDONALD, M. 2000. A start-up of her own. *U.S. News & World Report,* May 15, 34–42.

MCELHANEY, K. B., AND J. P. ALLEN. 2001. Autonomy and adolescent social functioning: The moderating effect of risk. *Child Development* 72 (Jan./Feb.): 220–35.

MCELVAINE, R. S. 1993. *The great depression: America, 1929–1941.* New York: Times Books.

MCFARLANE, M., S. S. BULL, AND C. A. RIETMEIJER. 2000. The Internet as a newly emerging risk environment for sexually transmitted diseases. *Journal of the American Medical Association* 284 (July 26): 443–46.

MCGINN, D., AND J. E. HALPERT. 1998. Final farewells. *Newsweek,* Dec. 14, 60–62.

MCGINNIS, T. 1981. *More than just a friend: The joys and disappointments of extramarital affairs.* Upper Saddle River, NJ: Prentice Hall.

MCGOLDRICK, M., AND J. GIORDANO. 1996. Overview: Ethnicity and family therapy. In *Ethnicity and family therapy,* 2nd ed., eds. M. McGoldrick, J. Giordano, and J. K. Pearce, 1–27. New York: Guilford.

MCGOLDRICK, M., M. HEIMAN, AND B. CARTER. 1993. The changing family life cycle: A perspective on normalcy. In *Normal family processes,* 2nd ed., ed. F. Walsh, 405–43. New York: Guilford.

MCGONAGLE, K. A., R. C. KESSLER, AND I. H. GOTLIB. 1993. The effects of marital disagreement style, frequency, and outcome on marital disruption. *Journal of Social and Personal Relationships,* 10 (Aug.): 385–404.

MCGRATH, D. 2003. Magazines still promote domestic chores as women's work. *Women's E-News.* www.womensenews.org/article.cfm/dyn/aid/

1280/context/outrage, Apr. 5 (accessed Apr. 7, 2003).

MCGUINESS, T., AND L. PALLANSCH. 2000. Competence of children adopted from the former Soviet Union. *Family Relations* 49 (Oct.): 457–64.

MCGUIRE, M. 1996. Growing up with two moms. *Newsweek,* Nov. 4, 53.

MCKAY, M. M. 1994. The link between domestic violence and child abuse: Assessment and treatment considerations. *Child Welfare* 73 (Jan./Feb.): 29–39.

MCKELVEY, L. M., H. E. FITZGERALD, R. F. SCHIFFMAN, AND A. VON EYE. 2002. Family stress and parent–infant interaction: The mediating role of coping. *Infant Mental Health Journal* 23 (Feb.): 164–81.

MCKINLAY, J. B., AND H. A. FELDMAN. 1994. Age-related variation in sexual activity and interest in normal men: Results from the Massachusetts male aging study. In *Sexuality across the life course,* ed. A. S. Rossi, 261–85. Chicago: University of Chicago Press.

MCLANAHAN, S. 2002. Life without father: What happens to the children? *Contexts* 1 (Spring): 35–44.

MCLANAHAN, S., AND L. BUMPASS. 1988. Intergenerational consequences of family disruption. *American Journal of Sociology* 94 (July): 130–52.

MCLANAHAN, S., I. GARFINKEL, N. E. REICHMAN, AND J. O. TEITLER. 2001. Unwed parents or fragile families? Implications for welfare and child support policy. In *Out of wedlock: Causes and consequences of nonmarital fertility,* eds. L. L. Wu and B. Wolfe, 202–28. New York: Russell Sage Foundation.

MCLANAHAN, S., AND G. SANDEFUR. 1994. *Growing up with a single parent: What hurts, what helps.* Cambridge, MA: Harvard University Press.

MCLANAHAN, S. S., J. A. SELTZER, T. L. HANSON, AND E. THOMSON. 1994. Child support enforcement and child well-being: Greater security or greater conflict? In *Child support and child well-being,* eds. I. Garfinkel, S. S. McLanahan, and P. K. Robins, 239–56. Washington, DC: Urban Institute.

MCLANE, D. 1995. The Cuban-American princess. *New York Times Magazine,* Feb. 26, 42–43.

MCLOYD, V. C., A. M. CAUCE, D. TAKEUCHI, AND L. WILSON. 2001. Marital processes and parental socialization in families of color: A decade review of research. In *Understanding families into the new millennium: A decade in review,* ed. R. M. Milardo, 289–312. Minneapolis: National Council on Family Relations.

MCLOYD, V. C., AND J. SMITH. 2002. Physical discipline and behavior problems in African American, European American, and Hispanic children: Emotional support as a moderator. *Journal of Marriage and Family* 64 (Feb.): 40–53.

MCNAMARA, R. P., M. TEMPENIS, AND B. WALTON. 1999. *Crossing the line: Interracial couples in the South.* Westport, CT: Greenwood.

MCNEELY, C., ET AL. 2002. Mothers' influence on the timing of first sex among 14- and 15-year olds. *Journal of Adolescent Health* 31 (Sep.): 256–65.

MCPHARLIN, P. 1946. *Love and courtship in America.* New York: Hastings House.

MCRAE, S. 1999. Cohabitation or marriage? Cohabitation. In *The sociology of the family,* ed. G. Allan, 172–90. Malden, MA: Blackwell.

MCROY, R. G. 1999. *Special needs adoptions: Practice issues.* New York: Garland.

MCWHORTER, J. H. 2001. Toward a useable black history. *City Journal,* 11 (3), Summer. www.cityjournal.org/html/11_3_toward_a_usable.html (accessed July 11, 2003).

MEAD, G. H. 1934. *Mind, self, and society.* Chicago: University of Chicago Press.

MEAD, G. H. 1938. *The philosophy of the act.* Chicago: University of Chicago Press.

MEAD, G. H. 1964. *On social psychology.* Chicago: University of Chicago Press.

MEAD, L. M. 1996. Work requirements can transform the system. *Chronicle of Higher Education,* Oct. 4, B6.

MEAD, M. 1935. *Sex and temperament in three primitive societies.* New York: Morrow.

MEIER, A. M. 2003. Adolescents' transition to first intercourse, religiosity, and attitudes about sex. *Social Forces* 81 (Mar.): 1031–52.

MEKOS, D., E. M. HETHERINGTON, AND D. REISS. 1996. Sibling differences in problem behavior and parental treatment in nondivorced and remarried families. *Child Development* 67 (Oct.): 2148–65.

MELOSH, B. 2002. *Strangers and kin: The American way of adoption*. Cambridge, MA: Harvard University Press.

MELTZER, N., ED. 1964. *In their own words: A history of the American Negro, 1619–1865*. New York: Crowell.

MELZER, S. A. 2002. Gender, work, and intimate violence: Men's occupational violence spillover and compensatory violence. *Journal of Marriage and Family* 64 (Nov.): 820–32.

MENARD, S. 2002. *Short- and long-term consequences of adolescent victimization*. Washington, DC: U.S. Department of Justice.

MENDEL, D. 2002. A family affair. In *Advocasey*, 12–19. Baltimore: Annie E. Casey Foundation.

MENDELSOHN, K. D., L. Z. NIEMAN, K. ISAACS, S. LEE, AND S. P. LEVISON. 1994. Sex and gender bias in anatomy and physical diagnosis text illustrations. *Journal of the American Medical Association*, Oct. 26, 1267–70.

MERGENBAGEN, P. 1994. Job benefits get personal. *American Demographics* 16 (Sep.): 30–38.

MERGENBAGEN, P. 1996. The reunion market. *American Demographics* 18 (Apr.): 30–34, 52.

MERTEN, D. E. 1996. Going-with: The role of a social form in early romance. *Journal of Contemporary Ethnography* 24 (Jan.): 462–84.

MESSNER, M. A. 2002. The focus on equity misses the real issues. *Chronicle of Higher Education*, Dec. 6, B9-B10.

MESTEL, R. 2003. Birth by test tube turns 25. *Los Angeles Times*, July 24. www.latimes.com/la-sci-invitro24jul24,1,250338.story (accessed July 25, 2003).

METTS, S. 1994. Relational transgressions. In *The dark side of interpersonal communication*, eds. W. R. Cupach and B. H. Spitzberg, 217–39. Hillsdale, NJ: Erlbaum.

MEYER, D. R., AND M. CANCIAN. 1997. Life after welfare. *Population Today* 25 (July/Aug.): 4–5.

MIALL, C. 1986. The stigma of involuntary childlessness. *Social Problems* 33 (Apr.): 268–82.

MIALL, C. E. 1987. The stigma of adoptive parent status: Perceptions of community attitudes toward adoption and the experience of informal social sanctioning. *Family Relations* 36 (Jan.): 34–39.

MICHAEL, R. T., AND C. BICKERT. 2001. Exploring determinants of adolescents' early sexual behavior. In *Social awakening: Adolescent behavior as adulthood approaches*, ed. R. T. Michael, 137–73. New York: Russell Sage Foundation.

MICHAEL, R. T., J. H. GAGNON, E. O. LAUMANN, AND G. KOLATA. 1994. *Sex in America: A definitive study*. Boston: Little, Brown.

MIEDZIAN, M. 1991. *Boys will be boys: Breaking the link between masculinity and violence*. New York: Anchor.

MIELL, D., AND R. CROGHAN. 1996. Examining the wider context of social relationships. In *Social interaction and personal relationships*, eds. D. Miell and R. Dallos, 267–318. Thousand Oaks, CA: Sage.

MIHESUAH, D. A. 1998. American Indian identities: Issues of individual choices and development. *American Indian Culture and Research Journal* 22 (2): 193–226.

MILES, T. 2003. Don't expect AIDS vaccine before 2009, experts say. Reuters. http://story.news.yahoo.com/news?tmpl=story&u=/nm/20030618/hl_nm/aids_vaccine_dc_2 (accessed June 20, 2003).

MILKIE, M. A., AND P. PELTOLA. 1999. Playing all the roles: Gender and the work–family balancing act. *Journal of Marriage and the Family* 61 (May): 476–90.

MILKMAN, R. 1976. Women's work and the economic crisis: Some lessons from the Great Depression. *Review of Radical Political Economics* 8 (Spring): 73–97.

MILLER, B. 1995. Household futures. *American Demographics* 17 (Mar.): 4, 6.

MILLER, B. C. 1986. *Family research methods*. Beverly Hills, CA: Sage.

MILLER, B. C. 2002. Family influences on adolescent sexual and contraceptive behavior. *Journal of Sex Research* 39 (Feb.): 22–26.

MILLER, K. S., R. FOREHAND, AND B. A. KOTCHICK. 1999. Adolescent sexual behavior in two ethnic minority samples: The role of family variables. *Journal of Marriage and the Family* 61 (Feb.): 85–98.

MILLER, W. L., AND B. F. CRABTREE. 1994. Clinical research. In *Handbook of qualitative research*, eds. N. K. Denzin and Y. S. Lincoln, 340–52. Thousand Oaks, CA: Sage.

MILLER-PERRIN, C. L., AND R. D. PERRIN. 1999. *Child maltreatment: An introduction*. Thousand Oaks, CA: Sage.

MILLNER, D., AND N. CHILES. 1999. *What brothers think, what sistahs know: The real deal on love and relationships*. New York: Morrow.

MILLS, R. J., AND S. BHANDARI. 2003. Health insurance coverage in the United States: 2002. U.S. Census Bureau, Current Population Reports, p60-223. www.census.gov/prod/2003pubs/p60-223.pdf (accessed Oct. 9, 2003).

MIN, P. G. 2002. Korean American families. In *Minority families in the United States: A multicultural perspective*, 3rd ed., ed. R. L. Taylor, 193–211. Upper Saddle River, NJ: Prentice Hall.

MINTON, L. 1995. Stepfamilies. *Parade Magazine*, Feb. 26, 24–25.

MINTZ, S., AND S. KELLOGG. 1988. *Domestic revolution: A social history of American family life*. New York: Free Press.

MIRANDE, A. 1985. *The Chicano experience: An alternative perspective*. Notre Dame, IN: University of Notre Dame Press.

MISRA, D., ED. 2001. *Women's health data book: A profile of women's health in the United States*, 3rd ed. Washington, DC: Jacobs Institute of Women's Health and The Henry J. Kaiser Family Foundation.

MITCHELL, A. A. 2002. Infertility treatment: more risks and challenges. *New England Journal of Medicine* 346 (Mar. 7): 769–70.

MITCHELL, B. A., AND E. M. GEE. 1996. "Boomerang kids" and midlife parental marital satisfaction. *Family Relations* 45 (Oct.): 442–48.

MOEN, P. 1992. *Women's two roles: A contemporary dilemma*. Westport, CT: Auburn House.

MOGELONSKY, M. 1996. The rocky road to adulthood. *American Demographics* 18 (May): 26–35, 56.

MOHR, J. 1981. The great upsurge of abortion, 1840–1880. In *Family life in America: 1620–2000*, eds. M. Albin and D. Cavallo, 119–30. St. James, NY: Revisionary Press.

MONASTERSKY, R. 2003. Scientists find genetic link to depression. *Chronicle of Higher Education*, July 18. http://chronicle.com/daily/2003/07/2003071803n.htm (accessed July 19, 2003).

MONEY, J., AND A. A. EHRHARDT. 1972. *Man & woman, boy & girl*. Baltimore: Johns Hopkins University Press.

MONTGOMERY, M. J., E. R. ANDERSON, E. M. HETHERINGTON, AND W. G. CLINGEMPEEL. 1992. Patterns of courtship for remarriage: Implications for child adjustment and parent–child relationships. *Journal of Marriage and the Family* 54 (Aug.): 686–98.

MONTGOMERY, M. J., AND G. T. SORELL. 1997. Differences in love attitudes across family life stages. *Family Relations* 46 (Jan.): 55–61.

MOORE, D. M. 2003. Half of young people expect to strike it rich. Gallup Poll Analysis. www.gallup.com/poll/releases/pr030311.asp (accessed Aug. 21, 2003).

MOORE, D. W. 2003. Poll analysis: Family, health most important aspects of life. Gallup News Service, Jan. 3. www.gallup.com/poll/releases/pr030103.asp (accessed Jan. 5, 2003).

MOORE, J., AND H. PACHON. 1985. *Hispanics in the United States*. Upper Saddle River, NJ: Prentice Hall.

MOORE, K. A., AND J. F. ZAFF. 2002. Building a better teenager: A summary of "what works" in adolescent development. Washington, DC: Child Trends. www.childtrends.org/PDF/K7Brief.pdf (accessed Aug. 23, 2003).

MOORE, M. 2001. In Turkey, "honor killing" follows families to cities. *Washington Post*, Aug. 8, A1, A14.

MOORE, M. R., AND P. L. CHASE-LANSDALE. 2001. Sexual intercourse and pregnancy among African American girls in high-poverty neighborhoods: The role of family and perceived community environment. *Journal of Marriage and Family* 63 (Nov.): 1146–57.

MOORE, P., WITH C. P. CONN. 1985. *Disguised*. Waco, TX: Word Books.

MOORE, R. L. 1998. Love and limerence with Chinese characteristics: Student romance in the PRC. In *Romantic love and sexual behavior: Perspectives from the social sciences*, ed. V. C. deMunck, 251–88. Westport, CT: Praeger.

MORAHAN, L. 2002. "Morning-after" pill available at some DoD clinics. CNSNews, June 3. www.cnsnews.com/ViewPentagon.asp?Page=/Pentagon/archive/200206/PEN20020603a.html (accessed Aug. 18, 2003).

MORALES, E. 1996. Gender roles among Latino gay and bisexual men: Implications for family and couple relationships. In *Lesbians and gays in couples and families: A handbook for therapists*, eds. J. Laird and R.-J. Green, 272–97. San Francisco: Jossey-Bass.

MORELL, C. M. 1994. *Unwomanly conduct: The challenges of intentional childlessness*. New York: Routledge.

MORGAN, D. I., ED. 1993. *Successful focus groups: Advancing the state of the art*. Thousand Oaks, CA: Sage.

MORGAN, P. D. 1998. *Slave counterpoint: Black culture in the eighteenth-century Chesapeake & lowcountry*. Chapel Hill: University of North Carolina Press.

MORGAN, R. 2002. The men in the mirror. *Chronicle of Higher Education*, Sep. 27, A53–A54.

MORGAN, R. 2002. States split on asking divorced parents to pay for children's tuition. *Chronicle of Higher Education*, Aug. 16, A28.

MORGAN, S. P., D. N. LYE, AND G. A. CONDRAN. 1988. Sons, daughters, and the risk of marital disruption. *American Journal of Sociology* 94 (July): 110–29.

MORGAN, W. L. 1939. *The family meets the depression: A study of a group of highly selected families*. Westport, CT: Greenwood.

MORGENTHAU, T. 1997. The face of the future. *Newsweek*, Jan. 27, 58–60.

MORIN, R. 1994. How to lie with statistics: Adultery. *Washington Post*, Mar. 6, C5.

MORRIS, B. 2002. Trophy husbands. *Fortune*, Oct. 12, 79–98.

MORRIS, C. L. 2002. Stepping in, stepping up: Raising your spouse's kids is a role that takes time and nurturance. *Washington Post*, July 20, C10.

MORRIS, M. 2003. Love in a hurry. *Baltimore Sun*, Jan. 12, 1N, 4N.

MORRIS, M. C., ET AL. 2002. Dietary intake of antioxidant nutrients and the risk of incident Alzheimer disease in a biracial community study. *Journal of the American Medical Association* 287 (June 26): 3230–37.

MORRISON, D. R., AND A. J. CHERLIN. 1995. The divorce process and young children's well-being: A prospective analysis. *Journal of Marriage and the Family* 57 (Aug.): 800–12.

MORSE, J. 2002. An RX for teen sex. *Time*, Oct. 7, 62–65.

MOSBY, L., AND A. W. RAWLS. 1999. Troubles in interracial talk about discipline: An examination of African American child rearing. *Journal of Comparative Family Studies* 30 (Summer): 489–522.

MOSCICKI, E. K. 1994. Gender differences in completed and attempted suicides. *Annals of Epidemiology* 4 (Mar.): 152–58.

MOSHER, W. D., AND W. F. PRATT. 1991. Fecundity and infertility in the United States: Incidence and trends. *Fertility and Sterility* 56 (Aug.): 192–93.

Motherhood today: A tougher job, less ably done. 1997. Pew Research Center for the People & the Press. www.people-press.org/momrpt.htm (accessed Oct. 5, 1997).

Mothers work. 2000. *Public Perspective* 11 (July/Aug.): 23.

MOTT, F. L., L. KOWALESKI-JONES, AND E. G. MENAGHAN. 1997. Paternal absence and child behavior: Does a child's gender make a difference? *Journal of Marriage and the Family* 59 (Feb.): 103–18.

MOWRER, E. R. 1972. War and family solidarity and stability. In *The American family in World War II*, ed. R. A. Abrams, 100–106. New York: Arno and New York Times. (Originally published in *Annals of the American Academy of Political and Social Science* 229, Sep. 1943.)

MOYNIHAN, D. P., ED. 1970. *Toward a national urban policy*. New York: Basic Books.

MUELLER, M. M., AND G. H. ELDER, JR. 2003. Family contingencies across the generations: Grandparent–grandchild relationships in holistic perspective. *Journal of Marriage and Family* 65 (May): 404–17.

MUI, A. C., N. G. CHOI, AND A. MONK. 1998. *Long-term care and ethnicity*. Westport, CT: Auburn House.

MUI, A. C., AND N. MORROW-HOWELL. 1993. Sources of emotional strain among the oldest caregivers: Differential experiences of siblings and spouses. *Research on Aging* 15 (Mar.): 50–69.

MULHAUSER, D. 2001. State Supreme Court finds sex bias in firing at U. of Northern Colorado. *Chronicle of Higher Education*, Dec. 5. http://chronicle.com/daily/2001/12/2001120501n.htm (accessed Dec. 6, 2001).

MULLER, T., AND T. J. ESPENSHADE. 1985. *The fourth wave: California's newest immigrants*. Washington, DC: Urban Institute.

MULSOW, M., Y. M. CALDERA, M. PURSLEY, A. REIFMAN, AND A. C. HUSTON. 2002. Multilevel factors influencing maternal stress during the first three years. *Journal of Marriage and Family* 64 (Nov.): 944–56.

MUMME, D. L., AND A. FERNALD. 2003. The infant as onlooker: Learning from emotional reactions observed in a television scenario. *Child Development* 74 (Jan./Feb.): 221–37.

MUNCY, R. L. 1988. Sex and marriage in utopia. *Society* 25 (Jan./Feb.): 46–48.

MUNDELL, E. J. 2002. Bye, bye love: How men, women dish out rejection. ABC News, Feb. 5. http://abcnews.go.com/wire/Living/reuters20020205_536.html (accessed Feb. 6, 2002).

MUNDELL, E. J. 2003. No sex until marriage? Don't bet on it, study finds. Reuters Health, June 23. www.reutershealth.com/en/index.html (accessed Aug. 3, 2003).

MUNDY, L. 2003. A special kind of poverty. *Washington Post*, Apr. 20, W8.

MUNTER, C. 1984. Fat and the fantasy of perfection. In *Pleasure and danger: Exploring female sexuality*, ed. C. Vance, 225–31. Boston: Routledge & Kegan Paul.

MURDOCK, G. P. 1967. Ethnographic atlas: A summary. *Ethnology* 6, 109–236.

MURPHY, D. 2002. Need a mate? In Singapore, ask the government. *Christian Science Monitor*, July 16, 1, 10.

MURPHY, M., K. GLASER, AND E. GRUNDY. 1997. Marital status and long-term illness in Great Britain. *Journal of Marriage and the Family* 59 (Feb.): 156–64.

MURRAY, C. I. 2000. Coping with death, dying, and grief in families. In *Families & change: Coping with stressful events and transitions*, 2nd ed., eds. P. C. McKenry and S. J. Price, 120–53. Thousand Oaks, CA: Sage.

MURRAY, J. E. 2000. Marital protection and marital selection: Evidence from a historical-prospective sample of American men. *Demography* 37 (Nov.): 511–21.

MURRY, V. M., P. A. BROWN, G. H. BRODY, C. E. CUTRONA, AND R. L. SIMONS. 2001a. Racial discrimination as a moderator of the links among stress, maternal psychological functioning, and family relationships. *Journal of Marriage and the Family* 63 (Nov.): 915–26.

MURRY, V. M., A. P. SMITH, AND N. E. HILL. 2001b. Race, ethnicity, and culture in studies of families in context. *Journal of Marriage and the Family* 63 (Nov.): 911–14.

MURSTEIN, B. I. 1974. *Love, sex, and marriage through the ages*. New York: Springer.

MURSTEIN, B. I., JR., R. MERIGHI, AND S. A. VYSE. 1991. Love styles in the United States and France: A cross-cultural comparison. *Journal of Social and Clinical Psychology* 10 (Spring): 37–46.

MUSICK, K. 2002. Planned and unplanned childbearing among unmarried women. *Journal of Marriage and Family* 64 (Nov.): 915–29.

MYERS, S. M., AND A. BOOTH. 1999. Marital strains and marital quality: The role of high and low locus of control. *Journal of Marriage and the Family* 61 (May): 423–36.

NAKAZAWA, D. J. 2003. A new generation is leading the way. *Parade Magazine*, July 6, 4–5.

NAKONEZNY, P. A., R. D. SHULL, AND J. L. RODGERS. 1995. The effect of no-fault divorce law on the divorce rate across the 50 states and its relation to income, education, and religiosity. *Journal of Marriage and the Family* 57 (May): 477–88.

NARDI, P. M., AND D. SHERROD. 1994. Friendship in the lives of gay men and lesbians. *Journal of Social and Personal Relationships* 11 (May): 185–99.

NASS, G. D., R. W. LIBBY, AND M. P. FISHER. 1981. *Sexual choices: An introduction to human sexuality*. Belmont, CA: Wadsworth.

National adoption attitudes survey: Research report. 2002. Dave Thomas Foundation for Adoption. www.cdc.gov/nccdphp/drh/ART00/PDF's/ART2000.pdf (accessed Aug. 17, 2003).

NATIONAL ADOPTION INFORMATION CLEARINGHOUSE. 2002. Pros and cons of each type of adoption for the involved parties. U.S. Department of Health & Human Services. www.calib.com/naic/pubs/f_openadoptablepros.cfm and www.calib.com/naic/pubs/f_openadoptablecons.cfm (accessed Aug. 17, 2003).

National Cancer Institute posts on Web site "revised" online fact sheet on abortion, breast cancer. 2003. The Henry J. Kaiser Family Foundation, Mar. 25. www.kaisernetwork.org/daily_reports/rep_repro.cfm#16771 (accessed Mar. 28, 2003).

NATIONAL CENTER ON ADDICTION AND SUBSTANCE ABUSE. 2001. *National survey of American attitudes on substance abuse VI: Teens*. Columbia University. www.casacolumbia.org/usr_doc/52809.pdf (accessed Aug. 25, 2003).

NATIONAL CENTER ON ADDICTION AND SUBSTANCE ABUSE. 2003. National survey of American attitudes on substance abuse VIII: Teens and parents. Columbia University. www.casacolumbia.org/usr_doc/2003_Teen_Survey.pdf (accessed Aug. 25, 2003).

NATIONAL COALITION FOR THE HOMELESS. 2002. National estimates of homelessness. www.nationalhomeless.org/howmany.pdf (accessed Sep. 10, 2003).

NATIONAL COALITION FOR THE HOMELESS. 2003. Illegal to be homeless: The criminalization of homelessness in the United States. www.nationalhomeless.org/civilrights/crim2003/report.pdf (accessed Sep. 12, 2003).

NATIONAL COMMISSION ON CHILDREN. 1991. *Beyond rhetoric: A new agenda for children and families*. Washington, DC: U.S. Government Printing Office.

NATIONAL EMPLOYMENT LAW PROJECT. 2003. Unemployment insurance: Specific worker initiatives. www.nelp.org/docUploads/ib194%2Epdf (Sep. 11, 2003).

NATIONAL LOW INCOME HOUSING COALITION. 2003. *Out of reach 2003: America's housing wage climbs*. www.nlihc.org/oor2003 (accessed Sep. 11, 2003).

NATIONAL RESEARCH COUNCIL. 1998. *Violence in families: Assessing prevention and treatment programs*. Washington, DC: National Academy Press.

National sexual health survey shows many women avoid discussing HIV/AIDS, STDs with partners, health providers. 2003. Kaiser Family Foundation. www.kaisernetwork.org/daily_reports/rep_index.cfm?DR_ID=18326 (accessed June 20, 2003).

Necessary compromises: How parents, employers, and children's advocates view child care today. 2000. Public Agenda Online. www.publicagenda.org/specials/childcare/childcare.htm (accessed Sep. 29, 2000).

Need for sustained HIV prevention among men who have sex with men. 2002. Centers for Disease Control and Prevention. www.cdc.gov/hiv/pubs/facts/msm.pdf (accessed June 20, 2003).

NEFT, N., AND A. D. LEVINE. 1997. *Where women stand: An international report on the status of women in over 140 countries, 1997–1998*. New York: Random House.

NELSON, G. 1994. Emotional well-being of separated and married women: Long-term follow-up study. *American Journal of Orthopsychiatry* 64 (Jan.): 150–60.

NESMITH, C. 2001. Strategies against abuse must reflect culture. *Women's E-News*, Aug. 3. www.womensenews.org/article.cfm/dyn/aid/188 (accessed Aug. 5, 2001).

NEUFELD, J., J. R. MCNAMARA, AND M. ERTL. 1999. Incidence and prevalence of dating partner abuse and its relationship to dating practices. *Journal of Interpersonal Violence* 14 (Feb.): 125–37.

NEUGARTEN, B. L., AND K. K. WEINSTEIN. 1964. The changing American grandparents. *Journal of Marriage and the Family* 26 (May): 199–204.

New Alzheimer projections add urgency to search for prevention, cure. 2003. Alzheimer's Association, Aug. 18. www.alz.org/Media/newsreleases/current/081803evans.htm (accessed Oct. 8, 2003).

NEWACHECK, P. W., R. E. K. STEIN, L. BAUMAN, AND Y.-Y. HUNG. 2003. Disparities in the prevalence of disability between black and white children. *Archives of Pediatrics & Adolescent Medicine* 157 (Mar.): 244–48.

NEWPORT, F. 1996. Americans generally happy with their marriages. *Gallup Poll Monthly* (Sep.): 18–22.

NEWPORT, F. 2001. Americans see women as emotional and affectionate, men as more aggressive. *Gallup Poll Monthly* 425 (Feb. 2001): 34–38.

NEWPORT, F. 2003. *Six out of 10 Americans say homosexual relations should be recognized as legal*. Gallup News Service, May 15. www.gallup.com/poll/releases/pr030515.asp (accessed May 16, 2003).

Newspaper content: What makes readers more satisfied. 2001. Readership Institute: Media Management Center at Northwestern University. www.readership.org/content/editorial/data/what_content_satisfies_readers.pdf (accessed May 23, 2003).

NG, F. 1998. *The Taiwanese Americans*. Westport, CT: Greenwood.

NICHD EARLY CHILD CARE RESEARCH NETWORK. 1999a. Child care and mother–child interaction in the first 3 years of life. *Developmental Psychology* 35 (Nov.): 1399–461.

NICHD EARLY CHILD CARE RESEARCH NETWORK. 1999b. Child outcomes when child care center classes meet recommended standards for quality. *American Journal of Public Health* 89 (July): 1072–77.

NICHD EARLY CHILD CARE RESEARCH NETWORK. 2000. Characteristics and quality of child care for toddlers and preschoolers. *Journal of Applied Developmental Science* 4 (3): 116–35.

NICHD EARLY CHILD CARE RESEARCH NETWORK. 2003. Does amount of time in child care predict socioemotional adjustment? *Child Development* 74 (July/Aug.): 976–1005.

NICOLOSI, A., ET AL. 1994. *The efficiency of male-to-female and female-to-male sexual transmission of the human immunodeficiency virus: A study of 730 stable couples. Epidemiology* 5 (Nov.): 570–75.

NIE, N. H., AND L. ERBRING. 2000. Internet and society: A preliminary report. www.stanford.edu/group/siqss/Press_Release/Preliminary_Report-4-21.pdf (accessed Aug. 4, 2000).

Nigerian girl sues over forced marriage. 2002. BBC News, Sep. 7. http://news.bbc.co.uk/2/hi/world/africa/2242842.stm (accessed Sep. 8, 2002).

Night shift puts serious dent in family life. 1996. Ann Landers column. *Baltimore Sun*, Dec. 9, 3D.

NIKKAN, J., AND L. FURMAN. 2000. *Our boys speak: Adolescent boys write about their inner lives*. New York: St. Martin's.

1997 Assisted re-productive technology success rates: National summary and fertility clinic reports. 1999. Centers for Disease Control and Prevention. www.cdc.gov/nccdphp/drh/art97/pdf/art97.pdf (accessed Sept. 21, 2000).

NISSINEN, S. 2000. *The conscious bride: Women unveil their true feelings about getting hitched.* Oakland, CA: New Harbinger.

N.J. finds welfare "family cap" fails to reduce additional births. 1997. *Baltimore Sun,* Sep. 12, A3.

NOCK, S. L. 1998. *Marriage in men's lives.* New York: Oxford University Press.

NOLAN, J., M. COLEMAN, AND L. GANONG. 1984. The presentation of stepfamilies in marriage and family textbooks. *Family Relations* 33: 559–66.

NOLEN-HOEKSEMA, S., AND J. LARSON. 1999. *Coping with loss.* Mahwah, NJ: Erlbaum.

NOLEN-HOEKSEMA, S., J. LARSON, AND C. GRAYSON. 1999. Explaining the gender difference in depressive symptoms. *Journal of Personality and Social Psychology* 77 (Nov.): 1061–72.

NOLLER, P. 1984. *Nonverbal communication and marital interaction.* New York: Pergamon.

NOLLER, P., AND M. A. FITZPATRICK. 1993. *Communication in family relationships.* Upper Saddle River, NJ: Prentice Hall.

NONNEMAKER, L. 2000. Women physicians in academic medicine: New insights from cohort studies. *New England Journal of Medicine* 342 (Feb. 10): 399–405.

NOONAN, M. C. 2001. The impact of domestic work on men's and women's wages. *Journal of Marriage and Family* 63 (Nov.): 1134–45.

NORTHRUP, C. 2001. *The wisdom of menopause: Creating physical and emotional health and healing during the change.* New York: Bantam.

NORTON, A. J., AND L. F. MILLER. 1992. *Marriage, divorce, and remarriage in the 1990s.* U.S. Census Bureau, Current Population Reports, P23–180. Washington, DC: U.S. Government Printing Office.

NOWINSKI, J. 1993. *Hungry hearts: On men, intimacy, self-esteem, and addiction.* New York: Lexington.

Number of new HIV cases up 7.1% among men who have sex with men. 2003. Kaiser Family Foundation, July 23. www.kaisernetwork.org/daily_reports/rep_index.cfm?DR_ID=19040 (accessed Aug. 2, 2003).

NURIUS, P. S., J. NORRIS, L. A. DIMEFF, AND T. L. GRAHAM. 1996. Expectations regarding acquaintance sexual aggression among sorority and fraternity members. *Sex Roles* 35 (7/8): 427–44.

NUTA, V. R. 1986. Emotional aspects of child support enforcement. *Family Relations* 35 (Jan.): 177–82.

NYE, F. I., AND F. M. BERARDO, EDS. 1981. *Emerging conceptual frameworks in family analysis.* New York: Praeger.

OATES, R. K., AND R. S. KEMPE. 1997. Growth failure in infants. In *The battered child,* 5th ed., eds. M. E. Helfer, R. S. Kempe, and R. D. Krugman, 374–91. Chicago: University of Chicago Press.

OBEIDALLAH, D. A., AND F. J. EARLS. 1999. *Adolescent girls: The role of depression in the development of delinquency.* Washington, DC: U.S. Department of Justice.

O'DONNELL, P., S. STEVENSON, V. S. STEFANAKOS, AND K. PERAINO. 1999. Click and split. *Newsweek,* Nov. 22, 8.

OFFNER, P. 2002. What's love got to do with it? *Washington Monthly,* Mar., 15–19.

OGGINS, J., J. VEROFF, AND D. LEBER. 1993. Perceptions of marital interaction among black and white newlyweds. *Journal of Personality and Social Psychology* 65 (Sep.): 494–511.

OGINTZ, E. 1994. Is Grandma always the best babysitter? *Parents* (Sep.): 139.

OGUNWOLE, S. U. 2002. *The American Indian and Alaska Native population: 2000.* U.S. Census Bureau. www.census.gov/prod/2002pubs/c2kbr01-15.pdf (accessed Apr. 13, 2003).

O'HARE, W. P. 2002. Tracking the trends in low-income working families. *Population Today* 30 (Aug./Sep.): 1–3.

OKIE, S. 1997. Immigration law arouses adopters' opposition. *Washington Post Health Supplement,* July 1, 7.

OLDENBURG, D. 1996. Guys and dolls. *Washington Post,* Dec. 13, C5.

Older Americans 2000: Key indicators of well-being. 2000. Federal Interagency Forum on Aging-Related Statistics. www.agingstats.gov/chartbook2000/OlderAmericans2000.pdf (accessed Oct. 28, 2000).

OLECK, J. 2000. The kids are not all right. *Business Week,* Feb. 14, 74, 78.

OLIVER, M. L., AND T. M. SHAPIRO. 2001. Wealth and racial stratification. In *America becoming: Racial trends and their consequences,* Vol. 2, eds. N. J. Smelser, W. J. Wilson, and F. Mitchell, 222–51. Washington, DC: National Academy Press.

OLLENBURGER, J. C., AND H. A. MOORE. 1992. *A sociology of women: The intersection of patriarchy, capitalism and colonization.* Upper Saddle River, NJ: Prentice Hall.

OLSON, D. H., AND A. K. OLSON. 2000. *Empowering couples: Building on your strengths.* Minneapolis: Life Innovations.

OLSON, D. H., AND A. OLSON-SIGG. 2002. Overview of cohabitation research: For use with PREPARE-CC. Life Innovations. www.lifeinnovation.com/pdf/ccoverview.pdf (accessed July 15, 2003).

OLSON, H. C., M. J. O'CONNOR, AND H. E. FITZGERALD. 2001. Lessons learned from study of the developmental impact of parental alcohol use. *Infant Mental Health Journal* 22 (May/June): 271–90.

OLSSON, K. 2003. Up against Wal-Mart. *Mother Jones* (Mar./Apr.): 53–59.

O'MARA, R. 1997. Who am I? *Baltimore Sun,* June 29, 1J, 4J.

ONO, H. 1998. Husbands' and wives' resources and marital dissolution. *Journal of Marriage and the Family* 60 (Aug.): 674–89.

OOMS, T. 2002. Marriage-plus. Center for Law and Social Policy. www.clasp.org/DMS/Documents/1023290035.07/marriage_plus.pdf (accessed Aug. 10, 2003).

OOMS, T. 2002. Strengthening couples and marriage in low-income communities. In *Revitalizing the institution of marriage for the twenty-first century,* eds. A. J. Hawkins, L. D. Wardle, and D. O. Coolidge, 79–100. Westport, CT: Praeger.

OPPENHEIMER, V. K. 2003. Cohabiting and marriage during young men's career-development process. *Demography* 40 (Feb.): 127–50.

ORCHARD, A. L., AND K. B. SOLBERG. 1999. Expectations of the stepmother's role. *Journal of Divorce & Remarriage* 31 (1/2): 107–23.

ORDOÑEZ, R. Z. 1997. Mail-order brides: An emerging community. In *Filipino Americans: Transformation and identity,* ed. M. P. Root, 121–42. Thousand Oaks, CA: Sage.

ORENSTEIN, P. 1994. *Schoolgirls: Young women, self-esteem, and the confidence gap.* New York: Doubleday.

ORENSTEIN, P. 1995. Looking for a donor to call dad. *New York Times Magazine,* June 16, 26–35, 42–58.

ORENSTEIN, P. 2000. *Flux: Women on sex, work, kids, love, and life in a half-changed world.* New York: Doubleday.

ORNISH, D. 1998. *Love & survival: The scientific basis for the healing power of intimacy.* New York: HarperCollins.

OSHERSON, S. 1992. *Wrestling with love: How men struggle with intimacy with women, children, parents and each other.* New York: Fawcett Columbine.

OSOFSKY, J. D. 1999. The impact of violence on children. *Domestic Violence and Children* 9 (Winter): 33–49.

OSTROWIAK, N. 2001. *Motherhood is not a rehearsal: Bottom-line mentoring for parents.* Hampton, GA: Southern Charm.

O'SULLIVAN, L. F., AND E. S. BYERS. 1993. Eroding stereotypes: College women's attempts to influence reluctant male sexual partners. *Journal of Sex Research* 30 (Aug.): 270–82.

OSWALD, R. F. 2002. Resilience within the family networks of lesbians and gay men: Intentionality and redefinition. *Journal of Marriage and Family* 64 (May): 374–83.

OUTCALT, T. 1998. *Before you say "I do:" Important questions for couples to ask before marriage.* New York: Perigee.

Outrage over marriage deal unsettles blood debt. 2002. *Baltimore Sun,* July 26, 24A.

OYSTERMAN, D., L. GANT, AND J. AGER. 1995. A socially contextualized model of African American identity: Possible selves and school persistence. *Journal of Personality and Social Psychology* 69: 1216–32.

OYSTERMAN, D., N. RADIN, AND R. BENN. 1993. Dynamics in a three-generational family: Teens, grandparents, and babies. *Developmental Psychology* 29 (3): 564–73.

PAASCH, K. M., AND J. D. TEACHMAN. 1991. Gender of children and receipt of assistance from absent fathers. *Journal of Family Issues* 12 (Dec.): 450–66.

Pakistani girl describes punitive gang-rape. 2002. *Baltimore Sun,* July 4, 13A.

PALMORE, E. B. 1999. *Ageism: Negative and positive.* New York: Springer.

PAPANEK, H. 1979. Family status production. *Signs* 4: 775–81.

PAPERNOW, P. L. 1993. *Becoming a stepfamily: Patterns of development in remarried families.* San Francisco: Jossey-Bass.

PARAMESWARAN, L. 2003. Battered wives often recant or assume blame. *Women's E-News,* Aug. 2. www.womensenews.org/article.cfm/dyn/aid/1468 (accessed Aug. 4, 2003).

PARCEL, T. L., AND E. G. MENAGHAN. 1994. *Parents' jobs and children's lives.* New York: Aldine de Gruyter.

Parenting skills: 21 tips & ideas to help you make a difference. 2000. Office of National Drug Control Policy. Washington, DC: National Clearinghouse for Alcohol and Drug Information.

PARK, R. L. 2003. The seven warning signs of bogus science. *Chronicle of Higher Education,* Jan. 31, B20.

PARKE, R. D. 1996. *Fatherhood.* Cambridge, MA: Harvard University Press.

PARKER, R., AND C. CÁCERES. 1999. Alternative sexualities and changing sexual cultures among Latin American men. *Culture, Health, & Sexuality* 1: 201–6.

PARKER, S. 1996. Full brother–sister marriage in Roman Egypt: Another look. *Cultural Anthropology* 11 (Aug.): 362–76.

PARMELEE, L. F. 2002. Among us always. *Public Perspective* 13 (Mar./Apr.): 17–18.

PARNELL, T. F., AND D. O. DAY, EDS. 1998. *Munchausen by proxy syndrome.* Thousand Oaks, CA: Sage.

PARSONS, T., AND R. F. BALES. 1955. *Family, socialization and interaction process.* Glencoe, IL: Free Press.

Participation sets record for fourth straight year. 2002. National Federation of State High School Associations. www.nfhs.org/press/participation%20survey02.htm (accessed May 15, 2003).

PASCUAL, P. 1999/2000. More foster families, fewer children entering care. *Advocasey* 1 (Fall/Winter): 4–7, 9–10.

PASUPATHI, M. 2002. Arranged marriages: What's love got to do with it? In *Inside the American couple: New thinking/new challenges,* eds. M. Yalom and L. L. Carstensen, 211–35. Berkeley: University of California Press.

PATNER, M. M. 1990. Between mothers and daughters: Pain and difficulty go with the territory. *Washington Post,* Nov. 8, C5.

PATTATUCCI, A. M. L., AND D. H. HAMER. 1995. Development and familiality of sexual orientation in females. *Behavior Genetics* 25 (5): 407–20.

PATTERSON, C. J. 2001. Family relationships of lesbians and gay men. In *Understanding families into the new millennium: A decade in review,* ed. R. M. Milardo, 271–88. Minneapolis: National Council on Family Relations.

PATTERSON, C. J. 2002. Lesbian and gay parenthood. In *Handbook of Parenting,* 2nd ed., Vol. 3: *Being and becoming a parent,* ed. M. H. Bornstein, 317–38. Mahwah, NJ: Erlbaum.

PATTERSON, J. M. 2002. Integrating family resilience and family stress theory. *Journal of Marriage and Family* 64 (May): 349–60.

PATTERSON, J., AND P. KIM. 1991. *The day America told the truth: What people really believe about everything that really matters.* Upper Saddle River, NJ: Prentice Hall.

PATZ, A. 2000. Will your marriage last? *Psychology Today* 33 (Jan./Feb.): 58–63.

PAUL, P. 2001. Childless by choice. *American Demographics* 23 (Nov.): 45–50.

PAUL, P. 2002. Make room for granddaddy. *American Demographics* 24 (Apr.): 41–45.

PAUL, P. 2002. Shacking up. *American Demographics* 24 (Jan.): 45.

PAUL, P. 2002. *The starter marriage and the future of matrimony.* New York: Villard.

PAULOZZI, L. J., L. E. SALTMAN, M. P. THOMPSON, AND P. HOLMGREEN. 2001. *Surveillance for homicide among intimate partners: United States, 1981–1998.* Centers for Disease Control and Prevention. www.cdc.gov/mmwr/PDF/SS/ SS5003.pdf (accessed Sep. 18, 2003).

PAULOZZI, L., AND M. SELLS. 2002. Variation in homicide risk during infancy: United States, 1989–1998. *Morbidity and Mortality Weekly Report* 51 (Mar. 8): 187–89.

PAULSON, A. 2003. The changing face of love. *Christian Science Monitor*, Jan. 15, 11–15.

PAULSON, A. 2003. Debate on gay unions splits along generations. *Christian Science Monitor*, July 7, 1, 4.

PAULSON, A. 2003. Hazing case highlights girl violence. *Christian Science Monitor*, May 9, 4.

PAULSON, A. 2003. New dating game: Hit the keyboard, checklist in hand. *Christian Science Monitor*, Feb. 14, 1, 3.

PAULSON, A. 2003. States grapple with gay rights and definition of the family. *Christian Science Monitor*, Mar. 6, 2–3.

PAULSON, R. J., ET AL. 2002. Pregnancy in the sixth decade of life: Obstetric outcomes in women of advanced reproductive age. *Journal of the American Medical Association* 288 (Nov. 13): 2320–23.

PAYNE, B. K. 2000. *Crime and elder abuse: An integrated perspective.* Springfield, IL: Charles C. Thomas.

PAZ, J. J. 1993. Support of Hispanic elderly. In *Family ethnicity: Strength in diversity*, ed. H. P. McAdoo, 177–83. Thousand Oaks, CA: Sage.

PEARSON, J. C. 1985. *Gender and communication.* Dubuque, IA: Wm. C. Brown.

PEARSON, P. 1997. *When she was bad: Violent women and the myth of innocence.* New York: Viking/Penguin.

PEAVY, L., AND U. SMITH. 1994. *Women in waiting in the westward movement: Life on the home frontier.* Norman: University of Oklahoma Press.

PEDDLE, N., C.-T. WANG, J. DIAZ, AND R. REID. 2002. Current trends in child abuse prevention and fatalities: The 2000 fifty state survey. Prevent Child Abuse America. www.cdc.gov/mmwr/ PDF/SS/SS5003.pdf (accessed Sep. 15, 2003).

PEELE, S., WITH A. BRODSKY. 1976. *Love and addiction.* New York: New American Library.

PENHA-LOPES, V. 1995. "Make room for daddy": Patterns of family involvement among contemporary African American men. In *American families: Issues in race and ethnicity*, ed. C. K. Jacobson, 179–99. New York: Garland.

PEPLAU, L. A., R. C. VENIEGAS, AND S. M. CAMPBELL. 1996. Gay and lesbian relationships. In *The lives of lesbians, gays, and bisexuals: Children to adults*, eds. R. C. Savin-Williams and K. M. Cohen, 250–73. New York: Harcourt Brace.

PÉREZ, L. 1992. Cuban Miami. In *Miami now! Immigration, ethnicity, and social change*, eds. G. J. Grenier and A. Stepick III, 83–108. Gainesville: University Press of Florida.

PÉREZ, L. 2002. Cuban American families. In *Minority families in the United States: A multicultural perspective*, 3rd ed., ed. R. L. Taylor, 114–30. Upper Saddle River, NJ: Prentice Hall.

PERITZ, I. 2003. Miracle birth signals male moms? *Toronto Globe and Mail*, Aug 15, A14.

PERKINS, F., T. LUSTER, F. A. VILLARRUEL, AND S. SMALL. 1998. An ecological, risk-factor examination of adolescents' sexual activity in three ethnic groups. *Journal of Marriage and the Family* 60 (Aug.): 660–73.

PERRIN, E. C. 2002. Technical report: Coparent or second-parent adoption by same-sex parents. *Pediatrics* 109 (Feb.): 341–44.

PERRY, T., C. STEELE, AND A. HILLIARD III. 2003. *Young, gifted and black: Promoting high achievement among African-American students.* New York: Beacon.

PERRY-JENKINS, M., AND K. FOLK. 1994. Class, couples, and conflict: Effects of the division of labor on assessments of marriage in dual-earner families. *Journal of Marriage and the Family* 56 (Feb.): 165–80.

Perspectives. 2001. *Newsweek*, June 18, 17.

PERTIG, J. 1994. A weighty problem. *American Health* (Jan./Feb.): 82.

PESSAR, P. R. 1995. *A visa for a dream: Dominicans in the United States.* Boston: Allyn & Bacon.

PETERSEN, W. 1966. Success story, Japanese American style. *New York Times Magazine*, Jan. 6, 20ff.

PETERSON, J. L., J. J. CARD, M. B. EISEN, AND B. SHERMAN-WILLIAMS. 1994. Evaluating teenage pregnancy prevention and other social programs: Ten stages of program assessment. *Family Planning Perspectives* 26 (May): 116–20, 131.

PETERSON, K. S. 2002. Having it all, except children. *USA Today*, Apr. 7, 2D.

PETERSON, K. S. 2003. Search for a soul mate, or love the one you're with? *USA Today*, May 28. www.usatoday.com/life/2003-05-28-soul-mates_x.htm (accessed May 29, 2003).

PETERSON, S. 2002. Gender meanings in grade eight students' talks about classroom writing. *Gender and Education* 14 (Dec.): 351–66.

PETTERSON, S. M., AND A. B. ALBERS. 2001. Effects of poverty and maternal depression on early child development. *Child Development* 72 (Nov./Dec.): 1794–813.

PETTYS, G. L., AND P. R. BALGOPAL. 1998. Multigenerational conflicts and new immigrants: An Indo-American experience. *Families in Society: The Journal of Contemporary Human Services* 79 (July/Aug.): 410–22.

PEWEWARDY, C. 1998. Fluff and feathers: Treatment of American Indians in the literature and the classroom. *Equity & Excellence in Education* 31 (Apr.): 69–76.

PHILLIPS, L. E. 1999. Love, American style. *American Demographics* 21 (Feb.): 56–57.

PHINNEY, J. S. 1996. Understanding ethnic diversity. *American Behavioral Scientist* 40 (Nov./Dec.): 143–52.

PHINNEY, J. S., C. CANTU, AND D. KURTZ. 1997. Ethnic and American identity as predictors of self-esteem among African American, Latino, and white adolescents. *Journal of Youth and Adolescence* 26: 165–85.

PHINNEY, J. S., B. HORENCZYK, K. LIEBKIND, AND P. VEDDER. 2001. Ethnic identity, immigration, and well-being: An interactional perspective. *Journal of Social Issues* 57: 493–510.

PHINNEY, J. S., I. ROMERO, M. NAVA, AND D. HUANG. 2001. The role of language, parents, and peers in ethnic identity among adolescents in immigrant families. *Journal of Youth and Adolescence* 30 (Apr.): 135–53.

PIAGET, J. 1932. *The moral judgment of the child.* New York: Harcourt, Brace.

PIAGET, J. 1950. *The psychology of intelligence.* London: Routledge & Kegan Paul.

PIAGET, J. 1954. *The construction of reality in the child.* New York: Basic Books.

PIAGET, J. 1960. *The child's conception of the world.* London: Routledge.

PIERRE, R. E. 2001. Suffrage and umbrage. *Washington Post*, Oct. 16, A2.

PIERRE, R. E. 2003. Northwest tribe struggles to revive its language project: A challenge for Klallam, others as native speakers age. *Washington Post*, Mar. 31, A3.

PILL, C. J. 1990. Stepfamilies: Redefining the family. *Family Relations* 39 (Apr.): 186–92.

PILLEMER, K., AND J. J. SUITOR. 1991. Will I ever escape my child's problems? Effects of adult children's problems on elderly parents. *Journal of Marriage and the Family* 53 (Aug.): 585–94.

PIÑA, D. L., AND V. L. BENGSTON. 1993. The division of household labor and wives' happiness: Ideology, employment, and perceptions of support. *Journal of Marriage and the Family* 55 (Nov.): 901–12.

PINDERHUGHES, E. E., K. A. DODGE, J. E. BATES, G. S. PETTIT, AND A. ZELLI. 2000. Discipline responses: Influences of parents' socioeconomic status, ethnicity, beliefs about parenting, stress, and cognitive-emotional processes. *Journal of Family Psychology* 14: 380–400.

PINSOF, W. M. 2002. The death of "till death us do part": The transformation of pair-bonding in the 20th century. *Family Process* 41 (Summer): 135–57.

PIOKOWSKI, C. S., AND D. HUGHES. 1993. Dual-earner families in context: Managing family and work systems. In *Normal family processes*, 2nd ed., ed. F. Walsh, 185–207. New York: Guilford.

PIORKOWSKI, G. K. 1994. *Too close for comfort: Exploring the risks of intimacy.* New York: Plenum.

PITTMAN, F. 1990. *Private lies: Infidelity and the betrayal of intimacy.* New York: W.W. Norton.

PITTMAN, F. 1999. *Grow up! How taking responsibility can make you a happy adult.* New York: Golden Books.

PLATERIS, A. A. 1973. *100 years of marriage and divorce statistics: 1867–1967.* Rockville, MD: National Center for Health Statistics.

PLECK, J. H. 1993. Are "family-supportive" employer policies relevant to men? In *Men, work, and family*, ed. J. C. Hood. Thousand Oaks, CA: Sage.

PLOTNIKOFF, D. 1994. Sexism and bias pollute cyberspace. *Baltimore Sun*, Aug. 24, 6D.

POE, L. M. 1992. *Black grandparents as parents.* Berkeley, CA: L.M. Poe.

Police in Iran crack down on vice: Valentine's Day. 2003. *Baltimore Sun*, Feb. 13, 12A.

POLIT, D. F., AND T. FALBO. 1987. Only children and personality development: A quantitative review. *Journal of Marriage and the Family* 49 (May): 309–25.

POLLACK, W. 1998. *Real boys: Rescuing our sons from the myths of boyhood.* New York: Henry Holt.

POLLARD, K. M., AND W. P. O'HARE. 1999. America's racial and ethnic minorities. *Population Bulletin* 54 (Sep.): 1–48.

POMFRET, J. 2000. Among Chinese, a low-key gay liberation. *Washington Post*, Jan. 24, A1, A18.

POMFRET, J. 2001. In China's countryside, "it's a boy!" too often. *Washington Post*, May 29, A1.

PONG, S.-L. 1997. Family structure, school context, and eighth grade math and reading achievement. *Journal of Marriage and the Family* 59 (Aug.): 734–46.

PONIEWOZIK, J. 2002. The cost of starting families. *Time*, Apr. 15, 56–57.

POPE, J. R., H. G. R. OLIVARDIA, AND J. BOROWIECKI. 1999. Evolving ideals of male body image as seen through action toys. *International Journal of Eating Disorders* 26 (July): 65–72.

POPENOE, D. 1996. *Life without father: Compelling new evidence that fatherhood and marriage are indispensable for the good of children and society.* New York: Free Press.

POPENOE, D., AND B. D. WHITEHEAD. 2002. *Should we live together? What young adults need to know about cohabitation before marriage: A comprehensive review of recent research*, 2nd ed. New Brunswick, NJ: The National Marriage Project, Rutgers University. http://marriage. rutgers.edu/Publications/swlt2.pdf (accessed July 12, 2003).

POPENOE, D., AND B. D. WHITEHEAD. 2003. *The state of our unions, 2003: The social health of marriage in America.* The National Marriage Project, Rutgers University. http://marriage.rutgers. edu/Publications/SOOU/SOOU2003.pdf (accessed July 4, 2003).

POPULATION REFERENCE BUREAU. 1990. *America in the 21st century: Social and economic support systems.* Washington, DC.

POSNER, J. K., AND D. L. VANDELL. 1994. Low-income children's after-school care: Are there beneficial effects of after-school programs? *Child Development* 65 (Apr.): 440–56.

POTTHOFF, S. J., L. H. BEARINGER, C. L. SHAY, N. CASSUTO, R. W. BLUM, AND M. D. RESNICK. 1998. Dimensions of risk behaviors among American Indian youth. *Archives of Pediatrics & Adolescent Medicine* 152 (Feb.): 157–63.

POTTS, L. 2003. PBS looks at how oral contraceptives changed women's lives. www.abqjournal. com/paperboy/ia/scitech/837405scitech02-22-03. htm (accessed Feb. 23, 2003).

POWELL, E. 1991. *Talking back to sexual pressure.* Minneapolis: CompCare.

Pregnancy discrimination charges. 2002. Equal Employment Opportunity Commission. www.eeoc. gov/stats/pregnanc.html (accessed Sep. 14, 2003).

PRESSER, H. B. 2000. Nonstandard work schedules and marital instability. *Journal of Marriage and the Family* 62 (Feb.): 93–110.

PRESSER, H., AND A. COX. 1997. The work schedules of low-educated American women and welfare reform. *Monthly Labor Review* 120 (Apr.): 25–35.

PREUSS, U. W., ET AL. 2003. Predictors and correlates of suicide attempts over 5 years in 1,237 alcohol-dependent men and women. *American Journal of Psychiatry* 160 (Jan.): 56–63.

PREVITI, D., AND P. R. AMATO. 2003. Why stay married? Rewards, barriers, and marital stability. *Journal of Marriage and Family* 65 (Aug.): 561–73.

PRICE, J. A. 1981. North American Indian families. In *Ethnic families in America: Patterns and variations,* 2nd ed., eds. C. H. Mindel and R. W. Habenstein, 245–68. New York: Elsevier.

PRICE, J. 2001. Court bans man from having more kids. *Washington Post,* Nov. 23. www.washingtonpost.com/wp-dyn/articles/A7012-2001Nov23.html (accessed Nov. 24, 2001).

PRICE, R. H., J. N. CHOI, AND A. D. VINOKUR. 2002. Links in the chain of adversity following job loss: How financial strain and loss of personal control lead to depression, impaired functioning, and poor health. *Journal of Occupational Health Psychology* 7 (4): 302–12.

PRIDONOFF, J. A. 1994. Is the right-to-die movement a danger? *Washington Post Health Supplement,* Oct. 18, 19.

Primary and secondary syphilis: United States, 2000–2001. 2002. Centers for Disease Control and Prevention. www.cdc.gov/mmwr/preview/mmwrhtml/mm5143a4.htm (accessed June 18, 2003).

PRIMUS, W., AND K. DAUGIRDAS. 2000. *Improving child well-being: Focusing on low-income non-custodial parents in Maryland.* Baltimore: Abell Foundation.

PROCTOR, B. D., AND J. DALAKER. 2002. *Poverty in the United States: 2001.* U.S. Census Bureau, Current Population Reports, P60-219. www.census.gov/prod/2002pubs/p60-219.pdf (accessed Apr. 14, 2003).

PROCTOR, B. D., AND J. DALAKER. 2003. *Poverty in the United States: 2002.* U.S. Census Bureau, Current Population Reports, P60-222. www.census.gov/prod/2003pubs/p60-222.pdf (accessed Oct. 5, 2003).

Projections of the resident population by age, sex, race, and Hispanic origin: 1999 to 2100. 2000. U.S. Census Bureau, Population Division. www.census.gov/population/projections/nation/detail/d2001_10.pdf (accessed Oct. 11, 2003).

PRUETT, K. D. 1987. *The nurturing father: Journey toward the complete man.* New York: Warner.

PRUSHER, I. R. 2000. Housemaids' woes spur Kuwait to review labor law. *Christian Science Monitor,* May 30, 1, 9.

PRUSHER, I. R. 2001. South Korea: Gay confession ignites debate. *Christian Science Monitor,* Jan. 17, 7.

PTACEK, J. 1999. *Battered women in the courtroom: The power of judicial response.* Boston: Northeastern University Press.

PURKAYASTHA, B. 2002. Rules, roles, and realities: Indo-American families in the United States. In *Minority families in the United States: A multicultural perspective,* 3rd ed., ed. R. L. Taylor, 212–24. Upper Saddle River, NJ: Prentice Hall.

PUTNEY, N. M., AND V. L. BENGSTON. 2001. Dynamics of social relationships in midlife. In *Handbook of midlife development,* ed. M. E. Lachman, 528–69. New York: Wiley.

PUZONE, C. A. 2000. National trends in intimate partner homicide: United States, 1976–1995. *Violence against Women* 6 (Apr.): 409–26.

PYKE, K. D. 1994. Women's employment as a gift or burden? Marital power across marriage, divorce, and remarriage. *Gender and Society* 8 (Mar.): 73–91.

PYKE, K., AND S. COLTRANE. 1996. Entitlement, obligation, and gratitude in family work. *Journal of Family Issues* 17 (Jan.): 60–82.

QU, L., AND R. WESTON. 2001. Starting out together through cohabitation or marriage. *Family Matters* 60 (Spring/Summer, 2001): 76–79. Australian Institute of Family Studies. www.

aifs.org.au/institute/pubs/fm2001/fm60/lx.pdf (accessed July 10, 2003).

QUEEN, S. A., R. W. HABENSTEIN, AND J. S. QUADAGNO. 1985. *The family in various cultures,* 5th ed. New York: Harper & Row.

QUICK, B. 1992. Tales from the self-help mill. *Newsweek,* Aug. 31, 14.

QUICK, D. S., P. C. MCKENRY, AND B. M. NEWMAN. 1994. Stepmothers and their adolescent children: Adjustment to new family roles. In *Stepparenting: Issues in theory, research, and practice,* eds. K. Pasley and M. Ihinger-Tallman, 119–25. Westport, CT: Greenwood.

QUILL, T. E. 1993. *Death and dignity: Making choices and taking charge.* New York: Norton.

QUINN, W., AND M. ODELL. 1998. Predictors of marital adjustment during the first two years. *Marriage & Family Review* 27 (1/2): 113–30.

QUINTANA, S. M., AND V. M. VERA. 1999. Mexican American children's ethnic identity, understanding of ethnic prejudice, and parental ethnic socialization. *Hispanic Journal of Behavioral Sciences* 21 (Nov.): 387–404.

QURESHI, R. B. 1991. Marriage strategies among Muslims from South Asia. In *Muslim families in North America,* eds. E. H. Waugh, M. Abu-Laban, and R. B. Qureshi, 185–211. Edmonton: University of Alberta Press.

Race and ethnicity in 2001: Attitudes, perceptions, and experiences. 2001. The Henry J. Kaiser Family Foundation. www.kff.org/content/2001/3143/RacialBiracialToplines.pdf (accessed Apr. 3, 2003).

RAFFAELLI, M., AND S. GREEN. 2003. Parent–adolescent communication about sex: Retrospective reports by Latino college students. *Journal of Marriage and Family* 65 (May): 474–81.

RAINE, A., C. REYNOLDS, P. H. VENABLES, AND S. A. MEDNICK. 2002. Stimulation seeking and intelligence: A prospective longitudinal study. *Journal of Personality and Social Psychology* 82 (Apr.): 663–74.

RAINIE, L., AND D. PACKEL. 2001. More online, doing more. Pew Internet Project: Internet tracking report. www.pewtrusts.com/pdf/vf_pew_internet_population_report.pdf (accessed Sep. 23, 2001).

RAJ, A., AND J. G. SILVERMAN. 2002. Intimate partner violence against South Asian women in greater Boston. *Journal of the American Medical Women's Association* 57 (Apr.): 111–14.

RALEY, R. K., AND J. BRATTER. 2000. Not even if you were the last person on Earth! How marital search constraints affect the likelihood of marriage. Department of Sociology, University of Texas at Austin, unpublished paper.

RAMIREZ, O., AND C. H. ARCE. 1981. The contemporary Chicano family: An empirically based review. In *Explorations in Chicano psychology,* ed. A. Baron, 3–28. New York: Praeger.

RAMU, G. N. 1989. Patterns of mate selection. In *Family and marriage: Cross-cultural perspectives,* ed. K. Ishwaran, 165–78. Toronto: Wall & Thompson.

RANDLE, W. 1998. So far from home. *Essence* (Sep.): 76, 176.

RANK, M. R. 1987. The formation and dissolution of marriages in the welfare population. *Journal of Marriage and the Family* 49 (Feb.): 15–20.

RANKIN, R. P., AND J. S. MANEKER. 1985. The duration of marriage in a divorcing population: The impact of children. *Journal of Marriage and the Family* 47 (Feb.): 43–52.

RANKIN, S. R. 2003. *Campus climate for gay, lesbian, bisexual, and transgender people: A national perspective.* National Gay and Lesbian Task Force Policy Institute. www.kff.org/content/2001/3193/LGBSurveyReport.pdf (accessed June 10, 2003).

RAPAPORT, J. 2000. Good life goals. *Christian Science Monitor,* July 6, 14.

RAPHAEL, J. 1995. Welfare women, violent men. *Christian Science Monitor,* Apr. 20, 20.

RATHUS, J. H., AND K. D. O'LEARY. 1997. Spouse-specific dependency scale: Scale development. *Journal of Family Violence* 12 (June): 159–68.

RAYBECK, D., S. DORENBOSCH, M. SARAPATA, AND D. HERRMAN. 2000. The quest for love and meaning in the personals. Unpublished paper.

RAYMO, J. M. 2003. Premarital living arrangements and the transition to first marriage in Japan. *Journal of Marriage and Family* 65 (May): 302–15.

RAYMOND, C. 1990. Studies of abortion's emotional effects renew controversial scholarly debate. *Chronicle of Higher Education,* Feb. 2, A6, A7.

REARDON, D. C., J. R. COUGLE, V. M. RUE, M. W. SHUPING, P. K. COLEMAN, AND P. G. NEY. 2003. Psychiatric admissions of low-income women following abortion and childbirth. *Canadian Medical Association Journal* 168 (May 13): 1253–56.

REARDON-ANDERSON, J., R. CAPPS, AND M. E. FIX. 2002. The health and well-being of children in immigrant families. Urban Institute. www.urban.org/UploadedPDF/310584_B52.pdf (accessed Apr. 4, 2003).

REAY, A. M., AND K. D. BROWNE. 2001. Risk factors for caregivers who physically abuse or neglect their elderly dependents. *Aging and Mental Health* 5 (1): 56–62.

RECTANUS, L., AND M. GOMEZ. 2002. Worker protection: Labor's efforts to enforce protections for day laborers could benefit from better data and guidance. United States General Accounting Office. www.gao.gov/new.items/d02925.pdf (accessed Apr. 13, 2003).

REDBOOT, D. L., AND S. M. PANDYA. 2002. Before the boom: Trends in long-term supportive services for older Americans with disabilities. Public Policy Institute, Washington, DC. http://research.aarp.org/health/inb60_trends.pdf (accessed Oct. 10, 2003).

REGAN, P. 2003. *The mating game: A primer on love, sex, and marriage.* Thousand Oaks, CA: Sage.

REGAN, P. C., AND E. BERSCHEID. 1999. *Lust: What we know about human sexual desire.* Thousand Oaks, CA: Sage.

REID, J. 1993. Those fabulous '50s. *Utne Reader* 55 (Jan.): 18–19.

REILLY, P. R. 2000. *Abraham Lincoln's DNA and other adventures in genetics.* New York: Cold Spring Harbor Laboratory.

REIMER, S. 1999. Sex questions show how little our kids know. *Baltimore Sun,* Sep. 9, 1e, 4e.

REINISCH, J. M., WITH R. BEASLEY. 1990. *The Kinsey Institute new report on sex: What you must know to be sexually literate.* New York: St. Martin's.

REIS, S. D., AND P. P. HEPPNER. 1993. Examination of coping resources and family adaptation in mothers and daughters of incestuous versus nonclinical families. *Journal of Counseling Psychology* 40 (1): 100–108.

REISBERG, B., ET AL. 2003. Memantine in moderate-to-severe Alzheimer's disease. *New England Journal of Medicine* 348 (Apr. 3): 1333–41.

REISBERG, L. 2000. 10% of students may spend too much time online. *Chronicle of Higher Education,* June 16, A43.

REISS, I. 1960. Toward a sociology of the heterosexual love relationship. *Marriage and Family Living* 22 (May): 139–45.

REISS, I. L. 1971. *The family system in America.* New York: Holt, Rinehart & Winston.

REISS, I. L., AND G. R. LEE. 1988. *Family systems in America,* 4th ed. New York: Holt, Rinehart & Winston.

REITMAN, V. 2002. Self-immolations on rise in Afghanistan. *Los Angeles Times,* Nov. 17. www.latimes.com/news/printedition/asection/la-fg-burn17nov17004438,0,7399916.story?coll=la%2Dnews%2Da%5Fsection (accessed Nov. 18, 2002).

RENN, J. A., AND S. L. CALVERT. 1993. The relation between gender schemas and adults' recall of stereotyped and counterstereotyped televised information. *Sex Roles* 28 (7/8): 449–59.

RENNISON, C. M. 2001. *Intimate partner violence and age of victim, 1993–99.* Washington, DC: U.S. Department of Justice.

RENNISON, C. M. 2002a. *Criminal victimization 2001: Changes 2000–01 with trends 1993–2001.* Washington, DC: U.S. Department of Justice.

RENNISON, C. M. 2002b. *Hispanic victims of violent crime, 1993–2000.* Washington, DC: U.S. Department of Justice.

RENNISON, C. M. 2002c. *Rape and sexual assault: Reporting to police and medical attention,*

1992–2000. Washington, DC: U.S. Department of Justice.

RENNISON, C. M. 2003. *Intimate partner violence, 1993–2001.* Washington, DC: U.S. Department of Justice.

RENNISON, C. M., AND S. WELCHANS. 2000. *Intimate partner violence.* Washington, DC: U.S. Department of Justice.

RENTERÍA, R. A. 2000. A vibrant Latino presence in Washington, DC. *Footnotes* 28 (May/June): 1, 41.

RENZETTI, C. M. 1992. *Violent betrayal: Partner abuse in lesbian relationships.* Thousand Oaks, CA: Sage.

RENZETTI, C. M., AND D. J. CURRAN. 1995. *Women, men, and society,* 3rd ed. Boston: Allyn & Bacon.

REPAK, T. A. 1995. *Waiting on Washington: Central American workers in the nation's capital.* Philadelphia: Temple University Press.

REPETTI, R. L., S. E. TAYLOR, AND T. E. SEEMAN. 2002. Risky families: Family social environments and the mental and physical health of offspring. *Psychological Bulletin* 128 (Mar.): 330–66.

Report cards for parents proposed in Lebanon, Pa. 2003. *Baltimore Sun,* Feb. 7, 3A.

RESTAK, R. 2002. All in your head. *Modern Maturity,* Jan./Feb., 60–66.

RETSINAS, G. 2003. Hospital to pay $5.4 million in sex harassment lawsuit. *New York Times,* Apr. 10, A21.

RETSINAS, J. 1988. A theoretical reassessment of the applicability of Kübler-Ross's stages of dying. *Death Studies* 12 (3): 207–16.

Reuters highlights a Chinese periodical targeting gay men that discusses "taboo" subjects of homosexuality and HIV/AIDS. 2002. The Henry Kaiser Family Foundation, Oct. 1. www.kaisernetwork.org/daily_reports/rep_index.cfm?hint=1&DR_ID=1781 (accessed June 12, 2003).

REVELL, J. 2003. Bye-bye pension. *Fortune,* Mar. 17, 65–74.

REYNOLDS, A. J., AND D. ROBERTSON. 2003. School-based early intervention and later child maltreatment in the Chicago longitudinal study. *Child Development* 74 (Jan./Feb.): 3–26.

REYNOLDS, A. J., J. A. TEMPLE, D. L. ROBERTSON, AND E. A. MANN. 2001. Long-term effects of an early childhood intervention on educational achievement and juvenile arrest: A 15-year follow-up of low-income children in public schools. *Journal of the American Medical Association* 285 (May 19): 2339–46.

RHEINGOLD, H. L. 1969. The social and socializing infant. In *Handbook of socialization theory and research,* ed. D. A. Goslin, 779–90. Chicago: Rand McNally.

RHOADES, E. R. 2003. The health status of American Indian and Alaska Native males. *American Journal of Public Health* 93 (May): 774–78.

RICE, G., C. ANDERSON, N. RISCH, AND G. EBERS. 1999. Male homosexuality: Absence of linkage to microsatellite markers at Xq28. *Science* 284 (Apr. 23): 665–67.

RICHARD, D. 2002. Love me tender. *Contemporary Sexuality* 36 (Mar.): 3–6.

RICHARDSON, C. R., P. J. RESNICK, D. L. HANSEN, H. A. DERRY, AND V. J. RIDEOUT. 2002. Does pornography-blocking software block access to health information on the Internet? *Journal of the American Medical Association* 288 (Dec. 11): 2887–94.

RICHARDSON-BOUIE, D. 2003. Ethnic variation/ethnicity. In *International encyclopedia of marriage and family,* 2nd ed., Vol. 2, ed. J. J. Ponzetti, Jr., 525–30. New York: Macmillan.

RICHEY, W. 1997. Girls, boys, sports, and fairness. *Christian Science Monitor,* Oct. 3, 1, 4.

RIDEOUT, V., C. RICHARDSON, AND P. RESNIK. 2002. See no evil: How Internet filters affect the search for online health information. The Henry Kaiser Family Foundation. www.kff.org/content/2002/3294/Internet_Filtering_exec_summ.pdf (accessed June 10, 2003).

RIESSMAN, C. K. 1990. *Divorce talk: Women and men make sense of personal relationships.* New Brunswick, NJ: Rutgers University Press.

RILEY, G. 1991. *Divorce: An American tradition.* Lincoln: University of Nebraska Press.

RIMER, S. 2002. Sex advice enlivens newspapers on campus. *New York Times,* Oct. 14, A25.

RINGLE, K. 1999. Unamicable partners. *Washington Post,* Mar. 15, C1, C7.

RISMAN, B., AND P. SCHWARTZ. 2002. After the sexual revolution: Gender politics in teen dating. *Contexts* 1 (Spring): 16–24.

RISTOCK, J. L. 2002. *No more secrets: Violence in lesbian relationships.* New York: Routledge.

RIVERS, C. 2001. Study: Young people seeking soul mates to marry. *Women's E-News,* June 20. www.womensenews.org/article.cfm/dyn/aid/588/context/archive (accessed July 15, 2003).

RIVERS, C. 2002. Pop science book claims girls hard-wired for love. *Women's E-News,* June 28. www.womensenews.org/article.cfm/dyn/aid/952 (accessed June 29, 2002).

ROAN, S. 2003. The mind's role comes into focus: Knowledge of the profound connection between emotions and physical well-being is increasingly put to practice. *Los Angeles Times,* Jan. 20. www.latimes.com/features/health/la-he-psychosomatic20jan20.story (accessed Jan. 22, 2003).

ROBERTS, C. M. 2001. The view from 90. *Washington Post Health Supplement,* Jan. 23, 15–16.

ROBERTS, D. F., U. G. FOEHR, V. J. RIDEOUT, AND M. BRODIE. 1999. *Kids & media @ the new millennium.* Washington, DC: The Henry Kaiser Family Foundation.

ROBERTS, L. J. 2000. Fire and ice in marital communication: Hostile and distancing behaviors as predictors of marital distress. *Journal of Marriage and the Family* 62 (Aug.): 693–707.

ROBERTS, S. V. 1994. The blue-collar blues. *U.S. News & World Report,* Nov. 7, 32.

ROBIN, R. W., B. CHESTER, J. K. RASMUSSEN, J. M. JARANSON, AND D. GOLDMAN. 1997. Prevalence, characteristics, and impact of childhood sexual abuse in a southwestern American Indian tribe. *Child Abuse & Neglect* 21 (Aug.): 769–87.

ROBINSON, J. P., AND G. GODBEY. 1999. *Time for life: The surprising ways Americans use their time,* 2nd ed. University Park: Pennsylvania State University Press.

ROBINSON, M. 2003. Dial to pay $10 million in sexual harassment suit. *Chicago Sun Times,* Apr. 29. www.suntimes.com/output/business/29dial.html (accessed May 6, 2003).

ROBINSON, R. B., AND D. I. FRANK. 1994. The relation between self-esteem, sexual activity, and pregnancy. *Adolescence* 29 (Spring): 27–35.

ROBINSON, S. 2002. Casting stones. *Time,* Sep. 2, 36–37.

ROBINSON-WHELEN, Y. T., R. C. MACCALLUM, L. MCGUIRE, AND J. K. KIECOLT-GLASER. 2001. Long-term caregiving: What happens when it ends? *Journal of Abnormal Psychology* 111 (Nov.): 573–84.

ROCHE, T. 2002. The Yates odyssey. *Time,* Jan. 28, 40–50.

ROCHE, W. F. JR., AND W. MARIANO. 2002. Trapped in servitude far from their homes. *Baltimore Sun,* Sep. 15, 1A, 12A–15A.

RODBERG, G. 1999. Woman and man at Yale. www.culturefront.org/culturefront/magazine/99/spring/article.5.html (accessed Aug. 29, 2000).

RODGERS, A. Y., AND R. L. JONES. 1999. Grandmothers who are caregivers: An overlooked population. *Child and Adolescent Social Work Journal* 16 (Dec.): 455–66.

RODGERS, J. L., P. A. NAKONEZNY, AND R. D. SHULL. 1997. The effect of no-fault divorce legislation on divorce rates: A response to a reconsideration. *Journal of Marriage and the Family* 59 (Nov.): 1026–30.

RODGERS, K. A. 1999. Parenting processes related to sexual risk-taking: Behaviors of adolescent males and females. *Journal of Marriage and the Family* 61 (Feb.): 99–109.

RODGERS, K. B., AND H. A. ROSE. 2002. Risk and resiliency factors among adolescents who experience marital transitions. *Journal of Marriage and Family* 64 (Nov.): 1024–37.

RODRIGUEZ, J. M., AND K. KOSLOSKI. 1998. The impact of acculturation on attitudinal familism in a community of Puerto Rican Americans.

Hispanic Journal of Behavioral Sciences 20 (Aug.): 375–90.

ROE, K. M., AND M. MINKLER. 1998. Grandparents raising grandchildren: Challenges and responses. *Generations* 22 (Winter): 25–32.

ROGERS, M. F. 1999. *Barbie culture.* Thousand Oaks, CA: Sage.

ROGERS, S. J. 1999. Wives' income and marital quality: Are there reciprocal effects? *Journal of Marriage and the Family* 61 (Feb.): 123–32.

ROGERS, S. J., AND D. D. DEBOER. 2001. Changes in wives' income: Effects on marital happiness, psychological well-being, and the risk of divorce. *Journal of Marriage and Family* 63 (May): 458–72.

ROGERS, S. J., AND D. C. MAY. 2003. Spillover between marital quality and job satisfaction: Long-term patterns and gender differences. *Journal of Marriage and Family* 65 (May): 482–95.

ROHDE, D. 1994. Golden-aged athletes go for the gold. *Christian Science Monitor,* July 8, 10–11.

ROHNER, R. P., S. L. BOURQUE, AND C. A. ELORDI. 1996. Children's perceptions of corporal punishment, caretaker acceptance, and psychological adjustment in a poor, biracial southern community. *Journal of Marriage and the Family* 58 (Nov.): 842–52.

ROHNER, R. P., AND R. A. VENEZIANO. 2001. The importance of father love: History and contemporary evidence. *Review of General Psychology* 5 (4): 382–405.

ROHTER, L. 2003. Chile inches toward a law that would make divorce legal. *New York Times,* Sep. 29, A4.

Romance on the Web. 2003. *Newsweek,* May 12, E20.

ROMERO, G. J., AND G. E. WYATT. 1999. The prevalence and circumstances of child sexual abuse among Latina women. *Hispanic Journal of Behavioral Sciences* 21 (Aug.): 351–67.

ROPER STARCH WORLDWIDE, INC. 1994. *Teens talk about sex: Adolescent sexuality in the 90s.* New York: Sexuality Information and Education Council of the United States.

ROPER STARCH WORLDWIDE, INC. 1996. *The 1995 Virginia Slims Opinion Poll.* Storrs: The Roper Center, University of Connecticut.

Roper youth report. 1999. Who's going to stay home with the kids? Nearly 2 in 5 teen girls say it will be their husbands. www.roper.com/news/content/news156.htm (accessed Aug. 25, 2000).

ROSE, S., AND I. H. FRIEZE. 1993. Young singles' contemporary dating scripts. *Sex Roles* 28 (May): 499–509.

ROSEN, B. C. 1982. *The industrial connection: Achievement and the family in developing societies.* New York: Aldine.

ROSEN, K. H. 1996. The ties that bind women to violent premarital relationships: Processes of seduction and entrapment. In *Family violence from a communication perspective,* eds. D. D. Cahn and S. A. Lloyd, 151–76. Thousand Oaks, CA: Sage.

ROSEN, K. H., AND S. M. STITH. 1993. Intervention strategies for treating women in violent dating relationships. *Family Relations* 42 (Oct.): 427–33.

ROSEN, R. 2003. Sentenced to stoning. *San Francisco Chronicle.* http://sfgate.com/cgi-bin/article.cgi?f=/c/a/2003/03/31/ED88060.DTL (accessed Mar. 31, 2003).

ROSENBERG, D. A. 1997. Unusual forms of child abuse. In *The battered child,* 5th ed., eds. M. E. Helfer, R. S. Kempe, and R. D. Krugman, 413–30. Chicago: University of Chicago Press.

ROSENBERG, J. 1993. Just the two of us. In *Reinventing love: Six women talk about lust, sex, and romance,* eds. L. Abraham, L. Green, M. Krance, J. Rosenberg, J. Somerville, and C. Stoner, 301–7. New York: Plume.

ROSENBLATT, P. C. 1994. *Metaphors of family systems theory: Toward new constructions.* New York: Guilford.

ROSENBLATT, P. C., T. A. KARIS, AND R. D. POWELL. 1995. *Multiracial couples: Black & white voices.* Thousand Oaks, CA: Sage.

ROSENBLATT, P. C., AND R. A. PHILLIPS, JR. 1975. Family articles in popular magazines: Advice to writers, editors, and teachers of consumers. *Family Coordinator* 24 (July): 267–71.

ROSENFELD, M. J. 2002. Measures of assimilation in the marriage market: Mexican Americans 1970–1990. *Journal of Marriage and Family* 64 (Feb.): 152–62.

ROSENTHAL, C. J. 1985. Kinkeeping in the familial division of labor. *Journal of Marriage and the Family* 47 (Nov.): 965–74.

ROSENZWEIG, P. M. 1992. *Married and alone: The way back.* New York: Plenum.

ROSIN, M. B. 1987. *Stepfathering: Stepfathers' advice on creating a new family.* New York: Simon & Schuster.

ROSS, C. E., AND J. MIROWSKY. 1999. Parental divorce, life-course disruption, and adult depression. *Journal of Marriage and the Family* 61 (Nov.): 1034–45.

ROSS, C. E., J. MIROWSKY, AND K. GOLDSTEIN. 1991. The impact of the family on health: The decade in review. In *Contemporary families: Looking forward, looking back,* ed. A. Booth. Minneapolis: National Council on Family Relations.

ROSS, S. M. 1996. Risk of physical abuse to children of spouse abusing parents. *Child Abuse & Neglect* 20 (July): 589–98.

ROTHMAN, B. K. 1984. *Hands and hearts: A history of courtship in America.* New York: Basic Books.

ROTHMAN, E. K. 1983. Sex and self-control: Middle-class courtship in America, 1770–1870. In *The American family in social-historical perspective,* 3rd ed., ed. M. Gordon, 393–410. New York: St. Martin's.

ROTHMAN, S. M. 1978. *Women's proper place: A history of changing ideals and practices, 1870 to the present.* New York: Basic Books.

ROUSE, L. 2002. *Marital and sexual lifestyles in the United States: Attitudes, behaviors, and relationships in social context.* New York: Haworth.

ROWE, J., AND R. KAHN. 1997. *Successful aging.* New York: Pantheon.

ROWLAND, M. 1994. Love and money the second time around. *Working Woman* (Aug.): 22, 24.

RUBIN, L. B. 1985. *Just friends: The role of friendship in our lives.* New York: Harper & Row.

RUBIN, L. B. 1994. *Families on the fault line: America's working class speaks about the family, the economy, race, and ethnicity.* New York: HarperCollins.

RUDOLPH, K. D., K. D. KURLAKOWSKY, AND C. S. CONLEY. 2001. Developmental and social-contextual origins of depressive control–related beliefs and behavior. *Cognitive Therapy and Research* 25 (Aug.): 447–75.

RUHM, C. J., AND J. L. TEAGUE. 1997. Parental leave policies in Europe and North America. In *Gender and family issues in the workplace,* eds. F. D. Blau and R. G. Ehrenberg, 133–56. New York: Russell Sage Foundation.

RUSSELL, C. 1999. Only 10% of day care is rated excellent. *Washington Post,* Feb. 23, 8–9.

RUSSELL, D. E. H. 1990. *Rape in marriage.* Bloomington: Indiana University Press.

RUSSO, F. 2002. That old feeling. *Time,* Feb. 13, G1–G3.

RUSSO, N. F., AND A. J. DABUL. 1997. The relationship of abortion to well-being: Do race and religion make a difference? *Professional Psychology: Research and Practice,* Vol. 28 (Feb.): 28–31.

RUSSO, N. F., J. D. HORN, AND S. TROMP. 1993. Childspacing intervals and abortion among blacks and whites: A brief report. *Women & Health* 20 (3): 43–51.

RUST, B. 2000. Walking the plain talk. *Advocasey* (Spring/Summer): 1–11.

RUTTER, V. 1994. Lessons from stepfamilies. *Psychology Today* (May): 30–33, 60ff.

RYAN, M. 1993. Undercover among the elderly. *Parade Magazine,* July 18, 8.

RYAN, M. P. 1983. *Womanhood in America: From colonial times to the present,* 3rd ed. New York: Franklin Watts.

RYAN, S., J. MANLOVE, AND K. FRANZETTA. 2003. *The first time: Characteristics of teens' first sexual relationships.* Washington, DC: Child Trends.

SAAD, L. 1994. Public has cold feet on health care reform. *Gallup Poll Monthly* (Aug.): 2–5.

SAAD, L. 2002. Fewer blacks say anti-white sentiment is widespread in black community. Gallup News Service, June 18. www.gallup.com/poll/releases/pr020618.asp (accessed June 20, 2002).

SAAD, L. 2003. *Roe v. Wade* has positive public image. Gallup News Service, Jan. 20. www.gallup.com/poll/releases/pr030120.asp (accessed Jan. 21, 2003).

SABATELLI, R. M., AND S. BARTLE-HARING. 2003. Family-of-origin experiences and adjustment in married couples. *Journal of Marriage and Family* 65 (Feb.): 159–69.

SABBAGH, S. 1996. Introduction: The debate on Arab women. In *Arab women: Between defiance and restraint,* ed. S. Sabbagh, xi–xxvii. New York: Olive Branch.

SADKER, M., AND D. SADKER. 1994. *Failing at fairness: How America's schools cheat girls.* New York: Scribner's.

SAFER, J. 1996. *Beyond motherhood: Choosing a life without children.* New York: Pocket Books.

SAFILIOS-ROTHSCHILD, C. 1977. *Love, sex, and sex roles.* Upper Saddle River, NJ: Prentice Hall.

SAGIRI, Y. 2001. *United National Indian Tribal Youth, Inc.* Washington, DC: U.S. Department of Justice.

SAITO, L. T. 2002. *Ethnic identity and motivation: Socio-cultural factors in the educational achievement of Vietnamese American students.* New York: LFB Scholarly Publishing.

SALDANA, D. H., AND A. M. DASSORI. 1999. When is caregiving a burden? Listening to Mexican American women. *Hispanic Journal of Behavioral Sciences* 21 (Aug.): 283–301.

SALTZMAN, A. 1993. Family friendliness. *U.S. News & World Report,* Feb. 22, 59–66.

SALTZMAN, A. 1999. From diapers to high heels. *U.S. News & World Report,* July 26, 57–58.

SALUTER, A. F. 1994. *Marital status and living arrangements: March 1993.* U.S. Census Bureau, Current Population Reports, Series P20–478. Washington, DC: U.S. Government Printing Office.

SALUTER, A. F. 1996. Marital status and living arrangements: March 1995 (Update). U.S. Census Bureau, Department of Commerce, Economics and Statistics Administration.

SANCHEZ, M. 2003. Fast-food industry introduces some young women to sexual harassment. www.kansascity.com/mld/kansascitystar/news/opinion/5791290.htm.

SANCHEZ, R. 1999. Abortion foes' Internet site on trial. *Washington Post,* Jan. 15, A3.

SANCHEZ-WAY, R., AND S. JOHNSON. 2000. Cultural practices in American Indian prevention programs. *Juvenile Justice* 7 (Dec.): 20–30.

SANDAY, P. R. 1990. *Fraternity gang rape: Sex, brotherhood, and privilege on campus.* New York: New York University Press.

SANDBERG, J. F., AND S. L. HOFFERTH. 2001. Changes in children's time with parents, U.S. 1981–1997. *Demography* 38 (3): 423–36.

SANDBERG, J. G., R. B. MILLER, AND J. M. HARPER. 2002. A qualitative study of marital process and depression in older couples. *Family Relations* 51 (July): 256–64.

SANDEFUR, G. 1996. Welfare doesn't cause illegitimacy and single parenthood. *Chronicle of Higher Education,* Oct. 4, B7–B8.

SANDER, J. 1991. *Before their time: Four generations of teenage mothers.* New York: Harcourt Brace Jovanovich.

SANDLER, L. 2003. Veiled and worried in Baghdad. *New York Times,* Sep. 16. www.nytimes.com/2003/09/16/opinion/16SAND.html?th (accessed Sep. 17, 2003).

SANDS, R. G., AND R. S. GOLDBERG-GLEN. 2000. Factors associated with stress among grandparents raising their children. *Family Relations* 49 (Jan.): 97–105.

SANTELLI, J., ET AL. 2003. The measurement and meaning of unintended pregnancy. *Perspectives on Sexual and Reproductive Health* 35 (Mar./Apr.): 94–101.

SANTELLI, J. S., L. D. LINDBERG, J. ABMA, C. S. MCNEELY, AND M. RESNICK. 2000. Adolescent sexual behavior: Estimates and trends from four nationally representative surveys. *Family Planning Perspectives* 32 (4): 156–65, 194.

SANTROCK, J. W., K. A. SITTERLE, AND R. A. WARSHAK. 1988. Parent–child relationships in stepfather families. In *Fatherhood today: Men's*

changing role in the family, eds. S. P. Bronstein and C. P. Cowan, 144–65. New York: Wiley.

SAPOLSKY, R. 2000. It's not "all in the genes." *Newsweek,* Apr. 10, 68.

SAPORTA, S. 1991. Miscellany: Old maid and dirty old man: The language of ageism. *American Speech* 66 (Fall): 333–34.

SARCH, A. 1993. Making the connection: Single women's use of the telephone in dating relationships with men. *Journal of Communications* 43 (Spring): 128–44.

SARMIENTO, S. T. 2002. *Making ends meet: Income-generating strategies among Mexican immigrants.* New York: LFB Scholarly Publishing.

SARWAR, B. 2002. Brutality cloaked as tradition. *New York Times,* Aug. 6. www.nytimes.com/2002/08/06/opinion/06SARW.html?todaysheadlines (accessed Aug. 7, 2002).

SAVE THE CHILDREN. 2003. *State of the world's mothers: Protecting women and children in war and conflict.* www.savethechildren.org/sowm2003/index.shtml (accessed Aug. 22, 2003).

SAVIN-WILLIAMS, R. C., AND E. M. DUBÉ. 1998. Parental reactions to their child's disclosure of a gay/lesbian identity. *Family Relations* 47 (Jan.): 7–13.

SCHAEFER, C. E., AND T. F. DIGERONIMO. 1999. *How to talk to teens about really important things: Specific questions and answers and useful things to say.* San Francisco: Jossey-Bass.

SCHAFER, S. 1999. At-home business, with pleasure. *Washington Post,* Oct. 4, A1, A4.

SCHECTER, S., AND A. GANELY. 1995. *Domestic violence: A national curriculum for family preservation practitioners.* San Francisco: Family Violence Prevention Fund.

SCHEMO, J. 2002. Women who lead colleges see slower growth in ranks. *New York Times,* Dec. 8. www.nytimes.com/2002/12/09/education/09COLL.html?tntemail0 (accessed Dec. 9, 2002).

SCHERER, R. 2003. Relaxing can wait, as retirees flood job market. *Christian Science Monitor,* Aug. 21, 1–2.

SCHLOSSER, E. 2002. Making it work. *Mother Jones* (Sep./Oct.): 68–73.

SCHMIDLEY, D. A. 2001. *Profile of the foreign-born population in the United States: 2000.* U.S. Census Bureau, Current Population Reports, Series P23-206. www.census.gov/prod/2002pubs/p23-206.pdf (accessed Mar. 1, 2003).

SCHMIDLEY, D. 2003. *The foreign-born population in the United States: March 2002.* U.S. Census Bureau. www.census.gov/prod/2003pubs/p20-539.pdf (accessed Apr. 4, 2003).

SCHMITT, D. P., AND D. M. BUSS. 2001. Interpersonal relations and group processes: Human mate poaching—tactics and temptations for infiltrating existing mateships. *Journal of Personality and Social Psychology* 80 (June): 894–917.

SCHMITT, E., AND M. MOSS. 2003. Air Force investigated 54 assaults in 10 years. *New York Times,* Mar. 7. www.nytimes.com/2003/03/07/national/07CADE.html?th (accessed Mar. 8, 2003).

SCHNEIDER, E. C., A. M. ZASLAVSKY, AND A. M. EPSTEIN. 2002. Racial disparities in the quality of care for enrollees in Medicare managed care. *Journal of the American Medical Association* 287 (Mar. 13): 1288–94.

SCHNEIDER, H. 2000. Egyptian women given faster route to divorce. *Washington Post,* Apr. 14, A16–A17.

SCHORR, M. 2001. Gay and lesbian couples do well at parenting. Excite News, Aug. 28. news.excite.com/news/r/010828/17/health-parenting (accessed Aug. 29, 2001).

SCHRADER, S. M., M. J. BREITENSTEIN, J. C. CLARK, B. D. LOWE, AND T. W. TURNER. 2002. Nocturnal penile tumescence and rigidity testing in bicycling patrol officers. *Journal of Andrology* 23 (Nov./Dec.): 927–34.

SCHRECK, L. 1999. Adolescent sexual activity is affected more by mothers' attitudes and behavior than by family structure. *Family Planning Perspectives* 31 (July): 200–201.

SCHROF, J. M. 1994. A lens on matrimony. *U.S. News & World Report,* Feb. 21, 66–69.

SCHROF, J. M. 1999. Who's guilty? *U.S. News & World Report,* May 17, 60–62.

SCHROF, J. M., WITH B. WAGNER. 1994. Sex in America. *U.S. News & World Report,* Oct. 17, 75–81.

SCHULMAN, K. A., ET AL. 1999. The effect of race and sex on physicians' recommendations for cardiac catheterization. *New England Journal of Medicine* 340 (Feb. 25): 618–26.

SCHULTZ, S. 2000. Talk to kids about drugs? Parents just don't do it. *U.S. News & World Report,* Feb. 7, 56–57.

SCHVANEVELDT, P. L., B. C. MILLER, E. H. BERRY, AND T. R. LEE. 2001. Academic goals, achievement, and age at first sexual intercourse: Longitudinal, bidirectional influences. *Adolescence* 36 (Winter): 767–87.

SCHWAB, R. 1998. A child's death and divorce: Dispelling the myth. *Death Studies* 22 (July/Aug.): 445–68.

SCHWARTZ, D. J., V. PHARES, S. TANTLEFF-DUNN, AND J. K. THOMPSON. 1999. Devin body image, psychological functioning, and parental feedback regarding physical appearance. *International Journal of Eating Disorders* 25: 339–43.

SCHWARTZ, F. N. 1989. Management women and the new facts of life. *Harvard Business Review* 89 (Jan./Feb.): 65–76.

SCHWARTZ, M. J. 2000. *Born in bondage: Growing up enslaved in the antebellum South.* Cambridge, MA: Harvard University Press.

SCHWEBEL, A. I., M. A. FINE, AND M. A. RENNER. 1991. A study of perceptions of the stepparent role. *Journal of Family Issues* 12 (Mar.): 43–57.

SCHWEITZER, M. M., ED. 1999. *American Indian grandmothers: Traditions and transitions.* Albuquerque: University of New Mexico Press.

SCINTO, L., ET AL. 1994. A potential noninvasive neurobiological test for Alzheimer's disease. *Science,* Nov. 11, 1051–54.

SCOMMEGNA, P. 2002. Increased cohabitation changing children's family settings. *Population Today* 30 (Oct.): 3, 6.

SCOTT, D., AND B. WISHY, EDS. 1982. *America's families: A documentary history.* New York: Harper & Row.

SEAGER, J. 2003. *The Penguin atlas of women in the world.* New York: Penguin.

SECCOMBE, K. 2002. "Beating the odds" versus "changing the odds": Poverty, resilience, and family policy. *Journal of Marriage and Family* 64 (May): 384–94.

SEDLACK, A. J., D. FINKELHOR, H. HAMMER, AND D. J. SCHULTZ. 2002. *National estimates of missing children: An overview.* Washington, DC: U.S. Department of Justice.

Seek spouse in India? Take out an ad. 1989. *Baltimore Sun,* June 7, F6.

SEEMAN, T. E., B. H. SINGER, C. D. RYFF, G. D. LOVE, AND L. LEVY-STORMS. 2002. Social relationships, gender, and allostatic load across two age cohorts. *Psychosomatic Medicine* 64 (May/June): 395–406.

SEFF, M. A. 1995. Cohabitation and the law. *Marriage & Family Review* 21 (3/9): 141–68.

SEGAL, J. 1989. 10 myths about child development. *Parents* (July): 81–84, 87.

SEGAL, L., AND Z. SEGAL. 1991. Does spanking work? *Parents* (Mar.): 188.

SEGAL, U. A. 1991. Cultural variables in Asian Indian families. *Families in Society* 72 (Apr.): 233–42.

SEGURA, D. A. 1994. Working at motherhood: Chicana and Mexican immigrant mothers and employment. In *Mothering: Ideology, experience, and agency,* eds. E. N. Glenn, G. Chang, and L. R. Forcey, 211–33. New York: Routledge.

SELIGMANN, J., AND P. ROGERS. 1994. The pressure to lose. *Newsweek,* May 2, 60–61.

SELTZER, J. A. 2001. Families formed outside of marriage. In *Understanding families into the new millennium: A decade in review,* ed. R. M. Milardo, 466–87. Minneapolis: National Council on Family Relations.

Sexually transmitted disease surveillance. 2001. Centers for Disease Control and Prevention. www.cdc.gov/std/stats (accessed July 13, 2003).

SHAABAN, B. 1995. The muted voices of women interpreters. In *Faith and freedom: Women's human rights in the Muslim world,* ed. M. Afkhami, 61–77. Syracuse, NY: Syracuse University Press.

SHAH, S. 2002. Judge rules rape of aboriginal girl "traditional." *Women's E-News,* Dec. 1. www.womensenews.org/article.cfm/dyn/aid/1126 (accessed Dec. 4, 2002).

SHAKIR, E. 1997. *Bint Arab: Arab and Arab American women in the United States.* Westport, CT: Praeger.

SHAPIRO, J. P. 1997. Death rights. *U.S. News & World Report,* Jan. 13, 21–27.

SHAPIRO, L. 1990. Guns and dolls. *Newsweek,* May 28, 57–65.

SHARIFZADEH, V.-S. 1997. Families with Middle Eastern roots. In *Developing cross-cultural competence: A guide for working with children and families,* eds. E. W. Lynch and M. J. Hanson, 441–82. Baltimore: Paul H. Brookes.

SHARMA, A. 2003. India takes steps to expel illegal Muslim immigrants. *Christian Science Monitor,* Mar. 4, 7.

SHARMA, O. P. 2001. 2001 census results mixed for India's women and girls. *Population Today* 29 (May/June): 1–3.

SHATZKIN, K. 1996. Battered wife wants husband to keep job. *Baltimore Sun,* Dec. 7, A1, A4.

SHATZKIN, K. 1999. A better message on teen pregnancy. *Baltimore Sun,* Nov. 9, 1A, 8A.

SHATZKIN, K. 2000. Perdue violated wage statute. *Baltimore Sun,* Feb. 29, C1.

SHAVER, P., C. HAZAN, AND D. BRADSHAW. 1988. Love as attachment. In *The psychology of love,* eds. R. J. Sternberg and M. L. Barnes, 68–99. New Haven, CT: Yale University Press.

SHEA, J. A., AND G. R. ADAMS. 1984. Correlates of romantic attachment: A path analysis study. *Journal of Youth and Adolescence* 13 (1): 27–44.

SHELDON, K. M., A. J. ELLIOT, Y. KIM, AND T. KASSER. 2001. What is satisfying about satisfying events? Testing 10 candidate psychological needs. *Journal of Personality and Social Psychology* 80 (Feb.): 325–29.

SHELTON, B. A. 1987. Variations in divorce rates by community size: A test of the social integration explanation. *Journal of Marriage and the Family* 49 (Nov.): 827–32.

SHERMAN, L. 1992. *Policing domestic violence: Experiment and dilemmas.* New York: Free Press.

SHIMOMURA, M. 1990. Japan: Too much mommy-san. *New Perspectives Quarterly* 7 (Winter): 24–27.

SHINAGAWA, L. H., AND G. Y. PANG. 1996. Asian American panethnicity and intermarriage. *Amerasia Journal* 22 (Spring): 127–52.

SHIPLEY, S. 1997. Making vows last longer in Louisiana. *Christian Science Monitor,* July 1, 14.

SHUEY, K., AND M. A. HARDY. 2003. Assistance to aging parents and parents-in-law: Does lineage affect family allocation decisions? *Journal of Marriage and Family* 65 (May): 418–31.

SIDEL, R. 1998. *Keeping women and children last: America's war on the poor.* New York: Penguin.

SIEGEL, A. F. 2000. Court rules lesbian ex can seek visitation. *Baltimore Sun,* May 3, 1A, 7A.

SILBERSTEIN, L. R. 1992. *Dual-career marriage: A system in transition.* Hillsdale, NJ: Erlbaum.

SILLIMAN, B., AND W. R. SCHUMM. 2000. Marriage preparation programs: A literature review. *The Family Journal: Counseling and Therapy for Couples and Families* 8 (Apr.): 133–42.

SILVERMAN, J. G., A. RAJ, L. A. MUCCI, AND J. E. HATHAWAY. 2001. Dating violence against adolescent girls and associated substance use, unhealthy weight control, sexual risk behavior, pregnancy, and suicidality. *Journal of the American Medical Association* 286 (Aug. 1): 572–79.

SILVERMAN, P. R. 2000. *Never too young to know: Death in children's lives.* New York: Oxford University Press.

SILVERMAN, R. E. 2003. Provisions boost rights of couples living together. *Wall Street Journal,* Mar. 5, D1.

SILVERSTEIN, M., AND X. CHEN. 1999. The impact of acculturation in Mexican American families on the quality of adult grandchild–grandparent relationships. *Journal of Marriage and the Family* 61 (Feb.): 188–98.

SIMMONS, A. M. 1998. Here beauty is measured in pounds. *Baltimore Sun,* Oct. 24, 2a.

SIMMONS, R. 2002. *Odd girl out: The hidden culture of aggression in girls.* New York: Harcourt.

SIMMONS, T., AND M. O'CONNELL. 2003. *Married-couple and unmarried-partner households: 2000.* U.S. Census Bureau. http://landview. census.gov/prod/2003pubs/censr-5.pdf (accessed Apr. 20, 2003).

SIMMONS, T., AND G. O'NEILL. 2001. *Households and families: 2000.* U.S. Census Bureau. www.census.gov/prod/2001pubs/c2kbr01-8.pdf (accessed Apr. 20, 2003).

SIMON, J. P. 1996. Lebanese families. In *Ethnicity and family therapy,* 2nd ed., eds. M. McGoldrick, J. Giordano, and J. K. Pearce, 364–75. New York: Guilford.

SIMON, R. J. 1993. *The case for transracial adoption.* Washington, DC: American University Press.

SIMON, R. J., AND H. ALTSTEIN. 2000. *Adoption across borders: Serving the children in transracial and intercountry adoptions.* Lanham, MD: Rowman & Littlefield.

SIMON, S. 2003. Custom poetry for Valentine's Day. *Baltimore Sun,* Feb. 14, 9A.

SIMONELLI, C. J., T. MULLIS, A. N. ELLIOTT, AND T. W. PIERCE. 2002. Abuse by siblings and subsequent experiences of violence within the dating relationship. *Journal of Interpersonal Violence* 17 (Feb.): 103–21.

SIMONS, R. L., & ASSOCIATES. 1996. *Understanding differences between divorced and intact families: Stress, interaction, and child outcome.* Thousand Oaks, CA: Sage.

SIMONS, R. L., C. JOHNSON, J. BEAMAN, AND R. D. CONGER. 1993. Explaining women's double jeopardy: Factors that mediate the association between harsh treatment as a child and violence by a husband. *Journal of Marriage and the Family* 55 (Aug.): 713–23.

SIMONS, R. L., C. JOHNSON, AND R. D. CONGER. 1994. Harsh corporal punishment versus quality of parental involvement as an explanation of adolescent maladjustment. *Journal of Marriage and the Family* 56 (Aug.): 591–607.

SIMONS, R. L., K.-H. LIN, L. C. GORDON, R. D. CONGER, AND F. O. LORENZ. 1999. Explaining the higher incidence of adjustment problems among children of divorce compared with those in two-parent families. *Journal of Marriage and the Family* 61 (Nov.): 1020–33.

SIMPSON, A. 1995. The Social Security pie: Save a piece for the kids. *Christian Science Monitor,* Mar. 10, 19.

SINGER, L. T., ET AL. 2002. Cognitive and motor outcomes of cocaine-exposed infants. *Journal of the American Medical Association* 287 (Apr. 17): 1952–60.

SINGER, R. 2001. Violence against young girls rises. *Christian Science Monitor,* Mar. 28, 6.

SIWOLOP, S. 2002. In Web's divorce industry, bad (and good) advice. *New York Times.* www.nytimes.com/2002/11/24/business/yourmoney/24DIVO.html?todaysheadlines (accessed Nov. 25, 2002).

SKINNER, D. A., AND J. K. KOHLER. 2002. Parental rights in diverse family contexts: Current legal developments. *Family Relations* 51 (Oct.): 293–300.

SKOLNICK, A. 1991. *Embattled paradise: The American family in an age of uncertainty.* New York: Basic Books.

SLADE, M. 1985. Treating parents as children. *New York Times,* May 13, C5.

SMALL, S. A., AND D. KERNS. 1993. Unwanted sexual activity among peers during early and middle adolescence: Incidence and risk factors. *Journal of Marriage and the Family* 55 (Nov.): 941–52.

SMALLEY, S., AND B. BRAIKER. 2003. Suffer the children. *Newsweek,* Jan. 20, 32–33.

SMEEDING, T., L. RAINWATER, AND G. BURTLESS. 2000. United States poverty in a cross-national context. www.lisproject.org/publications/liswps/244.pdf (accessed Sep. 12, 2003).

SMITH, C. S. 2002. Kandahar journal. Shh, it's an open secret: Warlords and pedophilia. *New York Times,* Feb. 21, A4.

SMITH, D. 2003. *The older population in the United States: March 2002.* U.S. Census Bureau, Current Population Reports, P20-546. www.census.gov/prod/2003pubs/p20-546.pdf (accessed Oct. 11, 2001).

SMITH, K. 2000. *Who's minding the kids? Child care arrangements: Fall 1995.* Current Population

Reports, P70-70. Washington, DC: U.S. Census Bureau.

SMITH, K., B. DOWNS, AND M. O'CONNELL. 2001. *Maternity leave and employment patterns: 1961–1995.* U.S. Census Bureau, Current Population Reports, P70-79. www.census.gov/prod/2001pubs/p70-79.pdf (accessed Sep. 10, 2003).

SMITH, K. R., C. D. ZICK, AND G. J. DUNCAN. 1991. Remarriage patterns among recent widows and widowers. *Demography* 28 (Aug.): 361–74.

SMITH, M. C., L. R. VARTANIAN, N. DEFRATES-DENSCH, P. C. VAN LOON, AND S. LOCKE. 2003. Self-help books for parents of adolescents, 1980–1993. *Family Relations* 52 (Apr.): 174–79.

SMITH, P. K., AND L. M. DREW. 2002. Grandparenthood. In *Handbook of parenting,* 2nd ed., Vol. 3: *Being and becoming a parent,* ed. M. H. Bornstein, 141–72. Mahwah, NJ: Erlbaum.

SMITH, S. 2002. How the balancing act disadvantages women in the workplace. *Sociologists for Women in Society* 19 (Fall): 19–20.

SMITH, T. W. 1994. Can money buy love? *Public Perspective* 5 (Jan./Feb.): 33–34.

SMITH, T. W. 1999. The emerging 21st century American family. www.norc.uchicago.edu/online/emerge.htm (accessed Aug. 12, 2000).

SMITH, T. W. 2000. *Taking America's pulse II: A survey of intergroup relations.* Survey conducted for the National Conference for Community and Justice and Bank of America. fdncenter.org/pnd/20000516/003375.html (accessed Oct. 2, 2000).

SMITH, T. W. 2001. Ties that bind: The emerging 21st century American family. *Public Perspective* 12 (Jan./Feb.): 34–37.

SMITH, W. L. 1999. *Families and communes: An examination of nontraditional lifestyles.* Thousand Oaks, CA: Sage.

SMOCK, P. J. 1993. The economic costs of marital disruption for young women over the past two decades. *Demography* 30 (Aug.): 353–71.

SMOCK, P. J. 1994. Gender and the short-run economic consequences of marital disruption. *Social Forces* 73 (Sep.): 243–62.

SMOCK, P. J., AND S. GUPTA. 2002. Cohabitation in contemporary North America. In *Just living together: Implications of cohabitation on families, children, and social policy,* eds. A. Booth and A. C. Crouter, 53–84. Mahwah, NJ: Erlbaum.

SMOLAK, L., M. P. LEVINE, AND F SCHERMER. 1999. Parental input and weight concerns among elementary school children. *International Journal of Eating Disorders* 25: 263–71.

SNIPP, C. M. 1996. A demographic comeback for American Indians. *Population Today* 24 (Nov.): 4–5.

SNIPP, C. M. 2002. American Indians: Clues to the future of other racial groups. In *The new race question: How the census counts multiracial individuals,* eds. J. Perlmann and M. C. Waters, 189–214. New York: Russell Sage Foundation.

SNOWDON, D. 2001. *Aging with grace: What the nun study teaches us about leading longer, healthier, and more meaningful lives.* New York: Bantam.

Solitaire set continues to grow. 2003. Population Reference Bureau. www.prb.org/solitaireset (accessed July 11, 2003).

SOLOMON, K., AND P. A. SZWABO. 1994. The work-oriented culture: Success and power in elderly men. In *Older men's lives,* ed. E. Thompson, Jr., 42–64. Thousand Oaks, CA: Sage.

SOLOMON, R. C. 2002. Reasons for love. *Journal for the Theory of Social Behaviour* 32 (Mar.): 1–28.

SOLOT, D., AND M. MILLER. 2002. *Unmarried to each other: The essential guide to living together as an unmarried couple.* New York: Marlowe & Company.

SOLTERO, J. M. 1996. *Inequality in the workplace: Underemployment among Mexicans, African Americans, and whites.* New York: Garland.

SOMERS, M. D. 1993. A comparison of voluntarily childfree adults and parents. *Journal of Marriage and the Family* 55 (Aug.): 643–50.

SOMERVILLE, F. P. L. 1994. Their faith offers better feminism. Muslim women say—rights with protection. *Baltimore Sun,* Feb. 15, 4B.

SOMMERS, C. H. 2000. *The war against boys: How misguided feminism is harming our young men.* New York: Simon & Schuster.

SONG, J. 2002. Aging immigrants find different "home." *Baltimore Sun,* May 22, 1A, 12A.

SONTAG, D. 2002. Fierce entanglements. *New York Times Magazine,* Nov. 17, 52.

SORENSEN, E., AND C. ZIBMAN. 2000. Child support offers some protection against poverty. Washington, DC: Urban Institute. newfederalism. urban.org/pdf/b10.pdf (accessed Oct. 21, 2000).

SOUTH, S. J., K. D. CROWDER, AND K. TRENT. 1998. Children's residential mobility and neighborhood environment following parental divorce and remarriage. *Social Forces* 77: 667–93.

SPAKE, A. 1998. Adoption gridlock. *U.S. News & World Report,* June 22, 30–37.

Speaking a language other than English. 2001. U.S. Census Bureau. www.census.gov/acs/www/Products/Ranking/C2SS/R03T050.htm (accessed Mar. 2, 2003).

SPEARS, G. 1994. Estate-planning musts for blended families. *Kiplinger's Personal Finance Magazine* 48 (Dec.): 91–96.

SPENCER, R. F., AND J. D. JENNINGS. 1977. *The Native Americans: Ethnology and backgrounds of the North American Indians.* New York: Harper & Row.

SPIEKER, S. J., N. C. LARSON, AND L. GILCHRIST. 1999. Developmental trajectories of disruptive behavior problems in preschool children of adolescent mothers. *Child Development* 70 (Mar.): 443–58.

SPITZE, G., J. R. LOGAN, G. DEANE, AND S. ZERGER. 1994. Adult children's divorce and intergenerational relationships. *Journal of Marriage and the Family* 56 (May): 279–93.

SPRECHER, S. 1999. "I love you more today than yesterday": Romantic partners' perceptions of changes in love and related affect over time. *Journal of Personality and Social Psychology* 76 (Jan.): 46–53.

SPRECHER, S. 2001. Equity and social exchange in dating couples: Associations with satisfaction, commitment, and stability. *Journal of Marriage and Family* 63 (Aug.): 599–613.

SPRECHER, S., A. BARBEE, AND P. SCHWARTZ. 1995. "Was it good for you, too?": Gender differences in first sexual intercourse experiences. *Journal of Sex Research* 32 (1): 3–15.

SPRECHER, S., AND K. MCKINNEY. 1993. *Sexuality.* Thousand Oaks, CA: Sage.

SPRINGEN, K. 2003. Bringing up baby. *Newsweek,* Jan. 27, 72.

SPRINGEN, K., AND D. NOONAN. 2003. Sperm banks go online. *Newsweek,* Apr. 21, E14–E15.

SQUIER, D. A., AND J. S. QUADAGNO. 1988. The Italian American family. In *Ethnic families in America: Patterns and variations,* 3rd ed., eds. C. J. Mindel, R. W. Habenstein, and R. Wright, Jr., 109–37. New York: Elsevier.

SQUIRES, S. 1995. What to do when your child asks about sex. *Washington Post Health Supplement,* Sep. 12, 10–13.

SRIVASTAVA, S., O. P. JOHN, S. D. GOSLING, AND J. POTTER. 2003. Development of personality in early and middle adulthood: Set like plaster or persistent change? *Journal of Personality and Social Psychology* 84 (May): 1041–53.

ST. JEAN, Y., AND J. R. FEAGIN. 1998. *Double burden: Black women and everyday racism.* Armonk, NY: M.E. Sharpe.

STACEY, J. 2003. Gay and lesbian families: Queer like us. In *All our families: New policies for a new century,* 2nd ed., eds. M. A. Mason, A. Skolnick, and S. D. Sugarman, 144–69. New York: Oxford University Press.

STACEY, J., AND T. J. BIBLARZ. 2001. (How) does the sexual orientation of parents matter? *American Sociological Review* 66 (Apr.): 159–83.

Stalking. 2000. www.ncvc.org/SPECIAL/stalking.htm (accessed Aug. 30, 2000).

STANLEY, S. M., H. J. MARKMAN, AND S. W. WHITTON. 2002. Communication, conflict, and commitment: Insights on the foundations of relationship success from a national survey. *Family Process* 41 (Winter): 659–75.

STANNARD, D. E. 1979. Changes in the American family: Fiction and reality. In *Changing images of the family,* eds. V. Tufte and B. Myerhoff, 83–98. New Haven, CT: Yale University Press.

STAPLES, R. 1988. The black American family. In *Ethnic families in America: Patterns and*

variations, 3rd ed., eds. C. H. Mindel, R. W. Habenstein, and R. Wright, Jr., 303–24. New York: Elsevier.

STARK, M. 1998. *What no one tells the bride.* New York: Hyperion.

STARR, A. 2001. Shotgun weddings by Uncle Sam? *Business Week,* June 4, 68.

State of the world's mothers 2003: Protecting women and children in war and conflict. 2003. Save the Children. www.savethechildren.org/sowm2003/index.shtml (accessed May 25, 2003).

STAUSS, J. H. 1995. Reframing and refocusing American Indian family strengths. In *American families: Issues in race and ethnicity,* ed. C. K. Jacobson, 105–18. New York: Garland.

STEIL, J. M. 1997. *Marital equality: Its relationship to the well-being of husbands and wives.* Thousand Oaks, CA: Sage.

STEIN, M. D. 1998. Sexual ethics: Disclosure of HIV-positive status to partners. *Archives of Internal Medicine* 158 (Feb. 9): 253–57.

STEIN, P. J., ED. 1981. *Single life: Unmarried adults in social context.* New York: St. Martin's.

STEIN, R. 2003. AIDS cases in U.S. increase. *Washington Post,* July 29, A1.

STEIN, R. 2003. More parents bring baby to bed. *Washington Post,* Jan. 14, A11.

STEIN, T. J. 1996. Child custody and visitation: The rights of lesbian and gay parents. *Social Service Review* 70 (Sep.): 435–50.

STEINBACH, A. 1995. Custody wars. *Baltimore Sun,* Mar. 13, 1D–2D.

STEINBERG, L., AND J. S. SILK. 2002. Parenting adolescents. In *Handbook of parenting,* 2nd ed., Vol. 1: *Children and parenting,* ed. M. H. Bornstein, 103–33. Mahwah, NJ: Erlbaum.

STEINDORF, S. 2002. Women make the team, but less often coach it. *Christian Science Monitor,* Mar. 12, 13, 16.

STEINMETZ, S. 1978. The battered husband syndrome. *Victimology* 2 (3/4): 499–509.

STENSON, J. 2002. Morning-after pill not offered in many U.S. rape cases. Yahoo! News, May 6. http://story.news.yahoo.com/news?tmpl=story&u=/nm/20020506/hl_nm/birthcontrol_rape_1 (accessed June 12, 2003).

STENSON, J. 2003. Secret to romantic intimacy: Skip the nagging. Reuters News, Feb. 13. http://reuters.com/newsArticle.jhtml?type=healthNews&storyID=2224935 (accessed Feb. 14, 2003).

STEPP, L. S. 2003. Sex in high school and college: What's love got to do with it? *Washington Post,* Jan. 19, F1.

STERK-ELIFSON, C. 1994. Sexuality among African-American women. In *Sexuality across the life course,* ed. A. S. Rossi, 99–126. Chicago: University of Chicago Press.

STERNBERG, R. J. 1986. A triangular theory of love. *Psychological Review* 93 (2): 119–35.

STERNBERG, R. J. 1988. *The triangle of love.* New York: Basic Books.

STETS, J. E. 1993a. Control in dating relationships. *Journal of Marriage and the Family* 55 (Aug.): 673–85.

STETS, J. E. 1993b. The link between past and present intimate relationships. *Journal of Family Issues* 14 (June): 236–60.

STEVENS, D., G. KIGER, AND P. J. RILEY. 2001. Working hard and hardly working: Domestic labor and marital satisfaction among dual-earner couples. *Journal of Marriage and Family* 63 (May): 514–26.

STEVENS, G. V. 1997. A retreat on children's well-being. *Christian Science Monitor,* Aug. 22, 18.

STEWART, A. J., A. P. COPELAND, N. L. CHESTER, J. E. MALLEY, AND N. B. BARENBAUM. 1997. *Separating together: How divorce transforms families.* New York: Guilford.

STEWART, S. D. 1999. Nonresident mothers' and fathers' social contact with children. *Journal of Marriage and the Family* 61 (Nov.): 894–907.

STEWART, S. D. 2003. Nonresident parenting and adolescent adjustment. *Journal of Family Issues* 24 (Mar.): 217–44.

STIEHM, J. 1997. Marriage long-distance style. *Baltimore Sun,* July 7, 1A, 6A.

STILLARS, A. L. 1991. Behavioral observation. In *Studying interpersonal interaction,* eds. B. M.

Montgomery and S. Duck, 197–218. New York: Guilford.

STINNETT, N., AND J. DEFRAIN. 1985. *Secrets of strong families.* Boston: Little, Brown.

STOCKEL, H. H. 1991. *Women of the Apache nation.* Reno: University of Nevada Press.

STODDART, T., AND E. TURIEL. 1985. Housework: It isn't going to go away. *Philadelphia Inquirer*, Sep. 1, 11, 14.

STOLBA, A., AND P. R. AMATO. 1993. Extended single-parent households and children's behavior. *Sociological Quarterly* 34 (3): 543–49.

STOLLEY, K. S., AND A. E. HILL. 1996. Presentations of the elderly in textbooks on marriage and family. *Teaching Sociology* 24 (Jan.): 34–45.

STOLZENBERG, R. M. 2001. It's about time and gender: Spousal employment and health. *American Journal of Sociology* 107 (July): 61–100.

STONE, B. 2001. Love online. *Newsweek*, Feb. 19, 46–51.

STONE, L., AND N. P. McKEE. 2002. *Gender and culture in America,* 2nd ed. Upper Saddle River, NJ: Prentice Hall.

STONE, R., AND C. WASZAK. 1992. Adolescent knowledge and attitudes about abortion. *Family Planning Perspectives* 24 (Mar./Apr.): 52–57.

STRAIT, S. C. 1999. Drug use among Hispanic youth: Examining common and unique contributing factors. *Hispanic Journal of Behavioral Sciences* 21 (Feb.): 89–103.

STRASBURGER, V. C. AND B. J. WILSON. 2002. *Children, adolescents, & the media.* Thousand Oaks, CA: Sage.

STRATTON, J. L. 1981. *Pioneer women: Voices from the Kansas frontier.* New York: Simon & Schuster.

STRAUS, M. A. 1993. Identifying offenders in criminal justice research on domestic assault. *American Behavioral Scientist* 36 (May): 587–600.

STRAUS, M. A., ED. 2001. *Beating the devil out of them: Corporal punishment in American families and its effects on children,* 2nd ed. Somerset, NJ: Transaction Publishers.

STRAUS, M. A., AND C. FIELD. 2000. Psychological aggression by American parents: National data on prevalence, chronicity, and severity. Paper presented at the meeting of the American Sociological Association, Washington, DC, Aug. 15. www.unh.edu/frl/cts27G1.pdf (accessed Sep. 24, 2000).

STRAUS, M. A., AND J. H. STEWART. 1999. Corporal punishment by American parents: National data on prevalence, chronicity, severity, and duration, in relation to child and family characteristics. *Clinical Child and Family Psychology Review* 2 (June): 55–70.

STRAUS, M. A., AND C. L. YODANIS. 1996. Corporal punishment in adolescence and physical assaults on spouses in later life: What accounts for the link? *Journal of Marriage and the Family* 58 (Nov.): 825–41.

STRAUSS, G. 2002. Good old boys' network still rules corporate boards. *USA Today.* http://story.news. yahoo.com/news?tmpl=story&u=/usatoday/20021101/bs_usatoday/4585244 (accessed Nov. 2, 2002).

STRAW, G., L. O'CONNOR, AND D. GANN. 1999. The AARP grandparenting survey: The sharing and caring between mature grandparents and their children. American Association of Retired Persons. research.aarp.org/general/grandpsurv.pdf (accessed Oct. 28, 2000).

Strict new rules help pare recipients from welfare rolls. 1999. *Baltimore Sun*, Mar. 29, 7A.

STRIEGEL-MOORE, R. H., ET AL. 2003. Eating disorders in white and black women. *American Journal of Psychiatry* 160 (July): 1326–31.

STROCK, M. 2002. Depression. National Institutes of Mental Health. www.nimh.nih.gov/publicat/depression.pdf (accessed Oct. 9, 2003).

STROUP, A. L., AND G. E. POLLOCK. 1999. Economic consequences of marital dissolution for Hispanics. *Journal of Divorce & Remarriage* 30 (1/2): 149–66.

STRUPP, J. 2002. Study: Fewer women hold top editor jobs. Associated Press, Sep. 18. www.editorandpublisher.com/editorandpublisher/headlines/article_display.jsp?vnu_content_id=1695560 (accessed Sep. 20, 2002).

SUGG, D. K. 2000. Subtle signs of heart disease in women are often missed. *Baltimore Sun*, Jan. 25, 1A, 13A.

SUGGS, W. 2001. Top jobs in college sports still go largely to white men, study finds. *Chronicle of Higher Education*, Aug. 3, A42.

Suicide and suicidal behavior. 2000. National Center for Injury Prevention and Control. www.cdc.gov/ncipc/pub-res/FactBook/suicide.htm (accessed Oct. 19, 2000).

SULLIVAN, A. D., K. HEDBERG, AND D. W. FLEMING. 2000. Legalized physician-assisted suicide in Oregon: The second year. *New England Journal of Medicine* 342 (Feb.): 598–604.

SUM, A., ET AL. 2002. Left behind in the labor market: Labor market problems of the nation's out-of-school, young adult populations. Prepared for Alternative Schools Network, Chicago. www.nupr.neu.edu/2-03/left_behind.PDF (accessed Sep. 8, 2003).

SUM, A., N. FOGG, AND P. HARRINGTON. 2002. Immigrant workers and the great American job machine: The contributions of new foreign immigration to national and regional labor force growth in the 1990s. Prepared for National Business Roundtable, Washington, DC. www.nupr.neu.edu/12-02/immigration_BRT.PDF (accessed Apr. 12, 2003).

Summary of recent studies on the wage gap between men and women professors. 2000. American Association of University Professors, Washington, DC. www.aaup.org/wstudy.htm (accessed Oct. 15, 2000).

SUN, Y. 2001. Family environment and adolescents' well-being before and after parents' marital disruption: A longitudinal analysis. *Journal of Marriage and Family* 63 (Aug.): 697–713.

SUN, Y., AND Y. LI. 2002. Children's well-being during parents' marital disruption process: A pooled time-series analysis. *Journal of Marriage and Family* 64 (May): 472–88.

SURO, M. D. 1997. Child-friendly divorce: Counselors try to keep kids together when families fall apart. *Washington Post Health Supplement*, Aug. 26, 10–12, 15.

SURO, R. 1994. Study of immigrants finds Asians at top in science and medicine. *Washington Post*, Apr. 18, A6.

SURO, R. 1998. *Strangers among us: How Latino immigration is transforming America.* New York: Knopf.

SUTTON, C. T., AND M. A. BROKEN NOSE. 1996. American Indian families: An overview. In *Ethnicity and family therapy*, 2nd ed., eds. M. McGoldrick, J. Giordano, and J. K. Pearce, 31–54. New York: Guilford.

SUTTON, P. D. 2003. Births, marriages, divorces, and deaths: Provisional data for January 2003. *National Vital Statistics Reports* 52 (Sep.): 1–3.

SWAIN, S. O. 1992. Men's friendships with women: Intimacy, sexual boundaries, and the informant role. In *Men's friendships*, ed. P. M. Nardi, 153–72. Thousand Oaks, CA: Sage.

SWAN, S. H., E. P. ELKIN, AND L. FENSTER. 1997. Have sperm densities declined? A reanalysis of global trend data. *Environmental Health Perspectives* 105 (Nov.): 1228–33.

SWANBERG, J. E., AND T. K. LOGAN. 2003. Intimate partner violence and employment: A qualitative study of rural and urban women. *Family Focus* (Mar.): F8-F9.

SWEDLUND, A. C. 1993. Review of *Anatomy of love: The natural history of monogamy, adultery, and divorce* by H. E. Fisher (New York: Norton, 1992). *American Anthropologist* 95 (Dec.): 1053–54.

SWIFT, E. K., ED. 2002. *Mental health: Culture, race, and ethnicity. A supplement to mental health: A report of the surgeon general.* Rockville, MD: U.S. Department of Health and Human Services.

SWINFORD, S. P., A. DEMARIS, S. A. CERNKOVICH, AND P. G. GIORDANO. 2000. Harsh physical discipline in childhood and violence in later romantic involvements: The mediating role of problem behaviors. *Journal of Marriage and the Family* 62 (May): 508–19.

SZABÓ, X. P., AND M. J. T. BLANCHE. 1997. Perfectionism in anorexia nervosa. *American Journal of Psychiatry* 154 (Jan.): 132.

SZEGEDY-MASZAK, M. 1993. Dating passages. *New Woman* 23 (Mar.): 85–88.

SZINOVACZ, M. E., ED. 1998. *Handbook on grandparenthood.* Westport, CT: Greenwood.

SZYMANSKI, L. A., A. S. DEVLIN, J. C. CHRISLER, AND S. A. VYSE. 1993. Gender role and attitudes toward rape in male and female college students. *Sex Roles* 29 (1/2): 37–57.

Taboo no more: Workplace romances. 2000. *Christian Science Monitor*, Feb. 14, 14.

TAKAGI, D. Y. 2002. Japanese American families. In *Minority families in the United States: A multicultural perspective*, 3rd ed., ed. R. L. Taylor, 164–80. Upper Saddle River, NJ: Prentice Hall.

TALVI, S. J. A. 2002. "Deadbeat" dads—or just "dead broke"? *Christian Science Monitor*, Feb. 4, 20.

TAM, V. C.-W., AND D. F. DETZNER. 1998. Grandparents as a family resource in Chinese-American families: Perceptions of the middle generation. In *Resiliency in Native American and immigrant families*, eds. H. I. McCubbin, E. A. Thompson, A. I. Thompson, and J. E. Fromer, 243–64. Thousand Oaks, CA: Sage.

TAMARACK, L. I. 1986. Fifty myths and facts about incest. In *Sexual abuse of children in the 1980s: Ten essays and an annotated bibliography*, ed. B. Schlesinger. Buffalo, NY: University of Toronto Press.

TAN, C. L.-L. 2002. With Asian eyes, the crease is the crux of the matter. *Baltimore Sun*, June 23, 1N, 9N.

TANAKA, J. 1997. There's no place like home, unless it's the office. *Newsweek*, July 7, 14.

TANNEN, D. 1990. *You just don't understand: Women and men in conversation.* New York: Ballantine.

TANNEN, D. 1994. *Talking 9 to 5: Women and men at work.* New York: Quill.

TANNER, R. 2002. Security for battered women studied. Yahoo! News, Aug. 6. http://story.news.yahoo.com/news?tmpl=story2&cid=534&ncid=534&e=10&u=/ap/20020806/ap_on_re_us/protection_orders_1 (accessed Aug. 8, 2002).

TANNER, R. 2003. Fewer women are in state legislatures. Associated Press, Jan. 30. http://story.news.yahoo.com/news?tmpl=story&u=/ap/20030130/ap_on_re_us/women_in_office_1 (accessed Feb. 1, 2003).

TANUR, J. M. 1994. The trustworthiness of survey research. *Chronicle of Higher Education*, May 25, B1–B3.

TARMANN, A. 2002. International adoptions. *Population Bulletin* 57 (Dec.): 22–23. Washington, DC: Population Reference Bureau.

TATARA, T. 1998. *The national elder abuse incidence study.* The National Center on Elder Abuse and the American Public Humane Services Association. www.aoa.gov/abuse/report/main-pdf.htm (accessed Oct. 19, 2000).

TAVRIS, C. 1992. *The mismeasure of woman.* New York: Simon & Schuster.

TAVRIS, C. 2002. Are girls really as mean as books say they are? *Chronicle of Higher Education*, July 5, B7–B9.

TAVRIS, C. 2003. Mind games: Psychological warfare between therapists and scientists. *Chronicle of Higher Education*, Feb. 28, B7–B9.

TAYLOR, R. L. 2002. Minority families and social change. In *Minority families in the United States: A multicultural perspective*, 3rd ed., ed. R. L. Taylor, 252–300. Upper Saddle River, NJ: Prentice Hall.

TEACHMAN, J. D. 1991. Contributions to children by divorced fathers. *Social Problems* 38 (Aug.): 358–70.

TEACHMAN, J. D. 2002. Childhood living arrangements and the intergenerational transmission of divorce. *Journal of Marriage and Family* 64 (Aug.): 717–29.

TEACHMAN, J. D., K. PAASCH, AND K. CARVER. 1996. Social capital and dropping out of school early. *Journal of Marriage and the Family* 58 (Aug.): 773–83.

TEACHMAN, J. D., L. M. TEDROW, AND K. D. CROWDER. 2001. The changing demography of America's families. In *Understanding families into the new millennium: A decade in review*, ed.

R. M. Milardo, 453–65. Minneapolis: National Council on Family Relations.

TEACHMAN, J. D., J. THOMAS, AND K. PAASCH. 1991. Legal status and the stability of coresidential unions. *Demography* 26 (Nov.): 571–86.

TEFFT, S. 1995. A rush to rock the cradle—of girls. *Christian Science Monitor*, Aug. 2, 1, 8.

TENENBAUM, H. R., AND C. LEAPER. 2003. Parent–child conversations about science: The socialization of gender inequities? *Developmental Psychology* 39 (Jan.): 34–47.

TERESI, D. 1994. How to get a man pregnant. *New York Times Magazine*, Nov. 27, 54–55.

TERGESEN, A. 2001. Cutting the knot—but not the benefits. *Business Week,* July 16, 87–88.

TERGESEN, A. 2003. Take the boys. *Business Week,* Apr. 23, 105.

TERZIEFF, J. 2002. Pakistan's fiery shame: Women die in stove deaths. *Women's E-News,* Nov. 1. www.womensenews.org/article.cfm/dyn/aid/1085/context/cover (accessed Nov. 3, 2002).

TESORIERO, H. W. 2002. "Without this ring. . . ." *Time,* Mar. 16, F9–F10.

TESSIER, M. 2003. Sexual assault pervasive in military, experts say. *Women's E-News.* www. womensenews.org/article.cfm/dyn/aid/1273/context/cover, Apr. 5 (accessed Apr. 6, 2003).

The big picture. 2000. *Business Week,* Mar. 20, 10.

The color line—still. 2001. *U.S. News & World Report,* July 23, 15.

The great divide: Female leadership in U.S. newsrooms. 2002. American Press Institute and Pew Center for Civic Journalism. www. americanpressinstitute.org/curtis/Great_Divide. pdf (accessed May 18, 2003).

The marriage movement: A statement of principles. 2000. www.marriagemovement.org/html/report.html (accessed Aug. 2, 2000).

The ties that bind. 2000. *Public Perspective* 11 (May/June): 10.

The world's women 2000: Trends and statistics. 2000. New York: United Nations.

THOMAS, A. J., AND S. L. SPEIGHT. 1999. Racial identity and racial socialization attitudes of African American parents. *Journal of Black Psychology* 25 (May): 152–70.

THOMAS, E. 2003. The war over gay marriage. *Newsweek,* July 7, 30–31, 40–43.

THOMAS, J. L. 1994. Older men as fathers and grandfathers. In *Older men's lives,* ed. E. H. Thompson, Jr., 197–217. Thousand Oaks, CA: Sage.

THOMAS, W. I., AND F. ZNANIECKI. 1927. *The Polish peasant in Europe and America,* vol. 2. New York: Knopf. (Originally published 1918 by the University of Chicago Press.)

THOMAS-LESTER, A. 1994. Carrying on: A joyless time for the grieving. *Washington Post,* Dec. 15, D5.

THOMPSON, L., AND A. J. WALKER. 1991. Gender in families. In *Contemporary families: Looking forward, looking back,* ed. A. Booth, 76–102. Minneapolis: National Council on Family Relations.

THOMPSON, P. M., ET AL. 2003. Dynamics of gray matter loss in Alzheimer's disease. *Journal of Neuroscience* 23 (Feb. 1): 994–1005.

THOMSON, E. 1997. Couple childbearing desires, intentions, and births. *Demography* 34 (Aug.): 343–54.

THORNBERRY, T. P., C. A. SMITH, C. RIVERA, D. HUIZINGA, AND M. STOUTHAMER-LOEBER. 1999. *Family disruption and delinquency.* Washington, DC: U.S. Department of Justice, Office of Justice Programs, Office of Juvenile Justice and Delinquency Prevention.

THORNTON, A. 2001. The developmental paradigm, reading history sideways, and family change. *Demography* 38 (Nov.): 449–65.

THORNTON, A., AND W. RODGERS. 1987. The influence of individual and historical time on marital dissolution. *Demography* 24 (Feb.): 1–22.

THORNTON, A., AND L. YOUNG-DEMARCO. 2001. Four decades in attitudes toward family issues in the United States: The 1960s through the 1990s. *Journal of Marriage and the Family* 63 (Nov.): 1009–37.

THORNTON, E. 1994. Video dating in Japan. *Fortune,* Jan. 24, 12.

THORNTON, J., AND D. WHITMAN WITH D. FREEDMAN. 1992. Whites' myths about blacks. *U.S. News & World Report,* Nov. 9, 41–44.

TICHENOR, V. J. 1999. Status and income as gendered resources: The case of marital power. *Journal of Marriage and the Family* 61 (Aug.): 638–60.

TIGER, L. 1999. *The decline of males.* New York: Golden Books.

TILLY, J., S. GOLDENSON, AND J. KASTEN. 2001. *Long-term care: Consumers, providers, and financing: A chart book.* Urban Institute. www.urban. org/pdfs/LTC_Chartbook.pdf (accessed Oct. 11, 2003).

TIMMER, S. G., AND T. L. ORBUCH. 2001. The links between premarital parenthood, meanings of marriage, and marital outcomes. *Family Relations* 50 (Apr.): 178–85.

TJADEN, P., AND N. THOENNES. 2000a. *Extent, nature, and consequences of intimate partner violence: Findings from the National Violence against Women Survey.* Washington, DC: U.S. Department of Justice, Office of Justice Programs.

TJADEN, P., AND N. THOENNES. 2000b. Prevalence and consequences of male-to-female and female-to-male intimate partner violence as measured by the National Violence against Women Survey. *Violence against Women* 6 (Feb.): 142–61.

TJADEN, P., N. THOENNES, AND C. J. ALLISON. 1999. Comparing violence over the life span in samples of same-sex and opposite-sex cohabitants. *Violence and Victims* 14 (Winter): 413–25.

TOHID, O. 2003. Pakistanis abroad trick daughters into marriage. *Christian Science Monitor,* May 15, 1, 7.

TOLIVER, S. D. 1998. *Black families in corporate America.* Thousand Oaks, CA: Sage.

TORO-MORN, M. I. 1998. The family and work experiences of Puerto Rican women migrants in Chicago. In *Resiliency in Native American and immigrant families,* eds. H. I. McCubbin, E. A. Thompson, A. I. Thompson, and J. E. Fromer, 277–94. Thousand Oaks, CA: Sage.

TOSA, M. 1998. *Barbie: Four decades of fashion, fantasy, and fun.* New York: Abrams.

TOTH, J. F., JR., AND X. XU. 1999. Ethnic and cultural diversity in fathers' involvement: A racial/ethnic comparison of African American, Hispanic, and white fathers. *Youth & Society* 31 (Sep.): 76–99.

TOTH, J. F., AND X. XU. 2002. Fathers' child-rearing involvement in African American, Latino, and white families. In *Contemporary ethnic families in the United States: Characteristics, variations, and dynamics,* ed. N. V. Benokraitis, 130–40. Upper Saddle River, NJ: Prentice Hall.

TOUSIGNANT, M. 1994. Bogged down in Bucharest. *Washington Post,* Oct. 26, B1, B5.

TOWER, R. B., S. V. KASL, AND A. S. DAREFSKY. 2002. Types of marital closeness and mortality risk in older couples. *Psychosomatic Medicine* 64: 644–59.

TOWNSEND, N. 2002. *Marriage, work, and fatherhood in men's lives.* New Brunswick, NJ: Rutgers University Press.

Traditional families account for only 7 percent of U.S. households. 2003. Population Reference Bureau. www.prb.org (accessed July 11, 2003).

TRAFFORD, A. 1997. Getting tough on divorce not the same as getting real. *Washington Post Health Supplement,* Aug. 26, 6.

TRAVIS, R., AND V. KOHLI. 1995. The birth order factor: Ordinal position, social strata, and educational achievement. *Journal of Social Psychology* 135 (Aug.): 499–508.

TREAS, J., AND D. GIESEN. 2000. Sexual infidelity among married and cohabiting Americans. *Journal of Marriage and the Family* 62 (Feb.): 48–60.

TRENT, K. 1994. Family context and adolescents' expectations about marriage, fertility, and nonmarital childbearing. *Social Science Quarterly* 75 (June): 319–39.

TRIMBLE, J. E., AND B. MEDICINE. 1993. Diversification of American Indians: Forming an indigenous perspective. In *Indigenous psychologies,* eds. U. Kim and J. W. Berry, 133–51. Newbury Park, CA: Sage.

TROTTER, R. J. 1986. Failing to find the father-infant bond. *Psychology Today* (Feb.): 18.

TRUMBULL, D. A., AND D. RAVENEL. 1999. Spare the rod? New research challenges spanking critic. *Family Policy,* Family Research Council, Jan. 22.

TRUMBULL, M. 1995. Demographics, computers multiply Asian-language media in the U.S. *Christian Science Monitor,* July 24, 13.

TSAI, D. T., AND R. A. LOPEZ. 1997. The use of social supports by elderly Chinese immigrants. *Journal of Gerontological Social Work* 29 (1): 77–94.

TSAI, G., AND J. GRAY. 2000. The eating disorders inventory among Asian American college women. *Journal of Social Psychology* 140 (Aug.): 527–29.

TSAI, J. L., D. E. PRZYMUS, AND J. L. BEST. 2002. Toward an understanding of Asian American interracial marriage and dating. In *Inside the American couple: New thinking/new challenges,* eds. M. Yalom and L. L. Carstensen, 189–210. Berkeley: University of California Press.

TUCKER, M. B., R. J. TAYLOR, AND C. MITCHELL-KERNAN. 1993. Marriage and romantic involvement among aged African Americans. *Journal of Gerontology: Social Sciences* 48 (3): S128–32.

TUCKER, R. K. 1992. Men's and women's ranking of thirteen acts of romance. *Psychological Reports* 71: 640–42.

TURCOTTE, P., AND A. BÉLANGER. 1997. *The dynamics of formation and dissolution of first common-law unions in Canada.* Ottawa: Statistics Canada.

TURNBULL, S. K., AND J. M. TURNBULL. 1983. To dream the impossible dream: An agenda for discussion with stepparents. *Family Relations* 32: 227–30.

TURNER, M. A., S. L. ROSS, G. C. GALSTER, AND J. YINGER. 2002. *Discrimination in metropolitan housing markets: National results from Phase I HDS 2000.* The Urban Institute. www. huduser.org/Publications/pdf/Phase1_Report. pdf (accessed Apr. 6, 2003).

TUROW, J., AND L. NIR. 2000. *The Internet and the family 2000: The view from parents, the view from kids.* Annenberg Public Policy Center, University of Pennsylvania. http://appcpenn.org/finalrepor_fam.pdf (accessed Aug. 13, 2000).

TUTTLE, W. M., JR. 1993. *Daddy's gone to war: The Second World War in the lives of America's children.* New York: Oxford University Press.

TWENGE, J., AND W. CAMPBELL. 2003. "Isn't it fun to get the respect that we're going to deserve?" Narcissism, social rejection, and aggression. *Personality and Social Psychology Bulletin* 29 (2): 261–72.

TWENGE, J. M., W. K. CAMPBELL, AND C. A. FOSTER. 2003. Parenthood and marital satisfaction: A meta-analytic review. *Journal of Marriage and Family* 65 (Aug.): 574–83.

2000 Assisted reproductive technology success rates: National summary and fertility clinic reports. 2002. Centers for Disease Control and Prevention. www.cdc.gov/nccdphp/drh/ART00/PDF's/ART2000.pdf (accessed Aug. 2, 2003).

TYLER, T. R., AND R. A. SCHULLER. 1991. Aging and attitude change. *Journal of Personality and Social Psychology* 61 (5): 689–97.

TYRE, P. 2003. Divorce: From bad to worse. *Newsweek,* July 21, 49–50.

TYRE, P., AND D. MCGINN. 2003. She works, he doesn't. *Newsweek,* May 12, 45–52.

Tyson Foods goes to trial in hiring case. 2003. *Washington Post,* Feb. 6, 9A.

TYSZKOWA, M. 1993. Adolescents' relationships with grandparents: Characteristics and developmental transformations. In *Adolescence and its social worlds,* eds. S. Jackson and H. Rodriguez-Tomé, 121–43. East Sussex, UK: Erlbaum.

TZENG, O. C. S. 1993. *Measurement of love and intimate relations: Theories, scales, and applications for love development, maintenance, and dissolution.* Westport, CT: Praeger.

U.S. CENSUS BUREAU. 1997. Money income in the United States: 1996 (with separate data on valuation of noncash benefits). Current Population Reports, P60-197. Washington, DC: U.S. Government Printing Office.

U.S. CENSUS BUREAU. 1999. *Statistical abstract of the United States, 1999,* 119th ed. Washington, DC: U.S. Government Printing Office.

U.S. CENSUS BUREAU. 2001. Households by type and size. Current Population Survey. www.census.gov/population/socdemo/race/api/ppl-146/tab05.pdf (accessed Apr. 22, 2003).

U.S. CENSUS BUREAU. 2002. *Statistical abstract of the United States: 2002.* Washington, DC: U.S. Government Printing Office.

U.S. CENSUS BUREAU. 2003. Detailed list of languages spoken at home for the population 5 years and over by state: 2000. www.census.gov/population/cen2000/phc-t20/tab05.pdf (accessed Apr. 22, 2003).

U.S. COMMISSION ON CIVIL RIGHTS. 1984. *Comparable worth: Issues for the '80s,* Vol. 1. Washington, DC: U.S. Government Printing Office.

U.S. CONSUMER PRODUCT SAFETY COMMISSION. 2001. *Home playground equipment–related deaths and injuries.* Washington, DC. www.cpsc.gov/library/playground.pdf (accessed Aug. 27, 2003).

U.S. DEPARTMENT OF EDUCATION. 2002. Degrees and other formal awards conferred. National Center for Education Statistics. http://nces.ed.gov/pubs2003/2003060c.pdf (accessed July 5, 2003).

U.S. DEPARTMENT OF HEALTH AND HUMAN SERVICES. 1996. *National Center on Child Abuse and Neglect. Third national incidence study of child abuse and neglect: Final report (NIS-3).* Washington, DC: U.S. Government Printing Office.

U.S. DEPARTMENT OF HEALTH AND HUMAN SERVICES. 1997. *National Center on Child Abuse and Neglect. Child maltreatment 1995: Reports from the states to the National Child Abuse and Neglect Data System.* Washington, DC: U.S. Government Printing Office.

U.S. DEPARTMENT OF HEALTH AND HUMAN SERVICES. 2000. *Child maltreatment 1998: Reports from the states to the National Child Abuse and Neglect Data System.* Washington, DC: U.S. Government Printing Office.

U.S. DEPARTMENT OF HEALTH AND HUMAN SERVICES. 2003a. Child maltreatment: 2001. www.acf.hhs.gov/programs/cb/publications/cm01/cm01.pdf (accessed Sep. 14, 2003).

U.S. DEPARTMENT OF HEALTH AND HUMAN SERVICES. 2003b. Overview of findings from the 2002 National Survey on Drug Use and Health. www.samhsa.gov/oas/NHSDA/2k2NSDUH/2k2SoFOverviewW.pdf (accessed Sep. 21, 2003).

U.S. DEPARTMENT OF JUSTICE. 2001. Crime in the United States, 2000. FBI National Press Office. www.fbi.gov/pressrel/pressrel01/cius2000.htm (accessed May 11, 2003).

U.S. DEPARTMENT OF JUSTICE. 2001. *Stalking and domestic violence: Report to Congress.* Washington, DC: Government Printing Office.

U.S. DEPARTMENT OF LABOR. 2000. The employment situation: September 2000. www.bls.gov/news.release/pdf/empsit.pdf (accessed Oct. 16, 2000).

U.S. SENATE SPECIAL COMMITTEE ON AGING, AMERICAN ASSOCIATION OF RETIRED PERSONS, FEDERAL COUNCIL ON THE AGING, AND U.S. ADMINISTRATION ON AGING. 1991. *Aging America: Trends and projections, 1991.* Washington, DC: Department of Health and Human Services.

UCHITELLE, L. 2003. Blacks lose better jobs faster as middle-class work drops. *New York Times,* July 12. www.nytimes.com/2003/07/12/business/12RACE.html?th (accessed July 13, 2003).

UDRY, J. R. 1993. The politics of sex research. *Journal of Sex Research* 30 (May): 103–10.

UHLENBERG, P., AND J. B. KIRBY. 1998. Grandparenthood over time: Historical and demographic trends. In *Handbook on grandparenthood,* ed. M. Szinovacz, 23–39. Westport, CT: Greenwood.

UMAÑA-TAYLOR, A. J., AND M. A. FINE. 2003. Predicting commitment to wed among Hispanic and Anglo partners. *Journal of Marriage and Family* 65 (Feb.): 117–39.

UMBERSON, D., K. L. ANDERSON, K. WILLIAMS, AND M. D. CHEN. 2003. Relationship dynamics, emotion state, and domestic violence: A stress and masculinities perspective. *Journal of Marriage and Family* 65 (Feb.): 233–47.

UMBERSON, D., AND C. L. WILLIAMS. 1993. Divorced fathers: Parental role strain and psychological distress. *Journal of Family Issues* 14 (Sep.): 378–400.

Underage drinkers at higher risk of brain damage than adults, American Medical Association report reveals. 2002. American Medical Association. www.alcoholpolicysolutions.net/pdf/RUDC_dec_nr.pdf (accessed Sep. 17, 2003).

UNDERWOOD, R. C., AND P. C. PATCH. 1999. Siblicide: A descriptive analysis of sibling homicide. *Homicide Studies* 3 (Nov.): 333–48.

UNITED NATIONS. 2002. *International migration report 2002.* www.un.org/esa/population/publications/ittmig2002/2002ITTMIGTEXT22-11.pdf (accessed Apr. 15, 2003).

UNIVERSAL LIVING WAGE. 2002. Clearing the air: Myths and concerns. www.universallivingwage.org (accessed Sep. 9, 2003).

UPCHURCH, D. M., C. S. ANESHENSEL, J. MUDGAL, AND C. S. NCNEELY. 2001. Sociocultural contexts of time to first sex among Hispanic adolescents. *Journal of Marriage and Family* 63 (Nov.): 1158–69.

UPCHURCH, D. M., L. A. LILLARD, AND C. W. A. PANIS. 2001. The impact of nonmarital childbearing on subsequent marital formation and dissolution. In *Out of wedlock: Causes and consequences of nonmarital fertility,* eds. L. L. Wu and B. Wolfe, 344–80. New York: Russell Sage Foundation.

UPCHURCH, M., C. S. ANESHENSEL, C. A. SUCOFF, AND L. LEVY-STORMS. 1999. Neighborhood and family contexts of adolescent sexual activity. *Journal of Marriage and the Family* 61 (Nov.): 920–33.

UPDEGRAFF, K. A., S. M. MCHALE, A. C. CROUTER, AND K. KUPANOFF. 2001. Parents' involvement in adolescents' peer relationships: A comparison of mothers' and fathers' roles. *Journal of Marriage and Family* 63 (Aug.): 655–68.

UTTAL, L. 1999. Using kin for child care: Embedment in the socioeconomic networks of extended families. *Journal of Marriage and the Family* 61 (Nov.): 845–57.

VACCARINO, V., ET AL. 2002. Sex differences in hospital mortality after coronary artery bypass surgery: Evidence for a higher mortality in younger women. *Circulation* 105 (Feb. 18): 1176–81.

VAKILI, B., ET AL. 2002. Sex-based differences in early mortality of patients undergoing angioplasty for first acute myocardial infarction. *Circulation* 104 (Dec. 18): 3034–38.

VALDEZ, E. O., AND S. COLTRANE. 1993. Work, family, and the Chicana: Power, perception, and equity. In *The employed mother and the family context,* ed. J. Frankel, 153–79. New York: Springer.

Valentine's a "worthless" day? 2002. Reuters News, Feb. 14. http://story.news.yahoo.com/news?tmpl=story&u=/nm/20020214/od_nm/saudi_dc_1 (accessed Feb. 15, 2002).

Valentine's day story. 2003. Agence France Presse, Feb. 13. http://ippfnet.ippf.org/pub/IPPF_News/News_Details.asp?ID=2615 (accessed Feb. 15, 2003).

VALENZUELA, A., JR. 2000. Working on the margins: Immigrant day labor characteristics and prospects of employment. www.weingart.org/institute/research/colloquia/pdf/DayLaborerStudy.pdf (accessed Apr. 20, 2003).

VAN BAARSEN, B., AND M. I. B. VAN GROENOU. 2001. Partner loss in later life: Gender differences in coping shortly after bereavement. *Journal of Loss and Trauma* 6: 243–62.

VAN BIEMA, D. 1997. Sparse at seder? *Time,* Apr. 26, 67.

VAN DER WERF, M. 2001. How much should colleges pay their janitors? *Chronicle of Higher Education,* Aug. 3, A27–A28.

VANCE, E. B., AND N. N. WAGNER. 1976. Written descriptions of orgasm: A study of sex differences. *Archives of Sexual Behavior* 5: 87–98.

VANDELL, D. L., K. MCCARTNEY, M. T. OWEN, C. BOOTH, AND A. CLARKE-STEWART. 2003. Variations in child care by grandparents during the first three years. *Journal of Marriage and Family* 65 (May): 375–81.

VANDELLO, J. A., AND D. COHEN. 2003. Male honor and female fidelity: Implicit cultural scripts that perpetuate domestic violence. *Journal of Personality and Social Psychology* 84 (May): 997–1010.

VANDERPOOL, T. 1999. Retirement communities for the PhD set. *Christian Science Monitor,* Nov. 22, 3.

VANDERPOOL, T. 2002. Tribes move beyond casinos to malls and concert halls. *Christian Science Monitor,* Oct. 22, 2–3.

VANDEWATER, E. A., AND J. E. LANSFORD. 1998. Influences of family structure and parental conflict on children's well-being. *Family Relations* 47 (Oct.): 233–330.

VANDIVERE, S., K. TOUT, J. CAPIZZANO, AND M. ZASLOW. 2003. *Left unsupervised: A look at the most vulnerable children.* Washington, DC: Child Trends. www.childtrends.org/PDF/UnsupervisedRB.pdf (accessed Aug. 23, 2003).

VARTANIAN, T. P., AND J. M. MCNAMARA. 2002. Older women in poverty: The impact of midlife factors. *Journal of Marriage and Family* 64 (May): 532–48.

VEATCH, R. M. 1995. Death and dying. In *Ethics applied,* ed. M. L. Richardson and K. K. White, 215–43. New York: McGraw-Hill.

VEEVERS, J. 1980. *Childless by choice.* Toronto: Butterworth.

VEGA, W. A. 1995. The study of Latino families: A point of departure. In *Understanding Latino families: Scholarship, policy, and practice,* ed. R. E. Zambrana, 3–17. Thousand Oaks, CA: Sage.

VEMER, E., M. COLEMAN, L. H. GANONG, AND H. COOPER. 1989. Marital satisfaction in remarriage: A meta-analysis. *Journal of Marriage and the Family* 51 (Aug.): 713–25.

VENEMA, S. 2003. Gay wedding announcements a growing trend. *Women's E-News,* Jan. 5. www.womensenews.org/article.cfm/dyn/aid/1170/context/cover (accessed Jan. 11, 2003).

VENTURA, S. J., C. A. BACHRACH, L. HILL, K. KAYE, P. HOLCOMB, AND E. KOFF. 1995. The demography of out-of-wedlock childbearing. In *Report to Congress on out-of-wedlock childbearing,* v–xxii. Hyattsville, MD: Centers for Disease Control and Prevention, National Center for Health Statistics.

VENTURA, S. J., S. C. CURTIN, AND T. J. MATHEWS. 2000. Variations in teenage birth rates, 1991–98: National and state trends. *National Vital Statistical Reports* 48, Apr. 24, Centers for Disease Control and Prevention. www.cdc.gov/nchs/data/nvs48_6.pdf (accessed Sep. 22, 2000).

VENTURA, S. J., B. E. HAMILTON, AND P. D. SUTTON. 2003. Revised birth and fertility rates for the United States, 2000 and 2001. *National Vital Statistics Reports* 51 (Feb.): 1–29. www.cdc.gov/nchs/data/nvsr/nvsr51/nvsr51_04.pdf (accessed Sep. 4, 2003).

VENTURA, S. J., J. A. MARTIN, S. C. CURTIN, T. J. MATHEWS, AND M. M. PARK. 2000. Births: final data for 1998. *National Vital Statistics Reports* 48, Mar. 28, Centers for Disease Control and Prevention. www.cdc.gov/nchs/data/nvs48_3.pdf (accessed Sep. 22, 2000).

VENTURA, S. J., K. D. PETERS, J. A. MARTIN, AND J. D. MAURER. 1997. Births and deaths: United States, 1996. *Monthly Vital Statistics Report* 46 (1), Suppl. 2. Hyattsville, MD: National Center for Health Statistics.

VERGHESE, J., ET AL. 2003. Leisure activities and the risk of dementia in the elderly. *New England Journal of Medicine* 348 (June 19): 2508–16.

VICK, K. 1998. Letter from Lagos: Abiola: A man of many parts and many wives, *Washington Post,* July 14, A9, A11.

VIDEON, T. M. 2002. The effects of parent–adolescent relationships and parental separation on adolescent well-being. *Journal of Marriage and Family* 64 (May): 489–503.

VINICK, B. H. 1997. Stepfamilies in later life: What happens to intergenerational relationships? Paper presented at the American Sociological Association Annual Meeting, Toronto.

VINICK, B. H. 2000. Sexuality among older couples: Perceptions of spouse and self. In *With this ring: Divorce, intimacy, and cohabitation from a multicultural perspective,* eds. R. R. Miller and S. L. Browning, 111–26. Stamford, CT: JAI.

VISHER, E., AND J. VISHER. 1982. *How to win as a stepfamily.* New York: Dembner.

VISHER, E. B., AND J. S. VISHER. 1988. *Old loyalties, new ties: Therapeutic strategies with stepfamilies.* New York: Brunner/Mazel.

VISHER, E. B., AND J. S. VISHER. 1993. Remarriage families and stepparenting. In *Normal family processes,* 2nd ed., ed. F. Walsh, 235–53. New York: Guilford.

VISHER, E. B., AND J. S. VISHER. 1996. *Therapy with stepfamilies.* New York: Brunner/Mazel.

VISSING, Y. 2002. *Women without children: Nurturing lives.* New Brunswick, NJ: Rutgers University Press.

VOGEL, S. 2003. U.S. awards lesbian 9/11 compensation for loss of partner. *Washington Post,* Jan. 23, B1.

VOGLER, C., AND J. PAHL. 1994. Money, power and inequality within marriage. *Sociological Review* 42 (May): 263–88.

VON HIPPEL, W., L. A. SILVER, AND M. E. LYNCH. 2000. Stereotyping against your will: The role of inhibitory ability in stereotyping and prejudice among the elderly. *Personality & Social Psychology Bulletin* 26 (May): 523–59.

VOSS, K. W. 2003. New anti-violence campaigns aim at boys, young men. *Women's E-News,* Feb. 28. www.womensenews.org/article.cfm/dyn/aid/1237 (accessed Mar. 3, 2003).

VOTRUBA-DRZAL, E. 2003. Income changes and cognitive stimulation in young children's home learning environments. *Journal of Marriage and Family* 65 (May): 341–55.

VUCHINICH, S. 1987. Starting and stopping spontaneous family conflicts. *Journal of Marriage and the Family* 49 (Aug.): 591–601.

VUCHINICH, S., E. M. HETHERINGTON, R. A. VUCHINICH, AND W. G. CLINGEMPEEL. 1991. Parent–child interaction and gender differences in early adolescents' adaptation to stepfamilies. *Developmental Psychology* 27 (4): 618–26.

WACHTER, K. W. 1997. Kinship resources for the elderly. *Philosophical Transactions: Biological Sciences* 352 (Dec. 29): 1811–17.

WADE, C., AND S. CIRESE. 1991. *Human sexuality,* 2nd ed. New York: Harcourt Brace Jovanovich.

WAGEMAAR, T. C., AND R. D. COATES. 1999. Race and children: The dynamics of early socialization. *Education* 120 (Winter): 220–36.

WAGNER, B. 1998. Who has abortions. *U.S. News & World Report,* Aug. 19, 8.

WAGNER, D. 2003. Firing pregnant workers a trend. *The Arizona Republic,* Jan. 24. www.tucsoncitizen.com/local/1_24_03eeoc.html (accessed Jan. 29, 2003).

WAITE, L. J., ED. 2000. *The ties that bind: Perspectives on marriage and cohabitation.* New York: Aldine de Gruyter.

WAITE, L. J., D. BROWNING, W. J. DOHERTY, M. GALLAGHER, Y. LUO, AND S. M. STANLEY. 2002. *Does divorce make people happy?* Findings from a study of unhappy marriages. Institute for American Values. www.americanvalues.org/UnhappyMarriages.pdf (accessed Sep. 24, 2003).

WAITE, L. J., AND M. GALLAGHER. 2000. *The case for marriage: Why married people are happier, healthier, and better off financially.* New York: Broadway.

WAITE, L. J., AND K. JOYNER. 2001. Emotional satisfaction and physical pleasure in sexual unions: Time horizon, sexual behavior, and sexual exclusivity. *Journal of Marriage and Family* 63 (Feb.): 247–64.

WAITE, L. J., AND L. A. LILLARD. 1991. Children and marital disruption. *American Journal of Sociology* 96 (Jan.): 930–53.

WAKIN, D. J. 2002. A count of U.S. Jews sees a dip; others demur. *New York Times,* Oct. 9, A20.

WALCZAK, L., ET AL. 2000. The politics of prosperity. *Business Week,* Aug. 7, 96–108.

WALDMAN, S., ET AL. 1994. Welfare booby traps. *Newsweek,* Dec. 12, 34–35.

WALKER, J. 1990. Genetic parents win custody of baby: California judge also denies surrogate mother visitation rights. *Washington Post,* Oct. 23, A4.

WALKER, L. 1978. Treatment alternatives for battered women. In *The victimization of women,* eds. J. R. Chapman and M. Gates, 143–74. Beverly Hills, CA: Sage.

WALKER, L. 2003. College classes on human sexuality face heightened scrutiny. *Christian Science Monitor,* July 22, 17.

WALKER, L. E. A. 2000. *The battered woman syndrome,* 2nd ed. New York: Springer.

WALKER, R. 1999. Canada rethinks its Medicare. *Christian Science Monitor,* Dec. 14, 1, 8.

WALKER, T. 1993. Chinese men embrace divorce. *World Press Review* 40 (Oct.): 48.

WALKER, W. D., R. C. ROWE, AND V. L. QUINSEY. 1993. Authoritarianism and sexual aggression. *Journal of Personality and Social Psychology* 65 (5): 1036–45.

WALLACE, H. 1996. *Family violence: Legal, medical, and social perspectives.* Boston: Allyn & Bacon.

WALLER, G. 2001. Family court system hurts mothers. *Women's E-News,* Sep. 7. www.womensenews.org/article.cfm/dyn/aid/641 (accessed Sep. 9, 2001).

WALLER, W. 1937. The rating and dating complex. *American Sociological Review* 2 (Oct.): 727–34.

WALLERSTEIN, J. S. 2003. Children of divorce: A society in search of policy. In *All our families: New policies for a new century,* 2nd ed., eds. M. A. Mason, A. Skolnick, and S. D. Sugarman, 66–95. New York: Oxford University Press.

WALLERSTEIN, J. S., J. M. LEWIS, AND S. BLAKESLEE. 2000. *The unexpected legacy of divorce: A 25 year landmark study.* New York: Hyperion.

WALSH, A. 1991. *The science of love: Understanding love and its effects on mind and body.* Buffalo, NY: Prometheus.

WALSH, F., ED. 1993. *Normal family processes,* 2nd ed. New York: Guilford.

WALSH, M. W. 2002. Number of women in upper ranks rises a bit. *New York Times,* Nov. 19. www.nytimes.com/2002/11/19/business/19WOME.html?tntemail0 (accessed Nov. 20, 2002).

WALSH, W. 2002. Spankers and nonspankers: Where they get information on spanking. *Family Relations* 51 (Jan.): 81–88.

WALSTER, E., E. BERSCHEID, AND G. W. WALSTER. 1973. New directions in equity research. *Journal of Personality and Social Psychology* 25 (2): 151–76.

WALTHER, A. N. 1991. *Divorce hangover.* New York: Pocket Books.

WALZER, S. 1998. *Thinking about the baby: Gender and transitions into parenthood.* Philadelphia: Temple University Press.

WANG, P. 1993. What every woman should know about stockbrokers. *Money* (June): 14–16.

Want ad proves a woman's worth is never done. 1997. Ann Landers column. *Baltimore Sun,* Sep. 20, 3D.

WARREN, E., AND A. W. TYAGI. 2003. *The two income trap: Why middle-class mothers & fathers are going broke.* New York: Basic Books.

WASSERMAN, G. A., ET AL. 2003. *Risk and protective factors of child delinquency.* Washington, DC: U.S. Department of Justice.

WATANABE, M. E. 2002. Scientist couples do the two-job shuffle. *The Scientist,* Apr. 1. www.the-scientist.com/yr2002/apr/prof1_020401.html (accessed Apr. 5, 2002).

WATKINS, G. 2002. Inuit ingenuity finds a warm reception. *Christian Science Monitor,* Oct. 2, 14.

WATKINS, M. L., S. A. RASMUSSEN, M. A. HONEIN, L. D. BOTTO, AND C. A. MOORE. 2003. Maternal obesity and risk for birth defects. *Pediatrics* 111 (May): 1152–58.

WATKINS, T. H. 1993. *The great depression: America in the 1930s.* New York: Little, Brown.

WATSON, J. A., AND S. A. KOBLINSKY. 1997. Strengths and needs of working-class African-American and Anglo-American grandparents. *International Journal of Aging and Human Development* 44 (2): 149–65.

WATSON, T., J. P. SHAPIRO, J. IMPOCO, AND T. M. ITO. 1996. Is there a "gay gene"? *U.S. News & World Report,* Nov. 13, 93–96.

WATTERS, E. 2001. The way we live now: In my tribe. *New York Times,* Oct. 14. www.nytimes.com/2001/10/14/magazine/14WWLN.html (accessed Oct. 14, 2001).

WEATHERFORD, D. 1986. *Foreign and female: Immigrant women in America, 1840–1930.* New York: Schocken.

WEBER, L., T. HANCOCK, AND E. HIGGINBOTHAM. 1997. Women, power, and mental health. In *Women's health: Complexities and differences,* eds. S. B. Ruzek, V. L. Olesen, and A. E. Clarke, 380–96. Columbus: Ohio State University Press.

WEBSDALE, N. 1999. *Understanding domestic homicide.* Boston: Northeastern University Press.

WEIBEL-ORLANDO, J. 1990. Grandparenting styles: Native American perspectives. In *The cultural context of aging,* ed. J. Sokolovsky, 109–25. Westport, CT: Greenwood.

WEIL, A. 2002. *Ten things everyone should know about welfare reform.* Minneapolis: National Council on Family Relations.

WEINER-DAVIS, M. 2003. *The sex-starved marriage: A couple's guide to boosting their marriage libido.* New York: Simon & Schuster.

WEIR, F. 2000. Adoptions stalled: Reform or red tape? *Christian Science Monitor,* June 16, 1, 8.

WEIR, F. 2002. East meets West on love's risky cyberhighway. *Christian Science Monitor,* June 11, 1, 7.

WEISS, C. H. 1998. *Evaluation research: Methods for assessing program effectiveness,* 2nd ed. Upper Saddle River, NJ: Prentice Hall.

WEISS, M. J. 2001. The new summer break. *American Demographics* 23 (Aug.): 49–55.

WEISS, M. J. 2003. Great expectations. *American Demographics* 25 (May): 27–35.

WEISS, R. 2000. Limited pay for egg donors advised. *Washington Post,* Aug. 4, A5.

WEISSMAN, R. X. 1999a. *Los niños* go shopping. *American Demographics* 21 (May): 37–39.

WEISSMAN, R. X. 1999b. That magical night. *American Demographics* 21 (May): 80.

WELLNER, A. S. 2002. The female persuasion. *American Demographics* 24 (Feb.): 24–29.

WELLNER, A. S. 2003. The wealth effect. *American Demographics* 24 (Jan.): 35–47.

WELLNER, A. S. 2003. Whither online focus groups? *American Demographics* 25 (Mar.): 31.

WELTER, B. 1966. The cult of true womanhood: 1820–1860. *American Quarterly* 18 (2): 151–74.

WENNERAS, C., AND A. WOLD. 1997. Nepotism and sexism in peer review. *Nature* 387 (May): 341–43.

WERTHEIMER, R. 2003. *Poor families in 2001: Parents working less and children continue to lag behind.* Child Trends. www.childtrends.org/PDF/PoorFamiliesRB.pdf (accessed Sep. 11, 2003).

WEST, C., AND D. H. ZIMMERMAN. 1987. Doing gender. *Gender and Society* 1 (June): 125–51.

WESTHOFF, C., L. PICARDO, AND E. MORROW. 2003. Quality of life following early medical or surgical abortion. *Contraception* 67 (1): 41–47.

WESTOFF, L. A. 1977. *The second time around: Remarriage in America.* New York: Viking.

WESTON, L. P. 2001. You get safety with CDs, but certainly not 10% a year. *Baltimore Sun,* July 29, 3D.

WETZSTEIN, C. 2003. Abstinence education gains record funding. *The Washington Times.* www.washtimes.com/national/20030324-2400260.htm (accessed Mar. 25, 2003).

WHEELER, C. G. 1993. 30 years beyond "I have a dream." *Gallup Poll Monthly* (Oct.): 2–8.

WHEELER, L. 1998. Excavation reveals slaves as entrepreneurs. *Washington Post,* Oct. 13, B3.

WHIPPLE, E. E., AND C. A. RICHEY. 1997. Crossing the line from physical discipline to child abuse: How much is too much? *Child Abuse & Neglect* 21 (May): 431–44.

WHITAKER, D., J. MILLER, AND S. KIM. 2000. Parent–adolescent discussions about sex and condoms: Impact on peer influences of sexual risk behavior. *Journal of Adolescent Research* 15 (Mar.): 251–73.

WHITBECK, L. B., AND D. R. HOYT. 1999. *Nowhere to grow: Homeless and runaway adolescents and their families.* New York: Aldine de Gruyter.

WHITBECK, L. B., K. A. YODER, D. R. HOYT, AND R. D. CONGER. 1999. Early adolescent sexual activity. *Journal of Marriage and the Family* 61 (Nov.): 934–46.

WHITE, J. W., AND J. A. HUMPHREY. 1994. Women's aggression in heterosexual conflicts. *Aggressive Behavior* 20 (3): 195–202.

WHITE, J. W., AND D. M. KLEIN. 2002. *Family theories,* 2nd ed. Thousand Oaks, CA: Sage.

WHITE, L. 1992. The effect of parental divorce and remarriage on parental support for adult children. *Journal of Family Issues* 13 (June): 234–50.

WHITE, L., AND J. G. GILBRETH. 2001. When children have two fathers: Effects of relationships with stepfathers and noncustodial fathers on adolescent outcomes. *Journal of Marriage and Family* 63 (Feb.): 155–67.

WHITE, L. K. 1991. Determinants of divorce. In *Contemporary families: Looking forward, looking back,* ed. A. Booth, 150–61. Minneapolis: National Council on Family Relations.

WHITE, M. 2003. What's your favorite way to say "be mine": Card, candy, flowers? *Christian Science Monitor,* Feb. 12, 20.

WHITEFORD, L. M., AND L. GONZALEZ. 1995. Stigma: The hidden burden of infertility. *Social Science and Medicine* 40 (Jan.): 27–36.

WHITEHEAD, B. D. 1996. The decline of marriage as the social basis of childrearing. In *Promises to keep: Decline and renewal of marriage in America,* eds. D. Popenoe, J. B. Elshtain, and D. Blankenhorn, 3–14. Lanham, MD: Rowman & Littlefield.

WHITEHEAD, B. D. 2002. *Why there are no good men left: The romantic plight of the new single woman.* New York: Broadway.

WHITEHEAD, B. D., AND D. POPENOE. 2001. *The state of our unions 2001: The social health of marriage in America.* The National Marriage Project, Rutgers University. http://marriage.rutgers.edu/Publications/SOOU/NMPAR2001.pdf (accessed July 12, 2003).

WHITEMAN, S. D., S. M. MCHALE, AND A. C. CROUTER. 2003. What parents learn from experience: The first child as a first draft? *Journal of Marriage and Family* 65 (Aug.): 608–21.

WHITING, J. B., AND R. E. LEE III. 2003. Voices from the system: A qualitative study of foster children's stories. *Family Relations* 52 (July): 288–95.

WHITSETT, D., AND H. LAND. 1992. The development of a role strain index for stepparents. *Families in Society: The Journal of Contemporary Human Services* 73 (Jan.): 14–22.

Who gets the most time off? 2000. *Christian Science Monitor,* July 3, 12.

WHYTE, M. K. 1990. *Dating, mating, and marriage.* New York: Aldine de Gruyter.

WICKRAMA, K. A. S., F. O. LORENZ, R. D. CONGER, AND G. H. ELDER, JR. 1997. Marital quality and physical illness: A latent growth curve analysis. *Journal of Marriage and the Family* 59 (Feb.): 143–55.

WIDOM, C. S,. AND M. G. MAXFIELD. 2001. *An update on the "cycle of violence."* Washington, DC: U.S. Department of Justice.

WIEHE, V. R. 1997. *Sibling abuse: Hidden physical, emotional, and sexual trauma,* 2nd ed. Thousand Oaks, CA: Sage.

WIEHE, V. R., WITH T. HERRING. 1991. *Perilous rivalry: When siblings become abusive.* Lexington, MA: Lexington.

WIENER, L. 2003. Age has its rewards. *U.S. News & World Report,* June 23, 32.

WIIST, W. H., AND J. MCFARLANE. 1998. Severity of spousal and intimate partner abuse to pregnant Hispanic women. *Journal of Health Care for the Poor & Underserved* 9 (Aug.): 248–61.

WILCOX, S., ET AL. 2003. The effects of widowhood on physical and mental health, health behaviors, and health outcomes: The women's health initiative. *Health Psychology* 22 (5): 1–9.

WILCOX, W. B. 2002. Sacred vows, public purposes: Religion, the marriage movement and marriage policy. The Pew Forum on Religion and Public Life. http://pewforum.org/publications/reports/marriagepolicy.pdf (accessed Mar. 3, 2003).

WILKIE, J. R., M. M. FERREE, AND K S. RATCLIFF. 1998. Gender and fairness: Marital satisfaction in two-earner couples. *Journal of Marriage and the Family* 60 (Aug.): 577–94.

WILKINSON, T. 2000. Midwest by moonlight: Low pay means two jobs. *Christian Science Monitor,* Aug. 16, 1, 5.

WILLIAMS, D. R. 2003. The health of men: Structured inequalities and opportunities. *American Journal of Public Health* 93 (May): 724–31.

WILLIAMS, L. 2002. Hispanic female athletes few and far between. *New York Times.* www.nytimes.com/2002/11/06/sports/othersports/06LATI.html?todaysheadlines (accessed Nov. 7, 2002).

WILLIAMS, N. 1990. *The Mexican American family: Tradition and change.* New York: General Hall.

WILLIAMS, T. K., AND M. C. THORNTON. 1998. Social construction of ethnicity versus personal experience: The case of Afro-Amerasians. *Journal of Comparative Family Studies* 29 (Summer): 255–84.

WILLIAMS, W. M. 2001. Women in academe, and the men who derail them. *Chronicle of Higher Education,* July 20, B20.

WILLINGER, M., C.-W. KO, H. J. HOFFMAN, R. C. KESSLER, AND M. J. CORWIN. 2003. Trends in infant bed sharing in the United States, 1993–2000. *Archives of Pediatrics & Adolescent Medicine* 157 (Jan.): 43–49.

WILLIS, S. L., AND J. D. REID, EDS. 1999. *Life in the middle: Psychological and social development in middle age.* San Diego, CA: Academic Press.

WILLIS, W. 1997. Families with African American roots. In *Developing cross-cultural competence: A guide for working with children and families,* eds. E. W. Lynch and M. J. Hanson, 165–202. Baltimore: Paul H. Brookes.

WILSON, B. F., AND S. C. CLARKE. 1992. Remarriages: A demographic profile. *Journal of Family Issues* 13 (June): 123–41.

WILSON, C. 2001. Living single grows in USA. *USA Today,* Oct. 23, D1.

WILSON, G. 1990. The consequences of elderly wives caring for disabled husbands: Implications for practice. *Social Work* 35 (Sep.): 417–21.

WILSON, J. Q. 1993. The family-values debate. *Commentary,* Apr. 1, 24–31.

WILSON, J. Q. 2002. *The marriage problem: How our culture has weakened families.* New York: HarperCollins.

WILSON, R. 1999. An MIT professor's suspicion of bias leads to a new movement for academic women. *Chronicle of Higher Education,* Dec. 3, A16–A18.

WILSON, S. 2002. The health capital of families: An investigation of the inter-spousal correlation in health status. *Social Science & Medicine* 55 (Oct.): 1157–72.

WILTENBURG, M. 2002. Minority. *Christian Science Monitor,* Jan. 31, 14.

WINCH, R. F. 1958. *Mate selection: A study of complementary needs.* New York: Harper & Row.

WIND, R. 2003. Policies to promote marriage target out-of-wedlock births but ignore unintended pregnancy among married women. The Alan Guttmacher Institute, May 30. www.agi-usa.org/pubs/archives/nr_gr060203.html (accessed Aug. 20, 2003).

WINEBERG, H. 1991. Intermarital fertility and dissolution of the second marriage. *Social Science Quarterly* 75 (Jan.): 62–65.

WINEBERG, H. 1994. Marital reconciliation in the United States: Which couples are successful? *Journal of Marriage and the Family* 56 (Feb.): 80–88.

WINEBERG, H. 1996. The prevalence and characteristics of blacks having a successful marital reconciliation. *Journal of Divorce & Remarriage* 25 (1/2): 75–86.

WINEBERG, H., AND J. MCCARTHY. 1993. Separation and reconciliation in American marriages. *Journal of Divorce & Remarriage* 20: 21–42.

WINER, E. L., AND L. BECKER, EDS. 1993. *Premarital and marital contracts: A lawyer's guide to drafting and negotiating marital and cohabitation agreements.* Chicago: American Bar Association.

WINGERT, P., AND J. F. LAUERMAN. 2000. Parents behaving badly. *Newsweek,* July 24, 48–49.

WINK, W. 1979. Homosexuality and the Bible. *Bridges Home.* www.bridges-across.org/ba/wink.htm.

WINNER, K. 1996. *Divorced from justice: The abuse of women and children by divorce lawyers and judges.* New York: Regan.

WINTON, C. A. 1995. *Frameworks for studying families.* Guilford, CT: Dushkin.

WISEMAN, R. 2002. *Queen bees and wannabes: A parent's guide to helping your daughter survive cliques, gossip, boyfriends, and other realities of adolescence.* New York: Crown.

WISSOW, L. S. 2000. Suicide among American Indians and Alaska Natives. In *American Indian health: Innovations in health care, promotion, and policy,* ed. E. R. Rhoades, 260–80. Baltimore: Johns Hopkins University Press.

WISSOW, L. S. 2001. Ethnicity, income, and parenting contexts of physical punishment in a national sample of families with young children. *Child Maltreatment* 6 (May): 118–29.

WITT, G. E. 1998. Vote early and often. *American Demographics* 20 (Dec.): 23.

WITTENBURG, M. 2003. Warehousing our children. *Christian Science Monitor,* June 19, 14–16.

WIZEMANN, T. M., AND M.-L. PARDUE, EDS. 2001. *Exploring the biological contributions to human health: Does sex matter?* Washington, DC: National Academy Press.

WMST-L. 2002. Women's studies e-mail list. research.umbc.edu/~korenman/wmst/wmst-l_index.html.

WOLCHIK, S. A., A. M. FENAUGHTY, AND S. L. BRAVER. 1996. Residential and nonresidential parents' perspectives on visitation problems. *Family Relations* 45 (Apr.): 230–37.

WOLCOTT, J. 2000. Finding Mrs. Right (and all the little Rights). *Christian Science Monitor,* Feb. 23, 15–17.

WOLCOTT, J. 2001. Dinnertime in America. *Christian Science Monitor,* Sep. 5, 15–17.

WOLCOTT, J. 2003. Single moms find roommates. *Christian Science Monitor,* Mar. 12, 11, 14.

WOLF, D. L. 1997. Family secrets: Transnational struggles among children of Filipino immigrants. *Sociological Perspectives* 40 (3): 457–82.

WOLF, R. S. 1996. Elder abuse and family violence: Testimony presented before the U.S. Senate Special Committee on aging. *Journal of Elder Abuse & Neglect* 8 (1): 81–96.

WOLFE, L. 1981. *The Cosmo report.* New York: Arbor House.

WOLFINGER, N. 1999. Trends in the intergenerational transmission of divorce. *Demography* 36: 415–20.

WOLFINGER, N. 2000. Beyond the intergenerational transmission of divorce: Do people replicate the pattern of marital instability they grew up with? *Journal of Family Issues* 21: 1061–86.

WOLFSON, E. 1996. Why we should fight for the freedom to marry: The challenges and opportunities that will follow a win in Hawaii. *Journal of Gay, Lesbian, and Bisexual Identity* 1 (1): 79–89.

Woman gives birth using her dead husband's sperm. 1999. *Baltimore Sun,* Mar. 27, 5A.

Women and smoking: A report of the surgeon general. 2001. Centers for Disease Control and Prevention. www.cdc.gov/tobacco/sgr/sgr_forwomen/Executive_Summary.htm (accessed May 19, 2003).

Women and Social Security. 2003. Social Security is important to women. Social Security Administration. www.socialsecurity.gov/pressoffice/factsheets/women-alt.htm (accessed Oct. 9, 2003).

Women in red! Equal pay day is April 15. 2003. National Organization for Women, Apr. 4. www.now.org/issues/economic/alerts/04-04-03.html (accessed Apr. 8, 2003).

Women in the United States: March 2000. U.S. Census Bureau, PPL-121. www.census.gov/population/www/socdemo/ppl-121.html.

WONG, B. 1998. *Ethnicity and entrepreneurship: The new Chinese immigrants in the San Francisco Bay area.* Boston: Allyn & Bacon.

WONG, P. 1993. *Child support and welfare reform.* New York: Garland.

WOOD, D. B. 2002. As homelessness grows, even havens toughen up. *Christian Science Monitor,* Sep. 21, 1, 4.

WOOD, D. B. 2002. New era of snooping parents. *Christian Science Monitor,* Feb. 21, 1, 4.

WOOD, H. M., B. J. TROCK, AND J. P. GEARHART. 2003. In vitro fertilization and the cloacal–bladder exstrophy–epispadias complex: Is there an association? *Journal of Urology* 169 (Apr.): 1512–15.

WOOD, J. T. 2002. *Gendered lives: Communication, gender, and culture,* 5th ed. Belmont, CA: Wadsworth.

WOODARD, E. H., IV, AND N. GRIDINA. 2000. *Media in the home: The fifth annual survey of parents and children, 2000.* Philadelphia: University of Pennsylvania, Annenberg Public Policy Center.

WOODS, R. D. 1996. Grandmother roles: A cross cultural view. *Journal of Instructional Psychology* 23 (Dec.): 286–92.

WOODWARD, K. L., AND K. SPRINGEN. 1992. Better than a gold watch. *Newsweek,* Aug. 24, 71.

Work at home in 2001. 2002. U.S. Department of Labor. www.bls.gov/news.release/homey.nr0.htm (accessed Sep. 14, 2003).

Working longer, working better? 1999. International Labour Organization. www.ilo.org/public/english/bureau/inf/magazine/31/work.htm (accessed Oct. 11, 2000).

Working women: Equal pay: Ask a working woman. 2000. AFL-CIO. www.aflcio.org/women/survey1.htm (accessed Oct. 15, 2000).

WORLD HEALTH ORGANIZATION. 2002. AIDS epidemic update. UNAIDS, Dec. www.unaids.org/worldaidsday/2002/press/update/epiupdate_en.pdf (accessed June 18, 2003).

WRIGHT, C. I., AND L. S. FISH. 1997. Feminist family therapy: The battle against subtle sexism. In *Subtle sexism: Current practices and prospects for change,* ed. N. V. Benokraitis, 201–15. Thousand Oaks, CA: Sage.

WRIGHT, J. 1997. Motherhood's gray area. *Washington Post,* July 29, E5.

WRIGHT, J. C., A. C. HUSTON, AND K. C. MURPHY. 2001. The relations of early television viewing to school readiness and vocabulary of children from low-income families: the Early Window Project. *Child Development* 72 (Sep./Oct.): 1347–66.

WRIGHT, J. M. 1998. *Lesbian step families: An ethnography of love.* New York: Haworth.

WTULICH, J. 1986. *Writing home: Immigrants in Brazil and the United States, 1890–1891.* Boulder, CO: East European Monographs.

WU, L. L. 1996. Effects of family instability, income, and income instability on the risk of a premarital birth. *American Sociological Review* 61 (June): 386–406.

WU, L. L., L. L. BUMPASS, AND K. MUSICK. 2001. Historical and life course trajectories of nonmarital childbearing. In *Out of wedlock: Causes and consequences of nonmarital fertility,* eds. L. L. Wu and B. Wolfe, 3–38. New York: Russell Sage Foundation.

WU, L. L., AND E. THOMSON. 2001. Race difference in family experience and early sexual initiation: Dynamic models of family structure and family change. *Journal of Marriage and Family* 63 (Aug.): 682–96.

WU, Z. 1994. Remarriage in Canada: A social exchange perspective. *Journal of Divorce & Remarriage* 21 (3/4): 191–224.

WU, Z., AND M. S. POLLARD. 2000. Economic circumstances and the stability of nonmarital cohabitation. *Journal of Family Issues* 21 (Apr.): 303–28.

XU, X., C. D. HUDSPETH, AND S. ESTES. 1997. The effects of husbands' involvement in child rearing activities and participation in household labor on marital quality: A racial comparison. *Journal of Gender, Culture, and Health* 2 (3): 171–93.

YAGAMINE, Y. 2002. Single in Japan. *New York Times,* Mar. 24. www.nytimes.com/2002/03/24/international/europe/24MARR.html?ex=10 1797 (accessed Mar. 25, 2002).

YANCEY, A. K., J. M. SIEGEL, AND K. L. MCDANIEL. 2002. Role models, ethnic identity, and health-risk behaviors in urban adolescents. *Archives of Pediatrics & Adolescent Medicine* 156 (Jan.): 55–61.

YARNALL, K. S. H., ET AL. 2003. Factors associated with condom use among at-risk women students and nonstudents seen in managed care. *Preventive Medicine* 37 (Aug.): 163–70.

YELLOWBIRD, M., AND C. M. SNIPP. 2002. American Indian families. In *Minority families in the United States: A multicultural perspective,* 3rd ed., ed. R. L. Taylor, 227–49. Upper Saddle River, NJ: Prentice Hall.

YESALIS, C. E., C. K. BARSUKIEWICZ, AND M. S. BAHRKE. 1997. Trends in anabolic–androgenic steroid use among adolescents. *Archives of Pediatrics & Adolescent Medicine* 151 (Dec.): 1197–207.

YEUNG, W. J., J. F. SANDBERG, P. E. DAVIS-KEAN, AND S. L. HOFFERTH. 2001. Children's time with fathers in intact families. *Journal of Marriage and Family* 63 (Feb.): 136–54.

YIN, S. 2002. Off the map: Looking for love. *American Demographics* 24 (Feb.): 48.

YOKOTA, F., AND K. M. THOMPSON. 2000. Violence in G-rated animated films. *Journal of the American Medical Association* 283 (May 24/31): 2716–20.

YOON, I.-J. 1997. *On my own: Korean businesses and race relations in America.* Chicago: University of Chicago Press.

YOSHIHAMA, M., A. L. PAREKH, AND D. BOYINGTON. 1991. Dating violence in Asian/Pacific communities. In *Dating violence: Young women in danger,* ed. B. Levy, 184–95. Seattle: Seal.

YOUNG, K. 2001. *Tangled in the Web: Understanding cybersex from fantasy to addiction.* Bloomington, IN: 1st Books Library.

YOUNG, M. H., J. D. SCHVANEVELDT, S. L. K. LINDAUER, AND P. L. SCHVANEVELDT. 2001. Understanding AIDS: A comparison of children in the United States and Thailand. *Family Relations* 50 (Oct.): 393–401.

YU, H.-Y. 2002. Salomon ordered to pay $3 mil in discrimination case. Bloomberg News, Dec. 14. www.quote.bloomberg.com (accessed Sep. 10, 2003).

YU, Y. 1995. Patterns of work and family: An analysis of the Chinese American family since the 1920s. In *American families: Issues in race and ethnicity,* ed. C. K. Jacobson, 131–44. New York: Garland.

ZAFF, J. F., J. CALKINS, L. J. BRIDGES, AND N. G. MARGIE. 2002. *Promoting positive mental and emotional health in teens: Some lessons from research.* Washington, DC: Child Trends. www.childtrends.org/PDF/K5Brief.pdf (accessed Aug. 23, 2003).

ZAGORSKY, J. L. 2003. Husbands' and wives' view of the family finances. *Journal of Socio-Economics* 32 (May): 127–46.

ZAIDI, A. U., AND M. SHURAYDI. 2002. Perceptions of arranged marriages by young Pakistani Muslim women living in a Western society. *Journal of Comparative Family Studies* 33 (Autumn): 495–514.

ZAL, H. M. 1992. *The sandwich generation: Caught between growing children and aging parents.* New York: Plenum.

ZAPLER, M. 1995. States may be next battleground for human-embryo research. *Chronicle of Higher Education,* Jan. 20, A24.

ZARIT, S. H., AND D. J. EGGEBEEN. 2002. Parent–child relationships in adulthood and later years. In *Handbook of parenting,* 2nd ed., Vol. 1: *Children and parenting,* ed. M. H. Bornstein, 135–61. Mahwah, NJ: Erlbaum.

ZELLNER, W. 2002. A Texas-size case of discrimination? *Business Week,* Mar. 18, 14.

ZHANG, Z., AND M. D. HAYWARD. 2001. Childlessness and the psychological well-being of older persons. *Journal of Gerontology: Social Sciences* 56B: S311–20.

ZHOU, J.-N., M. A. HOFMAN, AND D. F. SWAAB. 1995. A sex difference in the human brain and its relation to transsexuality. *Nature* 378 (Nov. 2): 68–70.

ZHOU, M., AND C. L. BANKSTON III. 1998. *Growing up American: How Vietnamese children adapt to life in the United States.* New York: Russell Sage Foundation.

ZILL, N., AND C. W. NORD. 1994. *Running in place: How American families are faring in a changing economy and an individualistic society.* Washington, DC: Child Trends.

ZIMBALIST, A. 2000. Backlash against Title IX: An end run around female athletes. *Chronicle of Higher Education,* Mar. 3, B9–B10.

ZIMMERMAN, T. S., K. E. HOLM, AND S. A. HADDOCK. 2001. A decade of advice for women and men in the best-selling self-help literature. *Family Relations* 50 (Apr.): 122–33.

ZITO, J. M. ET AL. 2003. Psychotropic practice patterns for youth. *Archives of Pediatrics & Adolescent Medicine* 157 (Jan.): 17–25.

ZITO, J. M., D. J. SAFER, S. DOS REIS, J. F. GARDNER, M. BOLES, AND F. LYNCH. 2000. Trends in the prescribing of psychotropic medications to preschoolers. *Journal of the American Medical Association* 283 (Feb. 23): 105–1030.

ZUCKERMAN, D. 2000. Child care staff: The low-down on salaries and stability. National Center for Policy Research for Women & Families. www.center4policy.org/wwf2.html (accessed Aug. 25, 2003).

ZUNIN, L. M., AND H. S. ZUNIN. 1991. *The art of condolence: What to write, what to say, what to do at a time of loss.* New York: HarperCollins.

ZURAVIN, S. J., AND F. A. DiBLASIO. 1996. The correlates of child physical abuse and neglect by adolescent mothers. *Journal of Family Violence* 11 (June): 149–66.

PHOTO CREDITS

NAME INDEX

SUBJECT INDEX